MARKETING MANAGEMENT

A Strategic Approach

The Irwin Series in Marketing
Consulting Editor
Gilbert A. Churchill, Jr.
University of Wisconsin, Madison

MARKETING MANAGEMENT

A Strategic Approach

Harper W. Boyd, Jr.
Donaghey Distinguished Professor of Marketing
University of Arkansas–Little Rock

Orville C. Walker, Jr.
James D. Watkins Professor of Marketing
University of Minnesota

Homewood, IL 60430
Boston, MA 02116

Developmental editor: Eleanore Snow
Project editor: Paula M. Buschman
Production manager: Carma W. Fazio
Photo researcher: Michael J. Hruby
Cover designer: Robyn Basquin
Cover photograph: © Michel Tcherevkoff
Compositor: Better Graphics, Inc.
Typeface: 10/12 Melior
Printer: R. R. Donnelley & Sons Company

Library of Congress Cataloging-in-Publication Data

Boyd, Harper W.
  Marketing management.

  Includes bibliographical references.
  1. Market—Management. I. Walker, Orville C.
II. Title.
HF5415.13.B669   1990   658.8   89–35302
  ISBN 0-256-05827-X
  ISBN 0-256-08400-9 (International student ed.)

Printed in the United States of America
1 2 3 4 5 6 7 8 9 0 DO 6 5 4 3 2 1 0 9

PREFACE

We may be a bit biased, but we see marketing as one of most important and most exciting of all the business functions. One reason for this perception was expressed by Peter Drucker more than four decades ago when he wrote that marketing is not really a separate function at all; it is the whole business seen from the point of view of its final result, that is, from the customer's viewpoint. More recently, Fred Webster—the executive director of the Marketing Science Institute—reinforced this broad view of the importance and scope of marketing by wondering "is there any difference between a good *manager* and a good *marketer?*"[1] He went on to predict that marketing as a stand-alone function will become extremely rare in the typical organization of the future. Instead, marketing—in the sense of doing what is necessary to serve and satisfy customers—will become everybody's business, at least within those organizations that survive and prosper in an increasingly competitive climate.

Of course, even when the day-to-day responsibility for marketing activities is diffused across employees in every part of the organization, someone still has to plan, coordinate, and control those activities. That "someone" might be a traditional product or marketing manager, a vice president of marketing, a general manager of a business unit, or even a team of managers drawn from a variety of functional areas. Regardless of who bears the responsibility, the *process* of managing an organization's marketing efforts is the central focus of—and provides the underlying structure for—this book.

But it is also important to recognize that the marketing management process does not occur in a vacuum. Most organizations have corporate and business-level strategies that establish guidelines concerning objectives to be attained, directions for future growth, and how the organization will compete and seek to gain a sustainable advantage in the marketplace. These guidelines impose constraints on the range of marketing strategies and activities a marketing manager can pursue within the larger strategic context of his or her organization. But, on the other hand, marketing managers are also uniquely positioned to provide information and insights for the development of corporate and business strategies because they straddle the boundary between the external environment and the inner-workings of the firm. Thus as organizations seek to become more customer oriented, and face ever more hostile and rapidly changing competitive environments, the marketer's role in strategy formulation is likely to increase.

---

[1] Frederick E. Webster, Jr., "It's 1990—Do You Know Where Your Marketing Is?" MSI White Paper (Cambridge, Mass.: Marketing Science Institute, April 14, 1989), p. 6.

Similarly, while marketing managers play a crucial role in translating the firm's strategies into action programs designed to win customer acceptance and competitive advantage in specific markets, they do not implement those programs all by themselves. Effective execution requires cooperative and coordinated efforts across many other functional areas. Thus, the range of viable strategic marketing programs available to a manager is constrained by the resources and functional competencies available within his or her organization. And the successful implementation of a chosen program depends on the marketer's ability to win the cooperation and support of people in other functional areas.

WHY WE WROTE THIS BOOK

As the above discussion suggests, we see marketing as the epicenter of both the strategic and operational life of an organization. The marketing management process is intimately linked with strategic decisions made at higher organizational levels and with the operational decisions and actions taken in other functional departments. And it is these internal linkages—together with its direct links to the external market and competitive environment—that make marketing such a challenging and exciting field.

Unfortunately, most of the existing marketing management textbooks tend to treat marketing management as a stand-alone business function. While they do a good job of describing the concepts, tools, and techniques involved in the marketing management process, they pay only scant attention to the web of internal strategic and operational relationships that surround that process. As a result, they fail to convey some of the true importance—and the intellectual excitement—of marketing in today's organizations.

A focus on the marketing management process

Our desire to present a broader and more realistic view of marketing's strategic and operational roles and relationships within the firm was our major motivation for writing this book. But from the beginning we also realized that the primary focus of a good marketing management text must be the marketing management process itself. Short-changing a discussion of that process in order to devote more attention to surrounding relationships and issues would be like throwing out the baby to make room for more bath water.

Thus, this book is structured around the steps involved in the analytical and decision-making processes involved in formulating, implementing, and controlling a stragetic marketing program for a given product-market entry. It includes chapters on all the topics one expects to find in a marketing management text: chapters on customer, competitor, and environmental analysis, market segmentation, market targeting, competitive positioning, the 4 Ps of product, price, promotion, and place (distribution), implementation, and control. Like most existing texts, this book includes separate chapters or sections on the tools of marketing research, demand estimation, and industry analysis. But we have also made a concerted effort to discuss specific applications of those tools in substantive chapters where each is most relevant (e.g., copy testing methods are discussed in detail in the chapter on advertising). Each of these "traditional" chapters presents a thorough discussion of the major issues, concepts, and techniques relevant to the marketing of both goods and services, while avoiding where possible encyclopedic lists and arcane models of limited practical use. It should therefore provide the student with a solid foundation of knowledge about what is involved in developing and implementing strategic marketing programs.

A unique focus on strategic and interfunctional relationships

What makes this book different from—and a bit longer than—other texts is that it ranges beyond the traditional discussion of the marketing management process to discuss how marketing interacts with other levels of strategy and with other functional departments within an organization. Specifically, it includes an examination of three sets of relationships that are given little or no attention in other texts.

1. **The relationships among corporate, business-level, and marketing strategies.** As mentioned, managers responsible for developing and implementing marketing strategies for specific products and target markets are also uniquely qualified to provide insights and information needed to formulate competitive strategies at the business and corporate levels of the organization. And, as organizations strive to become more customer oriented, the marketing manager's role in strategic planning is likely to increase. At the same time, those higher-level strategic decisions often impose guidelines and constraints on the marketing manager's freedom of action when designing marketing strategies and programs for individual products or services.

   This book examines this complex set of relationships among the different levels of strategy in several ways. First, Chapter 2 presents a general discussion of the hierarchy of strategies found in most multiproduct organizations, their interrelationships, and the marketer's role in helping to formulate strategies at different organizational levels. A more specific discussion of the linkages between business-level competitive strategies and marketing strategies appropriate for individual product-markets within the business unit is provided in Chapter 11. Finally, each of the chapters discussing the individual elements of a strategic marketing program (the 4 Ps) examines how decisions about those program elements should fit the business's competitive strategy.

2. **Relationships between marketing strategy and the strategic environment.** Most texts talk in general terms about how the marketing strategy for a given product or service should fit the characteristics of the market and competitive

environment. But they usually do not provide much detail concerning the specific kinds of strategic marketing programs that are best suited to different strategic contexts. Nor do they discuss the specific tactical decisions and actions necessary to effectively carry out each program.

In contrast, this book provides an entire section of four chapters that discusses the marketing strategies and tactics best suited to specific strategic situations. Those situations are defined both in terms of market characteristics as defined by the stage in the product life cycle, and by the product's relative competitive position. Thus, Chapter 19 discusses marketing strategies for new product-market entries. Chapter 20 examines strategies for growth markets—both share maintenance strategies for market leaders and growth strategies for low-share followers. Strategies for mature and declining markets are analyzed in Chapter 21. Finally, global marketing strategies are detailed in Chapter 22.

3. **Relationships between marketing and other functional areas.** A marketing manager's ability to effectively implement a strategic marketing program depends in large measure on the cooperation and competence of other functional areas within the organization. Consequently, we devote substantial attention to the interfunctional implications of specific strategic marketing programs. Each of the marketing strategies appropriate for particular strategic circumstances described in Chapters 19 through 22 are also examined in terms of the requirements they impose on other functional departments such as product and process R&D, production, quality control, logistics, finance, and cost control. In addition, Chapter 23 provides an overview of the functional competencies required to effectively implement different competitive and marketing strategies. It also discusses organizational mechanisms appropriate for coordinating efforts and resolving conflicts across functional areas.

Making marketing management "sing and dance"

We believe that the addition of material related to the above sets of relationships has produced a fringe benefit. By describing marketing management within the broader context of an organization's strategic circumstances and operational concerns we think this book conveys more of the challenge and excitement experienced by marketing managers in the real world. We have tried to further enhance the interest level for students and their involvement with real and familiar examples. This book incorporates hundreds of up-to-date examples that demonstrate marketing practices as they are applied to industrial as well as consumer products, services as well as goods, and not-for-profit organizations as well as business firms.

To further enhance student interest and involvement, every chapter begins with a mini-case example that serves to introduce and illustrate the major concepts discussed in that chapter. These introductory examples are referred to at several appropriate places throughout each chapter—and sometimes in subsequent chapters—to help the student see the relationships among concepts and their relevance to real problems.

THE INTENDED AUDIENCE FOR THIS BOOK

This book was primarily designed for use in the introductory marketing management course at the graduate level. It is particularly well suited for such a course because it provides a thorough foundation in the basic concepts and techniques of marketing management for those students who will take additional courses in marketing. It should also be well received by students majoring in other disciplines because it presents a detailed examination of the strategic role of marketing and its relationships with other functional areas.

The book's discussion of the linkages among the various levels of strategy and its detailed coverage of strategic marketing programs appropriate for various specific situations also makes it useful for courses in strategic marketing at either the graduate or advanced undergraduate level. In such courses the instructor might focus students' attention on the chapters dealing with the analyses necessary for formulating marketing strategies (Chapters 1–11) and those examining specific strategies and their implementation (Chapters 19–23). The remaining chapters focusing on the individual elements of the marketing mix can then be assigned selectively or reserved for student review.

FEATURES APPROPRIATE FOR DIFFERENT TEACHING APPROACHES

This book and its package of supporting materials were designed to fit a variety of teaching approaches. Instructors who emphasize the lecture–discussion approach will find ample material for either a quarter or semester course. For those who prefer case-oriented instruction, the book provides a solid foundation of concepts and techniques and—while no cases are included—the *Instructor's Manual* (written by Les Dlabay of Lake Forest College) lists cases (as well as other materials such as video tapes) from a variety of sources keyed to the major topics in each chapter.

Many other features of the book and its supporting materials are designed to stimulate student interest and involvement and to facilitate the instructor's teaching performance. These features include:

- **Discussion questions at the end of each chapter designed to provide a vehicle for meaningful student exercises or class discussions.** Rather than being simple review questions that ask students to regurgitate answers found in the chapter, many of the questions in this book are more application-oriented. They often take the form of mini-cases that reflect actual company problems.

- **Computer-based problems for use as student exercises.** A set of 10 problems involving various issues in the formulation and implementation of a strategic marketing program for a hypothetical product is available. Computer discs containing the data sets relevant to these problems are available to adopters, along with documentation and instructions for students plus solutions for the instructor.

♦ **Suggestions for coordinating a variety of marketing strategy simulation games with the material in the text.** The strategic focus of this text makes it a perfect companion for several existing strategy simulation games. The Instructor's Manual includes a detailed discussion of how the text material can be integrated with a number of such games.

♦ **Color transparencies that go beyond the exhibits presented in the text.** A set of 100 color transparencies are available to adopters. While some of these transparencies reproduce important exhibits found in the text, others provide original graphic representations of concepts and relationships described—but not depicted—in the book. Still others present advertisements for real products and services whose content illustrates concepts discussed in each chapter. Suggestions for incorporating these original materials in lectures or class discussions are included with the transparencies.

♦ **An extensive Manual of Tests and computerized test bank.** A Manual of Tests containing about 2,000 multiple-choice and short-answer questions is available to adopters. A unique feature of the Manual of Tests is the inclusion of a detailed rationale for the answers to many of the more difficult questions. The Manual of Tests, written by Daryl McKee and Mark Johnston of Louisiana State University, has been thoroughly reviewed to ensure relevant questions with accurate answers. Computest, a computerized version of the multiple-choice questions, is also available to adopters.

ACKNOWLEDGMENTS

A book like this is never solely the work of the authors whose names appear on the cover. Instead, there are many people who aid and abet such an enterprise, and whose contributions must be acknowledged.

First, we thank our faculty colleagues in our respective schools for their wise counsel and advice. We particularly thank Bob Ruekert of the University of Minnesota for his many contributions to research on the implementation of marketing strategies, the material he provided for the promotion chapters, and for his unflagging encouragement and emotional support. We are also especially indebted to Jean-Claude Larréché for his many valuable contributions to the preparation of this manuscript. Jean-Claude is Professor of Marketing and Director of the Strategic Marketing Institute at INSEAD in Fontainebleau, France. In particular, the chapters concerning the environment, market segmentation, and market targeting and positioning benefited from his help. Finally, Bill Dillon of the University of South Carolina offered valuable suggestions for the marketing research chapter.

We are also grateful to our friends in industry. Our conversations with them over the years have done much to improve our understanding of how marketing works in the real world and have produced many of the most interesting examples in this book. We especially thank:

- Cathy Brink, Ellen Pearl, and Steve Zuber at Pillsbury
- Linda Keefe at 3M
- Tom Hartley at Union Carbide
- John Kier, Danish business executive
- Steve Goldberg, restaurant owner and entrepreneur

Academicans—even those in marketing—are sometimes not very customer-oriented, particularly when it comes to writing textbooks. We have made a concerted effort to avoid such a heresy. Consequently, we offer special thanks to our many students for their patience in serving as guinea pigs during the classroom testing of parts of this book at various stages of its development. Their critical comments and useful suggestions helped make this a better book. Similarly we greatly appreciate the work of the following colleagues who reviewed this manuscript.

- Sharon Beatty
  University of Alabama
- Joseph Bellizzi
  Arizona State West
- Naser Bodiya
  University of Detroit
- Lon Camomile
  Colorado State
- Daniel Darrow
  Ferris State College
- Andrew Forman
  Hofstra University
- J. Robert Foster
  University of Texas-El Paso
- David Georgoff
  Florida Atlantic University
- Robert Harmon
  Portland State University
- Paula Haynes
  University of Tennessee-Chattanooga
- Richard Leventhal
  Metro State College
- Marilyn Liebrenz-Himes
  George Washington University
- David Ludington
  Mount Berry College
- Thomas Mahaffey
  Siena College
- Daryl McKee
  Louisiana State University
- Donald Norris
  Miami University-Ohio
- A. Ben Oumlil
  Louisiana Tech University
- Richard Spiller
  California State University-Long Beach
- Ron Taylor
  Mississippi State
- Gerard Tellis
  University of Southern California
- R. Dale Wilson
  Michigan State University
- Rebecca Yates
  University of Dayton

Their insightful criticisms, comments, and suggestions all greatly aided our efforts to make this book a useful tool for teaching and learning.

We owe a large debt of gratitude to Professor Gil Churchill of the University of Wisconsin-Madison—the Consulting Editor for Irwin's marketing series—for acting as the "product champion" for this project from the very beginning, and for his active participation and wise counsel throughout the book's development. We appreciated the encouragement of our good friend Jeanne Teutsch during the early stages of the project. We also thank the staff at Richard D. Irwin, Inc. for their invaluable assistance in turning a rough manuscript into an attractive and readable book. In particular, Eleanore Snow—our Senior Developmental Editor—has earned our heartfelt appreciation and respect for her administrative skill in coordinating the many people and activities involved in producing a finished book, for her excellent editorial taste and wisdom, and for her unflagging encouragement and gentle prodding. If not for Eleanore this book would still be a disorganized jumble of manuscript pages strewn around Little Rock and Minneapolis.

We also salute Roberta Moore for her skill in helping prepare the manuscript. She always responded with good grace no matter how many times she was asked to revise a chapter "one more time."

Finally, we thank Virginia Boyd for her tolerance in putting up with a preoccupied husband, and Amy and Kristen Walker for demonstrating by their example that there is more to life than manuscripts and deadlines. This book is dedicated, with love, to them.

Harper W. Boyd, Jr.
Orville C. Walker, Jr.

Contents in Brief

Contents

SECTION II Market opportunity analysis   **76**

3   Analyzing the macroenvironment   78

4   Consumer markets and buying behavior   110

MARKETING MANAGEMENT

A Strategic Approach

SECTION

An overview of marketing management

Chapter ◇ 1

Marketing and the marketing management process

RUBBERMAID—CREATIVE MARKETING OF HOMELY PRODUCTS

How do you make a silk purse out of a sow's ear? Rubbermaid, Inc., does it all the time—wringing substantial growth in sales and profits from a utilitarian line of dish drainers, plate scrapers, microwave utensils, and other plastic housewares. It accomplishes this feat largely through savvy marketing—listening intently to customers and retailers and spending millions on marketing research, product development, and consumer promotion. The housewares industry is characterized by slow market growth and intense competition; and yet Rubbermaid's sales doubled and earnings tripled from 1980 to 1986. By 1988, sales reached $1.19 billion.

Part of Rubbermaid's strategy for growth is to continually improve the design of existing products; for example, revising the design of its ice trays to make it easier to remove the cubes. Another major company focus is new-product and new-market development. Thus, the firm launches nearly 200 new products annually, one third of which are new from the ground up. Many of these are targeted at segments not previously served by the company. Rubbermaid reports an unusually high success rate (90 percent) for its new-product introductions. This success is attributed to continual monitoring of consumer preferences and lifestyles, competitive actions, and the concerns of retailers.

Rubbermaid's marketing managers keep a careful eye on the firm's competitors but do not try to match competitors' prices. Rubbermaid commands premium prices because of its products' uniqueness and high quality. The keystone of the company's consumer promotion efforts is extensive network TV advertising that features the firm's new products and stresses superior product quality. Rubbermaid also provides generous allowances to retailers to help support price promotions and co-op advertising in local markets. In addition, the company maintains a field salesforce to service—and to win more shelf space from—its existing retailers and to expand the number of stores carrying the firm's products. This high level of service and promotional support plus high retail margins generated by higher prices enabled Rubbermaid to increase its retail accounts from 60,000 in 1980 to 100,000 in 1987.

Source: Based on material found in Alex Taylor III, "Why the Bounce at Rubbermaid?" *Fortune*, April 13, 1987, pp. 77–78.

Rubbermaid's success at marketing an unexciting line of products in a mature market illustrates the critical importance of marketing in today's business organizations. A stronger market orientation will become even more important to most firms as the world marketplace becomes more crowded—and competitive. High-level managers in leading U.S. corporations report that their greatest challenge is formulating and implementing marketing strategies.[1] Executives in leading European companies also indicate a primary concern with formulating marketing strategies that will enable them to surpass competitors in satisfying consumers' needs.[2]

MARKETING ACTIVITIES AND THEIR CHARACTERISTICS

The importance of marketing in a company's ongoing success can better be understood and appreciated when you consider the activities it embraces. In essence, marketing anticipates and measures the importance of needs and wants of a given group of consumers and responds with a flow of need-satisfying goods and services. Accomplishing this requires the firm to:

- Target those markets most compatible with its resources
- Develop products that meet the needs of the target market better than competitive products
- Make the products readily available
- Develop customer awareness of the problem-solving capabilities of the company's line of products
- Obtain feedback from the market about the success of company products and programs.

One important characteristic of marketing as a business function is its focus on customers and their needs. When properly done, such focusing enables firms to enjoy success over time by exploiting changes in the marketplace, by developing products that have demonstrable superiority over what is currently available and thus fill a strong need, and by using a more integrated approach to their total operations. Rubbermaid, for example, has prospered by being market oriented. Its chief executive officer says the company's success formula is simple: "We absolutely watch the market, and we work at it 24 hours a day."[3]

Peters and Austin find just two ways of being successful over the long haul: either take exceptional care of your customers via superior service or

---

[1] *Business Planning in the Eighties: The New Competitiveness of American Corporations* (New York: Yankelovich, Skelly, & White, 1984). This study was conducted for Coopers & Lybrand.

[2] Jean-Claude Larréché, William W. Powell, and Hardy Deutz Ebeling, *Key Strategic Marketing Issues for the 1990s* (Fontainbleau, France: INSEAD, 1987).

[3] Alex Taylor III, "Why the Bounce at Rubbermaid?" *Fortune*, April 13, 1987, p. 78.

offer them superior quality.[4] These two basics must be practiced by everyone in the organization. "Thus, customer courtesy means courtesy from the accounting department, the purchasing department, and the engineers as well as from the salespeople. Quality, too, is an all-hands operation. The winners stun us not by their cleverness but by the fact that each and every aspect of the business is just a touch better than the norm."[5]

THE RELATIONSHIP OF MARKETING TO BUSINESS STRATEGY AND OPERATIONS

If we define business strategy largely as directing the firm's resources to provide the best fit between the firm and its environment—and further, to obtain a lasting competitive or differential advantage—then it should be clear that marketing plays an important role in strategy formulation. As one researcher notes, "The hallmarks of modern marketing are customer orientation and a long-range, or *strategic*, viewpoint that make an organization responsive to its everchanging environment."[6] In Exhibit 1-1, Nike's chief executive officer discusses the impact of the changing environment in that firm.

Marketing also plays a key role in development of operational (action) plans that are designed to implement a given strategy. In many, if not most, multiproduct companies, these plans are drafted within the marketing department. For example, a large consumer goods company assigns the responsibility for developing and implementing programs designed to build product volume and profit to a manager in the marketing department. This manager has specific responsibilities toward the product (to ensure its competitive superiority within certain cost constraints), advertising (making certain the advertising copy provides the maximum selling power and the media schedule delivers the message to the target audience in the most effective and efficient manner), merchandising (executes and evaluates sales promotions that are cost-effective), and adjustments to the plan during the fiscal year to deliver the required sales volume. These major responsibilities are detailed in an annual plan (complete with budget) that is updated quarterly.

THE DEVELOPMENT OF MARKETING SYSTEMS IN SOCIETY

Consider the Tiwi, an extremely primitive people living in the wilds of northern Australia. With the family as the center of Tiwi life, the household is the principal economic unit of their society. Each household is a self-sufficient production unit. Tiwi women gather vegetables, roots, grubs, worms,

---

[4] Tom Peters and Nancy Austin, "A Passion for Excellence," *Fortune*, May 13, 1985, p. 20.

[5] Ibid.

[6] Frederick E. Webster, Jr., *Industrial Marketing Strategy* (New York: John Wiley & Sons, 1984), p. 1.

EXHIBIT 1♦1

Nike and environmental change

CEO Philip H. Knight in discussing the impact of environmental change on Nike noted that: For at least a decade, running was America's primary fitness activity. An entire industry was born which supplied shoes to runners, racers, and those who wore running shoes as part of a major fashion trend. Nike grew because of an understanding of the needs of runners. We lead the industry in innovative technology to increase performance and reduce injury. As the fashion conscious consumer began to wear running shoes, Nike was there to meet the incredible demand. Slowly, two things began to happen.

First, the growth in the number of runners tapered off. Although running had been *the* fitness activity, it became simply a component in diversified fitness programs. People, for example, who used to run 30 miles per week were running 20 miles, swimming two miles, and perhaps lifting weights as well. In addition, aerobics, bicycling, tennis, racquetball, and soccer replaced the growth we once saw in running. . . .

Secondly, with this diversification there occurred a dramatic decline in the use of running shoes for fashion or casual wear. Running shoes were replaced with more traditional leather footwear and court and aerobic footwear.

We discovered that we were not sensitive enough to the shift, and let our product line wander too far into an area we call "athleisure." We have now intentionally pulled back from this area.

Nike is a sports company. Our innovation, our technology, and our talents are best suited for providing for the needs and demands of athletes. We didn't belong in the fashion industry, outside of sports, and some of our attempts there just don't work. We no longer will be chasing fashion—style and attractiveness will follow from a functional approach.

Source: Nike, Inc., 1985 annual report, p. 4.

and other delicacies from the surrounding countryside. The most experienced food gatherers are older women (often widows) who become the first wives of the young males. First wives supervise food gathering and other production activities of the younger women who subsequently join the household as additional wives of the polygamous men. The men contribute to their households' well-being by hunting and fishing.[7]

Because of their subsistence-level lifestyle and the self-sufficiency of each household, the Tiwi are one of the last remaining societies in which marketing activities are seldom undertaken.

But even the Tiwi have learned the benefits of specialization and division of labor. The women concentrate on gathering and preparing vegetables and insects; the males specialize in hunting and fishing. Increased division and specialization of labor is one of the most important changes that occurs as societies move from a primitive economy toward higher levels of economic

---

[7] Charles W. M. Hart and Arnold R. Pilling, *The Tiwi of North Australia* (New York: Holt, Rinehart & Winston, 1960).

EXHIBIT 1 ◆ 2

Examples of countertrading

> Because many countries have little cash to spend (third-world countries collectively owe more than $1 trillion), U.S. companies have had to engage in complex countertrade deals. For example, to sell copiers and printers in Brazil, Xerox sells Brazilian steel to Europe and venetian blinds to the United States. PepsiCo exports frozen broccoli and canned pineapple from Mexico to the United States to help local bottlers buy Pepsi concentrate. The Sudan pays for its Pepsi concentrate with sesame seeds. Boeing often bolsters the sales of its aircraft by offering to invest in local industry or a locally produced commodity.

Source: Louis Kraar, "How to Sell to Cashless Buyers," *Fortune,* November 7, 1988, p. 147.

development. Even though increased specialization helps improve a society's overall standard of living, it leads to a different problem: specialists are no longer self-sufficient. Artisans who specialize in making pots become very skilled and efficient at pot making, producing a surplus of pots; but they do not make any of the many other goods and services they need to survive and improve their lifestyle. A society cannot reap the full benefits of specialization, then, until it develops the means to facilitate the trade and exchange of surpluses among its members.

Social mechanisms to facilitate exchange

At the simplest level, exchanges occur through barter, where one producer trades surplus goods directly for another's surplus. The problem is that barter is time consuming and inefficient. Traders must seek out others who both produce the goods they want and are likely to want their goods. Then they must negotiate a mutually acceptable bargain. Despite these problems, a shortage of hard currency in many countries has caused a resurgence of barter, or countertrade, in international trade (see Exhibit 1–2 for examples of countertrading). Approximately 40 percent of all trade with Communist-bloc countries is in the form of barter.[8]

Early in the development of most economies, people evolve mechanisms that reduce their reliance on individual barter agreements and improve the efficiency of exchange. **Central marketplaces** spring up to reduce the time and travel involved in trade. Another social development facilitating exchange is **money.** This provides buyers and sellers with a standard unit of value and a common medium of exchange. Money frees traders from the necessity of finding others who currently have what they want and want

---

[8] We examine the marketing implications of this trend in Chapter 22. Also see John W. Dizard, "The Explosion of International Barter," *Fortune,* February 7, 1983, pp. 88–95.

EXHIBIT 1 ♦ 3

Effect of a distributor on number of exchanges between manufacturers and customers

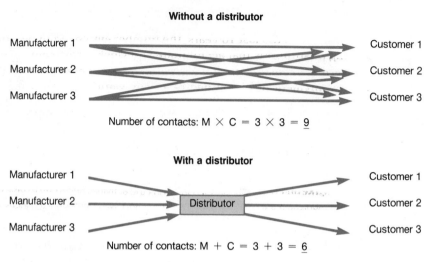

Without a distributor

Number of contacts: M × C = 3 × 3 = 9

With a distributor

Number of contacts: M + C = 3 + 3 = 6

what they have. Sellers need only to find someone willing to buy their goods or services at acceptable prices.

Institutions to facilitate trade

As a society's economy continues to grow and develop, more and more exchange transactions must occur for people to obtain the desired assortment of products and services. Another social mechanism then emerges to help them deal with this increasing volume and complexity of trade: A system of institutions specializing in activities facilitating exchange. Traders buy up the surpluses of producers, store them in inventory, and then offer customers a diverse assortment of goods for purchase in a single transaction. By reducing the transactions each person must engage in to obtain a desired assortment of goods and services, traders increase the overall efficiency of exchange. Exhibit 1–3 shows how fewer contacts and individual exchanges are required when a distributor is present.

Continued growth and diversification of a society's economic outputs stimulate an even faster growth in specialized institutions that distribute those outputs. In the United States, for example, the number of people employed in distribution increased substantially faster than the number of production workers since the turn of the century. Transportation and warehousing firms moved increasing volumes of goods from factories to buyers. Advertising agencies emerged to help manufacturers and retailers communicate information about available products and services to potential buyers. The number and variety of these exchange specialists has grown to such extent that today about 35 percent of our total workforce is engaged in the marketing and distribution of goods and services, rather than in their production. In the last 10 years, the number employed in retailing and wholesaling (institutions that accumulate and stock assortments of goods for sale to a variety of customers) has increased by about one third, while manufacturing employment has remained relatively static.[9]

MARKETING'S ROLE IN SOCIETY—FACILITATING EXCHANGE

Our discussion of the evolution of society's economic system provides some clues about what marketing is and the role it plays in society.

Marketing is a social process involving the activities necessary to enable individuals and organizations to obtain what they need and want through exchanges with others.

Conditions necessary for exchange

Many exchanges are necessary for individuals and organizations to reap the benefits of the specialization that accompanies and facilitates economic development. But such exchanges do not happen automatically. These conditions must be met before an exchange transaction occurs:

- There must be at least two parties.
- Both parties must offer something of value (e.g., money, goods, services, an idea).
- Both parties must be aware of the existence of the other; both must be capable of communication and delivery.
- Both parties must be free to accept or reject the other's offer.
- Both parties must be willing and able to negotiate terms of exchange that they find acceptable. In other words, both parties must believe that the exchange creates benefits or value.

The conditions necessary for an exchange can be met only after the parties themselves—or some exchange specialist—have successfully performed several tasks. These include identifying potential exchange partners, developing offerings, communicating information, delivering products, and collecting payments. This is what marketing is all about. Before we take a closer look at specific marketing activities and how they are planned and implemented by marketing managers, we will discuss some terms and concepts in

---

[9] U. S. Department of Labor, Bureau of Labor Statistics, *Employment and Earnings* (Washington, D. C.: U. S. Government Printing Office, August 1986), pp. 43–53.

our definition of marketing and the conditions necessary for exchange. Specifically, let's examine the following questions:

1. Who are the *parties* involved in exchange transactions? Which organizations and people market things, and who are their customers?
2. Which *needs and wants* do parties try to satisfy through exchange, and what is the difference between the two?
3. Which *things* can be exchanged? Can exchanges involve intangible as well as tangible products?
4. How does exchange create *value*? Why is a buyer better off and more satisfied following an exchange?
5. How do potential exchange partners become a *market* for a particular good or service?

1. Who markets and who buys? The parties in an exchange

Virtually every organization and individual with a surplus of *anything* engages in marketing activities to identify, communicate, and negotiate with potential exchange partners. Of course, some are more aggressive—and perhaps more effective—in their efforts than others. When thinking of extensive marketing efforts aimed at stimulating and facilitating exchange, we think first of the activities of goods manufacturers (Chrysler, Procter & Gamble, IBM), service producers (American Express, CBS, 20th Century Fox), and large retailers (Sears, K mart, Bloomingdale's).

Museums, hospitals, theaters, universities, and other social institutions—whether for-profit or nonprofit organizations—also carry out marketing activities to attract customers, students, and donors. In the past, their marketing efforts were not very extensive or well organized. Now increasing competition, changing customer attitudes and demographics, and rising costs have caused many nonprofit organizations to look to more extensive marketing efforts to solve their problems. For example, in the mid-1970s, less than 1 percent of the nation's 7,000 hospitals had a marketing director. A decade later, the proportion had increased to about 15 percent and was growing rapidly. Exhibit 1–4 describes the activities of the Guthrie Theater, which recognized the growing importance of marketing for nonprofit organizations.

Customers

Both individuals and organizations seek out goods and services obtained through exchange transactions. **Ultimate consumers** buy goods and services for their own personal use or the use of others in their immediate household. These are called **consumer goods and services. Organizational customers** buy goods and services (1) for resale (as when a retailer buys several gross of Levi jeans or K mart buys Rubbermaid's line of kitchen utensils for resale to individual consumers); (2) as inputs to the production of other goods or

EXHIBIT   1 ♦ 4

Marketing the Guthrie Theater

The Guthrie Theater in Minneapolis is one of the largest and most respected repertory theaters in the country. The very fact that it has been a large and successful theater for more than two decades, however, gives rise to a financial problem. It is difficult for a theater like the Guthrie to attract grant monies from foundations or government agencies because those funding sources tend to concentrate on supporting small, young organizations struggling to attain audience recognition. Consequently, the Guthrie's goal is to attain 70 percent of its $8 million operating budget from ticket sales, with much of the remainder coming from individual donations. To achieve this goal, the theater must average 80 percent of capacity over some 345 performances each year. This is no small feat in a metropolitan area boasting more than 30 professional theater organizations (and many more amateur groups) serving a total population of about 2 million. Consequently, a number of years ago the Guthrie hired a director of marketing who works with three full-time staff people and many part-time volunteers. To attract customers and donations the Guthrie has developed a very sophisticated marketing program involving the following elements:

♦ Extensive market research focused both on current customers and the general public to track changing tastes and entertainment consumption patterns. Data from these studies are used to develop other parts of the theater's marketing efforts, and for input when the creative director and the theater board choose a schedule of plays for the next season.

♦ A strong advertising program utilizing a variety of broadcast and print media and an annual budget of approximately $500,000 to generate awareness of, and interest in attending, the theater's offerings.

♦ An annual direct mail campaign targeted at selected up-scale ZIP code areas and an extensive telephone campaign aimed at all past theater attendees encourage season ticket sales.

♦ Innovative pricing programs to increase attendance at off-peak performances, such as Wednesday matinees and weeknights. They offer price discounts to selected price-sensitive customer segments such as senior citizens and students for those performances.

♦ Programs to improve the distribution of the theater's offerings, such as organized theater tours for senior citizen groups and a traveling troupe of actors that presents selected plays in small communities far from the Minneapolis main stage.

Source: The Guthrie Theater Annual Report, 1983–84.

services (as when Ford buys sheet steel to be stamped into car body parts); or (3) for use in the day-to-day operations of the organization (as when a university buys paper and typewriter or computer printer ribbons). These are called **industrial goods and services.**

Individuals and organizations have different needs and wants to satisfy through exchange transactions, and they go through different decision processes when seeking exchange partners and choosing transactions. For example, consumers make many purchases on their own. Organizational purchase decisions, however, are often made or influenced by a group or team representing different functional departments such as engineering, purchasing, and finance. Also, consumer markets typically consist of many more—and more geographically dispersed—potential customers than organizational markets. Because of such differences, some marketing strategies and tactics are more appropriate and successful for consumer markets; others work better when selling to organizations.[10] Throughout this book we examine differences in the buying behavior of these two types of customers, and the marketing strategies and programs relevant for each.

2. Customer needs and wants

Needs are the basic forces that drive customers to take action and engage in exchanges. An unsatisfied **need** is a gap between a person's actual and desired states on some physical or psychological dimension. Abraham Maslow argues that consumers are motivated by a five-level need hierarchy. He believes that lower-level (physiological) needs must be satisfied before a person can try to activate higher-level needs, such as those involving self-esteem or self-actualization.[11]

Thus, we all have *basic physical needs* critical to our survival, such as food, drink, warmth, shelter, and sleep. We also have *social and emotional needs* critical to our psychological well-being, such as *security, belonging, love, esteem,* and *self-fulfillment.* Those needs that motivate the consumption behavior of individuals, however, are few and basic. They are not created by marketers or other social forces; they flow from our basic biological and psychological makeup as human beings.

Organizations also must satisfy needs to assure their survival and well-being. Shaped by the organization's strategic objectives, these needs relate to the resource inputs, capital equipment, supplies, and services necessary to meet those objectives.

Wants reflect a person's desires or preferences for specific ways of satisfying a basic need. Thus, a person wants particular products, brands, or services to satisfy an unsatisfied need. A person is thirsty and wants a Coke. A person is tired and wants a vacation in Florida. A company needs office

---

[10] One recent study suggests that differences between organizational and individual consumers account for more of the variation in the performance of a given business strategy across different firms than any other environmental or organizational variable. See Donald C. Hambrick and David Lei, "Toward an Empirical Prioritization of Contingency Variables for Business Strategy," *Academy of Management Journal* 28 (1985), pp. 763–88.

[11] Abraham H. Maslow, *Motivation and Personality,* 2nd ed. (New York: Harper & Row, 1970). Also see William Wilkie, *Consumer Behavior* (New York: John Wiley & Sons, 1986), pp. 320–24.

space and its top executives want an office at a prestigious address in midtown Manhattan.

Basic needs are relatively few; but people's many wants are shaped by social influences, their past history, and consumption experiences. Different people, then, may have very different wants to satisfy the same need. Everyone *needs* to keep warm on cold winter nights, for instance. But some people *want* electric blankets, while others prefer old-fashioned down comforters. These individual differences in wants to satisfy basic needs are very apparent in the consumption differences across cultures or social groups within a society. For example, South Sea Islanders satisfy their hunger and warmth needs by wanting far different foods and clothing than North Americans. Within our own society, upper social classes and income groups satisfy their financial security needs by investing in stocks and bonds. The lower classes opt for savings accounts and real estate.

This distinction between needs and wants helps put into perspective the charge that "marketers create needs," or that "marketers make people want things they don't need." Neither marketers nor any other single social force can create needs deriving from the biological and emotional imperatives of human nature. On the other hand, marketers—and many other social forces—influence people's wants. Indeed, a major part of a marketer's job is to develop a new product or service and then to stimulate customer wants for it by persuading people it can help them better satisfy one or more of their needs. For example, homeowners might buy a home security system to satisfy their need for personal safety.

3. Products and services—the focus of exchange

Products and services help satisfy a customer's need when they are acquired, used, or consumed. **Products** are essentially tangible physical objects (such as cars, watches, and computers) that provide a service. For example, a car provides transportation; a watch tells the time. **Services** per se are less tangible and, in addition to being provided by physical objects, can be provided by *people* (doctors, lawyers, architects), *institutions* (the Roman Catholic Church, the United Way), *places* (Disney World and the south of France), and *activities* (a contest or a stop-smoking program).

Indeed, a single consumer might consider a variety of tangible and intangible products as possible solutions to a particular need. For instance, suppose the rigors of academic life have tired you out and you want to relax. What products might satisfy your need? You might buy a new album for your stereo or purchase a tennis racket with the intention of learning a new sport (physical objects). What services might satisfy your need? You might go to a baseball game or see a play *(people)*, take a trip to Florida *(place)*, volunteer your services to the Boy Scouts *(institution)*, or read a book or go swimming *(activities)*.

EXHIBIT   1 ◆ 5
Consumers buy benefits, not products

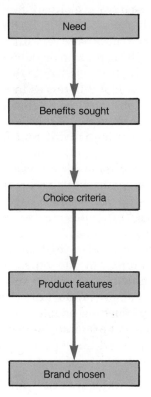

4. How exchanges create value

Customers buy benefits, not products

When people buy products to satisfy their needs, they are really buying the **benefits** they believe the products provide rather than the products per se. For instance, you buy headache relief, not aspirin. The specific benefits sought vary across customers depending on the needs to be satisfied and the situations where products are used. Because different customers seek different benefits, they use different choice criteria and attach different importance to product features when choosing models and brands within a product category. (This is diagrammed in Exhibit 1–5.) For example, a car buyer with strong needs for social acceptance and esteem might seek a socially prestigious automobile. Such a buyer would likely attach great importance to criteria relating to social image and engineering sophistication and would seek product features like a 16-valve turbocharged engine, European-road-car styling, all-leather interior, and a state-of-the-art sound system.[12]

Product benefits determine value and satisfaction

A customer's estimate of a product's benefits and capacity to satisfy specific needs and wants determines the value he or she will attach to it. Generally, after comparing alternative products and brands, consumers choose those they think provide the most value, or need-satisfying benefits, per dollar. This is why Rubbermaid constantly strives to improve the benefits its products offer to consumers. The firm can charge premium prices because the consumers perceive its products offer superior benefits.

Of course, customers' estimates of products' benefits and value are not always accurate. For example, after buying an air-conditioning installation for its premises, a company may find that the product's cost of operation is higher than expected, its response time to changes in the outside temperatures is slow, and the blower is of insufficient strength to properly heat or cool certain remote areas in the building.

A customer's ultimate *satisfaction* with a purchase, then, depends on whether the product actually lives up to expectations and delivers the anticipated benefits. This is why customer services—particularly those occurring *after* a sale, such as delivery, installation, operating instruction, and repair—are often critical for maintaining satisfied customers. Exhibit 1–6 gives an example of how General Electric attempts to make it easy for its customers to complain or make inquiries.

EXHIBIT 1 ◆ 6
GE's Answer Center

General Electric's Answer Center—located in Louisville, Kentucky—handles about 3 million calls per year and costs more than $8 million to operate. Service representatives have direct access to a data bank of some 750,000 answers pertaining to over 8,500 products and thus can "solve" 90 percent of all complaints or inquiries on the first call to the toll-free number. In 1988, about 700,000 callers were referred to GE dealers. Surveys reveal that 95 percent of all callers are satisfied with the service; and those who complain are often converted into more loyal buyers. The center generates more than twice the return that GE expected.

Source: Patricia Sellers, "How to Handle Customers' Gripes," *Fortune,* October 24, 1988, p. 88.

---

[12] We investigate consumer decision processes and the linkages among needs, benefits, and choice criteria in greater detail in Chapter 4.

Also, it is essential that companies handle customer complaints effectively. The average business never hears from 96 percent of its dissatisfied customers. This is unfortunate, for 50 percent of those who complain would do business with the company again if their complaint were handled satisfactorily—95 percent if the complaint were resolved quickly.[13] According to research on this subject, a company can make a substantial return on the money it invests in handling complaints and inquiries. Manufacturers of consumer durables such as refrigerators and washing machines, for example, realize an average return of 100 percent. For banks, it can be as high as 170 percent—even more in retailing.[14]

And, such paybacks do not even consider the losses in patronage resulting from the bad word of mouth spread by unhappy customers. It is estimated that customers are twice as likely to talk about their bad experiences as their good ones.

Sellers should focus on needs—not products

Preoccupation with products and their features may cause the firm to become vulnerable to competitors' new products that better satisfy customer *needs*. Indeed, to the best of its ability, the firm should constantly strive to find ways to *better* serve the basic need(s) it has targeted. This created obsolescence is made necessary by the appearance of new technologies and the fact that basic needs endure over long periods.[15] Thus, pharmaceutical companies continuously strive to develop better drugs to deal with high blood pressure, cholesterol, and cancer. An example of a company too occupied with its product and its features was Baldwin Locomotive. At the end of World War II, Baldwin was the world's most efficient manufacturer of locomotives. Unfortunately, it continued to focus on steam rather than on diesel fuel or electricity as a source of power and eventually went out of business.

5. Defining a market

A **market** consists of (a) *individuals and organizations who* (b) *are interested and willing* to buy a particular product to obtain benefits that will satisfy a specific need or want, and who (c) have the *resources (time, money)* to engage in such a transaction. There are situations where the market is sufficiently homogeneous that a company can practice undifferentiated mar-

---

[13] Patricia Sellers, "How to Handle Customers' Gripes," *Fortune*, October 24, 1988, p. 88.

[14] Karl Abrecht and Ron Zemke, *Service America* (Homewood, Ill.: Dow Jones-Irwin, 1985), p. 6.

[15] Theodore Levitt, *The Marketing Imagination* (New York: The Free Press, 1986), pp. 1–19.

EXHIBIT 1 ♦7

How General Foods segments the coffee market

General Foods, long the leader in coffee sales, does an excellent job of segmenting the market and featuring a variety of coffee brands designed to appeal to the unique needs of each segment. Thus, General Foods' Maxwell House is positioned as a home breakfast coffee, its Sanka as a decaffeinated coffee to be enjoyed both at home and in restaurants, and its Brim as the office market's decaffeinated product. In addition, the company produces a line of specialty coffees such as Swisse Mocha, Orange Cappuccino, and Cafe Amaretto for people who want a coffee with a unique flavor.

Source: Jagdish N. Sheth, *Winning Back Your Market* (New York: John Wiley & Sons, 1985), pp. 29–30.

keting. That is, it attempts to market a single line of products using a single marketing program. But because different people have different needs, wants, and resources, the entire population of a society is seldom a viable market for a single product or service. Also, people or organizations often seek different benefits to satisfy different needs and wants from the same type of product. (For example, one car buyer may seek social status and prestige while someone else wants economical basic transportation).

The total market for a given product category thus is often fragmented into several distinct **market segments.** Each segment contains people who are relatively homogeneous in their needs, wants, and the product benefits they seek. And, each segment seeks a different set of benefits from the same product category. (See Exhibit 1–7 for an example of how General Foods segments its coffee market.)

Much strategic marketing management involves a seller trying to determine the following points in an effort to define the market to be targeted:

a. Which customer needs and wants are currently not being well satisfied by competitive product offerings.

b. How desired benefits and choice criteria vary across potential customers and how to identify the resulting segments by demographic variables such as age, sex, lifestyles, or some other characteristics.

c. Which segments to target, and which product offerings and marketing programs appeal most to customers in those segments.

d. How to position the product to differentiate it from competitors' offerings and give the firm a sustainable competitive advantage.

Exhibit 1–8 provides an example of a company that has been uniquely successful in segmenting its market, determining what segments to target, and positioning its products.

Before discussing strategic marketing management in more detail, we need to examine the specific activities or functions that must be performed before an exchange transaction can occur between a buyer and a seller.

EXHIBIT 1 ◆ 8

Example of market targeting and positioning

> The North Face Company produced a line of backpacking and mountaineering
> equipment designed to appeal to climbers, backpackers, and occasional campers. Its line
> consisted of sleeping bags, parkas and other outdoor clothing, tents, and backpacks. The
> target market for these products consisted of a limited number of individuals who regularly
> and seriously engaged in such activities and had high expertise in terms of the equipment
> they purchased. These individuals were referred to as *technocrats* and were thought to
> influence the buying decisions of the average outdoors enthusiast.
>
> To satisfy the needs of the technocrat segment for sleeping bags, management
> reasoned that its products had to be superior to competitive products in durability and the
> optimal trade-off between warmth and weight. The quality of down used, the nylon thread
> count, the unique coil zippers, and the hand-stitching were the key points of difference.
> Further, the company followed a stringent zero-defect, quality-control program and offered
> a guarantee against any defects.

Source: Robert T. Davis, Harper W. Boyd, Jr., and Frederick E. Webster, Jr., *Marketing Management Casebook* (Homewood, Ill.: Richard D. Irwin, 1984), pp. 307–8.

Earlier we defined marketing as a "process involving the activities necessary for individuals and organizations to obtain what they need and want through exchanges with others." Decisions about how those necessary activities should be performed, and *who* performs them, constitute the basic building blocks of strategic marketing programs.

MARKETING FUNCTIONS AND INSTITUTIONS

The advantages of specialization and the economies of large scale dictate that most goods are produced in large plants, farms, or mines. These goods, however, are purchased in small quantities and consumed days or months later by thousands of different customers in different locations. For exchanges to occur between a producer and all those customers, the product, money, and information must flow back and forth across space and time. Exhibit 1–9 illustrates the flows involved in the distribution and exchange of products. Exhibit 1–10 outlines the various business functions that must be performed for such movements of goods, money, and information.

Flows and functions

Buying and selling functions are directly associated with negotiating an exchange of ownership—or the flow of title—between a seller and a prospective buyer. Buying activities include searching for, gathering information about, and evaluating alternative products, services, and suppliers; and negotiating a purchase agreement. The selling function involves identifying

EXHIBIT   1 ◆ 9
Flows necessary for exchange

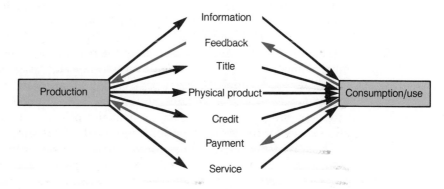

and seeking out potential buyers, determining an asking price, negotiating terms of sale, and similar activities.

Someone must ship the product from where it is produced to the locations where customers want to buy and use it, and store adequate inventories to satisfy customers' needs when they are ready to buy. The physical product flow thus requires **transportation and storage** functions associated with the physical handling and movement of goods. Rubbermaid, for example, is

EXHIBIT   1 ◆ 10
Functions/activities necessary for an exchange transaction

Flows	*Necessary functions/activities*

Title	◆ Selling
	    Identification of potential customers, negotiation
	◆ Buying
	    Identification and evaluation of suppliers, negotiation

Physical product	◆ Transportation ◆ Storage
Information	◆ Marketing communications Advertising, personal selling, sales promotion, publicity
Feedback	◆ Marketing research ◆ Environmental scanning ◆ Competitive intelligence
Credit and payment	◆ Financing Credit policies, billing, collection
Service	◆ Customer services Installation, repair, training, alterations, complaint handling

building a new distribution center in Phoenix, Arizona, to better serve its western markets.

Before an exchange can occur between two parties, each must have some information about the other. They must each know the other exists, what they have to offer, and what they are likely to want in return. Customers seldom have perfect information about the marketplace—and therefore they must somehow obtain it. This information flow to potential customers largely occurs through the **marketing communications** activities of advertising, personal selling, and sales promotion. Thus, Rubbermaid supports its products with network TV commercials and provides its retailers generous allowances for in-store promotions and local advertising.

The ultimate success of a producer depends on its ability to determine the needs, desired benefits, and choice criteria of potential customers in one or more market segments—and to then design product offerings and marketing programs that meet their wants. Thus, a seller must not only learn about its customers but also other aspects of the market environment—competitors' actions, social trends, and legal developments. Sellers obtain this feedback flow of information through a variety of **marketing research, environmental scanning,** *and* **competitive intelligence** activities. Rubbermaid spends a great deal of money on consumer research to determine customer satisfaction with its products and reaction to new-product concepts.

Because most transactions in our economy involve the exchange of goods or services for money rather than barter, financial flows—the extension of credit and the collection of payments—are also necessary. Sellers' **financial** activities stimulate demand when customers are unable or unwilling to pay the entire purchase price in one lump sum. They also facilitate the storage function by helping wholesalers or retailers finance inventories until the goods can be sold.

Finally, potential customers are often reluctant to finalize an exchange without some assurance that they will receive full value for their money. Therefore, many sellers provide **customer service** activities to reduce the risk customers must assume when making purchases. Warranties (Chrysler's 7 years or 70,000 miles) and return policies (Remington's "shaves as smooth as a blade or your money back") reduce risks, while alterations (men's suits), installation (new boilers), training (new commercial aircraft), and repair (major appliances) ensure that customers remain satisfied for the life of the product.

Who does what?—the system of marketing institutions

One of the few eternal truths in marketing is that "you can eliminate the middlemen, but you can't eliminate their functions." In other words, for exchanges of goods and services to take place, all of the preceding functions and activities must be performed by *someone*. The question is, who?

The buying function is always performed by the customer, of course. In some cases, the customer also undertakes many of the other exchange activities. This applies to both buyers of consumer (household) and industrial products. An example of the former is the consumer who shops at a Sam's Wholesale Club unit (a division of Wal-Mart), which charges an annual membership fee and restricts patronage to good credit risks. Such units are typically located outside of or near the city limits and feature a variety of both large and small consumer durables, TVs, tires, furniture (both office and home), clothing, jewelry and watches, and commercial packs of food, including some meats. Terms are cash, including checks, and carry. Customers even have to bag their purchases.

A Sam's customer pays a lower price (Sam's operates on a gross margin of only 8 to 10 percent) than at competing outlets. But the consumer must pay the out-of-pocket costs of performing a number of marketing activities, such as getting the products home and storing the excess product in the commercial-size pack.

There are also the opportunity costs of the individual's time. **Opportunity costs** are the financial or psychological costs of having to forgo other activities to spend the time completing exchange transactions. For example, if Sam's customer preferred to stay home and do something else (say, watch football on TV), then the opportunity costs of driving across town to shop at Sam's might be high.

In recent years, the time pressures on households where both spouses work outside the home have increased the opportunity costs of performing many marketing activities.[16] Increasingly, such consumers are willing to pay higher prices to have some firms in the marketing system perform more exchange activities. On the other hand, there are times when consumers enjoy the shopping process. When this occurs, the consumers do not experience any opportunity costs associated with shopping. In fact, they may gain psychological benefits (even when marketing activities do not result in a purchase transaction).

Marketing activities may also be performed by institutional buyers, as when an automotive repair shop buys a spare part from a cash-and-carry automotive parts wholesaler. The repair shop finances its own purchase and transports the part in its own truck.

In some cases, producers distribute goods or services directly to final customers, bypassing other wholesale or retail middlemen. Producers undertake marketing and distribution activities by storing large inventories, hiring an extensive company salesforce, or relying on catalogs or other

---

[16] Valarie A. Zeithaml, "The New Demographics and Market Fragmentation," *Journal of Marketing* 49 (Summer 1985), pp. 64–75; Valarie A. Zeithaml and Leonard Berry, "The Time Consciousness of Supermarket Shoppers," Working Paper (College Station: Texas A&M University, 1986).

direct-marketing methods to contact customers and generate sales. They also fund advertising and promotional programs, finance customers' purchases, arrange for delivery, and provide post-sale services. Avon's marketing of cosmetics through thousands of part-time door-to-door sales representatives and IBM's marketing of mainframes are both good examples of such direct, vertically integrated distribution systems. Such systems are most likely to be used:

♦ By makers of industrial goods with few potential customers and large average orders.
♦ When unique product characteristics or requirements make it difficult for a manufacturer to find outside wholesalers or retailers capable of performing necessary functions (e.g., sales engineering for a high-tech product).
♦ Where a producer finds it strategically important to maintain tight control over marketing and distribution activities.[17]

Except for these situations, most goods in our economy are distributed through multiple institutions or "middlemen" commonly referred to as **marketing channels** or **channels of distribution.** Each institution specializes in only a part of the functions and activities necessary to facilitate transactions with potential customers. We will examine these institutions in more detail in Chapter 13. Suffice for now to say that marketing intermediaries fit into one of the following categories:

♦ **Merchant wholesalers** take title to the goods they sell and sell primarily to other resellers (retailers), industrial, and commercial customers rather than to individual consumers.
♦ **Agent middlemen,** such as manufacturers' representatives and brokers, also sell to other resellers and industrial or commercial customers, but they do not take title to the goods they sell. They usually specialize in the selling function and represent client manufacturers on a commission basis.
♦ **Retailers** sell goods and services directly to final consumers for their personal, nonbusiness use.
♦ **Facilitating agencies,** such as advertising agencies, marketing research firms, collection agencies, and railroads, specialize in one or more marketing functions on a fee-for-service basis to help their clients perform those functions more effectively and efficiently.

Costs and benefits of marketing functions

The final selling price of the product reflects the costs of performing the activities necessary for exchange transactions. Those costs vary widely across different products and customers. They account for a relatively high

---

[17] Robert W. Ruekert, Orville C. Walker, Jr., and Kenneth J. Roering, "The Organization of Marketing Activities: A Contingency Theory of Structure and Performance," *Journal of Marketing* 49 (Winter 1985), pp. 13–25.

proportion of the price of frequently purchased consumer package goods such as cereals and cosmetics. Extensive transportation, storage, and promotion activities facilitate the millions of consumer purchases that occur every year. On average, roughly 50 percent of the retail price of such products is made up of marketing and distribution costs; one half represents retailer margins and the other, the marketing expenses of the manufacturer and wholesale middlemen.[18] On the other hand, marketing costs for non-technical industrial goods, such as sheet steel or basic chemicals, are much lower because they are sold in large quantities directly to a small number of regular customers.

Though both individual and organizational customers pay for the marketing activities of manufacturers and their middlemen, they are still usually better off than if they were to undertake all the functions themselves. This is true for two reasons: First, the purchasing, storage, promotion, and selling activities of wholesalers and retailers allow customers to buy a wide variety of goods from a single source in one transaction, thereby increasing **transactional efficiency**. For example, a consumer may buy a week's groceries on a single trip to a supermarket.

A second benefit of an extensive marketing system is that specialization of labor and economies of scale lead to **functional efficiency.** Manufacturers and their agents can perform the exchange activities more cheaply than individual customers. A railroad, for instance, can ship a load of new tires from a plant in Akron to a wholesaler in Tucson more cheaply than an individual consumer in Arizona could transport them in the family station wagon.

From the customer's viewpoint, then, the increased transactional and functional efficiency of exchange produced by members of the marketing system increases the value—the **utility/price** relationship—of goods and services. A product has greater utility for a potential customer when it can be purchased with a minimum of risk and shopping time **(possession utility),** at a convenient location **(place utility),** and at the time the customer is ready to use the product **(time utility).**

The efficiencies and utilities produced by a well-developed marketing and distribution system become obvious when considering what life would be like without it. For example, even though the Soviet government is currently pressing for economic reforms, Russian consumers still expend an enormous amount of time and effort in locating and purchasing desired goods. The comments of a *New York Times* correspondent quoted in Exhibit 1–11 illustrate the impact of the limited Soviet marketing system's reduced

---

[18] William J. Stanton, *Fundamentals of Marketing*, 6th ed. (New York: McGraw-Hill, 1987), p. 7.

EXHIBIT 1 ♦ 11

Some disadvantages of the Soviet marketing system

> Americans groan about the continual bombardment of their senses by ads and
> commercials on television and in their press. But they might reconsider if exposed for a
> while to the consumer blackout in Russia. Lack of the most basic consumer information is
> one of the most enervating and crippling facets of Russian life. It is the main reason why
> Russian sidewalks are constantly populated by shoppers earnestly plodding from store to
> store with their string bags and briefcases, engaged in an unending hit-or-miss lottery,
> hoping to stumble onto a find or to bump into some strange woman on the street and ask
> her where she got those good-looking oranges. . . . The shopper looking for choice meat
> or a stylish dress has no handy Yellow Pages to let her "fingers do the walking" nor the
> kind of specific daily supermarket or department store ads that in the West would tip her
> off where to shop. . . . Russians either get inside tips from well-placed friends or do
> without.

Source: Hedrick Smith, *The Russians* (New York: Ballantine Books, 1976), pp. 469–70. Copyright Times Books, a Division
of Random House, Inc.

choices and higher opportunity costs for consumers. This situation is little
changed today.

MARKETING MANAGEMENT

The marketing manager's role

What does the preceding discussion of flows and functions imply for the
development and management of marketing programs? Many activities facilitating customer purchases of a product are often contracted out to independent middlemen or agencies. The producer's managers have no formal
authority over these outsiders. Even those marketing and distribution-
related activities performed by the manufacturer are seldom all within the
domain of the marketing department or under the authority of a marketing
executive. At Pillsbury, for instance, a distribution department manages
transportation and storage activities while credit and accounts receivable
policies are handled by the financial controller's office. In reality, marketing
is—or should be—everybody's business, no matter what one's title or position in the organizational hierarchy.

Regardless of who has formal responsibility for them, however, exchange-
facilitating activities are important in determining the ultimate success or
failure of a product in the marketplace. By tailoring such activities to the
needs of a particular target segment, the firm can enhance a product's value
or utility to its customers. Also, by performing critical marketing activities
more effectively than anyone else, the firm can achieve a competitive advan-

tage.[19] For example, Crown Cork & Seal, a major producer of metal cans and crowns in the United States, is not limited to competing solely on the basis of product design, quality, or price. It also competes by maintaining close ties with its customers and by providing technical assistance at the customer's plant. From the top down, the organization is schooled to think the customer is always right.[20]

Producers of industrial goods also can compete by offering faster delivery (transportation function), a larger assortment (storage function), automatic order entry (selling and communications functions), more liberal credit terms and payment schedules (financing function), or more expert technical assistance or more liberal return policies (service functions).

Someone within the firm should be responsible for (a) evaluating the needs, wants, and purchasing patterns of a customer segment; (b) developing an integrated plan to facilitate purchase transactions by that segment, (c) designing a marketing channel system to carry out those activities, and (d) coordinating and monitoring the effectiveness of those activities over time. In many firms, marketing executives have these planning and coordinating responsibilities, even though actual performance falls outside the scope of their authority.

A definition of marketing management

Our discussion suggests that **marketing management** occurs whenever one party to an exchange transaction engages in planning, coordinating, implementing, and controlling the activities to facilitate an exchange. Thus

> **Marketing management** is the process of analyzing, planning, implementing, coordinating, and controlling programs involving the conception, pricing, promotion, and distribution of products, services, and ideas designed to create and maintain beneficial exchanges with target markets for the purpose of achieving organizational objectives.[21]

This definition describes the *content* of marketing management without fully capturing the exciting, dynamic nature of marketing as it is actually practiced in a company such as Rubbermaid. Exhibit 1–12 lists the activities

---

[19] The marketing and distribution activities that facilitate exchange are very consistent with the activities in a business's "Value Chain." Michael Porter argues outbound logistics, marketing and sales, and service are the basic building blocks for achieving and sustaining a competitive advantage. See Michael E. Porter, *Competitive Advantage* (New York: Free Press, 1985), chap. 2.

[20] C. Roland Christensen, Kenneth R. Andrews, Joseph L. Bower, Richard G. Hamermesh, and Michael E. Porter, *Business Policy: Text and Cases* (Homewood, Ill.: Richard D. Irwin, 1987), p. 184.

[21] For another—though very similar—definition, see "American Marketing Association Board Approves New Marketing Definition," *Marketing News*, March 1, 1985, p. 1.

EXHIBIT 1 ♦ 12

The marketing management process

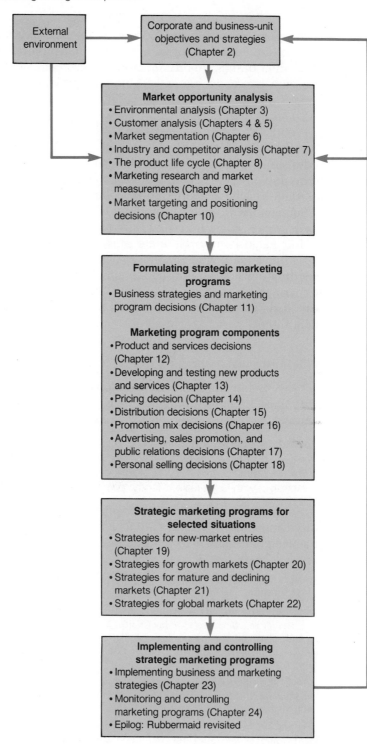

in the marketing management process; the remainder of this chapter briefly describes them. The diagram of marketing management activities in Exhibit 1–12 also serves as the organizational framework for the rest of this book.

THE MARKETING MANAGEMENT PROCESS

Corporate, business-unit, and marketing strategies

Most firms—particularly larger corporations with multiple divisions or business units—develop a hierarchy of interdependent strategies. Each strategy is formulated at different levels within the organization and deals with different sets of issues. For example, Rubbermaid's decision to seek growth through product improvements and new-product development and its acquiring of small firms that can benefit from its marketing and distribution strengths reflect its **corporate strategy.** This strategy provides direction on the company's mission, the businesses it should be in, and its growth policies. Charging premium prices for its housewares while justifying those prices with high product quality, an extensive line, and heavy promotion reflects a **business-level strategy,** which addresses the way the firm competes in the housewares industry. Finally, interrelated functional decisions about segments to target, designs and colors to include in the product line, promotions, prices, and retailer servicing all reflect Rubbermaid's **marketing strategy.** It is the plan for effectively pursuing the company's objectives within specific segments of the housewares market.

This suggests that marketing strategies and programs are not created in a vacuum. Instead, the marketing objectives and strategy for a particular product-market entry must be consistent with the direction and resources provided by the firm's corporate and business-unit strategies. And there should be a good fit—or internal consistency—among the various elements of the three levels of strategy. On the other hand, a major part of the marketing manager's job is to monitor and analyze customers' needs and wants and emerging opportunities and threats posed by competitors and trends in the external environment. Marketers thus often play a major role in providing inputs to—and influencing the development of—corporate and business strategies.[22] Chapter 2 describes in more detail the components of corporate and business strategies, and the roles that marketers play in shaping the strategic direction of their organizations and business units.

---

[22] Empirical support for this contention is provided by George S. Yip, *The Role of Strategic Planning in Consumer-Marketing Businesses*, Report 84–103 (Cambridge, Mass.: The Marketing Science Institute, 1984).

Market opportunity analysis

A major factor in the success or failure of strategies at all three levels is whether the strategy elements are consistent with the realities of the firm's external environment. Thus, the first step in developing a strategic marketing plan is to monitor and analyze the opportunities and threats posed by factors outside of the organization. This is an ongoing responsibility for marketing managers.

Environmental analysis

To understand potential opportunities and threats over the long term, marketers must first monitor and analyze broad trends in the economic and social environment. These include demographic, economic, technological, political/legal, and social/cultural developments. For example, Rubbermaid constantly monitors and attempts to forecast future oil prices because all of its products are made from petroleum-based plastics. Similarly, the early identification of broad social trends, such as the increase in small dwellings, is critical for helping the firm perceive new-product opportunities. Chapter 3 identifies a number of macro-environmental factors marketing managers should pay attention to. It discusses methods for monitoring, analyzing, and perhaps even influencing the impact of those factors on the future performance of their product-market entries.

Customer analysis and market segmentation

The primary purpose of marketing activities is to facilitate and encourage exchange transactions with potential customers. One of a marketing manager's major responsibilities, then, is to analyze the motivations and behavior of present and potential customers. What are their needs and wants? How do those needs and wants affect the product benefits they seek and the criteria they use in choosing products and brands? Where do they shop? How are they likely to react to specific price, promotion, and service policies? To answer such questions, a marketing manager must have some notion of the mental processes customers go through when making purchase decisions, and of the psychological and social factors that influence those processes. Chapter 4 thus discusses the processes and influences that shape consumers' buying behavior. Because some aspects of the purchase process differ for organizations, Chapter 5 examines the buying behavior of institutional customers.

Not all customers with the same needs seek the same products or services to satisfy those needs, however. Their purchase decisions may be influenced by different circumstances and variables. Similarly, customers purchasing the same product may be motivated by different needs, seek different benefits, and use different choice criteria. Rubbermaid realizes, for instance, that price-sensitive consumers are unlikely to buy the company's products because of its premium-price policy. Marketing managers must determine whether there are different segments of potential customers for their products and marketing programs and how those segments might best be defined, described, and appealed to. Chapter 6, therefore, examines dimensions and analytical techniques that can identify and define market segments in both consumer and organizational markets.

Industry and competitor analysis

Even the most appealing and well-designed marketing program has difficulty reaching its sales, market share, and profitability objectives when competitors offer target customers something even better. An important step, then, is to examine the strengths and weaknesses of existing and potential competitors. How might those competitors respond to the dynamics of the environment and to the firm's marketing actions in the future? This industry and competitor analysis is the subject of Chapter 7.

Of course, the competitive environment of an industry is not static, but can change dramatically over time. Rubbermaid's strategy of launching about 100 new products annually and constantly updating its mature products has enabled it to cope with a slow growth market that is constantly under attack from some 150 competitors and to generate substantial profits by charging premium prices. Chapter 8 explores the competitive dynamics of an industry, particularly emphasizing how competition and customers' buying patterns are likely to change as the industry or product-market moves through various life-cycle stages.

Market measurements and marketing research

Marketing managers must obtain objective information about potential customers and the strengths and weaknesses of competitors. Rubbermaid spends millions on marketing research, much of which goes for product development and new designs. The company never test markets for fear of tipping off its competitors. Instead, it conducts user panels, brand awareness studies, and other such research.

If managers are to make informed decisions, research information must be converted into estimates of the sales volume and profit the firm might reasonably expect a particular marketing program to generate within a given market segment. Chapter 9 discusses techniques and methods for collecting and analyzing market research information and for measuring the market potential and likely sales volumes of particular market segments. The specific research methods that marketing managers use to make decisions about elements of a marketing program—such as what price to charge or which advertising media to use—will be examined in more detail in chapters dealing with each of those program decisions.

Market targeting and competitive positioning

After examining customer needs, alternative market segments, and competitive strengths and weaknesses, the manager must decide which segments represent attractive and viable opportunities, and which of those opportunities the firm can satisfy in a way that gives it a sustainable advantage over potential competitors. In other words, the manager must select a target market segment in which to focus a strategic marketing program. Chapter 10 examines some of the considerations in selecting target markets and choosing the competitive positioning for a product within those markets.

Formulating strategic marketing programs

Designing an effective strategic marketing program for a product-market entry involves three interrelated sets of decisions:

1. The manager must set specific objectives to be accomplished within the target market, such as sales volume, market share, and profitability goals. Those objectives must be consistent with the firm's corporate and business-unit strategic objectives, yet specific enough to enable management to monitor and evaluate the product-market entry's performance over time.
2. The manager must decide on an overall marketing strategy to appeal to customers—and to gain a competitive advantage—in the target market. The strategy must be consistent with the firm's capabilities, its corporate and business-unit strategies, and the product-market objectives.
3. The manager must then make decisions about each element of the tactical marketing program used to carry out the strategy. These decisions must be internally consistent and integrated across all elements of the marketing program.

Specifying marketing objectives and strategies

The first step in developing strategic marketing programs is to specify the objectives to be pursued and the overall marketing strategy to be used in each product-market. However, these are partly dictated by corporate and business-unit objectives, strategies, and resource deployments. At Rubbermaid, for instance, the sales and profit objectives for a particular product such as a dish drainer—and the price, product quality, and promotional expenditures associated with it—are all influenced by the firm's goals of 15 percent annual volume and earnings growth and by its high price–high quality competitive strategy. Chapter 11 examines generic business-level competitive strategies and the way they affect decisions about the marketing objectives and programs for product-market entries within the business unit.

Marketing program components

Dozens of specific tactical decisions must be made in designing a strategic marketing program for a product-market entry. These decisions fall into four categories of major marketing variables that a manager has some ability to

EXHIBIT 1 ◆13

Decisions within the four elements of the marketing mix

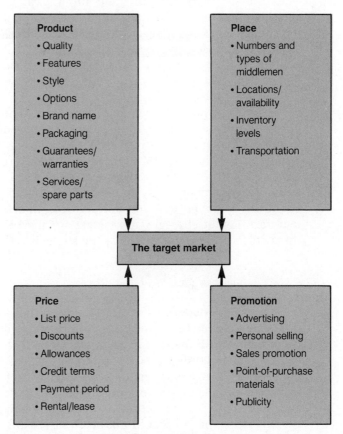

control over the short term. Often called the 4 Ps, the "controllable" elements of a marketing program are the **product offering** (including the breadth of the product line, quality levels, and customer services); **price; promotion** (advertising, sales promotion, and salesforce decisions); and **place** (or distribution). Because decisions about each element should be consistent and integrated with decisions concerning the other three, the four components are often referred to as the marketing mix.

The marketing mix is the combination of controllable marketing variables that a manager uses to carry out a marketing strategy in pursuit of the firm's objectives in a given target market.

Exhibit 1–13 outlines some of the decisions that must be made within each of the four elements of the marketing mix. Chapters 12 through 18 discuss in more detail the various methods and criteria for making decisions about each of these program components.

Formulating strategic marketing programs for specific situations

The strategic marketing program for a particular product-market entry should reflect market demand and the competitive situation within the target market. As demand and competitive conditions change over time, the marketing strategy should also be adjusted. At Rubbermaid, for instance, advertising and promotion expenditures focus on building awareness and demand for new products. As these products become more mature, they receive less promotional support.

Demand and competitive conditions tend to change as product-markets grow and mature. Chapter 19 discusses strategies for entering new product-markets; Chapter 20 examines strategies appropriate for building or maintaining a product's share of a growing market. And Chapter 21 considers the strategies a firm might adopt in mature or declining product-markets. Finally, many companies try to expand by pursuing target markets in other countries. However, cultural and political differences across nations often require different strategic approaches for marketing success. Chapter 22, therefore, discusses global marketing strategies.

Implementation and control of the marketing program

A final critical determinant of a strategy's success is the firm's ability to implement it effectively. And this, in turn, depends on whether the strategy is consistent with the resources, organizational structure, coordination and control systems, and the skills and experience of company personnel.[23] In other words, managers must design a strategy to fit the company's existing resources, competencies, and procedures—or try to construct new structures and systems to fit the chosen strategy. Rubbermaid's emphasis on new-product development would not be so successful, for example, without its heavy expenditures for marketing research and an organizational structure encouraging communication and cooperation across functional areas throughout the development process. Chapter 23 discusses the structural variables, planning and coordination processes, and personnel and corporate culture characteristics related to the successful implementation of marketing strategies.

The final tasks in the marketing management process are determining whether the strategic marketing program is meeting objectives and adjusting the program when performance is disappointing. This evaluation and con-

---

[23] N. Venkatraman and John C. Camillus, "Exploring the Concept of 'Fit' in Strategic Management," *Academy of Management Review* 9 (1984), pp. 513–25.

trol process provides feedback to managers and serves as a basis for a market opportunity analysis in the next planning period. Chapter 24 examines ways to evaluate marketing performance and develop contingency plans when things go wrong.

SUMMARY

As a society develops economically, increasing specialization and division of labor necessitates exchanges of goods and services among its members. The purpose of marketing is to facilitate those exchanges. This social process involves activities enabling individuals and organizations to obtain what they need and want through exchanges with others.

Every organization or individual with a surplus of anything engages in marketing activities aimed at identifying, communicating, and negotiating with potential exchange partners. Thus, service and nonprofit organizations engage in marketing, as do manufacturing firms.

Both ultimate consumers and organizational customers seek out goods and services through exchange transactions. The purchases of both customers are motivated by their needs and wants. An unsatisfied need is a gap between a person's actual and desired state of being on some physical or psychological dimension. Wants reflect a person's desires or preferences for specific ways to satisfy a basic need.

Anything that satisfies a customer's need when it is acquired, used, or consumed is defined as a product. Thus, products include physical objects, services, places, organizations, people, activities, and ideas. When people buy products to satisfy their needs, they are really buying the benefits they believe products can provide. The degree to which the product actually delivers the expected benefits, in turn, helps determine the customer's ultimate satisfaction with the purchase.

Most goods and services are produced in large quantities but consumed later in small amounts by many customers in different locations. Therefore, the physical product, informa-

tion, and money must flow back and forth across space and time for exchanges to occur. Someone must perform marketing functions—such as transportation, storage, buying, selling, marketing communications, marketing research, financial, and customer service activities—to facilitate these flows. These marketing activities may be performed by the customer, but they are usually performed by the producer with the aid of a variety of specialist institutions, such as retailers, merchant wholesalers, agent middlemen, and/or facilitating agencies, who make up the distribution channel for a product. Customers pay for this specialization of marketing activities through higher prices. On the other hand, the marketing system increases transactional and functional efficiencies and enhances the time, place, and possession utilities the customer obtains from a transaction.

Marketing management is the process of analyzing, planning, implementing, coordinating, and controlling programs for the conception, pricing, promotion, and distribution of products, services, and ideas designed to create and maintain beneficial exchanges with target markets. Thus, the marketing management process involves the following steps:

1. Monitor and evaluate potential threats and opportunities in the external environment, including those shaped by market, competitive, social, economic and political/legal forces.

2. Assist in the development of corporate and business-unit strategies.

3. Develop marketing objectives and a strategic marketing program—including specification of the controllable components of

product, price, promotion, and place (distribution)—for a given product-market entry. These must fit the constraints of corporate and business-level strategies.

4. Implement, monitor, and control the strategic marketing program over time, making adjustments when performance falls short of objectives.

These steps in the marketing management process serve as the framework for the organization of the remainder of this book.

QUESTIONS

1. What is the difference between a customer's *need* and a customer's *want*? Which customer's wants (or benefits) might be met by each of the following products?

   a. Raisin Bran cereal

   b. A Rolex watch

   c. A physical checkup at the Mayo Clinic

   d. An IBM mainframe

2. You have just made a $100 contribution to the United Way. Was this an *exchange* transaction? If so, what was exchanged? Which need(s) or want(s) did you satisfy by making your contribution? Which marketing activities do managers of the United Way engage in to facilitate such transactions?

3. An urban family goes for a drive in the country on a beautiful autumn day. Along the way they stop at a roadside stand and purchase a bushel of apples. Which marketing *flows* had to occur for this transaction to take place? Which marketing *functions* were involved? In this example, who performed each of the necessary functions?

4. A second family purchased a bag of apples from their local supermarket. Who performed each of the necessary marketing functions involved in this transaction?

5. The family in question 4 paid a higher price per pound for their apples than the family in question 3. Does the purchase price reflect the total costs incurred by the two families in obtaining their apples? Why or why not? Did the family in 4 gain any additional *utilities* by purchasing their apples in a supermarket?

6. Using the Guthrie Theater as a specific example, how do you explain the recent increased interest in—and allocation of resources to—marketing activities by not-for-profit institutions? Which environmental changes or trends have helped stimulate this interest?

7. Some members of Guthrie Theater's management and staff expressed concerns about the increased customer orientation and attention to marketing activities that have occurred in recent years. What are some of those concerns? As a member of the theater's board of directors, how would you respond to those concerns? Which counterarguments would you make? Which actions would you recommend to minimize possible conflicts?

8. A small urban college is considering developing an evening adult education program. They have hired you as a marketing consultant. Your first task is to determine whether there is a viable *market opportunity* for such a program in the area. Without going into great detail about how you would obtain the necesssary information, describe the various factors or trends that you would examine in evaluating the potential for such a program.

9. Assuming that the college decides to go ahead with the adult education program described in question 8, which major decisions will have to be made concerning each component of the *marketing mix* as you develop a marketing plan to attract students to the program?

Chapter ◇2◇

The strategic role of marketing

THE GREAT COOKIE WAR

In 1981 retail sales of ready-to-eat pack-aged cookies in the United States amounted to about $2.5 billion.[1] Sitting at the top of this mound of cookie sales was Nabisco's biscuit group, with a 35 percent share of the national packaged cookie business. The biscuit group earned about $215 million in operating profits on sales of $1.4 billion in 1981, making it the largest U.S. business unit in the $5.8 billion-a-year Nabisco Brands Corporation.

Nabisco's strategy

During the late 1970s and early 1980s Nabisco's executives viewed the cookie business as a mature industry. The total tonnage of cookies sold did not grow significantly during that period. Most cookies were purchased by mothers for their children; and a declining birth rate meant there would be fewer kids to eat cookies—at least until the 1990s. The company's market research indi-cated that cookie-buying mothers wanted a wide variety and low prices. Nabisco offered a broad product line with good price-value compared to competitors. It could do this because its large market share helped the company achieve economies of scale and rela-tively low production costs.

Its well-established position enabled Nabisco to spend relatively little on consumer advertising and promotion: only about $12 million in 1981, just a little over 1 percent of sales. Nabisco's promotional efforts focused on quantity discounts and special offers to retailers to encourage them to devote more shelf and display space to the company's cookies. These efforts were imple-mented and supported by 3,000 com-pany salespeople, who called directly on retailers.

Grandma—What big teeth you have!

In May 1982, the Frito-Lay division of PepsiCo introduced Grandma's cookies into test market in Kansas City. The

---

[1] Based on a variety of sources: Ann M. Mor-rison, "Cookies Are Frito-Lay's New Bag," *Fortune*, August 9, 1982, pp. 64–67; Al Urbanski, "On with the $2.1 Billion Cookie War," *Sales & Marketing Management*, June 6, 1983, pp. 37–40; "The Monster that Looms over Cookie Makers," *Business Week*, August 8, 1983, pp. 89–92; "Re-warding the Victors of the Cookie Wars," *Business Week*, June 18, 1984, pp. 27–31; "How the Cookie Crumbles," *Marketing and Media Decisions*, August 1984, pp. 54–56, 114–18; Matthew Heller, "The Great Cookie War," *Madison Avenue*, January 1985, pp. 101–4; "Why Nabisco and Reynolds Were Made for Each Other," *Business Week*, June 17, 1985, pp. 34–35; Laurie Freeman, "P&G's Duncan Hines Tackles Grandma's," *Advertising Age*, December 16, 1985, p. 3; "Pepsi's Marketing Magic: Nobody Does It Better," *Business Week*, February 10, 1986, pp. 52–57; and George Lazarus, "The Cookie Crumbles at P&G," *Adweek*, March 17, 1986, p. 28.

continued

Frito folks saw ready-to-eat cookies as an attractive growth opportunity and concluded that aggressive consumer promotion could stimulate cookie sales and enable them to capture a substantial market share. They also felt that Nabisco had ignored a large potential market: adults who might buy high-quality cookies for themselves. This perception was reinforced by the fact that in-store bakeries and specialty cookie stores—like David's and Mrs. Field's—had begun to proliferate during the late 1970s. Further, market surveys revealed that many shoppers considered the available brands of packaged cookies too hard, too dry, and a poor value.

To tap the adult market, Frito-Lay tried to develop softer, moister cookies in more sophisticated flavors than the competition. The firm's efforts to produce such cookies were a disaster, however, so the company acquired Grandma's, of Beaverton, Oregon, which mass-produced soft, moist cookies. With Grandma's help the company was able to produce a line of 16 varieties that met its quality standards.

Grandma's cookies had a shelf life of from two to three months compared to about six months for competing brands. But this was not a major problem for Frito-Lay, which had one of the world's largest store-door distribution systems. Nearly 10,000 route salespeople delivered products to each store from three to eight times per week, stocked shelves, maintained displays, and took back whatever went stale. The salesforce was paid largely by commissions (10 percent of sales). The company believed it could use the same distribution system and salesforce for its new cookies.

The bulk of Grandma's promotional budget was aimed at the consumer. In addition to a heavy schedule of TV and print ads, the company distributed price-off coupons of up to 35 cents per package. Frito-Lay budgeted about $70 million for promotion during the first year, nearly double the total promotional expenditures for the entire cookie industry.

Frito-Lay invested another $70 million in production facilities, but Nabisco had lower costs because of greater economies of scale and integrated manufacturing operations. These cost disadvantages, plus the large promotion budget, forced Grandma's to price its cookies 20 percent to 25 percent higher than competing brands. The firm's managers felt this price differential was justified by their product's superior quality.

Grandma's performance in the Kansas City test market exceeded all expectations. The company captured a 20 percent share of total ready-to-eat cookie sales in Kansas City. Everything was bright and sunny in Grandma's kitchen—until January 1983 when the biggest potential cookie monster of them all—Procter & Gamble—turned up the heat.

continued

Duncan Hines—Not just cake mixes any more

Procter & Gamble had been working to develop a soft and moist cookie since 1979. Like Frito-Lay, P&G believed that cookies were underpromoted and that adults represented a lucrative untapped market. In addition, P&G executives believed their Duncan Hines brand, the market leader in the cake and cookie mix business, would be familiar to cookie consumers. Also like Frito-Lay, P&G had no experience in distributing cookies. To secure shelf space, it provided substantial introductory discounts. Unlike Nabisco and Frito-Lay, however, P&G distributed its cookies through grocery chain warehouses. These actions successfully gained retail distribution for the new cookie brand. Retailers allocated 8 to 12 feet of their cookie shelf space to Duncan Hines cookies by shrinking the space available for everyone else.

P&G also provided strong consumer promotional support. In the first weeks of the market test, it distributed free trial-size packages of Duncan Hines cookies to nearly 300,000 households in the Kansas City area, plus coupons offering as much as 35 cents off per package. P&G also reduced their list price by 30 cents. This promotional effort was backed by heavy TV advertising. As the product was rolled out into national distribution, P&G intended to use its financial strength to outmuscle the competition through advertising and promotion with a $100 million budget.

Competitive responses

Nabisco's managers quickly realized that they needed a new marketing strategy, including a new line of moist and chewy cookies. The firm formed a development team, headed by the company's president and including top marketing, R&D, and production executives, to coordinate a competitive response. The team quickly reformulated some of the company's old stand-bys—including an improved version of Chips Ahoy with twice as many chocolate chips.

The Nabisco team's most impressive accomplishment, though, was to develop and introduce an entirely new 15-variety line of crispy-chewy cookies into test markets a little more than a year after Grandma's cookies appeared in Kansas City. The new line was labeled Almost Home to reflect its positioning as cookies that taste almost as good as homemade. The introductory advertising campaign billed the cookies as "the moistest, chewiest, most perfectly baked cookies the world has ever tasted . . . well, almost."

The Almost Home line was backed with a consumer advertising and promotion budget that matched or exceeded those of Grandma's and Duncan Hines. Nabisco focused on retailers in

continued

an attempt to win back valuable shelf space. It offered retailers a discount on each case of Almost Home cookies during the introductory period. And it offered an additional 10 percent discount on *any other cookie or cracker promoted by Nabisco* to any retailer who would give Almost Home four feet of shelf space. Given the popularity of such Nabisco brands as Oreos, Fig Newtons, and Premium Saltines, virtually no retailers turned down the offer.

Keebler, the number two cookie firm with a 12 percent market share, refused to roll over and play dead when Frito-Lay and P&G elbowed their way into the business. It developed its own line of soft, moist cookies. But its new Soft Batch line did not reach test markets until April 1984.

Third-place Sunshine Biscuits, with an 8 percent market share, pursued a different strategy by deciding to steal a larger share of traditional hard-cookie buyers while no one was looking. To attract a larger share of traditional cookie customers, Sunshine downsized nine of its sandwich-type cookie brands and repriced them to sell for under a dollar a package.

Winners and losers

By early 1986 total retail sales of ready-to-eat cookies had grown by about $500 million as a result of the new products and heavier promotion. But the market shares held by major competitors were virtually the same as in 1981! Nabisco continued to lead with 30 to 40 percent

of total volume, including about one third of all soft-and-chewy volume accounted for by its Almost Home line. Keebler remained in second place with a share of about 14 percent; Sunshine held third with about 7 percent.

What happened to the big guys? Although P&G accounted for about 30 percent of soft cookie sales, its total market share amounted to only about 4 percent. And Grandma's fared even worse. The Frito-Lay brand clung to 2 percent of the market; but virtually all of its sales resulted from single-serving packages sold through vending machines and at checkout counters—a market segment that Grandma's had dominated before it was acquired by Frito-Lay.

One reason for the disappointing performance of Grandma's and Duncan Hines is that their managers overestimated the volume potential of soft, moist cookies. Retail sales peaked at about $400 million in 1984 and then declined to an estimated $275 million in 1986. Paradoxically, all the hoopla stimulated demand for the traditional ready-to-eat brands by some 15 percent.

Nabisco

Some critics contend that if Nabisco had been more aggressive at developing new products and promoting cookies it may have avoided the cookie war. Once Grandma's and Duncan Hines appeared in Kansas City, though, Nabisco's response was swift and aggressive. The firm used heavy consumer promotion

continued

concluded

to prop up demand for hard cookies while relying on trade deals and long-standing relationships with retailers to limit the erosion of its shelf space. Simultaneously, the organization of a high-level development team allowed Nabisco to catch up rapidly with new products that were equal in quality to its competitors'. More important, the firm effectively used its superior production capabilities, large salesforce, and strong retail relationships to complete a national roll-out of Almost Home cookies before either Grandma's or Duncan Hines.

Frito-Lay

Grandma's ran into quality problems early on. The company soon discovered that adults liked Duncan Hines' crispy-chewy cookies better than Grandma's. Thus, its early 20 percent share of the test market quickly fell below 10 percent after P&G showed up. Subsequently, the company went through several product reformulations. This slow start devastated the firm's chances for national success. To make matters worse, Frito-Lay's store-door delivery system did not work as well as expected. The firm's commissioned sales reps were reluctant to take time from their high-volume salty snack products to deal with the slower moving cookies.

Procter & Gamble

P&G executives publicly attributed much of the reason for their disappointing performance in the cookie business to illegal actions by their competitors. They brought suit against Nabisco, Frito-Lay, and Keebler for infringing on the company's patented crispy-chewy production process. The defendants, however, argued that the technology had been common knowledge; and P&G ultimately lost its court battle.

In any case, many outside analysts felt that P&G's problems were due in part to the firm's own actions. For one thing, P&G began the cookie wars with a very narrow product line, even though a broad selection of flavors was important for gaining repeat purchases. Also, while the firm thought distribution through retailers' warehouses would be an attractive selling point, many retailers felt it required too much labor. Finally, the speed and aggressiveness of the responses by the established firms caught P&G by surprise. As one P&G executive is reported to have told a private gathering, the firm's entry into the cookie business was like "walking into a chicken coop, only to find out there was an elephant in there!"

CORPORATE, BUSINESS, AND MARKETING STRATEGIES—
DIFFERENT ISSUES AT DIFFERENT ORGANIZATIONAL LEVELS

The turbulent history of the cookie industry illustrates some important points about what strategies are and the interrelationships among different strategy levels. The cookie wars highlight the importance of marketers and their insights into customers and competitors in formulating successful strategies at all organizational levels. And they point out some of the pitfalls to avoid when planning and implementing marketing strategies and programs.

As shown in Chapter 1, marketing managers' familiarity with customers, competitors, and environmental trends often means they play a crucial role in influencing strategies formulated at higher levels in the firm. For example, top corporate managers committed hundreds of millions of dollars to the cookie business because marketing analyses indicated that adult cookie consumers were dissatisfied with existing brands and that current competitors were underpromoting the product category.

Some firms systematically incorporate such market and competitive analyses into their planning processes. They also coordinate their activities around the primary goal of satisfying unmet customer needs. Such firms are *market oriented* and follow a business philosophy commonly called the *marketing concept.* Even though neither P&G nor Frito-Lay was very successful at selling cookies, such market-oriented firms are typically among the most successful at maintaining strong competitive positions in their industries over time.

Regardless of their influence in formulating corporate and business-level strategies, however, marketing managers' freedom of action is ultimately constrained by those higher-level strategies. The objectives, strategies, and action plans for a specific product-market are but one part of a hierarchy of strategies within the firm. Each level of strategy must be consistent with— and therefore is influenced and constrained by—higher levels within the hierarchy. The marketing program for Duncan Hines cookies, for instance, was consistent with a business strategy geared to competing with high-quality products supported by heavy advertising and promotion expenditures. Furthermore, it was made possible by a corporate decision to allocate substantial resources to the cookie business.

The next section of this chapter examines the nature of—and the interrelationships among—corporate, business-level, and marketing strategies. Then we explore some of the specific strategic decisions made at the corporate and business-unit levels and their implications for marketing. Finally, we discuss the marketer's role in formulating and implementing different levels of strategy and why that role can vary across organizations and business units within the same company.

Strategy: a definition

Although *strategy* first became a popular business buzzword during the 1960s, it continues to be the subject of widely differing definitions and interpretations. The following definition, however, captures the essence of the term:

> A **strategy** is a fundamental pattern of present and planned objectives, resource deployments, and interactions of an organization with markets, competitors, and other environmental factors.[2]

Our definition suggests that a strategy should specify (1) *what* is to be accomplished; (2) *where* (on which industries and product-markets it will focus); and (3) *how* (which resources and activities will be allocated to each product-market to meet environmental opportunities and threats and to gain a competitive advantage).

The components of strategy

More specifically, there are five components—or sets of issues—within a well-developed strategy.

1. **Scope.** The scope of an organization refers to the breadth of its strategic domain—the number and types of industries, product lines, and market segments it competes in or plans to enter. Decisions about an organization's strategic scope should reflect management's view of the firm's purpose or *mission.* This common thread among its various activities and product-markets defines the essential nature of what its business is and what it should be.

2. **Goals and objectives.** Strategies should also detail desired levels of accomplishment on one or more dimensions of performance—such as volume growth, profit contribution, or return on investment—over specified time periods for each of those businesses and product-markets and for the organization as a whole.

3. **Resource deployments.** Every organization has limited financial and human resources. Formulating a strategy also involves deciding how those resources are to be obtained and allocated, across businesses, product-markets, functional departments, and activities within each business or product-market.

---

[2] This is a slightly modified form of the definition in Charles W. Hofer and Dan Schendel, *Strategy Formulation: Analytical Concepts* (St. Paul: West Publishing, 1978), p. 25. However, our definition differs in that we view the setting of objectives as an integral part of strategy formulation whereas they see objective setting as a separate process. Because a firm or business unit's objectives are influenced and constrained by many of the same environmental and competitive factors as the other elements of strategy, however, it seems logical to treat both the determination of objectives and the resource allocations aimed at reaching those objectives as two parts of the same strategic planning process.

4. *Identification of a sustainable competitive advantage.* One important part of any strategy is a specification of *how the organization will compete* in each business and product-market within its domain. How can it position itself to develop and sustain a differential advantage over current and potential competitors? To answer such questions, managers must examine the market opportunities in each business and product-market and the company's distinctive competencies or strengths relative to its competitors.

5. *Synergy.* Synergy exists when the firm's businesses, product-markets, resource deployments, and competencies complement and reinforce one another. Synergy enables the total performance of the related businesses to be greater than it would otherwise be: the whole becomes greater than the sum of its parts.

The hierarchy of strategies

Explicitly or implicitly, these five basic dimensions are part of all strategies. However, rather than a single comprehensive strategy, most organizations have a hierarchy of interrelated strategies, each formulated at a different level of the firm. The three major levels of strategy in most large, multi-product organizations are (1) **corporate strategy,** (2) **business-level strategy,** and (3) **functional strategies** focused on a particular product-market entry.[3] In small, single-product-line companies, however, corporate and business-level strategic issues merge.

For example, in anticipation of the new Europe that will result from widespread economic deregulation—fostering a unified market of some 320 million people—Heinz is acting to increase its position in Europe. It plans to do so mainly by expanding sales volume and market share in its established food business, such as ketchup products and Weight Watcher meals (corporate strategy). The company plans to make itself the low-cost ketchup producer in Europe and has spent $250 million on plant expansions and ketchup-related acquisitions (business-unit strategy). Its marketing strategy consists of expanding ketchup sales in existing markets, entering new ones, and making its ketchup products readily available at the retail level everywhere in Europe.[4]

Our primary focus is on the development of marketing strategies and programs for individual product-market entries, but other functional departments—such as R&D and production—also have strategies and plans for

---

[3] The recognition of a hierarchy of strategies within a single firm is a relatively recent, but increasingly common, concept in both the strategic management and marketing literatures. For example, see Hofer and Schendel, *Strategy Formulation,* pp. 27–29; and George S. Day, *Strategic Market Planning: The Pursuit of Competitive Advantage* (St. Paul: West Publishing, 1984), p. 44. Business-level strategy is formulated by a business unit or division (more recently termed a *strategic business unit* or *SBU*). A discussion of the definition of such units as well as how a firm divides itself into SBUs appears later in this chapter.

[4] Gregory L. Miles, Frank J. Comes, and Ellen Wallace, "Heinz Squares Off against Its Arch Rival," *Business Week,* December 12, 1988, p. 58.

each of the firm's product-markets. Throughout this book, we also examine the interfunctional implications of product-market strategies, conflict across functional areas, and the mechanisms that firms use to resolve those conflicts.

Strategies at all three levels contain the five components mentioned earlier, but because each strategy serves a different purpose within the organization, each emphasizes different sets of issues. Exhibit 2-1 summarizes the specific focus and issues dealt with at each level of strategy; we discuss them in the next sections.

Corporate strategy

At the corporate level, managers must coordinate the activities of multiple business units and—in the case of conglomerates—even separate legal business entities. Decisions about the organization's scope and resource deployments across its divisions or businesses are the primary focus of corporate strategy. The essential questions at this level are: What business(es) are we in? What business(es) *should* we be in? and What portion of our total resources should we devote to each of these businesses to achieve the organization's overall goals and objectives? Thus, the highest managerial levels of both Frito-Lay and PepsiCo made the decisions to enter the cookie business and to invest more than $70 million in capital expenditures and another $70 million in advertising and promotion.

Attempts to develop and maintain distinctive competencies at the corporate level focus on generating superior financial, capital, and human resources; designing effective organizational structures and processes; and seeking synergy among the firm's various businesses. Synergy can become a major competitive advantage in firms where related businesses share corporate staff, R&D, financial resources, production technologies, distribution channels, or a common salesforce. Frito-Lay sought the latter synergy when it assigned Grandma's cookies to its existing salesforce and store-door distribution system.

Business-level strategy

How a business unit competes within its industry is the critical focus of business-level strategy.[5] A major issue in a business strategy is that of sustainable competitive advantage. What distinctive competencies can give the business unit a competitive advantage? And which of those competencies best match the needs and wants of the customers in the business's target

---

[5] Donald C. Hambrick, "Operationalizing the Concept of Business-Level Strategy," *Academy of Management Review* 5 (1980), pp. 567–75.

EXHIBIT 2 ♦ 1

Key components of corporate, business, and marketing strategies

Strategy components	Corporate strategy	Business strategy	Marketing strategy
Scope	♦ Corporate domain—"Which businesses should we be in?"	♦ Business domain—"Which product-markets should we be in within this business or industry?"	♦ Target market definition
			♦ Product-line depth and breadth
			♦ Branding policies
	♦ Corporate development strategy Conglomerate diversification (expansion into unrelated businesses) Vertical integration Acquisition and divestiture policies	♦ Business development strategy Concentric diversification (new products for existing customers or new customers for existing products)	♦ Product-market development plan
			♦ Line extension and product elimination plans
Goals and objectives	♦ Overall corporate objectives aggregated across businesses Revenue growth Profitability ROI (return on investment) Earnings per share Contributions to other stakeholders	♦ Constrained by corporate goals	♦ Constrained by corporate and business goals
		♦ Objectives aggregated across product-market entries in the business unit Sales growth New product or market growth Profitability ROI Cash flow Strengthening bases of competitive advantage	♦ Objectives for a specific product-market entry Sales Market share Contribution margin Customer satisfaction

segment(s)? For example, a business with low-cost sources of supply and efficient, modern plants might adopt a low-cost competitive strategy. One with a strong marketing department and a competent salesforce may compete by offering superior customer service.[6]

---

[6] Strategy is not doing whatever is necessary to beat the competition—rather, it's about finding ways to deliver more value to a firm's customers. It is also about how to avoid competition wherever possible. See Kenichi Ohmae, "Getting Back to Strategy," *Harvard Business Review*, November–December 1988, p. 149.

EXHIBIT 2 ◆ 1
(concluded)

Strategy components	Corporate strategy	Business strategy	Marketing strategy
Allocation of resources	◆ Allocation among businesses in the corporate portfolio ◆ Allocation across functions shared by multiple businesses (corporate R&D, MIS)	◆ Allocation among product-market entries in the business unit ◆ Allocation across functional departments within the business unit	◆ Allocation across components of the marketing plan (elements of the marketing mix) for a specific product-market entry
Sources of competitive advantage	◆ Primarily through superior corporate financial or human resources; more corporate R&D; better organizational processes or synergies relative to competitors across all industries in which the firm operates	◆ Primarily through competitive strategy; business unit's competencies relative to competitors in its industry	◆ Primarily through effective product positioning; superiority on one or more components of the marketing mix relative to competitors within a specific product-market
Sources of synergy	◆ Shared resources, technologies, or functional competencies across businesses within the firm	◆ Shared resources (including favorable customer image) or functional competencies across product-markets within an industry	◆ Shared marketing resources, competencies, or activities across product-market entries

Another important issue a business-level strategy must address is appropriate scope: How many and which market segments to compete in, and the overall breadth of product offerings and marketing programs to appeal to these segments. Finally, synergy should be sought across product-markets and across functional departments within the business. For example, P&G used the same brand name and salesforce to promote its packaged cookies and cake mix products.

Marketing strategy

As we discussed earlier, the primary focus of marketing strategy is to effectively allocate and coordinate marketing resources and activities to accomplish the firm's objectives within a specific product-market. Therefore, the critical issue of the scope of a marketing strategy involves specifying the target market(s) for a particular product or product line. Then, firms seek competitive advantage and synergy through a well-integrated program of marketing mix elements (primarily the 4Ps of product, price, place, promotion) tailored to the needs and wants of potential customers in that target market.

Our descriptions of corporate, business-level, and marketing strategies are not very specific about the decisions involved in formulating each strategy or the tools that managers might use in making such decisions. We have already discussed the decision sequence involved in formulating marketing strategies and programs. The next two sections, therefore, focus on specific strategic decisions made at corporate and business-unit levels.

✳ STRATEGIC DECISIONS AT THE CORPORATE LEVEL

To formulate a useful corporate strategy, top management must address four interrelated decisions: the overall scope and mission of the organization; company goals and objectives; a development strategy for future growth; and corporate resource allocation across the firm's various businesses.

Corporate scope—defining the organization's mission

To provide a sense of direction, a corporate mission statement clearly defines the organization's strategic scope. It answers such fundamental questions as: What is our business? Who are our customers? Which kinds of value can we provide these customers? and What should our business be in the future?[7] For example, a few years ago PepsiCo's mission focused on "marketing superior quality food and beverage products for households and consumers dining out." That clearly defined mission guided the firm's managers toward the acquisition of several related companies—Frito-Lay, Pizza Hut, and Taco Bell—as well as the divestiture of operations that no longer fit the firm's primary thrust.[8]

Factors that influence the corporate mission
Like any other strategy component, an organization's mission should fit both its internal characteristics, resources, and competencies, and the opportunities and threats in the external environment.

---

[7] Some organizations develop mission statements that go beyond a definition of the firm's strategic domain and include specific ethical principles or social values to which top management desires the organization to adhere. The Pillsbury Company, for example, recently completed a statement of "Mission and Values" that outlines its strategic business direction and guiding principles about how to treat its employees, customers, and members of the larger society (see *Pillsbury 1986 Annual Report*, p. 1). For the purpose of understanding a corporation's competitive strategy, however, we focus only on those aspects of mission statements that address the scope of a firm's product and market domain.

[8] "Pepsi's Marketing Magic: Nobody Does It Better," *Business Week*, February 10, 1986, pp. 52–57.

Some of the internal characteristics reflected in a firm's mission statement are its historical accomplishments; top management preferences; and shared values, myths, and symbols that, taken together, make up the company's culture.[9] A firm's mission must be compatible with its resources, distinctive competencies, and possible synergies across its various businesses. Thus, PepsiCo divested its Wilson Sporting Goods and North American Van Lines divisions in part because the firm's marketing and product development skills were not much of an advantage in the moving or sporting goods businesses.

Finally, a firm's mission statement takes into account the opportunities and threats in its external environment. In this sense, a mission statement represents both a response to environmental conditions and an attempt to control those conditions by spelling out which markets and competitors a firm will *avoid* confronting in the future.[10] For example, General Mills seriously considered entering the packaged cookie business with its well-known Betty Crocker brand. The crowded competitive conditions in that industry caused the firm's managers to reject that idea, however.

Criteria for defining the corporate mission

Several different criteria can be used to define an organization's strategic mission.[11] Many firms specify their domain in *physical* terms, focusing on *products or services* or the *technology* used. The problem is that such statements can lead to slow reactions to technological or customer demand changes. For example, Levitt argues that Penn Central's view of its mission as being "the railroad business" helped cause the firm's failure. Penn Central did not respond to major changes in transportation technology, such as the rapid growth of air travel and the increased efficiency of long-haul trucking. Nor did it respond to consumers' growing willingness to pay higher prices for the increased speed and convenience of air travel. Levitt argues that it is better to define a firm's mission as *what customer needs are to be satisfied and the functions the firm must perform to satisfy them.*[12] Products and technologies change over time, but basic customer needs tend to endure. Thus, if Penn Central had defined its mission as satisfying the transportation needs of its customers rather than simply being a railroad, it might have been more willing to expand its domain to incorporate newer technologies.

---

[9] Terrence E. Deal and Allan A. Kennedy, *Corporate Cultures* (Reading, Mass.: Addison-Wesley, 1982).

[10] John Child, "Organization Structure, Environment, and Performance: The Role of Strategic Choice," *Sociology*, 1972, pp. 1–22.

[11] For a more detailed discussion of the dimensions and variables that an organization might use in defining its mission, see David A. Aaker, *Developing Business Strategies* (New York: John Wiley & Sons, 1984), chap. 2.

[12] Theodore Levitt, "Marketing Myopia," *Harvard Business Review*, July–August 1960, pp. 45–56.

EXHIBIT 2 ◆ 2

Characteristics of effective corporate mission statements

	Broad	Specific
Functional Based on customer needs	Transportation business	Long-distance transportation for large-volume producers of low-value, low-density products
Physical Based on existing products or technology	Railroad business	Long-haul, coal-carrying railroad

One problem with Levitt's advice, though, is that a mission statement focusing only on basic customer needs can be too broad to provide clear guidance and can fail to take into account the firm's specific competencies. If Penn Central had defined itself as a transportation company, should it have diversified into the trucking business? Started an airline? As the upper right quadrant of Exhibit 2–2 suggests, the most useful mission statements focus on the customer need to be satisfied and the functions that must be performed to satisfy that need. They are *specific* as to the customer groups and the products or technologies on which to concentrate.[13] Thus, instead of seeing itself as being in the railroad business or as satisfying the transportation needs of all potential customers, Burlington Northern Railroad's mission is to provide long-distance transportation for large-volume producers of low-value, low-density products, such as coal and grain.

Corporate objectives

Confucius said that "For one who has no objective, nothing is relevant." Formal objectives provide decision criteria that guide an organization's business units and employees toward specific dimensions and performance levels. Those same objectives provide the benchmarks against which actual performance can be evaluated. One factor that shaped Frito-Lay's decision to enter the cookie business was a corporate objective of maintaining a high rate of sales growth through diversification. Since the sales and market share performance of Grandma's cookies fell far short of the firm's objectives, the company viewed the venture as a major failure.

---

[13] Derek Abell, *Defining the Business: The Starting Point of Strategic Planning* (Englewood Cliffs, N.J.: Prentice-Hall, 1980), chap. 3.

To be useful as decision criteria and evaluative benchmarks, corporate objectives must be specific and measurable. Therefore, each objective contains four components:

- A *performance dimension* or attribute sought.
- A *measure or index* for evaluating progress.
- A *target or hurdle* level to be achieved.
- A *time frame* within which the target is to be accomplished.

Exhibit 2–3 lists some common performance dimensions and measures used in specifying corporate as well as business unit and marketing objectives.

Multiple objectives

Most organizations pursue multiple objectives. This is clearly demonstrated by a study of the stated objectives of 82 large corporations. The largest percentage of respondents (89 percent) had explicit profitability objectives; 82 percent reported growth objectives; 66 percent had specific market share goals. More than 60 percent mentioned social responsibility, employee welfare, and customer service objectives; and 54 percent of the companies had R&D/new-product development goals.[14] These percentages add up to much more than 100 percent because most firms had several objectives.

Many firms face potential conflicts in trying to fulfill their objectives. For example, the investment and expenditure required to pursue growth in the long term is likely to reduce profitability and ROI in the short term.[15]

Managers can reconcile conflicting goals by prioritizing them. Another approach is to state one of the conflicting goals as a **constraint** or **hurdle.** Thus, a firm attempts to maximize growth subject to the ROI constraint.[16]

Corporate development strategy

Often, the projected combined future sales and profits of a corporation's business units and product-markets fall short of the firm's long-run growth and profitability objectives. There is a gap between what the firm expects to become if it continues on its present course and what it would like to become. This is not surprising, because some of its high-growth markets are likely to slip into maturity over time, and some of its high-profit mature businesses may decline to insignificance as they get older. Thus, to answer the critical question—Where is future growth coming from?—management must decide on a specific strategy to guide future corporate development.

---

[14] Y. K. Shetty, "New Look at Corporate Goals," *California Management Review* 12 (Winter 1979), pp. 71–79.

[15] Gordon Donaldson, *Managing Corporate Wealth* (New York: Praeger, 1984).

[16] For a more detailed discussion of the objective setting process in organizations, see Max Richards, *Setting Strategic Goals and Objectives* (St. Paul: West Publishing, 1986); or David A. Aaker, *Developing Business Strategies*, chap. 8.

EXHIBIT 2♦3

Common performance criteria and measures that specify corporate, business-unit, and
marketing objectives

Performance criteria	Possible measures or indexes
♦ Growth	$ sales Unit sales Percent change in sales
♦ Competitive strength	Market share Brand awareness Brand preference
♦ Innovativeness	$ sales from new products Percent of sales from product-market entries intro- duced within past five years Percent cost savings from new processes
♦ Profitability	$ profits Profit as percent of sales Contribution margin* Return on investment (ROI) Return on net assets (RONA) Return on equity (ROE)
♦ Utilization of resources	Percent capacity utilization Fixed assets as percent of sales
♦ Contribution to owners	Earnings per share Price/earnings ratio
♦ Contribution to customers	Price relative to competitors Product quality Customer satisfaction
♦ Contribution to employees	Wage rates, benefits Personnel development, promotions Employment stability, turnover
♦ Contribution to society	$ contributions to charities or community institutions Growth in employment

  * Business-unit managers and marketing managers responsible for a product-market entry often have
little control over costs associated with corporate overhead, such as the costs of corporate staff or R&D. It
can be difficult to allocate those costs to specific strategic business units (SBUs) or products. Consequently, profit objectives at the SBU and product-market level are often stated as a desired *contribution
margin* (the gross profit prior to allocating such overhead costs).

Essentially, a firm can go in two major directions in seeking future
growth: **expansion** of its current businesses and activities, or **diversification**
into new businesses, either through internal business development or acquisition. Exhibit 2–4 outlines some of the specific options a firm might
pursue while seeking growth in either of these directions.

EXHIBIT 2 ◆ 4

Alternative corporate growth strategies

	Current products	**New products**

Current markets	**Market penetration strategies**
	• Increase market share
	• Increase product usage
	   Increase frequency of use
	   Increase quantity used
	   New applications
		Product development strategies
		• Product improvements
		• Product-line extensions
		• New products for same market

New markets	**Market development strategies**
	• Expand markets for existing
	  products
	   Geographic expansion
	   Target new segments
		Diversification strategies
		• Vertical integration
		   Forward integration
		   Backward integration
		• Diversification into related
		  businesses (concentric
		  diversification)
		• Diversification into unrelated
		  businesses (conglomerate
		  diversification)

Expansion

One way current businesses expand is by increasing their share of existing markets. This typically involves making product improvements, cutting prices, or outspending competitors on such things as advertising and consumer or trade promotions. In an effort to gain share in the full-size pickup truck market at the expense of industry-leading Ford, Chevrolet made product changes. To dramatize these improvements, it committed substantial funds to support its aggressive advertising campaign. Such actions typically invite competitive reaction, however; and Ford responded with its own product upgrading and strong advertising program.[17]

A second approach encourages current customers to use more of the product, use it more often, or use it in new ways. Kraft Inc.'s advertising for its cheeses and salad dressings, for example, features appealing new recipes to encourage consumers to use more of its products more often.

---

[17] Joseph B. White, "Chevy Turns to Negative Ads in an Effort to Topple Ford as Pickup Truck Leader," *The Wall Street Journal*, December 13, 1988, p. 81.

A third way to expand is to develop product-line extensions or new-product offerings for existing customers. For example, Arm & Hammer successfully introduced a laundry detergent, an oven cleaner, and a liquid detergent. Each capitalized on baking soda's image as an effective deodorizer and on the Arm & Hammer brand name recognition.[18]

Finally, a firm can expand the markets for its current products, as when a domestic producer attempts to expand into foreign markets. For example, Morgan Stanley, a large New York-based investment bank, recently opened a Tokyo branch that is concerned primarily with equity trading.[19]

✳ Diversification

Firms also seek growth by diversifying their operations. This is riskier than the various expansion strategies because it requires moving into operations and customer groups unlike current businesses. Nevertheless, about two thirds of all Fortune 500 companies are diversified to one degree or another.[20]

Vertical integration is one way for corporations to diversify their operations. **Forward integration** occurs when a firm moves "downstream" in terms of the product flow—as when a manufacturer acquires a wholesaler or retail outlet. For example, both Coca-Cola and PepsiCo are buying some of their franchises not only because of their profitability but also because they facilitate the introduction of new products. **Backward integration** occurs when a firm moves "upstream" by acquiring a supplier. The Limited, Inc., is a group of about 2,500 specialty stores focusing on women's apparel. The company was one of the first apparel retailers to vertically integrate via its Mast Industries division, which has a worldwide network of manufacturers producing most of the company's merchandise.

Integration gives a firm access to scarce or volatile sources of supply or tighter control over the marketing, distribution, and servicing of its products. But it increases the risks inherent in committing substantial resources to a single industry. Also, the investment necessary for firms to vertically integrate often offsets the additional profitability generated by integrated operations, resulting in little improvement in return on investment.[21]

Related (or concentric) diversification occurs when a firm internally develops or acquires another business that does not have products or customers in common with its current businesses but that might contribute to

---

[18] J. J. Honomichl, "The Ongoing Saga of 'Mother Baking Soda,'"*Advertising Age,* September 20, 1982, pp. M2–M3.

[19] "How to Beat the Japanese," *U.S. News & World Report,* August 24, 1987, pp. 38–44.

[20] Richard P. Rumelt, *Strategy, Structure, and Economic Performance* (Boston: Harvard Business School, Division of Research, 1976).

[21] Robert D. Buzzell, "Is Vertical Integration Profitable?" *Harvard Business Review,* January–February 1983, pp. 92–102.

internal synergy through the sharing of production facilities, brand names, R&D know-how, or marketing and distribution skills. Thus, P&G developed its cookie business internally to take advantage of the popularity of its Duncan Hines brand and its massive promotional resources.

The motivations for **unrelated (or conglomerate) diversification** are primarily financial rather than operational. By definition, an unrelated diversification involves two businesses that have no commonalities in products, customers, production facilities, or functional areas of expertise. Such diversification most likely occurs when a disproportionate number of the firm's current businesses face decline due to decreasing demand, increased competition, or product obsolescence. The firm must seek new avenues to provide future growth. Other more fortunate firms may move into unrelated businesses because they have more cash than they need to expand their current businesses, or they wish to discourage takeover attempts.

Allocating corporate resources

Diversified organizations have several potential advantages over more narrowly focused firms. They have a broader range of areas in which they can knowledgeably invest. Also, their growth and profitability rates may be more stable because they can offset declines in one business with gains in another. This is true for service and not-for-profit organizations, such as a hospital that runs outpatient clinics, trains doctors and nurses, and conducts medical research, as well as for manufacturers. Even the managers of small companies with a single core business are likely to eventually face questions of how and where to diversify to achieve further growth.

In exploiting the advantages of diversification, though, corporate managers must make intelligent decisions about how financial and human resources should be allocated across the firm's various businesses and product-markets. **Portfolio models** have emerged as significant tools to help managers allocate corporate resources across multiple businesses. These models enable managers to classify and review their present and prospective SBUs by evaluating each business's competitive strength and the attractiveness of the markets it serves. Most companies engaged in serious strategic planning use one or more such models.[22]

The Boston Consulting Group's (BCG) growth-share matrix
One of the first—and best known—of the portfolio models is the growth-share matrix developed by the Boston Consulting Group in the late 1960s. It analyzes the impact of investing resources in different business units on the corporation's future earnings and cash flows. Each business unit is positioned within a matrix, as shown in Exhibit 2–5. The vertical axis indicates

----

[22] George Day, *Analysis for Strategic Market Decisions* (St. Paul: West Publishing Company, 1986), pp. 193–94.

✳ **EXHIBIT 2 ◆ 5**
BCG's market growth/relative share matrix

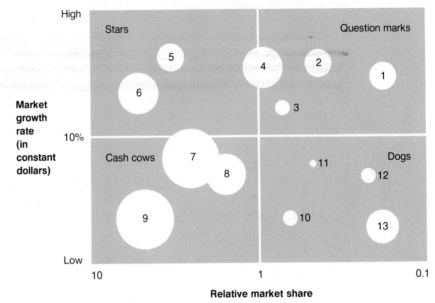

Source: Adapted from Barry Hedley, "Strategy and the Business Portfolio," *Long Range Planning* 10 (February 1977).

the industry's growth rate and the horizontal axis shows the unit's relative market share. Many companies have used the BCG model, including such well-known firms as Borg Warner, General Foods, and Black & Decker.

The growth-share matrix assumes that a firm must generate cash from businesses with strong competitive positions in mature markets. Then it can fund investments and expenditures in industries that represent attractive future opportunities. Thus, the **market growth rate** on the vertical axis is a proxy measure for the maturity and attractiveness of an industry. This model represents businesses in rapidly growing industries as more attractive investment opportunities for future growth and profitability. In Exhibit 2–5, an annual market growth rate of 10 percent is the cut-off level between fast- and slow-growing industries. This dividing line can vary, however, depending on a firm's objectives and available opportunities.

Similarly, a business's **relative market share** is a proxy for its competitive strength within its industry. It is computed by dividing the business's absolute market share in dollars or units by that of the leading competitor in the industry. Thus, in Exhibit 2–5 a business unit is in a strong competitive position if its share is equal to, or larger than, the next leading competitor's (i.e., a relative share of 1.0 or larger). But it is competitively weak if the leading competitor holds a larger share of the market. Finally, in the exhibit, the size of the circle representing each business unit is proportional to the

EXHIBIT 2◆6

Cash flows across businesses in the BCG portfolio model

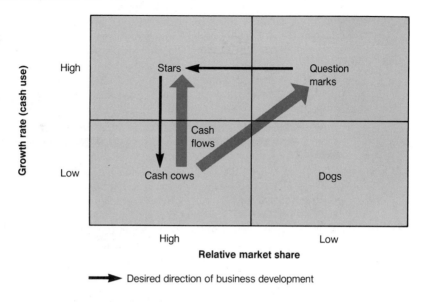

Desired direction of business development

unit's sales volume. Therefore, businesses 7 and 9 are the largest-volume businesses in this hypothetical company. Business 11 is the smallest.

Each growth-share matrix cell represents a different strategy position with different resource requirements.

● *Question marks*—Businesses in high-growth industries with low market shares (the upper right quadrant of Exhibit 2–5) are called question marks or problem children. Such businesses require large amounts of cash. Not only does the firm have to keep adding plant, equipment, and personnel just to keep up with the rapidly growing market, but it also needs even greater expenditures for marketing activities (or reduced margins) to build market share and catch the industry leader. If management successfully increases the share of a question mark business, it becomes a star. But if they fail, it eventually turns into a dog as the industry matures and the market growth rate slows.

● *Stars*—A star is the market leader in a high-growth industry. Stars are critical to the continued future success of the firm. As their industries mature they move into the bottom left quadrant and become cash cows. Paradoxically, although stars are critically important, they often are net users rather than suppliers of cash in the short run (as indicated by the possibility of a negative cash flow shown in Exhibit 2–6). The firm must continue to invest in such businesses to keep up with rapid market growth and support the R&D and marketing activities necessary to stave off competitors' attacks and maintain a leading market share.

● *Cash cows*—Businesses with a high relative share of low-growth markets are called *cash cows* because they are the primary generators of profits and cash in a corporation. Such businesses do not require much additional capital investments. Their markets are stable, and their share leadership position usually means they enjoy economies of scale and relatively high profit margins. The corporation can use the cash from these businesses to support its question marks and stars (as shown in Exhibit 2–6) in building more cash cows for the future. However, this does not mean that the firm should necessarily maximize the business's *short-term* cash flow by cutting R&D and marketing expenditures to the bone—particularly in industries where the business might generate substantial future sales. When firms attempt to harvest too much cash from such businesses they risk suffering a premature decline from cash cow to dog status, thus losing profits in the long term.

- *Dogs*—Low-share businesses in low-growth markets are called *dogs* because although they may throw off some cash, they typically generate low profits (or losses). And they often require more management time than they are worth. Divestiture is one option, although it can be difficult to find an interested buyer. Another common strategy is to harvest dog businesses. This involves maximizing short-term cash flow by paring investments and expenditures until the business is gradually phased out. In some cases, though, a case can be made for continuing to invest in a dog. One strategy is to focus the business on one or a few product-markets within the industry where the firm has some competitive strengths and can find profitable additional growth.

Exhibit 2–7 shows the use of the growth-share portfolio model by Black & Decker. Note that the company has only one question mark—Pacific International—and only one unit—McCulloch, which makes primarily chain saws—that might be classed as a dog.

Limitations of the growth-share matrix

Because the growth-share matrix uses only two variables as a basis for categorizing and analyzing a firm's businesses, it has significant limitations:

- *Interdependence among business units except for cash is a real danger*. There should be little cost and demand overlaps among any of the portfolio entries.
- *Market growth rate is an inadequate descriptor of overall industry attractiveness*. For one thing, market growth is not always directly related to profitability or cash flow. Some high-growth industries have never been very profitable because low entry barriers and capital intensity have enabled supply to grow even faster, resulting in intense price competition. Also, rapid growth in one year is no guarantee that growth will continue in the following year.
- *Relative market share is inadequate as a description of overall competitive strength and a determinant of profitability*. It is based on the assumption that an experience curve resulting from a combination of scale economies and other efficiencies gained through learning and technological improvements over time leads to continuing reductions in unit costs as a business's relative market share increases. A large relative market share within an industry does not *always* give a business a significant cost advantage—especially when the product is a low-value-added item, when different products within the business require different production or marketing activities, where different competitors have different capacity

EXHIBIT 2 ◆ 7

Growth-share matrix for Black & Decker—1976

	Business unit	Percent company business	Unit growth rate	Relative market share
Black & Decker corporate portfolio	1. European Power Tools	38%	14-15%	3.2x-4.0x
	2. U.S. Consumer Tools	20	7- 8	2
	3. McCulloch	14	10-11	.6 - .7
	4. U.S. Professional Tools	10	5- 6	1.25-1.75
	5. Pacific International	10	26	.3 - .4
	6. Canada	6	10	4
	7. Australia	2%	4.5%	5x

Source: Adapted from George S. Day, *Analysis for Strategic Market Decisions* (St. Paul: West Publishing, 1986), p. 170.

and utilization rates, or where some competitors are more vertically integrated or have lower cost suppliers than others.[23]

Market share is primarily the result of a company's strategy formulation and implementation; that is, a measure of success or failure.[24]

◆ *The outcomes of a growth-share analysis are highly sensitive to variations in how "growth" and "share" are measured.* Using information from 15 business units within a single firm, one study explored how their positions within a growth-share matrix would vary when different measures of growth and market share were used.

[23] David B. Montgomery and George S. Day, "Experience Curves: Evidence, Empirical Issues, and Applications," in *Strategic Marketing and Strategic Management*, eds. David Gardner and Howard Thomas (New York: John Wiley & Sons, 1984).

[24] Robert Jacobson argues that market share and profitability are joint outcomes from successful strategies and, further, that management skills likely have the greatest impact on profitability. See "Distinguishing among Competing Theories of the Market Share Effect," *Journal of Marketing*, October 1988, pp. 68–80.

The study used four measures of share and four measures of growth (both past and forecasted future growth). Only 3 of the 15 businesses ended up in the same quadrant of the matrix, no matter which measures were used. Four businesses fell into *all four* quadrants, depending on which measures were employed.[25]

A major measurement problem is how to define the industry and the relevant markets within it. For example, Mercedes-Benz has a small share of the total world auto market, but a substantial share of the luxury car market. Which is the most appropriate market definition to use?

♦ *Although the matrix specifies appropriate investment strategies for each business, it provides little guidance concerning how those strategies might best be implemented.* Even though the model suggests that a firm should invest cash in its question mark businesses, it does so without any consideration of whether the business can exploit any potential source of competitive advantage to successfully increase its share. Cash flow is not always related to either the location or direction of the business unit in the matrix.

Alternative portfolio models

A number of more detailed portfolio models have been developed by firms such as McKinsey & Company, General Electric, and Shell Oil. These models, typically referred to as *industry attractiveness-business position matrices* or *directional policy matrices,* rely on factors other than just market growth to judge the future attractiveness of different industries. They use multiple variables in addition to relative market share to judge the competitive strength and position of each business.

Exhibit 2–8 shows some of the factors that managers use to evaluate industry attractiveness and a business's competitive position. Corporate and business managers first select factors most appropriate for their firm and weight them according to their relative importance. They then rate each business and its industry on the two sets of factors. Next they combine the weighted evaluations into summary measures that are used to place each business within one of the nine boxes in the matrix in Exhibit 2–8. Businesses falling into boxes numbered 1 (where both industry attractiveness and the business's ability to compete are relatively high) are good candidates for further investment for future growth. Businesses in the 2 boxes should receive only selective investment with an objective of maintaining current position. Finally, businesses in the 3 boxes are candidates for harvesting or divestiture.

These multifactor models are richer and more detailed than the simple growth-share model. Consequently, they provide a more detailed picture of the likely future attractiveness and the competitive strengths and weaknesses of businesses, and more strategic guidance concerning how each business might best compete. They are also more useful for evaluating

---

[25] Yoram Wind, Vijay Mahajan, and Donald J. Swire, "An Empirical Comparison of Standardized Portfolio Models," *Journal of Marketing* 47 (Spring 1983), pp. 89–99.

✳ **EXHIBIT** **2 ◆ 8**

The industry attractiveness-business position matrix

Industry attractiveness

		High	Medium	Low
Business's competitive position	High	1	1	2
	Medium	1	2	3
	Low	2	3	3

1 Invest/grow
2 Selective investment/maintain position
3 Harvest/divest

Variables that might be used to evaluate:

Business's competitive position		*Industry attractiveness*	
Size	Distribution	Size	Profitability
Growth	Technology	Growth	Technological
Relative share	Marketing skills	Competitive intensity	sophistication
Customer loyalty	Patents	Price levels	Government regulations
Margins			

potential new product-markets. However, the multifactor measures in these models can be subjective and ambiguous, especially when managers must evaluate different industries on the same set of factors. Also, the conclusions drawn from these models still depend on the way industries and product-markets are defined.[26]

---

[26] For a more detailed discussion of the uses and limitations of "Market Attractiveness-Competitive Position" matrices, see G. S. Day, *Analysis for Strategic Market Decisions* (St. Paul: West Publishing, 1986), chap. 7.

STRATEGIC DECISIONS AT THE BUSINESS-UNIT LEVEL

The components of a firm involved in multiple industries or businesses are called **strategic business units,** or **SBUs.** Managers within each of these business units decide which objectives and strategies to pursue. Top-level corporate managers typically reserve the right to grant final approval of such decisions to ensure their overall consistency with corporate objectives and resource allocations across SBUs in the company portfolio. Lower-level general managers, however, conduct much of the analysis on which such decisions are based. These managers are more familiar with a given SBU's products and customers, and ultimately they are responsible for implementing its strategy.

The first step in developing business-level strategies, then, is for the firm to decide how to divide itself into SBUs. The managers of each SBU then must make recommendations about (a) the SBU's objectives and scope, (b) how resources should be allocated across its product-market entries and functional departments, and (c) which broad competitive strategy to pursue to build a sustainable competitive advantage in its product-markets.

Defining strategic business units

Ideally, strategic business units have the following characteristics:

* *A homogeneous set of markets to serve with a limited number of related technologies.* Minimizing diversity across an SBU's product-market entries enables the unit's manager to better formulate and implement a coherent and internally consistent business strategy.
* *A unique set of product-markets,* in the sense that no other SBU within the firm competes for the same customers with similar products. Thus, the firm avoids duplication of effort and maximizes economies of scale within its SBUs.
* *Control over those factors necessary for successful performance,* such as production, R&D and engineering, marketing, and distribution. This does not mean an SBU should not share resources—such as a manufacturing plant or a salesforce—with one or more other business units. But the SBU should determine how its share of the joint resource is used to effectively carry out its strategy.
* *Responsibility for its own profitability.*

As you might expect, firms do not always meet all of these ideals when designing business units. There are usually trade-offs between having many small homogeneous SBUs versus large but fewer SBUs that managers can more easily supervise.

What criteria should managers use to decide how product-markets can be clustered into a business unit? The three dimensions that define the scope and mission of the entire corporation also define individual SBUs:

   a. *Technical compatibility*; particularly with respect to product technologies and operational requirements, such as the use of similar production facilities and engineering skills.

   b. Similarity in the *customer needs* or the product benefits sought by customers in the target markets.

   c. Similarity in the *personal characteristics* or behavior patterns of customers in the target markets.

In practice, the choice is often between technical/operational compatibility on the one hand and customer homogeneity on the other. Frequently management defines SBUs by product-markets requiring similar technologies, production facilities, and employee skills. This minimizes the coordination problems involved in administering the unit.[27] In some firms, however, the marketing synergies gained from coordinating technically different products aimed at the same customer need or market segment outweigh operational considerations. In these firms, managers cluster product-market entries into SBUs based on similarities across customers or distribution systems. General Foods Corporation, for instance, includes Cool Whip and Jell-O in the same SBU even though they require different production technologies because they are marketed as dessert products.

The business unit's objectives

Corporate objectives are broken down into subobjectives for each SBU. In most cases, those subobjectives vary across SBUs according to their industry attractiveness, the strength of their competitive positions within those industries, and resource allocation decisions by corporate management. For example, managers may assign an SBU in a rapidly growing industry relatively high volume and share-growth objectives but lower ROI objectives than an SBU with a large share in a mature industry. Therefore, even though an SBU's manager may have substantial input, the unit's objectives are ultimately shaped by the strategic and resource allocation decisions of top corporate executives.

Breaking down overall SBU objectives into subobjectives for each product-market entry is often a major part of developing business-level strategy. Those subobjectives obviously must add up to the accomplishment of the SBU's overall objectives; yet they vary across product-market entries according to the attractiveness and growth potential of individual market segments and the competitive strengths of the company's product in each market. For

---

[27] Phillipe Haspeslagh, "Portfolio Planning: Uses and Limits," *Harvard Business Review*, January–February 1982, p. 65.

example, when it first introduced its Almost Home line, Nabisco's objective was to capture a large share of the soft and chewy cookie segment and fend off the competitive threats of P&G and Frito-Lay, even if the line did not break even for several years. At the same time, though, the company maintained high profitability goals for its established cookie brands to provide the cash required for Almost Home's introduction and to preserve corporate profit levels.

The business unit's competitive strategy

The essential question in formulating a business strategy is, How will the business unit compete to gain a sustainable competitive advantage within its industry? Achieving a competitive advantage requires a business unit to make two choices:

♦ What is the SBU's competitive domain or scope? Which market segments can it target, and which customer needs can it satisfy? These are stated in more general terms than is the case with marketing strategy. They serve as guidelines for the formulation of strategies for the individual product-market entries.
♦ How can the business unit distinguish itself from competitors in its target market(s)? What distinctive competencies can it rely on to achieve a unique position relative to its competitors?

Even though a business unit may contain a number of product-market entries, most analysts argue that the SBU should pursue the same competitive advantage in all of them. In this way it can take full advantage of its particular strengths and downplay its weaknesses. As Porter argues in his book on competitive advantage,

> If a [business] is to attain a competitive advantage, it must make a choice about the type of competitive advantage it seeks to attain and the scope within which it will attain it. Being "all things to all people" is a recipe for strategic mediocrity and below-average performance, because it often means that a [business] has no competitive advantage at all.[28]

Porter argues that a business might seek a competitive advantage on two dimensions: It can try to be the low-cost producer within its target segments, or it can differentiate itself by its product offering or marketing program. It can do this, for example, by offering a higher quality or more technically advanced product, more extensive promotion, broader distribution, or better customer service.

A business unit's strategic scope is defined broadly or narrowly. That is, it can pursue a wide range of market segments within its industry or focus on only one or a few target segments. As Exhibit 2–9 indicates, this suggests four

---

[28] Michael E. Porter, *Competitive Advantage* (New York: Free Press, 1985), p. 12.

Courtesy University of Chicago Medical Center

♦ Driving forces in the health-care industry environment are expected to lead to rapid growth in out-patient services and to increasingly sophisticated in-hospital treatment procedures. (Chapter 3)

John Thoeming/Irwin

Courtesy Dudley Riggs Brave New Workshop

♦ Dudley Riggs' strategy segmented the "hedonist" theatergoers attracted to satirical reviews and improvisations because there would be little direct competition for their patronage. (Chapter 6)

Courtesy Rubbermaid Incorporated

♦ Rubbermaid's successful strategy is to market a wide range of "homely" consumer and household products here and abroad. (Chapter 1)

TWO DELICIOUS PIZZAS
FOR ONE SPECIAL PRICE
AVOID THE NOID TWICE!

DOMINO'S
PIZZA
DELIVERS
FREE.

© 1987 Domino's Pizza, Inc.

DOMINO'S PIZZA GUARANTEES...

HOT & FRESH!

DOMINO'S

Steve Woit/Picture Group

◆ Domino's Tom Monaghan flips pizzas from store to customer's home in less than 30 minutes . . . taking advantage of his customers' tastes and buying behavior. (Chapter 4)

Generation to Generation.

Recyclable engineering materials today promise an even greater legacy than immediate reductions of costs and waste.

Generation and regeneration: from packaging to automotive to construction. The energy isn't lost. Our promise for the future. Advanced technology plastics offering long-term productivity and potential.

Recyclable. Reusable. Responsible.

For an informative outlook on recycling engineering plastics, request our free Recyclability Brochure today:
(800) 845-0600.

GE Plastics

Joe McNally/GE Aerospace, Valley Forge, PA

Courtesy General Electric Company

◆ General Electric, once known for its household appliances, has become an industrial giant whose wideranging products and services include plastics, communication satellites, and medical technology. (Chapter 5)

Steve Dunwell photo

EXHIBIT 2 ♦ 9

Generic business strategies

Source of competitive advantage

	Lower cost	Differentiation

Source: Adapted with permission of The Free Press, a Division of Macmillan, Inc. from *Competitive Advantage: Creating and Sustaining Superior Performance* by Michael E. Porter. Copyright © 1985 by Michael E. Porter.

generic strategies a business unit might adopt: (1) cost leadership across a broad range of product-market entries; (2) cost leadership focusing on a narrow group of target segments; (3) differentiation across a wide variety of segments; or (4) more narrowly focused differentiation.

Other authors have suggested additional ways to categorize business strategies.[29] No matter how the business is defined, though, the point here is that the strategy pursued by the SBU helps determine the marketing programs developed for its product-market entries and the relative influence of marketing managers in formulating and implementing strategic programs. We examine this relationship between business strategy and the strategic role of marketing in more detail later in this chapter.

Allocating resources within the business unit

Once SBU managers decide on the scope of product-market entries to pursue, they allocate the resources provided to the unit by corporate management across those product-markets. Because this allocation process is quite similar to allocating corporate resources across SBUs, many firms use the same portfolio analysis tools for both.

---

[29] For example, see Robert E. Miles and Charles C. Snow, *Organizational Strategy, Structure and Process* (New York: McGraw-Hill, 1978).

THE ROLE OF MARKETING IN FORMULATING AND IMPLEMENTING STRATEGIES

While developing a strategic marketing plan for a specific product-market entry, a marketing manager's range of choices is constrained by both corporate and SBU decisions.

The essence of strategic planning at all levels is identifying foreseeable threats to avoid and opportunities to pursue. The primary responsibility of any manager is to look outward continuously to keep the firm or business in step with anticipated changes in the environment. The lead role in meeting this responsibility is often played by marketing managers.[30] Because they occupy positions at the boundary between the firm and its customers, distributors, and competitors, marketing managers are usually most familiar with conditions and trends in the market environment.

Marketing managers thus often play an important role in strategic planning at the corporate, business-unit, and individual product-market entry levels. For example, see the wide-ranging participation and influence of marketing managers on strategic planning within SBUs at General Electric, as outlined in Exhibit 2–10. GE marketing managers have primary responsibility for—or are among the key participants in—formulating nearly all aspects of an SBU's strategy, as well as planning and implementing many of the functional program elements within the business unit's strategy.

Factors that mediate marketing's role in the formulation of strategy

Of course, marketing managers do not play as extensive a strategic role in all organizations as they do at General Electric. The more common tendency is to be inner-directed and to give unbalanced emphasis to internal aspirations, technological developments, and short-run efficiency considerations.[31] Among the many reasons why organizations are not always market-oriented are the following:

- Some managers hold a philosophical view that being market-oriented is not always in the best long-run interests of the firm or its customers.
- Competitive conditions may enable a firm to be successful in the short run without being particularly sensitive to market needs.
- The firm may suffer from strategic inertia—the automatic continuation of strategies successful in the past, even though current market conditions are changing.

---

[30] Day, *Analysis for Strategic Marketing Decisions*, pp. 2–3.

[31] Ibid., p. 3.

EXHIBIT   2 ♦ 10

Influence and participation of marketing managers at General Electric

Strategic planning activity	Marketing's role
Determination of SBU's objectives and scope	Key participant along with SBU's general manager
Environmental assessment (customers; economic, political, regulatory trends)	Primary contributor and a major beneficiary of the results
Competitive assessment (actual and potential competitors)	Primary contributor, working with other functional managers and staff planners
Situation assessment (inputs to portfolio analysis; industry and market attractiveness; firm and product position)	Primary contributor, working with staff planners and general manager
Objectives and goals	Key participant with other functional managers, including responsibility for measuring several performance indicators
Strategies	Major contributor to determination of SBU's competitive strategy; responsible for marketing strategy and for coordinating plans with other functional strategies

Key program elements	Marketing's role
Product-market development	Leadership role
Product quality	Leading responsibility for quality
Distribution	Primary responsibility
Technology	Varies according to the importance of technology to the product or service
Human resources	Responsible for functional area
Business development*	Key supporting role with strategic planning and manufacturing responsible for implementation
Manufacturing facilities	Typically, only limited involvement

   * Decisions to expand, improve, or contract the business.

Source: Adapted from a speech presented by Stephen G. Harrell (then of the General Electric Company) at the American Marketing Association Educators' Conference, Chicago, August 5, 1980. Mr. Harrell is currently a Partner in Megamark Partners, a consulting firm specializing in marketing and new-product development.

Criticisms of a market orientation

Business critics argue that a market orientation focusing on satisfying short-run customer wants may not serve the long-run interests of society.[32] Consumer desires and company goals often tend to ignore the social costs that business activities incur. For example, many consumers prefer the convenience of disposable soft-drink and beer containers. Such packages free manufacturers from having to collect, ship, and clean used containers. However, disposable bottles use substantially more resources than returnable bottles. Disposable containers also contribute to increased litter throughout our land.

Some critics argue that firms should broaden their business orientation to include a concern for long-run social interests. This view has been called the **societal marketing concept.** Firms following this market orientation would conduct a "social audit" to measure the long-term impact of their products and policies on society—instead of using profit and return on investment as their primary measures of success. A societal orientation is difficult to implement, however, and hard to sell to most stockholders and investors. Also, many businesspeople argue that such decisions should be made by our elected representatives, who can be recalled or voted out of office if the public does not agree with their decisions.

Another criticism of market-oriented firms is that they may not be very innovative in developing new products or technologies. Managers might tend to pursue minor product modifications and extensive promotional programs that satisfy customers and meet profit objectives in the short-run, but distract effort and resources from the pursuit of technological discoveries, unique products, or artistic achievement.[33]

Others argue, however, that technological innovation is not a sufficient criterion to justify the introduction of a new product. A customer or market orientation is still necessary, in that there must be an application for the new technology that fulfills a need perceived by a sufficient number of potential customers to constitute a viable market.

Competitive factors affecting a firm's market orientation

Often, managers only attend to customer demands and environmental conditions when competitive threats, declining demand, or environmental shocks force them to do so. Nabisco's failure to address the wants of adult cookie consumers until it was threatened by Frito-Lay and P&G is an example of how even strategically sophisticated companies can sometimes be lulled into complacency.

---

[32] For a discussion of this point of view, see Alan J. Resnick and Robert R. Harmon, "Consumer Complaints and Managerial Response: A Holistic Approach," *Journal of Marketing,* Winter 1983, pp. 86–97.

[33] Robert A. Hayes and William J. Abernathy, "Managing Our Way to Economic Decline," *Harvard Business Review,* July–August 1980, pp. 67–77.

Early entrants into newly emerging industries—particularly industries based on new technologies—are especially likely to be internally focused and not very market-oriented. This is because (a) product design and production problems tend to represent more immediate threats to the survival of such new firms; (b) there are likely to be relatively few strong competitors during the formative years of a new industry's life cycle; and (c) customer demand for the new product is likely to grow rapidly and outstrip available supply. Firms in such industries often espouse a **product or production-oriented** business philosophy.

They focus attention and resources on the functions of product and process engineering, production, and finance to acquire and manage the resources necessary for expansion. The firm is primarily concerned with producing more of what it wants to make, and marketing generally plays a secondary role in both formulating and implementing the firm's strategies.

A production orientation is illustrated by the early years of the Pillsbury Company. Charles Pillsbury founded his company in Minneapolis in 1869 because of the availability of high-quality wheat and cheap waterpower. The company's mission in those days was summarized as follows: "We are professional flour millers. Blessed with a supply of the finest North American wheat, plenty of waterpower, and excellent milling machinery, we produce flour of the highest quality. Our basic function is to mill high-quality flour."[34]

As industries grow and develop they tend to become more competitive. New firms are attracted to the industry by growing volumes and profits; and existing producers compete with improved product offerings and more efficient production processes. As a result, industry capacity often outstrips demand, forcing the industry's market environment to shift from a seller's market to a buyer's market. Consequently, firms tend to expend more effort and resources on selling activities to maintain a satisfactory volume of sales and profits.

A **sales-oriented** business approach focuses on aggressively selling what the firm wants to make rather than paying attention to customers' needs and developing product offerings and marketing programs tailored to those needs. This sales orientation characterized Pillsbury's approach to the flour business during the 1930s and 40s, when one of the company's executives is reported to have said, "We must hire salesmen to sell it [the flour] just as we hire accountants to keep our books."

The aggressive promotional tactics of a sales-oriented approach are easily matched by competitors. As industries mature and growth slows, competitive pressures often become even more intense. (This has been exacerbated in recent years by low-cost foreign competitors.) Thus, managers often

---

[34] Robert F. Keith, "The Marketing Revolution," *Journal of Marketing,* January 1960, pp. 35–38.

begin to pay more attention to customer needs and wants to find ways to differentiate the company's products and gain a competitive advantage.

When adopting a **market-oriented** business philosophy, the guiding principle becomes "it is more effective to make what customers want to buy than to sell them what we want to make."

A firm pays more attention to customer research *before* products are designed and produced.[35] It implements the concepts of market segmentation by adapting its product offerings and marketing programs to different target markets. Finally, these philosophical changes are often reflected in organizational changes. Marketing managers have a more active role in strategic planning and product development or in coordinating activities across functional departments to ensure that they are all consistent with the desires of target customers. Pillsbury reached this stage in the evolution of its business philosophy during the 1950s when it adopted a product management organization structure and redefined its mission as "providing high-value-added products to satisfy consumers' needs for quality foods, both at home and for dining occasions outside the home."[36]

> The philosophy that the *planning and coordination of all company activities around the primary goal of satisfying customer needs is the most effective means to attain a competitive advantage and achieve company objectives* has become widely known as the **marketing concept.**

No matter what the approach is called, a consistent focus on customers' needs and competitive circumstances in the market environment—and a willingness and ability to adapt company products and programs to fit changes in that environment—is characteristic of firms successfully maintaining a strong competitive position in their industries over time. Unfortunately, firms that have historically been product- or production-oriented cannot easily change to a market-oriented approach. Exhibit 2–11 outlines the differences in outlook between managers in production-oriented and market-oriented organizations.

---

[35] For a discussion of how being "market oriented" differs from "getting close to the customer," see Benjamin P. Shapiro, "What the Hell Is Market Oriented?" *Harvard Business Review*, November–December 1988, p. 119. Also see Franklin S. Houston, "The Marketing Concept: What It Is and What It Is Not," *Journal of Marketing*, April 1986, pp. 81–87.

[36] Because the U.S. economy has experienced different rates of industrial development and market growth at various times, some authors have associated historical periods with the business philosophy most prevalent during those times. Thus, the period of industrialization and development of new production technologies from the mid-1800s through the First World War is sometimes referred to as the era of "production orientation" in American business. The formal beginning of the "marketing concept" era is usually set in 1952 when General Electric first stated a customer-oriented philosophy. See Eric N. Berkowitz, Roger A. Kerin, and William Rudelius, *Marketing* (St. Louis: Times Mirror/Mosby, 1986), pp. 16–18.

EXHIBIT   2 ◆ 11

Differences between production-oriented and market-oriented organizations

Business activity or function	Production orientation	Marketing orientation
Product offering	Company sells what it can make; primary focus on functional performance and cost.	Company makes what it can sell; primary focus on customers' needs and market opportunities.
Product line	Narrow.	Broad.
Pricing	Based on production and distribution costs.	Based on perceived benefits provided.
Research	Technical research; focus on product improvement and cost cutting in the production process.	Market research; focus on identifying new opportunities and applying new technology to satisfy customer needs.
Packaging	Protection for the product; minimize costs.	Designed for customer convenience; a promotional tool.
Credit	A necessary evil; minimize bad debt losses.	A customer service; a tool to attract customers.
Promotion	Emphasis on product features, quality, and price.	Emphasis on product benefits and ability to satisfy customers' needs or solve problems.

Strategic inertia

In some cases, successful firms lose touch with their markets because managers are reluctant to tamper with strategies and marketing programs that worked in the past. They begin to believe that there is "one best way" to satisfy their customers. Strategic inertia is dangerous, for the simple reason that customers' needs and competitive offerings change over time. Staying successful requires constant analysis of and adjustments to changes in what customers want and value.[37] For this reason, formal strategic planning should be an on-going, frequent process. Information from marketing managers about threats and opportunities posed by changes in their target markets or competitors should serve as crucial inputs to that process.

---

[37] Thomas V. Bonoma, "Marketing Success Can Breed 'Marketing Inertia,'" *Harvard Business Review*, September–October 1981.

Factors mediating marketing's role in implementing strategy

Even when firms are market oriented, marketing activities are not always the most extensive or competitively crucial part of strategy implementation. During the cookie wars, for instance, Sunshine Biscuits successfully defended its market share with a low-cost strategy that appealed to traditional customers' desire for low prices. The implementation of that strategy, however, involved substantial cuts in many marketing activities and resources, such as consumer advertising, trade promotion, and new-product development.

As customer needs and competitive conditions change over time, a business's competitive strategy and marketing's role may also change. For example, when Allegheny Ludlum Steel Corporation introduced stainless steel in the 1930s, many potential customers were unaware of the product's many possible uses. Thus, the most important part of the product in those early days was not the steel itself, but the design and applications services that Allegheny's salesforce provided. Customers who had bought regular carbon steel in small quantities with low prices and fast delivery from local steel wholesalers were willing to pay higher prices for stainless steel and to buy larger quantities direct from the Allegheny mill with longer delivery times because they needed Allegheny's extensive customer services.

By the 1950s, Allegheny had educated customers to the point where they no longer needed the original cluster of customer benefits. The firm eventually responded by becoming less service oriented and more price oriented. It reduced its salesforce and began distributing through independent wholesalers to speed up deliveries and reduce costs. Thus, while remaining market oriented, the company simplified and streamlined its marketing program in response to changing customer needs.

SUMMARY

This chapter argues that a strategy should specify *what* is to be accomplished, *where* (which industries and product-markets to focus on), and *how* (allocating the resources and activities to each product-market to meet environmental opportunities and threats and to gain a competitive advantage). Consequently, there are five components within a well-developed strategy: (1) scope, or the desired breadth of the organization's strategic domain; (2) goals and objectives; (3) resource deployments—distribution of financial and human resources across businesses, product-markets, and/or functional departments and activities; (4) identification of a source of sustainable competitive advantage; and (5) specification of potential sources of synergy across business and/or functional departments.

Decisions about the organization's scope or mission, its overall goals and objectives, avenues for future growth, and resource deployments are the primary components of a corporate strategy. A mission statement provides guidance to an organization's managers about which market opportunities to pursue and which fall outside the firm's strategic domain.

Formal objectives guide a firm's business

units and employees toward specific dimensions and levels of performance by establishing benchmarks against which performance can be compared and evaluated.

The corporate development strategy addresses the question of future growth. A firm might pursue two primary growth directions: expansion of current businesses or diversification into new businesses. Finally, the firm's resources must be allocated across its various businesses in a way that reflects both the relative competitive strength of each business and variations in the attractiveness and growth potential of the markets they serve. Managers use portfolio models to make resource allocation decisions.

At the business-unit level, managers must make recommendations about (a) the SBU's objectives and scope, (b) how resources should be allocated across product-markets and functional departments within the SBU, and (c) which competitive strategy the unit should pursue in

attempting to build a sustainable competitive advantage in its product-markets. Decisions about an SBU's scope, objectives, and resource deployments are similar to—and should be consistent with—those made at the corporate level. The business unit's competitive strategy, however, should take into account the unit's unique strengths and weaknesses relative to competitors and the needs and wants of customers in its target markets.

When developing a marketing plan for a specific product-market entry, a marketing manager's range of choices is constrained by strategic decisions made at the corporate and business-unit levels. On the other hand, marketing managers often provide necessary information and analyses to the strategic planning process at higher levels of the organization. The extensiveness of the marketer's role in strategic planning is mediated, however, by the market (or customer) orientation of the firm and its top managers.

QUESTIONS

1. Which critical issues should be addressed at each of the following levels?
   a. Corporate strategy
   b. Business-level strategy
   c. Marketing strategy

2. How was the strategic marketing program for Grandma's cookies influenced or constrained by strategic decisions made at higher levels within Frito-Lay or perhaps within the firm's parent company, PepsiCo?

3. Many U.S. liberal arts colleges have historically offered an undergraduate degree in liberal arts (the product) to full-time 18- to 22-year-old students (the market). How might such a college attempt to expand its revenues by pursuing each of the different *expansion strategies* discussed in the chapter and outlined in Exhibit 2–4?

4. Which *diversification strategy* is illus-

trated by each of the following acquisitions? What synergies or benefits might each purchase produce?
   a. Pillsbury's acquisition of Totino's Pizza
   b. Sears' purchase of an interest in Whirlpool
   c. Philip Morris's acquisition of Miller Brewing Company
   d. Mobil Oil's acquisition of Montgomery Ward

5. A manufacturer of electrical components for industrial applications has five strategic business units (SBUs) shown in the table on page 74. Using the Boston Consulting Group portfolio model, evaluate the strength of the company's current and potential future condition. What strategies should it consider to improve its future position?

SBU	Sales ($ million)	Compet- itors	Sales of top 3 competitors ($ million)	Market growth rate
A	$1.0	7	$1.4, $1.4, $1.0	15%
B	3.2	18	3.2, 3.2, 2.0	20
C	3.8	12	3.8, 3.0, 2.5	7
D	6.5	5	6.5, 1.6, 1.4	4
E	.7	9	3.0, 2.5, 2.0	4

6. Critics argue that the BCG portfolio model sometimes provides misleading advice concerning how resources should be allocated across SBUs or product-markets. What are some of the possible limitations of the model? What might a manager do to reap the benefits of portfolio analysis while avoiding at least some shortcomings you have identified?

7. How are the basic *business philosophies or orientations* of a major consumer products firm such as General Mills and a small entrepreneurial start-up in a fast-growing, high-tech industry likely to differ? What are the implications of such philosophical differences for the role of marketers in the strategic planning processes of the two firms?

8. As the small entrepreneurial firm described in question 7 grows larger, its market matures, and its industry becomes more competitive, how should its business philosophy or orientation change? Why?

9. Which role should marketing managers play in helping to formulate business-level (SBU) strategies in a large diversified firm such as General Electric? What kinds of information are marketers best able to provide as a basis for planning? Which issues or elements of business-level strategy can such information help to resolve?

SECTION II

Market opportunity analysis

s we discussed in the first section, formulating and implementing strategic marketing programs for a given product-market entry requires selecting of target markets that represent attractive opportunities. Further, the firm must have the resources—business strengths—to exploit these opportunities in ways that give it an enduring competitive advantage. Thus, before any marketing strategies can be developed, the firm must undertake a market opportunity analysis. The process by which this analysis takes place is the focus of this section (Chapters 3 through 9).

The major steps in the market opportunity analysis emphasize that opportunities and threats derive primarily from the external environment. A favorable demand trend, the emergence of a new segment of some significance, a change in the relative importance of a channel of distribution, failure by a major competitor to follow recent industry price reductions, and improved process technology that can lower manufacturing costs are all examples of possible opportunities of some magnitude. Examples of threats—or problems—include the growth of a segment where your entry holds a low relative share, a general decline in prices when your company is a high-cost producer, increased direct selling by competitors when your salesforce is primarily oriented toward distributors, and the introduction of a lower-priced brand by a strong competitor.

Opportunities and threats can also come from *within* the firm. Opportunities include new and/or improved products, the development of a unique advertising program, and an ability to lower relative costs. But a deteriorating product quality, high relative costs, high turnover in the sales-force, poor product availability, and a weak service program are strong barriers to profitable growth.

The opportunity analysis process focuses on various environmental elements in an attempt to identify future opportunities and threats. We examine broad macroenvironmental forces and trends that might influence the entry's future objectives and action plans in Chapter 3. Chapters 4 and 5 analyze customer buying behavior goals (both for consumer and industrial goods) to determine what benefits different customers want from the product. How potential customers can best be clustered and the resulting market segments are described in Chapter 6. Industry and competitor analyses of competitive strengths and weaknesses and how the bases of competition are likely to evolve over time are discussed in Chapters 7 and 8. And the measurement of various markets, including the use of marketing research to help estimate the future value of the product-market entry, is examined in Chapter 9.

The outcome of a market opportunity analysis is a better understanding of what opportunities and threats must be addressed in each market. At this point the business unit's competitive strengths are combined with information about the market environment to develop marketing strategies, programs, and action plans aimed at taking advantage of the opportunities—or warding off the threats. This process begins with the decisions about which market segments the business should focus on as target markets, and how its product offerings should be positioned in each target market to gain a competitive advantage.

Chapter ⟨3⟩

Analyzing the macro-environment

TOMORROW'S HEALTH-CARE SYSTEM

In the 1990s, the U.S. health-care system will differ greatly from what it was in the 1980s. A number of driving forces will cause turmoil as the system goes through a period of radical structural changes. The key forces include an aging population, more sophisticated consumers, advances in technologies serving the system, a surplus of physicians and hospital facilities in some geographic areas, and federal, state, and local governments.

Health-care expenditures are expected to grow as much as 4 to 5 percent annually. The cost of health insurance will increase by at least 70 percent (in constant 1985 dollars) by the year 2000. A variety of outpatient services will experience rapid growth. Hospitals will become more sophisticated in their treatments, and admission expenditures per acute care will increase from $3,300 as was the case in 1985 to $5,000 for the year 2000. Hospital admissions will drop 10 percent—and total patient-days will decline even

more. Hospital outpatient services will grow from 16 percent to 25 percent of total hospital income. Health maintenance organizations (HMOs) and other contract group health services will almost double in coverage, from 18 percent to 35 percent. The system will continue to be fractionated; and a national health program is not likely to happen.[1]

This industry study illustrates the importance of the environment in generating opportunities and threats that affect an organization's objectives, strategies, and action plans. In the case of the health-care system, the number and type of players are numerous. They include private and not-for-profit hospitals and clinics, doctors, ambulatory services, pharmaceutical companies, medical instruments and equipment companies, insurance firms, drug wholesalers, and many more.

----

[1] Roy Amara, "Health Care Tomorrow," *The Futurist*, November–December 1988, pp. 16–20.

Interfacing with the marketplace and its competitors is of immediate concern to a firm. But it is critical that a firm also understand the macroenvironmental trends affecting the industry and the marketplace longer term if it is to exploit its opportunities and avoid its threats. Exhibit 3–1 shows how the environment interacts with the firm and its resources.

Environmental factors are more diverse, more difficult to monitor, less controllable, and less directly related to marketing actions than those stemming directly from the marketplace or competition. Environmental impact on one industry's future is illustrated by the following prediction:

> Intensified global competition, continued improvements in computer and telecommunications (technology), and accelerated deregulation (both abroad and in the United States) will impact the structure of the United States commercial banking industry dramatically. "By the early 1990s . . . nationwide consumer banking will become a reality in the United States. A few large firms will have coast-to-coast offices that take deposits, write mortgages, make auto loans, and issue credit cards. Large regional banks will continue expanding outside their home state. . . . By mid-decade no-holds-barred competition will spread as the legal walls separating commercial banking, investment banking, and insurance begin to crumble."[2]

Reactions to this scenario vary, depending on the financial institution and its size. Such giants as American Express, Citicorp, and Merrill Lynch probably see the next decade as one of opportunity, especially in the marketing of new financial services. The average commercial bank, on the other hand, is likely to view it as a hostile environment that threatens its very existence, given its expensive branch networks and many problem loans.

Myriad environmental changes emerge from a wide variety of sources over time. Many of these changes are largely irrelevant to a given firm; others significantly affect its competitive posture. The firm's challenge is to identify the key environmental factors that present opportunities and threats and are thus relevant in formulating marketing strategy and preparing action plans.

In this chapter, we present the main characteristics of the macroenvironment. We describe elements of the four major components of the marketing environment—the demographic/economic, political/legal, technological, and sociocultural environments. And we examine the strategic issue management process required to monitor and integrate environmental factors when formulating marketing strategies. Subsequent chapters narrow the search for opportunities and threats by focusing on the competitive environment (the industry and major competitors) and well-defined customer segments.

---

[2] Gary Hector, "The Money Game Will Get Brutal," *Fortune*, February 2, 1987, p. 43.

EXHIBIT   3 ♦ 1
Interaction of macroenvironment forces on firm's strategy

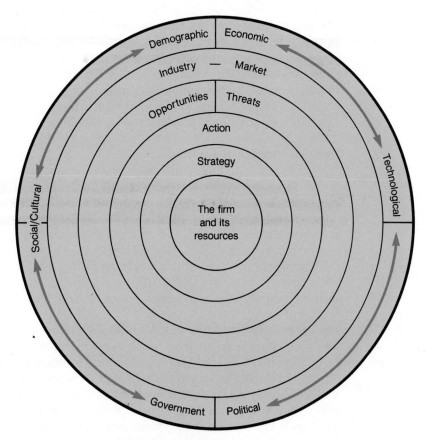

CHARACTERISTICS OF THE MACROENVIRONMENT

In the 1970s, the United States entered a period of increased environmental change that continues yet today. Raw material shortages, increasing international competition, consumerism, electronic technology, government regulation and deregulation: these forces continue to impact the formulation and implementation of marketing strategies and action plans. These changes no longer seem to be a temporary stage in the evolution of our society. Rather, they are an irreversible trend toward the increasing role of the macroenvironment in the formulation of marketing strategy.

Nature of the macroenvironment

Not only do the dynamics of the macroenvironment make it difficult to comprehend—but also the fact that it is *boundless*; that it conveys *signals* that are difficult to interpret as to their impact on marketing strategies; that it is for the most part *uncontrollable*; and that *special expertise* is required to understand it.

The boundlessness of the environment

Sources of *environmental* change are practically infinite and must be comprehensively and continuously monitored. Though such monitoring takes substantial time and effort, the probability of detecting a new element of importance to an individual marketing manager is relatively low. Consequently, it is rarely feasible for an individual marketing manager to have an ongoing, comprehensive understanding of the total environment.

Weak environmental signals

Factors external to the firm rarely evolve dramatically over a short time period. In most cases, detectable signals warn of the probable change in a market or a competitor. Signals arising from the environment, however, are less discernible than those generated by markets or competitors. They may, therefore, not be detected; and shifts in the environment may have already occurred when they are finally observed. One example is the formation of OPEC and its success in drastically raising oil prices. By producing a worldwide petroleum crisis, OPEC surprised even the largest oil companies—despite publicly available advance forecasts of Arab action.

The uncontrollable nature of environmental factors

The firm never has full control of any environmental factors; but it can respond in ways designed to take advantage of an opportunity or dampen the effects of a threat. An example of the first is the developing of food products that are cholesterol free—thereby turning a threat into an opportunity. When this cannot be done, and the threat is serious, then perhaps the only realistic solution is to disinvest in the business. For example, Corning Glass got out of the light-bulb glass business after 100 years because of declining demand, which the company thought it could do little to change.[3] Another alternative is to try to stop the event from happening, such as lobbying to prevent or delay the passage of legislation. This has been the case with legislation concerned with the sale of hand guns.

Or the firm could try to identify environmental trends likely to affect current product-market entries and then adjust the marketing mix to take advantage—or reduce the negative impact—of those changes. For instance, Ford increased the proportion of its ads placed in media with a high percentage of women readers in response to the fact that 30 percent of all car buyers in the mid-1980s were women, compared to only about 20 percent a decade earlier.[4]

---

[3] Myron Magnet, "Corning Glass Shapes Up," *Fortune*, December 12, 1982, p. 90.

[4] D. Walsh, "About Those New Women Consumers," *American Demographics*, October 1984, pp. 26–29.

The diversity of expertise required

By training and experience, marketing managers are generally prepared to understand and forecast the impact of changes in the marketplace or in the actions of competitors. On the other hand, analysis and understanding of macroenvironmental variables require expertise in many fields, including science, law, economics, and sociology. This makes an exhaustive and systematic monitoring of all environmental factors by the product or marketing manager neither feasible nor desirable. Marketers should, however, *participate* in the process and be primary beneficiaries of it.

CRITICAL COMPONENTS OF MARKETING'S MACROENVIRONMENT

Four components of the macroenvironment are particularly critical from a marketing viewpoint: the demographic/economic environment, the political/legal environment, the technological environment, and the sociocultural environment. Each of these is a driving force in the U.S. health-care system; for example:

* The aging population and the overcapacity in the system—both hospitals and doctors (the demographic/economic environment).
* The continued strong role played by the government in U.S. health care (the political/legal environment).
* New developments in the basic sciences (biology and chemistry) and in computers (the technological environment).
* The attitudes of consumers toward health-care costs (the sociocultural environment).

We will not provide an exhaustive overview of each of these environments but will discuss specific aspects of each that are important to marketing managers and show how changes in them affect marketing strategies.

The demographic/economic environment

The economy is the most pervasive component of the marketing environment. It is also the most analyzed, although our ability to fully comprehend and forecast changes in the economy remains limited. In an uncertain economic climate, the economic variables most likely to affect marketing activities are population demographics (particularly changes in age levels), the rate of economic growth, interest rates, and currency exchange rates. With the exception of the latter, these variables affect the objectives, strategies, and action plans of most, if not all, the organizations in the health-care system.

Demographics

The evolution of the population is a key environmental factor for marketers. It directly affects consumer markets and influences other economic forces. Exhibit 3–2 lists important U.S. demographic trends. Despite declining fer-

EXHIBIT   3 ♦ 2

Major U.S. demographic trends and their implications

1. U.S. population growth is slowing: 0.7 annual percentage increase during the 1990s versus 1.7 annual percentage increase during the 1950s.
   Implications: Declining number of births will lower the demand for such products and services as houses, major appliances, baby food, insurance, and medical care. The high birthrate following World War II served as a major force behind the high economic growth years of the 50s and 60s.

2. The United States is rapidly becoming a middle-aged society. By the year 2000, the 35–54 age group will represent the key consumer market on which to focus.
   Implications: This trend will increase the demand for travel, health foods, luxury goods, retirement services, and clothing. The demand for household goods, insurance, and housing will be reduced.

3. Growth will occur mostly in households making over $35,000, which will increase from about 27 percent of all households in 1980 to almost 45 percent in 1995.
   Implications: More demand for high-quality products and services. Greater variety of lifestyles.

4. The percentage of women in the labor force will increase. Over 50 percent of all wives will work; and a growing majority of preschoolers will have working mothers.
   Implications: Increased demand for automobiles by working women. Strong demand for a variety of child-care services—especially for infants and toddlers.

5. Three states are expected to account for over 50 percent of the total population increase: Florida (7.7 million), California (6.9 million), and Texas (6.5 million).
   Implications: More monies allocated for promotions (sales and advertising) in these states at the expense of low- or even negative-growth areas.

6. By the year 2000, blacks and Hispanics will total 36 million each. The two will represent over 25 percent of the total U.S. population.
   Implications: Greater importance of ethnic markets, leading to greater use of ethnic media. Greater demand for selected food and personal-care items.

Source: William Lazer, *Handbook of Demographics for Marketing and Advertising* (Lexington, Mass.: D. C. Heath and Company, 1987).

tility rates, the United States is far from experiencing zero population growth. According to the Bureau of the Census, the total U.S. population will grow to nearly 300 million by 2020—compared to 226 million in 1980. The absolute number of annual births should increase as baby boomers enter their childbearing years. U.S. births are expected to reach 4.4 million at the height of the new baby boom, compared to 3.6 million in 1980.

As the post-World War II baby boomers mature, the number of affluent households will increase substantially, which affects the purchase of many goods and services, because these are prime earning years and many households have two incomes. For example, the number of households headed by a person 35 to 54 years old will increase 40 percent—from 31 million in

EXHIBIT   3 ♦ 3

U.S. households headed by individuals aged 35–54 by total income:
1986 versus 2000 (in 1985 dollars)

	1986		2000	
	No.*	Percent	No.*	Percent
All households	31,099	100.0%	43,665	100.0%
Under $10,000	3,557	11.4	4,074	9.2
$10,000–$19,999	4,943	15.9	5,521	12.6
20,000–29,999	5,889	18.9	6,534	14.9
30,000–39,999	5,494	17.7	6,781	15.5
40,000–49,999	3,982	12.8	6,006	13.8
50,000–59,999	2,803	9.0	4,331	9.9
60,000–74,999	2,165	7.0	4,214	9.6
75,000 and over	2,266	7.3	6,205	14.2
Median income	$32,110		$38,410	

* Thousands.

Source: Thomas G. Exter, "Baby Boom Incomes," American Demographics, November 1987, p. 62.

1986 to 44 million in the year 2000. The median income of these households
is expected to rise from $32,110 to $38,410 after taking inflation into account.[5] Exhibit 3–3 shows the distribution of households by income group
for 1986 versus the year 2000.

The aging U.S. population will have a strong impact on the nation's
health-care system. The number of people over 75 years of age will increase
by about 35 percent by the year 2000. This group uses five to seven times the
medical services of the average total population.[6]

Consumer spending overall is expected to grow on average 2.5 percent
annually during the 90s—down from 2.7 percent in previous years. The
reason for this shift is that people save more as they get older—in part
because they do not have to make first-time outlays for big durables. New
household formations will remain at the current level of 1.3 million during
the 90s.

These figures mean a slowdown in the sales of items for the home. The
sale of automobiles is expected to remain essentially the same until the late
1990s. The sale of pharmaceuticals is expected to increase dramatically
during the 90s, due mainly to the presence of more older people. Travel and
recreation expenditures are expected to increase; thus, airlines, car rentals,

[5] Thomas G. Exter, "Baby Boom Incomes," American Demographics, November 1987, p. 62.
[6] Amara, "Health Care Tomorrow."

hotels/motels, entertainment, and health gear will benefit.[7] Personal-care products and services for older consumers will benefit from the demographic shifts. Some firms, such as Johnson & Johnson and Gillette, are already adjusting their product offerings and promotional programs to appeal to this growing age segment. As noted earlier, total health-care expenditures will increase dramatically in the 90s—causing medical insurance to increase by as much as 70 percent.

Growth

Economic growth is usually measured by the gross national product (GNP), which represents the sum total of all expenditures made on final products. The real growth in GNP (corrected for inflation) declined from 4.5 percent in the early 60s to 2.5 percent and less in the late 70s and early mid-80s. GNP is expected to grow at an average rate of 2.6 percent through the year 2000.[8]

The trend toward slower economic growth is due to several reasons. The high growth following World War II benefited from a number of positive factors such as a baby boom and an explosion of new technologies. But increased competition from abroad that negatively impacted employment, along with higher energy costs, has slowed economic growth. When slow growth is coupled with product maturity, competition heats up. Increasingly, products and sales strategies must be designed with that in mind.

Interest rates

At the beginning of the 80s, the prime interest rate in the United States reached high levels—around 20 percent. Since then it has declined dramatically to around 10 percent; some economists believe that interest rates will remain relatively low over the next several years. High interest rates adversely affect the market by restricting the financing capabilities of customers. They are particularly acute on the demand for consumer durables, such as housing, cars, and heavy appliances.

Currency exchange rates

Fluctuations in exchange rates may significantly change the relative price competitiveness of firms manufacturing in different countries. For example, the exchange rate between the U.S. dollar and the French franc changed from 4.48 to the dollar on January 6, 1981, to 9.69 on February 4, 1985—a difference of over 100 percent in about four years. By late 1988, it was about six. A weak currency improves the export opportunities of a firm; a strong currency places it at a disadvantage.

---

[7] Alex Taylor III, "What the Sober Spenders Will Buy," *Fortune*, February 2, 1985, pp. 35–38.

[8] Michael Brody, "The 1990s," *Fortune*, February 2, 1987, p. 22.

In the fall of 1988, the Japanese yen had appreciated some 60 percent against the dollar over a two-year period. Thus, to stay "even," Japanese car makers should have increased the retail price of their $10,000 cars to $16,000 and that of their $15,000 cars to $24,000. But the prices of Japanese car imports have increased considerably less than 60 percent, because the Japanese are fearful of losing market share.

International competition

The United States is the largest national market in the world, representing about 25 percent of the total world market for all products and services. In comparison, Japan is the second-largest market in the free world, with 10 percent of the total world market. The size of the U.S. market makes it a high-priority target for the business firms of most countries, but particularly those of Japan and Western Europe.

Today, about 25 percent of all automobiles sold in the United States are from abroad. Japan, in particular, has been able to successfully penetrate the U.S. market with cars as well as calculators, TVs and radios, motorcycles, binoculars, cameras, and digital watches. But Americans are also familiar with products from Europe, such as Norelco electric shavers (Holland), Volkswagen cars (Germany), Saab cars (Sweden), and Wedgwood china (England).

Businesses in the United States are increasingly seeking foreign markets. In 1987, over 100 U.S. firms had exports in excess of $4 billion each. For many of these firms, such as Black & Decker, Coca-Cola, Gillette, Polaroid, and Firestone, more than 50 percent of their earnings came from exports.[9] In recent years, the United States has experienced substantial deficits in its foreign trade—over $100 billion in 1987.[10]

Both opportunities and threats abound in world trade. Europe's decision to create a truly common market by 1992 with over 300 million consumers has posed a threat to many U.S. companies. The free flow of people, capital, and goods among the 12 nations of the European Economic Community (EEC) may trigger a move to protectionism. If so, then U.S. companies already in Europe (such as Ford, GM, IBM) will be better off than those simply exporting to the EEC. Consequently, direct investment in the EEC has increased dramatically, as shown in Exhibit 3–4. For example, Federal Express recently spent $250 million acquiring courier companies in Italy, West Germany, and Holland.[11]

---

[9] "The 100 Largest U.S. Multinationals," *Forbes*, July 25, 1988, pp. 248–50.

[10] *Survey of Current Business*, July 1988, p. 20.

[11] Richard I. Kirkland, Jr., "Outsider's Guide to Europe in 1992," *Fortune*, October 24, 1988, p. 124.

EXHIBIT 3 ◆ 4

Foreign direct investment in the European Community

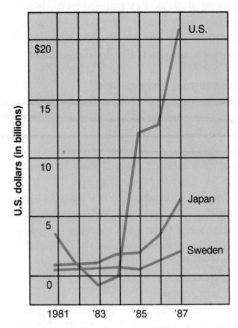

In Europe, *product standardization* across EEC-member countries will be one of the benefits of the 1992 deregulation. This prospect has made it possible for 3M to consolidate production and effect substantial cost savings. For many years, 3M produced a number of different product versions for various countries. But now, for example, one 3M plant produces all the videotapes and videocassettes for Europe.[12]

The political/legal environment

The political/legal environment includes all the factors controlled by public authorities. Its major element is legislation, which defines the regulatory environment within which business must operate. Its key distinctiveness is its ability to impose *mandatory* constraints on a firm's operations. Non-compliance with regulations exposes the firm to penalties and corrective actions imposed by administrative justice.

As with any other external force, the political/legal environment presents not only strategic threats to the firm, but opportunities also. New regulations

---

[12] Ibid., p. 122.

or deregulations may open new markets, such as the pollution or energy control markets. Or the political environment can destabilize an industry and enable more aggressive firms to improve their competitive posture.[13] In addition, other elements in the political/legal environment often present opportunities for business firms. Such is the case, for example, with taxes, subsidies, and government contracts.

Our review here includes the major elements of the political legal environment that have a potential impact on marketing activities; that is, government regulation and deregulation, other government influences, and the broad notion of political risk. All of these elements could conspire to impact the health-care system in a variety of ways. Will the federal government continue to press for increased regulation of the system? Will government continue to encourage competition within the system?

Government regulation

The intricacies and sheer number of laws and regulations make it difficult for marketing executives to fully comprehend the regulatory elements that may affect them. That this complexity has continually increased is shown in the number of new regulatory agencies created by the federal government— more than 35 since 1950.

A major area of government regulation concerns antitrust legislation, the purpose of which is to maintain and enforce competition. Because marketing activities impact a firm's competitive posture, they are a prime target of antitrust regulations. Firms operating in international markets must also be attentive to antitrust legislation in foreign countries. Of growing importance are the antitrust regulations of the European Economic Community. These regulations prohibit agreements between enterprises that restrict or distort competition within the Common Market and abuses of a dominant position in a market that affects trade between member states.

Consumer protection legislation

Consumer protection laws have centered primarily on product safety and information. Although the regulations deal for the most part with consumer goods, they also significantly affect industrial products used in their manufacture. These laws are enforced by more than 50 federal government agencies, the most prominent ones being the Food and Drug Administration (FDA) and the Federal Trade Commission (FTC).

The most significant element in the evolution of consumer protection legislation has been the increased recognition of the **strict liability** concept. This makes it possible for a seller to be held responsible for injuries caused by a defective product even though due care was exercised in its preparation

---

[13] For an analysis of opportunities created by regulation, see Barry M. Mitnick, "The Strategic Uses of Regulation—and Deregulation," *Business Horizons*, March–April 1981, pp. 71–83.

EXHIBIT 3 ◆ 5

Selected U.S. federal legislation of interest to marketers

Antitrust legislation

Sherman Antitrust Act (1890)

Forbids (1) "contracts, combinations or conspiracies in restraint of trade," and (2) "monopolies or attempts to monopolize" in interstate or foreign commerce.

Clayton Act (1914)

Supplements and attempts to overcome the vague wording of the Sherman Act by prohibiting certain specific practices (such as tying clauses and exclusive dealing contracts, interlocking directorates, and certain price discrimination) where the effect "may be to substantially lessen competition or tend to create a monopoly in any line of commerce." The act also provides that corporate managers who violate its provisions can be held individually responsible; exempts agricultural and labor organizations.

Federal Trade Commission Act (1914)

Created the FTC, a commission of specialists with broad powers to investigate possible violations of Section 5, which declares that "unfair methods of competition in commerce are unlawful." This provision has been widely applied to strike down such "unfair" marketing practices as false and misleading advertising claims. The commission can issue "cease and desist" orders to enforce its decisions.

Robinson-Patman Act (1936)

Amends the Clayton Act and outlaws (subject to certain specific defenses) prices that discriminate among buyers of goods "of like grade and quality" where the effect may be to "injure, destroy or prevent competition." Gives the FTC the right to limit quantity discounts, to forbid brokerage allowances except to independent brokers, and to prohibit promotional allowances except when made available to all dealers "on proportionately equal terms."

Wheeler-Lea Act (1938)

Prohibits unfair and deceptive acts and practices in interstate commerce regardless of whether competition is injured. Gives the FTC jurisdiction over the advertising of food and drugs.

Antimerger Act (1950)

Amends Section 7 of the Clayton Act by broadening the power to prevent corporate acquisitions where they may have a substantially adverse effect on competition.

Consumer Goods Pricing Act (1975)

Rescinds the provisions of the Miller-Tydings and McGuire acts by prohibiting resale price maintenance agreements between manufacturers and their resellers in interstate commerce.

---

and sale. Business firms' responsibilities under strict liability can be substantial: witness the millions of cars that automakers have been forced to recall over the years because of safety-related defects. Exhibit 3–5 summarizes some of the major federal antitrust and consumer protection legislation and their major provisions of importance to marketers.

Government deregulation

Government, business, and the general public have become increasingly aware of the negative effects of overregulation that protects inefficiencies, restricts entry by new competitors, and creates inflationary pressures. A

EXHIBIT 3 ◆ 5
(*concluded*)

Consumer protection legislation

Federal Food and Drug Act (1906)
Prohibits the manufacture, sale, or transport of adulterated or fraudulently labeled foods or drugs in interstate commerce (the act was supplanted by the Food, Drug, and Cosmetic Act in 1938). The Kefauver-Harris Amendment of 1962 establishes guidelines for the pretesting of drugs for safety and effectiveness, and for labeling of drugs by generic names.

Meat Inspection Act (1906)
Provides for the enforcement of sanitary standards in meat-packing firms and for federal inspection of companies selling meat in interstate commerce.

Automobile Information Disclosure Act (1958)
Prohibits dealers from inflating the manufacturer's price on new cars.

National Traffic and Safety Act (1958)
Provides for the setting of compulsory safety standards for automobiles and tires.

Fair Packaging and Labeling Act (1966)
Regulates the packaging and labeling of consumer goods, and requires manufacturers to state what the package contains, how much, and who made it. Permits voluntary adoption of uniform packaging standards within an industry.

Child Protection Act (1966)
Bans hazardous toys and other products for children; amended in 1969 to include products that pose electrical, mechanical, and thermal hazards.

Federal Cigarette Labeling and Advertising Act (1967)
Requires warnings on all cigarette packages and ads ("Warning: The Surgeon General has determined that cigarette smoking is dangerous to your health.") and bans advertising cigarettes on TV.

Truth-in-Lending Act (1968)
Requires lenders to state the true and complete cost of a credit transaction, prohibits the threat or use of violence in collecting loans, and restricts the amount of garnishments. Established a National Commission on Consumer Finance.

Fair Credit Reporting Act (1970)
Ensures that consumers' credit reports contain only recent, accurate, and relevant information, and that it will be confidential unless requested by a proper party for an appropriate reason.

Consumer Product Safety Act (1972)
Establishes the Consumer Product Safety Commission and authorizes it to set safety standards for consumer products and to impose penalties on firms that fail to uphold those standards.

Magnuson-Moss Warranty/FTC Improvement Act (1975)
Authorized the FTC to establish rules concerning consumer warranties and establishes means for consumers to gain redress of grievances (such as the "class action" suit). Also expands FTC's regulatory powers over unfair and deceptive acts and practices.

Equal Credit Opportunity Act (1975)
Outlaws discrimination in a credit transaction on the basis of sex, marital status, race, national origin, religion, age, or receipt of public assistance.

Fair Debt Collection Practice Act (1978)
Prohibits harassment of any individual and prohibits making false statements or using unfair methods when collecting a debt.

Toy Safety Act (1984)
Provides government with authority to recall dangerous toys quickly.

trend started in the 70s toward a reduction in the administrative and legal barriers to competition—a process called **deregulation.** This trend affects mainly economic regulations controlling the operations of specific industries. Industries that have been deregulated are passenger and cargo airlines, trucking, railroads, and telecommunications. Deregulation of banking and insurance is now underway.

The technological environment

Technology is a major source of change in today's world. It is the driving force behind the introduction of many new products and the development of many markets. By providing better substitutes, technology is also a major reason for the decline of some products and markets. Technology can have a substantial impact on the performance and competitive structure of an industry. For example, consider the effect of genetic engineering on pharmaceuticals, of transistors on telecommunications, of plastics on the use of metals, and of computers on about everything.

The total time required to effectively exploit a technological breakthrough can be divided into two parts. The first is the *incubation phase*, which begins when a basic discovery is made and ends with the recognition of its commercial potential. Second is *commercial development*, which ends with the commercial introduction of a new product based on the basic discovery. Dramatic acceleration has occurred in identifying the commercial potential of technological developments.[14] For instance, the incubation period for frozen foods was 74 years. It was only two years for integrated circuits. The time between ideas, invention, and commercialization will continue to decrease and new technologies—especially those pertaining to production—will be more quickly adopted.[15]

The importance of external technological change

Most companies try to develop new products internally through their R&D departments. But they are often affected by technological innovations that first occurred in other firms, including those outside their industry. U.S. R&D is still the most productive in the world, although in recent years, Japan, and to a lesser extent, West Germany and France have made considerable progress, for example, in robots and digital control systems (see Exhibit 3–6). More and better research is needed in the years ahead if the United States is to be successful in competing for global markets.[16] Specific signals

---

[14] Alvin Toffler, *Future Shock* (New York: Random House, 1970), p. 15.

[15] Marvin J. Cetron, Wanda Rocha, and Rebecca Luckens, "Into the 21st Century," *The Futurist,* July–August 1988, p. 30.

[16] Stuart Gannes, "The Good News About U.S. R&D," *Fortune,* February 1988, pp. 48–56.

EXHIBIT 3 ◆ 6

U.S. and world expenditures in research and development

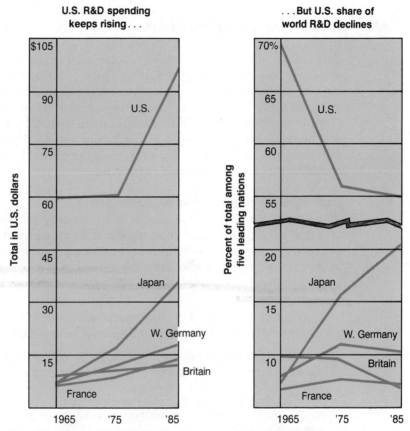

Source: Stuart Gannes, "The Good News About U.S. R&D," *Fortune*, February 1, 1988, p. 49. © Time Inc. All rights reserved.

that anticipate technological change include patents, trend analyses of product performance, industrial and governmental research budgets, or economic, political, and social pressures. These signals need to be carefully scrutinized, or substantial threats and opportunities may be overlooked—as in the following xerography example.

A report of Chester Carlson's first patent on xerography was spotted in *The New York Times* in 1940 by a young marketing man. Despite his efforts, he failed to interest IBM in Carlson's invention. In 1943, Eastman Kodak Company's technical publication, *Patent Abstracts*, published an abstract of the patent; but Kodak did not take any significant action. In October 1948, the little Haloid Company, which later became the Xerox Corporation, held a major demonstration in New York City. It received wide press coverage; but industry did not react. By 1965, copying was widely used. Xerox introduced its new high-speed model 2400 copier, which gave a new signal that the technology could also invade the duplicating and printing fields.[17]

Technological change and marketing

In addition to new products, technological developments have a wide impact on all marketing activities, including *communications* (by making available new media or new selling tools); *distribution* (by opening new channels or modifying the operations and performance of existing outlets); *packaging* (by allowing the use of new materials or designs); *marketing research* (by making feasible new data-gathering and analysis techniques); and *marketing decision making* (by offering improved procedures and computerized models). Exhibit 3–7 provides examples of how advances in telecommunications have affected marketing.

Intensification of technological development

In the past 10 to 12 years, we have seen an amazing number of new technologies that have brought such new products as videocassette recorders, compact discs, ever-more-powerful/ever-smaller computers, and highly effective genetically engineered vaccines. Many researchers predict technological progress between now and the year 2000 will be 10 times that experienced in the past 12 years.[18]

This intensification of technological progress has been colorfully described by Alvin Toffler in his well-known *Future Shock*:

> It has been observed, for example, that if the last 50,000 years of man's existence were divided into lifetimes of approximately sixty-two years each, there have been about 800 such lifetimes. Of these, fully 650 were spent in caves.
>
> Only during the last seventy lifetimes has it been possible to communicate effectively from one lifetime to another—as writing made it possible to do. Only during the last six lifetimes did masses of men ever see a printed word. Only during the last four has it been possible to measure time with any precision. Only in the last two has anyone anywhere used an electric motor. And the overwhelming majority of all the material goods we use in daily life today have been developed within the present, the 800th, lifetime.[19]

Even now our offices are being structured so as to interconnect over vast areas of space. FAX machines are revolutionizing the way offices communicate with one another. They are also affecting how whole industries operate: witness their effect on Federal Express, where in 1988 they si-

---

[17] James R. Bright, "Evaluating Signals of Technological Change," *Harvard Business Review*, January–February 1970, pp. 62–70.

[18] Bylinsky, "Technology in the Year 2000," *Fortune*, July 18, 1988, p. 92.

[19] Toffler, *Future Shock*, p. 15.

EXHIBIT 3 ♦ 7

Examples of effect of advances in telecommunications on marketing

1. Increase in the use of telephone interviews in marketing research because of decreasing cost of WATS lines and use of CRT displays and computer control of questionnaires.
2. Use of computers in tabulation and analysis of large quantities of data.
3. Use of supermarket scanners and in-home electronic recording of TV viewing to track audiences for TV programs and commercials by groups of households.
4. Increased ability to better target TV commercials due to increased TV station and program specialization.
5. Decrease in average inventories owing to automatic computer-based reorder systems.
6. Opportunity to shop by television. In 1987, some 43 million homes could engage in teleshopping.
7. Increased information available to consumers regarding price and purchase alternatives.

phoned off 20,000 to 30,000 letters nightly, forcing Fed Ex to emphasize its other services.[20]

Major technological innovations can be expected in a variety of fields, especially in biology, electronics/telecommunications, and man-made materials. We discuss each briefly.

The **biological revolution** is of fairly recent origins. By modifying the hereditary characteristics of bacteria, biologists have opened whole new areas of research concerned with such subjects as enhancing the body's ability to heal itself and the possibility of regrowing whole organs in the body. As noted earlier in the discussion of the health-care system of tomorrow, such new technologies will increase human beings' longevity and add substantial costs to the system. The cost of these new technologies will raise difficult ethical decisions about who gets to benefit from these new technologies and at what cost.

Some currently anticipated applications of this new technology include:[21]

♦ In *pharmaceuticals:* production of pure pharmaceutical substances such as insulin and interferon; production of human growth hormones to cure dwarfism and prevent muscle wastage; and introduction of powerful genetically engineered vaccines to eliminate many infectious diseases.

---

[20] Harriet Johnson Brackey, "It Makes Bold Push to Retain Market Share," *USA Today,* October 27, 1988, p. 1.

[21] For predictions about other potential applications of biotechnology and other new technologies, see "The Next Step: Twenty-Five Discoveries that Could Change Our Lives," *Science 85* (November 1985). For an example of how this technology has affected one company, see "Monsanto's New Regimen: Heavy Injections of Drugs and Biotechnology," *Business Week,* December 3, 1984, p. 64.

+ In *agriculture:* production of more resistant livestock and new species of animals; production of more resistant plants and new varieties generating their own fertilizer.
+ In *agricultural chemicals:* production of nonpolluting biological pesticides and insecticides.
+ In *animal foods:* production of protein by fermentation of algae or by the action of yeasts on hydrocarbons.
+ In *energy:* anaerobic production of methane by fermentation of algae; removal of sulfur from crude oil.
+ In *chemistry* and *metallurgy:* biological catalysts; bacteria capable of concentrating metals.
+ In *electronics:* production by genetically engineered bacteria of polymers modified to conduct electricity.

It is still too soon to comprehend all the ethical issues and potential applications of biotechnology. But it will probably affect other industries in addition to those previously listed; and it can be expected to have a deep long-term impact on our society.

Electronics have played an important role in our society since the 1950s. They were first used in such limited areas as computers, radio, and television. As technology improved, electronics contributed to the development of such new products as hand calculators, digital watches, automatic cameras, videogames, and microcomputers. By the year 2000, we can expect the following with respect to computers:[22]

+ Supercomputers that are 1,000 times more powerful than those of today. They are expected to do at least 4 trillion complex calculations a second—and the biggest may well cost $1 billion. Desktop workstations will have the power of present supercomputers.
+ Pocket-size computers that will respond to handwritten and human voice commands.
+ Electronic storage computers that can store up to 200 novels or nonfiction volumes, any one of which is available upon command.
+ Increasing use of the computer as an instrument of discovery; for example, simulating how the body reacts to a given disease or how an automobile handles before it is built.
+ More effective linkage of computers with other electronic machines; for example, as with medical diagnostic machines.
+ The arrival of the truly user-friendly computer.

Without computers, much of the progress in biology, electronics, and the development of new materials would not be possible.

Another area of particular importance is the increasing interaction between electronics and communications called **telecommunications.** This

---

[22] Bylinsky, "Technology in the Year 2000," pp. 92–96.

interaction allows for an easier transmission of data between persons, computers, and a variety of devices through cables, microwave relays, and satellites. In the near future, we can expect much-improved telephone lines permitting simultaneous transmission of voice, video, and data. The telephone of the year 2000 will allow picture-phone conferences in color, possess the ability to send and receive messages, and provide access to data sources. The rapid processing, analyzing, and presentation of data will facilitate the control and reappraisal of a firm's strategy and action plans.[23]

A third mega-technology has to do with such manufactured materials as high-performance plastics (which include composites based on carbon fibers) and superconducting ceramics. The plastics can be tailored for specific uses, but the two main areas of application are in cars and planes. General Motors anticipates that, within the next few years, 20 percent of its cars will have all-plastic bodies that will reduce weight, thereby increasing fuel economy. Composites made possible Voyager's nonstop round-the-world trip.

The new ceramics are lighter, stronger, and much more durable than many metals. They are currently used in knives, scissors, batteries, and artificial limbs. Engines and electronics will benefit most from the use of such materials. Nissan is using a ceramic turbo rotor in its 300ZX sports car because of its ability to tolerate temperatures up to 1500°C without lubrication.

Biomaterials made of plastics, composites, and ceramics are used to replace or augment bodily tissues, organs, and parts. Replacement joints and bone implants are now widely available, as are artificial tendons and ligaments. The implementation of artificial lenses is already widely practiced. Within a few years, synthetic human skin will help persons who are severely burned.[24]

The sociocultural environment

This environment represents the values, attributes, and general behavior of the individuals in a given society. Compared to economic, political, and technological changes, the sociocultural environment evolves slowly. People grow up in a system of values they tend to carry throughout their lifetimes. Transformations in the structure of society, in its institutions, and in the distribution of wealth occur gradually in democratic countries. Even so, we have in recent years seen a substantial change in individual values, family structure, minority rights, leisure-time activities, and conservation. These changes have impacted the sale of personal consumer products; advertising programs to accommodate more joint decision making; the creation

---

[23] Ibid., p. 96.

[24] Tom Forester, "The Materials Revolution," *The Futurist*, July–August 1988, pp. 13–20.

of special marketing programs for minority groups; the popularity of fast-food outlets; and the emergence of more energy-saving, reliable, and longer-lasting products. Changing demographics and variations in lifestyles will also affect the U.S. health-care system, as we have already noted. Next we discuss briefly two of the more important evolutionary trends—individual values and the family structure.

The evolution of individual values

North American society has traditionally been characterized by such values as the Puritan ethic of hard work, thriftiness, and faith in others and in institutions. In the 60s, however, a new social force emerged that did not entirely share these values. Instead of leaving the destiny of their country in the hands of their elders and institutions, the young—particularly college students—collectively fought for what they perceived to be good causes, such as civil rights, the end of the Vietnam war, and nonconformism. The young emerged as a new social force—sharing and defending a common set of new values even across national borders. This era is often referred to as the "Age of Us."

More recently, individual values shifted again for a variety of reasons, including "a new sense of lowered expectations, apprehensions about the future, mistrust of institutions, and a growing sense of limits."[25] Thus, individuals are becoming more concerned about self-actualization—the quality of life—than security. The meaning of work, relations with the opposite sex, and the importance of inner harmony are undergoing change as more people question the traditional ways of defining success.[26] As a consequence of this trend, marriages were postponed, birth rates dropped, divorce rates skyrocketed, and young women in the millions joined the labor force. One result of the declining birthrate will be a shortage of entry-level workers over the next decade. And increasingly we will find that consumers are preoccupied with maintaining economic stability in an environment perceived as hostile. Other changes include more concern about health, sexuality, travel, education, and creativity. Exhibit 3–8 lists the shift in values taking place in western societies.

The evolution of family structure

The traditional husband-dominated, closely structured family is less and less typical of our North American society. Children are becoming more autonomous and participate at an earlier age in many family decisions. A

---

[25] Daniel Yankelovich as quoted by Joseph T. Plummer, "Changing Values," *The Futurist*, January–February 1989, p. 8.

[26] Ibid., pp. 8–13.

EXHIBIT 3♦8

Shifting values in the western world

Traditional values	New values
Self-denial ethic	Self-fulfillment ethic
Higher standard of living	Better quality of life
Traditional sex roles	Blurring of sex roles
Accepted definition of success	Individualized definition of success
Traditional family life	Alternative families
Faith in industry, institutions	Self-reliance
Live to work	Work to live
Hero worship	Love of ideas
Expansionism	Pluralism
Patriotism	Less nationalistic
Unparalleled growth	Growing sense of limits
Industrial growth	Information/service growth
Receptivity of technology	Technology orientation

Developed Western societies are gradually moving away from traditional values and toward the emerging new values being embraced on an ever-widening scale, says author Plummer.

Source: "Changing Values: The New Emphasis on Self-Actualization," *The Futurist,* January–February 1989, p. 15.

more balanced allocation of power between husband and wife has also emerged. In part this has resulted from the fact that more women are more independent economically. Working parents' absence from the home has substantially reduced the interactions among family members and their cohesiveness. The increasing divorce rate has made one-parent households more common.

This evolution has considerably changed the buying process for many goods. The purchase of such major durables as housing, cars, furniture, and appliances is now often influenced by all family members. One study found that the influence of men on food purchases compared with that of women has risen from a low of 10:90 to as much as 50:50 in households where both spouses work. Consequently, many food firms are redirecting some of their marketing communications from media aimed primarily at women to those appealing to men and children.

STRATEGIC ENVIRONMENTAL ISSUE MANAGEMENT[27]

Most managers are aware of the importance of environmental analysis; but they also know the difficulties of monitoring it, and they lack management time to do so. They need a monitoring system that calls their attention only to relevant key environmental issues. Such an approach is called **strategic environmental issue management.** It consists of a four-stage process.[28]

1. *Environmental scanning:* This activity systematically seeks information about the various elements of the environment and detects new developments. Requiring special expertise and extensive information systems, it is usually performed by a central staff, such as a strategic planning service.
2. *Key environmental issue identification:* New environmental developments detected by a scanning system may have a significant impact on some activities of the firm. These are isolated for further consideration. In particular, key issues that have marketing implications are drawn to the attention of marketing executives.
3. *Impact evaluation:* The managers directly affected evaluate the potential impact of key environmental issues. A key environmental issue may represent a marketing opportunity or threat; managers must ascertain its short- and long-term implications.
4. *Formulation of a response strategy:* Given the foreseeable impact of a key environmental issue, managers must formulate an appropriate response strategy. The set of feasible response strategies includes a status-quo or wait-and-see position if the impact is not sufficiently significant or too uncertain.

Note the different organizational responsibilities for the various stages of the strategic environmental issue management process. Environmental scanning and identifying key issues are done at the corporate level by a special staff. Managers in different functions participate by providing information gathered as part of their normal activities. The output of these two stages are signals that are communicated to the appropriate areas of the firm for evaluation.

Impact evaluation and formulating a response strategy are the responsibility of the executives whose areas may be affected by specific issues. These managers should have the expertise needed to deal with such issues. Moreover, they are the ones who have to live with the consequences of their actions.

---

[27] This section has benefited from materials provided by Jean-Claude Larréché (Fontainbleau, France: INSEAD).

[28] See H. Igor Ansoff, "Strategic Issue Management," *Strategic Management Journal* 1 (1980), pp. 131–48.

EXHIBIT 3 ◆ 9

Alternative approaches to environmental scanning

	Irregular	*Regular*	*Continuous*
Nature of scanning activity	Ad-hoc studies	Periodically up-dated studies	Structured data collection and processing systems
Scope of scanning	Specific events	Selected elements	Broad range of environmental components
Impetus for activity	Crisis initiated	Problem areas	Planning process
Strategic orientation	Reactive	Proactive	Proactive
Time frame for data	Retrospective	Current and retro-spective	Current and pro-spective
Time frame for de-cision impact	Current and near term	Near term	Long term
Organizational re-sponsibility	Specially assigned teams	Various staff ser-vices	Environmental scanning unit

Source: Adapted from Liam Fahey and William R. King, "Environmental Scanning for Corporate Planning," *Business Horizons,* August 1977, pp. 61–71; and Liam Fahey, William R. King, and Vadake K. Narayanan, "Environmental Scanning and Forecasting in Strategic Planning—The State of the Art," *Long Range Planning,* February 1981, pp. 32–39.

Environmental scanning

As Exhibit 3–9 shows, there are three basic environmental scanning approaches.[29] The **irregular approach** consists of ad-hoc studies made only when specific events arise that may affect the firm. For the health-care industry this could cover a report on the growing problems of AIDS and their economic effects on hospitals. The **regular approach** consists of periodically updated studies of particular events of special interest. This approach enables the firm to be regularly informed on select issues so action can be taken before a crisis occurs. For example, the recent report prepared by the Institute for the Future was designed to present a comprehensive view of the U.S. health-care system over the next decade.[30] The **continuous approach**

---

[29] This typology of environmental scanning approaches was proposed by Liam Fahey and William R. King, "Environmental Scanning for Corporate Planning," *Business Horizons,* August 1977, pp. 61–71,

[30] Amara, "Health Care Tomorrow."

regularly monitors an array of environmental components and provides inputs to the normal planning process. One would assume that major health-care organizations (such as the American Medical Association) and large hospitals constantly monitor new drugs, new equipment, and new approaches to diagnosis and treatment.

Which of these three environmental scanning approaches is suitable for a given firm depends primarily on its potential vulnerability to environmental factors and on the strength of corporate resources. A firm's vulnerability depends to a large extent on the complexity and stability of its environment. Thus, a firm operating in a complex and dynamic environment is more vulnerable and requires a more complete scanning system than one operating in a simple and static environment.

Key environmental issue identification

In any given period many issues may be detected that could change the environment. Somehow the system must determine (1) the *probability* that an issue can materialize into an opportunity or a threat, and (2) the *degree of impact* it can have on the firm.

Initially, environmental issues are evaluated judgmentally on these two dimensions, using the information available to identify the more important issues. Each issue is then plotted on an opportunity/threat matrix that graphically shows their relative importance.[31] The matrix in Exhibit 3–10 contains 10 out of 101 potential events identified by a large New York City bank in the mid-70s. The probability of each occurring before 1985 was rated, as was its impact on the bank's market share and profitability. Environmental issues one and four, judged to have a high probability of occurring and a high impact level, actually did occur by 1985.[32]

The remaining 91 events posed a dilemma. Some were thought likely to occur and to have a small impact on the bank's share and profitability performance. Others were thought unlikely to occur—but if they did, to have a significant impact on performance. One solution is to add a limited number of issues with low probability and high impact to the analysis. In any case, managers should regularly monitor low probability/high impact issues as well as those with a high probability and low impact to determine if any priority changes need to be made.

---

[31] The opportunity/threat matrix was proposed by Philip Kotler, *Marketing Management*, 5th ed. (Englewood Cliffs, N.J.: Prentice-Hall, 1980), p. 281.

[32] This example is presented in Michael Palmer and Gregory Schmid, "Planning with Scenarios: The Banking World of 1985," *Futures*, December 1976, pp. 472–84.

EXHIBIT 3 ♦ 10

Opportunity/threat matrix

Probability of occurrence

Environmental issues:

1. Interstate barriers to banks are lowered.
2. Technological breakthroughs occur in information processing.
3. The cost of data manipulation falls.
4. Bank holding-company restrictions are eased.
5. Effective government ceilings exist on interest rates.
6. Antitrust actions are taken against large banks.
7. The correspondent network folds.
8. New York City loses its role as the country's commercial financial center.
9. Government regulation favors nonbank financial institutions.
10. Employers offer banking financial services to employees.

Source: Adapted from Michael Palmer and Gregory Schmid, "Planning with Scenarios: The Banking World of 1985," *Future,* December 1976, pp. 472–84. The probabilities of occurrence and degrees of impact are only illustrative.

Impact evaluation

Determining the impact of a key environmental issue requires that four basic questions be answered:

1. Does the issue represent an *opportunity* or a *threat* to the firm?
2. How *significant* will its impact be on the operations and performance of the firm?
3. What is the likely *timing* of its impact?
4. What are the *specific marketing areas* it will impact?

EXHIBIT 3 ♦ 11
Opportunity/threat profile

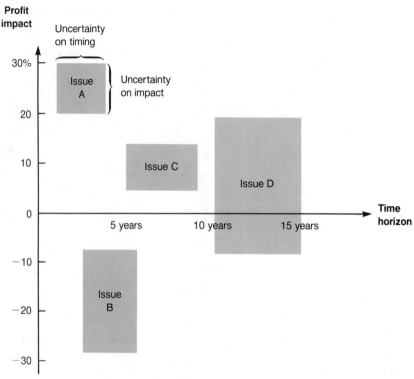

Source: © 1975 by The Regents of the University of California. Reprinted from *The California Management Review,* vol. 18, no. 2. By permission of The Regents.

Analysts can chart the first three considerations for key environmental issues on a graph called an *opportunity/threat profile* (see Exhibit 3–11). The horizontal axis of the graph corresponds to the estimated timing of the environmental event. (The width of the box indicates the extent of uncertainty about the timing.) The vertical axis represents its impact on a performance measure such as profits or market share. (The length of the box indicates the extent of uncertainty about the profit impact.) Environmental issues below the time horizon imply potential losses in performance; those above indicate gains.[33]

In Exhibit 3–11 issues A and C are opportunities, although A is more immediate and significant. Issue B represents a definite threat; but there is

---

[33] The opportunity/threat profile representation has been proposed by H. Igor Ansoff, "Managing Strategic Surprise by Response to Weak Signals," *California Management Review,* Winter 1975, pp. 21–33.

substantial uncertainty about its impact level. Issue D is remote in the future, and there is considerable uncertainty concerning both its timing and impact. It could either be a substantial opportunity or have a limited negative effect on the firm's profitability.

Of particular interest to the firm is the *relative* impact of a key environmental issue. That is, within the same industry some firms perceive a given event as an opportunity and others see it as a threat. For example, the energy crisis provided a major opportunity for Japanese and European automakers to increase their exports of fuel-efficient cars to the United States. It posed a severe threat, however, to U.S. manufacturers of larger, less fuel-efficient cars.

Formulation of response strategies

The expression *response strategy* indicates a response to an environmental issue—one not necessarily undertaken *after* the event. It includes *both* reactive and proactive strategies. This assumes a time interval between the identification of a key issue and the event it triggers. A **reactive strategy** is undertaken in response to a major environmental event, often in a crisis situation. A **proactive strategy** is formulated in response to a key environmental issue and in anticipation of its becoming an event.

A proactive strategy is usually more desirable than a reactive one. It avoids making pressure decisions and enables the firm to perform more in-depth analyses. Further, the greater the lead time, the broader the array of options. Reactive strategies benefit from more information being available and, consequently, less uncertainty about the event.

Exhibit 3–12 discusses and provides examples of six response strategies that can be fashioned in either a reactive or proactive mode. Most marketing strategies are more reactive than proactive; they derive from a set of environmental constraints already defined by management. Many consider adaptation to external forces the essence of the marketing concept. In recent years, more writers have advocated that marketing managers emphasize proactive response strategies whenever possible. They suggest changing the context in which the organization operates; that is, by extending the firm's influence over the environment. The present movement toward innovative, entrepreneurial management captures the essence of this perspective.[34] In brief, this approach emphasizes that "marketing is a significant force which the organization can call upon to create change and extend its influence over the environment."[35]

---

[34] Carl P. Zeithaml and Valarie A. Zeithaml, "Environmental Management: Revising the Marketing Perspective," *Journal of Marketing*, Spring 1984, p. 49.

[35] Ibid.

EXHIBIT   3 ♦ 12

Response strategies to environmental issues

1. **Opposition strategy:** The effectiveness of this strategy is limited because environmental factors are largely beyond the control of a firm. In some situations, a firm may,
   however, try to delay, attenuate, or otherwise influence an environmental force. Lobbying and corporate issue advertising are examples of opposition strategy used by some
   large firms to sensitize the public to their point of view and to influence the evolution of
   legislation. One example is the National Rifle Association, which opposes gun control
   legislation.

2. **Adaptation strategy:** Adaptations are often compulsory as, for example, is the case
   with legislation on product specifications, packaging, and labeling. Choices often exist,
   however, in the type and extent of adaptation. The danger is that if an adaptation strategy is pursued to the extreme, the environment (not management) sets the pace and
   scope of strategic change.
       For example, in response to mandatory fuel economy standards, a major strategy
   available to auto makers was to downsize existing fleets. This increased gas mileage
   while avoiding substantial retooling expenses.

3. **Offensive strategy:** Such a strategy uses the environmental issue to improve the
   firm's competitive position. A key environmental issue may have a destabilizing effect
   on an industry, which may create opportunities for the more aggressive firms. For example, because of increased cost, federal and state regulation, and risk, the operators
   of toxic waste dumps have been under economic pressure. Waste Management, Inc.,
   the nation's largest hazardous-waste company which owes much of its success to its
   large landfill business, is increasingly directing more of its research to innovative disposal methods, including biotechnology.*

SUMMARY

External analysis is concerned not only with the
market and the industry, but also with the environmental trends affecting them. Increasingly
the environment is difficult to understand. It is
boundless, conveys weak signals about its future
impact on marketing strategies, is largely uncontrollable, and requires a special expertise to understand.

The economic environment is most pervasive
in its impact on marketing. The elements most
likely to affect marketing strategies are demographics, growth, interest rates, and currency
exchange rates. The political environment includes all those factors controlled by authorities. The major factor is legislation that
defines the regulatory environment within

which business must operate. The influence of
the political/legal environment is not necessarily negative—opportunities may also be provided.

Technology can have a substantial impact on
the performance and competitive structure of an
industry. The pace of technological development has been increasing and promises to become even more intensive in the future. It is
difficult to predict the exact timing of a basic
discovery. Even so, it is possible to know that
certain fundamental breakthroughs are expected
in specific areas; that current scientific discoveries may lead to the development of new products; or that improvements in existing technologies are possible. Two technologies having

EXHIBIT   3 ♦ 12
(concluded)

4. **Redeployment strategy:** Faced with major environmental issues in one market, a firm may decide to redeploy its resources in other less-exposed areas. For example, tobacco companies such as Philip Morris and R. J. Reynolds have diversified into other consumer goods because of the environmental pressures concerning the health effects of cigarette smoking and the resulting less-attractive long-term prospects of their prime market.

5. **Contingency strategies:** One such strategy decreases the risk of being exposed to potentially harmful environmental events. For example, a search may be launched for substitutes for raw materials with volatile prices.

   Another contingency strategy designs alternative courses of action corresponding to the different possible evolutions of the environment. This involves isolating discrete environmental scenarios the firm may have to face in the future and designing appropriate responses for each. For example, given the possibility that the use of saccharin might be banned in drugs, cosmetics, soft drinks, and food, Plough, Inc., the maker of St. Joseph's Aspirin for Children and Maybelline Cosmetics, developed other sweetening agents that could be substituted for saccharin if necessary.†

6. **Passive strategy:** This strategy calls for not responding to an environmental threat or opportunity. For example, in the early days of modern consumerism, some corporations took major public action to oppose their critics—which only provided greater exposure to the issue and worsened their images. A better alternative would have been not to have taken *any* action until performing more complete analyses and formulating an appropriate response.

  * Ken Wells, "Toxic Waste Disposal Firms Enter High Technology Era," *The Wall Street Journal*, October 10, 1987, p. 27.
  † See "Drugmakers Seek a Substitute Sweetener," *Business Week*, December 11, 1978, p. 68 D-I.

Source: Jean-Claude Larréché, unpublished paper (Fontainbleau, France: INSEAD, 1980).

a significant influence on the future of our society are electronics/telecommunications and biology.

The sociocultural environment represents the values, attitudes, and general behavior of people in a given society. The evolution of this environment is slow compared to the other environments. Some of the more significant trends involve shifts in individual values toward self-realization and fulfillment, recognition of minority rights, changes in the family structure, increased leisure time, and more concern about conservation.

The strategic environmental issue management process consists of scanning the environment, identifying key environmental issues, evaluating their impact, and formulating a re-

sponse strategy. The latter can be fragmented into six response strategies having to do with opposition, adaptation, offensive action, redeployment, contingency planning, and doing nothing.

QUESTIONS

1. U.S. automobile companies have seen their share of the domestic auto market gradually shrink in recent years. There are many reasons for the declining competitive positions of these companies. Part of the problem can be traced to their failure to anticipate and adapt to major

changes in their macroenvironment. Such changes included the oil crisis of the mid-1970s, the increased competitiveness of foreign producers, and changing consumer attitudes about such things as the acceptability of small cars and the social acceptability of foreign-made products. Why did it take the American auto companies so long to identify such environmental trends and recognize their significance? What factors can make such environmental changes hard to anticipate?

2. Suppose you have been hired as a marketing consultant by Stouffer's Foods, the manufacturer of Stouffer's and Lean Cuisine frozen entrees. How might the *demographic trends* and the changes in *family structure* discussed in this chapter affect each of the "4 Ps" in Stouffer's strategic marketing program during the 1990s? What adjustments should the company be prepared to make to its marketing program?

3. In 1978 the U.S. airline industry was *deregulated*. As a result, the airlines were given more freedom to schedule their own routes and set their own prices. How did deregulation affect the role of marketing within the major air carriers? What elements of the marketing mix have become more or less important since deregulation?

4. How did the decline in the yen's value relative to the U.S. dollar during the late-1980s affect the Japanese auto companies' competitive strategies in the U.S. market? How did they adjust their marketing programs in response to the decline?

5. Experts at the Battelle Memorial Institute—a high-technology research firm and "think tank"—predict that microprocessors will someday enable automobiles to be equipped with radar capable of detecting oncoming crashes and then self-correcting the steering to avoid impact. What industries would be affected by such a *technological change*? How?

6. The president of a large manufacturer of household appliances, such as washing machines, dryers, and dishwashers, has asked you to develop a system for monitoring and evaluating the likely impact of major environmental trends. Briefly describe the major components you would include in such a *strategic environmental issues management* system. What major activities would be involved in the operation of such a system?

7. Suppose you have just been appointed the dean of your business school. Construct an *opportunities-threats matrix* for the school.

8. What kind of environmental *response strategy* does Philip Morris's acquisition of Miller Brewing Company and other food and beverage manufacturers illustrate? Describe two other strategies that Philip Morris might have pursued in response to the growing antismoking trend in America.

9. What is the difference between *proactive* and *reactive* environmental response strategies? Describe an example of a proactive strategy.

Chapter ◇4◇

Consumer markets and buying behavior

Domino Pizza Delivers

In 1960 Thomas S. Monaghan scraped together $500 to buy a tiny Italian restaurant near Eastern Michigan University, hoping to earn enough money to finance a degree in architecture.[1] Low volume and high operating costs eventually led him to focus on pizza, throw out the tables and chairs, and concentrate on a take-out and delivery service. His operation appealed to college students so successfully that by 1965 Monaghan had opened four more outlets near colleges and military bases and had begun selling franchises to other operators. Unfortunately, however, too-rapid expansion, strong competition, and lack of a sustainable competitive advantage pushed Monaghan to the edge of bankruptcy. A bank took over his business.

Monaghan went back to working in his restaurants, paid off his debts, and regained control of his business in 1971. This time, however, he decided to reduce his dependence on the college market and to seek a sustainable niche in the lucrative residential market. To define an effective marketing strategy, he researched the characteristics and attitudes of pizza consumers. After several studies, he found that: (1) the heaviest users of pizza were between 18 and 34 years of age; (2) many of these consumers preferred to have their pizzas delivered to their homes rather than eating in a restaurant; (3) the key choice criteria were good taste and prompt delivery; and (4) a large proportion of consumers were satisfied with the taste of the pizzas they were currently buying. There was, however, a great deal of dissatisfaction with the promptness and reliability of the delivery service.

Then, Monaghan says, "I began rebuilding by staking out a business niche—free delivery—and doing it better and faster than anyone else." His competitive strategy was to promise delivery of a hot pizza within 30 minutes after receiving a phone order—and to give the customer a free pizza if that promise was not kept. To ensure this strategy was implemented effectively, Monaghan spent millions on TV advertising and paid attention to many small details to improve the speed and efficiency of his operation. He also created strong incentives to motivate his delivery people to meet the 30-minute time limit.

The biggest incentive for good performance among delivery people is the opportunity to obtain their own Dom-

---

[1] Based largely on material found in Bernie Whalen, " 'People- Oriented' Marketing Delivers a Lot of Dough for Domino's," *Marketing News*, March 15, 1984, pp. 4ff; Wendy Zellner, "Tom Monaghan, the Fun-loving Prince of Pizza," *Business Week*, February 8, 1988, p. 90.

continued

concluded

ino's franchise. Indeed, the only way to get a Domino's franchise is to earn it by performing well as a delivery person and then working your way up through the company's management training program.

Monaghan's success in first identifying a benefit of importance to a well-defined segment of pizza consumers and then formulating and implementing a marketing program to deliver that benefit to the target market is evident in Domino's rapid rate of growth in recent years. The firm had 4,280 outlets by the end of 1987 and sales of nearly $2 billion.

Thomas Monaghan's experiences in turning Domino's near bankruptcy to a major success illustrates why examining the behavior of potential and existing customers—and the personal and social factors that influence their behavior—is an important step in analyzing the market opportunities for a product-market entry.

Customers engage in exchange transactions as a means to an end. They purchase products and services as potential solutions to their unsatisfied needs and wants. And customers purchase particular brands or deal with particular suppliers because those brands or suppliers are perceived to offer attributes or benefits—such as quick and reliable delivery of hot pizza—that are superior to those offered by competitors. Consequently, the more marketers can learn about customers' needs and wants and the attributes and benefits they perceive as important in satisfying those needs, the greater their ability to design product and service offerings that their customers find attractive and satisfying.

Customer decision making is essentially a problem-solving process. Most customers—whether individual consumers or organizational buyers—go through similar mental processes in deciding which products and brands to buy. Obviously, though, various customers often end up buying very different things. Their decisions are influenced by differences in their **personal characteristics** (their needs, the benefits they seek, their attitudes, values, past experiences, and lifestyles) and **social influences** (different social classes, reference groups, or family situations). Each of these factors can serve as a useful basis for defining unique but internally consistent segments of customers. For instance, Monaghan discovered that a large proportion of 18- to 34-year-olds liked to eat pizza at home, but were dissatisfied with the speed and reliability of home delivery from most pizza shops. Thus, the more marketers know about the factors affecting their customers' buying behavior, the greater their ability to define and target meaningful market segments. This also enables them to design marketing mix programs to fit the specific concerns and desires of those segments.

This chapter examines the mental processes that individual consumers go through when making purchase decisions, and the individual and environmental factors affecting those decisions. Our discussion provides a useful framework for choosing, organizing, and analyzing information about current and potential customers for a particular product or service. The next chapter discusses the decision processes and influences affecting the buying behavior of organizations.

CONSUMERS' PURCHASING DECISIONS

The decision-making processes consumers use when making purchases vary. As Exhibit 4–1 indicates, this process can be classified into four categories depending on (1) whether the consumer has a high or low level of

EXHIBIT   4 ♦ 1

Consumer decision making

Extent of involvement

	High	Low
Extended (information search; consideration of alternatives)	Complex decision making (cars, homes, vacations)	Variety seeking and impulse purchasing (cereals, cookies)
Routine (little information search; focus on one brand)	Brand loyalty (toothpaste, cologne, deodorant)	Inertia (canned vegetables, paper towels)

Extent of decision making

Source: From Henry Assael, *Consumer Behavior and Marketing Action,* 3rd ed. (Boston: Kent Publishing Company, 1987), p. 13. © by Wadsworth, Inc. Reprinted by permission of PWS-Kent Publishing Company, a division of Wadsworth, Inc.

product involvement and (2) whether the consumer finds it necessary to engage in an extensive search for information and evaluation of alternative brands or makes the decision routinely.[2] Different buyers may engage in different types of decision-making processes depending on how highly involved they are with the product. As the exhibit suggests, a high-involvement product for one buyer may be a low-involvement product for another.

High-involvement purchase decisions

High-involvement purchases involve products or services that are psychologically important to the consumer because they satisfy social or ego needs. The consumer takes the social and psychological risks of having family and friends say a purchase was foolish or inappropriate. There may also be financial risks—as well as the inconvenience—associated with an unsatisfactory product (including high service costs).

To reduce the risks associated with buying high-involvement, big-ticket items such as automobiles, homes, and household furnishings, which are purchased infrequently, many consumers engage in a **complex decision-making process.** They extensively search for information from various sources to evaluate alternative products or brands before making a purchase. In this way, buyers attempt to minimize the possibility of unforeseen negative consequences after the purchase.

Some frequently purchased products—such as deodorants, perfumes, toothpastes, and shaving creams—are also high-involvement purchases for many consumers. These products are tied to their egos and social needs and reflect their self-images. The frequency with which such products are purchased, however, enables consumers to judge which brand is best and to continue buying that brand with little thought given to alternatives. This decision process is referred to as **brand loyalty.** It grows out of the learning consumers acquire through experience. Many university students are likely to follow this process in selecting a brand of pizza such as Domino's.

Low-involvement purchase decisions

Because low-involvement products are not very important to consumers, the search for information to evaluate alternative brands is likely to be minimal. As a result, decisions to buy products such as cookies or cereals are often made within the store, either *impulsively* on the basis of brand familiarity or as a result of comparisons of the brands on the shelf. The consumers' involvement and their risks associated with making poor decisions are low for such products. Therefore, consumers are less likely to stay with the same

---

[2] H. Assael, *Consumer Behavior and Marketing Action*, 3rd ed. (Boston: Kent Publishing, 1987), pp. 12–14.

brand over time. They have little to lose by switching brands in a search for variety. Even so, many consumers develop loyalty to a given brand—as in the continued popularity of such low-involvement products as Wrigley Doublemint chewing gum and Gold Medal flour, which have been around for many years.

When a product is of little importance and there are few substantive differences among brands—as in salt and sugar—consumers continue to buy whatever brand is familiar or available without worrying whether it is the best choice. Such products are not deemed worth the time and effort of the decision process.

The decision processes involved in purchasing high- and low-involvement products are quite different. The following sections examine the mental steps involved in each decision process in more detail.

THE HIGH-INVOLVEMENT, COMPLEX DECISION-MAKING PROCESS

When purchasing high-involvement products or services, consumers go through a problem-solving process involving five mental steps: (1) problem identification, (2) information search, (3) evaluation of alternatives, (4) purchase, and (5) postpurchase evaluation. These five steps are diagrammed in Exhibit 4–2 and discussed in the context of the purchase of a new tennis racket by a hypothetical consumer, Virginia Lynn.

EXHIBIT 4 ◆ 2

Steps in the high-involvement, complex consumer decision-making process

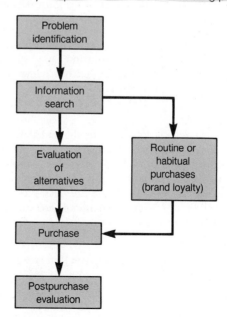

Problem identification

Consumers' purchase decision processes are triggered by unsatisfied needs or wants. Individuals perceive differences between ideal and actual states on some physical or sociopsychological dimension. This motivates them to seek products or services to help bring their current state more into balance with the ideal.[3]

We human beings are insatiable—at least with respect to our sociopsychological needs—but we are limited by time and financial resources. It is impossible for us to satisfy all our needs at once. We tend instead to try to satisfy the needs that are strongest at a given time. The size of the gap between our current and our desired state largely determines the strength of a particular need. A need can become stronger and be brought to our attention by a deterioration of our actual state or an upward revision of our ideal state.

A change in a consumer's actual state can occur for several reasons:

- For physical needs, a natural deterioration of the actual state occurs all the time. A person's body burns energy and nutrients. Thus, periodically we get hungry and tired and are motivated to find something to eat or go to sleep.
- A person's actual state may change as the result of the depletion of the current solution to a need. Our hypothetical consumer, Virginia Lynn, for instance, might be motivated to purchase a new tennis racket because the old one broke.
- In some cases, consumers can anticipate a decline in their actual state. If Virginia Lynn notices that her racket has a small crack in the frame, she might decide to buy another racket to have on hand if the old one breaks.

Similarly, a change in a consumer's desired state may occur for several reasons:

- The desired state may be revised upward because of new information or the development of a new solution for an old need. Thus, Lynn may have seen an ad for a new graphite racket with a wider head or noticed that a friend is playing better since purchasing such a racket. As a result, she may become dissatisfied with her present racket because she believes the new racket would improve her game.
- As one need is satisfied, the desired state on other need dimensions increases and becomes more demanding. For example, even though Lynn has been unhappy with her present racket for some months, she did not think about purchasing a new one until she had paid for necessary repairs to her car. Her need for dependable transportation outweighed her desire for a new racket; but once the first need was satisfied, the second demanded more attention.

---

[3] J. F. Engel, R. D. Blackwell, and Paul W. Miniard, *Consumer Behavior* (New York: Dryden Press, 1986), p. 28.

Information search

Having recognized that a problem exists, the consumer's next step is to refer to information gained from past experience and stored in memory for a solution. To continue with our example: If Lynn has purchased tennis rackets in the past (particularly if she has purchased them frequently or recently), she may believe that she already knows which brand is best. In such cases, as Exhibit 4–2 indicates, Lynn will make a routine purchase and forgo any further search for additional information or comparison of alternatives. However, Lynn may perceive that her past experience and stored information are inadequate for determining the best racket brand. Or she may see that substantial changes (new rackets introduced or price or design changes) have occurred since her last purchase. In either case, she will seek additional information.

How much information will a consumer seek?

People seek additional information about alternative brands until they perceive that the *costs* of obtaining more information are equal to the additional *value* or *benefit* derived from that information.[4] Information is valuable to consumers to the extent that it helps make a more satisfying purchase and avoids the negative consequences associated with a poor choice. Thus, consumers are likely to place a higher value on—and seek more—information when the purchase is important. This importance derives from (a) the strength of a person's need for the product; (b) the person's ego-involvement with the product; and (c) the severity of the social and financial consequences of making a poor choice. This is why people tend to seek more information about high-priced, socially visible products that reflect their self-image (cars, homes, clothing, and perhaps even tennis rackets) than for lower-priced products that other people seldom notice, such as furnace filters or paper towels.

Even when products are very expensive and ego-involving, some consumers are unlikely to conduct an exhaustive search for information before making a decision. Why? Because of the costs involved. Perhaps the biggest cost for most people is the **opportunity cost of the time** involved in seeking information. They give up the opportunity to use that time for other, more important or interesting activities, like working (more and more women are employed outside the home) or playing tennis. For some people, however, the opportunity costs of shopping are low, because they enjoy wandering through stores or scanning newspaper ads for bargains.

---

[4] Brian T. Ratchford, "Cost-Benefit Models for Explaining Consumer Choice and Information Seeking Behavior," *Management Science*, February 1982, pp. 97–212.

Another information search cost is the possible negative consequence of *delaying the decision too long*. **Delay costs** are a major reason why some home buyers stop searching for more alternatives. They fear the houses they like would be sold to someone else if they postponed a decision and continued looking for something better. Or perhaps the interest rates would go up. Finally, there are **psychological costs** involved in searching for information. Collecting information can be a frustrating task, often involving crowded stores and rude salespeople. Also, some consumers become frustrated and confused when they have a lot of complex information to evaluate before making a choice. Consequently they cut their information search short.

Sources of information

Assume that the purchase of a new tennis racket is important, ego-involving, and costly enough for Virginia Lynn to seek additional information before making a purchase. Which sources can she turn to? The three broad categories of information sources about alternative products, brands, and stores are personal, commercial, and public sources. **Personal sources** include family members, friends, and members of the consumer's reference groups. These would be very important in selecting a pizza to be delivered for a late snack at a university dorm. **Commercial sources** refer to various information disseminated by services, marketers, and manufacturers and their dealers. They include media advertising, promotional brochures, package and label information, salespersons, and various in-store information, such as price markings and displays. **Public sources** include noncommercial and professional organizations and individuals who provide advice for consumers, such as doctors, lawyers, governmental agencies, and consumer-interest groups.

Consumers are usually exposed to more information from commercial sources than from personal or public sources. However, many consumers are influenced more by personal sources when deciding which service, product, or brand to buy. (This is likely true with Domino's pizza.) Consumers do, however, use information from different sources for different purposes and at different stages within the decision process. In general, commercial sources perform an **informing function** for consumers. Personal and public sources serve an **evaluating and legitimizing function.** Thus, Lynn might rely on advertising, store visits, or discussions with salespeople to learn the brands of tennis rackets available, which features each brand offers, and how much each costs. But when it comes time to evaluate alternative brands and decide which is best suited to her game, Lynn is likely to seek the opinions of friends or the advice of the tennis pro.

Evaluation of alternatives

Consumers find it difficult to make overall comparisons of many alternative brands, because each brand might be better in some ways but worse in others. Instead, consumers simplify their evaluation task in several ways. First, they seldom consider all possible brands; rather, they focus on the **evoked set**—a limited number they are familiar with that are likely to satisfy their needs.

Second, consumers evaluate each of the brands in the evoked set on a limited number of **product dimensions or attributes.** They also judge the *relative importance* of these attributes, or the minimum acceptable performance of each attribute. The set of attributes used by a particular consumer and the relative importance of each represent the consumer's **choice criteria.** In the case of Domino's, the promptness and reliability of delivery are critical product attributes—to many consumers they are the most important ones. These, in turn, reflect the benefits wanted to satisfy the individual's needs and wants.

Third, consumers combine evaluations of each brand across attributes, taking into account the relative importance of those attributes. This multiattribute assessment of a brand results in an overall **attitude** toward that brand. The brand toward which consumers have the most favorable attitude is the one they are most likely to buy.

Product attributes and their relative importance

Consumers use many dimensions or attributes when evaluating alternative products or services. Virginia Lynn might compare prices, size and shape of the racket head, stiffness or durability of the materials used, and style or appearance. Exhibit 4–3 contains a more general list of product attributes that consumers might use to evaluate alternatives. Many product attributes can be identified; but consumers usually base their evaluations on half a dozen dimensions or less.

EXHIBIT 4♦3

Selected attributes consumers use to evaluate alternative products or services

Category	Specific attributes
Cost attributes	Purchase price, operating costs, repair costs, cost of extras or options, cost of installation, trade-in allowance, likely resale value.
Performance attributes	Durability, quality of materials, construction, dependability, functional performance (acceleration, nutrition, taste), efficiency, safety, styling.
Social attributes	Reputation of brand, status image, popularity with friends, popularity with family members (Do the kids like the taste of Oscar Mayer hot dogs?), style, fashion.
Availability attributes	Carried by local stores, credit terms, quality of service available from local dealer, delivery time.

Different consumers may use different sets of attributes to evaluate brands within the same product category. But even when two people use the same set of attributes, they may arrive at different decisions because they attach different importance to various attributes. Virginia Lynn is primarily interested in a new tennis racket with an intermediate-sized head and graphite frame to gain better control of her shots. A more casual player might attach greater importance to a low price and attractive style. Thus, consumers' personal characteristics and social influences—needs, values, personality, social class, and reference groups, among other things—help determine which attributes are considered and their relative importance. Environmental and situational factors also impact the perceived importance of various product benefits. When Steve Maxwell buys beer to drink while watching the late movie, for instance, he always buys the least expensive brand. Maxwell thinks there is little difference among brands. But when he buys beer for a party, Maxwell always buys a well-known, high-priced imported brand to win the approval of his friends. Thus, the use situation often determines a person's choice criteria.

Forming attitudes toward alternative brands

Even if two consumers use the same attributes and attach the same relative importance to them when evaluating product offerings, they may not necessarily prefer the same brand. They might *rate* the various brands differently on specific attributes. Differences in brand perceptions are based on past experience, the information collected, and how that information is perceived and processed. As we shall see later, consumers may also vary in the way they aggregate their evaluations across attributes when developing an overall attitude toward a brand.

Purchase

Even after a consumer has collected information about alternative brands, evaluated them, and decided which is the most desirable, the decision process still is not complete. The consumer must now decide *where* to buy the product. Choosing a source from which to buy the product involves essentially the same mental processes as does a product purchase decision. The source is usually a retail store but may also be a mail-order catalog like L. L. Bean or a teleshopping service. Consumers obtain information about alternative sources from personal experience, advertising, comments of friends, and the like. Then they use this information to evaluate sources on attributes such as merchandise carried, services rendered, price, convenience, personnel, and physical characteristics. Consumers usually select the source they perceive to be best on those attributes most important to them. Consumers whose experiences with a source are positive over time may develop **patronage loyalty** and routinely shop that source—similar to the way consumers develop brand loyalties.

Consumers who shop in a retail store intent on purchasing one brand sometimes end up buying something different. Virginia Lynn, for instance, fully intended to buy a Prince racket but emerged from the sporting goods store with a Wilson. This happens because the consumer's ultimate purchase can be influenced by factors within the store, such as out-of-stocks, a special display, or messages from a salesperson.

Postpurchase evaluation

After consuming or starting to use their products, consumers are satisfied with their purchases if there are adequate rewards (in the sense of good performance) given the effort and sacrifice required to obtain these products. Whether a particular consumer feels adequately rewarded following a purchase depends on two things: (1) the person's **aspiration or expectation level**—how well the product was expected to perform (delivery of a quality pizza while it is hot); and (2) the consumer's evaluation of *how well the product actually did perform* (the pizza arrived cold).

Consumers' expectations about a product's performance are influenced by several factors. These include the strength and importance of each person's need and the information collected during the decision-making process. In the case of Virginia Lynn, for example, a persuasive ad or an enthusiastic endorsement of Wilson rackets by a friend who is a good player may have caused her to expect her new racket to produce a greater improvement in her game than she would have otherwise expected. This suggests a danger in marketers using exaggerated claims in product advertising. Such claims can produce inflated expectations that the product cannot live up to—thereby resulting in dissatisfied customers.

Postpurchase dissonance

Even when a product performs as expected, consumers may doubt whether they made the best possible choices. Such doubts are called **cognitive dissonance.** This is most likely to occur when the purchase involves a product with which the consumer is highly ego-involved and when he or she must choose among almost equally attractive alternatives. Consumers are more likely to experience dissonance after buying big-ticket, socially visible items such as a new house, a car, or living room furniture than would typically be the case with pizza.

Doubts about whether the best possible choice has been made produce an uncomfortable psychological tension that consumers reduce in two ways. First, they can simply withdraw from their decision—take the product back and ask for a refund. A second way to reduce dissonance is for consumers to be convinced they really did make the best choice. Many people thus continue to seek information about their chosen brand *after* a purchase.

Thus, Virginia Lynn would pay particular attention to ads for Wilson rackets in the tennis magazine she receives monthly. She would also observe the various brands of rackets used by the better players at her club. In this way her attitude toward the chosen brand may become even more positive over time as her feelings of dissonance subside. Marketers play an active role in dissonance reduction by reinforcing consumers' purchase decisions. For example, follow-up letters can assure customers they made a wise choice and that the firm stands behind the product should anything go wrong.

LOW-INVOLVEMENT PURCHASE DECISIONS

Most purchase decisions are low in consumer involvement; the consumer does not consider the product or service sufficiently important to identify with it.[5] The consumer does not engage in an extensive search for information for such purchases or make a detailed evaluation of alternative brands. Instead, brand information is received *passively*. The consumer may see an ad for Green Giant vegetables on TV or hear a friend say that Green Giant products taste good, but does not interpret or evaluate such information. The consumer simply notices it and perhaps stores it away in memory with little additional processing.

Later, the consumer may identify a need because vegetables are running low. On the next trip to the supermarket, the consumer sees Green Giant vegetables on the shelf, recognizes the brand, and decides to buy several cans. The familiarity generated by exposure to past advertising and word-of-mouth information is sufficient to stimulate a purchase even though the consumer has not formed a strong attitude toward the brand. That is, the brand is regarded as relatively neutral because it is not associated with the consumer's self-image. This could be the case with the first purchase of a Domino's pizza.

After buying and using the product, consumers may decide that Green Giant vegetables are either reasonably good or bad. In either case they form a somewhat positive—or negative—attitude toward Green Giant products. This attitude may affect future purchases of canned vegetables. The important point, though, is that such brand evaluation occurs only after an initial purchase has been made. In complex decision making, consumers collect

---

[5] For a more complete review of what is known about low involvement purchase decisions and how they differ from complex decision making, see Engel et al., *Consumer Behavior*, chap. 2; J. C. Maloney and B. Silverman, eds., *Attitude Research Plays for High Stakes* (Chicago: American Marketing Association, 1979).

information, evaluate alternative brands, and then act according to well-formulated attitudes. In low-involvement purchasing, consumers act first and may (or may not) evaluate the brand later.

Inertia

As Exhibit 4–1 indicated, there are two low-involvement buying decisions. When there are few differences between brands and little risk associated with making a poor choice, consumers either buy brands at random or buy the same brand repetitively to avoid making a choice. Marketers must be careful not to confuse such repeat purchasing from inertia with brand loyalty. Consumers have no commitment to, or strong attitude about, the brand as the result of past learning and experience here. Thus, it is relatively easy for competitors to entice such customers to switch brands by offering cents-off coupons, special promotions, or in-store displays. Highly brand-loyal customers, on the other hand, resist such efforts due to their strong brand preference. For instance, a student who strongly prefers Domino's pizza over all other brands is less likely to use a coupon offering $1 off another brand than a student who perceives all pizzas to be equally satisfying.

Impulse purchasing and variety seeking

The second low-involvement purchase process is **impulse buying.** This buying behavior most likely occurs in product categories where consumers perceive substantial differences among brands. Some react to these differences by buying a variety of brands over time. However, their purchase decisions are not made as the result of complex decision-making processes. Instead, consumers impulsively decide to buy a different brand—though usually a brand name they are familiar with through passive exposure to advertising or other information—once they are in the store. Their motivation for switching brands is not dissatisfaction with a previous brand (as in the case of high-involvement products), but a desire for change and variety.

Marketing implications of low-involvement purchasing

Exhibit 4–4, on page 124, summarizes some of the differences in consumer decision- making processes and the factors influencing them. These differences suggest that the same strategies and program elements cannot be used for marketing low-involvement and high-involvement goods and services. Thus, target marketing, visual product differentiation, advertising copy, and media selection would be handled quite differently for high- versus low-involvement products or services.

EXHIBIT 4 ♦ 4

High-involvement versus low-involvement consumer behavior

High-involvement consumer behavior	Low-involvement consumer behavior
♦ Consumers are information processors.	♦ Consumers learn information at random.
♦ Consumers are information seekers.	♦ Consumers are information gatherers.
♦ Consumers represent an active audience for advertising.	♦ Consumers represent a passive audience for advertising.
♦ Consumers evaluate brands before buying.	♦ Consumers buy first. If they do evaluate brands, it is done after the purchase.
♦ Consumers seek to maximize expected satisfaction. They compare brands to see which provides the most *benefits* related to their needs and buy based on a multiattribute comparison of brands.	♦ Consumers seek an acceptable level of satisfaction. They buy the brand least likely to give them *problems* and buy based on a few attributes. Familiarity is the key.
♦ Personality and lifestyle characteristics are related to consumer behavior because the product is closely tied to the person's self-identity and beliefs.	♦ Personality and lifestyle are not strongly related to consumer behavior because the product is not closely tied to the person's self-identity and beliefs.
♦ Reference groups influence consumer behavior, because of the importance of the product to group norms and values.	♦ Reference groups exert little influence on consumer behavior because products are not strongly related to their norms and values.

Source: From Henry Assael, *Consumer Behavior and Marketing Action,* 3rd ed. (Boston: Kent Publishing Company, 1987), p. 96. © by Wadsworth, Inc. Reprinted by permission of PWS-Kent Publishing Company, a division of Wadsworth, Inc.

Product design and positioning

Highly involved consumers evaluate alternative brands according to choice criteria that reflect the **benefits** they seek to maximize the satisfaction of their needs and wants. In low-involvement purchasing, consumers more commonly seek brands that are least likely to give them problems. This is particularly true because brand evaluation occurs only after the product is purchased. If the product causes no problems in use, consumers may purchase the same brand again out of inertia. It may be effective, then, for manufacturers of low-involvement products to focus on product features that minimize any problems in using the product. A manufacturer of plastic trash bags, for instance, might focus on a strong, seamless bag that is not likely to rip and spill trash.

Advertising and promotion

Because low-involvement consumers are passive information gatherers, advertising should focus on a few main points to make it as easy as possible for them to gain familiarity and positive associations with a brand. For example,

Domino's spends $40 million a year on advertising—mostly to emphasize its delivery promise. Such advertising should also display the product and its package prominently and use symbols or imagery like The Jolly Green Giant and the Pillsbury Doughboy.[6]

Television, rather than print, should be the primary medium for advertising low-involvement products. TV is a low-involvement medium allowing passive learning without much mental effort on the consumer's part. Print media are more suitable if the audience is highly involved with the product and actively seeking information. The reader controls the pace of print media exposure and can absorb and reflect on more complex and detailed messages.[7]

Distinctive package design is important for low-involvement products. It helps consumers recognize brands they've seen advertised and makes these brands stand out on the store shelves.

Pricing

Many consumers buy low-involvement products based on price alone. Consequently, special sales or coupon offers can be effective in gaining a trial of such products. If no problems are experienced in using the product, consumers may continue to repurchase the brand out of inertia until a competitor offers an attractive price promotion. Until recently, Domino's had little competition in the eat-at-home pizza market. But now, such major players as Pizza Hut, Little Caesar's, and Godfather's are seeking a bigger share of this market. Discounting (two-for-one deals) is now common.[8]

Distribution

Extensive retail distribution is particularly important for low-involvement products because most consumers are not willing to search for—or expend extra effort to obtain—a particular brand. When a manufacturer's product is not in a store, customers are likely to substitute another brand.

Strategies to increase consumer involvement

In some cases, a firm may try to increase consumers' involvement with its brand as a way to increase revenues. Increased customer involvement can be attempted in several ways.[9] *The product might be linked to some involving issue*, as when makers of bran cereals associated their products with the

---

6 M. L. Rothschild, "Advertising Strategies for High- and Low-Involvement Situations," in Maloney and Silverman, eds., *Attitude Research Plays for High Stakes*, pp. 84–87.

7 See Michael L. Ray, *Advertising and Communication Management* (Englewood Cliffs, N.J.: Prentice-Hall, 1982), chap. 7.

8 Joan Lipman, "Pizza Makers Slug It Out for Share of Growing Eat-at-Home Market," *The Wall Street Journal*, January 12, 1988, p. 31.

9 Rothschild, "Advertising Strategies," pp. 84–87.

high-fiber diet that may reduce the incidence of colon cancer. Or *the product can be tied to a personally involving situation,* such as advertising a sleeping aid late in the evening when insomniacs are interested in finding something to help them sleep. Or *advertising might draw on basic social values* related to the consumer's self-identity: "Pepsi is the choice of the new generation!" Finally, *an important new feature might be added to an unimportant product*—as when Crest added fluoride and was positioned as a cavity-preventing toothpaste, or when Domino's promised delivery within 30 minutes and lived up to it.

PSYCHOLOGICAL AND PERSONAL INFLUENCES ON CONSUMER DECISION-MAKING PROCESSES

Even when two consumers have equal involvement with a product, they often purchase different brands for different reasons. The information they collect, the way they process and interpret it, and their evaluation of alternative brands are all influenced by psychological and personal characteristics. Some of the important psychological, or thought, variables that affect a consumer's decision-making process include **perception, memory, needs,** and **attitudes.** The consumer's personal characteristics, such as **demographic and lifestyle variables,** influence these psychological factors.

Perception and memory

Perception is the process by which a person selects, organizes, and interprets information.[10] When consumers collect information about a high-involvement product such as a tennis racket, they follow a series of steps, or a hierarchy of effects. **Exposure** to a piece of information such as a new product, an ad, or a friend's recommendation, leads to **attention,** then to **comprehension,** and finally to **retention** in memory. Once consumers have fully perceived the information, they use it to evaluate alternative brands and to decide which to purchase.

The perception process is different for low-involvement products. Here, consumers store information in their memories without going through the sequence of attention and comprehension. Exposure may cause consumers to retain enough information so that they are familiar with a brand when they see it in a store.[11]

Two basic factors—selectivity and organization—guide consumers' perceptual processes and help explain why different consumers perceive prod-

---

[10] For a more complete review of the processes involved in consumers' perception and processing of information, and the marketing implications of those processes, see J. R. Bettman, *An Information Theory of Consumer Choice* (Reading, Mass.: Addison-Wesley, 1979).

[11] H. E. Krugman, "Memory without Recall, Exposure with Perception," *Journal of Advertising Research* 17 (August 1977), pp. 7–12.

uct information differently. **Selectivity** means that even though the environment is full of product information, consumers pick and choose only selected pieces of information and ignore the rest. For high-involvement purchases, consumers pay particular attention to information related to the needs they want to satisfy and the particular brands they are considering for purchase. This **perceptual vigilance** helps guarantee that consumers have the information needed to make a good choice.

Consumers also tend to avoid information that contradicts their current beliefs and attitudes. This **perceptual defense** helps them avoid the psychological discomfort of reassessing or changing attitudes, beliefs, or behaviors central to their self-images. For example, many smokers avoid antismoking messages, or play down their importance, rather than admit that smoking may be damaging their health. For low-involvement products, consumers tend to selectively screen out much information to avoid wasting mental effort.

Organization simply means that consumers group information into various categories enabling them to better comprehend, remember, and use it in making subsequent decisions.

Selective perception

An average consumer is exposed to 300 to 600 ads every day—not to mention information from other sources such as salespeople and family members. Between 1967 and 1982 the number of ads about doubled; they are expected to double again by 1997.[12] Consumers must be selective in perceiving this information so they can cope with the clutter of messages. This selectivity occurs at each of the four stages in the perception process: exposure, attention, comprehension, and retention. We discuss each of these stages in greater detail in the chapter on advertising.

Memory limitations[13]

Even though consumers are selective in perceiving product information, they remember only a portion of the messages that they pay attention to and comprehend. You can see why this limitation of the human memory is of concern to marketers. Much marketing activity deals with communicating information to potential consumers to improve their attitudes toward a given brand—or at least increase their familiarity with the brand name—and influence their future purchases.[14] Screening out or forgetting much of that

---

[12] Leo Bogart, "Executives Fear Ad Overload Will Lower Effectiveness," *Marketing News*, May 25, 1984, pp. 4–5.

[13] This section has benefited from materials provided by Jean-Claude Larréché (Fontainbleau, France: INSEAD).

[14] Eric J. Johnson and J. Edward Russo, "Product Familiarity and Learning New Information," *Journal of Consumer Research*, June 1984, pp. 542–50.

information reduces the effectiveness of the marketing program. An important question, then, is: Why don't consumers remember more marketing information? And what can marketers do—if anything—to improve the memorability of their messages?

There are different theories of how the human memory operates; but most agree that it works in two stages. Information from the environment is first processed by the **short-term memory,** which forgets most of it within 30 seconds or less because of inattention or displacement by new incoming information. Some information, however, is transferred to **long-term memory,** from which it can be retrieved later. Long-term memory has a nearly infinite storage capacity; but the amount of product information actually stored there is quite limited, for the following reasons:

1. Selection perception screens out much product information before it even gets to short-term memory.
2. The limited capacity of short-term memory means that only a few pieces of information can be attended to and processed at any one time.
3. For a piece of information to be transferred to long-term memory for later recall, it must be *actively rehearsed and internalized.* It takes from 5 to 10 seconds of rehearsal to place a single chunk of information in long-term memory. This is a relatively long time compared to the fraction of a second necessary to perceive a piece of information. Therefore, new pieces of information swamp the old one before it can be transferred—unless consumers find it sufficiently relevant to warrant focusing their attention.[15]

This is why print media are good vehicles for communicating complex or technical information about high-involvement products to consumers. Readers can control the pace at which such information is received; and they can take the time necessary to comprehend, rehearse, and remember what is read. Similarly, this explains why TV advertising for low-involvement products should focus on a few simple pieces of information, such as brand name, symbol, or key product attributes, and be repeated frequently. Because consumers are unlikely to pay much attention to or rehearse such information, they must be exposed to the same message repeatedly before it registers in their long-term memories.

Perceptual organization

Another mental factor determining how much product information consumers remember and use is the way they organize the information. People do not view and remember each piece of information they receive in isolation. Instead, they organize information through the processes of categorization and integration. **Categorization** helps consumers process known informa-

---

[15] J. R. Bettman, "Memory Factors in Consumer Choice: A Review," *Journal of Marketing,* Spring 1979, pp. 37–53.

tion quickly and efficiently: "I've seen this ad before so I don't have to pay much attention." It also helps people classify new information by generalizing from past experience. An ad for a new cereal with a high vitamin and mineral content, for instance, is interpreted in light of consumers' experience with other nutritional cereals. This can cause a problem if consumers' experiences have not been very favorable: "Other nutritional cereals I've tried have tasted lousy, and this one probably does, too." Also, consumers tend to classify similar brands into a single category, causing them to overlook the unique attributes of a particular brand.

Integration means that consumers perceive separate pieces of related information as an organized whole. Think of a print ad, for instance. The picture, headline, copy, layout, and location in the magazine interact to produce a single overall reaction to the ad and the brand advertised. Similarly, consumers integrate information about various characteristics of a brand, such as its price and the retail stores that carry it, to form an overall image of the brand. Thus, a high-priced brand available only at specialty stores appears to have more prestige than a less expensive one stocked by K mart.

Effects of stimulus characteristics on perception

Consumers' personal characteristics—such as their particular needs, attitudes, beliefs, and past experiences with a product category—influence the information they pay attention to, comprehend, and remember. The characteristics of the message itself and the way it is communicated also influence consumers' perceptions. The ad's color, size, and position within a magazine or TV show influence consumers' attention to the message and the brand image the ad produces in consumers' minds. Such relationships are important in creating effective advertising campaigns, of course. We examine these factors in more detail in the advertising chapter.

One stimulus characteristic with broad marketing implications, however, is the concept of a **just noticeable difference (JND).** A person can discriminate between two objects only when they differ by more than a JND on at least one attribute. Ernst Weber, a 19th-century physiologist, discovered that the stronger or more intense one object or stimulus is, the larger the JND. Weber's law has implications for product positioning and pricing as well as for advertising.[16] For example, a price reduction of 50 cents on an item that previously sold for $5 may be sufficiently large for most consumers to notice; but a 50-cent reduction on a $20 item would probably fall below the JND. The net result of such a price cut would be a reduction in sales income without any compensating increase in sales volume.

---

[16] S. H. Britt and V. M. Nelson, "The Marketing Importance of the Just Noticeable Difference," *Business Horizons*, August 1976, pp. 38–40.

Needs and attitudes

An **attitude** is a positive or negative feeling about an object (say, a brand) that predisposes a person to behave in a particular way toward that object. Attitudes derive from a consumer's evaluation that a given brand provides the benefits necessary to help satisfy a particular need. These evaluations are multidimensional: consumers judge each brand on a set of dimensions or attributes, weighted by their relative importance.

Compensatory attitude models

Martin Fishbein pioneered a model that specified how consumers would combine evaluations of a brand across multiple attributes to arrive at a single overall attitude toward that brand.[17] His model is expressed as follows:

$$\text{Attitude}_A = \sum_{i=1}^{k} B_i I_i$$

Where:

Attitude_A = Consumer's overall attitude toward Brand A

B_i = Consumer's belief concerning the extent to which attribute i is associated with Brand A

I_i = The importance of attribute i to the consumer when choosing a brand to buy

k = The total attributes considered by the consumer when evaluating alternative brands in the product category

i = Any specific product attribute

Exhibit 4–5 applies the Fishbein model to consumer Virginia Lynn's evaluation of alternative tennis rackets. This model is **compensatory** because it assumes that Lynn's overall attitude toward a brand of racket is determined by the *weighted* sum of the ratings for that brand on all relevant attributes. Thus, a poor evaluation on one attribute is compensated for by a strong evaluation on another attribute. It also assumes that the brand with the highest total score is the one Lynn is predisposed to buy.[18]

---

[17] M. Fishbein, "A Behavior Theory Approach to the Relations between Beliefs about an Object and Attitudes toward the Object," in *Attitude Theory and Measurement*, ed. M. Fishbein (New York: John Wiley & Sons, 1967). There is also an extended version of the Fishbein model that includes social norms. For a discussion of the extended version, see J. Paul Peter and Jerry Olson, *Consumer Behavior: Marketing Strategy Perspectives* (Homewood, Ill.: Richard D. Irwin, 1987), pp. 214–25.

[18] For a discussion of the attitude-behavior relationship, see R. P. Bagozzi, "A Field Investigation of Causal Relations among Cognitions, Affect, Intentions, and Behavior," *Journal of Marketing Research*, November 1983, pp. 562–84.

EXHIBIT   4 ◆ 5

A multiattribute model of attitudes toward alternative tennis rackets

Our hypothetical consumer, Virginia Lynn, is interested in buying a new tennis racket with a large head, a stiff frame for good control, durable construction, attractive styling, and a reasonable price. However, as the table indicates, she considers head size and stiffness the most important attributes to look for. The other three criteria are of relatively less concern. On the basis of information gathered from advertising, conversations with friends and a tennis pro, and examination of various rackets in a sporting goods store, she evaluated three different tennis rackets on each of the five attributes. The table displays the results of Lynn's evaluations.

Product attribute	Importance weight (0–10)	Ratings		
		Brand A	Brand B	Brand C
Size of head	10	8	8	8
Stiffness	10	8	10	9
Durability	8	8	9	9
Style/Attractiveness	7	9	8	8
Low price	6	9	8	8

Using the formula in the text, Lynn's overall attitude score for Brand A equals $(10 \times 8) + (10 \times 8) + (8 \times 8) + (7 \times 9) + (6 \times 9) = 341$.

Her overall attitude scores for the other two brands are:

Brand B = 356
Brand C = 346

Consequently, Lynn prefers, and will be predisposed to buy, Brand B, the brand toward which she has the most positive attitude. Although head size was one of the most important attributes, it played no significant role in determining which brand she would buy. This is because there were no differences among the three brands on that attribute. Instead, the *determinant attribute*—the attribute that had the biggest impact in determining which brand our consumer would prefer—was stiffness.

Noncompensatory attitude models

As suggested by the compensatory model, the mental processes involved in forming an attitude are quite complex. That is because consumers must evaluate each alternative brand on each and every attribute. In some purchase situations—particularly with low-involvement products—consumers may adopt a simpler approach and evaluate alternative brands on only one attribute at a time. Such an approach is **noncompensatory** because a poor evaluation of a brand on one attribute cannot be offset by a strong evaluation on another. Exhibit 4–6 describes several noncompensatory approaches that

EXHIBIT 4 ♦ 6

Three noncompensatory models describing how consumers evaluate and form attitudes toward alternative brands

---

Lexicographic model

This model suggests that consumers evaluate alternative brands on the most important attribute first. If one brand appears clearly superior on that dimension, consumers select it as the best possible choice and the evaluation process ends. If no alternative brand stands out on the most important attribute, the consumer proceeds to evaluate them on the second most important attribute. This process continues until one brand is judged superior to all others on some attribute. In Exhibit 4–5, for instance, Lynn would have compared the three brands on the most important attribute (head size) only to find no differences. She then would have proceeded to the second most important attribute (stiffness) and discovered that Brand B was superior to both other brands, at which point her evaluation process would stop.

Conjunctive model

This model indicates that consumers compare alternative brands to some preconceived set of standards instead of comparing them to each other. Consumers have some minimum cut-off level in mind for each important attribute. They reject alternatives that fall below the minimum on any one of those attributes. Consumers favor the brand (or brands) that exceed the minimum requirements on all salient dimensions. Conjunctive evaluation does not pay attention to how high an alternative scores on any attribute as long as it exceeds the desired minimum. A high score on one attribute does not compensate for a below-minimum level on another.

Disjunctive model

Instead of setting minimum standards on different attributes and rejecting alternatives that do not meet all those minimums, consumers might set a high standard for one or a few attributes and then consider buying only those brands meeting or exceeding that standard. In our previous example, Lynn might have said that she would only buy a racket with the maximum possible degree of stiffness. In that case, Brand B (with a perfect rating of 10 on stiffness) would be the only brand Lynn would consider buying.

---

consumers use in evaluating and forming attitudes toward alternative brands.

Different consumers use different approaches in evaluating alternative brands, depending on the strength of their needs, their involvement with the product category, and the risk they associate with the purchase. Sometimes consumers employ a combination of approaches in making a single decision. They could use a noncompensatory approach to screen out undesirable product offerings followed by a more detailed compensatory evaluation of the remaining brands.[19]

Although the different attitude models provide insights into the ways consumers evaluate competitive product offerings, their implications for

---

[19] See, for example, David Grether and Louis Wilde, "An Analysis of Conjunctive Choice: Theory and Experiments," *Journal of Consumer Research*, March 1984, pp. 373–85.

marketers are similar. The models suggest that to design appealing product offerings and structure effective marketing programs, marketers must have some knowledge of (1) the attributes or decision criteria consumers use to evaluate a particular product category; (2) the relative importance of those attributes to different consumers; and (3) how consumers rate their brand relative to competitors' offerings on important attributes.

Attitude change

The multiattribute attitude models of consumer choice suggest various ways marketers might change consumer attitudes favorably toward their brands and away from competing brands. These are discussed briefly below.[20]

1. *Changing attitudes toward the product class to increase the total market—* thereby increasing sales for the particular brand. For example, a frozen-orange-juice seller once attempted to make its product acceptable as a refreshing drink throughout the day. This type of attitude change involves primary demand and is difficult to accomplish without a lowering of price designed to increase the cross-elasticities with substitute products.

2. *Changing the importance consumers attach to one or more attributes.* In recent years, any number of sellers have attempted to inform customers of the importance of the medical benefits derived from using their type of product. Cereal manufacturers, in particular, have been active in this regard. For example, they advertise that a cereal with a high fiber content can help prevent colon cancer or that an oat cereal helps lower cholesterol.

3. *Adding a salient product characteristic to the existing set.* For example, after many years of arguing that safety won't sell, auto manufacturers are now trying to outdo each other in this regard. Lee Iacocca, Chrysler Corporation Chairman, who was once strongly opposed to air-bag safety devices, is "now pledging to put them in all his U.S.-built cars by 1990. General Motors Corporation, meanwhile, is running ads playing up the formation of an in-house medical team dedicated to crash-injury research. And both companies are in a race with Ford Motor Company to offer state-of-the-art braking systems in more of their cars."[21]

4. *Improving the ratings of the salient product characteristics of a particular brand.* This is the most common attempt, particularly during the product introductory stage or when a product improvement has been made. For example, Procter & Gamble recently spent some $40 million to promote its Ultra Pampers Plus disposable diapers. Its advertising message focused on leakage protection. The TV commercials featured a new character, Dry Bear, and combined live action along with demonstrations and the animated bear to discuss the brand's new features.[22]

---

[22] Laurie Freeman, "P&G Takes Pampers on the Road," *Advertising Age*, November 2, 1987, p. 30.

[20] Harper W. Boyd, Jr., Michael L. Ray, and Edward C. Strong, "An Attitudinal Framework for Advertising Strategy," *Journal of Marketing*, April 1972, pp. 27–33.

[21] Joseph B. White, "U.S. Automakers Decide Safety Sells," *The Wall Street Journal*, August 24, 1988, p. 17.

5. *Lowering the ratings of the salient product characteristics of competing brands.* This can be attempted via comparative advertising, which has increased in recent years. For example, one nutritional cereal regularly compares the amount of vitamins and minerals its brand provides in an average serving with those provided by specific other brands.

Attitudes may also be changed by inducing the consumer to purchase a new brand rather than the preferred one, in the belief that attitudes will change to conform to behavior. For example, a price reduction for a shampoo might attract some buyers who at the time of purchase preferred other brands. Attitudes may change in favor of the brand most recently purchased, assuming satisfaction with that brand. This favorable situation can remain even after the price returns to normal. Attitude change may be helped along via the use of a well-known and respected spokesperson for the company, such as Bill Cosby, and a free product trial.

Demographics and lifestyle

Demographics and lifestyle—also called **psychographics**—are the personal characteristics that influence consumers' decision-making processes.

Demographics

Demographic characteristics—such as age, income, or education level—all influence (1) the nature of consumers' needs and wants; (2) their ability to buy products or services to satisfy those needs; (3) the perceived importance of various attributes or choice criteria used to evaluate alternative brands; and (4) consumers' attitudes toward and preferences for different products and brands. For example, older adults prefer conservative investments such as certificates of deposit, real estate, and bonds; have a greater need for convenience and health-related products; and spend less than younger age groups on clothing, transportation, and household furnishings.[23] The decision by Monaghan to focus on the eat-at-home pizza market translated into catering to a younger age group living in university towns or in neighborhoods characterized by substantial numbers of moderately priced apartments.

Lifestyles

Two people of similar age, income, education, and even occupations do not necessarily live their lives in the same way. They may have different opinions, interests, and activities. As a result, they are likely to exhibit different patterns of behavior—including buying different products and brands and using them in different ways and for different purposes. These broad patterns of activities, interests, and opinions—and the behaviors that result—

---

[23] George P. Moschis, *Consumer Socialization* (Lexington, Mass.: D. C. Heath & Co., 1982), pp. 196–97.

EXHIBIT   4 ◆ 7

Eight male psychographic segments

Group 1. *"The quiet family man"* (8 percent of total males)

He is a self-sufficient man who wants to be left alone and is basically shy. He tries to be as little involved with community life as possible. His life revolves around the family, simple work, and television viewing. He has a marked fantasy life. As a shopper he is practical and less drawn to consumer goods and pleasures than other men.

With low education and low economic status, he tends to be older than average.

Group 2. *"The traditionalist"* (16 percent of total males)

He is a man who feels secure, has self-esteem, and follows conventional rules. He is proper and respectable, regards himself as altruistic and interested in the welfare of others. As a shopper he is conservative, likes popular brands and well-known manufacturers.

With low education and low or middle socioeconomic status, he is a member of the oldest age group.

Group 3. *"The discontented man"* (13 percent of total males)

He is a man who is likely to be dissatisfied with his work. He feels bypassed by life, dreams of better jobs, more money, and more security. He tends to be distrustful and socially aloof. As a buyer, he is quite price-conscious.

He is a member of the lowest education and socioeconomic groups and is generally older than average.

Group 4. *"The ethical highbrow"* (14 percent of total males)

This is a very concerned man, sensitive to people's needs. Basically a puritan, he is content with family life, friends, and work, and is interested in culture, religion, and social reform. As a consumer he is interested in quality, which may at times justify greater expenditure.

He is well educated, of middle or upper socioeconomic status, and is middle-aged or older.

Group 5. *"The pleasure-oriented man"* (9 percent of total males)

He tends to emphasize his masculinity and rejects whatever appears to be soft or feminine. He views himself a leader among men. Self-centered, he dislikes his work or job and seeks immediate gratification for his needs. He is an impulsive buyer, likely to buy products with a masculine image.

He has a low education, is of the lower socioeconomic class, and is middle-aged or younger.

Group 6. *"The achiever"* (11 percent of total males)

This is likely to be a hardworking man, dedicated to success and all that it implies, social prestige, power, and money. He is in favor of diversity and is adventurous about leisure-time pursuits. He is stylish, likes good food, music, and so on. As a consumer he is status-conscious and a thoughtful and discriminating buyer.

He has a good education, high socioeconomic status, and is young.

Group 7. *"The he-man"* (19 percent of total males)

He is gregarious, likes action, seeks an exciting and dramatic life. He thinks of himself as capable and dominant and tends to be more of a bachelor than a family man, even after marriage. The products he buys and brands preferred are likely to have "self-expressive value," especially a "man of action" dimension.

He is well-educated, mainly middle socioeconomic status, and a member of the youngest of the male groups.

Group 8. *"The sophisticated man"* (10 percent of total males)

He is likely to be an intellectual, concerned about social issues, admires men with artistic and intellectual achievements. He is socially cosmopolitan with broad interests and wants to be dominant and a group leader. As a consumer he is attracted to the unique and fashionable.

He is the best educated and of the highest economic status of all groups. He is younger than average.

Source: Adapted from W. D. Wells, "Psychogenics: A Critical Review," *Journal of Marketing Research* 12 (May 1975), p. 201. Published by the American Marketing Association.

are referred to as *lifestyles.* We also discuss lifestyles at length in Chapter 6 on segmentation.

Examples of male lifestyle groups are shown in Exhibit 4–7. Broad types of products and benefits sought can be inferred from each of these lifestyle groups. For example, in Exhibit 4–7, the "quiet family man" group is likely to contain prospects for do-it-yourself equipment. The "outdoor people" and "adventurous" groups were prime targets for the advertising of International Harvester's four-wheel-drive recreational vehicle, Scout.

SOCIAL INFLUENCES ON CONSUMERS' DECISION-MAKING PROCESSES

Information and social pressures received from other people influence a consumer's needs, wants, evaluations, and product or brand preferences. Social influences are particularly apparent when consumers purchase high-involvement, socially visible goods or services. The social influences affecting consumers' purchase decisions include culture, subculture, social class, reference groups, and family. These five categories represent a hierarchy of social influences, ranging from broad, general effects on consumption behavior—such as those imposed by the culture we live in—to more specific influences that directly affect a consumer's choice of a particular product or brand. For a simplified view of this hierarchy of social influences, see Exhibit 4–8.

Culture

Culture is the set of values, beliefs, attitudes, and behavior patterns (customs and folkways) shared by the members of a society and transmitted from one generation to the next through socialization. Cultural values and beliefs tend to be relatively stable over time; but they can change from one generation to the next in response to changing conditions in society. For example, the baby boomers born between 1946 and 1960 have somewhat different values and behavior patterns than their parents. They tend to be more health conscious, to eat less red meat, to invest rather than save their money, to be more concerned with personal grooming, and to be more favorably disposed toward time- and labor-saving goods and services than their parents were at that age.

Cultural differences among countries create difficulties for international marketers, also. These differences can call for adapting the firm's marketing strategy to each local culture, particularly for such culturally sensitive products as food, clothes, and personal-care items. For example, Nestlé markets different coffees to the various European countries to accommodate local tastes. Some companies, however, use a standardized approach to their international marketing activities. They offer essentially the same product in all countries. Coca-Cola, Gillette, Toyota, and Mitsubishi (videocassette re-

EXHIBIT   4 ♦ 8

Simplified view of hierarchy of major social influences affecting consumer behavior

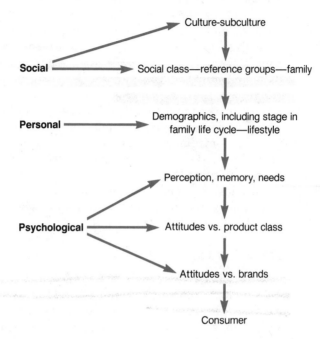

corders and television sets) use a standardized approach. International marketing is discussed in depth in Chapter 22.

Subculture

Americans are fond of referring to their nation as "the great melting pot." But many of the values and customs brought in by immigrants have never entirely melted. Thus, many groups of people in the United States share common geographic, ethnic, racial, or religious backgrounds. They continue to hold some values, attitudes, and behavior patterns that are uniquely their own. Such groups are referred to as **subcultures.**

There are, for example, 19 million U.S. Hispanics with $130 billion to spend annually. This fast-growing group—up 34 percent since 1980—is a puzzling market, partly because second- and third-generation Hispanics tend to perpetuate the culture their parents and grandparents had when they came to the United States. No other ethnic group has held on to its language so tenaciously, thereby making assimilation difficult.[24]

---

[24] Julia Liebach, "If You Want a Big New Market. . . ," *Fortune,* November 2, 1988, p. 181.

Social class

Every society has its status groupings. In our society, social status is based primarily on personal achievements as reflected in occupation, education, and source and amount of income. People associate most with others they view as their social peers. This creates a **social class** system that maintains certain barriers between people with different status rankings. It leads to commonalities in social attitudes, tastes, and preferences among individuals within a particular social class.

From a marketing manager's view, people in different social classes vary in many ways, including interpersonal relations, product usage, store patronage, and media usage. For example, people in the upper classes are targeted by marketers of financial investments, recreational apparel, and expensive imported cars. Working-class consumers are targeted for savings accounts, lower-priced apparel, and gadgets.[25] Because of its behavioral characteristics, social class is often used to segment a market for consumer goods. We discuss this further in Chapter 6.

Reference groups

Reference groups include both formal membership groups (the company one works for, one's church) and informal groups (friends who get together regularly to play cards). They can be groups that consumers currently belong to or groups to which they aspire. They can also be an individual who is considered an expert in the subject of interest. In any case, because consumers admire group members and want to win or maintain their acceptance, the group's norms and standards serve as a reference point for self-appraisal and as guides for purchasing behavior. Friends are considered to be one of the most reliable sources for information pertaining to products and services; advertising is usually considered one of the least reliable. Reference-group influence is strongest for luxury, high-involvement products consumed in socially visible situations.[26] In ordering a pizza or a late-night snack for the first time, college students would rely heavily on advice from their peer groups as to which brand to buy.

Family

The **family** is the most important source of social influence for most U.S. consumers. First, it serves as the primary socialization agent, helping members acquire the skills, knowledge, and attitudes to function as consumers in the marketplace. Consequently, the family has a great and lasting influence

---

[25] R. P. Coleman, "The Continuing Significance of Social Class to Marketing," *Journal of Consumer Research,* September 1983, pp. 183–94.

[26] W. O. Bearden and M. J. Etzel, "Reference Group Influence on Product and Brand Purchase Decisions," *Journal of Consumer Research,* September 1983, pp. 183–94.

EXHIBIT 4 ♦ 9

Examples of product classes associated with different types of family purchasing situations

Wife dominant	In 75 percent of families, wives decide how much to spend on food—and what individual food items to buy. Wives also dominate in decisions relating to furniture and small appliances.
Husband dominant	Husbands have a smaller array of products in which they specialize. These include life and auto insurance, lawn mowers, and tires.
Joint husband-wife	Examples include vacations, movies, and housing choices.
Autonomic	In these product categories, both husbands and wives make independent purchase decisions. The partner who makes most of these decisions varies across families. Examples include handling of financial resources, children's toys, men's clothing accessories, and living room drapes.

Source: From *Consumer Behavior* by William Wilkie, p. 188. Copyright © 1986 by John Wiley & Sons, 1986. Reprinted by permission of John Wiley & Sons.

on its younger members' attitudes toward various products, brands, and stores. It is likely that many of the products and services purchased by the "next generation" were influenced by parents—even grandparents. For example, one study found that nearly 65 percent of husbands in their 20s used the same insurance company as did their parents.[27]

Family members tend to specialize in the purchase of certain products either because of their interest or expertise or the role structure of the family. Basically, there are four kinds of family purchasing situations—wife dominant, husband dominant, joint wife-husband, and autonomic.[28] The latter applies to those products for which different families have different ways of purchasing. For examples of the kinds of products in each of the four categories, see Exhibit 4–9.

Family life cycle

When people leave home and start their own households, they progress through distinct phases of a **family life cycle.** The traditional cycle includes young singles, young marrieds without children; young marrieds with children; middle-aged marrieds with children; middle-aged marrieds without dependent children; older marrieds; and older unmarrieds. These stages are illustrated in Exhibit 4–10.

---

[27] Larry G. Woodson, Terry L. Childers, and Paul R. Winn, "Intergenerational Influences in the Purchase of Auto Insurance," in W. Locander, ed., *Marketing Look Outward* (Chicago: American Marketing Association, 1976), pp. 40–59; also see George P. Mosches, *Consumer Socialization* (Lexington, Mass.: D. C. Heath and Company, 1987), chap. 5.

[28] William Wilkie, *Consumer Behavior* (New York: John Wiley & Sons, 1986), p. 188.

EXHIBIT   4 ♦ 10

Modern family life cycle

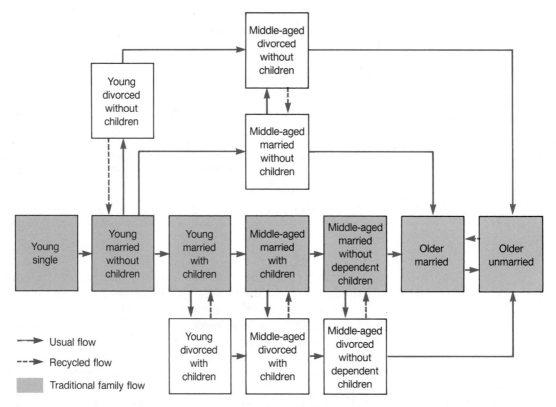

→ Usual flow

- - -▶ Recycled flow

▨ Traditional family flow

Source: Redrawn from Patrick E. Murphy and William A. Staples, "A Modernized Family Life Cycle," Reprinted with permission from *The Journal of Consumer Research* (June 1979), p. 17.

Each phase of the life cycle brings changes in family circumstances and purchasing behavior.[29] For example, young singles' purchases tend to concentrate on nondurable items, including food away from home, clothing, and entertainment. Young marrieds without children are typically more affluent because both spouses usually work away from home. They are a major market for such durables as automobiles, furniture, and appliances. Young marrieds with children probably have the least disposable income; but they are the major market for single-family dwellings, infant products and clothing, and child-care services. Middle-aged couples without children usually have the most discretionary income. They are a major market for

---

[29] Janet Wagner and Sherman Hanna, "The Effectiveness of Family Life Cycle Variables in Consumer Expenditure Research," *Journal of Consumer Research,* December 1983, pp. 281–91.

many luxury goods and services, such as expensive cars and international travel. Finally, the older marrieds and older unmarrieds typically have less disposable income, but are nevertheless an important market for health and medical products and services as well as hobby and craft items.

Of course, there are exceptions and elaborations of the "traditional" family life cycle—especially the growing number of single-parent families and affluent seniors. These groups are of increasing importance to marketers.

SUMMARY

Consumers' decision-making processes are classified largely on the basis of high versus low involvement with the product and how extensive the search for information is. High-involvement products relate to products or services psychologically important to the consumer. To reduce the psychological and financial risks associated with buying a high-involvement item, consumers engage in a complex decision-making process. The five major steps in the complex decision-making process are problem identification, information search, evaluation of alternatives, purchase, and postpurchase evaluation.

Most purchase decisions are low in consumer involvement; therefore, consumers do not engage in an extensive search for information or make a detailed evaluation of alternative brands. Rather, they receive brand information passively. In the main, the two low-involvement decisions are inertia versus impulse buying and variety seeking. Because of the differences in low-involvement and high-involvement goods, marketers must use different strategies and marketing program elements.

Buying behavior is strongly influenced by psychological and personal characteristics that vary across individual consumers. Some of the more important of these variables affecting consumers' decision-making processes are perception, memory, needs, and attitudes. These, in turn, are influenced by consumers' personal characteristics such as demographic and lifestyle variables.

Information and social pressures received from other people influence consumers' needs, wants, evaluations, and preferences for various products and brand names. This is particularly the case when consumers purchase high-involvement goods or services. The social influences are categorized as culture, subculture, social class, reference groups, and the family. These five categories represent a hierarchy of social influences ranging from broad effects on consumption behavior to the more specific influences that directly impact a consumer's choice of a particular brand.

QUESTIONS

1. Suppose that you are the product manager for Wrigley's Doublemint gum. For most consumers, chewing gum represents a *low-involvement* purchase. What are the implications of that fact for the decisions you must make concerning the (a) promotion, (b) distribution, and (c) price compo-

nents of the marketing program for your product?

2. Think back to a recent purchase you made involving a product or service costing more than $100 (e.g., a major article of clothing or a stereo). Using the framework outlined in Exhibit 4–2 and discussed in

the chapter, describe the *decision process* involved in making your purchase. What motivated your purchase? What were your thoughts at each stage in the decision process? What activities were involved?

3. In making the decision you described in question 2, what *kinds and sources of information* did you use? Which sources had the most influence on your final decision? Assuming that many other consumers behave as you did, what are the implications of your information search process for the design of a marketing program for the product or service you purchased?

4. As a marketing manager for Pepsi-Cola, you know that the purchase of a soft drink is a low-involvement purchase for most consumers. How might you try to *increase consumers' involvement* with your brand to increase their loyalty and reduce brand switching in your product category?

5. Many young consumers spread their candy bar purchases over different brands. They buy one brand on one purchase and a different brand on the next. Which purchase decision process does this sort of behavior suggest? What are the marketing implications of such behavior?

6. Examine the *attitudes* toward three brands of tennis rackets summarized in Exhibit

4–5. Suppose that a major segment of consumers hold attitudes similar to those of Virginia Lynn. Suppose further that you are the marketing manager for Brand C. Which actions could you take to improve consumers' attitudes toward your brand and increase your sales relative to the competition?

7. A very important *attribute* for most consumers when forming an attitude about an airline is the carrier's safety record. But airlines almost never mention safety in their advertising or promotional campaigns. Why not?

8. You are trying to identify target market segments for the following products and services. At what stage in the *family life cycle* are consumers most likely to purchase each item?
   a. Life insurance
   b. Home mortgage
   c. Baby furniture
   d. Caribbean cruise

9. What other *demographic and lifestyle variables* are likely to characterize consumers at each of the family life-cycle stages you identified in question 8? What do these characteristics imply for the "4Ps" involved in the marketing programs for each of the products and services listed in question 8?

Chapter ◇ 5

Organizational markets and buying behavior

GENERAL ELECTRIC: AN INDUSTRIAL GIANT

General Electric Company (GE) is one of America's industrial giants, with sales of $40.5 billion and net income of $2.9 billion in 1987.[1] Most people think of GE as a manufacturer of consumer goods, such as major appliances and TV sets. In reality, consumer products account for only about one fourth of GE's sales and profits. In 1987 GE sold its consumer electronics business (TVs, VCRs, and audio products) to Thomson S.A., a French electronics company. GE continues to manufacture major appliances, which represented just 12 percent of total sales in 1987. The bulk of the company's sales are made to other organizations rather than to individual consumers. For example, 11 percent of the firm's 1987 sales came from power systems and services, such as generators, transformers, and a nuclear service business. Another 9 percent of sales derived from technical products and services, including medical products such as the GE CAT Scan and other diagnostic imaging equipment. Aircraft engines, flight controls, and aerospace equipment accounted for nearly 30 percent of 1987 sales; and electrical motors, locomotives, and factory automation equipment generated another 12 percent. Finally, materials like high-performance plastics and Lexan resins brought in another 7 percent and NBC (National Broadcasting Company) 8 percent of sales.

The wide array of different products—and variations in the organizations and purchasing processes involved in buying those products—presents General Electric's divisions with different marketing opportunities and challenges. The firm's aerospace and aircraft engine businesses, for instance, depend heavily on a single group of customers—the U.S. Defense Department and the handful of defense contractors who build aircraft and electronic systems for the military. Consequently, volume fluctuates dramatically with changes in the U.S. government's defense policy and budget. The marketing program in these divisions relies heavily on the efforts of highly trained technical sales engineers who concentrate on only one or a few major customers, rather than on media advertising or other broadly focused forms of promotion. An extensive lobbying effort is also a part of GE's proactive strategy to influence government defense policy and smooth out fluctuations in its external environment.

On the other hand, many products sold by GE's materials division are commodities such as silicones and

---

[1] Sales and earnings information from the General Electric Company.

continued

concluded

basic plastics. They are sold as raw materials to manufacturers of a variety of products from automobiles to toys. Thus, GE relies on many wholesale distributors to reach end users in different industries. The firm must also pay close attention to the efficiency of its production and distribution operations to hold down costs and compete with low prices.

GE's experience is certainly not unique. Many marketers of goods and services make most or all of their sales to organizational rather than consumer markets. Indeed, about 16 million organizations—including manufacturers, farmers, governments, universities, and ballet companies—buy a variety of goods and services to stay in operation. This chapter discusses how institutional buyers go about making purchase decisions, the scope of organizational markets, and the goods and services such organizations buy.

We first compare the characteristics of industrial markets with those of consumer markets. Next, we examine organizational markets and purchasing behavior from two different perspectives. First, we take a micro view of organizational buying behavior. We examine the decision-making processes that organizations go through when deciding what to buy, who makes those purchasing decisions, and the organizational and environmental factors that influence them. We pay particular attention to the ways organizational purchasing processes differ from the consumer buying behavior we examined in Chapter 4.

Then the second half of the chapter takes a macro view of organizational markets and marketing, including an examination of different organizational customers and their characteristics. We examine several categories of goods and services purchased by such customers, along with some of the unique marketing considerations involved in selling products in each category.

COMPARING ORGANIZATIONAL AND CONSUMER MARKETS

Organizational markets (often referred to as *industrial* or *producer markets*) are, in the aggregate, about twice as large as consumer markets. Such markets consist of organizations that buy many of the same products and services as households do—for example, automobiles, computers, office supplies, paper products, transportation services, food, and furniture. Thus, marketing to such organizations is distinguished not on the basis of the nature of the product but by the nature of the customer and the buying processes used.

Organizational markets include resellers (retailers and wholesalers); goods producers (agriculture, mining, manufacturing); services—both consumer and business (such as those in the education, health, lodging, transportation, and amusement sectors); and the government—federal, state, and local. The federal government of the United States is the largest single buyer of goods and services in the world.

By definition, organizational buyers purchase goods and services for further production (raw materials and components), for use in operations (office supplies and insurance), and for resale to other customers (furniture and pharmaceuticals). In contrast, individuals and households buy for their own use and consumption. These two types of markets also differ in numerous other ways, including their demand characteristics, their market demographics, and their buyer-seller relationships (see Exhibit 5-1).

The derived demand characteristic of organization markets has led some companies to try to stimulate demand for their customers' products. For example, Du Pont regularly advertises clothing products made from its synthetic fibers. Fluctuating and cyclical demand have caused some producers of industrial goods to diversify into other products and markets in an effort to have more balanced sales.

The market demographics of industrial goods and services have a number of marketing strategy implications. They facilitate—often require—the use

EXHIBIT 5♦1

Differences between organizational and consumer markets

Demand characteristics
The demand for industrial goods and services is:
1. Derived from the demand for consumer goods and services.
2. Relatively inelastic—price changes in the short run are not likely to affect demand drastically.
3. More erratic, because small increases in consumer demand can, over time, strongly affect the demand for manufacturing plants and equipment.
4. More cyclical.

Market demographics
Organizational buyers, when compared to buyers of consumer goods, are:
1. Fewer in number.
2. Larger.
3. Geographically concentrated.
4. More apt to buy on specifications.

Buyer-seller relationships
Organizational markets are characterized by the following when compared to the markets for consumer goods:
1. Use of professional buying specialists following prescribed procedures.
2. Closer buyer-seller relationships.
3. Presence of multiple buying influences.

of **direct selling** with all its implications of personal selling, advertising, and physical logistics. Because continuing relationships are so important, services such as delivery, spare parts availability, and uniform product quality are emphasized.

Buyer-seller relationships can take many forms, including leasing, outright purchase using a variety of contracts, and customer financing by the seller. Because buyers depend on suppliers for an assured and continuing supply of a product and its servicing, the buyer-seller relationship is unusually close and extends substantially beyond simply the sale transaction. It is also marked by a complex buying process that affects the seller's formal organization structure as well as the qualifications of managers.

Webster, in his discussion of consumer versus industrial goods marketing, states that the latter involves more corporate and business strategy; its effectiveness depends to a much greater extent on how well marketing is integrated with the other business functions—manufacturing, R&D, inventory control, engineering, and finance. He goes on to state:

> By its very nature industrial marketing requires that all parts of the business be customer-oriented and that all marketing decisions be based on a complete and accurate understanding of customer needs.[2]

ORGANIZATIONAL BUYING DECISIONS AND PARTICIPANTS

Organizations purchase different kinds of goods and services for different purposes than consumers do. The crucial question from a marketer's viewpoint is whether organizations make their *purchase decisions* in different ways. What members of the organization are involved in making purchase decisions? Are the stages in the organizational buyer's decision-making process similar to those that consumers go through? How do the activities of the two types of buyers differ at each stage? Are organizational buyers influenced by environmental variables in the same ways as consumers?

Who makes organizational purchasing decisions?

Organizational purchasing often involves people from various departments. These participants in the buying process can be grouped as users, influencers, gatekeepers, buyers, and deciders.[3]

---

[2] Frederick E. Webster, Jr., *Industrial Marketing Strategy* (New York: John Wiley & Sons, 1984), p. 15.

[3] Frederick E. Webster, Jr., and Yoram Wind, *Organizational Buying Behavior* (Englewood Cliffs, N.J.: Prentice-Hall, 1972); and Frederick E. Webster, Jr., and Yoram Wind, "A General Model for Understanding Organizational Buying Behavior," *Journal of Marketing* 36 (April 1972), pp. 13–19.

Users

The people in the organization who must use or work with the product or service often have some influence on the purchase decision. For example, drill-press operators might request that the purchasing agent buy a particular brand of drills because they stay sharp longer and reduce down-time in the plant. Physicians, along with a variety of hospital laboratory specialists, would have substantial input into any decision relating to the purchase of GE's diagnostic imaging systems.

Influencers

Influencers provide information for evaluating alternative products and suppliers. They are usually technical experts from various departments within the organization. Influencers help determine which specifications and criteria to use in making the purchase decision, as do government specialists when it comes to the purchase of any of GE's large power-generating equipment involving nuclear energy.

Gatekeepers

Gatekeepers control the flow of information to other people in the purchasing process. They include the organization's purchasing agents and the suppliers' salespeople, as well as secretaries and receptionists. Gatekeepers influence a purchase by controlling the information reaching other decision makers. An organization does not decide to buy a new product, for example, unless information about its existence and advantages over alternatives is brought to the decision-makers' attention.

Buyers

The buyer is usually referred to as a **purchasing agent** or **purchasing manager.** In most organizations, buyers have the authority to contact suppliers and negotiate the purchase transaction. In some cases they exercise wide discretion in carrying out their jobs. In other firms, they are tightly constrained by specifications and contract requirements determined by technical experts and top administrators—as would have been the case in the purchase of factory automation equipment from GE by General Motors.

Deciders

The decider is the person with the authority to make a final purchase decision. Sometimes buyers have this authority; but often lower-level purchasing managers carry out the wishes of more powerful decision makers. When American Airlines ordered 80 jet aircraft engines from GE to power its new fleet of Boeing 767s, the final decision to do so was made by American's top-level executives.

The organizational buying center

For routine purchases with a small dollar value, a single buyer or purchasing manager may make the purchase decision. For many organizational purchases, though, several people from different departments participate in the decision process. The individuals in this group, called a **buying center,** share knowledge and information relevant to the purchase of a particular product or service.

A buyer or purchasing manager is almost always a member of the buying center. The inclusion of people from other functional areas, however, depends on what is being purchased. When the purchase is a major new installation, the high dollar value of the purchase usually dictates that the firm's chief executive and its top financial officer actively participate in the final decision. For purchases of key fabricating parts for the manufacture of the final product, R&D, engineering, production, and quality control people are likely to be added. For accessory equipment, such as new office equipment, an experienced user of the equipment (say, a secretary or office manager) might participate in the decision.

For an example of the roles played by the various individuals involved in the purchase or upgrading of a telecommunications system, see Exhibit 5–2. Note the addition of the initiator's role in the list of people involved in the buying situation. The composition of the buying center often varies by market segment. Exhibit 5–3 gives an example involving the marketing of dialysis treatment machines for use in treating kidney disorders and supplies to different market segments.

EXHIBIT 5 ◆ 2

Individuals in the buying process and their roles in the purchase or upgrading of a telecommunications system

Initiator	Division general manager proposes to replace the company's telecommunications system.
Decider	Vice president of administration selects, with influence from others, the vendor company to deal with and the system to buy.
Influencer	Corporate telecommunications department and vice president of data processing have important say about which system and vendor company to deal with.
Purchaser	Corporate purchasing department completes the purchase to specifications by negotiating or bidding.
Gatekeeper	Corporate purchasing and telecommunications departments analyze company's needs and recommend likely matches with potential vendors.
User	All division employees who use the telecommunications equipment.

Source: Adapted from Thomas V. Bonoma, *Marketing Management* (New York: The Free Press, 1984), p. 292.

EXHIBIT 5 ♦ 3

Composition of buying centers by segment for dialysis treatment machines and supplies

Dialysis machines are designed to treat end-stage renal disease (irreversible uremia), the fourth most common major health problem in the United States. The basic principles of treatment are passing a patient's blood through a disposable blood filter, where through the use of different pressure, urea and other waste matter are extracted from the blood, which is then returned to the patient's body. The process takes four to six hours and is normally undertaken three times a week.

There are three major market segments for a dialysis treatment machine. Each has a unique buying center, as follows:

1. *In-home patients:* The buying center for this segment includes the patient, the physician, the insurance company claims personnel, family members who assist in the treatment, professional nursing personnel who may visit the home to help, and certain state health personnel.

2. *Dialysis centers:* The buying center here includes the owner of the center, the physicians who practice there, the technicians and nursing personnel who oversee treatment, the third-party payers who must approve the treatment for reimbursement, and whatever local, state, and federal government agencies that are to oversee the quality and cost of the care.

3. *Hospitals:* These organizations are complex entities. Their buying center includes a board of directors (which often must approve any major equipment purchase); individual physicians who admit patients for care; the technicians and nurses who deliver the care; the administrator; financial officers who are especially concerned about capital expenditures, operating costs, and third-party reimbursement; purchasing personnel; and various committees of physicians, nurses, and administrative personnel who are concerned with such aspects of hospital operation as quality control, documentation of treatment, housekeeping, and relationships with other hospitals, especially in such areas of cooperation as the purchase of supplies.

Source: Robert T. Davis, Harper W. Boyd, Jr., and Frederick E. Webster, Jr., *Marketing Management Casebook* (Homewood, Ill.: Richard D. Irwin, 1984), pp. 43–56.

The participation of people from different functional departments—and their relative influence—also varies from stage to stage in the decision process. For example, engineering and R&D experts often exert the greatest influence on the specifications and criteria a new product must meet. The purchasing manager often has more influence in choosing among alternative suppliers. The buying center's makeup also varies with the experience the firm has had in buying particular products. The buying center tends to be smaller—and the relative influence of the purchasing agent greater—when reordering products the firm has purchased in the past.

Exhibit 5–4 illustrates these variations in the influence of buying center members. In a survey of 231 manufacturing firms, managers were asked to indicate the relative influence of people from various departments at different stages in the purchase of a component. As you can see in Exhibit 5–4, the

EXHIBIT 5 ◆ 4

The relative influence of representatives from various functional departments at different stages in purchase decisions

A. New buy

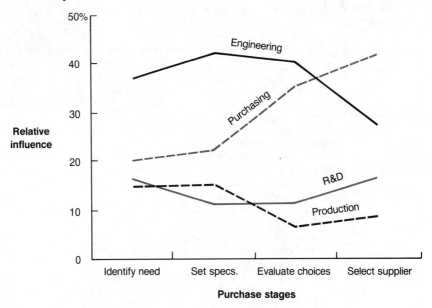

B. Straight rebuy

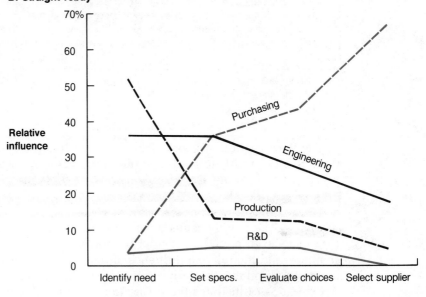

Source: Based on E. Naumann, D. J. Lincoln, and R. D. McWilliams, "The Purchase of Components: Functional Areas of Influence," *Industrial Marketing Management,* May 1984, pp. 113–22.

influence of different departments not only varied substantially across stages in the purchase process, but also depending on the decision being made.[4]

For example, in a new-buy situation, engineering exerted the most influence of any of the departments in identifying the need and setting specs; but purchasing had the greatest influence in selecting the supplier. In a straight rebuy, production has a strong relative influence in need identification but little relative influence in selecting the supplier.

Composition of the buying center

One of the selling firm's most important and difficult tasks is to determine the composition of the buying center within a potential customer firm. Then the seller can address appropriate promotional and personal selling efforts to all relevant members of the buying center, not just the purchasing agent. The marketer must answer four important questions about major organizational customers.[5]

1. Which individuals in the buying center are responsible for my particular product or service?
2. What is the relative influence of each member of this group?
3. What are the decision criteria of each member?
4. How does each member of the group perceive our firm, our products, and our salespeople?

Lucite Corporation's experience illustrates the importance of obtaining good answers to such questions.[6] The company's chemists discovered a puttylike adhesive useful for repairing worn machine parts. The firm named the product RC601 and tried to sell it to equipment designers as an adhesive to be used in manufacturing new equipment. Designers were reluctant to try an unproven new product, however, and RC601 bombed. By conducting some marketing research Lucite discovered that maintenance workers in manufacturing plants might influence their firms to try the new product. Maintenance workers indicated in interviews that they were willing to try anything that might help get broken down equipment back into production

---

[4] Earl Naumann, Douglas J. Lincoln, and Robert D. McWilliams, "The Purchase of Components: Functional Areas of Influence," *Industrial Marketing Management*, May 1984, pp. 113–22. Also see Gary L. Lilien and M. Anthony Wong, "An Exploratory Investigation of the Structure of the Buying Center in the Metal Working Industry," *Journal of Marketing Research*, February 1984, pp. 1–11; Wesley J. Johnston and Thomas V. Bonoma, "The Buying Center: Structure and Interaction Patterns," *Journal of Marketing*, Summer 1981, pp. 143–56; and Donald L. McCabe, "Buying Group Structure: Construction at the Top," *Journal of Marketing*, October 1987, p. 89.

[5] Thomas V. Bonoma, "Major Sales: Who Really Does the Buying?" *Harvard Business Review*, May–June 1982, pp. 111–19.

[6] Bill Abrams, "Consumer Product Techniques Help Lucite Sell to Industry," *The Wall Street Journal*, April 2, 1981, p. 27.

as soon as possible. Lucite renamed the product Quick Metal and targeted a promotional campaign at maintenance workers featuring the slogan, "Keeps machinery running until the new parts arrive." The maintenance workers passed along information and requests for the new product to production and purchasing personnel in their firms, and Quick Metal became a success.

Types of buying situations

Similar to consumers, organizational buyers learn from their past experiences. Three important and interrelated factors determine the buying task faced by an organization:

1. The newness of the problem and the relevant buying experience of decision makers in the buying center.
2. The information needs of the people in the buying center.
3. The number of new alternative products and/or suppliers to consider in making the purchase decision.[7]

Organizations encounter three kinds of buying tasks or situations: the straight rebuy, the modified rebuy, and new-task buying.[8]

A **straight rebuy** involves purchasing a common product or service the organization has bought many times before. Such purchases are often handled routinely by the purchasing department with little participation by other departments. Usually they show little interest in collecting additional information about alternative products or in seeking potential new suppliers. Such purchases are almost automatic, with the firm continuing to purchase proven products from reliable, established vendors. In straight rebuy situations, all phases of the buying process tend to be short and routine.

A **modified rebuy** occurs when the organization's needs remain unchanged, but buying center members are not satisfied with the product or the supplier they have been using. They may desire a higher quality product, a better price, or better service. Here buyers need information about alternative products and suppliers to compare with their current product and vendor. Therefore, the search for and evaluation of proposals and suppliers tends to be extensive. Modified rebuys present good opportunities for new suppliers to win the organization's business if they can offer something better than the firm's current vendor—such as GE did with its new energy-saving Halogen Performance Plus and high-color fluorescent lamps.

New-task buying occurs when an organization faces a new and unique need or problem. The buying center members have little or no experience

---

[7] Webster and Wind, *Organizational Buying Behavior* and "A General Model."

[8] Patrick J. Robinson, Charles W. Faris, and Yoram Wind, *Industrial Buying and Creative Marketing* (Boston: Allyn and Bacon, 1967). Also see Erin Anderson, Wujin Chu, and Barton Weitz, "Industrial Purchasing: An Empirical Exploration of the Buy Class Framework," *Journal of Marketing*, July 1987, pp. 71–86.

with such purchases; they must expend a great deal of effort to define specifications and collect information about alternative products and vendors. Each stage of the decision process is likely to be extensive, involving many technical experts and administrators. This was the case when McDonnell Douglas considered using GE's new jet aircraft engine—with its revolutionary power plant, featuring highly curved fan blades extending from the engine—as a component for its MD-91 commercial airplane.

The supplier's reputation for meeting delivery deadlines, providing adequate service, and meeting specifications is often a critical factor in selling a product or service to an organization for the first time. Because the buying center members have limited knowledge of the field they are entering, they may choose a well-known and respected supplier to reduce the risk of making a poor choice.

ORGANIZATIONAL PURCHASE DECISION-MAKING PROCESSES

As Exhibit 5–5 (on page 156) suggests, the stages in the organizational purchase decision-making process—at least for modified rebuy and new-task purchases—correspond quite closely with consumers' high-involvement purchases. However, the exhibit also suggests that some activities at each stage, and the execution of those activities, differ. More people are involved in organizational purchase decisions; the capability of potential suppliers is more critical; and the postpurchase evaluation process is more formalized. We examine other unique features of each stage of the organizational purchase decision process next.

Recognition of a problem or need

The organizational purchasing process starts when someone in the firm recognizes a need that can be satisfied by buying some product or service. The major characteristics of the stages in the organizational purchase decision-making process are discussed briefly below.

Organizational purchases result from product and operational needs

Consumers may buy things impulsively to satisfy psychological or social needs. Most organizational purchases, however, are motivated by the needs of the firm's production processes and its day-to-day operations. The primary purchasing objective is to increase the firm's profitability by buying goods and services that help it either reduce costs or increase revenues. Consequently, an organization's demand for goods and services is a **derived demand**—which, as we noted earlier, is derived from its customers' demands for the goods and services it produces. Ford's need for steel, tires, and interior fabrics, for instance, depends on the number of Ford cars purchased by consumers. Fluctuations in economic conditions can produce changes in the sales of an organization's goods or services—which, in turn, can result in

EXHIBIT 5 ◆ 5

Comparison of the decision processes for high-involvement consumer and organizational purchases

Stage in the buying decision process	Consumer purchase: a stereo system for a student	Industrial purchase: wooden poles for an electric utility
Problem recognition	Student doesn't like the sound of the stereo system now owned.	Operations department counts poles in inventory, concludes more are needed, and sends request to purchasing.
Information search	Student uses past experience, that of friends, ads, and *Consumer Reports* to collect information and uncover alternatives.	Purchasing department checks with operations and engineering departments to verify specifications for creosote-treated wood power poles.
Alternative evaluation	Alternative stereo systems are evaluated on the basis of salient and determinant attributes of what is desired in a stereo.	Purchasing and engineering personnel visit potential supplier's plant and assess (1) facilities, (2) financial status, (3) managerial capability, and (4) union situation. They drop any suppliers not satisfactory on these factors.
Purchase decision	A specific brand of stereo system is selected, the price is paid, and it is installed in the student's room.	They use (1) quality, (2) price, (3) delivery, and (4) technical capability as key buying criteria to select supplier. Then they negotiate terms and award a contract.
Postpurchase evaluation	Student reevaluates the purchase decision, may return stereo to store if it is unsatisfactory, and looks for supportive information to justify the purchase.	They evaluate suppliers using a formal vendor rating system and notify supplier if poles do not meet its quality standard. If problem is not corrected, they drop firm as a future supplier.

Source: Adapted from E.N. Berkowitz, R. A. Kerin, and W. Rudelius, *Marketing* (St. Louis: Times Mirror/Mosby College Publishing, 1986), p. 127. The material concerning the purchase of utility poles, in turn, was adapted from E. J. Wilson, "A Case Study of Repeat Buying for a Commodity," *Industrial Marketing Management,* August 1984, pp. 195–200.

rapid changes in production schedules and in accumulations or depletions in the firm's materials and parts inventories. As a result, the organization's purchase requirements for materials and parts can change dramatically in a short time.

Many different people can identify an organization's needs

In some cases need recognition may be almost automatic, as when a computerized inventory control system reports that an item has fallen below the reorder level, or when a piece of equipment wears out. In other cases, a need arises when someone identifies a better way of carrying out day-to-day operations. For example, a production engineer might recommend the purchase of a new machine that would increase production and reduce costs. Finally, changes in the organization's operations can create new needs. Top management may decide to produce a new product line. Or there may be changes in the firm's objectives, resources, market conditions, government regulations, or competition. Needs, then, may be recognized by many people within the organization, including users, technical personnel, top management, or purchasing agents.

Requirements planning

Instead of simply monitoring inventories and reordering when they run low, some firms attempt to forecast future requirements to plan their purchases in advance. Such requirements planning governs the purchase of raw materials and fabricating components as well as supplies and major installations. One result of such planning is the signing of long-term purchase contracts, particularly for products projected to be in short supply or to increase in price. Requirements planning can also lead to lower costs and better relations between a purchaser and its suppliers. When a supplier knows a buyer's requirements well in advance, both can carry less inventory.

Determining product specifications

An organization's need for particular goods and services is usually derived from its production or operating requirements. Therefore, those goods and services must meet specific technical requirements. Technical experts from the firm's R&D, engineering, or production departments thus are often involved early in the purchase process. When the firm needs a unique component or piece of equipment, it might even seek help from potential suppliers in determining appropriate specifications. For example, General Motors gave information about the performance and handling characteristics of its newly redesigned Corvette to Goodyear. Goodyear's engineers helped GM determine the ideal tire specifications for the new car, and then developed a new tire meeting those specifications.[9]

Search for information about products and suppliers

Value analysis

Once specifications for new equipment or component parts are developed, purchasing (and possibly other departments) performs a **value analysis.** This systematic reappraisal of an item's design, quality, and performance requirements helps to minimize procurement costs. It includes an analysis of the extent to which the product might be redesigned, standardized, or made

---

[9] Richard M. Hill, "Suppliers Need to Supply Reliably, in Volume, with Value Engineering Analysis, Market Data," *Marketing News*, April 4, 1980, p. 7.

EXHIBIT 5 ◆ 6

Checklist of value analysis questions

---

1. Can the item be eliminated?
2. If the item is not standard, can a standard one be used?
3. If it is a standard item, does it completely fit the application?
4. Does the item have greater capacity than needed?
5. Can the weight be reduced?
6. Is there a similar item in inventory that could be used?
7. Are closer tolerances specified than are necessary?
8. Is unnecessary machining performed on the item?
9. Are unnecessarily fine finishes specified?
10. Is commercial quality specified (commercial quality is usually most economical)?
11. Can the item be manufactured cheaper in-house? If it is being manufactured in-house, can it be bought for less?
12. Is the item properly classified for shipping to obtain the lowest rates?
13. Can cost of packaging be reduced?
14. Are suppliers being asked for suggestions to reduce cost?

Source: Adapted from *Industrial Marketing Strategy* by Frederick E. Webster, Jr., pp. 42–43. Copyright © 1984 by John Wiley & Sons, Inc. Reprinted by permission of John Wiley & Sons, Inc.

using less expensive production methods. Exhibit 5–6 offers a checklist of questions to ask. A cost analysis—an attempt to determine what the product costs a supplier to produce—is also often a part of a value analysis. Such information helps the purchasing agent evaluate alternative bids or negotiate favorable prices with suppliers.

Make-or-buy decisions

In some cases, a firm has the option of producing subassemblies components and some services, such as advertising and marketing research, internally or buying them from outside suppliers. Economic considerations usually dominate such decisions; however, other factors may also be important in the long run. For example, if there are only a few potential suppliers, the firm might become overly dependent on a single supplier and thus vulnerable to a strike, future price increases, or poor service.[10] Other considerations include the level of expertise required to design and manufacture the needed product, suppliers' reliability, the supplier's and the firm's capabilities for

---

[10] Robert W. Ruekert, Orville C. Walker, Jr., and Kenneth J. Roering, "The Organization of Marketing Activities: A Contingency Theory of Structure and Performance," *Journal of Marketing* 49 (Winter 1985), pp. 13–25.

continued product improvement and innovation, and the buyer's excess production capacity to make the needed product.

Information about potential suppliers

Because many larger firms formally evaluate supplier performance after purchases are made, they often have a wealth of information about suppliers' past performances in their files. Where new suppliers are being considered the purchasing department often engages in a substantial search for information to qualify a firm as a potential supplier. This might include an investigation of the firm's financial health and credit history, an examination of its reputation, and a visit to the firm to determine whether it has the capacity and quality standards necessary to fill the order. Information can come from personal as well as nonpersonal sources. Personal sources include sales personnel, trade shows, buying center members, other firms, and consultants. Nonpersonal services include catalogues, advertising, trade literature, direct mail, and training services.[11]

Evaluation and selection of suppliers

Similar to individual consumers, organizational buyers evaluate alternative suppliers and their offerings by a set of **choice criteria** reflecting the benefits the firm wants from the purchase. Once again, the criteria used and the relative importance attached to each attribute vary according to the goods or services being purchased and the characteristics and needs of the buyer. Always important to purchasing agents are the supplier's past performance and ability to meet quality standards and delivery schedules. The importance of other criteria varies depending on the technical complexity of the product. Price is critical for standard items such as steel desks and chairs; but for more technically complex items such as computers, a broader range of criteria enters the evaluation process, and price is relatively less important.

Some purchasing departments construct quantitative ratings of potential suppliers to aid in the selection process. These ratings look very much like the multiattribute, compensatory attitude model we discussed for individual consumers. The procedure involves selecting a set of salient attributes, each of which is assigned a weight reflecting its relative importance. Suppliers are then rated by summing their weighted scores across all attributes to obtain an overall score, as follows:

---

[11] Niren Vyas and Arch Woodside, "An Inductive Model of Industrial Supplier Choice Processes," *Journal of Marketing* 48 (Winter 1984), pp. 30–45. Also see Paul S. Busch and Michael J. Houston, *Marketing* (Homewood, Ill.: Richard D. Irwin, 1985), pp. 263–65.

Choice criteria	Importance weight	×	Rating for Supplier A	=	Score for Supplier A
Product quality	8		7		56
Product reliability	8		8		64
Delivery reliability	10		8		80
Price	7		10		70
Technical capability	5		6		30
Total score for Supplier A					300

Such ratings serve several useful purposes: They facilitate the comparison of alternative suppliers; they provide a basis for discussions with suppliers about their performance; and they control the number of qualified suppliers.

This step in the buying process and the previous steps seem to imply that the individuals making up the buying center respond only to economic arguments. Such is not the case. Industrial buyers are social entities in addition to being interested in the economics of the situation. Exhibit 5–7 gives an example of the importance of tapping the buyer's emotional feelings about the product. In general, the more similar the suppliers and their offerings, the more likely it is that social factors will affect the buying decision. Still, as Exhibit 5–7 shows, many suppliers would be better off if they understood that many industrial purchases are made on the basis of *both* emotion and logic.

Reciprocity
Another factor that can influence the selection of suppliers is **reciprocity.** It occurs when an organization favors a supplier who is, in turn, a customer or potential customer for the organization's own products or services. Reciprocity is the old concept of "you scratch my back and I'll scratch yours."

EXHIBIT 5 ◆ 7
Purchasing a business jet

> The CEO of a company that already owns a business jet is central in deciding whether to purchase a new one that costs several million dollars. But the CEO is strongly influenced by such individuals as the financial officer, the company's pilot, and the members of the board. The salesperson "who tries to impress both the CEO with depreciation schedules and the chief pilot will almost certainly not sell a plane if he or she overlooks the psychological and emotional components of the buying decision. 'For the chief executive,' observes one salesperson, 'you need all the numbers for support, but if you can't find the kid inside the CEO and excite him or her with the raw beauty of the new plane, you'll never sell the equipment. If you sell the excitement, you sell the jet.'"

Source: Thomas V. Bonoma, *Marketing Management* (New York: The Free Press, 1984), p. 284.

Even though reciprocity is relatively common in organizational purchasing, it can cause serious problems. One reason is it introduces a bias into the purchasing process. Reciprocity can also undermine the morale of purchasing and sales personnel by constraining the way they perform their jobs. Most important, reciprocal buying arrangements are illegal under certain conditions—particularly when they injure free competition among alternative suppliers.

The purchase

A good portion of all industrial buying involves a **purchasing contract**. This routinizes the buying decision, making it a straight rebuy situation. Webster describes three common contracts.[12] One is the **blanket purchase order** used for frequently purchased items such as office and janitorial supplies. Under such an arrangement, a supplier contracts to provide certain generic-type items at an agreed price. In contrast to a formal purchase order, the purchaser uses a simple release form to obtain the item, thereby saving paperwork.

A second common contract involves an **annual requirement purchasing arrangement.** It obligates a supplier to provide all that a buyer needs of a specific item at a given price. Sellers often grant quantity discounts based on the amounts actually bought. Again, buyers use a simple release form to procure the product. The third contract is a **stockless purchasing arrangement.** Here the supplier agrees to supply all a buyer's requirements for a specific item from a dedicated inventory available only to that customer. For example, a steel distributor agrees to keep a dedicated inventory of never less than five tons of special stainless steel sheeting for a manufacturer of kitchen sinks.

Contracts such as these enable a firm to standardize its purchasing activities across a multiplicity of locations. They also introduce cost savings through scale economies (quantity discounts) and a reduction in paperwork.

Expediting purchases

After an order has been placed with a supplier, the purchasing department must often expedite delivery of the goods. When a supplier falls behind schedule, the purchasing agent may be called upon to do whatever is necessary to speed up delivery. Thus, the firm avoids the negative consequences of not having materials or equipment available when needed.

---

[12] Frederick E. Webster, Jr., *Industrial Marketing Strategy*, p. 35. Some of the contracting procedures followed by government units are quite different. For more information about marketing to the government, see William Rudelius, "Selling to the Government," in *Handbook of Modern Marketing*, 2nd ed., ed. Victor Buell (New York: McGraw-Hill, 1985).

Performance evaluation and feedback

When a purchase is made and the goods delivered, the buyer's evaluation of both product and supplier begins. The buyer inspects the goods on receipt to determine whether they meet the required specifications. Later, the using department judges whether the purchased item performs to expectations. Similarly, the buyer evaluates the supplier's performance on promptness of delivery, product quality, and postsale service.

In many organizations this process is done formally, with written reports being submitted by the user department and other persons involved in the purchase. They use this information to evaluate proposals and select suppliers the next time a similar purchase is made. This formal evaluation and feedback process enables organizations to benefit from their purchasing mistakes and successes.

Environmental influences on purchase decision processes and procedures

Many of the same environmental factors affect organizational buyers in many of the same ways as consumers. In recent years these environmental variables have changed rapidly and dramatically. Technology, governmental regulations, and inflation have changed. In addition, shortages of energy and raw materials have made the organizational buyer's job more complex and more crucial to the continued success of the business unit.

Some organizations have been forced to adopt purchasing operations and procedures specially designed to cope with environmental uncertainty. This point is illustrated by a study that examined the procedures involved in buying 109 different products within 10 business firms.[13] A panel of experts examined the environmental factors affecting each purchase and classified them on a continuum from "stable and predictable" to "unstable and unpredictable." The study found that when the environmental variables affecting a purchase are highly unstable and hard to predict, the organization's purchasing procedures are more likely to have the following characteristics:

1. *More decentralized decision making.* When the purchasing environment is unstable, more technical experts are likely to have some influence on the purchase decision. Also, purchasing agents are more likely to specialize in buying one or a few items to develop the experience and expertise to make wise decisions in a changing environment.

---

[13] Joanne M. Klebba, *The Structure of the Purchasing Function as Determined by Environmental Uncertainty*, Ph.D. dissertation. Minneapolis: University of Minnesota.

2. *Fewer formal purchasing procedures.* Buyers are given more flexibility to respond to changing environmental and supply conditions. They are less constrained by rules and standard operating procedures.

3. *More professional purchasing personnel.* The people making purchases in a changing environment have more formal training, more experience, and are more active in professional organizations than those who purchase products not as critically affected by environmental factors.

Changes in a firm's internal environment can also affect its purchasing processes and procedures. For example, one internal change that has had a major impact on many organizations' buying procedures is the increased use of computers. Wilson and Mathews found that firms extensively using electronic data processing in their purchasing operations use fewer suppliers, evaluate suppliers' performances more frequently, and have more centralized purchase decision making than firms not using computers.[14]

THE IMPORTANCE AND SCOPE OF ORGANIZATIONAL MARKETS

Sixteen million organizational customers may not sound like much in comparison to 236 million consumers; but their economic importance is much greater than their numbers suggest. In fact, the total dollar value of exchange transactions involving organizational buyers is greater than the value of consumer purchases. Organizations buy in larger quantities and purchase more complex and expensive goods and services than consumers do. Also, several organizational exchanges are usually required to accumulate the equipment, parts, materials, and supplies necessary to produce one product or service for sale to consumers.

About half of all manufactured goods made in this country are sold to organizational buyers. The total value of these manufactured industrial goods is over $950 billion.[15] In addition, organizations buy nearly all of our minerals, farm, and forest products for further processing and manufacturing. These raw materials add at least $275 billion more to the total value of organizational purchases. Finally, nonhousehold buyers purchase many services—from advertising agencies, public accountants, lawyers, railroads, airlines, consultants, security firms, and others. The total value of such industrial services is impossible to estimate. Obviously, organizations repre-

---

[14] David T. Wilson and H. L. Mathews, "Impact of Management Information Systems on Purchasing Decision-Making," *Journal of Purchasing*, February 1971, pp. 48–56.

[15] Numerical data in this section are from *Statistical Abstract of the United States, 105th ed.* (Washington, D.C.: U.S. Department of Commerce, 1985); *County Business Patterns 1984* (Washington, D.C.: U.S. Department of Commerce, 1984); and the authors' calculations.

sent important markets for many products and services. But who are these nonhousehold customers? How many are there? And what do they buy?

Organizational customers

Nearly every organization buys at least some industrial goods and services. For descriptive purposes, though, organizational customers are grouped into distributive organizations or "resellers," goods producers, services producers, and governments. Exhibit 5–8 shows the approximate number of organizations in each category and their average size based on their total employees.

Resellers

Resellers include all retailers and wholesalers—some 1.8 million establishments employing 21 million people. Wal-Mart is an example of the former. It is the third-largest retailer in the United States—behind only Sears and K mart. Its 1,300 discount stores sell about $20 billion in goods each year. Resellers buy large quantities of goods for resale to other organizations or to consumers. Manufacturers distribute about two thirds of all consumer goods and 40 percent of industrial goods through independent wholesalers; and nearly all consumer goods are sold to consumers by retailers.

Resellers buy many products for use in their own operations. They buy large installations and pieces of equipment, such as store buildings, warehouses, computers, trucks, forklifts, and office equipment. They also buy supplies, such as invoice and sales receipt forms, heating fuel, and electricity. Finally, they purchase business services, including accounting, legal, advertising, and security. Thus, even though wholesalers and retailers are primarily concerned with purchasing goods for resale to other customers, they are themselves an important market for many industrial goods and services.

Goods producers

This category includes producers of raw materials (such as farms, forest products firms, and mines), building contractors, and manufacturers. Within this category, farms are the most numerous, but the smallest in the number of people employed. On the other hand, there are only about 350,000 manufacturing firms; but they are the largest employers (except for governments) with an average of 55 employees per firm. General Electric, Rubbermaid, and PepsiCo are all examples of manufacturing firms.

Goods producers are major purchasers of many kinds of installations and equipment, such as barns, factory buildings, combines, cranes, blast furnaces, milling machines, chain saws, and hand tools. They also buy supplies and services, such as cleaning supplies and accounting and financial services. In addition, manufacturers and building contractors are major custom-

EXHIBIT 5 ◆ 8

Organizational customers

Organization	Units*	Total employees	Average employees per unit
Resellers			
Retailers	1,409,531	16,080,830	11
Wholesalers	430,983	5,387,724	13
Goods producers			
Agriculture, forestry, fisheries	61,656	356,881	6
Mining	36,693	974,285	27
Contract construction	458,654	4,171,763	9
Manufacturing	350,740	19,325,352	55
Consumer and business services (partial list)			
Transportation, public utilities	198,147	4,675,385	24
Finance, insurance, real estate	477,750	5,783,225	12
Hotels, lodging places	48,125	1,200,435	25
Auto repair services, garages	126,129	626,067	5
Misc. repair services	56,116	310,095	6
Personal services	175,921	1,029,003	6
Misc. business services	241,569	3,833,744	16
Amusement, recreation	60,147	739,514	12
Medical, health services	384,288	6,202,435	16
Legal services	124,603	645,354	5
Educational services	29,282	1,476,430	50
Museums, zoos	2,006	32,911	16
Nonprofit membership orgs.	177,917	1,507,452	8
Governments			
Federal, state, and local	82,341	15,968,000	193

* For manufacturing organizations the term *unit* refers to a single *establishment* engaged in a distinct economic activity, such as a single factory. For nonmanufacturing organizations, *unit* refers to an *establishment or group of similar establishments under one control,* such as a chain of five dry cleaning stores owned by the same person.

Sources: Statistical Abstract of the United States, 105th ed. (Washington, D.C.: U.S. Department of Commerce, 1985), and *County Business Patterns 1984* (Washington, D.C.: U.S. Department of Commerce, 1984).

ers of raw materials producers. They buy raw materials such as iron ore, lumber, wheat, and cotton for use in making manufactured products and buildings. Finally, some manufacturers buy component parts from other manufacturers, as when Ford buys tires, batteries, and seat belts from suppliers.

Services producers

As our economy and our standard of living have grown over the years, the production and consumption of services have accounted for a large and growing proportion of our total economic activity. Today, more Americans are employed in the production and distribution of services than in the production of goods. Exhibit 5–8 lists a few of the vast array of service organizations in our economy. Examples include CitiCorp (commercial banking), American Express (financial), New York Life (insurance), Holiday Inns (lodging), Midas Muffler and Brake Shops (repair services), Snelling & Snelling Personnel Agency (personnel services), Walt Disney World (entertainment), Mayo Clinic (health), and Stanford University (education).

Services producers include: (1) retail service organizations selling consumer services, such as dry cleaners, taxi cab companies, restaurants, and theaters; and (2) facilitating agencies or business services—such as advertising agencies, trucking firms, and public accountants—selling their services primarily to other organizations. Both types of services producers buy a wide variety of goods and services for use in running their operations. Although they do not buy as many installations or heavy equipment items as goods producers, they do buy or rent office or store facilities, computers, and accessory equipment (copying machines, typewriters, cars, and trucks). Services producers are also a major market for supplies and business services. As the trend toward a service-oriented economy continues, we can expect services producers to be an even larger part of the market for industrial goods and services in the future.

Governments

Each year government buyers at federal, state, and local levels purchase nearly $900 billion worth of goods and services. Spending by the federal government alone accounts for about 8 percent of our country's gross national product. Spending by state and local governments accounts for another 10 percent. Purchases are made by open bid and negotiated contract. The former consists of a set of product specifications along with the number of items wanted for some stated time period. Qualified suppliers are asked to bid, and the lowest bidder is usually the winner. A negotiated contract results from a government unit working with one or more companies to determine the contract requirements and the terms.

The mix of goods and services purchased varies considerably across levels of government. Defense installations and equipment take a large proportion of the federal budget; educational expenditures account for a substantial amount of state and local purchases. Also, governments' purchases can change from year to year with changes in national priorities and legislative appropriations.

The SIC system: A tool for analyzing organizational markets

When contemplating which organizations might be potential customers for a particular product or service, a marketer needs detailed information to target specific firms and to find out where they are located and how they can be reached. A useful tool for making such detailed analyses of organizational markets is the **Standard Industrial Classification system (SIC),** a numerical classification scheme set up by the federal government. The SIC classifies organizations by their major activity or primary product or service produced. These groupings enable the federal government to collect, organize, and publish information (number of establishments and employees, and sales volume) for each group. The SIC also provides geographic breakdowns where possible.

The SIC system is organized around a numerical code that starts with broad categories such as food (SIC code 20) and apparel (SIC code 23). Most of these two-digit categories are further divided into three- and four-digit classifications of subindustries within the two-digit category.

In 1987, the SICs were revised to include a number of new four-digit industry codes, many of them affecting the way data are collected and published for the computer industry. Marketers now are able to identify prospects in manufacturing industries previously grouped under catchall categories such as SIC 3573—electronic computing equipment. In addition, four-digit classifications have been created for some high-growth services industries, some that are also computer related. Exhibit 5–9 (page 168) lists some of the newly created industry groups.[16]

The federal government uses the SIC to organize its Census of Business and other reports on U.S. economic activity. Marketers can use SIC codes to learn about current and potential customers. Once a firm knows which categories its current customers fall into, it can obtain SIC lists for potential customers that may want the same products or services. A firm can monitor government reports to track trends (such as growth rates) in specific industry categories.

The SIC does have some limitations, however. Because the government assigns each organization only one SIC code based on its primary product or activity, many divisions of large diversified companies get buried in inappropriate categories. And four-digit codes are not available for all industries in every geographic area because the government does not reveal data when fewer than three establishments exist in an area. Nevertheless, the SIC should not be overlooked as a low-cost first step for getting a handle on potential organizational customers.

---

[16] *Sales & Marketing Management,* May 1988, p. 32.

EXHIBIT   5 ◆ 9

Newly created industry groups

SIC	Description
3571	Electronic computers
3572	Computer storage devices
3575	Computer terminals
3577	Computer peripheral equipment
3695	Recording media (blank disks)
7371	Computer programming services
7372	Prepackaged software
7373	Computer integrated systems design
7374	Computer processing and data preparation services
7375	Information retrieval services
7376	Computer facilities management services
7377	Computer rental and leasing
7378	Computer maintenance and repair
7379	Computer related services not elsewhere classified
7291	Tax return preparation services
7334	Photocopying and duplicating services
7382	Security systems services
7841	Video tape rental
7991	Physical fitness facilities
8082	Home health care services
8741	Management services
8742	Management consulting services
8743	Public relations services
8748	Business consulting services not elsewhere classified

Source: Sales & Marketing Management 1988 Survey of Industrial & Commercial Buying Power.

GOODS AND SERVICES PURCHASED BY ORGANIZATIONAL BUYERS

A brief discussion of the goods and services sold to organizations is useful for two reasons: First, organizational buying processes vary substantially by types of products and services. Also, various industrial goods and services require different marketing strategies.

Marketers commonly classify industrial goods according to the uses made of the product by organizational purchasers. With this in mind, we can identify six categories of industrial goods and services: raw materials, component materials and parts, installations, accessory equipment, operating supplies, and business services. Exhibit 5–10 describes these categories and their major characteristics. We discuss their marketing implications next.

EXHIBIT 5 ◆ 10

Categories and characteristics of industrial goods and services

Category	Description	Characteristics	Examples
Raw material	Relatively unprocessed goods that become a portion of a final product	Limited supply, few producers, distribution is a key function, price is a critical competitive variable	Farm products (wheat, tobacco) and natural products (minerals, forests, fish, land)
Component parts and materials	Processed goods that become a portion of a final product	High-volume purchases, long-term contracts, fierce competition among suppliers, requires good service and nurturing of relationships with buyers	Working parts of a final product (engines, springs, ball bearings, microchips)
Installations	Major capital goods used to produce final product, but not part of the final product	Long-lasting, involved in production of many units of the final product over several years, involve large dollar outlays, capital budgeting committee involved in purchase decision, sold direct from manufacturer	Plant installations, manufacturing machinery (printing press, oil rig)
Accessory equipment	Finished goods that facilitate production of a final product	Enduring but less so than installations, more standardized, more frequently purchased and less costly than capital equipment, less complex buying; intermediaries may be involved	Trucks, typewriters, safety glasses, hand tools, conveyor belts, welding equipment
Operating supplies	Finished goods that facilitate repair, maintenance, and ongoing operations	Analogous to consumer convenience goods, frequently purchased and consumed in a short time; standardized; broad market; heavy use of channel intermediaries	Office supplies, fuel, janitorial supplies, repair parts
Business services	Provide special expertise to facilitate ongoing operations	Long-term relationships with customers; supplier's qualifications, experience and reputation critical to success; purchase decision often made by top executives	Security services, advertising agencies, law firms, public accountants, transportation agencies

Source: Adapted from Paul S. Busch and Michael J. Houston, *Marketing: Strategic Foundations* (Homewood, Ill.: Richard D. Irwin, 1985), p. 242.

Raw materials

Raw materials are goods receiving little or no processing before they are sold, except that necessary for handling and shipping. Purchased primarily by processors and manufacturers, they are inputs for making other products. The two types of raw materials are *natural products*, such as fish, lumber, iron ore, and crude petroleum; and *farm products*, such as fruits, vegetables, grains, beef, cotton, and wool. Processors and manufacturers purchase nearly all natural products and about 80 percent of all farm products. Retailers or consumers buy the remaining 20 percent of farm products directly without any processing.

Marketing implications

The supply of most natural products is limited; in recent years, there have been some shortages. Often only a few large firms produce particular natural products; and in some foreign countries those producers have been nationalized. Thus, these supply conditions can give producers the power to limit supplies and administer prices—as happened with the Organization of Petroleum Exporting Countries (OPEC). Such supply conditions have encouraged processors and manufacturers to seek ways to ensure adequate supplies for the future. This can be done by negotiating long-term purchase contracts at premium prices or through the purchase of the raw materials sources. For example, most of the large steel manufacturers own iron ore mining and processing operations.

Natural materials are generally bulky and low in unit value; therefore, producers try to minimize their handling and transportation costs. Distribution channels for natural materials thus tend to have few middlemen and most are marketed directly by the producer to processors and manufacturers.

The marketing problems associated with natural products are quite different than those of agricultural products produced by many relatively small farms located far from consumer markets. Also, many of these products are produced seasonally. The distribution channels for most agricultural materials thus involve many middlemen. They buy products from a large number of farmers, collect them in a central location (such as a grain elevator), and store them for shipment throughout the year to processors and exporters. There is little difference among the products grown by different farmers, making branding relatively unimportant. And there is usually little promotional activity, except for cooperative advertising campaigns funded by trade groups to stimulate primary demand for a product. Examples include a campaign to persuade health-conscious adults to drink more milk and clever TV ads to promote raisin consumption.

Component materials and parts

Similar to raw materials, component materials and parts are purchased by manufacturers as inputs for making other products. **Component materials** differ though, in that they have been processed to some degree before they are sold. Examples are the yarn purchased by a woolen mill to be dyed and woven into blankets, the steel purchased by an auto company to be pressed into fenders, and the flour bought by a bakery to be made into doughnuts. **Component parts** are manufactured items assembled as a part of another product without further changes in form. Examples are the batteries, tires, and windshields built into new cars, or the electric motors used in washing machines.

Marketing implications

Manufacturers buy most component materials and parts in large quantities; therefore, they are usually sold direct without the aid of middlemen. However, wholesale distributors sell to smaller manufacturers in some lines of trade.

To avoid disrupting production runs, sellers must ensure a steady, reliable supply of materials and parts. Reliability—particularly in on-time delivery and quality control—is becoming more essential as manufacturers move to just-in-time (JIT) inventory systems. These JIT systems reduce inventory to only a few days' or hours' supply. Consequently, highly detailed long-term purchase contracts are common for these items. The most important attributes for selecting a supplier of such goods are dependability, quality, service, and price. Branding and promotional activities are not very important, although some manufacturers have managed to establish reputations for quality, such as Timken roller bearings and Burlington fabrics.

Just-in-time is a management system that has important implications for marketing strategies and programs. It has as its objective the elimination of inventories at the customer's manufacturing site as well as those of the supplier. This objective requires that the product involved be perfect; that is, that the supplier deliver 100 percent quality (zero defect) products.

The JIT concept is based on the idea that value is added only by the actual work performed in producing a product—that other activities such as moving, storing, sorting, and counting do not add value—only cost. To many JIT experts, inventory is the worst evil because it hides problems that need to be solved, such as lead times, inadequate quality controls, machine breakdowns, and machine set-up time.[17] The results derived from a successful JIT program can be very impressive. In one such case, an electronics company operating in a mature industry reported a 30 percent increase in output per direct hour of labor, a 60 percent reduction in floor space devoted to production, a 15 percent decrease in waste, a 60 percent decrease in set-up time, and a 90 percent decrease in inventory costs.[18]

---

[17] Joe Statler, "Process in Control for Conformance," *Quality Progress*, April 1984, p. 67.

[18] Roy Dale Voorhees and John I. Coppett, "Marketing—Logistics Opportunities for the 1990s," *Journal of Business Strategy*, Fall 1986, p. 37.

A JIT system cannot be effectively implemented without a continuing and close working relationship between buyer and seller. Because JIT systems are costly to set up and force all concerned to work closely together, single sourcing often results. Further, once in place, the system tends to reinforce itself because each party has an investment in the other. Elco, a major producer of fasteners and precision metal components, is now the *sole* supplier of certain types of fasteners to IBM based on its ability to provide error-free components. It has a similar relationship with Control Data, Honeywell and Briggs & Stratton.[19]

Another part of the JIT system involves delivery. In some cases, it may be necessary to deliver product at frequent intervals—even daily. But it is not enough to deliver frequently—deliveries must be error-free in being on time (even to the hour of the day), undamaged, and the exact number required of the right product. Some suppliers have even relocated their factories to better serve their large customers. For example, Crown Cork & Seal, a major producer of metal cans, has located many of its production units close to its major customers, who are mainly concerned with packaging carbonated beverages.

Improvements in telecommunications technology has enabled suppliers to further integrate their marketing and distribution activities with their customers. Crown Zellerbach, for example, has a new sophisticated order-entry system that enables its customers not only to order directly, but also to obtain price and availability information on all of its products—forest products, pulp, paper, containers, packaging, and ore and gas.[20]

Because JIT involves long-term working relationships, decisions about how best to work with suppliers become inevitably tied to product design decisions. More and more buyers are bringing their suppliers into the design process early. For example, parts suppliers to the U.S. auto industry help establish vehicle performance objectives as well as design parts and processes. As a result of this new role (suppliers used to bid only after receiving a request), the number of parts manufacturers has been reduced by two thirds. Further, auto makers have received a better product at a lower cost. By placing more responsibility on its suppliers, Chrysler has been able to reduce its engineering costs by 50 percent while turning out a higher-quality product.[21]

---

[19] Elizabeth A. Haas, "Breakthrough Manufacturing," *Harvard Business Review*, March–April 1987, p. 79.

[20] Edward J. Hay, *Just-in-Time Production: A Winning Combination of Neglected American Ideas* (Lexington, Mass.: Rath & Strong, Management Consultants, N.D.).

[21] Robert J. Mayer, "Winning Strategies for Manufacturers in Mature Industries," *Journal of Business Strategy*, Fall 1987, p. 30.

JIT affects marketing strategy through a company's choice of its product-market entries by deciding which accounts to target. It places great emphasis on relationship marketing, which requires the successful integration of a supplier with its customers. It obviously changes the nature and scope of marketing programs with respect to such marketing elements as product, price, distribution, and promotion.

Installations

Installations are the buildings and major capital equipment manufacturers and services producers use to carry out their operations. These expensive, long-lived manufactured items help determine the scale of operations in the firms that purchase them. Examples are factory buildings constructed for a manufacturer, office buildings built for government agencies, computers used by the Internal Revenue Service, presses and welders bought by Ford, and airplanes purchased by United Airlines.

Marketing implications

The marketing of installations presents a real challenge because there are few potential customers and the average sale is very large. Every potential customer is critically important. Many installations are custom-made to fit a particular customer's needs; therefore, sellers must often provide some engineering and design services before making a sale. Often a long period of negotiation precedes the final transaction. Firms selling installations must usually provide many postsale services, such as installing the equipment, training the customer's personnel in its use, and providing maintenance and repair services.

Due to the small number of buyers, the large dollar volume of each sale, and the custom engineering involved, distribution is usually direct from producer to customer. Sometimes wholesale distributors provide replacement parts and repair services for equipment already in operation. For similar reasons, promotional emphasis is usually on personal selling rather than on advertising. High-caliber, well-trained salespeople are critically important in the marketing of installations.

Accessory equipment

Similar to installations, **accessory equipment** includes industrial machines and tools that manufacturers, services producers, and governments use to carry out their operations. The difference is that, although installations determine the scale of operations of the firms that buy and use them, accessory equipment has no such impact. Accessory equipment consists of tools and machines with relatively short lives and smaller price tags than most installations. They are supportive goods such as calculators, typewriters, desks, file cabinets, hand tools, and forklifts.

Marketing implications

Because this product category includes a wide range of specific items, it is hard to generalize about the most common or appropriate marketing strategies for accessory equipment. In some cases, as with Hyster forklifts and IBM office equipment, the producers sell accessory equipment directly. Their presale and postsale service requirements are substantial; and the dollar value of the average sale is high enough to justify direct distribution. In other cases, such as Black & Decker hand tools and 3M abrasives, producers use wholesale distributors extensively. Many different types of potential customers are scattered around the country; the average order size is often quite small; and the product does not require a great deal of technical service.

Personal selling, either by the producer's or a distributor's salesforce, is the most important promotional method used in selling accessory equipment. Most of the products in this category are standardized (not custom-made to the buyer's specifications). Because they are not technically complex, advertising and brand name promotions also are important in their marketing.

Operating supplies

Operating supplies do not become a part of the buyer's product or service, nor are they used directly in producing it. Instead, these supplies facilitate the buying organization's day-to-day operations. They are usually short-lived, low-priced items purchased frequently with a minimum of decision-making effort. Examples include heating fuel, floor wax, typing paper, order forms, paper clips, and pencils.

Marketing implications

Usually low in unit value, supplies are purchased in small quantities by a great many different organizations. Wholesale middlemen typically distribute such goods.

Price is usually the critical variable in marketing operating supplies. Competing products are quite standardized, and there is little brand loyalty. Personal selling by agents and distributors is also important.

Business services

Many business services producers—or facilitating agencies—have special areas of expertise used and paid for by other organizations. These include security and guard services, janitorial services, equipment repair services, public warehouses, transportation agencies, consulting and marketing research services, advertising agencies, and legal and accounting services.

Marketing implications

Services are intangible and are purchased *before* they can be evaluated by the buyer. Thus, the supplier's qualifications, past performance, and reputation become critical determinants of the success of the marketing effort. Price is less important in selling business services, because a lawyer or consultant with an outstanding reputation can often charge much more for a given service than one who is less well known.[22]

Because services are often tailored to the specific needs of a given customer, personal selling and negotiation are important elements in most services producers' marketing programs. This selling is often done by high-level executives in the service producer's organization—perhaps a vice president, or even the president. The negotiation process can be lengthy. For instance, an ad agency team spends months developing proposals and making presentations to a prospective client before finding out whether it has landed the new account. This selling task is often worth the effort, though, for once a relationship is established between a service supplier and a customer it tends to be maintained over a long time. Many companies employ the same law firm, accounting firm, or advertising agency for years or even decades.

SUMMARY

The total dollar value of purchases made by organizational buyers is greater than that of individual consumers. Organizations buy in larger quantities—and purchase more complex and expensive goods and services—than do consumers. Organizational customers can be grouped into four categories: distributive (reseller) organizations, goods producers, services producers, and governments. To determine potential customers for a particular product or service, a marketer needs to know which firms can be targeted, where they are located, and how they can be reached. A useful tool for making such a detailed analysis is the Standard Industrial Classification system (SIC).

Organizational buyers commonly classify industrial goods according to their uses. There are six categories: raw materials, component parts, installations, accessory equipment, operating supplies, and business services. Each of these requires a different marketing mix, partly because the buying process differs.

There are five participants in a buying center: users, influencers, gatekeepers, buyers, and deciders. One of the marketer's most important tasks is to identify which individuals in the buying center are responsible for a particular product, determine the relative influence of each, learn the decision criteria of each, and understand how each group member perceives the firm and its products.

The buying task is determined by three inter-

[22] Paul N. Bloom, "Effective Marketing for Professional Services," *Harvard Business Review*, September–October 1984, pp. 102–10; and Valarie A. Zeithaml, A. Parasuraman, and Leonard L. Berry, "Problems and Strategies in Services Marketing," *Journal of Marketing* 49 (Spring 1985), pp. 33–46.

related factors: (1) the newness of the problem to the decision makers; (2) the information needs of the people in the buying center; and (3) the number of new alternative products and/or suppliers to be considered. Based on these factors, there are three buying situations: straight rebuy, modified rebuy, and new-task buying. The decision-making process for the latter two are similar to that practiced by consumers making high-involvement purchases. The purchase decision stages are: problem recognition, information search, evaluation of alternatives, purchase decision, and postpurchase evaluation. Environmental factors—especially those that are unstable and hard to predict—obviously impact purchase procedures. The greater the instability, the more decentralized the decision making, the fewer the formal purchasing procedures, and the more professional the purchasing personnel.

QUESTIONS

1. Discuss the key characteristics of organizational buying that make it different from consumer buying.

2. Salespeople for firms such as Xerox and IBM who manufacture typewriters, copiers, and other office equipment often spend a good deal of their time talking with secretaries and office managers in the offices of potential customers. But those employees seldom have the authority to purchase major pieces of equipment. Is this an effective use of the salesperson's time? Why?

3. Suppose you are the vice president of marketing for the Sheldahl Corporation. The firm makes printed circuit boards and other electronic components for manufacturers in a variety of industries. General Motors is about to choose a supplier of printed circuits and wiring assemblies for a new car model it is going to produce for the first time next year. You would like to win the contract to supply those circuits and assemblies for Sheldahl. How are each of the following groups of people within GM likely to *influence* the firm's purchase decision concerning the new circuits and assemblies? At *which stages in the purchasing process* is each group likely to be most influential?
   a. R&D managers
   b. Product design engineers
   c. Production managers
   d. Purchasing managers

4. In view of your answers to question 3, outline the important elements of a marketing program for Sheldahl that would communicate the appropriate information at the appropriate time to each group involved in the purchasing decision at GM.

5. How would the relative influence of each of the four groups listed in question 3 change if the purchase decision involved a *straight rebuy* of a standardized component for an existing GM car model?

6. Purchasing managers at IBM have faced a very *unstable environment* in recent years. The firm has developed new product lines requiring a variety of new component parts and materials to be purchased from suppliers. The identity of those suppliers, in turn, keeps changing over time as new entrepreneurial start-ups emerge and as established firms make rapid technological advances in the design and production of components such as microchips and disk storage. How is this rapidly changing and unpredictable environment likely to affect the organization of IBM's purchasing function and the nature of the firm's purchasing procedures? What are the marketing implications for a firm that would like to become an approved supplier to IBM?

7. A foreign manufacturer of commercial ovens and other bakery equipment wants to identify the commercial bakeries in the United States, how big they are, and where

they are located as a basis for estimating the market potential for its products in the U.S. market. The firm has offered you a substantial fee to collect this information. Which *information source* would you turn to first? What information could you obtain from that source? What are the possible limitations of that information?

8. One of General Electric's divisions builds industrial robots and other computerized manufacturing equipment. What are some of the marketing challenges facing a manufacturer of this kind of *capital equipment*? What components of the division's marketing plan will be most critical in determining its success?

9. You are the marketing manager for the division at 3M Company that manufactures Post-it note pads. Which *industrial goods category* does this product fit into? What are the implications for the marketing program you would design for the product?

Chapter ◇ 6

Market segmentation

DUDLEY RIGGS AND THE BRAVE NEW WORKSHOP

Dudley Riggs is the fourth generation of a British circus family.[1] His grandfather was a contortionist and his mother and father did a flying trapeze act with the Ringling Brothers Circus. Riggs joined the family act in 1937 at the age of five and performed as an aerialist, acrobat, and juggler with circuses around the world. After a bad fall in 1953, he decided it was time to "run away from the circus and join a family."

In 1958 to use several espresso machines he had purchased in Italy years before, Riggs opened a coffeehouse near the University of Minnesota campus. At the coffeehouse Riggs and some friends put together an acting company that specialized in satirical reviews and improvisational humor. The Dudley Riggs' Brave New Workshop survived and grew largely on the strength of the talented young actors and writers Riggs discovered and helped develop. Several people, such as Al Franken and Tom Davis of NBC's "Saturday Night Live," went on to become well known nationally.

Even though the Brave New Workshop was relatively successful as small theaters go, Dudley Riggs was not satisfied. There were too many empty seats; and too many Twin Cities residents had never seen a performance at his theater. Riggs is not a marketing man; but he realized there was much to learn about his prospective audiences. The Brave New Workshop appealed to young people—particularly college students. But he had no other information about his audience or *why* they came to his theater. Nor did he know what other kinds of people might be potential customers.

Who attends the theater and why?

To help answer such questions, Dudley Riggs commissioned a market research study. One of the study's most interesting findings was that different people tend to spend their money on different forms of entertainment. (See Exhibit 6–1, p. 180.) The researchers concluded that Riggs should *not* try to attract all kinds of people to the Brave New Workshop. Promoting the theater to older people, those with low incomes, or those with low levels of education would probably be a waste of marketing effort. They recommended that Riggs concentrate his promotion and marketing efforts on people most likely to be theater-goers; people with characteristics similar to those outlined in Exhibit 6–1.

---

[1] Based on Schelly Braden, Catherine Brink, and Randall Hansen, "Live from Minneapolis: A Survey of the Potential Audiences of Dudley Riggs' Theaters," research paper (Minneapolis: University of Minnesota, 1978); and D. Hill, "Dudley Riggs: More than just that Coffeehouse Man," *Sun Weekender*, January 21, 1977, pp. 6–7.

continued

EXHIBIT 6♦1

Personal characteristics of people who attend various forms of entertainment

Personal characteristics	Movies	Jazz/rock/folk concerts	Ballet/symphony/ opera	Theater
Age	Young: Under 35	Very young: Under 25	Wide range: No relationship	Young to middle-aged: 26 to 45
Household income	Moderate: $7,000–15,000	Wide range: No relationship	Very high: Over $21,000	High: Over $16,000
Education	Wide range: No relationship	Moderate: High school or some college	Very high: College degree	High: At least some college
Occupation	Wide range: No relationship	Wide range: No relationship	White-collar/ professional	White-collar/ professional/ student

Source: Adapted from S. Braden, C. Brink, and R. Hansen, "Live from Minneapolis: A Survey of the Potential Audiences of Dudley Riggs' Theaters," research paper (Minneapolis: University of Minnesota, 1978), p. 11.

The data showed that theater-goers attend the theater for different reasons. The researchers found three types of theater-goers: the sociables, the intellectuals, and the hedonists, as shown in Exhibit 6–2. The *sociables* think of going to the theater primarily as a social event. They go with friends and prefer musicals or comedies. They often go to dinner theaters or to good, professional community theaters. The *intellectuals*, on the other hand, see theater-going as an educational experience. They want to see the classics or serious contemporary plays that have received good reviews. They prefer repertory and experimental theaters, or national touring companies, with first-rate acting. Finally, the *hedonists* go to the theater primarily to have fun. They prefer comedies, satirical reviews, and humorous improvisations. The hedonists, then, are more likely to attend improvisational theaters or see humorous plays and reviews presented by community and repertory theaters.

Target market and strategy recommendations

As might be expected, the researchers found that the Brave New Workshop attracted primarily hedonist theater-goers. The researchers thus recommended that Riggs' strategy should be to expand his audience within the hedonist group, because no other theater in the area presented the satirical reviews and improvisations that appealed to this group.

continued

EXHIBIT 6♦2

Characteristics of three types of theater-goers

Characteristics	The sociables	The intellectuals	The hedonists
Benefits sought from going to the theater	Night out with friends; social interaction; chance to dress up and get out of the house; light entertainment	Educational experience; chance to see well-known or reputable plays and high-quality acting	Having fun; topical humor; entertaining place to take date
Favored performances	Musicals, comedies	Classics, serious contemporary works	Comedies, satirical revues, improvisation
Favored theaters	Dinner theaters, community theaters	Repertory theaters, national touring companies, experimental theaters	Improvisational theaters, community theaters
Demographic and lifestyle characteristics	Wide range of ages and incomes; some college education; white-collar occupations; suburbanites	Age range 26–45; middle to upper income; college graduates; white-collar, professional occupations; attend other cultural entertainments, such as symphony concerts	Age range 16–35; single; low to moderate income; students or college graduates; white-collar occupations; also attend movies, rock concerts
Response to other marketing variables	Concerned about physical characteristics of theater—want a comfortable, "classy" evening; somewhat price conscious; convenient parking important; newspaper ads, reviews important information sources; listen to "beautiful music" and contemporary radio stations	Not concerned about physical features of theater; not sensitive to price; convenient parking important; reviews, newspaper ads important information sources; listen to classical, contemporary, and "beautiful music" radio stations	Not concerned about physical features of theater; sensitive to price; parking convenience less important, but locational convenience somewhat important; radio, newspaper ads, reviews important information sources; listen to rock and contemporary radio stations

Source: Adapted from S. Braden, C. Brink, and R. Hansen, "Live from Minneapolis: A Survey of the Potential Audiences of Dudley Riggs' Theaters," research paper (Minneapolis: University of Minnesota, 1978).

continued

concluded

The researchers suggested that the attitudes and awareness of the hedonists toward the Brave New Workshop could be improved through a promotional campaign explaining and demonstrating the satirical humor presented there. Further, they suggested that Riggs charge relatively low prices and promote the fact that people could attend a live performance at his theater for about the same price as going to a movie. Finally, to communicate these messages directly to the hedonist theater-goers, researchers recommended using both newspaper ads and radio spots on rock and contemporary stations.

SEGMENTATION, TARGETING, AND POSITIONING

The research findings and recommendations presented to Dudley Riggs illustrate three interrelated marketing concepts: market segmentation, target marketing, and product positioning. **Market segmentation** is the process of dividing a market into distinct subsets of customers. Each segment consists of people with similar needs and characteristics that lead them to respond in a similar way to a particular product offering and marketing program. In the Brave New Workshop example, the researchers first divided the total population into theater-goers and nongoers. They then segmented the theater-goers into three groups according to the benefits each group sought from attending a theater and the relative importance they attached to various choice criteria (such as price and location) they might use in deciding which theater to attend. They described each segment's demographic characteristics such as age, income, and education levels.

No single theater could satisfy the unique needs of all three segments of theater-goers; therefore, Dudley Riggs had to decide which segment to pursue as his target market. He decided to target the hedonist segment after evaluating the relative attractiveness of the three groups as to size, revenue potential, and growth rates. He also compared the strengths and weaknesses of the Brave New Workshop with the benefits sought by the customers in each segment and with other theaters competing for those customers. This process of deciding which segments to pursue is called **target marketing**.

Finally, **product positioning** involves designing a product offering and marketing program that creates a competitive advantage in the target mar-

EXHIBIT 6 ♦ 3

A satirical revue by The Brave New Workshop

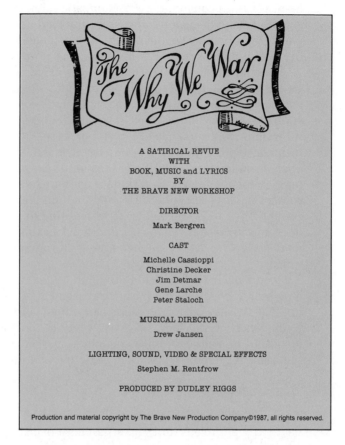

ket.[2] Researchers' recommendations urged Riggs to adopt a marketing program that would appeal to customers in the target segment (low prices and radio advertising). They also suggested stressing the unique characteristics of the Brave New Workshop (audience participation and an informal atmosphere). For evidence that the Brave New Workshop is alive and well, see the announcement of a new satirical revue produced by Dudley Riggs in Exhibit 6–3.

The remainder of this chapter examines the concept of market segmentation in more detail. First, we take a closer look at the rationale for segmenting

---

[2] For a discussion of market segmentation and positioning with reference to industrial markets, see Peter Doyle and John Saunders, "Market Segmentation and Positioning in Specialized Industrial Markets," *Journal of Marketing*, Spring 1985, pp. 24–32.

markets and its importance as a beginning step in formulating marketing strategies. Second, we examine some variables used to define market segments, both in consumer and organizational markets. Third, we discuss the analytical and decision processes involved in market segmentation. We particularly emphasize the pitfalls that plague marketers attempting to identify useful market segments and how those pitfalls might be avoided.

As demonstrated in the Dudley Riggs example, market segmentation is a prerequisite to target marketing and product positioning. Thus, after we have examined some methods for analyzing industry dynamics and the relative strengths and weaknesses of individual competitors (in Chapters 7 and 8), we examine the concepts of target market selection and product positioning in more depth (Chapter 10). For target market selection, this requires that once segments are identified, they must be analyzed to determine their relative attractiveness. Decisions must be made about the allocation of resources across segments. This may include not investing in any segments, serving only a few segments, or attempting to service most of them. Such decisions represent the most important ones made at the specific product-market level; and they impact strategy formulation as well as action planning.

Once a business has decided which segments to target, the next issue is how best to penetrate the individual segment. This requires offering a product that satisfies customer needs better than competing products can. Specifying such a product involves product positioning. (This subject is discussed immediately following target marketing.) Collectively these form the basis of Chapter 10, Market Targeting and Positioning Decisions.

WHY SEGMENT THE MARKET?

The past two chapters stressed that individual consumers or organizations have different needs and make purchase decisions influenced by different personal, social, and environmental factors. Where big-ticket installations are involved, such as the development of a new fighter plane or the construction of a custom-designed house, a firm may tailor its products and marketing programs for each customer.

Because markets are rarely homogeneous in benefits wanted, purchase rates, and price and promotion elasticities, their response rates vary depending on product and marketing program differences. Variations among markets in product preferences, size and growth, media habits, and competitive structures further impact the differences in their response rates. Thus, segmentation is a prerequisite to product and program development.

✳ Market aggregation

During the first 50 years of this century, most American firms—particularly manufacturers of consumer goods—pursued a strategy of market aggregation. They tried to maximize the efficiency of their production and marketing efforts by making one or a few standardized products and selling them to a mass market. Their major marketing strategy was to appeal to as many potential customers as possible. They relied on their efficiency to offer the lowest prices or provide the margins necessary to support substantial advertising and promotion efforts aimed at the mass market. Ford Motor Company was one of the first practitioners of market aggregation. During the 1910s and 1920s, Henry Ford concentrated on the mass production and mass marketing of a single, standardized car—the Model T. As volume increased and he realized greater economies of scale, Ford periodically reduced the price of the Model T. His assumption was that reduced prices would allow more and more consumers to afford cars. The market for the Model T would therefore continue to expand, and it would become increasingly difficult for other manufacturers to compete on a price basis. Many other manufacturers, such as Coca-Cola, Hershey, and Levi Strauss followed similar strategies. Until the 1950s, these were all essentially one-product companies.

Today, a market aggregation strategy is still appropriate where the total market has few differences in customer needs or desires. It is also appropriate where it is operationally difficult to develop distinct products or marketing actions to reach different customer segments. Relatively few product-markets meet these conditions in our economy; but some firms have pursued at least a partial aggregation strategy in recent years. For example, Stouffer's has defined two very broad customer segments for its frozen entrees: people who are watching their weight and people who are not. The company treats each of those broad groups as an aggregate market and does not attempt to segment them any further. As the firm's president pointed out when the Lean Cuisine line was introduced for the weight-watcher market, "There was no fancy target audience, because everyone wants to maintain their weight."[3] Thus, the firm directed a single line of Lean Cuisine products at all weight-conscious adults with a broad advertising appeal centered on the theme, "You'll love the way it looks on you."

✳Market segmentation

When customers are diverse, a single, standardized product does not appeal to many who need or want something different. Further, mass-marketing programs can be inefficient and ineffective when directed toward a heterogeneous group of potential customers. Much advertising and promotion is wasted, for example, because many recipients have no intention of buying the product. Thus, even though Ford's market aggregation strategy gave it the lowest manufacturing costs and the Model T was the lowest-priced car on the market, it eventually lost out to General Motors. Ford ignored changes in consumers' desires and disposable incomes during the 1920s. General Motors responded to those changes by offering a broad range of brands,

---

[3] "Bringing Stouffer's to TV," *New York Times*, May 3, 1982, p. D11.

styles, options, and prices to appeal to the varied needs and tastes of different car buyers.[4]

The growing importance of segmentation

Market segmentation has become increasingly important in developing business and marketing strategies for three reasons.[5] First, population growth has slowed, and many product-markets are mature or declining. This slower rate of market growth has sparked more intense competition for customers as firms—including aggressive foreign competitors—seek growth by wresting market share away from others (as in the color TV industry). To survive, firms are forced to pay more attention to the needs and desires of their customers. They must identify customer segments with different needs and target segments where they have greater strengths than the competition.

Second, other social and economic forces, such as expanding disposable incomes, higher education levels, and more awareness of the world through TV and other media, have produced customers with more varied and sophisticated needs, tastes, and lifestyles than ever before. Standardized products and mass-marketing campaigns are no longer as effective or as cost-efficient as they once were in many markets.

Third, many institutions and agencies facilitating the implementation of marketing programs have responded to increasingly diverse customer needs and tastes by broadening and segmenting their own services and operations. For example, retail organizations have added new stores and new methods of reaching consumers. These include Marshall Field's boutiques; superstores (Wal-Mart's Sam's Wholesale Clubs); discount houses (Dayton Hudson's Target Stores); and direct-marketing operations in which retailers send catalogs to preferred customers several times a year. Similarly, new advertising media have sprung up that appeal to narrow-interest groups, including special-interest magazines, radio programs, and cable TV channels. All of these developments have made it *more possible* for manufacturers and services producers to devise marketing programs focusing efficiently on precisely defined segments of the market.

The benefits of market segmentation

Market segmentation is the dominant strategy across firms in most industries today. There are several reasons for this popularity:

* *Segmentation reflects the realities faced by firms in most markets.* Economic and social forces have caused increased diversity in the needs and behaviors of customers.

---

[4] For one of the earliest statements about market segmentation, see Wendell R. Smith, "Product Differentiation and Market Segmentation as Alternative Marketing Strategies," *Journal of Marketing*, July 1956, pp. 3–8.

[5] Philip Kotler, "Marketization: The Art of Creating Market-Driven Businesses." Paper presented to the Marketing Science Institute, Boston, February 1986.

 Segmentation helps in the design of products and marketing programs that are most effective for reaching homogeneous groups of customers. For example, by identifying and focusing on the hedonistic theater-goers, Dudley Riggs could develop a pricing policy geared to their economic circumstances, select advertising media to effectively reach them, and design advertising appeals tailored to their unique interests.

 Segmentation can identify opportunities for new-product development. Often, a careful analysis of various segments of potential customers reveals one or more groups whose specific needs and concerns are not being well satisfied by existing competitive offerings. Such uncovered segments may represent attractive opportunities for the development of new products or innovative marketing approaches.

 Most important, segmentation can improve the strategic allocation of marketing resources. The strategic benefits of segmentation are sometimes overlooked. Well-defined segments, when coupled with specific products, serve as potential investment centers for a business. Few businesses have the resources or competitive strengths to pursue all segments within a given market. Even when they do, they must still determine the appropriate allocation of resources across segments. Most dramatically successful business strategies are market-segmentation based and concentrate resources in attractive segments.[6] Segmentation should concentrate on subdividing markets into areas in which investments can gain a long-term competitive advantage.

IDENTIFICATION OF MARKET SEGMENTS

There is no single way to segment a market. Virtually all of the variables discussed in the previous two chapters could influence consumers or organizations to desire and purchase different products. Any variable might be useful in distinguishing separate customer segments. For any specific market, the seller typically has to try a variety of such variables, singly and in combination, before finding the best way to view the market's structure. The variable or variables used to segment a market should correspond to the demand functions present if true market segments are to be identified. Because individual demand functions cannot be readily determined, different firms may have different perceptions of a market's structure—which, in turn, could well lead to different strategies.[7]

Marketers divide segmentation variables broadly into four major categories for both consumers and industrial markets.

1. *Customer needs.* Both consumers and organizations may buy similar products to satisfy different needs. This is reflected in the fact that they will seek different benefits from the product and use different choice criteria when deciding which brand to purchase. Also, a customer may seek different benefits

---

[6] Bruce D. Henderson, *Henderson on Corporate Strategy* (Cambridge, Mass.: ABT Books, 1979), p. 8.

[7] Peter R. Dickson and James L. Ginter, "Market Segmentation, Product Differentiation, and Marketing Strategy," *Journal of Marketing*, April 1987, pp. 1–10.

from a product, depending on the situation in which he or she plans to use or consume it.

2. *Product-related behavioral descriptors* reflect the behavior of customers toward a specific product. Relevant descriptors for both customer and industrial markets include product usage, loyalty, purchase predisposition, and purchase influence.

3. *Person- or firm-related behavioral descriptors* provide a better understanding of how a customer *behaves* in buying situations. These include consumers' lifestyles or personality traits and the purchasing structure or buying situations for organizations. Innovativeness and the willingness to buy new products are relevant to both consumer and industrial markets.

4. *Demographic descriptors* describe customers by characteristics such as age or income or the size of the industrial sector in which a firm is located. Geographic location is a physical descriptor common to both consumer and industrial markets. Demographic descriptors are objective and are widely available from public sources.

Generic market segmentation variables

Generic market segmentation variables are descriptors used to identify both consumer and industrial markets. Exhibit 6–4 lists the more common descriptors along with examples of each.

Customer needs

Customer needs are expressed in *benefits sought* from a particular product or service.[8] Individual customers do not have identical needs; and they attach different importance to the benefits offered by different products. In the end, the product that provides the "best" bundle of benefits—given the customer's particular needs—is most likely to be purchased.

As we discussed earlier, purchasing is a problem-solving process. Consumers evaluate product or brand alternatives on the basis of their desired characteristics and how valuable each characteristic is to the consumer. Marketers therefore can define segments on the basis of different choice criteria, both in the presence or absence of different characteristics and the different importance weights attached to each.

For example, the toothpaste market has traditionally been divided into four benefit segments—decay prevention, brightness of teeth, breath freshness, and taste. More recently, the removal of plaque has become another criteria. Different customer groups have different choice criteria for these benefits or product characteristics; and they can be further identified on the basis of other descriptors. The firm can choose which benefits to incorporate

---

[8] The importance of benefit segmentation was originally advocated by Russell I. Haley, "Benefit Segmentation: A Decision-Oriented Research Tool," *Journal of Marketing*, July 1968, pp. 30–35.

EXHIBIT   6 ◆ 4

Generic market segmentation descriptors

Customer needs descriptors	*Examples*
Benefits sought	Reliability, performance, convenience, economy, prestige
Product-related behavioral descriptors	
Product usage	Nonuser, light user, heavy user
Loyalty	Strong, medium, none
Purchase predisposition	Unaware, aware, knowledgeable, interested, positively disposed, intending to buy
Purchase influence	Buyer, user, prescriber
Person- or firm-related behavioral descriptors	
Innovativeness	Innovators, early adopters, early majority, late majority, laggards
Demographic descriptors	
Geographic location	Region, states, metropolitan areas, urban or rural areas

into its product—and to what extent. Such brands as Crest, Ultra Brite, Aqua Fresh, and Viadent have targeted different benefit segments. The latter bills itself as "the original plaque-fighting toothpaste with fluoride."

In industrial markets, customers consider relevant benefits that include product performance in different use situations, on-time delivery, credit terms, economy, spare parts availability, and training. Different customers have different choice criteria. For example, in the disposable paper cup market, some industrial buyers want service; others are primarily concerned with cost and credit terms.[9]

Note that benefits wanted must be linked to usage situations. There is ample evidence that usage often strongly affects product choice and substitutability.[10] Thus, the appropriateness of product attributes varies across different usage environments.[11] Any attempt to define viable segments must

---

[9] "Maryland Cup Sells More than just Paper Cups," *Business Week*, June 23, 1978, p. 104.

[10] Rajendra K. Srivastava, "Usage Situation Influences on Perceptions of Product Market: Theoretical and Empirical Issues," *Advances in Consumer Research*, ed. Kent Monroe (Chicago: Association for Consumer Research, 1981), pp. 32–37.

[11] George S. Day, Allan D. Shocker, and Rajendra K. Srivastava, "Identifying Competitive Product-Markets: A Review of Customer-Oriented Approaches," *Journal of Marketing*, Fall 1979, pp. 8–19.

recognize this fact, particularly with consumer goods. For example, the appropriateness of drinking beer or a soft drink, coffee, a gin and tonic, or wine varies across situations—as with or after a meal, when playing tennis or golf, immediately after work, while watching TV, or at a formal dinner party.

Product usage

In many markets, a small proportion of potential customers represents a high percentage of all purchases. In fact, about 20 percent of the users of most product classes account for 80 percent of total consumption. This is the case with soft drinks, many packaged food products, and beer. A special analysis is usually required to identify heavy, light, and nonusers in more tangible descriptors. For instance, heavy cola drinkers tend to be in their teens and live in the South.

In industrial markets, the customers are better known; and heavy users, often called *key accounts*, are easier to identify. For example, major airlines, banks, and insurance companies are heavy users of large-scale computer systems with many peripheral devices. These customers are easy to identify by name and location.

Loyalty

Current users of a product differ in their loyalty for a given brand or supplier. Customers show their degrees of loyalty by their successive purchases over time. In industrial markets, sellers can often directly observe this; in consumer markets, identifying loyal customers requires marketing research. As might be expected, the relative importance of the loyal and nonloyal segments varies widely among markets. The challenge to each firm is to protect its loyal customers while attracting new ones.

Purchase predisposition

Potential customers may not use a product for a variety of reasons: They may not be aware of the product or know all of its qualities. Maybe they are not satisfied by existing offerings. Perhaps they have intended to buy but never took the necessary action, or are simply not interested in this product.[12] These reasons reflect different predispositions toward the purchase of a product. A market segmentation scheme based on product knowledge and purchase predisposition can identify the nonusers who are most likely to become future buyers. For example, knowledgeable nonusers who intend to buy, say, a high-fiber cereal are the most likely to become future users. Knowledgeable nonusers who do not intend to buy, on the other hand, would probably represent a low potential.

---

[12] First developed for advertising purposes, this elaboration of purchase predispositions is known as the "hierarchy of effects." See Robert J. Lavidge and Gary A. Steiner, "A Model for Predictive Measurement of Effectiveness," *Journal of Marketing*, October 1961, pp. 59–62.

Purchase influence

Market segmentation by sources of purchase influence is relevant for both consumer and industrial markets. Many products used by various family members are purchased by the wife; but as we saw in Chapter 4, joint husband-wife decisions are becoming more common. Children's products, prescription drugs, and gifts are clearly influenced by a variety of individuals. In industrial markets, several individuals or organizational units with varying degrees of influence participate in the buying center.

For example, in the computer market, the purchasing role of the computer staff has been recognized by all manufacturers. The ease with which salespeople can talk to the technical specialists of prospective clients has led some computer manufacturers to focus exclusively on the computer staff. Computer acquisition decisions are, however, often strongly influenced by managers who place more emphasis on reliability than on technological sophistication—a fact long recognized by IBM.

Innovativeness

Individuals and organizations vary in their capacity and desire to innovate. This is particularly so for the adoption of new products. Exhibit 6–5 presents generalizations about major differences between early and late adopters in consumer markets. In organizational markets, suppliers can identify innovative firms by their reputations or from their experiences in dealing with them. For example, a new antibiotic prescription drug is most apt to be adopted early on by younger and better educated (more specialized) doctors

EXHIBIT 6 ◆ 5

Major differences between early and late adopters

	Early adopters	*Late adopters*
Age	Younger	Older
Income	Higher	Lower
Education	Higher—more specialized	Lower—less specialized
Social	Higher status	Lower status
Occupation	More prestigious	Less prestigious
Media and sources of information	Greater exposure to more media and variety of information sources	Less exposure to fewer media and less variety of sources plus more reliance on personal sources
Cosmopolitan contacts	More nonlocal personal contacts	Essentially local personal contacts

who read more medical journals and who attend more medical meetings than do other doctors.

From a marketing strategy viewpoint, identifying and understanding differing characteristics of innovative and late-adopting customers can be useful at various stages in a product's life cycle. It is particularly helpful when designing advertising appeals, selecting advertising media, and scheduling sales calls. An understanding of the innovative customer is particularly important for firms about to introduce a new product into the marketplace. We examine these customer segments in more detail later in the text when we discuss marketing strategies for new product-markets.

Geographical location

Markets can be easily segmented by geographical location, using counties, standard metropolitan statistical areas, states, and regions. The philosophy underlying geographic segmentation is that alternative locations may represent different sales potentials, growth rates, customer needs, servicing costs, or competitive structures. Different regions of the United States have different cultures, climates, and resources that influence the use of media and the purchase of certain products and services.[13]

Geographical segmentation is critical to the allocation of resources to the personal selling and advertising activities. Ordinarily, an analysis is made of the contents of each of the areas of interest using demographic variables such as age, income, and education along with the number of such individuals residing there. These data are particularly helpful in determining the relative potential of a given area for consuming a particular product.[14]

In recent years, considerable evidence suggests that geography can be an important indicator of what people buy:

> Northeasterners and Midwesterners prefer chicken noodle and tomato soups, but in California cream of mushroom is number one. Pepperpot soup sells primarily in the Philadelphia area, and cream of vegetable on the West Coast. People in the Southwest drive more pick-up trucks, people in the Northeast more vans, and Californians like high-priced, imported cars such as BMWs and Mercedes-Benzes. Texans drive big cars, New Yorkers like smaller ones. New Hampshirites drink more beer per capita than other Americans. The anxious denizens of Atlanta consume more aspirin and antacids a head, and the sweet-toothed Mormons of Salt Lake City eat more candy bars and marshmallows.[15]

Some companies use census data to segment the country into areas as small as or smaller than those covered by a ZIP code on the assumption that

---

[13] Lynn R. Kahle, "The Nine Nations of North America and the Value Basis of Geographic Segmentation," *Journal of Marketing*, April 1986, pp. 37–47.

[14] This combining of geography and demographics is sometimes referred to as *geodemographics*. See Art Weinstein, *Market Segmentation* (Chicago: Probus, 1987), pp. 81–85.

[15] Thomas Moore, "Different Folks, Different Strokes," *Fortune*, September 16, 1985, p. 68.

people with similar cultural backgrounds and value systems tend to cluster together. Claritas is one of several companies that produces and sells population profiles of ZIP codes for such geographic areas. For example, when requested to provide data on upwardly mobile black households, Claritas pulled together 160 neighborhoods identified by ZIP code boundaries (such as the Crenshaw-Imperial district in Los Angeles and Maywood, a Chicago suburb). The areas identified were at least 60 percent black and above the national average in the percent of families earning $15,000 to $50,000 a year and more.[16]

Segmentation descriptors specific to consumer markets

The segmentation categories here include lifestyle and social class, which are behavioral in nature, and demographics. Exhibit 6-6 shows examples of each of the descriptors we discuss next.

EXHIBIT 6 ◆ 6

Segmentation descriptors specific to consumer markets

Segmentation criteria	Examples of categories
Behavioral descriptors	
Lifestyle or psychographics	Traditionalist, family-oriented, hedonist, sophisticated, sports activist, outdoors person
Social class	Upper-upper, lower-upper, upper-middle, middle class, working class, lower class, lower-lower
Demographic descriptors	
Age	Under 2, 2-5, 6-11, 12-17, 18-24, 25-34, 35-49, 50-64, 65 or over
Sex	Male, female
Family life cycle	Young, single; newly married, no children; youngest child under 6; youngest child 6 or over; older couples with dependent children; older couples without dependent children; older couples retired; older, single
Income	Under 10,000; $10,000-14,999; $15,000-24,999; $25,000 or over
Occupation	Professional, manager, clerical, sales, supervisor, blue-collar, homemaker, student, unemployed
Education	Some high school, graduated high school, some college, graduated college
Race and ethnic origin	Anglo-Saxon, black, Italian, Jewish, Scandinavian, Hispanic, Oriental, white

---

[16] Eugene Carlson, ''Population-Data Firms Profit by Pinpointing Special Groups,'' *The Wall Street Journal*, October 15, 1985, p. 35.

EXHIBIT 6 ◆ 7

Lifestyle dimensions

Activities	Interests	Opinions
Work	Family	Themselves
Hobbies	Home	Social issues
Social events	Job	Politics
Vacations	Community	Business
Entertainment	Recreation	Economics
Club membership	Fashion	Education
Community	Food	Products
Shopping	Media	Future
Sports	Achievements	Culture

Source: Adapted from Joseph T. Plummer, "The Concept and Application of Lifestyle Segmentation," *Journal of Marketing,* January 1974, pp. 33–37. Published by the American Marketing Association.

Lifestyle

This descriptor, also referred to as **psychographics,** seeks to group consumers on the basis of their activities, interests, and opinions (AIOs). For a listing of the specific variables included in each of these categories, see Exhibit 6–7. As we noted in Chapter 4, lifestyle provides one of the more informative descriptions of consumers' behavior.

To obtain lifestyle data (sometimes referred to as *psychographic* data), consumers are usually asked to indicate the extent to which they agree or disagree with a series of statements. The statements are listed in random order on the questionnaire, so respondents are not likely to discern any meaningful pattern. The statements are designed to measure specific attitudes, opinions, or beliefs. Exhibit 6–8 shows some sample statements that might be used to measure such things as price consciousness, fashion consciousness, self-confidence, new brand trying, and enthusiasm for art. For each attitude, activity, belief, and so on that the researchers are trying to measure, there will be several statements on the questionnaire.

One general lifestyle typology has been developed by Stanford Research Institute's (SRI) Value and Lifestyle (VALS) program. The original VALS was set forth in 1978 and consisted of nine segments, each intended to describe a unique way of life. The segments were organized along a hierarchy of needs and, for the most part, reflected a young population with people in their 20s and 30s.[17]

---

[17] This section is based on material obtained from the VALS Program, SRI International (Menlo Park, Calif.: 1989) and an article by Martha Farnsworth Riche entitled "Psychographics for the 1990s," which appeared in the July 1989 issue of *American Demographics,* pp. 25–31.

EXHIBIT 6 ◆ 8

Psychographic variables and sample statements

Psychographic variable	Sample statement
Price conscious	I shop a lot for "specials."
Fashion conscious	My outfits are usually of the latest style.
Self-confidence	I am more independent than most people.
New brand trier	Often I buy a new brand just to see what it is like.
Arts enthusiast	I enjoy ballet.

Source: Adapted from William R. Darden and William D. Perreault, Jr., "Identifying Interurban Shoppers: Multiproduct Purchase Patterns and Segmentation Profiles," *Journal of Marketing Research,* February 1975, pp. 51–60. Published by the American Marketing Association.

But things have changed, raising questions about the validity of using values and lifestyles as the basis for the VALS segmentation scheme. The aging of the American population and its increased diversity, the decline in consumers' expectations for the future, the growing assortment of products, the changing retail structure, and the expanding diversity of media have all conspired to fragment values and lifestyles to a point where SRI no longer felt it could predict consumer behavior.

SRI's revised program (VALS 2) is based on a conceptual framework consisting of two dimensions—self-orientation and resources. The first dimension seeks to describe the way people search for and acquire products and services. According to VALS, they are motivated by one of three powerful self-orientations—principle, status, or action. Principle-oriented consumers are guided by their beliefs or principles, while status-oriented consumers are strongly influenced by the actions and opinions of others. Action-oriented individuals are guided by a need for either social or physical activity, variety, or risk-taking.

Resources, the second dimension, refers to the full range of physical, psychological, and material means as well as the capacities consumers can draw on. Thus, resources include income, education, health, self-confidence, intelligence, energy level, and eagerness to buy. As would be expected, resources typically increase from youth through middle age and diminish with old age.

By combining the two dimensions, VALS identifies and elaborates eight consumer segments, each of which has distinct behavior and decision-making patterns. The segments are about equal in size so that each represents a viable target. VALS 2 consists of a network of interconnected segments with neighboring types having similar characteristics. Exhibit 6–9 shows this network. A description of each of the segments appears in Exhibit 6–10.

EXHIBIT 6 ◆ 9

The VALS™ 2 network

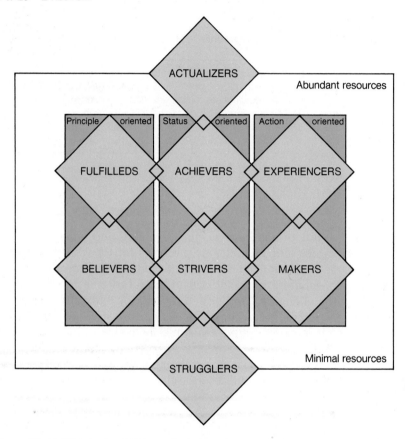

Source: "The VALS™ 2 Typology," *SRI International,* July 1989. Reprinted with permission of SRI International.

Social class

Every society has status groupings largely based on similarities in income, education, and occupation. From these similarities come social attitudes that characterize a particular class. Researchers have documented the values of different social classes as they relate to a wide range of areas. Thus, knowing a buyer's social class can help the seller infer certain behavior relevant to the marketing of a given product. This is particularly true of advertising, where higher social classes are more critical of advertising messages, appreciate humor and sophistication, react better to individualized messages, and look down on ads that stress economy and savings. Lower classes are more receptive to strongly visual, practical, and down-to-earth advertising that shows activity.

EXHIBIT 6 ♦ 10

Characteristics of VALS 2 consumer segments

Consumer type	*Values and lifestyles*
♦ **Actualizers:**	These are successful, sophisticated, active, "take-charge" people with high self-esteem and abundant resources. They are interested in growth and seek to develop, explore, and express themselves in a variety of ways. Actualizers are among the established and emerging leaders in business and government. They have a wide range of interests, are concerned with social issues, and are open to change. Their lives are characterized by richness and diversity.
♦ **Fulfilleds (principle-oriented):**	Such individuals are mature, satisfied, well informed, comfortable, reflective, and for the most part, well educated. Their leisure activities center around the home. Fulfilleds have incomes that allow for many choices. They are conservative, practical consumers who look for value, durability, and functionality in the products they buy.
♦ **Believers (principle-oriented):**	These are conservative, conventional people with concrete beliefs based on traditional, established codes: family, church, community, and the nation. As consumers, they are conservative and predictable, favoring American products and established brands. Their education, income, and energy are modest but adequate to meet their needs.
♦ **Achievers (status-oriented):**	People in this segment are successful and work-oriented and in control of their lives. They value structure, predictability, and stability over risk, intimacy, and self-discovery. Work provides them with a sense of duty, material rewards, and prestige. Achievers live conventional lives, are politically conservative, and respect authority. As consumers, they favor established products and services.
♦ **Strivers (status-oriented):**	They seek motivation, self-definition, and approval from the world around them. They are unsure of themselves and low on economic, social, and psychological resources and thus are deeply concerned about the opinions and approval of others. Money defines success for strivers who don't have enough of it. Strivers are impulsive and easily bored. They tend to emulate those who own more impressive possessions, which are generally beyond their reach.
♦ **Experiencers (action-oriented):**	These are young, vital, enthusiastic, impulsive, and rebellious people. They want variety and excitement, savoring the new, the off-beat, and the risky. Experiencers combine an abstract disdain for conformity and authority with an awe of others' wealth, prestige, and power. They enjoy exercise, sports, and social activities; further, they are avid consumers and spend much of their income on clothing, fast food, music, movies, and videos.
♦ **Makers (action-oriented):**	These are practical people with constructive skills who value self-sufficiency. They live within a traditional context of family, practical work, and physical recreation and have little interest in anything outside of that context. Movers experience the world by working on it—building a house, raising children, fixing a car, or canning vegetables. Makers are politically conservative and suspicious of new ideas. They are unimpressed by material possessions other than those with a practical or functional purpose (e.g., tools, pick-up trucks, or fishing equipment).
♦ **Strugglers:**	These are people who are poor, ill-educated, low-skilled, without strong social bonds, aging, and concerned about their health. They are often despairing and passive and are primarily concerned with security. They are cautious consumers who represent a very modest market for most goods and services. They are loyal to favorite brands.

Source: Adapted from "The VALS™ 2 Typology" (Menlo Park, Calif.: VALS Program, SRI International, 1989).

EXHIBIT   6 ◆ 11

Characteristics of American social classes

Upper-upper	0.3% of the population; socially elite with inherited wealth; do not engage in conspicuous consumption, but per capita expenditures are large and can be an important market for travel, housing, and jewelry; important as a reference group.
Lower-upper	1.2% of the population; new social elite; current professional and corporate leaders; can be very wealthy/nouveau riche; spend freely on products that serve as power/success status symbols; excellent market for expensive automobiles, elegant homes, large boats, planes, and fine furs and jewelry.
Upper-middle	12.5% of the population; remaining college graduate managers and professionals; value money both for status and lifestyle it can buy; more interested in books and magazines than TV; interested in status brands and stores; serve as markets for travel, books, good homes and furniture, and well-made styled clothes.
Middle-middle	32% of the population; white-color/blue-collar workers; technicians; aspire to live in a better neighborhood; prize education for their children; appreciate good brand names; good market for home furnishings, travel, and fashion merchandise.
Working class	38% of the population; average income; skilled and semi-skilled workers; single largest class; strong family orientation; very patriotic; highly structured roles for family members; emphasize day-to-day living.
Lower class	9% of the population; unskilled workers; live close to poverty level; not on welfare; some minorities included; average family size larger than other classes; spend disproportionate amount of income on appliances and color TV.
Lower-lower	6% of the population; many on welfare and living in poverty; many minorities; many single-parent households; reside in slums; few own homes; very low educational levels; live largely for today; rely heavily on name brands; heavy consumers of television.

Source: Adapted from an exhibit in R. P. Coleman, "The Continuing Significance of Social Class to Marketing," *Journal of Consumer Research* 10 (3), September 1983, pp. 265–80.

Exhibit 6–11 (p. 199) shows the values and consumption patterns of each of the seven social classes. For example, the middle classes tend to place more value on education, family activities, cleanliness, and being up to date than do lower-class families. Different classes hold different attitudes toward the purchase of products or services relating to such activities as investments, travel, home decoration, child rearing, entertainment, hobbies, and health.

Demographic descriptors

Demographic descriptors (age, sex, income), while the only specific and readily available data from reputable sources such as government census data, do not relate *directly* to consumer behavior; thus, they are not the most relevant bases for segmentation. Their primary use is to identify consumers who have been clustered according to other criteria, such as heavy cola drinkers or anti-plaque toothpaste users. These descriptors are helpful also in market-segmentation analysis when their relationship to purchasing behavior is obvious—as with products used exclusively by children or men or by certain professionals or ethnic groups. How many such descriptors to use or in what combination depends largely on the situation. Several demographic descriptors of the type discussed below, plus geography, are usually used to help describe market segments for a consumer good. But lifestyle, family life-cycle, and social-class descriptors are more relevant as a way of segmenting consumer markets because of their greater power to predict buying behavior for a given product or service.

Age.   The age variable runs a predictable course. That is, if we know the age distribution of the population as of a certain date, and estimates of births and deaths, we can reliably predict the size of various age groups at a future date. When these data are coupled with buying behavior in the marketplace, the implications for marketing become clear. For example, some 77 million Americans were born between 1946 and 1964. As many of them approach middle age, they gain substantial purchasing power. Thus, the number of people 35 to 44 years of age will increase 26 percent to 43 million by 1997. Further, the purchasing power of this group will grow by $195 billion, to $939 billion. In the years ahead, these aging baby boomers will affect the sales of such products as quality convenience foods, home furnishings, travel, educational services, and cars (mini-vans). Advertisers are learning how to cope with this aging of America and embrace middle age. Some, for example, are using such well-preserved TV stars as Linda Evans, Joan Collins, and John Forsythe to sell their products and services.[18]

Because age correlates with key events such as college attendance, marriage, and biological functions (puberty, childbearing) it is one of the more frequently used descriptors. The purchase and use of many products vary

---

[18] Faye Rice, "Wooing Aging Baby Boomers," *Fortune,* February 1, 1988, p. 67. For a discussion of some of the other consequences of the aging of the baby boomers, see Cheryl Russell, *100 Predictions for the Baby Boom* (New York: Plenum Books, 1987). For details concerning expenditures made by people 55 years and older, see William Lazer and Eric H. Shaw, "How Older Americans Spend Their Money," *American Demographics,* September 1987, pp. 36–41.

substantially by age group.[19] For example, families with a younger household head spend, on average, proportionately *less* on medical and personal care, food, and recreation, and *more* on clothing, home furnishings, appliances, and automotive products than do older household heads. These differences are not only a function of income, but also of differing needs and attitudes arising from biological differences and the presence of children.

Sex.   The sex descriptor has implications not only for biological reasons but also because of the roles assigned to men and women in our society. In recent years the increase in women in the workforce has changed former inferences about the role of women as stay-at-home homemakers. It has also increased the demand for convenience foods and appliances, automobiles (second car), child-care services, and cosmetics. A recent study showed that women buy 45 percent of new cars sold in the United States and influence another 40 percent. Toyota reports that women buy 56 percent of its cars. In addition to targeting women in their advertising, manufacturers are working with their dealers to find ways to attract women to their showrooms. Hyundai, for example, is designing its dealerships similar to shopping malls.[20] And motor oil is now sold in supermarkets due to the impact of women purchasers.

Family life cycle.   The concept of family life cycle attempts to predict buying behavior by combining age, marital status, and the presence of children. As we saw in Chapter 4, the family life cycle describes the various stages in the formation, growth, and decline of the family unit; i.e., the effect of the passage of time on consumption. Part of these effects is due to age (biological needs change as do activities); part is because income increases; part is because situations change with reference to the nature and scope of the family unit.[21] For examples of the kinds of purchasing behavior associated with each of the stages in the family life cycle, see Exhibit 6–12.

Each stage differs in its purchasing behavior. Young marrieds, for instance, are heavy buyers of small appliances, furniture, and linens. When children arrive, the family unit purchases insurance, baby foods, washers, and dryers. Large families (three or more children), while declining in importance, account for 20 percent of the dollars spent for food, clothing, and education in the United States and 8 percent of all housing and enter-

---

[19] For an interesting discussion of how age will affect the market for eyeglasses and contact lenses, see Thomas Exten, "Options for Optometrists," *American Demographics*, December 1988, p. 38.

[20] Freida Curtindale, "Marketing Cars to Women," *American Demographics*, November 1988, pp. 29–31.

[21] William L. Wilkie, *Consumer Behavior* (New York: John Wiley & Sons, 1986), pp. 192–98.

EXHIBIT 6 ◆ 12

Examples of purchasing behavior associated with each stage in the family life cycle

Stage	Buying behavior examples
1. Young singles under age 35.	Spend mostly on cars, entertainment, clothes, convenience items—"mating game" products/services.
2. Newly married/young married without children.	Much spending activity; accounts for large percentage of purchases of furniture, stereos, sterling flatware, travel, and jewelry.
3. Full Nest I—youngest child under 6 years of age; account for some 25 percent of population.	This stage accompanied by high level of debt as purchases are made of housing, furniture, appliances, insurance, and "baby expenses," such as medical, toys, and furniture.
4. Full Nest II—youngest child over 6 years of age; account for about 13 percent of population.	Better financial position than before; buy larger-size packages of food and personal-care items. Children exercise heavy influence on such purchases as bicycles, sporting goods, and entertainment.
5. Full Nest III—Older couples with mid-teen children still at home; account for some 15 percent of population.	Family financial position continues to improve; higher purchase rate of durables because of replacement and more multiple purchases for spouse and teen use (e.g., TV, stereo, and cars).
6. Empty Nest I—older couples with no children living at home; account for 6 percent of population.	Higher income and lower expenses than before; greater expenditures for travel, home improvements, and recreation.
7. Empty Nest II—older couples, no children living at home, and head retired; account for 5 percent of population.	Sharp drop in income because of retirement; strong market for medical products and services.
8. Solitary Survivor—lower income and older; account for 2 percent of population.	Increased medical needs—decreasing expenditures on durables, clothes, and recreation.

Source: William D. Wells and George Gubar, "Life Cycle Concept in Marketing Research," *Journal of Marketing Research,* November 1966, pp. 355–63. Also see William L. Wilkie, *Consumer Behavior* (New York: John Wiley & Sons, 1986), pp. 194–98.

taining expenditures.[22] As the children grow, purchases include educational services and materials and bigger cars. When the children leave home, new activities—including vacations—become more feasible.

Income.   The availability of money to support needs and wants is, of course, a prerequisite to effective demand. This descriptor is best defined as total family income, given the large number of two-income families. Although income is an important descriptor, it is most helpful when combined with other descriptors such as age and the presence of children.

The low-income segment is attractive because of its size—over a third of all households in 1987 earned less than $15,000 a year. Retail chains that target this segment have grown rapidly in recent years. For example, Dollar General operates over 1,300 small stores primarily in rural and inner-city areas. Over 90 percent of the items the stores stock (clothing and household items including irregulars and manufacturers' over-runs) retail for less than $10.[23] At the other extreme are the products targeted for the affluent segment. For example, American Airlines' magazine *Private Clubs* is designed to "attract readers with an average household income of $144,000, the sort of people who don't bother reading menu prices."[24]

Occupation.   The occupation descriptor can relate directly to needs for specific products. For example, Hewlett-Packard has designed hand-held calculators specifically for engineers and financial analysts. The increase in the working women segment has created needs for goods and services such as financial services, convenience products, business wardrobes, and special-interest magazines aimed at this segment.

Education.   Income and education are closely related; but income alone rarely explains spending behavior. The education level of consumers has, for example, a strong effect on the purchase of travel, books, magazines, insurance, and photographic equipment. Some firms have found it profitable to target certain education groups. AT&T, Campbell Soup, Chesebrough-Pond's, and American Express cultivate the 12.5 million college-student market, for example; and Procter & Gamble promotes its Head & Shoulders shampoo to high school students.[25]

---

[22] Diane Crispell, "Three's a Crowd," *American Demographics,* January 1989, p. 35.

[23] Hank Gilman, "Selling It to the Poor," *The Wall Street Journal,* June 24, 1985, p. 1.

[24] Ronald Alsop, "Wealth of Affluent Magazines Vie for Advertisers' Attention," *The Wall Street Journal,* January 9, 1986, p. 2.

[25] Ronald Alsop, "Firms Send Brands to College to Cultivate New Consumers," *The Wall Street Journal,* July 31, 1986, p. 23.

EXHIBIT 6 ♦13

Examples of successful marketing to the U.S. Hispanic market

---

* Metropolitan Life increased sales of insurance to Hispanics more than 150 percent in 1988 with nationwide Spanish-language ads. The company chose to use Latin actors rather than Snoopy, the cartoon mainstay of its English-language ads.
* Adolph Coors Co. has built Hispanic market share in part by sponsoring festivals celebrating such holidays as Columbus Day in Miami and Cinco de Mayo in Los Angeles.
* Best Foods' Mazola corn oil captured two thirds of the national Hispanic market with a five-year Spanish-language campaign promoting what Hispanic consumers want in corn oil: good taste, not low cholesterol.

Source: Julia Lieblich, "If You Want a Big New Market—," *Fortune,* November 21, 1988, p. 181. © Time Inc. All rights reserved.

Race and ethnic origin.   For certain products and services, race is an important descriptor, even though some behavior is less determined by race per se than by differences in income, education, and culture. In the United States, many companies offer special products and use different communication programs to appeal to blacks, Italians, Jews, Hispanics, Orientals, and others. For examples of successful marketing to the large and growing U.S. Hispanic market, see Exhibit 6–13.

Segmentation descriptors specific to industrial markets[26]

Industrial markets are segmented in two stages. The first, **macrosegmentation,** divides the market according to the organizational characteristics of the customers.[27] The second stage, **microsegmentation,** groups customers by the characteristics of the individuals who influence the purchasing decision.

The generic segmentation descriptors discussed earlier illustrate the distinction between these two stages. Product usage and geographic location are characteristics of the organization and are used for macrosegmentation purposes. Purchase influence, benefits sought, loyalty, and purchase predispositions relate to the behavior of individuals involved in the purchasing decision and are microsegmentation descriptors.

---

[26] For an interesting discussion on how to segment markets served by high-tech companies, see James D. Hlvacek and B. C. Ames, "Segmenting Industrial and High-tech Markets," *Journal of Business Strategy,* Fall 1986, p. 39.

[27] The distinction between these two stages is discussed in Ronald E. Frank, William F. Massey, and Yoram Wind, *Market Segmentation* (Englewood Cliffs, N.J.: Prentice-Hall, 1972), pp. 91–94.

EXHIBIT   6 ♦ 14

Segmentation descriptors specific to industrial markets

Segmentation descriptors	*Examples of categories*
Macrosegmentation	
Adoption process	Early, late adopters
Purchasing structure	Centralized, decentralized
Buying situation	New purchase; modified rebuy; straight rebuy
Industrial sector	Standard Industrial Classification (SIC)
Company size	Large; medium; small
Microsegmentation	
Personal characteristics	
Hierarchical position	Low; middle; high
Role in purchasing process	Specification; product evaluation; financial; final decision
Decision-making style	Normative; conservative; emotional
Demographics	Age; education; area of expertise

The segmentation descriptors commonly used for industrial markets are purchasing structure, buying situation, industrial sector, and company size at the macrosegmentation level—and personal characteristics of the buying center members at the microsegmentation level. See Exhibit 6–14 for examples of these variables that we discuss next.

Adoption process

The adoption decision process for industrial products is similar to that for consumer products, including the decision stages of awareness, interest, evaluation, trial, and adoption. Early adopters are likely to be among the larger firms in the industry because they are better able to afford the necessary investment and the risk of being an innovator. Thus, for example, the early adopters of new models of jet aircraft were the larger, faster-growing airlines that had more borrowing capacity than later adopters. Firms that adopt earlier also spend more on R&D and tend to have presidents who are younger and better educated.[28]

---

[28] Frederick E. Webster, Jr., *Industrial Marketing Strategy* (New York: John Wiley & Sons, 1984), pp. 136–47.

Purchasing structure

The *degree of centralization* of the purchasing structure is of particular interest. In some companies, a central purchasing department coordinates all buying activities. In others, organizational units such as plants or R&D labs assume their own buying responsibilities. The extent to which purchasing is centralized affects the level of authority, knowledgeability, geographic dispersion, and concerns of the buyers, as well as the relationships between buyers and users.

In a centralized structure, the buyer is likely to consider all transactions with a given supplier on a global basis, emphasize cost savings, and minimize risks. In a decentralized situation, the buyer is apt to be more sensitive to the user's need, emphasize product quality and fast delivery, and be less cost conscious. This is the case with the trans-Atlantic containerized freight business. The more centralized the buying function, the greater the emphasis on costs—in contrast to decentralized structures, where more emphasis is placed on fast and reliable delivery.

Buying situation

As we saw in Chapter 5, three distinct buying situations can be identified. A **straight rebuy** is a recurring situation handled on a routine basis. A **modified rebuy** occurs when some element (such as price or delivery schedules) has changed in a client-supplier relationship. A **new buying situation** is one that has not arisen before and may require considerable information gathering and the evaluation of alternative suppliers.

Industrial sector

A widely used approach in macrosegmentation is to group customers by the industrial sector in which they perform their activities. It is often based on the Standard Industrial Classification (SIC) system described in Chapter 5.

Macrosegmentation by industrial sector is a convenient way to classify customers into well-defined groups for which statistical data are readily available. It is particularly valuable if the segments differ significantly in other criteria more directly linked to the formulation of strategy, such as product usage or benefits sought.

Company size

Marketers often divide an industrial market into small, medium, and large organizations according to total sales, in the belief that such a measure of size will correlate with the purchase of their product. Since customers' total sales likely derive from many product lines, it is important to use a sales measure closely tied to the magnitude of their purchases. In lieu of sales, some sellers use number of employees as a measure of size.

Because of the typical concentration of sales (70 to 80 percent) in a limited number of buyers (10 to 20 percent of all customers), segmentation by size (importance) is critically important. This can be a powerful segmentation scheme because company size is, in addition to extent of product usage, often related to benefits sought, purchasing influence, purchasing structure, and servicing costs. For example, large organizations usually have more sophisticated inventory control, maintenance, and R&D programs than smaller ones. There may be, therefore, better opportunities to develop stronger ties with smaller companies than with larger companies on the basis of support systems. Sometimes a single firm will be large enough to be treated as a single segment in and of itself—say, Ford as a buyer of steel.

Personal characteristics

The more important of these are the hierarchical position, role in the purchasing process, decision-making style, and the demographic characteristics of the individuals participating in the decision. The *hierarchical* position may vary widely—from a mail clerk selecting an air freight carrier to a chief executive officer making the final decision on a major computer investment. Individuals at different levels have different priorities, freedom of action, and attitudes toward risk.

The *role* of an individual in the purchasing process may be to define the buying specifications, evaluate the performance of proposed products, negotiate prices, or make the final decision. The *decision-making* style of an industrial buyer may be rational, conservative or risk adverse, or emotional and based on personal relationships.[29] Finally, industrial buyers may also differ in *demographics* such as age, education, or area of expertise. Knowledge of such characteristics is particularly important in the selection of advertising media such as specialized trade (e.g., *Water Well Journal*) or general management magazines such as *Business Week*.

THE SEGMENTATION PROCESS

The need for multivariate definitions

As we have noted, there are many ways of dividing a market into segments. Regardless of which way is chosen, it is necessary to identify market segments in terms of their descriptors (that is, to describe the characteristics of the prospective customers they contain). Selection of meaningful descriptors in a given market situation represents the first step in the market segmentation process.

---

[29] For a study of normative and conservative decision making by industrial buyers, see David T. Wilson, "Industrial Buyers' Decision-Making Styles," *Journal of Marketing Research*, November 1971, pp. 433–36.

The next step is concerned with determining whether and to what extent there are differences in the needs or benefits being sought by customers in the various segments. The benefits sought may vary—often substantially—by usage situation. This means the saliency of different product characteristics needs to be considered across the various usage environments. For example, the choice of whether to fly first class or tourist often depends upon whether the individual is traveling for business or pleasure. As we will discuss later, the first and second steps in the segmentation process are sometimes *reversed*. Thus, a market can first be segmented on the basis of different needs (different product attributes wanted) and then identified on the basis of demographic descriptors.

The third step in the segmentation process requires evaluating the present and future attractiveness of each segment. Typically, such measures as sales, growth, competition, and profitability are used to indicate the market attractiveness of each segment. Whatever the criteria used, they must be considered in terms of the resources required to exploit the opportunity relative to the firm's resource base. This step leads to market targeting and the formulation of a market-segmentation strategy that specifies the allocation of resources across segments. (Market targeting and positioning are discussed in Chapter 10.)

The segmentation variable or variables used should explain the differences in customers' buying behavior that requires differentiated marketing programs involving different products and marketing mixes. This is why benefits sought and product-specific behavioral variables are particularly useful for answering *strategic* questions, such as:

◆ *How many distinct product-markets might be developed within a particular industry?* In the theater-goers "industry," there were three distinct segments that had different needs: the sociables, the intellectuals, and the hedonists.

◆ *Which segments represent attractive opportunities in view of the customers' needs and the firm's competitive strengths and weaknesses?* The hedonists go to the theater primarily for fun and thus prefer comedies, satirical reviews, and humorous improvisations. The Brave New Workshop was the only theater presenting such fare.

◆ *Which segments are not currently being satisfied and therefore represent opportunities for new-product development?* Given its uniqueness, the workshop hoped to expand its audience by focusing on the hedonist group and publicizing the fact that it concentrated on satirical humor.

On the other hand, more general behavioral and physical descriptors are most useful for answering many of the *tactical questions* that arise when designing a marketing program to reach a particular product-market, such as:

◆ Which retail outlets or distributors should be included in the distribution channel?

◆ How should sales territories be designed and how frequently should salespeople call on different customers?

♦ What advertising media should be used?
♦ Which promotional appeals should be emphasized?

Marketers thus try to define segments using a combination of benefit, behavioral, and physical factors—even though this often requires the collection of marketing research data and the use of sophisticated statistical analyses.[30]

Collecting the necessary information

The processes that marketers use to collect the data identifying useful market segments vary according to the product and the strategic objective involved. For an existing product, it often makes sense to:

1. Divide customers on the basis of one or more product-specific behavioral variables; for example, heavy, light, and nonusers of the product category, or loyal users of the firm's brand, loyal users of other brands, nonloyal users, and nonusers.
2. Examine each of the categories derived from step 1 above for differences in benefits sought and such characteristics as demographics and lifestyle. The purpose here is to determine whether the user groups constitute distinct segments and whether additional subsegments exist. This requires marketing research data obtained from commercial sources or surveys conducted by the firm's own research department.

When the strategic objective is to identify possible opportunities for new-product development, a firm proceeds as follows:

1. Determine the needs or benefits sought by different customers.
2. Identify benefit segments that are not satisfied with current products; further, define those groups by behavioral and demographic descriptors. For both consumer and industrial products, the identification of benefit segments usually requires marketing research.

---

[30] For a more detailed discussion of issues in market segmentation and different approaches to segmenting markets, see Henry Assael and A. Marvin Roscoe, Jr., "Approaches to Market Segmentation Analysis," *Journal of Marketing*, October 1976, pp. 67–76; Yoram Wind, "Issues and Advances in Segmentation Research," *Journal of Marketing Research*, August 1978, pp. 317–37; Shirley Young, Leland Ott, and Barbara Feigin, "Some Practical Considerations in Market Segmentation," *Journal of Marketing Research*, August 1978, pp. 405–12; Terry Elrod and Russell S. Winer, "An Empirical Evaluation of Aggregation Approaches for Developing Market Segments," *Journal of Marketing*, Fall 1982, pp. 65–74; Peter R. Dickson, "Person-Situation: Segmentation's Missing Link," *Journal of Marketing*, Fall 1982, pp. 56–63; and Thomas V. Bonoma and Benson P. Shapiro, *Segmenting the Industrial Market* (Lexington, Mass.: Lexington Books, 1983).

For industrial markets, however, potential customers for a new product can sometimes be identified by a firm's salespeople, who encounter requests for applications that cannot be served by the firm's existing products. Indeed, industrial firms often work hand-in-hand with major customers to develop new products designed to meet those customers' needs.

Requirements for effective segmentation

An effective and useful segmentation scheme should define market segments that meet four criteria: *adequate size, measurability, accessibility,* and *differential response to marketing variables*. These criteria are defined in Exhibit 6–15 and discussed below.

Adequate size

When segmenting a market, the manager must make a trade-off. The more narrowly the segments are defined, the more homogeneous the customers within each segment are likely to be. This makes it easier to define their unique needs and to develop specific products and marketing programs to appeal to them. However, the more narrowly a segment is defined, the fewer customers and potential customers it contains. Economies of scale are sacrificed due to shorter production runs and a proliferation of marketing programs.

Analysts argue that some of the American auto industry's problems in recent years were due to the fact that auto makers tried to provide separate products and options for too many narrowly defined market segments to the detriment of their unit costs and profitability. Analysts point out, for example, that 69,120 option combinations were available on the 1982 Ford

EXHIBIT 6 ♦15
Requirements for effective segmentation

1. **Adequate size**—sufficient potential customers in each segment.
   Involves trade-off between customer homogeneity and scale effects.
2. **Measurability**—use of measurable variables as bases for segmentation.
   Need for combination of concrete and abstract descriptors.
3. **Accessibility**—segments defined to facilitate targeting of marketing efforts.
   Segmentation variables must identify members in ways that facilitate their contact.
4. **Differential response**—segments must respond differently to one or more marketing variables.
   Segmentation variables must maximize behavioral differences between segments.

Thunderbird compared to only 32 combinations available on the 1982 Honda Accord, including colors.[31]

Segments should be defined, then, so that they contain enough potential customers to provide sufficient sales revenue to make it worthwhile to develop separate products and marketing programs for one or more of those segments.

Measurability

Concrete, measurable variables are useful bases for segmenting markets. A great deal of information about such variables is often available from secondary sources. For instance, if a segment is defined as women between the ages of 18 and 45 who work outside the home, it would be relatively easy for the marketer to find information about the number of such women in the population. Other relatively available information includes their average household income, and the number who live in a particular metropolitan area, read a certain magazine, or watch a given TV show.

It is more difficult to obtain such information about a segment of customers defined by more abstract, hard-to-measure variables. If a firm defines a segment as male hypochondriacs, for example, it would probably have to conduct its own market survey. Perhaps it would also have to develop its own instrument for measuring hypochondria to determine what proportion of the male population are hypochondriacs and whether they differ from other people in their purchase behaviors or other personal characteristics. Such abstract variables can, however, provide useful information for designing product benefits and promotional appeals. The best segment definitions, therefore, include some combination of concrete and abstract descriptors.

Accessibility

Segmentation leads to increased marketing efficiency only if marketers define the segments so that unique marketing efforts *can* be directed at them. Ideally, the potential customers in a market segment should be concentrated in certain geographic areas, shop at particular stores, and attend to specific media. This would make them accessible through specially designed distribution and promotion strategies.

Unfortunately, many possible segmentation variables do not define accessible customer groups. That is, the variables do not identify customer groups in ways that facilitate accessing the segment members. Suppose, for example, that a firm attempts to market frozen weinerschnitzel to a target market defined as Americans of German descent. This market segment would not be very accessible because few unique advertising media or

---

[31] James Cook, "Where's the Niche?" *Forbes*, September 24, 1984, pp. 54–55; and John Koten, "Giving Buyers Wide Choices May Be Hurting Auto Makers," *The Wall Street Journal*, December 15, 1983, p. 33.

distribution channels are frequented by third- or fourth-generation German-Americans. They watch the same TV programs, read the same magazines, live in the same suburbs, and shop at the same stores as Americans whose ancestors came from Britain, France, or Sweden. Therefore, there would be no gain in marketing efficiency in designing a marketing program to reach this group of customers.

Differential response

Ultimately, the most important criterion for choosing market segmentation variables is that they should define groups of customers who respond differently to one or more of the controllable elements of marketing strategy. The variables should maximize the behavioral differences *between* segments while minimizing the differences among customers within a segment.

It is costly to develop unique products and marketing programs for separate market segments. Marketers can justify such specific programs by increases in marketing efficiency and effectiveness, but only if they reflect meaningful differences in needs, preferences, and attitudes across groups of customers.

SUMMARY

A market aggregation strategy is appropriate when most customers have similar needs and desires. When customers are more diverse, a single standardized product and marketing program does not appeal to many customers who need or want something different. Thus, a firm may lose sales it could have attained if it had offered a wider array of products and programs. Segmentation has become increasingly popular because it reflects the realities faced by firms in most markets, provides information necessary for designing products and marketing programs that are effective in reaching specific groups of customers, identifies opportunities for new product development, and improves the strategic allocation of marketing resources.

The process of segmentation consists of describing market segments in terms of the characteristics of their customers and identifying the different needs or benefits sought by those customers. The variables used to explain the differences in product purchases across segments are referred to as descriptors. Generic descriptors are relevant for both consumer and industrial markets. The more commonly used ones include benefits sought, product usage, loyalty, purchase predisposition, purchase influence, innovativeness, and geographical location.

Segmentation descriptors specific to consumer markets include age, sex, family life cycle, income, occupation, culture, and social class. Industrial markets need to be segmented in two stages. Macrosegmentation divides the market according to the organizational characteristics of the customer. Microsegmentation groups customers by the characteristics of those individuals who influence the purchasing decision. Product usage and geographical locations are examples of descriptors concerned with macrosegmentation while purchase influence, loyalty, and area of expertise are microsegmentation descriptors. The descriptors most commonly used specifically for industrial markets are the personal characteristics of the buying influentials at the micro level and purchasing structure, buying situation, industrial sector, and company size at the macro level.

To be effective and useful, the chosen segmentation scheme must meet four criteria: adequate size, measurability, accessibility, and differential response to marketing variables. The latter is the most important criterion. The variables should maximize the behavioral differences among segments while minimizing the differences among customers included in the same segment.

QUESTIONS

1. Extensive market segmentation is a relatively recent phenomenon. Until about the middle of this century many firms offered a single basic product aimed at the entire mass market (such as Coca-Cola or Levi jeans). But in recent years many firms—including industrial goods manufacturers and services producers as well as consumer products companies—have begun segmenting their markets and developing different products and marketing programs targeted at different segments. Which *environmental changes* have helped spark this increased interest in market segmentation? Which *advantages or benefits* can a firm gain from properly segmenting its market?

2. Is market segmentation always a good idea? Under which conditions, if any, might segmentation be unnecessary or unwise?

3. Can market segmentation be taken too far? What are the *potential disadvantages of oversegmenting* a market? What strategy might a firm pursue when it believes that the market has been broken into too many small segments?

4. Which *variables or descriptors* might be most appropriate for segmenting the markets for the following *consumer products and services*? Explain your reasoning.
   a. Lawn mowers
   b. Frozen entrees or dinners
   c. Breakfast cereals
   d. Financial services

5. Which *variables or descriptors* might be most appropriate for segmenting the markets for the following *industrial goods and services*? Explain your reasoning.
   a. Photocopiers
   b. Floor sweepers
   c. Truck leasing

6. A camera manufacturer has hired you as a consultant to identify major *benefit segments* in the camera market. Which major benefit segments do you think might exist in this market, without actually conducting consumer research? What other information would you want to collect about the potential customers in each segment to provide a useful basis for designing camera models and marketing programs that appeal to each segment?

7. How would you know whether the segmentation variables you identified in question 6 actually define effective and useful segments of customers? What criteria would you use to *evaluate the effectiveness* of your segmentation scheme?

8. Until a few years ago there was only one Coca-Cola. But in recent years the firm has segmented the market for cola-flavored soft drinks. How has Coca-Cola segmented the cola market? How has the firm attempted to appeal to each of those segments in (*a*) product attributes, (*b*) package design, and (*c*) advertising appeals?

9. Suppose you are the marketing manager for a large dinner theater in Minneapolis. Using the information in Exhibit 6–2, which segment or segments of theatergoers would you want to target? Why?

10. In view of your answer to question 9, which actions or policies would you recommend concerning:
    a. Design of the theater's physical facilities
    b. Types of plays to be offered
    c. Ticket prices
    d. Advertising and promotional programs

Chapter ⬥7⬥

Industry and competitor analysis

PEPSI, COKE, AND THE SOFT-DRINK WARS

The U.S. soft-drink industry comprises firms selling flavored carbonated drinks. Since World War II the industry has experienced explosive growth. Per capita sales are pushing 45 gallons a year—up some 250 percent since the early 60s—and retail revenues in 1984 were in excess of $26 billion. Analysts attribute this surge in demand to several factors, including a strong growth in real disposable personal income (especially during the 60s), a substantial increase in the number of teenagers, larger container sizes, heavy advertising, greater product availability, and lifestyle changes that include more fast foods.[1]

The industry is highly concentrated—six companies account for nearly 80 percent of total sales. Pepsi and Coke together account for about 60 percent. Private labels are relatively unimportant (less than 1 percent); and small local bottlers are fast disappearing.

In recent years the growth in U.S. demand has slowed due to a shift in demographics—the U.S. population is aging—and to sluggish growth in personal income. The industry also has achieved maximum distribution and has about exhausted its bottle-size limits. Even so, some segment opportunities still remain, including diet products for older people, a growing number of fast-food outlets, convenience stores, and the international scene.

As the market demand for soft drinks slowed, the competition increased—especially between Coke and Pepsi. This cola war is being fought on every front. Both companies have rolled out new products, such as Pepsi's Slice (a juice-added soft drink), at enormous expense. Coca-Cola even brought out New Coke, using a sweeter-tasting formula, in an attempt to hold off Pepsi's grow-

---

[1] Based on "The Soft Drink Industry in 1985," in C. Roland Christensen, Kenneth R. Andrews, Joseph L. Bower, Richard G. Hamermesh, and Michael E. Porter, *Business Policy* (Homewood, Ill.: Richard D. Irwin, 1987), pp. 277–305. Also see "Seven-Up Uncaps a Cola—and an Industry Feud," *Business Week*, March 22, 1981, p. 96; Ann B. Fisher, "Coke's Brand-Loyalty Lesson," *Fortune*, August 5, 1985, p. 44; Amy Dunkin, "Pepsi's Marketing Magic: Why Nobody Does It Better," *Business Week*, February 10, 1986, p. 82; "Wayne Calloway's Nonstop Cash Machine," *Forbes*, September 7, 1987, p. 35; Thomas Moore, "He Put the Kick Back into Coke," *Fortune*, October 26, 1987, p. 47; Jennifer Lawrence, "Cola Wars Move In-Store," *Advertising Age*, November 9, 1987, p. 4; Ford S. Worthy, "Pop Goes Their Profit," *Fortune*, February 15, 1988, p. 68; Paul Hemp, "Soft Drinks Get the Hard Sell in Europe," *The Wall Street Journal*, November 21, 1988, p. 84; and Ira Teinowitz, "Royal Crown Targets Adults," *Advertising Age*, December 3, 1988, p. 58

continued

ing popularity—especially among youths. Some three months after introducing New Coke, however, the company was forced to bring back its old "Classic" Coke. Today, Classic Coke outsells New Coke (now just plain Coke) about 10 to 1.

Both companies spend large sums on advertising. In 1987, Coca-Cola spent $141 million and PepsiCo $135 million in measured media (TV, radio, and print). These figures do not include in-store promotions and the like. Pepsi has relied on Michael Jackson and other celebrities to promote its products on TV. The large sums spent by the two cola leaders have made life difficult for the Royal Crown Cola Company, which has only a 2.9 percent market share of the soft-drink business. In late 1988, Royal Crown announced it would focus its $10 million advertising budget on adults—it would drop out of the competition for the teenage segment. Increasingly, the cola wars are moving into stores; and it is difficult to find a time when a Coke or Pepsi-Cola product is not being discounted.

There is also considerable action in the international market. To achieve greater sales, Pepsi recently bought Seven-Up's international division for $246 million, which increased its overseas sales by 20 percent. Even so, Coke's lead (it holds an 80 percent share of the European cola market) seems safe. Coke, too, is spending vast sums of money to take advantage of the increasing demand for soft drinks in Europe. This demand is due, in part, to the growth of fast-food outlets and the introduction of low-calorie soft drinks. With international per-capita consumption only 15 percent of U.S. consumption, Coke believes it should attempt to increase demand. If only modestly successful, Coke could double its present international size by the year 2000.

The war between Pepsi and Coke is waged primarily in food stores, where the two giants are about equal. Coke continues to dominate the fountain and vending segments. In the food-store segment, Pepsi and Coke have gained share (collectively, they hold about two thirds of this market) at the expense of smaller competitors. Thus, their sales increased by 7 percent in 1987, while the combined sales of Dr Pepper, Seven-Up, Royal Crown, and Cadbury-Schweppes decreased by about 9 percent. Exhibit 7–1 shows the shares of the U.S. market held by the various soft-drink companies.

Seven-Up and Dr Pepper have tried to reposition themselves with mixed results. The former promoted its product as the "uncola" drink—a substitute for the cola beverages that account for over 60 percent of industry sales. Dr Pepper repositioned itself from a regional to a national brand. Both restructured their franchise systems by using more Coke and Pepsi bottlers. In 1986, Hicks and Haas, a leveraged buy-out firm, bought Dr Pepper, Seven-Up, and A&W (primarily root beer) brands. Collectively, these brands account for some 12 percent of industry sales.

continued

concluded

EXHIBIT   7 ◆ 1

U.S. market shares held by various companies in the soft-drink industry (1987)

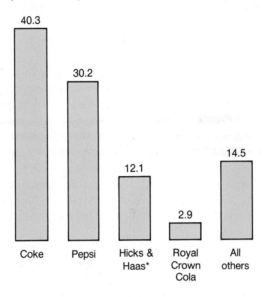

*Includes Dr Pepper, Seven-Up, and A&W

Source: Ford S. Worthy, "Pop Goes Their Profit," *Fortune,* February 15, 1988, p. 68; and Ira Teinowitz, "Royal Crown Targets Adults," *Advertising Age,* December 5, 1988, p. 58.

This industry example indicates how important the competitive environment is in strategy formulation. The major players in the soft-drink industry are clearly affected by the actions of each other as well as by their resources, including their market power. As an industry matures and its growth rate slows, companies are forced to pay increased attention to designing marketing strategies to exploit their competitors' weaknesses.

Two major considerations impact strategy formulation strongly: industry attractiveness and factors determining the firm's competitive position in the industry. It is not enough to determine industry attractiveness solely in terms of long-term profitability. We must also understand the forces that make it attractive or unattractive, such as changing demographics and lifestyle in the soft-drink industry. These forces critically influence the way the industry functions, where it is going, and what a business must do if it is to make money long term.

Industries vary substantially in their attractiveness. Some, such as medical lasers, are in robust health, full of opportunities and appear to have a bright future. Others, such as railroad locomotives, are stagnant or in decline. Industries also vary in their competitiveness. Some are so competitive that it is difficult for even a top sales performer to make large returns, as in children's shoes. The resources required to compete successfully also vary a great deal across industries.

The factors determining the position of a business within an industry evolve from the interaction of the strengths and weaknesses of a firm with those of its chief rivals—say, for instance, the position of Coke versus that of Pepsi-Cola. Knowing the competitive position, strategy, and the strengths and weaknesses of close rivals helps the firm to better anticipate what the rivals will do in the future and how they will respond to the firm's moves.

This chapter deals with the process of analyzing an industry in depth. The first step requires identifying the relevant industry and specifying strategic groups. The second step involves a structural analysis within an industry based on strategic groups; and the third examines the bases of competition. The final step is an analysis of close rivals—those within the same strategic group—to understand their competitive position, objectives and strategies, and their strengths and weaknesses. Exhibit 7–2 outlines the process.

IDENTIFICATION OF INDUSTRY AND STRATEGIC GROUPS

An industry analysis starts by defining the relevant industry and its strategic groups. This enables the firm to better position its offerings and anticipate the actions of close rivals.[2]

Industries comprise firms that produce similar products. This does not mean that all products in an industry are close substitutes for each other. Different market segments need different benefit bundles—and thus different products. Industry membership alone does not indicate which firms compete with each other nor the extent of their rivalry. Much depends on how the industry is defined and the level of aggregation used.

For example, the carbonated soft-drink industry produces colas, root beers, ginger ales, and fruit flavors. These products come in diet or regular form, and some are caffeine free. There are more than 50 soda concentrate producing and marketing firms in the United States, but the top four (Coca-Cola, Pepsi-Cola, Dr Pepper-Seven-Up, and Royal Crown) account for over 85 percent of industry sales. With the exception of Coke and Pepsi, these firms compete only on a limited basis involving one or more products.

---

[2] See Michael E. Porter, *Competitive Strategy* (New York: Free Press, 1980), pp. 129–45.

EXHIBIT   7 ◆ 2

Industry and competitor analysis process

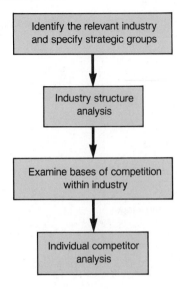

```
┌─────────────────────────────┐
│ Identify the relevant industry │
│ and specify strategic groups   │
└─────────────────────────────┘
              │
              ▼
┌─────────────────────────────┐
│     Industry structure       │
│         analysis             │
└─────────────────────────────┘
              │
              ▼
┌─────────────────────────────┐
│  Examine bases of competition │
│        within industry        │
└─────────────────────────────┘
              │
              ▼
┌─────────────────────────────┐
│    Individual competitor      │
│          analysis             │
└─────────────────────────────┘
```

We get a different alignment of products and firms if we define the soft-drink industry as consisting of carbonated *and* noncarbonated products. This definition adds fruit juices, vegetable juices, and bottled water to the list of products. (Note how in recent years both Pepsi and Coke have added sodas combined with fruit juices.) This higher level of aggregation adds several hundred firms to our industry listing—including Campbell Soup, Kraft, Libby's, Del Monte, General Foods, Welch, Hunts, and Perrier. Now the number of products, subtypes, market segments, and firms has become so huge that identifying competitors simply on industry membership is meaningless.

The data used to analyze an industry are well known. They include the number of firms, their sales, profitability, and market share; presence and degree of vertical integration (both forward and backward); channels of distribution; ease of entry and exit; and bases of competition. Where major segments are present, much of these data must be collected by individual segment.

The identification of strategic groups makes it easier for an analyst to learn more about the industry's structure. A **strategic group** consists of firms pursuing similar strategies; that is, employing a similar mix of strategy elements.

Because of this similarity, firms within the same group actively compete with one another. For example, Coke and Pepsi follow much the same strategy with respect to markets served, products and product line, price, channels, advertising, in-store promotions, and personal selling; thus, they

EXHIBIT   7 ◆ 3

Map of strategic groups in the U.S. chainsaw industry

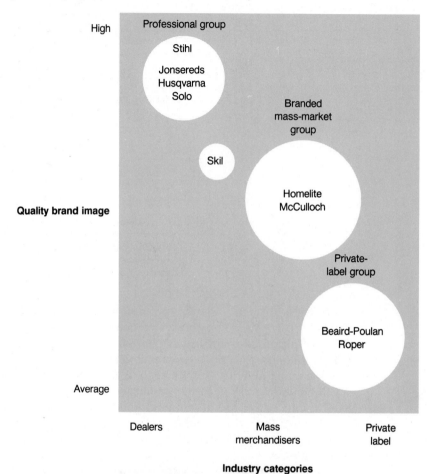

Source: George S. Day, *Strategic Market Planning* (St. Paul: West Publishing, 1984), p. 66.

constitute a strategic group. In contrast, Seven-Up and Dr Pepper sell essentially a single flavor to all market segments, using primarily Coke and Pepsi franchised bottlers. They use advertising and personal selling in ways similar to Coke and Pepsi but spend far less. For another example of strategic groups, see Exhibit 7–3.

A strategic group is analyzed in the hope that the firms in it are enough alike to react the same to environmental change and competitive moves. Using strategic groups facilitates the competitive analysis because each firm does not have to be analyzed separately. More important, it identifies close rivals who compete in similar ways.

The differences and similarities that define groups can involve any combination of strategic elements: markets served (increasingly this includes overseas markets), length of line (specialization), product differentiation and quality, branding, channels, technological leadership, integration, costs, price, service, and relationship to a parent company. Firms also differ in their objectives and in their structural characteristics (such as size and diversification). Thus, different groups emphasize different market segments and strategy mixes in their competitive relationships.

The more common elements used (often in combination) as the basis for identifying strategic groups are: markets served, products, and distribution. We discuss each of these elements below.

Markets served

Differences here can be based on the number and type of segments served. Only a few firms in a given industry attempt to service all major market segments with a variety of products and marketing programs. To serve all segments is very expensive; and firms that do are large and usually international in scope. In the soft-drink industry, only Coke and Pepsi attempt to serve all segments with a complete array of products sold in a variety of container types and sizes. Seven-Up—despite its efforts to market a noncola-type product—caters primarily to the market segment preferring a lemon-lime flavor. In the automotive industry, only Ford and General Motors would qualify as full-coverage companies. In contrast, a "specialist" strategic group that serves only the high-quality, expensive segment includes Mercedes-Benz, BMW, and Jaguar.

Firms are also often classed on the basis of their geographical markets: international, national, and regional/local. Coke and Pepsi are global; Dr Pepper and Seven-Up have limited overseas exposure. Banks can be classed as international or national; beer companies are often grouped on a national basis (Miller, Budweiser) or regionally (Stroh's, Olympia). Retail chains are often identified along geographic lines (Wal-Mart started out as a southern mass-merchandiser chain).

If served markets are defined by price, quality, or size preferences, then another important basis exists for setting up different strategic groups. For example, with the price/quality attribute many industries come to mind, including watches (Omega versus Timex); men's clothing (Oxford versus Kuppenheimer); motel chains (Hilton versus Days Inn). As to such attributes as product size, examples include such industries as computers (mainframe or PCs); diesel engines (over-the-road trucks or automobiles); motorcycles (heavy-duty police vehicles or racing bikes).

Products

The differences here can be expressed by product, length of line, price, product differentiation, or some combination thereof. These dimensions are similar to if not the same as those used to differentiate firms on the basis of markets served. An example of product differences is in the soft-drink industry, where only Pepsi and Coke market a full line of products including colas, flavored soft drinks, and carbonated juices. Another example is the gun industry, where companies produce handguns, long guns, or ammunition. The hand gun segment is dominated by Colt, Smith and Wesson, and Sturm, Ruger; in long guns and ammunition the leaders are Remington and Winchester.

Product differentiation, higher price, and a short line often go together. For example, Carpenter Technology makes highly sophisticated steel that sells for up to $15,000 a ton, 30 times the price of run-of-the-mill carbon steel. Dofasco dominates the Canadian sheet-steel market, turning out rust-resistant metals for autos, appliances, and other consumer goods.[3] Other product attributes include size (number of aircraft seats, truckload capacity), speed (printers), and power (diesel marine motors).

Distribution channels

Firms within the same industry often vary in their channels of distribution. Thus, Pepsi and Coke have elaborate franchise systems that are used by Dr Pepper and Seven-Up. Some tire companies are integrated forward (they control their own retail outlets, such as B. F. Goodrich). Others rely completely on independent and chain retailers (Dunlop and Michelin). Strategic groups can be defined on the basis of these distribution systems.

IDENTIFICATION OF POTENTIAL COMPETITORS

It is not sufficient to identify present competitors; a firm must also consider *potential* marketplace entrants. According to Aaker, the primary sources of new entrants are firms likely to do the following:

1. Expand their geographical market—as in the expansion of Wal-Mart to the East Coast.
2. Expand their product line—as when IBM entered the PC market.
3. Integrate forward—as when foreign and domestic steel mills buy steel service centers in the United States.
4. Integrate backward—as when a supermarket chain sets up its own private-label production activity (such as Safeway).

---

[3] "Some Steel Firms Profit in Declining Industry by Narrowing Product Lines," *The Wall Street Journal*, January 24, 1985, p. 4.

5. Seek a merger or buy-out because of inadequate resources to exploit an attractive market—as Hicks & Haas did in acquiring Dr Pepper, Seven-Up, and A&W, thereby becoming the third-largest soft-drink company in America.[4]

Strategic groups can be helpful in defining potential future competitors. For example, McKinsey studied the effects of deregulation on the brokerage, airline, trucking, railroad, and business terminals industries.[5] The study concluded that survivor firms (potential competitors) would belong to one of these three strategic groups:

1. Large full-line national companies featuring differentiated products at an attractive price: Merrill Lynch (brokerage), Delta (airlines), Consolidated Freight Ways (trucking), Burlington Northern (railroads), and Western Electric (business terminals).

2. Low-cost producers who are often new industry entrants after deregulation: Charles Schwab (brokerage), Midway Air (airlines), and Oki (business terminals).

3. Specialty (focused) firms with services targeting a particular market segment: Goldman Sachs (brokerage), Air Wisconsin (airlines), Ryder Systems (trucking), Santa Fe (railroads), and Northern Telecom (business terminals).

The evolution of a strategic group consisting of large, full-line competitors (group one above) usually takes place in three phases. In the first phase, smaller firms attempt to gain market share by merging so they can compete with the larger firms. This is what Hicks & Haas tried to do with its acquisitions. While all of its brands do not compete head-on with Pepsi and Coke, the merger does have some economies of scale and distribution synergies. In phase two, the strong firms make selective acquisitions to develop a full line of differentiated products and complete national coverage. This is what Pepsi hoped to accomplish by trying to acquire Seven-Up; but it was prevented in doing so by the federal government. Phase three involves interindustry mergers and acquisitions. For example, in the brokerage industry Sears purchased Dean Witter/Reynolds and Prudential acquired Bache Halsy Stuart.[6] Thus, firms currently in group one should keep a close watch on members of the other two groups to anticipate whether they might become members of group one through internal development or acquisition.

The second strategic group consists of the low-cost producers who entered the industry after deregulation. Their strategy consisted essentially of offering a minimum no-frills product line targeting the price-sensitive market segment. The third group consists of those companies offering a specialized service to a specifc customer group.

---

[4] David A. Aaker, *Strategic Market Management* (New York: John Wiley & Sons, 1984), p. 61.

[5] Donald C. Warte III, "Deregulation and the Banking Industry," *Bankers Magazine*, January–February 1982, pp. 76–85.

[6] Ibid.

INDUSTRY STRUCTURE ANALYSIS

The bases of competition and its intensity derive largely from the interplay of five competitive forces: present competitors, potential competitors, the bargaining power of buyers or customers, the bargaining power of suppliers, and substitute products. Exhibit 7–4 shows these forces, which we discuss next. Collectively, on an interactive basis they determine the industry's long-term attractiveness as measured by return on investment. The mix of forces explains why some industries are consistently more profitable than others. Also, these forces provide insights into which resources are required and which strategies should be adopted if the firm is to be successful in a given industry.[7]

The strength of the individual forces varies from industry to industry and over time within the same industry. In the soft-drink industry, the key forces are present competitors and substitute products—the latter in the form of coffee and tea. In the containerized ocean shipping industry, the threat of potential entrants and the rivalry between existing firms—on an international basis—are key forces. In the packaging industry, substitute products, such as metal cans, plastic containers, and paper cartons, dominate.

Present competitors

We are concerned here with the intensity and the form of the rivalry among existing firms within the industry. Rivalry occurs because a competitor acts to improve its standing within the industry or protects its position by

EXHIBIT   7 ♦ 4

The major forces that determine industry competition

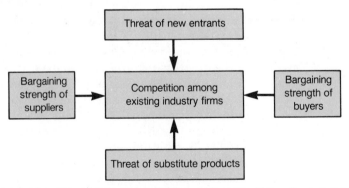

Source: Adapted from Michael F. Porter, "Industry Structure and Competitive Strategy: Keys to Profitability," *Financial Analysts Journal,* July–August 1980, p. 33.

---

[7] Based to a considerable extent on Michael F. Porter, "Industry Structure and Competitive Strategy: Key to Profitability," *Financial Analysts Journal,* July–August 1980, pp. 30–41.

reacting to moves made by other firms. Thus, firms are mutually dependent—what the firm does impacts others, and vice versa. This is certainly the case with Coke's and Pepsi's attempts to gain overall share via new products, massive advertising outlay, and almost continuous price deals.

Factors responsible for the intensity of competition within an industry include investment intensity, product differentiation, switching costs, industry growth, industry structure, and exit barriers. Each of these is discussed briefly below.

Investment intensity

By *investment intensity*, we mean the amount of fixed and working capital required to produce a dollar of sales. High intensity requires firms to operate at or near capacity as much of the time as possible. This puts a strong downward pressure on prices in an effort to attract business when demand slackens. Not surprisingly, high-investment-intensity businesses are on average much less profitable than businesses with a lower level of investment per dollar of sales (see Exhibit 7–5).[8]

EXHIBIT 7 ◆ 5

Return on investment by investment intensity

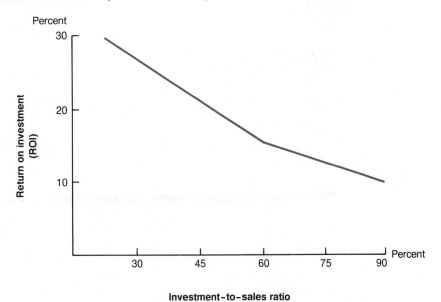

Investment–to–sales ratio

Source: Adapted with permission of The Free Press, a Division of Macmillan, Inc. from *The PIMS Principles: Linking Strategy to Performance* by Robert D. Buzzell and Bradley T. Gale. Copyright © 1987 by The Free Press.

---

[8] Robert D. Buzzell and Bradley T. Gale, *The PIMS Principles* (New York: Free Press, 1987), chap. 7.

The reason for this negative effect is that volume is essentially a prime determinant of profitability; price wars erupt when supply exceeds demand. In good years, when most companies operate at capacity, the industry may be quite profitable. But when the good and bad years are averaged, the overall result is a low return on investment. Examples of such industries include chemicals, steel, and metal containers.[9]

In the case of the soft-drink industry, large sums must be spent in advertising and promotion—thereby inhibiting potential new entrants and low-share holders. Investments in company-owned bottling plants can also be large. For instance, Coke's 49 percent share of Coca-Cola Enterprises (its own franchises) is worth about $1.3 billion.[10]

If capacity can be increased only in large increments (as in a new steel mill), the industry is apt to be subject to even more intense price competition. Further, if the plant size required for production efficiency increases due to improvements in process technology, larger firms opt for new plants—even though they increase the industry's capacity well beyond short-term demand.

Product differentiation and/or switching costs

The less differentiated the product, the more important price and service become. Thus, industries producing commodity products such as steel and aluminum are susceptible to price competition—and especially so when high-investment intensity is also present. If a product can be differentiated, then buyer loyalty reduces the likelihood of price reductions. As might be expected, price competition in the metal container industry is severe. The need for high utilization of expensive equipment coupled with the desire to avoid line changeovers led to high volume discounts on standard items. In the soft-drink industry, a sizable number of consumers see little difference between Coke and Pepsi; thus, discounting is prevalent in food stores. If a product can be differentiated, then buyer loyalty reduces the likelihood of price reductions. This has been the case with BMW and Mercedes-Benz automobiles.

Switching costs, or the costs of changing suppliers, inhibit competition. This is the case with changing computer mainframe hardware, for instance, because the software also has to be changed. Another example is the decision made by Roadway Services to challenge United Parcel Service's domination of the growing small-package delivery business. Roadway intends to use price as its primary weapon. But Roadway "will still have a tough time competing against UPS's untouchable reputation for reliability. Many ship-

---

[9] Ibid.

[10] Thomas Moore, "He Put the Kick Back into Coke," *Fortune*, October 26, 1987, p. 51.

ping managers are reluctant to switch to an unproven service. Says one: 'It would take an unbelievable arm-twist to get me to dump UPS.'"[11]

Once a fast-food chain has signed a contract to serve either Pepsi or Coke products, it is difficult to switch given the equipment investment and, more important, the association in the consumer's mind of the brand of soft drink sold and the name of the chain.

Industry growth
If industry growth is slow, then a firm's growth can only come by taking sales away from a competitor, as is increasingly the case in the metal can business. Coupled with high investment intensity and a lack of product differentiation, the lack of industry growth can be a particularly disruptive force leading to bitter warfare between large rivals.

Industry structure
The number of firms and their market-share positions have a strong effect on competition. If an industry has but a few competitors holding approximately equal shares, there is likely to be considerable instability, as no one firm clearly dominates or has the power to punish those who step out of line. This is the case in the soft-drink industry where Pepsi and Coke hold approximately the same market share in the food-store segment. While the two firms compete aggressively in the vending, fountain, and international areas, the war is mainly being fought in food stores.

Exit barriers
Exit barriers are factors that can keep companies engaged in a business despite negative profitability. Management's emotional ties to a particular business because of history and tradition ("we've always been in the printing business") and loyalty to employees and managers can become exit barriers. Foreign governments have prevented some firms from exiting an industry as a matter of national economic policy—as Sweden has done with its shipping industry.

Another reason firms stay in an industry—probably the most important reason—is that the fixed assets involved have little liquidation value or high conversion costs. Under such conditions the firm does better by continuing to operate the business than by exiting it. This was the case with certain large manufacturing businesses (such as farm equipment and the metal container business) where the assets were too large to be absorbed by a competitor and too specialized to be converted to another purpose. The fact that the business is often substantially in debt to the banks makes exiting even more difficult.

---

[11] Dan Cook, "Two Rivals Disturb United Parcel's 'Sheltered Life,'" *Business Week*, February 11, 1985, p. 34.

When the business is strategically interrelated to a firm's other businesses and considered a core unit, it is difficult to think of divestment even if the business is not profitable. For instance, even though 3M is losing money on its videotapes, it is reluctant to abandon the business. It sees electronic storage media as an essential part of its business and has a commitment to a full line of electronic memory products. This, of course, raises exit barriers—which, in turn, keeps the excess capacity in the industry and puts further pressure on price.

Potential competitors

A second major driving force affecting competition is a new industry entry. New competitors add new capacity to the industry, bringing with them a desire to gain market share, and making competition more intense. Experience effects, capital requirements, product differentiation, distribution channels, and switching costs all affect the likelihood of entry. Each of these is discussed below.

Experience effects

Strong economies of scale and learning effects make entry more difficult. It takes time to obtain the volume and learning required to yield a low relative cost per unit. This means that the entrant must accept a strong cost disadvantage from the outset and heavily subsidize the new entry. In the soft-drink industry, Pepsi and Coke enjoy economies of scale in their bottling operations as well as in their advertising, in-store promotions, and new products. These economies would make it extremely difficult for a new entry to compete successfully.

If the firms already present are vertically integrated, then it is even more expensive for new firms to enter. Also, if the existing firms share their output with related businesses, the problem of overcoming the cost disadvantage is made much more difficult. For example, a firm producing an electronic component used in its own TV and stereo lines has a potential cost advantage over a firm that does not have such integration. But integration can have a negative effect, as was the case with American car manufacturers compared to Japanese auto makers. The former bought up many of their component suppliers over the years and thus could not seek less expensive off-shore suppliers. This was not the case with the Japanese, who opted not to own their parts suppliers.

Capital requirements

If the industry requires heavy investment intensity at the outset (such as building a large plant with sophisticated equipment), then entry will be limited to large corporations that may well prefer to acquire an existing competitor. This was the case when Philip Morris acquired Seven-Up and spent large sums of money attempting to increase share at the expense of Pepsi and Coke.

Product differentiation

This factor typically favors established firms, because it leads to customer loyalty that results from product features, customer service, and/or promotion. Thus, a new entrant must not only develop a unique product, but also must spend heavily to develop favorable consumer attitudes toward it. Certainly this is true in the soft-drink industry, where existing firms have an enormous investment in brand identification and preference.

Distribution channels

Gaining distribution is particularly difficult and costly in some industries. Retailers are reluctant to add additional brands, given a scarcity of shelf space and the capital required for inventory. This is particularly true during the mature stage of the product life cycle. Industrial goods sellers find much the same problem with local or regional distributors. Thus, in either situation the entrant may find it difficult to persuade the accepted channels to stock and sell a new product without extra margins, trade allowances, and subsidizing of inventories through longer credit terms. This explains to a considerable extent why Pepsi and Coke are increasing their ownership of their domestic bottling networks. By doing so, the two companies improve their ability to move new products into the trade more quickly as well as to ensure the availability of older products.[12]

Switching costs

A buyer incurs these one-time costs in switching from one supplier to another. If these involve considerable monies, retraining of personnel, or risk, then the entrant must offer a substantially improved product or a much lower cost to get users to switch. Examples of switching costs include revising certain software programs when buying a new computer system; a retailer's costs in disposing of a substantial inventory when switching to a new line of expensive men's suits; retraining mechanics to service a new make of over-the-road truck; and the difficulties involved in switching to another cola brand by a fast-food chain.

---

[12] Timothy R. Smith, "Coke, Pepsi Seek Control over Bottling," *The Wall Street Journal,* July 3, 1986, p. 6.

Threat of substitute products

This is the third major force determining competition within an industry. Substitutes are alternative *product types* (*not* brands) that perform essentially the same function. Examples include gas for electricity, margarine for butter, and plastic for glass or metal containers. Substitute products put a ceiling on the profitability of an industry by limiting the price that can be charged—especially when demand exceeds supply. Substitute products that are a significant improvement in price or performance represent a considerable threat, assuming switching cost is not important. Thus, in the metal container industry, aluminum is a substitute for tin plate and constrains the prices charged by tin plate producers.

Bargaining strength of suppliers

The bargaining power of suppliers over firms in an industry is the fourth major determinant of industry competition. It is exercised largely through increased prices. And its impact can be significant. This is particularly the case when a limited number of suppliers service a number of different industries. Their power is increased if switching costs and the prices of substitutes are high. Suppliers are especially important when their product is a large part of the buyer's value added. For instance, the cost of tin plate is over 60 percent of the value added by producers of metal cans. Another example of the strength of suppliers is in the highly concentrated oil industry, which sells to a diverse group of industries. It sells a product that often represents a significant cost to the buyer and for which there is no close substitute product type. That is, it is usually expensive to convert to gas or coal. In the soft-drink industry, however, suppliers of sugar, flavors, and containers are largely undifferentiated and have little power. Suppliers of metal cans, for instance, are constrained from raising their prices too high by the ability of soft-drink and beer customers to integrate backward and produce their own containers.

Bargaining strength of buyers

An industry's customers constantly look for reduced prices, improved product quality, and added services, and thus can affect competition within an industry. Buyers play individual suppliers against one another in their efforts to obtain these concessions. This is certainly the case with some fast-food chains in their dealings with Pepsi and Coke. The extent to which buyers succeed in their bargaining efforts depends on several factors, including:

1. *Concentration.* A few buyers can account for a large portion of the supplier industry's sales, thereby bringing about certain concessions. For example, large food, beer, and soft-drink companies buy a high percentage of metal cans. Their

bargaining power is even stronger if suppliers have high investment costs, as in the metal container industry.

2. *Switching costs.* The presence of switching costs reduces the bargaining power of buyers.

3. *Threat of backward integration.* When buyers can threaten such integration, they can often demand and achieve certain concessions, as in the case of the soft-drink industry.

4. *Buyer profitability.* If buyers earn low profits and the product involved is an important part of their costs, then more aggressive bargaining is likely to take place. For instance, metal cans represent as much as 45 percent of a beverage manufacturer's cost. Thus, Coke and Pepsi are highly motivated to pressure their can suppliers to lower prices.

5. *Product importance.* When the purchased product or service is important to the performance of the buyer's product, the buyer's bargaining power is diminished. For example, highly sensitive, expensive electronic laboratory test equipment is critical to the R&D efforts of pharmaceutical firms—a fact that limits their bargaining power when dealing with the suppliers of such equipment.

Use of strategic groups in analyzing intraindustry competition

Earlier we noted that firms with similar strategies are likely to react much the same to environmental trends and competitive moves. Also, for those entering an industry, identifying and studying the various strategic groups would indicate which one to target. The same applies to firms in an industry seeking to enhance their long-term profitability by moving to another group—as Seven-Up tried (unsuccessfully) to do with its 7UP Gold drink aimed at cola drinkers. Further, knowledge of the characteristics of a given group provides insights into the bases of competition between and within the individual groups. This, in turn, indicates which resources are needed for success.

The barriers inhibiting the movement of firms among strategic groups are much the same as those inhibiting entry into the industry. The nature of these barriers explains why firms within the same industry have different levels of profitability and why some firms persist in using the same strategy even though it has not been highly profitable. Firms operating in groups with high mobility barriers should be more profitable than those with lower mobility barriers—it is more difficult for new or existing firms to enter. If it weren't for mobility barriers, less successful firms in the industry could quickly adopt the strategies used by the more successful ones. For instance, Dr Pepper might adopt the strategies of Coke and Pepsi, with their large franchise networks, long product lines, and strong brand images. Some firms have created their own unique strategic group, complete with high mobility barriers, and have prospered accordingly—for example, IBM (in its mainframe product features and service) and L'eggs pantyhose (supermarket distribution).

Other than the number of strategic groups—and their sizes—two major forces determine the extent of rivalry among groups. The first, and most important, is the **market interdependence** or substitution effects among groups; that is, the degree to which groups compete for the same customers or compete for customers in unique market segments. High interdependence leads to strong rivalry, as in the metal container and soft-drink industries.

The second important factor impacting rivalry is **product differentiation.** If the different groups pursue divergent product strategies, then the competition among groups is less than if high substitutability exists among offerings. In the metal container industry, can manufacturers do not compete head-on with foil manufacturers, for example. In the soft-drink industry, a substantial portion of consumers have switched from Seven-Up to Pepsi and Coke's cola products.

BASES OF COMPETITION

The key bases of competition represent what a business must do (what activities it must undertake) if it is to be successful. They are often referred to as **strategy elements,** and as such are important in strategy formulation, for they help to define which resources are needed.

The relative importance of the different bases of competition varies widely from industry to industry and across strategic groups within an industry. For example, the competitive bases in the computer and laundry detergent industries are very different. In the soft-drink industry, the more important elements include advertising, in-store promotions, product availability, and new-product development.

Typically, each element has several dimensions. For example, the product itself is always a critical strategy element that has much to do with success or failure in a given industry. Too often we think of product primarily on the basis of how its physical characteristics can be differentiated and ignore or minimize the importance of service features. Other important dimensions to consider are the extent to which a full line is needed and the importance of new products. These latter two dimensions, as well as container type and size, are important in the soft-drink industry.

A firm must consider what resources it needs to make a given strategy element successful. Product differentiation, for example, requires not only product engineering skills, but also management capabilities to decide which combination of product attributes is apt to be most successful. It takes other resources to effectively communicate the product's differences to the target audiences and to obtain the needed distribution. Unfortunately, Seven-Up has lacked these essential resources in its attempt to reposition its product as a strong cola substitute.

The sports shoe industry requires a number of operational strategy elements, including low-cost overseas sourcing (manufacturing). This requires decentralized quality control, plants in various countries to spread the risks, accurate forecasting to avoid overages and underages in production, funds or credit to finance the large buildup in preseason inventory, and strong physical logistics capabilities.

A large company—such as Nike—needs a full line of running, walking, exercise, basketball, and tennis shoes for men and women and perhaps children, at a variety of prices. This is necessary because of scale effects and the need of large retailers to carry a full line of sports shoes. R&D skills, a sense of style, and fashion trends are obviously important, too. Large advertising investments are necessary to presell the product, as mass merchandisers provide little sales support. Merchandising is also important here. The salesforce must be versatile enough to sell specialty shoe/sports stores, department stores, and mass merchandisers and be large enough to handle thousands of accounts.

The scope of a successful mass seller in this industry probably must be international to permit a varied response to acts of aggression by other international companies. An example is responding to a price cut here by a European company—such as Adidas—by cutting price in the aggressor's home country.

Competitive positioning

After assessing the forces affecting competition in an industry and how they affect the way firms compete, managers can better identify their own company's competitive strengths and weaknesses. Managers must take these into account when devising business-unit and marketing strategies for product-market entries in the industry.

At the business-unit level, managers can pursue either adaptive or proactive strategies. An *adaptive strategy* takes as given the competitive forces at work in the industry and tries to position the business unit so that its capabilities provide the best defense against those forces. A *proactive strategy* takes the offense and attempts to alter the balance of competitive forces through strategic moves, thereby improving the business's position relative to its competitors.[13] This is what Seven-Up tried to do with 7UP Gold.

Adaptive business strategy

An adaptive strategy weighs the business's strengths and weaknesses against the industry's existing competitive structure. It builds defenses against the major competitive forces or finds positions in the industry where the competitive forces are the weakest. Crown Cork & Seal did so by concentrating on "hard to protect" can applications that required special characteristics—such as beer cans and aerosol containers because of their active ingredients.

---

[13] Michael E. Porter, "How Competitive Forces Shape Strategy," *Harvard Business Review*, March–April 1979, pp. 137–45.

It also located its plants near its customers to save transport charges and provide overnight product availability.

Knowing a business's capabilities and the competitive forces at work in the industry can help a manager identify areas in which the business should confront competitors directly and those where it should not. Royal Crown Cola, for instance, does not have the promotion funds to confront Pepsi and Coke directly and thus has chosen to focus on adults rather than on teenagers, who are Coke and Pepsi's primary advertising target.

Dr Pepper's recent gains within the soft-drink industry show how a realistic assessment of business strengths and weaknesses when coupled with a sound industry analysis can produce successful marketing strategies. The company differentiated itself with a narrow line of beverages built around an unusual flavor. It then took advantage of its different flavor to "piggyback" on Coke and Pepsi bottlers who wanted a full line to sell to customers.

While it thus avoided confronting the giants in its product line and distribution network, Dr Pepper tackled them directly in its marketing program. Because of lower relative costs and the high value of a market-share point, Dr Pepper reasoned that a large advertising campaign would pay off. The campaign emphasized the product's uniqueness and helped to build strong brand identification and customer loyalty as well as stronger dealer support. Although these efforts only raised its share by a few points, its strategy of avoiding costly direct competition with major competitors has enabled it to establish an enviable earnings record.[14]

Proactive business strategy

When dealing with the forces that drive competition within an industry, a business can devise a strategy that takes the offensive—a strategy that attempts to alter the nature of competitive forces. For example, by making capital investments in large-scale facilities or in vertical integration, a firm can raise entry barriers and reduce the power of suppliers. Or its innovative marketing efforts can change the bases of competition and give the firm a competitive advantage through increased brand recognition and product differentiation. IBM's emphasis on customer service during the early days of the mainframe industry, for example, not only changed the nature of competition in that industry but also gave the company a differential advantage and a customer base that has remained loyal to this day.

Adapting to, or trying to change, the major competitive forces in an industry is an important concern when formulating a business strategy. It is also a critical part of a successful marketing strategy for an individual product-market entry. We devote Chapter 10 to a detailed discussion of competitive positioning at the product-market level.

---

[14] Ibid.

INDIVIDUAL COMPETITOR ANALYSIS

Exhibit 7–6 outlines the major steps in analyzing individual competitors. Following the identification of present and potential key rivals, this analysis consists of examining their characteristics, objectives, strategies, performance to date, and their strengths and weaknesses to gain insights into their future behavior. The purpose of this process is to predict the future behavior of each competitor. Managers need to assess the likelihood that each firm will change its strategy in response to dissatisfaction with its present position, changes in the environment, or moves made by other competitors. The evaluation process also helps management better understand a competitor's vulnerability, which can be an important source of opportunities to the firm.

Competitor's characteristics

Here managers are concerned with such characteristics as size of sales, profitability, market position or share, growth, financial strengths, relation to parent company, domestic versus foreign coverage, and specialization. The trend of a competitor's strategic business unit (SBU) and product-market entry sales and market share are of particular interest because—along with profitability data—they reveal the success of a competitor's strategy. When

EXHIBIT 7 ♦ 6
Competitor evaluation process

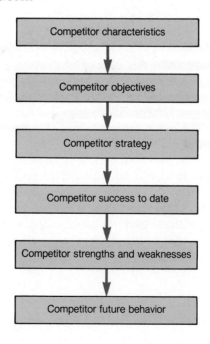

growth (or loss) is substantial over a short time, these data also provide insights into the stresses and strains to which the competitor's organization is being subjected. Under Philip Morris, Seven-Up not only lost share but also was a chronic money loser. Clearly, its strategy was not paying off. This fact did not go unnoticed by Coke or Pepsi as they sought to enhance their own shares of the lemon-lime market segment—a distant second to cola in popularity.

Analyzing the financial strengths of key competitors helps evaluate their durability or staying power. This is an especially important characteristic during periods of turmoil and strong competitive pressures. Financial strengths can be assessed on the basis of profitability, margins, cost trends, price/earning ratios, and other performance measures. Unfortunately, such data may not be available at the SBU level in any detail. Even so, knowing the financial condition of the parent helps assess the likelihood of its being able to finance high growth or a period of intense competitive action—especially when the SBU is losing substantial sums.

Along somewhat similar lines, knowing the relation of the SBU to the parent company is particularly important. The unit's assigned role and the parent's performance expectations strongly influence its response profile. Thus, a large and highly successful parent that has assigned an important strategic role to an SBU is likely to respond strongly to any competitive actions it perceives as threatening. Certainly this is true with Coca-Cola and PepsiCo, which overall have enviable earnings records and expect strong performances from their soft-drink SBUs.

Competitor's objectives

An analysis of a competitor's objectives is important for several reasons. It provides insights into whether the competitor is satisfied with its profitability and its current market position and, thus, how likely it is to retain its present strategy. It helps a firm predict how the competition will respond to changes in the environment, such as a sharp decrease in demand. And it is a predictor of how the firm will react to a particular strategic move made by a competitor.

Objectives usually include more than simply financial goals. Most also include competitive position (market share) and qualitative objectives—such as industry leadership in price, product technology, and social responsibility. Managers must know which trade-offs the company will make between these and its economic (profitability) objectives during times of stress. For example, at the *business-unit level* managers try to get answers to the following questions.[15]

---

[15] Based on Porter, *Competitive Strategy*, pp. 51–57.

1. What is the competitor's organizational structure, and what is the status of the unit with which we compete? Does the structure indicate the relative importance of any functional area? Does it provide insights into how and where decisions are made about such strategy elements as pricing and products?

2. What are the competitor's financial and market position objectives? How are trade-offs made between these objectives, especially short term verus long term? How does the competitor balance its rate of growth and return on assets managed?

3. What are the competitor's apparent expectations for some of its activities, and how do they affect its objectives? Does it think of itself as the market leader? The price leader? The technological leader? Is the competitor, in fact, the leader it perceives itself to be in a given field? What will it pay to remain a leader?

4. What incentive and control systems does the competitor use? How do these impact on its manager's response to competitive action?

5. What is the background of the competitor's key executives? What functional areas have they managed? What companies have they worked for? How much industry experience have they had?

6. What successes or failures of consequence has the competitor had recently? Will these affect future behavior? How?

7. Does the competitor have any commitments that may inhibit action? (Commitments may or may not be contractual, and include licensing, debt, and joint ventures.)

8. Does the competitor have any regulatory constraints on its behavior? (This constraint can be inferred, for example, when a large firm is reluctant to respond to the price moves made by a small competitor.)

In addition to these answers, the parent organization may directly or indirectly impose constraints on the behavior of its SBUs. Thus, the following questions need to be asked at the *corporate level* of the competitor: What are the objectives of the parent company, and how important is the SBU in helping attain these objectives? How successful has the parent been, and how does this affect its reaction to the SBU's performance? What strategic value does the SBU have in the parent's overall strategy? What is the economic relationship between the SBU and other SBUs? That is, to what extent do they involve shared costs or complementary products? How is the SBU management compensated, and what effect does this have on the behavior of the individuals involved? Does the parent have any regulatory, antitrust, or other constraints outstanding and, if so, how will they affect the actions of the SBU?

A portfolio analysis of the competitor's company can often provide answers to a good many of these questions. In particular, such an analysis should reveal how the competitor fits into the overall needs of the parent and how it relates to the firm's other SBUs (as in the area of shared costs). Thus, insights are often provided into the objectives of the competing business unit, how strongly it can defend its current market position, and the likelihood of any attempt to change its strategy.

Competitor's strategy

This component of competitor analysis reviews past and present strategies of each major competitor. Past strategies provide insights into failures and reveal how the firm engineered changes, especially in new product-market relationships. Such historical information helps anticipate which marketing mix strategy elements the competitor might emphasize in the future. Porter notes that it is important to ask whether the parent has used a general strategy with a number of its businesses that might be tried with this one. As an example, he uses BIC Pen, which employed a strategy comprising low price, mass-produced (standardized), disposable products that were heavily advertised. BIC used this strategy with its writing instruments, cigarette lighters, and—more recently—its disposable razors.[16]

Understanding the competitor's current marketing mix strategy elements is important in assessing its strengths and weaknesses. It leads to a better understanding of opportunities and threats and which of these to target for appropriate action. This is particularly the case when the strategy elements vary in their relative importance in achieving success.

Competitor's success to date

The next step is to evaluate how successful the competitor has been in achieving its objectives and carrying out its strategies. Profitability measures may be difficult to come by when the competitor is part of a large corporate entity, and even more difficult where specific product-market entries are concerned. It is often possible, however, to obtain reliable estimates of sales and market share even at the segment level from a variety of sources, including syndicated commercial service organizations. For example, A. C. Nielsen reports on a bimonthly basis the retail sales of a substantial number of product classes, such as frozen vegetables, baby foods, frozen poultry, and canned meats, by certain demographic and geographic breakdowns. Such data—especially when viewed on a trend basis—should give a good indication of how well the competitor is currently doing compared to its performance in prior years.

Another success indicator is the number of times the competitor has failed or succeeded in recent years. The memory of past successes or failures can impact a competitor's confidence for better or worse. In a similar vein, how has the competitor responded over the years to market and industry changes, including strategy moves made by other firms? Was there a response? How quickly? Was it a rational or emotional response? Was it effective?

---

[16] Porter, *Competitive Strategy*, p. 54.

EXHIBIT   7 ◆ 7

Analysis of strengths and weaknesses

Innovation	*Management*
R&D	Quality of top management
Technologies	Quality of middle management and
New-product capability	operating systems
Patents	Loyalty—turnover
Manufacturing	Quality of strategic decision making
Cost structure	*Marketing*
Equipment	Product quality
Access to raw material	Breadth of the product line
Vertical integration	Brand names
Workforce attitude and motivation	Distribution
Capacity	Retailer relationship
Finance—access to capital	Advertising/promotion skills
From operations	Salesforce
From net short-term assets	Service
Ability and willingness to use debt	Knowledge of customer's needs
financing	*Customer base*
Parent's willingness to finance	Size and growth of segments served
	Loyalty of customers

Source: From *Strategic Market Management,* by David A. Aaker, p. 66. Copyright © 1984 by John Wiley & Sons, Inc. Reprinted by permission of John Wiley & Sons, Inc.

Competitor's strengths and weaknesses

Knowledge of strengths and weaknesses derive to a considerable extent from the previous steps in evaluating competitors. This information is important—especially when tied to the competitor's objectives and strategies. Any evaluation of strengths and weaknesses must take into account the relative importance of the marketing mix strategy elements required to exploit the situation. Ideally, one would take advantage of a competitor's weakness using one's own strength. For a listing of areas that relate to strengths and weaknesses, see Exhibit 7–7.

Competitor's future behavior

The analysis thus far had as its objective assessing the competitor's likely future behavior in terms of its objectives and strategies. To develop a response profile for each key competitor, analysts ask the following questions, the answers to which should help a firm decide which competitors to target within each major segment as well as which strategies to use.

EXHIBIT 7 ◆ 8

Primary uses of competitive intelligence

---

1. Determine a competitor's corporate strategy.
2. Define competitor R&D activity.
3. Identify target acquisition companies.
4. Explore the market environment of an acquisition.
5. Provide financial information on a privately held corporation.
6. Provide biographical information on key executives.
7. Monitor competitor's product introductions.
8. Analyze the market for a product introduction.

Source: Reprinted from Richard Combs and John Moorehead, "The Quest for Corporate Excellence Begins with Competitive Intelligence," *Marketing News,* May 9, 1988, p. 11. Published by the American Marketing Association.

1. How satisfied is the competitor with its current position?
2. How likely is the competitor to change its current strategy? What specific changes will it make in individual strategy elements?
3. How much weight will the competitor put behind such changes?
4. What will likely be the response of other competitors to these moves? How will they impact the competitor initiating the changes?
5. What opportunities does the competitor provide its close rivals? Will these opportunities endure for some time or will they close down shortly?
6. How effective will the competitor be in responding to environmental change, including moves made by competitors? Which events and moves can it respond to well and which poorly? For each event or move, what retaliatory action is most likely?

Obtaining information about competitors

To answer questions like those indicated above requires a good deal of information (hereafter referred to as *intelligence*) about present and potential competitors—their past performance, current strategies, and future plans. Exhibit 7–8 lists the primary uses of competitor intelligence. Intelligence has increasingly become a management tool of considerable power—something American managers are just beginning to realize when compared to the Japanese. For examples of American intelligence gathering, see Exhibit 7–9.

Competitor intelligence is "highly specific and timely information about a corporation."[17] Almost all intelligence information needed by a company can be found in the public arena and thus can be collected without unethically engaging in cloak-and-dagger activities. By combining information from government publications, trade associations, competitors' annual re-

---

[17] Leonard M. Fuld, *Competitor Intelligence* (New York: John Wiley & Sons, 1985), p. 9.

EXHIBIT **7 ◆9**

Some examples of competitor intelligence

McDonnell Douglas recently had to decide whether to go ahead with a new generation of airliners driven by a rear prop-fan. Its decision hinged, to a considerable extent, on whether Boeing would proceed with a similar plane. A McDonnell Douglas team examined Boeing's annual reports, R&D spending, factory capacity, and the like, and concluded that Boeing could not produce such an airliner as cheaply or as quickly as McDonnell Douglas. As a consequence, the team recommended that McDonnell Douglas proceed with its development of the prop-fan jet (MD91); and management concurred. Shortly afterward, Boeing announced it would delay its development of a prop-fan plane.

In 1985, Coors introduced a wine cooler, which quickly failed. Management, however, still wanted to get into the wine cooler business and set up a task force to find out what kind of margins Gallo was experiencing with its wine coolers. Coors undertook a chemical analysis of Gallo's products to determine what wines and flavorings were used. It then priced out these ingredients. The findings showed that Coors could not compete against Gallo on price because Gallo was vertically integrated—it grew its own grapes. Coors decided not to reenter the wine cooler market.

Marriott sent an intelligence team around the country for six months to learn about the strengths and weaknesses of the major chains in the economy hotel business—a market it was considering entering. Members of this team would check into a room of an economy chain and proceed to test the bed, note the brand of soap and shampoo used, and determine the extent to which the walls were soundproof. After studying the detailed data about each major chain, Marriott budgeted $500 million to proceed with a new chain (Fairfield Inn), which it thought would beat the competition in every respect. The new chain was successful, averaging an occupancy rate 10 percentage points higher than the remainder of the industry.

Source: Brian Dumaine, "Corporate Spies Snoop to Conquer," *Fortune,* November 7, 1988, pp. 68–76. © 1988 Time Inc. All rights reserved.

ports and 10-K statements, a firm can generate reasonably accurate data about such important subject areas as sales volume, market share, a business's relative importance to its parent company, and a parent's overall financial resources. See Exhibit 7–10 (p. 242) for a list of intelligence sources.

One of the more common forms of competitive intelligence is reverse-engineering, which involves taking a competitor's product apart in an effort to learn everything possible about it, including its costs. Ford used this approach to develop its very successful Taurus and Sable models. After losing market share to one of Canon's copiers that retailed at a price less than Xerox's manufacturing cost, Xerox used reverse-engineering to stem the slide.[18]

For many consumer products—especially packaged food and household items—detailed information is available from syndicated commercial services. One of the best-known such services, the Nielsen Retail Index, pro-

---

[18] Brian Dumaine, "Corporate Spies Snoop to Conquer," *Fortune,* November 7, 1988, p. 76.

EXHIBIT 7 ♦ 10

Intelligence sources by subject area

1. **Company financials**
   Dun & Bradstreet report
   10-K
   Annual report
   State filing
   Published article
   Moody's
   Wall Street Transcript
2. **Market share**
   Literature search
   Simmons Market Research
     Bureau
   A. C. Nielsen Company
   Market studies
   EIS
   F&S Predicasts
3. **Company background**
   F&S indexes
   Standard & Poor's
   Dun & Bradstreet report
   Newspaper index
   Published articles
   Wall Street Transcript
4. **Industry background**
   Published articles
   Trade magazines
   U.S. Industrial Outlook
   Investment reports
   Value Line
   Special annual issues of
     industry handbooks

5. **Competitors**
   Standard & Poor's
   Thomas Register
   Industry buyer's guides
   Yellow Pages
   City directories
   Key magazines
   Associations
6. **Industry experts**
   Articles
   Key magazines
   Directory of Directories
   Associations
   Competitors
   Stockbrokers
   Consultants
   Government experts
   University professors
7. **Management personnel**
   Who's Who (General Industry)
   Local newspapers
   PR departments
   College alumni associations
   The Wall Street Journal
   New York Times
   Chamber of Commerce

8. **Foreign information**
   Consulates
   Embassies
   American–(foreign) Chamber
     of Commerce
   International Trade Commis-
     sion
   Special libraries
   International D&B
9. **Advertising information**
   Advertising Age
   ADTRACK
   Local newspapers
   LNA
   Advertising agencies
10. **Government experts**
    Washington researchers'
      guides
    FCC
    Department of Commerce,
      Bureau of Labor Statistics
    Environmental
      Protection Agency
    Federal Trade Commission

Source: Reprinted from Competitor Intelligence by Leonard M. Fuld, pp. 32–33. Copyright © 1985 by John Wiley & Sons, Inc. Reprinted by permission of John Wiley & Sons, Inc.

vides continuous sales data on grocery products, confectionery products, dairy products, frozen foods, alcoholic and nonalcoholic products, tobacco, health and beauty aids, housekeeping products, and paper products. Data are obtained every 60 days by auditing the inventories, purchases, and sales of a carefully selected sample of food stores, drugstores, and mass merchandisers.

Clients of the audit program receive regular reports of total sales of the applicable product class, sales of their own and competing brands, retail and wholesale prices, retail inventories, stores stocking the products, in-store promotional activity, and special manufacturing deals. These data are available for the total United States and by regions; by a client's sales territories; by types of retailer and ownership (chain versus independent); and by retail sales volume groups. Other major syndicated services include:

* National Purchase Diary—uses a consumer panel of some 15,000 households to report the purchase of food, household, and personal care products.
* Selling Areas-Marketing Inc. (SAMI/Burke)—provides movement data on more than 180,000 consumer products in more than 500 categories from warehouses to supermarkets, drugstores, and mass merchandisers.
* Nielsen Television Index—provides detailed information on the audiences of TV programs. Arbitron provides audience measurements on local TV, cable, and radio.
* Simmons' annual "Study of Media & Markets—reports exposure to all media (TV, radio, magazines, and newspapers) as well as product usage by brand and frequency of purchase.

Additional information about the effectiveness of competitors' past and current marketing efforts is often obtained as a by-product of a firm's own marketing research. For example, a survey designed to measure customer awareness and attitudes toward a firm's brand can collect similar information about major competitors' brands. Finally, a great deal of information about competitors' capabilities and activities is available from commerical sources other than syndicated services. Some 2,000 commercially available electronic data bases store information about firms in various industries. For example, one data base—called Investext—gives subscribers the full text of research reports prepared by securities analysts and investment bankers about companies.

Keeping tabs on competitors—particularly trying to anticipate their future strategic moves and reactions—has become so important that many larger firms have created staff departments to collect and analyze corporate intelligence. Some companies prefer to assign the task to specific individuals in their marketing research or corporate planning departments. In addition to collecting and analyzing information from secondary sources and the firm's own marketing research studies, such competitor intelligence units can obtain information by talking with a competitor's technical and management people at trade shows, companies that do business with competitors (for example, wholesalers), and former employees of competitors. Sometimes it is even possible to talk directly with present employees of competitors by using a consulting firm to do so.

SUMMARY

Understanding the competitive environment is an important part of any strategic market analysis. The competitive environment involves an industry analysis and an evaluation of individ-

ual close competitors. The former process consists of identifying the relevant industry including the specification of industry groups, an analysis of competitive forces, an industry structural analysis, and an evaluation of the bases of competition.

The bases and intensity on which companies compete derive from the interaction of existing and potential competitors, the bargaining power of customers and suppliers, and substitute products. These five forces are critical in determining the industry's long-term attractiveness; and they explain why some industries are more profitable than others. Their interplay also provides insights into what resources are required and what strategies should be adopted if a business is to be successful. A structural analysis *within* an industry to help determine which strategic group to target must consider mobility barriers, the rivalry between groups, the bargaining power of buyers and sellers, substitute products, and the industry's likely future structure.

An industry analysis must also identify and study the bases of competition that determine what the business must do to become successful. Strategy elements and their relative importance vary widely from industry to industry, across strategic groups within an industry, and by stage in the product life cycle. It is important to think of what resources a business must have to make a strategy element successful.

By analyzing present and potential key competitors, firms can better anticipate their future moves. The major steps in the competitor-evaluation process are identifying competitors and analyzing their characteristics, objectives, strategies, success to date, and strengths and weaknesses.

Certain questions should also be asked about the parent organization in an effort to understand the nature of any constraints placed on the activities of its SBUs. These include questions about the parent company's objectives and its success to date, the strategic value of the competitor SBU to the parent, the economic relations between the competitor SBU and other SBUs, the parent's generic strategy, how SBU managers are controlled and compensated, preferences for managers with certain backgrounds, and the presence of any regulatory or other constraints.

An analysis of the competitor's past and present strategies indicates successes and failures and helps in assessing its strengths and weaknesses. Firms should analyze strategies in terms of their elements, such as product and product line, price, channels, salesforce, advertising, postpurchase service, and merchandising.

The next step is to evaluate the competitor's success to date in light of its objectives and strategies. Then an analysis of the competitor's strengths and weaknesses is made using strategy elements as the basis for the investigation. And, finally, certain conclusions about the competitor's future behavior can be set forth. This centers mainly on how satisfied the competitor is with its current position and how it can respond to changes in the environment, including moves by its competitors. Such information is the basis for identifying and understanding opportunities and threats and helps firms decide which competitors to target in each major segment.

QUESTIONS

1. The frozen pizza industry has become increasingly competitive in recent years. Most major national and regional brands—Totino's, Jeno's, Tony's, and Tombstone—are owned by large food manufacturers such as Pillsbury. Major brands have experienced declining profit margins as a result of heavy trade and consumer promotions. What *industry characteristics* help explain the high *intensity of competition* in the frozen pizza business?

2. The U.S. steel industry has also experienced much more intense competition over the past decade or so. Were the same industry characteristics you identified as being responsible for the intense competition in the frozen pizza business (in question 1) also at work in the steel industry?

What additional or different industry factors impact the intensity of competition faced by U.S. steel manufacturers?

3. Why is the concept of *strategic groups* useful to a manager when developing a strategic marketing plan?

4. Which *criteria* might determine the brands in an industry belonging to the same strategic group? Apply the criteria you have identified to an industry you are familiar with—either a consumer goods, industrial goods, or services industry—and identify two distinct strategic groups in that industry. Which brands belong to each group?

5. How intense is the *rivalry between the two strategic groups* you identified in your answer to question 4? What major factors affect the intensity of that rivalry?

6. With cars priced well into six figures, Rolls-Royce stands virtually alone at the top end of the luxury sedan market. What *mobility barriers* are likely to make it difficult for any other firms to compete in the same strategic group with Rolls-Royce?

7. Suppose you are the marketing manager for Rolls-Royce. Even though the company currently has few—if any—direct competitors in its target market, you worry about *potential future entrants* to the luxury sedan market. Where are such competitors most likely to come from? What factors might enable or encourage a firm to become a competitor in your market?

8. Despite being the first entrant to the home videocassette recorder market and having an early cost advantage due to experience curve effects, Sony's Beta format VCRs no longer have much of a competitive position in the market. Using relevant *concepts of competition* discussed in the chapter, explain what happened to Sony.

9. Suppose you were a marketing assistant working on the Quaker Instant Oatmeal brand when General Mills decided to introduce Total Oatmeal in 1987. Your superiors have given you the task of evaluating the relative strengths and weaknesses of the new entrant and estimating the future marketing strategy that General Mills is likely to pursue in attempting to take market share away from your brand. What *information* would you attempt to obtain about General Mills and its new Total Oatmeal? *How would you obtain* that information?

Chapter ◇ 8 ◇

Industry dynamics and the product life cycle

MAINFRAME COMPUTERS—A CASE STUDY[1]

In the early 1940s, the first electronic digital computer was built at the University of Pennsylvania. It weighed 30 tons and was a thousand times faster than any analog machine. Sperry Rand bought the company that emerged from the work done at the university and produced the famous UNIVAC in 1950. Soon after, IBM, which had an established position in the office-machine market, began competing against Sperry Rand. IBM had marketing strengths, while Rand had technological leadership. In but a few years, IBM was the clear winner—and since then it has dominated the $150 billion-a-year computer business, the third-largest industry in the United States after automobiles and oil.

During the 50s and 60s, the industry's rapid growth was fueled largely by the sale of mainframe computers, made possible by the development of the transistor. Despite the introduction of minicomputers in the 60s and their subsequent popularity, mainframes continued to account for the bulk of industry sales in the 60s and 70s. Although numerous companies entered the computer industry during these years, IBM captured and maintained a 60 to 70 percent share of the mainframe market. Because of this domination, the industry was called Snow White (IBM) and the Seven Dwarfs—RCA, GE, Burroughs, UNIVAC, NCR, Control Data, and Honeywell. None of the dwarfs ever mounted a serious challenge to IBM.

By 1981 the sales of mainframe computers were about $14 billion. During the next few years, total computer sales increased dramatically—at a 24 percent compounded annual rate. This increase was due in no small part to a boom in microcomputers (personal computers). Sales of mainframes increased, but at a declining rate. These salad years were followed by a slump in industry sales that lasted through 1986. While sales have since improved, a return to the boom years is not likely. Increasingly, sales do not represent new systems, but rather replacements, upgrades, or enhancements of existing equipment. Some 56 percent of the mainframes sold in 1986 were replacements.

---

[1] Based on data contained in Al Ries and Jack Trout, *Marketing Warfare* (New York: McGraw-Hill, 1986), chap. 14; Alex Beam and Geoff Lewis, "The IBM-DEC Wars: 'It's the Year of the Customer,'" *Business Week*, March 30, 1987, p. 86; Standard & Poor's, *Industry Surveys*, October 1, 1987, p. C75; Stuart Gannes, "Tremors from the Computer Quake," *Fortune*, August 1, 1988, p. 43; and Stuart Gannes, "IBM and DEC Take on the Little Guys," *Fortune*, October 10, 1988, p. 108.

continued

concluded

The mainframe market has aged to a point where, in 1986, shipments fell by 5.5 percent. Nor is the worldwide outlook encouraging. Mainframe sales are forecasted to slow to an increase of about 4 percent annually through 1991. Revenues are expected to drop by 2.8 percent annually in the years ahead. Prospects for the United States are even less promising.

The main reason for this is the development of smaller and less expensive mini and personal computer systems that can do many jobs which were once the exclusive province of mainframes. Thus, many mainframe users are downsizing to smaller systems for selected applications. Further, some manufacturers of minicomputers have upgraded their machines so they can equal the processing power of mainframes—and do so at substantially lower cost. Digital Equipment Corporation (DEC) has been an aggressive leader in this regard.

The slowdown in sales of mainframes has further intensified competition and led to a shakeout involving three of IBM's oldest U.S.-based competitors. Burroughs acquired Sperry to form UNISYS; and Honeywell gave up its computer business to concentrate on its automation and control activities. Control Data has undergone substantial restructuring and has enacted stringent cost reductions, thereby significantly lowering its corporate cost structure. Mainframe plug-compatible manufacturers (AMADAHL and National Advanced Systems), which compete primarily on a price basis, have increased their share of worldwide shipments in recent years. IBM is introducing new mainframe models at shorter intervals, following more aggressive pricing practices, and has accelerated the introduction of product enhancements. All firms are placing increased emphasis on new-product development and personal selling.

Firms benefit greatly if they are among the first to adjust strategically to environmental change. This was the case early on with IBM, which took advantage of technological change to become the dominant computer company. It was later true with DEC, which took advantage of changing technology to create the minicomputer business.

Followers frequently find they are at a disadvantage in product development; the leader's product has become the standard against which other products are compared. The switching costs incurred by the leader's customers in changing to another supplier and the development and execution of an effective communication's strategy are other disadvantages followers experience. Thus, despite the reputation and resources of such companies as Burroughs, Honeywell, Sperry, National Cash Register (NCR), and Control

EXHIBIT   8 ◆ 1

U.S. vendors' market shares of worldwide large-scale computer systems—1986*

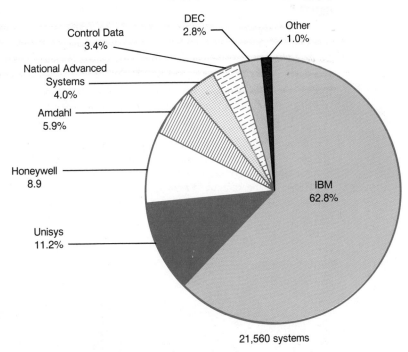

21,560 systems

* The large-scale market consists primarily of mainframes.

Source: Standard & Poor's, *Industry Surveys, Basic Analysis,* October 1, 1987, p. C79. Based on data provided by International Data Corporation.

Data, none was ever able to show impressive share gains against IBM. In fact, IBM still holds 62.8 percent share of U.S. vendors' worldwide sales of mainframes, as shown in Exhibit 8–1. With sales of $51.3 billion and net income of $4.8 billion in 1986, IBM accounted for 40 percent of U.S. total industry sales—and 70 percent of its profits. By comparison, DEC and UNISYS collectively had sales of $17 billion.

Environmental change that generates opportunities and threats for a firm is inevitable, given the evolution of an industry and its product-market relationships. There are many reasons why an industry or a segment thereof evolves over time. On the product side is the growing commonality of the technology and the increased difficulty of maintaining product differentiation. Also, over time the cost per unit declines because of scale and learning effects. Price reductions usually follow. On the market side, demand eventually slows. Consumers become knowledgeable about the product and its behavior under a variety of use conditions; and they form attitudes about the quality of various competing brands. Over time these forces impact the attractiveness of the industry and—more specifically—the product-market relationship, forcing the firm to change its objectives, strategies, and action plans. This was certainly the case in the computer industry.

The **product life cycle** is a concept that describes the sales and profit margin of a given product category over a prolonged period. The concept holds that a product's sales and profits change over time in a predictable manner—at least in the four distinct major stages of introduction, growth, maturity, and decline (see Exhibit 8–2). The usefulness of the product life cycle to managers has been summed up as follows:

> Sooner or later, new customers become scarce, their numbers offset by disappearance of old customers, except for population growth. Although some sellers have a far greater market share than others, large portions of the market will have little brand loyalty. Perceived differentiation (and the actuality itself, most likely) will have decreased greatly. . . . The offering is now becoming "yesterday's breadwinner," and resources need to be devoted to developing tomorrow's.[2]

EXHIBIT 8 ♦ 2

Generalized product life cycle

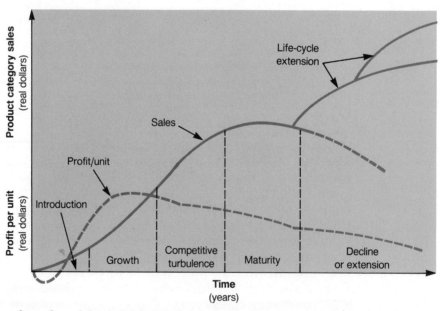

Source: George S. Day, *Analysis for Strategic Market Decisions* (St. Paul: West Publishing, 1986), p. 60.

---

[2] Charles R. Wasson, *Marketing Management: The Strategy, Tactics, and Art of Competition* (Charlotte, N.C.: ECR Associates, 1983), p. 92.

The implications of this statement of the product life-cycle concept from a management standpoint are threefold. First, the firm must generate new products or enter new markets to sustain its profitability over time. For example, as computer hardware matures and becomes less profitable, vendors are becoming more interested in the production of software. Worldwide software revenues are expected to increase at a 22 percent compounded annual growth rate into the early 90s, versus 7.1 percent for computer systems.[3]

Second, the objectives and strategy for a given product change as it passes through the various life-cycle stages. Thus, as the long-distance telephone business moved from growth to competitive turbulence, cost became the strategic variable. Because MCI paid higher connect charges to local telephone companies, it found itself at a disadvantage against AT&T.[4]

Third, the opportunities and threats in each stage are sufficiently well known to aid in the formulation of the most appropriate marketing mix for each stage. Thus, as the market for mainframe computers began to approach maturity. IBM accelerated its introduction of new models, enhanced its direct sales activities, and became more aggressive about price.[5]

This chapter first presents an overview of the product life-cycle concept, including its relationship to the diffusion of innovation concept and a description of its various stages. Second, we discuss the characteristics of each stage and their underlying dynamics in setting objectives, formulating strategy, and developing the most appropriate marketing mix. Third, we examine the investment implications of the product life cycle. And finally, we discuss its limitations.

A note of caution! It is not always easy to determine where a product is in the product life cycle. Nor can the life-cycle concept prescribe the specific action to take in each stage in the cycle. But, as a forward-looking concept, it describes the underlying forces that inhibit or facilitate growth and thus create opportunities and threats that have strategic implications.[6] The life cycle also is a moderating influence on the value of market-share position and the profitability consequences of strategic decisions.[7] Thus, the concept provides a rich framework within which to explore competitive actions and strategy options over time.

---

[3] Standard & Poor's, p. C76.

[4] "More Static on the Lines for an Expanding MCI," *Business Week*, November 5, 1984, p. 40.

[5] For an example of what happens when a company is not following the evolution of its market, see "Levi's: The Jeans Giant Slipped as Market Shifted," *Business Week*, November 5, 1984, p. 79.

[6] George Day, "The Product Life Cycle: Analysis and Application Issues," *Journal of Marketing*, Fall 1981, p. 65.

[7] Ibid.

OVERVIEW OF THE PRODUCT LIFE-CYCLE CONCEPT

The product life-cycle concept owes much to the **diffusion of innovations theory,** which explains the adoption process. Initially, the adoption of a new product or idea is limited by a lack of awareness. The result is that only a limited part of the total buying population purchases it in the **introductory stage.** As the product becomes better known—in part because of word-of-mouth from satisfied buyers—the number of adopters continues to increase **(growth stage)** until **market saturation** is reached (i.e., the maximum number have adopted). Then *repeat* rather than trial sales dominate. A product reaches the **mature stage** when the net adoption rate holds steady; that is, new adopters compensate for drop-outs. When the rate begins to decline, the product has reached its final or **decline stage.**

Exhibit 8–3 shows examples of products that appear to be at different stages in their product life cycles.[8] Thus, as of 1985, color TVs and audio systems appear to be in the mature stage. More recent data reveal that dollar sales for each remained about the same in 1986 and 87, which confirms this conclusion. VCRs were still in the growth stage in 1985 but have since entered the mature period, with sales of 15 million in both 86 and 87. Compact disc players, on the other hand, are still in the growth stage. Over 3 million units were sold in 1987—up 12 percent over 86. Sales in 88 were expected to reach 4 million.[9]

Some products have more than four product life-cycle stages. For strategic purposes, we add a fifth, referred to as the turbulent or **shakeout period**

EXHIBIT 8 ◆ 3

Product life cycle for some home electronic products

	Factory sales to dealers (in million units)				
	1981	*1982*	*1983*	*1984*	*1985**
Color TVs	11	11	14	16	16
VCRs	1	2	4	8	11
Audio systems	3	3	3	3	3
Compact disc players	—	—	.035	.208	.600
* estimated					

Source: Adapted from John Marcom, Jr., "Movie-Like Realism Could Put Sizzle in Home Market," *The Wall Street Journal,* June 4, 1985.

---

[8] David Cravens, *Strategic Marketing* (Homewood, Ill.: Richard D. Irwin, 1987), p. 243.

[9] Data since 1985 for all four electronic products were obtained from Standard & Poor's, pp. L16–17.

occurring at the end of the growth period—just before the advent of maturity. Shakeout is characterized by a rapidly decreasing growth rate that typically results in strong price competition. Many firms are forced to exit, as has been the case in the minicomputer industry in recent years.

The adoption process is concerned with the attitudinal changes consumers experience from the time they first learn about a new product until they adopt it. The consumer receives various stimuli about the new product from a variety of sources. These accumulate until the consumer responds by either accepting or rejecting the product. The five adoption stages are:

1. The **awareness stage:** Consumers are exposed to the new product but lack the interest to learn more about it.
2. The **interest stage:** Consumers are motivated to find out more about the product but remain uncommitted in assessing its value.
3. The **evaluation stage:** Consumers mentally rehearse the uses of the product and the results obtained.
4. The **trial stage:** Consumers actually use the product—preferably on a limited basis to minimize risk.
5. The **adoption stage:** Consumers use the product on a continued basis.

The rate at which people move through the adoption stages largely depends on the new product's relative advantage over existing products versus possible barriers to its use. These include its **risk** (cost of product failure or dissatisfaction, such as for a color TV); its **simplicity** (ease of use, as in computerized process controls that require a change in manufacturing facilities); the **extent** to which it lends itself to small-scale trial (e.g., most food and personal-care items); and the **ease** with which its core concept can be communicated (such as for a new type of soft drink or a new type of consumer savings instrument). These barriers to adoption provide insights into the shape of the product life-cycle curve. For instance, new breakfast cereals move rapidly to maturity compared to a new personal computer, which can take many years.

Life-cycle curves

Many products do not go through the product life-cycle curve shown in Exhibit 8–2. A high percentage of new products abort after an unsatisfactory introductory period.[10] Fads—such as hula hoops and pet rocks—have unusually short life cycles, even when they are successful. The shape of their life-cycle curve is similar to an inverted v ($\wedge$). Other products seemingly

---

[10] There are a variety of estimates regarding the percentage of new-product failures, ranging from as low as 15 percent to as high as 90 percent. Much depends upon when a new-product project is canceled. According to Booz, Allen, and Hamilton (*Management of New Products*, 1981), 46 percent of the total funds spent on new products goes for products that fail or are abandoned.

EXHIBIT 8 ◆ 4

Product life-cycle curves

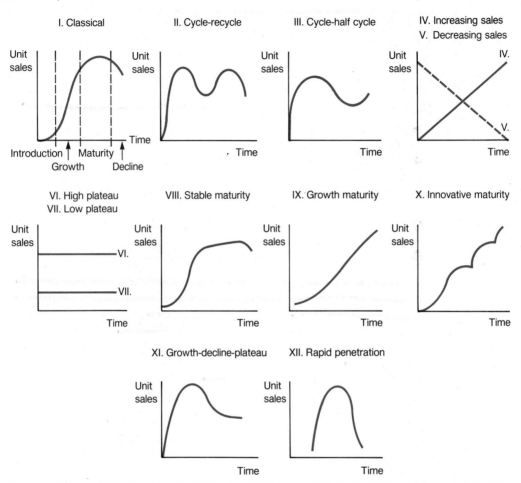

Source: John E. Swan and David R. Rink, "Effective Use of Industrial Product Life-Cycle Trends" in *Marketing in the '80s,* eds. Richard P. Bagozzi et al. (Chicago: American Marketing Association, 1980), pp. 198–99.

never die (scotch whiskey, TVs, and automobiles). There is considerable variation between and even within industries in the shape of the life-cycle curve. Indeed, as Exhibit 8–4 shows, 12 different curves have been identified.

In general, only one or very few curves typify an industry, as shown in Exhibit 8–5. The most common curve is the classical type, followed by the cycle-recycle curve. Consumer durables tend to follow the classical curve, although many major household appliances (such as refrigerators and washing machines) have never entered the decline stage. Drug products present the most complex patterns, using almost all cycles. Even here, however, the

EXHIBIT   8 ◆ 5

Product life-cycle curves classified by industry and product

Industry and product	Industry PLC
Consumer durables	
Televisions, automobiles, refrigerators	Classical
Consumer nondurables	
Drugs	Cycle-recycle (classical, increasing and decreasing sales, high and low plateau, cycle-half cycle)
Cigarettes	Classical
Household supplies	Cycle-recycle (classical)
Personal-care products	Cycle-recycle (classical)
Food products	Classical (cycle-recycle, stable, growth, and innovative maturity, increasing and decreasing sales, growth-decline plateau)
Industrial	
General engineering products	Classical
Fluid measuring devices	Cycle-recycle
Automobile components	Classical
Petrochemicals	Classical
Industrial chemicals	Classical (increasing sales, rapid penetration)

Source: John E. Swan and David R. Rink, "Effective Use of Industrial Product Life-Cycle Trends," in *Marketing in the '80s,* eds. Richard P. Bagozzi et al. (Chicago: American Marketing Association, 1980), p. 199.

cycle-recycle curve seems to be the most common. Industrial products have been found to typically follow the pattern of sales depicted by the classical curve. Product life cycles for industrial goods are longer than those for consumer goods.[11]

A surge in demand during the mature period, or recycling, can occur for many reasons. These include an increase in the price of a close substitute; a disproportionate increase in the size of a prime market segment caused by demographic shifts or increased purchases by one or more end-user industries; reduced prices resulting from lower raw material costs; or a basic shift in derived demand. The latter can result from a change in lifestyle, as has occurred with more women working outside the home. Often a given style may, after going into eclipse, regain its popularity. This has been the case with clothing (short skirts and men's double-breasted suit coats). **Innovative maturity** occurs when new types or subtypes introduced within a product class experience considerable sales success (say, more nutritional and natural fiber ready-to-eat cereals).

---

[11] Hans B. Thorelli and Stephen C. Burnett, "The Nature of Product Life Cycles for Industrial Goods Businesses," *Journal of Marketing,* Fall 1981, p. 105.

Definitions of products and markets

The usefulness of the product life-cycle concept requires understanding what is meant by a product and a market. A product may have several life cycles; it depends on the number of different customer needs and customer groups it serves. Defining products and markets is made even more difficult by the fact that they can be summed in a variety of ways to form several different levels of aggregation. We first address product hierarchies, which comprise at least three levels: product class, product type, and brand.

Product class

A *product class,* or *product category,* includes products that are essentially substitutes for satisfying the same need. A need can be defined broadly; but a product class includes different product types designed to satisfy more precise needs within the overall need structure. This has been the case with the computer industry which features three major product types (mainframes, minis, and micros), each of which is designed to satisfy different needs. Thus, a need must be defined with some degree of specificity, or the broad set of products involved will be meaningless. For instance, we would not ordinarily use the need for transportation as the basis for defining a product class, because the products involved—cars, planes, bicycles, trains, trucks, barges, and taxis—are each designed to serve a specific set of needs. Rather, we would define product classes largely around *each* of these transportation modes. For an example of a consumer durable product class life cycle, see Exhibit 8–6. While total sales of still cameras appear to be declining slowly, some camera types are still growing; for example, 35 mm cameras accounted for 55 percent of the U.S. market in mid-1987, up from 35 percent two years earlier.[12]

Product classes are defined on the basis of operational criteria like similar manufacturing processes, raw materials, physical appearance, or function. These criteria have generally wide acceptance because they appear to be easy to implement.[13] It is not surprising, then, that most industries have a reasonably precise definition of a product class and that sales and product data are reported on the basis of such definitions.

The more generic the need to define a product class, the higher the aggregation level of products within that class (e.g., all desserts versus pecan pie), and the more stable the product life-cycle curve. Basic needs change slowly, and the effect of substitution, or cross elasticity, has been lessened by the level of aggregation used. However, the more the product class is defined by generic need, the less useful it is for strategic planning, which identifies opportunities and threats for specific product-market relation-

---

[12] Standard & Poor's, p. L45.

[13] George S. Day, Allan D. Shocker, and Rajendra K. Srivastava, "Customer-Oriented Approaches to Identifying Product Markets," *Journal of Marketing,* Fall 1979, p. 8.

EXHIBIT   8 ♦ 6

Camera sales and pictures taken by amateurs

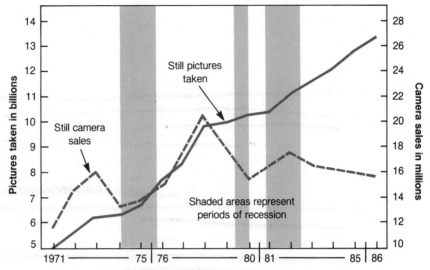

Source: Standard & Poor's, *Industry Surveys,* March 10, 1988, p. L45. Data obtained from *Wolfman Report* published by *Modern Photography.*

ships. This is certainly the case in the computer industry. For example, supercomputers are used mainly for computationally intense scientific and engineering problems, such as forecasting, geographical and petroleum exploration, nuclear research, and aircraft design.

Product type

Product types are subsets of the product class, containing items that are technically the same, although they may vary in any number of ways, including appearance and price.

The level assigned to a given product depends on the breadth of the product-class definition. In the case of cereals, for example, the product types would be defined as hot or cold (ready-to-eat cereals). Hot cereals would include at least two *subtypes* (regular and instant). Cold cereals would include regular, presweetened, natural, and nutritional. Regular cereal could be further broken down into such categories as corn flakes, shredded wheat, and bran. Other examples of product hierarchies comprising several levels abound, especially when different processing technologies are involved. This is the case with frozen, canned, fresh, dehydrated, or freeze-dried food items where use conditions vary substantially; and where multiple segments exist based on taste or flavors (e.g., carbonated beverages).

Product life cycles are particularly relevant when they reflect the effect of major forces at work in an industry—that is, those relating to market competition and technology. In the case of computers, this would argue for an analysis of the life cycles of the three product types—mainframes, minis, and microcomputers. Each serves a different market segment (although overlap is increasing); different companies are involved with each (only IBM produces all types); and each type emphasizes a somewhat different technology.

Brands

This product level uses some form of identification (i.e., name, sign, or symbol) intended to identify the goods or services of one seller and differentiate them from competitors. These typically exist at the product type or subtype level. Bic, Tylenol, and Maxwell House are examples. They can be differentiated in a variety of ways, some physical and others largely perceptual. Ordinarily, brands are close substitutes for each other within the same product type or subtype. Their sales curves differ, therefore, from that of the product class or product type because of differences in the competitive actions taken by different brands. Vlasic pickles, for instance, have outperformed the industry in part because of their advertising.

Brands typically are an aggregation of stock keeping units (SKUs), consisting of items with different package types, sizes, colors, or accessories. Ordinarily, a brand's sales history is considerably more volatile than that of the product type or subtype because it depends on management's strategic decisions, marketing expenditures, and competitive action.[14]

Market hierarchies

A market hierarchy is more complex than a product hierarchy because of the numerous ways markets can be segmented. At the outset we need to link products and markets. Earlier we urged that this be done by defining customer needs in terms of usage requirements related to product features. Choice criteria ordinarily discriminate on the basis of several product characteris. Therefore, we can define the market for a given product type or subtype as those consumers with similar choice criteria.

Knowing what choice criteria consumers have, however, is not sufficient. We need to identify which consumers have which criteria for targeting purposes. The resulting customer groups are, of course, referred to as **market segments,** which—as we saw in Chapter 6—need to be described using such descriptors as demographics, lifestyle, and location. As Exhibit 8–7 shows, the market hierarchy can vary substantially in the number of levels involved.

Firms differ in the levels they target; but the trend clearly is toward greater specificity—that is, to target at the lower levels in the hierarchy. In recent

---

[14] See Nariman K. Dhalla and Sonia Yuspeh, "Forget the Product Life-Cycle Concept," *Harvard Business Review,* January–February 1976, pp. 102–12.

EXHIBIT 8 ◆ 7

Illustration of a market hierarchy for a consumer product

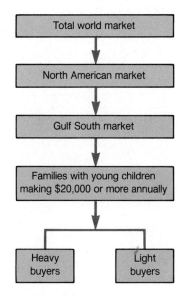

years, Hewlett-Packard has formed marketing groups with narrow specialties, such as promoting computing gear, that help make customers' sales
departments more productive. Its salespeople are being trained more intensively in such areas as financial services, wholesale distribution, and local
governments—all of which needed greater sales penetration. Largely because of such efforts, H-P computer sales have shown increases of about 15
percent annually.[15] Not unlike the product hierarchy, the nature and scope
of the product life-cycle curve varies depending on which market level is the
basis for defining the target market. That is, the higher the level of aggregation, the more apt the curve is to change slowly.

CHARACTERISTICS AND IMPLICATIONS OF THE PRODUCT LIFE-CYCLE STAGES

The various stages of the product life cycle present different opportunities
and threats to the firm. By understanding the characteristics of the major
stages in the product life cycle, the firm can make better decisions not only
about its objectives and strategies, but also about its action plans.

We have already discussed the variations in demand that occur across
life-cycle stages through the diffusion and adoption of innovations. We focus

---

[15] Jonathan B. Levine, "Mild-Mannered Hewlett-Packard Is Making Like Superman," *Business Week*, March 7, 1988, p. 110.

EXHIBIT 8 ◆ 8

Expected characteristics and responses by major product life-cycle stages

Stage characteristics	Stages in product life cycle				
	Introduction	Growth	Shakeout	Mature	Decline
Market growth rate (constant dollars)	Moderate	High	Leveling off	Insignificant	Negative
Technical change in product design	High	Moderate	Limited	Limited	Limited
Segments	Few	Few to many	Few to many	Few to many	Few
Competitors	Small	Large	Decreasing	Limited	Few
Profitability	Negative	Large	Low	Large for high market-share holders	Low
Firm's normative responses					
Strategic marketing objectives	Stimulate primary demand	Build share	Build share	Hold share	Harvest
Product	Quality improvement	Continue quality improvements	Rationalize*	Concentrate on features	No change
Product line	Narrow	Broad	Rationalize*	Hold length of line	Reduce length of line
Price	Skimming versus penetration	Reduce	Reduce	Hold or reduce slightly	Reduce
Channels	Selective	Intensive	Intensive	Intensive	Selective
Communications	High	High	High	High to declining	Reduce

* Eliminate weaker items.

now on their implications for developing strategic market objectives and marketing programs. However, our discussion is only a broad overview (see Exhibit 8–8). In later chapters, we conduct a more detailed and comprehensive examination of specific marketing strategies and programs to pursue at each product life-cycle stage—after we have examined in more depth the positioning and marketing-mix decisions that must be made in formulating such strategies.

Introductory stage

There is a vast difference between pioneering a product class and a product type or subtype. The former is more difficult, time consuming, expensive, and involves greater risk. The introductory period, in particular, is apt to be long—even for relatively simple product classes such as packaged food products. Because product type and subtype entries usually emerge during the late growth and maturity stages of the product class, they have shorter introductory and growth periods. For example, unit sales of microcomputers grew at a 56 percent compounded rate for the 1981–86 period. Unit growth is expected to level off to about 5.7 percent annually during the 1986–91 period.[16]

Once the product is launched, the firm's goal should be to move it through the introductory stage as quickly as possible. Research and engineering are critical to ensure a quality product. So is manufacturing capacity to provide adequate supply. Where service is important the firm must be able to provide it promptly (as in postpurchase service and spare parts availability). IBM has excelled in this over the years.

The length of the product line is likely to be relatively short. The limited product line during the introductory period accelerates the firm's learning curve. It reduces production set-up costs and holds down the inventories of the seller and its channel intermediaries.

For sophisticated industrial products, the initial market consists mainly of large companies with enough resources to risk adoption, the technical capabilities to objectively evaluate the merits of the new product, and the most to gain if it works out well. Many innovators involve such target companies in their R&D work not only to test the product, but also because the potential customer's involvement facilitates adoption.

For most consumer products, the initial targeted audience is millions of households widely dispersed geographically. To encourage consumers to try and keep buying their products, marketers use a combination of methods, including heavy demonstration-oriented TV advertising, in-store demonstrations, free samples, coupons, and special introductory prices. The firm must also obtain distribution, in-store displays, and ample shelf space to provide product availability. To do so, it is usually necessary to engage in extensive direct selling to the larger outlets and to provide incentives to the trade. Small wonder that some firms spend tens of millions of dollars launching a new consumer product!

A firm is either an innovator or a follower. If it is the latter, it can choose when to enter the market—at least up to a point. Ordinarily, a follower monitors the progress of the innovator not only to measure the evolution of the demand function, but also to learn from the innovator's mistakes. The follower hopes to find a better product and more effective ways to market it. During this monitoring period, the follower maintains an active R&D and engineering program and a stand-by production and marketing plan. When it appears certain that the innovator's product will break out of the introductory period in the near future, the follower must be ready to launch its

---

[16] Standard & Poor's, p. C87.

product. To wait longer runs the risk of substantial costs and an uphill battle to gain share.

Pricing (introductory stage)

This decision is critical for new products despite the fact that reliable estimates of demand and costs are hard to come by. The problem is made more difficult if the product is new to both the industry and the market. As one writer notes:

> All potential users of the product are unknown, and no comparative market experiences exist—no channels of distribution, no mark-ups, and no production and marketing cost experiences. Customers will question the product's functioning, reliability or durability, the extent of future improvements and how such improvements will affect the product, and the extent, if any, to which prices will be reduced later.[17]

Another difficulty is the influence of the product life cycle on the new product's competitive status. As the product passes through the various stages, changes occur in its promotion, price elasticities, and its production and distribution costs. The actual price level is affected strongly by a variety of factors: the product's value to the end user; how quickly it can be imitated by competitors; the presence of close substitutes; and the effect of price on volume (elasticity) and thus, in turn, on costs.

Pricing strategies should, of course, be related to the firm's objectives. A firm may wish to attain a certain market share, maximize product profits, or maximize the sales and profits of the entire product line. Basic strategy choices involve skimming and penetration. Skimming is designed to obtain as much margin per unit as possible. This enables the company to recover its new-product investments more quickly. Such a strategy is particularly appropriate in niche markets and where consumers are relatively insensitive to price. Penetration pricing enables the firm to strive for quick market development and makes sense when there is a steep experience curve, a large market, and abundant competition.[18] But either strategy is constrained by the prices of competitors' products and close substitutes, the price-setting practices of wholesalers and retailers, possible cannibalization of other line items, and government regulations such as the Robinson-Patman Act.

Promotion (introductory stage)

During the introductory period, advertising and salesforce expenditures are typically high when expressed as a percentage of sales. For the mass marketing of small-value household consumer goods, such as those sold through supermarkets, the advertising and promotion—excluding personal selling—

---

[17] Kent B. Monroe, "Techniques for Pricing New Products and Services," in *Handbook of Modern Markerting*, ed. Victor P. Buell (New York: McGraw-Hill, 1986), pp. 32–42.

[18] Price strategies are discussed in detail in Chapter 14.

to sales ratio is high. For industrial goods, personal selling costs are apt to be much higher than advertising costs.

The communications task at the outset is to build awareness of the new product's uniqueness; that is, its ability to better serve the customer's need. The market for many consumer products is large and dispersed, making the cost of developing awareness via media advertising high. Further, promotional expenditures such as in-store displays, premiums, coupons, samples, and off-list pricing required to obtain product availability and trial are substantial. This was dramatically illustrated by the cookie wars described in Chapter 2. For industrial products, the time required to develop awareness of the product's uniqueness is often extensive, given the number of people in the buying center and the complexity of the buying systems. For example, in order to sell its new superminicomputer to John Hancock Mutual Life Insurance Company, DEC increased the number of staffers assigned to the account from one to five—the same number as IBM.[19]

Distribution (introductory stage)

The importance of channel intermediaries during the introductory stage varies substantially from consumer to industrial goods. The latter are often sold on a direct basis; but with few exceptions consumer goods use one or more channel intermediaries. Product availability is particularly important with consumer goods, given the large amounts spent on promotion to make consumers aware of the product and to induce trial. Distribution is easier if the company uses the same channels as for its other products and has a successful track record with new-product introductions.

Growth stage

This stage starts with a sharp increase in sales—the product literally takes off. The time duration of this stage—especially that of rapid growth—is apt to be short, a few years at most for consumer goods. Early in the growth stage, competitors are most likely to enter the market. These new firms increase primary demand through their promotion efforts.

Important product improvements continue in the growth stage, but at a slower rate, for the product is moving toward technological maturity. Increased product or brand differentiation occurs primarily in product features as firms compete for market share. Not surprisingly, the product line expands during this stage. One important reason for the substantial growth in sales during this stage is the addition of new segments through lower prices and product differentiation. Some color TV producers, for example, expanded to over 40 models during the growth stage to appeal to different

---

[19] Alex Beam and Geoff Lewis, "The IBM-DEC Wars: It's 'The Year of the Customer.'"

demographic and lifestyle segments. The increased number of models slows, at least temporarily, the effects of scale and learning on per-unit costs.

During the growth stage, and especially during the latter part, the firm takes whatever action it can to extend this stage of the product life cycle. This is particularly true for the dominant firm. Extending the life cycle requires constant search for new segments, strong emphasis on improved product quality and new features, and sensitivity to any shifts in the relative importance of different distribution channels. In addition, the firm should try to increase product sales to present users. The manufacturers of mini-computers—most notably DEC—have extended the life cycle of this product type by offering 32-bit superminicomputers that achieve the processing powers of mainframes.

Two classic examples of life-cycle extension are Jell-O and Scotch brand tape, whose efforts to generate more frequent and more varied usage were quite successful. Jello-O increased its number of flavors and promoted the product as a salad base. 3M made its Scotch brand tape easier to use by packaging it in a variety of dispensers and by developing a colored, water-proof, and decorative line for packaging gifts.[20]

Pricing (growth stage)

Prices tend to decline during the growth stage (in real versus inflated dollars); and price differences between leading brands decrease. This has been the case in the computer industry. The extent of the decline in price depends on several favors, including cost-volume relationships, industry concentration, and the volatility of raw material costs. In cases where growth is so strong it outpaces demand, there is little or no pressure on prices; indeed, the situation may enable sellers to charge premium prices. If the industry is capital-extensive and entry is delayed, the innovator can often charge a significant premium.

Promotion (growth stage)

Advertising and personal selling in the growth stage become more concerned with building demand for a company's brand (selective demand) rather than demand for the product class or type (primary demand). Firms pay considerable attention to building favorable attitudes toward the brand on the basis of its unique features. Communications are also used to help cultivate new segments and to retain the loyalty of present buyers. Even though these expenditures tend to remain high throughout the growth stage, they often decline as a percentage of sales owing to the rapid growth in sales.

---

[20] Theodore Levitt, "Exploit the Product Life Cycle," *Harvard Business Review*, November–December 1965, p. 93.

Distribution (growth stage)

Especially for consumer goods, distribution assumes considerable importance during the growth stage. This is particularly true for companies using selective distribution. With only limited outlets in a given market area, the retailer's support is critical in selling the product. Retailers must often engage in specialized selling and servicing, as with pianos, high-priced stereos, and expensive 10-speed bikes. Selective distribution can also apply to nonretail intermediaries such as wholesalers/distributors, manufacturer reps, and brokers. Thus, it affects both consumer and industrial goods sellers. During the growth stage both industrial and consumer goods sellers hope to build a channel or a direct-sales system that provides maximum product availability and service at the lowest cost. If this can be accomplished, rivals are placed at a disadvantage, even to the extent of excluding them from some markets. A brand must attain some degree of success in advance of the mature stage, because during that stage channel members tend to disinvest in less-successful brands.

Shakeout period

At the end of the growth period and prior to entering the mature stage, most industries experience a shakeout period. The reasons for this period are summarized as follows:

> The lustily booming sales of the rapid growth phase of any introduction tends to overstimulate competitive entries, to bring into the market too many brands, too many models, and far too much production capacity. Once the sales climb slows down, and long before it stops, these surpluses of brands, models, and capacities must be squeezed and eliminated. The market cannot survive them all. Surviving sellers will be those whose previously well-executed marketing mix has established preferences at both dealer and consumer levels.[21]

The shakeout period is usually signaled by a drop in the overall growth rate. This turbulent period is often marked by substantial price cuts designed to move excess inventories at manufacturer and dealer levels and, for some firms, maintaining sufficient sales volume to stay alive. When the weaker competitors exit the market, the stronger firms increase their market shares. Thus, major changes in the industry's competitive structure occur during shakeout, as we saw in the computer industry discussed earlier. The firm's objective is not only survival, but also to emerge with an even more entrenched position, including a higher market share.

---

[21] Chester P. Wasson, *Dynamic Competitive Strategy and Product Life Cycle* (St. Charles, Ill.: Challenge Books, 1974), p. 219.

To a considerable extent, what happens to the firm during the shakeout period has been predetermined by how well the brand has been positioned in relation to its targeted segments, distribution, and relative costs per unit. During shakeout, however, a firm must make every effort to rationalize its product line by pruning weaker items and maintaining aggressive R&D and engineering activities. It must also emphasize creative promotional pricing, and strengthen its channel relationships, including efforts to reduce stock-carrying costs.

Mature stage

When sales plateau, the product enters the mature stage, which typically lasts for some time. Most products now on the market are in the mature stage—a fact of considerable importance to marketing.

Stability in terms of demand, technology, and competition characterizes maturity. Buyers are knowledgeable about what the product will and will not do. Industry leaders are now primarily concerned with market position. Strong market leaders, because of lower per-unit costs and the lack of any need to expand their facilities, should enjoy strong profits and high positive cash flows. Even so, the challenges to management are substantial. There is always the possibility of changes in the marketplace, the product, the channels of distribution, and the nature and scope of competition. The latter has been particularly important to U.S. manufacturers in recent years, given the increased flow of goods into America from Japan and West Germany.

The possibility of some change in demand increases the longer the mature stage lasts. If the firm does not respond successfully to the change but its competitors do, then a change in industry structure of some significance may occur. Change presents opportunities and threats; and because it occurs infrequently during the mature stage, a failure to exploit it may condemn the company to a lower share with fewer profits for a considerable time. But even so, the constraints of technical and market maturity are significant; and the decision options for marketing activities are narrowed.

Because of technical maturity, the various brands in the marketplace become more similar; therefore, any significant breakthroughs by R&D or engineering can have a substantial payout. One option is to add value to the product that benefits the customer. This can be done by improving the ease of use with a new container (such as an aerosol can) or by incorporating labor-saving features (such as adding an automatic icemaker to a refrigerator) or by selling systems rather than single products (adding extended service contracts). IBM has increased the versatility of its mainframes as well as their speed and memory capabilities. The extent to which a firm properly positions its brand with respect to quality during the earlier stages determines the brand's ability to withstand price erosion. Increasingly, service (including prompt delivery) becomes a way of differentiating the offering.

Marketing mix changes (mature stage)

Promotion expenditures and prices tend to remain stable during the mature stage. But the nature of the former is apt to change: media advertising for consumer goods declines and in-store promotions, including price deals, increase. The price premium attainable by the high-quality producer tends to erode. The effect of experience on costs and prices becomes smaller and smaller. Competition may force prices down—especially when the two leading competitors hold similar shares. Distribution and shelf facings become increasingly important, as does effective cost management. From a marketing point of view, this means increased attention to pruning weak items from the product line, harvesting share in market segments that are declining rapidly, and redeploying resources to growth segments.

Recycling

Thus far, we have been talking about the mature stage in a generalized way. As we saw in Exhibit 8–4, a product may, after years of maturity, again experience growth. This situation, called **recycling,** can occur for a variety of reasons. A change in raw material costs that lowers the price of the product or increases the price of a substitute product is one. Or a shift in the demand because of environmental change is another. One example was the increased demand for home insulation following the dramatic increase in energy costs. Yet another reason for a recycling is innovation that triggers new product types or subtypes. Examples here include the superminicomputer, nutritional ready-to-eat cereals, presweetened ready-to-eat cereals, corn oil or polyunsaturated margarines, and new types of dog food. In such cases, advertising expenditures and prices for the new product type follow essentially the same pattern as during the regular growth stage.

Firms can sometimes revive products to a point where a whole industry is recycled. This has happened with mature industries, such as motorcycles, watches, radios, and cameras, through product modifications, price reductions, and extensive advertising programs.

Decline stage

Eventually most products—especially product types, subtypes, and brands—enter the decline stage of the product life cycle. The decline may be gradual, as has been the case with certain canned vegetables and hot cereals; or it can be extremely fast, as in the sales decline in some prescription drugs. The sales pattern may also be one of decline and then petrification at a low level of sales as a small residual segment still clings to the use of the product. An example would be the small segment that still prefers tooth powder over toothpaste or gel. In any event, products enter the decline period for various reasons. The two most important are the introduction of technologically superior substitutes and a shift in consumer tastes, values, and beliefs.

Examples of technological advances are electric over manual typewriters, processed over natural fibers, and jet over piston airplane engines. Examples of consumer shifts include preferences for cholesterol-free margarine over butter, most fashions, and enrollments in schools of business over liberal arts programs.

As sales decline, costs increase—due in part to the firm's inability to fully utilize its production resources. Radical attempts are made to reduce costs and the firm's asset base, perhaps by selling or converting part of the business. But even so, many firms vacate the industry. This, in turn, temporarily increases the sales of firms that remain, delaying their exit for some time. Stronger firms, under certain circumstances, can prosper reasonably well for a substantial part of the decline stage. Much rests on the shape of the decline curve. If it is steep and uninterrupted (as with steam locomotives), then little can be done. If it is a steep decline followed by a plateau (as with baby food), then some firms can adjust. If the firm is strong in some segments vacated by its competitors, then it may experience a sufficient increase in market share to compensate for loss of sales volume elsewhere.

Marketing mix changes (decline stage)

Marketing expenditures, especially advertising, usually decrease as a percentage of sales in the decline stage. The extent to which prices decline—if at all—depends upon a number of factors. Prices tend to remain stable if the rate of decline is slow, there are some enduring profitable segments, there are low exit barriers, customers are weak and fragmented, and there are few single-product competitors. Conversely, aggressive pricing (even below cost) is apt to occur when decline is fast and erratic, there are no strong unique segments, there are high exit barriers, a number of large single-product competitors are present, and customers have strong bargaining power.[22] For consumer goods, marketing activity centers on persuading distributors and dealers to continue to stock the item even though they may not promote it. For industrial products the problem may center around maintaining the interest of the salesforce in selling the item.

Harvesting or withdrawal (decline stage)

Harvesting has as its objective an increase in cash flow—short term. It can be accomplished in three ways: Milking, which implies taking out of the business all but the most essential investments over time; internal transfer of assets; and sale of the business or its assets. In any milking operation, management looks for ways to reduce assets, costs, and the number of items in the product line. In attempting the latter, it is suggested that:

---

[22] Kathryn Rudie Harrigan and Michael E. Porter, "End-Game Strategies for Declining Industries," *Harvard Business Review*, July–August 1983, pp. 111–20.

Candidates for product pruning can be identified by a full cost allocation of all expenses. During such calculations, it is necessary to estimate both the degree to which dropping the product may cause loss of sales of other products and the fixed expenses that will continue after the product is dropped. Once a product is identified as a candidate for pruning, a last attempt still should be made to save it, either through asset reduction or price increases.[23]

This approach to milking is best suited to high-margin products. For low-margin products it is usually not possible to regain a profitable posture by either a cost- or asset-reduction program. Early withdrawal would seem to be the best course of action here. The problem lies in predicting what competitors will do. If they vacate, then the surviving firms may benefit—even prosper—at least for the short term. A slowly declining market such as coffee may still be so large that it continues to attract strong competition among rival firms.

INVESTMENT IMPLICATIONS OF THE PRODUCT LIFE CYCLE

The product life-cycle model is a framework that signals the timing of opportunities and threats; thus, it directs investments across and within the firm's product-market relationships. In this section we are primarily concerned with the aggregate level of investments. By matching the entry's market position objective with the investment level required, the profits, and cash flows associated with each stage in the product life cycle, we can better visualize the interrelationships (see Exhibit 8–9, p. 270). As one would expect, there is a high correlation between the market and industry characteristics of each stage, the market share objective, and the level of investment that strongly impacts cash flow.

Investments during introductory and growth stages

Because the introduction of a new product requires large investments in production and marketing, most firms sustain a rather sizable short-term loss. As the product moves into the growth stage, sales increase rapidly and, hence, substantial investments continue. Profitability is depressed because facilities have to be built in advance to ensure supply. The firm with the largest share during this period should have the lowest per-unit costs due to scale and learning effects. If it chooses to decrease its real price proportionate to the decline in its costs, it dries up the investment incentives of would-be entrants and lower-share competitors. At the same time, it lowers its own profitability and increases its cash flow problems. It has every incentive to

---

[23] Charles W. Hofer and Dan Schendel, *Strategy Formulation/Analytical Concepts* (St. Paul, Minn.: West Publishing, 1978), p. 175.

EXHIBIT 8 ◆ 9

Relationship of market position objective, investment levels, profits, and cash flow to individual stages in the product life cycle

Stage	Strategic market objective	Investments	Profits	Cash flows
Introduction	For both innovators and followers, accelerate overall market growth and product acceptance through awareness, trial, and product availability	Moderate to high for R&D, capacity, working capital, and marketing (sales and advertising)	Highly negative	Highly negative
Growth	Increase competitive position	High to very high	High	Negative
Shakeout	Improve competitive position	Moderate	Low to moderate	Low to moderate
Mature	Maintain position	Low	High	High
Decline	Harvest	Negative	Low	Moderate

hold or increase share during this period and to make the required investments to do so.

The innovating firm likely sees its share erode substantially during the growth stage. It must nevertheless still make large investments, for even though it is losing share, its sales are increasing. New entrants and low-share sellers are at a substantial disadvantage here. They must not only invest to accommodate market growth but also to gain market share. If low-share sellers do not gain share, they will continue to be at a relative cost disadvantage with high-share firms. This situation is aggravated as prices decline to a point where low-share firms may not survive the industry shakeout.

Investments during mature and decline stages

As the product enters the mature stage, the larger-share sellers should be able to reap the benefits of their earlier investments. This is particularly so with the leader, who should have lower relative costs. Given that the price is sufficient to keep the higher-cost sellers in business, that growth investments are no longer needed, and that most competitors may no longer be striving to gain share, the leader's profitability and positive cash flows should be substantial. But this does not suggest that the leader no longer needs to make investments. It would be shortsighted not to make every effort to reduce manufacturing costs by improving the plant and its equipment, standardizing common component parts, and improving the efficiency of marketing and physical logistics. R&D and process engineering expenditures should also be continued at a high level.

The generalized product life-cycle model portrays a profitability trend that peaks during the latter part of the growth stage. This is largely based on price competition resulting from overcapacity. But one study of over 1,000 industrial businesses found that despite declining margins, overall profitability does not decline during maturity. The more mature businesses spent less on marketing and R&D and most likely were working with a lower asset base because of depreciation.[24]

In the decline stage, the firm's normative decision is to cease making investments—indeed, cash may be removed from the business if at all possible. But, under certain conditions, a firm may increase its investments in a declining market (that is, when several firms exit, leaving one or more enduring segments open). The extent to which this happens depends on the rate at which total industry sales fall and the firm's response. If the firm plans to liquidate the business, the investment in that particular product-market relationship goes to zero. If it is a milking operation, then the investment—particularly in working capital—will be reduced substantially.

INDUSTRY DRIVING FORCES AND THE PRODUCT LIFE CYCLE

The product life-cycle (PLC) concept has received considerable criticism over the years. The criticism centers around its inability to forecast demand for a specific product and the lack of conclusive evidence to support the bell-shaped curve that depicts a product's movement through the PLC stages.

A major problem with the PLC concept is that it does not specify which forces drive the product through its cycle and what this means in a competitive situation. Because of the great variations across products and markets, it is not surprising that different products have different life cycles. Thus, the concept's major strength is that it represents "a versatile framework for organizing contingent hypotheses about strategy alternatives . . . and directing management's attention toward anticipation of the consequences of the underlying dynamics of the served market."[25]

Undoubtedly a variety of forces drives a firm's objectives, strategies, and plans of action for a given product as it proceeds from introduction through maturity to decline. If we understood these forces, we could anticipate the proximity of the next stage in the product's life cycle and better understand its characteristics. We discuss the more common driving forces briefly next.[26] They may affect the existing PLC in a number of ways, including the

---

[24] Thorelli and Burnett, "The Nature of Product Life Cycles," p. 105.

[25] Day, "The Product Life Cycle," p. 64.

[26] Michael E. Porter, *Competitive Strategy* (New York: Free Press, 1980), chap. 8.

speed at which the product moves from stage to stage, the importance of a particular strategy element such as price, and the severity of the shakeout stage. They can also act to start a new cycle—as might happen with the emergence of a new product type or a new buyer segment.

1. *Changes in the market's long-term growth rate.* This is a strong force; it directly impacts investment decisions, especially those relating to capacity and growing market share. The rate of change has a direct bearing on the intensity of competition. Market growth rates are a result of: (1) changing consumer demographics; (2) changes in the lifestyle and values of the relevant buyer groups; (3) changes in the price or quality of a substitute or complementary product; (4) extent to which a market is penetrated; and (5) product innovation.

2. *Changes in buyer segments.* A change in segmentation can derive from the same product being used by different consumers or the same consumers using the product differently. The significance of such change lies not only in its impact on demand, but also on its effect on *all* the marketing mix elements. Consider, for example, what selling a personal computer to households meant to IBM in product development, servicing, pricing, channels of distribution, salesforce, and advertising activities.

3. *Diffusion of proprietary knowledge.* Learning about basic product technology occurs over time among all industry members. It is particularly important among buyers and rival firms. The major issues are the rate at which such diffusion occurs and to what extent it can be used by buyers to integrate vertically or by new firms to enter the industry. Also, as a result of technology diffusion, products become more alike—thereby increasing the importance of price.

4. *Innovation.* Three kinds of innovation individually and collectively represent major forces of change within an industry: product, marketing, and process innovation. Product innovation is important because it can increase demand. It can also enhance product differentiation, thereby affecting the entry of new firms. Almost always, product innovations of any consequence have a strong effect on marketing activities and costs. Examples of product innovations severely impacting an industry include the digital watch and high-speed printer.

   Marketing innovations include the use of new channel intermediaries, new advertising themes and media, and new selling methods. These can affect an industry's structure by increasing demand and affecting scale economies which, in turn, affect mobility barriers. For example, retail institutions' use of telemarketing to enter new geographical markets has made the industry more competitive.

   Changes in manufacturing processes can have a strong effect on an industry and particularly on barriers to entry. Such innovations can change per-unit costs, minimum efficient plant size, desirability of integration, and scale economies.

5. *Product differentiation.* Over time, once-differentiated products become more like commodities. This affects promotional and price elasticity as well as production and distribution costs. Industries vary in the rate at which this

trend occurs. For instance, digital watches quickly became commodities, while it took many years before the mainframes of the various manufacturers became virtually indistinguishable from one another and price, software, and service became the determinants of sales.

6. *Risk reduction.* Emerging industries are characterized by considerable uncertainty in such important factors as ideal product configuration, market size, rate of demand increase, costs, and buyer characteristics. Understandably, firms have difficulty in deciding which strategy to adopt. There is substantial risk of failure at this time. Over time the uncertainties are reduced; and the surviving firms having adopted successful survival strategies that increase competition. Risk reduction also makes entry easier.

7. *Changes in costs and efficiency.* Experience effects resulting from both scale and learning can cause per-unit costs to decline. When such effects are strong, entry is more difficult and there is strong competition for market share. The more important cost inputs relate to wages, materials, capital, and physical logistics. Changes in these inputs affect prices and, therefore, demand—as well as industry costs, which, in turn, affect scale economies and investments in plants and machinery. A change in exchange rates can also strongly impact competition.

8. *Entry and exit.* Both can be strong forces triggering a change in the industry's structure. Entry by large firms well established in other industries can bring an increase in competition and change the way competition is waged. Such was the case when Philip Morris entered the beer industry by buying the Miller Brewing Company. It then changed the industry's structure by introducing a light beer that impacted the life cycle of regular beer. And, it invested large sums in TV advertising to support light beer. Exit also changes structure by enabling the dominant firms to become even more so.

9. *Change in government policies and regulations.* These can be strong driving forces on entry, costs, bases of competition, and profitability. Examples include deregulation of the airline and trucking industries, changes in the medical benefits provided by Medicare, and regulations on automobile safety.

Because PLCs are integrated systems, a change in one of these forces is likely to trigger changes in others, thus affecting the characteristics of individual stages. For example, a product innovation may increase demand, thereby increasing economies of scale, making entry more difficult, and on and on.

Because many of the changes inherent in the forces discussed above have been occurring more rapidly in recent years, the life cycles are becoming shorter for many products. A study comparing new consumer durables for 1965–79 and 1922–42 found that the introductory time period was substantially shorter for the later period. Thus, such products as calculators, coffeemakers, curling irons, digital watches, and slow cookers introduced between 1965 and 1979 all had introductory periods of two years or less. In comparison, hot plates, irons, toasters, vacuum cleaners, and heating pads introduced between 1922 and 1942 had introductory periods lasting at least 6 years and in most cases more than 12.[27] As noted earlier, VCRs and color TVs have moved rather quickly to maturity, while compact disc players moved through the introductory stage in but a few years.[28] It is much more difficult to manage a short and dynamic product life cycle than a longer, more stable one.

SUMMARY

The product life-cycle concept holds that a product's sales change over time in a predictable manner through the distinct major stages of introduction, growth, shakeout, maturity, and decline. The PLC's implications are that new products sustain a firm's profitability over time and that the objectives and strategies for a product change as it passes through the various stages.

The product life cycle owes much to the diffusion of innovation concept, which explains the adoption process experienced by consumers from the time of first hearing about a product until they adopt it. The five adoption stages include awareness, interest, evaluation, trial, and adoption. Not all individuals move through the adoption process at the same time; thus, adopter segments continue over time.

Not all products go through the typical, or classical, S-shaped life cycle curve. Even within industries the shape of the curve varies considerably. Of the 12 curves, the most common is the classical type, followed by the cycle-recycle. The latter occurs because a price increase in a close substitute, demographic shifts, price decrease, or a basic shift in derived demand restarts the cycle.

The usefulness of the PLC concept depends on an understanding of the definitions of a product and a market. Definitional problems concerning both abound. The product hierarchy consists of the product class, product type, product subtype (where appropriate), and brand. The higher the level of aggregation, the more stable the product life-cycle curve and the more its usefulness is constrained in strategic planning. The structure of a market hierarchy is more complicated than that of a product. Ideally, analysts segment customers on the basis of their usage requirements coupled with product features. The resulting groups are further identified using a variety of descriptors such as demographics, lifestyle, and geography for consumer products. End-user industry, account type, and geography are the descriptors used for industrial products.

Because the characteristics of the product life-cycle stages vary substantially, the firm needs to consider changing its objectives and strategies for a given product-market relationship. These, in turn, impact the level of investment and cash flow. The life-cycle concept cannot prescribe which specific action to take for each stage in the cycle; however, it does provide a framework within which to explore alternative objectives and strategies.

The product life-cycle concept has been criticized for its failure to forecast demand as well as for its bell-shaped curve. But products and markets do evolve and the concept is valuable in

---

[27] William Qualls, Richard W. Olshavsky, and Ronald E. Michaels, "Shortening of the PLC—An Empirical Test," *Journal of Marketing*, Fall 1981, p. 77.

[28] David Cravens, "Strategic Forces Affecting Marketing Strategy," *Business Horizons*, September/October 1986, pp. 77–86.

stimulating managers to think of how the evolution affects the firm's objectives, strategies, and action plans for a given product-market entry. Various major forces impact the demand for an entry, the industry, competitors, and the product. They include long-term growth rates, changes in buyer segments, diffusion of proprietary knowledge, innovation, product differentiation, risk reduction, changes in costs and efficiency, entry and exit, and changes in government policies and regulations.

QUESTIONS

1. Suppose you are the product manager responsible for Whirlpool's line of trash compactors. After more than 10 years, the product has yet to gain acceptance by many consumers. Using the *diffusion of innovations* theory discussed in the text, explain why trash compactors have achieved such poor market penetration. What does this imply concerning the shape of the rest of the trash compactor's life-cycle curve?

2. A few years ago, pet rocks were a *fad* and basic Levi's or Wranglers blue jeans were a *fashion* among younger consumers. Graph the life-cycle curves of the two products on the same chart. How do the two curves differ from one another? What are the major marketing implications for each product?

3. Although Levi's basic blue jeans experienced a period of increased popularity and sales growth a few years ago, the product's life-cycle curve has undergone several "cycle-recycle" phases throughout its history (see curve 2 in Exhibit 8–4). Which factors might account for this life-cycle pattern?

4. Several manufacturers of aseptic packaging (a new paper package that preserves milk and other liquids without refrigeration) have formed a trade association to jointly advertise and promote the merits of such packaging. In light of the life-cycle concept, does their action make sense? Why?

5. Suppose you are the U.S. marketing manager for Pioneer compact disc players. The U.S. market for compact disc players is in the *growth stage* of its life cycle. What are the implications for the decisions you must make about each of the "4Ps" when designing a strategic marketing program for your product line?

6. The U.S. market for color TVs is *mature* and has experienced relatively little growth in recent years. If you were the marketing manager for Sony's color TVs, what marketing strategy would you recommend?

7. Falling birthrates in many communities have caused *declining revenues* for the pediatric medicine departments of local hospitals. Because most hospitals must offer a full range of services, however, they cannot liquidate their pediatrics departments. If you were a hospital administrator, what alternative strategy would you pursue concerning your pediatrics department?

8. How are a product's *profitability and return on investment* likely to change as it moves through the stages of its life cycle? Why do those changes occur?

9. In the United States, both color TVs and automobiles are mature consumer products. But color TVs went from the introductory to the maturity stage of the life cycle in a much shorter time than automobiles. What *industry characteristics or forces* account for this *variation in the length* of the earlier stages of the two products' life cycles?

Chapter ◇ 9

Marketing research and market measurements

FORD TAURUS AND SABLE: REAL WINNERS

Ford's Taurus and its sister car, the Mercury Sable, have been the company's best sellers since its Mustang in the 1960s. Their success is the result of a project that cost $3 billion and stressed quality and the satisfaction of consumer wants and needs. At the outset, Ford used "reverse engineering" to identify the best car features in existence so many of them could be incorporated into its Taurus and Sable cars. It tore down some 50 midsized cars, including the Honda Accord and Toyota Corolla. Ford found, for example, that the Toyota Supra had the most accurate fuel gauge.

In addition to this research, Ford conducted many market studies that led to the adoption of new features, such as painting oil dipsticks yellow for ease of identification. Other studies focused on ways to make the cars more comfortable and easier to drive. Differ-ent kinds of seats were tested with both men and women drivers of different ages; and dashboard instruments and controls were tested to determine ease of use. The studies found, for example, that the best way to turn on the headlights was to turn a large dial located on the left side of the steering column—and that's where it is in Taurus and Sable.

When the cars were ready to be presented to the public, many other marketing research studies were made to determine how best to position the new cars in the consumer's mind and what advertising messages to use.[1]

---

[1] Russell Mitchell, "How Ford Hit the Bull's Eye with Taurus," *Business Week*, June 30, 1986, pp. 69–70. Reprinted by special permission, copyright © 1986 by McGraw-Hill, Inc. Also see, "This Time, Ford Had a Better Idea," *U.S. News & World Report*, December 15, 1986, p. 54.

As the Ford Taurus project illustrates, data about the marketplace are critically important in the development of new products—particularly one as complex as an automobile. Ford managers analyzed substantial quantities of data before deciding on the Taurus project, as they sought answers to such questions as why consumers were rejecting American cars in favor of Japanese models and what was the potential for midsized cars over the next 5 to 10 years. Thus, the search for market opportunities and threats demands the generation of large quantities of data. Some of these data will already exist in the form of secondary source data; others must be collected for the task at hand through specific marketing research.

Marketers rely on research throughout the marketing management process, particularly for such purposes as market targeting, product positioning, strategy formulation, developing marketing plans and marketing programs, and controlling marketing operations. Understandably, research that provides accurate market measurements (both present and future) is critical to the firm's success. Thus, the measurement of market potential and sales forecasting are among the most common activities undertaken by a marketing research unit. These types of market measurements are discussed following an examination of marketing research. The chapter closes with an overview of decision support systems (DSS).

MARKETING RESEARCH

Annual U.S. marketing research expenditures total between $3 and $4 billion. Studies by Market Facts, Inc., show that a substantial majority of responding companies report their marketing research expenditures will increase in the years ahead. Arthur C. Nielsen, Jr., past chairman of the A. C. Nielsen Company, estimates the marketing research industry is doubling in size every five years.[2] Many consumer goods firms spend as much as 1 percent of sales on this activity. It seems clear that marketing research is destined to play an increasingly important role in marketing decision making.

The American Marketing Association defines **marketing research** as "the function which links the consumer, customer, and public to the marketer through information—information used to identify and define marketing opportunities and problems; generate, refine, and evaluate marketing actions; monitor marketing performance; and improve understanding of marketing as a process." Most large firms have marketing research departments that undertake a variety of studies. Almost all companies of any size do research on their products and markets, including market potential, market

---

[2] "Marketing Research Growth Chronicled by Pioneer," *Marketing News*, November 21, 1986, p. 28; and *Practices, Trends, and Expectations for the Marketing Research Industry: 1987* (Chicago: Market Facts, Inc., April 1987).

EXHIBIT 9 ♦ 1

Percentage of consumer companies using marketing research for various applications*

Application	Percent of companies using marketing research
1. New-product screening or new-concept evaluation	95
2. Tracking studies to measure brand acceptance or usage	92
3. Advertising pretesting or copy pretesting	83
4. Basic marketing strategy studies	82
5. Consumer product testing	82
6. Product optimization or product design studies	65
7. Advertising campaign testing	61
8. Test marketing of new products in laboratories	54
9. In-store test marketing of new products	51

* Based on a sample of 84 large companies.

Source: *Practices, Trends, and Expectations for the Marketing Research Industry: 1987* (Chicago: Market Facts, Inc., April 1987), p. 13.

share, sales analysis, and forecasting. Industrial goods companies do more business trend and ecology studies than consumer goods companies; the latter do more research on new products, advertising, merchandising, and packaging.[3]

Exhibit 9–1 shows the percentages of companies that report using marketing research for nine different applications. For the most part, these are concerned with new products (such as Taurus) and advertising. We discuss these and other specific applications—as well as the techniques involved—in more detail in later chapters and confine our discussion here to a general overview of the marketing research process.

If research findings are to be helpful to managers in solving a particular problem, they must be relatively error-free. A research project must, there-

---

[3] Dik W. Twedt, ed., *1983 Survey of Marketing Research* (Chicago: American Marketing Association, 1983), pp. 41–44.

EXHIBIT 9 ♦ 2

Steps in the marketing research process and potential sources of error

Steps	Potential error
1. Problem formulation	Management identifies the wrong problem or defines it poorly.
2. Determining information needs and data sources	Management fails to identify the specific information needed for decision making or the researcher uses the wrong source.
3. Research design, including questionnaire	Ambiguous questions or poor experimental designs result in invalid responses.
4. Sample design and size	Sample procedures result in the selection of a biased sample.
5. Data collection	Errors are caused by nonrespondents, by poor selection of respondents, by the interviewer, or by the nature of interviewer/respondent interaction.
6. Tabulation and analysis	Errors occur while transforming raw data from questionnaires into research findings.

go back & answer quest/help solve problem

Source: Adapted from Table 2–2, "Research Process Steps and Potential Sources of Error That Can Cause Problems in Achieving Scientific Methodology," in Harper W. Boyd, Jr., Ralph Westfall, and Stanley F. Stasch, *Marketing Research: Text and Cases,* 7th ed. (Homewood, Ill.: Richard D. Irwin, 1989), p. 39.

fore, be designed to minimize the magnitude of the overall error. A brief discussion of the six major steps in the research process follows. Exhibit 9–2 lists the steps and potential sources of error. To minimize error, valid and reliable research methods that emphasize accurate measurements and objectivity on the part of the investigator must be used.[4]

Problem formulation

In specifying the problem—or opportunity—to be addressed by a research study, the decision maker and the researcher must work closely together. The researcher needs answers to such questions as, Who is the real decision maker? What are the limits on his/her authority to take action on the problem or opportunity being studied? What are the decision maker's objectives? What are the alternative courses of action? The more in-depth the above questions are answered, the more likely it is that a research plan will be developed that provides the needed information at the lowest possible cost.

---

[4] For a detailed discussion of research methods and their applicability to marketing problems, see Harper W. Boyd, Jr., Ralph Westfall, and Stanley F. Stasch, *Marketing Research,* 7th ed. (Homewood, Ill.: Richard D. Irwin, 1989).

Determining information needs and specifying data sources

Once the problem has been formulated, the decision-making manager should specify exactly what information should be obtained and from what sources. This helps determine the relative importance of the alternative sources of information and enables the researcher to better structure the research design to obtain the required reliability.

Yet another advantage to this requirement is that it gives the manager an idea of the kinds of information obtainable from the research. Among other things, this helps prevent unrealistic expectations on the part of the manager. Only rarely does research provide conclusive evidence as to what is or is not the "right" answer. More typically, it provides a set of clues—bits of information that often appear inconsistent. From these—and prior information—the marketing manager has to make a decision.

The researcher can evaluate the usefulness of the listed information by anticipating the study findings and then trying to answer the question, What will management do if these are the findings? Some findings may suggest courses of action that the firm cannot undertake. For example, if limited financial resources will prevent the firm from taking any action regardless of what the findings are, then there is no reason to undertake a research study.

Data sources

For each piece of information specified, the most reliable source should be sought out. Frequently the best source is not available or cannot be interviewed; for example, a report on how five-year-olds think and feel about a cereal product. Nevertheless, the marketing researcher should ensure that the most reliable available sources are contacted—not just the most accessible ones.

All data come from sources internal to the firm or from external sources. External sources can be further divided into primary and secondary sources, as shown in Exhibit 9–3. **Internal data** are generated by such departments as marketing, accounting, and production in the course of their normal operating activities and are particularly important in the compilation of sales and cost data.

External secondary data are collected by other organizations. They have the obvious advantage of saving both time and money; but their use may create problems. Data must be compatible with the needs of the study at hand; although in most cases, secondary-source data were collected with a different objective in mind. Thus, the fit of the data to the study at hand may be jeopardized. Also, the data may not be current, the units of measurement may not meet the researcher's requirements, or the class intervals may be too broad. For example, the secondary data may use households rather than families, manufacturing establishments instead of retail companies, or reporting at 10-year intervals when a more narrowly defined reporting period is wanted.

EXHIBIT　9♦3

Sources of marketing management information

Internal to the firm	*External to the firm*
Sales and costs broken down by products, markets, and types of marketing activities (advertising, promotion, personal selling, public relations)	Primary sources 　Consumers 　Retailers/wholesalers 　Other business firms Secondary sources 　Government publications 　Trade association publications 　Commercial services 　Other publications

The largest collection of statistics produced in this country originates with the Bureau of the Census. Almost all of the censuses are of value to marketing researchers and are especially important in the preparation of market potentials and forecasts. There are eight censuses: Agriculture, Construction, Housing, Manufactures, Population, Retail Trade, Service Industries, and Wholesale Trade. Most are taken every 5 years, except for Population, which is mandated every 10 years.

The growing demand for marketing data has given rise to an increasing number of companies that make a business of collecting and selling such information. These companies—almost all of which are concerned with consumer goods—fall into one of two categories. Some restrict themselves to research on specific problems faced by their clients, such as advertising copy testing. The other group collects certain marketing data on a continuing basis and sells it by subscription to all buyers.[5]

One well-known retail sales data service is the Nielsen Retail Index. It provides continuous sales data on grocery and dairy products, frozen foods, alcoholic and nonalcoholic products, tobacco, health and beauty aids, housekeeping products, and paper products. Data are obtained by auditing the inventories, purchases, and sales of a carefully selected sample of food, drug, and mass-merchandise stores. Reports include the sales of major brands in a product category, retail inventories, retail and wholesale prices, retail margins, percentage of stores stocking, and special deals.

In recent years, technology has made it possible for purchase and advertising data to come from a single source. That is, marketers know what

---

[5] See "The Nation's Top 50 Research Companies Profiled," in *Advertising Age*, May, 23, 1988.

EXHIBIT 9 ♦ 4

One source fits all

Overnight scanner results so advertisers can make daily media mix adjustments? Satellite transmission of selected ads to target households? Computer keyboards hooked to TV sets so consumers can signal their immediate reactions to trial ads?

These are a few of the wonders the future may hold as single-source research comes into its own. At A. C. Nielsen, single-source means SCANTRACK, a system that started out in 1979 as a replacement for the old Nielsen food index tracking business. Today, SCANTRACK is national with about 3,000 stores in 39 separate major markets (to jump to 50 by the end of this year). But what's exciting about the system is its marriage to household panels and data on frequency of TV commercials. Right now, Nielsen's Monitor Plus monitors TV commercial occurrence in 15 markets and its 500-member household panels are set up in the three major metros: New York, Chicago, and Los Angeles. And household purchasing data isn't limited to grocery store shopping with SCANTRACK. Each household has an individual hand-held scanner to keep track of all purchases that have UPC codes.

Evenutally all this data will come together for advertisers in five databases: store, therefore sales, data; store environment data, such as which products are displayed or run feature ads and what prices are set; coupon *distribution,* as well as redemption; TV commercial viewing; and household response.

"We're trying to find out what specific factors trigger consumer purchase," says Nielsen VP of business development Paul Schmitt. "You've got the manufacturer pumping all these stimuli into households to get them to buy specific products; on the other side, you have the retail store pumping stimuli to get them to shop in that store. So it's not just price, it's not just retailer advertising, display, coupons, TV advertising, or print ads—it's all of them. If we can measure all the stimuli and measure all the consumer response, we can build a model to look at all the influences."

Obviously, processing all this data is an enormous task—and one that Schmitt doesn't take lightly. "It's going to take a long time to develop the diagnostic ability to really analyze all this information, but single-source isn't just a phase. It's going to be around for a long time."

Source: Leslie Brennan, "Quick Study," *Sales & Marketing Management,* March 1988, p. 52.

brands a household buys and what advertising it has been exposed to. For a brief discussion of one-source research, see Exhibit 9–4.

After locating a possible secondary source, researchers must assess its reliability. They must answer the question, How good are the data? If the source specifies the data-collection method used, it can serve as the basis for the evaluation. If it does not, then researchers are forced to judge the quality of the research on the basis of other factors. These include the research sponsor (say, the federal government or a trade association); the purpose for which the study was made (was it self-serving, as is the case with many media audience studies?); and how the data were collected (by mail or personal interview).

Research design

After specifying the information needed and the sources, the next step is to determine the research design. The two major research designs are **exploratory research,** which uses secondary data, case studies, and interviews with knowledgeable people, and **conclusive research,** which comprises descriptive and experimental studies.

Exploratory-research designs

Researchers use exploratory-research studies to learn more about the nature and scope of the problem and to investigate the more likely solutions. Thus, exploratory research is a preliminary step to be followed by conclusive research that tests the relevant findings. Flexibility is the key to the investigation; that is, the investigator is free to pursue ideas as they emerge in the investigation.

There are several ways of doing exploratory research. The easiest is to study pertinent secondary-source data, including reports from research organizations furnishing continuing data. Another is to analyze, in depth, several cases consisting of organizations or key individuals. By making an intensive study of one or more pertinent organizations, one can more easily perceive relationships and understand the "why" behind those relationships. For example, a company faced with problems in selling through distributors might study two or three of its best and two or three of its poorest distributors to identify and understand their essential differences.

Many, if not most, large consumer goods firms use focus groups to explore a given subject area. A focus group comprises 6 to 12 consumers brought together to discuss a given topic. Many research organizations have elaborate facilities that permit discussions to be tape recorded or videotaped and allow marketing executives to watch the proceedings on closed-circuit TV or through one-way mirrors. This has enabled marketers to get a better feeling of consumer attitudes and reactions to the product or advertising in question.

Focus group research is designed to provide insights into some of the complex, subtle aspects of the interaction between consumers and a company's advertising and sales activities. Findings are essentially qualitative in nature—not quantitative measures of, say, how consumers perceive and react to a company's product or advertising efforts. The use of focus groups has spread to include a variety of organizations, other than producers of household packaged goods, as Exhibit 9–5 shows.

Conclusive-research designs

Researchers use conclusive-research designs to test alternative solutions to the problem. Descriptive studies (using the statistical method), often referred to as "survey" research, is the more commonly used design. Determining the

EXHIBIT 9 ◆ 5

Focus groups gain wider usage

As a rock critic for the *Hartford Courant,* Frank Rizzo is used to appraising others' performances. Earlier this year he listened in as a dozen readers of the Connecticut paper
candidly evaluated his.

Unaware of Mr. Rizzo's presence behind a one-way mirror, one reader objected to a
negative review of a concert by Ozzy Ozbourne, a rock star famous for once biting the
head off a live bat. Another disliked Mr. Rizzo's panning of Dan Fogelberg, whom the
critic calls "Barry Manilow for the younger set."

When Mr. Rizzo emerged at the end of the hour-long session, he says, the readers
were "pretty embarrassed." But he assured them that their remarks—both positive and
negative—had been useful. In fact, he feels their heated comments convinced the paper's
editors and administrators, who were also listening in, that his work is widely read. The
paper, for its part, is considering holding similar sessions on a regular basis.

Mr. Rizzo's readers made up what is known as a focus group. Such panels have long
served as an important research tool for consumer-goods companies interested in gaug-
ing the appeal of specific products. But in recent years, focus groups have won a wide
variety of new fans. Newspapers, for example, are using them as a guide in planning new
features, improving graphic design and even deciding how to approach certain stories.
Lawyers are using them to test arguments before a trial. Universities are using them to
tailor their recruiting efforts and fund drives, and public-service organizations are finding
them helpful in determining how to allocate funds.

Source: Amanda Bennett, "Once a Tool of Retail Marketers, Focus Groups Gain Wider Usage," *The Wall Street Journal,*
June 3, 1986, p. 33.

demographic and attitudinal characteristics of heavy purchasers, occasional
purchasers, and nonbuyers of a defined product class is one example. Obtaining brand-awareness levels and preferences for certain brands by different kinds of consumers is another. And determining the buying process and
the role of buying influentials in the purchase of an industrial product is a
third example of descriptive research design.

Experimental research studies have the advantage of permitting the researcher to show cause-and-effect relationships between the variables—
something that can only be inferred from descriptive studies. In essence,
such a design tests a given hypothesis (e.g., a new package design will
increase sales) in a setting where all conditions are controlled except the
relationship between the new package (the experimental variable) and sales
(the dependent variable).

The experimental design method has some serious disadvantages that
limit its usefulness in marketing. These include the fact that most experiments can measure only immediate results because respondents typically
will not cooperate over long periods of time. Also, experiments are expen-

sive; they use small samples that may not be representative of the national market; and they have difficulty holding all other variables constant. They can pose severe administrative problems (getting and maintaining cooperation of the subjects involved); and they can be audited by competitors.[6]

Data collection

The two basic ways of collecting marketing research information are through questioning and observation. **Questioning** is the most common way—almost any problem can be attacked using it; and problems involving attitudes, knowledge, and buying intentions can be approached *only* by using this method. Also, many behaviors cannot be observed because they do not happen on a planned basis. Imagine trying to observe how two people took care of their cars throughout an entire year! With direct questioning, however, the interviewer can take the initiative by going to the respondents rather than waiting for the event to take place.

Unfortunately, collecting data through direct questioning has some substantial disadvantages, too. Respondents often refuse to cooperate. Or they may not be able to remember the information wanted. Or they may be biased by the interviewing process and not want to report things that reflect poorly on their intelligence.

The problem of preparing a questionnaire is deceptive. Does a question mean the same thing to Smith in California as it does to Jones in New York? Will it mean the same to either of them that it means to the researcher? Questionnaires must be carefully designed and tested to produce useful measures—despite the fact that questionnaire construction is still more of an art than a science.

Interviewing respondents is one of the major sources of error in the typical research project. In telephone and personal interviews, an interviewer selects the person to interview, asks questions, and records the answers. Errors can occur at each step. Electronic and computer developments are helping organize and mechanize some aspects of the process, thereby reducing some types of errors—but perhaps adding some new ones, too. The growing concern with privacy in our society and the growing number of telephone and mail intrusions are causing more respondents to refuse to cooperate, thus adding a serious source of potential error. People who agree to participate in a study may not be representative of the population of interest.

Observation is the other method of collecting data. This process recognizes and notes people, objects, and actions, rather than asking for informa-

---

[6] For a discussion of the more common experimental designs, see Boyd et al., *Marketing Research*, pp. 136–61.

tion. Probably less than 1 percent of individual research projects use the observational method. But many of the larger syndicated research services rely on observation to collect data. Development of the Universal Product Code and scanning at supermarket checkout counters have increased the importance of observation as a marketing research method.

Questioning methods

Information can be gathered by questioning respondents through personal interviews, over the telephone, or via mail questionnaires. For years, the majority of all marketing research studies was conducted by personal interviews at the respondent's home. This is no longer the case, however. Telephone and personal interviews at shopping centers now dominate, primarily because they are less expensive and appear to give satisfactory results. For a rating of the various questioning methods on a number of factors, see Exhibit 9–6.

The data-collection step probably contributes more to the overall data error than any other in the research process. Errors derive from nonresponse by some respondents; selection errors by the interviewer; the way the interviewer stimulates responses from the respondent, including wording of the questions; interpretation and recording of answers; and interviewer cheating. Using the telephone is the best way to control the sample, but even here, to complete 100 interviews with randomly selected telephone homes can require 300 telephone numbers and 900 dialings. See the breakdown in Exhibit 9–7.

EXHIBIT 9 ◆ 6

Rating of different methods of communication on selected factors

Factor	Telephone	Mail	Personal at home	Personal at shopping center
1. Quality of information	Excellent	Excellent	Good	Good
2. Quantity of information	Limited	Limited	Excellent	Excellent
3. Control of sample	Excellent	Poor	Good	Poor
4. Response rates of sample	Fair	Fair	Fair	Fair
5. Supervision of fieldwork	Excellent	None	Fair	Good
6. Time required	Fast	Slow	Slow	Fair
7. Cost	Low	Low	High	Medium
8. Versatility	Fair	Fair	Excellent	Excellent

Source: Harper W. Boyd, Jr., Ralph Westfall, and Stanley F. Stasch, *Marketing Research: Text and Cases,* 7th ed. (Homewood, Ill.: Richard D. Irwin, 1989), p. 223.

EXHIBIT   9 ◆ 7

Disposition of telephone calls to sample 5,346 numbers in metropolitan Chicago

Final disposition	*Percent*
1. Number not in service	33.0
2. Completed interview	33.7
3. No answer after 10 calls	2.7
4. Business or inappropriate number	10.7
5. Foreign language required	2.5
6. No one older than 18	.3
7. Selected respondent never reached	4.2
8. Refusal by household or selected individual	10.3
9. Breakoff during interview	1.8
10. Other	.6

Source: Paul J. Lavrakas, *Telephone Survey Methods* (Beverly Hills, Calif.: Sage Publications, 1987), p. 76.

Sample design and size

The sample design determines how respondents are identified and selected. Along with sample size, the design impacts strongly on the cost of the study and the magnitude of any error contained in the findings. In any sampling operation, the first problem is to *define the universe* or population being studied. This is the group that contains all the items that the researcher wants to study—for example all households in the continental United States. To make our definition of this universe operational, we would have to define "households" in such a way that interviewers could identify them while actually conducting the study. The universe also must be defined in a time period—for example, "all households in the continental United States during the month of August 1987."

A second problem is defining the variables or attributes being studied. Assume that a publisher of college textbooks wanted to determine how college and university faculty members ranked the publisher versus its competitors on such attributes as number of titles, unit sales, readability of its books, and the reputation of its authors. A number of variables here must be defined. For example, under colleges and universities, are junior colleges to be included? And under faculty members, are lecturers faculty members? Graduate assistants? Clearly, even such a seemingly simple market study requires precise definitions of the variables.

A third problem is to choose the sample design; that is, the method to be used to select the sample units such as faculty members, in our example. Two alternative designs can be used—probability or nonprobability. **Probability sampling** ensures that every unit in the universe has a known probability of being selected. Probability sampling is the only method that enables the researcher to measure the reliability of the data collected from the sample.

Nonprobability sampling methods do not provide every unit in the universe with a known probability of being included in the sample. Thus, the results cannot be generalized with any degree of certainty to a larger population—the sampling universe. This selection process is not objective; a unit is included because the researcher thinks it should be, because it is convenient, or because a quota of units has been set (say, households having a certain total income, or of a specific race, or family size). **Quota sampling** attempts to structure the sample so that the characteristics of its units parallel those of the universe. That is, the sample of individuals contains the same age, sex, or income distribution as does the universe from which it is drawn. The individual sampling units are not, however, selected at random.

Tabulation and analysis

When the fieldwork is finished, the completed data forms must be processed to yield the information the project was designed to collect. The forms are edited to ensure that the instructions were followed, that all questions were asked or observations made, and that the resulting data are logical and consistent within each form. Next, researchers prepare the data for tabulation. This means they assign the data to various categories, coding it so that the responses can be put on computer cards or tapes, and then tabulated and analyzed.

In the tabulation and analysis function, researchers establish procedures to transform the raw data into the information needed. The data must be arrayed in tabular form, percentages and averages computed, and comparisons made between different classes, categories, and groups. In some cases sophisticated statistical analytical techniques are required. Whatever the actual procedures used to process the raw data, the end result should be information that agrees with the list of needed information defined in step two of the marketing research process.

Specification of the information needed is, in many ways, the most critical step in the research process. It follows from an understanding of the problem involved and what's at stake if the problem is—or isn't—solved. The data-collection form, the tabulation and analysis, and the written report (including recommendations) flow directly from the information needed step.

TYPES OF RESEARCH NEEDED AT DIFFERENT STAGES OF THE PRODUCT LIFE CYCLE

The kinds of information required and the problems to be addressed change as the market and competitive situations change at different stages in the product's life cycle. As a result, a marketing manager may find different kinds of marketing information useful as the product matures. Exhibit 9–8

EXHIBIT 9 ♦ 8

Examples of types of research studies by stage of product life cycle

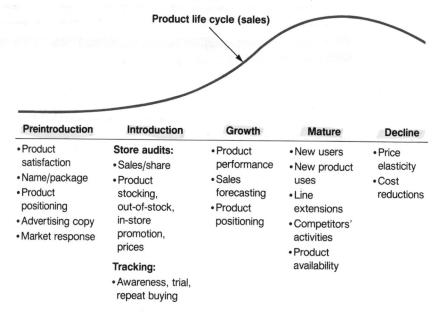

Preintroduction	Introduction	Growth	Mature	Decline
• Product satisfaction	**Store audits:**	• Product performance	• New users	• Price elasticity
• Name/package	• Sales/share	• Sales forecasting	• New product uses	• Cost reductions
• Product positioning	• Product stocking, out-of-stock, in-store promotion, prices	• Product positioning	• Line extensions	
• Advertising copy			• Competitors' activities	
• Market response			• Product availability	
	Tracking:			
	• Awareness, trial, repeat buying			

provides examples of the various kinds of research commonly conducted at each stage of the product life cycle.

In the preintroduction stage, the marketing manager primarily needs to determine the likelihood of market acceptance of the new product. Hence, the primary objectives of marketing research activities undertaken at this stage are designed to ensure that if the product is introduced, it has a good chance of meeting management's performance objectives. Thus, **product testing** is common at this stage as managers try to determine whether a new product can deliver the proposed benefits better than products now on the market. Similarly, **name/package testing** is often done with consumer products to determine whether the name is pronounceable and distinctive and whether the package provides the desired image. **Copy testing** is also common at this stage to determine if the advertising is understandable and believable. Finally, **test marketing** may be done to find out who buys the product and how often.

During the introductory stage, two basic types of marketing research studies, both aimed at assessing how well the new product is performing, are useful. **Store audits** provide retail sales/share data on the new product and on competitors as well as information about out-of-stocks, in-store promotions, and prices. **Tracking,** the second kind of study, consists of periodic (monthly or quarterly) waves of consumer interviews designed primarily to provide information on awareness, trial, and repeat buying by different market segments.

Marketing research studies conducted during the growth stage of the product life cycle focus mainly on the **performance of the new product** versus competitive products. **Sales forecasting** becomes increasingly important as management tries to identify loyal customers and their likely volume of purchases over time. Tracking studies continue to be important, especially with respect to competitive products. Another popular study involves **product positioning.** Does the product appeal to the target market? Does the advertising communicate the appropriate product benefits?

The mature stage calls for marketing research directed at finding opportunities that might stimulate new interest in the product. Typically, studies concerned with finding **new users (segmentation)** and **new uses for the product** will be conducted. Research may be undertaken to probe the possibility of introducing a **line extension.** Also, the effects of any significant moves made by major competitors—especially with respect to new products or product modifications and new advertising campaigns—will be monitored. **Product availability studies** (out-of-stocks and shelf facings) are yet another important type of research undertaken during the mature stage.

Large expenditures on marketing research are not characteristic of the decline stage. The marketing manager may, however, commission research studies that will help to cope with declining demand, including those concerned with **price elasticity** and **cost reduction.**

Marketing research covers a wide variety of studies designed to help marketing managers formulate and implement marketing strategies. As the above discussion indicates, certain research studies are more effective during specific stages in the product's life cycle. However, the typology contained in Exhibit 9–8 is presented only as a general guideline. Given the dynamics of product-markets, marketers may find it desirable to undertake a particular kind of study at any stage in the life cycle.

MARKET MEASUREMENT: THE DEMAND ESTIMATION PROCESS

Market measurements are critical in determining which markets to target (opportunity analysis); what resources to allocate to each (market planning); and whether the firm's sales performance on a segment-by-segment basis is satisfactory (control and reappraisal). The Milwaukee Machine Company example in Exhibit 9–9 describes the research one company undertook to determine the attractiveness of its market segments. It analyzed geographical sales territories, type of product, size of company, and age of machine. Exhibit 9–10 indicates the variation in the company's performance in market share across sales territories.

EXHIBIT 9 ♦ 9

Milwaukee Machine: Measuring the market

The Milwaukee Machine Company, with annual sales in excess of $300 million, primarily produced turning and boring machines selling for $20,000 or more. New management established ambitious growth objectives that led to an evaluation of the company's distribution system as well as individual distributors. In so doing, management noted a lack of information on the market potential of individual sales territories. The company then decided to undertake a research study to appraise its distributors and to assist the distributors to increase sales. This study was to provide a base for setting objectives, formulating strategies, and developing marketing plans.*

Because replacement sales were a significant part of the market for machine tools, management felt it essential to inventory installed machines by type, age, and manufacturer at the county level. The data could then be aggregated to provide information for individual sales territories.

Using a variety of sources (such as trade association membership lists), management discerned the number of large and small plants, or prospects, by county. The company next measured the average inventory of installed machines by size of plant. It selected a probability sample from a list of companies maintained by Dun & Bradstreet and conducted a telephone survey with the sample plants. Only 6 percent of the plants refused to cooperate. With a national average inventory for each large and small plant and the number of both large and small plants in each county, it was possible to project total inventories by type and age of machine by sales territory (accumulation of counties).

*These are machines used for working metal. A boring machine literally forms holes in a metal object, while a turning machine functions like a lathe; i.e., it holds a piece of metal and rotates it against a tool that shapes it.

Source: Harper W. Boyd, Jr., Ralph Westfall, and Stanley F. Stasch, *Marketing Research: Text and Cases,* 6th ed. (Homewood, Ill.: Richard D. Irwin, 1985), p. 813.

Any attempt to measure the demand function for a given product requires that we proceed step by step through the demand estimation process outlined in Exhibit 9–11 on page 294. The first step specifies the time period(s) involved—next year, three years hence, or 1995. The second step identifies the product levels of interest—the product class (for Milwaukee Machine, machine tools), the product type (turning machines), the product subtype (turret lathes), and the brand (Milwaukee). Each of these levels has a different demand function. The higher the level of aggregation, the greater the demand, as expressed in physical or monetary units.

Step three defines the markets involved, which contain all the actual and potential buyers of the product. The descriptors used here are the same as those discussed earlier in the market segmentation chapter. Wherever possible, the descriptors should correlate not only with interest in the product, but also with the ability to buy it. Milwaukee Machine's market consisted of

EXHIBIT 9 ♦ 10

Inventory of all turning machines in use and Milwaukee brand sales of turning machines by age and sales territory*

	All turning machines			Turning machines 0–5 years old		
Territory	Territory inventory	Milwaukee sales	Sales as percent of inventory	Territory inventory	Milwaukee sales	Sales as percent of inventory
1	1,500	466	31%	156	46	30%
2	2,828	445	16	374	83	22
3	145	48	33	17	8	47
4	397	109	27	69	27	39
5	822	309	38	56	40	71
6	789	207	26	77	20	26
7	597	207	35	65	23	35
8	3,881	996	26	351	134	38
9	937	215	23	82	29	35
10	179	98	55	21	13	62

*Inventory refers to machines in use in the various plants within a territory.

Source: Harper W. Boyd, Jr., Ralph Westfall, and Stanley F. Stasch, *Marketing Research: Test and Cases,* 6th ed. (Homewood, Ill.: Richard D. Irwin, 1985), p. 815.

two major parts—replacement and new plants or expansion of existing ones. Our example was concerned only with replacement and included such viable descriptors as present brand owned and age of machine. In addition, the telephone interview obtained data on which brand would be purchased next. Step four further clarifies the market of interest by specifying its geographical boundaries. Milwaukee Machine sought data at the national and sales-territory levels.

Step five consists of making assumptions about the marketing environment—the presence or absence of the more important uncontrollable factors (such as the economy or technology) affecting the demand for the product. Firms also make assumptions about the marketing programs used by other firms in the industry to stimulate both primary and selective demand (step six). In the machine tools example, the company believed that distributors were a critical component of its growth plans and assumed that such was also the case for its competitors. Step seven, an estimate of the market potential, industry sales, and sales by customer type are all outputs of the preceeding six steps.

The demand, therefore, for a specific product for a given time is determined by the response of a particular group of actual and prospective customers (the markets served) to the interaction of uncontrollable factors

EXHIBIT 9 ♦ 11

The demand estimation process

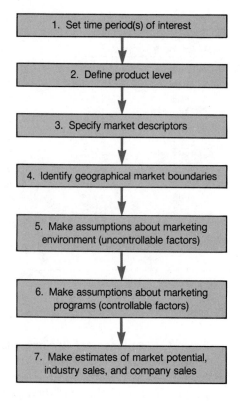

such as inflation and controllable factors such as product quality, advertising, and price.

MARKET POTENTIAL VERSUS MARKET FORECASTS

The demand estimation process yields any number of results depending on the conditions set forth in the various steps. After defining the product and market and setting the time period, marketing managers are particularly interested in knowing the effect of different levels of industry marketing program expenditure on market demand.

Exhibit 9–12 shows the response function for a product-market entry in a particular marketing environment. The curve shows how market demand responds to increases in the monies spent on industry marketing programs, such as some mix of new-product development, direct selling, and advertising. The **market demand minimum** is based on the assumption that some level of sales would occur even without any industry promotion (say, in

EXHIBIT 9 ◆ 12

Demand response function for a product-market entry given a particular marketing environment

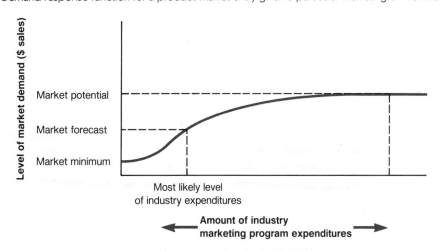

replacements for worn-out machines). As more monies are spent on industry programs, higher demand levels should result—first at an increasing rate and then at a decreasing rate, as the curve shows—until the **market potential** is reached. Between the market minimum and market potential is the **market forecast**—a demand estimate based on the most likely level of industry expenditures on the marketing programs currently in effect. Much of the remainder of this chapter discusses how these three measures are derived and used.

DEFINITION AND USES OF MARKET POTENTIAL

Market potential is an estimate of the *maximum possible sales of a product, a group of products, or a service for an entire industry during a stated period.* This definition contains two critical elements: the idea of *maximum opportunity* and the proviso that it pertains to *all sellers* of a similar good rather than to any particular firm. Thus, the current level of industry sales is not likely to be the "maximum possible," because industry firms may not be marketing their products effectively. And the market environment may change, increasing demand. The market potential is achieved only when all customers with reasonable use opportunities for the product are buying it to the fullest extent. This implies that market potential is seldom achieved, because it is rarely profitable for the firms involved to raise expenditure levels to the market saturation point.

Market potentials are conditional on certain assumptions made by the firm. Consider, for example, the market potential for large (over 36-inch) color TV sets during the late 1980s. Before estimating market potential, firms would have to make assumptions about available screen sizes, price, perceived reliability, warranties and service contracts, and picture quality. A significant change in any of these factors could make a great difference in the potential market for large color TVs.

Uses of market potential data

As we saw in the Milwaukee Machine Company example, data about the sales potential in different market segments can help a firm decide which markets to target. Market potential data are also the basis for allocating the firm's resources across segments. Their most frequent use in marketing is the allocation of salespersons and advertising across geographical areas—hence the need by Milwaukee Machine to gather data at the sales territory level. Market potential data are used geographically in six major ways. All assume substantial variations in market potential across space.

1. *Determination of market entry.* Before a firm decides to enter a new market by expanding its geographic outreach, it should consider the product's present and future potential in the new area.

2. *Location and size of new sales offices, warehouses, and plants.* The potential of various areas is one of several essential criteria employed in reaching decisions on locations for new facilities. The size of each facility depends on the extent of its geographical coverage, which again is a matter of adding up potentials.

3. *Determination of trade channels.* Knowing the potential of an area can help a firm make better decisions about its trade channels, including the alternative of selling directly. Potential is also pertinent in deciding how many middlemen to use in an area.

4. *Determination of sales territories.* If a sales territory has too large a potential, a salesperson cannot handle it and sales may be lost. Conversely, if the territory has too small a potential, the salesperson may be underutilized and consequently too costly. The definition of a sales territory should not be based solely on its potential, however, but should also take into account such factors as distance between accounts and average size of accounts.

5. *Determination of sales quotas.* A **quota** is the amount of sales (in dollars or units) a salesperson or agent should achieve for a given product group in a given market for a stated time. It is a *goal* and is frequently a basis for compensation. A sales quota does not necessarily have to be tied to the area's potential; it could, for example, be tied chiefly to last year's sales. But in the long run, a sales quota should in some way reflect the potential of the area.

6. *Allocation of advertising efforts.* This use of geographic potential is similar to that of allocating personal selling effort. Many mass advertisers of consumer products base the allocation of media advertising expenditures to a considerable extent on the relative market potentials of individual geographic areas.

Limitations to use of market potential

Potentials do not reveal the competitive structure of a market and the firm's ability to exploit it. For example, Chicago may have a high potential for a given firm; but the competition may be so firmly entrenched that the monies required to obtain an improved brand share would be too great. Actually, market responsiveness is a function of the potential, the competitive structure, *and* the firm's input into the market. Thus, the firm must realistically assess its own abilities—including its managerial ability and financial resources.

The firm must augment its market potential data with information about the competitive structure of the individual markets. One firm, for example, obtains the following information about each of its markets:

1. Brands in the market and the brand share of each.
2. Trend of each major brand's market share over the past several years.
3. Amount of money spent by the major brands in advertising currently and over the past several years.
4. Price structure.
5. Distribution structure with particular reference to the leading retail outlets and exclusive distribution franchises.
6. Availability and cost of prime time local station television time.

These data are then combined with the company's sales experience in the market plus the data on market potential. The results form the basis for this firm's allocation of its sales resources across its various markets.

MEASUREMENT OF ABSOLUTE POTENTIAL

There are two basic ways to determine market potentials. The first is sales-oriented, based on current sales of the industry in question and related industries. It is called an **aggregated approach.** The second is customer-oriented, in which estimates are built up from information on the use opportunities of various customer classes. It is called a **disaggregated approach.** We examine these approaches next.

Sales-oriented methods

One way to estimate the potential for a given product is to look at the present sales of the industry. This provides a *lower limit* for the potential. Often, management judgment determines the *upper limit*, the maximum amount of sales increase that could possibly be expected given the lowest possible price and maximum promotional effort. The marketing manager of a certain brand of color TV sets, for instance, might believe that 20 percent of the households can be persuaded to buy two rather than one set in a stated time interval. This would suggest that the market potential for color TVs is 1.2 times industry sales for the period in question.

Sometimes a more refined approach determines which substitute products could be replaced by the product and estimates the percentage of inroads that could be made on each substitute. This approach also estimates the sales of each of these products and determines the market potential by multiplying the percentage and sales figures for each product and summing the results.

Customer-oriented methods

The accuracy of market-oriented estimates can be increased by estimating each segment's potential separately. This allows management to analyze the product's various use opportunities in more detail than if only the aggregate of all customers were considered. They evaluate the tastes and habits of individual consumer groups in relation to competing products. For industrial goods, a detailed economic analysis of the advantages of using one or another substitute can be made. The overall estimate of market potential is obtained by summing the estimates for the various segments.

In a study of the market potential for a new copying machine that could copy one line at a time by an electrostatic process, analysts determined that the following classes of customers represented potential buyers: research libraries, general libraries, abstracting services, and mail-order houses, where the machine might be used to aid order entry. They interviewed representatives from each group of buyers to determine (1) whether the proposed application was feasible for them; (2) whether cost versus benefits made purchase of the machine economically sound; (3) what the buying process and noneconomic obstacles to buying would be; (4) whether the potential buyers seemed interested in the product; and (5) if so, to what extent. Their study showed that the product did not have a viable potential in any of the user classifications.

The outcome of this research shows the importance of a consumer-oriented approach. The new machine appeared to have great promise when viewed generally; but it was dominated by individual specialized substitutes at the segment level. This situation could not have been uncovered without a customer-oriented approach to estimate the market potential.

RELATIVE MARKET POTENTIALS

Some of the problems inherent in defining and estimating market potentials are alleviated when the firm is primarily concerned with allocating a fixed quantity of marketing resources among alternative segments—say, geographic areas. Here it is often sufficient to determine the *relative market potentials*. Suppose, for example, that a manufacturer of industrial equipment is setting up a new salesforce. Research determined that New York represents 12.5 percent of the U.S. market potential and Chicago 6.25 percent. Management might then reason that New York should have twice as many salespeople as Chicago.

There are two major ways of deriving relative market potential: the direct-data method and the use of corollary data. We discuss both in this section.

Direct-data method

The direct-data method assumes management accepts the present level of industry sales in each geographical area or segment as a valid measure of relative potential. This assumes that the true potential, while probably greater than present industry sales, is proportional to sales in the various areas. Thus, the direct-data method of determining geographic potentials is simply to find the percentage that each area contributes to total industry sales.

The primary data sources for this approach are usually government publications or industry figures published by trade associations. The data may also come from syndicated marketing research services, such as A. C. Nielsen, or from a company's own market surveys. Typically, the given data are arranged to conform to the firm's own sales territories. Researchers express the potential for each territory as a percentage of the total. This percentage is then applied to the firm's total volume to derive a company potential for each territory.

Exhibit 9–13 shows the results of such a comparison for the Milwaukee Machine Company for eight sales territories. Note that the data pertain only to turning machines and that the total number in use was assumed to be a reliable indicator of the relative potential (worth) of each sales territory. Column 1 indicates the number of existing machines by sales territory. Column 2 states these existing machines as a percent of all U.S. machines. Column 3 (which equals column 2 × total company sales) refers to the distribution of company sales—if they followed the industry pattern by territory. The exhibit reveals company strength in territories 1, 5, and 7 and a weakness in territory 2.

The implications of situations in which a company finds its sales under potential are not difficult to understand. But what about those in which it is over? To infer that the company should pull back from the strong areas and transfer the saved money to the weak areas would be foolish. It does not take into account the cost of acquiring an additional increment of sales in an "under" area versus the cost of a similar increment in an "over" area. One can easily imagine situations where it would be easier to acquire additional sales in an area where the company already had a share higher than its national share than to acquire more sales in a low-share area.

Exhibit 9–13 shows the distribution of past industry sales of turning machines and reflects the past actions of all companies in the industry. But

EXHIBIT   9♦13

Comparison of industry and company unit sales of all turning machines by selected sales territories

Sales territory	(1) Industry sales	(2) Percent of United States	(3) Company potential*	(4) Actual company sales	(5) Over/under potential
1	1,500	3.76%	297	466	+169
2	2,828	7.10	562	445	−117
3	145	.36	28	48	+20
4	397	.99	79	109	+30
5	822	2.06	162	309	+147
6	789	1.98	157	207	+50
7	597	1.50	119	207	+88
.	—	—	—	—	—
.	—	—	—	—	—
.	—	—	—	—	—
.	—	—	—	—	—
34	371	.93	73	65	−8
Total	39,794	100.00%	7,912	7,912	

* Column 2 applied to company sales of 7,912 turning machines.

Source: Based on data in the Milwaukee Machine Company case in Harper W. Boyd, Jr., Ralph Westfall, and Stanley F. Stasch, *Marketing Research: Text and Cases,* 6th ed. (Homewood, Ill.: Richard D. Irwin, 1985), pp. 813–15.

the cost of acquiring sales is not shown, and trend data are conspicuously absent. Such data would obviously help management arrive at better decisions in allocating its resources across segments. Assume that the following additional data about sales in territories 1 and 2 were available:

	1984	1985	1986	1987	1988
	Company share of industry potential				
Territory 1	25.10%	26.33%	28.57%	29.86%	31.06%
Territory 2	18.30	19.20	18.30	16.50	15.73
	Cost per unit of acquiring sales				
Territory 1	$1,500	$1,250	$1,250	$1,200	$1,200
Territory 2	2,000	2,200	2,350	2,350	2,725

One could argue that the probability of a payout from additional investments would be greater in Territory 1 than Territory 2, because the company apparently has more going for it there. A deeper analysis should identify what these success factors are and the likelihood of their continuing. The point is that a market potential analysis ultimately raises more questions than it answers. It is only a beginning—but an important one.

The principal advantage of using industry sales data to measure market potential is that actual sales results are being used. The method is straightforward and does not require as much detailed analytical work as other methods. Its primary limitation is that the data are usually expressed as past sales. Changes in the industry's marketing inputs or in the environment may not be revealed; yet these changes can shift demand and need to be taken into account.

Corollary-data method

The corollary-data method of measuring market potential is based on the premise that, if one series of data (industry sales) is closely related to a second series (number of persons employed), the distribution of the second series by market areas (sales territories) can indicate the distribution of the first series in the same market areas.

Single-factor index

The simplest corollary-data method is the single-factor index. Researchers use it most successfully when the two items have a derived or complementary demand; for example, the number of industrial workers and the demand for paper toweling. Population and household income data are often used as single-factor indexes in lieu of corollary sales data. This method makes the assumption that such data explain the relative demand for a given consumer item. For example, if twice as many households are in Area A as Area B, then the reasoning is that Area A has twice the potential. *Sales & Marketing Management* annually reports the number of households in four income groups by counties in the United States.[7] For many products, this income breakdown is better than using total income or number of households. For example, a company selling a high-priced consumer durable may wish to consider the geographic distribution of only the highest-income households, as opposed to using the geographic distribution of total income.

The problem with using the corollary-data method is the difficulty of determining the degree of correlation between the related series and the sales of the product under investigation. Ideally, determining the fit would call for a comparison of the related series with industry sales—but if industry sales were available for all areas, there would be no reason to worry about a related series. In addition, it is not possible to validate the usefulness of a related series by comparing it with company sales. Because the aim is to discover where company sales differ from potentials based on industry sales,

---

[7] See the "Survey of Buying Power," *Sales & Marketing Management*, August 1988.

a corollary series to company sales would rarely check out. For a few products, industry sales are available at the state level and can corroborate the merit of a related series. If the fit is good at the state level, it may be reasonable to assume that the related series is adequate to distribute the potential by counties.

Multiple-factor indexes

As the name indicates, multiple-factor indexes use a combination of two or more factors to estimate relative market potentials. Individual companies may develop these for their own purposes, or they might use a general index such as the buying-power index published by *Sales & Marketing Management*. The use of such an index is based on the assumption that several factors affect the sales of a product in a given market. These factors must be represented and properly weighed in the index. However, in practice it is usually difficult to obtain a measure for each factor and to determine its relative importance. Regression analysis, discussed later in this chapter, is often used for this purpose. As with the single-factor index, the problem of validating the appropriateness of the final index also arises. Does it truly represent the relative market potential for a product?

Exhibit 9–14 illustrates the construction of a multiple-factor index involving only two factors: number of production workers and value added by manufacture. The production workers series is assigned twice as much weight as the value-added series, on the assumption that the data are more current. The SIC weights shown in column 8 indicate the relative purchasing power of each industry group. The weights can be obtained from either a market survey or an analysis of the company's sales records.

In Exhibit 9–14, the weighted multiple index is derived from a process that uses two sets of weights—one involving the two factors (production workers and value added) and the other involving the relative importance of each SIC group. The validity of the final potential measure therefore depends not only on the factors selected, but also on the weights used.

This example used the standard industrial classification system (SIC) discussed in Chapter 5 to obtain the basic data. Once a firm determines to which SIC groups its product is sold, it can ascertain from government reports the number of workers employed by each group. The workers in the target SIC groups are then totaled by counties, and the figure for each county divided by the U.S. total to derive percentages.

The buying-power index (BPI) published by *Sales & Marketing Management* is probably the best-known general index of consumer purchasing power in the United States. The BPI combines three factors—retail sales, income, and population—and assigns retail sales a weight of 3, income a weight of 5, and population a weight of 2. Analysts reduce these three factors to percentages of the U.S. total for each county, and weight each percentage. Then they divide the sum of the weighted potentials by 10 (the sum of the

EXHIBIT 9 ♦ 14

A multiple factor index for determining market potentials for an industrial product for the Cleveland Metropolitan Area

SIC code (1)	Industry (2)	Production workers		Value added		Production workers and value added percents combined* (7)	SIC weights† (8)	Weighted multiple index‡ (9)
		Number (000) (3)	Percent of U.S. total (4)	Dollars (millions) (5)	Percent of U.S. total (6)			
349	Miscellaneous fabricated metal	4.2	.021%	274.7	.024%	.066%	.10	.0066%
354	Metalworking machinery	7.5	.038	485.3	.043	.119	.18	.0214
355	Specialized industrial machinery	2.1	.019	130.4	.018	.056	.06	.0034
371	Motor vehicles	7.8	.016	609.8	.018	.050	.38	.0190
372	Aircraft and parts	3.0	.010	268.6	.009	.029	.020	.0058
							.92	.0562%

.0562/.92 = market potential = 6.11%

* Column 7 is derived from the percentages in columns 4 and 6 with column 4 being weighted twice as much as column 6.

† Column 8 gives the relative weighted value of each SIC group where the weights reflect the proportion of total sales of the product sold to the industry. These weights come from the company's internal sales records or from industry sales data when available.

‡ Column 9 is derived by multiplying column 7 by column 8.

Source: 1982 Census of Manufactures, Geographic Area Series (Washington, D.C.: Department of Commerce, 1985).

weights); and the result provides an index of the potential for the county. For example, the buying-power index for an area is determined as follows:[8]

$$BPI = 3(R) + 5(I) + 2 (P)$$

where

R = the percentage of total retail sales
I = the percentage of disposable income
P = the percentage of U.S. population.

A general index such as this is not intended to measure the potential for any specific product and must, therefore, be used with care. The BPI, for example, would be a poor index on which to base estimates of relative potential

---

[8] Ibid.

for antifreeze, because temperature, a major determinant of demand, is not an index factor.

SALES FORECASTING

The sales forecast is the basis for most business planning. Such important areas of decision making as production and inventory scheduling, planning of plant and equipment investments, personnel requirements, raw material purchases, advertising outlays, salesforce expenditures, and cash-flow needs depend on the sales forecast. Any significant error in the forecast, then, could have far-reaching and serious consequences.

Managers base the company's sales forecast by market segment on the estimated impact of a specific marketing plan plus certain assumptions about the marketing environment. If we substitute company sales for the market forecast and company marketing program for the industry marketing program in Exhibit 9–12, we have a visual representation of a company's sales forecast. In practice, a company's sales forecast for a particular product-market entry derives from, first, a forecast pertaining to the macroenvironment and, second, an industry forecast. It is important to forecast the demand for that part of the industry, or the strategic group, to which the product belongs.

Company sales forecasts can be subjective or objective. We discuss both types next.[9]

Subjective methods

One of the more simple methods of forecasting sales is to use the judgment, opinions, or intentions of knowledgeable individuals, both outside and inside a company. Regarding the latter, such forecasting can use inputs from a number of different organizational levels—for example, executives, regional managers, and sales representatives. Probably the most common forecasts in use today are forecasts made by executives.[10]

Over the years judgment forecasting of the sales of a company's product has been improved by requiring a more intense review of the buying situa-

---

[9] A thorough discussion of these techniques is found in Vithala R. Rao and James E. Cox, Jr., *Sales Forecasting Methods: A Survey of Recent Developments* (Cambridge, Mass.: Marketing Science Institute, 1976). Also see the evaluation made by Spiros Makendakis and Steven C. Wheelwright, "Forecasting Issues and Challenges for Marketing Management," *Journal of Marketing*, October 1977, pp. 24–36, esp. pp. 30–33.

[10] Management judgment forecasting systems have received considerable attention in recent years, especially ways of reducing bias. For a discussion of forecasting design features to detect, measure, and reduce forecasting bias, see Mark M. Moriarty, "Design Features of Forecasting Systems Involving Management Judgments," *Journal of Marketing Research*, November 1985, pp. 353–64. Also, see Jean-Claude Larréché and Reza Moinpour, "Managerial Judgment in Marketing: The Concept of Expertise," *Journal of Marketing Research*, May 1983, pp. 110–21.

tion in the field. For example, with major industrial goods it would be important to take into account the decision-making process as well as the decision-making environment. The latter includes key influentials, their choice criteria, and the attributes of competitive brands.[11]

Jury of executive opinion

Some firms begin with executive forecasts, using a **jury of executive opinion.** A number of executives make independent forecasts of sales for the next period—usually a year. These executives have considerable factual data available on which to base their forecasts; and presumably, they possess mature judgment. Then the chief executive of the company considers the various estimates and makes a final decision. A better procedure is to bring the group together to discuss their estimates. This may bring out new ideas and lead some individuals to modify their previous estimates.

The jury method has the advantage of simplicity and of representing a number of different viewpoints; but it may fail to properly consider factors that may impact future sales. One study found that the total error in subjective forecasts resulted from two effects: the error associated with the expertise of the individuals involved and the contagion effect—the tendency of individuals to be systematically biased by factors that influenced all their forecasts.

The study concluded that subjective forecasts should be studied on a trial basis to determine the relative magnitude of the two error sources. If the *expertise error* is relatively large, then the forecasters can be given more information about the individual components of the forecast—for example, trend data on key accounts. If the *contagion effect* is relatively high, then "management should be wary of the use of supplementary information of a general nature. Economic indicators . . . are especially likely to introduce this type of bias if forecasters are urged to consider them."[12]

Salesforce estimates

Salesforce estimates are another common method of forecasting—despite the fact that the salesforce may be biased by quota-based commission programs toward low estimates. The actual process by which a final sales forecast is derived using this method varies substantially among firms. Sales representatives may be asked to state the probabilities of selling various quantities of each product to their present and prospective customers. To help them make better forecasts, they likely receive inputs from sales supervisors, product managers, company economists, and marketing researchers.

---

[11] Jerome E. Scott and Stephen K. Keiser, "Forecasting Acceptance of New Industrial Products with Judgment Modeling," *Journal of Marketing*, Spring 1984, pp. 54–67.

[12] Richard Staelin and Ronald E. Turner, "Error in Judgmental Sales Forecasts Theory and Results," *Journal of Marketing Research*, February 1973, pp. 15–16.

This help should include projections of the general economic climate, activities of competitors, and the planned activities of the firm. In some cases sales reps may be given a forecast for their territories and asked to "adjust it"; or they may be given a range within which sales will probably fall and asked to indicate a most likely figure.

For short-term or quarterly forecasts, it is likely that sales reps can do a better job than sophisticated objective methods—particularly during volatile times. Salesforce knowledge of the probable demand of major accounts for a product over the next several months is about the only basis on which a firm—especially those selling industrial products—can adjust its plans (including those concerned with product and inventories) to the dynamics of the marketplace. Even so, few companies use estimates prepared by their salesforce without some adjustments. Salespeople are apt to be unduly optimistic or pessimistic and often deprecate the impact on sales of other parts of their company's marketing program. Also, there is always the possibility that some will deliberately underestimate demand to obtain a low sales quota.

Buyer intentions

Another way to estimate future demand is to survey prospective consumers about their buying intentions. This is done by a number of research organizations for durable goods (including cars and houses) and certain industrial goods such as machine tools, plants, and some services. Questions are asked about the probability the respondent will purchase a given product or service during the next 6 or 12 months. A probability scale is used to facilitate the consumer's response, ranging from 0 (no chance) to 1.0 (certain) with such intermediate points as .20 (little chance), .40 (fair chance), .60 (good chance), and .80 (excellent chance). Such surveys also determine the respondent's ability to buy and expectations about the general economy. These plus the intentions data are combined to form a consumer confidence measure. The primary reason such surveys are undertaken is to anticipate changes in demand for certain products.

Objective methods

Objective methods are quantitative in nature and range in complexity from relatively simple trend extrapolations to the use of sophisticated mathematical models. More and more companies are using advanced methods in which a computer correlates a host of relationships.

Trend analysis via extrapolation

A simple objective forecasting method is the extrapolation of past sales trends. This method assumes that sales for the coming period will equal the current level or will change to the same degree they did from the prior period to the current one. Simple predictive models are more reliable than might at first be thought—especially for very short-term periods of a month or a quarter under stable conditions. This forecasting method assumes that analysts can identify and measure some past pattern in sales that reflects accurately what will happen in the coming period. Thus, the forecasting task centers on quantifying the trend or tendency in such a way as to project it into the future.

For example, using historical data on total births per 1,000 and current population statistics, analysts can forecast the births in the coming year. If annual consumption rates per infant for strained fruits are known, then a reasonably good short-term forecast for this product can be made. In trend analyses, each time series is made up of four factors—long-term trend, cyclical variations, seasonal variations, and irregular variations. If the pattern of these factors is at all well-developed, each can be separated from the others. The first three can then be projected to determine the sales pattern for the future.

Regression analysis

Regression analysis is used in sales forecasting to measure the relationship between a company's sales and other economic variables. For example, auto makers may find their sales are related to personal income—when incomes go up, car sales go up; and when incomes go down, sales drop. To use this relationship in forecasting sales, the manufacturers must determine the degree of relationship. If income rises 10 percent, do car sales rise 10 percent, 30 percent, 2 percent? Regression techniques enable the producers to estimate the relationship between changes in income and changes in car sales.[13]

The discovery of a relationship between sales and one or more other factors helps to forecast sales. But the analyst's problem is merely shifted from forecasting sales to forecasting the other factors. However, this indirect approach has two advantages. First, because factors such as general economic series and personal income are forecast by many people, a firm can take advantage of the forecasts of experts. Second, in some cases a lead-lag relationship may exist between a series and the company's sales. Income changes may precede changes in auto sales by six months, for example. When such a relationship exists, the correlation with the related series has a direct advantage. A building supply company, for example, has found a high correlation between the sales of its products and building contracts awarded. Because sales lag about five months behind building contracts, the firm can easily forecast its sales five months into the future.

---

[13] John M. McCann and David J. Reibstein, "Forecasting the Impact of Socio-Economic and Demographic Change on Product Demand," *Journal of Marketing Research*, November 1985, pp. 415–23.

DECISION SUPPORT SYSTEMS (DSS)

In recent years, the latest generation of management information systems (MIS), **decision support systems (DSS),** has rapidly gained in popularity. This is due in part to the growing availability of microcomputers and user-friendly software. Originally, MIS procedures led to the presentation and analysis of a regular series of reports to assist marketing decision making. It required an evaluation of each manager's needs, capabilities, and decision-making style. It was extremely difficult to gain any consensus about what data were wanted, how they should be analyzed and presented, and with what frequency. Thus, almost no report formats satisfied all users. Developers were forced to use compromise reports that rarely satisfied anyone. Or they had to tailor the system to meet the unique needs of each manager—an expensive and time-consuming task.

Another problem with MIS involved the dynamics inherent in the operations of such a system. New product-market entries, changes in competitors, realignment of sales territories, and changing managers necessitated a great deal of reprogramming. This, too, required considerable time and effort.

Decision support systems attempt to bypass these problems by designing systems that permit each user to manipulate the data to conduct any analysis desired—from simply adding a set of numbers to a sophisticated statistical analysis. A DSS uses dialog systems that permit managers to explore the data banks using system models to generate reports for their specific needs. Managers can query the computer and, based on the answer, ask another question. This can be done at a terminal rather than asking for a computer printout. For example, a marketing manager who notes that sales are down in a given region can ask the computer whether sales for the product type are down, if the company's brand is losing share, and if so, to which competitors, or if the decline is confined to a specific type of retailer.

DSS are highly flexible and action-oriented. They enable managers to follow their instincts in solving a problem and to do so on-line. Serving the needs of different managers, they are more adaptable to the changing environment. In brief,

> Decision support systems are small-scale interactive systems designed to provide managers with flexible, responsive tools that act, in effect, as a staff assistant, to whom they can delegate more routine parts of their job. DSSs support, rather than replace, a manager's judgment. They do not impose solutions and methods, but provide access to information, models, and reports, and help extend the manager's scope of analysis.[14]

This concept, when applied to marketing decisions, leads to the definition of a **marketing decision-support system (MDSS)** as "a coordinated collection of data, systems, tools, and techniques with supporting software

---

[14] Peter G. W. Keen and M. S. Scott Morton, *Decision Support Systems: An Organizational Perspective* (Reading, Mass.: Addison-Wesley, 1978), p. 1.

and hardware by which an organization gathers and interprets relevant information from business and environment and turns it into a basis for marketing action."[15] Thus, the primary purpose of an MDSS is to help management gain a better understanding of the business environment and what action to take regarding it. An MDSS has the processes required to select and store the data coming from marketing, production, and accounting, as well as from external sources. It also includes the statistical routines that permit the user to perform the kind of analyses desired. In addition to performing such simple tasks as calculating averages and doing cross-tabulations, the system enables the user to employ various statistical techniques to find any important relationships in the data (such as multiple regression analysis, discriminant analysis, and factor analysis).

There is every reason to believe that MDSS will increase in popularity in the near future. Increased competition forces managers to make more decisions more quickly. And the dynamics of the environment make it imperative that managers detect new opportunities and threats early on.[16] Technological advances that substantially increased computer power at a lower cost and the widespread availability of relatively simple analytic computer language make these systems more attractive.[17] The new systems will be concerned with what responses are obtained with what kinds of inputs; for example, what level of awareness resulted from X expenditures of dollars on advertising.

SUMMARY

The search for market opportunities and threats requires analysis of considerable data, some of which is collected via marketing research. Most large companies have their own marketing research departments; and almost all companies do research on products and markets. These and other kinds of research information are collected using a six-step process: (1) formulating the problem; (2) determining information needs and data sources; (3) specifying the research design, including preparation of the questionnaire; (4) determining the sample design and sample size;

(5) collecting data; and (6) doing the tabulation and analysis.

Market measurement is concerned with the development of market potentials and sales forecasts. Market potential is the maximum sales possible for a specific product or service in a specified time period given the probable marketing environment and industry marketing programs. The primary use of market potential data lies in the allocation of marketing resources (especially salesforce and advertising) across geographical areas. Market potentials should not,

---

[15] John D. C. Little, "Decision Support Systems for Marketing Managers," *Journal of Marketing,* Summer 1979, p. 22.

[16] George S. Day, *Analysis for Strategic Market Decisions* (St. Paul: West Publishing 1986), chap. 8.

[17] William J. Bruns, Jr., and F. Warren McFarlan, "Information Technology Puts Power in Control Systems," *Harvard Business Review,* September–October 1987, pp. 89–94.

however, be thought of as the sole or even the most important guide for allocating marketing efforts, because they do not reveal the competitive structure of a market and the firm's ability to exploit it.

There are two basic ways to determine absolute market potential. The first method is based on current industry sales. The second is based on estimates prepared and aggregated from information on the use opportunities presented by the various market segments. The latter method is more difficult, but improves the accuracy of the market-potential estimates.

Some problems inherent in estimating market potentials can be alleviated by using relative measures. Researchers derive relative data using the direct data method or the corollary data method. The latter uses either a single factor or multiple factors to estimate the relative value of each segment.

Sales forecasts are essential to business planning. There are two forecasts—subjective and objective. The former includes forecasts made by executives and the salesforce. Objective methods involve the use of statistics, the application of which ranges in complexity from simple trend extrapolations to the use of sophisticated mathematical models.

In recent years decision support systems (DSS) have gained in popularity because of their ability to bypass the problems of standard report formats and the dynamics of change associated with a brand or product. DSS permit users to manipulate data to conduct any analysis desired. Such systems are highly flexible and action-oriented; they enable managers to follow their instincts when attempting to solve a problem.

QUESTIONS

1. Suppose you are the marketing research manager for a large consumer package goods manufacturer. One of the firm's product managers tells you that her brand has been losing market share in recent months and asks you to *design a research study* to find out why. Describe the step-by-step procedure you would follow in designing the study. Which decisions will you have to make at each step in the design process?

2. A local theater company wants to know whether current season-ticket holders would prefer more comedies or more serious dramas next season. Because program decisions must be made soon, the information must be collected quickly. But the research budget is limited. Which *survey questioning method* (i.e., mail, phone, personal interviews) would you recommend using to collect the information? What limitations might that method impose on the study?

3. Given that *absolute market potential* almost always exceeds actual industry sales, why do marketers bother to make potential estimates? Discuss four decisions that a marketer of industrial grinding machinery might make based on such potential estimates.

4. Suppose that the firm in question 3 discovers that the market potential for grinding machinery is twice as great in Cleveland as it is in Memphis. Should twice as many salespeople be assigned to Cleveland as Memphis? What additional information would you like to have before making a final decision?

5. To more effectively allocate promotional expenditures and sales efforts, the marketing manager for Stouffer's Lean Cuisine frozen entrees would like to know the *relative market potential* for such products in every county in the United States. What variables would you include in a *multifactor index* for measur-

ing relative potential? Explain your rationale for including each variable. Where might you find up-to-date information about each of the variables in your index?

6. In the multifactor index you developed for question 5, would you *weight* all the variables equally? If not, which variables do you think should be given relatively more weight and why?

7. A small snowmobile manufacturer wants to add two new dealerships in a northern region of a midwestern state. Given the following information about the counties in the region, where would you recommend locating the two new dealerships?

8. What are the dangers involved in using *salesforce estimates* to forecast a product's future sales? Under which conditions are such estimates most likely to be accurate and useful?

9. How are the newer *marketing decision support systems* different from the earlier management information systems developed by many large firms? Why are line marketing managers likely to become heavier users of such systems in the future?

County	Popula-tion (000)	Total snow-mobile sales ($000)	Firm's snow-mobile sales ($000)
A	161.3	1,400	93
B	13.4	70	19
C	72	227.5	36
D	261.7	1,417.5	180.5
E	16.2	875	418
F	56.2	1,155	77.5
Totals:			
Counties	580.8	5,145	824
State	3,583.4	14,000	1,600

Chapter ◇ 10

Market targeting and positioning decisions

MARRIOTT HOTELS: CHANGING STRATEGY FOR FUTURE GROWTH

In the period from 1974 to 1987, the Marriott Corporation's revenues from its hotel, restaurant, food service, and theme-park businesses climbed from $691 million to more than $6.5 billion. During the same period, earnings grew at a compound annual rate of about 20 percent. The company manages the largest number of hotel rooms in the United States and is a major operator and franchisor of restaurants, including Big Boy, Roy Rogers, and Howard Johnson.

The company's hotel division accounted for much of this impressive growth. It produced 41 percent of Marriott's sales and over half its 1987 profits. During the past decade the chain spent several billion dollars building new hotels; and its room count increased from 14,110 to 102,893. Until recently, Marriott aimed most of its new hotels at a single segment of the lodging market: upscale business travelers and convention-goers willing to spend from $70 to $90 per night for relatively spacious rooms and consistently good service in fashionable hotels located in large cities. To help ensure a high level of service, Bill Marriott—the firm's CEO—spent much of his 70-hour workweek "managing by walking around," surveying one of his hotel's breakfast preparations at 6:15 A.M. or inspecting hotel rooms, much as the company's ads portrayed him. The firm also developed a strategy of selling its new hotels to outside owners while retaining contracts to manage them. This strategy enabled faster growth and paid bigger fees while allowing Marriott tighter control over its service than if it had relied on franchise contracts like many other hotel chains.

Because of the firm's rapid growth, however, by the mid-1980s it became clear that it would be difficult for the firm to continue to achieve its goals of 20 percent annual growth in revenues and profits and a 20 percent annual return on equity. Marriott's managers projected that growth in the upscale lodging segment would slow to about 2 percent per year by the end of the 1980s. With a projected 80,000 to 90,000 such rooms by then, Marriott would have trouble finding blue-chip locations for more hotels. Even with an 80 percent occupancy rate (one of the highest in the industry), it was clear that the firm either had to find some way to pick up the slack or scale back its objectives.

Marriott decided to continue growing by moving into several additional segments of the lodging market. Frederic V. Malek, the executive vice president who headed Marriott's hotel division, came up with the Courtyard concept as a vehicle for new growth. A Courtyard is a 150-room hotel that is one step down from a traditional Marriott and comparable to a Holiday Inn.

continued

concluded

It is designed to appeal to the more cost-conscious business traveler and middle-income family willing to spend from $35 to $60 per night for a comfortable room.

The midprice segment of the lodging market was overcrowded with competitors. But Marriott's research showed that travelers were unhappy with the quality and appearance of the 20- to 30-year-old chain outlets serving this segment. By putting up new residential-style hotels with bigger rooms, Marriott thought it could steal business from those competitors. Also, by using cookie-cutter designs, building the hotels in groups of 10 or 12 around a single metropolitan area, using common management teams for these "clusters," and minimizing service, Marriott thought it could also reduce overhead and offer lower rates than most of its midpriced competition.

To test the new concept, Marriott opened three Courtyards around the Atlanta area in 1983. They charged $48 a night for a single room (compared to about $57 at a nearby Holiday Inn) and achieved occupancy rates of over 90 percent while drawing only a few customers from the traditional Marriott hotels nearby. Based on those results, the company spent substantial sums building (as of January 1, 1988) 76 Courtyard hotels with 10,979 rooms.

Bill Marriott's multimillion-dollar investment decision was made with full awareness that—by refurbishing their old midprice chains—competitors might win back customers, especially since the low mortgage rates the competitors carried from days gone by would help them cut prices. But Bill Marriott apparently outmaneuvered the competition. A redesign of the old hotels was not considered worthwhile by many owners. Further, the small size of the Courtyards didn't pose a sufficient threat for competitors to spend the large sums required to renovate their properties.

In recent years, Marriott has continued to grow by pursuing additional market segments. Thus, after considerable research, the company has entered the budget market with its Fairfield Inns (under $35 a night). Marriott intends to have 50 to 60 such inns in operation by the late 80s or early 90s. It recently announced it would spend $1 billion over the next five years expanding its Residence Inn extended-stay lodging chain. Currently, it operates 106 such properties with 12,269 rooms. It also plans to open six "catered living" communities for older adults. These communities (called Brighton Gardens) will each have about 100 suites and a nursing care facility of 20 to 25 beds.[1]

---

[1] Drawn largely from S.W. Crawford, "Quality Key Ingredient to Marriott Success," *Advertising Age*, August 20, 1984, p. 4; "Bill Marriott's Grand Design for Growth: Upscale and Down in the Lodging Market," *Business Week*, October 1, 1984, pp. 60–62; Amy Dunkan, "Cheap Dreams: The Budget Inn Boom," *Business Week*, July 14, 1986, pp. 76–77; Tom Ichniowski, "Hey Little Spender, Have These Motels Got a Deal for You," *Business Week*, November 2, 1987, p. 63; Jeffrey A. Trachtenberg, ed., "When Cheap Gets Chic," *Forbes*, June 13, 1988, pp. 108–9; Standard & Poor's, *Industry Survey*, March 10, 1988, pp. 232–35; and Standard & Poor's, *Standard NYSE Stock Reports*, January 17, 1989.

MARKET TARGETING AND POSITIONING

The Marriott example illustrates the central role played by two interrelated decisions in the formulation of a business's marketing strategy. The first of these decisions concerns **market targeting—determining which segment or segments within a market the firm will direct its marketing efforts toward.** Once this decision has been made, marketers are then faced with the question of **market positioning—designing a marketing program and product that a segment's customers will perceive as desirable, and that will give the firm a differential advantage over current and potential competitors.**

These two strategic decisions are the focus of this chapter. In the next section we examine criteria and procedures for evaluating (1) the attractiveness of different market segments, and (2) the business's strengths and capabilities relative to the customer needs and the competitors in each segment. These two analyses help a manager prioritize various market segments and decide which are most attractive.

Of course, a business may not have the resources or the capabilities to target all of the high-potential segments within a market. Thus, the firm may focus on only one substantial target segment—as Marriott did from the mid-1970s into the early 80s—or it may target several smaller segments where it anticipates future growth. In any case, a strategic decision must be made about how many and which segments to target. As customer needs, company resources and objectives, or competitor actions change over time, the target market strategy may have to be adjusted. Marriott did this when it expanded into a second target market with its new Courtyard hotels and more recently into several other target markets with its Residence Inns, Fairfield Inns, and the planned Brighton Gardens. The third section of this chapter, then, examines alternative target market strategies.

Once the target segment is chosen, the critical question is: How can the business position its offering so that customers perceive it as providing desired benefits—and at the same time gain an advantage over current and potential competitors? Thus, the choice of a market position is a strategic decision with implications not only for how the firm's product or service should be designed, but for the design of the other elements of the marketing program associated with that product as well. Marriott's Courtyard concept, for instance, was positioned to attract customers and gain a competitive advantage by promoting larger rooms in newer, more attractive hotels while relying on operating efficiencies to hold costs and prices below the competition's. The last section of this chapter, then, examines some criteria and analytical techniques for identifying attractive positions in a given target market and discusses positioning strategies that a business might pursue.

EVALUATING POTENTIAL TARGET MARKETS

As we saw in Chapter 6, most firms no longer aim a single product and marketing program at the mass market. Instead, they break that market into homogeneous segments on the basis of meaningful differences in the benefits sought by different groups of customers. Then they tailor products and marketing programs to the particular desires and idiosyncrasies of each segment. But not all segments represent equally attractive opportunities for the firm. To prioritize segments by their potential, marketers must evaluate their future attractiveness and their firm's strengths and capabilities relative to the segments' needs and competitive situations.

Analyzing and prioritizing potential target markets

Rather than allowing each business unit or product manager to develop an approach to evaluate the potential of alternative market segments, it is often better to apply a common analytical framework across segments. With this approach, managers can compare the future potential of different segments using the same set of criteria and then prioritize them to decide which segments to target and how resources and marketing efforts should be allocated. One useful analytical framework managers can use for this purpose is the **market attractiveness/business position matrix,** a portfolio model discussed briefly in Chapter 2.[2] At the corporate level managers use such models to allocate resources across businesses, or at the business-unit level to assign resources across product-markets. We are concerned with the second application here.

Exhibit 10–1 outlines the steps involved in developing a market attractiveness/business position matrix for analyzing current and potential target markets. Underlying such a matrix is the notion that managers can judge the attractiveness of a market (its profit potential) by examining market, competitive, and environmental factors that may influence that profitability. Similarly, they can estimate the strength of the firm's competitive position by looking at the firm's capabilities or shortcomings relative to the needs of the market and the competencies of likely competitors.

The first steps in developing a matrix, then, are to identify the most relevant variables for evaluating alternative market segments and the firm's competitive position regarding them, and to weight each variable in importance. Note, too, that Exhibit 10–1 suggests conducting a forecast of *future changes* in market attractiveness or competitive position in addition to, but

---

[2] In addition to Chapter 2, for material concerning the uses and limitation of the market attractiveness/business position matrix see George S. Day, *Analysis for Strategic Market Decisions* (St. Paul: West Publishing, 1986), chap. 7; and David E. Hussey, "Portfolio Analysis: Practical Experience with the Directional Policy Matrix," *Long Range Planning,* August 1978, pp. 2–8.

EXHIBIT   10 ♦ 1

Steps in constructing a market attractiveness/business position matrix for evaluating potential target markets

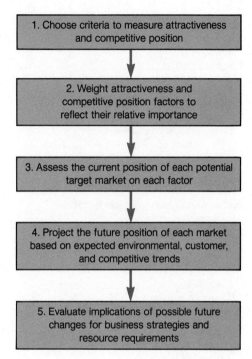

separately from, an assessment of the current situation. This reflects the fact that a decision to target a particular segment is a strategic choice that the firm will have to live with for some time into the future.

Step 1: choose criteria to measure market attractiveness and competitive position

An evaluation of the attractiveness of a particular market and of the strength of the firm's current or potential competitive position in it builds naturally on the kind of opportunity analysis discussed in the previous chapters in this section. Managers can assess both dimensions on the basis of information obtained from analyses of the environment, customer segments, competitive situation, and market potential estimates.

Factors underlying market attractiveness

As Exhibit 10–2 indicates, managers judge the attractiveness of a current or potential target market on the basis of four broad sets of variables. **Market factors** reflect the characteristics of the customers making up the market in

EXHIBIT 10 ♦ 2

Factors underlying market attractiveness and competitive position

Market attractiveness factors	Competitive position factors
Market/customer factors	**Market position factors**
Size (dollars, units)	Relative market share
Market potential	Rate of change in share
Market growth rate	Perceived actual or potential
Stage in life cycle	differentiation (quality/service/price)
Diversity of competitive offerings	Breadth of current or planned
(potential for differentiation)	product line
Customer loyalty/satisfaction	Company image
with current offerings	
Price elasticity	
Bargaining power of customers	
Cyclicality/seasonality of demand	
Economic and technological factors	**Economic and technological factors**
Investment intensity	Relative cost position
Industry capacity	Capacity utilization
Level and maturity of technology	Technological position
utilization	Patented technology (product or
Ability to pass through effects	manufacturing)
of inflation	
Barriers to entry/exit	
Access to raw materials	
Competitive factors	**Capabilities**
Industry structure	Management strength and depth
Competitive groupings	Financial
Substitution threats	R&D/product development
Perceived differentiation among	Manufacturing
competitors	Marketing
Individual competitors' strengths	Salesforce
	Distribution system
	Labor relations
	Relations with regulators
Environmental factors	**Interactions with other segments**
Regulatory climate	Market synergies
Degree of social acceptance	Operating synergies

Source: Adapted from George S. Day, *Analysis for Strategic Market Decisions* (St. Paul: West Publishing, 1986), pp. 198–99; and Derek F. Abell and John S. Hammond, *Strategic Market Planning: Problems and Analytical Approaches* (Englewood Cliffs, N.J.: Prentice-Hall, 1979), p. 214.

question—the benefits they seek, their satisfaction with current product offerings, their power relative to suppliers—and factors that might shape the market's future volume potential, such as its overall size, growth rate, and the life-cycle stage. Marriott was attracted to the budget segment (Fairfield Inns) because it was the fastest-growing part of the hotel market. In 1987, it accounted for 18 to 20 percent of the total number of rooms—up from 8 percent in 1980.

Economic and technological factors examine the capital and technology a firm needs to compete in the market, plus structural variables—such as entry and exit barriers—that help shape long-term competitiveness and profit potential. Marriott has long experience in operating hotels and an outstanding reputation for service. Its expansion program is largely self-financing because it sells the properties it builds (at a profit) and retains their management.

Competitive factors measure the number and strengths of existing competitors in the market and consider the possibility of future competitive changes through the appearance of substitute products. With strong chains seeking to exploit the budget market (155,000 rooms built in 1986), Marriott, as a leading player in the hotel industry, believed it had little option but to enter this growth segment, since growth in its upscale market had leveled off.

Finally, **environmental factors** reflect broad social or political constraints on the firm's ability to compete profitably in a market, such as governmental regulations or special-interest groups.

Each of the factors, shown in the left column of Exhibit 10–2, can either increase or decrease the attractiveness of a market. Unfortunately, the relationship between a factor and market attractiveness is often complex; it can vary across industries and business units. For example, look at Exhibit 10–3, an evaluation of the attractiveness of the market for heavy-duty clutches. The market comprises manufacturers of off-road equipment such as bulldozers and heavy dump trucks used in construction. A business unit of a large industrial corporation undertook this analysis. The unit itself was a relatively small-scale producer of component parts, such as clutches, joints, pumps, and injection systems. We might think that larger market segments represent more attractive opportunities than small ones; but the analysis in Exhibit 10–3 assigns the highest attractiveness rating to a small market segment. Why? Because the business unit's limited resources forced it to look for peripheral market segments big enough to produce reasonable sales volumes, but not so large as to attract major clutch manufacturers, such as Borg-Warner and Bendix, which would be difficult to compete against.

The first step in evaluating the relative attractiveness of current and potential market segments, then, is to identify the determinants of attractiveness that are appropriate for a given industry from the firm's perspective. One caveat is that the factors used to judge market attractiveness should be relevant to all of the markets considered as possible targets. Such com-

EXHIBIT   10◆3

Assessment of attractiveness of the market for heavy-duty clutches

Factor	Rating	× Weight	= Score	Rationale
1. Market size	5*	7†	35	Not big enough to attract large competitors
2. Growth rate	3	8	24	Approximately equal to growth in GNP or lower
3. Cyclicality	2	6	12	Follows construction cycle
4. Structure of competition	4	9	36	Only a few competitors with a strong commitment; rest treat it as a secondary business
5. Stability of competition	5	8	40	High barriers to entry; customers unlikely to integrate backward
6. Customer bargaining power	2	8	16	Customers pressuring for major cost reductions
7. Potential for differentiation	4	10	40	Opportunity to offer improved quality and service
8. Inflation resistance	3	6	18	Limited potential to pass through material price increases
9. Social/political/regulatory climate	4	8	32	No apparent threats
Total score			253 (Out of a possible 450)	

* Ratings are on a 5-point scale, with 5 = Very attractive and 1 = Very unattractive.
† Weights range from 1 to 10, with 10 = Very important

parability is essential if the aggregate attractiveness scores are to be a valid basis for rank ordering alternative markets.

Factors underlying competitive position

The right side of Exhibit 10–2 displays factors managers might use to evaluate a business's current or potential competitive position within a given target market. Once again, these factors reflect the information discussed in earlier chapters dealing with customer, industry, and competitor analysis. The **market position factors** are most appropriate for evaluating markets that the business is already in; they reflect the strength of the firm's current share position and product offerings compared to existing competitors. **Economic and technological factors** can indicate either the business's current or potential competitive advantages or shortcomings in low production costs (capacity use and process technology), or sustainable product differentiation (superior product technology or patent protection). The business's **capabilities** might reflect operational strengths or weaknesses relative to competitors—such as a more extensive distribution channel or more limited financial resources to support future growth.

Finally, managers should consider the possible positive or negative **interactions across multiple target markets.** Such interactions—or synergies—result from sharing operational activities and resources across markets (say, the use of a common salesforce to cover two or more target markets). Or they can result from the carryover effects of customer perceptions from one market to another. For example, Honda felt that its reputation for quality and reliability in the small-car market would carry over and provide a competitive advantage when it decided to enter the residential lawnmower market. Marriott, on the other hand, must have had some worries about whether its venture into the budget market (despite using different names) would hinder its upscale hotel business.

Once again, not all of the factors listed in Exhibit 10–2 are likely to be relevant for judging the competitive position of all businesses in all markets. The managers involved must choose factors likely to be most critical for achieving a strong competitive position—the *key success factors*—across the various markets being considered as possible targets.[3]

Step 2: weight the factors according to their relative importance

The factors measuring market attractiveness and competitive position are seldom of equal importance to the managers involved; and the weights assigned should reflect these differences. In Exhibit 10–3, for instance, the business-unit managers' concern with avoiding larger competitors caused them to weight factors related to the competitiveness of the market heavily, just as Marriott was greatly concerned with the rate of growth of the budget segment and the kinds of chains entering it. However, the precision of the composite scores should not obscure one important fact: the whole evaluation process is subjective and judgmental.

Step 3: assess a market's current position in the matrix

After the managers in our heavy-duty clutch example had rated the off-road equipment market on each attractiveness factor, they multiplied each factor score by an importance weight. As Exhibit 10–3 shows, they obtained a composite attractiveness score of 253 points out of a possible 450. This score suggests that the market was moderately attractive. A similar analysis to assess the unit's competitive position in this market showed very positive results. The firm had entered the off-road equipment market some years before. It currently held the largest share of that market as a result of high

---

[3] For examples of key success factors across a variety of industries, see Kenichi Ohmae, *The Mind of the Strategist* (New York: McGraw-Hill, 1982), chap. 3.

EXHIBIT   10♦4

Location in the market attractiveness/business position matrix of the off-road equipment manufacturers market for heavy-duty clutches

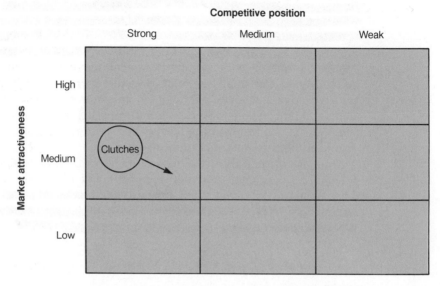

Note: When two or more segments are positioned in the matrix, the size of the circles that represent them are
drawn in proportion to the total volume or potential available in each market.

Source: Adapted from material found in G.S. Day, *Analysis for Strategic Market Decisions* (St. Paul: West Publishing,
1986).

product quality, consistent product innovation, and low costs due to a
highly computerized production process. As a result, management considered their competitive position to be very strong. Exhibit 10–4 shows the two
ratings for attractiveness and competitive position reflected in the market's
position within the matrix.[4]

Step 4: project the future position of a market

Forecasting a market's future is more difficult and more speculative than
assessing its current state. Managers should first determine how the market's
attractiveness is likely to change over the next three to five years. The
starting point for this assessment is the life-cycle analysis we discussed in
Chapter 8, including consideration of possible shifts in customer needs and
behavior, the entry or exit of competitors, and changes in their strategies.
Also, managers must address a number of broader issues, such as possible

---

[4] To aid comparisons across segments when two or more segments are positioned in the
matrix, the size of the circles that represent them should be drawn proportional to the total
volume or potential available in each market.

changes in product or process technology, shifts in the economic climate, the impact of social or political trends, and shifts in the bargaining power or vertical integration of customers. Because judgments about such future changes are highly speculative, it may be best to describe the future attractiveness of a market in several alternative scenarios.

The next question for managers to answer is how the business's competitive position in the market is likely to change—assuming that it responds effectively to projected environmental changes but does not undertake any initiatives requiring a change in basic strategy. The expected changes in both market attractiveness and competitive position can then be plotted on the matrix in the form of a vector (arrow) that reflects the direction and magnitude of the expected changes. Exhibit 10–4 shows this for our heavy-duty clutch example. The management team felt that the attractiveness of the market would decline slightly. Slowing growth and reductions in profitability would result from increased pressure for lower prices by the larger customers in that market. And they forecasted a slight decline in the firm's competitive position due to a narrowing of its technological superiority over competitors.

Step 5: evaluate implications for choosing target markets and allocating resources

Before considering a desirable candidate as a new target market, managers should evaluate a segment as strongly positive on at least one of the two dimensions of market attractiveness and potential competitive position, and rate it at least moderately positive on the other. In Exhibit 10–5 (page 324) this includes markets positioned in any of the three cells in the shaded upper-left corner of the matrix. However, a business may decide to enter a market that currently falls into one of the middle cells if: (1) managers believe that the market's attractiveness or their competitive strength is likely to improve over the next few years; (2) they see such markets as stepping-stones to entering larger, more attractive markets in the future; or (3) where shared costs are present, thereby benefiting another entry.

The market attractiveness/business position matrix, as a portfolio model, offers general guidance for strategic objectives and allocation of resources for segments currently targeted and suggests which new segments to enter. Exhibit 10–5 summarizes generic guidelines concerning strategic objectives and resource allocations for markets falling in each of the nine cells of the matrix. Note that the general thrust of these guidelines conforms to the basic ideas we discussed in Chapter 2. Managers should concentrate resources in attractive markets where the business is securely positioned, use them to improve a weak competitive position in attractive markets, and disengage from unattractive markets where the firm enjoys no competitive advantages. Unfortunately, this approach has limitations in being based on subjective judgments while appearing to be precise.

EXHIBIT   10 ◆ 5

Implications of alternative positions within the market attractiveness/business position matrix for target market selection, strategic objectives, and resource allocation

Competitive position

	Strong	Medium	Weak
High	**DESIRABLE POTENTIAL TARGET** **Protect position** • Invest to grow at maximum digestible rate • Concentrate on maintaining strength	**DESIRABLE POTENTIAL TARGET** **Invest to build** • Challenge for leadership • Build selectively on strengths • Reinforce vulnerable areas	**Build selectively** • Specialize around limited strengths • Seek ways to overcome weaknesses • Withdraw if indications of sustainable growth are lacking
Medium	**DESIRABLE POTENTIAL TARGET** **Build selectively** • Emphasize profitability by increasing productivity • Build up ability to counter competition	**Manage for earnings** • Protect existing strengths • Invest to improve position only in areas where risk is low	**Limited expansion or harvest** • Look for ways to expand without high risk; otherwise, minimize investment and focus operations
Low	**Protect and refocus** • Defend strengths • Seek ways to increase current earnings without speeding market's decline	**Manage for earnings** • Protect position • Minimize investment	**Divest** • Sell when possible to maximize cash value • Meantime, cut fixed costs and avoid further investment

Market attractiveness (vertical axis label)

Sources: Adapted from material found in G.S. Day, *Analysis for Strategic Market Decisions* (St. Paul: West Publishing Co., 1986), p. 204; D.F. Abell and J.S. Hammond, *Strategic Market Planning: Problems and Analytical Approaches* (Englewood Cliffs, N.J.: Prentice-Hall, 1979); and S.J. Robinson, R.E. Hitchens, and D.P. Wade, "The Directional Policy Matrix: Tool for Strategic Planning," *Long Range Planning* 11 (1978), pp. 8–15.

TARGETING STRATEGIES

A firm or business unit with limited resources often identifies more desirable potential target markets than it can pursue. The choice among desirable targets is even more difficult when one is a large, attractive market in which the firm has the potential for only a moderately strong competitive position versus a smaller and less desirable market where the firm could be a leader. For some situations quantitative models help managers select a combination

EXHIBIT 10 ✦ 6
A market selection model to aid managers in choosing target markets

The **market selection model (MSM)** is an optimization model developed to help managers choose target markets that maximize the achievement of a set of objectives specified by the manager while accounting for possible resource constraints. Managers use it to select an optimal set of target markets from among many possible end-user markets, where an end-user market is defined as any customer or customer group (market segment) characterized by a single profile of attributes.

To apply the model, managers must describe each end-user group or market segment by a set of attributes such as growth, revenue, net income, return on investment (ROI), and cash flow. Cyclicality and timing of production demand may also be attributes of interest if a manager is seeking to "smooth out" production to avoid exceeding capacity constraints. A key feature of the MSM is specifying functions that aggregate the attributes across end-user markets. For example, a function might provide an estimate of total business-unit revenue after aggregating the revenues that would be produced by all end-user markets if the unit's resources were allocated across all markets.

Given a set of end-user markets each described in the attribute profile, the MSM helps managers address such questions as the following:

♦ Which set of end-user markets should be targeted to match a desired profile of *aggregate* market attributes; for example, to achieve a desired overall mix of revenue, growth, and ROI?

♦ Which set of end-user markets will produce an aggregate level of performance that falls within specified minimum and maximum constraints on one or more attributes; for example, producing growth above a certain minimum level but not exceeding the rate at which the business can expand its production capacity?

♦ Which set of end-user markets will maximize (or minimize) performance on some aggregate attribute while holding other attributes within specified ranges?

Source: Andris Zoltners and Joe Dodson, "A Market Selection Model for Multiple End-Use Products," *Journal of Marketing* 47 (Spring 1983), pp. 76–88. Also see George S. Day, *Analysis for Strategic Market Decisions* (St. Paul: West Publishing Co., 1986), chap. 8.

of target markets that optimize the accomplishment of management's objectives while taking into account resource constraints. Exhibit 10–6 describes one such **market selection model (MSM).**

When managers in a division of a large commercial bank used the MSM, it indicated that of the 12 market segments then being targeted one should be dropped, one cut back, and several others should receive increased emphasis. By following the MSM's guidelines, the division reduced its staff size, and its profits rose by 5 percent.[5] Whether it is made qualitatively or with quantitative assistance, however, the decision about which markets to pur-

---

[5] Andris Zoltners and Joe Dodson, "A Market Selection Model of Multiple End-Use Products," *Journal of Marketing* 47 (Spring 1983), pp. 76–88.

sue and which to ignore is a strategic choice. It must take into account the business's resources and capabilities, its competitive strategy, and its objectives for volume growth and profitability.

Target market selection strategies

A number of strategies can help guide a manager's choice of target markets. Three of the most common of these are **mass-market, niche-market,** and **growth-market** strategies.

Mass-market strategy

A business pursuing a mass-market strategy can do so in two ways. First, it can ignore any segment differences and design a single product and marketing program that will appeal to the largest number of consumers. This is often referred to as **undifferentiated marketing,** the primary objective of which is to capture sufficient volume to gain economies of scale and a cost advantage. This strategy requires substantial resources—including production capacity—and good mass-marketing capabilities. Consequently, it is favored by larger business units or by those whose parent corporation provides substantial support. For example, when Honda first entered the American and European motorcycle markets, it targeted the high-volume segment consisting of buyers of low-displacement, low-priced cycles. Honda subsequently used the sales volume and scale economies it achieved in that mass-market segment to help it expand into smaller, more specialized segments of the market.

A second approach to the mass market is to design separate products and marketing programs for the different segments. This is called **differentiated marketing.** For example, Marriott did this with its various hotel chains. While such a strategy can generate more sales than an undifferentiated strategy, it also increases costs—in product design, manufacturing, inventory, and marketing (especially promotion).

Niche-market strategy

This market strategy involves serving one or more segments that—while not the largest—consist of substantial numbers of customers seeking somewhat specialized benefits from the product or service. Such a strategy is designed to avoid direct competition with larger firms that are pursuing the bigger segments. It may not require maximum cost efficiencies because it enables the business to differentiate itself using a specific technical or marketing advantage. Hewlett-Packard has followed a niche strategy in the hand-held calculator industry. By concentrating on developing programmable calculators capable of complex mathematical functions, the firm has attained a substantial share of high priced segments containing scientists, engineers, architects, and financial analysts. In this way, H-P has avoided direct competition with the Japanese firms that dominate the popular-priced, four-function calculator market.

Growth-market strategy

Businesses pursuing a growth-market strategy target one or more fast-growth segments, even though they may not currently be very large. This strategy is most compatible with an objective emphasizing future volume growth rather than short-term profits or ROI. It is a strategy often favored by smaller competitors to avoid direct confrontations with larger firms while building volume and share for the future. However, such a strategy usually requires strong R&D and marketing capabilities to identify and develop products appealing to newly emerging user segments, plus the resources to finance rapid growth. Digital Equipment has successfully pursued this strategy in the minicomputer industry. Over the years DEC has established strong positions in several emerging segments characterized by special new applications of minicomputer systems, such as engineering work stations for computer-assisted design activities.

The problem, however, is that fast growth—if sustained—attracts large competitors. This happened to DEC when IBM entered the minicomputer business. The goal of the defender (DEC) is to have developed an enduring competitive position via its products, service, distribution, and costs.

POSITIONING DECISIONS[6]

The success of a product offering within a chosen target market depends on how well it is **positioned** within that market; that is, how well it is perceived to perform relative to competitive offerings and customers' needs in the target segment. Positioning, therefore, has to do with the perceived fit between a particular product offering and the target market. Generally, the better the fit between a product offering and the targeted customers' needs, the larger the market share it can obtain.

The current position of a product offering relative to competitors might be assessed solely on the basis of how the various offerings compare on some set of *objective, physical characteristics*. For example, the typical Marriott Hotel might be compared to Hilton and Hyatt hotels on such things as room prices, size of the average room, amenities such as indoor pools or health clubs, the "free" services offered, and the size of the staff. In some cases this **physical product positioning analysis** provides useful information to the marketer. This is particularly true in the early stages of identifying and designing new product offerings. If no existing competitors occupy a strong

---

[6] This section has benefited from materials provided by Jean-Claude Larréché (Fontainbleau, France: INSEAD).

position on one or more physical attributes, there may be an opportunity to develop a new product emphasizing that attribute, thereby differentiating it from the other offerings on the market.

During the 1970s, for instance, several entrepreneurs noticed that none of the hotel chains offered room rates below $25 per night. Such prices were usually only available from old, unattractive independent motels in out-of-the-way locations. These entrepreneurs felt that new motels could be built cheaply by using standardized designs and low-cost materials, and that land costs could be minimized by seeking isolated locations conveniently near major highways. By combining low construction costs with a no-frills, low-service operation, they believed that such hotels could be profitable charging rates below $25. They felt these motels would appeal to substantial numbers of independent businesspeople who travel without the benefit of an expense account and to moderate income vacationers. As a result, new franchised chains—such as Super 8 and Days Inns—emerged to successfully capture a niche in the low-priced lodging market segment.

A simple comparison of alternative offerings on their physical dimensions alone usually does not provide a complete picture of their relative positions, however. This is because *positioning ultimately takes place in customers' minds*. Even though a product's physical characteristics, its package, brand name, price, and ancillary services can be designed to achieve a particular position in the market, customers may attach less importance to some of those characteristics—or perceive them differently—than the firm expects. Also, as we saw in Chapter 4, customers' attitudes toward a product are often based on social or psychological attributes not amenable to objective comparison, such as perceptions of the product's esthetic appeal, sportiness, or status image. In other words, Al Ries and Jack Trout—two advertising executives who popularized the concept of positioning—argue that positioning has more to do with how the product is positioned in the consumer's mind than with the product per se.[7] Consequently, **perceptual positioning analyses**—whether aimed at discovering opportunities for new-product entries or at evaluating and adjusting the position of a current offering—require inputs from marketing research about the perceptions and attitudes of customers and potential customers.

STEPS IN THE POSITIONING PROCESS

The process of determining the perceived positions of a set of product offerings and evaluating strategies for positioning a new entry or repositioning an existing one involves the steps outlined in Exhibit 10–7. First, managers must select a relevant set of competing offerings. For step 2 they must

---

[7] Al Ries and Jack Trout, *Positioning: The Battle for Your Mind* (New York: McGraw-Hill, 1982).

EXHIBIT 10 ◆ 7

Steps in the positioning process

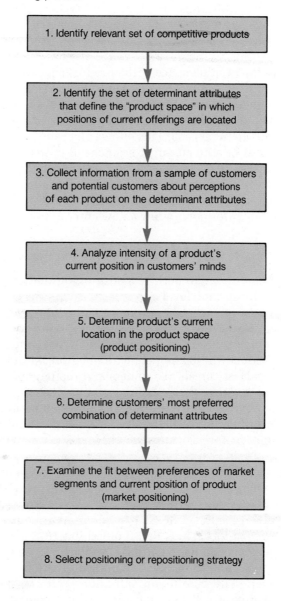

1. Identify relevant set of competitive products

2. Identify the set of determinant attributes that define the "product space" in which positions of current offerings are located

3. Collect information from a sample of customers and potential customers about perceptions of each product on the determinant attributes

4. Analyze intensity of a product's current position in customers' minds

5. Determine product's current location in the product space (product positioning)

6. Determine customers' most preferred combination of determinant attributes

7. Examine the fit between preferences of market segments and current position of product (market positioning)

8. Select positioning or repositioning strategy

identify a set of critical or determinant product attributes. *Determinant attributes* are physical or sociopsychological dimensions important to at least some customers and clearly differentiating among competing brands. Such attributes help determine which brand a given customer prefers; therefore, they are very relevant for defining the product space in which the positions of alternative offerings can be located. Step 3 involves collecting information from a sample of customers about their perceptions of the various offerings. In step 4, researchers analyze this information to determine the **intensity** of a product's current position in customers' minds (how familiar are customers with the product, and does it occupy a predominant position in their minds on at least one determinant attribute). The **location in the product space** of the product's position relative to those of competing products is analyzed in step 5. The customer's most preferred combination of determinant attributes must next be ascertained, which requires the collection of further data (step 6). These preferences can also be located within the product space. This allows an examination of the fit between the preferences of a given target segment of customers and the current positions of competitive offerings (step 7). And finally, in step 8, the degree of fit between the positions of competitive products and the preferences of various market segments can be examined as a basis for choosing a successful strategy for positioning a new entry or for repositioning an existing product.

Step 1: identify a relevant set of competitive products

Analysts can undertake a positioning analysis at either the **product category** or the **brand** level. A positioning analysis at the product category level examines customer perceptions about types of products they might consider as substitutes to satisfy the same basic need. Suppose, for example, that a company is considering introducing a new instant breakfast drink.[8] The new product would compete with other breakfast foods, such as bacon, eggs, and breakfast cereals. To understand the new product's position in the market, the manager could obtain customer perceptions of the new-product concept relative to likely substitute products on various determinant attributes. Part A of Exhibit 10–8 shows a product positioning map constructed from this information. The two attributes defining the product space in this instance were price and convenience of preparation. The proposed new drink occupies a distinctive position relative to the other alternatives because customers perceive it as a comparatively low-cost, convenient breakfast food.

Once competitors introduce similar brands into the same product category, a marketer needs to find out how a brand is perceived compared to its competitors. Thus, Part B of Exhibit 10–8 shows the results of a positioning analysis conducted at the brand level. It summarizes customer perceptions concerning three existing brands of instant breakfast drinks. Notice, however, that two different attributes define the product space in this analysis: relative price per ounce and calorie content. This brand-level analysis is very useful for helping marketers understand a brand's competitive

---

[8] Adapted from Paul S. Busch and Michael J. Houston, *Marketing: Strategic Foundations* (Homewood, Ill.: Richard D. Irwin, 1985), pp. 429–30.

EXHIBIT 10 ♦ 8

Product category and brand positioning

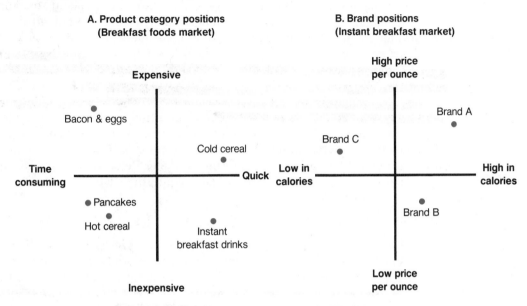

A. Product category positions
(Breakfast foods market)

B. Brand positions
(Instant breakfast market)

Source: Adapted from Paul S. Busch and Michael J. Houston, *Marketing: Strategic Foundations* (Homewood, Ill.: Richard D. Irwin, 1985), p. 430.

strengths and weaknesses in the marketplace and for determining whether the brand should be repositioned to differentiate and strengthen its position. The danger in conducting *only* a brand-level positioning analysis, though, is that it can overlook threats from possible substitutes in other product categories.

Step 2: identify determinant attributes that define the product space

Why did the analyst use different product attributes to locate the positions of product categories and brands in Exhibit 10–8? How did the analyst decide which attributes were most relevant for conducting the two analyses? We saw in Chapters 4 and 5 that individual consumers or organizational buyers can use a number of product attributes to evaluate products and brands. However, only a limited subset of those attributes are *salient;* that is, at least some customers are aware of them and actually use them when evaluating alternatives. But the *importance* attached to those salient attributes by customers often varies. For instance, while the brands of soap or shampoo provided by a hotel may be a salient attribute for many consumers when evaluating hotels, most are unlikely to attach a great deal of importance to that attribute when deciding which hotel chain to patronize. But an important attribute may not play a very big role in determining which brand a consumer prefers if all of the alternatives are perceived to be about equal on that dimension. As another example, deposit safety is an important attribute to consider when choosing a bank; but most consumers perceive all banks to be about equally safe. Consequently, deposit safety is not a *determinant* attribute. It does not play a major role in helping customers to differentiate among the alternatives and determine which bank they prefer.

Marketers should use only determinant attributes, then, to define the product space in a positioning analysis. The question is, how can a marketer find out which product dimensions are determinant attributes? The answer depends on the analytical technique the marketer uses. Choosing an appropriate statistical technique can help the marketer determine which of the important attributes are truly determinant in guiding customers' choices.

Step 3: determine customers' perceptions

Several techniques help marketers collect and analyze customers' perceptions about the competitive positions of alternative products or brands and identify the determinant attributes underlying those perceptions. These include: (1) factor analysis, (2) discriminant analysis, (3) multiattribute compositional models, and (4) multidimensional scaling. Exhibit 10–9 (pages 334–35) briefly describes these methods along with their relative advantages and disadvantages.[9] The primary advantage of the multidimensional scaling approach is that it allows determinant attributes to be inferred from customer perceptions about the similarities and differences among product offerings. The analyst does not have to identify the relevant attributes beforehand. However, the underlying dimensions discovered by such techniques can be difficult to interpret. Also, the scaling techniques require

---

[9] For a more technical discussion of how these techniques work, the data that must be collected as inputs for the different analyses, and their statistical strengths and weaknesses, see Gilbert A. Churchill, Jr., *Marketing Research: Methodological Foundations*, 4th ed. (Chicago: Dryden Press, 1987), chap. 16. For extensive critical reviews of past marketing applications of these different approaches see John R. Hauser and Frank S. Koppleman, "Alternative Perceptual Mapping Techniques: Relative Accuracy and Usefulness," *Journal of Marketing Research*, November 1979, pp. 495–506; and John W. Keon, "Product Positioning: TRINODAL Mapping of Brand Images, Ad Images, and Consumer Preference," *Journal of Marketing Research*, November 1983, pp. 380–92. Also see Paul E. Green, J. Douglas Carroll, and Stephen M. Goldberg, "A General Approach to Product Design Optimization via Conjoint Analysis," *Journal of Marketing*, Summer 1981, pp. 17–37; Michael R. Hagerty, "Improving the Predictive Power of Conjoint Analysis," *Journal of Marketing Research*, May 1985, pp. 168–84; Thomas W. Leigh, David B. MacKay, and John O. Summers, "Reliability and Validity of Conjoint Analysis and Self-Explicated Weights," *Journal of Marketing Research*, November 1984, pp. 456–63; and Paul E. Green, "Hybrid Models for Conjoint Analysis: An Expository Review," *Journal of Marketing Research*, May 1984, pp. 184–93.

special computer programs and are subject to statistical limitations when there are only a few product or brand alternatives to be positioned.

Step 4: analyze the intensity of a product's current position

Ries and Trout point out that in many markets served by similar brands, no one brand achieves any distinctiveness in customers' minds. In other words, none has a very *intense* position in the minds of customers. Ries and Trout argue that the marketer's task is to achieve an intense, distinctive position for a brand so that it is thought of first and evaluated as the best brand on at least one determinant attribute by customers preparing to make a purchase. Consequently, the first step in analyzing the current position of an existing brand is to assess the intensity of that position.[10]

The first question marketers must answer when examining the intensity of a brand's position is: How strongly do customers associate the brand with the product category? Will consumers associate Marriott's Brighton Gardens with retirement communities complete with a nursing-care facility? If most customers are not aware of the brand, it obviously does not have a very intense position in their minds. When customers think about a product class, one or two brands usually come to their minds first: Xerox in copiers, IBM in computers, Kleenex in facial tissues, and Hertz—followed perhaps by Avis, National, and Budget—in rental cars. The brand that most customers think of first when considering a product category has the most intense position in the market. This **top-of-mind awareness** is particularly important for low-involvement products where most consumers do not search for information or compare alternatives before making a purchase. One easy way to measure the intensity of a brand's association within a product category is to compare the proportion of "first mentions" it receives relative to other brands using *unaided brand recall*. (Customers are asked to name all the brands they can think of in a product category within a specified time limit without any prompting from the interviewer.)

Perhaps more important, the positioning intensity of a brand also depends on how strongly customers associate it with one or more determinant attributes when deciding which brand to buy. The brand that establishes a dominant position in customers' minds on one or more of these attributes is also likely to achieve a dominant position in market share. For instance, a large segment of consumers consider decay prevention to be a critical attribute when buying toothpaste. Many brands have similar fluoride ingredients and are now endorsed by the American Dental Association as effective decay fighters. Crest, however, was the first brand to seek and receive such an endorsement—a fact that Procter & Gamble has promoted heavily over the years. Consequently, Crest has the strongest positioning as a

---

[10] Ries and Trout, *Positioning.*

EXHIBIT 10 ◆ 9

Alternative methods for analyzing customers' perceptions of the competitive positions of different products or brands

---

1. Factor analysis

To employ factor analysis, the analyst must first identify the salient attributes consumers use to evaluate products in the category under study. The analyst then collects data from a sample of consumers concerning their ratings of each product or brand on all attributes. The factor analysis program then determines which attributes are related to the same underlying construct ("load" on the same factor). The analyst uses those underlying constructs or factors as the dimensions for a product space map, and the program indicates where each product or brand is perceived to be located on each factor.

Advantages are that the analyst can use both objective and subjective attributes; and the dimensions of the product space are relatively easy to determine and interpret. Disadvantages include the fact that the analyst must identify salient attributes before collecting data; and the factors identified are a function of the attributes used in data collection. For example, if one attribute is asked repeatedly in several related forms (e.g., rating cars on miles per gallon, fuel efficiency, acceleration), that attribute shows up as a major underlying factor (e.g., a "fuel efficiency" dimension). Thus, factors can be as much a function of the attributes examined as of product characteristics consumers actually hold to be important.

For examples of factor analysis applied to product and market positioning, see John R. Hauser and Glen Urban, "A Normative Methodology for Modeling Consumer Response to Innovations," *Operations Research* 25 (July–August 1977), pp. 579–619; and Joel Huber and Morris B. Holbrook, "Using Attribute Ratings for Product Positioning: Some Distinctions Among Compositional Approaches," *Journal of Marketing Research* 16 (November 1979), pp. 507–15.

2. Discriminant analysis

Discriminant analysis requires the same input data as factor analysis. The discriminant analysis program then determines consumers' perceptual dimensions on the basis of which attributes best differentiate—or discriminate—among brands. Once again, those underlying dimensions can be used to construct a product space map; but they are usually not as easily interpretable as the factors identified through factor analysis. Also, as with factor analysis, the underlying dimensions may be more a function of the attributes used to collect consumer ratings than of the product characteristics that consumers actually consider to be most important.

For examples of the use of discriminant analysis in product positioning, see Richard M. Johnson, "Multiple Discriminant Analysis Applied to Marketing Research," *Market Facts, Inc.*, January 1970; and Edgar A. Pessemier, *Product Management: Strategy and Organization* (New York: Wiley/Hamilton, 1977), pp. 234–41.

---

decay-preventing toothpaste and holds the biggest share of the toothpaste market.

Strategies for intensifying a product's perceived position

It is difficult to establish strong associations between a brand and more than one, two—or at most, three—attributes. This is particularly true for low-involvement products that people do not spend much time thinking about.

EXHIBIT   10 ♦ 9
(*concluded*)

3. Multiattribute compositional models (conjoint measurement)

Conjoint measurement determines which combination of a limited number of attributes is most preferred by consumers. The technique is helpful for identifying appealing new product designs and important points that might be included in a product's advertising. Although it can provide some insights about consumer preferences, however, it cannot provide information about how consumers perceive the positioning of existing products in relation to product dimensions. In other words, it is not very useful for product positioning analysis because it does not show how similar two products are perceived to be on underlying determinant attributes.

For examples of marketing applications of conjoint measurement, see John R. Hauser and Steven M. Shugan, "Intensity Measures of Consumer Preference," *Operations Research* 28 (March–April 1980), pp. 278–320; and Paul E. Green, "Hybrid Models for Conjoint Analysis: An Expository Review," *Journal of Marketing Research* 21 (May 1984), pp. 155–69.

4. Multidimensional scaling

Unlike the other techniques where the underlying dimensions identified depend on the attributes supplied by the researcher when collecting data, multidimensional scaling produces dimensions based on consumer judgments about the similarity of—or their preferences for—the actual brands. These underlying dimensions are thought to be the basic affective dimensions that consumers actually use to evaluate alternative brands in the product class. Multidimensional scaling programs that use similarities data construct geometrically spaced maps on which the brands perceived to be most similar are placed close together. Those that use consumer preferences produce joint space maps that show consumer ideal points and then position the most preferred brands close to those ideal points.

Unfortunately, the underlying dimensions of the maps produced by multidimensional scaling can be difficult to interpret. Also, the dimensions identified are only those dimensions that already exist for currently available brands. This makes the technique less useful for investigating new-product concepts that might involve new characteristics. Finally, the technique is subject to statistical limitations when the number of alternative brands being investigated is small. As a rule of thumb, such techniques should only be applied when at least eight or more different products or brands are being examined.

For examples of multidimensional scaling applications to product and market positioning analysis, see Paul E. Green, Yoram Wind, and Henry J. Claycamp, "Brand-Features Congruence Mapping," *Journal of Marketing Research* 12 (August 1975), pp. 306–13; and John W. Keon, "Product Positioning: TRINODAL Mapping of Brand Images, Ad Images, and Consumer Preference," *Journal of Marketing Research* 20 (November 1983), pp. 380–92.

Thus, most brands that have been successful at establishing intense positions in customers' minds have concentrated on only one or a few critical dimensions, as P&G did with Crest. As another example, since introducing Lite beer, Miller has consistently stressed three attributes: fewer calories, less filling, and tastes great. Even without explicitly mentioning diet or weight reduction, Miller has managed to convey an image of ruggedness by using retired athletes in its TV commercials.

But what if a competing brand already occupies the dominant position on the attribute that is most important for a majority of consumers? Competing head-on with a competitor on a dimension where the other brand is already perceived to occupy a strong position is difficult at best, and usually ineffective. A better option is to concentrate on an attribute not strongly associated with the dominant brand, and to position the challenger as a feasible substitute under certain situations or for a peripheral segment of the market. Avis pursued one of the most successful positioning strategies based on this principle during the 1970s, when the firm admitted "We're number two, so we try harder." Avis did not try to dislodge Hertz from its number-one position by claiming it was better on all dimensions. Instead it focused on one attribute—customer service—and succeeded in making inroads into Hertz's market share, as well as those of smaller competitors.

Constraints imposed by an intense position

Marketers should not only seek an intense position for their brands, but also keep in mind that attaining such a position can impose some constraints on future strategies. For one thing, an intense position is very difficult to change. If shifts in the market environment should cause customers to reduce the importance they attach to a current determinant attribute, it can be difficult for a brand that has an intensely perceived position on that attribute to reposition itself. This problem has plagued Sears for a number of years. In view of the prosperity and sophisticated tastes of the baby boom generation, Sears has attempted to trade-up many of its soft goods and fashion lines. But this has been difficult to accomplish because of the firm's strong perceived position as a low-priced mass merchandiser.

Another danger associated with an intensely positioned brand is the temptation to overexploit that position by using the brand name on line extensions and new products. The danger here is that the new products may not fit the original positioning and the brand's strong image may become diluted. Scott Paper provides an example of the problems caused by diluting a brand's position with new products. After achieving a strong position in the toilet tissue market with its Scott brand, the firm introduced a variety of other paper products with such names as ScotTowels, ScotTissue, Scottkins, and Babyscott. None of these new products achieved a strong position of its own and only served to dilute the positioning intensity of the Scott brand name. Procter & Gamble took advantage of this fact to capture the number-one share in the toilet tissue market with the Charmin brand. As Trout and Ries point out, "The housewife could write Charmin, Kleenex, Bounty, and Pampers on her shopping list and know exactly what products she was going to get. 'Scott' on a shopping list has no meaning."[11]

---

[11] Ibid.

Step 5: analyze the product's current relative position

How does a marketer know if a brand occupies a strong position on a particular attribute? The only way to find out is to collect information through marketing research and analyze it using the techniques in Exhibit 10–9. An example of what can be done with such information is shown in Exhibit 10–10. It shows the results of a sample of consumers' ratings of a number of automobile brands on several attributes, analyzed with a discriminant analysis program. The analysts designated the two underlying determinant attributes as "conservative/appeals to older people versus sporty/spirited performance/appeals to young people" and "practical/affordable versus classy/distinctive looking." Since the attributes the analysts chose to have consumers use in rating the brands influenced these dimensions, the true meaning is open to interpretation.

EXHIBIT 10 ✦ 10

Product positioning map of selected automobile brands

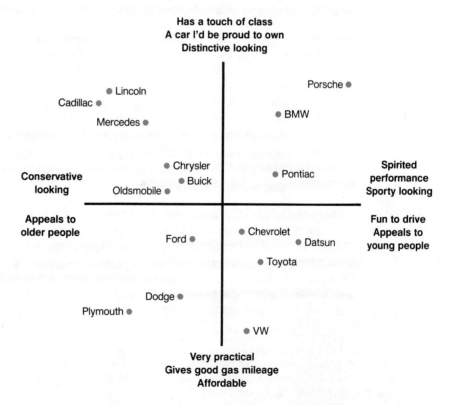

Source: John Koten, "Car Makers Use 'Image' Map as Tool to Position Products," *The Wall Street Journal,* March 22, 1984, p. 31.

Some brands—such as Porsche and Volkswagen—occupy relatively isolated positions away from any of the other brands included in the analysis; others occupy positions relatively close together in consumers' minds, such as Oldsmobile, Buick, and Chrysler. Because brands positioned near one another are considered by consumers to be relatively similar, the degree of substitutibility and the intensity of competition between such brands is likely to be greater than for those that occupy widely divergent positions. In a study of the scotch whiskey market, for instance, the amount of brand switching between the two brands with the closest positions was 10 times greater than for the pair perceived to be least similar.[12] Consequently, the perceived similarity between Oldsmobile and Buick in consumers' minds is a problem for General Motors because it suggests those two divisions of the company are waging a marketing war more against each other than the competition.

Competitive gaps

The product positioning analysis in Exhibit 10–10 also provides useful information about possible opportunities for the development of a new brand, or for repositioning an existing brand to differentiate it more clearly. This can be accomplished by examining the positioning map for competitive gaps—empty spaces where no existing brand is currently located. In Exhibit 10–10, for instance, there is such a gap in the "Affordable/Appeals to Young People" quadrant at the lower right side of the map. Such a gap may represent an opportunity for acquiring a distinctive position by developing a new entry that is perceived to offer good performance and sporty styling at a low price, or by repositioning an existing brand along those attributes. Of course, such gaps may exist simply because a particular position is either *impossible* for any brand to attain due to technical or marketing constraints, or *undesirable* in the sense that very few customers would purchase a brand with that particular set of attributes.

Limitations of product positioning analysis

The analysis depicted in Exhibit 10–10 is usually referred to as **product positioning** because it indicates how alternative products or brands are positioned relative to one another in customers' minds. The problem with this analysis, though, is that it does not tell the marketer which positions are most appealing to customers. For existing brands, such attractiveness can be inferred from current sales volumes and market shares. The position oc-

---

[12] Volney J. Stefflre, "Market Structure Studies: New Products for Old Markets and New Markets (Foreign) for Old Products," in *Applications of the Sciences in Marketing*, eds. Frank Bass, Charles W. King, and Edgar A. Pessemier (New York: John Wiley & Sons, 1969), pp. 251–68.

cupied by the share leader is obviously more appealing to more customers than the positions occupied by lesser brands. But this analysis fails to answer two important questions:

1. Is there one or more "open" positions—gaps in the competitive map where no current product or brand is located—that would be even more attractive to customers and provide a competitive advantage for a new brand, or for an existing brand that could be repositioned to occupy that location?
2. Do customers in different market segments prefer products or brands with different attributes and positions?

To answer such questions, analysts must explicitly measure customers' preferences and locate them in the product space along with their perceptions of the current positions of existing brands. This is commonly called a **market positioning** analysis.

Step 6: market positioning—determine customers' most preferred combination of attributes

There are two ways analysts can measure customer preferences and include them in a positioning analysis. First, survey respondents might be asked to think of the ideal product or brand within a product category—a hypothetical brand possessing the perfect combination of attributes (from those customers' viewpoints). They could then rate their ideal product and existing products on a number of attributes. Then analysts could use discriminant or factor analysis to plot the position of ideal points and existing brands within the same product space. An alternative approach is to ask respondents to not only judge the degree of similarity among pairs of existing brands, but to also indicate their degree of preference for each brand on a rating scale. Multidimensional scaling techniques can then locate the respondent's ideal point relative to the positions of the various existing brands on the product space map.

Whichever approach analysts use, the result will look something like Exhibit 10–11 (page 340), which shows a hypothetical cluster of ideal points for one segment of automobile consumers. As a group, this customer segment (which presumably can afford to buy a luxury car) would seem to prefer BMW to any other brand on the map because the closer the position of a given brand to a customer's ideal point, the greater the probability that the customer will prefer and purchase that brand. However, there are several reasons why not all the customers in this segment are likely to purchase a BMW every time they buy a car. First, the ideal points of some customers are actually closer to the Porsche brand. Those customers will slightly prefer Porsche to BMW. Also, customers whose ideal point is equidistant between

EXHIBIT   10 ◆ 11

Product positioning map of selected automobile brands with the ideal points of a segment of automobile customers

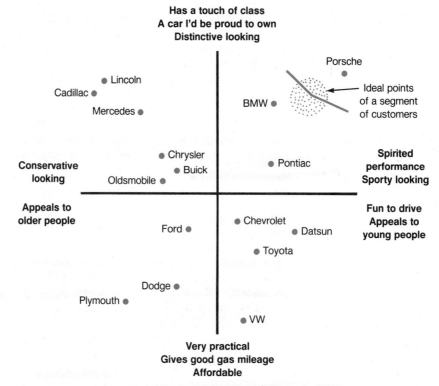

Source: Adapted from John Koten, "Car Makers Use 'Image' Map as Tool to Position Products," *The Wall Street Journal,* March 22, 1984, p. 31.

the two brands are likely to be relatively indifferent to them. Finally, customers may sometimes purchase brands somewhat farther away from their ideal—particularly when buying low-involvement nondurable goods or services—to assess the qualities of new brands, to reassess older brands from time to time, or just for the sake of variety.

Step 7: define market positioning and market segmentation

As we saw in Chapter 6, one important criteria for defining market segments is differences in the benefits sought by different customers. Because differences between customers' ideal points reflect variations in the benefits they seek, a market positioning analysis can *simultaneously identify distinct*

EXHIBIT   10 ◆ 12

Market positioning map of selected automobile brands

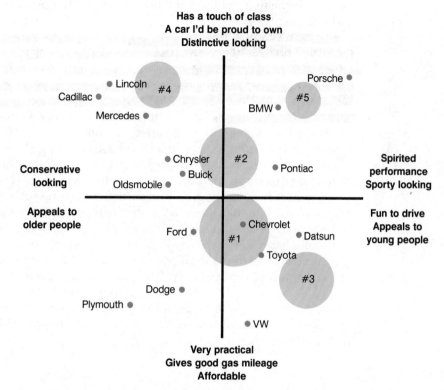

Source: Adapted from John Koten, "Car Makers Use 'Image' Map as Tool to Position Products," *The Wall Street Journal*, March 22, 1984, p. 31.

market segments as well as the perceived positions of different brands. When customers' ideal points cluster in two or more locations on the product space map, each cluster can be considered a distinct market segment.[13] For analytical purposes, each cluster is represented by a circle that encloses most of the ideal points for that segment; and the size of the circle reflects the relative proportion of customers within a particular segment. Exhibit 10–12

---

[13] When using preference data to define market segments, however, the analyst should also collect information about customers' demographic characteristics, lifestyles, product usage, and other potential segmentation variables. This enables the analyst to develop a more complete picture of the differences among benefit segments. As shown in Chapter 6, such information can be useful for developing advertising appeals, selecting media, focusing personal selling efforts, and designing many of the other elements of a marketing program that can be effective in appealing to a particular segment.

shows the sample of respondents in our automobile example grouped into five distinct segments defined on the basis of hypothetical clusters of ideal points. Segment 1 contains the largest proportion of customers; segment 5 the smallest.[14]

By examining the preferences of customers in different segments together with their perceptions of the positions of existing brands, analysts can learn much about (1) the competitive strength of different brands in different segments, (2) the intensity of the rivalry between brands in a given segment, and (3) the opportunities for gaining a differentiated position within a specific target segment. For example, BMW occupies a strong and relatively unchallenged competitive position among consumers in segment 5. Chevrolet, Ford, and Toyota appear to have an intense rivalry for the preferences of many consumers in segment 1. On the other hand, none of the brands occupies a strongly attractive position with respect to the preferences of customers in segment 3. This segment may represent a good opportunity for the development of a new brand or the repositioning of an existing brand. For example, even though customers in segment 3 are probably splitting their purchases between Toyota, Datsun (Nissan), and VW, a new brand positioned closer to the ideal points of customers in the segment would take sales from all of those brands. The sales volume such a new brand would generate could be estimated by examining the current volume of purchases of the existing brands by segment 3 customers and the distances between the average ideal point of segment 3 customers and the positions of an existing and a new brand.[15]

---

[14] The map in Exhibit 10–12 shows five distinct preference segments but only one set of perceived product positions. The implication is that consumers in this sample were similar in the way they perceived existing brands, but different in the product attributes they preferred. This is the most common situation; customers tend to vary more in the benefits they seek than in how they perceive available products or brands. Sometimes, however, various segments may perceive the positions of existing brands quite differently. They may even use different determinant attributes in assessing those positions. Under such circumstances, a marketer might construct a separate market positioning map for each segment. An example of this situation is a study of the positioning of different pharmaceutical brands. Researchers discovered that two segments of doctors differed dramatically in their perceptions of the side effects of various brands as well as in their preferences for those brands. See Lester A. Neidell, "The Use of Nonmetric Multidimensional Scaling in Marketing Analysis," *Journal of Marketing*, October 1969, pp. 37–43.

[15] Some sophisticated statistical techniques have recently been developed for making more precise forecasts of the sales volumes likely to be generated by new brands. For a technical review of such techniques, see Richard Schmalensee and Jacques-Francois Thisse, "Perceptual Maps and the Optimal Location of New Products," Technical Working Paper, Report 86–103 (Cambridge, Mass.: The Marketing Science Institute, 1986).

Step 8: select positioning strategies[16]

The final decision about where to position a new brand—or whether to reposition an existing one—should be based on *both the market targeting analysis* we discussed earlier and the results of a *marketing positioning analysis.* The position chosen should match the preferences of a particular market segment and take into account the current positions of competing brands. It should also reflect the current and future attractiveness of the target market (its size, expected growth, and environmental constraints) and the relative strengths and weaknesses of competitors. With this in mind, several positioning strategies can be considered. Some of the more common ones include: **monosegment positioning, multisegment positioning, imitative positioning, defensive positioning,** and **anticipatory positioning** strategies.

Monosegment positioning

As the name suggests, monosegment positioning involves developing a product and marketing program tailored to the preferences of a single market segment. Continuing with our automotive example, for instance, a firm might attempt to position its brand within the circle representing the ideal points of customers in segment 3. Successful implementation of such a strategy would give the brand an obvious advantage within the target segment. However, it would not generate many sales from customers in other segments with divergent preferences. This strategy thus is best used in conjunction with the mass-market targeting strategy discussed earlier.

Multisegment positioning

An alternative positioning strategy is to attain a position between two or more smaller segments, similar to the position of Datsun (Nissan) between segments 1 and 3 in Exhibit 10–12. Such a position should enable the brand to attract customers from both segments. This is a good strategy to consider when the target segments are relatively small, because it provides an opportunity to gain greater economies of scale. It also involves a smaller total investment than trying to position separate brands against each segment.

Imitative positioning

In more mature markets a new brand (or an older brand that is being repositioned) might pursue a position closely similar to that of an existing successful brand, in the hopes that it can divert a substantial number of customers away from the older brand. This is the positioning strategy that

---

[16] This classification of positioning was developed by Jean-Claude Larréché (Fontainbleau, France: INSEAD).

Marriott is pursuing with its new Courtyard Hotels in attempting to win customers in the middle-priced lodging segment away from entrenched competitors such as Holiday Inn. Such an imitative strategy results in direct confrontation with a competitor, however. It is unlikely to be very successful unless the firm has a distinctive advantage over that competitor—such as lower costs, better service, and/or a better salesforce.

Defensive positioning

When an existing brand occupies a strong position in a market segment, it may be vulnerable to the imitative strategy we just discussed. The firm may attempt to preempt such a competitive move by introducing a second similar brand positioned to appeal to the same market segment. Procter & Gamble has followed such a positioning strategy over the years in a number of product categories. For instance, the firm has seven brands of laundry detergent, such as Tide and Bold III, several of which occupy similar positions in consumers' minds. Such a strategy cannibalizes the market of the established brand and results in higher investments and lower economies of scale. The justification is that it is better in the long run for a firm to compete with itself than to lose customers to other firms.

Anticipatory positioning

In some cases a firm might position a brand in a location where there is currently no strong customer preference if it is convinced that a substantial number of customers will eventually develop a need or preference for such a product. For example, when Seymour Cray began developing the Cray-1 supercomputer in 1972, marketing research suggested that the total market would only absorb about 90 such computers. But Cray was convinced that when firms and government agencies realized the advantages of such high-performance machines, they would find new uses for them and demand would continue to expand.[17] When the strategist's assumptions are correct about the future evolution of market demand—as Cray was—this positioning strategy enables a firm to preempt a leading position in a market segment with substantial long-term potential. But when the strategist's assumptions are wrong, the firm can face a difficult economic situation for an extended period.

SUMMARY

This chapter focused on two interrelated decisions that constitute the first steps toward the formulation of a strategic marketing program for a product-market entry: *market targeting* and *market positioning*.

The *market attractiveness/business position*

---

[17] Tom Alexander, "Cray's Way of Staying Super-Duper," *Fortune*, March 18, 1985, pp. 66–76.

matrix provides a useful analytical framework to help managers decide which market segments to target and how to allocate resources and marketing efforts. The first step in applying such a matrix is for the manager to identify a relevant set of variables underlying the attractiveness of alternative market segments. This typically involves selecting variables related to four broad sets of factors: market factors, economic and technological factors, competitive factors, and environmental factors. Similarly, the manager must decide on a relevant set of variables to judge the firm's relative competitive position within the market segment. These competitiveness variables typically include items related to market position factors, economic and technological factors, the business's capabilities, and interactions or synergies across multiple target markets.

After managers have weighted these factors according to their relative importance, they can rate the attractiveness of alternative market segments and the strength of the firm's competitive position within each of those segments. Because a firm or business unit has limited resources, however, it often identifies more attractive potential target markets than it is capable of pursuing. Consequently, a *targeting strategy* must be developed to guide managers' choices of alternative target markets in a manner consistent with the firm's objectives, resources, and competitive strengths. The most common targeting strategies include mass-market, niche, and growth-market strategies.

The market segments targeted by a business are likely to change over time in response to changing customers' needs, competitive actions, and the firm's own objectives and resources.

Because a product offering's position in the marketplace is ultimately determined by how customers perceive it relative to alternative offerings, a *positioning analysis* requires inputs from marketing research concerning those customers' perceptions and attitudes. Managers can conduct such an analysis at either the product or brand level. The manager's first step is to identify a relevant set of competing offerings. Then, the manager identifies a set of determinant product attributes. These attributes define the product space in which alternative offerings are located. Finally, the manager collects information about customer perceptions of the alternative offerings. Managers use this information to determine the *intensity* of a product's current position in customers' minds. They can also analyze it using factor analysis, discriminant analysis, multiattribute compositional models, or multidimensional scaling to determine the product's perceived location in product space relative to the positions of alternative offerings.

The manager can also map information about customer preferences or ideal points along with their perceptions of current offerings. This *market positioning analysis* enables managers to identify market segments by examining clusters of customer preferences. It can provide useful information about the competitive strength of different brands in different segments, the intensity of rivalry between brands in a given segment, and opportunities for gaining a differentiated position with respect to a specific target segment. Using this information managers can develop a *positioning strategy*. Such strategies commonly include monosegment, multisegment, imitative, defensive, and anticipatory positioning.

QUESTIONS

1. How would you describe the market segment that is the *target market* for Marriott's Courtyard Hotels described at the beginning of the chapter? Which specific variables or trends would you want to examine in evaluating the *attractiveness* of that target market?

2. Evaluate Marriott's *competitive position* in the Courtyard Hotels' target market. Who are the firm's major competitors? How would you estimate their relative strengths and weaknesses?

3. What is the difference between a *growth-market* targeting strategy and a *niche* tar-

geting strategy? What capabilities or strengths should a business have to implement a growth-market targeting strategy effectively?

4. Which market targeting strategy was Honda pursuing when it first entered the U.S. market with its low-priced Civic automobile? How has its strategy changed over the years?

5. What determines the *intensity* of a product's perceived position in the marketplace? What might be done to increase the intensity of the position of a brand that currently holds a relatively small market share, such as Saab in the automobile market or Clinique in the cosmetics market?

6. Judging from the information presented at the beginning of this chapter, which *posi-* *tioning strategy* is Marriott pursuing with its Courtyard Hotels? What competitive strengths or capabilities must a firm have to implement such a strategy successfully?

7. Examine the market positioning map of automobile brands in Exhibit 10–12. Where on that map is the best place for a firm to try positioning a new brand if it is pursuing a *monosegment positioning strategy*? What are the advantages and limitations of such a strategy?

8. In terms of positioning strategy, what is the rationale for the fact that Nabisco offers many different brands within the cracker category, each of which is perceived as being only slightly different from the others? What are the advantages and limitations of such a strategy?

SECTION III

Developing strategic marketing programs

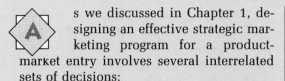s we discussed in Chapter 1, designing an effective strategic marketing program for a product-market entry involves several interrelated sets of decisions:

1. The manager must select a target market segment by deciding which segment represents attractive and viable opportunities, and which opportunities the firm has the capabilities and resources to satisfy in a way that gives it a sustainable advantage over potential competitors.

2. The manager must decide on an overall marketing strategy to appeal to customers—and to gain a sustainable competitive advantage—in the target market. The objectives and methods of competition incorporated in this marketing strategy should be consistent with the firm's capabilities and its higher level corporate and business-unit strategies and objectives.

3. The manager must then make decisions about each element of the tactical marketing program that will carry out the strategy. These decisions must be internally consistent and integrated across all elements of the marketing program.

In the preceding section we discussed the market, competitive, industry, and life-cycle factors that help define and influence the attractiveness of potential target markets. Then, in Chapter 10, we discussed methods of deciding which market segments to target and what competitive position to pursue in each segment. The last two sets of decisions involved in designing a strategic marketing program are the focus of the next section.

MARKETING STRATEGY DECISIONS

Once a target market has been selected and a competitive position decided, the next step is to develop a strategic marketing program. However, product-market objectives and strategic marketing programs are influenced and constrained by higher level corporate and business-unit objectives and strategies. This is because different functional areas—and different activities within a specific functional area, such as marketing—are more critical determinants of the success of some business strategies than others. Consequently, Chapter 11 examines *generic business-level competitive strategies* and the way such strategies affect decisions about the marketing objectives and programs appropriate for specific product-market entries within business units.

MARKETING PROGRAM COMPONENTS

Managers make dozens of specific tactical decisions in designing strategic marketing programs for product-market entries. These are related to the major marketing variables that they have some ability to control over the short term. Collectively, these decisions determine the design of the marketing plan or *marketing mix*—the combination of controllable marketing variables that managers use to carry out a marketing strategy in pursuit of the firm's objectives in a given target market.

The remaining chapters in this section examine some of the options available to managers in making choices about each component of the marketing mix, some of the analytical methods and criteria that they can use to make those decisions, and the strategic situations under which different alternative actions are likely to be most appropriate. Chapter 12 begins with an examination of *product decisions*, including decisions about the breadth of the product line, quality levels, and customer services provided with the product. Chapter 13 then discusses some of the special concerns and analytical techniques associated with the

development and introduction of *new products*. Chapter 14 deals with *pricing decisions*, and Chapter 15 with issues involved in the design and management of *distribution channels*.

Chapter 16 examines strategic and tactical decisions concerning the *promotion mix*. Because there are a variety of tools that marketing managers might use to promote products under different strategic circumstances, however, two additional chapters focus on decisions involving those tools. Chapter 17 examines *advertising, sales promotion, and public relations decisions*, while Chapter 18 discusses decisions involved in managing *personal selling efforts*.

Chapter ⟨11⟩

Business strategies and marketing program decisions

BUSINESS STRATEGIES AND MARKETING PROGRAMS AT 3M

The Minnesota Mining and Manufacturing Company, better known as 3M, began manufacturing sandpaper eight decades ago.[1] Today it is a leader in more than 100 technical areas from fluorochemistry to optical recording that produced $9.4 billion in sales and nearly a 25 percent return on capital employed in 1987.

As might be expected, 3M is organized into a large number of strategic business units (SBUs) . The company consists of 44 such units organized into four sectors or groups: the Industrial and Electronic Sector, making such products as pressure-sensitive tapes, abrasives, adhesives, and electronic connectors; the Life Sciences Sector, consisting of such diverse businesses as pharmaceuticals and reflective materials, both of which are designed to contribute to the health and safety of people; the Information and Imaging Technologies Sector, concerned with the areas of commercial graphics and audio visuals, magnetic media, and imaging systems; and the Commercial and Consumer Sector, responsible for Post-it brand repositionable notes and Scotch brand Magic Transparent Tape.[2]

3M has acquired several smaller firms over the years to fill out a product line or to gain some particular technical expertise. But the company's growth strategy has always focused primarily on internal new-product development, emphasizing improved products for existing customers and new products for new markets. Indeed, one formal objective assigned to *every* business unit is to obtain at least 25 percent of annual sales from products introduced within the last five years. The company supports this demand for a continuous flow of new products with an R&D budget of over $560 million, more than 6.5 percent of total revenues.

Differences in customers' needs, product life-cycle stages, and the maturity of technologies across industries, however, leads the various business units to pursue their growth objective in different ways. The Industrial Tape business unit, for example, operates in an industry where, for the most part, both the basic technologies and the customer segments are mature and relatively stable. Growth results from extending the scope of adhesive tech-

---

[1] Based on *The 3M Company, 1988 Annual Report* (St. Paul: The 3M Company, 1987); A. Johnson, "The 3M Company: Organized to Innovate," *Management Review,* July 1986, pp. 38–39; and "3M's Aggressive New Consumer Drive," *Business Week,* July 16, 1984, pp. 114–22.

[2] For a definition of strategic business units (SBUs), see Chapter 2.

continued

nology (e.g., attaching weather-stripping to auto doors and panels to truck trailers), finding new ways to use existing technologies (a stronger focus with respect to key markets), and expanding internationally.

In contrast, the firm's Health Care unit markets a broad range of innovative medical devices (such as a powered bone stapler), pharmaceuticals (a new drug to control irregular heartbeat), and dental products (tooth-colored fillings). Its product development efforts, therefore, concentrate on designing totally new products directed at new markets.

These differences are also reflected in the competitive strategies 3M's business units pursue. For instance, the company's tapes hold a commanding share of most market segments, even though it charges higher prices and earns bigger margins than its competitors. As a result, the Industrial Tape unit is primarily concerned with maintaining its share position in existing markets while preserving or even improving its profitability. Its competitive strategy is to differentiate itself on the basis of high product quality and excellent customer service.

On the other hand, the Health Care unit's competitive strategy is to avoid head-to-head competitive battles by being the technological leader in the industry and introducing a constant stream of unique products. This focus means, however, that it must devote substantial resources to R&D and to the stimulation of primary demand to build viable markets for those products.

Thus, its primary objective is volume growth. Health Care must sacrifice some short-run profitability to fund the product development and marketing efforts needed to accomplish that goal.

These differences in market environments and business-level competitive strategies and objectives also influence the strategic marketing programs for the various product-market entries within the 3M business units. For instance, most of 3M's tapes are mature products in established markets—therefore, 3M spends few resources on advertising or sales promotion for tape products. However, the business unit does maintain a large, well-trained, technical salesforce that provides valuable technical assistance to customers and feedback to the firm's R&D personnel for potential new applications and ideas for product modifications and improvements. The unit also maintains substantial inventories of tapes in company distribution centers throughout the world to ensure rapid delivery—another critical aspect of good service in the tape industry.

In contrast, the pioneering nature of many of the Health Care unit's products and services calls for more extensive promotion programs to generate customer awareness and stimulate primary demand. The unit thus devotes a relatively large proportion of its revenues to advertising in technical journals aimed at physicians, hospital administrators, and medical technicians. It also supports a large technical sales-

continued

concluded

force that spends much of its time demonstrating new products and prospecting for new accounts in addition to
servicing existing customers. Finally,
the unit also is a relatively heavy user

of marketing research services, such as
those concerned with the testing of new
product concepts, product use tests,
and forecasting the demand for new
product-market entries.

THE CONCEPT OF STRATEGIC FIT

The situation at 3M illustrates a point made in Chapter 2: Firms with
multiple businesses usually have a hierarchy of strategies extending from
the corporate level down to the individual product-market entry. This hierarchy is shown in Exhibit 11–1. The corporate strategy addresses such issues
as the firm's mission and scope and the directions it will pursue for future
growth. Thus, 3M's corporate growth strategy focuses on developing new
products and new applications for the firm's existing products.

The primary strategic question addressed at the business-unit level is,
How should we compete in this business? 3M's Industrial Tape business
unit attempts to maintain its commanding market share and high profitability by differentiating itself on the basis of high quality and good customer service. The Health Care unit seeks high growth via aggressive new-
product and market development. Finally, a strategic marketing program is
developed for each product-market entry that includes allocating marketing
resources and activities to accomplish the SBU's objectives. Thus, most of
the Health Care unit's marketing programs allot relatively large expenditures
for marketing research and introductory advertising and promotion campaigns. Their aim is to achieve sales growth through new-product and
market development.

One key reason for 3M's continuing success is that all three levels of
strategy have almost always been characterized by good internal and external consistency, or **strategic fit.** 3M's managers have usually done a good job
of monitoring and adapting their strategies to the market opportunities,
technological advances, and competitive threats in the company's external
environment. The firm's marketing and sales managers play a critical role in
not only developing market-oriented strategies for individual products, but
also in influencing and helping to formulate corporate and business-level
strategies that are responsive to the external environment. At the same time,
those strategies are usually internally compatible. Each strategy fits with

EXHIBIT 11 ♦ 1

Strategy hierarchy

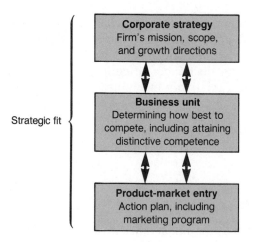

those at other levels as well as with the unique competitive strengths and competencies of the relevant business units and the company as a whole.[3]

Fit with the external environment

Because marketing managers occupy positions at the boundary between the firm and its customers, distributors, and competitors, they are usually most familiar with conditions and trends in the market environment. Thus, they typically bear the primary responsibility for monitoring and interpreting environmental threats and opportunities. Their knowledge and expertise often enables them to play an influential role in strategic planning at the corporate and business-unit levels as well as for their own individual product-market entries. This is particularly true for consumer goods organizations; but it is also true for more market-oriented industrial goods and services organizations.[4]

These firms often rely on a "bottom-up" planning process that begins with an analysis of potential opportunities and threats at the individual product-market level. They formulate marketing strategies for each product-market entry and then aggregate them to serve as a starting point for the

---

[3] For a more detailed discussion of strategic fit and the external and internal variables influencing the effectiveness of a firm's strategies, see N. Venkatraman and James Camillus, "The Concept of 'Fit' in Strategic Management," *Academy of Management Review* 9 (1984), pp. 513–25.

[4] George S. Yip, "The Role of Strategic Planning in Consumer-Marketing Businesses," Working Paper 84–103 (Cambridge, Mass.: Marketing Science Institute, 1984).

resource allocation decisions that must be made at the business-unit level. SBU plans, in turn, serve as a springboard for the formulation of corporate strategies. Thus, a firm's corporate and business-unit domain, objectives, and resource allocation decisions may be adjusted periodically to fit new market opportunities or competitive threats identified by marketing managers operating at the product-market level, as reflected by the target market and market positioning analyses and decisions discussed in the last chapter.

Fit with internal capabilities and strategies

No matter how well a strategy fits the firm's market and competitive environment, though, it will not be successful unless the company can carry it out effectively. Thus, the strategy should fit the company's internal capabilities, its resources, organizational structure, policies, and operating procedures. 3M is *able* to pursue a corporate strategy of internal growth through the development of high-tech products and applications partly because it has substantial financial resources. Add to that a large staff of competent scientists and engineers, excellent technical sales and marketing capabilities, and a corporate culture and reward system that encourages product innovation. Firms that lack any of these essential capabilities find it difficult to successfully pursue corporate growth through internal new-product development. They are better off adopting a growth strategy more consistent with their own internal capabilities, such as aquiring a new business. Thus, explicit consideration of such company strengths and limitations should be part of the analysis pertaining to target market decisions.

BUSINESS STRATEGIES

As mentioned earlier, the essential strategic question at the SBU level is, How are we going to compete within this industry? Thus, SBU strategies are primarily concerned with allocating resources across functional areas and product markets to give the unit a sustainable advantage over its competitors. As we have seen, however, the SBU's functional capabilities and resources and the customer and competitive characteristics of its industry determine the viability of competitive strategies. A growth strategy based on aggressive line extensions or product improvements, for example, is only likely to work if the SBU's R&D and product engineering resources are better than its competitors'. And a strategy of competing with low prices only makes sense if the SBU's procurement, manufacturing, and distribution operations are at least as efficient as everyone else's. Consequently, most SBUs pursue a single competitive strategy—one that fits their market environments and internal strengths—across all or most of the product-markets in which they compete. The question is, What alternative strategies are available to a business unit? What are the basic, or generic, competitive strategies most SBU's choose to pursue?

Generic business-level competitive strategies

Researchers have identified general categories of business-level competitive strategies based on overall patterns of purpose, practice, and performance in different businesses. Porter distinguishes three strategies that businesses pursue to gain and maintain competitive advantages in their various product-markets: (1) *overall cost leadership;* (2) *differentiation*—building customer perceptions of superior product quality, design, or service; and (3) *focus*, in which the business avoids direct confrontation with its major competitors by concentrating on narrowly defined market niches. Porter describes firms that lack a distinctive strategy as being "stuck in the middle," and predicts that they will perform poorly.[5]

Miles and Snow identified another set of business strategies based on a business's intended rate of product-market development (new-product development, penetration of new markets).[6] They classify business units into four strategic types: *prospectors, analyzers, defenders*, and *reactors*. Exhibit 11–2 describes each of these business strategies briefly. As you can see, businesses pursuing a *prospector strategy* focus on growth through the development of new products and markets. 3M's Health Care business unit illustrates this. *Defender businesses* concentrate on maintaining their positions in established product-markets while paying less attention to new-product development—as is the case with 3M's Industrial Tape business unit. The *analyzer strategy* falls in between these two. An analyzer business attempts to maintain a strong position in its core product-market(s) but also seeks to expand into new—usually closely related—product-markets. Finally, *reactors* are businesses with no clearly defined strategy.

Even though both the Porter and Miles and Snow typologies have received popular acceptance and research support, neither is complete by itself. For example, a *defender business unit* could pursue a variety of competitive approaches to protect its market position, such as offering the lowest cost or differentiating itself on quality or service. Thus, we have combined the two typologies in Exhibit 11–3 (page 360) to provide a more comprehensive overview of business strategies. The exhibit classifies business strategies on two primary dimensions: the unit's desired rate of product-market development (expansion) and the unit's intended method of competing in its established product-markets.

Of course, each of our strategic categories could be further subdivided according to whether a business applies the strategy across a broadly defined product-market domain or concentrates on a narrowly defined segment where it hopes to avoid direct confrontation with major competitors (i.e., the

---

[5] Michael E. Porter, *Competitive Strategy* (New York: Free Press, 1980). Also see Michael E. Porter, *Competitive Advantage: Creating and Sustaining Superior Performance* (New York: Free Press, 1985).

[6] Robert E. Miles and Charles C. Snow, *Organizational Strategy, Structure, and Process* (New York: McGraw-Hill, 1978).

EXHIBIT   11 ♦ 2

Summary definitions of Miles and Snow's four business strategies

---

Prospector

- Operates within a broad product-market domain that undergoes periodic redefinition.
- Values being a "first mover" in new-product and market areas, even if not all of these efforts prove to be highly profitable.
- Responds rapidly to early signals concerning areas of opportunity; and these responses often lead to new rounds of competitive actions.
- Competes primarily by stimulating and meeting new market opportunities, but may not maintain strength over time in all markets it enters.

Defender

- Attempts to locate and maintain a secure position in relatively stable product or service areas.
- Offers relatively limited range of products or services compared to competitors.
- Tries to protect its domain by offering lower prices, higher quality, or better service than competitors.
- Usually not at the forefront of technological/new-product development in its industry; tends to ignore industry changes not directly related to its area of operation.

Analyzer

- An intermediate type; makes fewer and slower product-market changes than prospectors, but is less committed to stability and efficiency than defenders.
- Attempts to maintain a stable, limited line of products or services, but carefully follows a selected set of promising new developments in its industry.
- Seldom a "first mover," but often a second or third entrant in product-markets related to its existing market base—often with a lower cost or higher quality product or service offering.

Reactor

- Lacks any well-defined competitive strategy.
- Does not have as consistent a product-market orientation as its competitors.
- Not as willing to assume the risks of new-product or market development as its competitors.
- Not as aggressive in marketing established products as some competitors.
- Responds primarily when it is forced to by environmental pressures.

Source: Adapted from R. E. Miles and C. C. Snow, *Organizational Strategy, Structure and Process* (New York: McGraw-Hill, 1978).

focus strategy of Porter). Although this is a useful distinction to make, it is more germane to a discussion of the business's target market strategy—as discussed in Chapter 10—than to its competitive strategy. Most businesses compete in a consistent way (at least in terms of basic dimensions) across all of their product-markets, whether their domain is broad or narrow.

Exhibit 11–3 describes only six business strategies rather than the eight that one might expect. One reason for this is that we view *reactor* and *prospector business units* as two homogeneous categories.

Evidence suggests that a substantial number of businesses fall into the *reactor* category. One study, for instance, found that 50 out of 232 businesses

EXHIBIT   11 ♦ 3

Combined typology of business-unit competitive strategies

Emphasis on new product-market growth

Heavy emphasis ⟵————————————————⟶ **No emphasis**

		Prospector	Analyzer	Defender	Reactor
Competitive strategy	Differentiation	Units primarily concerned with attaining growth through aggressive pursuit of new product-market opportunities	Units with strong core business; actively seeking to expand into related product-markets with differentiated offerings	Units primarily concerned with maintaining a **differentiated** position in mature markets	Units with no clearly defined product-market development or competitive strategy
	Cost leadership		Units with strong core business; actively seeking to expand into related product-markets with low-cost offerings	Units primarily concerned with maintaining a **low-cost** position in mature markets	

examined could be classified as *reactors.*[7] However, these businesses do not have well-defined or consistent approaches to *either* new-product or market development or to ways of competing in their existing product-markets. As a manager of Sheldahl, Inc.—a firm that designs and manufactures flexible circuit boards and other components for the electronics and defense industries—complained in a discussion with one of the authors,

> Our division is a reactor in the sense that we are constantly changing directions and getting into new areas in response to actions taken by our competitors or special requests from large customers. We are like a job-shop; we take on new projects without ever asking whether there will be a viable future market for what we are doing. Consequently, neither our volume growth nor our profitability has been as good as it should have been in recent years.

Because *reactors* have no clear competitive strategy, we largely ignore them in the remainder of this discussion.

Prospectors are also shown as a single strategic category in Exhibit 11–3 because the desire for rapid new-product or market development is the overriding aspect of their strategy. There is little need for a *prospector business* to consider how to compete in the new product-markets it devel-

---

[7] Charles C. Snow and Lawrence Hrbiniak, "Strategy, Distinctive Competence, and Organizational Performance," *Administrative Science Quarterly* 25 (1980), pp. 317–35.

ops. It usually faces little or no competition—at least not until those markets become established and other firms begin to enter. In 3M's Health Care SBU, for example, the marketing programs for many of its product-markets are aimed at generating awareness and stimulating primary demand. But there is relatively little concern with holding down costs or finding ways to differentiate the unit's products—for the simple reason that most of those products are unchallenged by any established competitors.

Underlying dimensions of different business strategies

In Chapter 2 we said that all strategies consist of five components or underlying dimensions: scope (or the breadth of the strategic domain or field of action); goals and objectives; resource deployments; a basis for achieving a sustainable competitive advantage; and synergy. The generic business strategies outlined in Exhibit 11–3 are defined largely on the basis of their differences on only one of these dimensions—the nature of the competitive advantage sought. However, each strategy has some important differences on the other four dimensions. Those underlying differences provide some useful insights about the conditions under which each strategy is most appropriate and about the relative importance of different functional activities—particularly marketing actions—in implementing them effectively.

Differences in scope

The breadth and the stability of a business's domain vary with different strategies; this can also affect the variables the firm uses to define its different businesses. At one extreme, *defender businesses* (whether *low-cost* or *differentiated*) operate in relatively well-defined, narrow, and stable domains where both the product technology and the customer segments are mature. A company can define and group related product-market entries into such business units on the basis of three sets of criteria: technical compatibility, the customer need to be satisfied, and similarity of customer characteristics and behavior patterns. For example, Pillsbury's Prepared Dough Products unit is a *differentiated defender* that consists of several product-market entries, such as Hungry Jack Biscuits and Crescent Rolls. All of the products in the SBU hold a commanding share of their product category, appeal to traditional households who want fresh-baked breadstuffs to complement meals served at home, and are based on the same dough-in-a-can technology. Consequently, the Prepared Dough SBU is largely self-contained in production facilities and marketing and distribution programs.

At the other extreme, *prospector businesses* usually operate in broad and rapidly changing domains where neither the technology nor customer segments are well-established. The scope and mission of such businesses—and the product-market entries within them—often must undergo periodic redefinition. It is usually impossible to organize such units using all three of the preceding criteria. Thus, *prospector businesses* are typically organized around either a core technology that might lead to the development of products aimed at a broad range of customer segments or a basic customer need that might be met with products based on different technologies. The latter is the approach taken by 3M's Health Care SBU. Its mission is to satisfy the health needs of a broad range of patients with new products and services developed from technologies drawn from other business units within the firm. Thus, it is developing innovative drug delivery systems using aerosols, adhesives, and other 3M technologies.

Analyzer businesses fall somewhere in between the two extremes. They usually have a well-established core business to defend; and often their domain and mission are primarily focused on that core business. However, businesses pursuing this intermediate strategy are often in industries that are still growing or experiencing technological changes. Consequently, they must pay attention to the emergence of new customer segments and/or new product types. As a result, managers must review and adjust the domain and mission of such businesses from time to time.

Differences in goals and objectives

Another important difference across generic business-level strategies with implications for the design and implementation of appropriate marketing programs is that different strategies often focus on different objectives. We saw in Chapter 2 that SBU and product-market entry objectives might be specified on a broad variety of criteria. To keep things simple, however, let's focus on only three performance dimensions of primary importance to both business-unit and marketing managers:

1. *Effectiveness:* The success of a business's products and programs compared to its competitors in the market. Effectiveness is commonly measured by such items as *sales growth* relative to competitors or *changes in market share.*

2. *Efficiency:* The outcomes of a business's programs relative to the resources used in implementing them. Common measures of efficiency are profitability as a percent of sales and *return on investment.*

3. *Adaptability:* The business's success in responding over time to changing conditions and opportunities in the environment. Adaptability can be measured in a variety of ways, but the most common ones are the *number of successful new products* introduced relative to competitors, or *the percent of sales accounted for by products introduced within the last five years.*

The problem is that no SBU—regardless of its competitive strategy—can simultaneously achieve outstanding performance on even this limited number of dimensions, because they involve substantial trade-offs. Good performance on one dimension often means sacrificing performance on another.[8] For example, developing successful new products or attaining

---

[8] Gordon Donaldson, *Managing Corporate Wealth* (New York: Praeger, 1984).

EXHIBIT   11 ◆ 4

Differences between different business strategies in scope, goals and objectives, resource deployment, and synergy

Dimensions	Low-cost defender	Differentiated defender	Prospector	Analyzer
◆ **Scope**	Mature/stable/ well-defined domain; mature technology and customer segments	Mature/stable/ well-defined domain; mature technology and customer segments	Broad/dynamic domains; technology and customer segments not well established	Mixture of defender and prospector strategies
◆ **Goals and objectives** Adaptability (new-product success)	Very little	Little	Extensive	Mixture of defender and prospector strategies
Effectiveness (increase in market share)	Little	Little	Large	Mixture of defender and prospector strategies
Efficiency (ROI)	High	High	Low	Mixture of defender and prospector strategies
◆ **Resource deployment**	Generate excess cash (cash cows)	Generate excess cash (cash cows)	Need cash for product development (question marks or stars)	Need cash for product development but less so than prospectors
◆ **Synergy**	Need to seek operating synergies to achieve efficiencies	Need to seek operating synergies to achieve efficiencies	Danger in sharing operating facilities and programs—better to share technology/marketing skills	Danger in sharing operating facilities and programs—better to share technology/marketing skills

share growth often involves large marketing budgets, substantial up-front investment, high operating costs, and a shaving of profit margins—all of which reduce ROI. This suggests that managers should choose a competitive strategy to maximize performance on one or two dimensions but expect to sacrifice some level of performance on the others, at least in the short term.

As Exhibit 11–4 indicates, *prospector businesses* can usually be expected to out-perform *defenders* on both new-product development and market share growth, while both *defender strategies* should lead to better returns on investment. *Differentiated defenders* likely produce higher returns than *low-cost defenders*, assuming that the greater expenses involved in maintaining their differentiated positions can be more than offset by the higher margins gained by avoiding the intense price competition low-cost competitors often face. The two *analyzer strategies* are not included in Exhibit 11–4 because they fall halfway between the polar extremes. Their performance can also be expected to fall between the levels produced by *prospectors* on the one side and *defenders* on the other.

The validity of the expected performance differences outlined in Exhibit 11–4 is supported by at least some empirical evidence. Hambrick found that businesses pursuing *defender strategies* significantly out-performed *prospector businesses* on return on investment and cash flow regardless of the environment faced. *Prospectors* generated significantly greater rates of market share growth—particularly in innovative or unstable environments.[9]

Differences in resource deployments

Businesses following different generic strategies also allocate their financial resources differently across product-markets, functional departments, and activities within each functional area. *Prospector*—and to a lesser degree, *analyzer*—businesses devote a relatively large proportion of their resources to the development of new product-markets. Because such product-markets usually require more cash to develop than they produce short term, businesses pursuing these strategies often need infusions of financial resources from other parts of the corporation. In portfolio terms, they are "question marks" or "stars."

Defenders, on the other hand, focus the bulk of their resources on preserving existing positions in established product-markets. These product-markets are usually profitable; therefore, *defenders* typically generate excess cash to support product and market development efforts in other business units within the firm. They are the "cash cows." Pillsbury's Prepared Dough Products SBU, for example, generated more than half of all the profits produced by the corporation's packaged foods operations in 1986. Much of those profits were subsequently reallocated to market and product development efforts—such as the introduction of microwave cake mix—carried out within other SBUs.

Marketing budgets tend to be the largest as a percent of an SBU's revenues when the business is pursuing a *prospector strategy*. They tend to be the

---

[9] Donald C. Hambrick, "Some Tests of the Effectiveness and Functional Attributes of Miles and Snow's Strategic Types," *Academy of Management Journal* 26 (1983), pp. 5–26.

smallest as a percent of sales under a *low-cost defender strategy*. We discuss this in detail later in the chapter.

Differences in sources of synergy

Different strategies emphasize different methods of competition and different functional areas and activities. And a given source of synergy also may be more appropriate for some strategies than for others. At one extreme, *low-cost defenders* should seek operating synergies that make them more efficient. Synergies that enable such businesses to increase economies of scale and experience-curve effects are particularly desirable. They help reduce unit costs and strengthen the basis of competitive advantage. The primary means of gaining such operating synergies is by sharing resources, facilities, and functional activities across product-market entries within the business unit or across related business units. Within Pillsbury's Prepared Dough Products SBU, for example, marketing managers for the various products developed a common "umbrella" advertising theme to promote all the SBU's products. They have also coordinated sales promotion efforts aimed at both consumers and the trade. These shared efforts have helped the SBU reduce the costs of advertising and the distribution and redemption of coupons.

At the other extreme, however, the sharing of operating facilities and programs may be an inappropriate way to gain synergy for a *prospector strategy*. And to a lesser extent, this is also true for *analyzer strategies*. Such sharing can reduce one unit's ability to adapt quickly to changing market demands or competitive threats. As one researcher points out,

> closely integrated operations [across SBUs] may produce synergy internally but at the expense of market fit . . . since changes in one [SBU] will ripple through others, heavy interdependence will reduce the desire and ability to change. Commitments to internally negotiated price structures and materials—as well as utilization and costing of joint resources, facilities and programs—limit the businesses' flexibility . . . [and] in markets that have frequent product technological changes, interdependence among [SBUs] makes adjustment harder.[10]

The lack of flexibility resulting from attempts to gain synergy through sharing operational resources and programs can make it difficult for *prospectors* and *analyzers* to successfully implement their chosen strategy. It is more appropriate for such businesses to seek synergy through the sharing of technology, engineering skills, or market knowledge—expertise that can help improve the success rate of their product development efforts. Thus, 3M's Health Care SBU attempts to find medical applications for new technologies developed in many of the firm's other business units.

---

[10] Carolyn Y. Woo, "Market-Share Leadership—Not Always So Good," *Harvard Business Review*, January–February 1984, p. 53.

EXHIBIT 11 ♦ 5

External factors favorable for the implementation of individual generic business strategies

External factors	Prospector	Analyzer	Differentiated defender	Low-cost defender
Market charac-teristics	Industry in intro-ductory or early growth stage of life cycle; many potential cus-tomer segments as yet uniden-tified and/or undeveloped.	Industry in late growth or early maturity stage of life cycle; one or more product offer-ings currently targeted at ma-jor customer segments, but some potential segments may still be un-developed.	Industry in matu-rity or decline stage of life cy-cle; current offerings tar-geted at all major seg-ments; sales primarily due to repeat pur-chases/replace-ment demand.	Industry in matu-rity or decline stage of life cy-cle; current offerings tar-geted at all major seg-ments; sales primarily due to repeat pur-chases/replace-ment demand.
Technology	Newly emerging technology; many applica-tions as yet undeveloped.	Basic technology well-developed but still evolv-ing; product modifications and improve-ments—as well as emergence of new compet-ing technolo-gies—still likely.	Basic technology fully developed and stable; few major modi-fications or improvements likely.	Basic technology fully developed and stable; few major modi-fications or improvements likely.

THE FIT BETWEEN GENERIC BUSINESS STRATEGIES AND THE EXTERNAL ENVIRONMENT

Different strategies pursue different objectives in different domains through different competitive approaches. This suggests that they will not all work equally well under the same environmental circumstances. The question is, which environmental situations are most amenable to the successful pursuit of each strategy? Exhibit 11–5 briefly outlines some major market, tech-nological, and competitive conditions—plus the business unit's strengths relative to its competitors—that are most favorable for the successful imple-mentation of each generic business strategy. We next discuss the reasons why each strategy fits best with a particular set of environmental condi-tions.

EXHIBIT 11 ♦5 *(concluded)*

External factors	Prospector	Analyzer	Differentiated defender	Low-cost defender
Competition	Few established competitors; industry structure still emerging; single competitor holds commanding share of major market segments.	Large number of competitors, but future shakeout likely; industry structure still evolving; one or more competitors hold large shares in major segments, but continuing growth may allow rapid changes in relative shares.	Small to moderate number of well-established competitors; industry structure's stable, though acquisitions and consolidation possible; maturity of markets means relative shares of competitors tend to be reasonably stable over time.	Small to moderate number of well-established competitors; industry structure stable, though acquisitions and consolidation are possible; maturity of markets means relative shares of competitors tend to be reasonably stable over time.
Business's relative strengths	SBU (or parent) has strong R&D, product engineering, and marketing research and marketing capabilities.	SBU (or parent) has good R&D, product engineering and marketing research capabilities, but not as strong as some competitors; has either low-cost position or strong sales, marketing, distribution, or service capabilities in one or more segments.	SBU has no outstanding strengths in R&D or product engineering; costs are higher than at least some competitors; SBU's outstanding strengths are in process engineering and quality control and/or in marketing, sales, distribution, or customer services.	SBU (or parent) has superior sources of supply and/or process engineering and production capabilities that enable it to be low-cost producer; R&D, product engineering, marketing, sales, or service capabilities may not be as strong as some competitors'.

Appropriate conditions for a prospector strategy

A *prospector strategy* is particularly well suited to volatile, unstable environments. Such volatility results from new or rapidly changing technology, shifting customer needs, or both. In either case, such industries tend to be at an early stage in their life cycles. There are often many opportunities for new product-market entries because many potential market segments are un-discovered or underdeveloped. Similarly, there are often few established competitors in such industries. *Prospector strategies* are common in industries where new applications—and customer acceptance—of existing technologies are still developing (such as the PC, computer software, and information technologies industries) and industries with rapid technological change (such as biotechnology, medical care, and aerospace).

Because they compete by seeking rapid growth through the early development of new products and/or new markets, the most successful *prospectors* are usually strong in two broad areas of competence: First, successful *prospectors* have outstanding competence in—and devote a large share of resources to—R&D, product engineering, and other functional areas related to the identification and conversion of new technology into innovative products. They also usually have strengths in marketing research, marketing, and sales. These functions are necessary for the identification and development of new market opportunities.

In some cases, even though *prospector businesses* are highly competent marketers, they may lack the resources necessary to maintain their early lead as product-markets grow and attract new competitors. For example, Minnetonka, which had sales of $151 million in 1987 compared with $95 million in 1986, has been the pioneer in several health and beauty-aid product categories, with brands like Softsoap and Check-Up plaque-fighting toothpaste. However, the firm has not been able to maintain its leading share position in these markets because competitors such as Procter & Gamble and Colgate-Palmolive introduced competing brands supported by advertising and promotion budgets much larger than Minnetonka could match. Realizing this, the company divested its Softsoap liquid soap, Sesame Street bubble bath and shampoo, and Village Bath Products. Minnetonka also sold its Check-Up oral care products. The firm survives by continuing to be a good *prospector*. It now relies for growth on new, higher-priced, upscale products available in limited distribution rather than fighting larger competitors for a bigger share of existing markets. For example, because of the success of its Obsession for Men fragrance, it followed with an Obsession for Men For-the-Hair program that includes shampoo, conditioner, styling gel and mousse, and hairhold (a fine hair spray). These products are licensed to Calvin Klein, taking advantage of that company's marketing resources. For a statement about the organizational consequences of Minnetonka's *prospector strategy*, see Exhibit 11–6.[11]

Appropriate conditions for an analyzer strategy

The *analyzer strategy* is a hybrid, incorporating parts of both *prospector* and *defender strategies*. On one hand, the *analyzer* is concerned with defend-

---

[11] Minnetonka Corporation, *Annual Report*, 1987.

EXHIBIT 11 ♦6

Minnetonka's organizational structure—statement by the president and chief executive officer

> Coupled with our first strategic decision to focus our resources on higher margin, upscale products, we have also chosen an organization plan that is more decentralized. Our four remaining business groups—Calvin Klein Cosmetics Corporation, the Fragrance Marketing Group, La Costa Products International and Minnetonka Medical—will all function as autonomous, entrepreneurial operations. While key managers of each group may share some support services and certainly will share ideas, these Minnetonka business leaders will have the freedom to act independently. As we develop new businesses or acquire others, they will share the same independence.
>
> This autonomous, entrepreneurial organizational style will allow Minnetonka people to utilize their creativity, take calculated risks, and be responsible for their own divisions. This in turn will permit flexibility and responsiveness to the marketplace.

Source: Minnetonka Corporation, *Annual Report,* 1987, p. 3.

ing—via low costs or differentiation in quality or service—a strong share position in one or more established product-markets. At the same time, the business must pay attention to new-product development to avoid being leapfrogged by competitors with more advanced products or being left behind in newly developing application segments within the market. The *analyzer strategy* is particularly appropriate for well-developed industries that are still experiencing some growth and change, due to evolving customers' needs and desires or continuing technological improvements.

Commercial aircraft manufacturing is an example of such an industry. Both competitors and potential customers are few and well-established. But technology continues to improve; the increased competition among airlines since deregulation has changed the attributes those firms look for when buying new planes; and mergers have increased the buying power of some customers. Thus, Boeing's commercial aircraft division has had to work harder to maintain its 50 percent share of worldwide commercial plane sales. Although the firm continues to enjoy a reputation for producing high-quality, reliable planes, it has had to make price concessions and increase services to customers to stave off threats from competitors like the European Airbus consortium. For example, in one deal with American Airlines, Boeing agreed to lease rather than sell more than $2 billion worth of planes and to allow American to cancel the leases with as little as 30 days' notice. At the same time, the firm's commercial aircraft division is engaged in a product development effort with a budget of more than $2 billion aimed at producing a new generation of airplanes to recapture the technological lead enjoyed by Airbus's new A-320 jet.[12]

---

[12] Kenneth Labich, "Boeing Battles to Stay on Top," *Fortune,* September 28, 1987, pp. 64–72.

One problem with an *analyzer strategy* is that few businesses—even very large ones such as Boeing's commercial aircraft division—have the resources and competencies to successfully defend an established core business while also generating new products. Success on both dimensions requires strengths across virtually every functional area from R&D to marketing to production and quality control. Few businesses or their parent companies have such universal strengths relative to competition; therefore, *analyzers* are often not as innovative in new-product development as *prospectors*. Nor are they as profitable in defending their core businesses as *defenders*. Thus, in addition to having its technological lead eroded, Boeing's commercial aircraft division also saw its market share fall from 70 percent in 1981 to 50 percent in 1987 and its earnings as a percent of revenues slump dramatically. Revenues have since improved substantially, but only because of a strong increase in demand for commercial jetliners.

Appropriate conditions for a defender strategy

A *defender strategy* makes sense only when a business has something worth defending; it is most appropriate for units with a profitable share of one or more segments in a relatively mature, stable industry. A *defender* may initiate some product improvements or line extensions to protect and strengthen its position in existing segments; but it devotes few resources to R&D. A *defender strategy* works best in industries where the basic technology is not very complex or where it is well-developed and unlikely to change dramatically over the short run. Pillsbury's Prepared Dough Products SBU, for instance, has introduced a number of line extensions over the years; but most have been reconfigurations of the same basic dough-in-a-can technology, such as Soft Breadsticks.

Differentiated defenders

To effectively defend its market position by differentiation, a business must be strong in functional areas critical for maintaining a differential advantage over time. For a differentiation based on a superior product, those functional areas include production, process engineering, quality control, and perhaps product engineering to develop product improvements. Interestingly, successful differentiation of its offerings on the quality dimension has a strong impact on a business's return on investment—a critical performance objective for *defenders*. The positive correlation between quality and ROI holds true even after allowing for the effects of market share and investment intensity. As Exhibit 11–7 shows, the pretax return on investment is higher in all businesses for firms selling above-average and highest-quality products than for firms selling average or below-average quality offerings.

Regardless of the basis for differentiation, marketing tends to be an impor-

EXHIBIT   11 ◆ 7

Quality and pretax ROI by business type

| | | Quality level (percent average ROI) | | | |
	Lowest	Below average	Average	Above average	Highest
Consumer durables	16%	18%	18%	26%	32%
Consumer nondurables	15	21	17	23	32
Capital goods	10	8	13	20	21
Raw materials	13	21	21	21	35
Components	12	20	20	22	36
Supplies	16	13	19	25	36

Source: Robert D. Buzzell, "Product Quality," Pimsletter no. 4 (Cambridge, Mass.: The Strategic Planning Institute, 1981), p. 5.

tant function for the effective implementation of a *differentiated defender strategy.* Marketing activities that track changing customers' needs and competitive actions and communicate the product offering's unique advantages through promotional and sales efforts to help maintain customer awareness and loyalty are particularly important.

Low-cost defenders

Successful implementation of a *low-cost defender strategy* requires the business to be more efficient than its competitors; it must lay the groundwork for such a strategy early on during the industry's growth stage. Achieving and maintaining the lowest per-unit cost usually means that the business has to seek large volume from the beginning—through some combination of low prices and promotional efforts—to gain economies of scale and experience. At the same time, such businesses must also invest in more plant capacity in anticipation of future growth and in state-of-the-art equipment to minimize production costs. This combination of low margins and heavy investment can be prohibitive unless the parent corporation can commit substantial resources to the business or substantial sharing of facilities, technologies, and programs with other business units is possible.

The *low-cost defender's* need for efficiency also forces the standardization of product offerings and marketing programs across customer segments to achieve scale effects. Thus, such a strategy is usually not as effective in fragmented markets with many segments desiring customized offerings as it is in commodity industries such as basic chemicals, steel, or flour, or in industries producing low-technology components such as electric motors or valves.

Changing strategies at different stages in the life cycle

A business's objectives and competitive strategy may have to change over time as the product category—and the business's competitive position within it—mature and stabilize. Thus, a *prospector strategy* is most appropriate during the early stages of a product category's life cycle as a business attempts to build a successful product line and quickly increase its market share. As the industry matures and the competitive environment stabilizes, *analyzer*—and ultimately *defender*—*strategies* become more appropriate as the business turns to maintaining and reaping the benefits of its hard-won market position in the form of higher ROI and cash flows.

The problem is that the effective implementation of different business strategies not only requires different functional competencies and resources, but also different organizational structures, decision-making and coordination processes, reward systems, and even personnel. Because such internal structures and processes are hard to change quickly, it can be very difficult for an entire SBU to make a successful transition from one basic strategy to another.[13] For example, many of Emerson Electric's SBUs historically were successful *low-cost defenders*. But accelerating technological change in their industries caused the corporation to try to convert them to *low-cost analyzers* who would focus more attention on new-product and market development.[14] The attempted change has provided mixed results, however.

In view of the implementation problems involved, some firms do not try to make major changes in the basic competitive strategies of their existing business units. Instead, they might form entirely new *prospector SBUs* to pursue emerging technologies and industries rather than expecting established units to handle the new-product development efforts. As individual product-market entries gain successful positions in well-established markets, some firms move them from the *prospector unit* that developed them to an *analyzer* or *defender unit* that is better suited to reaping profits from those entries as their markets mature. Finally, some firms that are technological leaders in their industries may divest or license individual product-market entries as they mature rather than trying to defend those entries in the face of increasing competition and eroding margins. This approach is commonly taken by such companies as 3M and DuPont; we discuss it further in Chapter 21.

---

[13] Although there is disagreement about how they occur, most people who have studied the transitions from one strategy to another within businesses agree that it takes at least several years for them to be implemented successfully. See, for example, James B. Quinn, *Strategies for Change: Logical Incrementalism* (Homewood, Ill.: Richard D. Irwin, 1980); and Danny Miller and Peter H. Friesen, *Organizations: A Quantum View* (Englewood Cliffs, N.J.: Prentice-Hall, 1984).

[14] "Emerson Electric: High Profits from Low Tech," *Business Week*, April 4, 1983, p. 2.

MARKETING IMPLICATIONS OF DIFFERENT BUSINESS STRATEGIES

Business units typically incorporate several distinct product-markets. The marketing manager for a given entry monitors and evaluates the environmental situation faced by that product and develops a marketing program suited to its situation. However, the manager's freedom to design such a program is constrained by the competitive strategy of the business unit. This is because different strategies focus on different objectives and seek to gain and maintain a competitive advantage in different ways. As a result, different functions within the SBU—and different activities within a given functional area, such as marketing—are critical for the success of different strategies.

There are, therefore, different functional "key factors for success" inherent in the various generic business strategies.[15] This constrains the individual marketing manager's freedom of action in two basic ways. First, because different functions within the business unit are more important under different strategies, they receive different proportions of the SBU's total resources. Thus, the SBU's strategy influences the *amount of resources committed to marketing*—and ultimately the budget available to an individual marketing manager within the business unit. Second, the SBU's strategy influences both the *kind of market and competitive situation* that individual product-market entries within the unit are likely to face *and the objectives they are asked to attain*. We discuss these constraints and their implications for the design of marketing programs within an SBU in greater detail in the following sections.

Implications for marketing policies and program components

It is somewhat risky to draw broad generalizations about how specific marketing policies and program elements might "fit" within different business strategies. Even though a business strategy is a general statement about how an SBU chooses to compete in an industry, that unit may comprise a number of different product-market entries facing different competitive situations in different markets. Thus, there is likely to be a good deal of variation in marketing programs—and in degrees of freedom for individual marketing managers in designing those programs—across products within a given SBU. Still, a business strategy *does* set a general direction for the target markets it will pursue and how the unit will compete in those markets. It does have some influence on marketing policies that cut across product-markets and on the demand stimulation and competitive positioning tasks specific product-market entries are likely to face. This, in turn, can impact

---

[15] For a more detailed discussion of key factors for success in implementing different strategies, see Kenichi Ohmae, *The Mind of the Strategist* (New York: McGraw-Hill, 1982), chap. 3.

EXHIBIT 11 ♦ 8

Differences in marketing policies and program components across businesses pursuing different strategies

Marketing policies and program components	Strategy		
	Prospector	Differentiated defender	Low-cost defender
Product policies			
♦ Product line breadth relative to competitors	+	+	−
♦ Technical sophistication of products relative to competitors	+	+	−
♦ Product quality relative to competitors	?	+	−
♦ Service quality relative to competitors	?	+	−
Price policies			
♦ Price levels relative to competitors	+	+	−
Distribution policies			
♦ Degree of forward vertical integration relative to competitors	−	+	?
♦ Trade promotion expenses as percent of sales relative to competitors	+	−	−
Promotion policies			
♦ Advertising expenses as percent of sales relative to competitors	+	?	−
♦ Sales promotion expenses as percent of sales relative to competitors	+	?	−
♦ Salesforce expenses as percent of sales relative to competitors	?	+	−

Key: + Greater than the average competitor
 − Smaller than the average competitor
 ? Uncertain relationship between strategy and marketing policy or program component

the marketing program elements appropriate within a particular business strategy. Exhibit 11–8 outlines some of the differences in marketing policies and program elements that occur across businesses pursuing different strategies.

Product policies

One set of marketing policies defines the *nature of the products* the business concentrates on offering to its target markets. These policies concern the *breadth* or *diversity* of product lines, the general *level of technical sophistication* of those products, and the target *level of product quality* relative to competitors. *Prospector businesses* rely heavily on the continuing development of unique new products and the penetration of new markets as their primary competitive strategy. Policies encouraging broad, more technically advanced products lines than competitors should be positively related to their performance on the critical dimension of share growth. For example, 3M's Health Care SBU pursues growth by developing a broad range of medical products based on new technologies adapted from other units in the company.

Quality is difficult to define—it can mean many different things to consumers. Even so, it is an important determinant of business profitability.[16] Hambrick suggests that in product-markets where technical features or up-to-the-minute styling are key attributes in customers' definitions of quality, high-quality products may play a positive role in determining the success of a *prospector strategy*. On the other hand, in markets where the critical determinants of "quality" are reliability or brand familiarity, the maintenance of relatively high product quality is likely to be more strongly related to the successful performance of *defender businesses*, particularly those following a *differentiated defender strategy*.[17]

Differentiated defenders compete by offering more or "better" choices to customers than their competitors. For example, 3M's commercial graphics business, a large supplier of sign material for truck fleets, is making inroads into custom signs. Until recently, the use of film for individual signs was not economical. But the use of computer-controlled knives and a new Scotch brand marking film produce signs of higher quality than those that are hand-painted—and at a lower cost. Success in developing relatively broad, technically sophisticated product lines, then, should be positively related to the long-term ROI performance of those businesses. However, such policies are inconsistent with the efficiency requirements of a *low-cost defender strategy*. Broad and complex product lines lead to short production runs and large inventories. Maintaining technical sophistication in a business's products requires continuing investments in product and process R&D. Consequently, the adoption of such policies is expected to be much less common in *low-cost defender businesses*.

Instead of—or in addition to—competing on the basis of product characteristics, businesses can distinguish themselves on the *quality of service* they offer. Such service might take many forms, including engineering and design services, alterations, installation, training of customer personnel, or maintenance and repair service. A policy of high service quality is particularly appropriate for *differentiated defenders*; it offers a way to maintain a competitive advantage in well-established markets. Thus, 3M has joined

---

[16] Robert Buzzell, "Product Quality," *Pimsletter no. 4* (Cambridge, Mass.: The Strategic Planning Institute, 1986).

[17] Hambrick, "Some Tests of the Effectiveness and Functional Attributes."

with Abbott Laboratories to offer over 5,000 heath-care products to hospitals using a single-source order entry, delivery, and service system.

The appropriateness of such a policy for *low-cost defenders*, though, is questionable if the customer satisfaction benefits are offset by the higher operating and administrative costs. Those higher costs may detract from the *low-cost defender's* ability to maintain the low prices critical to its strategy, as well as lowering ROI—at least in the short term. Even so, the low-cost firm would find it difficult to operate profitably if it did not have at least parity with respect to salient service attributes.

Similarly, the higher costs and administrative effort entailed by a high-quality service policy raises questions about the appropriateness of such a policy for *prospector businesses*. Efforts to improve service to existing customers may divert resources and attention from the more critical objective of new-product and market development.

Pricing policies

Successful adherence to a policy of offering *lower prices* than competitors should be positively related to the performance of *low-cost defender businesses*—for low price is the primary competitive weapon of such a strategy. However, a policy of meeting or beating competitors' prices is inconsistent with both *differentiated defender* and *prospector strategies*. The higher costs involved in differentiating a business's products on either a quality or service basis require higher prices to maintain profitability. It also gives customers additional value, for which higher prices can be charged. Similarly, the costs and benefits of new-product and market development by *prospector businesses* require and justify relatively high prices. Thus, adherence to a policy of low competitive prices is seldom characteristic of either *differentiated defenders* or *prospectors*.

Distribution policies

Some argue that *prospector businesses* should show a greater degree of *forward vertical integration* than *defender businesses*.[18] The rationale for this view is that the *prospector's* focus on new-product development requires superior market intelligence and frequent reeducation and motivation of distribution channel members. This can best be done through tight control of company-owned channels. However, these arguments seem inconsistent with the *prospector's* need for flexibility in constructing new channels for new products and markets. Indeed, attempting to maintain tight control over channel member behavior is a more appropriate policy for *defenders* who are trying to maintain strong positions in established markets. It is particularly true when *defenders* rely on good customer service to differentiate

---

[18] Miles and Snow, *Organizational Strategy, Structure, and Process*; and Hambrick, "Some Tests of the Effectiveness and Functional Attributes."

themselves from competitors. Consequently, it seems more likely that a relatively high degree of forward vertical integration will be found among *defender businesses* (particularly *differentiated defenders*), while *prospectors* will rely more heavily on independent channel members—such as manufacturer's representatives or wholesale distributors—to distribute their products.[19] Also, *prospector businesses* focus on introducing new products into new markets where success is uncertain and sales volumes are small in the short run. They are likely to devote a larger percentage of sales to *trade promotions*, such as quantity discounts, liberal credit terms, and other incentives, to induce cooperation and support from their independent channel members.

Promotion policies

Extensive marketing communications also play an important role in the successful implementation of both *prospector* and *differentiated defender strategies*. The form of that communication, however, may differ under the two strategies. *Prospectors* must constantly generate awareness, stimulate trial, and build primary demand for new and unfamiliar products. High *advertising and sales promotion expenditures* seem likely to bear a positive relationship to the new-product and share-growth success of such businesses. In 1988, 3M sponsored the Winter and Summer Olympic Games. Its purpose was to build brand awareness on a worldwide basis and to strengthen ties with potential customers.

Differentiated defenders, on the other hand, are primarily concerned with maintaining the loyalty of established customers by adapting to their needs and providing good service. These tasks can best be accomplished—particularly in industrial goods and services industries—by an extensive, well-trained, well-supported salesforce. Therefore, *differentiated defenders* are likely to have higher *salesforce expenditures* than competitors.

Finally, *low-cost defenders* appeal to their customers primarily on price. Thus, high expenditures on advertising, sales promotion, or the salesforce would detract from their basic strategy and may have a negative impact on their ROI performance. Consequently, such businesses are likely to make relatively low expenditures as a percent of sales on those promotional activities.

The marketing programs for individual product-market entries within a particular business unit may vary a good deal on some or all of the 4Ps. Within the constraints imposed by the business's strategy, individual marketing managers usually have a wide range of strategic options to choose from when developing a marketing plan. The nature of those options, their

---

[19] Although Hambrick argued for the reverse relationship, data from his study of 850 SBUs actually support our contention that defenders have more vertically integrated channels than prospectors. See Hambrick, ibid.

relative advantages and weaknesses, and the conditions where each is most appropriate are the topics of the remaining seven chapters in this section.

SUMMARY

To be successful, the marketing program for a given product-market entry must be compatible with the internal capabilities, resources, management processes, and procedures of the firm, as reflected in the higher-level strategies pursued by the corporation and the business unit of which the entry is a part. The major question addressed by a business-level strategy is, How are we going to compete within our industry? Such strategies focus on how to allocate resources across product-markets and functional areas within the business to gain a sustainable advantage over competitors. Researchers have identified general categories of business-unit strategies based on observations of how those SBUs compete within their industries. We combined the classification schemes of Porter and Miles and Snow to arrive at a typology of six business strategies: (1) prospector, (2) differentiated analyzer, (3) low-cost analyzer, (4) differentiated defender, (5) low-cost defender, and (6) reactor.

Businesses pursuing a prospector strategy are primarily concerned with attaining rapid volume growth through the development and introduction of new products and by attaining a leading share of new markets. This strategy is particularly appropriate for industries in the introductory or early growth stages of their life cycle where technology is rapidly changing, market segments are largely unidentified or undeveloped, and the competitive structure is still in flux.

At the other extreme, defender businesses are primarily concerned with maintaining an already strong position in one or more major market segments in industries where the technology, customer segments, and competitive structure are relatively well developed, stable, and mature. Their major objective is usually to gain and sustain a substantial return from their businesses. Differentiated defenders try to

do this by maintaining an advantage based on premium product quality or superior customer service. Low-cost defenders seek economies of scale, attempt to minimize unit costs in production and marketing, and compete largely on the basis of low price.

The analyzer strategies fall in between prospectors and defenders. Such strategies are most commonly found in industries that are in the late growth or early maturity stages of their life cycles where, although the industry is largely developed, some technological changes, or shifts in customers' needs, or competitive structure are still occurring. Because the analyzer is a hybrid strategy, it is difficult to make many generalizations about the implications of this strategy for the allocation of resources across functional departments, or for the design of marketing programs for individual product-market entries within such businesses.

Reactors are businesses that operate without any well-defined or consistently applied competitive strategy. Although reactors are found in all industry environments, they react to changing circumstances in an ad hoc, unsystematic way. Reactor businesses tend not to perform as well on any dimension as units with more consistent strategies. Thus, it is impossible to draw conclusions about how such businesses are likely to market their products.

Most business units incorporate multiple product-market entries. Although those entries face different market and competitive situations, their marketing programs likely face the constraints and influence of the SBU's overall competitive strategy.

Successful prospector businesses tend to be competent in—and allocate a relatively large proportion of their resources to—functional areas directly related to new-product and market development, such as R&D, product engineering, marketing, sales, and marketing research. *Differentiated defenders* also spend substantial resources on marketing and sales to maintain a strong product quality or customer service position. But *low-cost defenders* usually allocate relatively few resources to any of these functions to hold down costs and prices.

The competitive thrust of a business unit's strategy influences and constrains marketing policies and program components—such as the breadth of the product line, pricing policies, and the size of advertising and promotion budgets. Thus, while marketing managers often play a crucial role in formulating the SBU's strategy, that strategy subsequently imposes constraints and direction on the marketer's decisions about the marketing program for a specific product-market within the SBU.

QUESTIONS

1. Compare and contrast the *prospector* and *low-cost defender* business strategies discussed in this chapter on each of the following strategic dimensions:
   a. Scope
   b. Objectives
   c. Deployment of resources
   d. Sources of synergy

2. The 3M Company's Industrial Tape SBU pursues a differentiated defender strategy in an industry where both the basic technologies and the customer segments are relatively mature and stable. Is the objective imposed by top management of obtaining 25 percent of sales from products introduced within the last five years an appropriate *objective* for such an SBU? What do you think top management hopes to accomplish by imposing such an objective on the Industrial Tape SBU? What are the potential disadvantages or dangers involved in imposing such an objective?

3. If you were the general manager of the 3M Industrial Tape SBU discussed in question 2, which objectives would you argue are most appropriate for your business unit in view of its strategy and its external environment? Why?

4. Historically, each division in General Motors (i.e., Chevrolet, Pontiac) competed with a strategy aimed at (a) maintaining its current position within the automobile market by aggressively marketing and making annual improvements to its exist-

ing line of car models, and (b) simultaneously working to develop new models that would incorporate more advanced technologies and designs. How would you categorize this strategy in terms of the *types of business strategies* discussed in the chapter? What are the strengths and limitations of such a strategy?

5. Several years ago General Motors created the Saturn division and charged it with developing an entirely new line of cars incorporating the latest advancements in product and production technology. What kind of *business strategy* is the Saturn division expected to pursue? How might the creation of this new division help overcome some of the limitations of GM's traditional business-unit strategy that you identified in your answer to question 4?

6. Suppose you have been the marketing manager for 3M Company's Industrial Tape SBU as described in question 2. You have just been informed that you are being transferred to a similar position within the company's Health Care SBU, a business unit that pursues a *prospector strategy* aimed at the rapid development of new products for emerging markets. Would you see the transfer as a positive step in the development of your career? How are your *responsibilities* and your *decision-making influence* likely to change as a result of the transfer?

7. You are the marketing vice president for a

small firm whose success is dependent on pioneering the development of new personal-care products. What are the *implications of this business strategy for designing distribution channels* for the company's products? How would you gain the support of independent channel intermediaries to encourage them to carry and promote your new products?

8. Which *areas of functional competence* are critical for the continued success of the type of business described in question 7? As marketing vice president, what role would you and your subordinates play in determining the firm's future success?

9. You are the marketing manager for the generic products division of a major pharmaceutical manufacturer. Your division uses the corporation's excess manufacturing capacity to produce generic prescription drugs—drugs whose patents have expired and can thus be manufactured by any company that wishes to produce them. Your division is a *low-cost defender* that maintains its position in the generic drug market by holding down its costs and selling generic products to distributors and pharmacies at very low prices. What are the implications of this business strategy for each of the 4Ps in the strategic marketing program you would develop for your division?

Chapter 12

Product and services decisions

GM REVS UP ITS PRODUCT LINE

In 1981, GM engineers studied a large number of foreign and domestic cars with highly successful customer satisfaction records in an effort to determine what competition its own midsize cars would face several years out. In the process, management was shocked to learn how far GM's engineering was behind its major rivals.[1]

In 1984, GM decided to try to leapfrog the competition with a new car line, code-named "GM-10." Several years and $5 billion later, the new line was ready for its debut. If it is not successful, the company's 37 percent share of the U.S. auto market will tumble even further from the 44 percent it held a few years ago (as shown in Exhibit 12–1). The GM-10 cars were designed to help GM regain some of its lost share of the U.S. middle to upper-middle-class market—a traditional GM stronghold.

Despite one of the most expensive marketing launches in GM's history, the Buick Regal, Oldsmobile Cutlass, and Pontiac Grand Prix GM-10 cars are not likely to cure GM's problem—company earnings lag behind Ford's, which has only two thirds GM's revenues. While good, the GM-10s have no major technological or styling advances, even though the Pontiac Grand Prix was named the 1988 Motor Trend Car of the Year.

The GM-10 line, as well as other GM cars, must overcome several serious handicaps. Not the least of these is the fact that all brands of GM-10 cars use the same chassis. How can the three

EXHIBIT 12 ♦ 1

General Motors market share (1983–1987)

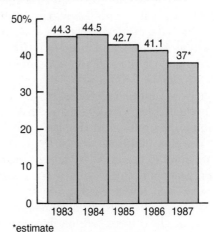

*estimate

---

[1] Based on Dale D. Biess and Doron P. Levin, "GM Readies New Line Aimed at Regaining Midsize Auto Sales," *The Wall Street Journal,* May 1, 1987, p. 1; General Motors 1987 *Annual Report;* Raymond Serafin, "How GM Is Shifting Gears," *Advertising Age,* January 4, 1988, pp. 1, 42; Thomas Moore, "For General Motors," *Fortune,* February 15, 1988; Jacob M. Schlesinger, "GM Seeks Revival of Buick and Olds," *The Wall Street Journal,* April 12, 1988, p. 37.

continued

brands be differentiated enough to meet the demands of an increasingly fragmented market? In an effort to do so, the GM-10 cars do not share any exterior metal skins, and the only common interior is the carpeting. Divisional integrity is supported through divisional marketing reps who were part of the product development teams, so that styling, features, and functions follow divisional themes. Even so, there is considerable similarity—enough so that some industry observers question whether GM has really escaped from its look-alike problem of the early 1980s.

Another handicap is that the GM-10 cars entered the midsize market nearly two years after Ford's highly successful Taurus and Sable. Some industry analysts think the Ford cars represent the look of the future, which forces GM into a me-too position. Further, weak GM profits caused by the massive reorganization of its vehicle operations to produce the GM-10s, plus increased competition, forced a reduction in the project's budget—which delayed the four-door and station-wagon models. As one Ford executive noted, "You just can't take three two-door cars and expect to turn around a company that large."[2] Because this cutback diminished the economies of scale, the per-car costs are higher than expected.

In the four years since GM decided to leapfrog its rivals, competition from both domestic and foreign auto companies has increased. Product planning and development have become more sophisticated as automakers strive to make their models distinctive. Targeting a car to a niche has become more important.[3]

For example, more and more producers are entering the luxury car segment, which is expected to boom as baby boomers move into their peak earning years. This segment has over 60 models, compared to 40 a few years back. This increase in competition has hurt not only the European luxury carmakers such as BMW, Jaguar, and Mercedes-Benz, but also domestic producers, including GM. Thus, Cadillac and the higher-priced models of Oldsmobile, Buick, and Pontiac are expected to have to fight hard to maintain share.[4] Another example of targeting is the Suzuki Samurai minijeep (base price $7,500), aimed at young, outdoorsy buyers while Chevrolet's S-10 Blazer ($11,588) is more upscale, with

---

[2] Jacob M. Schlesinger and Bradley A. Sterta, "GM-10 Cars Are Off to a Sluggish Start," *The Wall Street Journal*, June 17, 1988, p. 17; and James B. Treece, "Now Carmakers Are Really Burning Rubber," *Business Week*, January 9, 1989, p. 69.

[3] Melinda Grenier Guiles, "Upscale Drive: Competition Groups in U.S. Market for Luxury Autos," *The Wall Street Journal*, August 25, 1987, p. 29.

[4] Ibid.; also, see William J. Hampton, "Sporty Cars for the Family," *Business Week*, June 23, 1986, p. 164; and John Bussey, "Toyota to Enter Luxury Auto Market in U.S.," *The Wall Street Journal*, August 25, 1987, p. 5.

continued

concluded

nearly half its buyers earning $50,000 annually.[5] The Samurai has not been identified in its ads as a car, truck, or sport/utility vehicle—but simply as an inexpensive, fun machine. Of late, Samurai sales have dropped, largely because of Consumers Union's "not acceptable" rating. The reason given for the rating was the vehicle's tendency to roll over.[6]

---

[5] James B. Treece, "Why All Those City Folks Are Buying Pickups," *Business Week*, July 13, 1987, p. 102.

[6] "Suzuki Acts to Right Slipping Samurai Sales," *Advertising Age*, July 25, 1988, p. S-10.

Once a firm decides which markets to target, the single most important activity is product development. To a considerable extent, success here determines the firm's profitability—both short and long term. In many cases, the product serves as the basis for gaining a sustainable competitive advantage. It is a strong force in determining the character of the marketing mix. It affects the nature and scope of the other elements—price (level), channels of distribution (activities required), and advertising (message). It also affects such other functional areas as production, R&D, and engineering.

This chapter is concerned with the management of the firm's product line and its individual products. First, we define a product. Then we discuss various product classifications to show how a product's characteristics can affect how it is marketed. This is followed by a section dealing with the constraints on product strategies—notably those concerned with targeting and positioning, the business unit's strategy, and the product life cycle. In subsequent sections, we discuss product quality, product line and individual product decisions, and the marketing of services. New-product development is the subject of the next chapter.

WHAT IS A PRODUCT?

A **product** can be defined as anything that satisfies a want or need in terms of use, consumption, or acquisition. Thus, products include objects (TVs, radios, cars), services (medical, educational), places (New York, Moscow), people (Ronald Reagan, Bruce Springsteen), activities (entering a contest or visiting a weight-loss clinic), and ideas (have you hugged your kids today?).

Products should be thought of as problem solvers. They are purchased because of the benefits they provide—not because of the product per se. For example, a student who buys a hand-held calculator is buying a way to solve certain statistical problems and ensure accuracy of certain functions and speed. This means that what is important is how the *consumer* perceives that the product can satisfy a need, not how the *seller* sees the product. The seller must turn these benefits into a tangible product comprising features or attributes, packaging, brand name, and design or styling. Thus, a Hewlett-Packard hand-held calculator has numerous physical features (a number of functions, speed, and memory) that are packaged in a small, durable plastic box and sold under the H-P name.

The product offering is further augmented by such services as warranties, delivery, installation, and postpurchase service. In the case of H-P hand-held calculators, this would include a warranty, an instruction manual, and a traveling case. By thinking of a product in terms of benefits wanted, which are translated into a tangible product and augmented by such services as warranties, aftersale service, credit, delivery, and installation, it is easier for a firm to develop a total product package that better fits the needs of the target market.

PRODUCT CLASSIFICATIONS

Consumer goods can be divided into a number of subgroups based on how consumers think, feel, and shop for products. An understanding of these classes or groups is important in developing strategies and action plans.

Consumer goods

Consumer goods fall into four subgroups: convenience goods, shopping goods, specialty goods, and unsought goods. These subgroups vary primarily in the amount and kind of effort consumers exert in buying the products involved. Because of this, each type requires a different strategy involving a different set of strategy elements. For an indication of what mix items are stressed and examples of each type, see Exhibit 12–2.

Convenience products are typically purchased with as little effort as possible, frequently, and in small quantities. Usually convenience items are low in price and available in a variety of retail outlets. Convenience goods can be further subdivided into staple goods, impulse goods, and emergency goods. **Staple goods** are purchased on a regular basis and include most food items. **Impulse goods** are purchased without any planning prior to entering a store. The product itself, its packaging, and in-store displays are important in the sale of impulse items. **Emergency goods** are those needed to fill an unexpected need. They tend to be purchased immediately without shopping and often at a higher price. An example is the purchase of a pain reliever to treat a headache.

EXHIBIT 12 ◆ 2

Marketing strategy implications of consumer goods classification

	Examples	Strategy elements stressed
Convenience goods	Dentifrice, soap, razor blades, magazines, many packaged food products	Maximum distribution (product availability), consumer advertising (awareness and brand recognition), merchandising (in-store displays)
Shopping goods	Color TVs, cars, major appliances, homes	Available in limited number of stores, personal selling important, limited to extensive advertising, seller often offers financing, warranties, and postpurchase service
Specialty goods	Musical instruments, stereo equipment, some brands of men's clothing	Limited distribution, high price, strong advertising to promote brand uniqueness and where available locally
Unsought goods	Certain medical services, personal liability insurance, encyclopedias	Strong promotion, including personal selling

Shopping goods are products consumers ordinarily spend considerable effort to buy. Consumers shop around to compare competing products' features and prices before making a purchase. Compared to convenience goods, shopping goods are more expensive, available in substantially fewer stores, and rely heavily on personal selling.

Specialty products are sufficiently important to persons that they make a special effort to purchase them. In many cases consumers are not willing to accept a substitute for the preferred product. Retailers are especially important to the success of specialty goods; and thus marketers of such goods usually limit their distribution in an effort to get strong local sales support.

Unsought goods are products that consumers do not yet know about or they know about them but haven't considered buying them. For instance, the microwave was an unsought good to most consumers until they were made aware of the product. An example of a known but unsought consumer good is a set of encyclopedias—most people opt not to buy a set for home use. Unsought goods typically require considerable marketing effort, especially advertising and personal selling.

Overlap

Various groups of consumers position the same goods in different categories. Thus, to some individuals, dress shirts, tennis shoes, stereo equipment, and lawnmowers are shopping goods, while to others they are specialty goods. A convenience good to one consumer may be a specialty product to another in that the individual would not purchase a substitute if the desired product was not in stock.

Industrial goods

Industrial goods are classified in terms of their cost as well as how they fit into the buyer's production process (how they are to be used). Using such criteria, there are six categories of industrial goods and services: raw materials, fabricated materials and parts, installations, accessory equipment, supplies, and business services. Because we described each of these goods in some length in Chapter 5, they are not discussed here.

PRODUCT STRATEGY CONSTRAINTS

Earlier steps in the marketing management process constrain the business unit's product strategy. Market targeting (based on market attractiveness and business strengths) and market positioning (based on choice criteria) play a strong role with respect to the composition of the product line and the attributes of a given product. Business strategies of the type discussed in Chapter 11 derive from the characteristics of the targeted markets, their needs and wants in terms of products, and the competitors now serving these markets. Thus, it should not be surprising that business-level strategy strongly affects product strategy. But time changes the environment in which the business unit competes, forcing a revision in the business-unit strategy, which, in turn, affects product strategy. Thus, a product's life cycle also constrains its strategy.[7]

INFLUENCE OF MARKET TARGETING STRATEGIES ON PRODUCT DECISIONS

Different market targeting strategies have different effects on the firm's product line and the individual product's attributes. As we saw earlier, target market strategies can include mass-market, niche, and growth-market strategies. Targeting the **mass market** calls for emphasizing the larger market segments. As we saw in Chapter 10, this can be accomplished by using either a differentiated or an undifferentiated product strategy. Thus, the impact is mainly in terms of the length of the product line and the number of different

---

[7] For an interesting discussion of the relationship among segmentation, product differentiation, and strategy, see Peter R. Dickinson and James L. Ginter, "Market Segmentation, Product Differentiation, and Market Strategy," *Journal of Marketing*, April 1987, pp. 1–10.

marketing programs used. If an *undifferentiated strategy* is used, then the product's features would attempt to accommodate the choice criteria of the larger segments only. The hope would be that scale economies would enable the firm to price one or more of its items low enough to attract some consumers from segments with different choice criteria.

A *differentiated strategy* calls for developing products and programs tied to the needs of market segments that comprise the total market. GM uses such a strategy in its efforts to cover the whole market. For decades, GM divisions served as a price ladder; the first-time car buyer bought a Chevrolet and, as the customer became more affluent, he or she moved up to Pontiac, then Oldsmobile, next Buick, and finally Cadillac. The company is putting into place an updated differentiated strategy based on a new market segmentation scheme comprising some 19 segments.[8]

A **niche strategy,** a favorite of smaller firms, consists of selecting narrow segments that require special technical or marketing expertise. In the case of technical expertise, the product line is likely to be short and individual products specialized. For example, Chemfix Technologies is a small firm ($5 million in sales) in the hazardous-waste disposal industry. Chemfix has found a small but profitable market in converting toxic organic sludges (such as refinery wastes) into a nontoxic, easy-to-dispose-of clay.[9]

A **growth-market strategy** targets segments that are expected to expand—even if the segments are not very large at the present time. Product strategy here should reflect a firm's R&D capabilities, a strong marketing expertise, and the financial resources needed to fund growth. For example, the growing hazardous-waste disposal and treatment business is undergoing a technology revolution as it turns to more sophisticated ways to deal with harmful substances. One company, Waste Management, capitalizing on this, has developed a freeze-crystallization process that strips pesticides from tainted water, thereby solving water-pollution problems.[10]

EFFECT OF POSITIONING STRATEGIES ON PRODUCT DECISIONS

How a product is positioned affects its attributes. If a firm adopts a **single (mono) segment positioning strategy,** then the product is tailored to meet that segment's choice criteria and give it an advantage over competing products. If a firm undertakes a **multisegment positioning strategy,** then the selection of the product's attributes is a compromise that attempts to meet the choice criteria of all the segments involved and to beat the competing products.

---

[8] Raymond Serafin, "How GM Is Shifting Gears."

[9] Ken Wells, "Toxic-Waste Disposal Firms Enter High Technology Era," *The Wall Street Journal,* October 10, 1986, p. 27.

[10] Ibid.

Given the dynamics of the environment, including changes in a product's technology and moves made by competitors, it is not surprising that old brands have to be *updated* and possibly *repositioned*. This is particularly true in relation to competitive offerings. GM provides a good example of this kind of problem. By blurring the differences between Oldsmobile and Buick through look-alike styling and downsizing, GM hurt the sales of both brands. Collectively, the two dropped from a share of 20.2 percent in 1984 to 12.4 percent in 1987. GM is currently engaged in repositioning both cars.[11]

Sometimes a firm adopts an **imitative strategy** by targeting a position similar to a competitor's successful brand. It is difficult to be successful using this strategy unless the imitator has a distinct advantage—such as better access to channel intermediaries and a stronger salesforce or a lower price. For example, over the years a number of companies have undertaken a frontal attack on IBM, only to fail.

In a **defensive positioning strategy,** a firm with a successful brand introduces a second similar brand in an effort to preempt a competitor's imitative strategy. This is similar to a **flanker** or **fighting brand,** which counters the moves made by competitors by offering certain price and advertising concessions to retailers to take the heat off the major brand. For example, Hanes introduced its First to Last brand of pantyhose largely to protect its L'eggs brand against Kayser-Roth's No-Nonsense brand and Burlington's Active brand, both of which retailed for substantially less than L'Eggs. First to Last was introduced at about the same price and advertised as a durable and long-lasting product. Its intent was to slow the acceptance by supermarkets of the competing brands.

Anticipatory strategy calls for positioning a product in anticipation of a change in a segment's needs. Thus, a product is designed to fit a segment's future choice criteria. Zenith, for example, entered the big-screen market with a 45-inch model in the hope that when sales took off, Zenith would have a strong entry.

Generic business strategy constraints

As we saw in Chapter 10, business strategies are primarily concerned with answering the question of how the SBU will compete in a given industry with the objective of obtaining a sustainable advantage over rival firms. The typology used to classify business strategies was based on two dimensions: (1) the degree of emphasis placed on product-market development, and (2) the method chosen to compete in the unit's established product-markets. The first clearly says something about the importance of product develop-

---

[11] Raymond Serafin, "How GM Is Shifting Gears," and Jacob M. Schlesinger, "GM Seeks Revival of Buick and Olds."

ment, while the second is concerned with maintaining a low cost or having a higher product quality or better service than competitors. The four strategy types that emerged using these criteria were prospectors, analyzers, defenders, and reactors. Our concern here is with the first three.

Prospector strategies center on new-product development, which encourages broad and technically advanced lines. *Analyzers* are concerned with defending their established businesses, by using either a low-cost approach or by differentiating their product offerings on the basis of quality and service. They also pay some attention to new-product development to avoid being left behind by competitors. *Defender strategies* are similar to those of an analyzer, except defenders devote fewer resources to the development of new products, have—on average—smaller product lines, and wherever possible differentiate themselves from competitors via service. In summary, these three major types of business strategies constrain a firm's product strategy with respect to its breadth, technical sophistication, quality, and service.

Product life-cycle constraints

Different business strategies work better under different environmental conditions. Thus, strategy selection must take into account the different stages in the product life cycle. Prospector strategies are best suited to industries in an early stage of their life cycle. Analyzer strategies, on the other hand, are appropriate for the latter part of the growth stage, where the industry is well developed but still experiencing some growth and technological changes. Defender strategies apply best to the mature stage in the life cycle.

PRODUCT QUALITY[12]

As we have seen, one common way in which both analyzer and defender SBUs attempt to differentiate their established products is by offering superior quality. A variety of studies linking quality to profitability and market-share position have alerted managers to quality's competitive potential. These studies, coupled with the success of high-quality Japanese products

---

[12] This section has benefited from Robert D. Buzzell, "Product Quality," *Pimsletter no. 4* (Cambridge, Mass.: The Strategic Planning Institute), 1986; Bradley T. Gale and Richard Klavans, "Formulating a Quality Improvement Strategy," *Pimsletter no. 3* (Cambridge, Mass.: The Strategic Planning Institute), 1984; Phillip Thompson, Glenn DeSouza, and Bradley T. Gale, "The Strategic Management of Service Quality," *Pimsletter no. 33* (Cambridge, Mass.: The Strategic Planning Institute), 1985; Mark Chussel and Sidney Schoeffler, "Pricing High-Quality Products," *Pimsletter no. 5* (Cambridge, Mass.: The Strategic Planning Institute), 1985; and David A. Garvin, *Managing Quality* (New York: The Free Press, 1988).

EXHIBIT   12 ♦ 3

Samples of U.S. companies that have launched quality programs

---

♦ **Florida Power & Light** reduced power outages substantially even though most other utilities had long ago decided it couldn't be done.

♦ **Shearson Lehman Hutton** cut in half the time it takes to redeem customer bonds and, in the process, upped the accuracy of those transactions from 80 to 98 percent.

♦ **Whistler,** a large seller of radar detectors, increased the approval rate of products coming off its assembly lines from 75 to 99 percent, thereby saving hundreds of jobs from going to overseas manufacturing plants.

Source: Joel Dreyfuss, "Victories in the Quality Crusade," *Forbes,* October 10, 1988, p. 80.

and the quality failures of some American products (leading to well-publicized product liability suits) and government pressures, have led many U.S. companies to adopt a strategic quality management program.[13] These programs have increasingly stressed the importance of looking at quality from the customer's point of view; and many companies have now incorporated quality into their strategic planning process. For a sampling of U.S. companies that have successfully implemented a quality program, see Exhibit 12–3.

In recent years, quality has been redefined using a comparative basis (relative to competitive products) in contrast to fixed, internal standards. Further, it was recognized that customer satisfaction had to be measured on a set of product attributes over the product's lifetime. These changes required the use of marketing research, which made strategic quality management programs even more expensive. But the payout can be significant: there is little question that quality is positively correlated with profitability (see Exhibit 12–4). This can be accomplished by increasing sales, charging higher prices, and/or reducing the number of defects and field failures, thereby cutting manufacturing and service costs.

Dimensions of quality

The effect of quality on market share is likely to depend on the definition of quality. If *quality* is defined as reliability, superior esthetics (how a product looks and feels), or conformance (degree to which the product meets prescribed standards), then the relationship to market share is apt to be positive. If, however, product quality is defined in terms of superior performance or

---

[13] The National Highway Traffic Safety Administration, the Environmental Protection Agency, and the Consumer Product Safety Commission recalled some 29 million product units in 1978 versus 7 million in 1973. Product liability suits filed in federal district courts have been increasing at an annual rate in excess of 25 percent; see Garvin, *Managing Quality,* pp. 21–27.

EXHIBIT 12 ♦ 4
Product quality and profitability

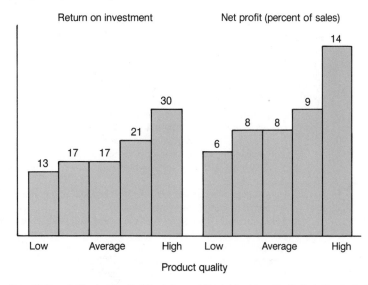

Source: Robert D. Buzzell, "Product Quality," *Pimsletter no. 4* (Cambridge, Mass.: The Strategic Planning Institute, 1986), p. 3.

more features, then the product is likely to be more expensive to produce and will sell in smaller amounts because of a higher price.[14] Exhibit 12–5 gives an overview of the eight dimensions of quality. Collectively, "they cover a broad range of concepts. Several of the dimensions involve measurable product attributes; others reflect individual preferences. Some are objective and timeless; others shift with changing fashions. Some are inherent characteristics of goods, while others are ascribed characteristics."[15]

Quality strategy

Because quality is multidimensional, products can be differentiated in many ways. The buyer behavior models discussed in Chapter 4 recognize that multiple choice criteria may be used to select a given product from a number of alternatives. But as noted in Chapter 4, the consumer's choice criteria are typically limited to fewer than eight product dimensions or attributes. Thus, a company does not have to use all eight quality dimensions to compete.

This implies that many companies will do better to focus on a limited number of quality dimensions rather than to seek high performance on most

---

[14] Garvin, *Managing Quality*, pp. 76–77.

[15] Ibid., p. 60.

EXHIBIT   12 ◆ 5

The eight dimensions of quality

---

1. *Performance* has to do with a product's basic operating characteristics. For an automobile, this translates into such traits as acceleration, miles per gallon, ease in handling, and comfort. What traits are important as well as how important depends upon the individual and the use environment.
2. *Features* are secondary product characteristics that are designed to enhance the product's basic functioning. In cars, examples include rear window defroster, power steering, cruise control, and white-wall tires.
3. *Reliability* is the probability that a product will perform satisfactorily over a given period. Because of the cost of repair and downtime, reliability is an extremely important dimension for automobiles and heavy machinery.
4. *Conformance* is the extent to which a product's operating characteristics meet certain specifications.
5. *Durability* is a measure of the life of a product. It has both technical (replacement) and economic (repair costs) dimensions.
6. *Serviceability* is concerned with the speed and ease of obtaining competent repair.
7. *Esthetics* has to do with how a product looks, feels, sounds, tastes, and smells. These ratings are subjective and are related to how the consumer perceives quality.
8. *Perceived quality* frequently results from the use of indirect measures since the consumer may lack or not understand information about a product's attributes. Thus, perceptions may derive from such cues as price, brand name, advertising, reputation, and country of origin.

Source: David A. Garvin, *Managing Quality* (New York: The Free Press, 1988), pp. 49–60.

or all dimensions. This assumes, however, that the dimensions selected are compatible with the choice criteria of the targeted segment or segments. For example, Japanese automobile manufacturers have stressed reliability (low number of repairs of their products). As a result, American consumers have given Japanese cars a high quality rating, even though they rate poorly, relative to American cars, on safety (performance) and corrosiveness (durability).

American producers of durable goods have often emphasized quality dimensions that are relatively unimportant to consumers; for example, car esthetics and features rather than reliability and conformance. Americans tend to tie product features to technological advances, while the Japanese emphasize refinements in the present technology. Even now, some U.S. car manufacturers seem overly enamored with features that will enable the driver to

> Step behind the wheel, turn the key, and . . . be pampered. The rearview mirrors automatically flip to the positions you want, the seat and back shift to accommodate your anatomical contours, the radio locks into your favorite station, and a message screen lights

up to remind you of your next appointment. Tell the navigation system where you're headed and it maps out the best route on a color video screen. If you hit a stretch of potholes, the suspension immediately adjusts for a smoother ride.[16]

Consumers can only hope that such features are not gimmicks that require frequent and expensive repairs—and that they are not provided at the expense of improved reliability.

A business's quality strategy is influenced by its decisions concerning what quality dimensions to emphasize in a given product. This determination derives in large part from the targeting and positioning steps taken earlier—especially positioning, which is concerned with the attributes needed to make a product succeed in the target market. The fact that American manufacturers have received low marks on quality reveals either a lack of marketing research or that they have been ineffective in implementing their quality strategies.

Two extremes in quality strategy are much in evidence: the expensive, high-quality products that embrace a large number of quality dimensions and are targeted at a limited market, and the lower-quality, lower-priced products incorporating few quality dimensions and aimed at the mass market. Examples of high-quality products include Mercedes-Benz and BMW cars, Rolex watches, and Steuben glass, as well as many handcrafted products. Yamaha, a Japanese manufacturer of pianos, has recently challenged Steinway, which has turned out handcrafted pianos for years and been considered the quality leader. Yamaha did so by focusing on reliability and conformance, while Steinway emphasized artistry and uniqueness.[17]

BRANDING

Branding identifies and helps differentiate the goods or services of one seller from those of another. It consists of a name, sign, symbol, or some combination thereof. A **brand name** is the part that can be vocalized (BIC, Levi's, Sony). A **brand mark** is something that cannot be verbalized, such as a symbol, design, or unique packaging (the Buick eagle, McDonald's arches, and the Pillsbury Dough Boy). A **trademark** is simply a brand or some part of a brand that legally belongs exclusively to a given seller.

Branding is important to consumers because it simplifies shopping, helps to ensure quality, and often satisfies certain status needs. Sellers also benefit from branding. It fosters a continuing relationship with consumers (brand

---

[16] William J. Hampton, Mel Gross, Deborah C. Wise, and Otis Port, "Smart Cars," *Business Week*, June 13, 1988, p. 68.

[17] Garvin, *Managing Quality*, p. 64.

loyalty), which protects the seller against competition. And it facilitates the introduction of new products.

Favorable branding conditions

Branding is particularly important when it is difficult for the consumer to measure the product's quality (both physical features and service) objectively. Examples of hard-to-measure quality branded products include TV sets, automobile tires, motor oils, and pianos. Branding is also important for status products (Omega watches or Gucci loafers) or when the brand connotes a favorable user stereotype (Clairol hair coloring or Nike running shoes).

Other favorable conditions include a sufficient-size market to warrant the cost of branding, the opportunity to physically differentiate the product so that it performs better for consumers, and the ease of physically branding the product (for example, some fresh fruits and vegetables are hard to physically brand).

Manufacturer versus distributor brands

Brands are classified as **manufacturer** (also known as **national brands**) or **distributor brands** (typically known as **private labels**), depending on who is responsible for their naming, pricing, promotion, and quality control. Either wholesalers or retailers can develop distributor brands. Manufacturer brands are typically the more popular brands in most product classes. They include such familiar names as Gillette razor blades, L'eggs panty hose, Miller beer, Tide detergent, Zenith televisions, and Xerox copiers. The sponsors of national brands ordinarily emphasize quality, spend heavily on advertising and merchandising, and price their product 15 to 20 percent above distributor brands. The branding of commodities is also increasing. For example, Excel Beef Corporation is putting its name on a line of 33 fresh beef items.[18]

Two somewhat countertrends are now in operation regarding national brands. The first is the declining share held by big name brand products in a product class because of the fractured marketplace. More and more product classes are being dominated by a collection of lesser-known brands.[19]

On the other hand, consumer household goods companies are being acquired at handsome prices because of the value of their brand names. Thus, P&G paid 2.6 times the book value of Richardson-Vicks, while Philip

[18] Shannon Thurmond, "Excel Puts Its Brand on Beef Line," *Advertising Age*, October 5, 1987, p. 91.

[19] Regis McKenna, "Marketing in an Age of Diversity," *Harvard Business Review*, September–October 1988, p. 88.

Morris bought General Foods for 3.5 times the book value. The reasons for these acquisitions are the increasing expense to create a well-known brand and the low success rate of new products. Thus, buying popular brands can be a shortcut to profitability. Of 24 leading consumer brands in 1923, 19 were still the leaders 50 years later.[20]

Distributor brands are not usually well-advertised brands. Their distribution is restricted to a limited number of stores and, in many cases, geographical areas. Examples of such brands are Lucerne (Safeway dairy products) and Kenmore (Sears major appliances). Distributor brands have been thought of as having less quality than national brands, but a number of exceptions have appeared recently. For example, A&P introduced its Master Choice, a line of fancy private-label foodstuffs that seeks to cash in on the increased demand for gourmet products.[21]

Branding strategies

A company has a number of branding strategy options, one of which is to brand name each individual product or to use a family brand name. **Individual branding** requires the company to provide each product with a distinctive name. This type of branding is practiced by such firms as Procter & Gamble (Tide, Luvs, Crest, Pringles), General Foods (Post cereals, Jell-O, Gaines dog food), and PepsiCo (Pepsi, Slice, Mountain Dew).

Individual brands reduce a company's risk, in that a failure is not readily associated with the firm's other products. Further, it enables a firm to compete via multibrand entries within the same product class. This is an increasingly popular practice—as in dog foods, soaps and detergents, razor blades, and automobiles. The underlying assumption is that the firm can capture a higher collective market share with multibrand entries.

In some cases, a firm launches a second brand with the objective of eventually replacing the present product. It uses a new brand name rather than offering the consumer an improved product under the old name— partly because attitudes toward the old product have matured to a point where they would be extremely difficult (and costly) to change and partly because some segments are slow to give up the old product.

Family branding uses the same brand name to cover a group of products. There are several variations of family branding, including its use primarily with related items (Campbell soups and Sears' Kenmore appliances); its use with all company items regardless of whether they are related (General Electric and H. J. Heinz); and the use of a family name combined with individual product names (Kellogg's Raisin Bran).

---

[20] Paul B. Brown, Zachary Schiller, Christine Dugas, and Scott Seredon, "New? Improved?" *Business Week*, October 21, 1985, p. 108.

[21] Alix M. Freedman, "A&P to Sell a Private-Label Food Line to Compete against Top-Shelf Brands," *The Wall Street Journal*, June 2, 1988, p. 28.

The major arguments for using family branding are reduced costs and transfer of customer satisfaction from one product to another bearing the same name. The latter makes it easier to launch product modifications such as new package sizes and types or new flavors and varieties and new products as when Nike extended its brand to cover athletic clothing. Family branding can also increase the impact of shelf facings in stores and make feasible the promotion of a product line comprising many low-volume items.

Under certain conditions, family branding is not a good strategy. For instance, when the family brand covers products that vary in quality, consumers become confused about what quality to expect. Also, extending a brand name to an inadequate product may tarnish the quality reputation of the entire line.

Yet another strategy involves the use of a **no-brand brand name.** Examples include generic, no-frill, unbranded, lower-quality food and household products sold through supermarkets. These items recorded their highest sales in the United States in 1982 when inflation was rampant. Since then, the no-brands have declined in popularity to about a 2 percent share of total food sales, even though they sell for up to 40 percent less than national brands.[22]

A **multiple brands strategy** represents a situation where a company deliberately decides to compete against itself. This strategy is sometimes useful for increasing a company's overall share of the market and its profits despite cannibalization. A business sometimes finds itself with multiple brands when a new formulation of an old product is placed in the marketplace and the old one is not discontinued. We are not, however, referring to such situations here, but rather to strategies involving competing brands, private branding, and the sale by a company of its own original equipment manufactured (OEM) components to competitors. Examples include General Motors (Buick versus Oldsmobile versus Pontiac), Ford (Mercury versus Ford), General Electric in major appliances (the GE brand versus Hotpoint), and Procter & Gamble (Crest versus Gleem toothpaste).

Another strategy option is to produce **private labels.** The most common situation is where a company manufacturing and selling a product under its own brand name produces essentially the same product, with differences primarily in appearance and features, for sale under another company's name. This is a fairly common practice in a variety of product categories including major appliances, tires, textiles, packaged food products, and consumer electronics. Thus, Whirlpool produces major appliances for Sears; General Electric did the same for J. C. Penney; and Coca-Cola supplies A&P with Minute Maid Orange Juice (its own brand) as well as with the orange juice A&P sells under its own label.

---

[22] Amy Dunkin, "No-frills Products: 'An Idea Whose Time Has Gone,'" *Business Week*, June 17, 1985, p. 64.

Strong retailer brands have become very important in the soft goods trade. Ralph Lauren, Coach, and a number of European retailers such as Burberry and Laura Ashley have opened their own U.S. stores—some under franchise—selling only their merchandise. Traditional retailers have responded aggressively. Macy's has increased its private-label sales from 6 percent of total sales to 20 percent since 1980. Over 70 percent of sales are private-label merchandise for The Limited, which has become one of the largest sellers of women's apparel in the United States.[23] On the other hand, note also that Sears—long the stronghold of private labels—has reversed itself and is now selling national brands (Levi's, Yamaha, Magnavox, and Kodak).

For many years, many companies rejected private labeling on the basis that it would lower the image of their regular brand. This no longer seems to be the case. A firm undertakes a private-label product-line strategy not only to increase sales but also to lower per-unit costs because of scale and learning effects. It enables a firm, therefore, to compete more effectively with its own brand. And, if successful in obtaining a high share for its own brand, it should be able to hold its private-label business because of its low *relative* per-unit costs. Private labeling permits the firm to enter a new segment—often of some considerable worth—at a low cost and with little risk.

PACKAGING

A product's package serves three functions—protecting, facilitating, and promoting the product. The protecting function is critical. The package must protect the product in transport and in storage at the factory, wholesaler, retailer, and consumer levels. Protecting an item under a variety of temperatures and moisture conditions as well as against being crushed or dropped during handling is no small undertaking.

Increasingly, packages are becoming an extension of the product and a way to identify and differentiate products. Packaging facilitates use of the product, as in aerosol cans, no-drip spouts, disposable and unbreakable bottles, and resealable containers. Packaging can also increase product safety, as shown by child-proof tops on drugs and tamper-resistant packages.

Packaging can give a firm's product strong promotional support at the point of purchase. Compared with advertising, many more potential customers may see the package and at more opportune times. More and more sellers are attempting to develop a common package design for their products, creating a greater impact on the consumer (for example, Kellogg's cereals on supermarket shelves). Because consumers purchase a high percentage of supermarket items on impulse, packaging is especially important for such items. L'eggs panty hose is an example of an impulse item whose package was instrumental to its success in the marketplace.

---

[23] Walter J. Salmon and Karen A. Cmar, "Private Labels Are Back in Fashion," *Harvard Business Review*, May–June 1987, p. 99.

Because of increasing competition among brands within stores, more attention is being paid to packaging. In the final analysis, "a successful package walks a slim line between fitting into its product category and capturing the consumer's attention. The design must convey an identity that says, 'I am a soup or a detergent' in a way that is instantly recognizable, memorable, enticing, and believable."[24]

SERVICING PRODUCTS

The service provided with a product can include a variety of activities, depending on the product and its use environment. The more common service attributes that are part of a product offering include:

- Delivery reliability, including lead time
- Warranty
- Repair and maintenance, including response time, spare parts availability, and effectiveness
- Fast price quotations
- Speedy order processing

- Efficient complaint handling
- Credit availability
- Prompt inquiries handling
- Buyer personnel training
- Prompt claim settlement

Companies that excel at providing service find it to be a considerable competitive advantage. In most markets, it is a significant part of a firm's quality rating; in many, it is more important than the product itself. Service is not just a competitive tool; it also strongly affects the overall level of profitability. The more service-sensitive the market, the greater the profitability (see Exhibit 12–6). To be effective, a firm's service program must set performance standards and monitor its service performance regularly. For example, American Airlines has set forth specifications on a number of service attributes (e.g., phones must be answered within 20 seconds 80 percent of the time and doors opened within 70 seconds after an airplane is parked). The company also uses consumer surveys and reports from consultants to keep management updated on how consumers view the quality of their service program versus those of competing airlines.[25]

PRODUCT-LINE STRATEGY DECISIONS

Companies must review their product lines at regular intervals to determine whether they have the potential for future growth and profitability. Because of environmental dynamics (including the actions of competitors), the sales and profitability of individual items in the lines change over time. A peri-

---

[24] Frederick Mittleman, "Packaging—If It's Good—Makes the Sale," *Marketing News*, September 26, 1988, p. 17.

[25] Thompson et. al., "The Strategic Management of Service Quality."

EXHIBIT 12 ◆6
Profits are high in markets where services are important

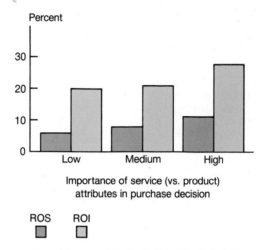

Source: Phillip Thompson, Glenn DeSouza, and Bradley T. Gale, "The Strategic Management of Service Quality," *Pimsletter no. 33* (Cambridge, Mass.: The Strategic Planning Institute, 1985), p. 4.

odic market analysis helps firms determine how successfully their product lines are satisfying the demand of the various market segments they serve. Exhibit 12–7 provides an example of such an analysis prepared for a major container shipping company showing the size of the targeted commodity segments, company sales, and company market share. The exhibit reveals that the company's performance is weak in all segments except motor vehicles and copper, and possibly wine and machinery. What does this reveal about the company's line of service offerings and its relative strengths and weaknesses? Is the weak performance due to a weak product line or to poor marketing support or both? Are new service offerings needed? If so, what features should they possess? To get a better view of the situation, we need to project the data—particularly the value of each segment—into the future. If the tonnage of motor vehicles and parts declines, the company's overall performance would suffer drastically.

In addition to a market analysis, a firm should make a product-line analysis. Because individual products vary in sales and profits, it is important to note the present and future contributions of each (see Exhibit 12–8). In the exhibit, products 4 and 5 account for only 22 percent of sales but 44 percent of profits, while product 1 with 31 percent of sales accounts for only 18 percent of profits. Can anything be done to improve the profits performance of product 1? Can the sales of products 4 and 5 be increased without engaging in strong price competition? Is product 4 vulnerable to competitive actions or the advent of an unfavorable demand trend?

EXHIBIT 12 ♦ 7

Market share of selected commodities exported from West Germany to United States—1982

Commodity	Total tons shipped	Tons shipped by company	Company market share
Wine	30,944	3,275	10.6%
Beer	101,088	3,572	3.5
Organic chemistry	57,071	4,043	7.1
Inorganic chemistry	68,290	5,083	7.4
Plastics	30,927	2,012	6.5
Refactory materials	40,232	2,425	6.0
Iron and steel	65,225	3,139	4.8
Copper	19,064	3,608	18.9
Machinery	101,595	12,372	12.3
Motor vehicles and parts	53,820	24,649	45.8
Total	568,256	64,279	11.3

Source: Adapted from Exhibit 3, North Star Shipping Company (Fontainebleau, France: INSEAD, The European Institute of Business Administration, 1983).

Length of product line

The question of whether the product line is too short or too long concerns target markets and the way the company wants to position itself over time. Much also depends on which stage of the product life cycle is involved.

A short product line is desirable in the short term, given the difficulties of managing a long line. Further, it should be more profitable, given the economies of scale and the learning curve. In the long term, however, a short line comes under fire as competitors segment the market and develop more specialized markets. To survive and prosper, short lines must be uniquely positioned against competitors; and the firm must be able to maintain the line's differential advantage.

Firms lengthen their product lines in an effort to grow by catering to more segments and to minimize competitive threats to small lines. Thus, many firms attempt to sell a line that targets a large number of segments. Examples include General Motors in automobiles, Caterpillar in road building machinery, and Procter & Gamble in laundry detergents. The problem is that as a line increases, it becomes more difficult to position individual products to prevent undue cannibalization. Cannibalization by a new product reduces the scale effects on the older product, thus affecting the net profitability of the line.

Aside from the short line/long line strategy issue, other product line decisions include line filling, line stretching, line extension, and product abandonment. All but the last involve adding to the length of the present line.

EXHIBIT   12 ♦ 8

Example of a product-line analysis

Product item	Percent of total sales	Percent of total net profits
1	31%	18%
2	18	11
3	15	11
4	12	28
5	10	16
6	8	8
7	6	8
	100%	100%

Line filling

This strategy lengthens the product line by adding items *within* the present range. It is done to satisfy more customers, to increase sales and profits, to placate dealers who want a full-line supplier, and to ward off competitors. RCA color television is an example of line filling: during the growth period of the product life cycle it more than doubled its number of TV models, most of which had features positioning them within its existing line. Most automobile manufacturers, both domestic and foreign, have added to their lines to a point where consumers can choose from over 300 different types of cars and light trucks—and this does not include variations within each line.

Because of the temptation to add items, line filling may result in too long a line from an economic viewpoint; hence the need for a periodic product-line analysis.

Line stretching

This strategy involves lengthening the product line beyond its current range of variables such as size and price. Aircraft manufacturers have typically expanded the size of their jets—as McDonnell Douglas lengthened its DC8 and DC9. Line stretching may be up or down or both. An upward stretch can also consist of trading up, as in the addition of higher price lines. Sears has traded up many of its soft goods lines over the years. Most Japanese auto makers have traded up in an effort to tap the high-priced market—Honda's Acura, Toyota's Lexus, and Nissan's Infinite. An upward stretch is not without its risks, however. Upper-end competitors may retaliate by entering the lower-end market; and consumers may not believe that the company can really produce the higher quality products.

A downward stretch involves adding products to serve the lower end of the market. For example, IBM added a line of minicomputers and later a line of personal computers to not only better serve present customers but also to serve new customers. American car manufacturers have emphasized the smaller-car component of their lines in recent years. The risks involved with a downward stretch are that competition may counterattack by moving into the higher end; channel intermediaries may not support the move because of lower margins; and consumers may feel that the lower quality of the new lower-end products diminishes the company's overall quality image.

Firms practice two-way stretches when they have a midrange offering and seek market dominance by expanding both up and down. In recent years Mercedes-Benz has followed this strategy by adding more expensive as well as less expensive, smaller car models. Both up and down line-stretching strategies are essentially incremental. Firms can thus exploit their current technological, manufacturing, and marketing resources, reducing the risks inherent in the introduction of new products.

Line extension

This strategy consists of introducing new products that differ significantly from those in the existing line, certainly more than just by size and price. In the commercial jet airplane industry, Boeing initiated an upward product-line stretching strategy based on its 727 model. It proposed a lengthened 200-passenger version of the 727—the 727-300—to United Airlines, which, after considerable study, refused the offer. Boeing then settled for a product-line extension with its B757, B767, and B777 models. Although this strategy required a considerably higher investment than the product-line stretching strategy initially considered, the three new models were designed to use common components, which substantially reduced the resources required.[26]

A product-line extension strategy involves greater costs and financial risks than product-line filling or stretching strategies. It provides, however, an extended technological base for the firm and is more likely to tap new market segments. It also provides a new anchor point in the product space from which product-line filling or stretching strategies can be based. The danger of the other strategies is the cannibalization of existing products. This is less apt to happen with a product-extension strategy.

Brand extension

While similar to line stretching and extension, brand extension is sufficiently different to warrant a separate discussion. It consists of two strategies. First, it can refer to the extension of an existing brand name, by using it to introduce new varieties of the original product (say, Tide with Bleach and Lite Citrus Hill). The second strategy extends a popular brand by using it with new products in related product categories (such as Crest Tartar Con-

---

[26] Louis Kraar, "Boeing Takes a Bold Plunge to Keep Flying High," *Fortune*, September 25, 1978, pp. 42–50.

trol Mouth Rinse, 3 Musketeers Ice Cream Bar, and Breyers'—known for its high-quality ice cream—new line of All-Natural jams, jellies, and preserves). The reasoning for brand extension is that they save big money in advertising and promoting the new product and get faster trial by consumers and better acceptance by retailers.[27]

Dropping products

All too often a company permits weak products to remain in the product line despite the high opportunity costs of keeping them. In many cases a firm rationalizes its continuation of certain items on the basis that sales at least cover direct costs. But this attitude fails to take into account that such products often consume a disproportionate amount of management time, divert the salesforce from items with a greater potential, and may cause consumers to have negative thoughts about the entire line.[28]

Substantial profits often result from a reduction in the size of a product line. For example, a Dutch company was losing money, reputation, and market share with its line of wire products such as hangers, kitchen gadgets, strainers, and baskets. It reduced its catalog from 1,400 to 400 items and concentrated on items with comparatively high value added. With this strategy the company once again became profitable and assumed a dominant market-share position. By 1992, General Motors is hoping to cut its number of models to 133—a 23 percent reduction from 1986—by reducing overlap.[29]

Product systems

This strategy is of post-World War II origin. It consists of selling a product, complementary products, and service as a package. For example, some airlines sell vacation packages that include airfare, rental car, hotel accommodations, meals, sight-seeing tours, and entertainment. Complex undertakings such as data processing and information retrieval also lend themselves to product systems. Many of the larger mainframe companies sell not only computers but also software, operating systems, preventative maintenance (including emergency repairs), financing, and employee training as well.

A product-system strategy requires a strong compatibility between the various components of the system. When properly implemented such a strategy produces scale economies (in contrast to individual consumers

---

[27] Martin Friedman, "A Brand by Any Other Name Would Not Sell as Sweet," *Adweek*, October 10, 1988, p. 35.

[28] Large companies with diverse product lines are apt to employ a formal decision process that is sequential and uses prescribed procedures. See George J. Avlonitis, "Product Elimination Decision Making: Does Formality Matter?" *Journal of Marketing*, Winter 1985, p. 41.

[29] Raymond Serafin, "How GM Is Shifting Gears," p. 42.

attempting to put together their own systems), and a closer, more enduring relationship between buyer and seller. Implementing a product system successfully requires an in-depth understanding of customers' needs, a well-trained, high-level salesforce, and sufficient funds to finance the sale of a system that often involves a time-consuming process.

SERVICES[30]

The service component of the U.S. economy accounts for over 70 percent of all nonfarm jobs and some two thirds of all economic activity, compared to 21 percent for manufacturing. Since 1969, services have added some 30 million jobs, while manufacturing employment has stayed relatively constant at 19 million for the past 20 years. Services outpace manufacturing in capital spending by nearly $50 billion, corporate profits by over $25 billion, and international trade, where they rang up a small profit, compared to a huge merchandise deficit.[31] As the number of two-wage-earner families increases (currently nearly 50 percent of the total), time becomes a critical factor. This, coupled with an increase in family income, has generated a substantial increase in the total amount spent on all services. For these and other reasons, we can expect services to grow at a 10 percent or more annual rate. Most of the new jobs in the future will be in the service sector.

> Want someone to fetch a meal from a local restaurant? In Austin, Texas, you can call Eat-Out-In. Plants need to be watered? In New York, you can call the Busy Body's Helper . . . "We'll find it, we'll do it, we'll wait for it" chirps Lois Barnett, the founder of Personalized Services in Chicago. She and her crew of six will walk the dog, shuttle the kids to Little League, or wait in line for your theater tickets.[32]

But what is a service? Traditionally, we have associated services with nonmanufacturing businesses, even though services may be an indispensable part of a goods producer's offering (such as postpurchase servicing of consumer durables). As we noted earlier, service is critical to building a profitable long-term relationship with customers—regardless of whether it is in a product- or nonproduct-based industry. Thus, almost all businesses are engaged in service to a greater or lesser extent. Does this mean there is no difference between the marketing of services and the marketing of goods? The answer is that there is a substantial difference, which we will discuss in the remainder of this section.

---

[30] For a more detailed discussion on services, see Christopher H. Lovelock's *Services Marketing* (Englewood Cliffs, N.J.: Prentice-Hall, 1984), pp. 1–9.

[31] John S. McClenahen and Perry Pascarella, "America's New Economy," *Industry Week*, January 26, 1987, pp. 26–32.

[32] Mark N. Vamos, Gregory L. Miles, and Mary J. Pitzer, "Presto!" *Business Week*, April 27, 1987, p. 86.

To better understand this difference, it helps to think of services as *intangibles* and goods as *tangibles*. The former can rarely be experienced in advance of the sale, while tangible products can be directly experienced—even tested—before purchase.[33] Using this distinction, a *service* can be defined as "any activity or benefit that one party can offer to another that is essentially intangible and does not result in the ownership of anything. Its production may or may not be tied to a physical product."[34]

The above definition applies to a variety of economic activities including entertainment, health care, retailing, food services, transportation, utilities, wholesalers, communications, finance, insurance, real estate, lodging, and a host of business services such as accounting, consulting, legal, and engineering. In addition, there are a variety of personal services—for example, recreation, barbering, and housekeeping. The public sector offers such diverse services as the military, police and fire departments, postal service, regulatory agencies, courts, and schools. The not-for-profit sector offers an assortment of services through churches, museums, libraries, hospitals, charities, and schools. Exhibit 12–9 lists some of the largest for-profit service companies.

EXHIBIT 12 ◆9

Examples of for-profit service companies

◆ **Transportation**	◆ **Lodging**
American Airlines	Marriott
Federal Express	Hyatt
Union Pacific	Holiday Inns
◆ **Communications**	◆ **Accounting, consulting, marketing**
AT&T	**research**
MCI	Arthur Anderson
Sprint	Booz, Allen & Hamilton
◆ **Utilities**	A. C. Nielsen
New England Electric System	◆ **Entertainment**
Pacific Gas and Electric	MGM
Arkansas-Louisiana Gas Company	New York Yankees
◆ **Finance and insurance**	NBC
Citicorp	
Merrill Lynch	
Prudential-Bache	

---

[33] Theodore Levitt, *The Marketing Imagination* (New York: Free Press, 1986), pp. 94–95.

[34] Philip Kotler and Gary Armstrong, *Principles of Marketing* (Englewood Cliffs, N.J.: Prentice-Hall, 1989), p. 575.

Classification of services

Services are usually classified according to what they provide, as specified by the Standard Industrial Classification (SIC) code. But this tells us very little about the production and delivery of a given service, because the SIC system is oriented toward goods and not services. Because of this, a variety of classifications have emerged. One classification system is based on the evolution of services as follows:[35]

1. *Unskilled personal services:* This category includes housekeeping, janitorial work, and street cleaning and originated in a traditional society.

2. *Skilled personal services:* These emerged as society became more industrialized—as it passed out of the subsistence stage, needs arose for government services, repair (fix-it) businesses, and retail/wholesale specialists.

3. *Industrial services:* As products became more plentiful, highly skilled specialists appeared, such as lawyers, accountants, consultants, and marketing researchers.

4. *Mass consumer services:* Discretionary income gave rise to any number of consumer service industries that flourished because of scale effects. These include national and international transport, lodging, fast-food, auto rental, and entertainment companies.

5. *High-tech business services:* The growth in the use of sophisticated technologies has created a need for new services as well as more efficient older ones. Thus, in recent years, we have seen a rapid growth in repair services relating to information processing, telecommunications, and other electronic products. The cost of such repairs is expected to reach $76 billion in the early 1990s.

Services have also been classified by whether they are **equipment-** or **people-based.** The former includes automated services (automated bank tellers), equipment operated by relatively unskilled operators (car washes), and equipment operated by skilled operators (airlines). People-based services vary by the degree of expertise required; that is, those involving unskilled labor (maids) versus professionals (lawyers and doctors).

Another way of classifying services is by the **extent of customer contact** involved. Examples of high-contact services include health care and education; low-customer-contact services include credit ratings and movie theaters. Services also differ as to whether they are provided by a **public** or a **private (for-profit) organization** and whether they are directed at the **consumer (household) market** or the **business sector.** All of these classifying services influence the way in which services are marketed.

---

[35] Karl Abrecht and Ron Zemki, *Service America* (Homewood, Ill.: Dow Jones-Irwin, 1985), p. 10.

Impact of service characteristics on marketing management[36]

Our definition of a service centered on the word *intangible*, which was used as a way of differentiating a service from a good. The degree to which a service is **intangible** affects the getting and keeping of customers. Because prospective customers have difficulty experiencing (seeing, touching, feeling, smelling) the service offering in advance, they are forced to buy promises. But promises are also intangible; hence, marketers need to make them tangible to prospective buyers. Thus, metaphors and similes become surrogates for the tangibility that is lacking. This explains the solid, reassuring decor of bank offices and law offices; the professional-looking lab coats and uniforms worn by a hospital staff; the neat, cheerful uniforms of fast-food restaurant employees; and the elegant decor and atmosphere of upscale shops and hotels. These things become the tangible evidence of the intangible service being offered.[37]

A further difficulty with *intangibility* is that consumers often don't know what criteria to use in evaluating a service. How do you rate a stockbroker's advice *before* you follow it? Or a travel agency? Or a repair or fix-it service? Typically, consumers approach the consumption of services with optimistic expectations. Disappointment is all too easy to come by under these conditons.

A second service characteristic that affects marketing is **perishability**; that is, because a service is an experience, it cannot be inventoried. Motel rooms and airline seats not occupied, idle telephone capacity, and the unused time of physicians and lawyers cannot be reclaimed. Further, when demand exceeds capacity, customers must be turned away, because no backup inventory is available. Thus, service organizations must do everything possible to anticipate peak loads and to fit demand to capacity. The two main ways of coping with this problem are to manipulate demand and/or supply:

1. *Manipulating demand.* This can be done in a variety of ways, including price, advertising, and the sale of other goods or services. Thus, for example, car-rental firms, hotels, airlines, and movie theaters run specials offering the same service at different times for a lower price.

   Some organizations have tried to smooth demand by advertising extensively to get consumers to change their habits. One example is the U.S. Postal Service's campaign to mail Chistmas cards and packages early. And some service operators have added other goods and services to better use their facilities; for example, cleaning establishments that handle laundry and fast-food outlets that serve breakfast.

---

[36] See Valarie A. Zeithaml, A. Parasuraman, and Leonard L. Berry, "Problems and Strategies in Services Marketing," *Journal of Marketing*, Spring 1985, p. 33.

[37] Levitt, *The Marketing Imagination*, p. 97.

2. *Manipulating supply.* This can be done by training employees to handle multiple tasks, substituting machines for labor (as banks have done with automatic teller machines), cooperating with other similar service organizations, and using part-time or paraprofessional employees.

A third service characteristic is the physical presence of the customer in the services system. Services are sold first, then simultaneously produced and consumed. The amount of **customer contact** is important to determine because it affects every service production and delivery decision. Thus, high-contact service systems (transportation and banking) are more difficult to manipulate than low-contact systems because the customer is more involved in the process, affecting the time of demand and the nature and quality of the service.[38] Exhibit 12–10 shows the more important of these decision areas and the considerations generated by high- and low-contact systems. The four conclusions deriving from this exhibit follow.

1. There is considerable uncertainty about the day-to-day operations of high-contact systems because the customer in one way or another can disrupt the production system; for instance, the need for emergency service from a hospital can overload operating room facilities.
2. Rarely does the supply of a high-contact service equal demand at any one time—not only because of the difficulty in making reliable forecasts, but also because of last-minute changes by the customer; for example, the cancellation of hotel reservations. Low-contact services can better match supply and demand by structuring a resource-oriented schedule such as the development of credit reports.
3. Because high-contact service workers interact with customers, their behavior can directly affect customer satisfaction/dissatisfaction with the service.
4. It is rarely possible to set up an efficient production schedule for high-contact services because customers cannot be programmed.[39]

The conclusion we can draw from this is: it is very difficult to rationalize the operations of a contact system. Technological devices can do some jobs performed by direct-contact workers; but worker attitudes, facility environment, and customers' attitudes still determine the ultimate quality of the service experience.[40]

A fourth service characteristic has to do with **variability.** Because of the human element, service quality varies depending upon who provides it and when. It is a difficult problem to overcome for firms that operate multiple service units such as banks, hotels, airlines, car rental companies, and retail stores. Delivering a uniform experience to customers of the Marriott Hotel group is much more difficult than buying and selling a Zenith TV.

---

[38] Richard B. Chase, "Where Does the Customer Fit into a Service Operation?" *Harvard Business Review*, November–December 1978, p. 173.

[39] Ibid., p. 139.

[40] Ibid., p. 140.

EXHIBIT 12 ♦ 10

Major design considerations in high- and low-contact systems

Decision	High-contact system	Low-contact system
Facility location	Operations must be near the customer.	Operations may be placed near supply, transportation, or labor.
Facility layout	Facility should accommodate the customer's physical and psychological needs and expectations.	Facility should enhance production.
Product design	Environment as well as the physical product define the nature of the service.	Customer is not in the service environment so the product can be defined by fewer attributes.
Process design	Stages of production process have a direct immediate effect on the customer.	Customer is not involved in majority of processing steps.
Scheduling	Customer is in the production schedule and must be accommodated.	Customer is concerned mainly with completion dates.
Production planning	Orders cannot be stored, so smoothing production flow results in loss of business.	Both backlogging and smoothing are possible.
Worker skills	Direct work force comprises a major part of the service product and so must be able to interact well with the public.	Direct work force need only have technical skills.
Quality control	Quality standards are often in the eye of the beholder and hence variable.	Quality standards are generally measurable and hence fixed.
Time standards	Service time depends on customer needs, and therefore time standards are inherently loose.	Work is performed on customer surrogates (e.g., forms), and time standards can be tight.
Wage payment	Variable output requires time-based wage systems.	"Fixable" output permits output-based wage systems.
Capacity planning	To avoid lost sales, capacity must be set to match peak demand.	Storable output permits selling capacity at some average demand level.
Forecasting	Forecasts are short term, time-oriented.	Forecasts are long term, output-oriented.

Source: Reprinted by permission of the *Harvard Business Review.* An exhibit from "Where Does the Customer Fit into a Service Operation?" by Richard B. Chase (November–December 1978). Copyright © 1978 by the President and Fellows of Harvard College; all rights reserved.

To overcome this problem as well as to increase supplier productivity, Levitt suggests services be industrialized.[41] This can be done in three ways as follows.

1. *Use of hard technologies:* This involves substituting machinery and/or tools for people. Examples include automatic bank tellers, automatic toll collectors at subway entrances, vending machines, and bank credit cards, such as Visa and American Express, that make it easy to grant loans to reliable customers.

2. *Use of soft technologies:* This is primarily concerned with the improvement of task performance in a systematic way. This ensures the delivery of a high-quality service under almost any set of conditions. This approach is not new; witness the use of self service to replace clerk services in supermarkets. It is the solution used by McDonald's, Pizza Hut, Marriott Hotels, and H&R Block as well as the providers of prepackaged vacation tours, off-the-shelf insurance programs, and payroll deduction savings.[42]

3. *Hybrid technologies:* These function by using hard equipment in conjunction with planned industrial systems to obtain greater efficiency. Levitt cites as examples limited-service, fast, low-priced automobile repair businesses that specialize in mufflers and brakes (Midas). Another of his examples is the radio-controlled ready-mix concrete truck routing, rerouting, and delivery system.[43]

A fifth characteristic of service businesses is that they do not require the same **physical distribution channels** as manufacturing firms do. Rather, they use some combination of the service factory, retail outlet, or the point of consumption. For example, a restaurant, barber, and dentist combine all three, while a dry cleaner that sends its clothes out functions mainly as a retail outlet. This means that service businesses find it necessary to engage in more and different contacts with their customers than is the case with manufacturing firms. This fact has some important marketing implications.[44]

- *Internal marketing:* Because service businesses often involve frequent contact between producers and consumers, the quality of service is tied to human performance. Thus, special attention must be paid to *all* those individuals contacting the customer. Banks, hotels, airlines, and many hospitals spend a considerable amount of time and money to motivate their employees to better serve actual and prospective customers.

- *Customizing:* Because of the nature of services, businesses can often provide customized service. This enables a better fit between a customer's needs and the service received. Examples include travel agencies that prepare special itineraries for individual travelers and financial firms that develop individualized portfolios.

---

[41] Levitt, *The Marketing Imagination,* pp. 56–61.

[42] Ibid.

[43] Ibid., pp. 38–39.

[44] Leonard Berry, "Big Ideas in Services Marketing," *Journal of Consumer Marketing,* Spring 1986, pp. 47–51.

♦ *Tangibility:* Because services cannot be examined, they are hard to evaluate. A service business, therefore, needs to make its offerings more tangible. This can be done by:

  a. *Using the facilitating products as quality indicators* (e.g., type of aircraft and the decor and furnishings of hotels/motels, restaurants, banks, and nursing homes). Because service businesses frequently distribute their service, they uniquely control the environment in which consumption takes place.

  b. *Creating a tangible representation of the service,* as is the case with credit cards such as American Express Gold Card.

  c. *Tying the marketing of services to the marketing of goods.* The sales of H&R Block, a firm that specializes in income tax preparation, benefit substantially from its association with Sears.

Professional services[45]

Marketing has become increasingly important to such professionals as dentists, doctors, lawyers, accountants, engineers, and architects. Many of these professions are now overcrowded and have, in recent years, experienced declining public images because of high fees and lawsuits. The federal government has now made it possible for some professions to use media advertising to promote their specialties. The presence of "retail" doctors, dentists, and legal outlets in suburban malls is no longer a novelty. Nor are the newsletters, media ads, and other forms of promotion used by these professionals.

Bloom notes that professional services have unique characteristics requiring that they be marketed differently than tangible products. Exhibit 12–11 shows the more important ones, which we discuss briefly here:

  1. *Ethical and legal constraints.* Despite a substantial reduction in the constraints on the use of marketing, most professional services still face many ethical and legal restraints imposed by national, state, and local government agencies, associations, certification boards, and others. These inhibit the use of marketing services, particularly advertising. To make certain that its marketing program is not violating any ethical and legal standards, the professional service firm would do well to set up peer review and self-regulation programs. It should also educate clients in what constitutes acceptable behavior.

  2. *Buyer uncertainty.* Because professional services do not have tangible characteristics, it is difficult for a buyer to make an evaluation before and after buying them. Indeed, buyers often don't even know whether they need a professional service and are shy about finding out. Buyers also may have erroneous ideas about what the service should cost and the benefits they should receive. Professional service managers should educate prospective customers in the need for professional services, attributes to consider in evaluating suppliers, how to communicate with professionals, and what to expect from them. This

---

[45] Based on Paul N. Bloom, "Effective Marketing for Professional Services," *Harvard Business Review,* September–October 1984, p. 102.

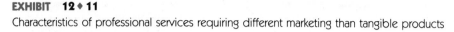

EXHIBIT   12 ◆ 11

Characteristics of professional services requiring different marketing than tangible products

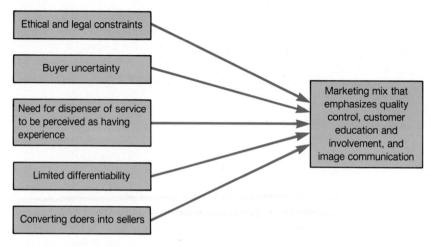

can be done in a variety of ways, including advertising and brochures. In recent years some car repair services have tried to provide guidelines for selecting a given type of service. And law firms have paid for advertising spots in which they explain the rights of individuals in legal situations.

3. *Need to be perceived as having experience.* Because of their own inexperience in dealing with professionals, most prospective buyers use the firm's past experience as an indicator of its expertise. This characteristic inhibits a firm's expansion; and any attempt to do so requires the hiring of people who have the experience needed, merging (or working with) firms that have the desired experience, or reducing the fees charged.

4. *Limited differentiability.* Because most professional services are difficult to differentiate, many have tried clever advertising, such as dentists who "cater to cowards." A better approach is to emphasize the firm's collective and individual experience, specialization, and special procedures. The latter includes the degree of involvement by high-level professionals, service accessibility, use of high-tech support equipment, and follow-up.

5. *Converting "doers" into "sellers."* Personal selling is critically important in the marketing of any professional service. Prospective buyers prefer to be solicited by those individuals who perform the service, not by salespersons they will not see again. This poses a problem, for many professionals feel that selling is demeaning. About all that can be done here is to get professionals to understand the need for selling, to train them in basic selling skills, and to make selling financially rewarding.

Coping with these problems is neither easy nor inexpensive. Most smaller service organizations cannot hire experienced marketing professionals, but must develop the requisite skills in-house. Even larger service firms find it difficult to commit resources to marketing research, to train staff members, and to educate prospective buyers and present clients.

SUMMARY

This chapter focuses on managing a firm's individual products and its product line. A product is a problem solver; and the consumer is buying benefits.

Marketers must consider various product classifications because products and their characteristics determine many marketing activities. The most common consumer goods classification consists of four subgroups based on the way they are purchased—convenience, shopping, specialty, and unsought. Marketers class industrial goods in terms of their costliness and how they are used. There are six categories of industrial products—raw materials, fabricated materials and parts, installations, accessory equipment, supplies, and business services.

How a firm positions a product governs product attribute decisions. In our dynamic environment, it is not surprising that "old" brands must be updated (or repositioned) from time to time. An imitative positioning strategy implies that the product has essentially the same attributes as the brand currently serving the segment. A defensive strategy often calls for the introduction of a similar second brand. An anticipation strategy calls for the product to fit future choice criteria in the hope that the targeted segment will grow substantially.

Other important product decisions involve packaging, services, and branding. Branding is a way to differentiate the goods or services of one seller from another. It is particularly important when consumers have difficulty measuring the product's quality objectively. Marketers class brands as manufacturer or distributor. In recent years retailers have become increasingly aggressive in promoting their own brands. The two major types of branding are individual versus family brands.

Product-line decisions require an ongoing analysis of individual products and their markets. Marketers must make decisions about length of the line, line filling, line stretching, line extension, and product abandonment; product overlap (competing brands, private label, and sale of own components); trading up and down; and product systems. Management should consider the product life cycle before making any changes in the line.

The development of services is becoming more and more important. Product managers must understand the differences between services and goods as to tangibility, quality control, customer involvement, inventories, and distribution channels. Each of these has important marketing implications.

QUESTIONS

1. What are the major *want-satisfying benefits* that customers are likely to receive from the following products?
   a. Cars
   b. Raincoats
   c. Fountain pens
   d. Contribution to the United Way
   e. Attending a serious play

2. Some men consider a business suit a *shopping good*, while others view such a product as a *specialty good*. How are the shopping and purchase behaviors of the two groups likely to differ? Why?

3. Suppose you are the marketing manager for Ralph Lauren's line of designer women's fashions. You believe that your

products are *specialty goods* in the eyes of most potential customers. What does this fact imply for each of the following areas of your strategic marketing program?

a. Price policy
b. Distribution
c. Promotion

4. The Pontiac division of General Motors has adopted a *market targeting strategy* aimed at the *peripheral segment* of the automobile market consisting of younger consumers who are interested in sporty and expressive cars. How has this strategy affected the division's decisions concerning the breadth of its product line and the design and features of individual products in its line?

5. Campbell Soup Co. has introduced fresh mushrooms under its brand name, and other firms are considering marketing other branded fresh foods. Does *branding* really make sense for such products? What are the pros and cons? What should Campbell do to avoid some of the possible pitfalls involved?

6. When Honda introduced a line of luxury cars to the U.S. market it decided to use a new brand name, Acura, along with a new and independent dealer network and marketing program rather than treating the new cars as part of the Honda line. What were the advantages and disadvantages of this *branding strategy*?

7. Even though the firm decided not to use the Honda brand when it introduced the new models described in question 6, the introduction can still be seen as an attempt to *stretch* the company's *product line.* What do you think motivated this strategic move? Which risks were involved?

8. The educational programs offered by your business school or college can be classified as *high-contact services.* What does this imply for:

a. Product design (i.e., the development of courses, programs, facilities)
b. Quality control
c. The development of a marketing program to attract new students

9. Doctors, lawyers, and other professionals have become increasingly active in recent years in marketing their services. Which unique characteristics or concerns make such *professional services* different from tangible products? What are the implications of those differences for the design of effective marketing programs for professional services?

Chapter 13

Developing and testing new products and services

COOKING UP NEW PRODUCTS IN THE FOOD INDUSTRY

Food companies such as General Foods, Campbell Soup, and Sara Lee have responded to the thought that "after a tough day at work, many people might like to come home to a fancy dinner of Caribbean chicken curry or scrod cooked in white wine. If these delicacies were fresh rather than frozen and took only a few minutes to prepare, people might even pay white-tablecloth prices for them."[1] These and other such companies are busy developing new, fresh, refrigerated meals to be sold through supermarkets.

General Foods' new Culinova line is designed to appeal to "consumers who are too tired to cook and too tired to go out—or who have no time for either—but still want a nice dinner."[2] Culinova's refrigerated entrees (Filet Mignon Madagascar, Sole with Saffron Sauce) individually retail for up to $7. Although consumers like the product concept, many have not been willing to pay the price.

Another major problem has been the short shelf life of these products. Campbell Soup couldn't cope with this problem and was forced to withdraw its Fresh Chef line of refrigerated soups, sauces, and salads from national distribution. It is now testing a new line of refrigerated entrees. But there are other problems. For one thing, retailers aren't paying enough attention to these products that require frequent restocking.

And consumers are often confused by the new specialties—and their labels. What is Monterey Garden Ravioli? Manufacturers seem to be confused by the elegant versus the esoteric.

Even the less exotic premium frozen dinners have experienced unit sales declines of 10 percent and more—a lot of dollars, given industry sales of $3.5 billion in the frozen main-meals category. All this has led manufacturers to drop lines and items and emphasize lower-priced, high-nutrition meals—a return to the TV dinner of yesteryear. A number of things conspired to cause this, including mediocre quality, growing availability of a wide array of reasonably priced refrigerated and hot prepared foods from restaurants and supermarkets, and the presence of so many products in the frozen case that consumers never developed brand loyalty.

To counter these problems and to blunt the success of the budget-priced brands, Stouffer reduced prices on its

---

[1] Based on Alex M. Freedman, "Food Firms' Fresh Approach: Elegant Refrigerated Entrees," *The Wall Street Journal*, June 18, 1987, p. 29; and Alex M. Freedman, "Glamour of Upscale Foods Fade as Buyers Return to Basics," *The Wall Street Journal*, December 15, 1987, p. 29.

[2] Freedman, "Food Firms' Fresh Approach."

continued

concluded

resized Dinner Supreme brand and emphasized nutrition. Campbell upgraded its Le Menu line (at no increase in price), dropped some items, and introduced LightStyle dinners. The latter are designed to meet the dietary guidelines of the American Heart Association and National Academy of Sciences, with less than 30 percent of their calories coming from fat. The new dinners also feature lower sodium and cholesterol levels.

NEW-PRODUCT SPENDING

The previous example illustrates some of the problems inherent in developing new products as well as the perseverance of companies striving to launch successful new products. More and more firms have learned that growth and survival depend largely on how well they succeed in adding new products to their lines.

The large amounts spent annually on R&D are evidence of management's concern with new products. Over the past 10 years, American companies have increased their spending on new-product research by 17 percent per year—a rate substantially exceeding inflation. In 1987 they spent nearly $50 billion. Seven companies spent more than $1 billion on R&D in 1987— General Motors ($4.1), IBM ($3.9), Ford ($2.3), AT&T ($2.3), General Electric ($1.3), Du Pont ($1.2), and Eastman Kodak ($1.0).[3] Further evidence of management's concern about new products is that marketing managers spend an estimated 21 percent of their time on this activity.[4]

Exhibit 13–1 shows the number of new products introduced from 1978 to 1987. These figures vary, though, depending on the reporting source. For instance, A. C. Nielsen reports a much greater number of new food items— over 6,000—in 1987 alone. Why the substantial difference? The answer lies in part in how manufacturers define a *new product*. There are a number of ways to classify such products. One of the simpler systems breaks new products into four major types: new to the world, new to the firm, product-line extensions, and product improvements. Only a small percentage of products are "new to the world." Most are either product-line extensions or

---

[3] Dana Siwolop, "Research Spending Is Building Up to a Letdown," *Business Week*, June 11, 1987, pp. 139–40. Also, see "R&D Spending Moves up Smartly despite Corporate Turmoil," *The Wall Street Journal*, June 11, 1987, p. 1.

[4] *Management of New Products* (New York: Booz, Allen & Hamilton, 1982).

EXHIBIT 13 ♦ 1
New-product introductions by industry

	Foods	Drugs	Cosmetics	Durables	Tools	Industrial	Toys/ games	Gadgets	Total
1987	2,814	1,476	802	382	452	624	749	4,781	12,080
1986	2,875	1,487	814	372	456	611	768	4,733	12,116
1985	2,314	1,340	734	358	431	592	754	3,642	10,165
1984	2,209	1,314	722	361	462	576	732	3,519	9,895
1983	2,307	1,401	743	347	484	598	740	3,782	10,402
1982	2,213	1,229	713	469	586	587	685	3,461	9,668
1981	2,142	1,142	693	452	493	613	653	3,212	9,400
1980	2,107	1,087	610	460	502	704	641	3,010	9,121
1979	1,860	810	420	310	430	503	645	2,970	7,948
1978	1,640	964	501	407	447	584	611	2,840	7,994
1987–86 change	−2%	−0.7%	−0.1%	+2.6%	−0.9%	+2%	−2%	+1%	−.03%
10-year change	+42%	+35%	+37%	−6%	+1%	+6%	+18%	+40%	+34%

Source: New Product Development Newsletter, December 1987.

product improvements.[5] In Exhibit 13–1, the 2,814 new food products excluded new flavors, line extensions, and the like—which probably means an almost equal number were of these types, given the Nielsen estimate of over 6,000.[6]

NEW-PRODUCT SUCCESS

Estimates of new-product failures range from as low as 15 percent to as high as 90 percent. This variation in failure rates is due, in part, to the fact that some studies examine the proportion of new-product concepts or ideas that fail to achieve commercial success, while others focus only on products that fail after being introduced into the market. The consulting firm of Booz, Allen & Hamilton estimates that out of every seven ideas that enter the new-product process only one emerges as a commercial success. And further, 46 percent of the total funds spent on new-product development by U.S. industry goes for products that fail or are abandoned.[7] On the other hand, Crawford estimates that 30 to 35 percent of marketed new products fail, while Hopkins reports that about 40 percent of industrial new products fail in the marketplace.[8]

Variations in failure estimates are also influenced by how the new product is defined, the type of product, and the channels involved. For example, the failure rate for new food items is substantially higher than for other products, like pharmaceuticals.[9]

Even when a new product passes the test of commercialization and makes it into the marketplace, the question of whether its managers will consider it a success depends on the magnitude of the objectives they set for the product. In other words, success is a matter of degree. In that sense, very few new products achieve overwhelming success. Of the many thousands of new food products introduced since 1970, for instance, only 25 have experienced retail sales of over $100 million annually. Only six of these brands were introduced since 1980. All 25 were introduced by well-known consumer goods companies, and none could be considered "new to the world" products (see Exhibit 13–2).[10]

---

[5] This classification is discussed in some depth in Chapter 19, which is concerned with the strategy options for new market entries.

[6] Calvin L. Hodock, "Nine Sure-Fire Ways to Cook Up New Ideas," *Sales & Marketing Management*, August 1988, p. 42.

[7] *Management of New Products.*

[8] C. Merle Crawford, *New Products Management* (Homewood, Ill.: Richard D. Irwin, 1987), p. 21; and David S. Hopkins, *New Product Winners and Losers*, Conference Board Report 773, 1980.

[9] Crawford, *New Products Management.*

[10] Ed Russell, Jr.; Anthony J. Adams; and Bill Boundy, "High-Tech Test Marketing at Campbell Soup Company," *Journal of Consumer Marketing*, Winter 1986, p. 71.

EXHIBIT   13 ◆ 2

Leading new food brands introduced from 1970 to 1986

Brand	Manufacturer	Annual retail ($ million)
◆ Lean Cuisine	Nestle	$447
Chunky Soup	Campbell	270
◆ LeMenu	Campbell	238
Minute Maid Refr. Orange Juice	Coca-Cola	224
Maxwell House Master Blend	General Foods	185
◆ Kool Aid Sugar Free	General Foods	171
Yoplait Refrigerated Yogurt	Yoplait	167
Prego Spaghetti Sauce	Campbell	165
Brim Coffee	General Foods	156
◆ Dinner Classics	Armour	155
Tender Vittles Cat Food	Ralston Purina	130
Weight Watcher Single Dishes	Heinz	115
Tyson Frozen Fried Chicken	Tyson Foods	114
◆ Chewy Cereal Meal Bars	Quaker Oats	113
Folgers Flaked Coffee	Procter & Gamble	112
◆ Equal Diet Sweetener	Searle	110
Pringles Potato Chips	Procter & Gamble	106
Stove Top Stuffing Mix	General Foods	106
Swanson Hungry Man Dinners	Campbell	106
Tasters Choice Decaf.	Nestle	104
Stouffers Frozen Pizza	Nestle	104
Cheerios Honey Nut	General Mills	103
Stouffers Oriental Entrees	Nestle	101
Meow Mix	Ralston Purina	96
Mighty Dog	Carnation	94

◆ Represents new brands introduced since 1980.

Source: Ed Russell, Jr., Anthony J. Adams, and Bill Boundy, "High-Tech Test Marketing at Campbell Soup Company," *Journal of Consumer Marketing,* Winter 1986, p. 72. Basic data obtained from SAMI on warehoused brands; does not include store-door brands like Dorito's.

It is becoming increasingly difficult to introduce new products success-fully, given the maturity of many basic technologies, shorter product life cycles, increasing competition, government regulations, and the increased costs of the new-product development process. Urban et al. identify 12 reasons for new-product failures, as shown in Exhibit 13–3. The biggest cause of failure is the introduction of me-too products that sell for the same or a higher price but do not outperform products already on the market.[11]

---

[11] Glen L. Urban, John R. Hauser, and Nikhilesh Dholakia, *Essentials of New Product Management* (Englewood Cliffs, N.J.: Prentice-Hall, 1987), pp. 37–38.

EXHIBIT 13 ♦ 3

Reasons for new-product failure

---

1. Demand for this type of product is insufficient.
2. Company capabilities do not match product requirements.
3. Product is a poor idea that offers nothing new.
4. Product does not offer better performance.
5. Perceived attributes of the product are not unique or superior.
6. Product fails to generate expected channel support.
7. Product sales are overestimated.
8. Competitors copy product quickly and effectively.
9. Consumers' preferences change before product is successful.
10. Key environmental factor changes.
11. Profit margins are poor and costs are high.
12. There are intraorganizational conflicts and poor management practices.

Source: Glen L. Urban, John R. Hauser, and Nikhilesh Dholakia, *Essentials of New Product Management,* © 1987, pp. 37–38. Adapted by permission of Prentice Hall, Inc., Englewood Cliffs, N.J.

Even when a new product avoids the many pitfalls and achieves acceptance in the marketplace, it may still have difficulty producing a desirable return on the firm's investment. Companies make most new-product investments with the expectation that they will pay out within the following three to five years. In fact, many new products take 5 to 10 years to simply get to the marketplace.[12] In any event, once a product is launched (the average cost for a new-product introduction is $15 million) the firm does not have a great deal of time to recover its investment. This is due to both the rapidity of technological change and the speed with which competitors generally follow an innovation with similar products.[13]

Given the high risk involved, there must be strong reasons why firms spend large amounts of time and money on new-product development. Most of them relate to external forces that impact a firm's sales, profitability, and competitive-position objectives. Marketers can identify many of these forces by market opportunity analysis, especially analyses of changes in the firm's macro-environment. Changes in technology are among the most important driving forces in new-product development because of their impact on existing products and a shortening of the product life cycle. Other macro-environment factors impacting the development of new products are government regulations, changing costs of raw materials, demographics, and life-

---

[12] Glen L. Urban and John R. Hauser, *Design and Marketing of New Products* (Englewood Cliffs, N.J.: Prentice-Hall, 1980), pp. 42–46.

[13] "Most New Products Start with a Bang, End Up as a Bomb," *Marketing News,* March 27, 1987, p. 36.

style. The introduction of new products by competitors may force a firm to respond with its own entry. Customers and suppliers can also be strong forces in causing a firm to develop new products, as we shall see later in this chapter.

In spite of the many problems and threats involved, some companies have been consistently successful over the years in developing new products. These firms include such well-known American companies as American Airlines, Apple Computer, Campbell Soup, General Electric, Intel, Merck, Minnesota Mining & Manufacturing, and Philip Morris. As one writer points out, all are

> convinced of the need to innovate. . . . No matter how the companies are on purely technical advances, they are uniformly devoted to marketing. Their people believe that markets can speak and routinely treat bureaucratic considerations . . . as entirely subservient to the goal of listening carefully to their customers.[14]

All of these companies limit their search for new-product ideas to areas that their resources will permit them to exploit. Further, all approach new-product development in a cautious, systematic way. This chapter examines such a systematic new-product development process, which consists of five major steps: setting objectives, opportunity identification, product design, testing, and product commercialization. This process is designed to avoid the pitfalls inherent in new-product development.[15]

THE NEW-PRODUCT DEVELOPMENT PROCESS

The basic objective of the new-product development process is to identify new-product opportunities that can be successfully commercialized at the greatest return on the funds invested and that are compatible with the firm's resources—both financial and managerial. Exhibit 13–4 shows this process. It is much more than just a simple sequence of steps, for it is iterative, and each step is dependent on the previous one. It applies essentially to new products that are not brand extensions, new flavors, or packaged in new or different-size containers.

Step one involves choosing a strategy and setting objectives for a firm's new-product development effort. Firms cannot implement the new-product development process successfully without a viable set of objectives and a well-articulated product strategy. The business must set certain criteria by which new products are selected. These include minimum sales revenues and market share, being an innovator or a follower, fit with present channels of distribution, and quality level.

---

[14] Stratford P. Sherman, "Eight Masters of Innovation," *Fortune*, October 25, 1984, p. 66.

[15] Glen L. Urban et al., *Essentials of New Product Management*, pp. 36–39. Also, see Calvin L. Hodock, "RX for New Product Survival," *Marketing Communications*, February 1986, p. 27.

EXHIBIT   13 ◆ 4

New-product development process

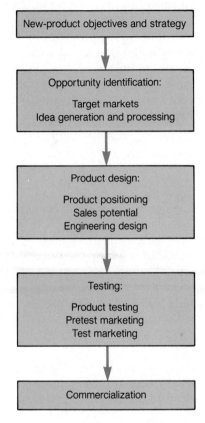

Source: Glen L. Urban, John R. Hauser, and Nikhilesh Dholakia, *Essentials of New Product Management,* © 1987, p. 26. Adapted by permission of Prentice-Hall, Inc., Englewood Cliffs, N.J.

As we saw in Chapter 12, product strategy derives largely from the firm's business strategies that emerge from the market targeting and positioning process. Thus, the new-product strategy should reflect the objectives of the firm as well as its resources. The firm's product-line strategy (line filling versus line extension) also constrains the new-product development process from the outset.

Step two, opportunity identification, results from analyses of the macroenvironment, the industry, and close competitors; the product life cycle; and customer segmentation. These subjects have already been covered in earlier chapters, so we do not deal with them again here. Rather, we *assume* that the firm has already identified its opportunities in the form of which markets to target and knows the choice criteria of each. The discussion of step two focuses instead on idea generation and processing.

Step three deals with converting an idea into a product design using marketing and engineering skills. Product positioning based on consumer preferences and using perceptual maps is important here. We covered these subjects in an earlier chapter, also, but will briefly examine them here from the point of view of new-product entries.

The fourth step involves testing customer reactions to the product. This process often begins with pretests in a laboratory setting in which both the product and its advertising are tested under simulated market conditions. If the pretest is successful, the firm may submit the product and its marketing action plan to a full-scale test market study. Commercialization, step five, follows a successful test market.

OBJECTIVES AND STRATEGIES FOR NEW PRODUCTS

The primary objective of most new-product development efforts is to secure future volume and profit growth; but a firm may have other objectives as well. Two other common objectives have to do with maintaining the firm's present position as an innovator and defending current market share. Typically firms have several objectives for their new-product efforts. Objectives vary with the type of environment in which the business unit operates and its business strategy.

New-product development strategies can be classified as either reactive or proactive.[16] Conditions that affect the adoption of a reactive or a proactive strategy include market size and growth, protection of an innovation, competitive strengths and weaknesses, and the firm's market position. Note how these relate to the various business strategies discussed in Chapter 11. For example, prospector strategies would be more proactive than reactive, while a defender is just the opposite.

There are several *reactive strategies*:

♦ A *defensive strategy* adjusts a firm's existing products so they can better compete against a recently introduced competitive product.
♦ An *imitative strategy* quickly copies a new product.
♦ A *second-but-better strategy* improves on a competitor's new product.
♦ A *responsive strategy* reacts to consumer requests for a new or improved product.

Campbell and Stouffer have embraced all of these strategies in the premium end of the frozen-meal market. Both have experienced declining sales and a drop in market share. Given the size of the markets, it is not surprising they are making strong attempts with "new and improved" products to regain lost ground.

---

[16] This discussion of strategies is based on Urban et al., pp. 15–22.

Proactive strategies are designed to initiate change:

• An *R&D strategy* strives to develop superior technical products. IBM's R&D expenditures of nearly $4 billion in 1987 illustrate such a strategy. 3M mandates that its business units obtain 25 percent of their sales volume from products introduced within the past five years. Over 6.5 percent of sales is spent on R&D to achieve this figure.

• A somewhat similar approach is the *marketing strategy*, based on finding a consumer need and then developing a product to fill it. Procter & Gamble has used this marketing strategy with considerable success over the years.

• Another proactive strategy is *entrepreneurial* in nature. This is the way many large electronic firms like Hewlett-Packard and Digital Equipment are organized and managed to foster the development of new and improved products.

• The last proactive approach is *acquisition strategy*, whereby a firm "buys" new products to market. Raytheon is an example of this strategy in action, and so is Rubbermaid, which uses acquisitions as one source of growth.[17]

NEW-PRODUCT IDEAS AND THE IDEA-SCREENING PROCESS

Once the firm has identified and studied its target markets, its next task is to generate ideas of how best to exploit the opportunities in these markets. Ideas are not final products; but they are a useful starting point for the creation of a new product. Success in generating and processing new-product ideas depends on how well organized the search efforts are, how carefully the company's product strategy has been articulated (does the firm know what it is looking for?), and what sources are used. As we noted earlier, it is necessary to generate a substantial number of ideas to get one successful product. But firms are improving. In 1968 it took 58 ideas to obtain one winner—but only 7 in 1981.[18] However, part of the improvement may be due to U.S. firms tending to emphasize "safe" products in contrast to innovative high-risk products. (See Exhibit 13–5.)

In this section we discuss the most important sources for new-product ideas and then describe the idea-screening process. The end result of this step should be a number of alternative product concepts.

Sources of new-product ideas

The relative importance of the sources of new-product ideas varies, depending on the company, industry, and the extent to which the product is really new. In addition to "by accident," we discuss the more important sources of new-product ideas next.

---

[17] Alecia Swasy, "Rubbermaid Moves beyond the Kitchen," *The Wall Street Journal*, February 3, 1989, p. 82.

[18] *Management of New Products.*

EXHIBIT   13 ◆5

The decay curve for new-product ideas

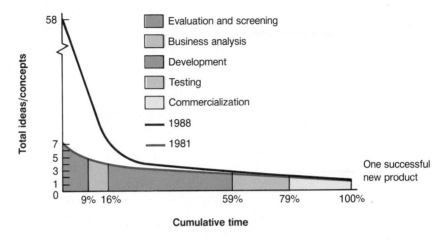

Cumulative time

Customers

This source is particularly important for new industrial products.[19] In the scientific instrument field (e.g., chromatography), some 80 percent of the major innovations in performance are a result of input from users. The same is true in process manufacturing. In both industries some innovations were so important the users actually commissioned manufacturers to undertake development work.[20] Firms can also identify customers' needs by using marketing research, sales reports, user-group discussions, and by following up complaints about present product performance. Hodock reports that such products as odorless antiperspirants, overnight spray-on oven cleaner, pizza dough used with your own toppings, and an inner tray for a cookie package came from listening to consumers.[21] Focus groups are also an excellent way to learn more about consumer needs as they relate to a new-product idea.

Company personnel

These individuals often provide helpful suggestions for new products—especially product-line additions and product improvements. The most important in-company sources are members of the R&D or engineering staff,

---

[19] Eric Von Hipple, "Users as Innovators," *Technology Review*, January 1978, pp. 3–11.

[20] Eric Von Hipple, "The Dominant Role of Users in the Scientific Instrument Innovation Process," *Research Policy*, July 1976, pp. 212–39; and Eric Von Hipple, "Transferring Process Innovations from User-Innovators to Equipment Manufacturing Firms," *R&D Management*, October 1977.

[21] Hodock, "Nine Sure-Fire Ways to Cook Up New Ideas," p. 41.

sales personnel, product managers, advertising personnel, and marketing researchers.

Channels of distribution

The industrial distributor who works closely with its customers can be particularly helpful in suggesting product modifications or line extensions to present products. These ideas can then be checked with end-use customers. For example, Black & Decker recently introduced a heavy-duty reciprocating power saw that can cut through plaster walls. The new product was suggested by one of B&D's distributors.[22]

Competitors

Competitive products are frequently a source of new-product ideas. In many cases a firm has no option but to respond to a new competitive product with one of its own. This is particularly true when a firm's major product is at risk—like the response of Zenith and others to RCA's color television.

Sometimes a firm must respond to a competitive entry because of its impact on per-unit costs. This is especially true when a competitor moves into a new market with a modification of an existing product—or introduces a new item that has sufficient synergy with an established product to lower per-unit costs. The problem is compounded when the new market is large and fast growing and costs are substantially affected by scale economies. This occurred a few years ago when car manufacturers first started using products from the semiconductor industry. Because this was a large, fast-growing market, the firm that could capture and hold a major share of the auto industry would benefit in lower per-unit costs for semiconductors it sold into other markets. This was a compelling reason for most firms in the semiconductor industry to enter the automotive market segment aggressively.

Government agencies

The U.S. Patent Office of the Department of Commerce regularly lists patents available for licensing or sale. It also lists government-owned patents available on a nonexclusive, royalty-free license basis and dedicated patents that can be used without charge. Research findings published by various federal and state agencies may also furnish new-product ideas.

---

[22] Christopher S. Eklund, "How Black & Decker Got Back in the Black," *Business Week*, July 13, 1987, p. 86.

Miscellaneous sources

These include trade magazines, trade associations, advertising agencies, marketing research firms, consultants, commercial laboratories, and university and institute laboratories.

Overseas products—particularly those sold in supermarkets—can be an important source of new-product ideas. This has been the case with pump dispensers for toothpaste (Germany), cookies (England), and body fragrance (France). Recently, Product Initiatives, a new-products consulting company located in Toronto, began offering a service that will select 50 products from overseas each quarter and survey 400 consumers to measure the products' acceptability. A combination window-cleaner and bug-killer spray from South Africa and a carbonated bubble bath from Japan are examples of products that did well.[23]

The above discussion suggests that product ideas often come from sources other than potential customers. In such cases, the firm should be sure to assess likely customer reaction to the idea before proceeding too far with product development. Indeed, according to one R&D researcher, "R&D isn't worth anything alone; it has to be coupled with the market. The innovative firms are not necessarily the ones that produce the best technological output, but the ones who know what is marketable."[24] Thus, an assessment of the marketability of a potential new product should be one part of the screening process.

Screening new-product ideas

The idea-screening stage is the decision point where more new-product projects are killed than anywhere else in the development process. It is a critical decision, because a *go* decision means committing resources to a new-product project. It is a difficult decision because little reliable information is available on the proposed product's market, its costs, and the nature of the investment required. Screening is an investment decision made without concrete financial data.[25] It is also a critical decision in that "too weak a screening procedure fails to weed out the obvious 'losers' or 'misfits,' with the resulting misallocation of scarce resources and the start of a creeping commitment to the wrong projects. In contrast, too 'rigid' a screening results

---

[23] Ronald Alsop, "U.S. Concerns Seek Inspiration for Products from Overseas," *The Wall Street Journal,* January 3, 1985, p. 17.

[24] As quoted in Urban and Hauser, *Design and Marketing of New Products,* p. 29.

[25] Robert G. Cooper and Ulrike de Brentaini, "Criteria for Screening New Industrial Products," *Industrial Marketing Management,* August 1984, p. 149.

in many viable and worthwhile projects being rejected, and perhaps is even more costly to the firm in lost opportunities."[26]

Scoring models

Scoring models are a popular idea-screening tool. A **scoring model** forces managers to subject each project to a consistent and large set of review criteria. It requires management to state goals and objectives clearly and helps make a highly judgmental decision somewhat more objective. It also systematizes the review of projects.[27]

Scoring models are easy to use and low in cost. They are most applicable when only rough distinctions are required among projects.[28] One drawback is that scoring models are forced to rely on the subjective rating of managers; but their opinion at this stage in the new-product development process is all that is available. A further weakness is that some scoring criteria may not be independent of each other and hence are double-counted in the scoring.

NewProd screening model

Cooper proposes the use of a scoring model he calls the NewProd Screening Model.[29] It asks evaluators to rate a new-product idea on a large number of criteria using zero-to-ten rating scales. By combining the individual evaluators' scorings, researchers obtain a product score which, in turn, indicates the likelihood of success. The items used and the weights assigned to each were determined after an examination of some 200 projects. The model has been validated and can predict a product's success or failure about 84 times out of 100.

NewProd's screening criteria consist of four major dimensions, the most important of which concerns the product's *marketability.* To be successful, a product must first have a differential advantage in design, features, quality, or economic advantage to the end user. A second area is *market attractiveness,* which is concerned with the size of the market opportunity (high or low growth) and competitive intensity. The latter measures the ease with which a firm can exploit the market opportunity.

The third major dimension is *project-company resource compatibility.* It includes synergies in management, salesforce, production, engineering, and R&D activities. Newness to the firm is a strong negative factor here. The fourth major criterion is *product scope.* Specialized products targeted at a limited market do less well than more standardized broad-appeal products.

---

[26] Robert G. Cooper, "Selecting Winning New Product Projects: Using the NewProd System," *Journal of Product Innovation,* March 1985, p. 35.

[27] W. E. Souder, "A Scoring Methodology for Assessing the Suitability of Management Science Models," *Management Science* 18 (1972), pp. 526–43.

[28] Cooper, "Selecting Winning New Product Projects," p. 37.

[29] Ibid., pp. 37–44.

EXHIBIT   13 ♦ 6

Scoring model

(1)	(2)	(3) Very good (10)		(4) Good (8)		(5) Average (6)		(6) Poor (4)		(7) Very poor (2)		(8)	(9)
Subfactor	Subfactor weight	EP	EV	EP	EV	EP	EV	EP	EV	EP	EV	Total EV	Subfactor evaluation
Product superiority	1.0	0.1	1.0	0.2	1.6	0.5	3.0	0.2	0.8	—	—	6.4	6.4
Unique features for users	1.0	0.1	1.0	0.2	1.6	0.4	2.4	0.2	0.8	0.1	0.2	6.0	6.0
Reduces customers' costs	3.0	0.3	3.0	0.4	3.2	0.2	1.2	0.1	0.4	—	—	7.8	23.4
Higher quality than competitors	1.0	0.1	1.0	0.2	1.6	0.5	3.0	0.2	0.8	—	—	6.4	6.4
Does unique task for user	2.0	0.5	5.0	0.4	3.2	0.1	0.6	—	—	—	—	8.8	17.6
Priced lower than competing products	2.0	—	—	0.2	1.6	0.5	3.0	0.3	1.2	—	—	5.8	11.6
	10.0												

Proposed Product: Product X
Area: Product marketability

Evaluated by: William Jones

Total value of factor 71.4

Note: EP = estimated probability as judged by management. EV = expected value, computed by multiplying the rating's numerical value by the estimated probability.

Source: Subfactors taken from Robert G. Cooper, "Selecting Winning New Product Projects: Using The NewProd System," *Journal of Product Innovation*, March 1985, p. 39. Reprinted by permission of the publisher. Copyright 1985 by Elsevier Science Publishing Co., Inc. Also, see John T. O'Meara, Jr., "Selecting Profitable Products," *Harvard Business Review*, January–February 1961, p. 86.

Screening procedure

The process of rating a new-product idea consists of seven steps as follows (see Exhibit 13–6 for how this process works):

1. Set forth the major areas or dimensions that firms should consider such as product marketability and market attractiveness.
2. Divide each major area into subfactors. Researchers can, for example, break product marketability into subfactors of "product superiority versus competing products," "product has unique features," and "product reduces customer costs." (See column 1, Exhibit 13–6.)
3. Weight each major area to indicate its relative importance. Do the same for each of the subfactors. (Note the subfactor weights in column 2 of Exhibit 13–6.)
4. For each subfactor, estimate the probability that the product's performance would be described as "very good," "good," "average," "poor," or "very poor." These probabilities appear under the EP (estimated probability) columns of Exhibit 13–6.
5. Multiply each probability figure by the numerical value assigned to the rating; for example, "very good" has a rating of 10. The results of each multiplication appear under the EV (expected value) headings in columns 3 to 7 of Exhibit 13–6.

6. Multiply the total expected value for each subfactor (column 8) by the subfactor's weight (column 2) to obtain the figures in column 9. The sum of this column represents the value assigned to the product marketability area.

7. Compute a total index for the new product by repeating this procedure for each of the other major areas and then weighting each factor by the value assigned in step 3.

Clearly, this procedure has both advantages and disadvantages. The system's merit lies in forcing whoever is involved in the evaluation of the new product to identify relevant criteria and to quantify the value of each. Its disadvantage stems from the possibility that the overall summary rating may mask major disadvantages, which, if discovered, would reveal the product proposal to be undesirable.

Final screening

Ideas that survive the preliminary screening are then submitted for a final screening. This typically involves a formal study dealing with the addition of a new product that must consider (1) the product's market potential; (2) the extent to which the company can exploit this potential; (3) the costs associated with the effort; and (4) the rewards to be obtained. If this analytical procedure is well structured, the idea may be terminated at any stage in the process. That is, it is not necessary to perform the entire screening procedure before rejecting the idea. The depth to which the investigation is carried depends on the complexity of the product, how much the company already knows about the market and the production of the proposed product, and the risks involved. At the final-screening stage most companies begin to treat the idea as a project, assign it a schedule, and set up a budget for planning and analysis. Because economic analyses can cost thousands of dollars, companies must enforce proper management controls. The first step in the final screening of a new-product idea involves a forecast of the market potential for each market segment. For a totally new or radically improved product, management should estimate an array of potentials based on different prices and different assumptions about the entry of competitors into the marketplace. Probabilities should be assigned to these different estimates.

Step two is to estimate what share of the market the company can obtain. This again involves making certain assumptions about company marketing activities, competitive reactions, and cost limitations. Thus, the second and third steps in the analysis are intertwined. The third step in the procedure is to set up a limited number of possible marketing plans and to estimate the effect each will have on company sales under certain environmental conditions. For example, if a company has two different advertising campaigns with different appeals and weights each based on different assumptions about the major competitor's reaction, it should note the effect of each on sales, costs, and margins.

If these steps are well executed, it should be possible to obtain reasonably good estimates of the marketing costs involved. To these must be added all other costs associated with the new product, including its development costs, investments in plant and equipment, and working capital. Managers can then compare the total cost against the expected sales volume and aggregate the product's "profit" over the time period being considered (step four). Finally the resulting rate of return can then be compared with the requirements of alternative proposals as well as those of the company.

PRODUCT DESIGN

After identifying the target market, its needs, and one or more ideas that the screening process suggests might successfully satisfy those needs, the next step is to design the new product. This requires a process that starts with the key benefits to be provided by the product and ends with an engineering design for the product (see Exhibit 13–7). The critical parts of this process are product positioning, determining the product's potential, and specifying the engineering design.

EXHIBIT   13 ◆ 7
New-product design process

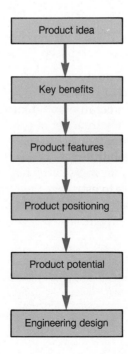

Given the product idea, managers must develop a statement of key benefits, which, in turn, helps them specify the necessary product features. Once this is done, they can position the product against competitors and the needs of the marketplace. Urban et al. suggest that the key benefits be identified in a statement called the **Core Benefit Proposition (CBP).**[30] This simple and direct statement facilitates an identification of essential product features. Examples of the CBP include:

- *Tylenol pain reliever:* "Effective, fast, and long-lasting relief without an upset stomach."
- *Corby Classic Pants Press:* "As efficient as any butler—and far less costly."

The ideal CBP states what is being offered to consumers, what they should derive from it, and why this is important—all in terms of consumer benefits. The CBP serves as the driving force behind R&D's development of a product that provides the desired benefits. Marketing is then challenged to find ways to best communicate these benefits to the targeted market.

The market segmentation process facilitates development of the initial core benefit proposition by clustering actual and potential customers by benefits wanted in the form of ideal choice criteria (set of features wanted). Even so, management must determine which product features are necessary to fulfill the CBP and whether these features will make the product unique in the eyes of the targeted audience. This requires that the seller know how consumers will perceive the new product (consumer perceptions), how they will compare it to existing products (consumer preferences), and the probability it will be purchased (consumer choice).

Consumer perceptions

To determine how potential customers will perceive the new product, managers must prepare a list of product features relevant to the CBP. The list of possible features emerges largely from company marketing and R&D managers augmented by small group or focus interviews.[31]

Once they have a list of features wanted, managers can determine how much relative importance customers attach to each. Probably the most common way to do so is through the use of reasonably simple scales admin-

---

[30] Urban et al., *Essentials of New Product Management*, pp. 155–58.

[31] For a discussion of how to develop and refine the CBP, see Edward F. McQuarrie and Shelby M. McIntyre, "Focus Groups and the Development of New Products by Technologically Driven Companies: Some Guidelines," *Journal of Product Innovation Management*, March 1986, p. 40.

istered by interviewers to a sample of potential buyers. The following is an example of a relative-importance scale for three product attributes of a new garden tractor:

	Not important									Very important	
	0	**1**	**2**	**3**	**4**	**5**	**6**	**7**	**8**	**9**	**10**
Silencer	—	—	—	—	—	—	—	—	—	—	—
Electric starter	—	—	—	—	—	—	—	—	—	—	—
Pneumatic tires	—	—	—	—	—	—	—	—	—	—	—

Such scaling not only profiles combinations of attributes most and least wanted, but can also yield information on how various types of consumers differ in their relative rankings of attributes.

If the new product will be introduced into an established product category, a sample of consumers representing the target market should be asked to rate brands on the extent to which each brand possesses each attribute of importance. From this information a weighted combination of those attributes that discriminate the most between products is determined. Following this, the average scores of each of the products or brands of interest on each dimension can be plotted on a space map. The greater the proximity between any two brands, the more consumers perceived them as being alike. Such a map shows not only which attributes are determinant, but also how a new product with certain features will be perceived relative to existing brands. Exhibit 13–8 shows such a map for pain relievers. A pain reliever is considered "effective" if it provides strong, fast, long-lasting relief. It is "gentle" if it does not cause upset stomach or heartburn. In Exhibit 13–8, Excedrin is positioned as the most effective pain reliever and Tylenol as the most gentle. As shown in the exhibit, there is a viable positioning opportunity for a product that is *both* highly effective and very gentle.[32]

Consumer preferences and choice

The preceding process describes the way consumers perceive the product space for a given product. But the marketer still needs to know how consumers compare the new product to existing ones and the probability that consumers will buy the new one. This requires having consumers describe their "ideal product" using the same attributes employed in the previous

---

[32] Urban et al., *Essentials of New Product Management,* p. 105.

EXHIBIT 13 ◆ 8
Perceptual map for pain relievers

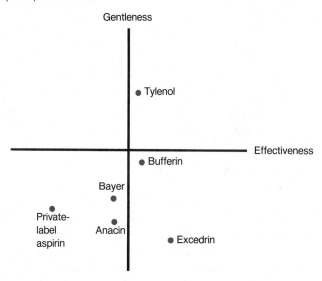

Source: Glen L. Urban, John R. Hauser, and Nikhilesh Dholakia, *Essentials of New Product Management,* © 1987, p. 105. Adapted by permission of Prentice-Hall, Inc., Englewood Cliffs, N.J.

step, and then locating these ideal points on the perceptual map. Exhibit 13–9 is an illustration of consumers' ideal points for pain relievers. Note that they cluster into two benefit segments. The space map shows which segments are most apt to buy which brands (those nearest the circle). The proximity of a brand to the center of a circle relative to the proximity of other brands determines the probability of purchase. Thus, there appears to be a substantial opportunity for our proposed new brand.

Sales potential

The need for an accurate sales forecast of the new product increases as it goes through the development process. At this stage only a small amount of money has been invested. What is needed is simply an indication of whether the product will likely be a dud, a moderate success, or a substantial hit. Later on, more accurate forecasts will be needed.

The perception and preference analyses should, when coupled with management's intuition, provide some crude but satisfactory sales forecasts. If one knows where the product will be positioned against competitive products and how close it will be to a given cluster of ideal points, it should be possible to estimate what the range of the new product's sales and brand share will be. Because management probably has a good idea of the sales and

EXHIBIT 13 ♦9

Positioning of proposed new product versus two benefit clusters for pain relievers

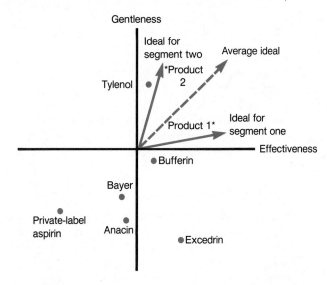

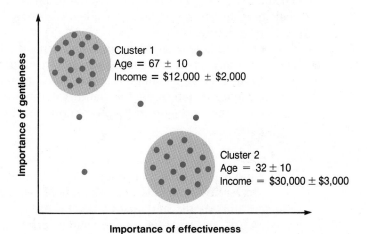

Source: Glen L. Urban, John R. Hauser, and Nikhilesh Dholakia, *Essentials of New Product Management,* © 1987, pp. 134–37. Adapted by permission of Prentice-Hall, Inc., Englewood Cliffs, N.J.

share of the "nearest" brand, it can use them to estimate the sales revenues of the new product, assuming it achieves its intended position.

The consumer research conducted to obtain the perception and preference data can also obtain intent-to-buy information. This can be done by scaling answers to the question:

All things considered, what are the chances that you will try this product?									
0– 10 No chance	10– 20	20– 30	30– 40	40– 50	50– 60	60– 70	70– 80	80– 90	90– 100 Certain

In using such data, the seller must keep in mind that all that is needed is simply a go/no go decision before proceeding to the next step in the new-product development process.

Engineering design

Having developed the core benefit proposition; determined the perception, preference, and probable choice of the new product; specified the mix of physical characteristics (and their levels) needed to fulfill the CBP; and prepared a preliminary sales forecast, a seller must then undertake the final engineering of a physical product that will deliver the benefits promised. Further, the design (appearance) of the product must communicate its physical characteristics. For example, a heavy-duty pick-up truck must appear to be a long-lasting, rugged vehicle.

Once an engineering design has been specified, it should be possible to estimate the cost of producing the new product under different volume assumptions. Using estimated marketing costs and the potential sales data, management can determine the viability of the project and decide whether to proceed to the next step in the new-product process—testing.

TESTING

Urban and Hauser note that predictions become less uncertain as tests come closer to reality; but costs also increase. Therefore, a good testing strategy balances uncertainty and cost by careful use of sequential testing.

As a first step in this testing sequence, researchers often examine the various components of its marketing program—such as the physical product, advertising, and price—individually before testing the entire strategy.

Once the components are tested, the entire marketing program can be examined in laboratory simulations, with consumer panels, and/or statistical models. These pretests eliminate many failures at low cost without revealing the product to competitors. But they still do not deal with reality. The final stage of testing involves a test market.[33]

---

[33] Urban and Hauser, *Design and Marketing of New Products*, p. 363.

Testing should not only reduce risk; it should also help improve the product and its marketing mix—thereby enhancing the product's success and its long-term profitability. Three kinds of testing can help meet the objectives: product testing, pretest marketing, and test marketing.

Product testing

The purpose of **product testing** is to make certain the product delivers the desired benefits and to provide data for improving the product and/or reducing its costs. There are a number of ways to test a product. But it is critically important that whichever way is used, the test results indicate how the products will perform under *actual use* conditions.

Laboratory tests and the use of experts

Lab tests can often accurately measure the performance of certain types of products under a variety of conditions. Certain uses can be simulated and many performance questions answered in a relatively short time in lab tests. For example, truck engines can be run continuously for long periods on a test stand. Toasters can be "popped up" thousands of times to test the ruggedness of the mechanism involved. And painted boards can be exposed to heat and light to gain information about a paint's longevity. Despite the obvious advantages of speed, cost, and controlled conditions, however, lab tests cannot totally replicate the product's actual use conditions, including the presence of human operators. For example, the next generation of car electronic devices, such as a dashboard video screen that shows road conditions ahead, traction control to prevent tires from spinning on slippery roads, and pressure sensors that warn drivers when their tires need air, can all be tested in the laboratory; but they will still need to undergo extensive consumer tests because of the variations in use environments and operators.

Another way to test new products is to use a **panel of experts.** This is often the case with foods, where experts evaluate taste and aroma to make sure the new product lives up to its benefits-offered claims. Or firms can test different recipes to determine which is best. The advantage of such tests is their relative low cost and the speed with which they can be done. The problem is that the experts may not accurately reflect the views of the actual consumers.

Consumer tests

Many subtle factors determine whether consumers ultimately like or dislike a new consumer product. Coca-Cola discovered the difficulty of replicating the real world in a use test when its new-formula Coke was released in April 1985. The company felt certain it would be a sure-fire success, based on the overwhelming results of taste tests done with nearly 200,000 consumers. But Coke failed to measure the psychological impact of tampering with a successful 99-year-old soft drink.[34] The company was eventually forced to bring back the original formula, relabeled Classic Coke.

Consumer tests can vary from relatively informal **in-house use tests** (where a sample of employees is asked to use the product and then fill out a questionnaire) to highly structured **blind-paired comparison tests** (where the consumer does not know the brands involved). In recent years, sensory evaluation, as used by such companies as Campbell, has progressed from simple taste-test panels to elaborate computer analyses. Some companies use employee volunteers to evaluate the taste, smell, and feel of their products; and they spend considerable time and money to select individuals who can discriminate between the taste or smell of various ingredients at certain levels of intensity. They also train evaluators to identify and discriminate among hundreds of flavors and to match taste sensation to common descriptive words. While in-house testing is no substitute for consumer testing, it does screen out product ideas with limited potential.[35]

When the new product is designed to replace an existing one, or when the product's competitors can be readily determined, researchers can use blind-paired comparison tests. This test places two different products with a sample of prospective users, who are asked to use the two products under normal conditions and to indicate which one they like best and why. If the new product must be tested against a number of competitive products, it is necessary to conduct several paired comparison tests. For example, a regional fast-food chain developed a fried breaded catfish fillet sandwich for possible adoption by its operating units. After conducting numerous taste tests among its employees, church groups, and high school clubs, the chain developed three formulations to test among a qualified (as to use of fast-food restaurants and recent eating of fish) group of respondents. The best research design for such a test consisted of the use of three matched samples of respondents, each testing a different combination of two of the three alternatives.[36]

We can see, then, that the results of blind-paired comparison tests are often difficult to analyze. First and foremost, these tests cannot replicate all the choices available in the marketplace. Second, the use situation is artificial, in that the consumer tries two products, one after the other. Third, the statistics obtained from the tests may be misleading or ambiguous. Assume A is preferred by only 25 percent. What does this mean? If the 25 percent *very strongly* preferred the product over the alternative product,

---

[34] See Ronald Alsop, "Coke's Flip-Flop Underscores Risks of Consumer Taste Tests," *The Wall Street Journal*, July 18, 1985, p. 25.

[35] "What They Taste Is What We Get," *Report*, a quarterly publication of RJR Nabisco, Inc., 2nd quarter 1986, p. 11.

[36] If we label the three alternatives A, B, and C, then group one would test A and B, group two would test A and C, and group three, B and C.

then product A may be a real winner. On the other hand, a respondent may merely be stating a mild preference; or if the respondent is unable to discriminate between the two, the choice made may be by chance. If A and B are relatively similar, the problem of random choices by nondiscriminating subjects is very real.[37] Despite these limitations, blind-comparison tests indicate whether a product has any substantial limitations under actual usage conditions.

Firms can test consumer durable and industrial products if actual usage conditions can be realistically simulated. For example, consumers can be asked to evaluate different interior configurations of refrigerators, the comfort of a ride in several different automobiles, and which power mower is easiest to use. Engineers can be asked which machine prototype is best in size, positioning of controls, and safety. Unfortunately, sometimes, even the largest companies fail to test properly. Exhibit 13–10 tells why IBM's PCjr failed.

Test marketing

In this procedure a company attempts to test on a small basis the commercial viability of a marketing plan for a new or modified product. The purpose of such a test is to estimate the sales and profitability potentials in the new product and to identify and correct problems with the marketing plan and the product itself before its full-scale introduction. Most major food and household product companies use test marketing extensively.

The cost of test marketing is not trivial—it ranges from $500,000 to $3 million or more. There is also the question of how reliable the test findings

EXHIBIT 13 ◆ 10

Why IBM's PCjr was an underachiever

Even though the PCjr was IBM's first consumer product, it was never adequately tested. The development team was more concerned about making sure the PC did not take sales away from larger units than whether it met the consumer's needs. It ended up as a compromise with such inadequacies as a toylike keyboard that made it unsuitable for word processing and a limited memory compared to competitors. IBM did conduct consumer tests, but primarily to find out whether consumers could easily run the machines—not to find out if it had the features needed for success.

Source: "How IBM Made 'Junior' an Underachiever," *Business Week,* June 25, 1984, pp. 106–7.

---

[37] Bruce S. Buchanan and Donald G. Morrison, "Measuring Simple Preferences: An Approach to Blind, Forced Choice Product Testing," *Marketing Science,* Spring 1985, p. 93. This article discusses alternative ways of designing blind product tests to separate random choices from real preferences.

are. According to one source, there is a 50-50 chance that the test results will fall within ±10 percent of the national performance.[38] Another disadvantage is that competitors can audit test markets thereby limiting the time advantage of the innovator. For example, Calgon went national with Cling Free, used in clothes dryers to eliminate static cling, before P&G's similar product, Bounce, was out of test marketing.

Pretest market research

Given the problems and costs of test marketing, it is understandable why efforts in recent years have focused on the development of low-cost alternatives to the traditional full-scale test market operation. Typically marketers refer to these as **laboratory test markets;** they are mostly applicable to packaged consumer products, including food items. The procedure measures the process by which a consumer adopts a new product: the three major steps of awareness, trial, and repeat buying.

In the lab procedure, respondents representative of the target audience see commercials about the new product in a TV program. Then they are given the option of buying the product in a simulated store also stocked with competing brands. They take the product home; and researchers make follow-up interviews to determine the extent of satisfaction (including preference over their regular brand) and repurchase intentions. Such a usage test is often extended by giving the respondents a chance to repurchase the test brand (using their own money), which is then delivered to them.[39] These tests cost between $30,000 and $50,000 and take from 10 to 14 weeks to complete.

About 200 new products have used the **Assessor model,** which follows the preceding procedures. A comparison of pretest market and test market share data—where available—showed an average deviation of only about one half of one share point.[40]

Pretesting industrial goods

Because of the nature of the industrial market, buyers and sellers often work closely together in developing new products. Sellers can often obtain valuable reactions to product features by presenting their proposed working specifications to potential users. It is usually not too difficult for a manufac-

---

[38] "To Test or Not to Test," *The Nielsen Researcher* 30, no. 4 (1972), pp. 3–8.

[39] For the methodology involved in such studies, see Trevor Watkins, "The Practice of Product Testing in the New Product Development Process: The Role of Model-Based Approaches," *European Journal of Marketing* 18 (November 6/7, 1984), pp. 14–19. Laboratory testing discussed here can also judge the success of a competitor's new product. See Peter Mimmaugh, "Reverse Simulation Preempts Competitors' Test Markets," *Marketing News,* June 19, 1987, p. 12.

[40] Urban et al., *Essentials of New Product Management,* pp. 225–26.

turer to obtain answers from users, because the latter typically have a lot to gain as a result of the development work. Further, users respond to questions in technical terms, thereby making misunderstandings less likely to occur than in tests of consumer goods.

Potential buyers are often willing—indeed anxious—to test new industrial products under actual operating conditions. Some buyers conduct these tests on their own premises and encourage members of the seller's development group to be present during the testing. Or the selling company may test the product in its own lab and ask prospective buyers to witness and comment on the tests. Discussions following such demonstrations are usually quite helpful. Industrial goods can also be tested at trade shows and sales presentations. The trade-show method consists of displaying and demonstrating the product to obtain measures of interest and buying intentions. Sales demonstrations present the product to a sample of prospective customers in an effort to learn how many would purchase it. Such forecasting methods, while overly simplistic, have value in determining the extent to which the new product is liked or disliked. The results are most valuable when responses are clustered at either extreme of liking or disliking.

Full-scale test marketing

The nature and extent of such research depends largely on how much confidence management has in its proposed national marketing plan. For example, if management is insecure about the product's initial retail price, then it should include provisions for testing alternative prices in the test market research. Thus, the company must first develop its *national* marketing plan for the new product and then replicate it in miniature for the test. (Sometimes a company will test more than one national marketing plan to determine which is best.) Companies frequently make the mistake of planning the test-marketing operation first and later expanding it into a national plan—only to find that what was done locally cannot be achieved at the national level. (For example, it may be too costly to sustain a high level of media expenditures or personal selling efforts nationally.)

The ultimate objective of any market test is to obtain an estimate of sales for at least the first year of national operation for some level of promotional expenditure—a difficult undertaking, given that most test markets use only three or four small cities. Firms obtain sales estimates by measuring the rate at which consumers are induced to try the new product and the number of consumers making repeat purchases. The market-test research design should break down such data by type of promotional expenditure as well as by level of expenditure. This makes it possible to test the various methods of sampling or dealing used to induce trial to determine which expenditure is most effective. Different levels of advertising intensity can also be tried and their effect on sales measured. The critical point here is not to test any strategy that is not part of one or more national marketing plans. The more variables to be tested, the more difficult and expensive is the test marketing.

Another important objective is to determine the reaction of the trade. Apparently Holly Farm's recent test market for its new full-cooked roasted chicken failed to do so. While the test market identified strong support for the product, it failed to detect the concerns of retailers, which centered on the chicken's short shelf life. Many retailers have dropped it because they have only five days to sell the product.[41]

Firms obtain test market data using a variety of research instruments, including store audits, continuous consumer panels, and personal telephone interviews. Increasingly, companies are using electronic minimarket tests that reduce the $2 to $3 million costs of a traditional two-city test market substantially and provide the needed data faster. Such electronic market tests typically cost between $400,000 and $500,000.

There are several electronic test-market services, including AdTel, Nielsen, and Information Resources Inc.'s BehaviorScan. IRI pioneered the technology and monitors the purchasing and viewing behavior of a sample of households in eight small cities across the United States. Panel members show their identification cards at the supermarket check-out. A scanner records their purchases and the data are sent directly to a central computer. Panel householders are increasingly using a hand-held wand that reads the bar codes on purchases as a substitute for in-store scanners.

IRI monitors all family TV sets to determine which programs and commercials are watched. Commercials for the new product are sent into specially designated homes. A manufacturer can also manage to test in-store promotions and the amount of shelf space used. IRI can also measure the impact of such individual promotional activities as samples and coupons.[42] Because such research comes from a single source (the household), the effect of a marketing variable (price, advertising copy, advertising weight, and coupons) either individually or in combination on the sales of a new product can be more readily determined.

Determining the length of a test market

In general, the test should last long enough to permit buyers who have purchased the product once to make at least two and possibly three repurchases. The heart of any sales estimate lies in the measurement of repeat purchases. Sellers often assume that the product in question has a unique quality that can be demonstrated in the first experience with the product. This leads to placing the major research emphasis on the rate at which *initial purchases* are made rather than on *repeat purchases*. But this can be a dangerous assumption, because management inevitably is favorably biased toward the product.

---

[41] Arthur Buckler, "Holly Farm's Marketing Error: The Chicken that Laid an Egg," *The Wall Street Journal*, February 9, 1988, p. 34.

[42] Aimee L. Stern, "Test Marketing Enters a New Era," *Dun's Business Month*, October 1985, p. 86.

Many products have enjoyed a high rate of trial but were unsuccessful when introduced on a national scale. One example is Pringles potato chips. Pringles' initial failure has often been attributed to the decline in quality that occurred when the product had to be produced in quantities large enough for national distribution.[43] Many consumers tried the product but then refused to repurchase it. Later, an improved version became successful.

Another example concerns a nonliquid temporary hair coloring that consumers used by inserting a tube of solid hair dye into a special comb. " 'It went to market and it was a bust,' a company spokesperson recalls. On hot days when people perspired, any hair dye excessively applied ran down their necks and foreheads. 'It just didn't occur to us to look at this under conditions where people perspire,' he says."[44]

Deciding what to measure

In addition to measuring sales, research should attempt to measure the following variables, as well.

1. *Advertising effectiveness.* Researchers should determine the rate at which target consumers become aware of the new product, the amount of time they retain the message, and their degree of knowledge about the product's characteristics. These factors affect the rate of adoption and the rate of subsequent purchases (see point 5).

2. *Effectiveness of an introductory offer.* Many companies rely on an introductory offer to accelerate consumer trial of the new product. They can determine the effectiveness of this offer by ascertaining whether consumers know about it and whether they availed themselves of it.

3. *Effectiveness of a trade offer.* Many companies give the trade a special incentive (such as an extra margin) to stock a new product. The effectiveness of this offer can easily be judged from information provided by the salesforce. The salesforce can also report any other difficulties experienced in getting cooperation from the trade.

4. *Share of the total market.* This is the new product's volume in units or dollars expressed as a percentage of the total volume for the product class involved. It is also essential to discover the effect of the new product on total sales of the product class. Does it increase total sales—expand the market—or does it obtain its share wholly by taking sales away from other brands? Is any particular brand being especially hurt by the new product? This latter information alerts the company to possible competitive retaliation.

5. *Characteristics of buyers, rate of adoption, and repeat-purchase rates.* These data are essential in estimating future sales. The data on the characteristics of

---

[43] A source that discusses this is Damon Darden, "Faced with More Competition, P&G Sees New Products as Crucial to Earnings Growth," *The Wall Street Journal*, September 13, 1983, pp. 37, 53.

[44] Roger Recklefs, "Success Comes Hard in the Tricky Business of Creating Products," *The Wall Street Journal*, August 23, 1978, pp. 1, 27.

households provide clues as to what audience groups are buying and to what extent; that is, who are the heavy buyers?

6. *Reasons for not adopting or for discontinuing usage.* Obviously, this information is vital. From the research conducted under point 5, it should be possible to locate consumers who fall into various user categories and to interview them in depth.

Projecting the results

If the company's market share, total sales, and repeat-buying measurements clearly exceed expectations, there is no reason not to proceed with national distribution. But such successful market-test results are not always achieved. Usually, it is difficult to project the results in a way that provides an accurate estimate of first-year sales. To make such a projection for a frequently purchased product, it is necessary to know the rate at which consumers are first attracted to try the new product, the number of first buyers who buy a second time, the number of second buyers who buy a third time, and so on.

It is difficult to forecast future sales, because the demand for a new product typically rises rapidly, then peaks and declines to a lower level. This situation is depicted graphically in Exhibit 13–11. Many more consumers try the product than eventually adopt it. The challenge is to look beyond the hump in the sales curve and estimate the level of sales after the effects of the product's introduction subside. The objective is to predict the sales level as early as possible from the test market results. The present state of the art allows reasonably accurate forecasts to be made between three and six months after introduction.

COMMERCIALIZATION

The last step in the new-product development process, **commercialization,** requires considerable coordination among the various functional areas— especially marketing, production, and physical distribution. Large sums are invested not only in manufacturing, but also in marketing. One large company recently spent over $60 million in media advertising alone to introduce a new coffee. Because marketing is responsible for making the product available and the target audience aware of the product and its unique set of attributes, its role is indispensable.

Before launching the new product, the firm usually requires the group responsible for it to prepare a detailed plan (complete with budget) stating the firm's long-term objectives for the product (sales, profitability, and competitive position), the strategy to attain these objectives (including the mix of strategy elements), and the action plan designed to make the selected strategy operational.

There are a number of different commercialization strategy options. One is concerned with the *scale of entry*. Some companies typically enter a new

• 3M organizes its many SBUs into four sectors or groups, including the Industrial and Electronic Sector, which makes products such as adhesives, and the Commercial and Consumer Sector, which is responsible for such products as Scotchgard and Post-it notes. (Chapter 11)

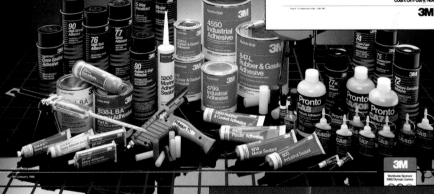

Courtesy 3M Company

Courtesy General Motors Corporation

• The Pontiac Grand Prix, 1988 Motor Trend Car of the Year, was an entry in the GM–10 line General Motors produced in an effort to recapture some of the middle- to upper-middle-class automobile buyers' market. (Chapter 12)

A & P POLICY:

Always do what is honest and fair for every customer.

RAINCHECK:

If an advertised special is sold out ask the Manager for a Raincheck. It entitles you to the same item at the same special price the following week. Or if you wish we'll give you a comparable item at the same special price.

GUARANTEE:

A&P offers an unconditional moneyback guarantee. No matter what it is, no matter who makes it, if A&P sells it, A&P guarantees it.

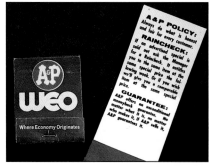

◆ In the early 1970s, A&P's WEO ("Where Economy Originates") strategy—designed to reverse the firm's declining market share and profits by drastically reducing prices—backfired when major competitive food chains strengthened their positions in nonprice areas. (Chapter 14)

Courtesy Campbell Soup Company

◆ To meet the demands of consumers' changing lifestyles, Campbell Soup introduced Low Sodium and Special Request varieties of its best-selling brands to appeal to segments with special dietary needs or preferences. Stouffer's frozen Dinner Supreme is aimed at the upscale, health-conscious segment. (Chapter 13)

Reprinted by permission of Stouffer Foods Corporation

Courtesy Toro

◆ Significant factors in Toro's successful distribution strategy are the firm's return to its traditional dealer network and its reliance on Toro retailers to provide postsale service on Toro equipment. (Chapter 15)

BARTLES & JAYMES
Summer Extravaganza
With 3 Big Events

EVENT NO. 1 • MEMORIAL DAY

Frank and Ed Life-Size Replica Offer

★ VERY HIGH *consumer demand*
★ NEVER BEFORE *available to the general public*
★ EXCLUSIVELY *offered at your* STORE DISPLAY
★ PROOF-OF-PURCHASE *generates* INCREASED SALES *(required in most states)*
★ OFFERED BY MAIL *for $14.95 plus $5.00 shipping and handling*

CARTON RIDER WITH COUPONS

Point-Of-Sale

★ STOPPING POWER *with stunning stop-action photography*
★ MOUTH WATERING *bottle shots*
★ REFRESHING *splash of cool blue water*
★ 4 FLAVORS *cover about 80% of wine cooler sales*

SPECTACULAR ON 100 CASE DISPLAY

WHEN ORDERING PLEASE SPECIFY

Description	Code No.	Size	Description	Code No.	Size
Spectacular	900BJC-007-7376	40"W x 38½"H	Coupon Pad	900BJC-017-7376	5½"W x 3⅝"
Cut Case Card	900BJC-004-7277	28"W x 17½"H	Proof of Purchase Coupon Pad	900BJC-017-7384	2⅝"W x 3½"
Banner	900BJC-006-7276	28"W x 17½"H	Display Prizer	Furnished upon request only	
Stand-up Offer Carton Rider	900BJC-014-7282	13"W x 17½"H	Pouch Display Prizer	Furnished upon request only	
			Berry Display Prizer	Furnished upon request only	

"Ed reminded me to tell you that BARTLES & JAYMES PREMIUM WINE COOLER goes great with Pizza!"

Thank you for your support

BARTLES & JAYMES
Premium WINE COOLER

◆ Bartles & Jaymes' successful promotion mix strategy launched the brand into first place in the wine-cooler market and became a classic in U.S. promotional history. (Chapter 16)

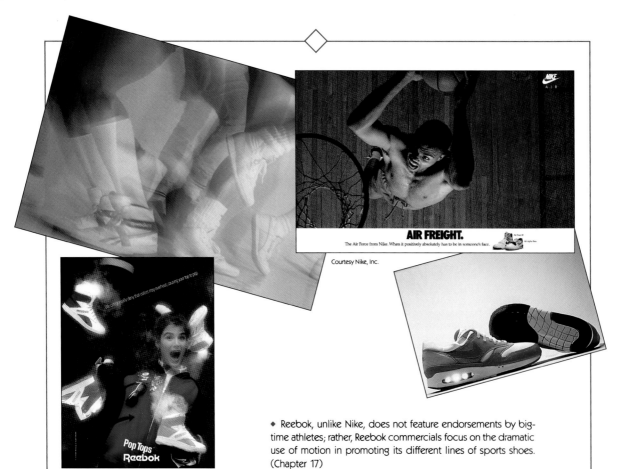

AIR FREIGHT.

The Air Force from Nike. When it positively absolutely has to be in someone's face.

Courtesy Nike, Inc.

Pop Tops
Reebok

Reprinted by permission of Reebok International Ltd.

◆ Reebok, unlike Nike, does not feature endorsements by big-time athletes; rather, Reebok commercials focus on the dramatic use of motion in promoting its different lines of sports shoes. (Chapter 17)

WILKINSON SWORD® MERCHANDISING PROGRAMS

From the moment Wilkinson Sword products enter your stores, we help support your sales efforts with everything from in-store displays to national advertising. Wilkinson Sword's merchandising works for *you!*

Point-of-Sale Displays—These easy-to-assemble displays are perfect for promotions and off-shelf featuring.

National Consumer Advertising—Multi-media advertising and promotional efforts increase awareness and encourage sales throughout the year.

Sales Support Material—Wilkinson Sword provides a variety of materials to help support your sales efforts—selling sheets, brochures, posters and ad slicks.

WILKINSON SWORD

Printed in U.S.A. Form No. 1142-06-89
© 1989 Wilkinson Sword, Inc.
P.O. Box 48117, Atlanta, GA 30062

◆ Wilkinson Sword's retail merchandisers support the firm's salesforce with programs offering national advertising, in-store displays, and other sales support materials to retailers who stock the Wilkinson products. (Chapter 18)

EXHIBIT   13 ♦ 11

A typical sales curve for a new convenience product

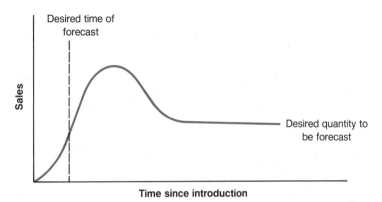

market on a small scale to enable them to avoid costly failures. For example, GE slowly introduced a new and highly promising heat-resistant specialty plastic, producing it only in small quantities in the firm's existing plants. Only after IBM approved its use in computer circuit boards did GE move to invest considerable sums in building a full-scale plant.

An alternative to this limited approach is to enter the market on a full-scale basis; that is, to seek national distribution as soon as possible. Because of the rapidity with which rivals can imitate a company's new product and the substantial scale economies to be achieved in both advertising and promotion, this strategy is often adopted by manufacturers of food and personal-care items.

Another strategy has to do with *ownership and control* of the new product. One option here is licensing, which is what Minnetonka did with its Obsession fragrance for men. Because Minnetonka didn't have the resources to exploit the product, the company licensed it to Calvin Klein. Yet another option is to sell the product, which is what Marriott did with its individual Courtyard Inns while still continuing to manage them. And there is the franchising option—a favorite of many service operators, such as those selling fast foods. The most common option, however, is to retain ownership of the new product and assume complete responsibility for its marketing.

During a product launch a control system attempts to measure at frequent intervals and on a geographical basis data similar to that obtained in the test market. The type of information tracked is shown in Exhibit 13–12.

APPLYING THE NEW-PRODUCT DEVELOPMENT PROCESS TO SERVICES

Despite the differences between physical objects and services, the new-product development process can also be applied to services. This is particularly true with the first three steps, which are concerned with objectives and

EXHIBIT 13 ◆ 12

Types of information tracked during product launch

◆ Sales	◆ Share of market
◆ Product availability—stores stocking and inventories by type and size of store	◆ Advertising effectiveness
	◆ Actions of leading competitors
◆ Effectiveness of each trade offer	◆ Source of share gains—competitors that lost share
◆ Consumer awareness	◆ Reasons for/against trial and adoption
◆ Trial—including source, such as coupons, introductory price, other incentive offers	
◆ Repeat-purchase rates by consumer demographics	

strategy, opportunity identification (idea generation and screening), and conversion of an idea into a product design. These steps are taken seriously by many sophisticated and successful companies, as in the way Marriott made its decision to enter the moderate-priced segment of the hotel industry, Scandinavian Airlines designed its first-class business service, McDonald's added to its food offerings, and American Express introduced its platinum credit card.

Implementation of the fourth step—testing—can pose problems for some new services. The presence of the consumer in the service system makes it difficult to turn out a service that is uniform or consistent. Service companies try to get around this problem in a variety of ways, as we noted in Chapter 12. They use *machines* (automatic bank tellers, coin-operated vending machines, electrocardiograms, and automatic car washes); *"soft" technology,* which substitutes structured preplanned systems for personal operators and may include special hardware (McDonald's and other fast-food restaurants, Book-of-the-Month Club, H&R Block, and American Express prepackaged vacation tours); and systems often referred to as *hybrids,* which combine *"hard" technology* with detailed industrial systems (Midas Muffler and radio-controlled ready-mix concrete truck routing).[45] The more a new service can be industrialized, the more it can be tested in ways similar to those used to test products, such as the testing of an automatic teller in labs as well as by a sample of bank customers and finally via a full-scale test market.

Most large for-profit service organizations extensively test a new service before adopting it on a full-scale commercial basis. For instance, McDonald's

---

[45] Theodore Levitt, *The Marketing Imagination* (New York: Free Press, 1986), pp. 56–59.

constantly tests new food and beverage offerings and restaurant layouts. In early 1989, it tested a new upscale format in one of Houston's fancier areas designed to appeal to the power-lunch crowd of busy executives. The new format comes equipped with an electronic stock ticker, plug-in phone jacks at some tables, and a fax machine; but the main entree is still McDonald's regular fare.[46] As another example, Marriott surveyed business travelers as to their preferences in room size and layout before designing its moderately priced Courtyard Inns. Later, it built several of these inns to test economic viability before going national. The three major TV networks regularly test the market for a new show with a pilot offering before committing to the production of 12 to 18 episodes.

But not all services can be industrialized; and not all service companies operate multiple units that facilitate the testing of a new service. Thus, it is difficult to test a highly labor-intensive service such as a new legal service, a new therapy program for drug addicts, or a new family financial advisory service being offered locally, even when professionals are used. If such services have been offered elsewhere, then the results can be studied to pinpoint the success determinants—they become the test market. At the very least, the success determinants can be concept-tested among members of the potential market.

Commercialization of new services can be conducted in ways similar to those used for new products. Thus, they can be franchised (fast-food), licensed (software), and sold but continue to be managed (hotels); and they can be introduced nationally or on a region-by-region basis.

SUMMARY

The development of new products is an expensive and difficult undertaking. Only a relatively small percentage of new products is successful. Firms introduce new products to increase sales and profits, to take advantage of changes in the environment (technology and demographics), and to counter competitors' moves. New products fail if they are me-too products, are incompatible with company strengths, have too small a market, have inadequate channel support, if buyer tastes change, or if strong competing products enter the market.

The new-product development process consists of four major steps: opportunity identification, product design, testing, and commercialization. Firms cannot implement this process without a well-articulated set of objectives and a detailed product strategy. Opportunity identification is first concerned with the markets targeted and, second, with product ideas that derive from a variety of sources. Ideas are screened using selected weighted criteria.

Designing the product starts with an acceptable idea and ends with an engineered product. The process generates product features from key benefits, positions the proposed product, estimates the product's potential, and provides an engineering design.

---

[46] "McDonald's Goes after Power Lunch Crowd," *Arkansas Gazette*, March 13, 1989, p. I–1.

Product tests include laboratory, panel of experts, and consumer tests. Companies must make certain that the tests replicate the product's actual use environment.

Following such tests, the company engages in test marketing in which it tests on a small-scale basis the commercial viability of a marketing plan for the new product. The two types of test marketing are pretests and full-scale. Pretesting uses a lab setting to measure awareness, trial, and repeat buying. Full-scale testing is expensive and, in addition to measuring sales, attempts to measure advertising effectiveness, product availability, effectiveness of trade of-

fers, share of market, buyer characteristics, and reasons for discontinuing usage. Increasingly such tests use electronic mini-test markets rather than the more traditional test markets.

Commercialization is the last step in the new-product development. It requires a detailed plan complete with sales forecasts and budgets covering a several-year period. The marketing plan serves as the basis for the plans developed by the other functional areas. The first-year plan should call for a continuation of much of the same kinds of information obtained in the full-scale test market.

QUESTIONS

1. The Toro Company is a leading manufacturer of outdoor power equipment, such as lawnmowers and snowblowers, for both consumer and commercial markets. Much of the firm's recent revenue growth, however, has come from its line of small outdoor appliances—line trimmers and garden hose reels. The company wants to expand its outdoor appliance line by developing several new products. You have been put in charge of *identifying ideas for potential new additions to the line*. How would you develop a list of such ideas? What sources of information would you turn to and why?

2. Now that you have developed a number of new-product ideas for possible inclusion in Toro's line of appliances described in question 1, your task is to *screen* those ideas and identify those with sufficient potential to justify further development. Devise a *screening procedure*. What dimensions would be important to evaluate as part of that procedure? Which members of Toro management would you ask to participate in the screening process?

3. Define a *core benefit proposition*. How should the core benefit proposition developed for a product relate to (a) the selec-

tion of a target market, and (b) the positioning of the product?

4. Develop a *core benefit proposition* for a local professional theater company (either a company you are familiar with or one you make up). To effectively communicate and deliver the core benefit to potential play-goers, what decisions would have to be made concerning (a) the selection of plays to be offered, (b) the theater's physical facilities and customer services, and (c) the theater's marketing program?

5. You are the marketing vice president of the Tennant Company, a major manufacturer of industrial cleaning equipment and supplies. The firm's engineers have designed a new sweeper that promises to be more effective at cleaning up oil and metal shavings than any other product currently on the market. The product might appeal to manufacturers in a variety of industries involving the cutting and shaping of metal. How would you find out whether potential customers are interested in such a product and what its potential sales volume is likely to be?

6. The new formula for Coca-Cola was much preferred by consumers in *blind paired-comparison taste tests*, yet when the com-

pany replaced its "classic" formula with the "new Coke" customers abandoned the brand in such numbers that the firm was eventually forced to offer both versions. Why did consumer testing fail to predict customer reactions in this case? What kind of testing might Coca-Cola have done to obtain more complete information about consumers' potential reactions?

7. An increasing number of consumer product manufacturers are forgoing *full-scale test marketing* of their new products. They either rely on pretest market research or go directly from consumer tests to commercialization. What accounts for this trend? What are the disadvantages of full-scale test markets? What risks do companies take by relying solely on consumer tests or pretest market research?

8. A regional manufacturer of ice cream products developed a new brand based on the low-fat Italian dairy dessert called *gelato*. The new product incorporated original Italian recipes and flavorings; it was positioned to compete with super premium ice creams such as Haägen Dazs. The company *test marketed* the product in one midwestern city and it was so encouraged by the first two months of test market sales that it immediately proceeded to a regional roll-out. Unfortunately, after initial sales success, the product's volume quickly declined and it was eventually pulled from the market. Why did the product's test market results fail to predict its eventual decline? What additional information could the firm have collected during the test market that may have helped it predict the new brand's eventual market performance more accurately?

Chapter ⟨14⟩

Pricing decisions

A&P'S COSTLY LOW-PRICE STRATEGY

George Huntington Hartford began the Great Atlantic and Pacific Tea Company in 1859 when he opened a tea shop in New York City.[1] Bypassing the tea wholesalers, Hartford purchased large quantities of tea directly from importers; and he thus could sell tea to consumers at prices substantially lower than those of his competitors. As the business prospered, he opened more shops and added coffee, spices, and other staple grocery items to the inventory. In 1912 the company introduced "cash-and-carry" stores, which did away with home delivery and customer credit and featured low prices. By 1916 A&P had expanded to 1,000 stores. By 1930 the firm was the world's largest grocery retailer with more than 19,000 stores and over $1 billion in sales.

Unfortunately, A&P's fantastic sales growth was accompanied by the growth of conservative management practices and complacency. The firm was slow to respond to the emergence of larger and more efficient supermarkets in the 1930s, aggressive merchandising practices—such as offering trading stamps —in the 40s, and the addition of high-margin nonfood items in the 50s. The company was also reluctant to build stores in suburban shopping center locations because of the high rents. As a result, it eventually found itself holding a large proportion of small, aging stores in deteriorating urban neighborhoods. To make matters worse, management became careless about store maintenance and customer service. As a result, sales volume began to fall in the early 1970s. The firm's market share slumped drastically from a high of 21 percent in 1963 to only 12 percent by 1971. Although the firm was still profitable, profits fell greatly in the early 1970s.

A dramatic change in strategy

When he took over as A&P's chairman and CEO in 1971, William J. Kane felt that only drastic action could reverse the firm's decline. Thus, early in 1972, A&P converted thousands of stores

---

[1] Based on "A&P's Ploy: Cutting Prices to Turn a Profit," *Business Week*, May 20, 1972, pp. 76–78; "A&P Counts the Cost of its Pyrrhic Victory," *Business Week*, April 28, 1973, pp. 117–19; "Price and Pride on the Skids," *Time*, December 12, 1977, p. 79; Robert F. Hartley, *Marketing Mistakes*, 3d ed. (New York: John Wiley & Sons, 1986), chap. 15; Thomas T. Nagle, *The Strategy and Tactics of Pricing* (Englewood Cliffs, N.J.: Prentice-Hall, 1987), pp. 124–25; *The Great Atlantic & Pacific Tea Company, Inc., Annual Report 1986* (Montvale, N.J.: A&P Inc., April 14, 1987); Bill Saporito, "Just How Good Is the Great A&P?" *Fortune*, March 16, 1987, pp. 92–93; and Robert T. Grieves, "Back to the Future," *Forbes*, May 30, 1988.

continued

across the country to something called "Where Economy Originates" or WEO for short. Although most of the stores were *not* remodeled, they made two major changes:

* They reduced merchandise assortments from an average of 11,000 items in the conventional A&Ps to about 8,000 in the WEO stores. This action increased inventory turnover and reduced costs; but it also reduced the number of sizes and brands customers could choose from.
* They lowered prices on 90 percent of the merchandise. The reductions for some items amounted to only a few cents, but overall they reduced store margins dramatically. WEO margins ran between 9 and 13 percent, compared to average supermarket margins of 20 to 22 percent.

A&P promoted the new strategy with a heavy advertising campaign and a profusion of signs and banners in each WEO store. It hoped that the low prices would lure more customers and that volume would rise fast enough to more than offset the lower margins.

Competitive reactions

The good news for A&P was that its WEO strategy did produce a sales volume increase of $800 million and a 1 percent increase in market share in 1972. The bad news was that the volume gain did not make up for the reduction in margins. The firm lost more than $51 million for the year.

One reason A&P's substantial price cuts did not attract more new customers and greater volume was because its major competitors reacted quickly and aggressively. Firms such as Safeway were already more efficient than A&P due to their newer, larger stores and more modern distribution facilities. Consequently, they could meet or beat all of A&P's price cuts, match A&P's volume and market share gains, and still remain profitable.

Other major chains such as Jewel successfully bucked the WEO campaign by strengthening their competitive position in nonprice areas. Jewel extended store hours from 8 A.M. to midnight, stocked a greater variety of nonfood items, and added frills like free bus transportation for elderly shoppers.

Most of the sales gains achieved by A&P and its large competitors came at the expense of smaller chains that did not have the economies of scale or the financial resources to match the WEO price cuts. Because A&P was the largest grocer in the world, however, those small competitors were in a good position to claim that the WEO campaign was anticompetitive and illegal. In fact, several competitors filed lawsuits.

The consequences

A&P was beset on all sides: by stockholder pressure to cut losses, by competitors' lawsuits, and by an inflationary economy that brought rapid increases in food costs. It ended the price war in early 1973 by returning margins to normal levels, although the WEO signs and advertising continued promi-

continued

concluded

nently. The question was whether the volume gains it had achieved with WEO would last. Unfortunately, time proved the strategy a failure. Sales did rise to $6.7 billion; and profits reached $12.2 million with the return to higher prices in 1973. But in 1974 the firm lost a whopping $157 million, was unseated as the sales leader in grocery retailing by Safeway, and was slapped with a $32.7 million settlement in a price-fixing suit.

In spite of efforts to prune its oldest and least efficient stores and correct its other operating problems, the firm continued to lose share and bleed red ink. Many A&P shareholders were eager to bail out and, when West Germany's largest grocery retailer tendered an offer in 1979, George Huntington Hartford's proud tea company fell into foreign hands.

By the late 1980s, A&P was in the black with over 1,200 stores generating some $9 billion in sales. This was achieved by closing hundreds of obsolete stores, renovating 75 percent of the remainder, building 100 new ones, and acquiring some 400 others. A&P's current merchandising strategy is to provide a supermarket for all the various kinds of shoppers: conventional A&Ps (called Superfresh in some cities) for middle-class shoppers; warehouse-style Sav-A-Centers for economy-minded shoppers; and Future Stores, which feature gourmet foods and electronic services for exclusive neighborhoods. Despite all these changes, however, the company trails the industry by $199 in sales per square foot and in sales per store per week—$130,000 versus the $206,500 national average. A&P also lags the industry in store size, inventory turnover, and pretax profit margins.

STRATEGIC PRICING ISSUES

A&P's disastrous experience with its price cutting program illustrates a basic tenet of business and marketing strategy: **a quick change in a single element of the marketing mix cannot overcome basic and pervasive competitive weaknesses in a poorly conceived—or poorly executed—strategy.** In some cases, short-term price cuts may be needed for a troubled firm to survive and buy time to shore up its basic strategic and operational weaknesses. In A&P's case, however, its price-cutting approach actually made it more difficult to repair its underlying shortcomings. Fewer revenue dollars were available to remodel aging stores, build larger and more efficient stores in growing neighborhoods, upgrade management talent, and otherwise improve the firm's ability to attract customers and operate efficiently.

A&P compounded a number of mistakes with its decision to launch its WEO program; and they all amounted to violations of a principle we have preached in several earlier chapters. The new pricing program **did not fit with either the firm's internal capabilities or the constraints imposed by the external environment.** Internally, the low-price strategy failed to resolve the more basic weaknesses of an unfocused and poorly implemented business strategy. And it ignored the fact that A&P was *not* the most efficient grocery retailer in its markets. Thus, it would have been impossible for the firm to win a prolonged price war.

Externally, the low-price program did fit the desires of many older and lower-income consumers in A&P's market areas. And it was successful in attracting $800 million in additional sales. Unfortunately, population was declining in the low-income neighborhoods where many A&P stores were located. That, plus the limited disposable incomes of many of their customers (and potential customers), made it difficult to generate enough additional volume to offset the lower margins.[2] Still, the WEO program might have lured enough new customers if other factors in the environment had not changed. What *should* have been unthinkable, though, was A&P's assumption that its competitors would allow such a threat to go unchallenged. Indeed, the aggressive responses of competitors on both price and nonprice dimensions—and an increasingly inflationary economy and constraints imposed by the antitrust laws—sealed the doom of the WEO program.

All of this suggests that pricing decisions must be based on a careful analysis of both internal and external factors. The next section of this chapter examines the steps in the **price setting process.** Then we examine the decisions involved in adapting prices to variations in market circumstances. The last section of the chapter is concerned with issues involved in initiating and responding to competitive price changes.

THE PRICE SETTING PROCESS

Price has not always been one of the most critical elements of a firm's marketing strategy. During the first two thirds of this century, rapid population growth fueled steadily increasing demand. Economic growth pushed up disposable incomes. Rapid technological change produced myriad new and differentiated products. During that period, nonprice factors—product design, good distribution, and effective advertising and promotion—were often the most important determinants of sales success. Indeed, one survey

---

[2] One analyst estimates that, given the low contribution margins and the variable labor costs involved, A&P would have needed to gain a 33 percent volume increase—or an additional $1 billion in revenue growth over what they actually achieved in 1972—just to break even. See Thomas T. Nagle, *The Strategy and Tactics of Pricing,* p. 125.

during the 1960s found that marketing executives did not rate price among the top five variables critical to a firm's marketing success.[3]

In recent years, however, things have changed dramatically in many industries. Extended periods of inflation, slower population growth, the maturing of many basic industries, and the increased aggressiveness of low-cost global competitors have made many markets more price competitive. Indeed, a recent survey ranked price and price competition as the number one problem facing marketers in the mid-1980s.[4]

Important considerations in setting a price

A manager's pricing freedom is constrained by a number of factors (see Exhibit 14–1). First, the firm's costs determine the *floor* to the range of feasible prices—at least for anything other than the very short term. A company obviously must cover its costs in the long run to make a profit and

EXHIBIT 14 ♦ 1

Major considerations in setting a price

Price too high; little or no demand

↑

Price ceiling

• Nature of demand in target market

• Business and marketing strategy

Range of feasible prices

• Product differentiation

• Competitors' prices

• Prices of substitutes

• Product costs

Price floor

↓

Price too low; no profit possible

---

[3] Jon G. Udell, "How Important Is Pricing in Competitive Strategy?" *Journal of Marketing*, January 1964, pp. 44–48.

[4] "Segmentation Strategies Create New Problems among Marketers," *Marketing News*, March 28, 1986, p. 1.

survive. At the other extreme, the price sensitivity of demand for the product or service determines the *ceiling* for the range of acceptable prices. Beyond some price level most potential customers seek less costly substitutes or simply do without the product or service. Regent Air discovered this when it attempted to sell luxury flights from Los Angeles to New York at more than $1,000 one way.[5]

Where should managers set a product's price within the range of feasible prices? There are a number of ways to calculate a price; but whichever one is used should take situational factors into account. Such factors include (1) the business strategy and the other components of the marketing mix; (2) the extent to which the product is perceived to differ from competitive offerings in quality or level of customer service; (3) competitors' costs and prices; and (4) the availability and prices of possible substitutes.

A step-by-step procedure

Given the variety of factors to consider when setting a price, the following paragraphs describe—and Exhibit 14–2 diagrams—a step-by-step procedure for managers to follow. This process is particularly appropriate for first-time pricing decisions—as when a firm introduces a new product or enters a bid for nonroutine contract work. It includes several steps involving detailed analyses of demand, costs, and the competition. First, however, managers should establish a pricing objective consistent with the firm's business and marketing strategies.

Strategic pricing objectives

The strategic pricing objective should reflect what the firm hopes to accomplish with the product or service in its target market. When the business strategy, the target market, and the positioning strategy for the product are all clearly defined, then formulating objectives and policies for the marketing program elements—including price—can be relatively simple. For instance, Cadillac's Allanté is a luxurious two-seat sport convertible designed to appeal to upscale consumers and to compete with the most prestigious European models. Its relatively high $55,000 base price is consistent with the car's prestige positioning and target customers' high disposable incomes.

The business strategy, market positioning, and marketing program elements should be consistent with one another and fit the circumstances the product faces within the firm and in its target market. We examine marketing objectives for different market and competitive situations, and their implications for the marketing mix components in more detail in Chapters 19, 20, and 21. But to clarify the role of price in different marketing programs, we

---

[5] Horace Sutton, "Nothing but Blue Skies," *Madison Avenue*, June 1984, p. 72.

EXHIBIT   14 ◆2

The price setting decision process

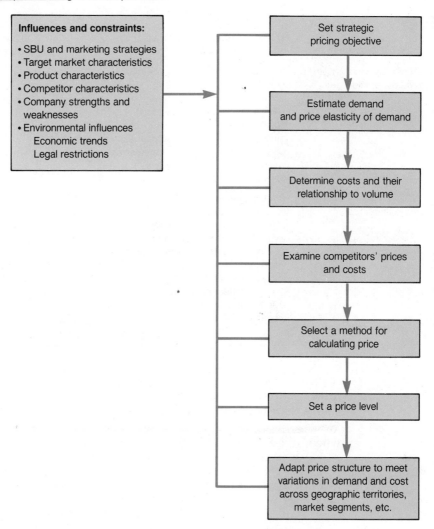

Influences and constraints:

• SBU and marketing strategies
• Target market characteristics
• Product characteristics
• Competitor characteristics
• Company strengths and
   weaknesses
• Environmental influences
      Economic trends
      Legal restrictions

Set strategic
pricing objective

Estimate demand
and price elasticity of demand

Determine costs and their
relationship to volume

Examine competitors' prices
and costs

Select a method for
calculating price

Set a price level

Adapt price structure to meet
variations in demand and cost
across geographic territories,
market segments, etc.

discuss some strategic pricing objectives next and summarize them in Exhibit 14–3. The exhibit also suggests the conditions under which each is appropriate and the implications for choosing a price level within the range of feasible prices.

Maximize sales growth

When a firm is an early entrant into a new product-market with the potential for substantial future growth, its objective may be to maximize its product's rate of sales growth (in units). This suggests it should set a relatively low

EXHIBIT 14 ◆3

Strategic pricing objectives

Objective	Conditions where most appropriate	Implications for relative price level
Maximize sales growth and penetration	Product-market is in introductory or growth stage of life cycle; firm is early entrant; target customers are sensitive to price; firm has low-cost position and is pursuing a low-cost business strategy; firm can gain experience-curve effects with increasing volume; low price may preempt potential competitors.	Set relatively low price—slightly above costs; penetration pricing policy aimed at winning new customers, expanding realized demand, and capturing as large a market share as possible.
Maintain quality or service differentiation	Product market is in growth or maturity stage of life cycle; firm's offering is perceived to have a quality or service advantage over competitive offerings; firm does extensive advertising to maintain the product's quality image; firm has high costs; firm is pursuing differentiated defender strategy; target customers are relatively insensitive to price.	Set price high relative to competitors to cover high production, distribution, and advertising costs; price high to reinforce prestige image.

price to attract as many new customers as quickly as possible and to capture a large share of the total market before it becomes crowded with competitors. This low-priced strategy is called **penetration pricing**. It is appropriate when, in addition to a large market:

1. Target customers are relatively sensitive to price.
2. The firm's costs are low compared to competitors' and the SBU is pursuing a low-cost strategy.
3. Production and distribution costs per unit are likely to fall substantially with increasing volume.
4. Low prices may discourage potential competitors from entering the market.

Texas Instruments (TI) has been a consistent practitioner of volume-based penetration pricing over the years. TI entered a variety of product categories during the 1970s—including digital watches, calculators, and personal computers. It built large and efficient plants, set prices as low as possible to build growth and market share, then cut prices further as costs fell with rising volume to preempt or drive out competitors. In each case, TI enjoyed early success only to be blindsided by uncontrollable events. In all three businesses, competitors undercut TI's low-cost position and experi-

EXHIBIT 14♦3

(concluded)

Objective	Conditions where most appropriate	Implications for relative price level
Maximize current profit		
♦ Skimming	Product-market is in introductory or early growth stage of life cycle; firm is the first entrant; firm is pursuing a prospector strategy; firm has limited capacity; advanced technology or other barriers prevent immediate entry by competitors.	Set price very high to appeal to only the most price-insensitive customer segment; as market matures and competitors enter, firm can (a) reduce price to attract new segments, or (b) withdraw from the product-market.
♦ Harvesting	Product-market is in late maturity or decline stage of life cycle; firm is pursuing differentiated defender strategy; there is no basis (e.g., product improvements, increased promotion) to sustain product demand or competitive position into the future; product is cash cow funding growth in other product-markets.	Set price to maintain margins and maximize profit or return on investment even though some customers may switch to competitive brands or substitutes.
Survival	Firm's product has a weak competitive position, but major shortcomings are correctable; firm needs to buy time and maintain cash flow to make necessary adjustments; product-market is still in growth or maturity stage of life cycle.	Reduce price, perhaps even below total cost, as long as price covers variable costs and makes a contribution to overhead.
Social objectives	Firm is a not-for-profit organization; costs are subsidized in part by tax revenues or contributions; one or more segments need the product or service but are unwilling or unable to pay full costs.	Set low price, perhaps below total cost for some segments, to stimulate or subsidize demand.

ence-curve advantages by shifting to off-shore production in countries with low wage rates, such as Korea and Hong Kong. In addition, consumer tastes changed in some of TI's markets. Many customers soon lost interest in low-cost digital watches. They increased their demand for more sophisticated, stylish, and expensive timepieces that reflected their individual tastes and social status.[6] TI's problems reflect a major risk inherent in using low prices

---

[6] Faye Rice, "Wooing Aging Baby-Boomers," *Fortune*, February 1, 1988, pp. 68–77.

to achieve maximum sales growth in the short term as a base for future profits. If market, competitive, or technological conditions change, those future profits may never be realized.

Maintain quality or service differentiation

When a firm has a strong competitive position based on superior product quality or customer service, its primary pricing objective is to generate sufficient revenue to maintain that advantage. Such a firm usually asks a premium price for its product for two reasons: First, it needs additional revenue to cover the R&D, production, distribution, and advertising costs it takes to maintain both the reality and the perception of superior quality or service. Second, customers are usually willing to pay more for a superior offering. A premium price policy is appropriate when the product's SBU pursues a differentiated defender strategy, and when target customers are more sensitive to variations in product quality or service than to price.

Firms with higher quality product lines that require more expensive materials and production processes, heavy R&D expenditures, and new-product introductions can charge prices that typically exceed the higher costs. Consumers unfamiliar with a new product may use the higher price as an indicator of higher quality. Further, a company with a reputation for high quality can charge higher prices because high quality decreases the elasticity of demand.[7]

The basic rationale is that a high price is consistent with the other marketing mix variables in implementing a quality or service differentiation strategy. A high price supports increased product development efforts, more effective distribution systems, and more extensive advertising and promotion efforts involved in such a strategy. Empirical findings illustrate this tendency toward internal consistency among marketing mix elements—including price. In a study of 227 consumer products businesses, Farris and Reibstein found that brands with product quality and advertising budgets higher than competitors' could also obtain the highest prices. Conversely, brands with low quality and low advertising expenditures charged the lowest prices. Also, the positive relationship between advertising budgets and prices held most strongly for market-share leaders defending well-established positions, products in the later stages of their life cycles, and low-cost items.[8]

---

[7] Stephen Land, "How Price Premiums and Discounts Affect Performance," *Pimsletter no. 7* (Cambridge, Mass.: The Strategic Planning Institute, 1979); David A. Garvin, *Managing Quality* (New York: Free Press, 1988), pp. 70–74; and Y. K. Shetty, "Product Quality and Competitive Strategy," *Business Horizons*, May–June 1987, pp. 46–52.

[8] Paul W. Farris and David J. Reibstein, "How Prices, Expenditures, and Profits Are Linked," *Harvard Business Review*, November–December 1979, pp. 173–84.

Maximize current profit: skimming

When firms pioneer the development of a new product-market, sometimes their pricing objective is to maximize short-run profits. They adopt a **skimming price policy,** setting the price very high and appealing to only the least price-sensitive segment of potential customers. This can also be accomplished over time, as in "periodic discounting," when the seller prices high at the beginning of each period and low at the end. Examples include off-season travel fares, peak-load pricing by utilities, and markdowns of fashion goods.[9] Skimming is particularly appropriate for businesses pursuing prospector strategies involving investments in the development and commercialization of a stream of new products. Such businesses may not have the production capacity to fill a large initial demand for any one new product. They must try to recoup their development costs quickly so they can fund the next generation of new-product ideas. Skimming works best when the new product involves proprietary technology, when the higher price reinforces the image of a superior product, or when other barriers discourage competitors from quickly entering the market and undercutting the pioneer's price. Skimming is most relevant to a small market because a large market is more apt to attract competitors.

As the product-market matures and the entry of competitors becomes a threat, the pioneer can adopt one of two strategic responses: Some firms begin to reduce their prices—often by introducing lower-cost versions of the original product—to appeal to broader, more price-sensitive segments of the market and build market share before competitors arrive on the scene. This is the approach followed by Polaroid over the past several decades. Each time the firm introduced a new camera, it first marketed a high-priced version and then gradually brought out simpler, lower-priced models to attract a wider range of customers and discourage potential competitors. When competitors enter and prices and margins begin to fall, other firms adopt the second strategic response and simply withdraw from the product-market. They usually do this by licensing their brand to another manufacturer or by divesting the business entirely. This is a common strategy among technological innovators like 3M and Du Pont.

Maximize current profit: harvesting

At the other end of the life cycle, some product-markets decline rapidly as customer preferences change or new technologies and substitute products are introduced. Often it is too late to divest the product and earn a reasonable return, so firms facing this situation adopt a **harvesting** strategy to maximize short-term profits before demand for the product disappears. This typically involves cutting marketing, production, and operating costs of the product,

---

[9] Gerald J. Tellis, "Beyond the Many Faces of Price: An Integration of Pricing Strategies," *Journal of Marketing*, October 1986, p. 146.

while setting a relatively high price to maintain margins and maximize profits.[10] The opportunity to accomplish this ideal state depends largely upon exit barriers. If large barriers are present, then competitors will exert a downward pressure on prices. If few barriers are present, then marginal competitors will exit and falling supplies may drive prices up.

The risk of maximizing short-run profits for a declining product is that demand can decline even faster in the long term as price-sensitive customers switch to competing brands or substitute products. Therefore, this is an appropriate strategy only where there is no way—such as by making product improvements or increasing promotion—to sustain market demand and the item's competitive position very far into the future. It is also appropriate when the product is a cash cow funding the development of more rapidly growing product-markets that eventually replace the declining item. Thus, General Foods maintained high margins on Dream Whip dry topping mix in the face of declining demand to fund expansion of its Cool Whip brand's share of the growing frozen toppings market.[11]

Unfortunately, some businesses pursue an objective of maximizing current profit even though the product may have years of stable, or even increasing, demand left. Such a policy is shortsighted. It often leads to a premature decline in market share and volume; and it sacrifices long-term performance for short-run gains.

Survival

Sometimes businesses with an established product in a market expected to grow or experience stable demand well into the future run into trouble due to strategic mistakes, such as failing to adapt to customers' changing desires or to competitive threats, or building excess capacity. If such mistakes are correctable, the firm may adopt a pricing objective of simply keeping the product alive while strategic adjustments are made. Because short-term profits are less important than survival for such products, this situation usually demands a low price to attract enough demand to keep the plant operating and maintain cash flow. So long as the price covers variable costs and at least contributes to fixed costs, the firm may be able to buy time to correct its competitive weaknesses. This was the objective behind the large rebates that Lee Iacocca offered buyers when he took over as president of the

---

[10] To truly maximize current profit, the product's price should be set exactly at the point where the marginal revenue gained from the last item sold equals the marginal cost of producing and selling that item. In reality, however, many firms do not have adequate knowledge of their demand and cost functions to determine the profit maximizing price with such precision. This is especially true when market and competitive conditions are rapidly changing.

[11] Fred Wiersema, "General Foods Corporation—Dessert Toppings Strategy," Case 9-580-046 (Cambridge, Mass.: Harvard Business School, 1979).

ailing Chrysler Corporation in the early 1980s. In a different yet related sense, Eastern Airlines, crippled by a machinist strike for most of its routes, cut its Washington–New York shuttle fares from $99 to $49 one way. While Eastern was able to run a full shuttle schedule, even this drastic cut didn't turn out crowds.[12] Eastern eventually filed for bankruptcy and sold its shuttle to Donald Trump.

Social objectives

Some organizations may forgo possible profits—at least among some price-sensitive customer segments—by offering a low price to those customers to achieve some broader social purpose. This is most common among not-for-profit organizations like performing arts organizations and public hospitals—especially if subsidized by government agencies, foundations, or private contributions and not relying on sales as their sole source of revenue. In reality, they are simply shifting the price "reduction" burden to organizations or individual contributors who are willing to subsidize one or more price-sensitive segments to achieve some social purpose. For example, performing arts organizations often offer substantial discounts to students. This is not just a strategy for building loyal future audiences. It also provides intellectual benefits to a customer group that would otherwise be unable to afford them.

Estimating demand

Demand sets the ceiling on the range of feasible prices for a product. It falls to zero when the price rises too far—or only a small number of people are willing to pay for the product. Even before that ceiling is reached, however, the total number of customers willing to buy during a given period varies according to the price charged. The familiar **demand curve** depicts this variation in the quantity demanded at different prices. (For example, see the demand curves (a) and (b) in Exhibit 14–6 on page 471.)

In most cases there is an inverse relation between a product's price and the quantity demanded: the higher the price, the less people want to buy. Thus, the typical demand curve has a negative, or downward, slope. However, prestigious products (such as expensive wines and liquors) and those whose quality is difficult to objectively judge sometimes have positively sloping demand curves. Some customers use price as an indicator of the prestige or quality of such products; and they are induced to buy more as the price increases.

---

[12] Doug Carroll and Jim Fresche, "Eastern Adds Flights, Loses Passengers," *USA Today,* March 14, 1989, p. 1B.

EXHIBIT 14 ◆ 4

Factors affecting customers' sensitivity to price

Buyer's perceptions and preferences	
Unique-value effect	Customers are less price-sensitive when they perceive the product or service provides unique benefits; there are no acceptable substitutes.
Price-quality effect	Customers are less price-sensitive when they perceive the product or service offers high quality, prestige, or exclusiveness.
Buyer's awareness of and attitude toward alternatives	
Substitute-awareness effect	Customers are less price-sensitive when they are relatively unaware of competing brands or substitute products or services.
Difficult-comparison effect	Customers are less price-sensitive when it is difficult to objectively compare the quality or performance of alternative brands or substitutes.
Sunk-investment effect	Customers are less price-sensitive when the purchase is necessary to gain full benefit from assets previously bought.
Buyer's ability to pay	
Total-expenditure effect	Customers are less price-sensitive when their expenditure for the product or service is a relatively low proportion of their total income.
End-benefit effect	Customers—particularly industrial buyers purchasing raw materials or component parts—are less price-sensitive when the expenditure is a relatively small proportion of the total cost of the end product.
Shared-cost effect	Customers are less price-sensitive when part of the cost of the product or service is borne by another party (e.g., when part of the cost of medical services is covered by health insurance, or when a salesperson's travel costs are covered by an expense account).
Inventory effect	Customers are less price-sensitive in the short run when they cannot store large quantities of the product as a hedge against future price increases.

Source: Thomas T. Nagel, *The Strategy and Tactics of Pricing*, © 1987, pp. 73–76. Adapted by permission of Prentice-Hall, Inc., Englewood Cliffs, N.J.

Factors affecting customers' price sensitivity

The demand curve sums the reactions of many potential buyers to the alternative prices that might be charged for a product. The curve's degree of slope reflects the fact that different buyers have different sensitivities to the product's price.

Nagle identified specific factors influencing variations in sensitivity to price across customers and products. These factors are summarized in Exhibit 14–4. Each factor reflects three more basic phenomena that determine customers' willingness and ability to pay for a good or service. First, buyers' willingness to pay a given price for a product is influenced by their perceptions and preferences: their needs, desires, awareness of, and attitude toward, the item in question.

Second, the price, availability, and attractiveness of alternative brands and substitute products affect buyers' willingness to buy the product. So do the prices of complementary items that customers must buy to gain full value from the product. For example, the high price of gasoline in the mid-1970s reduced consumers' willingness to pay high prices for large automobiles. Finally, the size of their incomes relative to the price influences customers' ability to pay for a product or service. An example of how one firm determined customers' price sensitivity to a new herbicide is given in Exhibit 14–5.

Price elasticity of demand

The larger the proportion of price-sensitive customers in a product's market, the more sensitive overall demand is to a change in the product's price. This degree of responsiveness of demand to a price change is referred to as the **price elasticity of demand.** Consider, for example, demand curve a in Exhibit 14–6. Note that the slope of this demand curve is relatively flat. Thus, a price increase from P_1 to P_2 leads to a relatively large drop in the quantity demanded from Q_1 to Q_2. This means that demand for the product is **price elastic.** For demand curve b the curve's slope is relatively steep. Therefore, the same price increase leads to a relatively small decline in the quantity demanded from Q_1' to Q_2'. Thus, demand for the product in diagram b is **price inelastic.**

EXHIBIT   14 ◆ 5

Determining price sensitivity for a new herbicide

A company had developed a strong potent herbicide, but didn't know if it could charge a high enough price to meet its profit objectives in the highly competitive herbicide market. To find out, it undertook a study to determine the new product's sensitivity to competitive price moves. After defining the new product's target market in terms of crops planted, 601 soybean and cotton farmers who dedicated at least 200 acres to these crops and who had used herbicides during the past growing season were surveyed. Respondents were asked to assess the relative importance of the different attributes they used to select a herbicide (their choice criteria). Next, they were asked to evaluate the major brands of herbicides on these same attributes. This information served as the basis for estimating the price elasticity of each brand, including the cross-elasticities between all brands. The results showed that price was not the only determinant of purchase—that value in terms of extent of control over the four most common weeds was also important. The study also revealed that some farmers equated low price with low quality. The end result was that the company stayed with its original pricing strategy.

Source: Reprinted from Diane Schneidman, "Research Method Designed to Determine Price for New Products, Line Extensions," *Marketing News,* October 23, 1987, p. 11. Published by the American Marketing Association.

The following formula calculates the price elasticity of demand for a product or service:

$$\text{Price elasticity of demand } (E) = \frac{\textbf{Percent change in quantity demanded}}{\textbf{Percent change in price}}$$

If, for instance, a seller raised the price of a product by 2 percent and demand subsequently fell by 6 percent, the price elasticity of demand for that product would be -3 (with the minus sign reflecting the inverse relationship between price and demand), indicating substantial elasticity. Conversely, if a 2 percent price increase produced only a 1 percent decline in the quantity demanded, then price elasticity is $-1/2$, indicating that demand is inelastic. If a 2 percent price increase leads to a 2 percent decline in quantity, price elasticity is **unitary.** In such a case the seller's total revenue stays the same because the smaller quantity sold is offset by the higher price.

The relationship between price elasticity and total revenue is of interest to marketing managers. When demand for a product is elastic, the manager might consider lowering the price (but not below costs). Assuming that other variables such as the prices of substitute products do not change, the total revenue would increase. On the other hand, the manager of a product with inelastic demand might consider raising its price to increase total revenue, because the increased revenue per unit would more than offset the decline in volume.

Tellis studied price elasticity across more than 200 different brands and markets. His findings indicate price elasticity is significantly negative and some eight times larger than advertising elasticity. However, his analysis suffered in its failure to take into account quality, the presence of which should make markets less price sensitive.[13] Also, the degree of price elasticity in the demand for a product often depends on the direction and size of the price change, however. Demand may be inelastic for a small price change, but elastic for a more dramatic change. For example, after years of slow sales, the laptop computer has become inexpensive enough to trigger a large market—one approaching $1 billion. A portable full-function machine that cost $8,000 a few years ago now sells for less than $2,000.

Demand may also be inelastic for a price cut, but elastic for a price increase of similar magnitude. Long-run elasticity may also be different from elasticity in the short run. Buyers may stay with a current supplier after a price increase because the increase is too small to notice, or they are preoccupied with other issues, or simply because changing suppliers takes time. But eventually they may switch to a lower-cost alternative. In such a case, demand is more elastic in the long run than in the short term. Such differ-

---

[13] Gerard Tellis, "The Price Elasticity of Selective Demand: A Meta-Analysis of Econometric Models of Sales," *Journal of Marketing Research*, November 1988, pp. 331–41.

ences between long- and short-run elasticities suggest that marketers should not be too hasty in judging the total effect of a price change.

Of course, price elasticities vary widely across product categories and across brands within a product category. For example, experiments suggest that brands of cola, coffee, and snack and specialty foods are generally price elastic, with $E = -1.5$ to -2.5. Most categories of fruits and vegetables, on the other hand, are price inelastic with Es of about -0.8.[14] Similarly, Neslin and Shoemaker found that the overall ready-to-eat cereal market is price inelastic ($E = -0.36$); but that the presweetened cereals within the category are price elastic ($E = -1.97$). They concluded that when prices of presweetened cereals are raised, consumers substitute low-sugar and granola cereals rather than skipping cereals entirely.[15] This helps explain why cereal manufacturers like Kellogg and General Mills maintain product lines with a balanced mix of presweetened, low-sugar, and granola brands.

EXHIBIT   14 ♦ 6

Elastic, inelastic, and shifting demand curves

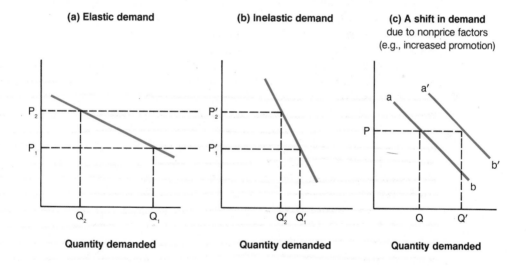

(a) Elastic demand   **(b) Inelastic demand**   **(c) A shift in demand**
due to nonprice factors
(e.g., increased promotion)

---

[14] For example, see Ronald C. Curhan, "The Effects of Merchandising and Temporary Promotional Activities on the Sales of Fresh Fruits and Vegetables in Supermarkets," *Journal of Marketing Research*, August 1974, pp. 286–94; and Gerald J. Eskin and Penny H. Baron, "Effects of Price and Advertising in Test-Market Experiments," *Journal of Marketing Research*, November 1977, pp. 499–508.

[15] Scott A. Neslin and Robert W. Shoemaker, "Using a Natural Experiment to Estimate Price Elasticity: The 1974 Sugar Shortage and the Ready-to-Eat Cereal Market," *Journal of Marketing*, Winter 1983, pp. 44–57.

Methods for estimating demand

Many firms—particularly larger ones—attempt to estimate the demand curves for their products through marketing research. This is easier said than done, though, for two reasons: First, laboratory or test-market experiments can provide insights into the price-demand relationship for a product; but such methods usually do not reflect the likely reactions of competitors to different prices or changes in price over time. Underestimating the aggressiveness and impact of such reactions is one reason A&P's WEO program failed so dramatically.

A second problem researchers encounter when trying to empirically estimate demand curves is that *effects of nonprice factors*—such as changes in economic conditions or in other components of the marketing mix—must be controlled or measured. Changes in nonprice variables affect demand by causing the demand curve to shift. An increase in the product's advertising budget or in the disposable income of the population, for example, might shift the demand curve for the product to the right, as shown in Exhibit 14–6. A shift in the demand curve from ab to $a'b'$ causes the quantity demanded to increase from Q to Q' even though the price stays the same. Thus, if a firm conducted a test market in which it increased advertising expenditures at the same time it lowered prices, researchers could not tell how much increased volume was due to the sensitivity of demand to price and how much was a result of the heavier advertising.

Keeping these two problems in mind, there are a number of ways for marketers to estimate a product's demand curve. One approach is to survey a sample of consumers, or bring them into a laboratory setting, and ask them how much of the product they would buy at different possible prices. The artificiality of this approach, however, and the fact that respondents are not required to "put their money where their mouth is" leads to questions about the validity of the findings.[16] A more realistic experiment conducted by Bennett and Wilkinson took place in an actual retail setting. They systematically varied the prices of several products sold in a discount store and observed the sales results.[17] Multiple test markets can also be used to estimate the demand curve for a new product. The firm can set different prices in test cities matched in economic conditions and population demographics; then they can observe differences in quantities sold across those cities. The expense of such multiple test markets, however, limits their feasibility to only the largest firms and consumer products with great future potential. Nagle reviews these and other demand estimation approaches in more detail in his recent book.[18]

---

[16] John R. Nevin, "Laboratory Experiments for Estimating Consumer Demand—A Validation Study," *Journal of Marketing Research*, August 1974, pp. 261–68.

[17] Sidney Bennett and J. B. Wilkinson, "Price-Quantity Relationships and Price Elasticity under In-Store Experimentation," *Journal of Business Research*, January 1974, pp. 30–34.

[18] Thomas T. Nagle, *The Strategy and Tactics of Pricing*, chap. 11.

Estimating costs

Demand sets the ceiling on the range of feasible prices a firm might charge for a product; but costs determine the floor. The product's price must cover the costs of producing and marketing it, at least in the long run, as well as a fair return for the resources invested and the risk assumed by the company.

Cost categories

A firm's costs take two forms: fixed and variable. **Fixed costs** (or **overhead**) are constant in the short term, regardless of production volume or sales revenue. They include rent, interest, heat, executive salaries, and functional departments—such as purchasing and R&D—needed to support the products made by the firm. Because total fixed costs remain constant in the short term regardless of volume, the **fixed cost per unit** of a product declines as a firm produces and sells more of the product in a given period.

Variable costs vary in total magnitude directly with the level of production; but they remain constant *per unit*, regardless of how many units are produced. They involve such things as the costs of materials, packaging, and labor needed to produce each unit of the product.

Total costs equal the sum of fixed and variable costs for a given level of production. The product's price must cover this total cost figure—divided by the number of units produced—if it is to be economically viable in the long run.

Measuring costs

The firm's cost accounting system provides managers with information about the fixed and variable costs associated with each of the company's products. Even though it is a relatively simple matter to measure each product's variable costs, fixed costs present a problem. The analyst has the option of using full costing (which involves allocating indirect costs) or direct costing (often referred to as the contribution margin approach because it takes into account only variable costs). These topics are covered in depth in Chapter 24, and will not be discussed here.

Examining the impact on a product's contribution is a useful way to evaluate the economic viability of marketing program components directly linked to a specific product. However, it does not provide enough detailed information for a manager to judge whether a given price is adequate to cover the total costs incurred by that product. Consequently, many firms are beginning to revise their cost accounting systems to provide more accurate product cost information to managers. They often develop multiple systems for financial reporting, cost control, and product cost measurement purposes.[19]

---

[19] For example, see H. Thomas Johnson and Robert S. Kaplan, *Relevance Lost: The Rise and Fall of Management Accounting* (Cambridge, Mass.: Harvard Business School Press, 1987).

Cost and volume relationships

A product's average cost per unit—and the price necessary to cover that cost—varies with the quantity produced. Managers should take two different volume-cost relationships into account when making pricing decisions. The first relationship involves **economies of scale.** In the short run, scale economies result from more complete use of available capacity. In the long run, companies can gain further economies by constructing larger and more efficient facilities. For example, suppose that General Electric has a dishwasher plant designed to produce 1,000 dishwashers per day. Exhibit 14–7(a) shows the U-shaped short-run average cost (SRAC) curve typically associated with such a fixed-size plant. The average cost per unit is high if few units are produced; but it falls as production approaches the plant's capacity, because fixed costs are spread over more units. This is why excess capacity is anathema to the profitability and competitive cost position of a product—particularly in mature, commodity-like product categories where margins tend to be low. If, however, GE tries to produce more than 1,000 units in its plant, average costs per unit would rise. The overworked machinery would break down more often, workers would get in each other's way, and other inefficiencies would occur.

In the long term, if GE believes that demand justifies producing more than 1,000 units per day it would be better off building a larger, more efficient plant. Exhibit 14–7(b) shows the increasing economies of scale associated with such a plant. The SRAC curve of a plant with a targeted capacity of 2,000 units per day is lower than that of the 1,000-unit plant. Consequently, the long-run average cost (LRAC) falls as firms build bigger plants. At very large capacity levels, however, LRAC typically begins to rise because of the increasing administrative and coordination costs associated with very large-scale production.

The second volume-cost relationship involves the **experience curve**—the fall in production and marketing costs per unit as a firm gains accumulated experience. Regardless of a firm's plant size, its average costs per unit decline as it gains experience over time. Its production workers discover efficient shortcuts; procurement costs fall; and the accumulated impact of past advertising and marketing efforts may enable the firm to succeed with smaller per-unit marketing expenditures. We discussed these experience curve effects on product costs—and their marketing implications at different stages of the product's life cycle—in Chapter 8.

Analyzing competitors' costs and prices

To achieve a desired strategic competitive position for a product or service in its target market, the manager must take competitors' costs and prices into account. To successfully implement a low-cost strategy, for instance, the manager must be sure that the product's costs are truly lower than any competitor's, and that those lower costs are reflected in the product's rela-

EXHIBIT   14 ◆ 7

Costs per unit and the economies of scale

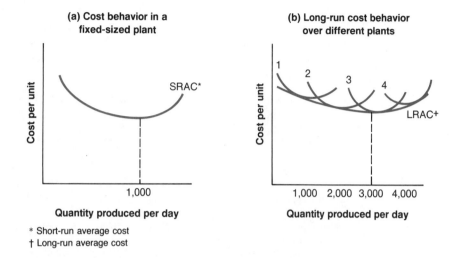

**(a) Cost behavior in a
fixed-sized plant**

**(b) Long-run cost behavior
over different plants**

* Short-run average cost
† Long-run average cost

tive price. Thus, the manager needs to learn and track the price, cost, and relative quality of each competitor's offer.

An example of the importance of tracking competitors' costs and prices is provided by Sears, Roebuck. Sears recently announced a change in its pricing strategy to combat discount stores. At an ever-increasing rate, consumers visited Sears only when the giant retailer ran sales. In 1988, only 45 percent of Sears' domestic revenues came from items sold at their regular price. In some months, Sears was lowering prices on as many as 8,000 items. The new pricing strategy is what the trade calls "everyday low pricing"— something Wal-Mart has long practiced. Thus, Fruit of the Loom men's briefs now sell for the same price as at Wal-Mart; a DieHard battery is priced 14 percent lower than before; and a child's car seat sells for 31 percent less than the old price. Sears test marketed its new price strategy in Wichita, Kansas, before going national with it in all of its 825 U.S. stores (see Exhibit 14–8). Unfortunately, Sears' costs are higher than its competitors. But because the company's managers were aware of this fact, they were able to make some adjustment in Sears' operations to make this new strategy more viable. The firm greatly reduced the number of items in many lines of merchandise to reduce inventory costs and increase turnover. Also, it increased the percentage of national brands it carries to about 40 percent (compared to 15 percent before the change)[20] to avoid price comparisons with discounters' off-brand merchandise.

---

[20] Francine Schwadel and Michael J. McCarthy, "New Sears Strategy on Display in Wichita," *The Wall Street Journal,* November 17, 1988, p. B1; and "Sears Switches Pricing Strategy to Combat Discounters," *The Wall Street Journal,* November 1988, p. B1.

EXHIBIT 14 ◆ 8

New look for prices at Sears

a. Sears prices in Wichita, Kansas, test market, before and after new pricing strategy was implemented on Sept. 30, 1988.

Item	Old regular price	Old sale price	New price
One-Step infant car seat	$ 64.99	$ 49.99	$ 44.96
Matchmate twin sheet sets	16.99	11.99	11.99
Kenmore gas grill	199.99	159.99	159.49
Hug-Alon hosiery	1.79	1.29	1.36
Conair hair dryer	19.99	16.99	17.96
Kenmore freezer	319.99	299.99	299.99

b. New Sears prices vs. the competition

Item	Sears	Penney	Wal-Mart	Ward	Target
Levi 501 jeans men	$ 19.96	$ 19.99	N.A.	N.A.	N.A.
Vanderbilt one-ounce eau de toilette spray	15.96	15.50	$ 13.84	$ 15.50	$ 13.95
Fruit of the Loom men's underwear (three-pack)	3.96	N.A.	3.96	N.A.	3.99
Prestone antifreeze	7.62	N.A.	7.47	7.99	7.99
Sealy mattress queen size	549.95	557.75	N.A.	549.99	N.A.
Lego basic building set	9.99	N.A.	9.57	9.99	9.99
Etch a Sketch	8.99	N.A.	6.97	8.99	8.99
Monopoly	8.99	N.A.	8.97	9.99	6.99

N.A. = Not available

Source: Francine Schwadel and Michael J. McCarthy, "New Sears Strategy on Display in Wichita," The Wall Street Journal, November 17, 1988, p. B1.

As we saw in Chapter 7, there are a number of ways to collect and analyze such information. The firm's own salespeople or periodic store checks can track competitive price information. Market surveys can collect customers' perceptions of the relative quality and value of competitive offerings. Competitors' costs, however, are harder to estimate. But past employees of competitors, joint suppliers, or the use of reverse engineering to disassemble competing products and estimate the cost of materials and production processes can often provide such information.

Methods for setting a price level

By combining all of the demand, cost, and competitor information collected in the preceding steps, managers can arrive at a price for the product or service. Given the complexity of the concerns involved in setting a price—and the frequent incompleteness of information about demand and costs—managers often rely on simplifying heuristics or rules of thumb to set list prices. Although these "practical" pricing methods are unlikely to produce an optimal—or profit maximizing—price, they are all based on a set of relevant considerations. These various pricing methods fall into three categories: cost-oriented pricing, competition-oriented pricing, and demand or customer-oriented pricing.

Cost-oriented methods

Perhaps the simplest, and most commonly used, pricing method is to add a standard markup to the cost of the product. This kind of **cost-plus** or **markup pricing** does not explicitly consider the price sensitivity of demand nor the pricing practices of competitors. But it is convenient and easy to apply—important considerations when a firm faces hundreds or thousands of pricing decisions each year, as in the case of retail stores and wholesaling institutions. It is also widely used among firms that must submit competitive bids for a variety of projects, as is the case with construction firms.

The typical procedure for determining price under the markup approach is to first calculate the cost per unit by adding variable cost to fixed costs divided by an expected level of unit sales:

$$\text{Unit cost} = \text{Variable cost} + \frac{\text{Fixed cost}}{\text{Expected unit sales}}$$

To find the price, add a desired markup on retail to the unit cost (or divide unit cost by 1 − the desired percent markup):

$$\text{Markup price} = \frac{\text{Unit cost}}{(1 - \text{Desired percent markup on retail})}$$

Suppose, for instance, that a small-appliance manufacturer produces a line of electric coffee makers and expects to sell 50,000 in the coming period. Fixed costs of $500,000 are associated with producing the coffee makers, and variable costs are $10 per unit. The unit cost for each coffee maker would be:

$$\text{Unit cost} = \$10 + \frac{\$500,000}{50,000} = \$10 + \$10 = \$20$$

Suppose further that the manufacturer wants to earn a markup (or margin on selling price) of 30 percent. The markup price would be:

$$\text{Markup price} = \frac{\$20}{(1 - .30)} = \frac{\$20}{.7} = \underline{\$28.57}$$

This approach largely ignores the price sensitivity of demand. It assumes a level of sales *before* the price is set. Furthermore, if the manager's assumption about likely sales volume is wrong, the desired markup is not achieved. A shortfall in units sold would mean that fixed costs would be spread over fewer units and the realized markup would be smaller than desired.

In the distributive trades, retailers and wholesalers simply add standard markups to what they paid for the item to attain a margin sufficient to cover overhead and provide a profit. These standard markups do not explicitly consider variations in demand. However, they have evolved over time in a way that reflects general variations in price sensitivity across products. In other words, there is a great deal of variability in the size of standard markups across products. In supermarkets, for instance, markups on selling price range from as low as 10 percent on baby foods to more than 50 percent on some toiletries and greeting cards.[21] The products with the lowest markups tend to be frequently purchased, commodity-like items for which many consumers make price comparisons. They also tend to be products for which promotional pricing (special deals and discounts) is frequently used. These facts suggest that the standard margins generally reflect variations in consumers' price sensitivity of demand.

Rate-of-return or **target return pricing** is similar in principle to, but somewhat more sophisticated in practice than, markup pricing. This cost-oriented approach brings one more cost element into the pricing decision; namely, the cost of capital tied up in producing and distributing the product. The objective is to set a price yielding a target rate of return on investment. This pricing approach is common at GM and other automobile companies that price their cars to achieve a target of 15 to 20 percent return on investment. It is also popular with regulated firms—such as public utilities—that must justify their prices by showing that they result in a "fair" return on their invested capital.

Operationally, this pricing approach demands that managers (1) estimate the unit sales volume of the product; (2) figure unit costs (variable costs plus overhead attributable to the product); (3) estimate the amount of capital involved in producing and selling the product; and (4) select a target rate of return on investment. They can then determine the price as follows:

$$\text{Target return price} = \text{Unit cost} + \frac{\text{Desired percent return} \times \text{Capital invested in product}}{\text{Unit sales}}$$

For example, suppose our small-appliance manufacturer has invested $1 million in facilities and equipment to produce and distribute its coffee makers and wants to make a 20 percent return on that investment. The target return price for each coffee maker would be:

$$\text{Target return price} = \$20 + \frac{.20 \times \$1,000,000}{50,000 \text{ units}} = \$20 + \frac{\$200,000}{50,000} = \$24$$

When managers make these estimates accurately, the target return method results in a more rational pricing decision than the simpler markup method. As typically practiced, however, this method does not explicitly consider the interaction between alternative prices and demand.

---

[21] "Supermarket 1986 Sales Manual," *Progressive Grocer*, July 1986.

EXHIBIT 14 ♦9

Break-even chart showing break-even and target return volume

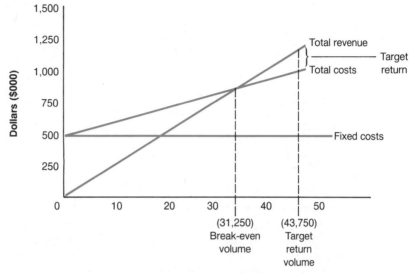

Sales volume in units (000)

What happens if the price is set on the basis of an overly optimistic sales estimate? As with markup pricing, the realized return falls below the target level, because fixed costs have to be covered by a smaller unit volume. The impact of such variations in volume can be examined by preparing a **break-even analysis.** Suppose our appliance manufacturer decided to price its coffee makers at $26. With variable costs of $10 per unit and fixed costs of $500,000, the break-even chart in Exhibit 14–9 indicates that the product's **break-even volume** is 31,250 units—the volume necessary to just cover total costs. To calculate this result, use the following formula:

$$\text{Break-even volume} = \frac{\text{Fixed cost}}{\text{Price} - \text{Variable cost}} = \frac{\$500,000}{\$26 - \$10} = 31,250 \text{ units}$$

If we also consider the $1 million of capital invested in the product and the manufacturer's target return of 20 percent (or $200,000), the chart shows that the firm must sell 43,750 to achieve the desired return. Break-even analysis can also calculate break-even and target return volumes at different price levels. Exhibit 14–10 indicates how these volumes vary for our product example over a range of prices. Break-even analysis, however, suffers from the same limitations as other cost-oriented pricing methods. It does not explicitly consider the price sensitivity of demand or the likely reactions of competitors. Therefore, managers must rely on their own judgment to decide how likely it is that the product's actual volume will reach or exceed the break-even level associated with each alternative price.

EXHIBIT 14 ♦ 10

Break-even and target return volumes for alternative selling prices

Selling price	Fixed costs ($000)	Per-unit average variable cost	Target return ($000)	Break-even volume (units)	Target return volume (units)
$18	$500	$10	$200	62,500	87,500
20	500	10	200	50,000	70,000
24	500	10	200	35,714	50,000
26	500	10	200	31,250	43,750
28	500	10	200	27,778	38,889
30	500	10	200	25,000	35,000

Competition-oriented methods

In some industries companies key their pricing decisions to what competitors are charging and pay less attention to their own costs or demand schedules. (See Exhibit 14–11 for an interesting example of competitive pricing involving U.S. and Japanese car manufacturers.) This is not to say that their prices are always the same as their competitors'; some firms may add a premium or discount their price below the average for the industry. As industry prices change over time, these relationships tend to continue. Such competition-oriented pricing is common in industries where it is difficult to accurately determine unit costs. It is also found in mature industries where little product differentiation and a few strong competitors make it difficult for one firm to change its price without precipitating a competitive reaction. Under such circumstances, a common industry price structure reflects the collective wisdom about what price will yield a fair return and minimizes the chances of a price war jeopardizing the profits of all industry firms.

Firms that pursue competition-oriented pricing approaches do not entirely ignore cost or return on investment considerations. Instead, they try to control costs to make adequate returns at prices consistent with those of competitors. But if this cannot be done (e.g., because the firm is less efficient), the target rate of return may well be the factor that is changed.

In some cases, firms adopt a **going-rate** or **competitive parity** pricing approach, where they try to maintain prices equal to those of one or more major competitors. This is common in oligopolistic industries with little product differentiation and a few large competitors, as in steel, paper, and fertilizer. Price virtually ceases to be a controllable element of the marketing mix under such circumstances. No firm can increase its price without some assurance that others will follow, because most customers would switch to lower-priced competitors. Similarly, a firm would be reluctant to price below the competition lest other companies also cut their prices and reduce profits for all concerned. Consequently, prices are usually quite stable in

EXHIBIT 14 ♦ 11

American car manufacturers raise prices behind Japanese as yen increases

From 1985 to 1988, the yen nearly doubled in value against the dollar, thereby driving up the price of Japanese cars to record levels. The Big Three American firms followed suit, choosing increased profits over increased share. In the mid-1980s, the dollar was worth some 240 yen, which made Japanese cars a bargain here. Then came the weaker dollar, selling for only 120 yen. The Japanese countered by limiting their U.S. sales, resulting in a sell-out even at somewhat higher prices. (The Japanese set prices at a level that will not hurt market share drastically.) U.S. automakers responded by raising their prices— and the market share of domestically produced cars changed very little. Profits of the Big Three totaled $9.5 billion in 1987—a near record—despite a record multitude of consumer incentives. According to a study by the U.S. International Trade Commission, American consumers paid extra billions because competition in the auto industry was curbed.

Source: John Bussey, "Did U.S. Car Makers Err by Raising Prices when the Yen Rose?" *The Wall Street Journal,* April 18, 1988, p. 1.

such industries until a **price leader** decides an increase in industry prices is necessary to meet increased costs and maintain returns.

The ability of a firm to be a price leader whose pricing decisions are emulated by other companies is not determined solely by its size or market share. The leader also tends to be one of the most efficient firms in the industry; that is, one of the last to feel the need for a price increase. Often leaders are also perceived to have good marketing expertise, and have had past success in making price increases "stick." Even so, there is no guarantee that a given price leader can maintain its position over time. "Follower" firms are particularly likely to cut prices below the leader during periods of overcapacity and to increase prices faster than the leader during periods of high inflation. For instance, many members of OPEC refused to abide by the prices urged by Saudi Arabia during the mid-1980s to maintain their own production volumes in the face of softening world demand for oil.

In industries where product quality, service, or availability varies across brands, a firm may still base its pricing on what its competitors are charging, but try to hold its prices either below or above the competition. Such **discount** or **premium price policies** usually reflect differences in positioning strategies. A firm pursuing a low-cost strategy with a product positioned at the low end of the quality spectrum typically tries to maintain a price below most competitors. For example, cut-rate gasoline brands usually sell for five to seven cents a gallon less than the national brands in many large markets. On the other hand, cosmetics firms differentiating their brands on the basis of high quality and social prestige set prices substantially above their mass-market competitors.

Competition-oriented pricing also dominates when firms must engage in

competitive bidding. It is common in the sale of heavy equipment, construction contracts, and government defense projects. Firms submit bids influenced by their expectations of how their competitors will bid as well as by their estimate of the costs and profits involved. The higher its bid, the more profit the firm can make, but the lower its chances of winning the contract. Conversely, the lower its bid, the better its chances of winning, but the lower its potential profits.

The **expected value** of a particular bid describes the net effect of the two opposite effects of price on profit and the probability of winning. Suppose a firm faces a situation where a bid of $100,000 would yield a high probability of winning the contract—say .8—but would produce only a small profit of $5,000. The expected value of such a bid would be .8 × $5,000 = $4,000. On the other hand, a higher bid of $120,000 would have only a .5 chance of winning but would produce $12,500 in profit. The expected value of this bid is $6,250.

Submitting bids that maximize expected value makes sense for large firms that bid on many projects. Such a strategy maximizes total profits in the long run. However, small firms that bid only occasionally, or that need a particular project to stay in business, may be wiser to place bids low enough to have a high probability of winning even though they may not be tremendously profitable.

Customer-oriented methods

Demand or customer-oriented pricing practices focus on the key issues of the sensitivity of demand to variations in price. Once again, firms using such practices do not ignore costs or competitive actions. But they tend to adjust their costs (through product design and reductions in marketing effort) to set prices that reflect customer expectations in their target market. Such practices include customary pricing, price lining, psychological pricing, and promotional pricing. All of these are particularly popular in consumer nondurable product categories where the price sensitivities of thousands of potential consumers must be considered.

In some product categories all manufacturers are compelled to charge a single **customary price** for their product—a price dictated by customer expectations. Candy bars, for example, sold for many years at a customary price of 10 cents. When increasing costs put pressure on manufacturers' margins, they elected to reduce the size of the bar rather than upset customers' expectations by raising the price. Eventually, of course, continuing cost increases made it necessary to increase prices. A similar customary price phenomenon exists with many other consumer convenience goods, such as soft drinks, chewing gum, and certain cosmetics.

Price lining is another common customer-oriented pricing practice, especially among retailers. It involves selling all products in a category or department at one of several predetermined "price points" or levels. Each price line represents a different level of quality. For example, different brands of men's shirts in the same store might be priced at $14.95, $19.95, and $24.95. This practice helps customers make quality comparisons, assuming the price differences can be easily associated with differences in quality, including the number and type of features offered. It also simplifies pricing decisions for the retailer and guides the retail buyer in deciding which brands to purchase for the department or store.

The rationale for price lining is that consumers often use price information as a basis to make judgments about a brand's relative quality, performance, or prestige. This is particularly true when customers have little past experience with the product or lack the expertise to make more objective quality comparisons, as when the product is technically complex.[22] Firms in such product categories sometimes use **psychological pricing** to help establish a market position for their brand and to appeal to consumers' noneconomic needs. For example, Heublein successfully repositioned its Popov brand of vodka by substantially raising its price. The 8 percent price increase reduced the brand's market share by 1 percent; but it produced a 30 percent increase in profit.[23]

Another common psychological pricing practice is called **odd pricing.** For instance, a product or service might be priced at $29.95 instead of $30.00, 19 cents instead of 20, or $39,950 instead of $40,000. Odd prices convey the psychological impression of a lower price. No one doubts that many consumers see through this practice. First impressions are often important determinants of purchase behavior, however, especially for convenience goods. And odd prices often create a better first impression than the corresponding, slightly higher even-numbered prices would.[24]

A final demand-oriented pricing practice is the use of **promotional pricing** to transmit a message about the product in conjunction with, or sometimes in lieu of, advertising or other forms of promotional activity. The most common form of promotional pricing is the familiar **sale:** the offer of a reduced price on the product for a limited time. In addition to reducing the real cost to the buyer, such promotional prices represent "something different"—and thus stand a better chance of gaining the customer's attention and

---

[22] For a more detailed review of this price-perceived quality relationship, see Kent B. Monroe, "Buyers' Subjective Perceptions of Price," *Journal of Marketing Research*, February 1973, pp. 70–80; and David M. Gardner, "Is There a Generalized Price-Quality Relationship in an Experimental Setting?" *Journal of Advertising Research*, August 1981, pp. 49–52.

[23] Jeffrey H. Birnbaum, "Pricing of Products Is Still an Art, Often Having Little Link to Costs," *The Wall Street Journal*, November 25, 1981, p. 25.

[24] Zarrell V. Lambert, "Perceived Price as Related to Odd and Even Price Endings," *Journal of Retailing*, Fall 1975, pp. 13–22.

motivating prompt action. Promotional pricing is particularly common in seasonal product categories—such as clothing, skis, and snowblowers—where manufacturers and retailers want to reduce excess stocks at the end of each season to minimize their investment in carry-over inventory. It can also stimulate increased purchases among current customers or consumer trial of a new brand or one attempting to increase its market share.

ADAPTING PRICES TO VARIATIONS IN MARKET CIRCUMSTANCES

Even though determining a product's price level is a complicated process, most firms do not stop with the choice of a single list price. Instead, the final step in the pricing process is usually to develop a **price structure** that adapts the price to variations in cost and demand across geographic territories, types of customers, and items within the product line.

Geographic adjustments

Firms with only one or a few plants must adjust their prices for the variations in transportation costs of selling to customers in different parts of the country. One approach is called **FOB origin pricing:** the manufacturer places the goods "free on board" a transportation carrier. At this point the title and responsibility passes to the customer, who pays the freight from the factory to the destination. Advocates argue that this is the fairest way to allocate freight charges: each customer picks up its own costs. The disadvantage, though, is that the manufacturer may be at a cost disadvantage when trying to sell to customers in distant markets.

The opposite alternative is **freight absorption pricing.** Here the seller picks up all or part of the freight charges. New competitors trying to penetrate new markets and smaller competitors in maturing industries trying to increase their share sometimes use this approach. Their rationale is that if they can obtain more business, their average unit costs will fall enough to compensate for the high freight costs.

Most firms use a compromise approach to deal with variations in transportation costs. One method is **uniform delivered pricing,** where a standard freight charge—equal to the average freight cost across all customers—is assessed every customer, regardless of location. This lowers the overall cost to distant customers, but raises costs for customers near the company's plant. Nevertheless, the approach is popular, because it is easy to administer and enables the firm to maintain a single nationally advertised price. **Zone pricing** is another compromise approach that falls between FOB and uniform delivered pricing. Here the company divides the country into two or more pricing zones. It charges all customers within the same zone the same delivered price; but a higher price is set for distant zones than for those closer to the plant.

Discounts and allowances

Firms relying on independent wholesalers and retailers to distribute their products must adjust their list prices to motivate and reward these firms to perform needed marketing activities. We discuss programs for gaining reseller support in more detail in the next chapter, but briefly describe price discounts and allowances—basic tools used in creating such programs—in the next sections.

Trade discounts

To induce wholesalers and/or retailers to carry a product and perform their usual marketing activities in its support, manufacturers must offer **trade (or functional) discounts** from the suggested retail list price. Such discounts vary, depending on the intermediary's wholesale or retail level in the channel and the specific activities they are expected to perform. A manufacturer who distributes stereo speakers through a channel of independent wholesale distributors and retailers, for instance, might have a suggested retail price of $100 for each speaker and a trade discount schedule of 50/15. The 50 represents the percent discount from list price offered to retailers who carry the product. The 15 is the discount offered to the wholesaler. Thus, a retailer would pay $50 for each speaker ($100 − [.5 × $100]). The wholesaler would pay the manufacturer $42.50 ($50 − [.15 × $50]). In effect, when sellers abide by the suggested list price the trade discounts reflect the margins earned by the wholesalers and retailers in the channel of distribution.

Quantity discounts

To encourage channel members, or even ultimate customers, to purchase more of the product, a manufacturer might offer a price reduction for ordering in large quantities. (See Exhibit 14–12 for United Parcel Service's quantity discount program.) The **quantity discount** often increases as order size increases. For example, a firm might offer no additional discount on orders of 50 units or less, a 2 percent discount off list on orders of 51 to 100 units, 4 percent off on orders of 101 to 500 units, and 5 percent off on orders of more than 500 units. To avoid charges of illegal price discrimination against smaller purchasers, the size of such discounts should be justified by the cost savings that manufacturers gain by filling larger orders. These savings include reductions in per-unit selling, order processing, transportation, and inventory carrying costs. In addition to cost savings, quantity discounts help move more inventory closer to the ultimate customer, thereby encouraging

EXHIBIT   14 ♦ 12

United Parcel Service offers volume discounts on certain deliveries

United Parcel Service's new incentive program for its large customers (a polite way of talking about quantity discounts) will reduce the cost of domestic service for its "Next Day Air" from $8.50 an item to either $7.50 or $7.00, depending on average weekly volume over a 13-week period. Analysts say the move clearly positions UPS (which holds a 10 percent share of the overnight delivery market) in a battle with Federal Express (which holds a 50 percent share). A Federal Express spokeswoman says Fed Ex has no plans to retaliate because it relies on service, not price, to sell its service.

Source: "United Parcel Offers Volume Discounts on Certain Deliveries," The Wall Street Journal, October 2, 1988, p. 37.

more impulse purchases and reducing the probability of stock-outs occurring among wholesalers or retailers in the distribution system.

Cash discounts

A **cash discount** is a price reduction to encourage customers to pay their bills promptly. A common example of such a discount is "2/10, net 30." This means that payment in full is due within 30 days, but the buyer can deduct 2 percent from the price if payment is made within 10 days. Such discounts are found across a wide variety of industries. They help reduce the capital the seller has tied up in accounts receivable and lower collection costs and bad debts.

Seasonal discounts

A **seasonal discount** is a price reduction to encourage customers to buy a good or service during periods when demand is normally low. Their purpose is to smooth out variations in production schedules and inventories from period to period. For example, ski manufacturers offer seasonal discounts to encourage their retailers to place orders and stock merchandise during the spring and summer. Hotels in large cities also offer weekend rates to offset the shortage of business travelers.

Allowances

Allowances are similar to discounts in that they are inducements to encourage channel members or final customers to engage in specific behaviors in support of the product. One common example in consumer durable goods categories—particularly automobiles—is the **trade-in allowance.** This is essentially a price reduction granted to customers for turning in an old item when buying a new one. Such allowances help customers recoup the value from their used products and thereby encourage more frequent replacement purchases.

Promotional allowances offered to channel intermediaries encourage them to provide promotional support for a product. Cooperative advertising programs, for instance, reward distributors or retailers for advertising the product at the local level. Other promotional allowances may induce retailers to devote more shelf space to the product or to encourage middlemen's salespeople to provide more aggressive selling support.

Discriminatory pricing adjustments

Discriminatory pricing occurs when a firm sells a product or service at two or more prices not determined by proportional differences in costs. The motivation for doing this is usually to take advantage of differences in the price sensitivities or preferences of various customer segments. Specific discriminatory price adjustments include:

* **Image pricing.** Some manufacturers use different packaging and promotional campaigns—and different prices—to market the same basic product to different market segments. Their purpose is to create a more sophisticated or upscale image for the product in those segments where image is important, while appealing to other segments with a low price or other more objective appeals. For example, Evian markets mineral water in bottles holding from 8 to 32 ounces for drinking. The firm also sells one-ounce spray atomizers containing the same mineral water for use as a moisturizer when applying or removing makeup. One ounce of Evian water is nearly 10 times more expensive than the 8-ounce bottles.
* **Time pricing.** Prices might be adjusted seasonally, across days of the week, or across hours of the day to capitalize on predictable fluctuations in demand over time. Movie theaters, for instance, often charge higher prices for evening shows than for early matinees.
* **Location pricing.** The same product or service might be priced differently at various retail locations to capitalize on local demand or the intensity of competition. Even within a single theater, seats in some locations are typically more expensive because many theater-goers are willing to pay more to sit near the stage. Football end-zone seats and baseball bleacher seats are usually less expensive than seats with a better view or closer to the action.
* **Customer segment pricing.** Perhaps the most common discriminatory pricing practice is to charge different prices to customer segments that differ in their willingness or ability to buy. Many arts organizations, for example, offer lower prices to senior citizens whose fixed incomes might otherwise prohibit their attendance.

Sometimes the product line price adjustments discussed in the next section are also discriminatory. This is the case when the prices of different models in a line vary more widely than the costs associated with producing and marketing them.

Conditions allowing discriminatory adjustments

First, it is not always possible or wise to set different prices for essentially the same product. For such a discriminatory pricing policy to work, there must obviously be identifiable customer segments with different price sensitivities. Second, the customer segments must either be physically separated from one another or the firm must institute control procedures to insure that the segment paying the lower price cannot resell the product to customers paying the higher price. Obviously, too, the cost to the manufacturer of segmenting and monitoring the market should not exceed the extra revenue generated by the discriminatory pricing. And the firm should be confident that resentment among customers asked to pay the higher price, or competitive conditions in the market, will not leave it vulnerable to competitive attacks in the high-price segments. Finally, the firm should pay careful attention to the legal restrictions involved in price discrimination.

Legal considerations

Price discrimination is not the legal issue today that it was in the past. It is important to note, however, that the Robinson-Patman Act outlaws price discrimination among buyers of goods of "like grade and quality" where the effect may be to "injure, destroy or prevent competition." Because individual consumers buy goods and services for their own use and are not competing with one another, the law usually does not prevent discriminatory pricing of consumer goods at the retail level because there is no injury to competition. To legally offer different prices for the same product to retailers, distributors, or industrial buyers, however, one of two basic conditions should be met: Either the manufacturer must be sure that the buyers being quoted different prices are not in direct competition because they are operating in different geographic areas or at different channel levels so there will be no injury to competition. Or the difference in prices offered must be justified by differences in the cost of doing business with the different buyers. This cost defense, for example, is the rationale for offering the quantity discounts mentioned in the preceding section. Because transportation and order processing costs are usually lower for large orders, firms can legally pass those cost savings on to the buyer as a discount or lower price.

In addition to price discrimination, the Sherman Act prohibits both horizontal and vertical price fixing. In the case of the former, competitors agree to maintain a given price. The latter involves an agreement between manufacturers and retailers to sell products at a certain price. The Miller Tyding Act (1937) was passed to permit such vertical price fixing; but in 1976, Congress passed the Consumer Goods Pricing Act, which made such pricing once more illegal. Predatory pricing is also illegal under the Sherman Act because it involves selling below cost to drive one or more competitors out of the market.

Product-line pricing adjustments

Pricing decisions become even more complicated when a firm produces a line of several models or styles that potential customers perceive as bearing some relationship to one another. In such cases, firms should adjust the prices of various models to reflect customers' perceptions of their relative value. For example, Ford prices its basic Escort model substantially below its more prestigious Thunderbird.

In theory, producers should determine the prices for all the products in the line simultaneously, taking into account not only the price elasticity of demand for each model, but also the cross-elasticities among them. A **cross-elasticity** is the percentage change in sales of one product induced by a 1 percent change in the price of another product that is assumed to be a close substitute. Because of the difficulties in estimating such cross-elasticities, however, firms seldom use this approach. About the best that managers can do is to price each item separately and then adjust those prices to reflect the likelihood that customers will trade up or down and will perceive the prices of the related items to be fair and reasonable.

For example, consider a refrigerator manufacturer who must set prices for a variety of makes and models. If the price of the cheapest model in the line is too high, customers may not see much difference between it and the next best model. As a result, sales of the cheapest model may be cannibalized by the higher-priced one. If the price of the cheapest model is too low, however, the likelihood that customers will be willing or able to trade up to the better version is reduced. Airlines have traditionally not discounted first-class fares because of their belief that businesspeople and well-to-do passengers weren't concerned about how much they paid for wider seats and extra service. But the differential has widened so much between transcontinental first class and discounted coach fares (for example, $1,500 versus $200) that airlines have experienced a large decline in the number of first-class passengers. As a result, more and more airlines are reducing first-class fares in an effort to win passengers back.[25]

INITIATING AND RESPONDING TO PRICE CHANGES

As a product moves through the various stages of its life cycle, the manager is likely to face occasions when a price increase or price cut must be considered. Similarly, the firm may have to decide how to respond to price

---

[25] Roy J. Harris, Jr., "Airlines Cutting First-Class Fares to Win Back Profitable Customers," *The Wall Street Journal*, February 20, 1986, p. 21.

changes initiated by its competitors. Questions about when to initiate—or how to respond to—price changes are usually interrelated with the design of other elements of the strategic marketing program and affected by variables that shape the broader business strategy of the firm or SBU. We examine the role of price as a component of strategic marketing programs for different market and competitive conditions in more detail in Chapters 19, 20, and 21. To clarify the dynamic nature of competitive pricing decisions over time, however, we briefly discuss some specific issues managers should consider when deciding whether to initiate or respond to price changes in an established product category.

Initiating price changes

Several circumstances might lead a firm to consider cutting its price, even though such action might risk precipitating a price war. These include:

* The emergence of **excess capacity** as the market matures and the rate of growth slows. To cover high fixed costs, the firm may have to generate increased volume. But if it cannot gain such increases with product improvements, more promotion, or other nonprice methods, it may have to consider lowering price.
* A related circumstance is the **loss of market share,** particularly when the market is still growing. To preserve its competitive position and be able to reap future profits, the firm may try to stave off in-roads by lower-priced competitors by reducing its own prices. Thus, American auto companies relied heavily on rebates, discounts, and other price reduction mechanisms in the mid-1980s in an attempt to reverse their loss of share to lower-priced foreign competitors.
* A more proactive reason for cutting prices is an attempt by a low-cost firm to preempt or drive out less-efficient competitors and thus **increase its market share.** This was the strategy adopted by Texas Instruments in the digital watch business when it tried to benefit from experience-curve effects to lower its costs and prices and capture an increasing share of the market.

On the other hand, some circumstances might provoke a firm to increase its prices, even though such action risks placing the firm at a competitive price disadvantage. These situations include:

* High rates of **inflation** in the economy. Inflation necessitates price increases to cover rising costs of production and marketing. And it makes such increases more competitively viable, because all firms in the industry likely feel the same pressure on their margins.
* When a firm cannot fill all of its orders due to **excess demand,** it must consider raising its prices or allocating the available supply among its customers in some way, or both. The concern with sharply raising prices under such conditions is the possible negative reaction from customers who may feel that the firm is taking advantage of them. This could lead to a loss of market share over the long term.
* A more proactive reason for raising a product's price is an attempt by the firm to **reposition the product** toward the "high quality" or "prestige" end of the market.

As we noted earlier, this was the approach taken by Heublein when it repositioned its Popov brand as a high-quality vodka.

Customers' reactions to price changes

One thing that complicates the decision about whether to initiate a price change is that customers do not always perceive such changes in the way managers might expect.[26] Instead of viewing a price cut as a positive event, some customers might see it as an indication that (a) the product is about to be replaced by a newer model; (b) the product's quality has been cut; (c) the firm itself is in financial difficulty and may not be around to supply parts and service in the future; (d) other customers do not like the product and it is not selling well; or (e) the price will fall farther in the future. Any of these perceptions can reduce or eliminate any anticipated volume increase as a result of the price cut.

Similarly, a price increase is not always seen as a *negative* factor by potential buyers. They may view the increase as an indication that (a) the product is becoming popular and may be hard to obtain unless the customer acts quickly; (b) shortages are developing that will make the item more difficult to buy in the future; or (c) other customers see the item as an attractive value. These variations in perceptions underscore the value of preliminary market research into the price sensitivities of customers and their likely reactions to a price change before such a decision is implemented.

The importance of using research to understand customers' reactions to a possible price change is increased by the fact that some observers believe brand loyalty has declined sharply in recent years. Consumers no longer deal with business on a highly personal basis; they have little attachment to a favorite supermarket, gas station, or department store. A favorite brand can be bypassed in favor of a comparable product that is on sale at 25 cents less. In brief, consumers are less emotional and are looking for a deal, which makes price more and more of a competitive weapon.[27]

Competitors' reactions to price changes

A firm should also attempt to predict its competitors' reactions before initiating a price change. This is particularly true in mature markets with few competitors and little differentiation across brands. These are the conditions where competitors are most likely to match a price cut or to refuse to follow a

---

[26] Monroe, "Buyers' Subjective Perceptions of Price."

[27] John Koten, "Product Loyalty Lasts as Long as the Best Price," *The Wall Street Journal*, August 7, 1986, p. 21.

price increase unless inflationary cost pressures force them to follow the leader.

A firm might try to predict a competitor's response to a price change in two ways. Firms with a consistent response policy always react in the same way; and their future behavior, therefore, is quite predictable. In this situation, a firm needs to track the competitor's reactions to past price changes in the industry to gain insights into how it will respond to a future change. One task commonly assigned to marketing assistants at Procter & Gamble is to track each competitor's reactions to price changes, promotional discounts, and other price adjustments over time. They analyze this information to determine whether a given competitor's reactions tend to be consistent and predictable.

Some firms treat each price change by a competitor as a unique situation; they react according to their perception of their own self-interest at the time. Their likely response to future price changes is much less predictable. The only way to judge how such a competitor might respond is to guess how it might interpret what is in its own self-interest. Firms can do this by using the information collection techniques discussed in Chapter 9 to determine the competitor's current financial position, its recent sales results, production capacity, customer loyalty, and corporate objectives. In general, if the competitor is pursuing a market-share growth or maintenance objective, it is more likely to react aggressively to a price change than if it is attempting to maintain or increase its return on investment.

Responding to price changes

As subsequent chapters show, market leaders frequently face aggressive price cutting by smaller firms trying to build their own market shares. IBM's commanding share of the personal computer market, for instance, was substantially eroded during the mid-1980s due largely to aggressive price competition from makers of low-cost clones. The market leader can choose to react in one of several ways. First, it can simply match the lower prices of its competitors. However, this is only feasible if its costs are actually as low as those of its most efficient competitor, or if it has the financial strength to outlast those smaller firms. Such a response also risks lowering the profits for everyone in the industry for some time into the future.

A second response is to fight back on nonprice dimensions. The firm might try to maintain both price and market share by introducing product improvements, increasing promotion and selling efforts, or both. The viability of this response, of course, depends on the price sensitivity of customers in the target market and their willingness to pay a premium for better product quality.

A third response is for the leader to introduce a second "flanker" brand— one designed to cost less than the firm's premier product and priced to compete directly with products of smaller firms. This approach—if successful—can help preserve the leader's overall share without sacrificing the higher margins to be made on its premium brand.

The most appropriate response depends on the particular situation faced by the product: its stage in the life cycle, its relative importance in the firm's product portfolio, the likely intentions and resources of the competitors, the price sensitivity of potential buyers, and the firm's objectives. Unfortunately, a firm may not have much time to consider all options when a competitor initiates a threat. A quick response may be necessary to reduce the damage. This suggests a firm should consider its response to such threats *before* they actually occur by developing a set of contingency plans as part of its overall planning process.

SUMMARY

Managers faced with pricing decisions for a product or service need to consider five sets of issues: First, they should specify a pricing objective that is consistent with the overall strategy and the other elements of the marketing program planned for the product. Such an objective might be to (1) maximize sales growth, (2) maintain the quality or service differentiation of the product, (3) maximize current profit through a skimming strategy, (4) maximize current profit through a harvest strategy, (5) survive in the short term, or (6) achieve some social objective.

Next, managers must determine the price sensitivity of potential buyers and the nature of the demand curve for the product. The more inelastic the demand, the higher the company can set its price without suffering an offsetting reduction in volume. Similarly, the more elastic the demand for the product, the greater the volume increase obtained with a lower price. The relationship between quantity demanded and various price levels effectively sets the ceiling for the range of feasible prices.

On the other hand, the firm's costs of producing and marketing the product determine the floor of the range of viable prices in the long run. Total product costs must be covered if the product is to remain economically viable over time. Those total costs consist of the variable costs directly associated with producing each unit of the product and an allocation of fixed costs or overhead (the size of which varies per unit as volume increases or declines).

The firm must also examine its competitors' costs and prices before setting its own. This is particularly important in mature industries where there is relatively little differentiation among competing brands.

Once managers have gathered this information and analyzed it, they can choose a method for setting the product's basic list price. Such methods can be cost-oriented, competition-oriented, or customer-oriented.

An overall price level or list price must usually be adapted to variations in market conditions. First, adjustments must reflect the transportation costs involved in selling to customers in widespread geographical areas. Managers also make adjustments to encourage middlemen at different channel levels to support the product and perform necessary marketing functions. These adjustments include trade, quantity, cash and seasonal discounts, and allowances for activities such as local promotion and advertising.

Finally, when a firm considers changing its price over time, it must consider the likely reactions of both customers and competitors. Customer perceptions of the true meaning of the change influence their reactions. Competitors are likely to react in either a predictable manner due to well-established policy or unpredictably according to their perception of their own self-interest at the time.

The firm that faces a price change initiated by a competitor should try to figure out that competitor's strategic intent and the likely duration of the change before deciding how to react. If a quick response is necessary, the firm should prepare contingency plans that specify desired responses for possible future threats.

QUESTIONS

1. Under which market and competitive conditions are each of the following *pricing objectives* most appropriate for a business to consider?
   a. Maximize sales growth through penetration pricing
   b. Maximize current profit through skimming pricing
   c. Maximize current profit through harvesting

2. Firms sometimes set a low price in a new product-market (penetration pricing) to discourage potential competitors from entering the market. Can you think of any circumstances where a company might deliberately want to attract competitors to a new market and set a high price to help accomplish such an objective?

3. What is *price elasticity?* Distinguish between price elastic demand and price inelastic demand. What are the pricing implications of each elasticity condition?

4. Suppose executives estimate that the unit variable cost for their firm's videocassette recorder is $100, the fixed cost related to the product is $5 million annually, and the estimated sales volume for next year is 100,000 recorders. The firm has a target rate of return of 20 percent, and it has made capital investments totaling $4 million to produce and distribute its recorders. What price will the firm have to obtain for each recorder to achieve its target rate of return?

5. The manufacturer of videocassette recorders described in question 4 sells its recorders through electronics wholesalers, which in turn sell to retail stores. The manufacturer's *trade discount* policy is 40/20. What should be the suggested retail price for the firm's recorders? How much should the retailer have to pay for each recorder?

6. Tennant Company manufactures cleaning equipment for commercial applications. Its walk-behind electric floor waxer/buffer is priced at $350. The product's per unit variable cost is $200, and total fixed costs associated with the product are $3 million. How many units must Tennant sell to *break even?* How would the break-even volume change if the firm reduced the price of the product by $50?

7. A furniture manufacturer in North Carolina operates at a freight cost disadvantage relative to competitors in the western United States. Which methods of quoting prices could the firm adopt to make it more competitive in the western states? What are the possible disadvantages of each method?

8. Manufacturer A has experienced cost increases for its product in recent months. It would like to initiate a price increase, but only if its major competitors are likely to follow A's lead with price increases of their own. Which characteristics of Manufacturer A, and which market and competitive conditions, are most likely to encourage A's competitors to follow its lead in increasing prices?

9. Under which conditions are firms most

likely to adopt a *going-rate* or *com-petitive parity* method for determining their prices?

10. Ford Motor Company offers a number of automobile models in different price ranges. In addition to the usual cost and demand considerations, which other factors should the company consider when determining the relative prices for the various products in its line?

Chapter ⟨15⟩ | Distribution decisions

TORO TRIES TO CHANGE ITS DISTRIBUTION CHANNEL

After beginning life in 1914 as a manufacturer of tractor engines, the Toro Company entered the new market for gasoline-powered mowing equipment in the early 1950s. It quickly became a leading producer of lawn care and snow removal equipment for the residential market.[1] Toro attained success by pursuing a differentiation strategy: producing high-quality, dependable products and selling them to an upscale segment of homeowners at premium prices. It spent a relatively high percentage of revenues on TV and print advertising to persuade target customers to "trade up" to Toro products. Ads featured the long-running slogan, "Haven't you gone without a Toro long enough?"

Supporting this differentiation strategy were 59 wholesale distributors who recruited and helped maintain the support of more than 9,000 independent retail dealers, such as hardware stores and lawn and garden centers. The retailers played an important role in Toro's early success. They had to persuade customers that Toro's higher quality was worth its premium price; and they performed all postsale service on Toro equipment. The dealers' competence in servicing Toro equipment was enhanced by company training programs. And it was an important factor in building Toro's reputation as a producer of dependable equipment.

By the mid-1970s, however, the lawn mower and snow thrower markets were beginning to mature. Although Toro's market share remained high, its growth rate began to slow. To combat this trend, the company introduced several new products related to lawn care, such as trimmers, electric chain saws, and garden hoses. The firm also decided to expand its distribution channel. Mass merchandisers such as K mart and J. C. Penney had captured an increasing percentage of outdoor equipment sales. Toro's managers believed that by adding such retailers to its distribution channel it could capitalize on its extensive advertising and promotional efforts and capture an even bigger share of the maturing lawn mower and snow thrower markets.

At first, Toro directed its wholesale distributors to begin selling to mass merchandisers in their territories. The distributors were reluctant to do so, however, for fear of upsetting their traditional retail dealers. Those dealers believed they would lose substantial sales to the more aggressive pricing policies of the mass merchandisers. Conse-

---

[1] Based on Neil Harrison and Christina Cannon-Bonaventre, *The Toro Company (A)*, Case 9-582-032 (Cambridge, Mass.: The Harvard Business School, 1981); and *The Toro Company Annual Report, 1988* (Bloomington, Minn.: The Toro Company, Inc.).

continued

concluded

quently, Toro established a second distribution channel by contracting with manufacturers' reps to sell selected lawn mower and snow thrower models—and all the company's smaller appliances—directly to mass merchandisers.

By the early 1980s, Toro realized its expanded distribution channel was causing a number of problems. For instance, the traditional dealers were dissatisfied over being forced to compete on price with mass merchandisers when selling Toro products. Because many of those dealers carried several brands, they began to switch their selling efforts away from the Toro line. One of Toro's major competitors, Snapper, gained increased support among some of the traditional Toro dealers because it sold very little through mass merchandisers.

Another result of Toro's traditional dealers' dissatisfaction was a deterioration of postsale service. The mass merchandisers seldom had service departments; and the traditional retailers were reluctant to perform warranty service on products they had not sold. This reluctance took the form of long service delays or, in some cases, outright refusal to perform service work on Toro equipment that had not been purchased from the dealer—resulting in increasing numbers of dissatisfied Toro customers.

Toro also discovered problems with the way the mass merchandisers promoted and sold Toro products. The mass merchants offered little sales assistance or postsale service to potential customers. They promoted lawn mowers and snowblowers on a seasonal basis; but they marked prices down substantially at the end of the season to avoid carry-over inventory. Many chains used Toro products as promotional items to build traffic for their own private-label products. Both of these practices meant that Toro products were being heavily price promoted, which was not consistent with the firm's strategy of differentiating its brand on the basis of quality and service.

In 1983, after several years of losses, a new CEO and top-management team decided to return to the traditional dealer network and to drop mass merchandisers from their distribution channel. To win back the trust and cooperation of its distributors and dealers, Toro's president wrote them an open letter promising that the firm would never again abandon them in favor of mass-merchandising channels.

STRATEGIC DISTRIBUTION ISSUES

The decision to add mass merchandisers to Toro's channel was inconsistent with the firm's established strategy. Those retailers treated Toro's products as promotional items, slashing prices and providing little selling or service support. Worse, their addition to the channel eroded the loyalty and cooperation of the traditional dealers. These two distribution problems damaged the keystone of Toro's competitive strategy—the company's reputation for quality products and superior customer service. Not until the firm once again "rationalized" its distribution network by eliminating the mass merchants could it return to profitability. (Toro earned $20.0 million on sales of $609.2 million in 1987, for a 26.3 percent return on shareholders' equity.)

The Toro case also illustrates the two interrelated sets of decisions a firm must make about distributing its products or services: channel design and channel management. **Channel design** involves developing a channel structure that fits the SBU's strategy and the needs of the target market. These decisions focus on how long the channel should be and which types of institutions—and how many of each—should be included at each level.

Designing the ideal distribution system is one thing. But, as Toro discovered, convincing desirable wholesalers and retailers to carry a firm's products, and to actively support and help implement its marketing programs, can be another matter. **Channel management,** then, is the development of policies and procedures to gain and maintain the cooperation of the various institutions in the firm's distribution channels. Channel management decisions focus on selecting and recruiting channel members, motivating them to perform specific marketing activities, coordinating their efforts, assessing their performance, and resolving conflicts that arise. Channel management offers opportunities for companies to gain a considerable competitive advantage—as in what American Hospital Supply accomplished by linking hospitals with its warehouses via sophisticated computer-based systems.

We examine both channel design and channel management decisions in later sections of this chapter. To fully understand the issues involved, though, we must first discuss the wide variety of institutions a marketing manager has to choose from when designing a channel and the various functions they perform.

CHANNEL FUNCTIONS AND INSTITUTIONS

Channel flows and functions

As we saw in Chapter 1, *someone* must perform a number of marketing functions or activities before a producer and a customer can exchange goods or services.[2] Buying and selling functions pave the way for an exchange of title. Someone must engage in transportation and storage functions to facilitate the physical movement of the goods. Someone must communicate information to potential customers through advertising, personal selling, or

---

[2] To review the marketing flows and functions necessary to facilitate exchange transactions, see Exhibit 1–10, Chap. 1.

sales promotion to make them aware of the product and encourage them to
buy it. And marketing research must feed information about potential customers and their desires back to the producer. Financing functions aid the
flow of credit and payment. And someone must take care of services such as
installation and repair to ensure that customers receive full value from their
purchases.

Sometimes the customer undertakes most of the marketing activities in an
exchange—as when a family takes a drive through the country to buy
vegetables at a farmer's roadside stand. In other cases, a producer may
distribute goods or services directly to end users. Avon's marketing of
cosmetics and jewelry through mail-order catalogs and thousands of part-
time door-to-door sales reps is an example of such a direct, vertically integrated distribution system. In the great majority of cases, though, goods are
distributed through systems consisting of a variety of institutions or middlemen—retailers, wholesalers, agents, facilitating agencies—where each
one performs a part of the marketing functions. Thus, a **marketing channel
is the set of interdependent organizations involved in the process of making
a product or service available for consumption or use by consumers or
industrial users.**[3]

The rationale for marketing channels: costs versus benefits

Performing the marketing activities necessary to facilitate transactions costs
money. The final selling price of the product or service reflects these costs—
including margins paid to wholesalers and retailers and the manufacturer's
marketing expenses. Such costs vary widely across products and customers,
but they are often substantial. As we have seen, marketing costs account for
an average of roughly 50 percent of the retail price of consumer package
goods such as cosmetics and tennis balls.[4] About half of those costs represent the retailer's margin. The rest consists of the marketing expenses of the
manufacturer and wholesale middlemen. Although the marketing costs for
many industrial goods such as sheet steel or basic chemicals tend to be lower
because they are sold in large quantities to a small number of regular
customers, they can still account for 10 percent or more of the final selling
price.

Why should customers pay such high marketing costs? Wouldn't they be
better off buying directly from the manufacturer and bypassing middlemen
like wholesalers and retailers? Usually not. *It's a classic marketing truth that
although middlemen can be eliminated, someone must still perform all the
marketing functions.* Various sources of efficiency often enable some com-

---

[3] Louis W. Stern and Adel I. El-Ansary, *Marketing Channels*, 3rd ed. (Englewood Cliffs, N.J.:
Prentice-Hall, 1988), pp. 3–4.

[4] William J. Stanton, *Fundamentals of Marketing*, 6th ed. (New York: McGraw-Hill, 1987),
p. 7.

bination of middlemen to perform those functions at lower cost than either the customer or the manufacturer could by themselves. This is particularly true when a product must be distributed to large numbers of geographically dispersed customers.

Marketing channels that incorporate specialized middlemen improve marketing efficiency in several ways:

- *Functional efficiency:* Middlemen can often perform one or more marketing activities more efficiently than manufacturers or their customers because of their specialization and greater economies of scale. For example, a manufacturer's rep can spread costs across different manufacturers and perform the selling function at a lower cost per manufacturer than if each firm paid its own company salesperson.
- *Scale efficiency:* By purchasing large quantities of goods from manufacturers, storing them, and then breaking them down into the smaller quantities their customers prefer to purchase (sometimes referred to as **sorting**), wholesalers and retailers enable manufacturers and their customers to operate at their most efficient scale. Rather than having to make small production runs to fill the orders of individual customers, manufacturers can achieve the economies of large-scale production. And their customers can buy smaller quantities without having their capital tied up in large inventories.
- *Transactional efficiency:* By purchasing goods from a variety of suppliers and then storing, promoting, and selling them (sometimes referred to as **assorting**), wholesalers and retailers make it possible for customers to acquire wide assortments of products from a single source with one transaction. This reduces the time and effort that businesses and consumers must expend in finding and purchasing the goods they need—as when an auto mechanic can obtain the parts to repair different makes of cars with a single call to an auto parts wholesaler.[5]

However, not all middlemen perform a full range of marketing functions, including the financing of inventories and accounts receivables. And all middlemen are not equally efficient or effective under all market and competitive conditions. Thus, a major objective in designing a marketing channel is to find the most efficient combination of middlemen for the particular product-market—a channel that minimizes distribution costs but still reaches and satisfies target customers. This is sometimes easier said than done, though, because of the variety of institutions from which marketing managers can choose.

Channel institutions

There are four broad categories of marketing institutions that a manufacturer might include in the marketing channel for a product: merchant wholesalers, agent middlemen, retailers, and facilitating agencies. Exhibit 15–1 briefly

---

[5] For a graphic depiction of how a marketing intermediary can improve transactional efficiency, refer to Chapter 1, Exhibit 1–3.

EXHIBIT 15 ♦ 1

Institutions found in marketing channels

Institution	Definition
Merchant wholesalers	*Take title* to the goods they handle; sell primarily to other *re-sellers* (e.g., retailers), *industrial and commercial customers* rather than to individual consumers.
Agent middlemen	Include manufacturers' representatives and brokers. Also sell to other *resellers, industrial or commercial customers;* but *do not take title* to the goods. Usually specialize in the selling function and represent client manufacturers on a commission basis.
Retailers	Sell goods and services directly to *ultimate consumers* for their personal, nonbusiness use. Usually *take title* to goods they handle; are compensated by the margin between the price they pay for those goods and the price they receive from their customers.
Facilitating agencies	Include advertising agencies, marketing research firms, collection agencies, trucking firms, and railroads; *specialize in one or more marketing functions; work on a fee-for-service basis* to help clients perform those functions more effectively and efficiently.

defines each of these. Other terms—such as *distributor, jobber,* and *dealer*—are often used to refer to channel members. The first two usually refer to wholesalers, particularly those handling industrial goods. The term *dealer* may refer to either a wholesaler or a retailer.

Merchant wholesalers

These firms sell primarily to other resellers (retailers and other wholesalers) and industrial, commercial, and institutional customers, rather than to individual consumers. Merchant wholesalers take title to the goods they carry. These independent businesses are compensated by the margin between the prices they pay their suppliers and the prices they can obtain from their customers. There are currently about 340,000 merchant wholesaler establishments operating in the United States, accounting for over $1.5 trillion a year in sales.[6] For sales by kind of business, see Exhibit 15–2.

Wholesalers are of two general types: full-service and limited-service. **Full-service wholesalers** perform a wide range of marketing functions for their suppliers and customers. This includes buying, selling, transporting, storing, financing, and even advising customers on such things as inventory

---

[6] U.S. Department of Commerce, *U.S. Industrial Outlook,* January 1988 (Washington, D.C.: U.S. Government Printing Office, 1988), pp. 60–61.

EXHIBIT 15 ◆ 2

Estimated wholesale sales by kind of business—1987 ($000)

Total merchant wholesale trade (excluding farm product raw material)	
Durable goods, total	$739,277
Motor vehicles/auto parts, supplies	152,222
Furniture, home furnishings	24,702
Lumber, other construction materials	62,360
Electrical goods	96,031
Hardware, plumbing, heating supplies	47,472
Machinery equipment, supplies	192,173
Scrap, waste materials	*
Nondurable goods, total	781,550
Paper, paper products	44,741
Drugs, drug proprietaries, sundries	32,955
Apparel, piece goods, notions	45,283
Groceries, related products	235,033
Beer, wine, distilled alcoholic beverages	42,380
Miscellaneous nondurable goods	105,524
Tobacco, tobacco products	*
* Not available	

Source: Department of Commerce, U.S. Bureau of the Census, 1988, as reported in the *1989 Almanac* (Boston: Houghton Mifflin Company, 1989), p. 35.

control and accounting procedures. They are active in industries with many small manufacturers on one side and small independent retailers or commercial users on the other, such as hardware, drugs, and clothing.

One unique form of full-service wholesaler that has enjoyed relatively rapid growth in recent years is the **rack jobber.** To offer greater shopping convenience to their customers and to increase their own profit margins, many retailers—such as supermarkets and drugstores—have added nontraditional product lines such as magazines, housewares, and health and beauty aids to their stores. Because those retailers know little about merchandising such products, rack jobbers have prospered by not only performing a full range of wholesaling activities but also by taking over some of the retailers' functions as well. They often provide display racks and promotional materials for the retailer's store, stock the racks on a regular basis, and sell on consignment (which means they retain title to the merchandise and bill the retailer only for the goods actually sold).

One way wholesalers have managed to survive even in industries characterized by large manufacturers or commercial customers is by specializing only in functions they can perform more efficiently than anyone else. These **limited-service wholesalers** offer suppliers and customers cost savings by cutting out nonessential functions. For example, because most plumbers own their own trucks and buy supplies in small quantities for a particular

EXHIBIT   15 ♦ 3

Description of services rendered and examples of products carried by type of limited-service wholesaler

Type	Services provided	Products carried
Cash and carry	Inventory, some promotion and selling	Limited line of fast-moving items—plumbing supplies, auto parts, meats and fresh vegetables
Drop shipper	Selling, financing, some promotion	Bulk products—coal, lumber, and heavy equipment
Wagon wholesalers	Selling, delivery, inventory	Limited line of semiperishable merchandise—milk, bread, pastries, snack food
Mail-order wholesalers	Inventory, financing, selling	Limited line of nonperishable merchandise—specialty foods, cosmetics

Source: Louis W. Stern and Adel I. El-Ansary, *Marketing Channels* (Englewood Cliffs, N.J.: Prentice-Hall, 1988), p. 106; and Philip Kotler, *Marketing Management* (Englewood Cliffs, N.J.: Prentice-Hall, 1988), p. 572.

job, most plumbing supplies wholesalers operate on a cash-and-carry basis. They specialize in the buying and storage functions; but they require their customers to perform their own transporting and financing activities.

Other types of limited-service wholesalers (besides cash and carry) include drop shippers (sometimes referred to as a *desk jobber*), wagon (truck) wholesalers, mail-order wholesalers, and producer co-ops. For a description of services rendered by each and the types of products involved, see Exhibit 15–3.

Agent middlemen

Agents are also independent businesspersons or organizations; but their primary role is to represent other organizations in the sale or purchase of goods or services. Agents do not take title to—or physical possession of—the goods they deal in. Instead, they specialize in either the selling or buying function. They can be thought of as free-lance salespeople or purchasing agents who represent client organizations on a commission basis. Common types of agent middlemen include manufacturers' representatives, brokers, and import and export agents. All told, there are approximately 40,000 agent middlemen at work in our economy; and they generate over $230 billion in annual sales, or about 12 percent of all wholesale sales.[7]

Manufacturer's agents and sales agents are the two major types of agents

---

[7] Ibid.

used by producers. **Manufacturer's agents** (or **manufacturer's reps**) usually work for several manufacturers and carry noncompetitive, complementary merchandise in an exclusive territory.[8] They concentrate only on the selling function. Found in a wide variety of industries, they are particularly common where manufacturers do not produce broad enough product lines to support a company salesperson in a particular territory. Thus, manufacturer's reps are particularly common in the industrial equipment, automotive supply, footwear, and toy industries. In contrast, **sales agents** usually represent only one manufacturer and are responsible for the full range of marketing activities needed by that producer. They design promotional plans, set prices, determine distribution policies, and recommend product strategy. Because they have a wider range of responsibilities, their commissions are also usually much larger than those of manufacturer's reps. Sales agents are used primarily by small firms—or new start-ups—that have limited marketing capabilities. They are particularly common in the electronics, apparel, and home furnishings industries.

Brokers are independent firms or individuals whose purpose is to bring buyers and sellers together for an exchange. Unlike agents, brokers usually have no continuing relationship with a particular buyer or seller. They negotiate a single exchange between two parties and then move on to another transaction. Food brokers are an exception, in that their business is based on maintaining a continuous relationship with both manufacturers and retail buyers. The producers of seasonal products such as fruits and vegetables and the real estate industry use brokers extensively.

Purchasing agents typically have a long-term contractual relationship with their clientele. They not only buy for them, but also often receive, inspect, warehouse, and ship to buyers. **Resident buyers** are located in major apparel markets and provide helpful information to small retailers. They also obtain merchandise for their clients.

Manufacturers' sales branches and offices

These wholesaling operations are owned by a manufacturer and are found in such industries as trucking, farm machinery, automotive equipment and parts, major appliances, and plumbing. There are two types of sales branches —those that carry inventory and those that do not. Collectively, they account for about one third of total wholesale sales. The number of branches carrying inventory has reached its peak and may even be in decline.

Retailers

Retailers sell goods and services directly to final consumers for their personal, nonbusiness use. Because retailers usually take title to the goods they carry, their compensation is the margin between what they pay for the

---

[8] Stanley D. Sibley and R. Kenneth Teas, "The Manufacturer's Agent in Industrial Distribution," *Industrial Marketing Management*, November 1979, pp. 286–92.

merchandise and the prices they charge their customers. Retailing is a major industry in the United States, with more than 1.4 million retail establishments accounting for nearly $1.5 trillion in sales in 1987.[9]

Retail stores can be categorized in many different ways. For example, stores might be classified by the type of merchandise carried (supermarkets, drugstores), breadth of product assortments (specialty or department stores), pricing policies (discount or specialty stores), or the nature of the business's premises (mail-order retailers, vending-machine operators, traditional stores). One of the more useful classification schemes groups stores according to their **method of operation.** As Exhibit 15–4 shows, the characteristics of low-margin/high-turnover retailers vary substantially from their opposites—high-margin/low-turnover operators.

Low-margin/high-turnover retailers compete primarily on a price basis. To keep volume high while minimizing investments in inventory, such operations usually concentrate on fast-moving items—such as food, health and beauty aids, basic clothing items, and housewares—and carry a relatively limited selection in each product category. Examples of such retailers

EXHIBIT 15 ♦ 4

Retailers classified by margin and turnover

Low margin/ high turnover		High margin/ low turnover
Few services		Many services
Large variety, small assortments		Smaller variety, large assortments
Below market prices		Above market prices
National brands		Prestige brands, including their own
◄───►		
Hypermarkets and wholesale clubs (Wal-Mart)	Convenience stores 7-Eleven	Upscale jewelry stores and boutiques (Tiffany)
Mass-merchandise discounters (K mart)		Department stores
Supermarkets (A&P)		Upscale specialty stores (Marshall Field's)

Source: Adapted from Joseph B. Mason and Morris L. Mayer, *Modern Retailing: Theory and Practice* (Homewood, Ill.: Richard D. Irwin, Inc., 1987), p. 18.

---

[9] U.S. Department of Commerce, *U.S. Industrial Outlook,* January 1988, pp. 60–61.

include hypermarkets and wholesale clubs (Sam's), mass-merchandise discounters (K mart), and most supermarket chains.

To earn a profit, low-margin/high-turnover retailers must minimize their operating costs. Their focus on standardized, prepackaged merchandise often helps lower personnel costs by reducing or eliminating sales assistance within the store. It also enables them to centralize many purchasing and store operating decisions, thus reducing the administrative levels and personnel needed to manage the organization. Such operations typically also minimize their capital investment by operating out of free-standing, no-frills facilities near major traffic arteries—locations where land costs, rents, and taxes tend to be low.

At the other extreme, high-margin/low-turnover retailers differentiate themselves with unique assortments, quality merchandise, good customer service, and a prestigious store image. They focus on shopping or specialty goods, usually carrying a narrow range of product categories but offering deep assortments of styles and sizes within each category. They also emphasize prestigious national brands or exclusives unavailable in other stores. Tiffany's, for example, carries many one-of-a-kind crystal and jewelry items. This category includes most department stores and upscale specialty stores.

These operations must generate high margins to cover the costs of extensive, well-trained salesforces and a variety of customer services, such as alterations, delivery, and credit. Because they offer narrow and specialized assortments, they typically locate within clusters of retailers in shopping malls or downtown shopping areas. This way they can take advantage of the combined pulling power of those stores in attracting customers. Also, to enhance their image as prestigious stores offering quality merchandise, their facilities and fixtures tend to be stylish, luxurious, and costly.

Between the two extremes are the convenience stores (7-Eleven) and some specialty chains that abound in almost every area, including drugs (Payless), women's clothing (The Gap), shoes (Footlocker), hardware (Ace), and kitchen accessories (Rolling Pin).

Facilitating agencies

Many organizations provide services that help other firms perform marketing activities more effectively and efficiently. These commercial service firms, or **facilitating agencies,** are usually not involved directly in the exchange of goods. Instead, firms use them only when their special expertise facilitates a particular marketing task. Clients compensate these agencies by commissions or fees paid for their services. For example, a manufacturer or retailer might hire an outside advertising agency to help develop an advertising plan, create effective ads, and buy space in appropriate advertising media. Other facilitating agencies include marketing research firms, transportation agencies (airlines, railroads, trucking companies), public warehouses, mercantile and consumer credit reporting agencies, and collection agencies.

Facilitating agencies are usually involved in a marketing channel only on an as-needed basis; therefore we say little about them in this chapter. We focus instead on the more constant and enduring members of the channel—wholesalers, agent middlemen, and retailers—and how they should be combined and managed to form effective distribution systems.

RECENT TRENDS AMONG CHANNEL INSTITUTIONS

Trends in wholesaling

Arthur Andersen & Co. studied the wholesale industry and concluded total annual sales would grow in real terms at about 5 percent—a rate considerably higher than that forecast for the gross national product. In addition, the study predicted individual wholesale companies would become considerably larger—primarily by acquisition, but also through geographic expansion. Computers will play an increasingly important role as wholesalers strive to become more cost effective—especially so versus stock-carrying manufacturers' branches. Thus, by the early 1990s, a majority of wholesale firms will use on-line order-entry systems. More efficient purchasing and inventory control will result from on-line information systems.[10]

Trends in retailing[11]

Because of such strong demographic changes as the increasing number of two-wage-earner households, the aging of the baby boomers, and the slowing birthrate, the U.S. retail structure is changing dramatically. In recent years, there has been considerable innovation in retailing, not only in terms of new and imaginative institutions (hypermarts, warehouse clubs, TV home shopping, and electronic kiosks), but also dramatic changes in traditional retailing, including supermarkets, department stores, specialty stores, and catalog selling.

With a slowing of retail sales, little new shopping center construction (limiting stores' physical expansion), and greater emphasis on price, one can predict greater competition and more and more consolidation through mergers and acquisitions. And just as retailers have been integrating vertically toward suppliers, manufacturers have been moving toward the retail side. Esprit, Ralph Lauren, Benetton, and Liz Claiborne are but a few examples of manufacturers that have set up their own retail outlets.

---

[10] Arthur Andersen & Co., *Future Trends in Wholesale Distribution: A Time of Opportunity* (Washington, D.C.: Distribution Research and Education Foundation, 1987).

[11] This section has benefited not only from the specific sources cited in the footnotes, but also from "A Decade of Change 1978–1987," *Chain Store Age Executive*, November 1988, pp. 55–78; and Standard & Poor's, *Industry Surveys*, January 1989, p. R71 forward.

Retailing is also becoming a global business. Laura Ashley (British), Benetton (Italian), and IKEA (Swedish) are examples of European specialty chains that do their own manufacturing and have recently come to the United States. Correfour's, the French retailer with multibillion dollars in sales that pioneered the development of hypermarts, is opening a store in Philadelphia. British B.A.T. Industries owns Marshall Field's, Saks Fifth Avenue, Ivey's, and Breunner's; and Australia's Hooker Corp. has acquired Bonwit Teller, B. Altman, and Merksamer Jewelers. The Campean Corporation of Canada owns Allied Stores and Federated Department Stores. Marks and Spencer, a well-known British retail clothing chain, has bought Brooks Brothers, an upscale U.S. men's clothier. The American consumers' desire for distinctive merchandise coupled with the fragmentation of our national market has made this transfer of retailing from Europe possible.

Low-margin retailers[12]

The latest addition to the discount type of retailing is the **hypermart.** While less than a dozen are in operation in the United States, they appear to alter the consumers' buying habits and change the retail structure in large and small cities in which they exist. These enormous physical entities (over 200,000 square feet, about six times as large as a supermarket) are so big that stock clerks often wear roller skates. Sales in the Garland, Texas, hypermart operated by Wal-Mart are about evenly divided between food and nonfood items. The average transaction is about $40; and some 70,000 people within a 30-mile radius shop there in an average week. Sales are $2 to $3 million per week.

Hypermarts must generate more than $100 million in annual sales to be profitable. Wal-Mart is testing a scaled-down format, called *Super Centers* (140,000 square feet), that, while giving up some size benefits, would be simpler to operate—and less risky. For a comparison of hypermarkets, wholesale clubs, discount stores, and supermarkets on various economic and physical dimensions, see Exhibit 15–5.

General merchandise discounters (K mart, Target, Wal-Mart) carry broad assortments of both hard goods (auto accessories, housewares, small appliances, gardening tools) and soft goods. They emphasize national brands whenever possible and rely heavily on self-service. They depend on price to attract customers—either everyday low prices (Wal-Mart and, recently, Sears) or weekly sales promotions.

The larger discount chains are attempting to trade up—especially in their software lines. K mart, for example, is upgrading its merchandise, store appearance, and advertising to appeal to younger and wealthier customers.

---

[12] Based on Bill Saporito, "Retailers Fly into Hyperspace," *Fortune*, October 24, 1988, pp. 150–152; Todd Mason, Joseph Weber, and Stephen Phillips, "The Return of the Amazing Colossal Store," *Business Week*, August 11, 1988, p. 59; and Shannon Thurmond, "Sam Speaks Volumes about New Formats," *Advertising Age*, May 9, 1988, p. 3.

EXHIBIT   15 ♦ 5

Comparison of types of discounters and supermarts on various economic measures

	Hypermarket	Wholesale club	Discount store	Supermarket
Size (sq. ft.)	200,000	100,000	65,000	39,000
Weekly sales ($000)	1,750	1,000	150	250
Items stocked (000)	50	4.5	80	30
Gross profit margin (%)	15	11	28	24
Customers per week (000)	50	14.5	9.5	15.5
Average purchase ($)	35	70	16	16
Labor cost (% of sales)	5	4.5	10	12.5
Inventory (annual turns)	13	16	4	26

Source: Adapted from Bill Saporito, "Retailers Fly into Hyperspace," *Fortune,* October 24, 1988, p. 152.
Copyright © 1988 Time, Inc. All rights reserved.

Other changes engineered by discounters include setting up hypermarts, wholesale clubs, and specialty chains (books, drugs, sports); adding food to their present stores; and increasing current operations by adding new stores and increasing the size of the old ones.[13]

Warehouse clubs are cash-and-carry wholesalers catering to small businesses and individual consumers. In 1987, they had sales of $12 billion from 328 units—up from $1 billion in 1983. Business customers pay a small annual fee (retail customers pay an additional 5 percent above posted prices) to buy a variety of merchandise, including canned and frozen food, basic wearing apparel, major appliances, jewelry, office supplies, books, and auto supplies. The warehouse clubs typically carry a limited line of stock keeping units—about 4,000 to 5,000 compared to 60,000 to 80,000 for a regular, general merchandise discount store. Annual sales per store can reach as much as $70 to $80 million.

Supermarkets with sales of over $300 billion in 1987 are experiencing some difficulties because of declining birthrates, a drop in at-home eating, and increased competition from discounters such as hypermarts and wholesale clubs. Their answer to these problems has been to broaden their lines of merchandise to better satisfy today's shopper who wants variety, convenience, and service—all at a single source. Thus, supermarkets are building larger stores, opening new departments (wine, videocassette rentals, health and beauty aids, salad bars, flowers), and adding gourmet foods. Some (such as A&P) have even set up different groups of stores operating under different names to appeal to different market segments.

---

[13] Francine Schwadel, "K mart Is Trying to Put Style on the Aisle," *The Wall Street Journal,* August 9, 1988, p. 6.

Nondiscount retailers

Department stores, as traditional middle-of-the-road retailers, have suffered over the years for a variety of reasons, but primarily because of the growth in specialty and discount retailing. Sears and Penneys—two of the largest department store chains—have failed to keep pace because of their dependency on the traditional middle-class home-owning family, which is now in decline. Sears, in particular, tied its business to housing starts and home turnover. Unfortunately, an increasing number of families cannot afford individual home ownership.

Some **department store chains** (Dillard's, Macy's) have performed well by cutting costs, emulating specialty stores by embracing the concept of market segmentation, and repositioning themselves to cater to higher income individuals by offering upscale fashions, full assortments, and strong customer service. Success hinges on their ability to divide traditional departments into a number of boutiques (store-within-a-store), each targeting a different segment. Because designer and other brands of clothing have become so common, many department stores—and specialty stores as well—are turning to private labels. It is estimated that such merchandise represents half of all women's basic dresses and sportswear at such well-known stores as Macy's, May Co. (Los Angeles), and Famous Barr (St. Louis).[14]

Specialty retailers have been successful by targeting specific segments (The Gap, Benetton, Brooks Brothers, The Rolling Pin, The Athlete's Foot, and Toys 'Я' Us). F. W. Woolworth now makes a majority of its income from specialty stores selling athletic footwear, apparel, and deep-discount drugs. Sears recently bought into the specialty field by acquiring 41 optical superstores (Eye Care Centers) and Western Auto Supply, a $3 billion player in the auto-supply market.

Traditional specialty retailers are coping with the changing buying habits of men and women in a variety of ways. Examples include remodeling stores to cater to women shoppers (hardware and auto parts retailers) and adding new merchandise lines (offering of diet sandwiches and salads by convenience stores) and merchandising programs (men's fashion shows by department stores).[15] The increased cost of pharmaceuticals has stimulated the sale of drugs by mail. The American Association of Retired Persons (AARP) operates the largest U.S. mail-order pharmacy. It fills more than 6 million prescriptions a year and employs 125 registered pharmacists.[16] Super car

---

[14] Teri Agins, "Clothing Retailers Stress Private Labels," *The Wall Street Journal*, June 8, 1988, p. 31.

[15] Scott Kilman, "Retailers Change Their Stores and Goods, Looking to Cash In on New Buying Habits," *The Wall Street Journal*, September 8, 1986, p. 23.

[16] Walt Bogdanich, "Mail-Order Pharmacies' Sales Advance, Provoking an Outcry from Drug Stores," *The Wall Street Journal*, January 16, 1986, p. 25.

dealers represent the latest change in auto retailing. Numbering only 250 dealers out of a total of 25,000, they made 15 percent of all sales in 1986; and this was expected to reach 30 percent by 1990. The largest super-dealer, Potamkin, sold nearly 40,000 new cars and 26,000 used cars in a year, which added up to sales of about $800 million.[17]

Nonstore retailers (catalog and electronic operators) have seen sales increase in recent years. Catalog sales climbed to over $30 billion in 1988, but the rate of increase has slowed. The successes of such retailing rest mainly on convenience (in-home shopping) and finding goods not available in stores. But catalog overload (over 12 billion mailed in 1988), a rash of companies imitating the more successful ones (such as Lands' End and Sharper Image), and increased postal rates have forced the industry to consolidate. For example, General Mills sold its Talbots clothing catalog and stores to a Japanese retailer and its Eddie Bauer operation to Spiegel.[18] Even the Sears' catalog of over 1,000 pages is likely to give way to a family of specialty books.[19]

Home shopping via TV (American Shopping Network, Cable Value Network, QVC Network) had $1.75 billion in sales in 1987; and this was expected to double by 1991. Most buyers are women with above-average incomes and education attracted by convenience and low prices. Electronic terminals in kiosks, a variation of the automated bank teller, are expected to have a lively future—about $3 billion by 1991, with about 30,000 transaction units in operation.[20]

CHANNEL DESIGN ALTERNATIVES

Alternative consumer goods channels

Exhibit 15–6 diagrams four channel designs commonly used to distribute consumer products and services. Channel *A* involves direct distribution of a product or service from the producer to the consumer. Such direct channels currently are most common for industrial products. But they are also becoming more popular for distributing to ultimate consumers—particularly for products and services targeted at two-wage-earner households where time pressures make in-home shopping attractive. The sellers of audiocassettes and CDs, books, kitchen gadgets, home exercise devices, and even some services (financial) have used TV to promote sales using a toll-free telephone

---

[17] William J. Hampton, "The New Super Dealers," *Business Week*, June 2, 1986, p. 60.

[18] Francine Schwadel, "Catalog Overload Turns Off Consumers," *The Wall Street Journal*, October 28, 1988, p. B1.

[19] David Snyder, "Last Chapter for Big Catalog," *Advertising Age*, July 18, 1988, p. 26.

[20] Rifka Rosenwein, "Whir, Click, Thanks: Merchandisers Turn to Electronic Salesmen in 24-hour Kiosks," *The Wall Street Journal*, June 6, 1986, p. 23.

EXHIBIT   15 ◆6

Marketing channels for consumer goods and services

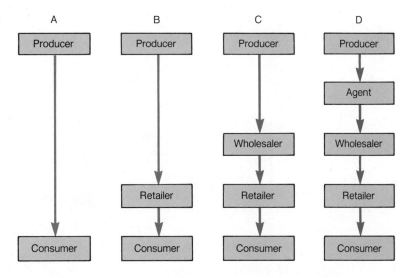

number. The growth of interactive cable TV and home computer networks is likely to make direct channels even more common in the future. Even consumer services can be distributed through direct channels—as when an insurance company maintains a salesforce and branch sales offices to distribute its financial services to consumers.

Channel *B* in Exhibit 15–6 involves the producer selling through a few select retailers who distribute products to a small target market, as in designer fashions. Such channels also occur when the producer distributes through Safeway, J. C. Penney, or other retail chains large enough to efficiently perform the buying, storage, and transportation functions otherwise performed by a wholesaler.

Channel *C*, involving both a wholesaler and a retailer, is most common for low-cost, frequently purchased items extensively distributed through a large number of retailers. Because many of those retailers are small, the cost to the manufacturer of dealing with them directly would be prohibitive. Toro distributes its lawn mowers through such a two-step channel. This channel system is also common for such things as packaged food items, liquor, and health and beauty aids.

Channel *D*, where an agent sells to wholesalers who in turn sell to retailers, is common where the manufacturer is too small—or its product line is too narrow—to justify a company salesforce. Firms also use such channels when they are entering an unfamiliar geographic market for the first time. For example, Mansar Products, Ltd.—a Belgian manufacturer of specialty jewelry—uses manufacturer's reps to sell to jewelry wholesalers in the United States.

EXHIBIT 15 ♦ 7

Marketing channels for industrial goods and services

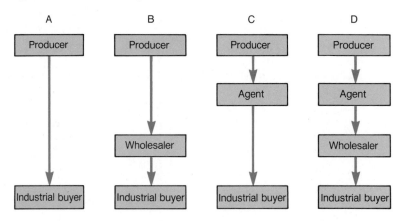

Alternative industrial goods channels

Exhibit 15–7 illustrates four alternative channel designs for distributing industrial goods. Direct distribution (channel *A* in the exhibit) is more common for industrial goods and services than for consumer goods and services. It is particularly popular when buyers are large and well-defined, the product is technically complex and of high unit value, and the selling function requires technical expertise and extended negotiation. For example, mainframe computers are usually sold through direct distribution.

Many industrial goods manufacturers distribute through wholesalers (industrial distributors), as in channel *B* in Exhibit 15–7. The manufacturer does lose some control over such activities as the negotiation of sales contracts, installation, and maintenance by using distributors. But a wholesaler can often improve distribution efficiency by lowering costs for such functions as selling, storage, and transportation. This is particularly likely when the product is standardized, there are many potential buyers with similar requirements, the average value of an order is small, and the item is easy to handle and store.[21] For example, 3M Company uses distributors for many low-tech products such as industrial tapes and abrasives.

Two other industrial goods channels involve the use of agents or brokers, either to sell directly to customers as in channel *C*, or to wholesalers as in channel *D*. Manufacturers too small to support a company salesforce most frequently use agents. Larger firms also employ agents to reach smaller or geographically dispersed customers. Agents can also develop new territories or product-markets where the firm has no experience. For example, Stake

---

[21] James D. Hlavacek and Tommy J. McCuistion, "Industrial Distributors—When, Who, and How," *Harvard Business Review* 61 (March–April 1983), pp. 96–101.

Fastener Company, a small producer of industrial fasteners, uses agents to call on its customers rather than employing a company salesforce.

Multichannel distribution

Companies are increasingly using multiple channels to reach their target segments. Some use **dual distribution** systems (two channels to reach two market segments)—as, for example, when a manufacturer of industrial goods uses wholesalers to sell and service small accounts and its own salesforce to handle large accounts. But given the increase in the number of target segments and channel alternatives, more and more companies are using more than two marketing channels. For example, a manufacturer of brake fluid distributes its product (a) directly via company salespeople to General Motors, Ford, and Chrysler for use in new cars; (b) through major oil companies that wholesale the fluid to their retail stations for consumers who bring their cars in for service; and (c) through auto parts wholesalers to retail auto parts stores to reach do-it-yourself consumers.

Horizontal market systems

This involves two or more unrelated companies pooling their resources in a program to take advantage of an opportunity. Such relationships are referred to as *symbiotic* and can take many forms, ranging from joint promotions to programs involving the marketing of products.

An example of a joint promotion is that by the manufacturers of Post Grapenuts cereals and Dannon yogurt. In a similar fashion, a business will offer a complimentary good involving another company—as, for example, when an airline offers a special deal with a rent-a-car firm or hotel. An example of a joint marketing program is Kraft serving as a channel of distribution for some of Pillsbury's food products that require refrigeration. Under this agreement (which started in the 1950s), Pillsbury takes responsibility for R&D, manufacturing, consumer advertising and sales promotion, field sales support, and pricing. Kraft is responsible for distribution, warehousing, delivery, trade advertising, product rotation, and shelf management. Joint responsibilities include inventory control, receivables, product recall, and deal communication.[22]

Channels for services

Producers of services and ideas also face the problem of making their outputs available to targeted customer segments. In some cases, this results in forward vertical integration involving decisions about branch outlets—as in

---

[22] Rajan Varadarajan and Daniel Rajaratnam, "Symbiotic Marketing Revisited," *Journal of Marketing*, January 1986, pp. 7–17.

bank services that are accessible through branch banks (some of which may be located in supermarkets) and automatic tellers. Another example is a hospital that establishes outpatient clinics to serve the specific health needs of various community segments, such as high-stress or drug- or alcohol-dependent groups.

Ordinarily, the marketing of services does not require the same kind of distribution networks as does the marketing of tangible products. Marketing channels for services tend to be short—direct from the creator or performer of the service to the end user. Thus, service retailers are emphasized because services are produced *and* distributed simultaneously in the presence of the consumer. Franchising (discussed later in this chapter) is an important channel system for the private sector.

Some services do require the use of longer channels, however. Health-care services use a variety of channel systems other than the traditional fee system employed by many doctors and hospitals in selling directly to the consumer. Health maintenance organizations (HMOs) sometimes use a vertically integrated system, where consumers pay a monthly charge to an organization (such as Baptist Medical Systems-HMO, Inc.) that coordinates the services of all health-care providers through a comprehensive facility that takes care of all the health-care needs of its constituents.[23] Hotels rely increasingly on indirect channels for their bookings. Intermediaries include travel agents who may deal directly with a hotel or contact another intermediary holding blocks of rooms, sales representatives who represent a number of noncompeting hotels or resorts, airlines that provide tour packages that include hotels, and automated reservation services that maintain a computerized inventory of available rooms travel agents can tap into for a fee.

Even the marketing of people and ideas necessitates the design of cost-effective channels for distributing information to target audiences and for collecting funds from supporters. United Way, for example, distributes ideas through private companies, service organizations, and individuals. Political ideas flow from national campaign coordinating committees to regional, statewide, and local committees.[24]

Backward channels for recycling

Recycling services have become increasingly important, given the growth of waste materials and the high costs associated with their disposal. Volunteer groups have been important in the recycling process—particularly in the collection and transport of waste to recycling plants. But the problem of disposing of waste materials is growing so fast that more commercial solu-

---

[23] Anne B. Fisher, "The New Game in Health Care," *Fortune*, March 4, 1985, p. 138.

[24] Patricia Sellers, "The Selling of the President in '88," *Fortune*, December 21, 1987, pp. 131–36.

tions must be found. In addition to traditional wholesalers and retailers, some specialized institutions now perform the marketing functions involved in recycling trash. These specialists include manufacturer-owned redemption centers and independent recycling centers. But on the whole, current backward channels are primitive and financial incentives inadequate. Somehow the consumer must be motivated to become a producer—the initiating force in the reverse distribution process of waste management.[25]

CHANNEL DESIGN DECISIONS

The design of a distribution channel is a major strategic decision neither frequently made nor easily changed. As summarized in Exhibit 15–8, it actually involves a series of interrelated decisions. It starts with (1) specifying channel objectives and proceeds through choices of (2) the desired number of retail outlets (for consumer goods and services), (3) the number of wholesale distribution points (wholesalers or company warehouses), and (4) the types of institutions to be used at each level of the channel. A number of internal company, market, and environmental factors influences each of these channel design decisions.

EXHIBIT   **15 ◆ 8**

Channel design decisions

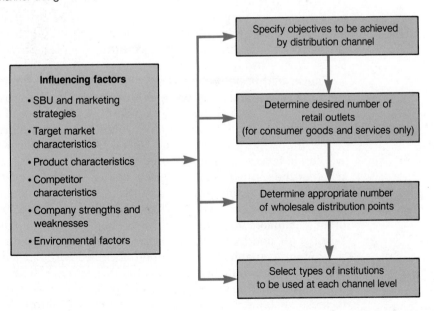

Channel objectives

As Exhibit 15–9 indicates, firms design distribution channels to accomplish one or more of the following objectives: (1) making the product available, (2) ensuring that promotional effort is devoted to the product, (3) providing a high level of customer service, (4) attaining the feedback of market information, and (5) providing cost-effectiveness. Each of these objectives is a measurable criterion to evaluate the performance of a particular channel. The exhibit summarizes ways channel performance can be measured for each objective. However, the appropriateness of each objective and the channel level at which the objective needs to be achieved varies with a number of factors, including the buying process used by the consumer and the nature of the product.

Product availability

The most important objective for any distribution channel is to make the product conveniently available for customers who want to buy it. For consumer goods, two aspects of availability must be considered: The first is to attain the desired level of coverage of appropriate retail outlets. Because retailers differ in size and the extensiveness of their trade territories, however, manufacturers should weight the contribution of each retailer to total product availability by its relative importance. This can be done on the basis of the retailer's percent of sales within the product category in question. The resulting figure is referred to as **effective distribution.** For example, a packaged food item may be carried by only 40 percent of the country's food stores. But it may have 70 percent effective distribution because it is handled primarily by large supermarkets accounting for a large proportion of the total sales of such products.

The second important aspect of availability for consumer products is the item's coverage and positioning within the store. One way to measure performance on this objective is to examine the percentage of available shelf or display space devoted to the brand, weighted by the importance of the store.

For industrial products—and for assessing channel performance at the wholesale level for consumer products—the relevant issue of availability is whether the industrial customer or retailer has the opportunity to place an order and obtain the product when it is needed. This is a question of the adequacy of market coverage. Firms can assess coverage by measuring how often customers in a territory are called on by company or distributor salespeople and by the time required to fill and deliver an order.

Product availability is an important objective for all distribution channels. The appropriate degree of availability varies with the characteristics of the product and the target customers—particularly the product's importance to those customers and the amount of time and effort they will expend to obtain it. For example, consumer convenience goods—such as packaged foods and health products—demand extensive availability. Most customers

EXHIBIT 15♦9

Distribution channel objectives and measurement criteria

Performance objective	Possible measures	Applicable product and channel level
Product availability		
♦ Coverage of relevant retailers	♦ Percent of effective distribution	♦ Consumer products (particularly convenience goods) at retail level
♦ In-store positioning	♦ Percent of shelf-facings or display space gained by product, weighted by importance of store	♦ Consumer products at retail level
♦ Coverage of geographic markets	♦ Frequency of sales calls by customer type; average delivery time	♦ Industrial products; consumer goods at wholesale level
Promotional effort		
♦ Effective point-of-purchase (P-O-P) promotion	♦ Percent of stores using special displays and P-O-P materials, weighted by importance of store	♦ Consumer products at retail level
♦ Effective personal selling support	♦ Percent of salespeoples' time devoted to product; number of salespeople receiving training on product's characteristics and applications	♦ Industrial products; consumer durables at all channel levels; consumer convenience goods at wholesale level
Customer service		
♦ Installation, training, repair	♦ Number of service technicians receiving technical training; monitoring of customer complaints	♦ Industrial products, particularly those involving high technology; consumer durables at retail level
Market information		
♦ Monitoring sales trends, inventory levels, competitors' actions	♦ Quality and timeliness of information obtained	♦ All levels of distribution
Cost-effectiveness		
♦ Cost of channel functions relative to sales volume	♦ Middlemen margins and marketing costs as percent of sales	♦ All levels of distribution

are unwilling to devote much effort to obtaining a particular brand. At the other extreme, immediate availability is less critical for unique and important products like consumer specialty goods or major industrial equipment and installations. Buyers are more willing to endure an extensive search process and wait for delivery of these products.

Market and competitive factors also influence a firm's *ability* to achieve a desired level of availability for its product. When demand is limited, or when the brand holds a small relative share of the total market, it may be difficult to find wholesalers or retailers willing to carry the product. The firm may have to offer extra incentives and inducements to achieve an adequate level of product availability. On the other hand, Nabisco's strong competitive position made it easier for the firm to attain extensive retail coverage and shelf space for its new Almost Home line of soft cookies. Environmental factors such as cultural differences across markets and the existence of enough appropriate middlemen can also affect a firm's ability to achieve the desired product availability. For example, Philip Morris and R. J. Reynolds were forced to invest in their own warehouses and employ their own salespeople to achieve adequate retail coverage for their cigarettes in the Brazilian market, which had few independent wholesalers to distribute such products.[26]

Promotional effort

Because the distribution channel is also the communications link between the firm and its customers, another common channel objective is to obtain strong promotional support from channel members for the firm's product. For consumer goods this often involves gaining retailers' cooperation for special in-store promotional events planned by the manufacturer, such as special displays and other point-of-purchase materials. One way to measure the achievement of such an objective is to calculate the percentage of retailers that agree to participate in such events. Once again, though, that percentage should be weighted by the retailers' relative importance.

Gaining broad retailer participation in in-store promotions can be particularly important for low-involvement, convenience goods. Many customers for such products do not engage in extensive decision making before entering the store, and they are unlikely to have strong loyalties to a specific brand. On the other hand, customers may be loyal to a particular store and shop there frequently. Point-of-purchase promotions can help draw their attention to a product and have a strong influence on their buying behavior.

Both the amount and the quality of personal selling effort that channel members devote to a product can be critical to marketing success. Strong selling support is particularly important when (1) firms are marketing technically complex and expensive consumer durables or industrial goods; (2)

---

[26] "Marketing Observer," *Business Week*, October 4, 1976, p. 104.

the market is highly competitive; and (3) a differentiated defender is trying to sustain a competitive advantage based on superior product quality or customer service. Under such conditions customers often rely on—and are influenced by—technical information and assistance from salespeople. When hardware retailers shifted their selling efforts to other brands in retaliation against Toro's use of mass merchandisers, for example, sales of Toro lawn mowers and snowblowers slumped rapidly.

The most obvious way to measure the degree of selling support being given a product is to examine the percentage of time devoted to the product by retailers' or distributors' salespeople. This can be difficult to determine accurately without conducting expensive field studies, though. Another measure of selling support is the degree to which middlemen's salespeople inform themselves about the product through participation in company training programs or the study of technical materials.

Customer service

Channel members can also play a crucial role in providing postsale service, including installation, customer training, and repair. Prompt and proficient service is a particularly important channel objective for makers of consumer durable goods and technically complex industrial products, such as computers and security systems. It is also a crucial objective for businesses pursuing a differentiated defender strategy and trying to preserve customer loyalty by offering superior service. For example, Toro achieved its leading market position in the outdoor equipment industry by offering excellent product quality and service. The reluctance of Toro's traditional dealers to service equipment they had not sold and the lack of service departments in most discount stores were major reasons Toro abandoned the use of mass merchandisers to distribute its products.

One common way to measure the achievement of a service objective is to monitor customers' complaints over time. Often firms set up a toll-free customer-assistance hotline. Another indicator of the service capability of a channel system is the number of service technicians that middlemen agree to send to company training programs.

Market information

Because middlemen are closer to the market than the manufacturer, firms often rely on their channel members for fast and accurate feedback of information about such things as sales trends, inventory levels, and competitors' actions. A high level of channel feedback is particularly important for firms in highly competitive industries characterized by rapid changes in product technology or customer preferences, such as the computer and fashion industries. Timely feedback is also crucial for firms pursuing prospector business strategies; they depend on the early identification of new-product and market development opportunities for their success.

New technologies, such as scanner systems in retail stores and comput-erized inventory control systems at both the retail and wholesale levels, enable middlemen to provide more accurate and timely market information than ever before. As we shall see, however, this improved ability to acquire and process market information has increased the power of large retailers and wholesalers over their suppliers. And it has raised new challenges for manufacturers as they attempt to coordinate and control the other members of their distribution channels.[27]

Cost effectiveness

Manufacturers naturally want to achieve their objectives at the lowest possi-ble cost. Thus the channel should be designed to minimize middlemen's margins and the other marketing costs necessary to achieve a firm's other channel objectives. The cost-effectiveness of the distribution channel is of particular concern to businesses pursuing low-cost analyzer or defender strategies. However, there is often a trade-off between channel costs and the level of control the manufacturer can exercise over the system. For example, the selling costs incurred for a given level of revenue are often lower when a manufacturer uses agent middlemen than when it maintains its own sales-force; but the firm has greater control over the efforts and activities of its own salespeople. A firm may use a more costly channel system in the belief that greater control will make its marketing efforts more effective and lead to volume and market share gains sufficient to offset those higher costs in the long run.

Wholesalers and retailers are also concerned with the cost-effectiveness of their dealings with alternative suppliers. Retailers are increasingly using a relatively new decision-support tool called **DPP—direct product prof-itability**—which supplements the use of gross margin analysis as a perform-ance measure.[28] DPP is obtained by taking gross margin dollars and adding any discounts or allowances to arrive at an adjusted gross margin figure. Direct product costs are next subtracted from this measure, leaving the direct product profit, often referred to as the *direct product profit contribution.*

While costs vary by product, they are typically incurred in the warehouse or distribution center, in transportation, in the store (receiving, stocking, selling, bagging, inventory, and space), and at headquarters (buying and paper processing). Cost data are collected from detailed studies of a retailer's operations; that is, the time required to receive a pallet of goods at the distribution center coupled with the wages of the person or persons in-

---

[27] Thayer C. Taylor, "The Great Scanner Face-Off," *Sales & Marketing Management*, Sep-tember 1986, pp. 43–46.

[28] This section is based on an article by Gary Robins, "Not Only for Groceries," *Stores*, July 1988, pp. 48–52. The initial use of DPP analysis started in supermarkets, but it is now spreading to mass and general merchandise retailers—hence the title of Robins' article.

volved. DPP can be used in many ways, including store layout and space allocations, product assortment, delivery method, product addition or deletion, and pricing.

K mart makes extensive use of DPP to better manage its operating costs, identify the most efficient channel, and identify items that are poor profit contributors. K mart plans to use DPP to evaluate different pricing strategies, new store layouts, and new advertising programs. It performs these analyses by using a DPP model developed by the International Mass Retailers Association. The model is essentially a preformatted spreadsheet that runs on a personal computer. The retailer enters the cost data about a given product and the computer performs the necessary calculations to generate a DPP figure. Exhibit 15–10 is an example of using DPP to determine the difference in direct product contribution of a product being handled through a distribution center and being drop-shipped.

The number of retail outlets

For consumer goods and services, achieving a desired level of product availability is largely a matter of selecting—and gaining the cooperation of— an appropriate number of retail outlets. There are three basic **strategies of**

EXHIBIT   15 ◆ 10

Distribution center versus drop-ship to store for men's jeans*

	Warehouse	Drop-ship
Retail	$19.95	$19.95
Less cost	11.50	11.95
Equals gross margin	$ 8.45	$ 8.00
Plus discounts and allowances:		
Payment discount	0.46	0.70
	$ 7.99	$ 8.70
Less direct handling costs		
Warehouse direct labor	0.55	0.00
Warehouse inventory expense	0.18	0.00
Warehouse operating expense	0.19	0.00
Transportation to stores	0.12	0.00
Retail direct labor	0.59	0.69
Retail inventory expense	0.18	0.16
Retail operating expense	0.22	0.25
Equals direct product profit	$ 5.96	$ 7.60

 * Example developed by Touche Ross & Co.

EXHIBIT 15 ♦ 11

Comparison of intensive, exclusive, and selective retail coverage strategies

	Retail coverage	Major strength	Major weakness	Products most appropriate for
Intensive	Maximum	Maximizes product availability	Lack of retailer support	Low-involvement consumer convenience goods
Exclusive	Single	Matches retailer clientele with target market; facilitates close cooperation with retailer	Risk of relying on single retailer	High-involvement specialty or shopping goods
Selective	Limited	Provides adequate coverage but not at expense of manufacturer-retailer cooperation	Difficult to implement given interstore competition, especially where discounts may occur	Infrequently purchased shopping goods

retail coverage that a manufacturer might pursue: intensive distribution, exclusive distribution, or selective distribution. Exhibit 15–11 compares the three strategies. The best strategy for a given product depends on the nature of the product itself, the target market being pursued, and the competitive situation.

Intensive distribution

When a manufacturer adopts an **intensive distribution strategy,** it uses the maximum possible number of retailers to distribute its product. This strategy is most appropriate for low-involvement convenience goods that consumers purchase frequently with a minimum of effort, such as candy, soft drinks, deodorant, and razor blades. Increasingly, low-involvement services—such as fast-food and eye examinations—are also being intensively distributed.

The advantage of an intensive distribution strategy is that it maximizes product availability. This generates greater product recognition, more impulse buying, and a larger market share due to the product's broad exposure to potential buyers. However, firms that adopt intensive distribution can also run into some implementation problems and cost disadvantages. Individual retailers may be more reluctant to carry the product or to cooperate fully with the manufacturer's marketing program than if they were given an exclusive right to carry the product in their territory. Gaining cooperation from a large proportion of available retailers can be a problem when total demand for the product is relatively small or when the brand is not the share leader in its product category. As Toro discovered, intensive distribution can also lead to conflicts between different types of retailers in the channel, and between those retailers and the manufacturer. Finally, if a company receives many small orders from an intensive network of small retailers, order processing and shipping costs can become exorbitant.

Exclusive distribution

At the other extreme, a manufacturer using an **exclusive distribution strategy** relies on only one retailer or dealer to distribute its product in a given geographic territory. This strategy is most appropriate when the product is a high-involvement specialty or shopping good that customers expend a good deal of time and effort to seek out and obtain, and when the product is targeted at a narrowly defined market niche. Exclusive distribution is also useful when a firm wants to differentiate its product on the basis of high quality, prestige, or excellent customer service. The main advantages of exclusive distribution are, first, that the manufacturer can choose retailers whose clientele and image match the target market and the positioning of the product. And second, the close cooperation with exclusive dealers facilitates implementing the producer's merchandising and customer-service programs. Indeed, there are often contractual agreements that spell out the promotional and service activities retailers agree to carry out in return for the exclusive right to sell the product in their territory. Examples of products that are exclusively distributed include Ethan Allen furniture, Curtis Mathes televisions, and Rolls-Royce automobiles.

The major disadvantage of exclusive distribution is the risk involved in relying on a single retailer for the success of the product's distribution and promotional program in each territory. This risk makes careful evaluation and selection of dealers, the development of explicit contract terms, and the monitoring of dealers' performance critically important.

Selective distribution

A **selective distribution strategy** is a compromise between the other two extremes. It uses more than one retailer, but fewer than all available retailers, in a geographic area. It is usually an appropriate strategy for shopping goods that customers buy infrequently and compare for differences in price and product features. Most brands of automobiles, Sansui audio components, and Calvin Klein sportswear are examples of products distributed selectively. Selective distribution is also necessary when the product is positioned so that some types of retailers are not appropriate. For example, Toro discovered that discounters and other mass-merchandise retailers did not fit the quality image and high customer service requirements of the firm's lawn mowers and snow throwers. Implementing this strategy, then, usually requires developing an explicit set of criteria—such as the store's price policy, customer image, annual sales volume, or financial strength—for deciding which available retailers to select.

Physical distribution and the number of distribution points

A central issue in designing a distribution channel is moving the product from the manufacturer's plant to its customers at the lowest possible cost while still satisfying those customers' demands for good service. It involves decisions about **physical distribution** (PD)—the activities involved in moving a product from the producer to customers. The importance of this issue to marketers is signified by the fact that, although PD costs vary widely across different firms and industries, on average they amount to more than 20 percent of sales.[29] In addition, one study indicates that industrial buyers rate PD performance (i.e., the speed and reliability of delivery) second only to product quality as a criterion for evaluating alternative suppliers.[30]

One critical decision that influences both PD costs and customer service levels is the number of distribution points or warehouses to be included in the channel system. A related decision concerns the type of institution to employ at each distribution point—company warehouses versus independent wholesalers, for instance. We discuss this in a later section.

Total cost concept

One objective of channel design is to minimize the **total costs** of distributing a firm's goods to its customers. The problem is the number of costs involved in PD—transportation, inventory, storage, sales lost due to stockouts, order processing costs—and that some costs trade off against others. For example, as inventory levels (and associated costs of capital and storage) increase, the costs of stockouts are likely to decrease.

As Exhibit 15–12 indicates, one common factor related to the levels of all of the elements of physical distribution cost is the number of distribution points in the system. The exhibit shows that, for a given level of customer service, as distribution points or warehouses increase, inventory, storage, and order processing costs also increase; but transportation and stockout costs go down. Thus, a firm determines the optimum distribution points for a channel system by the point where the *total of all related physical distribution costs is minimized*—even though none of the individual cost

---

[29] Roy D. Shapiro, "Get Leverage from Logistics," *Harvard Business Review*, May–June 1984, p. 124. Total physical distribution costs, on average, are made up of the following factors: transportation costs = 45 percent, cost of capital invested in inventory = 25 percent, storage (warehousing) costs = 20 percent, and order processing and management costs = 10 percent.

[30] "Changes in Segmentation, Distribution, Logistics, and Demand Analysis Challenge Industrial Marketers," *Marketing News*, June 26, 1981, p. 9.

EXHIBIT   15 ♦ 12

How physical distribution costs vary with the distribution points in the channel

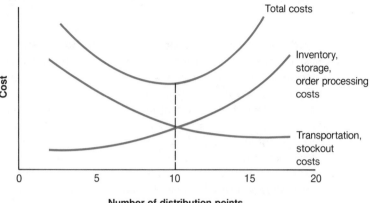

elements is as low as possible. In Exhibit 15–12, then, the channel should incorporate 10 distribution points for greatest efficiency.[31]

Customer service

It would be easy to reduce distribution costs if customer service could be ignored, but competition—and good sense—prevent this. The firm's objective, therefore, must be to minimize PD costs subject to the constraint of maintaining some target level of customer service.

From a PD point of view, **customer service** is the ability of the channel system to satisfy the needs of consumers, industrial users, or channel intermediaries (such as retailers) in order cycle time, dependability, communication, and convenience. **Order cycle time** refers to how long it takes the manufacturer (or a channel intermediary) to receive, process, and deliver an order. **Dependability** is the consistency or reliability of delivery. Studies indicate that this is the most important element of distribution service to customers—particularly for those who have implemented just-in-time delivery systems in an attempt to reduce their inventory costs.[32] **Communication** refers to a two-way link between buyer and seller that enables both parties to monitor service and to identify and resolve any problems at an early stage. Finally, the **convenience** dimension of service flows from the fact that the

---

[31] Mathematical programs can determine the optimal number and location of distribution points. See, for example, Alfred Kuehn and Michael J. Hamburger, "A Heuristic Program for Locating Warehouses," *Management Science*, July 1963, pp. 657–58.

[32] John J. Coyle and Edward J. Bardi, *The Management of Business Logistics*, 3rd ed. (St. Paul: West Publishing Company, 1984), pp. 95–101.

system is flexible enough to accommodate the special needs of different customers. If an important customer requires that all deliveries be made before noon, the distribution system should be adaptable enough to fulfill such a request.

Trade-offs between service and distribution costs

Firms often set written PD service standards as part of their marketing strategy. These standards serve as objectives and benchmarks for evaluating the channel's distribution performance. They should reflect the needs and preferences of target customers, the nature of the product, and the thrust of the business's strategy. For example, delivery standards are likely to be higher for firms making component parts for other manufacturers than for those manufacturing capital equipment. Businesses with differentiated defender strategies set more stringent standards than those following low-cost strategies. To illustrate such standards, one appliance manufacturer aims to deliver at least 95 percent of orders to its retail dealers within seven days of receipt of the order, be at least 99 percent accurate in filling orders, answer all dealer inquiries about order status within three hours, and hold damage to merchandise in transit to 1 percent or less.

Costs place an upper limit on the amount of service a firm can provide. The problem is that physical distribution costs grow at an increasing rate as service improves beyond minimum levels. One firm found, for instance, that increasing on-time delivery from a 95 percent rate to a 100 percent rate would triple its distribution costs. It would need more warehouses, incur increased order processing costs, and use more expensive modes of transportation (air freight instead of trucks or rail).[33] Thus, firms are faced with a trade-off between continuing to improve customer distribution service and containing their PD costs.

Types of institutions

A producer often must choose among channel configurations involving different institutions at one or more levels. For example, Dennison Fastener Company developed a plastic tie that could quickly bind together groups of wires in the inner-workings of complicated electronic components. The firm achieved initial success by selling its ties to the automotive original equipment manufacturer (OEM) market. A few company salespeople called directly on GM, Ford, and other major auto companies, convinced them to use the ties in making their new cars, and arranged for delivery direct from

---

[33] "The Basic Problem: Skyrocketing Costs," *Purchasing Week*, October 25, 1971, p. 18.

Dennison's plant. The firm's managers realized, however, that many other industries—such as computers and consumer electronics—were also potential markets for the product. The question was how to select channel institutions that would achieve the product availability, promotion, and customer service objectives necessary to penetrate those markets. Among the choices considered were:

- *Expand the company's salesforce.* Dennison could hire and train additional salespeople and have them contact all potential customers in a geographic territory. Or it could assign one or more salespeople to customers in each target industry. In either case, this option would necessitate developing several company warehouses or renting public warehouse space to maintain inventories and short order cycle times.

- *Use manufacturer's representatives.* The firm could contract with manufacturer's reps who sell other related products to companies in the target industries to sell its product. This option, however, would also require developing company warehouses or renting public warehouse space to handle storage.

- *Use wholesale distributors.* The firm could locate wholesalers selling related products to customers in the target industries and offer them sufficient margins (perhaps with exclusive territories and promotional support) to induce them to perform a full range of selling and distribution functions for the product.

- *Use a combination of institutions.* For example, Dennison could employ a few "key account" company salespeople to call on the largest potential customers and rely on distributors to cover all remaining customers.

Managers need to examine each of these alternatives against a set of **economic, control,** and **adaptive criteria** before making an appropriate choice.

Economic criteria

Each arrangement of channel institutions produces different levels of sales and costs. On the revenue side, most marketers believe that company salespeople are more productive than wholesalers or agents. This is largely due to the greater control the company has over their activities and effort (a contention that we examine in more detail later). However, this is not always the case. Because they spread their costs over a number of products, distributors and rep organizations can often field more salespeople in a given area than a manufacturer. They also have established relationships with customers, many of whom prefer to deal with salespeople offering a variety of products on a single call. Finally, depending on the margin or commission generated by the product relative to other lines, reps and distributors may be just as aggressive in selling the product as the manufacturer's own salespeople.

Even if an in-house salesforce would produce more volume than reps or distributors, it might also generate higher costs. Once they have projected sales revenues for alternative channels, managers must also evaluate the costs of performing the functions necessary to achieve those revenues. At a given level of sales volume they should compare the margins that would be paid to distributors to the costs involved if the firm took over the selling and distributive functions. Similarly, they should compare the costs of maintaining a company salesforce to the commissions earned by manufacturer's reps at various volume levels.

The fixed costs of a company's salesforce are typically higher than those involved in dealing with reps. This is due to higher administrative costs, capital investment in branch offices, and expenses for such things as travel and entertainment. However, the cost of using reps tends to rise faster as volume increases, because the commissions paid to reps for incremental units are usually higher than those paid to company salespeople. Thus, reps are usually more cost efficient at low levels of sales; but above some volume level an in-house salesforce becomes relatively more efficient. This helps explain why reps are most often used by smaller firms or in territories with limited sales potential where the likely volume is too small to justify a company salesforce.

Control criteria

One potential advantage of **vertically integrated channel arrangements** such as a company salesforce and company-owned warehouses is that selling and distributive activities can be more directly and thoroughly controlled than when a firm uses independent agents, distributors, or retailers. Because the people in a vertically integrated channel are company employees, the firm can select, train, and supervise personnel. It can establish operating procedures and policies and formal evaluation and reward mechanisms. And ultimately it can transfer or fire employees whose performance is not satisfactory.

Of course, manufacturers can also replace independent middlemen if their performance falls below expectations. But in many cases it is difficult for the manufacturer to tell whether the poor performance is due to a lack of effort or to factors beyond the intermediary's control, such as difficult competitive or market conditions. The company can monitor its employees' activities on a regular basis, but it is more difficult and costly to monitor the behavior of hundreds of independent middlemen. Also, it may be difficult for the manufacturer to find acceptable replacements for poorly performing middlemen. This is particularly true when a technically complex product requires specialized knowledge or capital investments to perform the channel functions effectively. For example, one reason Toro gave in to its dealers' demands to drop mass merchandisers was because those dealers would be nearly impossible to replace, especially because of their investments in and knowledge of repair service. Mass merchandisers did not offer product service, and the investments necessary for Toro to establish company-owned service centers were prohibitive. It would also have taken years to recruit and train new dealers to service Toro equipment. Under such conditions, the difficulty of replacing poor performers can make it difficult to control independent middlemen, thus increasing the attractiveness of vertical integration within the channel.[34]

Need for flexibility

Different channel designs involve different levels of commitment and loss of flexibility by manufacturers. Generally, vertically integrated systems are difficult to alter quickly—particularly when a firm has made substantial investments in physical and human resources, such as building warehouses and recruiting experienced salespeople. On the other hand, channels involving independent middlemen are often more flexible, especially if the firm did not have to sign long-term contracts to gain their support. Manufacturers facing uncertain and rapidly changing market or competitive environments (e.g., those with products in an early life-cycle stage, and prospectors rapidly developing new products) often rely on independent reps or wholesalers to preserve the adaptability of their distribution channels. Conversely, firms operating in relatively mature and stable markets, and defenders whose efficiency or good service is more critical than flexibility, might attach greater importance to the increased control inherent in vertical integration.[35]

CHANNEL MANAGEMENT DECISIONS

Designing the perfect channel to accomplish the firm's objectives in its target product-market is one thing. But actually getting the desired number of appropriate middlemen to carry the product and perform their functions consistent with the manufacturer's marketing strategy presents an entirely new set of challenges. This is particularly true for the conventional distribution channels that have been the primary focus of this chapter so far. A **conventional marketing channel** consists of an independent producer, agents, wholesalers, and/or retailers, each operating as a separate business entity primarily concerned with maximizing its own profits. One authority characterizes such conventional channels as "highly fragmented networks

---

[34] Based on the *transaction cost analysis theory* first developed in Oliver E. Williamson, *Markets and Hierarchies: Analysis and Antitrust Implications* (New York: Free Press, 1975). One critical assumption Williamson makes is that independent middlemen pursue their own self-interest—even at the expense of the manufacturers they represent—when they think they can get away with it. Because they most likely get away with self-interest-seeking behavior when it is difficult for manufacturers to evaluate their performance or to replace them for poor performance, Williamson argues that the transaction costs of using independent intermediaries is likely to be higher under such conditions than the costs of vertical integration. For empirical evidence in support of this contention, see Erin Anderson and Barton Weitz, "Make or Buy Decisions: Vertical Integration and Marketing Productivity," *Sloan Management Review*, Spring 1986, pp. 1–19.

[35] Robert W. Ruekert, Orville C. Walker, Jr., and Kenneth J. Roering, "The Organization of Marketing Activities: A Contingency Theory of Structure and Performance," *Journal of Marketing*, Winter 1985, pp. 13–25.

in which loosely aligned manufacturers, wholesalers, and retailers have bargained with each other at arm's length, negotiated aggressively over terms of sale, and otherwise behaved autonomously."[36] In such systems no one member has substantial control over the actions of the others. It can be difficult for a manufacturer to gain the cooperation of these middlemen or to coordinate their efforts in distributing its product.

In recent years, manufacturers—and in some cases large wholesalers and retailers like SuperValu and Sears—have sought ways to improve their control and coordination of the activities of their distribution channel members. As a result, several forms of vertical marketing systems have emerged. These **vertical marketing systems** (VMSs) are:

> professionally managed and centrally programmed networks pre-engineered to achieve operating economies and maximum market input. . . . These vertical marketing systems are . . . designed to achieve technological, managerial and promotional economies through the integration, coordination and synchronization of marketing flows from points of production to points of ultimate use.[37]

Firms have attempted to develop and manage such integrated VMSs in one of three ways: A **corporate VMS** uses the formal authority acquired by vertically integrating the system. A **contractual VMS** formulates agreements spelling out a coordinated set of rights and obligations for members of the system. An **administered VMS** uses the firm's economic position or expertise to provide inducements for cooperation from other members. Exhibit 15–13 diagrams the three VMSs—corporate VMSs, contractual VMSs, and administered VMSs.

Greater coordination and cooperation in all these VMSs lead to greater marketing effectiveness and distribution economies by virtue of their size, bargaining power, and the elimination of duplicated functions. As a result, VMSs have become the dominant form of channel arrangement, particularly in the distribution of consumer goods and services. The remainder of our discussion of channel management focuses on how firms can develop and maintain such systems. First, we discuss the three VMSs, their relative advantages, and the conditions under which each is most appropriate. Next, we examine the sources of power and the inducements and incentives that channel administrators use to gain the support of other system members. Finally, we identify possible sources of conflict in VMSs and some resolution mechanisms that firms use to preserve cooperation within their channels.

---

[36] Bert C. McCammon, Jr., "Perspectives for Distribution Programming," in *Vertical Marketing Systems*, ed. Louis P. Bucklin (Glenview, Ill.: Scott, Foresman, 1970), p. 43.

[37] Ibid.

EXHIBIT   15 ◆ 13

Vertical marketing systems

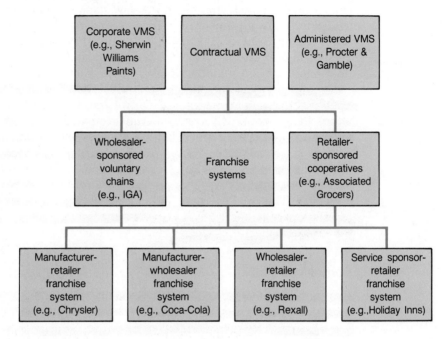

Corporate VMSs

In **corporate vertical marketing systems** firms achieve coordination and control through corporate ownership. In most cases, this is the result of vertical integration by a manufacturer of the functions at the wholesale—and perhaps even the retail—levels of the channel. For example, many industrial firms have their own salesforces, warehouses, or branch sales offices. Firms such as Sherwin-Williams in paints, Hartmarx in clothing, and Goodyear in tires and auto accessories also own their own retail outlets.

However, it is not always the manufacturer that controls the channel system through vertical integration. **Backward integration** occurs when a retailer or wholesaler assumes ownership of institutions that normally precede them in their distribution channels. Sears, for example, has an ownership interest in a number of manufacturers that are important suppliers of the firm's private label goods, including Whirlpool and DeSoto. Such integration is also common among large supermarket chains.

The primary advantage of these corporate systems is the tight bureaucratic control they afford the owner over personal selling, promotion, distribution, and customer service activities within the channel. Such control can be particularly important when the product is technically complex; specialized knowledge or facilities are needed to effectively sell, distribute, and/or service the product; and there are few capable independent middlemen available. Thus, a number of years ago Singer established company-owned retail sewing centers. Extensive educational programs to teach potential customers how to sew were essential to sell sewing machines; but independent retailers were reluctant to assume the cost of such programs.

One disadvantage of corporate systems is the large capital investment required for vertical integration. Only large, financially healthy firms can afford to develop such systems. And even those firms may find vertical integration unattractive from a purely financial point of view, because the average return on investment is often lower for wholesaling and retailing operations than it is in manufacturing. Also, we have seen that corporate systems are often not as flexible and adaptable as less formally structured channels. This makes them less viable for manufacturers operating in rapidly changing technological or market environments, and for businesses pursuing prospector strategies.

Contractual VMSs

In **contractual vertical marketing systems** independent firms at different levels of production and distribution coordinate their programs through legal contracts that spell out the rights and duties of each party. The intent is to obtain greater economies and market impact than they could achieve alone. Contractual VMSs have had the greatest growth of any channel system in recent years. There are many specific forms of contractual systems; but the three basic types include **wholesaler-sponsored voluntary chains, retailer cooperatives,** and **franchise systems.**

Wholesaler-sponsored voluntary chains
Wholesalers organize voluntary chains by getting independent retailers to sign contracts in which they agree to standardize their selling practices and to purchase a certain portion of their inventories from the wholesaler. This gives the wholesaler greater buying power in its dealings with manufacturers and enables the voluntary chain to compete more effectively with large corporate chains. The Independent Grocers Alliance (IGA), Western Auto, and Ben Franklin are among the best-known wholesaler-sponsored voluntaries.

Retailer cooperatives
Groups of independent retailers can also take the initiative and form their own cooperative chain organizations. Typically, they agree to concentrate their purchases by forming their own wholesale operations. In many cases they also engage in joint advertising, promotion, and merchandising programs. Profits are passed back to the member retailers in proportion to their

purchases. Such cooperatives are particularly common in the grocery field, where Associated Grocers and Certified Grocers are examples.

Franchise systems[38]

A channel member might coordinate two successive stages in the distribution channel by offering franchise contracts that give others the right to participate in the business provided they accept the agreement terms and pay a fee. Such contracts usually specify a variety of operational details—including which members of the system will perform specific functions and how—as well as mechanisms to evaluate members' performance and to terminate members who fail to perform adequately.

Franchising has great versatility. Such systems operate in almost every business area and cover a wide variety of goods and services, including the following:[39]

accounting and tax services	car washes	lawn care
art galleries	credit and collection	motels and hotels
auto rentals	employment agencies	pet stores
auto repair	entertainment	printing
auto accessories	fast food	real estate
beauty salons	food stores	retail stores
building services	health aids	schools
candy stores	ice cream	travel
carpet cleaning	laundry	vending machines

There are four major franchise systems.

- **Manufacturer-retailer franchise systems** account for the largest number of franchisees and the largest volume of sales. They are common in the automotive and petroleum industries. Chrysler, General Motors, Ford, and other automotive companies, for example, license independent dealers to sell and service their cars. Those dealers, in turn, must meet certain requirements and agree to conduct their operations according to a number of prescribed standards.

- **Manufacturer-wholesaler franchise systems** are exemplified by the soft-drink industry: Coca-Cola and Pepsi sell syrup concentrate to franchised wholesale bottlers who then carbonate, bottle, sell, and distribute soft drinks to retailers in their territories.

- **Wholesaler-retailer franchise systems** are similar to wholesaler-sponsored voluntary chains. But the retail franchisees agree to conduct and coordinate their operations according to detailed standards specified by the franchise agreement. Examples include Rexall drugstores and SuperValu supermarkets.

---

[38] Based on Stern and El-Ansary, *Marketing Channels*, pp. 332–48.

[39] Breton R. Schlender, "Working on the Chain Gang," *The Wall Street Journal*, May 19, 1986, p. 140.

♦ **Service sponsor-retailer franchise systems** are the most familiar to consumers. They develop when service firms contractually organize and coordinate entire systems for delivering their services to customers. Examples include McDonald's, Burger King, and Kentucky Fried Chicken in fast foods; Holiday Inns in lodging; Hertz and Avis in car rentals; Midas and Precision Tune in auto repair; and Manpower in employment services.

The popularity of franchise systems derives from their being able to offer consistent quality at a convenient location at a reasonable price. The start-up costs of a franchise vary from $300,000 for McDonald's to $6,500 for Jani-King (a commercial janitorial service). Franchisors receive an initial fee (typically between $10,000 and $25,000), a percentage of the franchisee's gross sales (about 5 percent), and—where applicable—rent on equipment, fixtures, and the building.

Franchise operations—both goods and services—had sales of $640 billion in 1988, a 30 percent increase over 1984. They now represent 34 percent of all retail sales and by the year 2000 may reach 50 percent as companies use this channel system as a way to reduce employee costs.[40] The faster-growing franchise industries include recreation, entertainment, and travel; construction and home services; nonfood retailing; restaurants; business services; and auto/truck rental services. This strong growth results from the continued shift from a manufacturing-based economy to a service one, consumer demand for consistent convenience and economy, increasing numbers of women and minorities interested in owning their own businesses, and expansion abroad.[41]

Administered VMSs

In an **administered vertical marketing system,** firms coordinate activities at successive stages of distribution through the informal guidance and influence of one of the parties (rather than through ownership or contractual agreements). The administrator—or channel captain—has typically been the manufacturer. In some cases, however, that role is performed by a large retailer or wholesaler, such as Sears. Usually the administration of such systems involves developing a detailed merchandising program in which the manufacturer spells out shelf-space arrangements, a promotional calendar, pricing policies, and guidelines for other activities to be followed by its wholesalers and retailers. Such programs have been implemented successfully by Nabisco in marketing its cookies and crackers; General Electric in major appliances; and Sealy with its Posturepedic mattresses.

---

[40] "Signal," *Fortune,* January 30, 1989, p. 14.

[41] Meg Whittemore, "Franchising's Future: More than $1.3 Trillion Sold," *Daily Market Digest,* April 28, 1986, p. 22.

The critical question, though, is how can a manufacturer convince independent middlemen to participate in and accurately carry out detailed merchandising plans when the firm neither owns nor enjoys contractual agreements with them? The answer is that successful channel administrators draw on their power within the system to induce cooperation from its other members.

Sources of channel power

Firm A has *power* over firm B to the extent that A can get B to do something that B would not do if left to its own devices.[42] The extent of firm A's power over B is inversely proportional to firm B's dependence on A to attain desired rewards or avoid unwanted consequences. **Sources** (or **bases**) **of power** within channel relationships include the following:

- **Economic power** exists when channel members perceive that a firm can mediate economic rewards for them if they follow its directives. Most often, those rewards take the form of increased sales and profits. Thus, the producer of a brand with the largest share or the most prestige in its product category can often gain the cooperation of distributors or retailers who believe that their efforts on behalf of the brand are likely to be rewarded with handsome sales and profits. Even producers of new or less-dominant brands can exercise economic power by offering additional rewards to other channel members, such as large margins, promotional allowances, or introductory discounts. Nabisco ensured adequate shelf space for its Almost Home soft cookies, for example, by offering an additional 10 percent discount on any Nabisco product to every retailer that agreed to devote four feet of space to the new line.
- **Coercive power** is based on a perception that one channel member will punish another for failure to cooperate. It is the inverse of economic power, since such punishments usually take the form of a reduction in or withholding of economic rewards. For example, a manufacturer might threaten to withdraw a retailer's exclusive territorial rights or its promotional allowances if the retailer's performance does not meet expectations. Coercive power should be used sparingly, though. Frequent threats of punishment often lead to conflict, resentment, and dissatisfaction among other channel members.[43]
- **Expert power** stems from a perception that one channel member has special knowledge or expertise that can benefit other members of the system. Because of the reputations of firms like General Mills and Procter & Gamble as savvy marketers, middlemen are often willing to abide by their merchandising suggestions. The assumption is that their programs are more likely to lead to sales success than anything the middlemen could come up with on their own. However, the recent proliferation of scanners in retail stores has increased the expert power of retailers.

---

[42] John F. Gaski, "The Theory of Power and Conflict in Channels of Distribution," *Journal of Marketing*, Summer 1984, pp. 9–29.

[43] Gary L. Frazier and John O. Summers, "Interfirm Influence Strategies and Their Application within Distribution Channels," *Journal of Marketing*, Summer 1984, pp. 43–55.

They now have more detailed and up-to-date information about local sales of individual brands and the effectiveness of specific promotions than the manufacturers have.[44]

+ **Referent power** is based on perceptions of the benefits and satisfactions that have been generated—and are likely to continue to be generated—from a long-term relationship with a channel member. A member that has received good service and earned substantial profits from a relationship with a manufacturer over the years may be willing to accede to its suggestions or requests, without demanding any additional rewards, simply to preserve the relationship into the future.

+ **Legitimate power** flows from the perception that one channel member has the right to make certain decisions or demands and to expect compliance from other members. Legitimate power is usually the result of ownership or contractual agreements. But in some instances it is based on "moral authority" or common beliefs about what is right and proper. For example, most middlemen would agree that a food manufacturer has the right to print expiration dates on its packages and to expect middlemen to pull out-dated packages off the shelves as a means of protecting the product's quality and the consumer's health.

Channel control strategies

A manufacturer might draw on a number of sources of power to gain the support and cooperation of independent middlemen. The ability to deliver economic rewards—either directly or by providing expert advice that improves those middlemen's economic performance—is crucial. But what can strengthen the perceptions of other channel members that carrying a manufacturer's product and following its merchandising program will benefit them economically? Two strategies manufacturers use to improve perceived economic power and to win better cooperation from other channel members are a pull strategy and a push strategy. These strategies are diagrammed in Exhibit 15–14.

Pull strategy

When pursuing a **pull strategy** a manufacturer focuses its marketing efforts primarily on building selective demand and brand loyalty among potential customers in its target market. A large proportion of the brand's marketing budget is spent on media advertising, consumer promotions, extended warranties and customer service, product improvements, line extensions, and other actions aimed at winning customer preference. If successful, such a strategy can "pull the product through" the distribution channel. Middlemen are virtually sure to make substantial sales and profits by carrying such a popular product and supporting the manufacturer's merchandising program. In other words, by building strong customer demand, the manufac-

---

[44] Taylor, "The Great Scanner Face-Off."

EXHIBIT   15 ♦ 14
Pull and push strategies

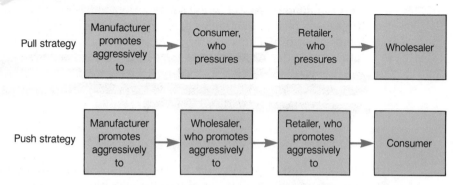

turer increases its ability to promise economic rewards in the form of large sales volumes to its channel members in return for their cooperation.

A manufacturer whose brand is already the share leader or the most prestigious brand in its category has substantial power to influence other channel members—particularly if the product is in the growth stage of its life cycle. But what if the manufacturer is introducing a new product with no past sales history? In such situations the use of a pull strategy to gain reseller support presents a unique challenge. To persuade potential wholesalers and/ or retailers to carry and support the new product, the manufacturer must somehow convince them that its marketing program can successfully build strong customer demand and loyalty for the new brand *before that program is initiated*. After all, the product must be available to customers when the advertising and promotion campaign begins. To persuade potential channel members that a new product's marketing efforts can result in substantial sales and profits, company salespeople make kick-off presentations in which they demonstrate the new product and describe the planned marketing program in detail. Prospective middlemen are often told the product's advertising and promotion budget, shown actual ads and the calendar of promotion events, and given any other information that might help convince them of the program's future viability, including test-market data that show strong results. Such efforts at persuasion are most likely to be successful when the manufacturer has substantial resources to devote to the new product's marketing program, is perceived to have a great deal of marketing expertise, and has an extensive track record of past new-product successes.

Push strategy

Smaller firms with limited resources, those without established reputations as savvy marketers, and those attempting to gain better channel support for existing products with relatively small shares and volumes often have difficulty achieving cooperation solely on the promise of future sales and profits.

In such situations firms must usually adopt a **push strategy** in which much of the product's marketing budget is devoted to more direct inducements to gain the cooperation of wholesalers and/or retailers. Typically, a manufacturer offers channel members a number of rewards, each aimed at motivating them to perform a specific function or activity on the product's behalf. The rationale is that direct inducements to channel members help push the product into the marketplace. By motivating more wholesalers or retailers to carry and aggressively promote and sell the product, more customers are exposed to and persuaded to buy it.

Incentives for motivating channel members

Manufacturers typically use a combination of incentives to gain reseller support and push their products through the channel, because different types of incentives are good for motivating resellers to perform different functions. By combining different rewards, manufacturers can tailor trade incentives to the specific marketing and distribution needs of a product and its target customers. Exhibit 15–15 lists a variety of reseller incentives along with the functional performance dimensions each is appropriate for motivating.

Incentives to increase reseller purchases and inventories

The reseller action most critical for a manufacturer to influence is purchasing behavior. For new products, the objective is simply to get wholesalers or retailers to carry and stock the new item. Manufacturers unable to build much pull for their products by stimulating selective demand often have to offer wholesalers and retailers more direct inducements to build distribution. They can offer higher margins than are typical for the product category. They can offer introductory discounts or buy-in (co-op) promotions for a limited time to encourage the initial adoption of the product. And they can agree to give selected wholesalers or retailers exclusive rights to the product in their local territory. (Of course, granting exclusive territories at the retail level is usually not a viable option for convenience goods requiring widespread distribution!)

Once a product has achieved an adequate level of distribution coverage, the manufacturer's purpose changes to one of shifting the *storage* of the product as close to the ultimate customer as possible by motivating resellers to purchase and stock larger quantities. This usually involves offering resellers periodic price discounts structured so that the size of the discount is tied to the quantity purchased. We examined a number of such discounting practices, including quantity discounts and seasonal discounts, in the last chapter. Other methods of stimulating volume purchases include **buy-back allowances,** where the producer offers a discount on a future second order based on the size of an initial order; and **free goods,** where the manufacturer rewards volume purchases with additional merchandise at no cost. Liquor

EXHIBIT 15 ♦ 15

Incentives for motivating channel member performance

Functional performance dimensions	Examples of channel incentives
Increased purchases/carry larger inventories	Larger margins, exclusive territories, buy-in promotions, quantity discounts, seasonal discounts, buy-back allowances, free goods, shelf-stocking programs
Increased personal selling effort	Sales training programs, instructional materials, incentive programs for channel members' salespeople
Increased local promotional effort ♦ Local advertising	Cooperative advertising; advertising allowances; print, radio, or spot TV ads for use by local retailers
♦ Increased display space	Promotion allowances tied to shelf space
♦ In-store promotions	Display racks and signs, in-store demonstrations, in-store sampling
Improved customer service	Service training programs, instructional materials, high margins on replacement parts, liberal labor cost allowances for warranty service

wholesalers, for instance, sometimes offer one free case of a brand for every ten cases purchased by a retailer.

Incentives to increase personal selling effort

For many industrial products and consumer durable goods, the quality and amount of personal selling effort devoted to the product by channel members are critical determinants of marketing success. To motivate and assist resellers in upgrading the knowledge and professionalism of their salespeople, manufacturers can provide instruction manuals, training seminars conducted at the middleman's home office or store, or more detailed training programs held at the manufacturer's headquarters.

Some manufacturers also attempt to increase the amount of effort their resellers' salespeople devote to their products by offering incentive programs directly to those sales personnel. Such programs are usually sales contests rewarding individual reseller salespeople if their sales of the manufacturer's product exceed some target level. The rewards may be monetary— sometimes called **push money** or **spiffs**—or in the form of merchandise or travel. However, manufacturers should obtain approval from each reseller before initiating such programs. Because most middlemen represent a number of manufacturers, they sometimes resent attempts by one supplier to gain a disproportionate allocation of their employees' time and effort.

Incentives to increase local promotional effort

Middlemen can play an important role in advertising and promoting a manufacturer's product in their local areas, particularly for consumer goods. Thus, many consumer products firms try to motivate their retailers to (1) increase the quantity and quality of local advertising featuring their products, (2) increase the amount of display space devoted to their brands, and/or (3) participate in in-store promotions.

To stimulate more local advertising, many manufacturers use cooperative advertising programs. They pay a percentage (say, 50 percent) of a retailer's expenses for local advertising up to some limit based on that retailer's sales of the product. For example, they might pay an amount equal to 2 percent of the retailer's annual sales of the brand. Many such programs also try to control the quality of local advertising by providing preproduced ads for a variety of different media, to which the retailer can simply add the name and location of the store.

When a manufacturer tries to up the volume of a retailer's purchases by offering volume-based discounts, it also hopes that more of the product will end up on that retailer's shelves, thereby increasing the display space devoted to the firm's brand. This does not always happen, however. Some manufacturers, thus, make their discount offers contingent on being given a specific amount of shelf space. For example, Nabisco offered a discount on any of its products to retailers who agreed to allocate four feet of space to its Almost Home cookies.

Another method for encouraging retailer promotional support is to induce them to participate in in-store promotions. Many manufacturers offer free racks, signs, and other materials for use in free-standing promotional displays. These are often in conjunction with volume discounts to further encourage dealers' participation. Some firms also make representatives available to conduct in-store demonstrations of the firm's products or to pass out free samples to shoppers.

Incentives to improve customer service

For consumer durables and many industrial products, manufacturers often rely on distributors or retailers to provide product-related services, such as installation and repair, to the final customer. One way for manufacturers to strengthen the quality of such service is to provide detailed instructional materials or company-sponsored training programs for their dealers' service technicians. Some firms—such as Toro in the outdoor power equipment industry—also offer relatively high margins on replacement parts to encourage dealers to keep an adequate supply of parts in inventory and liberal labor cost reimbursements for warranty service.

Channel conflicts and resolution strategies

Regardless of how well a manufacturer administers its channel system, or how many inducements it offers to gain cooperation, some amount of **channel conflict** is almost certain to arise from time to time. Indeed, some conflict is essential if members are to adapt to change. Conflict should result in more effective and efficient channel performance, *provided* it does not become destructive. Disagreements among channel members can occur for several reasons:

* **Incompatible goals.** Each channel member is interested in maximizing its own share of the total profits generated by the system. Consequently, manufacturers and middlemen frequently disagree over the size of margins and incentives offered at each channel level and over which members should bear the cost of performing specific functions such as inventory storage. Conflicts can also arise because the manufacturer is concerned with increasing the market share of its brand while its dealers want to offer an assortment of competing brands to satisfy a range of customers.

* **Unclear rights and responsibilities.** Sometimes a manufacturer's marketing policies are unclear to its middlemen. Or, they may seem to be incompatible with the traditional activities and expectations of those middlemen. For example, IBM uses its own company salesforce to sell personal computers to large business accounts. But its licensed retail dealers also call on such accounts. This has caused confusion and conflict about who should be calling on whom and who should get credit for major sales, as well as a good deal of duplication of effort within the channel.

* **Misperceptions and poor communication.** Sometimes conflicts arise when there are no substantive reasons for them to occur. This is because members at different channel levels can interpret events in very different ways. When Toro began selling direct to mass merchandisers, for instance, its distributors concluded that it was a first step toward the total elimination of the wholesale level in Toro's distribution channel. Even though Toro never intended to bypass its distributors, it took years of effort—and a major change in policy—to win back their support.

Because channel conflict is inevitable, the challenge is not to eliminate it but to minimize it and manage it better. Firms have pursued several approaches aimed at recognizing and resolving potential conflicts early before they cause a breakdown of cooperation in the system.[45]

* **Involve channel members in policy decisions.** Some companies have formed dealer advisory boards or survey a sample of middlemen on a regular basis to gauge their reactions to company policies and programs. Du Pont, for instance, has a Distributor Marketing Steering Committee that meets regularly to discuss problems and trends. And Parker Hannifin sends out an annual mail survey asking distributors to rate the company's performance on key dimensions.

---

[45] See James A. Nars and James C. Anderson, "Turn Your Industrial Distributors into Partners," *Harvard Business Review*, March–April 1986, pp. 66–71.

- ◆ **Increase interaction among personnel at all levels.** Increased contacts among the employees of a manufacturer and its middlemen can lead to an improved understanding of each party's problems and objectives and to more accurate and open communications. Thus, Square D—a manufacturer of electrical equipment—has its salespeople spend a day "working the counter" with each of its distributors to better understand the distributor's business. Dayco Corporation runs an annual week-long retreat where 20 company executives interact in seminars and outings with 20 distributor executives.

- ◆ **Focus on common goals.** When channel members can be persuaded to focus on a common purpose or a common external threat, such as foreign competition, they may be more willing to compromise their individual concerns for the good of the system. When Lee Iacocca became president of Chrysler, for instance, he gained dealer cooperation by stressing the common objective of survival in the face of threatening competitive and financial circumstances.

- ◆ **Mediation and arbitration.** Sometimes the use of outside administrative mechanisms such as third parties to mediate or arbitrate disputes is an effective method of resolving conflict. Successful action here rests on clarifying the issues, examining alternative solutions, keeping the parties in contact with each other, and encouraging agreement to certain proposals.

Legal constraints[46]

Effective channel management requires the use of power, but there are substantial legal constraints on how power may be used with respect to distribution channels. This is most apt to be the case when the firm uses an exclusive or selective distribution strategy and/or attempts to dictate how the channel intermediary will do business in connection with marketing the product.

In recent years, the courts have begun to use more of a rule-of-reason approach to potential offenses rather than finding specific practices inherently illegal. Even so, vertical relationships are covered by the major antitrust acts—Sherman, Clayton, and FTC. A brief discussion of the major nonprice legal constraints imposed by the federal government is presented below. Despite the increased number of state laws pertaining to the regulation of distribution, their variability makes it impossible to summarize them briefly.

1. *Exclusive dealing.* The requirement that a channel member sell or lease only the seller's products is illegal if the requirement substantially lessens competition.

2. *Tying contracts.* This requires a buyer to take products other than the one wanted and, with some exceptions, is illegal per se. **Reciprocity,** wherein a buyer refuses to do business with a supplier unless that firm buys its product, is

---

[46] This section draws heavily on Louis W. Stern and Adel I. El-Ansary, *Marketing Channels,* chap. 8.

similar to tying contracts and is illegal when coercion is involved and substantial commerce is affected.

3. *Territorial restrictions.* This involves the granting of a geographical monopoly to a buyer for a given product. The decision here rests on the effect of intrabrand restrictions on interbrand competition. **Resale restrictions** on type of customer the buyer can sell to are handled on much the same basis.

4. *Refusal to deal.* The right of a seller to select its customers—or to stop selling to one—is legal as long as it does not substantially lessen competition or foster a restraint of trade.

5. *Promotional allowances and services.* These must be offered to all resellers on proportionally equal terms and must be used for the purposes intended (e.g., advertising allowances must be used to pay for advertising).

6. *Incentives for resellers' employees.* Such incentives (e.g., push money) are generally acceptable, provided they do not injure competition substantially.

Vertical integration from within is legal if it does not lead to monopolization in restraint of trade. Vertical integration via merger or acquisition is typically viewed rather negatively if there is thought to be any chance competition will be substantially lessened.

SUMMARY

A marketing channel is the set of interdependent organizations involved in the process of making a product or service available for consumption or use by consumers or industrial users. Usually a number of specialized institutions are involved in a distribution channel because such specialization and division of labor increase the functional, scale, and transactional efficiencies of the performance of necessary marketing functions.

Among the types of institutions a manufacturer might include in the distribution channel are (1) merchant wholesalers who take title to the product and sell to other resellers, institutions, or industrial customers; (2) agent middlemen who also operate at the wholesale level but are paid by commission rather than taking ownership of the goods; (3) retailers who take title and sell to consumers; and (4) facilitating agencies—such as advertising agencies and trucking firms—that are employed on an as-needed basis and paid fees for their specialized services. Firms can organize one or more of these institutions into a channel for a specific product or service in a variety of ways. It is

becoming increasingly common for manufacturers to use multiple channel structures for distributing a single product in order to reach distinct target segments of customers.

Managing the distribution of a product or service requires a manufacturer to make two interrelated sets of decisions: those concerning channel design and those involving the management of the various institutions included within the channel. Major channel design decisions include (1) specifying the manufacturer's objectives for its distribution system; (2) determining the appropriate number of retail outlets; (3) deciding on physical distribution; and (4) choosing specific types of institutions for each level in the channel.

Channel management decisions are primarily concerned with improving the manufacturer's control and coordination of channel members' activities. To accomplish that purpose, some manufacturers (and a few large wholesalers and retailers) have vertically integrated to form *corporate vertical marketing systems* in which they have the formal authority to coordinate activities at various levels. Such systems are particularly common when the product is complex, specialized knowledge or facilities are required to sell or service the product, and few independent middlemen capable of performing the necessary activities are available.

Other firms have improved their control and coordination of channel activities by forming contractual vertical marketing systems, in which independent firms at various levels agree to legal contracts that spell out each party's rights and duties within the system. Marketers categorize such contractual systems into three basic types: wholesaler-sponsored voluntary chains, retailer cooperatives, and franchise systems.

Finally, through informal guidance and influ-ence, one of the parties coordinates administered vertical marketing systems. The channel administrator—who is usually a manufacturer but may be a large wholesaler or retailer—relies on its power within the system to motivate cooperation from the other members. Manufacturers attempt to improve their economic power to administer the distribution channel through: (1) a pull strategy in which consumer advertising and promotion efforts build selective demand for the product, and resellers are motivated by the promise of future sales and profits; or (2) a push strategy in which direct incentives—such as quantity discounts and cooperative advertising programs—are offered to induce cooperation from channel members.

QUESTIONS

1. Under what conditions is a manufacturer most likely to consider the use of *multi-channel distribution* for marketing a product? Describe an example of multi-channel distribution involving a consumer good or service.

2. A Swedish manufacturer of home entertainment equipment such as stereos and VCRs is interested in entering the U.S. market. What kinds of institutions should it consider including in its distribution channel in the United States? Why?

3. The president of a carpet manufacturer has asked you to look into the possibility of bypassing the firm's wholesalers (who sell to carpet, furniture, and department stores) and using company salespeople to sell directly to these stores. What caution would you voice on this matter and what information would you gather before making a recommendation?

4. How might a regional professional theater—such as the Guthrie Theater—attempt to gain more *extensive distribution* for its performances?

5. Calvin Klein jeans are *selectively distributed* through a limited number of fashionable department and specialty stores. Is this an appropriate channel design for such a product? Why or why not?

6. A few years ago, large manufacturers with well-known brands (e.g., General Foods or Procter & Gamble) held substantial *power* over even the largest retailers in their distribution channels. Today, large retailers such as the Safeway supermarket chain have the power to demand more rewards and support from major manufacturers. What has caused this change in the balance of power? What are the bases (or sources) of the retailers' power over their suppliers?

7. Why would an independent hardware store owner agree to become a member of a *cooperative chain*? What benefits would the store owner receive? How would the development and growth of the cooperative chain affect the balance of power in hardware distribution channels?

8. A cereal manufacturer is considering

using a *pull strategy* to gain extensive retail coverage for a new cereal brand targeted at health-conscious adults. Which characteristics and capabilities of the manufacturer can help determine its ability to successfully implement such a strategy?

9. A small and relatively unknown manufacturer of valves and fittings wants to induce large plumbing wholesalers to carry and promote its products. Which strategy should it pursue? Which specific *incentives* might it offer to wholesalers to gain their support?

10. There is often *conflict* between manufacturers and the retailers that distribute their products. What are some major causes of such conflicts? What can a manufacturer do to minimize or resolve these conflicts?

Chapter ◇ 16

Promotion mix decisions

BARTLES & JAYMES: GALLO'S CLASSIC PROMOTION

The scene has become a classic of American advertising—two frumpy-looking middle-aged men sitting on the porch of a farmhouse. One of them, Frank, does all the talking, while the other, Ed, sits quietly in the background. These two folksy, country bumpkins are, of course, Frank Bartles and Ed Jaymes, spokesmen for Bartles & Jaymes wine coolers.[1]

This advertising first entered the living rooms of America in 1985 with the introduction by Ernest and Julio Gallo of Bartles & Jaymes wine coolers. Gallo, the largest wine marketer in the United States, followed the lead of others such as Brown-Forman's California Cooler in developing a wine-and-fruit-based product that matched the trend toward lighter, natural, lower-alcohol beverages. What makes the Bartles & Jaymes story a classic in American promotional history is not the development of a unique product that captured American tastes, but the development and execution of a promotional strategy that launched the brand into first place in the wine cooler category.

From the outset Gallo declined to link this entry with its existing low-price image. Rather, it chose to develop a fictional company managed by characters created through media advertising. A major reason for the almost overnight recognition of Frank and Ed was the volume of advertising support Gallo gave this brand. In 1985 when Bartles & Jaymes was introduced, Gallo spent $17.4 million in advertising and in-store promotion.

EXHIBIT 16♦1

© Bartles & Jaymes Co., 1988.

The success of the Bartles & Jaymes advertising campaign was strongly reinforced by the effects of the massive

---

[1] Based on Brian Lowry, "One Gag That's Gone Too Far," *Advertising Age*, August 22, 1985; Julie Solomon, "Bartles and Jaymes Aren't Real Guys, But You Knew That," *The Wall Street Journal*, July 8, 1986; "How They Became King of Coolers," *Nation's Business*, October 1985; and Jaclyn Fierman, "How Gallo Crushes the Competition," *Fortune*, September 1, 1986, p. 31.

continued

concluded

amounts of "free advertising" gener-ated by the publicity that surrounded the campaign from the beginning. Gallo received media attention ranging from *The Wall Street Journal* to *People* mag-azine. The value of the publicity Gallo received from the press is difficult to assess; but it is reasonable to assume that this coverage was an important rea-son for consumers' favorable response to the brand.

Capturing consumers' attention and interest was certainly important; but Gallo also had to obtain the support of the retail distributors of wine coolers.

It did so with its large salesforce, which many feel is the best in the industry. Gallo uses a unique approach to the selling of its products at the retail level called "clean teams." It uses one sales-person per individual product line in each sales territory. A single liquor store, for example, may be visited by as many as eight Gallo sales reps. Given Gallo's overall strength—annual sales in excess of $1 billion coupled with strong advertising and publicity cam-paigns—it is not surprising that Bartles & Jaymes received prominent display at the retail level.

As this example illustrates, marketing consists of far more than develop-ing a good product, offering it to the target market at the right price, and making it readily available. Companies must also communicate a consider-able amount of information about their firm, its products, its price struc-tures, and its distribution system to a variety of audiences including consumers, intermediaries, and the media. *Marketing communications—typically and hereafter referred to as promotion*—can be a distinctive advan-tage that separates the product from its competitors. Certainly this seems to be the case with Bartles & Jaymes.

In this chapter, we begin by discussing the promotion mix and its major components. Then we examine the communication process—an under-standing of which is essential to the development and implementation of an appropriate promotion strategy. A discussion of the major determinants of the promotion mix follows. Finally, we present a framework for developing an effective promotion mix.

THE PROMOTION MIX

The term **promotion** has been defined in a variety of ways over the years. More recently it has been used interchangeably with the term **marketing communications** and, thus, has to do with persuading people to accept products, concepts, and ideas. **Promotion strategy** is a "controlled, inte-

grated program of communication methods and materials designed to present an organization and its products to prospective customers; to
communicate need-satisfying attributes of products to facilitate sales and
thus contribute to long-run profit performance."[2] The development of an
effective promotion strategy depends heavily on how well the company has
carried out earlier steps in the marketing management process—especially
those concerned with understanding buyers' behavior, market segmentation,
competitive analysis, target marketing, and product positioning.

Firms make their promotion strategies operational through the use of
advertising, personal selling, sales promotion, and public relations.[3] Definitions of these promotion mix components follow:

- **Advertising**—Any paid form of nonpersonal presentation and promotion of ideas,
  goods, or services by an identified sponsor.
- **Personal selling**—A process of helping and persuading one or more prospects to
  purchase a good or service or to act on any idea through the use of an oral
  presentation (person-to-person communication).
- **Sales promotion**—Incentives designed to stimulate the purchase or sale of a
  product—usually in the short term.
- **Public relations**—Nonpaid, nonpersonal stimulation of demand for a product,
  service, or business unit by planting significant news about it or a favorable
  presentation of it in the media.[4]

Collectively these are referred to as the **promotion mix.** (See Exhibit 16–2
for the kinds of activity involved.) Gallo's promotion mix emphasized advertising (especially television), personal selling to the trade (not only to obtain
stocking but in-store displays as well), and publicity. Incentives (sales promotions) at either the retail or consumer level are prohibited by laws in most
states for liquor, wine, and beer products.

Business strategy constraints

We noted earlier that business strategies set not only a general direction for
what target markets to pursue, but also how to compete in such markets.
These strategies affect the marketing program elements chosen to meet the
demand stimulation and competitive position tasks relating to individual
product-market entries.

Prospector and *differentiated defender* strategies require extensive promotion programs for their successful implementation. Because of their
heavy emphasis on new product-market entries, *consumer-goods prospec-*

---

[2] James F. Engel, Martin R. Warshaw, and Thomas C. Kinnear, *Promotional Strategy* (Homewood, Ill.: Richard D. Irwin, 1987), p. 6.

[3] The composition of the firm's promotion mix is strongly affected by whether the firm
follows a push or a pull strategy. This subject was discussed in Chapter 15.

[4] *Marketing Definitions: A Glossary of Marketing Terms* (Chicago: American Marketing
Association, 1960).

EXHIBIT   16 ◆ 2

Examples of promotional activities

◆ **Advertising:**	Print ads (newspaper and magazine), radio, television, billboard, direct mail, brochures and catalogues, signs, in-store displays, posters, and motion pictures.
◆ **Sales promotion:**	Coupons, sweepstakes, contests, product samples, rebates, tie-ins, self-liquidating premiums, trade shows, trade-ins, and exhibitions.
◆ **Public relations:**	Newspaper and magazine articles/reports, TV and radio presentations, charitable contributions, speeches, issue advertising, and seminars.
◆ **Personal selling:**	Sales presentations, sales meetings, sales training and incentive programs for intermediary salespeople, samples, and tele-marketing.

tors rely heavily on advertising and public relations to build awareness. They also use a variety of sales promotion activities (such as coupons and in-store displays) to obtain sampling and retailer support. *Industrial-goods prospectors,* on the other hand, rely primarily on a well-trained salesforce coupled with trade shows, public relations, and trade advertising.

Differentiated defenders, especially for industrial goods and services, are for the most part concerned with maintaining the loyalty of their existing customers. The salesforce thus dominates their promotion mix decisions. For consumer goods, much depends on whether the differentiation is concerned with something new relating to the product (including new brands, line extensions, and new packaging) or a change in distribution (say, setting up an on-line ordering system). The former, where a new brand is involved, necessitates a mix heavily dominated by advertising and sales promotion. If the change concerns a line extension or new packaging, then reliance is placed primarily on advertising, while the overall emphasis on promotion is considerably less. Where the change deals with something other than the product, then implementation is carried out primarily by the salesforce.

Low cost defenders, as might be expected, spend little on promotion. Such firms, regardless of whether they sell industrial or consumer goods, select personal selling as their main promotion expense, followed by trade advertising. Expenditures are as low as possible, given the need to minimize costs in order to protect ROI performance.

THE COMMUNICATION PROCESS

Before specifying the promotion mix for a product or service, marketers must understand the communication process—that is, how communication works. The essential elements of any communication are a **source** (the

EXHIBIT **16 ◆ 3**

The communication process

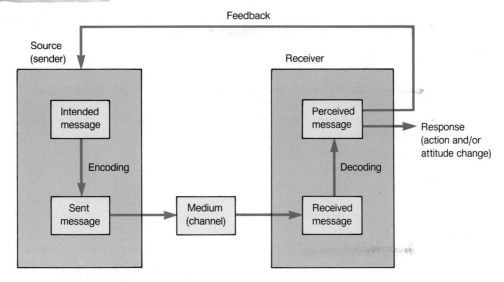

communicator), a **message** (a set of symbols), a **medium** (the communication channel), a **receiver** (the target audience), and a **response** (a set of reactions). Exhibit 16–3 shows these elements. Marketers begin with an idea or concept; for example, that Bartles & Jaymes is produced by a small California winery. They hope to communicate this idea to a specific audience; in this case, young, affluent members of the wine cooler market. They then transform the concept into a set of symbols understandable to the target audience like those in the TV ad—Frank and Ed sitting on the porch discussing their product. This process of transforming ideas into symbols is called **encoding**.

These sets of symbols or messages are then transmitted through alternate channels or media to the targeted audience. After receiving the message, the audience must change the symbols (the words or pictures) into an idea or concept to derive meaning from the communication. This activity by the receivers is **decoding**. For marketing communications to be effective, the source's encoding process must be similar to the receiver's decoding process. Because the source can encode—and the receiver can decode—only in terms of the experience each has had, the experience of the message senders and receivers must overlap if the message is to be effective.[5]

The process of communication concludes with an evaluation of the audience's reaction to the message sent. Through **feedback**, marketers attempt

---

[5] Wilbur Schramm, "How Communication Works," in *The Process and Effects of Mass Communication*, eds. Wilbur Schramm and Donald F. Roberts (Urbana: University of Illinois Press, 1971).

to find out whether the right audience received the message, whether they understood it, and whether it had any impact on how they think, feel, or act. Because time and distance usually separate the source and the receiver, marketers must often actively pursue feedback through marketing research.

Noise

The so-called **noise** in the system inhibits effective communication. People are bombarded by over 1,000 commercial messages each day along with all their other activities. These distractions are the noise in the system and serve not only to block the receipt of a message, but also can cause the receipt of a message different from what the sender intended. To make communication even more difficult, consumers engage in practices designed to protect themselves from receiving unwanted messages, understanding what action is wanted and why, and remembering what has been said. (See Exhibit 16–4.) In each of these areas researchers have reached the following conclusions:

Selective exposure. Most people expose themselves to messages and media that fit—are compatible with—their existing attitudes. Conversely, consumers avoid messages not compatible with their attitudes or that they find irritating or boring.

EXHIBIT 16 ♦ 4

Effect of consumer protection practices on message receipt and retention

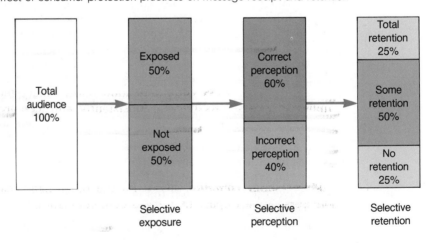

Results: Of the total audience, only 7.5 percent totally retained the message intended by the communicator (50% × 60% × 25%), while 15 percent retained some part of the message (50% × 60% × 50%). Note that these results say nothing about the number (percent) who correctly perceived the message, totally retained it, and experienced a change in attitudes of any magnitude. The results here would be even lower—perhaps much lower.

Selective perception. People may distort or misinterpret the intended meaning of a message when it differs from their attitudes. As might be guessed, the greater the change required in the attitudes of the respondents to make them accept the position advocated in the message, the more likely is the message to be distorted or rejected.

Selective retention. People tend to forget more quickly communications that are substantially at variance with their attitudes. At the same time, people remember for a longer time messages reinforcing their attitudes.

Research indicates that communications are most likely to be successful when they reinforce existing attitudes. They are somewhat likely to be successful if they cater to latent predispositions. And they are least likely to succeed when they run counter to existing or latent positions. Changing a person's attitudes or behavior is typically *not* likely via promotion. Exceptions occur where the attitude or behavior involved is of little consequence to the individual. For example, people who care little which brand of coffee they drink are more likely to be influenced to switch brands. If the mediating factors (predispositions and personal influence) are inoperative (people have not yet formed any negative attitudes about a new product), they may be influenced by a promotion for it. Or where the mediating factors favor change (say, friends start buying a new product), people are more likely to be influenced by the promotion about it.

It is difficult, therefore, for a communicator to develop a message that achieves its intended results. Only when much gain is likely with little effort and cost or risk is a message likely to be received, processed, and acted on.[6]

Mass versus interpersonal communications

As we noted earlier, the advertising, sales promotion, and publicity elements of the promotional mix rely on mass forms of communication. Personal selling, on the other hand, relies on interpersonal communication. As Exhibit 16–5 shows, there are important differences between these two types of communications. **Mass communication** allows marketers to reach large numbers of individuals quickly, consistently, and with great efficiency. For example, a prime-time network TV commercial reaches millions of viewers across the country with exactly the same message and at a very reasonable *price per exposure*. Unfortunately, such a commercial has a very high *absolute cost* both in producing the ad and in buying the airtime to show it.

Interpersonal communication, on the other hand, can provide much more persuasive impact than mass communication. The marketer is in a better position to communicate large amounts of information and complex information. The marketer can tailor messages to fit the specific differences of individuals in the audience and receive direct and clear feedback on the

---

[6] Ibid.

EXHIBIT 16 ♦ 5

Comparison of interpersonal and mass communication

Factor	Interpersonal communication	Mass communication
Reaching a large audience		
Speed	Slow	Fast
Cost per individual reached	High	Low
Influence on the individual		
Ability to attract attention	High	Low
Accuracy of message communicated	Low	High
Probability of selective screening	Relatively low	High
Clarity of content	High	Moderate to low
Feedback		
Direction of message flow	Two-way	One-way
Speed of feedback	High	Low
Accuracy of feedback	High	Low

Source: James F. Engel, Martin R. Warshaw, and Thomas C. Kinnear, *Promotional Strategy,* 6th ed. (Homewood, Ill.: Richard D. Irwin, 1987), p. 49.

effects of the communication on the receiver. But interpersonal communication has its limitations, too. It is not suited for a large, geographically diverse audience—and its per-exposure costs can be very high.

FRAMEWORK FOR DEVELOPING AN EFFECTIVE PROMOTION MIX

Because there are four distinct promotion mix components (advertising, personal selling, promotion, and publicity or public relations) each with its own unique strengths and weaknesses, developing an effective promotion mix is difficult. To facilitate this task, most companies follow a seven-step decision process similar to that shown in Exhibit 16–6.

Analyze the situation (step 1)

Marketing managers must acquire and analyze a great deal of information for a successful promotion program. Earlier steps in the marketing management process should provide much of the data required here. In general, managers need three kinds of information to perform a situation analysis—assessments of the consumer, the competitive situation, and the environment.

Assessments of the consumer

The effectiveness of the promotion process depends considerably on how well the target audience has been specified. The target audience can be current or past users of the company's product, heavy or light users of the

EXHIBIT **16 ♦ 6**
A decision sequence framework for marketing communications

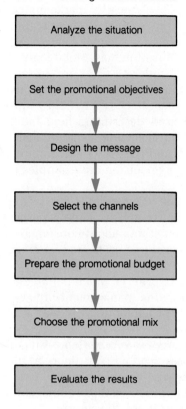

product, users of the product class or type, users of closely related substitute products, or buying influentials. The characteristics of the target audiences impact message formulation, the selection of communication channels, and the promotion mix. Managers classify the information they need to define and understand the target audience as descriptive, perceptual, and the buying process.

Descriptive information.   This type of information pertains to understanding who constitutes target audiences and how to describe such consumers or organizations. Chapter 6 on market segmentation discussed descriptors for consumer and industrial products. The more common ways of describing audiences for consumer goods are by such demographics as age, income, sex, geography, and education. Another useful way to describe consumers is by *lifestyle.* This is particularly helpful to those preparing the promotion message, because it provides insights into consumers' attitudes and values relative to a product class.

A third type of descriptive information involves *product-usage levels.* Categories of usage include users/nonusers, current/former users, and heavy/light users. Typically, marketers combine demographic and product-usage descriptors to profile a target audience. An example would be a heavy-user family where the female head is over 40 years of age, employed, has a high-school education, has a total family income of over $30,000, and where two children under 18 years are present.

For industrial goods marketers usually use a two-stage process to identify the target audiences. First, they identify the company or organization. Commonly used descriptors here include the company's SIC group, its size, product usage, and geographical location. Purchase influence, benefits wanted, and the sociodemographic characteristics of those participating in the buying decision are examples of second-stage descriptors.

Perceptual information. The second kind of information managers need to assess consumers is largely **perceptual** in nature. Thus, marketers must know something about consumers' familiarity with the product, how consumers evaluate products in a given product category (choice criteria), and how the company's product and competitive products are rated in terms of the choice criteria. Much perceptual information is derived from the step in the marketing management process that relates to product positioning discussed in Chapter 10.

Buying process information. The third category of information involves the **processes** used by consumers in the purchase and use of the product. Data concerning, for example, the buying decision process, where consumers expect to purchase the product, and how they search out sources of information about it are all relevant.

Assessments of the competitive situation
Chapter 7 on competitive analysis discussed the kinds of information needed here.

Assessment of the environments
The third part of the situation analysis involves examining the internal and external environments within which the promotional strategy must operate. From an internal perspective, the promotional strategy must be properly aligned with the company's objectives. It must certainly consider the financial resources available for promotion both short and long term. Similarly, the promotion strategy must be consistent with and complement the other elements in the marketing mix such as the product, its price, and the distribution system.

Factors in the external macroenvironment also constrain promotional activities. Chapter 3 discussed this type of analysis in depth. In the case of the Bartles & Jaymes brand as well as its other wine products, Gallo monitors changes in state laws pertaining to the sale and promotion of wines and changes in the minimum age for buying and consuming alcoholic beverages. The company is also vitally concerned with any technological changes that impact its containers. And Gallo follows with considerable interest American consumers' growing preference for lighter alcoholic products.

Set the promotional objectives (step 2)

Once managers complete a thorough situation analysis, the next step is to develop specific **promotional objectives.** Like any managerial process, the likelihood of a successful promotion is greatly enhanced if you know where you want to end up before you start. Specific promotion objectives make the job of developing message and media strategies much easier. They also provide the basis on which to evaluate the promotion once it is completed.

Sometimes changes in sales and market share are set as promotional objectives, but such changes are a function of the entire marketing program—not just the promotional mix. An exception is where the promotion requires an immediate response, such as direct-mail advertising and catalogs. Advertising that contains coupons can be evaluated based on coupon redemption. And the effectiveness of retail ads featuring sale merchandise can be determined by sales. Although difficult, sales effects of brand advertising can be determined through the use of test markets similar to those used to test new products.

Acceptable promotional objectives follow from the situation analysis and involve four key components: a statement defining the target audience; a statement of how the audience should change; a statement of how fast such a change should occur; and a statement as to the degree of change desired. Suppose you are introducing a new consumer food product—say, a line of frozen food items called Quick and Lite Dinner Entrees aimed at working women. A common promotional objective in such a situation would be to try to generate awareness (brand name and salient product features) for this new product. Thus, a possible promotional objective for this situation might be as follows:

> To create awareness of the new product among 50 percent of the working women between the ages of 25 and 50 with incomes of $25,000 or more within the next three months.

Notice that this brief statement includes each of the four components, albeit in rather brief form. The objective describes the target audience (working women ages 25–50 with incomes of $25,000 or more); how the marketer would like them to change (become aware of the new brand); by how much (from 0 percent of the target audience to 50 percent); and how fast (three months).

Objectives must be stated for each component within the promotion mix. Brief statements of what each of the promotion components is intended to accomplish follow.[7] They serve as the basis for setting objectives. We give a more detailed description of these objectives in the next chapter. Promotion component objectives are:

- **Advertising**—to communicate by building awareness, understanding, and belief in a product's salient characteristics.
- **Personal selling**—to make personal presentations and close the sale; also, to provide point-of-sale support.
- **Sales promotion**—to trigger action at the point-of-sale level.
- **Publicity**—to build support for the company and its product through nonpaid media.

Applied to the introduction of the Bartles & Jaymes brand, the statements might translate into the following objectives:

- *Advertising*—to build brand awareness to 35 percent of the wine cooler market.
- *Personal selling*—to place the product in 80 percent of the available retail outlets.
- *Sales promotion*—to place a life-size display of Frank and Ed in retail outlets representing 75 percent of the sales of wine coolers.
- *Publicity*—to place articles about the Bartles & Jaymes advertising campaign in magazines totalling 10 million in paid circulation.

These objectives should also indicate the demographics of the targeted consumer audience, the characteristics of the targeted retailers (size and type), and a timetable showing when each of the objectives should be accomplished.

Design the message (step 3)

Designing a successful message is a difficult task—if only because of the countless ways in which a marketer can construct the message. Yet the payouts from good messages versus poor ones are substantial. For example, simple changes in the wording of a print ad have been known to generate a substantial increase in sales for retail stores, mail-order houses, and direct-mail sellers.

All marketing communications involve some degree of information and persuasion. Each message, for example, involves a sponsor or a brand name, which is basically *informative*. And each message directly or indirectly advocates some change by the audience, which is basically *persuasive*. Which type of communication should dominate depends on the nature of the communication objective and the characteristics of the audience.

Messages can also be classed as being predominantly connotative or denotative. **Connotative messages** deal essentially with feelings and relationships (e.g., the Bartles & Jaymes wine cooler advertising). **Denotative**

---

[7] Engel et al., *Promotional Strategy*, p. 197.

messages are more literal and factual, as would be the case with most industrial goods advertising. Connotative messages reveal much more about the sender—including feelings and even emotional makeup. Rarely, however, is a message entirely connotative or denotative; it is usually a blend of the two. There are several types of message appeals—rational, emotional (including fear), moral, and humorous.

Rational and emotional appeals

Rational appeals show that the product can deliver the benefits wanted by the target audience. The message seeks to demonstrate the product's quality, reliability, and performance. Many such ads are organized to first arouse the audience's needs and then present a solution—the purchase of the sponsor's brand. For example, a recent ad appeared in the *New Yorker* magazine with the heading, "Beat Moles and Gophers without Guilt." It goes on to note that your garden may be victimized by moles, gophers, woodchucks, or other burrowing rodents, but "You can't surrender—poisoned traps might hurt the kids and pets—anyway, they'd make you feel like a murderer." The ad then presents its solution: a European import that fits in the ground over the rodent's tunnel. It emits a continuous electric pulse that drives the rodents so crazy they leave forever.[8] See Exhibit 16–7 for a print example of a rational ad. Ads that appeal to a consumer's economic needs are common, especially ads featuring price.

In recent years we have seen an increase in the use of **emotional appeals** that downplay product attributes and emphasize the good feeling derived from using the product. Bartles & Jaymes' advertising is of this type as is the Maxwell House coffee TV campaign, which has featured a young couple enjoying a cup of coffee in a romantic setting. (See Exhibit 16–8 for a print ad using essentially an emotional appeal.) Why this shift from the traditional message that featured the product's benefits? According to Assael, there are at least four reasons for this trend:

1. Advertisers have run out of rational things to say about their products.
2. Tighter advertising regulation has substantially reduced the claims that can be made in a product's behalf.
3. Rational appeals are often associated with a hard sell which, when used extensively, hurts the attention-getting power of the advertising.
4. Some products are low-involvement items that can be better remembered on an emotional basis.[9]

Fear appeals are often relied on to persuade consumers to use a product such as life insurance or mouthwash—or to *not* use a product such as drugs or cigarettes—as a way to avoid some unpleasant outcome feared by those

---

[8] *The New Yorker*, February 29, 1988, p. 95.

[9] Henry Assael, *Marketing Management* (Boston: Kent Publishing, 1985), pp. 325–26.

EXHIBIT 16 ♦ 7

Example of a rational appeal in a print ad

Courtesy First Chicago Corporation.

EXHIBIT 16 ♦ 8

Example of an emotional appeal in a print ad

© 1988 Ralston Purina Company.

consumers. Moderate fear appeals are more effective than very strong or very weak appeals. The former generates too much anxiety. In the words of Ray and Wilkie, "there is the possibility of defensive avoidance of the ad, denial of the threat, selective exposure or distortion of the ad's meaning, or a view of the recommendation as being inadequate to deal with so important a fear."[10] Whatever else the message communicates, it must propose a believable solution to the problem. An example of moderate fear advertising is Michelin's ads that portray a baby along with the message, "When you have so much riding on your tires."

Moral and humorous appeals

Some advertisers—mostly those concerned with social causes—use **moral appeals** to get people to take the appropriate action. Appeals made in behalf of United Way, Mothers Against Drunk Driving (MADD), and the Red Cross

---

[10] Michael L. Ray and William L. Wilkie, "Fear: The Potential of an Appeal Neglected by Marketing," *Journal of Marketing*, January 1970, p. 55.

EXHIBIT 16♦9

Example of the use of humor in a print ad

Courtesy Nabisco Brands USA. (This ad was used exclusively in health clubs.)

are examples of moral appeals. **Humor** often attracts attention and creates a positive attitude toward advertisers; but such ads must take care not to distract the reader or viewer from the real purpose of the message. An example is the TV commercial in which Frank Bartles and Ed Jaymes tell the audience how they put their orchard and vineyard together to make a premium wine cooler. "So Ed took out a second mortgage on his house," says poker-faced Frank, "and wrote Harvard for an MBA."[11] (See Exhibit 16–9 for another example of the use of humor in advertising.)

Select the channels (step 4)

Channel selection is concerned with how best to deliver the message. It is a three-step process: First, marketers decide which promotion components to use: advertising, personal selling, sales promotion, or publicity. Second, they choose the specific activities within each component. In advertising, this involves considering such media as TV, radio, newspapers, magazines, or billboards. A consumer sales promotion could consist of coupons, free samples, or premiums.

---

[11] Fierman, "How Gallo Crushes the Competition," p. 31.

EXHIBIT 16 ♦ 10

A comparison of promotional elements

	Scope	*Cost*	*Advantages*	*Disadvantages*
Advertising	Mass	Relatively in-expensive per contact	Allows expressive-ness and control over message	Hard to measure results
Personal selling	Personal	Expensive per contact	Permits flexible presen-tation and gains im-mediate response	Costs more than all other forms per contact
Sales promotion	Mass	Can be costly	Gains attention and has immediate effect	Easy for others to imitate
Publicity	Mass	Inexpensive	Has high degree of be-lievability	Not as easily controlled as other forms

Source: Adapted from David J. Rachman and Elaine Romano, *Modern Marketing* (Hinsdale, Ill: Dryden Press, 1980), p. 450.

Third, within each activity they must decide which specific vehicle to employ. Thus, in advertising this requires selecting a TV or radio program; while in personal selling they must find a salesperson with certain attributes. In sales promotion, they must decide about the coupon specifics—its value, size and color, message format, and how it will be delivered.

Each of the four components of the promotion mix has some advantages and disadvantages as channels for delivering promotional messages. These are summarized in Exhibit 16–10 and discussed below.

Product advertising

Most advertising efforts are concerned with stimulating the demand for a particular brand; for example, those campaigns promoting Coke, Tylenol pain reliever, Subaru cars, or Bartles & Jaymes wine coolers. For an example of product advertising, see Exhibit 16–11 for a unique in-store display consisting of a cardboard replica of Bartles (in the rocker) and Jaymes (holding the sign). **Brand advertising** helps increase the sales of the brand by getting consumers to switch from competitive brands, increasing consumption among present users, attracting nonusers of the product type, and maintaining sales from current users.

Most brand advertising focuses on stimulating **selective demand** for a particular product, in contrast to **primary demand,** which expands the market for a product type. However, brand advertising probably does stimulate some primary demand, particularly during the introductory and growth stages of the product life cycle.

EXHIBIT 16 ♦ 11

Retail display of Bartles and Jaymes

© Bartles & Jaymes Co., 1986; photo by John Harding.

Primary demand advertising typically is an industry's attempt to stimulate demand for its product. In recent years, many associations and agricultural cooperatives have promoted such items as cotton, wool, chicken, beef, and coal, and certain bank financial services. The National Pork Producers Council has undertaken an extensive promotional program, including TV advertising, depicting pork as "the other white meat" in an effort to convince consumers that pork is low in calories and cholesterol and that it contains important nutrients.[12] Although they are the exceptions, some companies also engage in primary demand advertising. For example, Campbell Soup once promoted "soup for lunch"; now, "soup is good food." Because Campbell holds an 80 percent share of the canned soup market, it stands to benefit substantially from any increase in the overall demand for soup.

---

[12] "Pork Producers Extend Campaign," *Marketing News*, February 29, 1988, p. 19.

Cooperative advertising is a joint effort by manufacturers and retailers to sell a particular product. The manufacturer typically takes the initiative by offering the retailer an advertising allowance (usually a small percentage of the dollar sales) to advertise its products locally—often in the Yellow Pages of the phone directory, in newspapers or on local radio or TV stations. This type of advertising is widespread among consumer goods firms.

Corporate advertising

Corporate advertising differs from product advertising in that its purpose is to benefit the corporation as a whole; that is, to enhance the company's image by building favorable attitudes toward the overall firm. Historically this advertising has been termed **institutional advertising.** Three major types of corporate or institutional advertising include issue advertising, investor-relations programs, and corporate image building.[13]

Issue advertising. Such advertising can support a given social issue in which a firm has a strong interest—or it can advocate a certain point of view on issues the firm thinks are threatening to its future. An example of the first is Anheuser-Busch's corporate advertising campaign called Operation Alert. It publicizes the company's series of programs designed to get people to be more responsible about their consumption of all alcoholic beverages. Programs the company has developed or supported include SADD (Students Against Driving Drunk), the Alert Cab program, "I'm Driving" (a designated-driver program), and "Know When to Say When."[14]

Most of the large tobacco companies have sponsored advocacy advertising in an effort to downplay the need for more government regulation of the tobacco industry. Major oil companies have done much the same to try to prevent the government from passing tax legislation unfavorable to the oil industry.

Investor relations programs. Such advertising is designed to generate awareness and build favorable attitudes among financial analysts and possible investors. For example, *The Wall Street Journal* carried a full-page ad sponsored by Safety-Kleen with the headline, "The only company that's had over 20 percent annual net earnings growth for 17 consecutive years." It also reported that 1987 net earnings grew 24.2 percent to $35,083,000; and earnings per share increased 23.3 percent to $7.06.[15]

---

[13] Thomas F. Garbett, "When to Advertise Your Company," *Harvard Business Review,* March–April 1982, p. 100.

[14] Full-page ad entitled "Operation Alert," in the *Harvard Business Review,* January–February 1988, p. 9.

[15] *The Wall Street Journal,* February 18, 1988, p. 19.

Corporate-image advertising. Corporate-image advertising establishes an identity for a corporation or changes an image held by its target audiences. An example is the campaign that seeks to identify Hitachi as the company with the goal: "in automotive electronics—and medicine, energy, and consumer electronics as well—to create and put into practice innovations that will improve the quality of life the world around." The ad attempts to establish Hitachi as a leader in automotive electronics technology.[16]

Personal selling

Personal selling is unique compared to other promotion types because it permits the company to meet with the customer face to face. This means that the message does not have to be prepared in advance; rather, it can be adapted as the meeting progresses. Thus, questions can be asked—and answered—about the product.

Much of Gallo's success is attributed to its aggressive salespeople who link the company to the retailer and have the last chance to influence the consumer to buy a Gallo product. The company has a 300-page training manual that "describes and diagrams every conceivable angle of the wine business. 'As a sales representative of Gallo Wine, . . . you are the [one] that Ernest and Julio Gallo depend on to sell retailers the merchandising ideas that sell Gallo Wine to consumers.' The manual contains sections on how to display Gallo products in stores, how much shelf space Gallo products should occupy, how to maintain shelves, and instructions on making the 'complete' sales call."[17]

Advertising and personal selling are more compatible than might be thought—at least under certain circumstances. Because the average cost per sales call is close to $200, many companies have turned to advertising—a lower cost medium—to perform certain selling functions. This is particularly true with many industrial goods (like a computer system) where there are a number of buying influentials scattered throughout the organization. Typically, the salesperson does not know these influentials or how important they are. Even if such information were available, the salesperson would have difficulty getting to see them all; and the costs involved would be substantial. Thus, advertising can be a useful vehicle for communicating with such individuals.

Corporate advertising is an important way to develop a company's reputation. And this, in turn, saves valuable time for both the prospect and the salesperson. Further, many industrial salespeople sell a relatively long line of products and find it impossible to cover all items in a single visit. Advertising, by covering the nature and scope of the line, can supplement the salespeople's efforts and provide them a greater opportunity to highlight

---

[16] *Fortune*, February 29, 1988, inside back cover.

[17] Jaclyn Fierman, "How Gallo Crushes the Competition," p. 28.

specific products. Advertising can also help accelerate the rate of adoption of a new industrial good by developing awareness and interest in potential customers before the salesperson arrives.

Sales promotion

Sales promotional activity is essentially short-term oriented compared to brand advertising, which seeks to build a favorable long-term brand image. Sales promotion consists of coupons, rebates, sweepstakes, refunds, free samples, and premiums. These incentives range in value from a few cents to thousands of dollars on new cars. Sellers direct sales promotions at the final consumer or at the trade (wholesalers and retailers). For an example of a major Burger King sales promotion, see Exhibit 16–12.

Expenditures on sales promotion are greater than for advertising—perhaps twice as much. Coupons are the most popular sales promotion for consumer goods. In 1985 companies issued over 180 billion coupons with a face value of some $50 billion. Consumers redeemed 6.5 billion coupons worth $2 billion. Sales promotion expenditures are increasing at a faster rate than advertising. Products are becoming less and less differentiated, and promotions help ensure shelf space. Media costs have increased to a level where many sellers reason that sales promotion offers a better buy. And sales promotion offers a way to reduce prices temporarily without changing list prices.[18] Trade allowances made to retailers by manufacturers are an increasingly important part of the manufacturer's promotion budget. One estimate put the amount of packaged merchandise sold to retailers on some kind of trade deal at over 80 percent.[19]

Public relations

Public relations is largely complementary to the other promotional activities. It consists of news releases and even films about the product and company. It may even include appearances by company executives. At its best, publicity provides an extra degree of credibility to a company and its products and does so at little cost.

An example of successful public relations was the introduction of the Cabbage Patch Kids doll in 1983; people were literally fighting to buy them as Christmas presents. The company persuaded Nancy Reagan to give Cabbage Patch dolls to two South Korean children when they returned home after undergoing heart surgery. Jane Pauley gave the dolls visibility on the "Today" show; and later they were featured on the "Tonight" show. Brooke Shields and Catherine Bach appeared as life-size Cabbage Patch dolls in a sketch on Bob Hope's TV Christmas special. Hospitals gave hundreds of

---

[18] Felix Kessler, "The Costly Coupon Craze," *Fortune,* June 9, 1986, pp. 83–84.

[19] William C. Johnson, "Sales Promotion: It's Come Down to 'Push Marketing,'" *Marketing News,* February 29, 1988, p. 8.

EXHIBIT   16 ◆ 12

Burger King launches $140 million game to aid sales

Burger King, the number two hamburger chain, hoped to generate huge traffic with its heavily advertised Triple Jump Checkers Game via awards to customers of $140 million in cash, cars, cruises, and food. The checkers game is similar to McDonald's highly successful "Monopoly" game in calling for customers to scratch off game pieces. A comparison of the stakes involved in the two games is presented below.

Prizes	McDonald's Monopoly	Burger King Checkers
Soft drink co-sponsor	Coca-Cola	PepsiCo
Automobile prizes	500 Oldsmobiles	75 Pontiacs
Travel prizes	Walt Disney World	Carnival Cruises
Apparel prizes	$1,000 Sears spree	None
Dream House prize value	$300,000	$200,000
Grand prize cash value	$2 million	$1 million
Estimated advertising/marketing support	$80 million	$30 million

The challenge is not to get the customer in the door, but to deliver once you get them there. McDonald's has done a good job of this, but Burger King has been inconsistent. Hence, according to one expert, Burger King may be putting the cart before the horse by spending so much on short-term sales promotions before improving the consistency of its operations.

Source: Richard Gibson, "Burger King Starting $140 million Game in Ploy to Aid Sales," *The Wall Street Journal,* September 23, 1988, p. 21; and Scott Hume, "Burger King Plays $140 Million on Promo Game," *Advertising Age,* September 19, 1988, p. 1

Cabbage Patch dolls to young patients as Christmas gifts from the company. Radio stations and newspapers played up these gifts. With such a publicity campaign, it's no wonder the dolls were a smashing success.[20]

Prepare the promotional budget (step 5)

This fifth step in the decision process in the development of the promotional mix is difficult and complex to execute. Ideally, a firm would answer the question of "How much should be spent on the promotional mix?" by measuring the marginal revenue from each additional dollar spent. The firm would continue to spend monies on promotion so long as the marginal revenues were greater than the marginal promotion costs. The difficulty is that only rarely can the firm estimate the marginal revenue. The reason is that sales are a function of many variables, of which promotion is only one.

There are a number of ways to determine the promotional budget, most of

---

[20] "Behind-Scenes Look at Cabbage Patch PR," *Advertising Age,* December 26, 1983, p. 2.

which work from the top down. This means managers determine the total amount to be budgeted and then allocate the amount to various components of the mix. These budget-setting methods include: (1) percentage of sales, (2) all that can be afforded, and (3) competitive parity. A fourth way is a bottom-up approach, called the objective-and-task method.

Percentage-of-sales method

Perhaps the most common way that firms set promotional budgets is to tie promotional expenditures directly to sales. Often, this year's budget is calculated as a simple percentage, such as 5 or 10 percent, of either last year's sales or anticipated sales this year. The amount can also be estimated using the unit of sale as the basis for determining the advertising budget. For example, some auto makers allocate $50 to $60 to advertising for each car sold.

Under this approach, sales volume determines promotional activity rather than planning the promotion budget to achieve some desired sales objective. Even though this is somewhat illogical, the percentage-of-sales method does have some advantages. It is very simple to calculate, and it is risk-adverse, because spending is linked to sales. It keeps the firm from getting too far out of line with what the industry as a whole is doing.

A study by Lilien, called ADVISOR, investigated how industrial marketers determined their advertising budgets. It found that such firms tended to use a two-step process. First, they decided on their marketing budget as a percentage of sales (M/S ratio). Second, they decided how much to spend on advertising as a percent of the marketing budget (A/M ratio). The advertising to sales percentage (A/S ratio) derives from multiplying the A/M and M/S ratios.

The average industrial goods firm budgeted about 7 percent of its anticipated net sales for its marketing activities and 0.6 percent of its net sales on advertising. The study also found that as the product moved through its life cycle, its M/S ratio fell; the higher the product quality, the higher the M/S ratio; the higher the product's market share, the lower the M/S ratio; the higher the concentration of sales in the hands of a relatively few customers, the lower the M/S ratio; and the higher the purchase frequency, the greater the M/S ratio. Industrial firms spent nearly two thirds of their advertising budget on media (41 percent) and direct mail, including brochures and catalogues (24 percent). Trade shows accounted for another 11 percent, and sales promotion added the final 24 percent. A second study (ADVISOR 2), extended the investigation to twice the number of products, and its findings confirmed the results of the first study.[21]

---

[21] Gary L. Lilien and John D. C. Little, "The ADVISOR Project: A Study of Industrial Marketing Budgets," *Sloan Management Review*, Spring 1976, pp. 17–31; and Gary L. Lilien, "ADVISOR 2: Modeling the Marketing Mix Decision for Industrial Products," *Management Science*, February 1979, pp. 191–204.

Unfortunately, while the percentage-of-sales method is commonly used, under some conditions it fails to provide much direction in setting promotional budgets. It doesn't work well for new brands or in situations where sales volume is volatile. Under these conditions, the firm tends to overspend when times are good and underspend when times are bad.

Affordable method

The basic premise of this method of budgeting is that the firm spends only available resources on promotional activities. All other necessary expenditures, such as production costs, personnel costs, and so forth, come first, and promotion receives what is left over. In good years, the firm may commit large amounts to promotion, but in bad years spend little or nothing. Of all methods considered here, the affordable method holds the least potential for making sound promotional decisions.

Competitive parity method

The third method for determining promotional budgets is to set the levels of promotional spending in a market equal to the firm's share of the market or somewhat larger if the firm is attempting to increase share; for example, if the firm's share of market was 20 percent, then the budget would be 20 percent of the total amount spent by the industry. This rather conservative method of budgeting tends to create stability in market shares among competitors. It does, however, have the advantage of at least considering competition. Share of market budgeting is often used in connection with new products where the rule of thumb is to spend one and a half times the share objective at the end of the first or second year.

This matching of relative expenditures among competitors can also lead to promotional wars, with each participant matching the actions of competitors. For example, in the past, major fast-food franchisors have gone through periods of heavy use of contests and sweepstakes. Once one chain started such promotional activity, others quickly followed to maintain market position. This method's main limitation is its failure to consider the other marketing mix elements and the buyer. These are the same disadvantages the other top-down methods have.

Objective-and-task method

Because the objective-and-task method avoids most of the flaws inherent in the top-down budgeting approaches, it is currently the most popular approach.[22] This is a relatively simple budgeting method to describe, because it essentially involves only three steps.

First, define promotional objectives as specifically as possible. Second,

---

[22] Charles H. Patti and Vincent Blasko, "Budgeting Practices of Big Advertisers," *Journal of Advertising Research*, December 1986, pp. 23–29.

EXHIBIT 16 ♦ 13

Applying the objective-and-task method to setting an advertising budget for a new wine cooler brand—a hypothetical example

---

1. **Establish a market-share goal.** By the end of the first year, achieve a 15 percent share of the estimated 40 million-case wine cooler market, which is expected to grow by 10 million cases per year into the early 1990s. This target of 6 million cases is to be obtained by attracting first-time wine cooler buyers and getting users to switch to the new brand. Assume some 10 million wine cooler drinkers and the net addition of 2.5 million new drinkers each year. The number of individual consumers needed to attain a 15 percent share is estimated to be 2 million.

2(a). **Determine the percent of the target audience that needs to be made aware of the new brand** in order to induce a trial and repeat usage rate (3 or more bottles) that will attract 2 million consumers. The agency estimates that 40 percent of those who try a bottle of the new brand will become long-term users. This means 5 million persons must try the product. The agency further assumes that 75 percent of those who become aware of the product will try it. This translates into a need to make 6.67 million—or some 53 percent of the 12.5 million total present and prospective buyers—aware of the brand.

2(b). **Determine the number of impressions needed** to obtain an awareness level of 53 percent followed by trial and repeat buying. The agency estimates that 35 impressions on average will be needed for each of 12.5 million individuals in the target audience to bring this about (less than one per week). Thus, the total number of impressions needed is 35 × 12.5 million = 437.5 million.

2(c). **Determine the number of gross rating points (GRPs) needed.*** Based on needed reach and repetition (35), assume 3,500 GRPs are needed.

3. **Determine the cost of the needed 3,500 GRPs.** The agency estimates an average cost per GRP of $4,000—hence, the advertising media budget would be $14 million. To this amount, the costs of ad production and marketing research have to be added.

* GRPs are computed by multiplying the *reach* by the average frequency. *Reach* means the different individuals (or households) exposed to an advertising schedule per time period—usually four weeks. Reach measures the unduplicated audience exposed to a media schedule and is typically expressed as a percent of the target audience. *Frequency* is a measure of the number of times on average a person or household receives an advertising measure. Thus, it is a measure of repetition. If we assume a reach of 70 percent and a need for an average frequency of 20, then a media schedule yielding 1,400 gross rating points would be needed.

---

determine the strategies and specific tasks necessary to meet those objectives. Third, estimate the costs of performing those tasks and budget accordingly. In the example in Exhibit 16–13, the promotional goal is to attain a 15 percent share of the wine cooler market, or about 2 million consumers (step 1). Steps 2(a)–2(c) outline the strategies and tasks needed to meet this objective. In step 3, the costs and media budget necessary to perform the strategies and tasks are estimated.

The objective-and-task method, though easy to describe, is difficult to implement. It has the advantage of forcing firms to set specific promotional objectives through careful analysis of the specific situation and is most effective when the results obtained from particular ads can be measured (e.g., the awareness generated among members of the target audience or the number of persons who would be exposed to the product via sampling). It also requires firms to approach promotional planning from an analytical point of view—even to the point of attempting to link marginal costs and marginal revenues. It assumes that management has some knowledge of the relationship between sales and advertising for the time period under consideration. Engel et al. note, however, that

> management frequently has no conclusive idea of how much it will cost to attain the objective or even whether or not the objective is *worth* attaining. What is the best way, for example, to increase awareness by 20 percent next year? Should a combination of network television, spot radio, and newspapers be used with hard-sell copy, or should these variables be changed?[23]

Choose the promotional mix (step 6)

Even within the same industry, companies vary in the way they allocate their resources to various components of the promotional mix. For example, Avon focuses mainly on personal selling and spends only about 1.5 percent of its sales on advertising. However, many major competitors in the cosmetic industry (like Noxell) spend as much as 20 percent of sales on advertising. Designing the promotional mix is complex in that the elements interact. A consumer sales promotion, such as a sweepstake, often requires advertising to inform the public and perhaps distributors about the promotion. The following factors largely determine the effectiveness of the mix components: (1) the objectives and resources of the firm; (2) the type of product involved; (3) the stage of the product life cycle; (4) market characteristics; and (5) other elements in the marketing mix.

Firm's objectives and resources

A firm's objectives and resources relative to those of its competitors impact the structure of the promotional mix. For example, a firm with a high sales growth objective is almost compelled to spend more on its promotional mix. A consumer goods firm seeking a rapid increase in short-term sales would emphasize advertising and sales promotion that rely on mass communications. These deliver messages much faster than interpersonal forms.

In a similar situation, an industrial producer using some advertising and trade shows would rely heavily on personal selling to large end users and, where appropriate, on the use of intermediaries' salespersons. It would ordinarily take longer for such a seller to generate a substantial increase in sales than it would for a consumer goods firm because of the latter's use of mass media.

---

[23] Engel et al., *Promotional Strategy*, p. 234.

The promotion mix is also affected by the amount of resources available. Small, start-up organizations—especially those selling industrial goods—tend to rely heavily on personal selling, because sales reps who work on commission (and thus are a variable cost) are readily available to sell to target companies. Mass-media advertising, on the other hand, is expensive up front, which restricts its use by such companies.

Type of product

The typical consumer goods company spends most of its promotional resources on advertising, followed by sales promotion, personal selling, and publicity. Industrial goods companies usually devote most of such funds to personal selling, followed by advertising, publicity, and sales promotion. Advertising is the most important mix element when the benefits to be communicated are relatively simple; there is need to develop awareness and comprehension of these benefits in a mass market; a brand name is involved; products are purchased frequently; and product specifications are reasonably standardized. It comes as no surprise that such large consumer goods companies as Procter & Gamble, General Foods, and General Mills each spend hundreds of millions of dollars on media advertising each year.

Personal selling dominates the promotional mix when the product is complex, bought on specification, expensive, involves negotiation over terms of the sale, needs demonstration, requires postpurchase service, and is sold to only a few customers. For the most part, such characteristics are typical of industrial goods, although they also apply to some major consumer durables.

Life cycle stage

Marketing strategies change as a product goes through its life cycle; therefore, it is not surprising that promotional objectives and the allocation of promotional resources across the promotional mix also change, as shown in Exhibit 16–14. Thus, for example, for consumer goods, advertising and sales promotion (in-store displays, coupons, samples) are important during the introductory stage and early in the growth stage to create awareness and induce trial. In the remainder of the growth period, advertising expenditures continue heavy in order to build brand loyalty. Sales promotion—especially that concerned with price—declines because prolonged discounting may cause some consumers to view the brand as one of low quality.

During the maturity stage, advertising continues to be important to maintain attitudes toward the product and encourage users of competitive brands to switch; but it frequently declines in importance as a percent of sales during this period. For many products, the importance of sales promotions increases over time—not to induce trial, but to get consumers to switch to the company's brand. Because of greater sensitivity to the trade, more pro-

EXHIBIT   16 ◆ 14

Promotion expenditures for a typical consumer good over the product life cycle

motions are directed at it in an effort to retain its support, especially in terms of shelf space. In the decline stage, the firm spends few promotional resources. Sales promotion is probably the dominant element in the promotion mix in the stage.

Market characteristics

When a large, widely dispersed market is targeted—as is typically the case for many consumer goods—the heavy use of advertising is economical. If the target market for an industrial good is small and geographically concentrated, then personal selling is the most economical promotional mix element, provided the average sale is sufficiently large.

The consumer's position in the purchase-decision process (buyer-readiness stage) also affects the promotional mix. Advertising is most important in the early stages. It is useful in building awareness and providing information consumers need to make a purchase decision; but it is less effective than personal selling in changing attitudes or behavior. Personal selling—and to some extent sales promotion—are more persuasive and more likely to alter the consumer's behavior, especially at the trial and adoption stages of the diffusion process. Evaluation and conviction are more strongly influenced by word-of-mouth communication from respected sources.

Other elements in the marketing mix

The elements of the marketing mix must work together to achieve marketing and organization objectives. Marketers should develop and manage the promotion mix, therefore, only after considering the other elements in the marketing mix. We have discussed how the product component influences the allocation of resources across the promotion mix. In addition firms must consider the pricing and distribution components.

Pricing can affect the promotional mix in a number of ways. As we noted earlier, the product's price and characteristics help form consumers' perceptions of quality. If, for example, the firm chooses a low-cost pricing and low-quality product strategy, the promotional strategy needs to be so aligned for consistency. The reverse is also true; high-quality products are often priced high on the assumption that price is an indicator of quality. Heavy reliance on sales promotions to both final consumers and distributors would likely result from such a set of marketing strategies.

The pricing strategy also is a key element in creating margins for the producer from which the promotion funds are derived. Low-margin products cannot support expensive promotions, because the potential return to the firm is not sufficient. Generic products in grocery chains are a good example of how such pricing strategies virtually eliminate any promotional activity.

Distribution strategies can also affect the allocation of promotional resources. Generally, the more complex the product's distribution network is, the greater the need for personal selling to develop and maintain a reseller organization. Sales promotion aimed at distributors increases as the intensity of distribution increases. Some advertising expenditures directed at resellers may even be needed to support the company's personal selling and sales promotion efforts.

Evaluate the results (step 7)

The final stage of the decision sequence framework is the evaluation stage. In this stage the marketer tries to find out whether the objectives of the promotional activity were met. Marketing research is often used to answer this question. For instance, in the Bartles & Jaymes example, Gallo could conduct a telephone survey after the promotional campaign had run for a designated period of time to determine whether the objective of generating a certain level of awareness among members of the target audience had been achieved. Further, the survey could determine what percent had tried the brand and of these how many had bought it two or more times. In this way management could obtain information about the relationship of trial to awareness. For example, assume a trial/awareness ratio of 25 percent and an awareness level of 50 percent among members of the target audience group. Under such conditions, management should seriously consider spending additional funds to increase awareness. This analysis can be made even more meaningful if repeat buying is considered.

Research can also provide important insights into whether the firm attained any of the distribution objectives. The number of stores stocking the product, weighted by their relative importance (sales), would be important information here. The information gathered helps management learn more about the effectiveness of the promotion mix, which serves all concerned to good advantage in the future.

SUMMARY

This chapter introduces the promotional element of the marketing mix. Marketers often need to communicate large amounts of information to customers and intermediaries; to do this they rely on the four elements of the promotional mix—advertising, sales promotion, publicity, and personal selling.

A simple model of communication describes the process by which marketing information is passed to the target audience. Communication involves a sender, who encodes messages and transmits them through a channel or medium. Receivers decode messages; and feedback completes the connection between the two parties.

The allocation of resources among the components in the promotional mix and within each component varies from firm to firm and from product to product. The key factors that influence this allocation are the objectives and resources of the firm, the type of product, customers' characteristics, and the other elements in the marketing mix.

The final section of this chapter proposed a decision sequence framework for developing and implementing marketing communications. First, the firm begins with a situation analysis that includes specifying the target market. Second, it formulates detailed promotional objectives. These must state how the marketer wants the target audience to change, how fast, and the degree of change desired. Such objectives must be set for each of the components of the promotion mix. The third step is formulating the message. There are two major types of messages—those dealing primarily with feelings and relationships (connotative) and those that are more literal and factual (denotative). Messages can use several types of appeals—rational, emotional, humorous, and moral.

The fourth step, channel selection, is concerned with delivering the message. Three steps are required here: deciding which promotion components to use, which activities within each promotion component to emphasize, and the most appropriate vehicle for each activity selected. The fifth step, determining the promotion budget, is a complex and difficult decision. Many firms use a top-down method. The more popular ones are percent of sales, affordable, and competitive parity. A fourth—and the preferred method—is the objective-and-task method, which represents a bottom-up approach. The sixth step is to choose the promotional mix. The last step is concerned with evaluation, as the marketer seeks to determine whether the objectives of the promotional mix were met. Typically, this requires the use of information obtained by marketing research.

QUESTIONS

1. IBM does a substantial amount of television advertising for its various computer products. On the other hand, Cray Research—the most successful builder of the supercomputers used by government agencies, the U.S. Weather Service, and large scientific research organizations—does no advertising on TV. In fact, Cray does very little advertising of any kind. Instead, the firm relies on the efforts of its small salesforce. Why do the two firms pursue such different *promotional strategies?*

2. Based on some comments made in the Kennedy-Nixon debates during the 1960 presidential campaign, some audience members concluded that Richard Nixon was "soft on communism." Nixon later said his comments had been misinterpreted. Discuss the factors that may lead someone to *misinterpret the message intended by a communicator.* What can

the communicator do to minimize the possibility of being misunderstood?

3. For many years Hershey did not advertise its candy bars. In spite of this, its sales continued to grow. Does this suggest that companies with excellent products do not need to do much promotion? Why?

4. You are the marketing manager for a major airline. How would you vary the emphasis among the *tools in your promotional mix* when designing promotional strategies for (a) individual consumers who travel for pleasure, and (b) corporate travel departments that select the airlines to be used by company employees?

5. Which appeals would you use in advertising a well-established, low involvement consumer package good like Kleenex? Why?

6. Which *sales promotion* tools would be most useful for the following products?
   a. a new brand of super premium ice cream
   b. 3M self-sticking Post-it™ note pads
   c. Skippy peanut butter

7. Several years ago the Union Pacific Company—the railroad people—conducted a *corporate promotional campaign* involving extensive advertising on prime-time TV. Because the firm offered virtually no consumer products or services, was such a campaign justified? What objectives might the firm have been trying to accomplish?

8. The advertising manager for a large firm asked you—the marketing vice president—to approve a $500,000 *increase in the advertising budget* for one of the company's products. She predicts that the additional advertising will produce a $2 million increase in the product's sales. What additional information would you ask for before making a decision?

9. An automobile company sets the advertising and promotion budget for one of its car lines by allocating a fixed number of dollars for each car it forecasts will be sold in the coming year. What are the advantages and limitations of this approach in determining a promotional budget?

Chapter ⟨17⟩

Advertising, sales promotion, and public relations decisions

REEBOK AND ITS ADVERTISING[1]

In 1979, Paul Fireman, a former fishing and camping equipment distributor, discovered Reebok (named after the African gazelle) at a trade show. At that time, J. W. Foster & Sons, a British family-owned company, was making Reeboks by hand for well-known runners throughout the world. Foster, founded in 1895, is the world's oldest athletic shoe company. It made the shoes worn by Britain's 1924 Olympic track team, immortalized in the movie "Chariots of Fire."

Freeman obtained a license to sell Reebok shoes in the United States but had little luck penetrating the market for high-priced running shoes. He ran out of money in 1981, but a British shoe distributor bailed him out with $77,500 in exchange for 56 percent ownership. In 1984, Fireman and his new partner bought Reebok from the Foster family for $700,000.

In the following years, Reebok sales and profits exploded, as shown in Exhibit 17–1. The stylish, brightly colored shoes were an instant hit with women and fast became standard equipment for trendy young consumers. In 1986, Reebok started buying TV time (primarily to help introduce its new athletic shoes) and increased its ad budget from about $7 million in 1985 to more than $10 million in 1986. But the spending on advertising was insignificant compared to the unsolicited music video endorsements from such entertainment giants as Mick Jagger, Lionel Ritchie, and Bruce Springsteen. Cybill Shepherd appeared at the Emmy Awards wearing a black dress and orange Reeboks.

In 1987, Reebok raised its advertising budget to over $30 million. Four themes were used: performance, new technology, "classic" sports shoes, and fashion. The TV spots featured sports shoes for basketball, sports conditioning, tennis, and walking, as well as PopTops, a new women's basketball

---

[1] This section is based on Lois Theruen and Amy Borrus, "Reeboks: How Far Can a Fad Run?" *Business Week,* February 24, 1986; "Walking," *The New Yorker,* February 16, 1987, pp. 27–29; J. N. Wiener, "Beatles Buy-Out," *New Republic,* May 11, 1987, pp. 13–14; Lois Helm, "Reebok's Recent Blisters Seem to Be Healing," *Business Week,* August 3, 1987; Pat Sloan, "Reebok Ad Budget Reaches New Height," *Advertising Age,* August 17, 1987, p. 44; Katherine Weisman, "The Air of Victory," *Forbes,* May 2, 1988, p. 8; Gretchen Morgenson, "Has the Runner Stumbled?" *Forbes,* September 19, 1988, pp. 118–19; Barbara Buell, "Nike Catches Up with the Trendy Frontrunner," *Business Week,* October 24, 1988, p. 88; "Nike Rushes in Where Reebok Used to Tread," *Business Week,* October 3, 1988, p. 42; Reebok International's *1987 Annual Report;* and Joseph Pereira, "Reebok Trails Nike in Fight for Teens' Hearts and Feet," *The Wall Street Journal,* September 23, 1988, p. 19.

continued

EXHIBIT 17◆1

Reebok net sales and income, 1983–87 ($ millions)

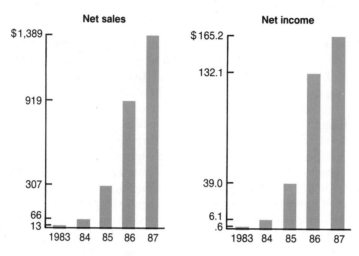

Source: Annual Report 1987, Reebok International (Canton, Mass.: 1988).

shoe. The campaign attempted to negate the perception of Reebok as a yuppie brand by positioning it for both serious athletes and for fashion-conscious shoppers less interested in fitness.

Reebok did not feature endorsements by big-time athletes as Nike did. Rather, its commercials "dramatically employed motion, whether it is on the basketball court, on a street full of walking shoes, or in a gym where blackouts and grunts of exercise are interspersed with shots of Reebok-clad feet and a weightlifter's upper body."[2] To promote PopTops, a more stylized commercial was used in an effort to "get the attention of its young and trendy female audience. In the spot, a

hydraulic lift raises a woman's skirt, coated with lacquer, to create the effect of a Japanese umbrella, while the woman's face becomes a rotating police light."

Reebok experienced record sales and profits in 1987, due in part to its acquisition of Avia, another athletic shoe company, and Rockport, a manufacturer of casual and walking shoes; its entry into sports clothing; and growing overseas sales. But in 1987, consumers began clamoring for performance—and

---

[2] Pat Sloan, "Reebok Ad Budget Reaches New Height," p. 44.

continued

this time Nike, which had been badly hurt by Reebok, was ready to respond. In the mid-1980s, Nike's Air Jordan basketball shoes were a tremendous success—the only ones inner-city kids would wear. But when this fad slowed, Nike had no replacement.

Nike's technological advantage over Reebok consisted of a gas-filled sac embedded in the heel of the shoe. This sac cushions feet as they bang against cement pavements, and it stays springy longer than conventional foam or rubber. In the past, Nike had not adequately promoted its shoes; nor had it realized athletic shoes didn't have to be ugly. But this time, aided by a smashingly successful $20 million ad campaign featuring the old Beatles' song "Revolution" that linked the technology with most of Nike's line of shoes, better fashion and bright colors, and an improved distribution system, Nike rebounded.

By the end of 1988, Nike had caught up with—perhaps surpassed—Reebok. It spent large sums of money on an advertising campaign that emphasized the air sac in the heel. One Nike shoe model even has a window in the heel that lets customers see the air sac; and in ads, light streams through this window. For an example of Nike's 1988 advertising featuring this technology, see Exhibit 17–2. Nike's current advertising campaign is called "Just Do It" and features serious-faced athletes puffing and sweating while working out (wearing Nike shoes, of course).

Reebok stresses performance and argues that just because its products are fashionable doesn't mean they can't perform. The shoes incorporate the Reebok Energy Return System, featuring Du Pont Hytrel tubes that compress on impact and—as they return to normal—give the wearer a lift. For an example of Reebok's 1988 advertising that describes this system, see Exhibit 17–3. Reebok's present campaign is called "U.B.U." and showcases a group of odd-looking characters in Reeboks doing such things as vacuuming an Oriental rug on a lawn while a voice in the background reads Emerson. This avant-garde advertising may go over the heads of most teenagers, according to an industry spokesman. Both Reebok and Nike also emphasize the importance of the inner-city market, as evidenced by their advertising (see Exhibit 17–4). The youth market is where the action is; consumers between the ages of 15 and 22 buy 30 percent of all athletic shoes; and they influence another 10 percent by example and word of mouth. On average, teens buy four pairs of athletic shoes a year compared to two for older consumers.[3]

But thus far, despite spending $70 million annually on advertising, Reebok seems to be losing ground to Nike

---

[3] Joseph Pereira, "Reebok Trails Nike in Fight for Teens' Hearts and Feet," p. 19.

continued

EXHIBIT 17 ◆ 2

Examples of Nike advertising in magazines and dealer ads

IF BO JACKSON TAKES UP ANY MORE HOBBIES, WE'RE READY.

Who says Bo has to decide between baseball and football? We encourage him to take up everything from basketball to cycling. And to train for them all in the Nike Air Trainer SC. A cross-training shoe with plenty of cushioning and support for a number of sports. Or should we say, a number of hobbies?

Air Trainer SC

TAKE THE HIGH ROAD.

The Air Max for men and women, with NIKE-AIR®, the cushioning that never gives in. Even if you do.

NIKE
AIR

DEALER NAME

Courtesy: Nike.

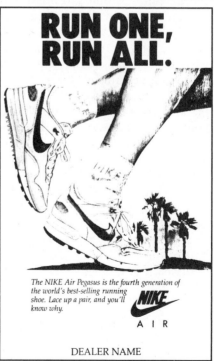

RUN ONE, RUN ALL.

The NIKE Air Pegasus is the fourth generation of the world's best-selling running shoe. Lace up a pair, and you'll know why.

NIKE
AIR

DEALER NAME

Examples of Reebok advertising in magazines and dealer ads

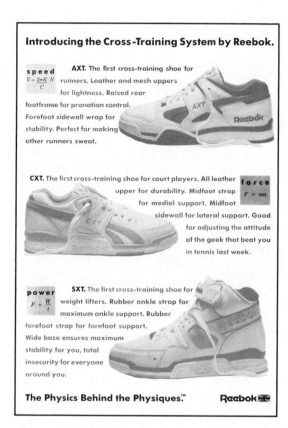

Introducing the Cross-Training System by Reebok.

speed
$$V = \frac{2\pi R}{C} N$$

AXT. The first cross-training shoe for runners. Leather and mesh uppers for lightness. Raised rear footframe for pronation control. Forefoot sidewall wrap for stability. Perfect for making other runners sweat.

CXT. The first cross-training shoe for court players. All leather upper for durability. Midfoot strap for medial support. Midfoot sidewall for lateral support. Good for adjusting the attitude of the geek that beat you in tennis last week.

force
$$F = ma$$

power
$$P = \frac{W}{t}$$

SXT. The first cross-training shoe for weight lifters. Rubber ankle strap for maximum ankle support. Rubber forefoot strap for forefoot support. Wide base ensures maximum stability for you, total insecurity for everyone around you.

The Physics Behind the Physiques.™

Reebok

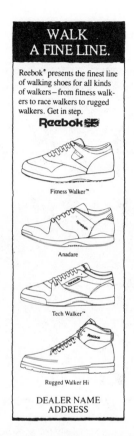

WALK A FINE LINE.

Reebok* presents the finest line of walking shoes for all kinds of walkers—from fitness walkers to race walkers to rugged walkers. Get in step.

Reebok

Fitness Walker™

Anadare

Tech Walker™

Rugged Walker Hi

DEALER NAME ADDRESS

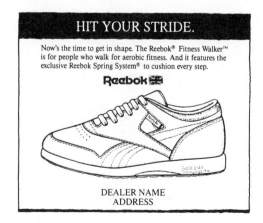

HIT YOUR STRIDE.

Now's the time to get in shape. The Reebok® Fitness Walker™ is for people who walk for aerobic fitness. And it features the exclusive Reebok Spring System® to cushion every step.

Reebok

DEALER NAME ADDRESS

Courtesy: Reebok.

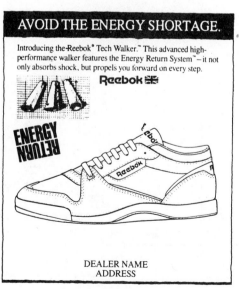

AVOID THE ENERGY SHORTAGE.

Introducing the Reebok® Tech Walker.™ This advanced high-performance walker features the Energy Return System™—it not only absorbs shock, but propels you forward on every step.

Reebok

ENERGY RETURN

DEALER NAME ADDRESS

EXHIBIT 17♦4

Examples of Reebok and Nike advertising to the inner-city market

Courtesy: Reebok.

Courtesy: Nike.

concluded

on performance and to L. A. Gear, a trendy newcomer to the athletic shoe industry, on fashion. As evidence of Reebok's troubles, analysts point to a decline in net income for the fourth quarter of 1988 to $6.7 million from $34.1 million in the same quarter in 1987. For all of 1988, net income was off $30 million despite an increase in sales from $1.4 to $1.8 billion.

Both Reebok and Nike had to make many decisions before undertaking the advertising programs just described. For the most part, these decisions are common to all advertising programs regardless of sponsorship.

Advertising is certainly one of the more important and most complex decision areas facing business executives. Advertising decisions are among the most difficult decisions to make, due largely to the difficulties of measuring advertising results. The effectiveness of advertising depends to a great extent on how well the company has specified its target markets, positioned the product relative to competitive products and the choice criteria of the target market, and formulated the marketing mix. Advertising's effectiveness is also heavily conditioned by the marketing decisions made about the product, price, channels, and personal selling—and, of course, the promotion mix. In this chapter, we focus on advertising—and sales promotion and public relations—as entities in their own right. We examine the decisions that have to be made after management has specified the role that each of these tools should play in the promotional mix for a given product or service.

Advertising decision making is concerned with setting objectives, deciding what the message should be and how to present it, choosing which media types and vehicles to use with what frequency, and evaluation—analyzing the effectiveness of the advertising program. Managers make all of these decisions within the context of an advertising budget, which must somehow relate sales or profits to advertising expenditures in some stated time period. This chapter examines these subjects and then discusses sales promotion and public relations (publicity) in a similar but more abbreviated fashion.

ADVERTISING EXPENDITURES

U.S. spending on advertising reached an estimated $118.8 billion in 1988—up some 8 percent from 1987—partly because of the effect of the Olympics and the national elections (see Exhibit 17–5). These spending figures include

EXHIBIT 17♦5

Estimated annual U.S. advertising expenditures, 1980–88 ($ millions)

	National	Local	Percent change from previous year
1980	29,815	23,735	—
1981	33,890	26,540	12.7%
1982	37,785	28,795	10.2
1983	42,525	33,325	13.9
1984	49,690	38,130	15.8
1985	53,355	41,395	7.9
1986	56,850	45,290	7.7
1987	60,625	49,025	7.4
1988	66,350	52,470	8.4

Source: Joanne Lipman, "Estimate for '88 U.S. Ad Spending Is Sliced by Prominent Forecaster," *The Wall Street Journal,* June 16, 1988, p. 24.

primarily TV and radio, print (newspapers and magazines), direct mail, and billboards. Advertising in the United States is expected to continue to grow as a percent of gross national product because of an increase in the number of new products, stable economic conditions, growth in the buying power of women, the greater number of people in prime buying years, and increased competition. Companies vary in their advertising spending because of their size and the type of products involved. Firms selling packaged food products, soaps and cleansers, automobiles, soft drinks, tobacco products, and telephone equipment are among the top spenders. Exhibit 17–6 shows that some of these firms spent over 10 percent of their sales on advertising.

Advertising expenditures overseas (essentially Europe) by both U.S. and foreign firms are expected to increase even faster than in the United States for the foreseeable future. In 1987, an estimated $95 billion was spent on advertising—up 19 percent from 1986. The reasons for this optimistic view of the future are strong economic growth, deregulation of European broadcasting, which will bring in more stations accepting advertising, and the removal of trade barriers by 1992, which will enable advertisers to use the same commercial across Europe.[4]

ADVERTISING OBJECTIVES

In Chapter 16 we discussed the objectives of the promotion mix. There is considerable similarity between promotion mix and advertising objectives, especially those relating to behavior. Thus, we build here on what was said earlier on this subject.

---

[4] Standard & Poor's *Industry Report,* January 1989, PM 36–38.

EXHIBIT 17 ◆ 6

Percentage of sales allocated to advertising by the top 25 advertisers ($ millions)

Category	Rank	Company	U.S. advertising expenditures	U.S. sales	Advertising as percent of U.S. sales
Automotive	20	Chrysler Corp.	$ 426.0	$20,489.0	2.1
	6	Ford Motor Company	648.5	50,034.0	1.3
	5	General Motors Corp.	839.0	91,343.0	0.9
Electronics	25	General Electric Co.	354.3	N/A	N/A
Food	13	BCI Holdings	535.9	5,809.0	9.2
	11	General Mills	551.6	N/A	N/A
	23	Kellogg Co.	374.1	2,269.0	16.5
	19	Kraft Inc.	438.0	6,278.3	7.0
	16	Pillsbury Co.	494.9	5,510.0	9.0
	17	Ralston Purina Co.	478.0	N/A	N/A
	4	RJR Nabisco	935.0	15,978.0	5.9
Pharmaceuticals	22	American Home Products Corp.	395.7	3,682.0	10.7
	21	Johnson & Johnson	410.7	3,970.0	10.3
	12	Warner Lambert	548.8	1,700.0	32.3
Retail	15	J.C. Penney Co.	496.2	14,117.0	3.5
	9	K mart Corp.	590.4	N/A	N/A
	3	Sears Roebuck & Co.	1,004.7	N/A	N/A
Restaurants	8	McDonald's Corp.	592.0	3,077.0	19.2
Soaps and cleaners	1	Procter & Gamble Co.	1,435.5	N/A	N/A
	14	Unilever N.V.	517.7	4,842.0	10.7
Soft drinks	24	Coca-Cola Co.	370.4	4,650.0	8.0
	10	PepsiCo Inc.	581.3	8,065.0	7.2
Telephone	18	American Telephone & Telegraph	439.9	N/A	N/A
Tobacco	2	Philip Morris Cos.	1,364.5	17,568.0	7.8
Wine, beer, and liquor	7	Anheuser-Busch Cos.	643.6	N/A	N/A

Source: Courtland L. Bovee and William F. Arens, *Contemporary Advertising,* 3rd ed. (Homewood, Ill.: Richard D. Irwin, 1989), p. 244.

It is not enough to say that the objective of advertising is to trigger behavior that will lead, in some way, to a sale. Rather, what is needed is a measurement of the *process* by which marketers achieve the desired response. The communication must attract the attention of the target group, be understood, and convince them that the product can meet their needs better than alternate products.

Communication hierarchy

A hierarchy of effects—unawareness, awareness, comprehension, conviction, and action—is a useful framework for stating advertising objectives.[5] The advertising hierarchy is similar to the stages of product adoption—awareness, interest, evaluation, trial, and adoption. The purpose of marketing is to move prospective buyers through this series of steps to the ultimate objective: namely, the purchase of the marketer's goods or services. Achieving the purchase objective is the responsibility of marketing, not just of advertising. But knowing the various adoption step categories enables the firm to better set its advertising objectives. Thus, if most prospects are aware of the product and its advantages but not convinced of its uniqueness, the next step—and hence the advertising objective—would be to create conviction. In such a situation it should be advertising's job to demonstrate product superiority and to create brand preference.

Another advantage of using the communication hierarchy as the basis for setting advertising objectives is that it is possible to measure the proportion of potential customers who are at each stage in the hierarchy. This means that advertising objectives can be set forth in numerical terms for a stated time period and pertaining to a defined audience group.

Building, changing, and reinforcing attitudes

Another way of stating advertising objectives has to do with influencing the *attitudes* of the target audience toward the brand in question versus competing brands or substitute products. Such an objective is based on buyer behavior models. Given the marketer's knowledge of how a brand compares with others, based on the target audience's choice criteria, advertising can be directed at building, changing, or reinforcing consumer attitudes about a brand's salient product characteristics.

Sellers may use advertising to reinforce rather than shift certain attitudes, as—for example—when the profile of one brand is almost identical with that of the consumer's ideal. On the other hand, they may want to reinforce some aspects of consumer beliefs while shifting others. The degree of difficulty associated with these objectives varies with each situation. In general, the stronger a particular belief, the harder it is to change. This is seen in the difficulties encountered in getting the driving public to "buckle up" in spite of the evidence of greatly reduced serious injury or death with seat belt use.

The length of time the consumer has held the belief and the degree to which it is linked to other attitudes and general perceptions of the environment are important. And, as we have noted, it is also difficult to change attitudes because consumers practice selective awareness, perception, and

---

[5] For an in-depth discussion of this hierarchy, see Courtland L. Bovee and William F. Arens, *Contemporary Advertising*, 3rd ed. (Homewood, Ill.: Richard D. Irwin, 1989), pp. 228–33.

attention. This makes it difficult for advertisers to expose consumers to the message, make them perceive what action is wanted and why, and then remember what was said, when the message differs from their current attitudes.

The three-order hierarchy models

Ray suggests that there are three behavioral hierarchies. First is the standard **learning hierarchy,** which we have been discussing: learn—feel—do (or awareness, comprehension, conviction, and action). This hierarchy is most relevant for describing the mental stages people go through when deciding to purchase relatively high-involvement consumer or industrial products. But it is not applicable to all purchase decisions, particularly when a buyer experiences dissonance over a choice among equally attractive alternatives, or when the decision focuses on a low-involvement product. Two other hierarchy models apply to such situations. One is the **dissonance-attribution hierarchy** consisting of action first, followed by attitude change and learning: do—feel—learn. A third is the **low-involvement hierarchy** consisting of a gross awareness followed by action and then attitude development: learn—do—feel.[6] To determine proper advertising objectives, marketers should undertake a situation analysis, which would indicate the most appropriate hierarchy to use. Following this, they can set advertising objectives.

The *learning hierarchy* posits that learning is a prerequisite to all subsequent responses. This hierarchy is most likely to occur when the audience is involved in the subject of the campaign, product differentiation exists, emphasis is on mass media, and the product is in the introductory or early growth stage of the product life cycle. The objectives here would center on one or more levels in the learning hierarchy (awareness, comprehension, conviction, or action) or a change in attitudes toward a product's salient characteristics.

The *dissonance-attribution hierarchy* is just the opposite. It applies to situations where people are forced to make a choice between two alternative products that are proximate in quality and price. In an effort to rationalize the buying decision, or reduce dissonance, people seek out favorable information about their choice—and avoid information unfavorable to it. Such situations occur when the audience has been involved, when there is little to differentiate one alternative from another, and when the product is in the mature stage of the product life cycle. Automobiles and other major consumer durables are the products that fit this hierarchy. Advertising objectives for such situations deal with consumers who have already purchased the product and need reinforcement relating to the present as well as future

---

[6] Michael L. Ray, *Advertising and Communication Management* (Englewood Cliffs, N.J.: Prentice-Hall, 1982), pp. 184–88.

purchases. Objectives are expressed in terms of conviction and attitudes favoring the seller's brand versus those of competitors.

The *low-involvement hierarchy* is typical of most TV viewers, in that they are often not involved with either the advertising or the subject area. Under such conditions, TV ads may not change attitudes. They may simply facilitate consumer learning about a brand so that in a purchasing situation for that product type the consumer recalls the brand name and purchases the item. Attitude change then occurs because of product experience. These situations feature low involvement of consumers, low differentiation between products, the use of mass media, and products in the mature stage of the life cycle. Awareness and recall are suitable advertising objectives for these situations.

THE SOURCE

The development of an advertising message and the selection of advertising media depend on the characteristics and predispositions of the target audience. Chapter 16 discussed the importance of audience segmentation and how to make this concept operational. For our purposes here, the terms *audience, destination, public,* and *segment* are synonymous. By the time marketers are ready to structure the advertising message, they should already know a great deal about the target audience as well as the hierarchical situation involved. Our interest here is the way the source (the seller) impacts the target audience.

In addition to referring to the seller, the source almost always includes the seller's **spokesperson**—the person delivering the message. For example, Ronald Reagan was once the spokesman for General Electric. Sometimes this spokesperson is not a celebrity or an announcer, but the owner or manager, as Lee Iacocca has been for Chrysler. In magazine and newspaper advertising, the **signal vehicle,** or **carrier**—the publication itself—is considered part of the source, as, for example, *The Wall Street Journal* and *New Yorker* magazine.

A source often consists of several entities, including the seller, the person delivering the message, and the medium. In some cases, it is possible to have an even greater number of sources—as, for example, when a retailer advertising a manufacturer's brand (two sellers) uses an announcer at a local TV station. In this discussion we treat media as **message (signal) carriers,** separate from the source. We recognize, however, that the media also function as sources; thus, we investigate their effect on the message.

Yet another source is embodied in the story line of the commercial. A typical example is the family pharmacist offering advice about which cold remedy to take to alleviate the sore throat, runny nose, and fever of the common cold.

Source credibility

The way the audience perceives the source influences the message's credibility and, consequently, the audience's attitudes following receipt of the message. This effect interacts with that caused by the information content of the message. Some sources attract greater attention than others and, hence, increase the number of consumers exposed to the message. Furthermore, some sources are better than others at presenting an unambiguous message. The most important factor, however, is **source credibility.** For example, Bill Cosby is generally considered a highly creditable source for Jell-O.[7] A great many things about a communication affect the credibility of the message. In addition to variables that relate directly to message content such as authority or expertise, audience attitudes can be affected by the communicator's appearance, presumed social class, and mannerisms.

The fairer and less biased the audience perceives the source to be, the more credible the message—and the more likely attitudes will shift toward the source's position. Research shows, furthermore, that the perceived fairness and trustworthiness of the source are more important than perceived expertise on the matter discussed. *Fairness* is much more effective than obvious propaganda. Another acceptable generalization is that the greater the ambiguity about the source's credibility and the greater the change in attitudes attempted, the higher the audience resistance. A source viewed as *responsible* is more apt to be successful in bringing about a substantial shift in attitudes.[8]

Sources and stages in the adoption process

Different sources are important for each of the different stages in the adoption process for a product. **Impersonal sources** (commercial mass media), for instance, are important in creating awareness; but **personal sources** are highly influential during the evaluation stage. As people move through the adoption process, they are more apt to value dialogs with credible sources. For example, a physician is more likely to turn to colleagues and journal articles than to commercial sources before deciding to adopt a new drug. Such professional sources are said to have a **legitimatizing role** in helping the doctor decide whether to adopt the new drug; that is, they sanction its use.

---

[7] "People Appreciate Good Ads, an Agency Survey Concludes," *The Wall Street Journal,* April 28, 1983, p. 33.

[8] For a fuller discussion of "source," see Ray, *Advertising and Communication,* pp. 303–9.

Word-of-mouth communication

Consumer attitudes are also affected by **opinion leaders.** These are persons whose advice is sought by individuals or by members of a social or business group on a given subject (say, the purchase of a new computer). The process by which opinion leaders obtain ideas from various sources and then transmit them to the rank and file of their group is often referred to as a two-step flow—a **trickle-down effect.** Word-of-mouth communication can be a powerful force—and especially so if the product or service involves a high economic or psychological risk. We noted earlier that personal influence is often pivotal in the valuative stage of the adoption of new products. The more unstructured and risky a decision is, the more important personal influence becomes.

Opinion leaders are generally perceived by their followers as having a strong interest and a special competency in a particular subject. Usually they are assumed to have access to up-to-date and sometimes unusual source material, much of which is obtained from others who reside outside the local area. Thus, whether they do or do not recommend a product verbally, an opinion leader can affect the decision-making process of a follower through purchase or use of a product.

Opinion leaders tend to conform closely to the norms of the social group to which they belong. Opinion leaders must be similar to their followers. Otherwise, they would not be approachable and, therefore, could not perform their word-of-mouth activities. Moreover, there is little overlapping among opinion leaders. Each subject area tends to have its own opinion leader within the group.

Some significant differences, however, exist between leaders and those who seek their advice. They may, for example, differ in their sources of information, social status, and innovativeness. Opinion leaders are likely to use more impersonal and a wider range of information. Their social status tends to be somewhat higher, although not enough to prevent their being accessible. They are apt to accept or reject new ideas in their own field faster than others.

Opinion leaders can be identified and targeted on the basis of such characteristics as the following:

* **Occupation**—for example, a financial advisor who recommends a certain stock; a tennis pro who uses a new type of racket; a county farm agent who reports negatively about a new weed killer.
* **Product ownership**—this must be coupled with perceived honesty in reporting satisfaction or dissatisfaction.
* **Education**—for example, highly specialized doctors from prestigious schools are often considered opinion leaders by their peers about new drugs and procedures.
* **Club membership**—for example, a person belonging to a camera club would be

considered by some as an opinion leader regarding a new type of camera, lens, or photographic process.

* **Special experiences**—for example, a person who has traveled extensively abroad should know which airline is best for overseas travel.

THE MESSAGE

A **message** is a summation of signs or signals attempting to convey one or more ideas. In advertising, it can be delivered by a TV or radio commercial, a billboard, a point-of-purchase display, or a print ad. In this context, the construction of a message depends on the other parts of the communication process, including the media used and the objectives of the communicators (the behavior they seek to induce). In this section, however, we treat messages as a separate part of the communications process, assuming that the decision designating the advertising objectives has already been made.

Symbols

Symbols are the heartbeat of the message. They portray complex emotional situations; as, for example, in a close-up of a grandmother receiving flowers on Mother's Day. Symbols, if at all effective, evoke anticipation of what can happen under certain conditions. If many symbols are used in a given message, many responses may be expected. Too many symbols, however, can cause confusion. Thus, the source should ordinarily strive to impart the desired message with as few symbols as possible. Short words in short sentences are easier to understand. The more involved the audience is with the product, however, the more likely they are to be receptive to a more complex message.

The receiver notes the whole message—the use of pictures, color, and space; the length of the commercial; and the quality of the production efforts. Consumers, for example, can tell a great deal about the character of a department store from the content of its ads even though they have never visited the store.

Message structure[9]

The success of any message depends not only on its content, but also on its structure. Researchers have studied a variety of structural factors, including two-sided versus one-sided messages, drawing conclusions, order of presentation, and message size.

---

[9] For a more complete discussion of this subject, see James F. Engel, Martin R. Warshaw, and Thomas C. Kinnear, *Promotional Strategy* (Homewood, Ill.: Richard D. Irwin, 1987), chap. 13.

Two-sided versus one-sided messages

The problem of whether it is more effective to present the pros and cons of a situation rather than only one side comes up often in advertising. Research indicates that two-sided presentations are generally more effective with those opposed to the position advocated by the communicator. One-sided presentations are more effective with those who already favor the position taken.

Two-sided communications have more effect on better-educated respondents; one-sided presentations have more effect on less-educated respondents. A two-sided message apparently has the effect of preparing people to adjust to counterarguments advanced at a later date. However, a two-sided message may also make them aware of product disadvantages they had not previously recognized.[10]

Drawing conclusions

Generally it is best to state a conclusion in the message; that is, to explicitly specify the action to be taken rather than let the audience draw its own conclusions. Actually, the advisability of stating a conclusion depends on the intelligence of the audience, the complexity of the subject matter presented, and the kind of communicator involved.[11] Thus, communications with complex arguments on impersonal subjects directed toward a mass market are usually more effective when the conclusion is made explicit for the audience.

Size of message unit

Because smaller message units are less expensive, the advertiser can run more small units for the same cost as fewer larger units. This begs the question of the extent to which message size relates to audience reactions. Usually, larger units attract more attention, not only because they appear more important but also because they can use more elaborate attention-getting devices. Just what the optimal size of a message should be is difficult to ascertain, due to the interaction of message size, the power of the message itself, and the effect of repetition on consumer learning.

The choice of message size is linked to the degree of consumer interest in the product. For low-interest, widely used commodity products, marketers use large-unit messages like a full-page ad in a magazine or a full 30-second TV spot. Conversely, if the message is of great interest to the target audience,

---

[10] The original research was reported in Carl Hovland, Arthur A. Lumsdine, and Fred D. Sheffield, *Experiments in Mass Communications* (New York: John Wiley & Sons, 1949), pp. 182–200.

[11] Carl I. Hovland and Wallace Mandell, "An Experimental Comparison of Conclusion-Drawing by the Communicator and by the Audience," *Journal of Abnormal and Social Psychology*, July 1952, pp. 581–88.

a smaller unit may suffice—say, a quarter-page ad. The choice of size also depends on the media used and the number of times the ad is repeated.

Television commercials are getting shorter and shorter. The reason is the increased costs of prime time. For instance, in the 1960s a 30-second commercial cost $15,000. In 1987 the cost for 30 seconds was as much as $400,000 for prime time. The 15-second commercial, virtually unknown a few years ago, now accounts for a third of all network commercials. "The challenge is to get the message across forcefully, memorably, and—as if that weren't task enough—faster than ever before."[12] One advertising agency took six months and half a million dollars to produce a 15-second commercial for a new cherry-flavored antacid tablet produced by Rolaids.[13]

Comparative advertising

Some advertisers attempt to provide meaningful information about their product by comparing it directly to a named competitor. Research on the effectiveness of such advertising indicates that it works primarily when the product has an important, recognizable advantage that ads can visually demonstrate. Typically the brand involved is trying to gain a bigger share at the expense of the leader. It may, however, be an also-ran trying to get consumers to perceive it in the same mind-set as the leader.[14] For example, Burger King attacked McDonald's hamburgers as having 20 percent less meat and for being fried rather than broiled.

In general, audiences perceive comparative ads to be less believable, less truthful, and less informative than ads that do not involve direct comparisons. Recall rates also tend to be lower for comparative ads. On the other hand, forceful comparative advertising has apparently helped increase the market shares of some brands—examples include Pepsi-Cola and Savin Copiers.[15]

Repetition

An advertiser may want to repeat its message for many reasons: to give added emphasis to previous messages; to keep the audience from forgetting the message; and to save the costs involved in producing new commercials. By far the major reason for repetition for most advertisers is to increase

---

[12] John Pfeiffer, "TV Commercials: Faster and Faster," *Smithsonian*, October 1987, p. 134.

[13] Ibid.

[14] Robert Levy, "Big Resurgence in Comparative Ads," *Dun's Business Month*, February 1987, p. 56.

[15] William L. Wilkie and Paul W. Farris, "Comparison Advertising: Problems and Potential," *Journal of Marketing*, October 1975, pp. 7–15; Philip Levine, "Commercials That Name Competing Brands," *Journal of Advertising Research*, December 1976, pp. 7–16; "Comparative Ads: Battles That Wrote Dos and Don'ts," *Advertising Age*, September 29, 1980, p. 64; and "Campaign: The Battle for Hamburger Hill," *Madison Avenue*, January 1983, p. 61.

audience retention of the message. The repetition required to prevent forgetting varies from message to message as well as among audience groups.
Indeed, **over-learning** sometimes occurs when the advertiser repeats a message too often within a given time period. When this happens, audience
members stop paying attention—and, of course, money is wasted.

Repetition is, nevertheless, clearly tied to learning. How to repeat most
effectively is the crucial question. Because most commercial messages are
surrounded by similar ones, repetition of a given message should be scheduled in concentrated bursts over a relatively short period (increasing the
probability of awareness and retention at that time)—rather than stretching
the same number of repetitions over a longer period. This is especially true if
much new learning must take place.[16]

ADVERTISING MEDIA

The media problem is basically one of selection and scheduling. Advertisers
must choose some combination of *reach* and *frequency* that will attain the
advertising objectives by delivering a given message to the desired target
audience. **Reach** is the number (or percent) of the target audience exposed to
a given media mix. **Frequency** is the number of times the target audience is
exposed to a message within a given time period. **Exposure** can be defined in
a number of ways and is elaborated on later in this section.

The large number of prospects for most consumer products and their wide
geographic dispersion make the problem of media selection complex. It is
further complicated by the great many media in which time or space can be
purchased, the varying options (such as size and color) available for each
medium, and the intricate systems of quantity discounts in the advertising
industry. These problems are less severe for industrial advertisers, but are
still present.

Media types

Exhibit 17–7 depicts the major types of mass media and their percentage of
the total 1987 advertising expenditures. Newspaper advertising was the
largest medium, with 26.8 percent of total expenditures, followed by network and cable TV (22.2 percent), direct mail (17.3 percent), radio (6.6
percent), and all others, including magazines and business papers (27.1
percent).[17] Each type of medium offers unique advantages to the advertiser;
but each also has limitations. Exhibit 17–8 (page 600) lists some of the
strengths and weaknesses of each medium.

---

[16] Herman Simon, "ADPULS: An Advertising Model with Wearout and Pulsation," *Journal
of Marketing Research*, August 1982, p. 354.

[17] *Advertising Age*, July 18, 1988, p. S–6.

EXHIBIT   17 ✦ 7

U.S. 1987 media advertising breakdown (percent of total)

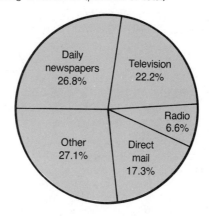

Source: Reprinted with permission from *Ad Age,* July 18, 1988, copyright Crain Communications, Inc.

Television is best at communicating images and symbols because it can demonstrate product usage and consumer reactions. It has enormous reach: almost all U.S. households have a TV set; and on an average day nearly 90 percent of these households watch one or more programs. TV commercials are even being aired via a liquid crystal screen attached to the handlebars of supermarket shopping carts.[18] Thus, TV is a particularly good medium to help sell a mass-market product. It is, however, an expensive one.

Less involving than television, radio offers economy and the opportunity for targeting. As mass marketing declines, radio offers the opportunity to focus on a specific audience, such as Hispanics, blacks, teenagers, and senior citizens. For instance, General Motors places Chevy truck ads on an all-night radio network to reach 650,000 long-haul truckers.[19] The average household owns several radios; and the average person listens to the radio more than three hours a day. Radio advertising suffers from the fact that it reaches people mostly when they are doing something else—working, driving, or walking. It is often used to reinforce TV advertising.

Print media are more involving than broadcast media. Readers control the advertising they read and take as much time as they wish to do so. Thus, print is effective in communicating specific information about a product. This is particularly important for most industrial products and high-involvement consumer goods. Magazines are increasingly specialized and are excel-

---

[18] "Coming to a Shopping Cart Near You: TV Commercials," *Business Week,* May 30, 1988, p. 48.

[19] Ronald Alsop, "More Firms Tune into Radio to Stretch Their Ad Budgets," *The Wall Street Journal,* July 17, 1986, p. 25.

EXHIBIT 17 ◆ 8

Comparative evaluation of advertising media

	Spot TV	Network TV	Spot radio	Network radio	Consumer magazines	Business publications	Sunday supplements	Daily newspapers	Weekly newspapers	Direct mail	Outdoor and transit	Point of purchase
Audience considerations												
Attentiveness of audience	M	M	M	M	M	M	M	M	M	M	W	W
Interest of audience	M	S	M	M	S	S	S	S	S	W	W	W
Offers selectivity to advertiser	W	W	M	M	S	S	W	W	W	S	W	W
Offers involvement	M	S	M	M	M	S	M	M	M	W	W	W
Avoids distraction	M	S	M	M	S	S	M	M	M	S	W	W
Offers prestige	M	S	W	M	S	S	S	M	W	W	W	W
Good quality of audience data	M	M	M	M	S	S	M	M	W	M	W	W
Timing factors												
Offers repetition	S	S	S	S	M	M	W	M	W	V	S	M
Offers frequency	S	S	S	M	M	M	W	M	W	M	S	M
Allows long message	M	M	M	M	S	S	S	S	S	S	W	W

Note: W = Weak, M = Medium, S = Strong, N = Not a factor for this medium, V = Varies from one vehicle to another within the medium.

lent for reaching specific audiences. One example is industry-specific magazines such as *Chain Store Age Executive*. Newspaper advertising consists mainly of retail advertising, although it is an important medium for national advertisers who want to communicate specific facts about their products.

Many large food companies are experimenting with high-tech ways to deliver messages to consumers while they are shopping. For example, Campbell Soup is testing an interactive video promotion system that dispenses coupons and recipes and acts as a store directory. Such computerized video delivery systems permit local audiences to be better targeted. Although primarily developed for supermarkets and drugstores, the technology can be used by any consumer service industry.[20]

---

[20] Laurie Freeman and Judann Dagnoli, "Point-of-Purchase Rush Is On," *Advertising Age,* February 8, 1988, p. 47.

EXHIBIT 17 ◆ 8
(concluded)

	Spot TV	Network TV	Spot radio	Network radio	Consumer magazines	Business publications	Sunday supplements	Daily newspapers	Weekly newspapers	Direct mail	Outdoor and transit	Point of purchase
Geographic considerations												
Offers geographic selectivity	S	W	S	W	M	M	S	S	S	S	M	S
Provides for local dealer "tags"	M	W	M	W	M	M	M	S	S	S	M	S
Creative considerations												
Permits demonstration	S	S	W	W	M	M	M	M	M	S	W	S
Provides impact	S	S	M	M	M	M	M	M	M	S	W	M
Permits relation to editorial matter	M	M	W	M	S	S	M	M	M	S	N	N
Control considerations												
Advertiser control of media content	W	M	W	M	W	W	W	W	W	S	N	N
Advertiser control of location	N	S	N	S	M	M	W	W	W	S	W	M
Mechanical and production factors												
Ease of insertion	M	S	M	S	S	S	M	M	W	S	M	W
High reproduction quality	M	M	M	M	S	S	S	V	V	S	V	S
Flexibility of format	M	M	M	M	S	S	W	N	N	S	M/W	W
Financial considerations												
Low total cost	M	W	M	W	W	W	M	S	S	W	M	M
High efficiency	M	S	S	M	M	M	M	M	W	S	S	W

Source: Adapted from Courtland L. Bovee and William F. Arens, Contemporary Advertising, 3rd ed. (Homewood, Ill.: Richard D. Irwin, 1989), pp. 392–93.

Direct marketing via advertising media

In recent years the use of direct marketing using advertising media has increased dramatically. Direct marketing is "an interactive system of marketing that uses one or more advertising media to effect a measurable response and/or transaction at any location."[21] This means that sellers use media to contact a specific person or household to generate some type of action (usually to buy a consumer product or service). Direct mail (including catalogs), interactive TV home shopping, and TV, radio, and print ads coupled with a toll-free telephone number are the major types of direct

---

[21] "Direct Marketing—What Is It?" Direct Marketing, June 1985, p. 20.

marketing.[22] Annual sales revenues generated by these forms of direct marketing are between $30 and $40 billion and are likely to continue growing rapidly for the indefinite future. This does not include the $25 to $30 billion raised annually by nonprofit organizations.

Direct marketing of the type described above has flourished in part because sellers have learned how to identify prospects. Computer records are kept of when prospects became customers and of all their purchases thereafter. Other factors that contributed to direct marketing's growth are the demands for more shopping convenience coming in part from working women, greater discretionary incomes, universality of credit cards, and the problems of driving to and parking at many retail stores. Direct marketing involves getting a response—typically the purchase of a product. Thus, it should not be used to develop awareness or to change attitudes.

Media audiences

Most media research measures the size and composition of the audience exposed to a specific media vehicle (say, "L.A. Law"). In print media, researchers measure vehicle exposure based on the number of individuals who read, as a minimum, some part of a particular vehicle. They use much the same definition to measure TV and radio audiences.

A **print medium audience** comprises people who report having read one or more editorial features of an average issue (not all issues are surveyed). Thus, there may be a substantial difference between the size of the audience of the issue carrying the ad and that of the average issue. When to interview is also a problem. If researchers conduct interviews too soon after an issue has been released, not everyone who ordinarily reads the magazine has had a chance to do so. Conversely, if interviews are delayed too long, some people may have forgotten having been exposed to the vehicle or will be confused as to where they read what. Interviewers collect demographic data concurrently with readership information. Some print media also report the ownership of certain products by members of their audience.

In **electronic media,** the need to define the geographic reach of a particular medium complicates the problem of measuring audiences. On the other hand, the fact that the time and duration of the broadcast are fixed simplifies the measurement problem. Through the use of an electronic recorder called a **passive meter,** researchers can measure the number of TV sets tuned to a given program. This machine records whether a set is on and provides a complete tuning record for a given time period. Researchers can estimate the total number of sets that are on at any given time, the channels to which they are tuned, and how long they are tuned to a given program. Advertisers,

---

[22] Both direct mail and interactive TV were discussed in Chapter 15 as a form of nonstore retailing.

therefore, obtain data on the average audience *per minute*. They can also obtain these and other data for each type of household in the viewing audience. Despite the objectivity of this measurement, it does not record the number of actual *viewers* and their characteristics.

Other methods of measuring the audiences of electronic media include **listening and viewing diaries, roster recall tests** ("Which of the following programs did you view or listen to yesterday?"), and **coincidental telephone calls.** All are significantly limited by sampling and nonresponse errors and the respondents' inability to remember the programs to which they were exposed. Status-related reporting biases are also limiting; people like to report seeing or listening to "good" programs and dislike reporting they watch TV for hours on end. The conditioning effect of keeping a diary is limiting, for it involves keeping a continuous record of listening or viewing choices.

Because both passive meters and diaries have audience measurement problems, researchers have made a considerable effort over the years to find a better system. A recent technological breakthrough—an import from Europe—is called a **People Meter.** This involves a remote control that sends signals to a small control box on top of a TV set. Household members push their assigned buttons every time they start or finish watching TV. The People Meter relays information about who is watching to a computer that has on file the age and sex of each household member. Researchers can transmit audience data at the individual level to subscribers within 24 hours.

The use of People Meters has its problems, too. Just because people push the buttons does not mean they are looking at the TV. Also, people (especially children and teenagers) are not always totally reliable in pushing buttons. Audience measures derived from the use of People Meters are somewhat lower for the more popular shows compared to measures obtained from diaries. Thus, for example, Bill Cosby's People Meter rating was about 10 percent less than his diary rating. This is an important difference, given that a 30-second spot on "The Bill Cosby Show" costs about $380,000.[23] Saturday-morning ratings of cartoon shows have fallen dramatically. A comparison of 1987 People Meter ratings to the previous year's diary ratings showed "Smurfs" supposedly was being watched by 33 percent fewer children.[24]

The growth in the use of VCRs and remote-control devices is beginning to cause TV audience measurement problems. So far the effects of such high-

---

[23] See Jeffrey A. Trachtenberg, "Anybody Home Out There?" *Forbes*, May 19, 1986, pp. 169–70; Peter Barnes and Joanne Lipman, "Networks and Ad Agencies Battle over Estimates of TV Viewership," *The Wall Street Journal*, January 1, 1987, p. 23; and David Lieberman, "The Networks' Big Headache," *Business Week*, July 6, 1987, pp. 26–28.

[24] Dennis Kneale and Peter W. Barnes, "For Saturday-Morning Kids' Shows the 'People Meter' Verdict Is Grim," *The Wall Street Journal*, December 28, 1987, p. 13.

tech products are not incorporated into audience ratings. There are two major ways in which these effects (called **zipping** and **zapping**) impact ratings. Zipping occurs when viewers use a VCR to record a program and then use the fast-forwarding mechanism to avoid the commercials during the playback. It is estimated that viewers zip past more than 50 percent of the commercials.

Zapping has to do with the use of a remote-control device to mute commercials or switch away from them completely. Because VCR and remote-control penetration will soon reach 60 to 70 percent of all U.S. TV homes, zapping is fast becoming a significant problem. After all, to most of us, the possibility of watching a TV program without commercials is certainly attractive![25]

Accumulation and duplication

A TV program or a magazine, after several shows or issues, often reaches an **accumulated audience** considerably larger than that for a single show or issue. This total is made up of individuals or households who have been exposed *one or more* times and, therefore, contains no duplications. (That is, a person who views two shows or reads two issues is counted only once.) The term **reach** refers to this unduplicated audience at any particular time, usually four weeks. It can be used in connection with a single media vehicle (e.g., several issues of a single magazine) or a media schedule comprising a number of vehicles. Reach is typically expressed as a percent of the target audience. Thus, if the target audience was 100,000 households and the media schedule reached 70,000, then the reach would be 70 percent. Ordinarily, costs rise at an increasing rate as higher levels of reach are sought.

Duplication occurs whenever a marketer purchases a second medium (e.g., a second medium type or a second issue of a given magazine or a second spot commercial). Some portion of the audience of the first medium is almost always part of the audience of the second medium. Assume that Medium A (TV) has an audience of 100,000 persons and Medium B (magazine), 90,000. If 40,000 of the persons exposed to Medium B are also members of A's audience, then buying the two media yields an *unduplicated audience* of 150,000—not 190,000. Some 40,000 of the 150,000 may receive two impressions. With a relatively long media schedule, the duplication problem can be immense. The more media vehicles used, the greater the problem of duplication becomes. Duplication is the basis for determining **frequency,** which is needed over time to obtain awareness and message retention. Reach and frequency determine the total advertising media expenditures.

---

[25] Barry M. Kaplan, "Zapping—The Real Issue Is Communication," *Journal of Advertising Research,* April/May 1985, pp. 9–14. Also see in the same issue, "Profiling Zappers" by Carrie Heeter and Bradley S. Greenberg (pp. 15–20) and "Channel Flickers and Video Speeders" by David A. Yorke and Philip J. Kitchen (pp. 21–25).

Media models[26]

Almost all media models basically seek to maximize some measure of advertising exposure that is assumed to impact sales. These models report, for a given advertising schedule, the number of individuals or households exposed to a medium and the number of times they are exposed. Because different schedules have different costs, advertisers divide the exposure "output" by the costs involved to obtain an effectiveness ratio.

Even if exposure can be predicted with reasonable accuracy, not all who are exposed are of equal value to the advertiser, however. Some may be heavy buyers, while others may not even be prospects. Further, how should successive exposures be weighted? Is the second exposure worth more than the third? How much more? How much time should elapse between exposures? How much forgetting takes place over time, and what is the variation in forgetting between different exposures? Even though most models seek to address these problems, they are handicapped by a lack of precise input data—especially that pertaining to duplication, forgetting, and accumulation.

Some models provide reach (extent of audience) and frequency of exposure for each media schedule. Others require that advertisers state their objectives in terms of reach and frequency by target segments. Then the model's output consists of a recommended media schedule by media vehicle, by time period, and by number of units purchased—plus information about the composition and size of the audience reached, the total number of impressions, the distribution of exposure frequencies, and the cost.

Some advertisers do research to obtain media exposure that they can tie directly to brand usage. They ask respondents to what extent they are exposed to specific media vehicles and which brands of an array of products they use. These data facilitate selecting a media schedule, because advertisers can specify a target audience (say, those using a given brand) and determine its exposure to various media vehicles.

FEEDBACK

Management must know to what extent the message was received by members of the target audience, whether it was understood and believed, and whether it had any effect on how the receivers thought or felt about the product. In many cases, management wants answers to these and similar questions about competitive products to make comparisons with its own product. Marketing research obtains such feedback information mainly by message testing.

---

[26] For more information on this subject, see Roland T. Rust, *Advertising Media Models* (Lexington, Mass.: D.C. Heath, 1986).

Message testing

Message testing is often called **copy testing.** It evaluates alternative ways for advertisers to present their messages to the target audience. For the most part researchers use measures concerned with recognition, recall, comprehension, believability, persuasion, and attitude change to judge advertising effectiveness. One study revealed that all 60 TV commercials in a specific test were misunderstood; further, that the average amount of miscomprehension was 30 percent.[27]

The discussion here is divided into two parts—tests made *before* the message is released on a full-run basis, and tests done *after* the copy is run in the prescribed media. The essential difference between these two types of tests is their purpose. If the objective is to improve the message prior to its full run, then the test is considered a before test despite the fact that the test may call for the copy to be run in one or several media. A basic problem is that "before" testing cannot measure long-term effects—and yet most attitudes change very slowly.

Before tests

No pretest of a message can simulate exactly the conditions of exposure and the long-run effect of repetition on a particular audience group. However, advertisers have a number of ways to test the effectiveness of an advertisement beforehand.

Memory tests.   Advertisers insert test ads into a dummied-up magazine or newspaper and tell respondents to read whatever interests them. Then they ask respondents which ads they remember and to "play back" as much of each as possible. Typically they ask additional questions about message credibility and product usage. Based on the results, they can determine the extent to which a given message gets through. Thus, advertisers can rate ads on how well they achieved the communicator's objectives. There is some question of the validity of these tests for well-known brands, however. Recall scores for these ads are more apt to reflect the brand's popularity than the message's structure and content.

Advertisers test TV commercials by exposing a finished commercial in one or more cities, and following up with several hundred phone interviews to obtain a recall score, that is, to find out how many remember the message. They compare the results with a standard or normative score obtained from similar studies. On this basis they either accept or reject the commercial. The

---

[27] Jacob Jacoby and Wayne D. Hoyer, "Viewer Miscomprehension of Television Communication—Selected Findings," *Journal of Marketing,* Fall 1982, pp. 12–17.

average score in one testing system is 24; a Meow Mix spot that featured a singing cat holds the record with a 74.[28]

Projective tests.   For such tests interviewers give an ad (usually in rough form) to respondents and use a variety of projective methods—including storytelling, word association, and sentence completion—to elicit responses. Through these techniques the interviewer finds out how readers of the ad perceived its content. By analyzing the data, researchers can tell which mental associations the ad triggered; what the reader saw (or did not see); what the reader thought was important and unimportant; and whether the message was understood in its entirety. Such tests are fairly simple to conduct, because they use an ad as a stimulus to provoke response. They are, however, difficult to interpret properly and require highly skilled interviewers.

Physiological tests.   These tests use specially designed machinery to measure physiological responses to advertising. Two of the oldest methods measure the *galvanic skin response* and *eye movements*. The first, through electrodes attached to the respondent's palms, measures the changes in perspiration as the subject sees or hears advertising messages. The second uses an eye camera to continuously record the activity of the eyes as they read a printed message. The machine records what first caught the attention of the respondent, the path followed as the reader proceeded through the ad, and whether they got hung up on any part of the ad.

A more recent device measures *pupil dilation*. When a person is viewing or listening to interesting or pleasant messages, the pupil dilates. Conversely, when a person is viewing boring or unpleasant materials, the pupil contracts. These changes in pupil diameter are not related to light intensity and are not controllable by the individual. By comparing the changes caused by the stimulus with those produced by a neutral source, researchers can obtain measurements of an ad's effectiveness. Pupil dilation is presumed to indicate a positive interest in the ad's message. Random pupillary variations indicate lack of interest; and contraction indicates dislike. This method suffers from the artificiality of the testing situation and the difficulty of interpreting the reasons for any recorded change. Much the same can be said for all physiological tests.

Sales tests.   Commercial research firms like BehaviorScan, operated by Information Resources, Inc., measure the effect of TV commercials through

---

[28] Bill Adams, ''Should 200 Viewers' Memories Decide Whether Ads Live or Die?'' *The Wall Street Journal*, July 24, 1980, p. 17.

the use of consumer panels located in a number of small cities. Purchases are recorded electronically by scanners at supermarket checkout counters by panel members using special ID cards. BehaviorScan can insert test TV commercials into TV programs at the individual panel household level. They select household samples on the basis of their purchase behavior history. Thus, the consumer panel becomes a single source of both purchase and viewing behavior, thereby enhancing its value. Because alternative ad treatments can be shown to different balanced samples at the same time, it is possible to measure the sales effect of one copy treatment against another based on actual purchase data.

Other TV commercial tests.   Several research methods are available to pre-test TV commercials. One is through the use of a trailer or rented space in a shopping mall. Prospective buyers are interviewed about their attitudes toward and use of various brands in one or more product classes. Then they are shown a series of commercials imbedded in a TV pilot program that presumably the audience has not seen. One or more of the commercials constitute the test ad or ads. After the viewing, respondents are given coupons that can be used to obtain any brand within a given product type at a mall store. By checking the redemptions and comparing them with the pre-exposed measures of the sample consumers' attitudes and use patterns, advertisers can gain insights into the test ad's influence on the consumer.

Theater tests are similar to the above, except the audience's reaction (positive/negative) to commercials is measured electronically during the showing via buttons the audience pushes to indicate "liking/disliking." Before and after measurements of brand preferences are also made to determine the effect of the test ad, which is one of a number of commercials inserted into a pilot TV program. The after test consists of respondents selecting gifts of their favorite brands in certain product classes.

On-air testing consists of using a VHF or a cable TV channel to air a given program in which the ad will appear. Respondents are either asked to view the program or are selected after the program has run. In either case, respondents who viewed the program are queried about the advertising to provide an evaluation of the commercial.

After tests

Measuring the effects of an advertising message *after* it has run is difficult because advertisers are confounded by the effects of the media used and the frequency with which the audience received the message. After tests tend to measure the effectiveness of the total advertising effort. Here we look at only those after tests used primarily to measure the message.

Advertisers design after tests in a number of ways, all of which rely on the respondent's memory. This raises the question of how soon after running the ad the measurement should be taken. Also, testing that relies on a single measure in time does not measure the commercial's maximum performance, since it does not reflect the learning that takes place with repeated exposure.

Recognition tests are the most popular postexposure testing method for print media. Advertisers design these tests to measure the extent to which advertising copy is noted and read. Field workers interview people who say they have read a given issue of a magazine. Each respondent goes through the issue pointing out what was seen and read. When the respondent reports seeing an ad, the interviewer asks which parts were read. The interviewer starts each interview at a random point within the issue, so that the ratings are not affected by respondent fatigue.

Recall tests are another common way to measure the effectiveness of an advertising message—especially a TV commercial—after it has been run. Respondents are typically aided in their recall. Interviewers show them a list of the advertisers and brands presented and ask which ones they have seen recently. In this way, interviewers obtain playbacks of the ad from the respondents.

The industry has long raised questions of whether recall and recognition tests provide adequate measures of memory. There is considerable evidence that both recall and recognition scores are sometimes inflated by over-reporting by respondents. Research indicates that recall scores are adequate for "thinking" commercials, but that they understate the effect of "feeling" commercials. Researchers can best measure the latter type of ad by using recognition tests.[29]

Other postexposure ways of measuring the effectiveness of the message include sales tests similar to those used to test new products, inquiries (possible when coupons are used or a toll-free telephone number is made available for placing orders), and measurements of attitudinal change. The latter typically involves before-after measures of the degree to which a given brand possesses certain salient features.

ADVERTISING BUDGETS

The problem of how much to spend on advertising is essentially the same as for the promotion mix. The effect of advertising on sales can be measured directly only when advertising offers consumers something they can learn about in no other way—such as via mail order. A typical advertising campaign interacts with the past and the present environment to produce sales. This continuous nature of the promotion process makes it hard to link sales to specific advertising expenditures. (And the large number of uncontrolled variables present further complicates matters.)

---

[29] Hugh A. Zielski, "Does Day-After Recall Penalize 'Feeling' Ads?" *Journal of Advertising Research*, February–March 1982, pp. 19–22.

We discussed several different approaches to budget setting for the promotion mix in Chapter 16. These are essentially the same alternatives available for determining how much to spend on advertising. As with the promotion mix, the objective-and-task approach is the best method to use.

Assume that the objective of advertising is modifying or maintaining attitudes toward the product. Any effect on attitudes is primarily a function of the source, the message (including the size of the message unit), the media type and vehicle, the frequency of message receipt, and the intervals between message receipts. If the best possible message is constructed, and if message unit size, media type, vehicle, and source are held constant, then the essential variables are *reach* and *frequency*.

Firms must make certain assumptions about how frequently a message must be received during a given period and how many periods are needed to maintain or increase levels of awareness or attitudes. They must also make certain assumptions about how the extent and timing of the change in attitudes or awareness relates to sales. This approach to determining the media component of the advertising budget shows how advertising must work if expenditures in this area are to have an effect on sales. And it specifies the assumptions firms must make to arrive at a budget. Exhibit 17–9 presents a simplified example of the use of the objective-and-task approach to set an advertising budget.

For industrial products, the case can be made for including the salesforce as an advertising medium, so that the firm can build a total communications model. Although there are no reasons conceptually why this cannot be done, management must make certain assumptions about the value of a personal sales call versus information received through other media.

SALES PROMOTION

The American Marketing Association defines **sales promotion** as "those marketing activities, other than personal selling, advertising, and publicity, that stimulate consumer purchasing and dealer effectiveness." Sales promotions typically offer an incentive to consumers and resellers to stimulate short-term demand for a product. Thus, it focuses on direct buyer behavior. Advertising, in contrast, typically focuses on factors leading to a sale, such as creating brand awareness or changing buyers' perceptions and attitudes toward the brand.

Importance of sales promotion

Industry expenditures for sales promotion exceeded $100 billion in 1986. From 1975 to 1985, sales promotion spending grew at a faster rate than advertising—an average of 12 percent versus 10 percent per year. Exhibit

EXHIBIT 17 ◆ 9

Applying the objective-and-task method to setting an advertising budget for a new brand of running shoe—a hypothetical example

1. **Establish a market share goal.** By the end of the first year, want a 15 percent share of the estimated 40-million-pair market, which is expected to grow by 5 million pairs per year into the early 1990s. This target of 6 million pairs (first year) is to be obtained by attracting first-time runners as buyers and getting present runners to switch to the new brand. Assume some 20 million present runners and the net addition of 2 million new runners each year. The number of individual consumers needed to obtain a 15 percent share by the end of the first year is estimated to be 3 million.

2. **Determine the percent of the target audience that needs to be made aware of the new brand in order to induce purchases of 6 million pairs.** The agency estimates 30 percent of those who become aware of the new product will buy it. This translates into a need to make 10 million present and prospective buyers aware of the brand (or some 46 percent of the 22 million total).

3. **Determine the number of impressions needed to obtain an awareness level of 46 percent followed by purchase.** The agency estimates 35 impressions on average will be needed for each of 10 million individuals in the target audience to bring this about over the year (less than one per week). Thus, the total number of impressions needed is $35 \times 10M = 35.0$ million.

4. **Determine the number of gross rating points (GRP) needed.*** Based on needed reach and repetition (35), assume 3,500 GRPs are needed.

5. **Determine the cost of the needed 3,500 GRPs.** The agency estimates an average cost per GRP of $4,000—hence, the advertising media budget would be $14 million. To this amount, the costs of ad production and marketing research would have to be added.

* GRPs are computed by multiplying the reach by the average frequency. Remember that reach is the number of different individuals (or households) exposed to an advertising schedule per some time period—usually four weeks. Reach measures the unduplicated audience exposed to a media schedule and is typically expressed as a percent of the target audience. Frequency is a measure of the number of times on average a person or household receives an advertising measure. Thus, it is a measure of repetition. If we assume a reach of 70 percent and a need for an average frequency of 20, then a media schedule yielding 1,400 gross rating points would be needed.

17–10 indicates various promotional activities and the relative importance of each based on expenditures. Note that meetings and conventions are twice as important as direct mail.

Expenditures for consumer promotions have increased in recent years, while those for trade promotions have decreased. Trade promotions are still the larger of the two, however. In 1986, packaged goods sellers allocated 29 percent of their promotion budgets to consumer promotions, 37 percent to trade promotions, and 34 percent to media advertising. Most consumer promotions use a combination of activities. An example is Quaker Oats' "Where's the Cap'n?" promotion that

EXHIBIT   17 ♦ 10
Sales promotion activities and percent of total expenditures

Sales promotion activity	Percent of total expenditures
Meetings and conventions	31%
Direct mail	16
Promotions and incentives	14
Point-of-purchase displays	12
Print, audiovisuals, and misc.	8
Promotion ad space	8
Exhibits and trade shows	6
Couponing	4

Source: Reprinted from Joe Agnew, "Burgeoning Sales Promotion Spending to Top $100 Billion," *Marketing News,* May 22, 1987, p. 8; published by the American Marketing Association.

offered a $1 million sweepstakes reward for the return of the Cap'n, who mysteriously vanished from the fronts of millions of cereal boxes in August 1985. The event was promoted via a multimedia blitz, including freestanding newspaper inserts, Sunday comics, TV, radio, and a PR campaign. As a result . . . consumers searched store shelves for the packages and clues.[30]

There are a number of reasons for the rapid growth of sales promotion over advertising. The more important ones include:

1. The growing product parity—lack of differentiation between brands.
2. Advertising media costs—especially those of TV—are so high that advertisers question their cost effectiveness versus certain sales promotion activities more and more. The increased clutter on TV and the growth in cable has also favored the use of sales promotion over TV advertising.
3. The growing number of price-sensitive consumers resulting from the strong inflation of the late 70s and early 80s.
4. Increased competition from not only other manufacturer brands but private labels as well.[31]

In addition to the above, marketing managers are often geared to the short run because their pay and bonuses are structured that way. Thus, they are more likely to use sales promotions to energize immediate sales than to invest in advertising aimed at improving a brand's image. Also, the effects of sales promotions are easier to measure than advertising.[32]

---

[30] Joe Agnew, "Burgeoning Sales Promotion Spending to Top $100 Billion," *Marketing News,* May 22, 1987, p. 18.

[31] Henry Assael, *Marketing Management* (Boston: Kent Publishing, 1985), p. 371.

[32] Felix Kessler, "The Costly Coupon Craze," *Fortune,* June 9, 1986, p. 83.

Consumer sales promotion

Marketers classify consumer sales promotions on the basis of their use with new products or established brands. For new products, they use sampling, couponing, and refunds most often. They use price-off promotions, premiums, and consumer contests or sweepstakes primarily for mature products.

While consumer promotion activity is important and growing, however, trade allowances made by manufacturers to retailers dominate manufacturers' promotional expenditures. Although manufacturers spend about 40 percent of all sales promotion money on consumer promotion, trade promotion accounts for 60 percent. More than 60 percent of the items sold by supermarkets are discounted and some 90 percent of all soft-drink sales volume goes at discount prices.[33]

Sampling

Sampling is an effective but expensive way to encourage trial of a new product. Large firms marketing a line of packaged food or personal-care products that are small, lightweight, and relatively inexpensive frequently use sampling. For example, when introducing Finesse shampoo, Helene Curtis distributed over 70 million free samples at a cost of $10 million.[34] Samples are most effective when the new product has some strong differentiating characteristics.

Coupons

The most popular consumer promotion is the coupon, which has experienced strong growth in recent years. As we saw in Chapter 16, packaged goods producers issued some 180 billion coupons with a face value in excess of $50 billion in 1985; consumers redeemed about 6.5 billion at a value of more than $2 billion.

Coupons are the major means by which sellers offer consumer price incentives. After they are redeemed, retail stores are reimbursed for their value plus a handling fee of about five cents per coupon. There are several reasons why coupons are so popular. First, coupons limit the price reduction to customers sensitive to the price deal. All other customers continue to pay the regular price. Second, coupons allow the manufacturer to dictate the time frame for the promotion. Third, since many products are losing their distinctiveness, the coupon offer may help to develop a selective demand for a brand.[35]

---

[33] William C. Johnson, "Sales Promotion: It's Come Down to 'Push Marketing,'" *Marketing News*, February 1988, p. 8.

[34] *Advertising Age*, November 28, 1985.

[35] Engel et al., *Promotional Strategy*, p. 447.

Rebates

Another way a seller can reduce the price of its product to encourage trial is through the money refund offer. Typically, such offers require the consumer to mail some proof of purchase to the manufacturer to receive some discount on the purchase. This type of promotion is often used to support retailers who then advertise the product at a price *less* the rebate.

Premiums

Manufacturers sometimes attempt to attract buyers by offering a product or service free or at a substantially reduced price to encourage the purchase of another product. For example, Pizza Hut might offer free Pepsi with the purchase of a large pizza. Some firms have successfully created premium campaigns that tie into the images of their brands. Marlboro has offered western hats and belt buckles that tie in with the "Marlboro country" advertising theme, for example. Premiums may even be to some degree self-liquidating—they pay for themselves by some charge to the consumer (as when the consumer sends in a package top and 50 cents for a premium). The primary purpose of a premium is to get consumers to switch brands in the hope of gaining repeat purchases.

Price-off promotions

One of the simplest sales promotions is to temporarily reduce the product's price. Sellers usually advertise price-off promotions and couple them with in-store displays. A similar popular promotion increases the amount of product provided while holding the price constant—like Pepsi's offer of 15 cans of soda for the normal price of a 12-pack. Price-off promotions may be the most effective way to boost sales temporarily. However, they suffer from several disadvantages. Often they only transfer future sales to the present as loyal customers stock up. Another problem is that competitors can easily copy them. Also, they may lead consumers to the notion that the product should be bought only below the suggested retail price. This is not the case, however, with a new product. In an effort to move finished-goods inventory on its new Spectra camera (priced at retail from $115 to $200), Polaroid offered to reduce its price to any consumer trading in a used camera. (See Exhibit 17–11 for an illustration of Polaroid's trade-in ad.)

Contests and sweepstakes

Firms add interest to ordinarily routine products with consumer contests and sweepstakes. In a consumer contest, buyers compete for prizes on the basis of skill. Sweepstakes, on the other hand, distribute prizes on the basis of chance.

Popular formats for contests include developing the best name for a new product or finding new uses for existing products, as in the famous Pillsbury

EXHIBIT   17 ♦ 11

Polaroid trade-in ad

Somewhere in your past is an old camera that doesn't collect wonderful memories anymore. It just collects dust.

But now it can help you collect something else. A sizeable savings on the Polaroid camera of the future.

Because your Polaroid dealer will give you $20 off the price of the amazing Polaroid Spectra System, or $25 off on the new Spectra System Onyx (the world's first transparent camera) just for trading in your old camera. Any old camera. Even if it's junk.

The way we look at it, you won't be losing a camera, you'll be gaining a complete photographic system.

One that features a precise autofocus system, full-information viewfinder, sophisticated light metering and quick recharge fill-flash that virtually guarantee a great shot every time.

So instead of collecting dust, you can collect the most brilliant, most lifelike instant pictures you've ever seen.

TRADE IN YOUR CAMERA OF THE PAST FOR POLAROID'S CAMERA OF THE FUTURE.

$20 SAVINGS
$25 SAVINGS

PolaroidSpectraSystem
WE TAKE YOUR PICTURES SERIOUSLY.

© 1987 Polaroid Corp."Polaroid,"® "Spectra and Onyx"™ Offer expires July 4, 1987.

Courtesy: Polaroid Corporation.

Bake-Off. Contests and sweepstakes effectively create interest and excitement for a product. And they can help gain the support of middlemen. Unfortunately, it is difficult to pretest these sales promotions. Further, they may attract a lot of professional participants.

Trade promotions

As we noted earlier, trade promotions are declining compared to the expenditures for consumer promotions, although they are still the larger of the two. There are a variety of ways manufacturers can stimulate resellers to improve their performance. These include training a distributor's salesforce, cooperative advertising and promotional allowances (including in-store promotions), and contests and incentives for sales personnel.

Reseller training programs

Training resellers' salespeople can be a profitable investment for manufacturers as well as for resellers. The primary training program objectives are to provide the reseller's salesforce with knowledge about the product and how it can best be sold through certain selling techniques. In some cases whole-salers' salespeople provide management advice to retailers. Selling aids, including sales literature and video tapes, often are part of such training programs.

Cooperative advertising and promotional allowances

In cooperative advertising programs, a manufacturer may pay a percentage of a reseller's expenses for local advertising based on the reseller's purchases from the manufacturer. For example, assume a retailer purchased $100,000 worth of product from a manufacturer whose co-op program paid 50 percent of local advertising up to 2 percent of purchases. In this case, the manufac-turer would pay up to $2,000 for local advertising, provided that amount was matched by the retailer.

The manufacturer typically provides the mats for the local newspaper ads and the finished radio and TV commercials. Such advertising is advan-tageous to the manufacturer for several reasons. It involves the reseller financially, and obtains local advertising at a lower cost than national adver-tising. It encourages the reseller to maintain adequate inventories. And it increases the likelihood that the seller will coordinate co-op advertising with point-of-purchase displays.

Manufacturers give **promotional allowances** when it is essential that retailers display products in a prescribed way. These allowances are de-signed not only to gain acceptance of the display, but also to maintain it over some specified period of time.

In-store promotions stimulate resellers to undertake certain activities such as setting up displays, undertaking cooperative advertising, and reduc-ing prices. They often tie together co-op advertising, sales kits, in-store promotions, and contests. Automobile manufacturers use such programs to promote their cars. **Contests and incentives** are designed to improve selling at the wholesale and retail levels. Prizes often consist of a pleasure trip abroad. Resellers sometimes object to such promotional activities because they may cause their salespersons to spend a disproportionate amount of time on one manufacturer's product line.

In summary, sales promotions can effectively obtain consumer trial and purchase of new products, increase purchase of existing products, create interest in routine product categories, and help support middlemen. But they suffer from several key limitations, which marketers must consider when designing sales promotion programs.

PUBLIC RELATIONS

The third element in the promotion mix that relies on mass communication is **public relations.** Dunn defines this activity as a promotional function that "uses two-way communications to mesh the needs and interests of an in-

EXHIBIT 17 ♦ 12

Key definitions in public relations

Public relations

Two-way communication to mesh the needs and interests of an institution or person with those of publics.

Publics

Any target audience tied together or distinguished by some interest or concern.

Public affairs

Planned effort to gain favorable reactions and influence opinion inside and outside an organization through actions and effective two-way communication; often emphasizes media and government publics.

Publicity

Planned program to obtain favorable media coverage of topics important to an organization.

Press agentry

Generating publicity through attention-getting devices (usually blatant) or publicity gimmickry.

Promotion

Marketing function used to build the image of a product or service through advertising, public relations, sales promotion, or personal selling.

Propaganda

Attempt at persuasion of target audiences at all costs, using unethical as well as ethical forms of communication.

Advertising

Nonpersonal, persuasive, paid communication through the media with sponsors or brands identified in the message.

Source: S. Watson Dunn, *Public Relations: A Contemporary Approach* (Homewood, Ill.: Richard D. Irwin, 1986), p. 5.

stitution or person with the needs and interests of the various publics with which that institution or person must communicate."[36]

Some key definitions in public relations are listed in Exhibit 17–12. Firms undertake public relations for a product (Cabbage Patch Kid Dolls); for a product class (cigars); for a company as a whole (Procter & Gamble's educational services department, which prepares laundering, food preparation, and personal-care kits for high school students); and for an industry (the National Beef Council). Exhibit 17–13 gives an example of the use of public relations to position a brand.

Publicity has several unique advantages. It is credible; most people feel the mass media would have no reason to carry favorable information about a

---

[36] S. Watson Dunn, *Public Relations: A Contemporary Approach* (Homewood, Ill.: Richard D. Irwin, 1986), p. 50.

EXHIBIT 17 ♦ 13

Example of the use of public relations to position a brand

Westwood Pharmaceuticals, Inc., a division of Bristol-Meyers, recently undertook a re-positioning strategy for its Keri brand of products. Westwood was well recognized for its outstanding skincare products and had strong contacts with dermatologists. As part of its longer-term growth plans, it decided to reposition Keri as not only an excellent skin-care product but also one that was essentially nonmedical. It hoped to do so by building a link between Keri and the lifestyle of confident and secure women.

The first phase of the program was to undertake a study among accomplished women selected from *Who's Who of American Women* to serve as the basis for "The Keri Report—Confidence and The American Woman," which would explore women's self-perception during the social changes of the past two decades. The results showed, among other things, there was a direct relationship between how women feel about their appearance and their overall sense of confidence.

The "Keri Report" was announced at a press conference in New York attended by more than 80 journalists and leaders of women's organizations. News coverage included a dozen nationally syndicated articles that appeared in hundreds of newspapers; articles in such major women's publications as *Vogue* and *Working Woman;* and radio and TV coverage in cities throughout the United States. The "Keri Report" generated over 12 million audience impressions and created a high brand awareness among consumers that was further enhanced by a four-page summary of the report that was sent to consumers.

A mall program planned for early release profiled a live TV show based on the report that would tie into the Keri product line. The show featured Judith Briles, author of a book on the report. Product samples, coupons, and distribution of the report summary were undertaken. The report also served as the basis for extensive research to develop a creative new concept for advertising the Keri brand in women's magazines.

Source: From David Finn, "Creative PR Can Help Position a Brand," reprinted from *Marketing News,* December 5, 1988, published by the American Marketing Association.

product unless it were true. Thus, public relations reinforces the firm's advertising campaign by increasing awareness and the believability of product claims. Publicity also makes it easier for the salesforce to present a case for the product. And it is low cost, in that there are few media costs. The major disadvantage is that publicity is beyond the company's control, not only as to whether the release will be run, but also what is said about the product.

Through public relations, firms communicate with a variety of publics. They include:

♦ The ultimate consumer—information about new products and new uses for old products.

♦ The financial community and stockholders—signalling the maintenance of or improvement in the company's profitability.

- The community—with "good citizen" information.
- Prospective employees—why the firm is a good place to work.
- Present employees—to develop pride in the company.
- Suppliers—good company with which to build an enduring relationship.

This listing of audiences suggests that publicity might be aimed at accomplishing different objectives among different groups. Such objectives range from simply increasing awareness of a company or its products to stimulating an actual response, such as sending for a free bulletin.

Firms also use public relations to cope with an unexpected shock. This was the case with the public relations campaign Johnson & Johnson mounted when seven people died from poisoned Tylenol capsules. J&J was able to restore confidence in the company and its Tylenol brand due in part to its responsible and well-orchestrated public relations program.

Public relations tools

The communication tools available to the public relations department range from news releases to hardbound books. We discuss the more common ones briefly here.[37]

Firms use **books, brochures, and pamphlets** extensively to communicate with their various audiences. These printed materials are particularly important in telling employees about a company's history, mission, and policies. **News releases** sent to print and electronic media announce a new product, the promotion of an executive, a gift to charity, and the like. Exhibit 17–14 shows the opinions of a sample of public relations executives concerning the best media vehicles to use for various news releases. Firms send their **annual reports** to stockholders and other interested parties. These reports contain financial information and management's statement about its performance. Firms send their **house publications** to employees or to external audiences including customers, stockholders, and dealers. Companies furnish **audiovisual materials** such as slides, films, and videocassettes without charge to theaters and a variety of organizations, including colleges and universities. Other publicity tools include speeches, posters, exhibits, letters, product inserts, events (such as the Kool Jazz tour), and open houses.

Considering the increase in TV commercials shown in a given program, and the high costs of most major media, firms will likely increase their use of the publicity component of the promotion mix. More and more companies are using public relations along with their advertising campaigns in an effort to add credibility to the claims made about the product.

---

[37] For a more detailed discussion, see Bovee and Arens, *Contemporary Advertising*, pp. 595–606.

EXHIBIT 17 ♦ 14

How public relations executives—both corporate and agency—rank the media

Asked how they rank the media if they have a very important and favorable corporate story to place, public relations executives responded as follows:

Corporate PR	PR agency
Most important medium:	
1. Newspaper	1. Business publications
Assuming the story could only be placed in newspapers:	
1. *The Wall Street Journal*	1. *New York Times*
2. *New York Times*	2. *The Wall Street Journal*
3. *USA Today*	3. *USA Today*
Assuming only general news magazines could be used:	
1. *Time*	1. *Time*
2. *Newsweek*	2. *Newsweek*
3. *U.S. News & World Report*	3. *U.S. News & World Report*
Assuming only business publications:	
1. *Business Week*	1. *Business Week*
2. *Fortune*	2. *Fortune*
3. *Forbes*	3. *Forbes*
Which TV news shows:	
1. "NBC Nightly News"	1. "NBC Nightly News"
2. "CBS Evening News"	2. "CBS Evening News"
3. "ABC World News Tonight"	3. "ABC World News Tonight"
Any other TV show:	
1. "Today"*	1. "Today"
"Good Morning America"*	2. "Good Morning America"
* Tied for first place	

Source: Reprinted with permission, from *Ad Age,* October 31, 1988, copyright © 1988 Crain Communications, Inc.

SUMMARY

Effective advertising decisions depend on how well the company has specified its target market, positioned the product, and formulated the marketing mix. Advertising is part of a company's communications mix along with personal selling, sales promotion, and public relations (publicity). The major advertising decisions have to do with setting objectives, deciding what the message should be and how to best present it, which media types and vehicles to use, and evaluating the effectiveness of the advertising program.

Advertising objectives are difficult to quantify. Somehow they must relate to the behavior needed to generate a sale. The marketing communications hierarchy can serve as the basis for setting advertising objectives although it is probably more useful to state them as building, changing, or reinforcing attitudes.

The source is an important part of the message, because source credibility influences the attitudes formed and held about a product. Different sources are important for each of the various stages in the product adoption process. The structure of a message also determines its effectiveness. Research shows that such factors as two-sided versus one-sided, drawing conclusions, and message size can impact a message's success.

Message testing consists of before and after tests. Before tests include memory tests, projective tests, physiological tests, and sales and inquiries tests. After tests measure the effectiveness of the total advertising effort, making it difficult to measure only the effect of the message. The two most common tests are recognition and recall.

Major media types include newspapers, TV, direct mail, radio, and magazines. In recent years, direct mail (including catalogs) and telemarketing have become prominent in direct marketing. Each has its own unique set of advantages and disadvantages, making it difficult to compare media on the basis of their effectiveness. Most media research is concerned with audience measurement. A print medium audience is defined usually on the basis of recall, while electronic recorders, diaries, roster recall, and coincidental telephone calls measure TV audiences. It is important to know as much as possible about a media vehicle's accumulated audience as well as the duplication within and between media.

The best way to set an advertising budget is to use the objective-and-task approach. This, in turn, requires that certain assumptions be made about reach and frequency relative to attaining the objective.

Sales promotions usually offer an incentive to consumers or resellers in an effort to stimulate short-term demand. There are two major types of sales promotions—those involving the consumer and those involving the trade. In recent years sales promotion spending has grown at a faster rate than advertising. More is spent on trade promotions than on consumer promotion, although the latter is becoming increasingly important.

Consumer promotion tools include sampling, coupons, refunds, premiums, price-off promotions, and contests and sweepstakes. Trade promotions include reseller training programs, cooperative advertising, promotional allowances, in-store promotions, and contests and incentives.

Public relations or publicity is an attempt to influence the attitudes of various publics toward the firm using the editorial content of the media to do so. Publicity may be undertaken for a product, a product class, or a company. Its major advantages are its low cost and its ability to enhance the credibility of the claims made for the product. When done properly, publicity helps the salesforce and the firm's advertising efforts. A wide variety of communication tools is available to the public relations department, ranging from news releases to videocassettes.

QUESTIONS

1. Steve's Ice Cream is a small ice cream chain that has slowly expanded from a single store in Boston to stores in cities on both coasts. Suppose Steve's is about to open a new store in Austin, Texas, near the University of Texas campus. UT students will be the primary target market for the new store. Which of the three *behavioral hierarchy models* discussed in the chapter do you think would be most appropriate to use as a basis for setting advertising objectives for Steve's new store? Why?

2. Using the hierarchy model you recom-

mended in question 1, outline a series of *promotional objectives* to move UT students through the various stages in the hierarchy.

3. Select two different advertisements with which you are familiar. Briefly describe each ad and state what you think the *objectives* of each ad are. Be explicit about any assumptions you make in formulating your answer.

4. Which *message structure* is employed in each of the two ads you described in question 3? Given what you think the objectives of the ads are, do you think they employ appropriate messages? Why?

5. If you were working for the ad agencies that created the two ads you selected in question 3, how would you recommend *testing the effectiveness* of the message in each ad *before* running the ads in the media? How would you test the effectiveness of the messages *after* the ads run in the media? What are the advantages and limitations of the tests you have recommended?

6. Suppose you are a consultant to a small consumer electronics firm that is about to introduce a sophisticated and relatively expensive new compact disc player. Which *media* would you recommend using for the introductory advertising campaign for the new product? Why?

7. In consumer packaged goods industries the proportion of the promotional budget spent on *consumer sales promotion* has increased in recent years while the proportion spent on media advertising has declined. How do you explain this trend? Is the trend likely to continue?

8. Suppose you own a chain of dry cleaning stores in a major city. Competition is intense and there is a good deal of customer switching among competing stores. Which *sales promotion tools* might you use to help increase the proportion of customers who return to your store for their dry cleaning needs?

9. Suppose you are the public relations director for a regional ice cream manufacturer. In the course of a regularly scheduled inspection, the Food and Drug Administration inspector discovers a low level of listeria—a bacteria that can cause illness in pregnant women and the elderly—in your plant. Although the low level of the bacteria makes it unlikely that anyone will become seriously ill, your firm decides to voluntarily remove all of the ice cream it has produced in the past week from store shelves and replace it only after the bacteria problem has been resolved. What *public relations steps* would you recommend to minimize the damage to the company's image and future sales by this voluntary recall effort?

Chapter ⟨18⟩

Personal selling decisions

WILKINSON SWORD USA BUILDS A NEW SALESFORCE

Until 1985 Wilkinson Sword USA, the U.S. arm of London-based Wilkinson Sword, Ltd., had no salesforce of its own.[1] For 30 years the marketer of razors, blades, and self-sharpening knives and scissors had relied on the salesforces of manufacturers of related products—such as Scripto—or independent manufacturers' reps and brokers to sell its products to supermarkets and drugstores. During the early years when the parent company provided strong advertising support, the system worked relatively well. Wilkinson achieved a peak share of 7.9 percent of the wet-shave market in 1974—a market currently estimated to be worth about $500 million wholesale.

The lack of a dedicated salesforce exacerbated Wilkinson USA's problems in the mid-1970s, when the parent company withdrew its advertising support to focus its resources on the European market. As Ronald Mineo, then Wilkinson USA's vice president of sales, points out, "Without ad support the product slips in the marketplace; and there was no salesforce to intervene. [Using] brokers, Wilkinson could not get the kind of focus our product lines require to compete efficiently. All our competitors [were] out there with their own salesforces." Consequently, Wilkinson's share of the U.S. market slipped to a mere 0.7 percent by the end of 1984.

In response to this poor market performance, its parent company reorganized Wilkinson USA. Armed with a $23.5 million budget for a two-year advertising campaign it received the go-ahead to create its own 34-person salesforce. The first step in organizing the new salesforce was account classification. Wilkinson USA identified 25 leading national supermarket, drugstore, and mass-merchandise chains as primary accounts to be called on by two national account sales managers stationed at the firm's Atlanta headquarters. Next it identified regional chains and assigned these to area sales managers, who were also responsible for supervising one or two territory sales representatives operating in their areas. Finally, Wilkinson USA assigned smaller local accounts to the territory sales representatives.

In a second related step, Wilkinson USA organized the salesforce geographically. It divided the country into three geographic divisions—east, west, and central—and assigned each division to a field sales manager responsible for planning and coordinating sales ac-

---

[1] Based on Rayna Skolnik, "The Birth of a Sales Force," *Sales & Marketing Management*, March 10, 1986, pp. 42–44.

continued

concluded

tivities in that division. Next, it divided each division into an average of five areas, each assigned to an area manager. Finally, it specified one or two territories within each area—each with its own sales rep.

As President Norman Proulx of Wilkinson Sword North America points out, "Organizing is the easy part. The hard part is finding the people." Thus, the third step was to recruit, select, train, and motivate the necessary salespeople. Wilkinson sought people with at least five years of selling experience with top health and beauty aids companies because "given where we were in the marketplace, we couldn't hire new recruits. We absolutely had to have people with basic selling experience behind them." Even those experienced salespeople, however, required training to become familiar with Wilkinson's products, policies, and procedures. Consequently, the costs of recruiting and training the new salesforce—together with salaries, bonuses, and selling expenses—totaled more than half a million dollars in 1985.

To attract experienced people to the new salesforce—and to motivate them once they were hired—Wilkinson offered a compensation package that was about 10 percent more generous than competitors'. In addition to a base salary, its field sales bonus program enabled sales reps to earn up to 60 percent additional compensation for good performance.

Finally, Wilkinson USA hired a new vice president for trade relations to represent the firm at trade shows and to deal with any unusual problems or conflicts arising with major retailers. The company also began hiring a group of retail merchandisers to support the salesforce by checking stocks at individual retail stores, building in-store displays, and checking pricing.

The switch to a company salesforce had begun to pay off by the end of the first year. By late 1985 Wilkinson had increased its share to 3.5 percent of the U.S. wet-shave market. It was well on its way toward the firm's ultimate objective of capturing a 10 percent share and becoming the country's number two seller of razors and blades.

STRATEGIC PERSONAL SELLING AND SALES MANAGEMENT ISSUES

As we saw in Chapter 16, personal selling is only one of the promotional tools that a marketing manager can use to communicate with potential customers. Each promotional tool has some unique advantages for communicating certain kinds of information to certain customers under specific conditions. Thus, decisions about *how many resources to allocate to the salesforce* relative to other promotional mix elements and *the strategic objectives to be pursued by the salesforce* both depend on the communications tasks that must be accomplished. In turn, the business's objectives and competitive strategy, its resources, the number and type of customers in its target market, its competitive position in the market, and the other components of its strategic marketing program influence these communications tasks. In Wilkinson's case, for instance, the firm's weak competitive position and spotty retail distribution made it necessary to seek more retail shelf space to support the company's plan to recapture market share with improved products and heavier promotion. Thus, Wilkinson allocated a substantial portion of its promotion budget to build a salesforce with experience in selling to supermarket and drugstore chains. The next section of this chapter further examines the relative importance and the objectives of personal selling in the context of a firm's promotional and marketing strategies.

The strategic situation a firm faces in a product-market—and the objectives it sets for its salesforce—influences the tasks and activities on which its sales personnel must focus. Salespeople do not spend all their time trying to persuade customers to buy goods or services. Firms include a wide range of other activities in a specific sales job. And they incorporate a variety of sales jobs in their salesforces. Therefore, we describe a *number of sales jobs and the kinds of activities they involve*—including the tasks necessary to make a sale—in a later section.

Simply providing a large budget and setting objectives for the salesforce, however, is no guarantee that its members will perform their role effectively. Similar to all other parts of the marketing program, the salesforce must be managed. **Sales management** involves three related sets of activities: sales planning, implementation of the sales program, and evaluation and control of sales performance. We describe each of these three aspects of sales management briefly in the following sections and examine each in more detail later in this chapter.

Sales planning involves deciding how the salesforce should allocate its efforts within the market. Firms make specific decisions about organizing the salesforce, defining sales territories, and formulating account management policies to guide the amount and kinds of effort salespeople devote to different types of customers. Thus, Wilkinson's sales plan reflected its decision to organize its salesforce both by geographic region and by type of customer, with salespeople at different levels in the hierarchy assigned to different types of accounts. For example, area sales managers called on regional chains and territory representatives were assigned to smaller local accounts.

Implementation of a sales plan requires that the individual salespeople have the aptitude, skills, knowledge, and motivation to do their jobs effectively. The manager must recruit and hire the appropriate kinds of people, provide them—through training and supervision—with an understanding of the products or services they are to sell and the tasks they must perform, and motivate them with attractive compensation and incentive programs.

Finally, the sales manager must periodically **evaluate the performance** of each sales rep to determine whether the plan is being effectively carried out. Frequent monitoring of performance gives the manager a basis for better control over the sales program. On discovering deviations from planned levels of performance managers can adjust the plan or take action, such as giving additional training or supervision to poor performers, to deal with the problem areas or to take advantage of opportunities.

STRATEGIC OBJECTIVES FOR THE SALESFORCE

The advantages of personal selling as a promotional tool stem largely from the fact that it involves face-to-face communication with a potential customer. Personal sales messages are often more persuasive than advertising or publicity in the mass media. The salesperson communicates with only one potential customer at a time and tailors the message to that customer's unique needs and interests. Because feedback is immediate, the representative often knows when a particular sales approach is not working and can switch to a different tack. Another advantage of face-to-face contact is that salespeople can transmit more complex and larger amounts of information than with other promotional tools. And because the salesperson is likely to call on the same customer many times, the rep can devote a great deal of time to educating that customer about the advantages and features of a product or service. The long-term contact in personal selling is particularly important when the product can be customized to fit the needs of an individual customer—as in the case of computer systems and insurance policies—or when the terms of the sale are open to negotiation.

The primary disadvantage of personal selling is that the sales representative can communicate with only a relatively small number of potential customers. Consequently, personal selling is much more costly per person reached than other promotional tools. The cost of a print ad often amounts to just a few dollars per thousand readers, for instance; but the cost of a single industrial sales call ranges between $140 and $210.[2]

Because the cost of personal selling is relatively high, the company should allocate a major portion of its promotion budget to the salesforce only when the communication objectives can be accomplished better by face-to-face selling than by any other promotional method. As Exhibit 18–1 indicates, the business's strategy and resources, the characteristics of the customers in the product-market, the product's competitive position, and the other elements of the strategic marketing program influence the communications objectives in a product-market. Those communication objectives, in turn, help determine both the emphasis and the proportion of available

---

[2] Richard Kern, "Measuring Sales Call Efficiency," *Sales & Marketing Management*, February 22, 1988, p. 12.

EXHIBIT 18 ◆ 1

Factors affecting the role, objectives, and content of personal selling

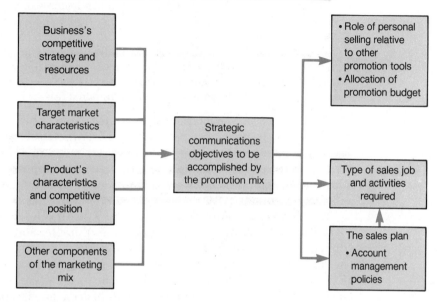

Source: Adapted from Gilbert A. Churchill, Jr., Neil M. Ford, and Orville C. Walker, Jr., *Sales Force Management* (Homewood, Ill.: Richard D. Irwin, 1985), p. 66.

resources that should be devoted to the salesforce relative to other promotional tools. They also determine the type of selling job and the specific activities the firm's salespeople should perform. Finally, the company should formulate its account management policies and other aspects of the sales plan to help direct the salespeople's efforts toward accomplishing the desired objectives.

Determinants of the role of personal selling

There are a few general conditions under which personal selling's overall role in the promotion mix is likely to be important. These conditions favor the unique advantages of face-to-face communication or minimize its cost disadvantage. Such conditions include:

◆ A technically complex product or service, particularly one that requires a good deal of presale or postsale service—such as systems design, installation, or user training—to enable customers to obtain full value.

◆ A target market consisting of customers that are relatively few in number, large in size, and/or geographically concentrated.

◆ The use of an extensive distribution network with substantial numbers of wholesale or retail dealers to be sold and serviced.

♦ Pursuit of a marketing strategy aimed at wresting market share away from established competitors. Since personal selling can be more persuasive than less personal methods—particularly when the product features or applications involved are complex—the salesforce often plays a critical role in implementing a share-building strategy.

♦ A limited amount of promotional resources available to the firm. The "catch 22" faced by smaller firms is that although media advertising costs less per person reached, the minimum outlay necessary to carry out a successful ad campaign is usually larger than the amount needed to support a reasonably effective salesforce.

Many of these characteristics seem more applicable to industrial goods markets than to consumer package goods. Thus, one might expect the promotional mixes of industrial goods producers to rely heavily on personal selling; those of manufacturers of consumer durables to contain a combination of advertising and personal selling; and those of consumer nondurable producers to stress advertising and consumer promotion.

The above expectations are supported by the findings of a survey in which executives of 336 industrial, 52 consumer durable, and 88 consumer nondurable goods manufacturers rated the relative importance of various promotional tools in their firm's marketing strategies. As the results shown in Exhibit 18–2 indicate, they considered personal selling more important and media advertising less important in industrial goods companies than in consumer nondurable firms. More interesting, though, is the fact that they viewed personal selling as the single most important promotional tool in all three types of businesses. Even though less complex consumer goods are aimed at target markets with large numbers of small customers, personal

EXHIBIT 18♦2

Perceived importance of promotional mix elements for different product types*

	Producers of		
Promotional tool	*Industrial goods*	*Consumer durables*	*Consumer nondurables*
Personal selling	69.2	47.6	38.1
Broadcast media advertising	0.9	10.7	20.9
Print media advertising	12.5	16.1	14.8
Sales promotion activities	9.6	15.5	15.5
Branding and promotional packaging	4.5	9.5	9.8
Other	3.3	0.6	0.9
Total	100.0	100.0	100.0

* Executives were asked to rate the relative importance of each tool using a scale of 100 points.

Source: Jon G. Udell, *Successful Marketing Strategies in American Marketing* (Madison, Wis.: Mimir Publishers, 1972), p. 47.

selling still plays a critical role. This is due to its importance in developing and maintaining wholesale and retail distribution for such products.

While the results of the original 1972 study might be questioned due to age, a replication conducted nearly 10 years later with a sample of almost 1,000 firms produced remarkably similar results.[3] This suggests that the role of personal selling in marketing strategy has remained quite constant over time in spite of all the environmental changes that occurred in the 1970s and 1980s.

Personal selling objectives

The strategic objectives for the salesforce can vary widely across companies facing different market and competitive situations. A firm's sales staff might be asked to focus on one or more of the following objectives: (1) winning acceptance of new products by existing customers; (2) developing new customers for existing products; (3) maintaining the loyalty of current customers by providing good service; (4) facilitating future sales by providing technical services to potential customers; (5) facilitating future sales by communicating product information to potential customers or influencers; and (6) gathering market information. Exhibit 18–3 summarizes these selling objectives, the specific activities involved in achieving them, and the conditions under which they are likely to be appropriate. Note too that several of these selling objectives—such as maintaining customer loyalty, providing technical service, and communicating product information—are all related to the broader marketing objective of *increasing sales to current customers.* The point to remember, though, is that the most appropriate role for the salesforce to play—and the objectives and activities it should pursue—in achieving that broader objective may vary depending on the nature of the product being sold and the competitive situation faced by the firm.

Winning acceptance for new products

Media advertising and sales promotion are often the most efficient tools for building customer awareness of a firm's new products. Personal selling may be necessary to induce trial, however—particularly if the products are complex or targeted at a few large industrial customers. Indeed, small entrepreneurial firms in high-tech industries such as medical products or computers usually have very limited resources for promotion but must effectively implement a prospector strategy to survive. Often they rely heavily on their salesforces to win market awareness and acceptance. Even for new consumer products the salesforce can be crucial for gaining acceptance within the distribution channel, especially if the firm has limited resources and must rely on a push strategy to build distribution.

---

[3] Clyde E. Harris, Richard R. Still, and Melvin R. Crask, "Stability or Change in Marketing Methods?" *Business Horizons,* October 1978, p. 35.

EXHIBIT 18♦3

Personal selling objectives

Objective	Activities involved	Conditions where appropriate
Winning acceptance for new products	Sales reps build awareness and stimulate demand for new products or services among existing or potential customers.	Business pursuing prospector strategy; potential customers large in size or few in number; company's promotional resources limited; firm pursuing "push" distribution strategy.
Developing new customers	Sales reps find and cultivate new customers and/or expanded distribution for business's products or services.	Target market in growth stage or firm wishes to increase share of mature market; potential customers large in size or few in number; company's promotional resources limited; firm pursuing "push" distribution strategy.
Maintaining customer loyalty	Sales reps work to increase value delivered to customers by providing advice or training on product use, expediting orders, and facilitating product service.	Business pursuing differentiated defender strategy; firm has large share of mature market and wants to maintain loyalty of existing customers; product technically complex and/or competition for distribution support is strong.
Technical service to facilitate sales	Sales reps work to increase value to customers by helping integrate product or service with customer's other equipment or operations and by providing design, installation, and/or training.	Product technically complex; customers (or dealers) relatively few in number and large in size; product or service can be customized to fit needs of individual customers; products sold as parts of larger system.
Communicating product information	Sales reps work to increase understanding of product's features and applications as basis for possible future sales and to educate people who may influence final purchase.	Product technically complex and/or in introductory or growth stage of life cycle; lengthy purchase decision process; multiple influences on purchase decision.
Gathering information	Sales reps provide reports on competitors' actions, customers' requests or problems, and other market conditions and conduct market research or intelligence activities.	Appropriate under all circumstances, but especially useful in industry introductory or growth stage, or when product technology or other factors are unstable; business pursuing a prospector strategy.

Developing new customers

The persuasive nature of face-to-face communication makes the salesforce a key factor in successfully implementing a strategy to increase market share or expand distribution for existing products by winning customers or shelf space away from competitors. This is particularly true, again, when the firm's resources are too limited to mount an aggressive pull strategy with heavy advertising and sales promotion. As we saw earlier, this was the major objective underlying Wilkinson Sword USA's decision to build its own salesforce.

Maintaining customer loyalty

The salesforce can also play a critical role in keeping current customers well satisfied through good service, training, and advice. Maintaining close working relationships between salespeople and their customers is very important for established firms in mature, competitive markets—particularly if their strategy is to defend their position by differentiation on the basis of excellent service. For example, much of IBM's success in commercial computer markets is due to its salespeople's excellent reputation for technical competence and good customer service.

Technical service to facilitate sales

Industrial purchasers have to be shown how new capital equipment can be effectively integrated into their operations. They must be assured that it can be installed with minimal disruption and that their personnel will be effectively trained in its use. Thus, the salesperson—or the sales support staff—may have to provide a wide range of technical services to facilitate the final sale and reduce the risk of a disruption in the customer's operations. This is particularly true for technically complex products that can be tailored to fit individual customers or that are incorporated into larger systems. Salespeople for mainframe manufacturers and telecommunications firms, for instance, often spend much more time providing engineering and systems design services than making sales presentations.

Communicating product information

In some situations communicating information about a company's products or services is the salesforce's primary objective. This is the case, for example, with detail salespersons in the pharmaceutical industry. Their job is to communicate information about prescription drugs to physicians. Although those physicians strongly influence ultimate sales by writing prescriptions for their patients, they do not make any purchases directly. Consequently, a detailer's job is not to make sales but simply to influence them through the effective communication of useful information. Similarly, salespeople in other industries often spend much time communicating to people in customer organizations—such as office managers or plant supervisors—who may influence a buying decision but lack direct authority to make a purchase.

Gathering information

Salespeople are always a useful source of information about customers' needs, preferences, and complaints, and about competitors' actions in the marketplace. But it is crucial for a firm to develop procedures for the systematic collection and reporting of such information in a developing and unstable market environment, or when a prospector strategy depends on the successful development of new products or applications.

TYPES OF SALES JOBS

Each of the above objectives demands a somewhat different set of activities from the salesforce. Because different firms pursue different objectives, the nature and content of the industrial sales job varies widely across companies. Researchers have classified sales jobs in more than 100 different ways.[4] The most useful classification scheme identifies four types of sales jobs found across a wide variety of industries.[5]

- **Trade selling**—the salesforce's primary responsibility is to gain and maintain support for the firm's products within the distribution channel by providing merchandising and promotional services to the channel members. Such salespeople also play a critical role in gaining distribution support for new products by making effective sales presentations to wholesale or retail buyers. As we saw in the Wilkinson USA example, some firms divide their trade selling activities between two positions: sales representatives concentrate on gaining acceptance for new products and expanded support for established products; **retail merchandisers** support the selling effort by providing merchandising and promotional services, such as building displays, in individual stores.

- **Missionary selling**—the salesforce's primary purpose is to build and maintain volume from current customers—and perhaps to facilitate new-product introductions—by giving purchase decision makers product information and service assistance. Missionary salespeople often do not make sales to customers directly but persuade them to buy the firm's products from wholesalers or retail suppliers. Examples include brewers' reps who call on bar owners and encourage them to order a particular brand of beer from the local distributor, and medical detailers who call on doctors as representatives of pharmaceutical manufacturers.

- **Technical selling**—the salesforce's primary objective is to increase business from both past and potential customers by providing technical product information and technical design and engineering services needed to facilitate sales. Sales engineers for machine-tool and telecommunications equipment manufacturers are examples of people engaged in technical selling.

- **New business selling**—the salesforce's primary responsibility is to identify, establish relationships with, and obtain business from new customers that the firm has

---

[4] For a brief summary of some classification schemes, see Alan J. Dubinsky and P. J. O'Connor, "A Multidimensional Analysis of Preferences for Sales Positions," *Journal of Personal Selling and Sales Management*, November 1983, pp. 31–41; and William C. Moncrief III, "Selling Activities and Sales Position Taxonomies for Industrial Salesforces," *Journal of Marketing Research*, August 1986, pp. 261–70.

[5] Derek A. Newton, *Sales Force Performance and Turnover* (Cambridge, Mass.: Marketing Science Institute, 1973), p. 5.

not dealt with before. This is a particularly important kind of selling in firms pursuing prospector strategies and in industries with rapidly changing technology and newly emerging product applications.

Each type of sales job involves different objectives and tasks; and each requires different skills and capabilities on the part of the salesperson. Thus, a firm's sales management policies—including its selection criteria, training programs, and compensation plans—must be consistent with its objectives and the kinds of selling activities necessary to achieve them. One set of activities, however, is common to nearly all kinds of sales jobs (with the exception of missionary selling); namely, the activities involved in actually making a sale to a customer.

STEPS IN THE SELLING PROCESS

A variety of conceptual schemes describes what salespeople do when attempting to make a sale. The essence of most of those schemes is that the selling process consists of six stages: prospecting for customers, opening the relationship, qualifying the prospect, presenting the sales message, closing the sale, and servicing the account. These steps are diagrammed in Exhibit 18–4 and discussed below.

EXHIBIT 18 ◆4
Stages in the selling process

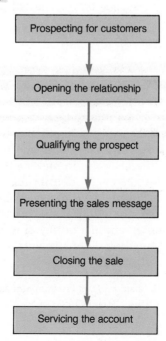

Prospecting for customers

Opening the relationship

Qualifying the prospect

Presenting the sales message

Closing the sale

Servicing the account

Prospecting for customers

In many types of selling, prospecting for new customers is critical. It can also be one of the most disheartening aspects of selling, however, especially for beginning salespeople. Prospecting efforts are often met with rejection, and immediate payoffs are usually minimal. Nevertheless, the ability to uncover potential new customers often separates successful from unsuccessful salespersons.

In some consumer goods businesses, prospecting for new customers simply involves cold canvassing—going from house to house knocking on doors. In most cases, though, the target market is more narrowly defined, and salespersons must identify prospects within that target segment. Salespeople use a wide variety of information sources to identify relevant prospects, including trade association and industry directories, telephone directories, other salespeople, other customers, suppliers, nonsales employees of the firm, and social and professional contacts.

New technologies—particularly various telemarketing systems—can also help salespeople identify and qualify potential new accounts. Many firms set up incoming Wide-Area Telecommunication Service (WATS) phone lines and publicize toll-free telephone numbers in their media advertising and other promotional material. When prospects call for more information about a product or service, an operator determines the extent of interest and whether the prospect meets the company's qualification standards for new customers. If so, the operator passes on information about the caller to the appropriate salesperson or regional office.

Opening the relationship

In their initial approach to prospective customers, the sales reps should accomplish two things: (1) determine who within the organization is likely to have the greatest influence and/or authority to purchase the product the rep is trying to sell; and (2) generate enough interest within the firm to obtain the information needed to qualify the prospect as a worthwhile potential customer.[6] An organizational buying center often consists of individuals who play different roles in making the purchase decision. Thus, it is important for salespersons to identify the key decision makers, their desires, and their relative influence. Indeed, when the purchase decision is likely to be very complex, involving many people within the customer's organization, the seller might adopt a policy of multilevel or **team selling.** Here members of relevant functional departments of the seller's firm—such as engineering,

---

[6] Benson P. Shapiro, *Sales Program Management: Formulation and Implementation* (New York: McGraw-Hill, 1977), p. 159.

production, and finance—talk to their counterparts in the customer's organization.

Qualifying the prospect

Before attempting to set up an appointment for a major sales presentation, sales reps determine whether prospects qualify as worthwhile potential customers. Obviously, if prospects do not qualify, sales reps can spend the time better elsewhere. Qualification is difficult for many salespeople, however. It requires them to put aside their eternal optimism and make an objective, realistic judgment about the probability of making a profitable sale.

The qualification process involves finding the answers to three big questions:

1. Does the prospect have a need for my product or service?
2. Can I make the people responsible for buying so aware of that need that I can make a sale?
3. Will the sale be profitable to my company?

Because so many kinds of information are needed to answer such questions, companies often involve their nonselling departments—such as the credit and collections department—in the qualification process. Also, company policies should guide the salesperson's judgment of whether or not a specific prospect qualifies as a customer. These policies might spell out minimum standards for such things as the prospect's annual dollar value of purchases in the product category or the credit rating that must be met before the prospect can be accepted as a customer. Some firms specify a minimum order size to avoid dealing with very small customers and to improve the efficiency of their order-processing and shipping operations.

Instead of turning down business from accounts that are too small to qualify for a face-to-face visit from a salesperson, many firms turn them over to an "inside" telemarketing salesforce that can service them more efficiently. The A. B. Dick Co. is a good example of a firm that uses telemarketing to service its smaller accounts. With more than 100,000 of its customers buying less than $200 of office supplies per year, the company realized it was not economically sound to have its field salespeople visiting those accounts regularly. By adopting a telephone direct-marketing effort to service low-volume customers, the firm could focus its field selling efforts on the larger institutional market. Coordinated with special mail promotions to maximize response, the telephone was used to sell and record orders directly. A first call to each small customer sought permission for later, regular phone contact. The initial results of the program were impressive. Ten percent of the companies contacted placed an order at the time of the initial call. Another 8 percent of these customers were discovered to have the potential for larger equipment and supply purchases. These accounts were qualified over the phone and passed along to the field salesforce for follow-up. Finally, 60 percent of all the customers contacted asked to become part of the continuing telephone sales program.[7]

Presenting the sales message

The presentation is the core of the selling process. Salespeople actually transmit the information and attempt to persuade prospects to become customers. Making good presentations is a critically important aspect of the sales job. Unfortunately, many salespeople do not perform this activity very well. In one survey of organizational buyers, for example, 40 percent of the respondents classified the presentations they generally witness as less than good.[8]

Different firms have widely differing policies for how sales presentations should be organized, what selling points should be stressed, and how force-fully the presentation should be made. Encyclopedia companies commonly train their door-to-door salespeople to deliver the same memorized, forceful presentation to every prospect. A person selling computer systems, on the other hand, may be trained in very low-key selling, to act primarily as a source of technical information and advice and do little "pushing" of the company's computers.

Much has been written about techniques for making effective sales presentations, and about methods for improving salespeople's ability to adapt their presentations to fit the interests and concerns of different customers.[9] New technologies—such as portable computers and video recorders—are also making it possible for salespeople to tailor more effective presentations to each customer.[10] Such topics are beyond the scope of this discussion.

---

[7] This and other examples of successful telemarketing programs can be found in Howard Sutton, *Rethinking the Company's Sales and Distribution Channels* (New York: The Conference Board, 1986). Also see William C. Moncrief, Charles W. Lamb, Jr., and Terry Dielman, "Developing Telemarketing Support Systems," *Journal of Personal Selling and Sales Management,* August 1986, pp. 43–49.

[8] Reported in Gilbert A. Churchill, Jr., Neil M. Ford, and Orville C. Walker, Jr., *Sales Force Management* (Homewood, Ill.: Richard D. Irwin, 1985), p. 88.

[9] Barton A. Weitz, Harish Sujan, and Mita Sujan, "Knowledge, Motivation, and Adaptive Behavior: A Framework for Improving Selling Effectiveness," *Journal of Marketing,* October 1986, pp. 174–91. Also see Robert E. Hite and Joe Bellizzi, "Differences in the Importance of Selling Techniques between Consumer and Industrial Salespeople," *Journal of Personal Selling and Sales Management,* November 1985, pp. 19–30.

[10] Thayer C. Taylor, "Marketers and the PC: Steady as She Goes," *Sales & Marketing Management,* August 1986, p. 53.

Interested readers are referred to one of the more specialized books on selling.[11]

Closing the sale

Closing refers to obtaining a final agreement to purchase. All the sales staffs' efforts are wasted unless clients "sign on the dotted line"; yet this is where many salespeople fail. It is natural, even within organizations, to delay making purchase decisions. But as the time it takes to close the sale increases, the profit to be made from the sale goes down, and the risk of losing the sale entirely increases. Consequently, the salesperson's task is to speed up the final decision. Often, this can best be done by simply asking for an order. "May I write that order up for you?" and "When do you want it delivered?" are common closings.

Servicing the account

The sales job is not finished when the sale is made. Sellers must provide many kinds of service and assistance to customers to ensure their satisfaction and repeat business. Unfortunately, this is another area where many salespeople do not perform very well. Sixty-one percent of the respondents in a survey of organizational buyers were dissatisfied with services after the sale. As one buyer said, "Service is the first thing that gets sold and the last thing delivered."[12]

Salespeople should follow up each sale to make sure that there are no problems with delivery schedules, quality of the goods, or customer billing. In addition, they often supervise the installation of the equipment, train the customer's employees in its use, and ensure proper maintenance. In most cases, salespersons must work closely with other departments in their firms to make sure that customers' interests are represented and that problems do not lead to dissatisfaction.

PLANNING THE SALES PROGRAM

Simply setting objectives and communicating them to the salesforce is no guarantee that individual salespeople will always allocate their efforts across activities and types of customers in ways consistent with those objectives. Some salespeople shy away from filling out reports and expediting orders, those mundane administrative and customer service activities that

---

[11] For example, see Carlton Pederson, Milburn Wright, and Barton A. Weitz, *Selling: Principles and Methods,* 9th ed. (Homewood, Ill.: Richard D. Irwin, 1988).

[12] Gilbert A. Churchill, Jr., et al., *Sales Force Management,* p. 90.

are not likely to result in immediate sales. This is particularly true if a large portion of their compensation is based on commissions. Others are reluctant to spend much time courting new customers, since the probability of making a sale is lower than when calling on existing accounts. Sales managers thus must develop detailed sales programs that organize and direct the firm's personal selling efforts to be consistent with its selling objectives and the other elements of its business and marketing strategies.

As Exhibit 18–5 indicates, planning a sales program involves four sets of decisions. First, the salesforce must be organized to facilitate the most efficient allocation of effort. Second, **account management policies** should be developed as guidelines for the way different types of customers are approached, persuaded, and serviced. Third, **deployment** decisions must be made to define territories and assign salespeople to those territories. Fourth, performance expectations—**quotas**—should be developed for each sales rep based on forecasted demand in that territory. When these four aspects of a sales program are well planned and clearly communicated, they help the sales staff understand the job requirements and the role they are expected to play in implementing the firm's strategy. That improved understanding, in turn, should help the sales staff achieve desired levels of performance.

Salesforce organization

There are several common bases for organizing sales efforts. Each has unique advantages that make it appropriate for a business under specific strategic circumstances. The first organizational issue to be resolved is the one that

EXHIBIT 18◆5

The strategic sales program

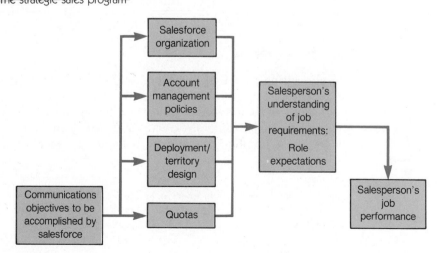

faced Wilkinson Sword USA: should it hire its own salespeople or use outside agents? We examined some of the economic, control, and adaptive criteria a firm might use to resolve such a make-or-buy decision in Chapter 15. When using a company salesforce, alternative organizational approaches are: by geographic area, by product type, by customer type, and by selling function.

Geographic organization

The simplest and most common way to organize a salesforce is to assign salespeople to separate geographic territories. Each salesperson is then responsible for performing all the activities necessary to sell all the products in the company's line to all types of customers in that territory. Exhibit 18–6 illustrates a geographic sales organization.

One of the geographic organization's major strengths is its relatively low cost. With only one salesperson in each territory, firms minimize travel time and expenses. Also, since only one sales rep calls on each customer, there is seldom any confusion about who is responsible for what or who the customer should talk to when problems arise.

The major disadvantage of this form of organization is that it does not provide any of the benefits of specialization and division of labor. Each salesperson becomes a jack-of-all-trades. Each must sell all the firm's products to all types of customers and be competent in performing a full range of selling activities.

Despite geographic organization's limitations, its simplicity and low cost make it very popular among smaller firms, particularly those with narrow,

EXHIBIT   18 ♦ 6

Geographic sales organization

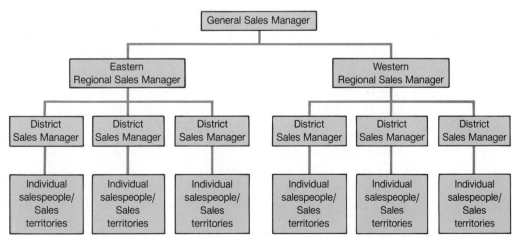

uncomplicated product lines, such as Wilkinson Sword USA. Although it is unusual for large organizations to rely exclusively on geographic organization, they do commonly use it in conjunction with other organizational forms. A firm might have two separate salesforces for different product lines, for instance; but each salesforce is likely to be organized geographically.

Product organization

Many larger firms have separate salesforces for each product—or related groups of products—in their product line (see Exhibit 18–7). Nearly every division at the 3M Company, for instance, has its own salesforce.

The primary advantage of a product organization is that salespeople become familiar with the technical attributes, applications, and effective selling methods associated with a specific type of product or service. It also enables sales management to control the allocation of selling effort across products. If management decides to devote more effort to a particular product line, it can simply assign more people to the appropriate salesforce.

Another major advantage of a product organization is the greater specialization it allows the salespeople; thus, it is most common among large multi-SBU firms with diverse product lines. This is particularly true when

EXHIBIT 18 ♦ 7

A salesforce organized by product type

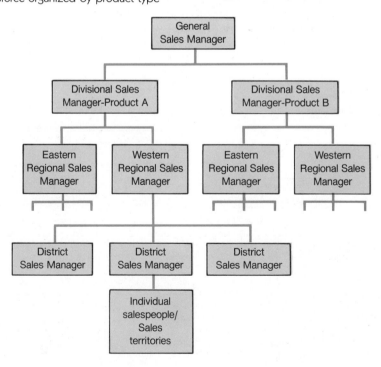

some of those lines are highly technical and require special expertise or different selling methods.

The major disadvantage of organizing by product is duplication of effort. Salespeople from different product divisions assigned to the same geographic territories may call on the same customers. For instance, a supermarket chain might deal with one Procter & Gamble sales rep when buying soap and detergent, a second P&G salesperson when purchasing food products like Pringles potato chips, and a third for paper products like Pampers. Such duplication leads to higher selling and administrative costs for the firm and possible confusion and frustration among its customers.

Customer organization

In recent years, increasing numbers of firms have organized their salesforces by customer type (see Exhibit 18–8). For example, General Electric at one time organized its salesforce by products (fan motors, switches). Later GE changed its structure to allow salespeople to specialize in a particular industry, such as air-conditioning manufacturers or auto makers. This approach is a natural extension of the concept of market segmentation. By specializing in serving a particular type of customer, a salesperson can better understand their unique needs and requirements. Managers can also control the allocation of selling effort to different markets by varying the size of the specialized salesforces.

The disadvantages of customer organization are the same as those of a product-oriented structure. When customer firms have different departments or divisions operating in different industries, two or more salespeople

EXHIBIT 18 ◆ 8

A salesforce organized by customer type

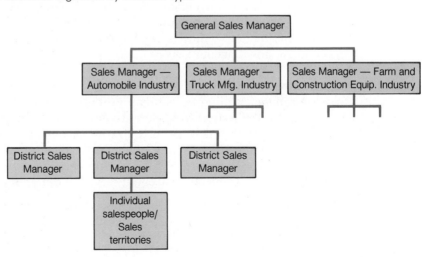

may end up calling on the same customer. This duplication of effort can lead not only to higher selling and administrative costs but also to customer confusion. Nevertheless, these structures are increasingly popular among large firms whose products have different applications in different industries, or who must use different selling approaches to reach different types of customers (as when products are sold to both the government and to private industry). It is also a useful organizational form when a firm's objectives include penetrating previously untapped markets.

One specific form of customer-oriented organization that has enjoyed a rapid recent increase in popularity is **national account management.** In this form a firm designates its largest customers or potential customers as national accounts (sometimes also called **key accounts** or **house accounts**) and assigns them to special high-level sales managers or sales teams. Xerox, for example, handles about 250 of its largest customers through a separate force of national account managers.

National account management is growing in popularity for several reasons: Mergers and acquisitions have produced greater concentrations of large firms in many industries. Some companies find that a mere 10 percent of their customers account for well over half their sales volume. Also, many large corporations are centralizing more of their purchases to increase their bargaining power over suppliers. Those suppliers, in turn, are forced to devote more attention to such customers. Finally, the typical sales representative may not always have sufficient authority or expertise to deal effectively with the high-level managers from various functional departments who constitute the buying centers in many large corporations.

Given this rationale, a firm's national account managers should have several characteristics. They should hold relatively high-level positions within the company hierarchy. They should have the knowledge and experience—or the technical support—to deal effectively with buying influences from different functional areas. And they should have the authority to coordinate the efforts of departments within their own company—such as R&D and production—playing crucial roles in meeting the requirements of the firm's national accounts.[13]

Organization by selling function

Because different selling tasks require different skills and abilities, it may make sense in some cases for different salespeople to specialize in different functions. One such functional organization has one salesforce prospecting for and developing new accounts, while a second maintains and services old customers. The Wilkinson Sword USA approach of hiring retail merchandisers to take over some of the account servicing duties and free salespeople

---

[13] Philip Maher, "National Account Marketing: An Essential Strategy, or Prima Donna Selling?" *Business Management*, December 1984, pp. 38–45.

to spend more time selling is another example of a functional organization. In view of the high costs of such structures, however, a functional organization is justified only when the complexity of the selling task or the effort required to service accounts increases the value of specialization.

Account management policies

In some firms, once salespeople are assigned to territories they decide how often to call on specific customers and how to deal with each customer. This has the advantage of maximizing the salesperson's flexibility to adjust to unique situations; but the problem is that sales reps do not always match their efforts to the sales and profit potential of the accounts in their territories. To overcome this problem, the sales plan in more sophisticated firms incorporates account management policies with guidelines for sales effort allocation across customers.[14]

The initial step in developing account management policies is to classify the accounts in each territory—or the products handled by the salesperson—into categories according to their sales potential, profitability, or importance to the firm's marketing plan objectives. Managers can then formulate policies to guide the amount of effort each salesperson devotes to each class of customers or products. For instance, they might instruct salespeople to call on high-potential "A" accounts at least once a month and to visit less important "B" accounts once every two months. Managers often formalize such policies further through separate volume or activity quotas for each category of customers or products and reinforce them by tying incentive bonuses or other rewards to meeting those quotas.

A firm's account management policies can also specify how to carry out sales calls on various categories of customers. Such policies detail such things as which members of the customer organization to contact, how frequently, and which appeals to emphasize to different members of the customer's buying center.

Territory design and deployment

Salesforce size and the number of territories

Before making intelligent decisions about the design of specific sales territories, managers must decide how many salespeople—and, thus, how many territories—are needed to cover the customers in a country or region. Most firms use the **workload approach** to establish salesforce size.[15] This ap-

---

[14] For a more detailed discussion of account management policies, see John M. Gwin and William D. Perreault, Jr., "Industrial Sales Call Planning," *Industrial Marketing Management* 10, 1981, pp. 225–34.

[15] For a discussion of alternative approaches for determining salesforce size and territory design, see Gilbert A. Churchill, Jr., et al., *Sales Force Management*, chap. 6.

proach builds on the account management policies discussed earlier and involves the following steps:

1. Using the account classification scheme specified in the firm's account management policies, determine how many potential customers are in each category. (Wilkinson Sword USA identified 25 national accounts, plus some large regional and smaller local accounts it wanted its salespeople to call on.)
2. Multiply the number of potential customers in each category times the desired call frequency specified by the firm's account management policies (i.e., number of calls per year for each type of customer). Add the totals across all customer categories to arrive at a total workload for the salesforce stated in total calls to be made in a year.
3. Estimate the average number of calls a salesperson can make in a year.
4. Determine the number of salespeople needed by dividing the total number of calls that need to be made by the average number of calls a salesperson can make in a year.

Suppose, for instance, that a firm identifies 1,000 A accounts that should be called on 24 times a year, and 2,000 B accounts requiring 12 calls per year. The annual workload would be 48,000 sales calls. If the average salesperson for the firm can make 1,000 calls in a year, the firm would need 48 full-time sales representatives.

Territory size

Managers design territories to either *equalize the workload* across members of the salesforce or to provide each salesperson with *equal sales potential*. When territories are approximately equal in sales potential, each sales rep has the same income opportunities, and the firm has a common benchmark for evaluating reps' performance. Persistent differences in sales across territories can be assumed to reflect differences in ability or effort among the salespeople assigned to those territories.

Because customers can vary greatly in size and density from area to area, territories designed to provide equal potential can vary widely in size. The potential wholesale sales of women's sportswear in Manhattan, for instance, exceeds the entire potential of North and South Dakota. Consequently, the New York City rep can cover all potential customers with much less travel time and effort than the rep in the Dakotas. One possible solution to this inequity is to pay the salesperson in the Dakotas extra compensation to make up for the extra effort required. But this would reduce the profitability of sales in that territory. A more common approach is to acknowledge that territories with similar potential differ in attractiveness—and use those differences when designing career paths for salesforce members. New recruits, for example, might be assigned to the least attractive territories. If they perform well, they might then be rewarded with a promotion to a territory requiring less travel and effort.

Alternatively, territories can be designed to equalize the workload in the number of calls to be made and the time and effort required to make them. Each rep can then cover that territory with equal effort. The problem with this approach is that such territories may provide very different sales potential. This can be a particular problem when firms compensate salespeople at least partly on commission, because territory assignments can greatly affect their ability to generate sales. Such territory assignments make it more difficult for managers to compare performance across salespeople. Once again, a firm might try to deal with these problems by paying a higher compensation rate to people in low-potential territories or by assigning those territories to the least experienced or lowest performing salespeople.

Regardless of the basis used to define territories, some adjustments in the shape and location of those territories are likely to be necessary to take into account such things as natural barriers and the adequacy of transportation. Many of these adjustments must rely on the experience and good judgment of the sales manager. However, a number of quantitative models and computer programs are available to assist managers in designing optimal territories on such criteria as geographic compactness, equalization of workload or sales potential, and travel time.[16]

Setting quotas

To provide still further guidance and encouragement in allocating sales efforts, many firms set quotas for each salesperson. Such quotas can specify goals in dollar sales, unit sales, profit margin, or specific activities; say, to make at least 24 presentations to prospective new customers during the year. They can break down by specific products in the line and/or by type of account. To give them more motivational impact, quotas are often used to determine incentive compensation with bonuses or other incentive rewards tied to the degree of quota attainment.

To be effective motivators, quotas should be attainable, easy for the salesforce to understand, and complete in incorporating the full range of performance dimensions on which the salespeople are evaluated. Attainability is an important attribute of good quotas; thus, the obvious starting point is to develop sales forecasts for each territory, product line, and/or customer group for which quotas are to be specified.

There is a good deal of controversy, however, about whether quotas should then be set somewhat higher than, equal to, or a little lower than the

---

[16] For example, see Andris A. Zoltners and Prabhakant Sinha, "Sales Territory Alignment: A Review and Model," *Management Science*, November 1983, pp. 1237–56; and Leonard M. Lodish, "Sales Territory Alignment to Maximize Profits," *Journal of Marketing Research*, February 1975, pp. 30–36.

forecast. The argument in favor of setting quotas higher than a realistic sales forecast is that, even though most salespeople may not attain them, they are spurred to greater effort than they would expend in the absence of such a "carrot." The problem is that when salespeople perceive their quotas are too high to attain with reasonable effort, they may simply not try. Worse, they may engage in undesirable practices to reach them. They might put undue pressure on customers at the end of the quota period to gain enough volume to meet their goals and thereby risk damaging the firm's long-term relationships with its customers. Or they may accept orders from customers who do not financially qualify to increase short-term volume—even though much of that volume may ultimately prove illusory. Such behavior was so common at Itel Corporation in the late 1970s, for example, that the firm nearly collapsed when forced to write off $226 million in revenues that proved to be uncollectible.[17]

In view of the potential dangers, few companies use quotas that greatly exceed their sales forecasts. In one Conference Board study, only 5 percent of the responding firms reported using such quotas. More than 80 percent said they set "realistic" quotas that correspond closely to forecasts of what sales should be with the expenditure of reasonable effort.[18] Of course, such firms might still provide an incentive for salespeople to exceed their quotas by offering higher rewards for sales over quota. For example, a firm might offer a 7 percent bonus to all salespeople who reach 100 percent of quota, a 10 percent bonus for sales reaching 105–110 percent of quota, and a 13 percent bonus for sales exceeding 111 percent of quota.

IMPLEMENTING THE SALES PLAN

There is no guarantee that even a very well-designed and clearly communicated sales plan can be carried out effectively. Good implementation requires that the members of the salesforce have both the ability and the desire to meet management's expectations. Thus, as Exhibit 18–9 indicates, implementing the sales program requires three more sets of management actions: First, management must **recruit and select** appropriate kinds of salespeople with the aptitude for effectively carrying out the activities involved in the job. Second, management must provide appropriate kinds and amounts of **training** to ensure that the salespeople have the knowledge and skills needed to do their jobs. Finally, management must design an attractive

---

[17] Marilyn Chase, "How a Red-Hot Firm in the Computer Business Overheated and Burned," *The Wall Street Journal*, February 22, 1980, p. 1.

[18] *Incentive Plans for Salesmen, Studies in Personnel Policy, No. 217* (New York: The National Industrial Conference Board, 1970), pp. 27–29.

EXHIBIT 18 ◆ 9

Implementing the strategic sales program

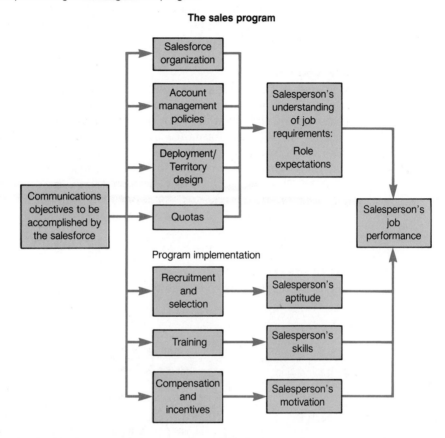

package of **compensation and other incentive rewards** to motivate the sales-force to expend the effort necessary to achieve good performance.

Recruitment and selection

Identifying and selecting personnel who have the aptitude for success is a critical part of a sales manager's job. Unfortunately, there are no sure-fire ways to identify such people. This fact is seen in the great variability in performance across salespeople hired by most firms. For example, one survey of more than 500 companies found that the top-performing 25 percent of their salespeople brought in about half their total sales volume. Another indication that good salespeople are hard to identify is their high rate of turnover, especially those who are relatively young and inexperienced. Of

16,000 salespeople who had been hired by the firms surveyed, only 68 percent were still with their companies after the first year—and only about 50 percent were expected to remain through the second year.[19] Given that it costs some firms more than $50,000 to recruit and train a single salesperson, such hiring mistakes can be extremely costly.

Selection criteria

No personality traits or individual characteristics are good predictors of sales success for all sales jobs. Indeed, one extensive review of past research found that no single variable could explain more than about 9 percent of the variation in sales performance across salespeople. Most personality variables were unable to explain more than 2 percent of that variation.[20]

Part of the problem is that different kinds of selling require different abilities. Thus, some personal characteristics and traits are likely to be critical for success in one type of selling position, but not in others. Returning to our discussion of types of selling jobs, Exhibit 18–10 summarizes

EXHIBIT   18 ◆ 10

Personal characteristics related to sales performance in different sales jobs

Sales job	Characteristics	
	Important	*Less important*
Trade selling	Age, maturity, empathy, knowledge of customers and business methods	Aggressiveness, technical ability, product knowledge, persuasiveness
Missionary selling	Youth, high energy, and stamina, verbal skill, persuasiveness	Empathy, knowledge of customers, maturity, previous sales experience
Technical selling	Education, product and customer knowledge—usually gained through training, intelligence	Empathy, persuasiveness, aggressiveness, age
New business selling	Experience, age and maturity, aggressiveness, persuasiveness, persistence	Customer and product knowledge, education, empathy

---

[19] Reported in Philip Kotler, *Marketing Management: Analysis, Planning, Implementation, and Control* (Englewood Cliffs, N.J.: Prentice-Hall, 1988), p. 673.

[20] Gilbert A. Churchill, Jr., Neil M. Ford, Steven W. Hartley, and Orville C. Walker, Jr., "The Determinants of Salesperson Performance: A Meta-Analysis," *Journal of Marketing Research*, May 1985, pp. 103–18.

research findings about salesperson characteristics that are important—and those that are relatively less important—in influencing success in trade selling, missionary selling, technical selling, and new business selling. Notice, for instance, that age, experience, and persistence are more relevant to new business selling than to technical selling. Prospecting for new customers requires people who have the self-confidence to deal with frequent rejection without becoming discouraged and giving up. On the other hand, intelligence, education, and product knowledge are particularly important for success in technical selling.

Because there are no general characteristics that make some people better performers in all types of sales jobs, the starting point in the recruitment process should be a thorough analysis of the job to be filled, including the development of a written job description. This provides a starting point for sales managers and experienced personnel staffers to develop a **statement of the job qualifications** a hiree should have, focused on the personal traits and abilities needed to perform the tasks and responsibilities involved in the job. In firms with large existing salesforces, managers could note the traits of the most successful salespeople for clues about factors that relate to their success.

Recruiting procedures

The next recruiting problem is to identify an appropriate pool of applicants. When a firm seeks—and is willing to pay a premium for—experienced candidates, it might directly contact salespeople working for firms in related industries, or ask a professional recruiting firm to do so. This was the approach followed by Wilkinson Sword USA when it set out to build its new salesforce. More commonly, however, sales managers ask their firm's personnel department to develop a pool of applicants who generally fit the selection criteria. This is done by asking other company employees for referrals, sending job descriptions to employment agencies, placing ads in newspapers, or recruiting on college campuses.

Selection procedures

Firms use a variety of types and sources of information to evaluate applicants and decide who best fits the qualifications needed for the job. These typically include personal interviews, personal history information from application forms, reference checks, and personality and aptitude tests. Sales managers generally perceive personal interviews and application forms as the most helpful sources for determining which applicants are best qualified. They view personality and aptitude test scores with more skepticism.[21] These perceptions are reflected in Exhibit 18–11, which summarizes the results of a survey of the selection procedures followed by 121

---

[21] Gilbert A. Churchill, Jr., et al., *Sales Force Management*, p. 376.

EXHIBIT   18 ♦ 11

Percentage of firms that use various tools for selecting salespeople

Selection items	Percentage of small firms	Percentage of large firms
Personal interviews	91%	96%
Application blanks	73	70
Personal reference checks	70	62
List of job qualifications	34	45
Job descriptions*	30	51
Psychological tests	22	32

* A statistically significant difference ($p < 0.05$) exists between the percentage of small and large firms that "extensively use" this sales management tool. In this survey, "small" firms were defined as those with annual sales of less than \$40 million (n = 74), and large firms were those with sales over \$40 million (n = 47).

Source: Reprinted from "A Survey of Sales Management Practices," by Alan J. Dubinsky and Thomas E. Barry, *Industrial Marketing Management* 11, p. 136. Copyright © 1982 by Elsevier Science Publishing Co., Inc.

industrial firms. The exhibit shows that large firms are more thorough in their use of job descriptions and personality tests as a part of their selection process than are smaller companies.

Training

In spite of the high costs, most firms see sales training as a critical activity for ensuring that their salespeople have the knowledge and skills necessary for success. Many firms have increased the amount of sales training in recent years as they try to keep up with the increasing size and sophistication of their customers, the growing complexity of their technologies, and faster new-product introductions. Indeed, the median training period for new salespeople in both consumer and industrial products firms was 22 weeks in 1987; and it was 27 weeks in firms selling services such as insurance and investment programs.[22]

In many firms, training does not stop once a new recruit is considered ready to take the field. Experienced salespeople are retrained periodically to upgrade their knowledge of new products and applications and to continually sharpen their selling skills. Such ongoing training programs are particularly important for businesses pursuing prospector strategies and those operating in industries with high rates of technological change and frequent new-product introductions. Thus, firms such as Union Carbide and 3M maintain their own training facilities for retraining salespeople on a regular basis.

---

[22] "1988 Survey of Selling Costs," *Sales & Marketing Management*, February 22, 1988, p. 49.

Sales training programs can be designed to accomplish a number of goals. These include increasing salespeople's knowledge and skills concerning the company's products and their applications, the company itself and its internal policies and procedures, the types of customers and competitive situations the salespeople face in the field, and effective selling methods. Unfortunately, the majority of firms stress only product knowledge and field training in their sales training programs. They are much less likely to focus on improving their salespeople's knowledge of the company, its customers, its competitors, or effective selling techniques. These shortcomings are particularly likely in the programs offered by smaller companies. Indeed, the limited resources available for sophisticated training helps explain why many smaller firms prefer to hire experienced salespeople.

There are a variety of methods used in sales training. These range in sophistication from simple lectures by a sales manager to such things as role-playing sessions and computerized programmed learning units.[23] Once again, however, the fact that only about 6 percent of smaller firms have programs conducted by a staff sales trainer or outside training firm suggests that most such firms rely on the simplest and most basic methods.

Finally, in view of the importance and the expense of sales training programs, one would expect firms to periodically evaluate their effectiveness. This can be done by measuring the attitudes of their salespeople toward the program and improvements in their product knowledge, selling skills, and performance in the field. Unfortunately, only about half of large firms—and fewer than 20 percent of smaller ones—make such evaluations. This suggests that there may well be a good deal of room for improvement in the effectiveness and impact of sales training in many American companies.

Compensation and rewards

Money is generally considered one of the most important, if not the single most critical, motivators for salespeople. Therefore, the design of an attractive compensation and reward package is an important determinant of a firm's ability to attract, retain, and obtain substantial effort from good salespeople. Designing such a package requires several important decisions: First, management must decide what overall **level of compensation** is needed to attract and satisfy salespeople with the qualifications needed to accomplish the firm's selling objectives. Second, they must determine whether that compensation should consist entirely of a **fixed salary,** plus expenses and fringe benefits, or whether some or all of the compensation will be in the form of a **variable incentive** tied to the salesperson's performance. Third, management must consider **nonfinancial rewards** for good performance—such as promotions and recognition programs.

---

[23] For an extensive discussion of sales training methods, see Gilbert A. Churchill, Jr., et al., *Sales Force Management,* chap. 12.

Level of compensation

Compensation varies substantially across different sales jobs and across companies. For example, in 1987, average salesperson compensation ranged from $36,200 in the plumbing and heating industry, to $52,200 in the construction industry, to $63,500 among firms selling computer services.[24] To compete for the best talent, then, a company must determine how much total compensation other firms in its industry or in related ones pay people in similar jobs. Then management can consciously decide whether to pay an amount equal to the average of what others are paying or to offer above-average compensation. Although some do so without knowing it few companies intentionally set their pay at below-average levels because below-average compensation generally cannot attract and hold good sales talent.

Whether a firm offers an average or premium level of compensation depends in part on its size and reputation. Big firms with good reputations and large salesforces, such as IBM and 3M, generally offer only average or slightly below-average compensation. Such firms attract good talent because of their reputations and because they are big enough to offer advancement into management. Also, such firms can afford to hire younger, inexperienced salespeople and put them through extensive sales training programs. On the other hand, smaller firms often must offer a compensation premium—5 to 10 percent above industry average—to attract experienced salespeople from other firms.

Types of compensation plans

The three major methods of compensating salespeople are straight salary, straight commission, and a combination of base salary plus incentive pay (commissions, bonuses, or both). In recent years the trend has been away from both straight salary and straight commission plans. Today, combination plans are the most common form of compensation in most industries, although the use of different plans varies greatly across industries. This suggests that all three types of plans have unique advantages for motivating specific kinds of sales performance under particular circumstances. The advantages and disadvantages of each type of plan—together with their frequency of use and the situations where each is most appropriate—are summarized in Exhibit 18–12 and discussed below.

Two sets of conditions favor the use of a **straight salary** compensation plan: The first is when management wants to motivate the salesforce to accomplish objectives other than short-run sales volume. The second is when the individual salesperson's impact on sales volume is difficult to measure in a reasonable time. Thus, a straight salary plan—or a plan offering a large proportion of fixed salary—is appropriate when the salesforce is expected to do many account servicing or other nonselling activities, such as

---

[24] "1988 Survey of Selling Costs," p. 40.

EXHIBIT 18 ♦ 12

Comparison of different compensation plans

	Straight salary	*Straight commission*	*Combination*
Frequency of use	18%	9%	73%
Especially useful	When compensating new salespersons; when firm moves into new sales territories that require developmental work; when salespersons need to perform many nonselling activities	When highly aggressive selling is required; when nonselling tasks are minimized; when company cannot closely control salesforce activities	When sales territories have relatively similar sales potentials; when firm wishes to provide incentive but still control salesforce activities
Advantages	Provides salesperson with maximum amount of security; gives sales manager large amount of control over salespersons; easy to administer; yields more predictable selling expenses	Provides maximum amount of incentive; by increasing commission rate, sales managers can encourage salespersons to sell certain items; selling expenses related directly to sales resources	Provides certain level of financial security; provides some incentive; selling expenses fluctuate with sales revenue; sales manager has some control over salesperson's nonselling activities
Disadvantages	Provides no incentive; necessitates closer supervision of salespersons' activities; during sales declines, selling expenses remain at same level	Salespersons have little financial security; sales manager has minimum control over salesforce; may cause salespeople to provide inadequate service to smaller accounts; selling costs less predictable	Selling expenses less predictable; may be difficult to administer

Source: Gilbert A. Churchill, Jr., Neil M. Ford, and Orville C. Walker, Jr., *Sales Force Management: Planning, Implementation, and Control,* 2nd ed. (Homewood, Ill.: Richard D. Irwin, 1985), p. 472; "Sales Pay Survey: Figures and Methods," *Management Briefing—Marketing* (New York: The Conference Board, October 1986), pp. 4–5; and Eric N. Berkowitz, Robert A. Kerin, and William Rudelius, *Marketing,* 2nd ed. (Homewood, Ill.: Richard D. Irwin, 1989), p. 511.

marketing research or stocking retailers' shelves. Such plans are particularly common in industries where design and engineering services are a critical part of the salesperson's job, as in the aerospace and other high-tech industries. Finally, salary plans are also necessary when the individual salesperson's efforts are difficult to link directly to sales volume, as in the case of missionary selling or situations where team selling is common.

The major limitation of straight salary plans is that financial rewards are not tied directly to any specific aspect of sales performance. Although management should attempt to give bigger salary increases each year to the best performers, the amount of those increases and the way performance is evaluated is subject to the whims of the managers who make the decisions. Consequently, salespeople may not have a clear understanding of what they must do to receive a desired increase in rewards. Also, salaries make sales compensation a fixed cost. This can be an advantage when volumes are high, but it is a disadvantage in recessionary times, or during an industry shakeout period, when a firm's short-term volume is falling.

Commission payments are usually based on a salesperson's dollar or unit sales volume. Some companies, however, base them on the profitability of sales to encourage their salespeople to concentrate on the most profitable products and customers. In any case, the direct link between sales performance and the salesperson's compensation is the primary strength of a commission compensation plan. Salespeople are strongly motivated to increase their productivity to increase their compensation—at least until they reach such high pay levels that additional increases are no longer worth the additional effort. Assuming that territories are properly designed with equal sales potential, commission plans also have a built-in element of fairness because good performers are automatically rewarded.

On the other hand, straight commission plans have some important limitations that have caused many firms to abandon them. Perhaps their most critical weakness is that management has little control over the salesforce. When all financial rewards are tied directly to sales volume, it is difficult to motivate salespeople to perform account management activities that do not lead directly to short-term sales. In addition, commissioned salespeople are more likely to "milk" current customers rather than prospect for new accounts, to overstock their customers, and to neglect service after the sale.

Combination compensation plans have become increasingly popular because they have most of the advantages—and avoid most of the limitations—of both straight salary and straight commission plans. The base salary gives the salesperson a stable income and gives management some capability to reward salespeople for performing customer servicing and administrative tasks. At the same time, the incentive portion provides direct rewards to motivate salespeople to improve their sales volume or profitability.

Combination plans add commissions, bonuses, or both to a base salary. A salary plus commission ties commissions to volume or profitability, as in a straight commission plan. On the other hand, a salesperson typically receives a bonus for surpassing some level of total sales or a quota, or some other aspect of performance. Also, the degree to which the salesperson exceeds the performance goal determines the size of the bonus. Thus, bonuses are additional incentives to spur salespeople to reach higher than average levels of performance.

One important question to consider when designing a combination plan is what percentage of total compensation should be accounted for by the incentive portion of the plan. If the incentive portion is too low, it lacks motivational impact on the salesforce. If it is too high (or even open-ended), the program may become extremely costly. Most authorities suggest that the incentive portion of a program should amount to about 25 to 30 percent of total gross compensation to be an effective motivator. Even though this is a reasonable rule of thumb, the actual percentage of incentive pay varies substantially across firms and industries. Also, a recent survey of more than 200 combination compensation plans found that the size of the incentive portion varied by type of plan. Incentive pay averaged only 11 percent of total compensation in salary-plus-bonus plans; but salary-plus-commission plans provided an average of 33 percent incentive pay.[25]

Nonfinancial rewards

Nonfinancial rewards can also motivate salespeople to produce good performance. One such reward—of particular importance to many younger salespeople—is the opportunity for advancement and promotion. Many new salespeople see selling as a training ground for sales or marketing management and are willing to work hard for a chance to be promoted. Some discover that not only do they like selling but also they would have to accept a cut in compensation with a "promotion" into management. They decide to stay in sales. Unfortunately for the others, there are often simply not enough opportunities in management to accommodate all the good performers in the salesforce. Besides, because selling and managing often require different skills, not all successful salespeople make good managers. To deal with these problems, many firms have developed dual career paths for their salespeople to maintain the motivating potential of promotion. One path leads to positions in the management hierarchy; the other leads to greater responsibilities within the salesforce itself, such as a better territory or a national account management position.

EVALUATION AND CONTROL

Managers collect and evaluate information about their salespeople's performance and compare these data to the plan's objectives and forecasts to determine how well the salesforce is doing. The purpose is much like that of navigating a ship at sea. By determining where the ship is relative to its destination, the captain can see how well the ship is doing and make necessary corrections when it is off course.

Companies use three approaches in monitoring the salesforce to evaluate and control sales performance.

1. **Sales analysis:** Managers monitor sales volume for each salesperson. In addition, they break down sales figures by geographic territory, by each product in the line, and by different types of customers. They compare results to the

---

[25] Charles A. Peck, *Compensating Field Sales Representatives, Report No. 828* (New York: The Conference Board, 1982), p. 14.

forecasts and quotas in the firm's sales plan to determine which salespeople are doing well and where adjustments may be needed.

2. **Cost analysis:** They can also monitor the costs of various selling activities such as travel and entertainment expenses. Managers often examine these across individual salespeople, districts, customers, and product types. However, this does present some difficult technical challenges about how certain costs, such as administrative costs and overhead, should be allocated. When put together with the results of a sales analysis, this procedure allows managers to evaluate the profitability of different territories, products, and customer types.

3. **Behavioral analysis:** When sales volume or profitability in a territory falls below expectations, managers may be uncertain as to the cause. Perhaps the salesperson in that territory is not working hard enough or is allocating effort to the wrong activities. Or the disappointing results could be due to factors beyond the salesperson's control, such as poor economic conditions or heavy competition in the territory. To gain a better understanding of the cause—and provide a better basis for taking corrective action—many managers believe it is necessary to monitor and evaluate the actual behavior of the salesperson as well as the *outcomes* of that behavior. They obtain much information for this kind of behavioral analysis from activity reports and call reports submitted by the salespeople themselves. In addition, some firms use self-rating scales, field observations, and supervisor ratings to compile the needed information.

Many of these methods apply equally well to the evaluation and control of entire marketing programs, not just the salesforce. Consequently, we examine this topic in more detail in Chapter 24.

SUMMARY

Decisions about how many resources to allocate to the salesforce relative to other elements of the promotional mix and the strategic salesforce objectives are influenced by various factors. These include the business's objectives and competitive strategy, its resources, the number and type of customers in its target market, its competitive position in the market, and the other components of its strategic marketing program. The objectives that a firm might set for its salespeople include: (1) winning acceptance of new products by existing customers; (2) developing new customers for existing products; (3) maintaining the loyalty of current customers by providing good service; (4) facilitating future sales by providing technical services; (5) facilitating future sales by communicating product information; and (6) gathering market information.

The strategic situation a firm faces in a product-market—and the objectives it sets for its salesforce—influence the kinds of tasks and activities on which its sales personnel must focus their efforts. A wide range of activities might be included in a specific sales job; and a variety of sales jobs might be incorporated in a firm's salesforce. This chapter discussed four types of selling jobs: trade selling, missionary selling, technical selling, and new business selling. Each type of job not only involves different activities, but also requires salespeople with different skills and personal characteristics.

Like all other parts of the marketing program, the salesforce must be managed. Sales management involves three related sets of activities: sales planning, implementation of the sales program, and evaluation and control of sales performance.

Sales planning involves deciding how the salesforce should allocate its efforts within the market. Managers must make specific decisions about organizing the salesforce, defining sales territories, formulating account management policies to guide the amount and kinds of effort salespeople devote to different types of customers, and setting quotas for each salesperson.

Implementation of a sales plan requires that the individual salespeople have the aptitude, skills, knowledge, and motivation necessary to do their jobs effectively. The manager must recruit and hire the appropriate kinds of people, train and supervise them so they understand the products or services they sell and the tasks they perform, and motivate them with attractive compensation and incentive programs. The three most common compensation plans for the salesforce are straight salary, straight commission, and combination plans providing a base salary and an incentive consisting of commissions, a bonus, or both. The combination plan has become most popular in recent years because it provides most of the advantages of the other two plans and has fewer limitations.

Finally, the sales manager must periodically evaluate the performance of each member of the salesforce to determine whether the sales plan is being effectively carried out. Frequent monitoring of performance gives the manager a basis for better control over the sales program. Three types of analysis monitor sales performance: sales analysis, cost analysis, and behavioral analysis. When managers discover deviations from planned levels of performance, they adjust the plan or take action such as giving additional training or supervising poor performers to deal with the problem areas or take advantage of opportunities.

QUESTIONS

1. A sales manager for a large consumer package goods firm argues that $250,000 should be cut from the media advertising budgets of the firm's various products and used to hire five more company salespeople. Her rationale is that at today's media prices five more salespeople can generate more sales volume than a quarter of a million dollars in advertising. How would you evaluate this argument? Under which conditions might the sales manager be right? Under what conditions might she be wrong?

2. The 100-member salesforce of the firm mentioned in question 1 calls on national, regional, and local supermarket chains. They are responsible for gaining authorization for purchases from the chain headquarters and winning shelf space in, and providing merchandising services to, individual stores in each chain. The company's product line consists of 10 varieties of cookies, 7 kinds of crackers, and 5 snack products. Suggest two ways in which such a salesforce might be organized. What are the benefits and limitations of each form of organization? Which would you recommend and why?

3. Which type of sales job are the salespeople working for the company described in questions 1 and 2 involved in? What objectives and activities are likely to be most important in such a job? What kind of skills and personal characteristics should the company look for when hiring new salespeople?

4. The Spano Company is a medium-sized manufacturer of electrical components that it sells to manufacturers in a number of industries. The firm's managers estimate that there are 500 large "A" customers and potential customers for its products who should be called on twice a month on average. There are another 500 medium-sized "B" accounts that should receive a monthly sales call and 1,200

smaller accounts that should be visited four times a year. Given that Spano salespeople have been averaging three sales calls per day over the past year, and that each salesperson gets two weeks of paid vacation, how many salespeople should the Spano company have on its payroll?

5. A manufacturer of computer systems targeted at engineering design firms compensates its salespeople primarily with a fixed salary, although it also pays a small bonus if the salesperson makes a specified number of proposals to potential new customers during the year. Does this compensation plan make sense for such a firm? Why or why not?

6. Describe a situation (type of product, target market, competitive strategy, etc.) where you would recommend that a salesforce be compensated by a straight commission. Explain the rationale for your recommendation.

7. A manufacturer of power equipment used by building contractors compensates its salespeople with a modest salary plus a substantial commission based on dollar sales volume. The compensation plan is open-ended in the sense that there is no limit to the amount of commission salespeople can earn. Indeed, some of the more experienced members of the company's salesforce earn well into six figures. The firm's rationale is that "we don't care how much we pay our salespeople, because their compensation relates to their volume of sales." What possible problems could result from this policy?

8. You are the marketing manager for a biotechnology firm that hopes to gain Food and Drug Administration approval for a large number of new prescription pharmaceuticals over the next several years. You are in the process of building a salesforce in anticipation of this flow of new products. Which objectives should that salesforce focus on? Which selling activities would be critical for accomplishing those objectives?

9. Given your answer to question 8, what kinds of people would you want to hire for your new salesforce and why? What kind of compensation package would you design to motivate those salespeople?

SECTION IV

Strategic marketing programs for selected situations

I n Section III we examined options available to a marketing manager for each marketing mix component. The next question is how those components should be combined into an effective and internally consistent strategic marketing program. As we saw in Chapter 11, the marketing programs for individual product-market entries are constrained and influenced by the overall competitive strategy, objectives, and resource allocations of the entry's business unit. Nevertheless, the manager usually has substantial freedom to design a program that fits the specific customer and competitive conditions of the target market. Of course, as we saw in Chapter 8, those conditions change over time as the market grows and matures and the competitive structure of the industry changes. The marketing objectives facing a product-market entry, and the marketing program most appropriate for accomplishing those objectives, also change over time. The chapters in this section, then, focus on the strategic marketing programs suited to the specific market and competitive situations a product commonly faces over its life cycle.

Despite the recent popularity of mergers, acquisitions, and conglomerate diversification, many firms focus primarily on attaining future growth by developing new products for existing markets, finding new applications and customer segments for existing products, or diversifying into new businesses that are somehow related to their current ones. Implementing such growth strategies requires the penetration and development of new product-markets.

Whether a firm is introducing an entirely new product or simply trying to market an existing product to a new group of customers, a major objective for the new entry is to gain a viable level of sales volume as quickly as possible. In this way the firm can recoup the heavy investments that are often involved in new-product or market development and establish a strong competitive position. Chapter 19 describes specific marketing programs for accomplishing these new-market entry objectives. It also discusses the important strategic question of whether it is better for a firm to be the pioneer in a new product-market or a fast-follower who tries to capitalize on the pioneer's shortcomings and mistakes.

As a product-market enters the growth stage of the product life cycle and additional competitors emerge, businesses face one of two strategic situations; they either find themselves as share leaders who must try to *maintain* their high relative share in the face of increased competition, or they are followers who must try to *increase* their share relative to the leader. Chapter 20 discusses a variety of specific marketing programs that businesses in growing markets might adopt to achieve either a share growth or a share maintenance objective.

A business that successfully builds market share during the early phases of an industry's life eventually sees many of its product-markets turn into cash cows as the industry matures and growth slows. Chapter 21 examines a number of marketing programs appropriate for products in mature markets.

Businesses that are not successful at attaining a commanding market share while a product-market is growing eventually find themselves in possession of a dog—a product with a small share of a mature or declining market. Chapter 21 also discusses the marketing implications of this situation.

Finally, declining rates of growth in domestic markets and increased threats from foreign competitors have combined in recent years to increase the attractiveness of foreign markets as potential avenues for future growth. Chapter 22 examines some of the unique strategic marketing issues encountered when a firm moves into global markets.

Chapter ◇ 19

Strategies for new-market entries

IBM: "BIG BLUE'S" STRATEGY FOR GROWTH

An executive at Fujitsu, Ltd.—Japan's largest computer manufacturer—offered the following observation about IBM: "In the world information processing market, we have to respect IBM. We are like the hunter that approaches the lion with rifle in hand. Suddenly, the lion kneels down. "Are you afraid?" the hunter asks. "No," the lion replies, "I'm just praying before eating." One reason even IBM's largest competitors felt threatened by the firm's voracious appetite was because its growth objectives were the most ambitious of any firm in history. In the early 1980s John R. Opel, then the firm's CEO, decreed that the firm should match or beat the information processing industry's growth in *all* market segments through at least the mid-1990s. Increases were expected to range from 12 percent per year in mainframes to 40 percent for personal computers and software. The firm managed to achieve these goals through 1985, reaching a sales volume of more than $50 billion. What made its competitors nervous, though, was the fact that if IBM continued to reach its growth objectives it would have reached $185 billion in sales by 1994.[1]

In trying to achieve such rapid growth, IBM pursued a full range of corporate growth strategies, although different business units within the firm planned to grow in different ways.

First, in older and more fully developed product-markets, IBM concentrated on various line extensions and product improvements. For example, it introduced a new generation of mainframe in 1986; and it brought out a line of faster and more powerful PCs in 1987. Part of the motivation for such changes was to enable IBM to defend its dominant position in established markets in the face of improved competitive products, such as Apple's Macintosh, and more aggressive price competition by manufacturers of PC clones. In addition, such product improvements—particularly when they involved the introduction of a whole new technological generation of products—helped sustain and even increase total volume in the product-market. The new technology made the computers owned by past customers obsolete and thus brought many of them back into the market. And the improved price-performance ratios of the new equipment attracted some new users with applications that were not previously cost effective.

[1] Based largely on Marilyn A. Harris, "IBM: More Worlds to Conquer," *Business Week*, February 18, 1985, pp. 84–98; "How IBM Is Fighting Back," *Business Week*, November 17, 1986, pp. 152–57; and "The Greatest Capitalist in History," *Fortune*, August 31, 1987, pp. 24–35.

continued

A second avenue for growth pursued by IBM's established businesses was new-market development—the pursuit of new customer segments and applications for existing products and services. One source of such growth was the expansion into international markets. IBM has aggressively pursued global markets for decades, with the result that international operations accounted for about 40 percent of its total sales volume in 1985. Growth plans called for even more aggressive development of global markets by most of IBM's businesses.

In addition to foreign markets, IBM targeted new or underdeveloped U.S. customer segments as sources of future growth for existing products and services. For example, it began marketing efforts aimed at winning more of the lucrative state contracts for PCs used in public schools, a market dominated by Apple. The firm has also tried to expand the customer base for its highly respected service unit by offering service for equipment made by other manufacturers. Besides having the potential for additional sales volume growth, such market development activities helped the firm reduce unit costs and increase the profitability of its existing products and services.

IBM's third path toward growth focused on developing new products for many of its current customer segments. These products involved entirely new technologies or designs. In some cases, they complemented and helped increase the utility of—and customer demand for existing products.

For example, IBM has long developed applications software for its computers. But it increased its efforts in this area so that more customers could use IBM machines for a greater variety of purposes.

The firm also pursued new products that were largely unrelated to current offerings. For example, the company targeted robotics and computer-integrated manufacturing systems as high-potential areas for future growth.

Finally, IBM focused on some areas for future growth that involved entirely new products for new applications and markets. Most of these efforts amount to related (or concentric)—as opposed to unrelated (or conglomerate)—diversification. One of its highest priority growth areas was the automated "office-of-the-future," which involved a variety of workstations tied to a telecommunications system. No single manufacturer can as yet put all of the elements of an automated office together. But this is exactly what IBM hoped to do to clinch a leading position in the booming office market estimated at about $30 billion per year. To develop this new market, however, IBM had to improve its capabilities in unfamiliar technical areas—such as telecommunications—and develop a tremendous amount of new software capable of tying together a variety of computers and communication devices. Thus the firm acquired several telecommunications companies, such as Rolm Corp. and Satellite Business Systems, and asked key company divi-

continued

concluded

sions to increase their programming staffs by 20 percent per year through the mid-1990s.

Making large investments in an undeveloped product area such as the "office of the future" was clearly risky, especially for a company that failed in its first two attempts to market integrated office networks.

As Exhibit 19–1 indicates, the risks were even greater than IBM realized. IBM's desire to be the pioneer in automated office systems represented a change in strategy. It usually had not been the first to enter new markets or to introduce innovative technologies. Instead, it often watched smaller innovators enter new markets first, evaluated their equipment and marketing programs, and observed customers' responses. If a new market showed signs of substantial future growth, IBM relied on improved product design, its reputation for reliability and service, and its superior marketing skills and salesforce to capture a commanding share of that market as a follower rather than the pioneer.

EXHIBIT   19 ♦ 1

IBM sells ROLM

In the mid-1980s, IBM paid $1.5 billion for ROLM and then spent $1 billion trying to turn the company around. Recently IBM sold ROLM for a little more than $1 billion to Siemens, the powerful West German electronics firm. This represented the third false start in the last 10 years for IBM in attempting to penetrate the telecommunications business which it sees as critical to its long-term welfare. ROLM was a model Silicon Valley start-up. Its computerized PBXs had revolutionized the industry by the late 1970s. Product development continued to be successful into the early 1980s when IBM purchased the company (1983). Shortly thereafter, growth stalled; AT&T and Northern Telecom caught up technologically; and margins dropped dramatically. IBM compounded the situation with its highly structured management of what was basically an entrepreneurial company. New-product development, and marketing in particular, suffered as ROLM employees sought greener pastures. As a result of its experience with ROLM, IBM will likely avoid buying companies to gain a foothold in a given market and instead invest in niche players and internal product development.

Source: Paul B. Carroll, "IBM's Telecommunications Effort with Rolm Unit Has Turned Sour," *The Wall Street Journal,* December 12, 1988, p. 33; and Robert D. Hof and John J. Keller, "Behind the Scenes at the Fall of ROLM," *Business Week,* July 10, 1989, p. 82.

SOME ISSUES CONCERNING NEW-MARKET ENTRY STRATEGIES

Not all of IBM's strategies to secure continued growth have been equally successful. Indeed, the firm's rate of growth in a number of markets slowed significantly during the late 1980s. We will examine the reasons for the firm's declining growth rate in one area—the commercial PC market—at the start of the next chapter. But IBM's various planned approaches toward securing future growth illustrates several important points about new-product and market development. We explore these further in the next sections of this chapter. First, growth strategies involve products that differ in their degree of "newness" from the perspective of both the company and its customers. If IBM is successful at developing the automated office, for example, the resulting products will be new to *both* the company and its customers. On the other hand, IBM's foray into robotics involves products new to IBM but not to its customers, because other manufacturers already offer such products. The planned expansion of IBM's service operation to owners of non-IBM systems would be a product offering that is new for those customers but is old hat for the company.

In Chapter 13 we focused on the problems and processes involved in developing and evaluating product offerings that are *new to the company*. This chapter examines marketing objectives and programs appropriate for introducing products and developing markets for offerings that are *new to the target customers*. Our primary focus is on programs used by the pioneer firm—or first entrant—into a particular product-market. We postpone our discussion of marketing programs appropriate for follower firms until the next chapter when we examine share building strategies.

IBM's wide variety of approaches to new-product and market development are all motivated by the common objective of increasing future volume and profit. But different strategies can achieve a variety of secondary objectives as well. For example, expanding the target markets for an *existing product* can reduce the unit costs and increase the profitability of that product. And major *product improvements* can help protect a firm's share position in existing markets in the face of increasing competition. Top management, then, must be explicit about its objectives for new-market entries in its various business units. Managers need guidelines for choosing appropriate development strategies. Later in this chapter we discuss some of the objectives that new entries can achieve and the conditions under which various objectives are appropriate.

Finally, new-product development can be expensive and risky. From 1980 to 1985, IBM spent $15 billion on R&D and engineering for new products and an additional $13 billion on the land, buildings, and equipment needed to produce them. As of 1985 it had yet to realize a payoff on nearly two thirds of that investment. There is no guarantee of ultimate success, as attested to by the firm's false starts in introducing the automated office.

This raises an intriguing strategic question: Is it better for a firm to be the pioneer in developing and introducing a new product (as IBM is attempting to be in the office-of-the-future) or to be a follower who watches other innovators bear the risks of product failure and marketing mistakes before joining the battle with its own entry (as IBM did in the PC market)? Before discussing some alternative marketing programs that pioneers might use to penetrate and develop new markets, we examine the conditions where pioneer and follower strategies each have the greatest probability of long-term success.

HOW NEW IS NEW?

A survey of the new-product development practices of 700 U.S. corporations conducted by the consulting firm of Booz, Allen & Hamilton found that the products those firms introduced from 1976 to 1981 were not all equally "new." The study identified six categories of new products based on their degree of newness as perceived by both the company introducing them and the customers in the target market. These categories are discussed below and diagrammed in Exhibit 19–2, which indicates the percentage of new entries falling in each category during the five-year study period. Notice that only 10 percent of all new-product introductions fell into the new-to-the-world category.[2]

* *New-to-the-world products:* True innovations new to the firm, creating an entirely new market (10 percent).
* *New product lines:* A product category new for the company introducing it, but not new to customers in the target market due to the existence of one or more competitive brands (20 percent).
* *Additions to existing product lines:* New items that supplement a firm's established product line. These items may be moderately new to both the firm and the customers in its established product-markets. They may also serve to expand the market segments appealed to by the line (26 percent).
* *Improvements in or revisions of existing products:* Items providing improved performance or greater perceived value brought out to replace existing products. These items may present moderately new marketing and production challenges to the firm, but unless they represent a technologically new generation of products, customers are likely to perceive them as similar to the products they replace (26 percent).
* *Repositionings:* Existing products targeted at new applications and market segments (7 percent).
* *Cost reductions:* Product modifications providing similar performance at a lower cost (11 percent).

Introducing a product that is new both to the firm and to target customers requires the greatest expenditure of effort and resources. It involves the

---

[2] *New Products Management for the 1980's* (New York: Booz, Allen & Hamilton, 1982).

EXHIBIT   19◆2

Categories of new products defined according to their degree of newness to the company and customers in the target market

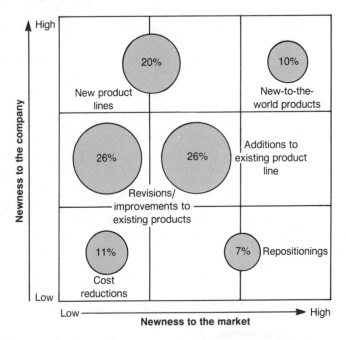

Source: New Products Management for the 1980s (New York: Booz, Allen & Hamilton, 1982).

greatest amount of uncertainty, due to the lack of information and experience with the technology and the target customers. And it presents the greatest risk of failure.

Products new to target customers but not to the firm (such as line extensions or modifications aimed at new customer segments or repositionings of existing products) are often not very innovative from a product design or operations viewpoint; but they may present a great deal of marketing uncertainty. The marketing challenge here—as with new-to-the-world products—is to build primary demand, making target customers aware of the product and convincing them to adopt it. This is the marketing problem we investigate in this chapter.

Finally, products new to the company but not to the market (such as new product lines, line extensions, product modifications, and cost reductions) often present fewer challenges for R&D and product engineering. There are earlier designs or competitors' products to study and learn from. However, these products can present major operations challenges in process engineering, production scheduling, quality control, and inventory management. As we saw in Chapter 13, one marketing challenge with this kind of new-product development is to develop an offering that fits customer needs and

◆ Some of IBM's strategies for growth include targeting new markets (such as placing IBM PCs in public schools), concentrating on line extensions and product improvements in older, more fully developed product-markets (such as computer-aided design and robotics), and developing new products and applications. (Chapter 19)

Courtesy International Business Machines Corporation

• The PC has come a long way since Jobs and Wozniak built the first Apple in Jobs' garage. Today, competitors race to improve and find new applications for existing products and to develop new entries in this growth market. (Chapter 20)

Courtesy Apple Computer, Inc.

Courtesy Compaq Computer Company

Photo Courtesy of Hewlett-Packard

Courtesy International Business Machines Corporation

Being selective has its rewards.

JOSTENS
AMERICA'S CLASS RING

Courtesy Jostens

◆ Jostens, a producer of class rings, predicted the decline of its primary market and successfully prepared for it with a market penetration strategy that included product modifications, line extensions, and a broadened price range. (Chapter 21)

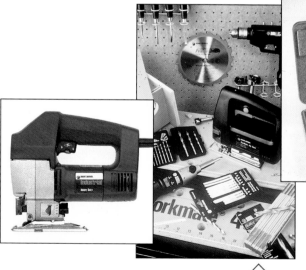

Courtesy of the Black & Decker Corporation

◆ Black & Decker designed its 2-speed cut-saw, its pendulum jigsaw, and other products to meet the needs of the lucrative European market. (Chapter 22)

Courtesy The Procter & Gamble Company

◆ Procter & Gamble has a number of different brands and line extensions in most of its business categories—as in its Crest toothpaste line, which now includes Sparkle Crest for kids. (Chapter 23)

Courtesy Wal-Mart Stores, Inc., Bentonville, Ark.

© Peter C. Poulides

◆ One reason for Wal-Mart's profitability, despite consistently pricing many products below those of their leading competitors, is their ability to control costs—even in hypermarts so large employees wear roller skates to stock the shelves. (Chapter 24)

the firm's capabilities and stands a reasonable chance of success in the marketplace. When the new product is introduced into the market, however, the primary marketing objective is to build selective demand and capture market share—convincing customers that the new offering beats the competition. We discuss marketing programs that a firm can use to meet these objectives in Chapter 20.

OBJECTIVES OF NEW-PRODUCT AND MARKET DEVELOPMENT

The primary objective of most new-product and market development efforts is to secure future volume and profit growth. The IBM case illustrates, however, that individual development projects may also accomplish other strategic objectives. When asked what strategic role was served by their most successful recent new entry, the respondents in the Booz, Allen & Hamilton survey mentioned eight strategic objectives. Exhibit 19–3 lists these objec-

EXHIBIT 19 ♦3

Strategic objectives attained by successful new-market entries

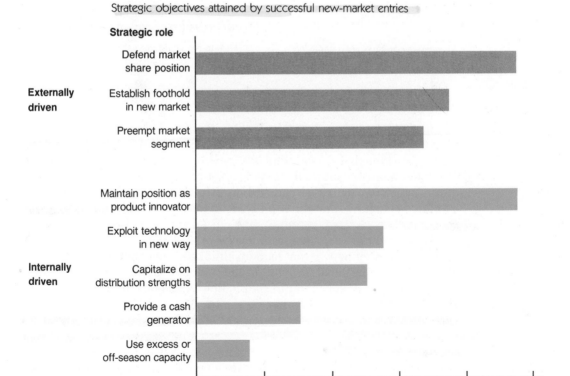

Source: *New Products Management for the 1980s* (New York: Booz, Allen & Hamilton, 1982), p. 11.

EXHIBIT 19◆4

New entries appropriate for different strategic objectives

Objective	New entry
Maintain position as a product innovator	New-to-the-world products; improvements or revisions to existing products
Defend a current market-share position	Improvements or revisions to existing products; additions to existing product line; cost reductions
Establish a foothold in a future new market; preempt a market segment	New-to-the-world products; additions to existing product line; repositionings
Exploit technology in a new way	New-to-the-world products; new product line; additions to or revisions of existing product line
Capitalize on distribution strengths	New-to-the-world products; new product line; additions to or revisions of existing product line
Provide a cash generator	Additions to or revisions of existing product line; repositionings; cost reductions
Use excess or off-season capacity	New-to-the-world product; new product line

tives and the percent of respondents that mentioned each one. The exhibit also indicates which objectives were focused on external concerns—such as defending market share—and which were driven by a desire to improve or build upon the firm's internal strengths. Notice, too, that most respondents indicated their new entry helped accomplish more than one objective.

Exhibit 19–4 shows that different types of new entries are appropriate for achieving different strategic objectives. For example, if the objective is to establish a foothold in or preempt a new-market segment, the firm must introduce a product new to that market, although it may not be entirely new to the company. On the other hand, if the objective is to improve cash flow by adding another cash generator, simple line extensions or product modifications that reduce unit costs may do the trick.

The business's objectives for its new entries influence the kind of strategy it should pursue and the marketing and other functional programs needed to implement that strategy. For instance, if a business is pursuing a prospector strategy and its objectives are to maintain a position as a product innovator and establish footholds in a variety of new product-markets, it should attempt to be the pioneer in as many of those markets as possible. And as we saw in Chapter 11, successful implementation of such a strategy requires the business to be competent in and devote substantial resources to R&D, product engineering, marketing, and marketing research.

On the other hand, if the business is defending an already strong market share position it may prefer to be a follower. It would then enter new product-markets after an innovator and rely on superior quality, better customer service, or lower prices to offset the pioneer's early lead. Such a strategy usually requires fewer investments in R&D and product development, though marketing and sales still are critical in implementing it effectively. A more detailed comparison of these alternative new-market entry strategies—pioneer versus follower—is the focus of the next section of this chapter.

MARKET ENTRY STRATEGIES: PIONEERS VERSUS FOLLOWERS

Even though IBM is one of the world's premier high-tech companies, it has usually not been a pioneer in the sense of being the first to enter new markets. For example, IBM did not enter the PC market until several other firms—including Apple, Commodore, and Tandy —had already established substantial sales volumes. But as a follower, IBM could rely on superior product performance, an extensive advertising and promotional effort, and an established reputation for reliability and customer service. It captured a commanding share of the PC market within a year of its entry. On the other hand, IBM appears to be committed to a pioneering entry strategy in the emerging automated office-of-the-future market. From a strategic viewpoint, which of the two entry approaches makes the most sense? Or do both entry strategies have particular advantages under different sets of conditions?

Pioneer strategy

Although they take the greatest risks and probably experience more failures than their conservative competitors, successful pioneers are handsomely rewarded, according to the conventional wisdom. It is assumed that competitive advantages inherent in being the first to enter a new product-market can be sustained through the growth stage and into the maturity stage of the product life cycle, resulting in a strong share position and substantial returns. This is particularly true when the pioneer can gain patent protection, since the firm enjoys a monopoly position for the life of the patent. One study of a cross section of industries with mature industrial products provides some support for this view. The study's results—summarized in Exhibit 19–5—indicate that firms that were pioneers in a product category and survived held an average market share of 30 percent when their indus-

EXHIBIT   19 ◆ 5

Average market shares at industry maturity of firms pursuing different market entry strategies

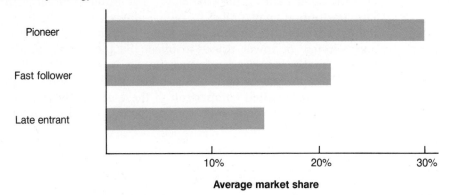

Market entry strategy

Source: Based on material in William T. Robinson, "Market Pioneering and Sustainable Market Share Advantages in Industrial Goods Manufacturing Industries," Working Paper, Purdue University, 1984.

tries reached maturity. This compared to average shares of 21 percent for followers and 15 percent for late entrants.[3]

Some of the potential sources of advantage available to pioneers are briefly summarized in Exhibit 19–6 and discussed below.[4]

1. *Economies of scale and experience.* Being first means the pioneer gains accumulated volume and experience and thereby lower per-unit costs at a faster rate than followers. This advantage is particularly pronounced when the product is technically sophisticated and involves high development costs, or when its life cycle is likely to be short with sales increasing rapidly during the introduction and early growth stages.

   As we shall see later, the pioneer can deploy the cost advantages that accrue to protect its early lead against followers. One strategy is to lower price; this can discourage followers from entering the market because it raises the volume necessary for them to break even. Or the pioneer might invest in additional marketing efforts to expand its penetration of the market, such as heavier advertising, a larger salesforce, or continuing product improvements or line extensions.

---

[3] William T. Robinson, "Market Pioneering and Sustainable Market Share Advantages in Industrial Goods Manufacturing Industries," Working Paper, Purdue University, 1984. Also see William T. Robinson and Claes Fornell, "Sources of Market Pioneer Advantages in Consumer Goods Industries," *Journal of Marketing Research* 22 (1985), pp. 305–17; and William T. Robinson, "Sources of Market Pioneer Advantages: The Case of Industrial Goods Industries," *Journal of Marketing Research* 25 (1988), pp. 87–94.

[4] The following discussion expands on material discussed in George S. Day, *Analysis for Strategic Market Decisions* (St. Paul: West Publishing, 1986), pp. 99–107; and Michael E. Porter, *Competitive Advantage* (New York: Free Press, 1985), pp. 181–91.

EXHIBIT   19 ◆ 6

Potential advantages of pioneer and follower strategies

Pioneer	Follower
◆ Economies of scale and experience	◆ Ability to take advantage of pioneer's positioning mistakes
◆ High switching costs for early adopters	◆ Ability to take advantage of pioneer's product mistakes
◆ Pioneer defines the "rules of the game"	
◆ Distribution advantage	◆ Ability to take advantage of pioneer's marketing mistakes
◆ Influence on consumer choice criteria and attitudes	◆ Ability to take advantage of pioneer's limited resources
◆ Possibility of preempting scarce resources	

2. *High switching costs for early adopters.* Customers who are early to adopt a pioneer's new product may be reluctant to change suppliers when competitive products appear. This is particularly true for industrial goods where the costs of switching can be high. Compatible equipment and spare parts, investments in employee training, and the risks of lower product quality or customer service make it easier for the pioneer to retain its early customers over time.

3. *The pioneer defines the "rules of the game."* The pioneer's actions on price, product quality, distribution, warranties, postsale service, promotional appeals, and budgets set standards that subsequent competitors must "meet or beat." If the pioneer sets those standards high enough, it can raise the costs of entry and perhaps preempt some potential competitors.

4. *Distribution advantages.* The pioneer possesses the most options in designing a distribution channel to bring the new product to market. This is particularly true for industrial goods where, if the pioneer exercises its options well and with dispatch, it should end up with a network of the best distributors. This can exclude later entrants from some markets. Distributors are often reluctant to take on second or third brands; especially when the product is technically complex and the distributor must carry large inventories of the product and spare parts, and invest in specialized training and service.

   For consumer packaged goods, it is more difficult to slow the entry of later competitors by preempting distribution alternatives. Nevertheless, the pioneer still has the advantage of attaining more shelf facings at the outset of the growth stage. By quickly expanding its product line following an initial success, the pioneer can appropriate still more shelf space, thereby making the challenge faced by followers even more difficult.

5. *Influence on customer choice criteria and attitudes.* The pioneer has the opportunity to develop a product offering with attributes closely linked to the choice criteria most important to the largest segment of customers, or to promote the importance of attributes that favor its brand. Thus, the pioneer's brand can become the standard of reference customers use to evaluate other brands. This can make it more difficult for followers with me-too products to convince customers that their new products are superior to the older and more familiar

pioneer. If the pioneer has successfully tied its offering to the most salient criteria of the largest group of customers, it also becomes more difficult for followers to differentiate their offerings in ways that are attractive to the mass-market segment. They may have to target a smaller peripheral segment or niche instead.

6. *Possibility of preempting scarce resources.* The pioneer may be able to negotiate favorable deals with suppliers who are eager for new business or who do not appreciate the size of the opportunity for their raw materials or component parts. If later entrants subsequently find those materials and components in short supply, they may be constrained from expanding as rapidly as they might like or be forced to pay premium prices.

The evidence suggests that these advantages can help a pioneer gain and maintain a competitive edge in a new market, but not all pioneers are successful at doing so. For one thing, some pioneers fail during the introductory stage of the product life cycle. Others disappear during the shakeout that typically occurs later in the growth period. As we discuss in the next section, in some cases—particularly where the pioneer is pursuing a prospector business strategy—a withdrawal during the shakeout period may be intentional and strategically planned. In other cases, it is simply the result of failure due to inadequate resources, poor product design, or marketing mistakes.

Even when the pioneer survives the shakeout period, it is not always able to convert its initial advantage into a continuing position of share leadership. The pioneer may lack the resources or competencies to keep up with rapid growth in the market and fully exploit the advantages of its early lead in the face of a competitive onslaught by strong followers. This has been the case, for instance, in the personal computer market. Even though early entrants like Apple, Tandy, and Commodore have survived and, in some cases, prospered, follower IBM is the current share and profit leader.

Follower strategy

The above observations suggest that there may be some advantages to letting other firms go first into a product-market. Let them shoulder the initial risks while observing their shortcomings and mistakes. Some of the possible advantages of such a follower strategy are briefly summarized in Exhibit 19–6 and discussed below.

1. *Ability to take advantage of the pioneer's positioning mistakes.* If the pioneer misjudges the preferences and purchase criteria of the mass-market segment or attempts to satisfy two or more segments at once, it is vulnerable to the introduction of more precisely positioned products by a follower. By tailoring its offerings to each distinct segment, the follower can successfully encircle the pioneer.

2. *Ability to take advantage of the pioneer's product mistakes.* If the pioneer's initial product has technical limitations or design flaws, the follower is in a

position to benefit by overcoming these weaknesses. Even when the pioneering product is technically satisfactory, a follower may gain an advantage in product enhancements. For example, Compaq captured a substantial share of the commercial PC market by developing a faster and more portable version of IBM's original machine.

3. *Ability to take advantage of the pioneer's marketing mistakes.* If the pioneer makes any marketing mistakes in introducing a new entry, opportunities are left open for later entrants. This is closely related to point 1, yet it goes beyond product positioning to the actual execution of the pioneer's marketing program. For example, the pioneer may lack adequate distribution, spend too little on introductory advertising, or use ineffective promotional appeals to communicate the product's benefits. A follower can observe these mistakes, design a marketing program to overcome them, and successfully compete head-to-head with the pioneer. As described in Exhibit 19–7, for instance, Compaq has achieved outstanding growth in the European market by building a strong network of independent dealers in local areas rather than adopting market pioneer IBM's strategy of using company salespeople.

4. *Ability to take advantage of pioneer's limited resources.* If the pioneer has limited resources for such things as production facilities or marketing programs—or fails to commit sufficient resources to its new entry—followers find few enduring constraints if they can and will outspend the pioneer to offset its early advantage.

Determinants of success for pioneers and followers

Our discussion suggests that a pioneering firm stands the best chance for long-term success in market share leadership and profitability (a) when the new product-market is insulated from the entry of competitors—at least for a

EXHIBIT   19 ◆ 7

COMPAQ's distribution strategy in Europe

COMPAQ Computer Corporation is the leading seller of IBM-compatible PCs with annual revenues of $3 billion—a 500 percent increase since 1986. One reason for its success is the surge in overseas sales which account for about half of the company's total revenues. European sales are up 57 percent from 1988, resulting in a market share of over 10 percent of the PC market—making it the number two firm there; and foreign sales may rise 60 percent in 1989. One of the reasons behind this outstanding performance is COMPAQ's dealer-only strategy that it perfected in the United States. It has a strong network of European dealers who rely on COMPAQ to be the best in developing PCs which use the latest technology. In return they give strong selling and service support which includes close working contacts with both large and small accounts.

Source: Mark Ivey and Geoff Lewis, "How COMPAQ Gets There Firstest with the Mostest," *Business Week,* June 26, 1986, p. 146; and Thane Peterson, "The Power behind COMPAQ's European Powerhouse," *Business Week,* June 26, 1989, p. 150.

while—by strong patent protection, by proprietary technology (a unique production process), or by substantial investment requirements, or (b) when the firm has sufficient size, resources, and competencies to take full advantage of its pioneering position and preserve it in the face of later competitive entries.

Polaroid Corporation is a pioneer that profited from the first situation. Strong patent protection has enabled the firm to grow from an entrepreneurial start-up to a $1.6 billion company with little direct competition. Kodak, the only firm that attempted to challenge Polaroid in the instant photography business, dropped out of the industry after losing a patent infringement suit in 1985. Consequently, Polaroid could grow and profit by introducing a steady but narrowly focused stream of product improvements. It supported those products with modest advertising and promotion and charged relatively high prices. However, the firm's insulated market situation led it to focus largely on the instant photography business rather than diversifying into other industries or product-markets. The firm's primary concern now is that instant photography is beginning to decline as consumers shift to products based on newer technologies, such as video recorders.[5]

McDonald's is a pioneer that succeeded by aggressively building on the foundations of its early advantage. Although the firm started small as a single hamburger restaurant, Ray A. Kroc—the company's founder—effectively used the franchise system of distribution to enable rapid expansion of McDonald's outlets with a minimum cash investment. That expansion plus stringent quality and cost controls, relatively low prices made possible by experience curve effects, heavy advertising and promotion, and product line extensions aimed at specific market segments (Egg McMuffin for the breakfast crowd and salads for health and diet-conscious adults) have all enabled the firm to maintain a commanding 40 percent share of the fast-food hamburger industry—more than double the share of Burger King, its largest competitor.[6]

On the other hand, a follower will most likely succeed when there are few legal, technological, or financial barriers to inhibit entry and where the follower has sufficient resources and competencies to overwhelm the pioneer's early advantage. IBM exploited this situation as a follower in the personal computer industry. Many smaller firms had already entered the business; but IBM could rely on a quality product with extensive software, buying power among component suppliers to hold down costs, extensive advertising, a strong salesforce with established contacts—particularly among potential business users—and an excellent reputation for reliability and good customer service. IBM quickly captured more than half the world-

---

[5] "Polaroid's Spectra May Be Losing Its Flash," *Business Week*, June 29, 1987, p. 31.

[6] Monci J. Williams, "McDonald's Refuses to Plateau," *Fortune*, November 12, 1984, pp. 34–40; and "McWorld?" *Business Week*, October 13, 1986, pp. 78–86.

EXHIBIT 19♦8

Marketing strategy elements pursued by successful pioneers, fast followers, and late entrants

These marketers . . .	*are characterized by one or more of these strategy elements:*
Successful pioneers	♦ Large entry scale ♦ Broad product line ♦ High product quality ♦ Heavy promotional expenditures

Successful fast followers	♦ Larger entry scale than the pioneer
	♦ "Leapfrogging" the pioneer
	    with superior:
	        product technology
	        product quality
	        customer service

Successful late entrants	♦ Focus on peripheral target markets or niches

wide PC market (although that market share was subsequently eroded somewhat by low-cost clones).[7]

A study conducted across a broad range of industries in the PIMS data base supports these observations. The study's findings are briefly summarized in Exhibit 19–8 and discussed in more detail below.[8]

The study found that regardless of the industry involved, pioneers able to maintain their preeminent position well into the market's growth stage had supported their early entry with the following marketing strategy elements:

♦ *Large entry scale*—successful pioneers had sufficient capacity, or could expand quickly enough, to pursue a mass market targeting strategy, usually on a national— rather than a local or regional—basis. Thus, they could expand their volume quickly and achieve the benefits of experience curve effects before major competitors could confront them.

♦ *Broad product line*—successful pioneers also quickly add line extensions or modifications to their initial product to tailor their offerings to specific market segments. This helps reduce their vulnerability to later entrants who might differentiate themselves by targeting one or more peripheral markets.

♦ *High product quality*—successful pioneers also offer a high-quality, well-designed product from the beginning, thus removing one potential differential advantage for later followers. Competent engineering, thorough product and market testing before commercialization, and good quality control during the production process are all important to the continued success of pioneers.

---

[7] "Who's Afraid of IBM?" *Business Week*, June 29, 1987, pp. 68–74.

[8] Mary L. Coyle, "Competition in Developing Markets: The Impact of Order of Entry," Ph.D. Diss., University of Toronto, 1986.

♦ *Heavy promotional expenditures*—characterizing the marketing programs of pioneers who continue to be successful are relatively high advertising and promotional expenditures as a percent of sales. Initially the promotion helps to stimulate awareness and primary demand for the new-product category, build volume, and reduce unit costs. Later, this promotion focuses on building selective demand for the pioneer's brand and reinforcing loyalty as new competitors enter.

The same study found that the most successful fast followers had the resources to enter the new market on a larger scale than the pioneer. Consequently they could quickly reduce their unit costs and offer lower prices than incumbent competitors. Some fast followers achieved success, however, by leapfrogging earlier entrants. These followers won customers away from the pioneer by offering a product with more sophisticated technology, better quality, or superior service (like IBM in the PC market).

Finally, the study found that some late followers also achieved substantial profits. These successful late entrants avoided direct confrontation with more established competitors by employing the kind of peripheral market targeting discussed in Chapter 10. They offered tailor-made products to smaller market niches and supported those products with high levels of customer service.

A more detailed discussion of the marketing strategies appropriate for followers is presented in the next chapter. Followers typically enter a market after it has begun to move into the growth stage of its life cycle, and they start with low market shares compared to the more established pioneer. Consequently, the next chapter's examination of marketing strategies for low-share competitors in growth markets is relevant to both fast followers and late entrants. The remainder of this chapter concentrates only on pioneers and the strategic marketing programs that might be successfully pursued by the first entrant in a new product-market.

STRATEGIC MARKETING PROGRAMS FOR PIONEERS

The preceding discussion suggests that the ultimate success of a pioneering strategy depends on the nature of the demand and potential competitive situation the pioneer encounters in the market, and on the pioneer's ability to design and implement an appropriate strategic marketing program. As we have seen, a pioneer's long-term success—in continued share leadership as well as profitability—depends on its ability to implement and maintain a *mass-market penetration* marketing strategy. This strategy requires getting potential customers to adopt the new product as quickly as possible to drive down unit costs and build a large contingent of loyal customers before competitors enter the market. The ultimate objective of such a strategy is to capture and maintain a commanding share of the total market for the new product. It is most successful when barriers inhibit or delay the entry of competitors (thus allowing the pioneer more time to build volume, lower unit costs, and establish a loyal customer base), or when the pioneer has resources or competencies that most potential competitors cannot match.

Exhibit 19–9 presents a detailed listing of specific circumstances favoring the use of a mass-market penetration strategy. Note that barriers to entry can result from a number of factors, including patent protection for the pioneer's technology, limited supply of materials or components, substantial investment requirements, or the fact that most potential competitors lack the resources to enter the market on a major scale.

Several competencies are germane to the successful implementation of a mass-market penetration strategy: product engineering and marketing skills, and the financial and organizational resources to expand capacity in advance of demand. In some cases, though, it is possible for a smaller firm with limited resources to successfully employ a mass-market penetration strategy if the market has a protracted adoption process and slow initial growth. Slow growth delays competitive entry because fewer competitors are attracted to a market where future growth appears to be questionable. This allows the pioneer more time to expand capacity. For example, even though Medtronic introduced heart pacemakers in 1960, it took nearly a decade for cardiologists to embrace the new technology in large numbers. Consequently, even though Medtronic was a small entrepreneurial firm, it could keep pace with the slow rate of volume growth and expand its capacity and product line sufficiently to maintain a leading position in the pacemaker industry.[9]

Even when a new product-market expands quickly, however, it may still be possible for a small firm with limited resources to be a successful pioneer. In such cases, however, the firm must define success in a more limited way. Instead of pursuing the objective of capturing and sustaining a leading share of the *entire* market, it may make more sense for such firms to focus their efforts on a single market segment. This **niche penetration** strategy can help the smaller pioneer gain the biggest bang for its limited bucks and yet avoid future direct confrontations with bigger and more accomplished competitors.

As Exhibit 19–9 suggests, a niche penetration strategy is most appropriate when the new market is expected to grow quickly and there are a number of different applications or benefit segments to appeal to. It is particularly attractive when there are few barriers to the entry of major competitors and when the pioneer has limited resources and competencies to defend any advantage it gains through early entry.

Stouffer is an example of this strategy. As the first to introduce high-quality, relatively expensive frozen entrees, the firm focused solely on the upscale, working adult segment of the market. Stouffer threw all available resources into expanding its product line, consumer advertising, and trade

---

[9] David H. Gobeli and William Rudelius, "Managing Innovation: Lessons from the Cardiac-Pacing Industry," *Sloan Management Review*, Summer 1985, pp. 29–43.

EXHIBIT 19 ◆ 9

Marketing objectives and strategies for new-product pioneers

Situational variables	Alternative marketing strategies		
	Mass-market penetration	Niche penetration	Skimming; early withdrawal
Market charac- teristics	◆ Large potential demand	◆ Large potential demand	◆ Limited potential de- mand
	◆ Relatively homoge- neous customer needs	◆ Fragmented market; many different applica- tions and benefit segments	◆ Customers likely to adopt product relatively slowly; long adoption process
	◆ Customers likely to adopt product relatively quickly; short diffusion process	◆ Customers likely to adopt product relatively quickly; short adoption process	◆ Early adopters willing to pay high price; demand is price inelastic
Product charac- teristics	◆ Product technology patentable or difficult to copy	◆ Product technology offers little patent pro- tection; easily copied or adapted	◆ Product technology offers little patent pro- tection; easily copied or adapted
	◆ Components or mate- rials difficult to obtain; limited sources of sup- ply	◆ Components or mate- rials easy to obtain; many sources of supply	◆ Components or mate- rials easy to obtain; many sources of supply
	◆ Complex production process; substantial de- velopment and/or investment required	◆ Relatively simple pro- duction process; little development or addi- tional investment required	◆ Relatively simple pro- duction process; little development or addi- tional investment required

promotion to obtain adequate shelf space; and all those efforts were focused on the singles segment. The firm has never attempted to expand into the higher volume (but lower margin) "quick, low-cost meals for the family" segment dominated by Swanson (a division of Campbell).[10]

Even when a firm has the resources and competencies necessary to sustain a leading position in a new product-market, it may choose not to. Competition is usually inevitable; and prices and margins tend to drop dramatically after followers enter the market. Some pioneers therefore opt for a **skimming** strategy while planning an early withdrawal from the market. This involves setting a high price for the new item and engaging in

---

[10] Kevin Higgins, "Meticulous Planning Pays Dividends at Stouffers," *Marketing News*, October 28, 1983, pp. 1, 20.

EXHIBIT 19 ◆ 9
(*concluded*)

Situational variables	Alternative marketing strategies		
	Mass-market penetration	**Niche penetration**	**Skimming; early withdrawal**
Competitor characteristics	◆ Few potential competitors	◆ Many potential competitors	◆ Many potential competitors
	◆ Most potential competitors have limited resources and competencies; few sources of differential advantage	◆ Some potential competitors have substantial resources and competencies; possible sources of differential advantage	◆ Some potential competitors have substantial resources and competencies; possible sources of differential advantage
Firm characteristics	◆ Strong product engineering skills; able to quickly develop product modifications and line extensions for multiple market segments	◆ Limited product engineering skills and resources	◆ Strong basic R&D and new-product development skills; a prospector with good capability for continued new-product innovation
	◆ Strong marketing skills and resources; ability to identify and develop marketing programs for multiple segments; ability to shift from stimulation of primary demand to stimulation of selective demand as competitors enter	◆ Limited marketing skills and resources	◆ Good sales and promotional skills; able to quickly build primary demand in target market; perhaps has limited marketing resources for long-term market maintenance
	◆ Sufficient financial and organizational resources to build capacity in advance of growth in demand	◆ Insufficient financial or organizational resources to build capacity in advance of growing demand	◆ Limited financial or organizational resources to commit to building capacity in advance of growth in demand

limited introductory advertising and promotion to maximize per-unit profits and recover development costs as quickly as possible. At the same time the firm may work to develop new applications for its technology, or the next generation of more advanced technology. Then when competitors enter the market and margins fall, the firm is ready to cannibalize its own product with one based on new technology or to move into new segments of the market.

The 3M Company is a master of the skimming strategy. According to one 3M manager, "We hit fast, price high (full economic value of the product to

EXHIBIT   19 ♦ 10

3M's skimming strategy in the casting tape market

> 3M developed the first water-activated synthetic casting tape to set broken bones in 1980, but by 1982 eight other companies had brought out copycat products. 3M's R&D people retreated to their labs and developed and tested 140 new versions in a variety of fabrics. In 1983, the firm dropped the old product and introduced a technically superior version that was stronger, easier to use, and commanded a premium price.

Source: Christopher Knowlton, "What America Makes Best," *Fortune,* March 28, 1988, p. 45.

the user), and get the heck out when the me-too products pour in." The new markets pioneered by 3M are often smaller ones of $10 to $50 million; and the firm may dominate them for only five years or so. By then it is ready to launch the next generation of new technology or to move the old technology into new applications.[11] An example of 3M's approach is described in Exhibit 19–10.

As Exhibit 19–9 indicates, skimming and early withdrawal can be used by either small or large firms. It is critical that the company have good R&D and product development skills so it can produce a constant stream of new products or new applications to replace older ones as they attract heavy competition. A firm pursuing this strategy plans to stay in a market only for the short term. Therefore it is most appropriate when there are few barriers to entry, the product is expected to diffuse rapidly, and the pioneer lacks the capacity or other resources necessary to defend a leading share position over the long haul.

Objectives of alternative pioneer strategies

Exhibit 19–11 outlines both the long-term and short-term strategic objectives that should be focused on by pioneers pursuing mass-market, niche penetration, or skimming strategies.

The long-term objective of a mass-market penetration strategy is to gain and hold a leading share of the new product-market throughout its growth and perhaps to even preempt competitors from entering the market. The short-term objective should be to maximize the number of customers adopting the new product as quickly as possible.

Both the short- and long-term objectives of a niche penetration strategy are largely the same as those of a mass-market penetration strategy. The one essential difference is that a firm pursuing a niche strategy tries to capture

---

[11] George S. Day, *Analysis for Strategic Marketing Decisions* (St. Paul: West Publishing, 1986), pp. 103–4.

EXHIBIT   19♦11

Objectives of strategic marketing programs for pioneers

Strategic objectives	Alternative strategic marketing programs		
	Mass-market penetration	Niche penetration	Skimming; early withdrawal
Short-term objectives	♦ Maximize number of triers and adopters in total market; invest heavily to build future volume and share.	♦ Maximize number of triers and adopters in target segment; limited investment to build volume and share in chosen niche.	♦ Obtain as many adopters as possible with limited investment; maintain high margins to recoup product development and commercialization costs as soon as possible.
Long-term objectives	♦ Attempt to preempt competition; maintain leading share position even if some sacrifice of margins is necessary in short-term as new competitors enter	♦ Maintain leading share position in target segment even if some sacrifice of short-term margins is necessary.	♦ Maximize ROI; withdraw from market when increasing competition puts downward pressure on margins.

and maintain a leading share of one or a few narrow segments rather than diffusing its limited resources across the entire market.

Finally, the long-term objective of a skimming strategy is to maximize returns before competitors enter the market. When increasing competition begins to reduce profit margins, many firms withdraw—by introducing a new generation of products or by moving to other markets or product categories. Thus, the short-term objective should be to gain as much volume as possible while simultaneously maintaining high margins to recoup development expenses and to generate profits quickly.

Marketing program components for a mass-market penetration strategy

As mentioned, the short-term objective of a mass-market penetration strategy is to maximize the number of customers adopting the new product as quickly as possible. This requires a marketing program focused on *(a) aggressively building product awareness and motivation to buy* among a broad cross section of potential customers, and *(b) making it as easy as possible for those customers to try the new product* (on the assumption that they will try it, like it, develop loyalty, and make repeat purchases). Exhibit 19–12 out-

EXHIBIT   19 ♦ 12
Components of strategic marketing programs for pioneers

Strategic objectives and tasks	Alternative strategic marketing programs		
	Mass-market penetration	Niche penetration	Skimming; early withdrawal
Increase customers' awareness and willingness to buy	♦ Heavy advertising to generate awareness among customers in mass market; broad use of mass media.	♦ Heavy advertising directed at target segment to generate awareness; use selective media relevant to target.	♦ Limited advertising to generate awareness, particularly among least price sensitive early adopters.
	♦ Extensive salesforce efforts to win new adopters; possible use of incentives to encourage new-product sales.	♦ Extensive salesforce efforts focused on potential customers in target segment; possible use of incentives to encourage new-product sales to target accounts.	♦ Extensive salesforce efforts, particularly focused on largest potential adopters; possible use of volume-based incentives to encourage new-product sales.
	♦ Advertising and sales appeals stress generic benefits of new-product type.	♦ Advertising and sales appeals stress generic benefits of new-product type.	♦ Advertising and sales appeals stress generic benefits of new-product type.
	♦ Extensive introductory sales promotions to induce trial (sampling, couponing, quantity discounts).	♦ Extensive introductory sales promotions to induce trial, but focused on target segment.	♦ Limited use, if any, of introductory sales promotions; if used, they should be volume-based quantity discounts.
	♦ Move relatively quickly to expand offerings (line extensions, multiple package sizes) to appeal to multiple segments.	♦ Additional product development limited to improvements or modifications to increase appeal to target segment.	♦ Little, if any, additional development within the product category.
	♦ Offer free trial, liberal return, or extended warranty policies to reduce customers' perceived risk of adopting the new product.	♦ Offer free trial, liberal return, or extended warranty policies to reduce target customers' perceived risk of adopting the new product.	♦ Offer free trial, liberal return, or extended warranty policies to reduce target customers' perceived risk of adopting the new product.

EXHIBIT   19 ◆ 12

(concluded)

Strategic objectives and tasks	Alternative strategic marketing programs		
	Mass-market penetration	Niche penetration	Skimming; early withdrawal
Increase customers' ability to buy	◆ Penetration pricing; or start with high price but bring out lower-priced versions in anticipation of competitive entries.	◆ Penetration pricing, or start with high price but bring out lower-priced versions in anticipation of competitive entries.	◆ Skimming pricing; attempt to maintain margins at level consistent with value of product to early adopters.
	◆ Extended credit terms to encourage initial puchases.	◆ Extended credit terms to encourage initial purchases.	◆ Extended credit terms to encourage initial purchases.
	◆ Heavy use of trade promotions aimed at gaining extensive distribution.	◆ Trade promotions aimed at gaining solid distribution among retailers or distributors pertinent for reaching target segment.	◆ Limited use of trade promotions; only as necessary to gain adequate distribution.
	◆ Offer engineering, installation, and training services to increase new product's compatibility with customers' current operations to reduce "switching costs."	◆ Offer engineering, installation, and training services to increase new product's compatibility with customers' current operations to reduce "switching costs."	◆ Offer limited engineering, installation, and services as necessary to overcome customers' objections.

lines a number of marketing program activities in each of the 4Ps that might help increase customers' awareness and willingness to buy or improve their ability to try the product. This is by no means an exhaustive list; nor do we mean to imply that a successful pioneer must necessarily engage in all of the listed activities. Marketing managers must develop programs combining activities that fit both the objectives of a mass-market penetration strategy and the specific market and potential competitive conditions faced by the new product.

Increasing customers' awareness and willingness to buy

Obviously, heavy expenditures on advertising, introductory promotions such as sampling and couponing, and personal selling efforts can all increase *awareness* of the new product among potential customers. This is the critical first step in the adoption process for a new entry.[12] The relative importance of these promotional tools varies, however, depending on the nature of the product and the number of potential customers. We saw in Chapter 16, for instance, that personal selling efforts are often the most critical component of the promotional mix for highly technical industrial products with a limited potential customer base. Media advertising and sales promotion are usually more useful for building awareness and primary demand for a new consumer good among customers in the mass market. In either case, when designing a mass-market penetration marketing program, the promotional efforts should be broadly focused to expose and attract as many potential customers as possible before competitors show up.

Firms might also attempt to increase customers' willingness to buy their products by reducing the risk they associate with buying something new. This can be done by letting customers try the product without obligation (as when car dealers allow potential customers to test-drive a new model), or by committing to liberal return or extended warranty policies for the product. When Lee Iacocca took over Chrysler, for instance, he decreed that all new car models should be introduced with the longest warranties in the industry to overcome the low-quality image of Chrysler products in the minds of potential customers.

Finally, a firm committed to mass-market penetration might also devote a lot of effort to broadening its product offerings to increase its appeal to as many market segments as possible. This would reduce its vulnerability to later entrants who could focus on specific market niches. It can be done through the rapid introduction of line extensions, product modifications, and additional package sizes.

Increasing customers' ability to buy

For customers to adopt a new product and develop loyalty toward it, they must be aware of the item and be motivated to buy. But they must also have the wherewithal to actually purchase it. Thus, to capture as many customers as soon as possible, a firm pursuing mass-market penetration will keep prices low (penetration pricing)—and perhaps offer liberal financing arrangements or easy credit terms during the introductory period.

Another factor that can inhibit customers' ability to buy is a simple lack of product availability. Extensive personal selling and trade promotions aimed at gaining adequate distribution are usually a critical part of a mass-market penetration marketing program. Such efforts should take place *before* the start of promotional campaigns—to ensure that the product is available as soon as customers are motivated to buy it.

---

[12] The following discussion builds on the literature concerning diffusion and adoption processes for new products. See the discussion in Chapter 13.

One factor that can inhibit the purchase of highly technical new products is that they may be incompatible with other related products or systems currently used by the customer. For example, many firms have been reluctant to buy Apple's Macintosh computers because they have made large investments in IBM software, which cannot be used with the Apple system; and their employees would have to be retrained to use the new system. In other words, a new product's lack of compatibility with other elements of an existing system can result in high switching costs for a potential adopter. The pioneer might reduce those costs by designing the product to be as compatible as possible with related equipment. It can also offer engineering services to help make the new product more compatible with existing operations, provide free installation assistance, and conduct training programs for the customer's employees.

Marketing program components for a niche penetration strategy

Because both the short- and long-term objectives are similar for niche and mass-market companies, the marketing program elements pursued by a niche penetrator are also likely to be similar to those discussed above for a mass-market penetration strategy. However, the niche penetrator should keep all of its marketing efforts clearly focused on the target segment to gain as much impact as possible from a limited budget. This point is clearly evident in the outline of program components in Exhibit 19–12. For example, although the same advertising, sales promotion, personal selling, and trade promotion activities are called for as in a mass-market program, more *selective* media, call schedules, and channel designs can direct those activities toward the target segment.

Marketing program components for a skimming strategy

As Exhibit 19–12 suggests, one major difference between a skimming strategy and a penetration strategy involves pricing policies. A relatively high price is appropriate for a skimming strategy to increase margins and revenues—even though some more price-sensitive customers may be reluctant to adopt the product at that price.[13] Introductory promotions then might best focus on customer groups who are least price sensitive and most likely to be early adopters of the new product. This can help hold down promotion costs and avoid wasting marketing efforts on less profitable segments. In many consumer goods businesses, a skimming strategy should focus on relatively upscale customer groups, who are often more likely to be early adopters and less price sensitive.

---

[13] This assumes that demand is relatively price inelastic. In markets where price elasticity is high, a skimming price strategy may lead to *lower* total revenues due to its dampening effect on total demand. See our discussion of price elasticity in Chapter 14.

Another critical element of a skimming strategy is the nature of the firm's continuing product development efforts. A pioneer that plans to leave a market when competitors enter should not devote much effort to expanding its product line through line extensions or multiple package sizes. Instead, it should concentrate on preparing the next generation of technology or on identifying new application segments; in other words, preparing its avenue of escape from the market.

Now that we have examined the strategies a pioneer might follow in entering a new market, we are left with two important strategic questions. Because the pioneer is by definition the early share leader in the new market, the first question is, What adjustments in strategy might be necessary for the pioneer to *maintain its leading share position* after competitors arrive on the scene? The second question is, What strategies might followers adopt to take business away from the early leader and *increase their relative share position* as the market grows? These two strategic issues are the focus of the next chapter.

SUMMARY

Not all new products are equally new. Only about 10 percent of the new-product introductions made by U.S. companies involve new-to-the-world products, truly new to both the company and the target customers. Many new entries—such as line extensions or modifications—are new to the customers in the target market but are relatively familiar to the company. Other new entries—new product lines, extensions of an existing line, or cost reductions—may be quite new to the company but not to the target customers. The firm that introduces products new to the target market must *build primary demand* by making potential customers aware of the new product and stimulating their willingness and ability to buy.

The primary objective of most new market entries is to secure future volume and profit growth for the firm. However, individual market development efforts often accomplish other secondary objectives as well: maintaining the firm's position as a product innovator; defending a current market share position in an industry; establishing a foothold in a future new market; preempting a market segment; or exploiting technology in a new way. Top management must clearly specify new-market entry objec-

tives for each SBU. If a prospector SBU's new entry objectives are to maintain a position as a product innovator and establish footholds in many new markets, its most appropriate new entry strategy is to be the *pioneer*—or first entrant—in as many new product-markets as possible. But if the SBU wants to defend a strong market share position, it often adopts a *follower* strategy whereby it enters new product-markets later and relies on superior product quality, better customer service, or lower prices to offset the pioneer's early lead.

Both pioneer and follower strategies offer unique potential sources of competitive advantage. A pioneering strategy is most likely to lead to long-term share leadership and profitability when the new market is insulated from the entry of competitors due to patent protection, proprietary technology, or other barriers, or when the pioneer has sufficient marketing resources and competence to maintain its early lead against competitive attacks. Pioneers are most likely to maintain their early market share lead when they can enter the new market on a large scale, quickly add line extensions, offer and sustain high product quality, and support their product introduction with heavy promotional expenditures. Followers are most successful when they can enter the market on a larger scale and attain lower per-unit costs than the pioneer, or when they can leapfrog the pioneer by offering a superior product or better service.

Alternative strategic marketing programs that are appropriate for a pioneer include a *mass-market penetration* strategy, a *niche penetration* strategy, or a *skimming* strategy. A mass-market penetration strategy aims at getting as many potential customers as possible to try the new product and develop brand loyalty before competitors can enter. The pioneer must maximize customers' *awareness* and increase their *willingness to buy* and their *ability to buy*. These actions require substantial resources, making a mass-market strategy most appropriate for larger businesses or when barriers slow competitive entry.

Pioneers with limited resources are better off adopting a niche penetration strategy. The marketing objectives and actions of a niche strategy are similar to penetration; but they focus on a smaller peripheral segment of customers where fewer resources are needed to defend the pioneer's early lead.

Finally, some technological leaders, particularly those pursuing a prospector strategy, may prefer to enter many new markets, attain as much profit as possible before competitors enter, and then withdraw as competition increases and margins erode. A skimming strategy incorporating relatively high prices and low marketing expenditures is appropriate for such firms.

QUESTIONS

1. Minnetonka, Inc., is a relatively small firm that has pioneered the development of consumer health and beauty products—such as Softsoap and Check-Up plaque-fighting toothpaste—over recent years. What potential advantages does being the pioneer in new product-markets provide a firm like Minnetonka in an industry dominated by giants such as Procter & Gamble and Colgate-Palmolive?

2. Not all new-market pioneers effectively take advantage of the potential benefits inherent in their early lead. What does the research evidence suggest that Minnetonka should do relevant to major elements of its marketing strategy to gain and maintain a leading share position in the new markets it enters?

3. Unfortunately, Minnetonka, Inc., has historically been one of those pioneers unable to sustain its early lead in many of the markets it enters. The firm's Check-Up toothpaste, for example, now trails both Crest and Colgate's plaque-fighting brands by a wide margin. What strategic factors might account for Procter & Gamble's and Colgate-Palmolive's success at capturing strong market shares as followers in the plaque-fighting toothpaste market?

4. Given the information contained in questions 1, 2, and 3, which business strategy does Minnetonka, Inc., appear to have been pursuing in recent years? Does its inability to maintain its early lead in new product-markets suggest its strategy should be changed? Why or why not?

5. With the exception of certain core businesses—such as adhesives and information storage technology—the 3M Company has often followed a strategy of withdrawing from markets in which it was the pioneer after other competitors enter and profit margins start to decline. It typically does this by licensing products to other firms. Under what kinds of market and competitive situations is such a withdrawal strategy most appropriate? What kinds of products do you think 3M is most likely to license to other firms?

6. For 3M to profitably implement a strategy of "skimming and early withdrawal" in a particular new product-market, what spe-

cific marketing objectives should it pursue in that market? What marketing actions would be appropriate for achieving those objectives?

7. When Frito-Lay introduced Grandma's soft cookies into a Kansas City test market, it fully expected—assuming the test market results were positive—to introduce the product to the national market with a mass-market penetration strategy. Given the information concerning the Grandma's product, the cookie market, and the competitive situation discussed in Chapter 2, did such a strategy make sense at the time?

8. Nabisco was a follower in the soft-cookie market. Its Almost Home line was not introduced for nearly a year after Grandma's and Duncan Hines. What marketing actions did Nabisco take that were consistent with a mass-market penetration strategy and that ultimately enabled Almost Home to capture the leading share of the soft-cookie market?

9. Sun Computer is a relatively small firm by computer industry standards. It has been very successful at capturing a substantial—and profitable—share of the market for specialized midsized computer systems used for computer-assisted design and engineering applications. Given the characteristics of the computer industry, do you think Sun's niche penetration strategy appropriate? Why or why not?

Chapter 20

Strategies for growth markets

WHO'S AFRAID OF IBM? THE BATTLE OVER THE GROWING COMMERCIAL PC MARKET

In the last chapter, we saw that International Business Machines Corporation has pursued very aggressive goals for future growth and has devoted substantial resources to the development of new products and markets.[1] However, while IBM has often been a pioneer in the sense of developing new applications and market segments for its equipment, the firm has not always been the technological leader in the computer industry. In some cases, IBM has followed smaller technological innovators into new-product categories and relied on superior product design, lower manufacturing costs, and more extensive promotion, sales, and customer service to capture a commanding share as those categories have grown. This was the case in the micro or personal computer category where several smaller competitors—such as Apple® and Atari®—were already established before IBM introduced its PC in 1981. Nevertheless, IBM's superior resources, including its marketing prowess, enabled it to capture an estimated 52 percent share of the worldwide sales of personal computers by 1983.

Although IBM was a follower in the introduction of the PC, it was a pioneer in the development of one major customer segment for such machines—business users. The notion of giving individual managers their own PCs did not really catch on until IBM's huge direct salesforce began promoting it to executives in large corporations and some business software packages—such as Lotus® 1-2-3®—were developed for IBM's PC. The business market for PCs grew at a rate of about 40 percent per year into the mid-1980s, and IBM captured the lion's share of that business.

IBM's success in the business market for PCs began to slip a bit, however, beginning in 1984. For one thing, although market growth continued to be healthy, it was slower than in the early years. Analysts estimated market growth to be about 10 percent worldwide in 1987. This slower growth and the entry of many smaller competitors combined to make the battle for market share more intense during the mid-1980s. As a result, IBM saw its share of the U.S. commercial market for PCs slip

---

[1] Based on Marilyn A. Harris, "IBM: More Worlds to Conquer," *Business Week*, February 18, 1985, pp. 84–98; "How IBM Is Fighting Back," *Business Week*, November 17, 1986, pp. 152–57; "Apple's Comeback," *Business Week*, January 19, 1987, pp. 84–89; Carol J. Loomis, "IBM's Big Blues: A Legend Tries to Remake Itself," *Fortune*, January 19, 1987, pp. 34–54; and "Who's Afraid of IBM?" *Business Week*, June 29, 1987, pp. 68–74.

continued

to slightly above 30 percent by 1986. Much of this decline was caused by the popularity of IBM clones—machines that performed at the same level and ran the same software as the IBM PC at a fraction of the cost. Small clone manufacturers undercut IBM's prices by buying standardized components from foreign suppliers, assembling their machines in offshore plants in low-wage countries such as Taiwan, avoiding high sales and marketing costs by using independent retailers or direct mail to generate sales, and offering little if any postsale service. A number of these firms wrested small shares of commercial PC volume away from the market leader. Apple, however, did not pursue this kind of low-cost competitive strategy, but successfully built its share of the business market at IBM's expense.

Apple—competing with differentiation and niche strategies

The original Apple II had neither the computing power nor a sufficient library of business software to attract major corporate customers. After IBM's success demonstrated the growth potential of the business market, however, Apple made several attempts to win a share of that business by introducing more powerful machines. Rather than attempting to compete head-to-head, however, Apple decided to leapfrog IBM. It designed the Macintosh with an entirely different operating system that appealed to business users by being more user friendly than other machines. Apple also implored leading software companies to write more extensive business software for the Mac.

And it developed an "open Mac" that can use the IBM PC software that many firms already have. Finally, the firm beefed up its sales and marketing efforts in the business market. While it continued to rely on independent computer retailers, such as Businessland, to sell its machines, Apple took a half-step toward a direct salesforce by placing 40 missionary salespeople around the country to help pair up retail dealers with large potential customers. It also created a 30-person government sales group to pursue the $1.6 billion federal microcomputer market.

Winning over established IBM customers was slow-going at first, so Apple focused extra efforts on specialized segments with needs that the Macintosh could satisfy better than IBM's PC. One such application segment was desktop publishing. In 1986 alone, Apple sold some 50,000 Macintosh publishing systems. Sales of the accompanying laser printers added another $150 million to Apple's revenues.

Apple's efforts to differentiate its machines technologically and to pursue underdeveloped market niches began to pay off, as Exhibit 20–1 shows. By 1986, Macintosh had captured a 7.5 percent share of all personal computer sales to U.S. commercial customers, and increased its earnings by more than 150 percent.

IBM strikes back

IBM, of course, did not sit idly by while competitors chipped away at its dominant position in the commercial PC market. The firm fought back in several ways: First, it embarked on an exten-

concluded

EXHIBIT **20 ♦ 1**

The results of Apple's strategy to capture an increased share of the commercial PC market

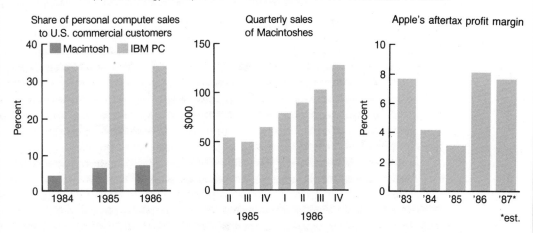

Source: Data from Goldman, Sachs & Co. estimates, Infocorp, and company reports.

Apple revived the Macintosh by concentrating on sales to business, and this helped its margins to bounce back.

sive cost-cutting campaign to help meet the threat of the cheaper clones. This involved improving the efficiency of its production processes and shifting 2,800 headquarters staffers back to branch sales offices. Second, IBM expanded its direct salesforce to a total of 10,000 people—twice as many as any other computer company—by reassigning personnel. It also reorganized that salesforce along industry lines to enable salespeople to become more familiar and maintain closer contact with customers in specific application segments. For example, one sales group concentrates on finance and brokerage firms in New York, while another focuses on the automobile manufacturers in Detroit.

Finally, the firm rushed the development of a new generation of PCs using a more advanced proprietary technology: the PS/2 line. It hoped that the greater power, expanded graphics capabilities, and improved user-friendliness of the new machines would win back customers from both Macintosh and the clones. IBM also anticipated that the proprietary technology of the PS/2 would make it more difficult for small competitors to make low-cost clones of the new equipment. Because the new line required a new generation of software, however, IBM risked losing some customers of its older equipment who might be reluctant to throw out their existing software to convert to the new system.

STRATEGIC ISSUES IN GROWTH MARKETS

IBM's experience in the commercial PC market, where it had to fight harder just to hold onto its leading position in the face of increasingly intense competition, is common to many firms. As we saw in Chapter 8, product-markets in the growth stage of their life cycles usually attract many competitive followers. Both conventional wisdom and the various portfolio models suggest that there are advantages inherent in quickly entering—and investing heavily to build share in—growth markets. But a market is neither inherently attractive nor unattractive simply because it promises rapid future growth. Managers must consider how the market and competitive situation in a product-market is likely to evolve, and whether their firms can exploit the rapid growth opportunities to establish a competitive advantage. The next section of this chapter examines both the market opportunities and the competitive risks often found in growing product-markets.

The primary strategic objective of the early share leader (who is usually the market pioneer) in a growth market is **share maintenance.** From a marketing view, the firm must accomplish two important tasks: (a) retain repeat or replacement business from its existing customers; and (b) continue to capture the major portion of sales to the growing number of new customers entering the market for the first time. As shown by IBM's actions in the commercial PC market, the leader might use any one—or a combination—of several marketing strategies to accomplish these marketing objectives. It can reduce its prices, make product improvements, expand its product line to appeal to newly emerging segments such as desktop publishing, and increase its marketing and sales efforts. The third section of this chapter explores strategic marketing programs—both defensive and offensive—that leaders might use to maintain market share in the face of rapid market growth and increasing competition.

A challenger's strategic objective in a growth market is usually to *build its share* by expanding its sales faster than the overall market growth rate. Firms do this by attracting existing customers away from the leader or other competitors, capturing a larger share of new customers than the market leader, or both. Once again, the history of the commercial market for PCs shows that challengers might use a number of strategies to accomplish these objectives. These include developing a superior product technology as attempted by Apple with its Macintosh, differentiating through product modification or line extensions as illustrated by Compaq, offering lower prices à la the IBM clones, or focusing on market niches where the leader is not well established, as Apple did in the desktop publishing segment. The fourth section details these and other **share-growth** strategies used by market challengers under different conditions.

The success of a firm's strategy during the growth stage is a critical determinant of its ability to reap profits—or even survive—as a product-market moves into maturity. Unfortunately, the growth stage is often short;

and increasingly rapid technological change and market fragmentation are causing it to become even shorter in many industries.[2] This shortening of the growth stage is of concern to many firms—particularly late entrants or those who fail to acquire a substantial market share—because as growth begins to slow during the transition to maturity, there is often a shakeout of marginal competitors. In the PC industry, for example, there were an estimated 150 manufacturers and another 300 or so firms producing add-on products, software, services, and support in 1982.[3] As the industry growth rate began to slow during 1984–85, a vast majority of those firms—including some very large companies such as Texas Instruments—failed, abandoned the industry, or were acquired by larger competitors. Thus, a manager's choice of marketing strategies for competing in a growing product-market should be made with at least one eye on building a competitive advantage that the business can sustain after growth slows and the market matures.

OPPORTUNITIES AND RISKS IN GROWTH MARKETS[4]

Why are followers attracted to rapidly growing markets? Conventional wisdom suggests that such markets present attractive opportunities for future profits because:

* It is easier to gain share when a market is growing.
* Share gains are worth more in a growth market than in a mature market.
* Price competition is likely to be less intense.
* Early participation in a growth market is necessary to make sure that the firm keeps pace with the technology.

Each of these propositions may be valid in general, but can be seriously misleading for a particular business in a specific situation. Many followers attracted to a market by its rapid growth rate are likely to be shaken out later when that growth slows, either because the preceding premises did not hold or they could not exploit growth advantages sufficiently to build a sustainable competitive position. By understanding the limitations of the assumptions about growth markets and the conditions under which they are most likely to hold, a manager can make better decisions about entering a market and the kind of marketing strategy likely to be most effective in doing so.

---

[2] Hans B. Thorelli and S. C. Burnett, "The Nature of Product Life Cycles for Industrial Goods Businesses," *Journal of Marketing*, Fall 1981, pp. 102–7.

[3] "The Coming Shakeout in Personal Computers," *Business Week*, November 22, 1982, pp. 72–78.

[4] For a more extensive discussion of the potential opportunities and pitfalls of rapidly growing markets, see: David A. Aaker and George S. Day, "The Perils of High Growth Markets," *Strategic Management Journal* 7 (1986), pp. 409–21; and George S. Day, *Analysis for Strategic Market Decisions* (St. Paul: West Publishing, 1986), chap. 4.

Gaining share is easier

The premise that it is easier for a business to increase its share in a growing market is based on two arguments: First, many new users are entering the market for the first time, and they have no established brand loyalties or supplier commitments. It is easier, then, for a new competitor to attract those users than to convert customers in a mature market. Second, established competitors are less likely to react aggressively to market share erosion as long as their sales continue to grow at a satisfactory rate.

There is some truth to the first argument. It usually *is* easier for a new entrant to attract first-time users than to take business away from entrenched competitors. To take full advantage of the situation, however, the new entrant must be able to develop a product offering that new customers perceive as more attractive than other alternatives, and it must have the marketing resources and competence to effectively persuade them of that fact. For instance, it took Apple three years and millions of dollars in marketing effort to overcome IBM's superior brand reputation and to begin to capture an increasing share of commercial PC customers for its Macintosh.

The notion that established competitors are less likely to react to share losses so long as their revenues are growing at an acceptable rate is more tenuous. It overlooks the fact that those competitors may have higher expectations for increased revenues when the market itself is growing. Capital investments and annual operating budgets are usually tied to those sales expectations; therefore, competitors are likely to react aggressively when sales fall below expected levels, whether or not their absolute volumes continue to grow. This is particularly true given that the leader's relative market share is likely to fall in the face of increased competition, even though its volume may continue to increase. As illustrated by the hypothetical example in Exhibit 20–2, the leader's market share drops from a high of 100 percent at the beginning of the growth stage to only 50 percent by the maturity stage, even though the firm's absolute volume shows steady growth.

Industry leaders often react forcefully when their sales growth falls below industry levels and their relative market share shows a substantial decline. For example, IBM's objective for the PC market was to equal or exceed the growth rate for the overall market. Thus, when the firm's revenue growth fell below the industry rate and its relative market share declined, IBM took aggressive actions—such as reducing prices and introducing the new PS/2 line—even though its absolute sales volume was still increasing.

Share gains are worth more in growth markets

The premise that share gains are more valuable when the market is growing stems from the expectation that the earnings produced by each share point continue to expand as the market expands. The implicit assumption in this

EXHIBIT 20 ◆2

Market shares of leader and followers over the life cycle of a hypothetical market

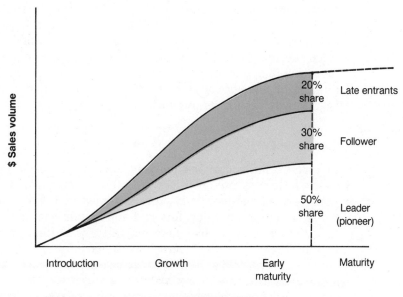

Source: Adapted from George S. Day, *Analysis for Strategic Market Decisions* (St. Paul: West Publishing, 1986), p. 100.

argument, of course, is that the business can hold its relative share as the market grows. The validity of such an assumption depends on a number of factors, including:

◆ *Future changes in technology or other key success factors.* If the rules of the game change, the competencies a firm relied on to capture share may no longer be adequate to maintain that share. A critical question in the commercial PC market, for example, is whether Compaq will continue to be successful following IBM's introduction of its new PS/2 computers. Compaq gained share by offering IBM-compatible machines with features or performance levels better than IBM's, but "Big Blue's" new proprietary technology makes it more difficult for Compaq to offer machines using IBM software.

◆ *Future competitive structure of the industry.* The number of firms that ultimately decide to compete for a share of the market may turn out to be larger than the early entrants anticipate, particularly if there are few barriers to entry. The sheer weight of numbers can make it difficult for any single competitor to maintain a substantial relative share of the total market.

◆ *Future fragmentation of the market.* As the market expands, it may fragment into numerous small segments, particularly if potential customers have relatively heterogeneous functional, distribution, or service needs. When such fragmentation occurs, the market in which a given competitor competes may shrink as segments are splintered away. The Macintosh desktop publishing package dealt a severe blow to IBM's ability to attract or hold customers in the publishing industry.

In addition to these possible changes in future market conditions, a firm's ability to hold its early gains in market share also depends on *how* those gains are obtained. If a firm captures share through short-term promotions or price cuts that can easily be matched by competitors and that may tarnish its image among customers, its gains may be short-lived. Witness the large number of manufacturers of IBM clones that failed once IBM reacted by aggressively cutting its own prices.

Price competition is likely to be less intense

In many rapidly growing markets, demand exceeds supply. The market exerts little pressure on prices initially; the excess demand may even support a price premium. Early entry provides a good opportunity to recover a firm's initial product development and commercialization investment relatively quickly. New customers may also be willing to pay a premium for technical service as they learn how to make full use of the new product. In contrast, as the market matures and customers gain more experience, the premium a firm can charge without losing market share slowly shrinks; it may eventually disappear if customers no longer perceive a meaningful value difference among competitors.[5]

However, this scenario does not hold true in every developing product-market. If there are few barriers to entry, or if the adoption process is protracted and new customers enter the market at a slow rate, demand may not exceed supply—at least not for very long. Also, the pioneer (or one of the earliest followers) might adopt a penetration strategy and set its initial prices relatively low to move down the experience curve as fast as possible or discourage other potential competitors from entering the market.

Early entry is necessary to maintain technical expertise

In high-tech industries many managers believe that early involvement in new-product categories is critical for staying abreast of technology. They feel that the early experience gained in developing and producing the first generation of products, and in helping customers apply the new technology, can put the firm in a strong position for developing the next generation of superior products. Later entrants, lacking such customer contact and production and R&D experience, are likely to be at a disadvantage.

In many cases, there is substantial wisdom in these arguments. Sometimes, however, an early commitment to a specific technology can turn out

---

[5] Irwin Gross, "Insights from Pricing Research," *Pricing Practices and Strategies* (New York: The Conference Board, 1979).

to be a liability. This is particularly true where a market might be served by multiple unrelated technologies, or when a newly emerging technology might replace the current one. Once a firm is committed to one technology, adopting a new one can be difficult. Management is often reluctant to abandon a technology in which it has made substantial investments, and it might worry that a rapid shift to a new technology will upset present customers. As a result, early commitment to a technology has become increasingly problematic in recent years due to the rapid rate of change in many growth industries and the shortening of technological life cycles.

The dangers inherent in being overly committed to an early technology are illustrated by Medtronic, the pioneer in the cardiac pacemaker industry. Medtronic waited too long to switch to a new lithium-based technology that enabled pacemakers to work much longer before being replaced. As a result, several Medtronic employees left the company and founded Cardiac Pacemakers, Inc., to produce and market the new lithium-based product. They quickly captured nearly 20 percent of the total market.[6] And Medtronic saw its share of the cardiac pacemaker market fall quickly from nearly 70 percent to 40 percent.

GROWTH MARKET STRATEGIES FOR MARKET LEADERS

For the share leader in a growing market, of course, the question of the relative advantages versus risks of market entry is a moot point. The leader is typically the pioneer—or at least one of the first entrants—who developed the product-market in the first place. Its strategic objective is to maintain its leading relative share in the face of increasing competition as the market expands. Share maintenance may not seem like a very aggressive objective, because it implies that the business is merely trying to stay even rather than forging ahead. But two important facts must be kept in mind: First, the dynamics of a growth market are such that simply maintaining a leading relative share position is usually a major challenge. The increasing number of competitors, the fragmentation of market segments, and the threat of product innovation from within and outside the industry make maintaining an early lead in relative market share very difficult.[7] The continuing need for investment to finance growth, the likely negative cash flows that result, and the threat of governmental antitrust action also make it difficult. For instance, even though Medtronic still holds the leading *relative share in the pacemaker market, the odds that it can ever recapture an absolute* share as large as the 70 percent held in the early days are very slim.

---

[6] Daniel H. Gobeli and William Rudelius, "Managing Innovation: Insights from the Cardiac-Pacing Industry," *Sloan Management Review* (Summer 1985), pp. 29–43.

[7] Philip Kotler and Paul N. Bloom, "Strategies for High Market-Share Companies," *Harvard Business Review*, November–December 1975, pp. 63–72.

This example also illustrates the second point: Share maintenance in a *growth market* means that the leader's sales volume must continue to grow at a rate equal to that of the overall market for the firm to stay even with its absolute market share. It may, however, be able to maintain a relative share lead even if its volume growth is less than the industry's.

Marketing objectives for share leaders

Share maintenance for a market leader involves two important marketing objectives: First, the firm must *retain its current customers*, to ensure that those customers remain brand loyal when they make repeat or replacement purchases. This is particularly critical for firms in consumer nondurable, service, and industrial materials and components industries where a substantial portion of total sales volume consists of repeat purchases. The second objective is to *stimulate selective demand among later adopters* to ensure that the leader continues to capture a large share—perhaps even an increased share—of the continuing growth in industry sales.

In some cases the market leader might pursue a third objective—namely, stimulating primary demand to help speed up overall market growth. This can be particularly important in product-markets where the adoption process is protracted due to the technical sophistication of the new product or high switching costs for potential customers.

The market leader is the logical one to stimulate market growth in such situations. Its large relative market share means that it has the most to gain from increased volume—assuming, of course, that it can maintain its relative share of that volume. However, expanding total demand—by promoting new uses for the product or stimulating existing customers' usage and repeat purchase rates—is often more critical near the end of the growth and early in the maturity stages of a product's life cycle. Consequently, we discuss marketing actions appropriate to this objecive in the next chapter.

Marketing actions and strategies to achieve share maintenance objectives

A business might take a variety of marketing actions to maintain a leading share position in a growing market. Exhibit 20–3 (page 708) outlines a lengthy though by no means exhaustive list of such actions and the specific marketing objectives each is best suited to help accomplish. Because share maintenance involves multiple objectives, and different marketing actions may be needed to achieve each one, a strategic marketing program usually integrates a mix of the actions outlined in the exhibit.

Not all of the actions outlined in Exhibit 20–3 fit or are consistent with one another. It would be fairly unusual, for instance, for a business to invest heavily in product improvements and promotion to enhance its product's high-quality image and simultaneously slash prices—unless it was trying to drive out weaker competitors in the short run with an eye on higher profits in the future. Thus, the activities outlined in Exhibit 20–3 cluster into five internally consistent strategies that a market leader might employ, singly or in combination, to maintain its leading share position: *a fortress or position defense strategy; a flanker strategy; a confrontation strategy; a market expansion or mobile strategy; and a contraction or strategic withdrawal strategy.* Exhibit 20–4 (page 710) diagrams this set of strategies. It is consistent with what a number of military strategies and some marketing authorities have identified as common defensive strategies.[8] To think of them as strictly defensive, though, can be misleading. Companies can use some of these strategies offensively to preempt expected future actions by potential competitors. Or they can improve the leader's ability to capture an even larger share of new customers who may enter the market in the future.

Which—or what combination—of these five strategies is most appropriate in a particular product-market depends as always on (a) the market's size and its customers' characteristics; (b) the number and relative strengths of the competitors or potential competitors in that market; and (c) the leader's own resources and competencies. Exhibit 20–5 (page 711) outlines the situations where each strategy is most appropriate, and the primary objectives for which they are best suited.

Fortress or position defense strategy

The most basic defensive strategy is to continually strengthen a strongly held current position—to build an impregnable fortress capable of repelling attacks by current or future competitors. This strategy is nearly always at least a part of a leader's share maintenance efforts. By shoring up an already strong position, the firm can improve the satisfaction of current customers and reduce their likelihood of switching to a competitor. At the same time it increases the attractiveness of its offering to new customers with needs and characteristics similar to adopters already using the firm's product.

Strengthening the firm's current position, then, makes particularly good sense when current and potential customers have relatively homogeneous needs and desires and the firm's offering already enjoys a high level of awareness and preference in the mass market. In some homogeneous markets a well-implemented position defense strategy may be all that is needed for share maintenance. This is particularly true if the leader commands more R&D and marketing resources and competencies than its current or potential competitors. Firms in this fortunate position have the luxury of taking a

---

[8] For a detailed discussion of these strategies in a military context, see Carl von Clausewitz, *On War* (London: Routledge & Kegan Paul, 1908), and B. H. Liddell-Hart, *Strategy* (New York: Praeger Publishers, 1967); for a related discussion of the application of such strategies in a business setting, see Philip Kotler and Ravi Singh, "Marketing Warfare in the 1980s," *Journal of Business Strategy*, Winter 1981, pp. 30–41.

EXHIBIT 20 ♦ 3

Marketing actions to achieve share maintenance objectives

Marketing objectives	*Possible marketing actions*
Retain current customers by:	
♦ Maintaining/improving satisfaction and loyalty	♦ Increase attention to quality control as output expands.
	♦ Continue product modification and improvement efforts to increase customer benefits and/or reduce costs.
	♦ Focus advertising on stimulation of selective demand; stress product's superior features and benefits; reminder advertising.
	♦ Increase salesforce's servicing of current accounts; consider formation of national or key account representatives to major customers; consider replacing independent manufacturer's reps with company salespeople where appropriate.
	♦ Expand postsale service capabilities; develop or expand company's own service force, or develop training programs for distributors' and dealers' service people; expand parts inventory; consider development of customer service hotline.
♦ Encourage/simplify repeat purchase	♦ Expand production capacity in advance of increasing demand to avoid stockouts.
	♦ Improve inventory control and logistics systems to reduce delivery times.
	♦ Continue to build distribution channels; use periodic trade promotions to gain more extensive retail coverage and maintain shelf-facings; strengthen relationships with strongest distributors/dealers.
	♦ Consider negotiating long-term requirements contracts with major customers.
	♦ Consider developing automatic reorder systems for major customers.
♦ Reduce attractiveness of switching	♦ Develop a second brand or product line with features or price more appealing to a specific segment of current customers (*flanker strategy*—see Exhibits 20-4 and 20-5).
	♦ Develop multiple-line extensions or brand offerings targeted to the needs of several user segments within the market (*market expansion* or *mobile strategy*).
	♦ Meet or beat lower prices or heavier promotional efforts by competitors—or try to preempt such efforts by potential competitors—when necessary to retain customers and when lower unit costs allow (*confrontation strategy*).

EXHIBIT   20 ◆ 3
(*concluded*)

Marketing objectives	Possible marketing actions
Stimulate selective demand among later adopters by:	
◆ Head-to-head positioning against competitive offerings or potential offerings	◆ Develop a second brand or product line with features or price more appealing to a specific segment of potential customers (*flanker strategy*).
	◆ Make product modifications or improvements to match or beat superior competitive offerings (*confrontation strategy*).
	◆ Meet or beat lower prices or heavier promotional efforts by competitors when necessary to retain customers and when lower unit costs allow (*confrontation strategy*).
	◆ When resources are limited relative to competitor's, consider withdrawing from smaller or slower growing segments to focus product development and promotional efforts on higher potential segments threatened by competitor (*contraction or strategic withdrawal strategy*).
◆ Differentiated positioning against competitive offerings or potential offerings	◆ Develop multiple-line extensions or brand offerings targeted to the needs of various potential user applications, or geographical segments within the market (*market expansion or mobile strategy*).
	◆ Build unique distribution channels to more effectively reach specific segments of potential customers (*market expansion or mobile strategy*).
	◆ Design multiple advertising and/or sales promotion campaigns targeted at specific segments of potential customers (*market expansion or mobile strategy*).

wait-and-see attitude when attacked by a competitor. Their position may be strong and appealing enough that they need not respond directly to aggressive competitors by cutting prices or increasing promotional budgets. H. J. Heinz—the share leader of the ketchup industry—is a good example of a firm with such a strong competitive position that it could weather a direct attack without altering its basic strategy or marketing program. Exhibit 20–6 (page 712) tells the story of Heinz's battle with Hunt's for share leadership in the ketchup market.

Most of the marketing actions listed in Exhibit 20–3 as being relevant for retaining current customers might be incorporated into a position defense strategy. Anything the business can do to (*a*) improve customer satisfaction and loyalty, and (*b*) encourage and simplify repeat purchasing, should help the firm protect its current customer base and make its offering more attractive to new customers. Some of the specific actions that Exhibit 20–3 indi-

EXHIBIT 20 ◆ 4

Strategic choices for share leaders in growth markets

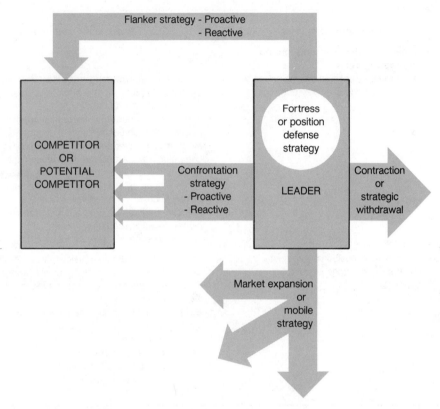

Source: Adapted from P. Kotler and R. Singh, "Marketing Warfare in the 1980's," *Journal of Business Strategy,* Winter 1981, pp. 30–41.

cates are appropriate for accomplishing these two marketing objectives are discussed in more detail below.

Actions to improve customer satisfaction and loyalty

The rapid expansion of output necessary to keep up with a growth market can often lead to quality control problems for the market leader. As new plants, equipment, and personnel are quickly brought on-line, bugs can suddenly appear in the production process. Thus, it is critical for the leader to pay particular attention to quality control during this phase. Most customers have only limited, if any, positive past experiences with the new brand to offset their disappointment when a purchase does not live up to expectations.

Perhaps the most obvious way for a leader to strengthen its position is to continue to modify and improve its product. This can reduce the oppor-

EXHIBIT 20 ◆ 5

Marketing objectives and strategies for share leaders in growth-market situations

Situational variables	Share maintenance strategies				
	Fortress or position defense	Flanker	Confrontation	Market expansion or mobile	Contraction or strategic withdrawal
Primary objective	Increase satisfaction, loyalty, and repeat purchase among current customers by building on existing strengths; appeal to late adopters with same attributes and benefits offered to early adopters.	Protect against loss of specific segment of current customers by developing a second entry that covers a weakness in original offering; improve ability to attract new customers with specific needs or purchase criteria different from those of early adopters.	Protect against loss of share among current customers by meeting or beating a head-to-head competitive offering; improve ability to win new customers who might otherwise be attracted to competitor's offering.	Increase ability to attract new customers by developing new product offerings or line extensions aimed at a variety of new applications and user segments; improve ability to retain current customers as market fragments.	Increase ability to attract new customers in selected high-growth segments by focusing offerings and resources on those segments; withdraw from smaller or slower growing segments to conserve resources.
Market characteristics	Relatively homogeneous market with respect to customer needs and purchase criteria; strong preference for leader's product among largest segment of customers.	Two or more major market segments with distinct needs or purchase criteria.	Relatively homogeneous market with respect to customers' needs and purchase criteria; little preference for, or loyalty toward, leader's product among largest segment of customers.	Relatively heterogeneous market with respect to customers' needs and purchase criteria; multiple product uses requiring different product or service attributes.	Relatively heterogeneous market with respect to customers' needs, purchase criteria and growth potential; multiple product uses requiring different product or service attributes.
Competitors' characteristics	Current and potential competitors have relatively limited resources and competencies.	One or more current or potential competitors with sufficient resources and competencies to effectively implement a differentiation strategy.	One or more current or potential competitors with sufficient resources and competencies to effectively implement a head-to-head strategy.	Current and potential competitors have relatively limited resources and competencies, particularly with respect to R&D and marketing.	One or more current or potential competitors with sufficient resources and competencies to present a strong challenge in one or more growth segments.
Firm's characteristics	Current product offering enjoys high awareness and preference among major segment of current and potential customers; firm has marketing and R&D resources and competencies equal to or greater than any current or potential competitor.	Current product offering perceived as weak on at least one attribute by a major segment of current or potential customers; firm has sufficient R&D and marketing resources to introduce and support a second offering aimed at the disaffected segment.	Current product offering suffers low awareness, preference and/or loyalty among major segment of current or potential customers; firm has R&D and marketing resources and competencies equal to or greater than any current or potential competitor.	No current offerings in one or more potential applications segments; firm has marketing and R&D resources and competencies equal to or greater than any current or potential competitor.	Current product offering suffers low awareness, preference, and/or loyalty among current or potential customers in one or more major growth segments; firm's R&D and marketing resources and competencies are limited relative to those of one or more competitors.

tunities for competitors to differentiate their products by designing in features or performance levels that the leader does not offer. As noted earlier, Compaq, for example, successfully stole a share of the commercial PC market by offering product features, such as portability, that were not available from IBM. A more aggressive product improvement effort on IBM's part may

EXHIBIT   20 ♦ 6

Heinz versus Hunt's: The advantage of a strong competitive position

---

In the mid-1960s Heinz had strengthened its leading share position in the ketchup market to 27 percent largely through emphasis on high product quality and heavy consumer advertising. Hunt's—with a 19 percent share—decided to directly attack the leader with a combination of new pizza and hickory flavors that it hoped would appeal to specific segments of ketchup users, heavy trade allowances to retailers to capture more shelf space, a price cut to 70 percent of Heinz's price, and an increase in its advertising budget to twice the amount spent by Heinz. Heinz's position was so strong, however, that Hunt's expensive attack failed to make any inroads into the leader's market share, even though Heinz did not bother to react to the attack. Heinz did not cut prices, increase advertising or trade allowances, or develop any line extensions. Yet when the dust settled, Heinz's share had increased to about 40 percent of the market. Heinz's strategy continues to be one of strengthening its current position in existing product categories by carefully controlling costs and quality and using its high margins to support advertising and promotional efforts as necessary to maintain consumer awareness and preference. The company's product development efforts are mostly directed at new markets—such as instant baby food and gourmet cat food—rather than toward line extensions or multiple brand offerings in its established markets.

Source: See "The H. J. Heinz Company (A)," Harvard Business School Case 9-569-011 M357; also see Bill Saporito, "Heinz Pushes to Be the Low-Cost Producer," *Fortune*, June 24, 1985, pp. 44–54.

have reduced its vulnerability to such competitive threats. Improvement efforts might also try to reduce unit costs to discourage low-price competition.

The leader should take steps to improve not only the physical product, but customers' perceptions of it as well. As competitors enter or prepare to enter the market, the leader's advertising and sales promotion emphasis should shift from the stimulation of primary demand to building selective demand for the company's brand. As we saw in Chapter 16, this usually involves the creation of appeals that stress the brand's superior features and benefits. The leader may continue sales promotion efforts to stimulate trial among later adopters but shift some of those efforts toward encouraging repeat purchases among existing customers. For instance, it might include cents-off coupons inside the package to give customers a price break on their next purchase of the brand.

For industrial goods, some salesforce efforts should shift from prospecting for new accounts to servicing existing customers. Firms that relied on independent manufacturer's reps to introduce their new products might consider replacing them with company salespeople to increase the customer-service orientation of their sales efforts. Firms whose own salespeople introduced the product might reorganize their salesforces into specialized groups focused on major industries or user segments—as IBM has done in the commercial PC market. Or they might give key account representatives the responsibility for servicing their largest customers.

A final step toward strengthening a leader's position as the market grows is to give increased attention to postsale service. Rapid growth in demand can not only outstrip a firm's ability to produce a high-quality product, but it can also overload the firm's ability to service customers who have problems with it. Obviously, this can lead to a loss of existing customers as well as negative word of mouth that might inhibit the firm's ability to attract new users. The growth phase thus often requires increased investments to expand the firm's parts inventory and hire and train service personnel. Firms that rely on distributors or retail dealers to service their products may need expanded training programs to help those dealers do adequate jobs.

Actions to encourage and simplify repeat purchasing

One of the most critical actions a leader must take to ensure that customers continue buying its product is to maximize its availability. It must reduce stockouts on retail store shelves or shorten delivery times for industrial goods. To do this, the firm must invest in plant and equipment to expand capacity in advance of demand; and it must implement inventory control and logistics systems adequate to provide a steady flow of goods through the distribution system. The firm should also continue to build its distribution channels. It must seek more extensive representation in retail outlets, more shelf facings in each store, or—in the case of industrial goods—gain representation by the best distributors or dealers in each market area. These actions not only increase the product's availability, but they can also help reduce competitive threats by making it more difficult for later entrants to gain an adequate share of limited shelf space or distributor support.

Some market leaders—particularly in industrial goods markets—can take more proactive steps to turn their major customers into captives and help guarantee future purchases. For example, a firm might negotiate requirements contracts or guaranteed price agreements with its customers to ensure their loyalty and preempt competitors. Concessions may have to be offered to win such agreements, however. These can involve substantial risks for the marketer if future market conditions are likely to be volatile. A less risky method of tying major customers to a supplier is for the selling firm to provide a computerized reorder system or channel information system. American Hospital Supply was one of the earliest adopters of this approach, as described in Exhibit 20–7.

Flanker strategy

One shortcoming of a fortress strategy is that a challenger might simply choose to bypass the leader's fortress and try to capture territory where the leader has not yet established a strong presence. This can represent a particular threat when the market is fragmented into two or more major segments

EXHIBIT 20 ♦ 7

American Hospital Supply's computerized reorder system

In the mid-1970s American Hospital Supply, a major wholesaler of medical supplies, offered to install the industry's first computer order terminals in the stockrooms of major hospitals. Because hospitals were accustomed to ordering supplies from salespeople making regular rounds, they at first accepted the system only as a hedge against emergencies. But stock clerks found the terminals more convenient than waiting for a salesperson to call; and they turned to American Hospital for everything from tongue depressors to blood analyzers. Rival distributors filed an antitrust suit, claiming the system represented an attempt to establish exclusive supply arrangements with major hospitals, but they lost the suit on appeal. By the mid-1980s American Hospital had become a $3.4 billion-a-year operation and was purchased in a friendly acquisition for nearly $4 billion by drug maker Baxter Travenol.

Source: Peter Petre, "How to Keep Customers Happy Captives," *Fortune,* September 2, 1985, pp. 42–46.

with different needs and preferences, and the leader's current brand does not meet the needs of one or more of those segments. A competitor with sufficient resources and competencies could develop a differentiated product offering to appeal to the segment where the leader is weak and thereby capture a substantial share of the overall market.

To defend against an attack directed at a weakness in its current offering (its exposed flank), a leader might develop a second brand (a flanker or fighting brand) to compete directly against the challenger's offering. In some cases this might involve trading up, where the leader develops a high-quality brand offered at a higher price to appeal to the prestige segment of the market. Honda did this with the development of the Acura. The new brand served not only to penetrate the higher-priced segment of the market, but also to help Honda hold on to former Accord owners who were beginning to trade up to more expensive European brands as they got older and earned higher incomes.

More commonly, though, a flanker brand is a lower-quality product designed to appeal to a low-price segment to protect the leader's primary brand from direct price competition. Pillsbury's premium-quality Hungry Jack brand holds the major share of the refrigerated biscuit dough market; however, a substantial number of consumers prefer to pay less for a somewhat lower quality biscuit. Rather than conceding that low-price segment to competitors, or reducing Hungry Jack prices and margins in an attempt to attract price-sensitive consumers, Pillsbury introduced Ballard—a low-priced flanker brand.

A flanker strategy is always used in conjunction with a position defense strategy. The leader simultaneously strengthens its primary brand while introducing a flanker to compete in segments where the primary brand is vulnerable. This suggests that a flanker strategy is only appropriate when the firm has sufficient resources to develop and fully support two or more entries. After all, a flanker is of little value if it is so lightly supported that a competitor can easily wipe it out.

Finally, a flanker strategy can be either proactive or reactive. The leader might introduce a flanker in anticipation of a competitor's entry, either to establish a strong position before the competitor arrives or to dissuade the competitor from entering. In some cases, however, the leader does not recognize the severity of the threat until a competitor has already begun to enjoy a measure of success. The leader may then be forced into a crash development program to introduce a flanker as quickly as possible to limit the damage. As you'll remember, this was the situation Nabisco found itself in when Frito-Lay and Procter & Gamble achieved strong test market results with their soft, chewy cookies.

Confrontation strategy

Suppose a competitor chooses to attack the leader head-to-head and attempts to steal customers in the leader's main target market. If the leader has established a strong position and attained a high level of preference and loyalty among customers and the trade, it may be able to sit back and wait for the competitor to fail, as Heinz did when Hunt's attacked its ketchup. In many cases, though, the leader's brand is not strong enough to withstand a frontal assault from a well-funded, competent competitor. Even mighty IBM, for instance, lost 20 market share points in the commercial PC market to competitors like Compaq—whose machines cost about the same but offered better features or performance levels—and to the clones who offered IBM-compatible machines at much lower prices. In such situations the leader may have no choice but to respond by confronting the competitive threat directly. If the leader's competitive intelligence is good, it may decide to move proactively and change its marketing program *before* a suspected competitive challenge occurs. A confrontational strategy, though, is more commonly reactive. The leader usually decides to meet or beat the attractive features of a competitor's offering—by making product improvements, increasing promotional efforts, or lowering prices—only after the challenger's success has become obvious.

The problem with simply meeting the improved features or lower price of a challenger is that such a strategy does nothing to reestablish a sustainable competitive advantage for the leader. A confrontation based largely on lowering prices creates an additional problem of shrinking margins for all concerned. Unless the leader's production costs fall with increasing volume and decreasing prices generate substantial new industry volume, a leader may be better off responding to price threats with increased promotion or product improvements while trying to maintain its profit margins. Evidence also suggests that in product-markets with high repeat purchase rates, the leader may be wise to adopt a penetration pricing policy in the first place.

This would strengthen its share position and may preempt low-price competitors from entering.[9]

One way to avoid the problems of a confrontation strategy is for the leader to try to reestablish the competitive advantage that has been eroded by challengers' frontal attacks. Often, the best way to accomplish this is to develop a new generation of products based on a more sophisticated technology and to offer expanded benefits to customers. This is the approach taken by IBM with the introduction of its PS/2 personal computers.

Market expansion or mobile strategy

A market expansion or mobile strategy is a more aggressive and proactive version of the flanker strategy. Here the leader defends its relative market share by establishing positions in a number of different market segments. This strategy's primary objective is to capture a large share of new customer groups who may prefer something different than the firm's initial offering. But it also can help keep potential competitors off balance and protect the firm from future competitive threats from a number of different directions. Such a strategy is particularly appropriate in fragmented markets with many smaller, heterogeneous customer segments, where the leader has the resources to undertake multiple product development and marketing efforts.

The most obvious way for a leader to implement a market expansion strategy is to pursue the development of line extensions, new brands, or even alternative product forms using similar technologies, to appeal to multiple market segments. For instance, Pillsbury holds a strong position in the refrigerated biscuit dough category; biscuit consumption is concentrated among older, more traditional consumers in the south. To expand its total market, to gain increased experience curve effects, and to protect its overall technological lead, Pillsbury developed a variety of other product forms that use the same refrigerated dough technology and production facilities but appeal to different customer segments. The expanded line includes crescent rolls, Danish rolls, and soft breadsticks.

A less expensive way to appeal to a variety of customer segments is to retain the basic product but vary other elements of the marketing program to make it relatively more attractive to specific users. Thus, a leader might create specialized salesforces to deal with the unique concerns of different user groups. Or it might offer different ancillary services to different types of customers, or tailor sales promotion efforts to different segments. This approach is becoming particularly popular in consumer package goods industries where there are substantial *regional* differences in customer tastes and preferences. Campbell Soup, for instance, has created regional product man-

---

[9] Robert J. Dolan and Abel P. Jewland, "Experience Curves and Dynamic Demand Models: Implications for Optimal Pricing Strategy," *Journal of Marketing*, Winter 1981, p. 52.

agers in some of its major product categories and given them their own promotional budgets. The managers can create promotional campaigns tailored to the specific product preferences and competitive challenges in their areas of the country.[10]

Contraction or strategic withdrawal

In some highly fragmented markets a leader may be unable to defend itself adequately in all market segments. This is particularly likely when the leader has limited resources compared to newly emerging competitors. The firm may then have to reduce or abandon its efforts in some segments to focus on areas where it enjoys the greatest relative advantages or that have the greatest potential for future growth. Even some very large firms may decide that certain segments are not profitable enough to continue pursuing and that they would be better off concentrating on more attractive segments. IBM made an early attempt to capture the low end of the home hobbiest market for personal computers with the introduction of the PC Jr., for example. Eventually it abandoned that effort to concentrate on the more lucrative commercial and education segments.

SHARE GROWTH STRATEGIES FOR FOLLOWERS

Marketing objectives for followers

Not all late entrants to a growing product-market have illusions about eventually subduing the leader and capturing a dominant share of the market. Some competitors—particularly those with limited resources and competencies—may simply seek to build a small but profitable business within a specialized segment of the larger market that has been overlooked by earlier entrants. As we saw in Chapter 19, this kind of *niche strategy* is one of the few entry options that small, late entrants can pursue with a reasonable degree of success.[11] If a firm can successfully build a profitable business in a small segment while maintaining a low profile and avoiding direct competition with larger competitors, it can often survive the shakeout period near the end of the growth stage and remain profitable throughout the maturity stage.

On the other hand, many followers—particularly larger firms that enter a product-market shortly after the pioneer—have more grandiose objectives. They often seek to displace the leader—or at least to become a more powerful competitor within the total market. Thus, their major marketing objective

---

[10] "Marketing's New Look," *Business Week*, January 26, 1987, pp. 64–69.

[11] Mary L. Coyle, "Competition in Developing Markets: The Impact of Order of Entry," Ph.D. Diss., University of Toronto, 1986.

is to attain *share growth*, and the size of the increased relative share sought by such challengers is usually substantial. It is rarely less than 50 percent of their current share and more often about a 100 to 150 percent increase.[12] The rationale for such aggressive goals is the expected relationship between market share and unit costs in the short run, and between share and ROI over the long term. General Electric, for instance, has adopted a formal policy of not continuing to compete in any business where it does not enjoy the leading relative share or cannot reasonably expect to attain a leading position in the foreseeable future.

Marketing actions and strategies to achieve share growth

A challenger with visions of taking over the leading share position in an industry has two basic strategic options, each involving somewhat different marketing objectives and actions. Where the share leader—and perhaps some other early followers—have already penetrated a large portion of the potential market, a challenger may have no choice but to *steal away some of the repeat purchase or replacement demand from competitors' current customers.* As Exhibit 20–8 indicates, the challenger can attempt this through marketing activities that give it an advantage in a head-to-head confrontation with a target competitor. Or it can attempt to leapfrog over the leader by developing a new generation of products with enough benefits to induce customers to trade in their existing brand for a new one. Secondarily, such actions may also help the challenger attract a larger share of late adopters in the mass market.

If the market is relatively early in the growth phase and no previous entrant has captured a commanding share of potential customers, the challenger can focus on *attracting a larger share of potential new customers* who enter the market for the first time. This may also be a viable option when the overall market is heterogeneous and fragmented and the current share leader has established a strong position in only one or a few segments. In either case, the primary marketing activities for increasing share via this approach are to *differentiate* the challenger's offering from those of existing competitors by making it more appealing to new customers in untapped or underdeveloped segments of the market.

Exhibit 20–8's list of possible marketing actions for challengers is not exhaustive; and it contains actions that do not always fit well together (page 720). The activities that do fit tend to cluster into five internally consistent strategies that a challenger might use singly or in combination to secure growth in its relative market share. As Exhibit 20–9 (page 722) shows, these five share growth strategies are: *frontal attack, leapfrog strategy, flanking at-*

---

[12] Charles W. Hofer and Dan Schendel, *Strategy Formulation: Analytical Concepts* (St. Paul: West Publishing, 1978), p. 163.

tack, encirclement, and *guerrilla attacks.* Many of these share growth strategies are mirror images of the share maintenance strategies we discussed earlier.

Which—or what combinations—of these five strategies is best for a particular challenger to use depends on market characteristics, the current positions and strengths of existing competitors, and the challenger's own resources and competencies. Exhibit 20–10 (page 723) briefly outlines the situations where each of the five strategies is likely to work best; we discuss them in greater depth in the following sections.

Deciding who to attack

When more than one competitor is already established in the market, one of the first decisions a challenger must make is which competitor, if any, to target. There are several options to consider:

- *Attack the market share leader within its primary target market.* This typically involves either a *frontal assault* or an attempt to *leapfrog* the leader through the development of superior technology or product design. It may seem logical to try to win customers away from the competitor with the most customers to lose, but this can be a dangerous strategy unless the challenger has superior resources and competencies that can be converted into a sustainable advantage. In some cases, however, a smaller challenger may be able to avoid disastrous retaliation by confronting the leader only occasionally in limited geographic territories through a series of *guerrilla attacks.*
- *Attack another follower who has an established position within a major market segment.* This also usually involves a *frontal assault,* but it may be easier for the challenger to gain a sustainable advantage if the target competitor is not as well established in the minds and buying habits of customers as the market leader.
- *Attack one or more smaller competitors who have only limited resources.* Because smaller competitors usually hold only a small share of the total market, this may seem like an inefficient way to attain substantial share increases. But by focusing on several small regional competitors one at a time, a challenger can sometimes achieve major gains without inviting retaliation from stronger firms. For example, by first challenging and ultimately acquiring a series of smaller regional brewers, G. Heilman and Sons has managed to become number three in total share of the domestic beer industry.
- *Avoid direct attacks on any established competitor.* In fragmented markets where one or more segments are not currently being satisfied by the leader or other major competitors, a challenger is often best advised to "hit 'em where they ain't." This usually involves either a *flanking* or an *encirclement* strategy where the challenger develops differentiated product offerings targeted at one large—or several smaller—segments where no competitor currently holds a strong position.

Deciding which competitor to attack necessitates a comparison of relative strengths and weaknesses—a critical first step in developing an effective share growth strategy. It can also help limit the scope of the battlefield, a particularly important consideration for challengers with limited resources.

EXHIBIT 20 ◆ 8
Marketing actions to achieve share growth objectives

Marketing objectives	Possible marketing actions

Capture repeat/replacement purchases from current customers of the leader or other target competitor by:
◆ Head-to-head positioning against competitor's offering in primary target market
	◆ Develop products with features and/or performance levels superior to those of the target competitor.
	◆ Draw on superior product design, process engineering, and supplier relationships to achieve lower unit costs.
	◆ Set prices below target competitor's for comparable level of quality or performance, but only if low-cost position is achieved.
	◆ Outspend the target competitor on promotion aimed at stimulating selective demand:
	    Comparative advertising appeals directed at gaining a more favorable positioning than the target competitor's brand enjoys among customers in the mass market.
	    Sales promotions to encourage trial if offering's quality or performance is perceptively better than target competitor's, or induce brand switching.
	    Build more extensive and/or better trained salesforce than target competitor's.
	◆ Outspend the target competitor on trade promotion to attain more extensive retail coverage, better shelf space, and/or representation by the best distributors/dealers.
	◆ Outperform the target competitor on customer service:
	    Develop superior production scheduling, inventory control, and logistics systems to minimize delivery times and stockouts.
	    Develop superior postsales service capabilities; build a more extensive company service force, or provide better training programs for distributor/dealer service people than target competitor.
	◆ If resources are limited, engage in one or more of the preceding actions (e.g., an advertising blitz, sales or trade promotions) on a sporadic basis in selected territories (*guerrilla attack strategy*).

Frontal attack strategy

Where the market for a product category is relatively homogeneous, with few untapped segments and one or more well-established competitors, a firm wanting to capture an increased market share may have little choice but to tackle a major competitor head-on. Such an approach is most likely to be successful when most customers do not have strong brand preferences or loyalties and when the challenger's resources and competencies—particu-

EXHIBIT   20 ◆ 8
(*concluded*)

Marketing objectives	Possible marketing actions

◆ Technological differentiation from target competitor's offering in its primary target market	◆ Develop a new generation of products based on different technology that offers a superior performance or additional benefits desired by current and potential customers in the mass market (*leapfrog strategy*).
	◆ Build awareness, preference, and replacement demand through heavy introductory promotion:
	    Comparative advertising stressing product's superiority.
	    Sales promotions to stimulate trial or encourage switching.
	    Extensive, well-trained salesforce; heavy use of product demonstrations in sales presentations.
	◆ Build adequate distribution through trade promotions and dealer training programs.

Stimulate selective demand among later adopters by: ◆ Head-to-head positioning against target competitor's offering in established market segments	◆ See preceding actions.
◆ Differentiated positioning focused on untapped or underdeveloped segments	◆ Develop a differentiated brand or product line with unique features or price that is more appealing to a major segment of potential customers whose needs are not met by existing offerings (*flanking strategy*). or ◆ Develop multiple line extensions or brand offerings with features or prices targeted to the unique needs and preferences of several smaller potential applications or regional segments (*encirclement strategy*). ◆ Design advertising, personal selling, and/or sales promotion campaigns that address specific interests and concerns of potential customers in one or multiple underdeveloped segments to stimulate selective demand. ◆ Build unique distribution channels to more effectively reach potential customers in one or multiple underdeveloped segments. ◆ Design service programs to reduce the perceived risks of trial and/or solve the unique problems faced by potential customers in one or multiple underdeveloped segments (e.g., systems engineering, installation, operator training, or extended warranties).

larly in marketing, R&D, and production—are equal to or greater than the target competitor's. But even superior resources are no guarantee of success when a challenger's frontal assault strategy merely imitates the target competitor's, as P&G discovered when it attacked Maxwell House in the coffee market. (See Exhibit 20–11 on page 724.)

To successfully implement a frontal attack, a challenger must find one or more ways to achieve a sustainable advantage over the target competitor. As

EXHIBIT   20♦9

Strategic choices for challengers in growth markets

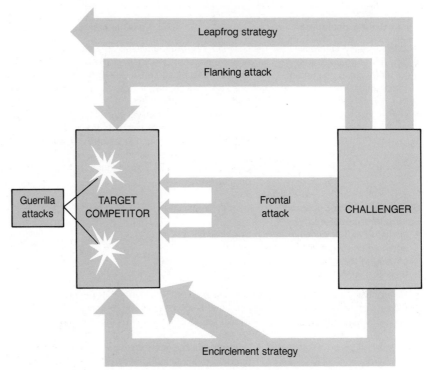

we have seen, such an advantage is usually based on attaining lower costs or a differentiated position in the market. If the challenger has a cost advantage, it can cut prices to lure away the target competitor's customers—as a number of the clone manufacturers have done to IBM in the commercial PC market. Or, it can maintain a similar price and use its higher margins to support more extensive promotion or increased R&D.

Challenging a leader solely on the basis of low price is a highway to disaster, however, unless the challenger really does have a sustainable cost advantage. Otherwise, the leader might simply match the lower prices until the challenger is driven from the market. The problem is that initially a challenger is often at a *cost disadvantage* due to the experience curve effects established competitors have accumulated. The challenger must have offsetting advantages in the form of superior production technology, established relations with low-cost suppliers, the ability to share production facilities or

EXHIBIT 20 ◆ 10

Marketing objectives and strategies for challengers in growth market situations

Situational variables	Share growth strategies				
	Frontal attack	**Leapfrog**	**Flank attack**	**Encirclement**	**Guerrilla attack**
Primary objective	Capture substantial repeat/replacement purchases from target competitor's current customers; attract new customers among later adopters by offering lower price or more attractive features.	Induce current customers in mass market to replace their current brand with superior new offering; attract new customers by providing enhanced benefits.	Attract substantial share of new customers in one or more major segments where customers' needs are different from those of early adopters in the mass market.	Attract a substantial share of new customers in a variety of smaller, specialized segments where customers' needs or preferences differ from those of early adopters in the mass market.	Capture a modest share of repeat/replacement purchases in several market segments or territories; attract a share of new customers in a number of existing segments.
Market characteristics	Relatively homogeneous market with respect to customers' needs and purchase criteria; relatively little preference or loyalty for existing brands.	Relatively homogeneous market with respect to customers' needs and purchase criteria, but some needs or criteria not currently met by existing brands.	Two or more major segments with distinct needs and purchase criteria; needs of customers in at least one segment not currently met by existing brands.	Relatively heterogeneous market with a number of small, specialized segments; needs and preferences of customers in some segments not currently satisfied by competing brands.	Relatively heterogeneous market with a number of larger segments; needs and preferences of customers in most segments currently satisfied by competing brands
Competitor's characteristics	Target competitor has relatively limited resources and competencies, particularly in marketing and R&D; would probably be vulnerable to direct attack.	One or more current competitors have relatively strong resources and competencies in marketing, but relatively unsophisticated technology and limited R&D competencies.	Target competitor has relatively strong resources and competencies, particularly in marketing and R&D; would probably be able to withstand direct attack.	One or more competitors have relatively strong marketing, R&D resources and competencies, and/or lower costs; could probably withstand a direct attack.	A number of competitors have relatively strong marketing, R&D resources and competencies, and/or lower costs; could probably withstand a direct attack.
Firm characteristics	Firm has stronger resources and competencies in R&D and marketing and/or lower operating costs than target competitor.	Firm has proprietary technology superior to that of competitors; firm has necessary marketing and production resources to stimulate and meet primary demand for new generation of products.	Firm's resources and competencies are limited, but sufficient to effectively penetrate and serve at least one major market segment.	Firm has marketing, R&D, and production resources and competencies necessary to serve multiple smaller segments; firm has decentralized and adaptable management structure.	Firm has relatively limited marketing, R&D, and/or production resources and competencies; firm has decentralized and adaptable management structure.

marketing efforts across multiple SBUs, or other sources of synergy before a low-price assault makes sense.

A similar caveat applies to frontal assaults based solely on heftier promotional budgets. Unless the target competitor's resources are substantially more limited than the challenger's, it can retaliate against any attempt to win away customers through more extensive advertising or attractive sales and trade promotions.

One possible exception to this limitation of greater promotional effort is the use of a more extensive and better-trained salesforce to gain a competitive advantage. A knowledgeable salesperson's technical advice and

EXHIBIT 20 ◆ 11

P&G's frontal assault on Maxwell House

> The dangers of launching a frontal assault with a me-too product and marketing program are illustrated by P&G's experience in the coffee market. P&G attacked General Food's Maxwell House coffee with Folger's, a brand that lacked the superior quality that P&G usually builds into its products. Maxwell House, tough to the last drop, fought back with increased advertising and consumer and trade promotions. Although Folger's managed to capture 25 percent of the coffee market, most of its gains were taken from smaller brands. And after seven years of battle, Folger's still had not achieved acceptable levels of profitability.

Source: Michael E. Porter, "How to Attack the Industry Leader," *Fortune,* April 29, 1985, pp. 153–66.

problem-solving abilities can add additional value to a firm's product offering, particularly in newly developing high-tech industries. And it can take years for a competitor to upgrade its salesforce in order to match such a move, whereas that competitor may be able to react immediately to lower prices or heavier promotional expenditures. IBM's extensive and highly competent company salesforce, for instance, gives it a competitive advantage in the commercial PC market that is difficult for its challengers to overcome. Thus, in industries where a challenger can use a more sophisticated and extensive company salesforce than its target competitor, it may be able to capture and sustain a substantial advantage.

In general, the conclusion that we must draw from the preceding discussion is that the best way for a challenger to effectively implement a frontal attack is to differentiate its product or associated services in ways that better meet the needs and preferences of many customers in the mass market. If those meaningful product differences can then be supported with strong promotion or an attractive price, so much the better; but usually the unique features or services the challenger offers are a foundation for a sustainable advantage. Thus, Compaq achieved a measure of success in its battles with IBM by developing a variety of product offerings with features, such as portability, that were unavailable on comparable IBM equipment, or that delivered better performance for the same price. Compaq has also made extensive use of marketing research to stay in close touch with changing customer needs. And it has invested a relatively large percentage of revenues in R&D to produce a continuing stream of product modifications and improvements to sustain its strategy over time.

Other factors can improve the chances for success of a frontal attack and should be explored when choosing a target competitor. They are *variables limiting the competitor's willingness or ability to retaliate.* The industry leader, for instance, may be reluctant to retaliate aggressively against a direct attack for fear of incurring the wrath of agencies that enforce antitrust laws.

Indeed, this has been a continuing restraint on IBM's competitive behavior in both the domestic and foreign computer markets. Similarly, a target competitor with a reputation for high product quality may be loath to cut prices in response to a low-price competitor for fear of cheapening its brand's image. And a competitor pursuing high ROI or cash flow objectives may be reluctant to increase its promotion or R&D expenditures in the short run to fend off an attack.[13]

Leapfrog strategy

A challenger stands the best chance of attracting repeat or replacement purchases from a competitor's current customers when it can offer a product that is differentiated from the competitor's offerings in an attractive way. It is logical to assume that the odds of success might be even greater if the challenger can offer a far superior product based on advanced technology or a more sophisticated design. This is the essence of a leapfrog strategy. It is an attempt to gain a significant advantage over the existing competition by introducing a new generation of products that significantly outperform, or offer more desirable customer benefits than, existing brands.

Such a strategy often carries the additional benefit of inhibiting quick retaliation by established competitors. Firms that have achieved some success with one technology are often reluctant to switch to a new one because of the large investments involved and a fear of disrupting current customers. Apple's development of the Macintosh—with its point-and-click operating system and user-friendly software—to challenge IBM's PC is a good example of a leapfrog strategy.

On the other hand, Apple's experience in trying to capture a larger share of the commercial PC market with the Macintosh also illustrates a possible limitation of the leapfrog strategy. The critical requirement for success is that the challenger have proprietary technology superior to that of established competitors as well as the product and process engineering capabilities to turn that technology into an appealing product. But the challenger must also have the marketing resources to effectively promote its new generation of products. The challenger must not only make potential customers aware that the new technology exists, but it must also convince customers already committed to an earlier technology that the new product offers sufficient benefits to justify the costs of switching. As Apple discovered, this conversion process can require years and millions of dollars of promotional effort to accomplish. To speed up the process, the challenger might develop sales promotion or customer service programs aimed at reducing the customer's switching costs. For instance, a Polaroid promotion offered buyers a $20

---

[13] For a more extensive discussion of factors that can limit a leader's willingness or ability to retaliate against a direct attack, see Michael E. Porter, *Competitive Advantage* (New York: Free Press, 1985), chap. 15.

trade-in on any old camera—whether it worked or not—toward the purchase of its new Spectra camera. For industrial goods, the offer of systems engineering services or product features that help potential customers integrate the new technology with their existing equipment and processes can encourage them to switch suppliers. Apple, for example, worked feverishly to develop its open Macintosh II system that can use IBM software. This product modification enables old IBM customers to preserve their earlier investments in IBM software while switching to the more user-friendly Macintosh hardware.

Flanking and encirclement strategies

Military historian Liddell-Hart, after analyzing battles ranging from the Greek Wars to World War I, concluded that only 6 out of 280 frontal assaults ended in victory for the attacker.[14] He concluded from this that it is usually wiser to avoid attacking an established adversary's point of strength and to focus instead on an area of weakened defenses. This is the basic premise behind both flanking and encirclement strategies. Both strategies avoid direct confrontations by focusing on market segments whose needs are not being satisfied by existing brands and where no current competitor has a strongly held position.

Flank attack

A flank attack is appropriate where the market can be broken into two or more large segments, where the leader and/or other major competitors hold a strong position in the primary segment, but where no existing brand fully satisfies the needs of customers in at least one other segment. A challenger may be able to capture a significant share of the total market by concentrating primarily on one large untapped portion of the market. This usually involves developing product features or services tailored to the needs and preferences of the targeted customers, together with appropriate promotional and pricing policies to quickly build selective demand.

The Japanese auto companies provide a good example of a flank attack. They first penetrated the U.S. car market by focusing on the low-price segment of the market where domestic manufacturers' offerings were limited and generally unappealing to a large segment of price-sensitive car buyers. Interestingly, domestic car manufacturers were relatively unconcerned by this flanking attack at first. They failed to retaliate very aggressively because the Japanese were pursuing a segment they considered to be rather small and unprofitable. History proved them wrong.

In some cases, a successful flank attack need not involve unique product features. Instead, the special needs of an untapped segment can sometimes

---

[14] Liddell-Hart, *Strategy*, p. 163.

be met simply by providing customer services or specially designed distribution channels. One major reason for the success of L'eggs panty hose, for instance, was the fact that it was the first brand distributed through an extensive channel of convenience goods retailers—such as supermarkets and drugstores—instead of more fashionable department and clothing stores. The greater shopping convenience provided by this new distribution channel appealed strongly to a growing segment of working women who also happened to be heavy users of panty hose.

Encirclement

An encirclement strategy involves targeting several smaller untapped or underdeveloped segments in the market simultaneously. The idea is to surround the leader's (or other major target competitor's) brand with a variety of offerings aimed at several peripheral segments. This strategy makes the most sense when the market is fragmented into many different applications segments or geographical regions with somewhat unique needs or tastes.

Once again, this strategy often involves developing a varied line of products with features tailored to the needs of different segments. For example, Apple originally developed the Macintosh in an attempt to attract the less technically sophisticated customers in the commercial PC market who desired a user-friendly computer. But as Exhibit 20–12 illustrates, the company then developed the desktop publishing segment by bringing out a high-quality laser printer to supplement the Macintosh system and by encourag-

EXHIBIT 20 ◆ 12

Apple's encirclement strategy

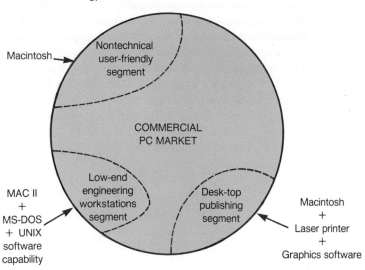

ing software producers to design the sophisticated graphics software desired by customers in that applications segment. Subsequently, Apple attacked the low-priced end of the market for engineering workstations by developing the more powerful Macintosh II and giving it the capability of handling the UNIX software popular for engineering applications. In some cases, though, minor variations in customer services, promotional appeals, or distribution channels may be all that is needed to capture various specialized segments.

Guerrilla attack

When all major segments of the market are already covered by well-established competitors, and the challenger's resources are relatively limited, then flanking, encirclement, or an all-out frontal attack may not be possible. In such cases the challenger may be reduced to making a series of surprise raids against its more established competitors. To avoid massive retaliation, such guerrilla attacks should be sporadic and perhaps directed against limited geographic areas where the target competitor is not particularly well-entrenched.

A challenger can choose from a variety of means for carrying out such guerrilla attacks. These include sales promotion efforts—such as coupon drops and merchandising deals (send in three box tops and receive a free magic decoder ring)—local advertising blitzes, and even legal action. Short-term price reductions through sales promotion campaigns are a particularly favored guerrilla tactic in consumer goods markets. They can target specific customer groups in limited geographic areas; they can be implemented quickly; and they are often difficult for a larger competitor to respond to, because that firm's higher share level means that a given discount costs it more in absolute dollars.[15]

In some cases the ultimate objective of a series of guerrilla attacks is not so much for the challenger to build its own share as it is to prevent a powerful leader from further expanding its share or engaging in certain aggressive acts that would be costly for the followers to respond to. Lawsuits brought by several smaller competitors over a range of activities can effectively slow down the leader's expansionist tendencies by diverting some of the leader's resources and attention. During the Burger Wars of the early 1980s, for example, a number of suits and countersuits were brought by Burger King, Wendy's, and McDonald's challenging the fairness and veracity of each other's advertising claims and other competitive practices.

---

[15] A. L. Stern, "New Marketing Game: Stealing Customers," *Dun's Business Month*, February 1985, pp. 48–50.

Empirical evidence

Several empirical studies conducted using the PIMS data base provide some empirical support for many of the managerial prescriptions we have discussed.[16] These studies compared businesses that achieved high market shares during the growth stage of the product life cycle or that increased their market shares over time with low-share businesses. In general, they found that the marketing programs and activities of businesses that successfully achieved increased market share differed from their less successful counterparts in the following ways:

♦ Share-gaining businesses typically developed and added more new products, line extensions, or product modifications to their line than low-share businesses.

♦ Businesses that increased the quality of their products relative to those of competitors achieved greater share increases than businesses whose product quality remained constant or declined.

♦ Share-gaining businesses tended to increase their marketing expenditures faster than the rate of market growth.

  Increases in both salesforce and sales promotion expenditures effectively produced share gains in both consumer and industrial goods businesses.

  Increased advertising expenditures were effective for producing share gains primarily in consumer goods businesses.

♦ Surprisingly, businesses that cut their prices more deeply than competitors did not achieve significant gains in market share.

These findings are consistent with many of our earlier observations. For instance, they underline the folly of launching a frontal attack solely on the basis of lower price. Unless the challenger has substantially lower unit costs—or the leader is inhibited from cutting its own prices for some reason—the challenger's price cuts are likely to be retaliated against and will, therefore, generate few new customers. On the other hand, frontal, leapfrog, flanking, or encirclement attacks based on product improvements tailored to specific segments are more likely to end in success—particularly when those attacks are supported with substantial promotional efforts.

Regardless of the strategies pursued by market leaders and challengers during a product-market's growth stage, the competitive situation often changes as the market becomes mature and its growth rate slows. As fewer new customers enter the market, competition to retain repeat business from current customers—and to strengthen share position by winning other firm's customers—becomes more intense. As we have seen, this change in market

---

[16] Robert D. Buzzell and Frederik D. Wiersema, "Successful Share-Building Strategies," *Harvard Business Review*, January–February 1981, pp. 135–43; and Carl R. Anderson and Carl P. Zeithaml, "Stages of the Product Life Cycle, Business Strategy, and Business Performance," *Academy of Management Journal*, March 1984, pp. 5–25.

and competitive conditions often leads to a shakeout within the industry, with less profitable firms either withdrawing from the market or being acquired by strong firms. Such changes also usually require the remaining competitors to adjust their objectives and to develop new strategic marketing programs to achieve them. In the next chapter we examine the environmental changes that occur as a market matures—and the marketing strategies that firms might use to adapt to those changes.

SUMMARY

Both conventional wisdom and the various portfolio models suggest that advantages can be gained by quickly entering—and investing heavily to build share in—growth markets. Among the commonly cited advantages inherent in the early and aggressive pursuit of growing markets are the beliefs that: (1) it is easier to gain share when a market is growing; (2) share gains are worth more when total volume is expanding rather than stable; (3) price competition is likely to be less intense in growing markets because demand often exceeds supply; and (4) early experience gained in developing products and applications for a growth market can give a firm the technical expertise needed to keep up with advancing technology.

Even though each of these premises is true in general, it is not always valid for every firm in every situation. If there are few barriers to entry or the adoption process is protracted, for example, price competition may be very intense even though the market is growing. Thus, a market does not always represent an attractive opportunity for a business simply because it promises rapid future growth. Managers must consider how the market and competitive situations are likely to evolve, and whether their firms can exploit the market's rapid growth to establish a sustainable competitive advantage.

The primary strategic objective of the early share leader (who is also typically the market pioneer) in a growth market is *share maintenance*. From a marketing view, the firm must accomplish two important tasks: (a) retain repeat or replacement business from its existing customers, and (b) continue to capture the major portion of sales to the growing number of new customers entering the market for the first time. Among the marketing strategies a firm might use either singly or in combination to maintain a leading share position are: (1) a fortress or position defense strategy, (2) a flanker strategy, (3) a confrontation strategy, (4) a market expansion or mobile strategy, and (5) a contraction or strategic withdrawal strategy.

A challenger's strategic objective in a growth market is usually to *build its share* by expanding its sales faster than the overall market growth rate. Challengers do this by stealing existing customers away from the leader or other competitors, capturing a larger share of new customers than the market leader, or both. Possible share growth strategies include: a frontal attack, a leapfrog strategy, a flanking attack, encirclement, and guerrilla attacks.

QUESTIONS

1. Many marketers believe that it is important to aggressively attempt to build market share during the growth stage of a product's life cycle because share growth is easier to attain—and share gains are worth more—when the market is growing. Which rationale underlies these beliefs? Under what circumstances might these

widely held beliefs prove to be misleading or false?

2. Stouffer Foods holds a commanding share of the growing market for low-calorie frozen entrees with its Lean Cuisine product line. To maintain its lead as the market continues to grow, what strategic marketing objectives should Stouffer focus on and why?

3. Given your answer to question 2, which specific marketing actions would you recommend for accomplishing Stouffer's objectives? Be specific with regard to each of the 4Ps in the firm's marketing program.

4. During the late 1970s General Foods' Cool Whip frozen dessert topping held nearly a two-thirds share of the market, but it was gradually losing share to low-priced private label competitors in many regional markets. Describe two strategies that General Foods might have adopted to defend its leading share position and the marketing actions necessary to implement them. Which of the two would you recommend and why?

5. Under which conditions might a share leader decide to withdraw from one or more market segments even though the overall market is growing? Describe an example of this withdrawal strategy.

6. As we saw at the beginning of the chapter, Compaq was a follower in the commercial PC market, yet it managed to capture a substantial and growing share of that market. Indeed, it was the fastest-growing firm in the history of the computer industry during the mid-1980s. How would you categorize the strategy Compaq used to achieve success against such a powerful leading competitor as IBM? Which marketing actions were the critical keys to the success of Compaq's strategy?

7. How would you characterize the early strategies of the major Japanese auto makers (e.g., Toyota, Nissan, and Honda) when they first entered the U.S. auto market in the 1960s and 1970s? What marketing variables do you think were critical to the ultimate success of their strategies?

8. If you had been the top marketing executive at General Motors during the early years of the Japanese invasion of the U.S. auto market, which strategy would you have recommended to defend GM's leading market share against this new competitive threat? Why do you think GM failed to adopt such a strategy at the time?

9. Under which circumstances might a firm appropriately consider adopting a guerrilla attack strategy? What are the dangers inherent in such a strategy?

Chapter 21

Strategies for mature and declining markets

JOSTENS—MAKING MONEY IN A DECLINING MARKET

Jostens, Inc., produces high school class rings and other merchandise used in incentive and reward programs.[1]

The company's primary products include class rings, yearbooks, graduation products, customized sales and service awards, custom imprinted sportswear, student photography packages, sports awards, customized products for university alumni, and computer-based educational products and services.

The firm's primary market has been shrinking since the last of the baby boomers left high school. U.S. high school enrollment has declined by almost 2 million since the 1976 peak of 15.7 million students. Nevertheless, as of 1988 Jostens had achieved increases in profits and revenues for 31 consecutive years. In its 1988 fiscal year, the firm earned profits of $44.4 million on revenues of $560 million.

One reason for the firm's success is that it saw the decline coming and prepared for it. Jostens' marketing research warned 20 years ago of the coming drop in high school enrollment. The firm avoided making heavy investments in expanded plants, increased personnel, and broadly focused marketing programs. Instead, it made its operation as lean and efficient as possible. Some of the firm's competitors were not so farsighted. They succumbed to problems of overcapacity during the industry shakeout that occurred as market growth slowed.

Jostens also decided not to pursue unrelated diversification but continued to focus on the industry it knew best. The firm did enter new markets it could appeal to with only minor modifications in the company's existing products and services, however.

Jostens' primary efforts to maintain growth and profits, however, focused on gaining greater revenues from the shrinking target market of high school students. Rather than aggressively attempting to pry more market share away from established competitors, which may have precipitated a price war and reduced everyone's profits, Jostens concentrated on getting a larger percentage of students to buy rings by introducing product modifications and line extensions.

Over the years, the firm has introduced a steady stream of product variations geared to changing student tastes and to more narrowly defined subsegments of the market. For instance, the company developed a variety of personalized rings that successively ap-

---

[1] The information in this case example was drawn largely from Jaclyn Fierman, "How to Make Money in Mature Markets," *Fortune*, November 25, 1985, pp. 46–53; and the Jostens 1988 *Annual Report*.

continued

concluded

pealed to the disaffected youth of the 1960s, the "Me generation" of the 1970s, and the new conformists of the 1980s. All told, the firm can provide 16,000 ring permutations by varying the metal and the cut, shape, and size of the stone. And that wide range of product alternatives does not take into account the variety of decorations available for the metal, such as carvings of football helmets, musical instruments, or school mascots. In broadening the range of its product offerings, the firm also broadened the range of prices—and increased the revenue per ring—it can command.

Extensive promotional and personal selling efforts also play a major role in Jostens' increased penetration strategy. "Our approach is to create desire," says Richard Fjellman, marketing director for high school products. The firm spends more than $500,000 a year teaching 500 salespeople how to communicate with, and inspire, high school ring committees. New recruits spend two weeks in training programs at the headquarters, and veterans periodically take refresher courses. The company has also invested over $4 million in "spirit-building" marketing tools, such as a film—"The Greatest Days of Your Life . . . So Far"—that try to boost students' self-esteem, stir up school loyalty, and stimulate demand for class rings.

STRATEGIC ISSUES IN MATURE AND DECLINING MARKETS

Many managers—particularly those in marketing—seem obsessed with growth. Their objectives tend to emphasize annual increases in sales volume, market share, or both. But the biggest challenge for managers in most U.S. companies over the next decade will be running businesses that compete in markets that grow slowly, if at all. The majority of products, like Jostens' class rings, are in the mature or decline stages of their life cycle. Their marketing managers face the task of developing strategic marketing programs for stable or declining markets.

But the situation is not always as depressing as it sounds, as Jostens' recent performance confirms. In many cases, managers can find new opportunities to make money as competitors leave the industry.

Issues during the transition to market maturity

A period of competitive turbulence almost always accompanies the transition from market growth to maturity in an industry. This period often begins after approximately half the potential customers have adopted the product and the *rate* of sales growth starts to decline. As growth slows, many competitors find they have excess production capacity. Competition becomes more intense as firms battle to increase volume, cover high fixed costs, and maintain profitability.

Many firms do not deal successfully with declining market growth rates. Such transition periods are commonly accompanied by a **shakeout,** during which weaker businesses fail, withdraw from the industry, or are acquired by other firms. The shakeout period is pivotal in influencing the continued survival of a brand and the strength of its competitive position during the later maturity and decline stages of the life cycle. The next section of this chapter examines in more detail the market and competitive pressures that commonly emerge during such periods. We also discuss some common strategic traps that can threaten a product's survival in an industry shakeout.

Issues in mature markets

As a market matures, total volume stabilizes, and replacement purchases rather than first-time buyers account for the vast majority of that volume. A primary marketing objective of all competitors in mature markets, therefore, is simply to hold their existing customers—to sustain a meaningful competitive advantage that will help ensure the continued satisfaction and loyalty of those customers. In earlier chapters we discussed two generic business strategies geared to defending a product's competitive position in a mature market—a low-cost defender strategy and a differentiated defender strategy. Thus, a product's financial success during the mature life-cycle stage depends heavily on the firm's ability to achieve and sustain a competitive advantage on lower delivered cost or some perceived product quality or customer service superiority.

Some firms tend to passively defend mature products while using the bulk of the revenues produced by those items to develop and aggressively market new products with more growth potential. This can be shortsighted, however. All segments of a market and all brands in an industry do not necessarily reach maturity at the same time. Aging brands like Jell-O, Johnson's baby shampoo, and Arm & Hammer baking soda experienced sales revivals in recent years because of creative marketing strategies. Thus, a share leader in a mature industry might build on a cost or product differentiation advantage and pursue a marketing strategy aimed at building additional volume by promoting new uses for an old product (such as using baking soda as a refrigerator deodorizer) or by encouraging current customers to buy and use the product more often. Product modifications or line extensions might also be pursued to attract additional customers. A later section of this chapter examines basic business strategies necessary for survival in mature markets and marketing strategies that might be used to extend a brand's sales and profits.

Issues in declining markets

Eventually, technological advances; changing customer demographics, tastes, or lifestyles; and devleopment of substitutes result in declining demand for most product forms and brands. As a product starts to decline, managers face the critical question of whether to divest or liquidate the business. Unfortunately, firms sometimes support dying products too long at the expense of current profitability and the aggressive pursuit of future breadwinners.

An appropriate marketing strategy can, however, produce substantial sales and profits even in a declining market. If few exit barriers exist, an industry leader might attempt to increase market share by aggressive pricing or promotion policies aimed at driving out weaker competitors. This is the strategy pursued by Jostens in the shrinking market for high school class rings. Or the leader might try to consolidate the industry by acquiring weaker brands and reducing overhead by eliminating excess capacity and duplicate marketing programs.

Alternatively, a firm might decide to harvest a mature product by maximizing cash flow and profit over the product's remaining life. This approach typically avoids any further capital investment in the brand and reduces R&D and marketing budgets. The last section of this chapter discusses specific marketing strategies for gaining the greatest possible returns from products approaching the end of their life cycle.

SHAKEOUT: THE TRANSITION FROM MARKET GROWTH TO MATURITY

Characteristics of the transition period

The transition from growth to maturity begins when the market is still growing but the rate of growth starts to decline, as shown in Exhibit 21-1. This declining growth either sparks—or occurs simultaneously with—other changes in the market and competitive environment. Such changes include the appearance of excess capacity, increased intensity of competition, increased difficulty of maintaining product differentiation, worsening distribution problems, and growing pressures on costs and profits. Weaker members of the industry—those with small market shares, high costs, or other competitive disadvantages—often bail out of the market or are acquired by larger competitors during this **shakeout stage.**

Excess capacity
During a market's growth stage, manufacturers must usually invest heavily in new plant, equipment, and personnel to keep up with increasing demand. Some competitors fail to anticipate the transition from growth to maturity, however, and their expansion plans eventually overshoot market demand. Thus, excess production capacity often develops at the end of the growth

EXHIBIT   21 ♦ 1

The transition or shakeout stage of the generalized product life cycle

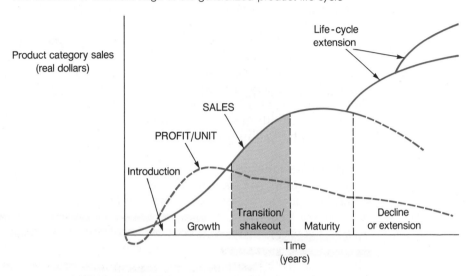

stage. This leads to a more intense struggle for market share as firms seek increased volume to hold down unit costs and maintain profit margins.

More intense competition

The intensified battle for increased volume and market share at this stage usually leads to price reductions and increased selling and promotional efforts. Firms modify products to appeal to more specialized user segments, make deals to produce for private labels, and take other actions that lower per-unit revenues, increase R&D and marketing costs, and put pressure on profit margins.

Difficulty of maintaining differentiation

As an industry's technology matures, the better and more popular designs tend to become industry standards, and the physical differences among brands become less substantial. The popularity of the VHS format among videocassette recorder customers, for example, eventually made it the industry standard, and Sony's alternative Beta format largely disappeared from the market. This decline in differentiation across brands often leads to a weakening of brand preference among consumers, further opens the door for private label products (store brands such as Kenmore appliances and Craftsman power tools), and makes it more difficult for even the market leaders to command premium prices for their products.[2] Such problems are magnified in a relatively homogeneous market with no undeveloped application or user segments that marketers might appeal to with a modified version of the basic product.

Diminishing product differentiation can also increase costs as firms seek differentiation in other ways, such as through improved service. As the products and prices offered by competing suppliers become more similar, many purchasing agents become increasingly concerned with service and its impact on their firms' costs. For instance, they may demand a higher level of delivery reliability (as in just-in-time [JIT] deliveries) to help reduce their cost of capital tied up in inventory.

Distribution problems

During an industry's transition from growth to maturity, channel members often become more assertive in ways that are particularly detrimental to smaller share competitors. As sales growth slows, for example, retailers may reduce the number of brands they carry in an effort to reduce inventory costs and space requirements. Much the same can happen at the wholesale/distributor level. Because any reduction in product availability has serious repercussions for a manufacturer, low-share firms often must offer additional trade incentives simply to hold their distribution coverage during this period. These additional expenses place low-share competitors at a further cost disadvantage compared to industry leaders.

Pressures on costs and profits

Costs typically increase and profits decline during shakeout, which increases the industry's instability and volatility. Some firms may decide that a strategy of continued growth is viable; others may opt for disinvestment. The choice of strategy largely depends on the strength of a firm's competitive position when shakeout begins and on its distinctive competencies.

Given their higher per-unit costs, smaller market share businesses often operate at a loss during transition. Some are ultimately forced to leave the industry. This is particularly likely with commodity-type products, when few unique market niches exist in which the firm can maintain a competitive advantage and when heavy investments in fixed assets are required and experience curve effects are high.

Firms that enter the transition period with high relative market shares are more likely to survive. Even these firms may experience a severe drop in profits, however. As the shakeout proceeds, the shares held by firms exiting the industry pass to the surviving firms, helping increase their volumes and lower per-unit costs. This does not necessarily mean, though, that the lead-

---

[2] Joel Dean, "Pricing Policies for New Products," *Harvard Business Review,* November–December 1976, pp. 141–53.

ers' market shares remain stable after shakeout. One study indicates that larger firms tend to lose share during market maturity because they fail to maintain their cost advantage.[3] We will discuss this danger in more detail later in this chapter.

Strategic traps during the transition period

A business's ability to survive the transition from market growth to maturity also depends to a great extent on whether it can avoid some common strategic traps.[4] Four such traps are summarized in Exhibit 21–2 and discussed below.

The most obvious trap is simply the **failure to recognize the events signaling the beginning of the shakeout period.** Many firms get into trouble because their capacity overshoots demand as growth slows. This drives up their unit costs and forces them to cut prices or increase promotion in an attempt to increase volume. The best way to minimize the impact of slowing growth is to accurately forecast the slowdown in sales growth and hold the firm's production capacity to a sustainable level. For both industrial and consumer durable goods markets, models can forecast when replacement sales will begin to outweigh first-time purchases—a common signal that a market is beginning to mature.[5] But in consumer nondurable markets—particularly those where growth slows as the result of shifting consumer preferences or the emergence of substitute products—the start of the transition period can be nearly impossible to predict.

A second strategic trap is for a business to **get caught in the middle during the transition period without a clear strategic advantage.** A business may survive and prosper during the growth stage even though it has neither differentiated its offering from competitors nor attained the lowest cost position in its industry. But during the transition period, such is not the case.

A third trap is the **failure to recognize the declining importance of product quality and the increasing importance of price or service.** Businesses that have built their success on quality often disdain aggressive pricing or marketing practices even though quality differentials typically erode as markets mature. At best, such firms delay meeting their more aggressive competitors head-on and end up losing market share. As we saw

---

[3] Robert D. Buzzell, "Are There 'Natural' Market Structures?" *Journal of Marketing*, Winter 1981, pp. 42–51.

[4] For a more detailed discussion of these "traps," see Michael E. Porter, *Competitive Strategy* (New York: Free Press, 1980), pp. 247–49.

[5] For a description of one such model used by a major manufacturer, see Stephen B. Lawton and William H. Lawton, "An Autocatalytic Model for the Diffusion of Educational Innovations," *Educational Administration Quarterly*, Winter 1979, pp. 19–46.

EXHIBIT 21 ◆ 2

Four common strategic traps firms can fall into during the shakeout period

1. Firm fails to anticipate transition from growth to maturity.
   ◆ Firms may make overly optimistic forecasts of future sales volume.
   ◆ As a result, they expand too rapidly and production capacity overshoots demand as growth slows.
   ◆ Their excess capacity leads to higher costs per unit.
   ◆ Consequently, they must cut prices or increase promotion in an attempt to increase their volume.
2. Firm is caught without a clear competitive advantage as growth slows.
   ◆ Many firms can succeed without a strong competitive advantage during periods of rapid growth.
   ◆ However, firms that do not have the lowest costs or a superior offering in terms of product quality or service can have difficulty sustaining their market share and volume as growth slows and competition intensifies.
3. Firm assumes that an early quality advantage will insulate it from price or service competition.
   ◆ In many cases, quality differentials become smaller as more competitors enter and initiate product improvements as an industry approaches maturity.
   ◆ If customers perceive that the quality of competing brands has become more equal, they are likely to attach greater importance to price or service differences.
   ◆ Failure to detect such trends can cause an early quality leader to be complacent and slow to respond to competitive threats.
4. Firm sacrifices market share in favor of short-run profit.
   ◆ A firm may cut marketing or R&D budgets or forgo other expenditures in order to maintain its historical level of profitability even though industry profits tend to fall during the transition period.
   ◆ This can cause long-run erosion of market share and further increases in unit costs as the industry matures.

in the last chapter, for instance, IBM's reluctance to compete with the clone manufacturers by lowering PC prices cost the firm substantial market share points as the demand for personal computers slowed during the mid-1980s.

Why should a firm not delay responding to the more aggressive pricing or marketing actions of its competitors? Because doing so leads to a fourth trap—**giving up market share too easily in favor of short-run profit.** Many businesses try to maintain the profitability of the recent past as markets enter the transition period. They usually do this at the expense of market share or by forgoing marketing, R&D, and other investments crucial for maintaining future market position. This tendency can be seriously shortsighted, particularly if economies of scale are crucial for the business's continued success during market maturity.

Of course, some firms may be forced into this trap because they do not have sufficient resources to match the actions of larger competitors. Minnetonka, Inc., the pioneer in several health and beauty aid product categories with brands like Softsoap and Check-Up plaque-fighting toothpaste, is a good example. The firm was unable to match the advertising and promotional expenditures of later entrants into those categories, such as Procter & Gamble and Colgate-Palmolive. Consequently, Minnetonka lost market share and profitability as each category matured, and thus sold off these products. The firm had to find new categories to pioneer in order to survive and grow.

BUSINESS STRATEGIES FOR MATURE MARKETS

The maturity phase of an industry's life cycle is often depicted as one of stability characterized by few changes in the market shares held by leading competitors and steady prices. The industry leaders, because of their low per-unit costs and little need to make further investments, enjoy high profits and positive cash flows. Those cash flows are harvested and diverted to other SBUs or products in the firm's portfolio that offer greater growth opportunities.

Unfortunately, this conventional scenario provides an overly simplistic description of the situation businesses face in most mature markets. For one thing, it is not always easy to tell when a market has reached maturity. Variations in brands, marketing programs, and customer groups can mean that different brands and market segments reach maturity at different times.

Further, as the maturity stage progresses, a variety of threats and opportunities can disrupt an industry's stability. Shifts in customer needs or preferences, product substitutes, increased raw material costs, changes in government regulations, or factors such as the entry of low-cost foreign producers or mergers and acquisitions can threaten individual competitors and even throw the entire industry into early decline. Consider, for example, the competitive position of Timex, a brand that dominated the low-price segment of the American watch market in the 1970s. First the appearance of imported digital watches and later a shift in consumer preferences toward more fashionable and prestigious brands buffeted the firm and eroded its market share.

On the positive side, such changes can also open new growth opportunities in mature industries. Product improvements (the development of high-fiber nutritional cereals), advances in process technology (the creation of minimills for steel production), falling raw materials costs, increased prices for close substitutes, or environmental changes (the increased demand for insulation in the energy crisis of the 1970s and early 80s) can all provide opportunities for a firm to dramatically increase its sales and profits. An entire industry can even experience a period of renewed growth.

Discontinuities during industry maturity suggest it is dangerously short-sighted for a firm to simply engage in the complacent milking of its cash cows. The Timex example shows how environmental and competitive threats can dislodge share leaders from their preeminent positions.[6] And recent evidence indicates even industry followers can substantially improve volume, share, and profitability during industry maturity if they can adjust their marketing objectives and programs to fit the new opportunities.[7] Thus, success in mature markets requires two sets of strategic actions: (1) development and maintenance of a clearly defined and well-implemented business strategy to sustain a competitive advantage, and (2) application of flexible and creative marketing programs geared to pursue growth or profit opportunities as conditions change in specific product-markets.

Strategies for maintaining competitive advantage

As we saw in Chapter 11, both **analyzer** and **defender strategies** may be appropriate for units with a leading—or at least a profitable—share of one or more major segments in a mature industry. The two strategies differ primarily in the emphasis given to new-product and market development. Analyzers and defenders are both concerned with maintaining a strong share position in established product-markets. But analyzers also do some product and market development in order to avoid being leapfrogged by competitors with more advanced products or being left behind in new applications segments. On the other hand, defenders may initiate some product improvements or line extensions to protect and strengthen their position in existing markets, but they spend relatively little on product R&D. Thus, an analyzer strategy is most appropriate for developed industries that are still experiencing technological change and may have opportunities for continued growth, such as the computer and commercial aircraft industries. The defender strategy works best in industries where the basic technology is not very complex or is unlikely to change dramatically in the short run, as in the food industry.

Both analyzers and defenders can attempt to sustain a competitive advantage in established product-markets through **differentiation** of their product offering (either on the basis of superior quality or service) or by maintaining a **low-cost** position. Evidence suggests the ability to maintain either a strongly differentiated or a low-cost position continues to be a critical determinant of success throughout both the transition and the maturity stage. One study examined the competitive strategies pursued by the two leading firms (in terms of return on investment) in eight mature industries characterized by slow growth and intense competition. In each industry, the two leading firms offered either the lowest relative delivered cost or the highest relative

---

[6] Buzzell, "Are There 'Natural' Market Structures?"

[7] Cathy Anterasian and Lynn W. Phillips, "Discontinuities, Value Delivery, and the Share-Returns Association: A Re-Examination of the 'Share-Causes-Profits' Controversy," distributed worker paper (Cambridge, Mass.: Marketing Science Institute, April 1988).

EXHIBIT 21 ◆ 3

The strategic competitive positions and return on investment percentages of firms in the U.S. heavy-duty truck industry

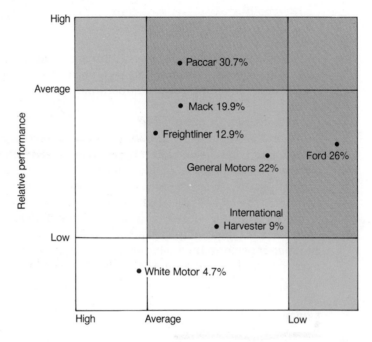

(The percentage next to each firm's name indicates its return on investment.)

Source: William K. Hall, "Survival Strategies in a Hostile Environment," *Harvard Business Review,* September–October 1980), p. 81.

product differentiation. In most cases, an industry's ROI leader opted for one of the strategies, while the second-place firm pursued the other. For example, Exhibit 21–3 shows the competitive positions and return on investment obtained by firms in the heavy-duty truck industry. Paccar, the ROI leader, offered the most highly differentiated (in terms of performance) product in the industry; while number two Ford had the lowest relative delivered cost. Generally, it is difficult for a business to pursue both low-cost and differentiation strategies at the same time. The low margins generated by a low-cost strategy usually cannot support efforts to maintain high differentiation over time.[8] Keep in mind, though, that a firm may have two or more SBUs focused on different industry segments or product-markets, and each SBU

---

[8] William K. Hall, "Survival Strategies in a Hostile Environment," *Harvard Business Review,* September–October 1980, pp. 75–85.

may pursue a different strategy. For instance, Daimler Benz has the lowest cost position in the European truck market but offers a highly differentiated automotive line in export markets.

Methods of differentiation

Differences in product designs, features, or performance are not the only ways a business can differentiate its offering. Customer service can also help maintain an advantage over competitors.

Dimensions of product quality[9]

To attain a sustainable competitive advantage in product quality, a firm must understand what **dimensions customers perceive to underlie differences in quality** across products. One authority identified eight such dimensions of product quality. These were originally listed in Exhibit 12–5 and are offered here in Exhibit 21–4 in a slightly different form to facilitate discussion.

European manufacturers of prestige automobiles, such as Mercedes-Benz and Porsche, have emphasized the first dimension of product quality— **functional performance.** These auto makers have designed cars that provide excellent performance on such attributes as handling, acceleration, and

EXHIBIT 21 ◆ 4

Dimensions of product quality

◆ **Performance**	How well does the washing machine wash clothes?
◆ **Durability**	How long will the lawn mower last?
◆ **Conformance with specifications**	What is the incidence of product defects?
◆ **Features**	Does an airline flight offer a movie and dinner?
◆ **Reliability**	Will each visit to a restaurant result in consistent quality?
	What percentage of the time will a product perform satisfactorily?
◆ **Serviceability**	Is the product easy to service?
	Is the service system efficient, competent, and convenient?
◆ **Fit and finish**	Does the product look and feel like a quality product?
◆ **Brand name**	Is this a name that customers associate with quality?
	What is the brand's image?

Source: Adapted from "What Does 'Product Quality' Really Mean?" by David A. Garvin, *Sloan Management Review,* Fall 1984, pp. 25–43, by permission of the publisher. Copyright © 1984 by the Sloan Management Review Association. All rights reserved.

---

[9] The following discussion is based on material found in David A. Aaker, *Strategic Market Management,* 2nd ed. (New York: John Wiley & Sons, 1988), chap. 11.

comfort. Volvo, on the other hand, has emphasized and aggressively promoted a different quality dimension—**durability.** A third quality dimension, **conformance to specifications** (or the absence of defects), has been a major focus of the Japanese auto makers. Until recent years, American car makers relied heavily on broad product lines and a wide **variety of features**—both standard and optional—to offset their shortcomings on some of the other quality dimensions.

The **reliability** quality dimension can refer to the consistency of performance from purchase to purchase or to a product's uptime, the percentage of time that it can perform satisfactorily over its life. Tandem Computers has maintained a competitive advantage based on reliability by designing computers with several processors that work in tandem, so if one fails, the only impact is the slowing of low-priority tasks. IBM cannot match Tandem's reliability because of its commitment to an operating system not easily adapted to the multiple-processor concept. Consequently, Tandem has maintained a strong position in market segments consisting of large-scale computer users—such as financial institutions and large retailers—for whom system downtime is particularly undesirable.

The quality dimension of **serviceability** refers to a customer's ability to obtain prompt and competent service when the product breaks down. For example, Caterpillar Tractor has long differentiated itself with a parts and service organization dedicated to providing "24-hour parts service anywhere in the world."

Many of these quality dimensions can be difficult for customers to evaluate, particularly for consumer products. As a result, consumers often generalize from quality dimensions that are more visual or qualitative—even if they are of lesser importance. Thus, the **fit and finish** dimension can help convince consumers that a product is of high quality. Buyers are likely to assume that if the product does not *look* high quality, it probably won't have the other more important quality attributes. On the other hand, they perceive attractive and well-designed products as generally high in quality, as witnessed by the success of the Krups line of small appliances. Similarly, the **quality reputation of the brand name**—and the promotional activities that sustain that reputation—can strongly influence consumers' perceptions of a product's quality. In pursuing a differentiation strategy based on quality, a business must understand what dimensions or cues customers use to judge quality and pay attention to the seemingly less important but more visible attributes of the product.

Dimensions of service quality

One series of studies of customer perceptions of service quality in industries such as retail banking, appliance repair, and securities brokerage identified a number of quality dimensions, eight of which are summarized in Exhibit 21–5 (page 746).

EXHIBIT 21 ♦ 5

Dimensions of service quality

♦ **Tangibles**	Physical facilities, equipment, and the appearance of personnel.
♦ **Reliability**	Ability to perform the promised service properly the first time.
	Consistency of service from purchase to purchase.
♦ **Responsiveness**	Willingness to help customers and provide prompt service.
♦ **Competence**	Knowledge and skill of employees and their ability to convey trust and confidence.
♦ **Credibility/trustworthiness**	The believability and honesty of employees.
♦ **Empathy**	The amount of caring, individualized attention the firm provides its customers.
♦ **Courtesy**	The friendliness of customer contact.
♦ **Communication**	Personnel listen to customers and attempt to understand their needs.
	The firm keeps customers informed in language they can understand.

Source: Based on A. Parasuraman, Valarie A. Zeithaml, and Leonard L. Berry, "A Conceptual Model of Service Quality and Its Implications for Future Research," Report 84–106 (Cambridge, Mass.: Marketing Science Institute, 1984); and A. Parasuraman, Valarie A. Zeithaml, and Leonard L. Berry, "SERQUAL: A Multi-Item Scale for Measuring Customer Perceptions of Service Quality," Report 86–108 (Cambridge, Mass.: Marketing Science Institute, 1986).

The quality dimensions listed in Exhibit 21–5 apply specifically to service businesses; but most of them are also relevant for judging the service component of a product offering. This pertains to both the objective dimensions related to the performance of the service delivery system—such as **reliability** and **responsiveness**—as well as to the more personal elements of service personnel performance, such as their **competence, empathy, courtesy,** and **communication.**

Improving customer perceptions of service quality

The key to a differentiation strategy based on providing superior service is to meet or exceed target customers' service quality expectations and to do it more consistently than competitors. The problem is that sometimes managers underestimate the level of those customer expectations, which can be unrealistically high. Therefore, a firm needs to both clearly identify target customers' wants with respect to service quality and define and communicate what level of service the firm intends to deliver. When this is done, customers have a more realistic idea of what to expect and are less likely to be disappointed with the service they receive. The major factors that determine a customer's expectations and perceptions concerning service quality and five gaps that can cause unsatisfactory service delivery are outlined in Exhibit 21–6 and discussed next.

EXHIBIT 21 ◆ 6

The determinants of perceived service quality

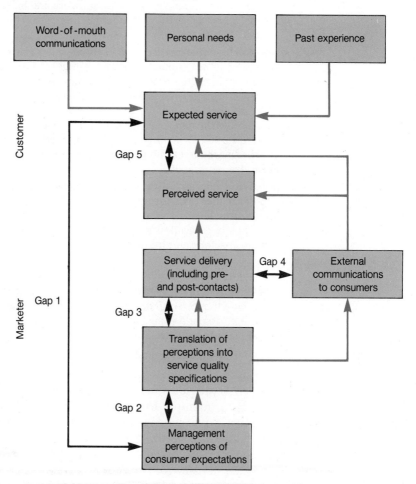

Source: Reprinted from A. Parasuraman, Valarie A. Zeithaml, and Leonard L. Berry, "A Conceptual Model of Service Quality and Its Implications for Future Research," *Journal of Marketing,* Fall 1985, p. 44. Published by the American Marketing Association.

1. **Gap between the customer's expectations and the marketer's perceptions.** Managers do not always have an accurate understanding of what customers want or how they will evaluate a firm's sevice efforts. The first step in providing good service, then, is to collect information—through customer surveys, evaluations of customer complaints, or other methods—to determine what service attributes customers consider important.

2. **Gap between management perceptions and service quality specifications.** Even when management has a clear understanding of what customers want, that understanding might not get translated into effective operating standards.

A firm's policies concerning customer service may be unclear, poorly communicated to employees, or haphazardly enforced. Unless a firm's employees know what the company's service policies are and believe that management is seriously committed to those standards, their performance is likely to fall short of desired levels.

3. **Gap between service quality specifications and service delivery.** Lip service by management is not enough to produce high-quality service. High standards must be backed by the programs, resources, and rewards necessary to enable and encourage employees to deliver good service. Employees must be provided with the training, equipment, and time necessary to deliver good service. Their service performance must be measured and evaluated. And good performance must be rewarded by making it part of the criteria for pay raises or promotions, or by other more direct inducements, in order to motivate the additional effort good service requires.

4. **Gap between service delivery and external communications.** Even good service performance may disappoint some customers if the firm's marketing communications cause them to have unrealistically high expectations. If the photographs in a vacation resort's advertising and brochures make the rooms look more spacious and luxurious than they really are, for instance, first-time customers are likely to be disappointed no matter how clean or well-tended those rooms are kept by the resort's staff.

5. **Gap between perceived service and expected service.** This results when management fails to close one or more of the other four gaps. It is this difference between a customer's expectations and his or her actual experience with the firm that leads to dissatisfaction.

The above discussion suggests a number of actions management can take to close the possible gaps and improve customer satisfaction with a company's service. To provide a more practical example, Exhibit 21–7 describes BellSouth Corp.'s attempts to implement a program aimed at improving customer service. Some goods manufacturers face an even more complex set of problems than those outlined above when they try to improve service to their customers. As discussed in Chapter 15, their ability to deliver good service may also depend on the design of their logistics systems and distribution channels, and on whether they can gain the cooperation and support of channel intermediaries in implementing their service policies.

Methods for maintaining a low-cost position

The experience curve is the most commonly discussed method for achieving and sustaining a low-cost position in an industry. But, as we argued earlier, a firm does not necessarily need a large relative market share in order to implement a low-cost strategy. The small clone manufacturers in the PC industry, for instance, found other ways to hold their costs below those of the industry leaders. Other means for obtaining a sustainable cost advantage include producing a no-frills product, using an innovative product design,

EXHIBIT 21 ♦ 7

BellSouth Corp.'s customer-oriented approach to improving service

Sometimes, listening to customers can trigger massive changes in an organization. BellSouth Corp. was reacting to customer input when it decided in 1985 to try to recombine its business services and its equipment sales and maintenance operations, which had been scattered into separate subsidiaries as part of the original Bell System divestiture plan.

The Atlanta-based telecommunications company found that customers were confused and irritated because they had to deal with different organizations for each different need. Many wanted to go back to the old days, before the court-ordered break-up, when business customers could handle everything with one call to the telephone operating company.

That, essentially, is what BellSouth has done, with the Federal Communications Commission's permission. On Jan. 1, it restored "one-stop shopping" for business customers, becoming the first of the Bell companies to recombine its services and equipment sales and maintenance staff completely under the FCC's new rules. "We took this step because customers have told us time and again over the past five years that this is what they wanted," says Jere Drummond, senior vice president-marketing for BellSouth.

BellSouth's decision to reintegrate, which took four years to implement, was an outgrowth of what the company calls its "Customer First" strategy. That strategy includes almost continual measurements of the satisfaction levels of the large, midsized, and small businesses and the residential customers it serves within its nine-state area.

Major customers are contacted in person or by mail every year. Some 2,000 midsized and small businesses are surveyed randomly each month. Still another survey, called the Telephone Service Attitude Measurement, tells the company each month what's on the minds of some 35,000 residential and business users with one or two telephone lines.

"We promise customers that we will do everything possible to provide faultless service and to stand behind the service we provide," explains Drummond. "We judge our performance by their standards, and one of those standards is being easy to do business with."

Source: Joan C. Szabo, "Service = Survival." Reprinted from *Nation's Business,* March 1989. Copyright 1989, U.S. Chamber of Commerce.

finding cheaper raw materials, automating production, developing low-cost distribution channels, and reducing overhead.[10]

A no-frills product

A direct approach to obtaining a low-cost position involves simply removing all frills and extras from the basic product or service. Thus, Yugo cars, warehouse furniture stores, legal services clinics, and grocery stores selling canned goods out of crates all offer lower costs and prices than their com-

---

[10] For a more detailed discussion of these and other approaches for attaining a low-cost position, see Aaker, *Strategic Market Management,* chap. 12.

petitors. This lower product cost is often sustainable because established differentiated competitors find it difficult to stop offering features and services their customers expect. However, those established firms may lower their own prices in the short run—even to the point of suffering losses—in an attempt to drive out a no-frills competitor that poses a serious threat. This was the response of the major airlines to inroads made by People Express. Thus, a firm considering a no-frills strategy needs the resources to withstand a possible price war.

Innovative product design

A simplified product design and standardized component parts can also lead to cost advantages. In the office copier industry, for instance, Japanese firms overcame substantial entry barriers by designing copiers that were extremely simple, with a fraction of the number of parts, compared to those of market-leading Xerox. Also, the copiers of Savin, Canon, and others incorporate readily available components as opposed to the customized components used in Xerox machines.

Cheaper raw materials

A firm with the foresight to acquire, or the creativity to find a way to use, relatively cheap raw materials can also gain a sustainable cost advantage. For example, Fort Howard Paper has achieved an advantage by being the only major papermaker to rely exclusively on recycled pulp. While the finished product is not so high in quality as paper from virgin wood, Fort Howard's lower cost gives it a competitive edge in the price-sensitive commercial market for toilet paper and other such products used in hotels, restaurants, and office buildings.

Innovative production processes

Although low-cost defender businesses typically spend little on *product R&D*, they often continue to devote substantial sums to *process R&D*. Innovations in the production process—including development of automated or computer controlled processes—can help them sustain advantages over competitors.

In some labor-intensive industries, a business can achieve a cost advantage—at least in the short term—by gaining access to inexpensive labor. This is usually achieved by moving all or part of the production process to countries with low wage rates, such as Taiwan, Korea, or Mexico. Unfortunately, because such moves are relatively easy to emulate, this kind of cost advantage may not be sustainable.

Low-cost distribution

When distribution accounts for a relatively high proportion of a product's total delivered cost, a firm might gain a substantial advantage by developing lower cost alternative channels. Typically, this involves eliminating, or shifting to the customer, some of the functions performed by traditional channels in return for a lower price. In the PC hardware and software industries, for example, mail-order discounters can offer low prices because they have fewer fixed costs than the retail stores with which they compete. However, they also do not provide technical advice or postsale service to their customers.

Reductions in overhead

Successfully sustaining a low-cost strategy requires that the firm pare and control its major overhead costs as quickly as possible as its industry matures. Many U.S. companies learned this lesson the hard way during the 1980s when high costs of old plants, labor, and large inventories left them vulnerable to more efficient foreign competitors and to corporate raiders.

Business strategy and performance

Analyzer—and particularly defender—businesses are mostly concerned with protecting their existing positions in one or more mature market segments. Their primary objective is usually to maximize profitability over the remaining life of those established product-markets rather than spending heavily to increase market share. Thus, financial dimensions of performance, such as return on investment and cash flow, are usually of greater interest to such businesses than more growth-oriented dimensions, like volume, market share, or new-product success.

Firms with the highest quality goods and services obtain higher pretax returns on investment across all types of industries than businesses with average or below-average quality offerings.[11] This positive relationship between quality differentiation and ROI appears to hold true regardless of a business's market share or investment intensity.[12] In other words, a business need not limit its focus to the relatively small "snob-appeal" segment of the market in order to make money with a high-quality strategy. Good products and good service can have mass appeal, as the Japanese auto makers have demonstrated.

Alternatively, low-cost producers can also prosper in mature markets. In all eight industries studied by Hall, for example, one of the two businesses with the highest ROIs in each industry was the firm with the lowest delivered cost position in that industry.[13] And, because factors other than the experience curve affect a business's unit costs, a firm does not necessarily

---

[11] To refresh your memory about the evidence of a positive relationship between relative quality and ROI performance, return to Exhibit 11–7 in Chapter 11.

[12] Robert Jacobson and David A. Aaker, "The Strategic Role of Product Quality," *Journal of Marketing*, October 1987, pp. 31–44.

[13] Hall, "Survival Strategies."

have to be a market share leader to successfully implement a low-cost strategy.

The major lesson to be learned, then, is that the choice between a differentiation or a low-cost business strategy is not the critical determinant of success in mature markets. What is critical is that one or the other strategy be chosen, clearly defined, and well-implemented. The businesses with the poorest financial performance during industry maturity—and those most vulnerable to environmental changes and threats—are those without any consistent strategy. They fail to provide either a differentiated offering or lower costs than their competitors.

MARKETING STRATEGIES FOR MATURE MARKETS

Marketing objectives

Since markets can remain in the maturity stage for decades, milking or harvesting mature product-markets by maximizing short-run profits makes little sense. Pursuing such an objective typically involves substantial cuts in marketing and R&D expenses, which can lead to premature losses of volume and market share and lower profits in the longer term. The business should strive during the early years of market maturity to maximize the flow of profits over the remaining life of the product-market. Thus, the most critical marketing objective is to maintain and protect the business's market share. In a mature market where few new customers buy the product for the first time, the business must continue to win its share of repeat purchases from existing customers.

Because different segments of a market mature at different times and environmental conditions can change over the mature phase of a product's life, there may be opportunities for additional volume growth. Thus, an important secondary objective for firms in many mature product-markets is to stimulate additional volume growth. Such an objective is particularly appropriate for industry share leaders because they often can capture a relatively large share of any additional volume generated. A firm might pursue several different marketing objectives to squeeze additional volume from a mature market. First, they can try to increase the product's penetration in one or more existing market segments by converting current nonusers into users. This is usually done by modifying the product offering to enhance its value to those potential customers. In a second approach, the firm increases the amount used by current customers through marketing actions that increase their frequency of use or promote new ways to use the product. Finally, the firm might try to expand into underdeveloped market segments by moving into new geographic areas (say, global marketing) or by developing a flanker brand or producing for private labels to appeal to more price-sensitive segments.

Marketing actions and strategies for maintaining current customers

In Chapter 20, we saw that holding current customers was an important marketing objective for maintaining market share in a growth market. A number of the share-maintenance marketing strategies discussed in that chapter continue to be relevant for firms as their markets mature. The appropriateness of those various strategies for a specific business unit depends, however, on whether it is a share leader in its industry or one of the smaller competitors.

Strategies for share leaders

For leading firms with a strong competitive position, perhaps the most obvious strategy is to continue to protect and strengthen that position through a **fortress defense.** Recall that such a strategy involves two sets of marketing actions: those aimed at improving customer satisfaction and loyalty, and those intended to encourage and simplify repeat purchasing.

For differentiated defender businesses, customer satisfaction and loyalty can be maintained and improved by continuing to pay strict attention to quality control and by making reasonable R&D expenditures for product improvements. Advertising should also continue to inform customers about product improvements and keep the brand name fresh in their memories. Thus, while the physical appearance of BMW's automobiles did not change dramatically throughout the 1980s, the firm made hundreds of technical improvements to its cars over the decade, such as anti-lock brakes. BMW heavily promoted those improvements as part of a campaign to enhance the firm's high-quality image.

A firm should also pay attention to the continued strengthening of customer service. For consumer goods, this might involve ongoing incentive and training programs for retail dealers or the expansion of company-owned service centers. For industrial goods, the firm might switch to more direct channels of distribution to gain better control over inventories, delivery times, and customer relations. It might also organize its salesforce into specialized groups focused on servicing major industries or applications segments, as IBM has done in the commercial PC market. Or it might develop national or key account executives to concentrate on servicing its largest customers.

For low-cost defenders, implementing a fortress defense largely means a continuing search for ways of maintaining a low delivered cost position within the industry. Although some expenditures on product R&D might continue to keep up with competitive improvements and to simplify the product and reduce its cost, the bulk of such expenditures should focus on process R&D to improve production efficiency. Such businesses can also look for ways to increase the efficiency of their sales and distribution systems (e.g., telemarketing for smaller accounts or the use of manufacturer's reps in territories with low sales potential) and to reduce overhead.

EXHIBIT 21 ♦ 8

Low costs allow greater market expenditures at Heinz

The H. J. Heinz Company worked diligently during the early 1980s to become the low-cost producer in a number of food categories. Between 1980 and 1985, the firm increased its gross profit rate (i.e., sales less the cost of goods) from 35.2 percent to 38.1 percent of sales, generating about $115 million in additional gross profit. About half of that came from lower costs and the rest from price increases. Heinz plowed 60 percent of the proceeds back into marketing, mostly for increased advertising and promotion. As a result, the firm has maintained a commanding lead in many of its mature markets. For instance, Heinz holds more than a 50 percent share of the ketchup and frozen french fries markets.

Source: Bill Saporito, "Heinz Pushes to Be the Low-Cost Producer," *Fortune,* June 24, 1985, p. 44.

A low-cost strategy does not necessarily mean the firm must always compete by offering the lowest prices. It might maintain prices at competitive levels and use some of its higher margins to support continued advertising and promotion programs aimed at preserving customer loyalty and stimulating repeat purchases. The H. J. Heinz Company provides an example of this approach, as described in Exhibit 21–8.

Regardless of its competitive strategy, a share leader in a mature market should also seek ways to simplify and encourage repeat purchasing by current customers. Maintenance of the firm's distribution coverage is critical here. Thus, firms often shift some promotional dollars from advertising into trade promotion as their markets mature. Businesses might also attempt to tie up major customers by offering long-term requirements contracts, just-in-time (JIT) delivery agreements, or computerized reorder systems like the one American Hospital Supply developed for its major hospital customers.

When confronted by aggressive low-cost competitors, a share leader may have no choice but to adopt either a **confrontation** or a **flanker strategy** to preserve its market share. In the airline industry, for instance, the major carriers confronted the low-price, no-frills challenge of People Express by matching the firm's low prices on directly competing routes. Even though the major lines lost money on those routes, their ability to subsidize those losses with income from other less competitive routes and their greater financial resources eventually enabled them to drive People Express into bankruptcy. On the other hand, Pillsbury's prepared dough SBU developed several low-priced flanker brands, such as Pillsbury Basic Biscuits and Ballard, to meet the threat posed by several regional and private lable producers to the unit's very profitable Hungry Jack line.

Strategies for low-share competitors

Small-share businesses can earn substantial profits in mature markets by focusing on marketing strategies that avoid prolonged direct confrontations with share leaders, such as a niche strategy or a guerrilla attack. A **niche**

strategy can be particularly effective when the target segment is too small to appeal to larger competitors or when the small-share firm can establish a strong differential advantage and brand preference among customers in the segment. For instance, even in an era when many people were reducing their alcohol consumption and turning to lighter beverages such as white wine, Jim Beam maintained a very profitable share of the small but loyal segment of bourbon drinkers. The family-run operation continued to pay close attention to product quality, remaining faithful to the traditional formula and production methods handed down through the family for generations. It promoted its quality image with $10 million of annual advertising focused on the target segment of bourbon drinkers through ads in carefully selected magazines. The company also avoided any attempts to diversify or expand its product line into areas that might lead to direct confrontations with the larger competitors in the liquor industry. As a result, Jim Beam earned about $40 million on sales of about $250 million in 1985.[14]

When the market is more homogeneous, or when one of the industry's larger competitors dominates all segments, a small-share firm may have little choice but to engage in a **guerrilla attack strategy.** The small-share firm launches sporadic raids against the customers of its more established competitors to preserve, or even marginally increase, its limited share of a mature market. To avoid massive retaliation, such raids should be limited in duration and directed against a limited number of geographic areas. Local advertising blitzes—and particularly regional sales promotion efforts such as coupon drops and merchandising deals—are effective tools for implementing a guerrilla attack. Such efforts can target specific customer groups in limited areas for a short time. They are difficult for larger competitors to respond to because cents-off promotions cost high-share firms more in absolute dollars.[15]

Marketing actions and strategies for extending volume growth

Even when total industry sales volume has been stagnant for a while, there may still be opportunities for a firm, particularly a share leader, to precipitate a renewed spurt of growth through aggressive marketing actions. A firm might use three different strategies, either singly or in combination, to do so: an **increased penetration strategy,** an **extended use strategy,** and a **market expansion strategy.** Exhibit 21–9 summarizes the environmental situations where each of these strategies is most appropriate and the objectives each is best suited for accomplishing. Exhibit 21–10 (page 758) outlines some spe-

---

[14] Fierman, "How to Make Money in Mature Markets," p. 50.

[15] A. L. Stern, "New Marketing Game: Stealing Customers," *Dun's Business Month,* February 1985, pp. 48–50.

EXHIBIT 21 ◆ 9

Situational determinants of appropriate marketing objectives and strategies for extending growth in mature markets

Situational variables	Growth extension strategies		
	Increased penetration	**Extended use**	**Market expansion**
Primary objective	Increase the proportion of users by converting current nonusers in one or more major market segments.	Increase the amount of product used by the average customer by increasing frequency of use or developing new and more varied ways to use the product.	Expand the number of potential customers by targeting underdeveloped geographic areas or applications segments.
Market characteristics	Relatively low penetration in one or more segments (i.e., low percentage of potential users have adopted the product); relatively homogeneous market with only a few large segments.	Relatively high penetration but low frequency of use in one or more major segments; product used in only limited ways or for special occasions; relatively homogeneous market with only a few large segments.	Relatively heterogeneous market with a variety of segments; some geographic areas, including foreign countries, with low penetration; some product applications underdeveloped.
Competitor characteristics	Competitors hold relatively small market shares; comparatively limited resources or competencies make it unlikely they will steal a significant portion of converted nonusers.	Competitors hold relatively small market shares; comparatively limited resources or competencies make it unlikely their brands will be purchased for newly developed uses.	Competitors hold relatively small market shares; have insufficient resources or competencies to preempt underdeveloped geographic areas or applications segments.
Firm characteristics	A market share leader in the industry; has R&D and marketing competencies to produce product modifications or line extensions; has promotional resources to stimulate primary demand among current nonusers.	A market share leader in the industry; has marketing competencies and resources to develop and promote new uses.	A market share leader in the industry; has marketing and distribution competencies and resources to develop new global markets or applications segments.

cific marketing actions a firm might employ to implement each of the strategies. We discuss them in more detail in the following paragraphs.

Increased penetration strategy

The total sales volume produced by a target segment of customers is a function of (1) the number of potential customers in the segment, (2) the product's penetration of that segment—that is, the proportion of potential customers who actually use the product, and (3) the average frequency with which customers consume the product and make another purchase. Where usage frequency is quite high among current customers but only a relatively small portion of all potential users actually buy the product, a firm might use a strategy aimed at increasing market penetration. It is an appropriate strategy for an industry's share leader because such firms can more likely gain and retain a substantial share of new customers than smaller firms with less well-known brands.

The secret to a successful increased penetration strategy lies in discovering why nonusers are uninterested in the product. Often the product does not offer sufficient value from the potential customer's point of view to justify the effort or expense involved in buying and using it. One obvious solution to such a problem is to **enhance the product's value** to potential customers by adding features or benefits, usually via line extensions. Jostens used this approach successfully. By expanding the number of designs and price ranges offered and promoting class rings as symbols and reminders of an important period in young people's lives, the firm greatly increased the proportion of high school students who buy rings.

A second way to add value to a product is to design and sell integrated systems that help improve the basic product's performance or ease of use. Both Apple and IBM, for instance, offer entire computer systems, which integrate the computer with software, disk drives, printers, and so on, for both individual and commercial users. Such capability gives these firms an advantage in attracting relatively uninformed buyers who are intimidated by the prospect of buying many individual pieces of equipment and trying to hook them all together.

A product's value may also be enhanced by offering services that improve its performance or ease of use for the potential customer. Since it is unlikely that people who do not know how to knit will ever buy yarn or knitting needles, for example, most yarn shops offer free knitting lessons.

Product modifications or line extensions will not, however, attract former nonusers unless the enhanced benefits are effectively promoted. For industrial goods, this may mean redirecting some sales efforts toward nonusers. The firm may offer additional incentives for new account sales or assign specific salespeople to call on targeted nonusers and convert them into new customers. For consumer goods, some combination of advertising to stimulate primary demand in the target segment and sales promotions to encourage trial, such as free samples or tie-in promotions with complementary

EXHIBIT 21 ◆ 10

Possible marketing actions for accomplishing growth extension objectives

Marketing strategy and objectives	Possible marketing actions

Increased penetration Convert current nonusers in target segment into users	◆ Enhance product's value by adding features, benefits, or services.
	 ◆ Enhance product's value by including it in the design of integrated systems.
	 ◆ Stimulate additional primary demand through promotional efforts stressing new features or benefits:
	   Advertising through selective media aimed at the target segment.
	   Sales promotions directed at stimulating trial among current nonusers (e.g., tie-ins with other products).
	   Some sales efforts redirected toward new account generation; perhaps by assigning some sales personnel as account development reps or by offering incentives for new account sales.
	 ◆ Improve product's availability by developing innovative distribution systems.

Extended use Increase frequency of use among current users	◆ Move storage of the product closer to the point of end use by offering additional package sizes or designs.
	 ◆ Encourage larger volume purchases (for nonperishable products):
	   Offer quantity discounts.
	   Offer consumer promotions to stimulate volume purchases or more frequent use (e.g., multipack deals, frequent flier programs).
	 ◆ Reminder advertising stressing basic product benefits for a variety of usage occasions.

Encourage a wider variety of uses among current users	◆ Develop line extensions suitable for additional uses or applications.
	 ◆ Develop and promote new uses, applications, or recipes for the basic product.
	   Include information about new applications/recipes on package.
	   Develop extended use advertising campaign, particularly with print media.
	   Communicate new application ideas through sales presentations to current customers.
	 ◆ Encourage new uses through sales promotions (e.g., tie-ins with complementary products).

products that nonusers currently buy, can be effective. In some cases, informative advertising can convert nonusers into customers without having to modify the product, especially when potential customers hold misconceptions or unjustifiably negative attitudes about the product. America's pork producers, for instance, have attempted to persuade health- and diet-conscious consumers to eat pork by promoting the fact that some cuts are relatively low in fat and calories and by positioning pork as the "other white meat."

EXHIBIT 21 ◆ 10
(concluded)

Marketing strategy and objectives	Possible marketing actions
Market expansion Develop differentiated positioning focused on untapped or under-developed segments	◆ Develop a differentiated flanker brand or product line with unique features or price that is more appealing to a segment of potential customers whose needs are not met by existing offerings *(see flanking strategy in Chapter 20)*. or ◆ Develop multiple line extensions or brand offerings with features or prices targeted to the unique needs and preferences of several smaller potential applications or regional segments *(see encirclement strategy in Chapter 20)*. ◆ Consider producing for private labels. ◆ Design advertising, personal selling, and/or sales promotion campaigns that address specific interests and concerns of potential customers in one or multiple underdeveloped segments to stimulate selective demand. ◆ Build unique distribution channels to more effectively reach potential customers in one or multiple underdeveloped segments. ◆ Design service programs to reduce the perceived risks of trial and/or solve the unique problems faced by potential customers in one or multiple under-developed segments (e.g., systems engineering, installation, operator trailing, extended warranties).

Finally, the benefits offered by some products may simply be too modest to justify much shopping effort for many potential customers. In such cases, development of more convenient or accessible distribution channels may expand market penetration. For instance, few travelers would go through the effort of calling an insurance agent to buy an accident policy for a single flight. But the sales of such policies are greatly increased by making them conveniently available through vending machines in airport terminals.

Extended use strategy

As noted earlier, the manager of General Foods' Cool Whip frozen dessert topping discovered that nearly three fourths of all households used the product, but the average consumer used it only four times a year and served it on only 7 percent of all toppable desserts. In such situations—good market penetration but low frequency of use—an extended use strategy may increase volume. This was particularly true in the Cool Whip case; the relatively large and homogeneous target market consisted for the most part of a single mass-market segment. Also, General Foods held nearly a two-thirds share of the frozen-topping market; and it had the marketing resources and competencies to capture most of the additional volume that an extended use strategy might generate. Its competition came largely from private labels and small regional producers.

One effective approach for stimulating increased frequency of use is to move product inventories closer to the point of use. This approach works particularly well with low-involvement consumer goods. Marketers know that most consumers are unlikely to expend additional time or effort to obtain such products when they are ready to use them. If there is no Cool Whip in the refrigerator when the consumer is preparing dessert, for instance, he or she is unlikely to run to the store immediately and will probably serve the dessert without topping.

One obvious way to move inventory closer to the point of consumption is to offer larger package sizes. The more customers buy at one time, the less likely they are to be out of stock when a usage opportunity arises. This approach can backfire, though, for a perishable product or when consumers perceive it as an impulsive indulgence. Thus, most superpremium ice creams, such as Häagen-Dazs or Frusen Glädjé, are sold in pint containers; most consumers want to avoid the temptation of having large quantities of such a high-calorie indulgence too readily available.

The design of a package can also help increase use frequency by making the product more convenient or easy to use. Examples include single-serving packages of Jell-O pudding to pack in children's lunches, packages of paper cups that include a convenient dispenser, and frozen-food packages that can go directly into a microwave oven.

Various sales promotion programs also help move inventories of a product closer to the point of use by encouraging larger volume purchases. Marketers commonly offer quantity discounts for this purpose in selling industrial goods. For consumer products, multi-item discounts or two-for-one deals serve the same purpose. Promotional programs also encourage greater frequency of use and increased customer loyalty in many service industries. Consider, for instance, the frequent flier programs offered by major airlines and the frequent guest programs promoted by large hotel chains.

Sometimes the product's characteristics inhibit customers from using it more frequently. If marketers can change those characteristics, such as difficulty of preparation or high calories, a new line extension might encourage customers to use more of the product or to use it more often. Frozen waffles and pancakes and low-calorie salad dressings are examples of such line extensions.

Finally, advertising can sometimes effectively increase use frequency by simply reminding customers to use the product more often. For instance, General Foods recently conducted a reminder campaign for Jell-O pudding that featured Bill Cosby asking, "When was the last time you served pudding, Mom?"

Another approach for extending use among current customers involves finding and promoting new functional uses for the product. Sometimes this does not even involve modifying the product, but simply promoting new ways to use it. Jell-O gelatin is a classic example, having generated substantial new sale volume over the years by promoting the use of Jell-O as an ingredient in salads, pie fillings, and other dishes.

Suggestions for new ways to use a product are promoted through a variety of methods. For industrial products, firms send technical advisories about new applications to the salesforce to present to their customers during regular sales calls. For consumer products, new use suggestions or recipes may be included on the package or in an advertising campaign. Print media advertising, in particular, can communicate more detailed information concerning the new application or recipe. Sales promotions, such as including cents-off coupons in ads featuring a new recipe, encourage customers to try a new application. To reduce costs, two or more manufacturers of complementary products sometimes cooperate in running such promotions. A recent ad promoting a simple Italian dinner, for instance, featured coupons for Kraft's Parmesan cheese, Pillsbury's Soft Breadsticks, and Campbell's Prego spaghetti sauce.

In some cases, slightly modified line extensions might encourage customers to use the product in different ways. Thus, Kraft introduced a jalapeno-flavored Cheese-Whiz in a microwavable container and promoted the product as an easy-to-prepare topping for nachos.

Market expansion strategy

In a mature industry with a fragmented and heterogeneous market where some segments are less well-developed than others, a market expansion strategy may generate substantial additional volume growth. Such a strategy aims at gaining new customers by targeting new or underdeveloped geographic markets (either regional or foreign) or new customer segments. Once again, the firms best suited for implementing such a strategy tend to be share leaders. But even smaller competitors can employ such a strategy successfully, as illustrated by the experience of the Baldor Company described in Exhibit 21–11.

Pursuing market expansion by strengthening a firm's position in new or underdeveloped domestic geographic markets can lead to experience curve benefits and operating synergies. The firm can rely on largely the same expertise and technology—and perhaps even the same production and distribution facilities—it has already developed. Unfortunately, domestic geographic expansion is often not viable in a mature industry because by that time the share leaders usually have attained national market coverage. Smaller regional competitors, on the other hand, might consider domestic geographic expansion as a means for improving their volume and share position. However, such a move risks retaliation from the large national brands as well as from entrenched regional competitors in the prospective new territory.

EXHIBIT 21 ◆ 11

Surviving a decade of foreign competition in a mature industry

> For the past decade, the U.S. electric motor industry has experienced poor sales. But un-
> like such big boys as General Electric, Reliance Electric, and Emerson Electric, a rela-
> tively small Fort Smith (Arkansas) company—Baldor—has emerged with record sales and
> profits as well as a higher market share. Since 1985, the company's sales have increased
> by 40 percent to an all-time high of $243 million while profits rose 53 percent. Baldor sur-
> vived and prospered by identifying undeveloped segments of potential industrial users and
> engineering highly specialized high-quality motors to meet the needs of those new market
> niches.
>
> For example, Baldor turns out explosion-proof motors for mining and gas applications,
> lint-proof motors for the textile industry, heart pumps for hospitals, large motors for the
> windshield wipers on battleships, and really big motors to roll steel. Such motors, while
> not sold in large quantities, do sell at premium prices. The company continues to explore
> new markets such as a "fitness" motor to turn jogger's treadmills and a wash-down motor
> that will survive dousings with the hot soapy waters used in canning mushrooms.

Source: Alan Farnham, "Baldor's Success: Made in the U.S.A.," *Fortune,* July 17, 1989, p. 101.

To get around the retaliation problem, a regional producer may try to
expand through the acquisition of small producers in other regions. This can
be a viable option when (1) the low profitability of some regional producers
enables the acquiring firm to buy their assets for less than the replacement
cost of the capacity involved, and (2) synergies gained by combining regional
operations and the infusion of resources from the acquiring firm can improve the effectiveness and profitability of the acquired producers. For
example, Heileman Brewing Company grew from the 31st-largest brewer in
the mid-1960s to the fourth-largest by the mid-1980s through the acquisition
of nearly 30 regional brands. Heileman now controls strong regional brands
such as Old Style, Carling, and Rainier, but because it has no strong national
brand, it has avoided antitrust opposition to its acquisition program. After
acquisition, Heileman maintains the identity of each brand, increases its
advertising budget, and expands its distribution by incorporating it into the
firm's distribution system in other regions. As a result, Heileman has
achieved a strong earnings record for two decades.

For share leaders in a mature domestic market, less-developed markets in
foreign countries often present a viable opportunity for geographic expansion. This kind of **global marketing** can be accomplished in a variety of
ways, from simply using agent middlemen to establishing wholly owned
subsidiaries in foreign markets. However, differences in the social, political,
and competitive environments across nations often necessitate modifications in the firm's strategic marketing programs. Because the issues involved

are both crucial and complex, the next chapter is devoted to a discussion of global marketing strategies.

In a different approach to market expansion, the firm identifies and develops new customer or application segments. Sometimes the firm can reach new customer segments by simply expanding the distribution system without changing the product's characteristics or the other marketing mix elements. A sporting goods manufacturer that sells its products to consumers through retail stores, for instance, might expand into the commercial market consisting of schools and amateur and professional sports teams by establishing a direct salesforce.

In most instances, though, the development of new market segments requires some modifications to the product to make it more suitable for the application or to provide more of the benefits desired by customers in the new segment. Thus, Jostens expanded its market by developing custom-designed rings, pins, and jackets for corporate incentive and recognition programs. When the firm pursues the development of one relatively large new segment, its marketing activities are very similar to those associated with the *flanking strategy* discussed in Chapter 20. When the firm attempts to expand into two or more underdeveloped segments at the same time, its marketing efforts will be similar to those of an *encirclement strategy*.

One danger in investing heavily to develop new customer or application segments is that other competitors might reap the lion's share of the benefits. This is especially true when the product involved is hard to differentiate. For example, Inco, the leading producer of nickel, developed a variety of new uses for nickel during the 1960s and 1970s, including applications in stainless steel for automobiles and appliances. But the additional market growth stimulated by these new applications attracted new competitors. Inco attempted to keep both its commanding market share and its margins by holding prices but differentiating its offerings with good technical service, quick delivery, and the ability to guarantee large quantity shipments. Nevertheless, the firm was vulnerable to lower-priced competitors and its market share slipped sharply.[16] Thus, a market expansion strategy is most suitable when the firm can be reasonably certain of gaining and maintaining a competitive advantage in the newly developed segments.

One final possibility for market expansion is to produce **private-label brands** for large retailers such as Sears or Safeway. Firms whose own brands hold relatively weak positions and which have excess production capacity find this a particularly attractive option. Private labeling allows such firms to gain access to established customer segments without making substantial

16 "Inco: Guarding Its Edge in Nickel While Starting to Diversify Again," *Business Week*, June 9, 1980, pp. 104–6.

marketing expenditures, thus increasing the firm's volume and lowering its per-unit costs. However, since private labels typically compete on the basis of low price—and their sponsors usually have strong bargaining power—producing private labels is often not a very profitable option unless a manufacturer already has a relatively low-cost position in the industry. It can also be a risky strategy, particularly for the smaller firm, because reliance on one, or a few, large private-label customers can result in drastic volume reductions and unit cost increases should those customers decide to switch suppliers.

For example, in the years following World War II, Norge was a major brand in the household-appliance industry. In the 1960s, however, the firm decided to manufacture private-label washers and driers for several mass merchandisers, including Montgomery Ward. Private labels eventually consumed such a large proportion of the firm's capacity and resources that it could not give adequate marketing support to the Norge brand. That brand's market share eventually shrunk to nothing, and the firm is now so dependent on its private label customers it would find it hard to survive if one or more of them switched to new suppliers.

STRATEGIES FOR DECLINING MARKETS

Most products eventually enter a decline phase in their life cycles when unit sales fall over a sustained period. As sales decline, excess capacity once again develops. As the remaining competitors fight to hold volume in the face of falling sales, industry profits erode. Consequently, the conventional wisdom suggests that declining products should either be divested quickly or harvested to maximize short-term profits. Not all markets decline in the same way or at the same rate of speed, however; nor do all firms have the same competitive strengths and weaknesses within those markets. Therefore, as in most other situations, the relative attractiveness of the declining product-market and the business's competitive position within it should dictate the appropriate strategy.

Relative attractiveness of declining markets

Jostens' experience shows that some declining product-markets can offer attractive opportunities well into the future, at least for one or a few strong competitors. In other product-markets, the potential for continued profits during the decline stage is dismal. The acetylene industry offers a good example of an unattractive declining market. Acetylene, a gas used for welding and other high-temperature applications, is rapidly being replaced by ethylene and other substitutes. Because acetylene is a commodity product with high fixed manufacturing costs, the remaining producers have engaged in protracted price wars in an attempt to hold volume. Rapidly declining volumes and low profits have driven most acetylene producers to seek ways of abandoning the industry as quickly as possible.[17]

Three sets of factors help determine the relative attractiveness of declining product-markets from a strategic point of view: **conditions of demand,** including the rate and certainty of future declines in volume; **exit barriers,** or the ease with which weaker competitors can leave the market; and factors affecting the **intensity of future competitive rivalry** within the market. The impact of each of these sets of variables on the attractiveness of declining market environments is summarized in Exhibit 21–12 and discussed below.

Conditions of demand

Demand in a product-market declines for a number of reasons. Technological advances produce substitute products (such as electronic calculators for slide rules), often with higher quality or lower cost. Demographic shifts lead to a shrinking target market (for example, baby foods). Customers' needs, tastes, or lifestyles change (the falling consumption of beef). Finally, the cost of inputs or complementary products increases and shrinks demand (the effects of rising gasoline prices on sales of recreational vehicles in the late 1970s).

The cause of a decline in demand can affect both the rate and the predictability of that decline. A fall in sales due to a demographic shift, for instance, is likely to be gradual, whereas the switch to a technically superior substitute can be abrupt. Similarly, the fall in demand as customers switch to a better substitute is predictable, while a decline in sales due to a change in tastes is not.

As Exhibit 21–12 indicates, both the rate and certainty of sales decline are demand characteristics that affect a market's attractiveness. A slow and gradual decline allows an orderly withdrawal of weaker competitors. Overcapacity does not become excessive and lead to predatory competitive behavior, and the competitors that remain are more likely to make profits than in a quick or erratic decline. Also, when most industry managers believe market decline is predictable and certain, reduction of capacity is more likely to be orderly than when there is substantial uncertainty about whether demand might level off or even become revitalized. For instance, because the market for high school class rings is largely shaped by demographic trends, Jostens and its competitors could accurately forecast a decline in future market potential. This not only gave Jostens time to develop an aggressive marketing strategy to improve its market share during the decline period, but it also lowered the odds that smaller competitors would stay in the industry due to false expectations of future growth.

---

[17] This example, as well as much of the following discussion, is based on material found in Kathryn Rudie Harrigan and Michael E. Porter, "End-Game Strategies for Declining Industries," *Harvard Business Review,* July–August 1983, pp. 111–20. Also see Kathryn Rudie Harrigan, *Strategies for Declining Business* (Lexington, Mass.: D.C. Heath, 1980).

EXHIBIT 21 ♦ 12

Factors affecting the attractiveness of declining market environments

	Environmental attractiveness	
	Hospitable	*Inhospitable*
Conditions of demand		
Speed of decline	Very slow	Rapid or erratic
Certainty of decline	100% certain predictable patterns	Great uncertainty, erratic patterns
Pockets of enduring demand	Several or major ones	No niches
Product differentiation	Brand loyalty	Commodity-like products
Price stability	Stable, price premiums attainable	Very unstable, pricing below costs
Exit barriers		
Reinvestment requirements	None	High, often mandatory and involving capital assets
Excess capacity	Little	Substantial
Asset age	Mostly old assets	Sizable new assets and old ones not retired
Resale markets for assets	Easy to convert or sell	No markets available, substantial costs to retire
Shared facilities	Few free-standing plants	Substantial and interconnected with important businesses
Vertical integration	Little	Substantial
Single-product competitors	None	Several large companies
Rivalry determinants		
Customer industries	Fragmented, weak	Strong bargaining power
Customer switching costs	High	Minimal
Diseconomies of scale	None	Substantial penalty
Dissimilar strategic groups	Few	Several in same target markets

Source: Kathryn Rudie Harrigan and Michael E. Porter, "End-Game Strategies for Declining Industries," *Harvard Business Review,* July–August 1983, p. 117.

Of course, not all segments of the market decline in sales volume at the same time or at the same rate. The number and size of enduring niches or pockets of demand, and the customer purchase behavior within them, also influence the continuing attractiveness of the market. When the demand pockets are large or numerous, and when the customers in those niches are brand loyal and relatively insensitive to price, competitors with large shares and differentiated products can continue to make substantial profits. For example, even though the market for cigars has been shrinking for years, there continues to be a sizable number of cigar smokers who prefer premium-quality cigars. Those firms with well-established positions at the premium end of the cigar industry have continued to earn above-average returns.

Exit barriers

The higher the exit barriers, the less hospitable a product-market will be during the decline phase of its life cycle. When weaker competitors find it hard to leave a product-market as demand falls, excess capacity develops and firms engage in aggressive pricing or promotional efforts to try to prop up their volume and hold down unit costs. Thus, exit barriers lead to competitive volatility.

Once again, Exhibit 21–12 indicates that a variety of factors influence the ease with which businesses can exit an industry. One critical consideration involves the amount of highly specialized assets. Assets unique to a given business are difficult to divest because of their low liquidation value. The only potential buyers for such assets are other firms that would use them for a similar purpose, which is unlikely in a declining industry—particularly one with substantial excess capacity. Thus, the firm may have little choice but to remain in the business or to sell the assets for their scrap value. This option is particularly unattractive when the assets are relatively new and not fully depreciated.

Another major exit barrier occurs when the assets or resources of the declining business intertwine with the firm's other business units, either through shared facilities and programs or through vertical integration. Exit from the declining business might shut down shared production facilities, lower salesforce commissions, damage customer relations, and increase unit costs in the firm's other businesses to a point that greatly damages their profitability.

Emotional factors can also act as exit barriers. Managers often feel reluctant to admit failure by divesting a business, even though it no longer produces acceptable returns. This is especially true when the business played an important role in the firm's history and when it houses a large number of senior managers.

Intensity of future competitive rivalry

Even when substantial pockets of continuing demand remain within a declining business, it may not be wise for a firm to pursue them in the face of future intense competitive rivalry. Exit barriers preventing weaker competitors from leaving the industry strongly influence the intensity of that future rivalry. Other factors also affect the ability of the remaining firms to avoid intense price competition and maintain reasonable margins: size and bargaining power of the customers who continue to buy the product; customers' ability to switch to substitute products or to alternative suppliers; and any potential diseconomies of scale involved in capturing an increased share of the remaining volume.

Divestment or liquidation

When the market environment in a declining industry is unattractive or when a business has a relatively weak competitive position, the firm may recover more of its investment by selling the business in the early stages of decline rather than later. The earlier the business is sold, the more uncertain potential buyers are likely to be about the future direction of demand in the industry and thus the more likely that a willing buyer can be found. Of course, the firm that divests early runs the risk that its forecast of the industry's future may be wrong. Thus, Raytheon sold its vacuum-tube business in the early 1960s even though transistors had just begun replacing tubes in radios and TV sets and there was still a strong replacement demand for tubes. By moving early, the firm achieved a much higher liquidation value than companies that tried to unload their tube-making facilities in the 70s, when the industry was clearly in its twilight years.[18]

Quick divestment may not be possible if the firm faces high barriers, such as interdependencies across business units or customer expectations of continued product availability. By starting early to plan for departure, however, the firm may be able to reduce some of those barriers before liquidation is necessary.

Marketing strategies for remaining competitors

The conventional wisdom suggests that a business that decides to remain in a declining product-market should pursue a harvesting strategy aimed at maximizing its cash flow in the short run. Such businesses actually have several other strategic options, however. They might attempt to maintain their position as the market declines, improve their position in order to become the profitable survivor, or focus efforts on one or more remaining demand pockets or market niches. Once again, the appropriateness of these strategies depends on factors affecting the attractiveness of the declining market and on the business's competitive strengths and weaknesses. Exhibit 21–13 summarizes the situational determinants of the appropriateness of each strategy. Some of the marketing actions that might be taken to implement them are discussed below and summarized in Exhibit 21–14 (page 770).

---

[18] Harrigan and Porter, "End-Game Strategies," p. 114.

EXHIBIT   21 ♦ 13

Situational determinants of appropriate marketing objectives and strategies for declining markets

Situational variables	Strategies for declining markets			
	Harvesting	**Maintenance**	**Profitable survivor**	**Niche**
Primary objective	Maximize short-term cash flow; maintain or increase margins even at the expense of a slow decline in market share.	Maintain share in short term as market declines, even if margins must be sacrificed.	Increase share of the declining market with an eye to future profits; encourage weaker competitors to exit.	Focus on strengthening position in one or a few relatively substantial segments with potential for future profits.
Market characteristics	Future market decline is certain, but likely to occur at a slow and steady rate.	Market has experienced recent declines, but future direction and attractiveness are currently hard to predict.	Future market decline is certain, but likely to occur at a slow and steady rate; substantial pockets of demand will continue to exist.	Overall market may decline quickly, but one or more segments will remain as demand pockets or decay slowly.
Competitor characteristics	Few strong competitors; low exit barriers; future rivalry not likely to be intense.	Few strong competitors, but intensity of future rivalry is hard to predict.	Few strong competitors; exit barriers are low or can be reduced by firm's intervention.	One or more stronger competitors in mass market, but not in the target segment.
Firm's characteristics	Has a leading share position; has a substantial proportion of loyal customers who are likely to continue buying brand even if marketing support is reduced.	Has a leading share of the market and a relatively strong competitive position.	Has a leading share of the market and a strong competitive position; has superior resources or competencies necessary to encourage competitors to exit or to acquire them.	Has a sustainable competitive advantage in target segment, but overall resources may be limited.

EXHIBIT 21 ◆ 14

Possible marketing actions appropriate for different strategies in declining markets

Marketing strategy and objectives	Possible marketing actions
Harvesting strategy Maximize short-term cash flow; maintain or increase margins even at the expense of market share decline.	◆ Eliminate R&D expenditures and capital investments related to the business. ◆ Reduce marketing and sales budgets. Greatly reduce or eliminate advertising and sales promotion expenditures, with the possible exception of periodic reminder advertising targeted at current customers. Reduce trade promotions to minimum level necessary to prevent rapid loss of distribution coverage. Focus salesforce efforts on attaining repeat purchases from current customers. ◆ Seek ways to reduce production costs, even at the expense of slow erosion in product quality. ◆ Raise price if necessary to maintain margins.
Maintenance strategy Maintain market share for the short term, even at the expense of margins.	◆ Continue product and process R&D expenditures in short term aimed at maintaining or improving product quality. ◆ Continue maintenance levels of advertising and sales promotion targeted at current users. ◆ Continue trade promotion at levels sufficient to avoid any reduction in distribution coverage. ◆ Focus salesforce efforts on attaining repeat purchases from current users. ◆ Lower prices if necesary to maintain share, even at the expense of reduced margins.

Harvesting strategy

The objective of a harvesting—or milking—strategy is to generate cash quickly by maximizing cash flow over a relatively short term. This typically involves avoiding any additional investment in the business, greatly reducing operating (including marketing) expenses, and perhaps raising prices. Since the firm usually expects to ultimately divest or abandon the business, some loss of sales and market share during the pursuit of this strategy is likely. The trick is to hold the business's volume and share declines to a relatively slow and steady rate. A precipitous and premature loss of share would limit the total amount of cash the business could generate during the market's decline.

A harvesting strategy is most appropriate for a firm holding a relatively strong competitive position in the market at the start of the decline and a cadre of current customers likely to continue buying the brand even after marketing support is reduced. Such a strategy also works best when the market's decline is inevitable but likely to occur at a relatively slow and

EXHIBIT   21 ♦ 14
(*concluded*)

Marketing strategy and objectives	Possible marketing actions
Profitable survivor strategy Increase share of the declining market; encourage weaker competitors to exit.	♦ Signal competitors that firm intends to remain in industry and pursue an increased share. Maintain or increase advertising and sales promotion budgets. Maintain or increase distribution coverage through aggressive trade promotion. Focus some salesforce effort on winning away competitors' customers. Continue product and process R&D to seek product improvements or cost reductions. ♦ Consider introducing line extensions to appeal to remaining demand segments. ♦ Lower prices if necessary to increase share, even at the expense of short-term margins. ♦ Consider agreements to produce replacement parts or private labels for smaller competitors considering getting out of production.
Niche strategy Strengthen share position in one or a few segments with potential for continued profit.	♦ Continued product and process R&D aimed at product improvements or modifications that will appeal to target segment(s). ♦ Consider producing for private labels in order to maintain volume and hold down unit costs. ♦ Focus advertising, sales promotion, and personal selling campaigns on customers in target segment(s); stress appeals of greatest importance to those customers. ♦ Maintain distribution channels appropriate for reaching target segment; seek unique channel arrangements to more effectively reach customers in target segment(s). ♦ Design service programs that address unique concerns/problems of customers in the target segment(s).

steady rate, and when rivalry among remaining competitors is not likely to be very intense. Such conditions help enable the business to maintain adequate price levels and profit margins as volume gradually falls.

Implementing a harvesting strategy means avoiding any additional long-term investments in plant, equipment, or R&D. It also necessitates substantial cuts in operating expenditures for marketing activities. This often means the firm should greatly reduce the number of models or package sizes in its product line in order to reduce inventory and manufacturing costs. The business should also seek improvements in the efficiency of sales and distribution. This often involves reducing the amount of attention and service paid to small marginal customers.

For industrial goods, a business might establish minimum order quantities to avoid the high processing and delivery costs associated with small purchases. It could service its smaller accounts through a telemarketing system rather than through its field salesforce; or it could assign its smaller customers to agent middlemen. For consumer goods, the business might move to a more selective distribution system by concentrating its efforts on the larger retail chains. The firm would substantially reduce consumer advertising and promotion expenditures, usually to the minimum level necessary to retain adequate distribution. Finally, the business should attempt to maintain or perhaps even increase its price levels to increase margins. A classic example of a harvesting strategy is that of Chase & Sanborn coffee, as described in Exhibit 21–15.

Maintenance strategy

In markets where future volume trends are highly uncertain, a business with a leading share position might pursue a strategy aimed at maintaining its market share, at least until the market's future becomes more predictable. In such a maintenance strategy, the business continues to pursue the same strategy that brought it success during the market's mature stage. This approach will probably result in reduced margins and profits in the short term, though; the firm is likely to have to reduce prices or increase marketing expenditures to hold its share in the face of declining industry volume. Thus, share maintenance should be considered only an interim strategy. Once it becomes clear that the market will continue to decline, the business should switch to a different strategy—such as harvesting, divestment, or a profitable survivor strategy—that will provide better cash flows and return on investment over the market's remaining life.

EXHIBIT 21 ◆ 15

Chase & Sanborn's harvesting strategy

In 1879, Chase & Sanborn was the first U.S. company to sell roasted coffee in sealed cans. The company became part of Standard Brands and dominated the coffee industry during the 1920s and 30s largely through heavy expenditures on radio advertising. After World War II, however, the slowing growth of coffee consumption, the development of instant coffee, and large and aggressive new competitors like General Foods' Maxwell House brand made Chase & Sanborn reluctant to continue the large marketing expenditures necessary to hold its market share. Consequently, it adopted a harvesting strategy. Advertising and promotional expenditures were gradually cut, and eventually stopped, while the brand's share slowly eroded. Finally, Standard Brands merged with Nabisco in 1981, and the coffee business was sold to a small Miami firm for $15 million.

Source: David Aaker, *Strategic Market Management,* 2nd ed. (New York: John Wiley & Sons, 1988), p. 284.

Profitable survivor strategy

An aggressive alternative for a business with a strong share position and a sustainable competitive advantage in a declining product-market is to invest enough to increase its share position and establish itself as the industry leader for the remainder of the market's decline. This kind of strategy makes most sense when the firm expects a gradual decline in market demand or when substantial pockets of continuing demand are likely well into the future. It is also an attractive strategy when a firm's declining business is closely intertwined with other SBUs through shared facilities and programs or common customer segments.

A profitable survivor strategy often makes it possible for a strong competitor to improve its share position in a declining market at relatively low cost because other competitors may be harvesting their businesses or preparing to exit. Once the firm has achieved a strong and unchallenged position, it can switch to a harvesting strategy and reap substantial profits over the remaining life of the product-market. The key to the success of such a strategy is to encourage other competitors to leave the market early, or at least to avoid costly competitive rivalries with the firm seeking to become the profitable survivor.

A firm might encourage smaller competitors to abandon the industry by being visible and explicit about its commitment to become the leading survivor. It should aggressively seek increased market share, either by cutting prices or by increasing advertising and promotion expenditures. It might also introduce line extensions aimed at remaining pockets of demand to make it more difficult for smaller competitors to find profitable niches. Thus, General Foods introduced a line of gourmet instant "international coffees" to the declining coffee market to preempt a small specialized niche. Finally, the firm might reduce its competitors' exit barriers to make it easier for them to leave the industry. This might involve taking over competitors' long-term contracts, agreeing to supply spare parts or to service their products in the field, or providing them with components or private-label products. For instance, large regional bakeries have encouraged grocery chains to abandon their own bakery operations by supplying them with private-label baked goods.

The ultimate way to remove competitors' exit barriers is to purchase their operations and either improve their efficiency or remove them from the industry to avoid excess capacity. With continued decline in industry sales a certainty, smaller competitors may be forced to sell their assets at a price low enough for the survivor to reap high returns on its investment. For example, White Consolidated Industries purchased a number of appliance brands such as Kelvinator, Philco, Westinghouse, and Frigidaire from firms that were strongly motivated to exit the sagging appliance industry. By paying favorable prices for each operation, streamlining product lines, and improving the efficiency of manufacturing and distribution operations, White returned each brand to profitability in a matter of months and captured the third-leading market share in the appliance industry.

Niche strategy

Even when most segments of an industry are expected to decline rapidly, a niche strategy may still be viable if one or more substantial segments will either remain as stable pockets of demand or decay slowly. The business pursuing such a strategy should have a strong competitive position in the target segment or be able to build a sustainable competitive advantage relatively quickly to preempt competitors. This is one strategy that even smaller competitors can sometimes successfully pursue because the assets and resources required can be focused on a limited portion of the total market. The marketing actions a business might take to strengthen and preserve its position in a target niche are similar to those discussed earlier concerning niche strategies in mature markets.

SUMMARY

An industry's transition from growth to maturity begins when approximately half the potential customers have adopted the product and, while sales are still growing, the rate of growth begins to decline. As growth slows, some competitors find themselves with excess production capacity. Other changes in the competitive environment, including a reduction in the degree of differentiation across brands and increased difficulty in maintaining adequate distribution, occur at about the same time. As a result, competition becomes more intense with firms either cutting prices or increasing their marketing expenditures as they battle to increase volume, cover high fixed costs, and maintain profitability.

This transition period is usually accompanied by a shakeout as weaker competitors fail or leave the industry. A number of strategic mistakes—or traps—increase the likelihood that a firm will be forced out of an industry during the transition period. These traps include: (1) failure to recognize that the market is becoming mature; (2) lack of a clearly defined competitive strategy; (3) failure to recognize the declining importance of product quality and the increasing importance of price and service; and (4) tendency to sacrifice market share in favor of maintaining short-term profits.

Success during the maturity stage of a product-market's life cycle requires two sets of strategic actions. First, managers should work to maintain and strengthen either the differentiation of the business's offerings on quality and/or service dimensions or its position as a low-cost competitor within the industry. The second strategic consideration during the maturity stage is to develop meaningful marketing objectives and a marketing strategy appropriate for achieving them. Since maturity can last for many years, the most critical marketing objective is to maintain and protect the business's market share. For share leaders, some variation of the fortress defense, confrontation, or flanker strategies discussed in Chapter 20 is often appropriate for achieving that objective. Smaller competitors, on the other hand, may have to rely on a niche or guerrilla attack strategy to hold their position.

Since different market segments may mature at different times and environmental conditions can change over the mature phase of a product's life, firms often find oportunities to extend the growth of seemingly mature product-markets. Thus, an important secondary objective for firms in many mature markets is to stimulate additional volume growth. Among the marketing strategies that might be used to accomplish that objective are: an increased penetration strategy, an extended use strategy, or a market expansion strategy focused on developing either new geographic territories (including global markets) or new applications segments.

Conventional wisdom suggests that declining products should either be divested or harvested to maximize short-term profits. However, some declining product-markets remain attractive enough to justify more aggressive marketing strategies. The attractiveness of such markets is determined by three sets of factors: (1) condi-

tions of demand, including the rate and certainty of future declines in volume; (2) exit barriers, or the ease with which weaker competitors can leave the market; and (3) factors affecting the intensity of future competitive rivalry. When a declining product market is judged to offer continuing opportunities for profitable sales, and when a business can maintain a strong competitive position within that market, managers might consider one of several strategic alternatives to divestment or harvesting. Those alternative strategies include: a maintenance strategy, a profitable survivor strategy, and a niche strategy.

QUESTIONS

1. Osborne Computer, manufacturer of the first portable personal computer, was one of the industry's early success stories. Yet when growth in the PC market began to slow in the mid-1980s, Osborne went bankrupt. What changes in the market and competitive environment commonly occur as an industry moves from growth to maturity that may have precipitated Osborne's downfall?

2. Without knowing the details, what strategic mistakes would you speculate Osborne may have made that would have contributed to the firm's financial failure during the shakeout period in the PC industry? What actions might the firm have taken to avoid such mistakes and survive the more intense competition of the transition period?

3. Throughout the 1980s, Delta held a leading position in customer satisfaction within the commercial airline industry. What dimensions of service quality do you think Delta emphasized to differentiate itself from competing airlines? What marketing actions did the firm take to reinforce and promote its high service quality image?

4. Savin is one of the lowest-cost producers in the office copier industry, even though its market share and production volume are smaller than industry leader Xerox. How is it possible for a relatively small-volume producer to achieve a low delivered cost position?

5. In the early 1970s, many firms in the frozen prepared foods industry believed the market had reached maturity. Population growth had slowed and the primary user segment for low-priced frozen TV dinners—families with young children—was beginning to shrink with the end of the baby boom. However, by pursuing an innovative and aggressive marketing strategy, Stouffers Foods propelled the industry into a period of renewed rapid growth. What strategy (or strategies) could Stouffers have used to stimulate additional market growth in frozen prepared foods? What marketing actions would the firm have to undertake to implement that strategy (or strategies)?

6. Suppose you were the marketing manager for General Foods' Cool Whip frozen dessert topping during the late 1970s. Marketing research indicates nearly three fourths

of all households use your product, but the average user buys it only four times a year, and Cool Whip is used on only 7 percent of all toppable desserts. What marketing strategy would you recommend to increase Cool Whip sales and why? What specific marketing actions would you propose to implement that strategy?

7. Even though the market for cola-flavored soft drinks was experiencing little growth during the 1980s, both Coca-Cola and PepsiCo introduced a large number of line extensions (New Coke, Classic Coke, Diet Coke, Cherry Coke, Caffeine-free Coke, and so on). What was the strategic rationale for these moves?

8. While we have seen that a business may have a number of other strategic options, the conventional wisdom suggests that a declining business should either be divested or harvested for maximum cash flow. Under what kinds of market and competitive conditions do each of these two conventional strategies make good sense? What kinds of marketing actions are typically involved in successfully implementing a harvesting strategy?

9. J. B. Kunz, the leading manufacturer of passbooks for financial institutions, saw its market gradually decline during the 1970s and 1980s because the switch to electronic banking was making its product superfluous. Nevertheless, the firm bought the assets of a number of smaller competitors, greatly increased its market share within its industry, and managed to earn a very high return on investment. What kind of strategy was the company pursuing? Why do you think the firm was able to achieve a high ROI in the face of industry decline?

Chapter ◇ 22

Strategies for global markets

BLACK & DECKER UPDATES ITS GLOBAL STRATEGY[1]

In 1985 Black & Decker, a U.S. company selling power tools and household appliances, had a $158.4 million loss. New management found an array of aging and inefficient plants around the world (the company had sales in some 100 countries), a line of products that were nonstandardized across countries, a lack of a strong product development effort, and a weak marketing program that included shabby sales activities. Aggressive overseas competitors—especially Japanese power tool makers led by Makita Electric Works—had penetrated the large U.S. market and obtained a 20 percent share.

Today Black & Decker is clearly "back," once more one of the world's leading marketing and manufacturing firms. In 1988 the company had record sales ($2.28 billion) and profits ($125.7 million). Exhibit 22–1 provides B&D's financial highlights for 1985–88. In 1988 B&D leveraged a sales gain of 18 percent into an increase in net earnings of 74 percent over 1987.

A crucial element in the plan that turned the company around was a worldwide product strategy that called for selling the same basic products across countries with relatively minor modifications. This forced the company to improve its product designs and reduce the number of parts per product. The decision to adopt a global strategy was based on the assumption that the western world is becoming increasingly homogenized and that differences between markets are becoming fewer and fewer—at least for the kinds of products Black & Decker produces.

Another reason for the company's progress, according to president and chief executive officer Nolan D. Archibald, was tied to excellence in marketing. He stated in the 1988 annual report:

> We have done two things very well—developing and aggressively supporting products with unique benefits and features that meet consumer needs, and ensuring that the quality of our products lives up to the Black & Decker name.[2]

Archibald goes on to note that an essential part of the company's success has to do with the gains made in working with customers. This was achieved through greater product availability and marketing programs tailored to the specific needs of each distribution

---

[1] Based on Christopher S. Eklund, "How Black & Decker Got Back in the Black," *Business Week,* July 13, 1987; Mary Lu Carnevale, "Black & Decker Goes to Full-Court Press," *The Wall Street Journal,* November 10, 1988, p. A8; *1988 Annual Report,* Black & Decker; and John Huey, "The New Power in Black & Decker," *Fortune,* January 2, 1989, p. 89.

[2] *1988 Annual Report,* Black & Decker, p. 4.

continued

concluded

EXHIBIT   22 ◆ 1

Financial highlights for Black & Decker Company, 1985–88

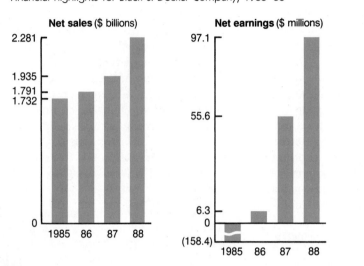

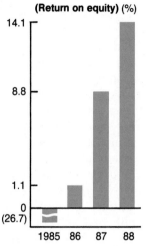

Source: Black & Decker, *1988 Annual Report.*

channel. In 1988 a leading trade magazine named Black & Decker the top supplier in its industry.

The company is also standardizing other elements in its marketing mix. Whenever possible, it uses similar advertising messages in the countries it serves, while recognizing that use of the various media types must vary because of their availability in individual countries. B&D also plans to use a strong salesforce geared to the different needs of its various channels of distribution.

Clearly, Black & Decker believes a global strategy of the kind described above is the wave of the future. It also believes a successful implementation of this strategy will enable it to launch new products that will further enhance its strong industry leadership position. CEO Archibald thinks the Black & Decker brand is strong enough to support not only power tools and small household appliances, but other consumer and commercial durables as well.

As the Black & Decker case illustrates, the internationalization of competition has become one of the most important challenges facing most firms today. Since the early 1950s, international trade has been growing at an explosive rate—substantially faster than world GNP (see Exhibit 22–2). This fact, coupled with an array of new international competitors, has caused a basic change in the nature and scope of the global competitive environment.

The question now facing large segments of American business is, What is the best way to compete in this new world order? The process by which this question can best be answered is similar to that used for domestic products. But there are some important differences. These differences affect a business's marketing objectives, marketing strategies, market entry strategies, and product-marketing programs. The chapter is organized around these subjects.

THE IMPORTANCE OF INTERNATIONAL TRADE

International trade has become increasingly important to American business. Foreign revenues of the 100 largest U.S. multinational corporations totaled $441 billion in 1987; and profits were $26.8 billion. Some of these firms derived more than 50 percent of their sales from overseas. Exhibit 22–3

EXHIBIT 22 ◆ 2

Growth of world trade

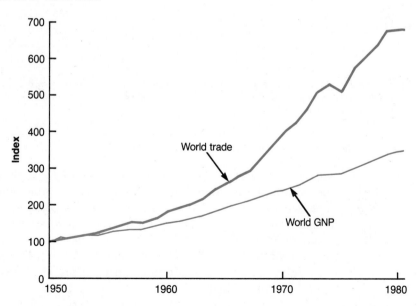

Source: Michael E. Porter, "Competition in Global Industries: A Conceptual Framework," in *Competition in Global Industries,* ed. Michael E. Porter (Boston: Harvard Business School Press, 1986), p. 16. Data from United Nations, *Statistical Yearbook,* various years. Reprinted with permission.

EXHIBIT 22 ◆ 3

The 15 largest U.S. multinationals

1987 rank	Company	Foreign revenue (mil)	(percent of total)	Foreign operating profit (mil)	(percent of total)	Foreign assets (mil)	(percent of total)
1	Exxon	$57,375	(75.1%)	$3,301[1]	(68.2%)	$37,742	(51.0%)
2	Mobil	31,633[2]	(60.5)	1,238[3]	(60.9)	20,110	(48.9)
3	IBM	29,280	(54.0)	3,330[1]	(63.3)	34,468	(54.1)
4	General Motors	24,091	(23.7)	1,919[1]	(54.0)	20,389	(23.4)
5	Ford Motors[4]	23,955	(32.8)	1,184[1]	(25.6)	24,077	(39.4)
6	Texaco	17,120	(49.8)	863	(P-D)	10,550	(31.1)
7	Citicorp	13,314	(48.4)	−2,293[1]	(201.5)	89,675[5]	(45.1)
8	E. I. du Pont de Nemours	11,651[6]	(38.2)	682[7]	(32.5)	7,757	(27.5)
9	Dow Chemical	7,431	(55.6)	1,278	(55.2)	7,037	(49.0)
10	Chevron	5,905	(22.7)	2,006	(60.5)	6,947	(20.2)
11	Procter & Gamble	5,524	(32.5)	951[1]	(29.1)	3,849	(28.1)
12	Eastman Kodak	5,265	(39.6)	815	(38.2)	5,014	(34.7)
13	Chase Manhattan	5,021	(46.7)	−1,438[1]	(160.7)	37,280	(37.6)
14	ITT[4]	4,891	(25.0)	384	(30.0)	5,908	(14.8)
15	Xerox[4]	4,852[2]	(32.1)	182	(31.7)	5,691	(24.3)

[1] Net income.   [2] Includes other income.   [3] Net income before corporate and net financing expenses.   [4] Includes proportionate interest in unconsolidated subsidiaries and affiliates.   [5] Average assets.   [6] Includes excise taxes.   [7] Operating income after taxes.   P-D: Profit over deficit.

Source: "The 100 Largest U.S. Multinationals," *Forbes,* July 25, 1988, pp. 248–49.

lists the 15 largest U.S. multinationals. Note that 8 of these firms generated more profits abroad than they did domestically—some with even less assets employed than in the United States. For example, General Motors has 23 percent of its assets abroad, but profits from its foreign operations were $1.9 billion, or 54 percent of total operating profits.[3] But small and medium-sized companies are also finding overseas markets an important source of growth and profits. Exhibit 22–4 provides an example of an export success story featuring a small business.

---

[3] "The 100 Largest U.S. Multinationals," *Forbes,* July 25, 1988, pp. 248–50. Also, see "Smoother Sailing Overseas," *Business Week,* April 18, 1986, p. 286.

EXHIBIT 22 ◆ 4

An export success story

> The POM Company of Russellville, Arkansas, the successor to Park-O-Meter, which developed the first coin-operated parking meter in 1935, is bigger overseas than it is at home. In 1981 POM began exporting parking meters to the newly industrialized countries that were beginning to experience crowded urban streets and limited parking resources. By requiring irrevocable letters of credit confirmed by a U.S. bank, the company has practically eliminated nonpayment risks.
>
>   Exports have grown 20 percent annually since 1982, and today the company is virtually tied for first place in the world market with a share of 42 percent. POM hopes to keep its momentum going with its introduction of the first solar-powered parking meter, which features a programmable timer driven by a microprocessor. The company is counting heavily on exports to double its annual sales of $10 million over the next several years.

In recent years, international trade has received much publicity, primarily because of the huge U.S. foreign trade deficit—over $100 billion annually as of the late 1980s (see Exhibit 22–5). In addition, foreign investment in the United States was $209.3 billion in 1986, while U.S. direct investment abroad was $259.9 billion.[4] The United States is the largest exporter in the

EXHIBIT 22 ◆ 5

U.S. trade in goods and services ($ billions)

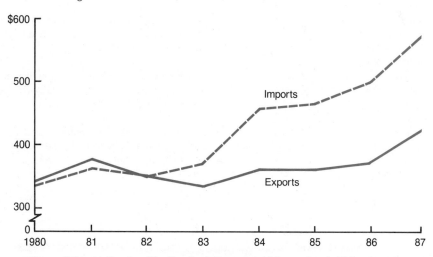

---

   [4] *Survey of Current Business,* August 1987, pp. 58, 85. For an interesting example of a successful investment in the United States by a Japanese company, see Stewart Toy, Neil Gross, and James B. Treece, "The Americanization of Honda," *Business Week,* April 25, 1988, p. 90.

EXHIBIT   22 ◆ 6

The world's top exporters by industry, 1986

Industries	1986 exports (in billions of U.S. dollars)	Outlook
Automobiles	$185.8	Japanese manufacturers will keep gaining ground—partly
Japan	29.1%	by building in the United States. Exports from U.S. car
W. Germany	20.7	makers will grow too.
United States	11.9	
Steel	$ 63.0	The United States is narrowing the Japanese cost advan-
Japan	21.0%	tage and will remain the world's No. 2 steel producer,
W. Germany	16.1	though a minuscule exporter.
France	9.2	
Apparel	$ 57.0	Pacific Rim producers will be the big winners. The U.S.
Italy	13.4%	industry will keep shrinking, but many manufacturers will
Hong Kong	11.6	prosper by filling niches.
Korea	9.2	
Telecom-		American makers will extend their dominance at the
munications	$ 41.6	market's high end as the world shifts to digital technology.
Japan	33.5%	Japan is gaining at the low end.
United States	11.1	
W. Germany	8.5	
Petrochemicals	$ 40.6	U.S. products are highly competitive, but Canada, Venezu-
W. Germany	16.5%	ela, and several low-cost Middle Eastern oil producers are
United States	14.8	expanding capacity.
Netherlands	10.4	
Plastics	$ 36.2	Oil-rich countries have a growing cost advantage in com-
W. Germany	21.3%	modity products. But U.S. export trade is booming in high-
United States	13.3	tech engineering plastics.
Netherlands	11.4	
Computers	$ 33.1	U.S. producers will remain dominant, though some sales
United States	30.9%	will come from new overseas subsidiaries. European and
Japan	19.7	Japanese shares may rise faster.
W. Germany	8.8	
Instruments	$ 30.6	A lead in software gives American producers the edge in
Japan	27.5%	sophisticated machines. Japanese and European rivals will
United States	18.3	set up factories in the United States.
W. Germany	15.7	

world, even though exports account for only about 10 percent of its gross national product. Many other countries, such as Japan, Great Britain, West Germany, and the Netherlands, export a much higher share of their gross national product.

American firms, both domestic and international, face increasingly strong competition from such foreign companies as Toyota, Siemens, Nestlé, Mit-

EXHIBIT   22 ♦ 6
(concluded)

Industries	1986 exports (in billions of U.S. dollars)	Outlook
Pulp and paper	$ 27.7	The U.S. industry, the world's biggest, is recapturing
Canada	19.2%	exports. Scandinavian costs are far higher. Canada mainly
Finland	14.5	ships low-value newsprint.
Sweden	13.0	
Aircraft	$ 26.1	America rules the skies, but Europe's Airbus Industrie is
United States	47.2%	aiming for 30% of the market by 1995. Many analysts think
France	16.9	it'll get it.
Britain	10.8	
Textiles	$ 23.4	The highly efficient and specialized U.S. industry should
Japan	16.3%	gain sales at home now that Japanese and European
W. Germany	15.4	producers have no big cost advantage.
Italy	14.6	
Pharmaceuticals	$ 20.0	A burst of new drugs and low production costs will fortify
W. Germany	16.0%	the U.S. market share. Foreign makers will expand produc-
United States	13.5	tion in the United States.
Switzerland	12.0	
Semiconductors	$ 18.1	Japan remains the champion cost cutter. Unless American
Japan	21.6%	companies shape up, the Japanese may grab 60% of the
United States	18.3	world market by 1995.
Malaysia	8.3	
Aluminum	$ 15.1	Europe and the United States will lose in primary produc-
W. Germany	13.3%	tion to Canada and Latin America. But the United States
Canada	12.0	will remain the biggest producer of finished metal.
Netherlands	7.0	
Machine tools	$ 13.2	Germany dominates the high end and Japan the low, but
Japan	27.3%	the United States will hold its own from now on. Japanese
W. Germany	24.3	companies will also build in America.
Switzerland	9.9	

Source: Sylvia Nasar, "America's Competitive Revival," Fortune, January 4, 1988, p. 47. Information provided by DRS/McGraw-Hill.

subishi, Hyundai, Imperial Chemical Industries, Nippon Steel, and Unilever. Because of its attractive market size, the United States is a prime target for many international companies. Successful U.S. sales coupled with sales elsewhere can provide economies of scale and learning effects that enable a foreign company to compete worldwide more aggressively. Despite their considerable domestic success, U.S. firms have not always succeeded overseas. Large firms like General Foods, General Motors, Kentucky Fried Chicken, and Campbell Soup have encountered sales and profitability problems in marketing their products abroad. Exhibit 22–6 lists the world's top exporters by industry.

THE INTERNATIONAL BUSINESS ENVIRONMENT

It is primarily because of strong environmental differences between countries that the international arena offers such a rich opportunity to develop strategy options. As Cateora notes,

> The key to successful international marketing is adaptation to the environmental differences that exist from one market to another. Adaptation is a conscious effort on the part of the international marketer to anticipate the influences of both the foreign and domestic uncontrollable environments on a marketing mix and then adjust the marketing mix to minimize the effects. The primary obstacle to success in international marketing is a person's self-reference criterion (SRC) in making decisions; i.e., an unconscious reference to one's own cultural values, experiences, and knowledge as a basis for decisions. The SRC impedes the ability to assess a foreign market in its true light.[5]

The best way to minimize the effect of SRC is to recognize its existence—especially in the ways the environments of the various countries differ not only among themselves, but also how they differ from the United States.

In order to select and prioritize target markets, a firm must analyze these different environments. An obvious but frequently overlooked one is a country's physical environment, including its geographical location. Physical factors such as the presence of extreme hot or cold temperatures, high humidity, unusual amounts of snow and rain, and even an overabundance of sand (as in the Middle East) can lead not only to needed differences in products, but also to the demand for a given product. For example, vehicles operating in Africa experience severe maintenance problems because of climate unless certain safeguards such as rustproofing and the use of heavy-duty electrical systems are taken.

Differences among countries in the demand for a particular product exist not only because of their physical environment, but also because of their legal, economic, political, cultural, competitive, and infrastructure environments. These differences are far greater than those existing between geographical segments within the United States.

Legal environment

Trade regulations can raise a firm's cost per transaction directly or indirectly by increasing the legal hurdles to entry. Countries have long enacted certain trade regulations to protect local industries, provide income, and inhibit the

---

[5] Philip R. Cateora, *International Marketing*, 7th ed. (Homewood, Ill.: Richard D. Irwin, 1990), chap. 1, in press.

flow of foreign exchange. Such regulations come in a variety of forms. The most common is the **tariff,** which imposes a tax on imported goods. Legal barriers also include a **quota** limiting the units or value of specific goods that can be imported in a given time period. For instance, at one time the United States set a quota on Japanese motorcycles. Quotas also may be voluntary, as when the Japanese auto industry put restraints on its exports to the United States. An **embargo** bans the import of certain goods. This is currently the case with many products previously exported to the United States by South Africa.

Indirect legal or quasi-legal barriers to trade consist of a variety of activities. They include customs and administrative entry procedures such as tariff classifications and documentation requirements; and restrictions on the quality of goods that may enter a country due to intergovernmental testing methods and packaging and labeling standards. They also include government participation in trade through procurement policies and export subsidies; and charges on imports such as credit discriminations, import deposit requirements, and administrative fees.[6] As countries lower their import duties, these legal barriers become more important.

Following World War II, the United States and 22 other countries sought to liberalize trade by reducing tariffs through the General Agreement on Tariffs and Trade (GATT). Since its origin in 1947, GATT has reduced tariffs seven times. Today the average tariff in the United States is about 8 percent, 10 percent in Western Europe, and 11 percent in Japan—compared to 50 percent and better for these countries before World War II.

Some countries have even banded together to form economic communities to reduce tariffs. The best known of these, the European Economic Community (EEC or the Common Market), seeks to eliminate trade barriers between member nations and generally to encourage economic integration. By 1992 the last trade barriers within the ECC are scheduled to be eliminated, resulting in a unified market of over 300 million consumers. At that time, the EEC will have to decide what approach to adopt regarding the rest of the world. Will it encourage protectionism? This question is being raised by large multinational companies throughout the world.[7] Since Black & Decker already has a strong presence in Europe, it is not likely to be affected by whatever policy the EEC adopts. Other economic communities include the Latin American Free Trade Association (LAFTA), the Central American

---

[6] A. D. Cao, "Non-Tariff Barriers to U.S. Manufactured Exports," *The Columbia Journal of World Business,* Summer 1980, p. 94.

[7] Richard I. Kirkland, Jr., "Outsider's Guide to Europe in 1992," *Fortune,* October 24, 1988, p. 121.

Common Market (CACM), and the Council for Mutual Economic Assistance (CMEA).

Economic, political, and cultural environments

These three environments strongly affect whether a country should be targeted and, if so, how a company should do business there. The **economic environment** has its primary impact on the demand function for a particular product. Thus, it is important for marketers to know about per capita income and the distribution of income (the purchasing power of various consumer groups). A country's stage of economic development (ranging from less developed to postindustrialized) greatly affects its purchasing power and income distribution.

The stability of a country's **political environment** must be considered both short and long term. Some U.S. companies have suffered considerable losses from political instability in such countries as Chile, Iran, Lebanon, and Libya. The extent to which a country relies on centralized planning and government ownership also must be considered because this is likely to affect an importer's freedom in pricing, distribution, and advertising.

In some cases, a company may still consider it worthwhile to export goods to a country experiencing considerable political instability, such as Iran, Argentina, and Libya. Ordinarily, a company would do so via export marketing rather than direct investment. Because of the Iran experience and an increase in political instability throughout the world, more and more international firms are undertaking formal political risk assessment studies to identify potentially high-risk countries and prepare contingency plans for emergencies.

A country's **cultural system** (values, beliefs, and norms) affects the way firms market their goods. This is particularly true with food, personal-care, and clothing items. For example, on average, Europeans consume less beef, more chicken and fish, less whiskey, more wine, less ice cream, fewer soft drinks, and more bread than Americans. Most African and Middle Eastern men do not shave as frequently as American men.

Music is an important part of all cultures, but the type of music that is accepted and liked varies substantially from one part of the world to another. A TV or radio commercial for Latin America would likely use a bossa nova rhythm or "salsa" beat, compared to a rock rhythm for North America. Differences in the meaning of certain words and symbols can affect advertising themes, brand names, and packaging. Pepsi, for instance, had to change its advertising theme "Catch that Pepsi spirit" in South America because *spirit* translates into Spanish as ghost.

Communication is both verbal and nonverbal. People from western nations tend to be verbal; people from Eastern nations tend to be nonverbal. Thus, the latter believe people will understand via nonverbal cues—they don't have to be told. A Japanese who responds to an American business person by smiling and nodding is not saying "yes" to a proposal but rather "I understand what you're saying—please continue."[8]

Competitive and infrastructure environments

Knowledge about the competitive environment of a particular country is important because it is likely that substantial differences exist among the various target countries. Thus, expectations about the outcome of investments made in different countries vary. Further, marketing programs need to be tailored to accommodate these different competitive conditions. For example, Nestlé was able to obtain a 60 percent market share for its instant coffee in Japan, in part because of weak domestic competition. This is in contrast to the United States, where Nestlé is in competition with two strong companies (General Foods and Procter & Gamble) and holds less than a 30 percent share.[9]

Differences in the infrastructures of the target countries have an important bearing on the extent to which a company will be forced to individualize its marketing programs. Particularly important here are the local transport system (including roads), media (to be discussed later in this chapter), and distribution. The latter is extremely important and includes not only the physical handling of goods, but also the buying and selling of goods among channel members, producers, and consumers. There is considerable difference among countries not only in the availability of certain channels, but also in the functions performed and how well they are performed. As a result, some companies have resorted to channels vastly different than those used at home. For example, Procter & Gamble uses mass merchandising in the United States and Europe but sells door to door in many developing countries. Channel power is stronger in Europe than in the United States because manufacturers like Black & Decker must rely on dealers for more local promotion, given the limited availability of TV and radio time.

Other important differences exist between U.S. channel systems and those in other countries, particularly in developing countries where middlemen—including retailers—are smaller, more specialized, and more numerous. These middlemen typically perform little aggressive selling, carry minimal inventories, frequently require financing, and often give preference to local products. Marketers are seeing considerable change in distribution systems across countries, however, especially in retailing. Supermarkets, automatic vending, and discount stores are increasingly commonplace in Europe and are making inroads in many large third-world cities.

---

[8] Warren J. Keegan, *Global Marketing Management* (Englewood Cliffs, N.J.: Prentice-Hall, 1989), chap. 4.

[9] Hirotaka Takeuchi and Michael E. Porter, "Three Roles of International Marketing in Global Strategy" in *Competition in Global Industries*, ed. Michael E. Porter (Boston: Harvard Business School Press, 1986), p. 114.

INTERNATIONAL MARKETING OBJECTIVES

A company's profitability objectives concerning foreign trade are much the same as for the domestic market. They include return on investment, return on assests managed, marginal contribution, growth, cash flow, and market share. Economic objectives should be specified for each foreign market and are likely to vary from country to country. A mature product in the United States may be a strong growth product in Spain and a new entry in Nigeria, for example. In addition, a number of the objectives firms might pursue in entering global markets aim at improving overall profitability by reducing costs, increasing revenues, or both.

One broad objective that a firm might pursue in global markets is an increase in scale economies. When such economies depend on volumes greater than those provided by the home market, a firm has a strong incentive to export because of the resulting cost advantages. Indeed, it may have no alternative if it is to remain cost competitive and retain its position within its industry. For example, the new shipbuilding facilities required for large vessels, such as tankers, have a minimum efficient size that substantially exceeds the needs of any one country.

A number of economic reasons other than size of production facilities may prompt a company to export. An important reason is a comparative advantage in factor cost or quality tied to the production of a given product. Thus, the firm's location in countries possessing such advantages is critical to the firm's world position. The relatively low cost of quality labor in Japan and, more recently, in South Korea, Singapore, and Taiwan has given these countries an economic advantage over the United States in the production of certain goods (shipbuilding, textiles, consumer electronics, and certain automobile models).

Other sources of global competitive advantage include logistical economies of scale (the use by the Japanese of specialized ocean-going bulk carriers to transport raw materials); R&D (pharmaceuticals, aircraft, computers); and marketing.[10] An example of the latter is Honda, which dominated the U.S. motorcycle market by convincing large numbers of Americans that riding motorcycles is fun and that its product was better than those of competitors. Honda did this by investing heavily in advertising, consumer promotions, trade shows, and a network of some 2,000 dealers. By expanding its line over time, Honda encouraged existing consumers to trade up. Eventually, Honda challenged and defeated its American and European competitors with a 750cc "superbike."[11]

But there are still other reasons a firm may go overseas. One is the desire to satisfy customers who are doing so. Thus, in the 1950s and 1960s, many

---

[10] Michael E. Porter, *Competitive Strategy* (New York: Free Press, 1980), chap. 13.

[11] Thomas Hout, Michael E. Porter, and Eileen Rudden, "How Global Companies Win Out," *Harvard Business Review*, September–October 1982, pp. 98–108.

U.S. advertising agencies set up offices in Europe to service their American clients who were exporting there. Japanese automobile companies with manufacturing facilities in the United States have encouraged some of their parts suppliers to do the same. Firms also enter overseas markets to earn foreign exchange and, in some cases, are subsidized by their governments to do so. Other reasons include countering demographic trends and disposing of excess stocks of goods. The marketing of U.S.-produced baby food to Central America because of declining U.S. birthrates is an example of this.

A company may also go international to retaliate against another global company by attacking in a market where the competitor is vulnerable. One way is to make price reductions in large markets, the cost of which requires using resources generated elsewhere in the world. If the competitor is only a domestic producer, it must respond by cutting the price on its entire volume, while the aggressor has to do so on just a part of its total sales.[12]

To prevent such attacks or to minimize their impact, a firm must have the capacity to strike back in markets where the competitor is vulnerable. For example, in the 1970s Michelin used resources generated in Europe to attack the American market. Goodyear, a major U.S. competitor, could have responded by lowering prices, but because of its larger share had more to lose. It chose to strike back in Europe, the major source of Michelin's cash flows. In so doing, Goodyear slowed Michelin's penetration of the U.S. market.[13]

INTERNATIONAL MARKETING STRATEGIES

Basically, the process for formulating international marketing strategies is the same as for formulating domestic marketing strategies. Both require a detailed understanding of the operating environment and an unbiased assessment of the firm's resources relative to those of competitors. But one basic issue differentiates international from national marketing strategies: to what extent should the firm develop its strategy on a country-by-country basis (a localized approach) in contrast to using the same strategy in all countries (a standard or global approach)?

Localization versus standardization

The localization marketing strategy argues that differences across countries require a tailored marketing program for each country. In contrast, a standardized strategy like the one Black & Decker has adopted holds that marketing skills and know-how can be transferred across countries and that much

---

[12] Gary Hamel and C. K. Prahalad, "Do You Really Have a Global Strategy?" *Harvard Business Review*, July–August 1985, pp. 139–48.

[13] Ibid.; also, see Craig M. Watson, "Counter-Competition Abroad to Protect Home Markets," *Harvard Business Review*, January–February 1982, p. 40.

can be gained through the standardization of marketing. Carried to the extreme, this would mean marketing the same product at the same price and using the same channels and sales and advertising programs throughout the world.[14]

Levitt has been a strong advocate for standardization or, as he terms it, the "globalization of markets." He argues that this is the wave of the future because of growing worldwide homogenization of needs that will lead to substantial economies of scale in such areas as production, logistics, and marketing, which, in turn, will lead to lower prices.[15]

While Levitt's global marketing argument may apply to products that enjoy strong scale and learning economies and are not highly culture-bound (consumer electronics, watches, electronic measurement instruments, cameras), there is considerable question about its applicability to many—if not most—consumer goods. Global advertising, in particular, is singled out as generally a failure "because it's often mind-numbingly dull. 'It's marketing to the lowest common denominator . . . vanilla marketing.'"[16] For an example of a company that tried global advertising, see Exhibit 22–7.

The reverse argument is that because most marketing activities are, of necessity, tied to buyer location, marketing cannot be standardized. But some marketing activities can be sufficiently standardized to gain a competitive advantage in the form of lower cost or improved differentiation. And sometimes the advantage may be achieved regionally if not globally. Some firms, including Black & Decker, are already standardizing their products, manufacturing, and marketing in Europe in anticipation of 1992 when customs and other barriers will be dropped, thereby making the European Economic Community a unified market.

Takeuchi and Porter note five types of marketing activities that offer the most potential for some form of centralization in one or a few locations. They believe the opportunities for centralization will increase in the future because of changing technology, buyer shifts, and the growth in global and regional media. The five activities are (1) production of promotional materials, (2) salesforce, (3) service support organization, (4) training, and (5) advertising media.[17] These marketing activities are discussed briefly below.

1. **Production of promotional materials.** Centralization of sales promotion materials (advertisements, brochures, posters, manuals) can generate scale economies as well as higher quality, based on accumulation of learning. Colgate-

---

[14] J. A. Quelch and E. J. Hoff, "Customizing Global Marketing," *Harvard Business Review*, May–June 1986, p. 60.

[15] Theodore Levitt, "The Globalization of Marketing," *Harvard Business Review*, May–June 1983, pp. 92–102.

[16] Joanne Lipman, "Marketers Turn Sour on Global Sales Pitch Harvard Guru Makes," *The Wall Street Journal*, May 12, 1988, p. 1.

[17] Takeuchi and Porter, "Three Roles of International Marketing."

EXHIBIT   22 ♦ 7

Parker Pens tries global marketing

In the early 1980s, Parker was making some 500 styles of pens in 18 plants scattered around the world. The company had local offices in about 150 countries, all of which created their own ads and packaging. As a result of adopting a global marketing strategy, Parker by 1984 had dropped the number of pen styles to 100 and the number of plants to 8. It adopted a single international ad campaign that was translated into myriad local languages.

Local managers resented that the U.S. company was mandating both the advertising and which agency to use. Profits dropped, and Parker had a $12 million loss in 1985. In 1986 the company was sold, and the executives who put the global program in effect were fired. In a short time, the company returned to profitability, and local managers again chose their own ads.

While global marketing was not the sole contributor to the company's problems, it was a major factor.

Source: Joanne Lipman, "Marketers Turn Sour on Global Sales Pitch Harvard Guru Makes," *The Wall Street Journal,* May 12, 1988, p. 8.

Palmolive Company, for example, recently introduced its new tartar-control toothpaste in some 40 countries. Each country could choose between two ads. U.S. viewers saw one in which little men were building a wall of tartar on giant teeth. Colgate estimates it saved $1 to $2 million in production costs for every country where the same TV commercial aired.[18]

2. **Salesforce.** A salesforce based in one country and serving a region or even the world can provide a company with a strong competitive advantage. This is especially the case with highly expensive, complex state-of-the-art projects such as the building of a new steel mill, jet aircraft engines, and major construction projects.

3. **Service support.** Service specialists can be centralized to a company's advantage much like a salesforce. Thus, highly skilled service personnel can serve as troubleshooters the world over and, in the process, provide valuable information to the home office design and production staff. Service specialists often work through subsidiaries, thereby providing a form of technical training.

4. **Training.** Centralization here can lead to important economies of scale in the production of training material, especially when sessions are videotaped and teleconferences are used. Centralized training also makes possible shared learning because of the varied backgrounds of those attending. IBM and Hewlett-Packard frequently use centralized training.

5. **Advertising.** Regional—even global—advertising is becoming more feasible with the growth in geographical coverage of general interest magazines, trade magazines, and television via satellite (sporting events). Airport posters and

---

[18] Joanne Lipman, "Marketers Turn Sour on Global Sales Pitch," p. 8.

airline magazines also provide access to certain kinds of international audiences. Also, the use of a single, centralized advertising agency can ease the
coordination task and help ensure high-quality advertising throughout the
world.

In real life, a firm's international strategy can fall anywhere on the continuum between complete localization and total standardization. In most
cases, the question to be answered is, What program items can be standardized and what are the consequences of doing so? Too often, strategy here is
viewed on an either/or basis—a matter of trade-offs, when, in reality it
should be thought of in terms of obtaining a competitive advantage. The
challenge, therefore, is how to satisfy local market needs better than competitors—and at a lower cost. This requires a discussion of marketing elements and their role in the formulation of marketing strategy, which we take
up later in this chapter.

Market-entry strategies[19]

Once a firm decides to sell its goods in a particular country, it must decide
which entry strategy to use. There are three major ways a company can enter
a foreign country. One is to export goods manufactured outside the target
country. A second is to transfer the technology and skills necessary to
produce and market the goods to an organization in the foreign country
through licensing or other contractual agreements. Finally, a firm might
transfer manufacturing and marketing resources through direct investment
in a foreign country. Since services cannot be produced independently of
consumption, a service company must use the second or third way to enter a
foreign country. These three types of entry break down into a number of
different modes, as shown in Exhibit 22–8.

Exporting
This is the simplest way to enter a foreign market because it involves the
least commitment and risk. Manufacturing remains in the home country—
and the firm may not even modify the product for export. Export may be
passive and sporadic, mainly involving the firm's surpluses, or **active** with
regular shipments to one or more countries.

Exporting can be direct or indirect. **Indirect exporting** involves less investment and risk than any other strategy. The firm makes no investment in
an overseas salesforce; rather, it relies on the expertise of international
domestic middlemen. The four major types of such middlemen are: (1)
export merchants who buy the product and sell it overseas for their own
account; (2) **export agents** (including trading companies) who sell on a

---

[19] This section is based on Franklin R. Root, *Entry Strategy for International Markets*
(Lexington, Mass.: D. C. Heath and Company, 1987), chaps. 1, 2, 3, and 5; and David A. Aaker,
Strategic Market Management (New York: John Wiley & Sons, 1984), chap. 16.

EXHIBIT   22 ◆ 8

Classification of entry modes

Export entry modes
  Indirect
  Direct agent/distributor
  Direct branch/subsidiary
  Other

Contractual entry modes
  Licensing   Management contracts
  Franchising   Construction/turnkey contracts
  Technical agreements   Contract manufacture
  Service contracts   Co-production agreements
                                         Other

Investment entry modes
  Sole venture: new establishment
  Sole venture: acquisition
  Joint venture: new establishment acquisition
  Other

Source: Franklin R. Root, *Entry Strategies for International Markets* (Lexington, Mass.: D. C. Heath & Company, 1987), p. 6.

commission basis; (3) **cooperative organizations** that export for several producers (especially those selling farm products); and (4) **export management companies** that, for a fee, manage a company's exporting activities.

Sellers begin using **direct exporting** when they have enough business abroad to warrant investing in marketing activities. Direct exporting does not use home-country middlemen, but may use foreign-based distributors/agents or set up operating units in the foreign country in the form of branches or subsidiaries.

Exporting is a viable entry strategy for a small firm with limited resources; or under conditions of considerable political risk, a small foreign market, or little or no political pressure to manufacture in the foreign market. As an example of political pressure, American politicians have repeatedly warned Japanese auto makers of the risks incurred by not locating manufacturing plants in this country.

Contractual entry modes

These nonequity arrangements involve the transfer of technology and/or human skills to an entity in a foreign country. In **licensing** arrangements, a firm offers the right to use its intangible assets (technology, know-how, patents, company name, trademarks) in exchange for royalties or some other form of payment. Licensing is less flexible than exporting, which can be expanded to include an overseas manufacturing facility whenever this becomes desirable. A firm also has less control over a licensee than over its own exporting or manufacturing abroad. Further, if sales turn out better than expected, the licensor's profits are limited by the licensing agreement. And, if it terminates its contract with the licensee, the licensor may find it has developed a competitor. Licensing is particularly appropriate, however, when the market is unstable and the licensing firm would have financial and marketing problems in penetrating the foreign market.

Franchising is similar but different from licensing—especially in motivation, services rendered, and duration. It grants the right to use the company's name, trademarks, and technology. Also, the franchisee typically receives help in setting up the franchise, its organizational structure, and its marketing. Franchising has been an attractive way for U.S. firms, especially service firms, to penetrate foreign markets at low cost and to couple their skills with local knowledge and entrepreneurial spirit. Most foreign countries have been reasonably receptive to this type of exporting because franchising involves local ownership. U.S. franchisers currently operate in most countries in the world. Fast-food companies have been especially aggressive globally. For example, McDonald's, Pizza Hut, Burger King, and Kentucky Fried Chicken have substantial overseas investments. With over 2,000 units in 450 foreign countries, McDonald's opened over 200 more in 1987. ServiceMaster launched over 500 home-cleaning franchises in Japan—in addition to winning contracts to do the housekeeping for 40 hospitals.[20]

Other contractual entry modes have increased in prominence in recent years, especially with the developing and communist countries. **Contract manufacturing** involves sourcing a product from a manufacturer located in a foreign country for sale there or elsewhere. This usually requires providing assistance to ensure that the product meets the desired standards. The advantages and disadvantages of using such an entry mode are similar to those of licensing. Contract manufacturing is most attractive when the local market is too small to warrant making an investment, export entry is blocked, and a quality licensee is not available.

A **turnkey construction contract** requires that the contractor make the project operational (up and running) before releasing it to the owner or, in some cases, provide services (such as worker training) after the project is completed. Since most such contracts are with host countries, they involve considerable risks. **Management contracts** give a company the right to manage the day-to-day operations of a local company. They are used primarily in conjunction with a turnkey operation or a joint venture agreement.

Industrial cooperation agreements (ICAs) include all kinds of contract arrangements between a western company and an organization in a communist country. The most common types of ICAs are licensing/technical as-

---

[20] Richard I. Kirkland, Jr., "The Bright Future of Service Exports," *Fortune*, June 8, 1987, p. 32. Also, see Joann S. Lubin, "For U.S. Franchisers, a Common Tongue Isn't a Guarantee of Success in the U.K.," *The Wall Street Journal*, August 16, 1988, p. 18.

sistance agreements and turnkey projects. Another type of ICA is **co-production,** where a western company provides technology know-how and components in return for a share of the output that the western partner agrees to market in the West. Maintaining quality is often a major problem in such agreements, however.

ICA agreements often call for the western company to accept payment in the form of locally produced goods. This practice is referred to as **countertrade** and may comprise as much as 10 percent of all world trade. It is discussed under the marketing mix section later in this chapter.

INVESTMENT OVERSEAS

This entry mode can be implemented in two ways—through joint ventures or sole ownership. The **joint venture** involves a joint-ownership arrangement (between, e.g., a U.S. firm and one in the host country) to produce and/or market goods in a foreign market. The extent of ownership for the U.S. firm can vary from a small percent to 50 percent. Joint ventures have more risk and less flexibility than either exporting or licensing. In recent years joint venture strategies have become increasingly popular as a way to avoid quotas and import taxes and to satisfy government demands to produce locally. For example, Brazil has an 85 percent local content requirement for automobile production. Joint ventures also have the advantages of sharing the investment costs and gaining local marketing expertise. Sometimes, the investment costs are too much for a single firm (say, for the development of a new generation of jet engines). Market access remains, however, the main reason for joint ventures. In almost all developing countries and in some developed ones, the governments require some local participation with foreign firms that operate in their country.

Marketers encounter a number of problems in their joint ventures. This is especially so when changes in the product-market portfolio of one partner make the joint venture less attractive—even unsatisfactory—to the other. The lack of flexibility may be especially difficult if one partner later wants to adopt a global strategy of direct investment to control all manufacturing and marketing.

If the results of a joint venture disappoint one of the parties, its commitment to making the venture successful may weaken. For example, when Mitsubishi became disappointed in the sales of its cars through Chrysler dealers, it set up its own dealers to handle sales of its other models in the United States. Another complicating factor can be one partner's desire for secrecy with its technology—especially when the parent firm's partner may benefit from the technology by applying it in another foreign country.

A **sole ownership** investment entry strategy involves setting up a production subsidiary in a foreign country. Ordinarily, the subsidiary makes its own operating decisions. The parent company provides the finances, R&D, product specifications, and production technology. Direct investment usually allows the parent organization to retain total control of the overseas operation and avoids the problems of shared management and loss of flexibility. Firms extensively using a direct investment strategy include General Motors, Procter & Gamble, General Foods, Hewlett-Packard, and General Electric. Many of the same reasons for using joint ventures apply to direct investments. This strategy avoids political resentment against an exporter exploiting a foreign market; and it is particularly appropriate when the politics of the situation require a dedicated local facility (as in communications equipment).[21]

High risks can be associated with direct investment. Such risks are classified as *macro*, which impact the total country, and *micro*, which affect only some industries and threaten profitability. Macro risks include changes in the political and economic environments ranging from armed revolution (as in Iran) to high inflation (as in Argentina). A change in market attractiveness, like a shift to negative growth, is an example of micro risk. Despite these risks, as Exhibit 22–9 shows, direct investments are accelerating. Executives everywhere have concluded that to capture customers who demand constant innovation and rapid, flexible response, they can no longer afford to export from a single country—or even a single continent.[22]

Sequential strategies

A company can follow a number of routes or paths in becoming a worldwide marketer.[23] By *route* we mean the order in which the firm enters foreign markets. Japanese companies provide an illustration of different global expansion paths. The most common expansion route involves moving from Japan to developing countries to developed countries. They used this path, for example, with automobiles (Toyota), consumer electronics (National), watches (Seiko), cameras (Minolta), and home appliances, steel, and petrochemicals.

At the outset, Japanese companies focused on their home market by producing products to replace those made elsewhere—primarily in the United States. Their government ably assisted them by limiting imports in a variety of ways. Eventually the Japanese dominated their own country with these products. This brought their manufacturing costs down substantially, enabling them to consider foreign markets.

Their initial thrust was toward the markets of developing countries, where they would find minimum competition and consumers less sensitive

---

[21] Aaker, *Strategic Market Management*, p. 291.

[22] Richard I. Kirkland, Jr., "Entering a New Age of Boundless Competition," *Fortune*, March 14, 1988, p. 46.

[23] The contents of this section derive largely from Somkid Jatusripitak, Liam Fahey, and Philip Kotler, "Strategic Global Marketing: Lessons from the Japanese," *Columbia Journal of World Business*, Spring 1985, pp. 47–53.

EXHIBIT 22 ♦ 9

Direct investment in other countries, including reinvested earnings

	U.S. dollars (millions)			
	1960	*1970*	*1980*	*1986*
United States	$2,940	$7,589	$19,220	$28,050
Japan	79	355	2,385	14,480
West Germany	139	876	4,180	8,999
Great Britain	700	1,308	11,360	16,691
Canada	52	302	2,694	3,254
France	347*	374	3,138	5,230
Italy	−17*	111	754	2,661

* 1961 data.

Source: Based on data from OECO as reported in Robert I. Kirkland, Jr., "Entering a New Age of Boundless Competition," *Fortune,* May 14, 1988, p. 46.

to quality and more sensitive to price than U.S. and European consumers. Prime Japanese targets thus included Southeast Asia and Latin America. Success there enabled the Japanese to further reduce their per-unit manufacturing costs, substantially improve product quality, and gain marketing experience to a point where they could concentrate on developed countries—especially the United States. The priority objective assigned to the U.S. market was not only to obtain further economies of scale, but also to gain recognition for Japanese products, which would make their penetration of European markets easier. Within the U.S. market the Japanese targeted specific segments not covered by American producers, like small cars.

This sequential strategy succeeded: by the early 1970s 60 percent of Japanese exports went to developed countries—more than half to the United States. Japanese exports to Europe increased from 13 percent in 1960 to 20 percent in 1979. Japanese cars hold nearly 12 percent market share in the UK; 20 percent share in Switzerland, Austria, Belgium, and the Netherlands; and 30 percent share in Denmark, Ireland, and Norway. Japanese motorcycles dominate Europe, as do its watches and cameras.

A second type of *expansion path* has been used primarily for high-tech products such as computers and semiconductors. For the Japanese it consists of first securing their home market and then targeting developed countries. Japan largely ignored developing countries in this strategy because of their small demand for high-tech products. When demand increased to a point where developing countries did become "interesting," Japanese producers quickly entered and established strong market positions.

In attempting to penetrate the U.S. computer market, IBM had the Japanese companies at a technological disadvantage. Thus, they relied on price and distribution to move their products. They followed much the same attack plan in Europe. When Japan entered selected developing countries (South Korea, Taiwan, Brazil), it used heavy price cuts (up to 50 percent) to quickly attain a strong market position.

INTERNATIONAL MARKETING MIX

Here again the major question is, To what extent can firms standardize the marketing plan and elements of the marketing mix across countries or localize them by individual countries? As one might guess, standardization is greatest for product features, branding, and packaging because of the substantial savings in manufacturing costs. And firms use similar distribution channels whenever possible to capitalize on the experience gained in serving a particular channel system. But often a substantial difference exists in the availability of certain channel intermediaries and in the quality with which they perform their functions between countries. This is especially so between developed and developing countries.

Pricing tends to be localized because of differences in both manufacturing and marketing costs, taxes, and the prices of competitive products. Advertising messages frequently must be adapted to local conditions due to cultural and language differences. Media allocations vary substantially among countries because of vast differences in media availability and, in the case of print media, the quality of reproduction.

Researchers have studied multinational companies marketing consumer packaged goods (food, drink, cosmetics, pharmaceutical products) to lesser-developed countries to determine the extent to which they standardized products across countries. The study found that, on average, management made about 4.1 changes per product out of a possible 9 changes. These include brand name, packaging protection, packaging esthetics, measurement units, labeling, ingredients, product features, package size, and usage instructions. Some 70 percent of the changes were market-oriented; 22 percent were mandated by the environment (measurement units, package size, need to use local materials, and labeling). Companies made the remaining 7 percent of the changes for miscellaneous reasons. Two thirds of all products transferred to lesser-developed countries retained their physical features.[24]

Product strategy

Regardless of whether a company adopts a standardized or a localized international marketing strategy, it must make sure its products are of the highest quality. Regardless of the kind of product involved "the pursuit of

---

[24] J. S. Hill and R. R. Still, "Adapting Products to LDC Tastes," *Harvard Business Review*, March–April 1984, pp. 92–101.

quality is no longer voluntary. If U.S. industry expects to win . . . more customers and market share, it has no choice but to improve its products. For the customer, quality is irresistible. For industry, it is essential."[25]

Assuming a company can produce a quality product, it has three major product options, based on the extent to which it modifies the product's physical dimensions. These options are:

1. **Market the same product to all countries (a "world" product).** This strategy requires that the physical product sold in each country be the same except for labeling and the language used in the product manuals. It assumes customer needs are essentially the same across national boundaries or can be made the same by offering a quality product at a relatively low price resulting from scale effects. This strategy can be successful when products are not culture sensitive and economies of scale are significant. Product examples include cameras, jet aircraft engines, basic steel, chemicals, plastics, memory chips, and many components.

2. **Adapt the product to local conditions.** This strategy keeps the physical product essentially the same. Only modifications that represent a small percentage of total costs are permitted, such as changes in voltage, packaging, and color. Examples include computers, copiers, over-the-road construction equipment, cars, calculators, and motorcycles.

3. **Develop a country-specific product.** In this situation the physical product is substantially altered (affects a significant part of total costs) across countries or groups of countries. Such a strategy is common with packaged food and personal-care items.

Producing a world product is not easy because it requires setting standards that reflect the conditions under which the product is used. Using a set of standards developed from U.S.-use conditions may not produce a product acceptable to the rest of the world and hence the need for marketing research. (For an example of adapting a product to the environments of target markets, see Exhibit 22–10.)

In a similar but somewhat different situation, it may be possible to create demand for a world product that would replace a line of country-specific products. This has been the Black & Decker strategy. Only a few years ago, the company consisted of

> a confederation of nearly sovereign fiefdoms. British managers developed and sold their own products in Britain, as did their French and German counterparts without any regard to global strategy. The tremendous overhead was not offset by any efficiencies or economies of scale. Worldwide the company made 100 different motors—the most expensive component of power tools. Today . . . it makes fewer than 20 and is aiming for five.[26]

---

[25] Christopher Knowleton, "What America Makes Best," *Fortune*, March 28, 1988, p. 53. This article lists the 100 products that America makes best.

[26] John Huey, "The New Power in Black & Decker," *Fortune*, January 2, 1988, p. 60.

EXHIBIT 22 ♦ 10

Boeing's rescue of the 737

Boeing designed its 737 to compete with McDonnell Douglas's DC-9; but its late entry into the market was not altogether successful. In the mid-70s the company was about to phase the 737 out, but decided to give it one more chance. Boeing turned to engineer Bob Norton to save the plane. Norton decided to target the Mideast, Africa, and South America. This required adapting the 737 to the aviation environment of the third world.

The major problems were that the runways in developing countries were too short and too soft because they were asphalt rather than cement, and pilots came in too hard, causing more wear and tear on the planes. Boeing redesigned the wings to permit shorter landings, added thrust to the engines for quicker takeoffs, redesigned the landing gear, and used low-pressure tires to make the plane stick to the ground when it touched down. Recently, the Boeing 737 became the best-selling commercial jet in history.

Source: Condensed from Andrew Kupfer, "How to Be a Global Manager," *Fortune,* March 14, 1988, p. 52.

Market segmentation is yet another way of facilitating the sale of physically similar products worldwide. This can be accomplished in three ways. The first involves selling to much the same segment in each country, for example, the high-income segment for expensive cars. A second approach calls for targeting diverse groups across countries using essentially the same physical product. Thus, the Canon AE-1 camera targeted young replacement buyers in Japan, upscale first-time buyers of this type of camera in the United States, and older and more knowledgeable replacement buyers in Germany. Once these segments were identified, Canon proceeded to develop a marketing program for each country.[27]

Pricing[28]

Companies find it difficult to adopt a standardized pricing strategy across countries because of fluctuating exchange rates; differences between countries in costs, competition, and demand; conflicting governmental tax policies plus government controls (such as dumping and price ceilings); and such other factors as transportation costs, differences in channels of distribution, and global accounts that demand equal price treatment regardless of location. Much also depends upon the firm's objective in its various markets, for example, penetration pricing versus market holding.

In general, a firm's pricing alternatives in a given market are the same as for the domestic market, although the factors favoring a given alternative

[27] Takeuchi and Porter, "Three Roles of International Marketing," pp. 107–41.

[28] Based on Keegan, *Global Marketing Management,* chap. 13.

will surely differ. As companies have expanded their overseas sales, an increasing number have set up decentralized operations in an effort to increase flexibility as well as to motivate local management. This, in turn, has led to an increase in **transfer pricing.** This can be implemented in several ways, including transfer at cost, at cost plus overhead and margin, at market price, and on an arm's-length basis (a price arrived at by unrelated parties). Because taxes vary across countries, companies often adjust their transfer prices to minimize income in high-tax countries and maximize it in low-tax countries. Governments have recognized this and have countered with programs designed to maximize their tax revenues.

Keegan proposes three global pricing alternatives. The first is an **extension/ethnocentric** policy, which sets the same price throughout the world with the customer absorbing all freight and import duties. Its virtue is its simplicity; but its weakness is its failure to take into account local market demand and competitive conditions.

The second pricing alternative is called **adaptive/polycentric.** It permits local management to establish whatever price is most desirable at any particular time. Although sensitive to local conditions, this policy may favor product arbitrage where differences in price between markets exceed the freight and duty costs separating the markets. There is also the question of whether the objectives of local management are the same as those of corporate management.

Invention/geocentric pricing is the third approach. It seeks to set an intermediate position, neither setting a single worldwide price nor relinquishing total control over prices to local management. This alternative recognizes the importance of both local factors (including costs) and the firm's market objectives. Thus, a firm might allow local managers to set a high price in countries where its product is well established, but require pricing below local costs to pursue a market-penetration objective in countries where its competitive position is weak. Another advantage is that this pricing policy enables price to be compatible with the other elements in the marketing program. It recognizes that price coordination by central management is necessary to prevent arbitrage and in dealing with international accounts. And it is the only approach that permits the company as a whole to take into account global markets and global competitors.

Countertrade transactions have increased in importance in recent years. Basically, the four types of countertrade are barter, compensation packages, counterpurchase, and buy-backs.[29] **Barter** involves a direct exchange of goods between two or more parties. The seller must be able to sell the bartered goods at a price sufficient to compensate for those traded to the other party. An example is trading Yugoslavian hams for commercial air-

---

[29] Stephen S. Cohen and John Zysman, "Countertrade, Offsets, Barter, and Buybacks," *California Management Review*, Winter 1986, pp. 41–56.

craft. **Compensation packages** involve some combination of products and cash—like selling machine tools to Yugoslavia and getting 25 percent cash and the remainder in work shoes.

Counterpurchase, the most popular form of countertrade, involves two contracts. First, the seller agrees to sell a product at a fixed price for cash. But this agreement is conditional on the seller agreeing to buy goods from the buyer over some future period of time for all or part of the amount in the first agreement. The second condition gives the seller time to sell the goods and thus makes this transaction preferable over barter. A **buy-back agreement** involves selling products that are used to produce other goods (say, a production system). The seller agrees to buy a certain amount of the output, and this is applied as a partial payment to the sale amount.

Channels[30]

Two major types of international channel alternatives are available to a domestic producer. The first is the use of domestic middlemen who provide marketing services from their domestic base. Because of their proximity, they are convenient to use, but suffer from their lack of knowledge about a foreign market and their inability to provide the kind of representation offered by foreign-based middlemen. Exhibit 22–11 summarizes the primary functions performed by the more important kinds of domestic middlemen who sell overseas.

Four of the domestic middlemen shown in this exhibit need to be discussed briefly because, for the most part, they are unique to international marketing. The first is the **export management company (EMC),** which is an important agent middleman for firms with small foreign sales. Operating under the name of the manufacturer, they represent and function as a low-cost marketing arm of a company. Their main services are providing contacts with overseas buyers and negotiating sales.

The second middleman that needs elaboration is the **manufacturer's export agent (MEA).** Unlike the EMC, the MEA does not serve as the client's export department, but rather has a short-term relationship that covers only a few countries. MEAs operate in their own name. Thus, a manufacturer might have one EMC but several MEAs.

Trading companies are yet another type of merchant intermediary that has only recently been emphasized by American firms. They provide extensive services, including the accumulation, transport, and distribution of a variety of goods typically to a number of countries close to one another (the Middle East). Japanese trading companies can be enormous in size and offer

---

[30] This section has benefited from Cateora, *International Marketing*, chap. 17; Louis W. Stern and Adel I. El-Ansary, *Marketing Channels* (Englewood Cliffs, N.J.: Prentice-Hall, 1988), chaps. 12, 14.

not only the traditional wholesale services, but also those involving the development of joint ventures, technical assistance, and even the production of goods. They offer one of the best ways of gaining access to the complicated Japanese distribution system.

Complementary marketers engage in piggybacking, which means they accept products for distribution other than their own that are noncompetitive yet complementary and thus enhance their distribution resources. Typically, most such business is undertaken on a purchase-resale basis. For example, Singer Sewing Machine Company sells fabrics, patterns, and notions—all of which it buys for resale.

Foreign middlemen

In contrast to dealing with domestic middlemen, a manufacturer may decide to deal directly with middlemen in foreign countries. This shortens the channel, thereby bringing the manufacturer closer to the market. This is particularly important in terms of information about the market. A major problem is that foreign middlemen are some distance away, and therefore more difficult to control than domestic ones. Since many middlemen—especially merchant middlemen—are prone to act independently of their suppliers, it is difficult to use them when market cultivation is needed.

The functions performed by both foreign agents and merchant middlemen are similar to those performed by American middlemen (see Exhibit 22–12). There is, however, considerable variation among foreign middlemen across countries as to how well the various functions are performed. Further, in some countries (those in Southeast Asia) trade is dominated by a small number of large powerful middlemen. This means a manufacturer must either transfer control of its product to such middlemen or set up its own system.

Retail structures in foreign countries vary tremendously because of differences in the cultural, economic, and political environments; for example, the size of retail stores increases as gross national product per capita increases. European retailing seems to be following a path similar to that pioneered by the United States with respect to store size, self-service, discounting, automation, and direct marketing. Even so, the average size store is still small by U.S. standards, which makes it difficult to sell to them directly. The use of consumer goods wholesalers is common, particularly in the emerging countries where small retailers are prevalent.

Channel problems[31]

Although the problems encountered by a manufacturer in establishing and maintaining a channel system overseas are similar to those experienced domestically, there are some important differences. First, the kind of chan-

---

[31] Stern and El-Ansary, ibid., pp. 552–56.

EXHIBIT 22 ◆ 11

Characterisitics of domestic middlemen serving overseas markets

Type of duties	Agents				
	EMC*	MEA†	Broker	Buying offices	Selling groups
Take title	No	No	No	No	No
Take possession	Yes	Yes	No	Yes	Yes
Continuing relationship	Yes	Yes	No	Yes	Yes
Share of foreign output	All	All	Any	Small	All
Degree of control by principal	Fair	Fair	Nil	Nil	Good
Price authority	Advisory	Advisory	Yes (at mkt level)	Yes (to buy)	Advisory
Represent buyer or seller	Seller	Seller	Either	Buyer	Seller
Number of principals	Few—many	Few—many	Many	Small	Few
Arrange shipping	Yes	Yes	Not usually	Yes	Yes
Type of goods	Mfd goods, commodities	Staples, commodities	Staples, commodities	Staples, commodities	Complementary to their own lines
Breadth of line	Specialty— wide	All types of staples	All types of staples	Retail goods	Narrow
Handle competitive lines	No	No	Yes	Yes—uses many sources	No
Extent of promotion and selling effort	Good	Good	One shot	n.a.	Good
Extend credit to principal	Occasionally	Occasionally	Seldom	Seldom	Seldom
Market information	Fair	Fair	Price and mkt conditions	For principal, not for mfr	Good

Note: n.a. = not available.
* Export management company.
† Manufacturer's export agent.

Source: Philip R. Cateora, *International Marketing,* 7th ed. (Homewood, Ill.: Richard D. Irwin, 1990), chap. 17, in press.

nel needed simply may not be available because of the country's low level of economic development (such as lack of refrigeration) or the presence of only state-controlled middlemen.

A second and related problem is that access may be difficult because existing middlemen have already been appropriated by other manufacturers (particularly local ones) via various arrangements, including financial and the exclusive use of private labels. This has often been the case with Japan.

A third problem is that once a channel is set up, it may be difficult to change because there are often strong barriers to the termination of a rela-

EXHIBIT 22 ◆ 11

(concluded)

	Merchants			
Norazi	**Export merchant**	**Export jobber**	**Importers and trading companies**	**Complementary marketers**
Yes	Yes	Yes	Yes	Yes
Yes	Yes	No	Yes	Yes
No	No	Yes	Yes	Yes
Small	Any	Small	Any	Most
Nil	None	None	Nil	Fair
Yes	Yes	Yes	No	Some
Both	Self	Self	Self	Self
Several per transaction	Many sources	Many sources	Many sources	One per product
Yes	Yes	Yes	Yes	Yes
Contraband	Mfd goods	Bulky and raw materials	Mfd goods	Complementary to line
n.a.	Broad	Broad	Broad	Narrow
Yes	Yes	Yes	Yes	No
Nil	Nil	Nil	Good	Good
No	Occasionally	Seldom	Seldom	Seldom
No	Nil	Nil	Fair	Good

tionship. In some countries (Norway), it is illegal to do so without evidence of incompetency. In some of the lesser-developed countries, terminating a powerful middleman can result in reprisals, including being barred from the marketplace.

A fourth problem is control, which is only partly due to distance. An international marketer will almost always use a variety of channel systems to penetrate and service its various markets, no two of which are identical. The problems of controlling this varied set of distribution systems are so numerous that many companies use a contractual entry mode (licensing or franchising) whenever possible to facilitate control.

EXHIBIT 22 ◆ 12

Characteristics of middlemen in foreign countries

		Agents		
Type of duties	*Broker*	*Manufacturer's representative*	*Managing agent*	*Comprador*
Take title	No	No	No	No
Take possession	No	Seldom	Seldom	Yes
Continuing relationship	No	Often	With buyer, not seller	Yes
Share of foreign output	Small	All or part for one area	n.a.	All one area
Degree of control by principal	Low	Fair	None	Fair
Price authority	Nil	Nil	Nil	Partial
Represent buyer or seller	Either	Seller	Buyer	Seller
Number of principals	Many	Few	Many	Few
Arrange shipping	No	No	No	No
Type of goods	Commodity, food	Mfd goods	All types mfd goods	Mfd goods
Breadth of line	Broad	Allied lines	Broad	Varies
Handle competitive lines	Yes	No	Yes	No
Extent of promotion and selling effort	Nil	Fair	Nil	Fair
Extend credit to principal	No	No	No	Sometimes
Market information	Nil	Good	Nil	Good

Note: n.a. = not available.

Source: Philip R. Cateora, *International Marketing,* 7th ed. (Homewood, Ill.: Richard D. Irwin, 1990), chap. 17, in press.

Despite these problems, international middlemen have not only increased in number, but have also become more adept at fulfilling their functions. Even so, the establishment and maintenance of an effective and efficient overseas distribution network remains one of the biggest challenges facing the international marketer.

Promotion

Advertising is extremely difficult to standardize across countries primarily because prospective consumers for a given product live in very different social, economic, and political environments. Exhibit 22–13 enumerates how the different types of environments affect promotion. Standardization is particularly difficult with message construction, where differences in product knowledge, benefit expectations, buying motives, and languages make the use of a standardized message across countries difficult, if not impossi-

EXHIBIT 22 ◆ 12
(concluded)

Merchants			
Distributor	**Dealer**	**Import jobber**	**Wholesaler and retailer**
Yes	Yes	Yes	Yes
Yes	Yes	Yes	Yes
Yes	Yes	No	Usually not
All, for certain countries	Assignment area	Small	Very small
High	High	Low	
			Nil
Partial	Partial	Full	Full
Seller	Seller	Self	Self
Small	Few major	Many	Many
No	No	No	No
Mfd goods	Mfd goods	Mfd goods	Mfd consumer goods
Narrow to broad	Narrow	Narrow to broad	Narrow to broad
No	No	Yes	Yes
Fair	Good	Nil	Nil usually
Sometimes	No	No	No
Fair	Good	Nil	Nil

ble. Even when the primary benefits remain intact across national boundaries, the transferability of an advertising message is still difficult because of language differences. For example, Parker Pen's message "You'll never be embarrassed with a Parker Pen" translates into Spanish as "You'll never be *pregnant* with a Parker Pen" because *embarazade* means pregnant in Spanish.

Traditional beliefs and contemporary behavior patterns inhibit message transferability. (Exhibit 22–14 compares American and Japanese advertising messages for the same product.) In some cases, the target audience may even be ignorant of a product's benefits. For example, Polaroid's Swinger, an inexpensive camera and the company's first entry in France, failed because the concept of instant photography was unkown there.

Further barriers to transferring the creative presentation intact include culture (response to humor based on exaggeration); competitive conditions; and execution (poor color reproduction in print ads). Even Coca-Cola, which has been cited as a prime example of standardized advertising, is now using considerable local flavor in its worldwide campaign.

EXHIBIT 22 ◆ 13

How different kinds of environments affect promotion across countries

Type of environment	Examples of effect
Social	Languages, culture, religion, and lifestyles vary substantially across most countries. For example, because attitudes differ regarding cleanliness, Gillette promotes its razors, deodorants, and other men's grooming products differently in the developing countries than in the United States.
Economic	Because of substantial variations in standards of living across countries as well as the distribution of wealth within countries, demand for a particular product varies, as does the way a product is perceived. For example, watches and pens are considered reasonably standard items in developed countries. Not so in the developing countries, however, where they are a sign of wealth and influence.
Political	Some countries (such as Russia) prevent the importation of some U.S. products under any conditions. Political control also determines what products can be advertised (pharmaceuticals, alcohol, airlines, and candy are forbidden in some Arabic countries); what media can be used (no TV advertising is permitted in Scandinavia); and what can be said about products (comparative advertising is not allowed in Germany).

While the TV commercials show a thousand children singing the praises of Coke, each McCann office was allowed to edit the film to include close-ups of a youngster from its market. There are at least 21 different versions of the spot running.[32]

Another difficulty in standardizing advertising has to do with the media. While much the same media types exist around the world, the extent to which prospective consumers are exposed to each type varies considerably. Thus, while most Americans, British, and Europeans own TVs, such is not the case in the developing countries. Also, as we noted in Exhibit 22–13, it may not be legal to use certain media for advertising. Even when it is legal, the media's availability may be severely restricted. Italy, for example, limits a TV commercial to 10 showings a year with no two exposures within a 10-day period. Billboards and movies are important media in the developing countries where high illiteracy exists.

---

[32] Julie Skeer Hill and Joseph M. Winski, "Good-bye Global Ads," *Advertising Age,* November 16, 1987, p. 22.

EXHIBIT 22 ♦ 14

Advertising messages—American style versus Japanese style

In the United States we might use music in a commercial to create mood and arouse emotion, while in Japan this is accomplished through the nuances of language. In the Japanese culture, images, feelings, and sensations can all be created through abstract word associations. To write a successful commercial in Japan, therefore, specific product features are not as important as the sensitivity of the wording, the actor's sense of intimacy, and a general good feeling.

Take the case of National Mini-refrigerators, a Japanese brand. If we planned to market this product to young, single, liberated women in the United States, we probably would use a very pragmatic approach, creating ads stressing the economical or space-saving characteristics of the product. Our ad might show the product in use and the headline, "Save Money. Buy a Mini."

Speaking to the same target group in Japan, the advertiser positioned the product in the background of the ad and, on the floor in the foreground, the mutilated photograph of a lost lover. The emotional copy written in Japanese characters reads: "There are nights when it's better to drink up rather than cry your eyes out. So set your heart at rest. Forget him. You have your Mini."

Source: Courtland L. Bovée and William F. Arens, *Contemporary Advertising,* 2nd ed. (Homewood, Ill.: Richard D. Irwin, 1986), p. 600.

EXPORTING OF SERVICES

America is the world's largest exporter of services—a record $48 billion in 1986. And most forecasters expect it to increase dramatically. America's strengths in selling services abroad lie largely in international transport, which has benefited from the weak dollar, thereby encouraging foreign travel in the United States; data processing and computer services, including software (some 15 of the world's largest 20 software producers are American); management skills in such industries as construction, health care, and business services (HCA, the biggest operator of private hospitals in the United States, owns 28 hospitals overseas); trash collection (Waste Management's overseas revenues are expected to increase by 25 percent each year over the next five years); and pop culture, including royalties from films and TV shows such as "Dallas."

McDonald's and other U.S. franchisors have expanded overseas at an ever increasing rate. International sales now account for 25 percent of McDonald's total revenues from over 2,000 units located around the world.[33] Direct mail, telephone marketing, marketing research, advertising,

---

[33] Kirkland, "Entering a New Age," pp. 32–38.

EXHIBIT 22 ◆ 15

The shrinking surplus in business services (U.S. balance on business-related[1] services trade, in billions of dollars)

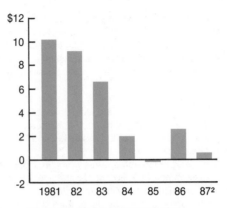

[1]Excludes government transactions
and investment income.

[2]Annualized, based on first nine months.

Source: Christopher J. Chipello, "Foreign Rivals Imperil U.S. Firms' Leadership in the Service Sector," *The Wall Street Journal,* March 21, 1988, p. 1.

and head hunting are other kinds of services exported successfully by American firms. International growth in financial services has been extensive, but Americans are experiencing difficulties here because four of the world's largest banks and four of the six largest securities houses are Japanese.[34]

American service firms are experiencing increased competition. The Japanese, having passed us in the international lending area, are now moving aggressively into construction, hotels, and travel services. The world's largest advertising agency is Saatchi & Saatchi of London. And European service companies are acquiring more and more U.S. companies; for example, U.K.-based Blue Arrow PLC acquired Manpower, Inc. (Milwaukee, Wisconsin), a leading supplier of temporary help. The U.S. surplus in services has dropped from $10 billion in 1981 to less than $1 billion in 1987 (see Exhibit 22–15).[35]

INTERNATIONAL MARKETING RESEARCH

Exporting firms can minimize the risks inherent in coping with the different environments present in their target countries through marketing research. More and more firms are using marketing research in their global operations.

---

[34] Ibid.

[35] Christopher J. Chipello, "Foreign Rivals Imperil U.S. Firms' Leadership in the Service Sector," *The Wall Street Journal,* March 21, 1988, p. 1.

Estimated world expenditures for all marketing/advertising/public opinion research for 1987 was estimated at $4.7 billion. The 25 largest worldwide research organizations accounted for nearly 55 percent of the total. Dun & Bradstreet, owner of A.C. Nielsen Co., is the biggest player with a market share of about 23 percent. The next largest company, Control Data Corporation of Minneapolis, holds a 6.9 percent share.[36]

International marketing research covers a broader range of subjects than does domestic marketing research. Often, researchers are asked to provide a wide range of information about the various environments of a number of countries the firm is considering entering. Such requests include information a domestic marketer would already know or could readily access, particularly if it was a U.S. company (e.g., data on economic, political, and cultural environments; distribution and transport systems; and regulations on products and packaging). Further, many foreign countries, especially third-world ones, provide little secondary source data about their various environments, and what information is available is lacking in reliability and recency.

Marketing researchers encounter special difficulties in international settings (see Exhibit 22–16 for an example). The same research techniques are used; but differences in the environments create serious problems, primarily in sampling and data collection. One problem involves a lack of recent data needed to structure a sample. In many countries up-to-date telephone directories, street directories, census tract data, and demographics are not avail-

EXHIBIT 22 ◆ 16

Example of marketing research problem resulting from cultural differences

Because of cultural and national differences, confusion can just as well be the problem of the researcher as the respondent. One classic misunderstanding that occurred in a *Reader's Digest* study of consumer behavior in Western Europe resulted in the report that France and West Germany consumed more spaghetti than Italy did. This rather curious and erroneous finding resulted from questions that asked about purchases of "packaged and branded spaghetti." Italians buy their spaghetti in bulk; the French and West Germans buy branded and packaged spaghetti. Since the Italians buy little branded or packaged spaghetti, the results underreported spaghetti purchases by Italians. However, the real question is, What did the researcher want to find out? Had the goal of the research been to determine how much branded and packaged spaghetti was purchased, the results would have been correct. However, because the goal was to know about total spaghetti consumption, the data were incorrect.

Source: Philip R. Cateora, *International Marketing* (Homewood, Ill.: Richard D. Irwin, 1987), p. 350.

---

[36] Jack J. Honomichl, "Top Worldwide Research Companies," *Advertising Age*, December 5, 1988, p. S–1.

able. Researchers often find that the use of certain survey communication methods are limited. In many of the developing countries, few households have telephones, for instance. Poor postal service and a lack of mailing lists raise serious obstacles to mail surveys in many countries. This is not the case in most European countries and Japan, however, where adults must register and provide certain demographic data.

Researchers also find respondents in many countries more difficult to interview than in the United States. One reason for this is that respondents suspect that the interviewer might be a tax agent! In some cultures women refuse to be interviewed by a stranger, and men won't talk to a female interviewer. A respondent's inability to articulate answers because of little or no education often compounds a lack of awareness of a given product and its use.

Although conducting survey research is ordinarily more difficult in the international arena, it is not impossible to do so. Firms need researchers experienced in dealing with the local environment in imaginative ways. More and more global companies now decentralize their research activities to accommodate this need.

SUMMARY

International marketing has become increasingly important to U.S. firms in recent years. International sales are not only an important source of profits, but also critical for some firms' survival because of the impact on scale effects and the ability to retaliate against competitive attacks without lowering profits drastically in the home market. International marketing follows many of the same principles as domestic marketing. There are, however, major differences between countries and the development of strategy options and marketing programs built on these differences.

In considering which foreign markets to target, a firm must analyze each country's physical, legal, economic, political, cultural, competitive, and infrastructure environments. Legal barriers come in a variety of forms, including tariffs and embargoes. There are also a variety of indirect legal barriers. The other environments affect demand as well as targeting, product positioning, and the development of marketing programs.

The latter depends heavily on the major marketing mix elements, all of which are strongly affected by the various environments.

Reasons for entering into overseas marketing include economies of scale that extend beyond the size of the home market, defending against a global competitor, and satisfying customers going international. Market-entry strategies include exporting (both direct and indirect); contractual, including licensing, franchising, and a variety of other types of agreements; and investment, which can be via joint or sole venture. Companies can mix these to service different overseas markets.

International trade strategies revolve for the most part around localization versus standardization. The extent to which a firm opts for one or the other strategy depends heavily on the product involved. Products enjoying strong experience effects and not highly culture-bound are candidates for standardized marketing. Achieving a commanding world competitive position involves not only low-cost manufacturing, but also a well-integrated distribution system.

Not unlike the formulation of an international strategy, the major question regarding the international marketing mix is the extent to which it can be standardized across countries. Standardization is greatest in product features, branding, and packaging because of manufacturing scale effects. Firms use similar channels whenever possible; but prices tend to be localized because of differences in cost and competition. Typically, advertising messages need to be adapted to local conditions.

The United States is the largest exporter of services in the world and is particularly strong in international transport, data processing and computer services, management skills, trash collection, pop culture, fast foods, and marketing services. U.S. firms are, however, experiencing increased competition. The American surplus in services slipped to less than $1 billion in 1987.

QUESTIONS

1. Suppose you are the marketing vice president for the Rubbermaid Company, a manufacturer of low-cost household utensils. You are considering expanding the market for your firm's product into South America, starting with Argentina. What potential *barriers* to success might your firm encounter in the Argentine market? What specific factors or questions relevant to each of those potential barriers would you want to investigate before making a final decision to enter the Argentine market?

2. What unique problems might you encounter in attempting to do the *marketing research* necessary to resolve some of the questions you identified in your answer to question 1? What actions would you take to avoid or overcome such problems?

3. Rubbermaid is a relatively small firm manufacturing a broad line of low-tech consumer products, such as garbage pails and plastic bowls, requiring relatively extensive distribution. It also has only limited experience in competing in foreign markets. What type of *market-entry strategy* would be best for Rubbermaid to follow if it decides to enter the Argentine market? Why?

4. IBM competes in the developed nations of Western Europe and in Japan largely through wholly owned subsidiaries. What are the advantages—and potential disadvantages—of this kind of *direct investment strategy* for entering foreign markets from IBM's point of view?

5. Theodore Levitt argues that the successful global competitors of the future will be those firms that move toward greater *standardization of products and marketing programs* across national markets. What is the rationale for Levitt's argument? Are there any types of products for which such standardization may not be appropriate?

6. The 3M Company views many of the more developed countries of Eastern Europe—such as East Germany and Hungary—as attractive potential markets for many of its industrial products. In the past, however, a lack of hard currency has constrained the volume of purchases that organizations in those countries could make from U.S. companies. Consequently, in recent years, 3M has engaged in extensive *countertrade agreements* to increase sales in Eastern Europe. Describe three types of countertrade arrangements and discuss

how each might be implemented by 3M in selling its products to East Germany.

7. In recent years, many large U.S., European, and Japanese advertising agencies have acquired smaller agencies or established subsidiaries in other developed countries. This merger activity enables large agencies to gain the expertise needed to adapt the advertising campaigns of their large multinational clients to the unique characteristics of different national markets. *Why are advertising campaigns often less standardized* across countries than the products they promote? What factors should be taken into account when adapting a campaign to consumers in another country?

SECTION V

Implementing and controlling strategic marketing programs

Earlier sections described the process by which a strategic marketing program for a product-market entry evolves. More specifically, Chapters 1 and 2 dealt with the objectives and strategies of the corporation as a whole and the applicable business unit; Chapters 3 through 9 with marketing opportunity analysis; and Chapters 10 through 18 with developing strategic marketing programs in general and Chapters 19 through 22 with programs for selected situations. This section comprises two chapters that discuss the implementation and control of marketing programs.

Formulating marketing strategies consistent with their resources is meaningless unless firms implement their strategies effectively and efficiently. Implementation varies depending on the strategy type selected, because different strategies have different objectives. Thus, Chapter 23 on implementation is initially concerned with how strategies vary in the ways they are expected to perform, as well as how they vary in requiring different functional strengths. Further, each of these strategy types affects the way the company structures its marketing organization.

Implementation requires developing a written plan of action for each product-market entry and each marketing unit, such as sales and personal selling. These plans derive from a specification of the strategy elements and, therefore, are tied directly to the fit between the firm's resources and market opportunities. They detail the marketing mix to be used in accordance with the determinants of sales and market share.

The final step in the marketing management process is to monitor and control the marketing program (Chapter 24). Marketers evaluate the performance of a product-market entry's strategic marketing program (complete with its plan of action) to determine if it is meeting its profitability and competitive position objectives—and to exercise control by adjusting the program when the performance is disappointing. The control discussion centers on the control process and each of its major components; for example, setting standards of performance. Following this is a description of the several marketing controls, including examples of each.

Chapter ◇ 23

Implementing business and marketing strategies

PROCTER & GAMBLE CHANGES ITS MARKETING ORGANIZATION[1]

In 1931 Neil H. McElroy, a young P&G advertising manager, persuaded his bosses to assign a single marketing "brand man" to each of the company's products. McElroy, who years later became the company's chairman, argued that the firm's struggling new Camay soap brand suffered from "too much Ivory thinking." He pointed out that the firm would grow faster by allowing each of its brands to compete independently in the market. One person should be given full responsibility for evaluating the market, developing marketing plans, and coordinating all the functional activities associated with a given brand.

Some P&G executives at first denounced his idea as "suicide"; but it soon took hold, and the first product management organization was born. The firm assigned young managers with high potential to manage individual brands. Each manager ran the brand as a competitive business. Although the brand managers had little formal authority and their decisions required approval from layers of superiors—often right up to the chief executive—they were the critical starting point for developing marketing and advertising strategy, planning sales promotions, and coordinating package design. Similarly, although the brand managers had

no authority over managers in other functional areas, such as R&D and manufacturing, they were responsible for coordinating activities of those functions to ensure consistency with the needs and desires of target customers and with the overall strategy for the brand.

The product management organization developed at P&G proved so successful that many other consumer products and services firms soon adopted it. And, usually with some modifications, a growing number of industrial goods companies adopted it as well. The product manager form of organization has proved particularly effective within large organizations with broad and diverse product lines, especially when a firm targets many of its products at growing markets. By serving as a vocal champion for the product, the product manager helps ensure that it receives the resources necessary to keep up with growing demand. And the manager plays an important role in

[1] The following case example is based on material found in Julie Solomon and Carol Hymowitz, "P&G Makes Changes in the Way It Develops and Sells Its Products," *The Wall Street Journal*, August 11, 1987, p. 1.

continued

planning and implementing the advertising, sales promotion, distribution, and other critical marketing activities.

The product manager structure has also been effective for coordinating new-product and new-market development efforts, especially in nondurable consumer goods industries. Here managers' familiarity with customer needs and preferences is often critical in identifying and addressing market opportunities. P&G's development of the product manager form of organization contributed greatly to the firm's ability to sustain the growth that made it the premier consumer package goods company with sales of $17 billion in 1987.

As both P&G's external environment and its internal character changed over the years, however, the firm has modified its product management structure. For one thing, the firm pursued market expansion strategies in growth markets and extended use and market development strategies in more mature markets. As a result, P&G now has a number of different brands and line extensions (e.g., regular Crest toothpaste, tarter-control Crest, and Gleem) in most of its business categories. In some cases, different brands target distinct segments of the market; but in others, they are direct competitors. Consequently, P&G has begun adding another layer of marketing managers above its product managers. These new category brand managers coordinate marketing strategies across related brands and allocate resources within the company's portfolio of products in a given business. This addition of higher-level group marketing managers or marketing directors to coordinate marketing

strategies across related products and brands has become common in many firms.

In addition to the proliferation of brands and line extensions, several other environmental factors have increased the fragmentation of P&G's maturing product-markets. Shifts in demographics and lifestyles, such as the increasing number of single-person households and the growing number of women working outside the home, have motivated the firm to introduce line extensions or new brands to appeal to more narrowly defined segments. This, in turn, has forced the development of individualized marketing programs.

Variations in customer tastes and preferences across geographic areas have also forced the firm to respond to regional differences in market and competitive conditions. P&G's Folgers coffee, for instance, faces more intense competition in the South, and must rely on more extensive sales promotion efforts there, because of the popularity of regional brands that cater to the Southern preference for strong and chicory-flavored coffees. Finally, P&G has lost some of its power to gain unquestioning cooperation from its retailers due to increased concentration in the supermarket industry (some major metropolitan areas are dominated by only one or a few supermarket chains) and the proliferation of scanners, which give retailers more timely data than manufacturers have about the sales of competing brands in their stores.

As a result of these changes, P&G

continued

concluded

now faces increasingly fragmented, variable, and demanding markets at both the retail and consumer levels. And the firm is changing its organization structure to increase its flexibility in dealing with those markets. For instance, it decentralized some decision-making and spending authority in some product categories by adding regional marketing managers who work directly with sales executives in a given region. These regional managers have the authority—and the budget—to develop and implement local sales or trade promotion programs geared to the unique market and competitive situations in their territories.

Another set of environmental changes has forced P&G to change its approach to new-product development. Historically, the firm's system called for entering markets slowly, studying all the angles, and then launching a superior product with a massive advertising and promotion campaign. The product manager played the central role in this process, being responsible for coordinating the activities of all other functional areas and for making sure all aspects of the new product and its marketing program fit the needs and benefits sought by target customers. But in today's faster-moving market, P&G has at times found itself beaten to the marketplace. Grandma's cookies were test marketed in Kansas City before P&G's Duncan Hines brand was ready for consumer trial, and Nabisco's Almost Home line beat Duncan Hines into national distribution.

Further, some of the firm's product lines have become more technically complex—both in terms of product design and the process technology involved in manufacturing. As a result, it has become more difficult for a single product manager to keep tabs on all the factors and decisions involved in developing such complicated products and bringing them to market in a timely and successful manner. When Pringle's potato chips were introduced, for instance, the product manager argued for the construction of new chip plants based on the product's success in one test market even though manufacturing and packaging managers warned that the uniformly shaped chip—packed in tennis-ball-style cans—would be too expensive. The product's high price, together with consumer reservations about its taste and texture, caused initial sales to fall far below projections and at least one of the new plants had to be closed.

To speed up the new-product development process and improve the coordination of those activities, P&G has moved to a greater use of "business teams." These teams bring together representatives of different functional areas as part of a group responsible for developing and introducing a new product. As one P&G executive explains, "Working on a team with 12 or 20 others, it takes longer to reach decisions, but once that's done you've got everybody you need in place to move a product to market faster." Thus, one P&G team rushed Ultra Pampers to market in just nine months, half the usual time.

ISSUES IN THE IMPLEMENTATION OF BUSINESS AND MARKETING STRATEGIES

The recent changes at P&G illustrate a point mentioned in Chapter 11: a business's success is determined by two aspects of strategic fit. First, its competitive and marketing strategy must fit the needs and constraints of the external market and the competitive environment. Second, the business must be able to effectively implement that strategy; its internal structure, policies, procedures, and resources must fit the demands of the strategy. As Exhibit 23–1 indicates, when a business cannot effectively implement its chosen strategy—even when that strategy is very appropriate for the circumstances it faces—trouble is likely to ensue. Worse, management may con-

EXHIBIT　23◆1

The combined effects of strategy selection and implementation

Strategy

	Appropriate (fits the market and competitive environment)	Inappropriate (does not fit the market or competitive environment)
Excellent	**Success** — Objectives for volume growth, market share, profits are met.	**Rescue or ruin** — Good implementation may mitigate poor strategy and give management time to adjust. But good implementation of poor strategy may also hasten failure.
Poor	**Trouble** — Poor implementation hampers performance. Management may conclude that strategy is inappropriate and switch to less appropriate strategy.	**Failure** — Cause of failure is hard to diagnose because poor strategy is masked by inability to implement.

Implementation

Source: Reprinted by permission of the *Harvard Business Review.* An exhibit adapted from "Making Your Marketing Strategy Work," by Thomas V. Bonoma (March–April 1984), Copyright © 1984 by the President and Fellows of Harvard College; all rights reserved.

clude the strategy was not appropriate, switch to a less desirable strategy, and ultimately depress the business's performance even further, possibly to the point of failure. On one hand, excellent execution may offset the negative effects of a poorly conceived, inappropriate strategy. But on the other hand, good implementation of the wrong strategy can speed the business along the road to failure.

Most of this book has focused on issues and methods relevant for analyzing the external environment and developing marketing strategies and programs that fit the environment faced by a business and its product-market entries. In this chapter, we turn our attention to questions of internal fit—the fit between a business's strategies and the organizational structures, policies, processes, and plans necessary to implement those strategies. Four major sets of internal variables affect a business's ability to implement particular strategies:

♦ The fit between the marketing strategies pursued in individual product-markets and the firm's higher-level corporate and business strategies.

♦ Administrative relationships between the SBU and corporate headquarters, such as the amount of autonomy the SBU's managers have, the extent to which the SBU must share facilities and functional area programs with other businesses within the firm, and the manner in which the SBU's managers are evaluated and rewarded by top corporate executives.

♦ The SBU's internal organization structure and coordination mechanisms, including such variables as the technical competence of the various functional departments within the SBU, the manner in which resources are allocated across functions, and the mechanisms used to coordinate and resolve conflicts among the departments.

♦ The contents of a detailed marketing action plan for each product-market entry.

These four sets of variables are diagrammed in Exhibit 23–2 and serve as a framework for the remainder of our discussion.

RELATIONSHIPS BETWEEN BUSINESS AND MARKETING STRATEGIES

As we discussed in Chapter 11, generic business-level strategies define how an SBU intends to compete in its industry. Exhibit 23–3 reviews the kinds of industry environments and the SBU objectives most appropriate for the pursuit of prospector, analyzer, differentiated defender, and low-cost defender strategies. Remember, though, that some businesses fail to develop any clearly defined or consistent competitive strategy. Such businesses are referred to as **reactors** because their competitive posture tends to change sporadically in response to the actions of other firms or environmental threats. Because it is impossible to generalize about how to effectively implement a strategy that does not exist or that changes from day to day, we will say no more about reactors in the rest of this chapter.

EXHIBIT   23 ◆ 2

Factors affecting the implementation of business and marketing strategies

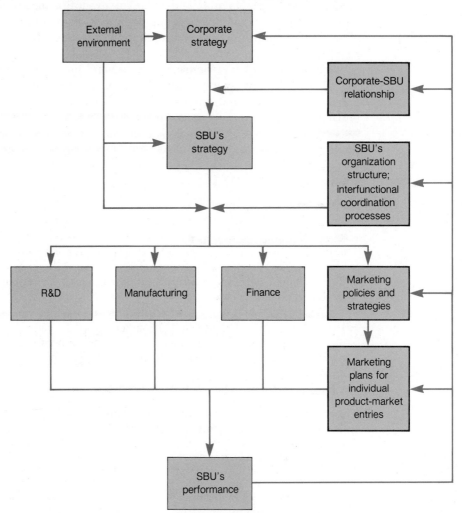

Appropriate marketing policies and strategies

An SBU may comprise a number of product-markets, each facing different demand and competitive situations. It is thus somewhat risky to generalize about what marketing policies and strategies at the product-market level best fit different business strategies. Still, an SBU's strategy does set a general direction for the types of markets to pursue, the way to compete in those markets, and the kinds of objectives to seek to attain. Also, the SBU's strategy

EXHIBIT 23 ◆ 3

The fit between business strategies, the environment, and SBU objectives

Situational variables and objectives	Business strategies			
	Prospector	Analyzer	Differentiated defender	Low-cost defender
Industry environment	Industry in the introductory or growth stage of its life cycle; relatively few competitors; technology still evolving.	Industry in growth or early maturity stage of its life cycle; substantial competition; technological advances or new-product applications still possible.	Industry in maturity or decline stage of its life cycle; substantial competition; technology is mature, but new applications may still be possible.	Industry in maturity or decline stage of its life cycle; substantial competition; technology is mature, but new applications may still be possible.
Appropriate SBU objectives	High increases in sales volume and market share; relatively large proportion of volume from new products and markets; relatively low ROI and cash flow.	Moderate increases in volume and share; some volume from new products and markets; moderate levels of ROI and cash flow.	Low increases in sales volume and market share; relatively little volume from new products, but some volume may be gained from new customers or markets; high ROI and cash flow.	Low increases in sales volume and market share; relatively little volume from new products or markets; moderate to high ROI and cash flow.

is—or should be—geared to the general market and competitive conditions it faces in its industry. Thus, the business's competitive strategy should influence the unit's general policies concerning such marketing program elements as relative product quality, price, and promotional levels.

Specific product-market strategies are most relevant for specific sets of market and competitive conditions and are also likely to be more appropriate within a limited range of business-level competitive strategies. For example, Pillsbury's prepared dough SBU is a differentiated defender in a mature, or possibly declining, portion of the food industry. The marketing strategies for virtually all of its core brands, such as Hungry Jack biscuits and Pillsbury Crescent rolls, involve a combination of (1) a fortress defense strategy focused on high product quality, premium prices, and extensive distribution to maintain share; (2) the development of flanker brands to protect against low-priced regional competitors; and (3) extended use strategies to increase volume among current users. Such marketing strategies are all consistent with the SBU's leading share position in the industry and its differentiated defender competitive strategy. But other marketing policies and strategies, such as substantial price cutting on its core brands or aggressive attempts to develop new-product categories, would not be. The relationships between different business strategies and the most appropriate marketing policies and strategies to implement them are summarized in Exhibit 23–4 and briefly discussed below.[2]

Marketing policies and strategies for prospector business

Prospector businesses rely on the continuing development of unique new products and the penetration of new markets as their primary competitive approach. Thus, policies encouraging broad and technically sophisticated product lines relative to competitors' should be positively related to their success on the critical volume and share growth dimensions of performance. Prospector businesses also need to budget relatively high advertising and sales promotion expenditures to stimulate primary demand; and they need to charge relatively high prices to cover their substantial R&D and marketing costs.

Prospectors in consumer goods and less technically complex industrial goods industries rely heavily on independent middlemen, such as manufacturers' reps and wholesalers, to maintain their flexibility to pursue a variety of different product-markets. Thus, they often must provide substantial trade promotion dollars to gain the support of those intermediaries. With more technically complex industrial products, however, prospectors may have to use highly trained company salespeople to provide the sales engineering and other up-front services necessary to induce potential customers to adopt new products or applications.

The kinds of marketing strategies pioneers use in developing new product-markets, such as mass-market penetration, niche penetration, and skimming strategies, are all commonly used by prospector businesses. As the prospector's industry moves into the growth stage, it may try to penetrate new user segments by adopting market expansion and encirclement strategies.

---

[2] While we have briefly discussed many of the specific actions involved in each of the program elements of various marketing strategies in previous chapters, space limitations and the broad strategic—rather than operational—focus of this book prevented us from covering many specific executional issues in much detail. For a more in-depth examination of executional issues, see Thomas V. Bonoma, *The Marketing Edge: Making Strategies Work* (New York: Free Press, 1985).

EXHIBIT   23 ♦ 4

The fit between business strategies and marketing programs

Appropriate marketing policies and strategies	Business strategies			
	Prospector	**Analyzer**	**Differentiated defender**	**Low-cost defender**
Product and service policies	Broad, technically sophisticated product lines; moderate to high quality and levels of service, especially sales engineering services.	Moderately broad and technically sophisticated product lines; service levels and quality indeterminant.	Relatively narrow but high quality and technically sophisticated product lines; high quality and levels of service.	Narrow, less technically sophisticated product lines; relatively low level and quality of service.
Price policy	Relatively high prices.	Relatively high prices.	Relatively high prices.	Relatively low to competitive prices.
Distribution policies	Little forward vertical integration; relatively high trade promotion expenses as a percent of sales.	Degree of forward vertical integration indeterminant; moderate to high trade promotion expenses as a percent of sales.	Relatively high degree of forward vertical integration; low trade promotion expenses as a percent of sales.	Degree of forward vertical integration indeterminant; low trade promotion expenses as a percent of sales.
Promotion policies	High advertising, sales promotion, and salesforce expenditures as a percent of sales.	Moderate advertising and sales promotion expenditures as a percent of sales; salesforce expenditures indeterminant.	Relatively low advertising and sales promotion expenditures as a percent of sales; high salesforce expenditures as a percent of sales.	Low advertising, sales promotion, and salesforce expenditures as a percent of sales.
Common marketing strategies	Mass-market penetration; niche penetration; skimming and early withdrawal; market expansion; encirclement.	Flanker strategy; market expansion; leapfrog strategy; encirclement; guerrilla attack.	Fortress defense; confrontation; flanker strategy; increased penetration; extended use; market expansion; profitable survivor strategy; maintenance strategy; niche strategy.	Fortress defense; confrontation; profitable survivor strategy; maintenance strategy; niche strategy; harvesting strategy.

Marketing policies and strategies for analyzer businesses

It is difficult to generalize about the marketing policies most appropriate for analyzer businesses; they simultaneously defend established product-markets and seek to develop new ones. One would expect, though, that such businesses should have at least moderately broad product lines, moderate to high prices, and high promotional expenditures relative to competitors in order to achieve their multiple objectives. Because analyzers typically operate in industries in the growth or early maturity stage, they commonly pursue growth-oriented marketing strategies. If the SBU is an industry share leader, it likely relies heavily on proactive market development strategies to maintain its position, such as market expansion or flanker strategies. A follower SBU may focus more effort on strategies such as leapfrog, encirclement, or guerrilla attack that rely on new-product or market development to increase its overall share.

Marketing policies and strategies for differentiated defenders

Because differentiated defenders typically operate in more mature, established markets, their product lines should be relatively narrow and clearly focused. But to maintain their differentiated position, such businesses must pay close attention to the quality of their products, services, or both. Their advertising and sales promotion expenditures may be relatively low as a percent of sales. However, they likely charge relatively high prices to be consistent with the high quality of their offerings and to cover the expenses of continuing product improvement and maintaining the salesforce needed to ensure good customer service. When operating in mature industries, differentiated defenders likely rely on marketing strategies geared to maintaining their share (fortress defense, confrontation, and flanker strategies) and to squeezing additional volume out of their markets (increased penetration, extended use, or market expansion strategies). As their industries decline, differentiated defenders may switch to profitable survivor, maintenance, or niche strategies, depending on the rate and nature of decline in their individual product-markets.

Marketing policies and strategies for low-cost defenders

Low-cost defenders are also likely to offer relatively narrow product lines to maximize the economies of scale accruing to each offering. Stringent cost cutting is also likely to result in moderate to low levels of product and service quality. Similarly, such businesses likely hold trade promotions to the minimum levels necessary to sustain adequate distribution and reduce advertising and sales promotion to maintenance levels. Such cost-reduction policies are often reflected in highly competitive prices. Like differentiated defenders, low-cost defenders will fight to hold their position in their mature product-markets by employing fortress or confrontation defense strategies. But they are less likely to engage in more proactive defensive moves requiring additional product or market development (such as flanker or market expansion strategies). Also, as their industries decline, low-cost defenders may more likely harvest individual product-markets, although their low-cost position can also allow them to be a profitable survivor if exit barriers are low.

We can conclude from the preceding discussion that while marketing managers often play a primary role in formulating an SBU's overall competitive strategy,[3] once that strategy is in place it constrains the kinds of marketing policies appropriate for the SBU to adopt. Those policies—together with the market and competitive situation the business faces and the objectives in its strategy—also limit the range of marketing strategies appropriate for the individual product-market entries within the SBU. Thus, effective implementation of a particular business strategy necessarily involves the implementation of a specific set of marketing policies and strategies as well. And the organizational structures, policies, and processes necessary for the effective implementation of a given competitive strategy— as discussed in the next two sections—also facilitate the implementation of the marketing policies and programs incorporated within that strategy.

ADMINISTRATIVE RELATIONSHIPS AND STRATEGY IMPLEMENTATION

In organizations consisting of multiple divisions or SBUs, the administrative relationships between the unit and corporate headquarters influence the ability of the SBU's managers, including its marketing personnel, to implement specific competitive and marketing strategies successfully.[4] As a study of the performance of 69 business units in 12 industries concluded, "Corporate managers can have as much impact on a business unit's performance by attending to its administrative ties to headquarters as they can by managing according to detailed strategic portfolio analyses."[5]

Three aspect of the corporate-business unit relationship can affect the SBU's success at implementing a particular competitive strategy.

1. The degree to which the unit's managers have the **autonomy** to make decisions independent of other parts of the company, particularly the home office.

---

[3] George S. Yip, "The Role of Strategic Planning in Consumer-Marketing Businesses," Working Paper #84-103 (Cambridge, Mass.: Marketing Science Institute, 1984).

[4] Much of the discussion in this section is based on material found in Orville C. Walker, Jr., and Robert W. Ruekert, "Marketing's Role in the Implementation of Business Strategies: A Critical Review and Conceptual Framework," *Journal of Marketing*, July 1987, pp. 15–33.

[5] Richard G. Hamermesh and Roderick E. White, "Manage beyond Portfolio Analysis," *Harvard Business Review*, January–February 1984, pp. 103–9.

2. The degree to which the unit **shares functional programs and facilities,** including marketing programs, such as a common salesforce or promotional programs, with other SBUs in a search for corporate synergies.

3. The manner in which the corporation **evaluates and rewards** the performance of the SBU's managers.

Exhibit 23–5 summarizes how these variables relate to the successful implementation of different business strategies. We discuss the rationale underlying these relationships below. Note, however, that analyzer strategies are not included in the following discussion. Because analyzers incorporate some elements of both prospector and defender strategies, the administrative arrangements appropriate for implementing an analyzer strategy typically fall somewhere between those best suited for the other two types. In order to simplify the following discussion, we will focus only on the polar types— prospector, differentiated defender, and low-cost defender strategies.

Business unit autonomy

Prospector business units likely perform better on the critical dimensions of new-product success rates and increased volume and market share when organizational decision making is relatively decentralized and the SBU's managers have substantial autonomy to make their own decisions. There are several reasons for this. First, more decentralized decision making allows the managers closest to the market, who should be first to recognize new opportunities, to make more major decisions on their own. Greater autonomy also enables the SBU's managers to be more flexible and adaptable. It frees them from the restrictions of standard rules and procedures imposed from above, allows decisions to be made with fewer consultations and participants, and disperses power. All of these help produce quicker and more innovative responses to environmental opportunities. Thus, when IBM decided to develop and introduce a PC, it established a new and separate development unit and located it in Atlanta, far from IBM's corporate headquarters, to help preserve its autonomy. Further, it gave the new unit largely free rein to design its own structure and procedures.

On the other hand, low-cost defender SBUs likely perform better on their critical dimensions of ROI and cash flow by keeping managers on a tight leash and giving them relatively little decision-making autonomy. For a low-cost strategy to succeed, the SBU must pay close attention to operational details, including the relentless pursuit of cost economies and productivity improvements through standardizing components and processes, routinizing procedures, and integrating functional activities across units. Such efficiencies are more likely to be attained when decision making and control are relatively centralized at the highest managerial levels.

The relationship between autonomy and the ROI performance of differentiated defenders is more difficult to predict. On one hand, because such businesses are defending existing positions in established markets and their

EXHIBIT 23 ♦ 5

Administrative factors related to the successful implementation of business strategies

Administrative factor	Type of business strategy		
	Prospector	Differentiated defender	Low-cost defender
SBU autonomy	Relative high level of autonomy is positively related to new-product success and volume and market share performance.	Moderate level of autonomy is related to high levels of ROI and market share maintenance.	Relatively low level of autonomy is related to high ROI and cash flow performance.
Shared programs and synergy	Relatively little synergy; SBU's volume and market share performance likely to be best when it shares few marketing, R&D, or manufacturing programs or facilities with other SBUs; an exception may be the sharing of distribution channels among consumer goods businesses.	Little synergy in areas central to SBU's differential advantage (e.g. R&D, marketing); programs in such areas should not be shared in order to preserve flexibility; sharing of programs or facilities in other functional areas may improve efficiency and ROI performance.	High levels of synergy; ROI performance is likely to be best when marketing, R&D, and manufacturing programs or facilities are shared with other SBUs.
Evaluation and reward systems	The greater the proportion of SBU managers' compensation accounted for by incentives based on unit's sales or share growth, the better the unit's performance.	The greater the proportion of SBU managers' compensation accounted for by incentives based on unit's profit or ROI, the better the unit's performance.	The greater the proportion of SBU managers' compensation accounted for by incentives based on unit's profit or ROI, the better the unit's performance.

Source: Adapted from Orville C. Walker, Jr., and Robert W. Ruekert, "Marketing's Role in the Implementation of Business Strategies," *Journal of Marketing,* July 1987, p. 31.

primary objective is ROI rather than volume growth, one might expect that the increased efficiency and tighter control associated with relatively low autonomy should lead to better performance. On the other hand, such businesses can maintain profitability only if they continue to differentiate themselves by offering superior products and services. As customers' wants change and new competitive threats emerge, the greater flexibility and market focus associated with greater autonomy may allow these businesses to more successfully maintain their differentiated positions, and higher levels of ROI, over time. These arguments suggest that the relationship between autonomy and performance for differentiated defenders may be mediated by the level of stability in their market and competitive environments, and by the proportion of offensive or proactive marketing strategies they employ in their various product-markets. Units operating in relatively unstable environments and pursuing more proactive marketing programs (such as extended use, market expansion, profitable survivor) likely perform better when they have relatively greater autonomy.[6]

Shared programs and facilities

Firms face a trade-off when designing strategic business units. An SBU should be large enough to afford and maintain critical resources and to operate on an efficient scale, but it should not be so large that its market scope is too broad or that "it is inflexible and does not respond quickly to customer needs, to the tactics of competition, and to its unique market opportunities."[7] Some firms attempt to avoid this trade-off between efficiency and adaptability by designing relatively small, narrowly focused business units, but then having two or more units share functional programs or facilities, such as common manufacturing plants, R&D programs, or a single salesforce. These firms believe the managers of such narrowly defined SBUs can stay in close contact with their customers and competitive environments while the sharing of programs simultaneously provides increased economies of scale and synergy across units.

Recent evidence suggests, however, that sharing resources across SBUs reduces their flexibility and innovativeness.[8] This poses a particular problem for prospector business units. Suppose, for instance, a business wants to introduce a new product, but it shares a manufacturing plant and a salesforce with one or more other SBUs. The business would have to negotiate a production schedule for the new product; and it may not be able to get sufficient quantities produced as quickly as needed if other units sharing the plant are concerned about maintaining sufficient volumes of their own products. It may also be difficult to train salespeople on the new product or to motivate them to reduce the time spent on established products in order to push the new item. Recall the difficulty Grandma's Cookies had in motivating the Frito-Lay salesforce to take time away from the profitable salty snack lines to sell cookies. Thus, prospector SBUs likely perform better on their primary objectives of new-product success, volume, and share growth when

---

[6] Ibid.

[7] E. Raymond Corey and Steven H. Star, *Organization Strategy: A Marketing Approach* (Boston: Division of Research, Graduate School of Business, Harvard University, 1971), p. 9.

[8] Robert W. Ruekert and Orville C. Walker, Jr., "The Sharing of Marketing Resources Across Strategic Business Units: The Effect of Strategy on Performance," Working Paper (Minneapolis, Minn.: Carlson School of Management, University of Minnesota, 1988). Also see Anil K. Gupta, "SBU Strategies, Corporate-SBU Relations, and SBU Effectiveness in Strategy Implementation," *Academy of Management Journal* 30 (1987), pp. 477–500.

they are relatively self-contained and share few functional programs or facilities with other units.

The one exception to this generalization may be the sharing of sales and distribution programs across consumer package goods SBUs. In such cases, a prospector's new product may have an easier time obtaining retailer support and shelf space if it is represented by salespeople who also sell established brands to the same retail outlets. For prospectors producing consumer durables or industrial goods, however, functional independence generally facilitates good performance. That is why successful prospector businesses, like most of the business divisions at 3M, control their own R&D budgets, manufacturing facilities, salesforces, and marketing programs.

On the other hand, the increased efficiencies gained through the sharing of functional programs and facilities often boost the ROI performance of SBUs pursuing low-cost defender strategies. Also, the inflexibility inherent in sharing is usually not a major problem for such businesses because their markets and technologies tend to be mature and relatively stable. Thus, Heinz, the cost leader in a number of food categories, uses a single salesforce to represent a wide variety of products from different business units when calling on supermarkets.

The impact of shared programs on the performance of differentiated defenders is more difficult to predict. However, such businesses must often be able to modify their products and their sales and marketing programs in response to changing customer desires or competitive actions in order to maintain their competitive advantage, and profitability, over time. Thus, it seems likely that greater functional independence in areas directly related to the SBU's differential advantage, such as R&D, sales, and marketing, is positively associated with the long-run ROI performance of such businesses. This is particularly true for SBUs pursuing proactive strategies, such as extended use or market expansion, in a number of product-markets. But greater sharing of facilities and programs in less crucial functional areas, such as manufacturing and distribution, may also help improve their efficiency and short-run ROI levels.

Evaluation and reward systems

Corporate executives periodically compare measures of each SBU's performance to its planned objectives as a means of evaluating and controlling the actions of that unit's managers. The SBU's managers, in turn, are motivated to achieve their planned objectives by bonuses or other financial incentives tied to their unit's performance. Such incentives are most commonly determined by one or more of the following aspects of an SBU's performance: (1) absolute unit profits or ROI, (2) degree of improvement in the unit's profit, (3) the unit's profit performance compared to the industry average, or (4) achievement of the unit's profit or ROI target or plan. Note that all of the above dimensions relate to the SBU's short-run financial performance. Incentive performance also often determines which business-unit managers will win promotions. Those managers typically remain in one position for only three to five years. These facts suggest that the most commonly used evaluation and reward systems encourage SBU managers to concentrate on short-run returns and adopt policies that may discourage innovation, the acceptance of risk, and the aggressive pursuit of growth for future returns.[9]

Reliance on evaluation and reward systems geared to short-run financial performance poses no major problems in SBUs pursuing defender strategies where most markets are stable and mature, or even in decline, and where ROI and cash flow are the most important performance objectives. Such incentive systems are likely to be counterproductive, though, when an SBU pursues a prospector strategy requiring some level of risk taking and innovativeness in the short run to achieve long-run success. In such businesses, evaluation and reward systems based on an increase in sales volume, market share, or the percentage of volume generated by new products (say, products introduced within the last five years) more likely motivate managers to engage in aggressive and innovative courses of action. Thus, P&G has historically employed an executive incentive system based solely on achieving planned sales volume targets, and 3M's system is based in part on volume generated by new products. Because many firms incorporate both prospector and defender SBUs, however, it is increasingly common for large corporations to adopt evaluation and reward systems based on some combination of volume and profitability.[10]

ORGANIZATIONAL STRUCTURE, PROCESSES, AND STRATEGY IMPLEMENTATION

Implementing any business strategy requires performing a number of different functions. But different strategies are appropriate for different market and competitive circumstances, emphasize different ways to gain a competitive advantage, and stress different objectives. Thus, a given functional area may be key to the success of one type of strategy but less critical for others. For instance, competence in new-product R&D is critical for the success of a prospector business, but less so for a low-cost defender. Regardless of their relative importance, though, all functional efforts must be coordinated. The inevitable conflicts that develop between functional departments must be resolved before any strategy can be successful. And once again, different organizational structures and conflict resolution mechanisms are appropriate for businesses pursuing different strategies. Thus,

---

[9] Alfred Rappaport, "Executive Incentives vs. Corporate Growth," *Harvard Business Review,* July–August 1978, pp. 81–88. Also see David Norburn and Paul Miller, "Strategy and Executive Reward: The Mis-Match in the Strategic Process," *Journal of General Management,* (1981), pp. 17–27.

[10] Norburn and Miller, ibid.

successful implementation of a given strategy is more likely when the business has the **functional competencies** demanded by its strategy and supports them with substantial **resources** relative to competitors; is **organized** suitably for its technical, market, and competitive environment; and has developed appropriate **mechanisms for coordinating efforts and resolving conflicts across functional departments.** Exhibit 23–6 summarizes the relationships between these organizational structure and process variables and the performance of different generic business strategies.

Functional competencies and resources allocation

We saw in Chapter 11 that competence in marketing, sales, product R&D, and engineering are all critical to the success of prospector businesses because those functions play pivotal roles in the development of new products and new markets. However, competence in these key functional areas will do an SBU little good, and will be hard to maintain, unless the business unit also supports them with adequate physical, financial, and human resources. Thus, prospectors likely perform better on their new-product success and volume and share growth objectives when these key functions are supported with budgets set at a larger percent of sales than their competitors'. For instance, Johnson & Johnson, a firm respected for its high rate of new-product innovation during the 1980s, spent $617 million, or about 8 percent of sales, on R&D in 1987. This was about double the average for all U.S. companies and five times the amount the firm spent 10 years earlier.[11]

Marketing, sales, and R&D managers are also closest to the changes occurring in a business's market, competitive, and technological environments. Therefore, in prospector SBUs the greater the input and influence those managers have in making strategic decisions the more successful the SBU is likely to be over time. This argues that "bottom-up" strategic planning systems, where the planning process is initiated by analyses and recommendations from lower-level product and functional managers, are particularly well suited to prospector businesses operating in relatively unstable environments.[12] Alternatively, when lower-level managers in prospector units are given little autonomy to initiate or modify their own policies and programs, they are less likely to respond effectively to environmental changes. For example, a recent study of British firms characterized by highly centralized, "top-down" strategic planning processes found that such firms were plagued by a lack of flexibility and were inhibited from responding quickly to changing market needs or environmental conditions. As a result,

---

[11] Kenneth Labich, "The Innovators," *Fortune,* June 6, 1988, p. 52.

[12] For a more detailed discussion of "top-down" versus "bottom-up" planning processes, see George S. Day, *Strategic Market Planning: The Pursuit of Competitive Advantage* (St. Paul: West Publishing, 1984), chap. 2.

EXHIBIT   23 ◆ 6

Organizational and interfunctional factors related to the successful implementation of business strategies

Organizational factor	Type of business strategy		
	Prospector	Differentiated defender	Low-cost defender
Functional competencies of the SBU	SBU will perform best on critical volume and share growth dimensions when its functional strengths include marketing, sales, product R&D, and engineering.	SBU will perform best on critical ROI dimension when its functional strengths include sales, financial management and control, and those functions related to its differential advantage (e.g., marketing, product R&D).	SBU will perform best on critical ROI and cash flow dimensions when its functional strengths include process engineering, production, distribution, and financial management and control.
Resource allocation across functions	SBU will perform best on volume and share growth dimensions when percent of sales spent on marketing, sales, and product R&D are high, and when gross fixed assets per employee and percent of capacity utilization are low relative to competitors.	SBU will perform best on the ROI dimension when percent of sales spent on the salesforce, gross fixed assets per employee, percent of capacity utilization, and percent of sales devoted to other functions related to the SBU's differential advantage are high relative to competitors.	SBU will perform best on ROI and cash flow dimensions when marketing, sales, and product R&D expenses are low, but process R&D, fixed assets per employee, and percent of capacity utilization are high relative to competitors.

firms like British Petroleum and Cadbury had suffered setbacks in their expansion strategies and heavy losses from failing to abandon or revise unsuccessful new ventures.[13]

In low-cost defender businesses, on the other hand, those functional areas most directly related to operating efficiency, such as financial management and control, production, process R&D, and distribution or logistics, play the most crucial roles in enabling the SBU to attain good ROI performance. Consequently, executives from those departments should have substantial influence on the strategic decisions made within such SBUs. "Top-down" planning systems in which the planning process is initiated by top business managers tend to be best-suited for low-cost defenders operating in relatively stable environments.

---

[13] Michael Goold and Andrew Campbell, "Many Best Ways to Make Strategy," *Harvard Business Review*, November–December 1987, p. 72.

EXHIBIT 23 ♦ 6
(concluded)

Organizational factor	Type of business strategy		
	Prospector	Differentiated defender	Low-cost defender
Decision-making influence and participation	SBU will perform best on volume and share growth dimensions when managers from marketing, sales, product R&D, and engineering have substantial influence on unit's business and marketing strategy decisions.	SBU will perform best on ROI dimension when financial managers, controller, and managers of functions related to unit's differential advantage have substantial influence on business and marketing strategy decisions.	SBU will perform best on ROI and cash flow when controller, financial, and production managers have substantial influence on business and marketing strategy decisions.
SBU's organization structure	SBU will perform best on volume and share growth dimensions when structure has low levels of formalization and centralization, but high level of specialization.	SBU will perform best on ROI dimension when structure has moderate levels of formalization, centralization, and specialization.	SBU will perform best on ROI and cash flow dimensions when structure has high levels of formalization and centralization, but low level of specialization.
Functional coordination and conflict resolution	SBU will experience high levels of inter-functional conflict; SBU will perform best on volume and share growth dimensions when participative resolution mechanisms are used (e.g., product teams).	SBU will experience moderate levels of interfunctional conflict; SBU will perform best on ROI dimension when resolution is participative for issues related to differential advantage, but hierarchical for others (e.g., product managers, product improvement teams, etc.).	SBU will experience low levels of inter-functional conflict; SBU will perform best on ROI and cash flow dimensions when conflict resolution mechanisms are hierarchical (e.g., functional organization).

Source: Adapted from Orville C. Walker, Jr., and Robert W. Ruekert, "Marketing's Role in the Implementation of Business Strategies," *Journal of Marketing*, July 1987, p. 31.

Because of the mature and relatively stable nature of most markets faced by low-cost defenders, relatively high expenditures on marketing, sales, and product R&D activities are not so critical for maintaining the SBU's competitive position. Further, they would simply raise costs and erode already thin margins. But to be successful, such businesses must employ their resources efficiently and work to improve their efficiency even further. Thus, the best-performing low-cost defenders spend a relatively large percentage of sales on process R&D to further improve production efficiency, have high fixed assets per employee (i.e., replace labor with more efficient capital equipment whenever possible), and operate their plant at near capacity.

Because differentiated defenders need to attain high returns on their established products, functional areas related to efficiency, particularly financial management, control, and production, are also critical areas for their success. Similarly, such units also seek to improve efficiency by continuing to invest in process R&D, making needed capital investments, and striving to maintain a high level of capacity utilization. But because they must also maintain their differential advantage over time, functional departments related to the source of that advantage—the salesforce, product R&D for SBUs with a technical product advantage, or marketing and distribution for SBUs with a customer service advantage—are also critical for the unit's continued success. Consequently, they need substantial resources, and their managers should play a major role in strategic decision making within the business unit.

Organizational structures

Three structural variables—formalization, centralization, and specialization—are important in shaping both an SBU's and its marketing department's performance within the context of a given competitive strategy. **Formalization** is the degree to which decisions and working relationships are governed by formal rules and standard policies and procedures. **Centralization** refers to the location of decision authority and control within an organization's hierarchy. In highly centralized SBUs or marketing departments, only one or a few top managers hold most decision-making authority. In more decentralized units, middle- and lower-level managers have more autonomy and participate in a wider range of decisions. Finally, **specialization** refers to the division of tasks and activities across positions within the organizational unit. A highly specialized marketing department, for instance, has a large number of specialists, such as marketing researchers, advertising managers, sales promotion managers, package designers, sales managers, and product managers, who direct their efforts to a narrowly defined set of activities.

High levels of formalization and centralization together with low levels of specialization likely promote relatively efficient performance within an SBU or its marketing department.[14] The top business unit or marketing manager can use his or her centralized authority to steer a common direction for the

---

[14] Robert W. Ruekert, Orville C. Walker, Jr., and Kenneth J. Roering, "The Organization of Marketing Activities: A Contingency Theory of Structure and Performance," *Journal of Marketing*, Winter 1985, pp. 13–25.

unit and keep overt conflicts to a minimum. Formal rules and procedures help routinize activities and hold down risks and administrative costs. The relatively small number of specialists also helps make such units more cost efficient. Such highly structured businesses should perform well on ROI and cash flow dimensions, making them particularly appropriate for SBUs pursuing low-cost defender strategies.

But highly structured business units and marketing departments are unlikely to be very innovative or quick to adapt to changing environmental circumstances. Adaptiveness and innovativeness are enhanced when (1) decision-making authority is decentralized, (2) managerial discretion and informal coordination mechanisms replace rigid rules and policies, and (3) more specialists operate within the unit. Thus, prospector business units and their marketing departments—which must both innovate and adapt quickly to changes—likely perform better on their critical new-product development and volume and share growth dimensions when they are decentralized, have little formalization, and are highly specialized.

Differentiated defenders must be efficient in order to achieve high ROIs, but adaptable enough to maintain their differential advantage as the environment changes. Thus, they likely perform best over time when their organization structures incorporate moderate levels of formalization, centralization, and specialization. Those departments most directly related to the source of a differentiated defender's competitive advantage (sales, marketing, and R&D), however, should be less highly structured than those more crucial for the efficiency of the unit's operations (production and logistics).

To achieve different levels of formalization, centralization, and specialization, an SBU or functional department must be designed in different ways and incorporate different types of managerial positions. Thus, the above discussion of structural variables has practical implications for designing an appropriate organization chart for a business pursuing a particular strategy. Before we discuss those implications, though, we must first examine some of the issues involved in coordinating activities across the functional departments within the SBU and in resolving the conflicts that develop across those departments.

Interfunctional coordination and conflict resolution mechanisms

Levels of interfunctional conflict

Because of their broad product-market domains and their emphasis on new-product and market development, prospector businesses often have a high degree of complexity and uncertainty in their operations. Their functional managers often must make unfamiliar decisions about how to adapt to unknown environments. Such complex and unfamiliar situations can result in substantial interfunctional conflict, particularly among departments that play interdependent roles in helping the business to adapt to new market and technological opportunities, such as marketing, sales, R&D, and production.[15]

On the other hand, low-cost defenders commonly operate in more narrowly defined domains and in more mature and stable environments. They usually have clearly defined operating procedures for holding down costs through routinization. Consequently, though functional managers may chafe under the rules and restrictions imposed by top management, low-cost defender businesses likely have less interfunctional conflict across departments than businesses pursuing other strategies.

Conflict resolution mechanisms

Regardless of its competitive strategy, every business has some degree of conflict among its functional departments. How can managers resolve those conflicts? While there are many variations, conflict resolution mechanisms fit into two broad categories. The first is a **hierarchical approach,** whereby top managers impose a solution, either by requiring adherence to formal rules and operating procedures or by judging on a case-by-case basis. The second is a **participative approach,** in which the parties themselves are expected to work out a mutually acceptable solution.[16] New-product development teams, such as those recently formed at P&G, are examples of the participative approach in practice.

Hierarchical resolution mechanisms are efficient because they reduce the amount of time and effort necessary to reach a decision, and they help ensure consistency in the relations across functional departments over time. Such efficiency and routinization are particularly helpful for low-cost defender businesses striving for high ROI objectives in relatively stable environments.

Participative approaches are less efficient because the parties involved typically require more time to work out their differences. But they often lead to a fuller understanding of, and more innovative solutions to, problems that cut across and cause conflict among functional departments. They are particularly appropriate for uncertain and nonroutine situations in which innovative, adaptive actions are called for[17]—situations most commonly faced by prospector businesses.

Once again, since differentiated defenders (and analyzers) need both efficiency and adaptiveness to maintain their differential advantage—and profitability—some combination of resolution mechanisms is appropriate.

---

[15] Robert W. Ruekert and Orville C. Walker, Jr., "Interactions between Marketing and R&D Departments in Implementing Different Business Strategies," *Strategic Management Journal,* 1987, pp. 233–48.

[16] John McCann and Jay R. Galbraith, "Interdepartmental Relations," in *Handbook of Organizational Design,* Vol. 2, ed. Paul C. Nystrom and William Starbuck (New York: Oxford University Press, 1981), pp. 60–84.

[17] Ibid.

Moderate use of participative methods can resolve conflicts among those areas directly involved in preserving the SBU's differential advantage. A greater reliance on rules, standard procedures, or top management fiat can deal with disputes in other operational areas.

Alternative organizational designs

Several common organizational designs incorporate differences in both the structural variables (formalization, centralization, and specialization) and in the mechanisms for resolving interfunctional conflicts discussed above. These include (1) functional, (2) product management, (3) market management, and (4) various types of matrix organizational designs.[18]

Functional organizations

The functional form of organization, as diagrammed in Exhibit 23-7 for both business-unit and marketing department levels, is the simplest and most bureaucratic design. At the SBU level, managers of each functional department (such as production or marketing) report to the general manager. Within the marketing department, managers of specific marketing activity areas (such as sales, advertising, or marketing research) report to the marketing vice president or director. At each level, the top manager coordinates the activities of all the functional areas reporting to him or her, often with heavy

EXHIBIT   23 ◆ 7

Functional organization of an SBU and its marketing department

---

[18] Barton Weitz and Erin Anderson, "Organizing and Controlling the Marketing Function," in *Review of Marketing, 1981*, ed. Ben M. Enis and Kenneth J. Roering (Chicago: American Marketing Association, 1981), pp. 134-42.

reliance on standard rules and operating procedures. Thus, this is the most centralized and formalized organizational form, and it relies primarily on hierarchical mechanisms for resolving conflicts across functional areas. Also, because top managers perform their coordination activities across all product-markets in the SBU, there is little specialization by product or customer type.

These characteristics make the functional form both simple and efficient. It is particularly appropriate for businesses whose products and markets are few and similar in nature, or those operating in relatively stable and predictable environments. Thus, functional organization structures are common among small entrepreneurial start-up firms producing only one or two products or services, and they are also appropriate for low-cost defender SBUs attempting to maximize their efficiency and profitability in mature or declining industries.

Product management organizations

When an SBU has a relatively complex environment and a large number of product-market entries, the simple functional form of organization is inadequate. A single manager finds it difficult to stay abreast of developments in —or to coordinate functional activities across—a variety of different product-markets. One common means of dealing with this problem is to adopt the kind of product management organization structure first developed by P&G. As Exhibit 23–8 illustrates, this form of organization adds an additional layer of managers to the marketing department (usually called product managers, brand managers, or marketing managers). Each of these managers has the responsibility to plan and manage the marketing programs—and to coordinate the activities of other functional departments—for a specific product or product line.

EXHIBIT 23 ◆ 8

A marketing department with a product management organization

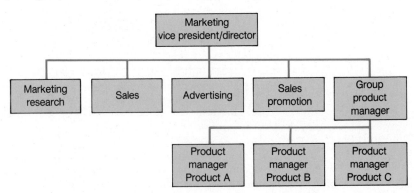

This product-management structure decentralizes decision making while increasing the amount of product specialization within the SBU. If the product managers also have substantial autonomy to develop their own marketing plans and programs, this structure can also decrease the formalization within the business. Finally, although the product managers are responsible for obtaining cooperation from other functional areas both within and outside of the marketing department, they have no formal authority over those areas. They must rely on persuasion and compromise—in other words, more participative methods—to overcome conflicts and objections when coordinating functional activities. These factors make the product management form of organization less bureaucratic than the functional structure. It is more appropriate then, for businesses pursuing differentiated defender and analyzer strategies, particularly when they operate in industries with complex and relatively unstable market and competitive environments.

Businesses that enact flanker, mobile, market penetration, or expansion marketing strategies as their industries mature often end up with a number of different brands in the same product category. In some cases, the different brands are aimed at different market segments; but they may also be direct competitors. To coordinate marketing strategies and allocate resources across such related brands, the product management form of organization typically includes one or more "group" or "category" marketing managers— as shown in Exhibit 23–8—on the level immediately above the product managers.

Product management organizations have a number of advantages, including: (1) the ability to identify and react more quickly to threats and opportunities faced by individual product-market entries, (2) improved coordination of functional activities within and across product-markets, and (3) increased attention to smaller product-market entries that might be neglected in a functional organization. Consequently, about 85 percent of all consumer goods manufacturers use some form of product management organization.[19]

Despite its advantages, the product manager type of organization also has its shortcomings. Although the product manager must rely on persuasion, compromise, and other more participative conflict resolution and coordination methods to develop effective programs for his or her product, such coordination does not always happen. The product manager may pay too little attention to the advice or concerns of managers in other functional departments—as happened during the introduction of P&G's Pringles potato

---

[19] Richard T. Hise and J. Patrick Kelly, "Product Managers on Trial," *Journal of Marketing*, October 1978, pp. 28–33; also see Jacob M. Duker and Michael V. Laric, "The Product Manager: No Longer on Trial," in *The Changing Marketing Environment*, ed. Kenneth Bernhardt et al. (Chicago: American Marketing Association, 1981), pp. 93–96.

chips—or the market, competitive, or technological environments surrounding the product may be too complex for a single manager to cope with. To make matters worse, product management is often the training ground for top management. Thus, successful product managers at firms like P&G are often promoted to larger-volume products or higher positions in the organization's hierarchy—and unsuccessful product managers are often dismissed—after spending only a year or two managing a given brand. This rapid turnover can lead to a short-term orientation on the part of the product manager, a lack of continuity in marketing programs over time, and perhaps repetition of past mistakes. As a result of these potential shortcomings, modifications to the product management form of organization have emerged in some SBUs in recent years. We examine two major types of modifications, market management and matrix organizations, next.

Market management organization

In some industries, a single product may be marketed to a large number of different markets where customers have very different requirements and preferences. A product manager may be unable to understand all of those markets well enough to develop and coordinate effective programs for each one. In such situations, an SBU might turn to a market management structure in which product managers are replaced with market managers responsible for planning and coordinating programs for one or more products aimed at a particular market segment. Pepsi-Cola, for instance, is sold through restaurants, fast-food outlets, and supermarkets. The syrup needed to make Pepsi is sold direct to institutions such as Kentucky Fried Chicken and Taco Bell. But marketing Pepsi to consumers for home consumption involves the use of franchised bottlers that process and package the product and distribute it to supermarkets. The intermediaries and marketing activities involved in selling to these markets are so different that it makes sense to have a separate market manager in charge of each.

Recently, some SBUs have adopted a combination of product and regional market management organizational structures. A product manager may have overall responsibility for planning and implementing a national marketing program for a product; but several market managers might also be given some authority, and an independent budget, to work with salespeople and develop promotion programs geared to a particular user segment or geographic market. This kind of decentralization, or regionalization, of marketing decision making has become a common organizational response by consumer products companies to increased geographic segmentation and the growing power of regional retailers. Campbell Soup Company was one of the first companies to add regional marketing managers to its organization;[20] but a number of other major firms, including Kraft, General Foods, and P&G,

---

[20] "Marketing's New Look," *Business Week*, January 26, 1987, pp. 64–69.

have since followed Campbell's lead. As another example, Frito-Lay's recent addition of regional managers is described in Exhibit 23–10.

Matrix organizations

When a business faces an extremely complex and uncertain environment, it may find a matrix form of organization appropriate. The matrix form is the least bureaucratic or centralized, and the most specialized, type of organization. It brings together two or more different types of specialists within a participative coordination structure. One example is the product-market form of organization used by some businesses (such as the textile fibers unit at Du Pont) that brings together both product and market managers. The product managers plan the sales and profits of a particular product and develop advertising, promotion, and pricing policies. They contact the market managers to determine sales estimates for their product in each market. The market managers develop specific customer segments. They identify new products or line extensions to fit the needs of their customers and sell existing products to their markets.

Another matrix form of organization gaining increased popularity is the product team. As illustrated in Exhibit 23–9, a team of representatives from a number of functional areas can be assembled for each product or product line. As a group, the team has the responsibility of agreeing on a business plan for the product and ensuring the necessary resources and cooperation from each functional area. As we saw in our discussion of P&G's experiences with such teams, this kind of participative decision making can be very inefficient; it requires a good deal of time and effort for the team to reach mutually acceptable decisions and gain approval from all the affected functional areas. But once reached, those decisions are more likely to reflect the expertise of a variety of functional specialists, to be innovative, and to be quickly and effectively implemented. Thus, the matrix form of organization particularly suits prospector businesses and managing new-product development within analyzer or differentiated defender businesses.

Matrix organizations such as product teams are particularly well suited for rapidly changing competitive situations that demand creative and inno-

EXHIBIT   23 ♦ 9

One example of a matrix organization: Product teams

Products	Functional departments					
	Product manager	Marketing research	Advertising	Production	R&D	Finance
Product A	(Team for product A)					
Product B						
Product C						

EXHIBIT   **23 ♦ 10**
Frito-Lay installs regional managers

> Frito-Lay set up a regional organization (six zones) in 1986 to implement local and regional trade and consumer promotions. In June 1989 the company—a division of PepsiCo and the nation's leading marketer of salty snack foods—created four business areas that replaced the six zones. Each business area is headed by a vice-president/general manager. This move will put more senior management in the field and consolidate responsibility for sales, promotion, advertising, and, possibly, even production within each area. Each vice-president will report to the Frito-Lay senior vice-president/marketing and sales, at headquarters. This latest organization is motivated by the desire to get closer to the trade and consumers with an organization that can respond quickly and decisively to regional competition.

Source: Jennifer Lawrence, "Frito Reorganizes," *Advertising Age* (June 26, 1989), p. 4.

vative decisions. This helps account for the popularity of this organizational form among advertising agencies. In most large agencies, a team of functional specialists is assigned to a client's account. The team is typically led by an account representative or manager; but it also includes members from several other functional departments. A typical account team includes one or more creative people (whose work is supervised by an art director in their own functional department), a media planner, buyers for print and broadcast media, and perhaps a marketing research person and an accountant to coordinate billing and keep an eye on the account's budget.

MARKETING ACTION PLANS

Despite the ritualistic overtones that accompany the preparation of any formal written plan, most firms believe "unless all the key elements of a plan are written down . . . there will always be loopholes for ambiguity or misunderstanding of strategies and objectives, or of assigned responsibilities for taking action."[21] Thus, preparation of written plans is a key step in ensuring the effective execution of a strategy because it spells out what actions are to be taken, when, and by whom.

Each functional department within a business—and perhaps even different areas within a functional department (e.g., sales and marketing research within the marketing department)—prepares annual plans detailing its intended role in carrying out the business's strategy. Our concern here, however, is with the annual marketing plan for a specific product-market entry. Much of this book has focused on the planning process, the decisions that must be made when formulating a marketing strategy and its various components, and the analytical tools managers might use in reaching those

---

[21] David S. Hopkins, *The Marketing Plan* (New York: The Conference Board, 1981), p. 2.

EXHIBIT 23 ♦ 11

Contents of an annual marketing plan

Section	Content
I. Executive summary	Presents a short overview of the issues, objectives, strategy, and actions incorporated in the plan and their expected outcomes for quick management review.
II. Current situation	Summarizes relevant background information on the market, competition, past performance of the product, and the various elements of its marketing program (e.g., distribution, promotion, etc.), and trends in the macroenvironment.
III. Key issues	Identifies the main opportunities and threats to the product that the plan must deal with in the coming year, and the relative strengths and weaknesses of the product and business unit that must be taken into account in facing those issues.
IV. Objectives	Specifies the goals to be accomplished in terms of sales volume, market share, and profit.
V. Marketing strategy	Summarizes the overall strategic approach that will be used to meet the plan's objectives.
VI. Action plans	This is the most critical section of the annual plan for helping to ensure effective implementation and coordination of activities across functional departments. It specifies: ♦ **What** specific actions are to be taken, ♦ **Who** is responsible for each action, ♦ **When** the action will be engaged in, and ♦ **How much** will be budgeted for each action.
VII. Projected profit-and-loss statement	Presents the expected financial payoff from the plan.
VIII. Controls	Discusses how the plan's progress will be monitored; may present contingency plans to be used if performance falls below expectations or the situation changes.

decisions. Consequently, we will say little more here about the processes or procedures involved in putting together a marketing plan. Instead, our focus is on what should be included in the plan and how its content should be organized and presented to best ensure that the strategy for a product-market entry will be effectively carried out.

Marketing plans across companies vary a good deal in content and organization.[22] In general, however, most annual marketing plans follow a format similar to that summarized in Exhibit 23–11 and discussed below. To help

---

[22] The results of a survey conducted with a broad sample of companies from different industries concerning the contents of their marketing plans and a number of examples of plan formats used by different types of firms are presented in David S. Hopkins, *The Marketing Plan*.

illustrate the kinds of information that might be included in each section of the plan, the contents of a recent annual marketing plan for a Pillsbury refrigerated bread dough, one of the smaller product lines within the firm's differentiated defender prepared dough products business unit, are summarized in Exhibit 23–12.[23]

Analysis of the current situation

This section summarizes relevant background information drawn from a detailed analysis of target customers, competitors, and macroenvironmental variables. It also reviews the recent performance of the product on such variables as sales volume, margin, and profit contribution. This information provides the foundation for identifying the key issues—the threats and opportunities—the product must face in the coming year.

Market situation

Here data are presented on the target market. Total market size and growth trends should be discussed, along with any variations across geographic regions or other market segments. Marketing research information might also be presented concerning customer perceptions (say, awareness of the brand) and buying behavior trends (e.g., market penetration, repeat purchase rate, heavy versus light users). As Exhibit 23–12 indicates, for instance, information about the market situation presented in the plan for Pillsbury's refrigerated bread dough (RBD) includes not only data about the size of the total market for dinner breadstuffs and Pillsbury's market share, but it also points out the low penetration and use frequency of RBD among potential users.

Competitive situation

This section identifies and describes the product's major competitors in terms of their size, market share, product quality, marketing strategies, and other relevant factors. It might also discuss the likelihood that other potential competitors will enter the market in the near future and the possible impact of such entry on the product's competitive position. Note, for instance, that while other Pillsbury brands are the primary competitors for RBD in the refrigerated dough category, the potential entry of a new low-cost competitor could dramatically change the competitive situation.

The macroenvironmental situation

This section describes broad environmental occurrences or trends that may have a bearing on the product's future. The issues mentioned here include

---

[23] While this example is based on the material contained in an actual marketing plan for a Pillsbury product, the name of the brand and some of the specific numbers included in this example have been disguised in order to protect proprietary information.

I. Analysis of current situation

A. Market situation

- The total U.S. market for dinner breadstuffs is enormous, amounting to about 10.5 billion servings per year.
- Specialty breads, such as whole grain breads, are growing in popularity, largely at the expense of traditional white breads.
- Pillsbury's share of the total dinner breadstuffs market, accounted for by several brands including Crescent rolls as well as refrigerated bread dough, is small, amounting to only about 2 percent of the total dollar volume.
- Since its introduction several years ago, refrigerated bread dough (RBD) has been able to achieve only low levels of penetration (only about 15 percent of all households have used the product) and use frequency (nearly two thirds of the product's volume comes from light users who buy only one or two cans per year).
- RBD consumption is concentrated in the northern states and during the fall and winter months (about 75 percent of volume is achieved from September through February).
- Marketing research results suggest consumers believe RBD is relatively expensive in terms of price/value compared to alternative forms of dinner breadstuffs.

B. Competitive situation

- RBD's share of the total dinner breadstuffs category is likely to remain low because of the wide variety of competing choices available to consumers.
- The largest proportion of volume within the category is captured by ready-to-eat breads and rolls produced by supermarket chains and regional bakeries and distributed through retail grocery stores.
- RBD's major competition within the refrigerated dough category comes from other Pillsbury products, such as Crescent rolls and Soft Breadsticks.
- There are currently no other national competitors in the refrigerated bread dough category; but Merico, a small regional producer, was recently acquired by a major national food manufacturer. Evidence suggests Merico may be preparing to introduce a competing product line into national distribution at a price about 10 percent lower than Pillsbury's.

C. Macroenvironmental situation

- Changes in American eating habits may pose future problems for dinner breadstuffs in general, and for RBD in particular:
  More meals are being eaten away from home, and this trend is likely to continue.
  People are eating fewer starchy foods.
  While total volume of dinner breadstuffs did not fall during the early 1980s, neither did it keep pace with population growth.
- Increasing numbers of women working outside the home, and the resulting desire for convenience, may reduce consumers' willingness to wait 30 minutes while RBD bakes, even though the dough is already prepared.
- Because RBD does not use yeast as a leavening agent, Food and Drug Administration regulations prohibit the company from referring to it as "bread" in advertising or package copy, even though the finished product looks, smells, and tastes like bread.

D. Past product performance

- While sales volume in units increased only slightly from 1986 to 1987, dollar volume increased by 24 percent due to a price increase taken in early 1987.
- The improvement to gross margin from 1986 to 1987 was even greater than the price increase due to an improvement in manufacturing costs.
- The improvement in gross margin, however, was not sufficient to produce a positive net margin due to high advertising and sales promotion expenditures aimed at stimulating primary demand and increasing market penetration of RBD.
- Consequently, while RBD showed improvement from 1986 to 1987, it was still unable to make a positive contribution to overhead and profit.

continued

EXHIBIT   23 ♦ 12
(*continued*)

II. Key issues
   A. Threats
   ◆ Lack of growth in the dinner breadstuffs category suggests the market is mature and may decline in the future.
   ◆ The large variety of alternatives available to consumers suggests it may be impossible for RBD to substantially increase its share of the total market.
   ◆ Potential entry of a new, lower-priced competitor poses a threat to RBD's existing share and may result in lower margins if RBD responds by reducing its price.
   B. Opportunities
   ◆ The largest percentage of RBD volume accounted for by light users suggests an opportunity of increasing volume among current users by stimulating frequency of use.
   ◆ Trends toward increased consumption of specialty breads suggests possible line extensions, such as whole wheat or other whole grain flavors.
   C. Strengths
   ◆ RBD has a strong distribution base, with shelf facings in nearly 90 percent of available retail outlets.
   ◆ RBD sales have proved responsive to sales promotion efforts (e.g., cents-off coupons), primarily by increasing purchases among existing users.
   ◆ The fact that most consumers who try RBD make repeat purchases indicates a high level of customer satisfaction.
   D. Weaknesses
   ◆ RBD sales have proved unresponsive to advertising. Attempts to stimulate primary demand have not been able to increase market penetration.
   ◆ Consumer concerns about RBD's price/value place limits on ability to take future price increases.

III. Objectives
   A. Financial objectives
   ◆ Achieve a positive contribution to overhead and profit of $4 million in current year.
   ◆ Reach the target level of an average of 20 percent return on investment over the next five years.
   B. Marketing objectives
   ◆ Maintain market share and net sales revenues at previous year's levels.
   ◆ Maintain current levels of retail distribution coverage.
   ◆ Reduce marketing expenditures sufficiently to achieve profit contribution objective.
   ◆ Identify viable opportunities for future volume and profit expansion.

---

any relevant economic, technological, political/legal, or social/cultural changes. As Exhibit 23–12 indicates, for example, lifestyle trends leading to more meals being eaten away from home and increased desires for convenience pose a threat to future demand for Pillsbury's RBD.

Past product performance

This part of the situation analysis discusses the product's performance on such dimensions as sales volume, margins, marketing expenditures, and profit contribution for several recent years. This information is usually presented in the form of a table, such as the one for RBD shown in Exhibit

EXHIBIT 23 ♦ 12
(concluded)

IV. Marketing strategy
   ♦ Pursue a **maintenance strategy** aimed at holding or slightly increasing RBD volume and market share primarily by stimulating increased frequency of use among current users.
   ♦ Reduce advertising aimed at stimulation of primary demand/penetration and reduce manufacturing costs in order to achieve profit contribution objective.
   ♦ Initiate development and test marketing of possible line extensions to identify opportunities for future volume expansion.

V. Marketing action plans
   ♦ Improve the perceived price/value of RBD by maintaining current suggested retail price at least through the peak selling season (February). Review the competitive situation and the brand's profit performance in March to assess the desirability of a price increase at that time.
   ♦ Work with production to identify and implement cost savings opportunities that will reduce manufacturing costs by 5 percent without compromising product quality.
   ♦ Maintain retail distribution coverage with two trade promotion discount offers totaling $855,000; one offered in October–November to support peak season inventories, and another offered in February–March to maintain inventories as volume slows.
   ♦ Reduce advertising to a maintenance level of 1,100 gross ratings points during the peak sales period of September to March. Focus copy on maintaining awareness among current users.
   ♦ Encourage greater frequency of use among current users through three sales promotion events, with a total budget of $748,000, that will stimulate immediate purchase:
     One free-standing insert (FSI) coupon for 15 cents off next purchase to appear in newspapers on September 19.
     One tear-off refund offer (buy three, get one free) placed on retailers' shelves during November.
     A $1 refund with proof of purchase offer placed in women's service books (i.e., women's magazines like *Good Housekeeping*) during March.

23–13. As the table indicates, even though RBD showed an improvement in gross margin due in part to reduced manufacturing costs, high advertising and sales expenditures prevented the product from making a positive contribution to overhead and profit in 1987.

Key issues

After analyzing the current situation, the product manager must identify the most important issues facing the product in the coming year. These issues typically represent either threats to the future market or financial performance of the product or opportunities to improve those performances. This section should also highlight any special strengths of the product or weaknesses that must be overcome in responding to future threats and opportunities. Some of the key threats and opportunities faced by Pillsbury's RBD together with the product's major strengths and weaknesses are summarized in Section II of Exhibit 23–12.

EXHIBIT 23 ♦ 13

Historical and projected financial performance of refrigerated bread dough product

Variable	1986	1987	Percent change 1986–87	Projected 1988	Percent change 1987–88
Sales volume					
(cases)	2,290M	2,350M	+3%	2,300M	(2%)
Net sales ($)	17,078M	21,165M	+24	21,182M	0
Gross margin ($)	6,522M	10,767M	+65	11,430M	+5
Gross margin/					
net sales	38%	51%	—	54%	—
Advertising and					
sales promotion ($)	11,609M	12,492M	+6	6,100M	(51)
Advertising & sales					
promotion/gross					
margin	178%	116%	—	53%	—
Net margin ($)	(5,087M)	(1,725M)	—	5,330M	—
Net margin/					
net sales	—	—	—	25	—
Product					
contribution ($)	(6,342M)	(3,740M)	—	4,017M	—

Objectives

Information about the current situation, the product's recent performance, and the key issues to be addressed can now serve as the basis for setting specific objectives for the coming year. Two types of objectives need to be specified. **Financial objectives** provide goals for the overall performance of the brand and should reflect the objectives for the SBU as a whole and its competitive strategy. Those financial goals must then be converted into **marketing objectives** that specify the changes in customer behavior and levels of performance of various marketing program elements necessary to reach the product's financial objectives.

The major financial and marketing objectives for Pillsbury's RBD are summarized in Section III of Exhibit 23–12. Sales volume and market share are not expected to increase, but the product is expected to make a $4 million contribution to overhead and profit through additional cost reductions.

Marketing strategy

Because there may be a number of different ways to achieve the objectives specified in the preceding section, the manager must now specify the overall marketing strategy to be pursued. It is likely to be one, or a combination of several, of the strategies discussed in Section IV of this book. Keep in mind that the marketing strategy selected must not only fit the situation and the objectives faced by the product, but it must also be consistent with the overall competitive strategy of the business unit.

The RBD product manager recommends that a **maintenance strategy** be pursued. The intense competitive situation, uncertainty over the possible entry of Merico, and the past inability of primary demand advertising to increase market penetration all suggest that it would be difficult to expand RBD's market by simply doing more of the same. Consequently, the recommended strategy seeks to maintain or slightly increase RBD volume and share primarily by stimulating repeat purchases among current customers. Reductions in advertising expenditures and continued improvements in manufacturing costs will be relied upon to help the brand achieve its profit contribution objective. In addition, it is recommended that development and test marketing of several line extensions (for example, whole wheat and a French-style loaf) be initiated in an attempt to identify viable opportunities for future volume expansion.

Action plans

The action plan is the most crucial part of the annual marketing plan for ensuring proper execution. Here the specific actions necessary to implement the strategy for the product are listed, together with a clear statement of who is responsible for each action, when it will be done, and how much is to be spent on each activity. Of course, actions requiring the cooperation of other functional departments should be included only after the product manager has contacted the departments involved, worked out any potential conflicts, and received assurances of support.

Some of the action programs specified for RBD are outlined in Section V of Exhibit 23–12. It is also common practice to display the relative timing of the various actions in the form of an events calendar detailing when each action is scheduled for the coming year.

Projected profit-and-loss statement

The action plan includes a supporting budget that is essentially a projected profit-and-loss statement. On the revenue side, it forecasts next year's sales volume in units and dollars. On the expense side, it reflects manufacturing, distribution, and marketing costs associated with the planned actions. This budget is then presented to higher levels of management for review and possible modification. Once approved, the product's budget serves as a basis for the plans and resource allocation decisions of other functional departments within the SBU, such as manufacturing and purchasing. The projected financial results of RBD's 1988 annual plan are summarized in the last column of Exhibit 23–13.

Controls

The final section of the plan outlines the controls used to monitor its progress during the year. The objectives and budget are usually broken down by quarter to allow management to review the results for each period and adjust the plan during the year, if necessary, to achieve the annual objectives. This section might also specify contingency plans to be implemented if specific threats or opportunities should occur during the year. The RBD product manager, for instance, recommended that no change in price or promotion programs be made during the year even if Merico should enter the national market. The rationale was that time would be needed to assess the magnitude of Merico's potential threat and to determine the most appropriate response. The issues and methods involved in controlling strategic marketing programs are examined in more detail in Chapter 24.

SUMMARY

For a business to be successful it must not only have competitive and marketing strategies that fit the demands of the external market and competitive environment, but it must also be capable of implementing those strategies effectively. The business's internal structure, resources, policies, procedures, and plans must fit the demands of its strategies. This chapter examined four aspects of internal fit critical for effective implementation: (1) the compatibility of strategies at different levels within the business, (2) the administrative relationships between the SBU and corporate headquarters, (3) the organization structure of the SBU and its interfunctional coordination mechanisms, and (4) the contents of annual marketing plans that detail the specific actions necessary to execute strategy in each of the SBU's product-markets.

Both the broad marketing policies guiding the development of marketing plans for individual product-markets and the specific marketing strategies pursued within those product-markets should be consistent with the SBU's overall competitive strategy. Pioneering marketing strategies, such as mass-market penetration, niche penetration, and skimming, are all common within prospector SBUs. Consequently, such SBUs should adopt marketing policies that encourage the development of broad and tech-

nically sophisticated product lines, relatively large promotional expenses, and relatively high prices. Differentiated defenders are likely to rely on marketing strategies geared to maintaining market share or to squeezing more volume from mature markets. Their marketing policies should encourage relatively narrow product lines with high product or service quality, moderate to low promotional expenditures, and relatively high prices. Finally, low-cost defenders are more likely to engage in reactive marketing strategies and to harvest product-markets as their industries move into decline. Their marketing policies should focus on narrow product lines of moderate quality, relatively low sales and promotional expenditures, and competitive prices.

Administrative relationships between an SBU and its corporate headquarters can influence its ability to implement different business and marketing strategies. Prospector businesses perform best when their managers have substantial autonomy to make independent decisions, when they share few functional programs or facilities with other SBUs, and when their evaluation and reward systems are primarily based on growth dimensions of performance such as increases in sales volume or market share. On the other hand, low-cost defender businesses perform best when their managers have relatively little autonomy, when there is substantial sharing of functional programs and facilities across SBUs, and when their evaluation and reward systems are focused primarily on financial dimensions of performance.

The SBU's organizational structure and the processes it uses to coordinate functional activities and resolve conflicts across departments also influence its ability to implement different strategies. Prospector businesses perform best when their structures feature low levels of centralization and formalization, have high specialization, and stress participative methods of interfunctional coordination and conflict resolution. Consequently, matrix forms of organizational design, such as interfunctional product teams or product and market management structures, are particularly well suited to such businesses. At the other extreme, low-cost defenders perform best when their structures provide high levels of centralization and formalization, have relatively little specialization, and stress hierarchical methods of coordination. Highly structured and bureaucratic organizational designs, such as those organized along functional lines,

are most appropriate for businesses pursuing low-cost defender strategies. While the product management form of organization is most commonly used, especially in consumer products businesses, it is most appropriate for businesses pursuing differentiated defender and analyzer strategies.

Finally, implementation is facilitated by the development of a detailed annual marketing plan for each product-market entry within the business unit. Such plans should contain (1) an executive summary, (2) a discussion of the current market and competitive situation and the product's past performance, (3) a summary of the key issues facing the product, (4) the objectives to be accomplished in the coming year, (5) the overall marketing strategy to be pursued, (6) the action plans detailing the specific activities involved in carrying out the plan, (7) a projected profit-and-loss statement, and (8) a summary of how the plan's performance is to be monitored and controlled. A detailed set of action plans is particularly crucial for effective implementation because it describes exactly what is to be done, by whom, when, and how much is to be spent on each activity.

QUESTIONS

1. What kinds of marketing strategies are most likely to be pursued by individual product-market entries within a low-cost defender SBU operating in a mature industry? Explain why you would expect to find this kind of consistent relationship between business and marketing strategies within most successful business units.

2. If you were the marketing director of the SBU described in question 1, what marketing policies would you establish to guide decisions concerning the business's products, prices, distribution channels, and promotional programs? Explain the rationale for those policies.

3. How should the marketing policies for a differentiated defender SBU differ from those you described in answering question

2? What is the rationale for those differences?

4. Suppose you have been offered the job of developing and managing a new medical products business unit for a major electronics manufacturer. The purpose of the new SBU will be to adapt technology from other parts of the company for medical applications (e.g., diagnostic equipment such as CAT scanners, surgical lasers, etc.) and to identify and build markets for the new products the unit develops. The new unit's performance over the next several years will be judged primarily on its success at developing a variety of new products and its rate of growth in sales volume and market share. Before accepting the job, what assurances would you seek from

the company's CEO concerning the administrative relationships to be established between the new SBU and corporate headquarters? Why?

5. Now that you have accepted the job described in question 4, you have been given a $50 million operating budget for the first year. Your first task is to staff the new unit and to allocate your budget across its various functional departments. While you obviously want to hire good people for every position, which departments require the most competent and experienced personnel, and which departments should receive relatively large shares of the available budget? Why?

6. As general manager, what type of organizational design would you select for the new SBU described in question 4? Justify your choice in terms of its ability to help the SBU implement its strategy and accomplish its primary objectives. What potential disadvantages—if any—might be associated with your chosen organization structure?

7. As the general manager of 3M's industrial tape division you are responsible for a business where the basic technology and the majority of product-markets are rela-

tively mature, but where new applications and product improvements are still possible. Consequently, you are pursuing a differentiated defender strategy. If you had the authority to design the structure for your SBU, what type of organizational design would you select? How would you characterize your choice in terms of the structural variables of centralization, formalization, and specialization? Why do you think this design most appropriate for your SBU?

8. Given your answer to question 7, how would potential conflicts between functional departments within the industrial tape SBU be resolved? Who would be responsible for coordinating the activities of the various functional departments for each of the SBU's product-market entries?

9. Using the information presented in the text's discussion of the marketing plan, develop a new and different marketing plan for Pillsbury's refrigerated bread dough. What new objectives, marketing strategy, and action plans would your new approach involve? In general terms, how would your new plan change the projected financial performance of the product in the next fiscal year?

Chapter ◇ 24

Monitoring and controlling marketing programs

COST CONTROLS PAY OFF AT WAL-MART[1]

Sam Walton of Bentonville, Arkansas, is one of the richest persons in the world. In 1988 he and his family owned 39 percent of Wal-Mart stock, worth nearly $7 billion. The company is a discount general merchandise retailer. Founded some 25 years ago, Wal-Mart had sales in excess of $15 billion in 1988. Its average annual return to investors from 1977 to 1987 was an amazing 46 percent. Because of this and its nearly 20-fold growth over the past 10 years, the company's market value well exceeds K mart's, despite being substantially smaller. Exhibit 24–1 compares Wal-Mart's net income to other leading retailers'.

In addition to 1,114 Discount City stores in 1988, the company operates over 80 Sam's Wholesale Clubs with sales of close to $3 billion. Sam's targets small business and low-risk groups of individual households. It operates on gross margins of 9 to 10 percent and stocks only about 3,500 items, in contrast to nearly 50,000 for a Discount City store. In addition, Wal-Mart operates three Hypermart USAs. which are five-acre "malls without walls," and a small chain of discount drugstores.

Wal-Mart is America's most admired retailer, and it ranks fifth on the list of the most admired large U.S. companies. If the recent past is any indication, Wal-Mart will be the largest—and most profitable—U.S. retailer in a few years.

Only K mart and Sears stand in its way. In 1989 the company planned to expand its retail square footage from 77.8 million to over 90 million.

> Construction [would] include 125 Wal-Mart stores, 18 Sam's Wholesale Clubs, two Dot Discount Drug Stores, and two Hypermart USA stores (one joint venture and one wholly owned). Expansions and relocations of 58 existing stores, including the relocation of three Wal-Mart stores into experimental combination supermarket/general merchandise stores to be operated as Wal-Mart SuperCenters, [were] also planned.[2]

Initially, Wal-Mart focused on small-town markets (largely in Oklahoma, Arkansas, and Missouri) that were ignored by the national discounters. It now operates stores in such major cities as Dallas, Houston, Kansas City, and St. Louis; but it still operates in only 25 states.

A major reason for Wal-Mart's success is its ability to control cost. Despite the substantial increase in the number

---

[1] Based on a case written by Clark Lawrence of the College of Business, University of Arkansas at Little Rock, in 1983 and revised in 1986; Wal-Mart's *1988 Annual Report*, and John Huey, "Wal-Mart—Will It Take Over the World?" *Fortune*, January 30, 1989, p. 52.

[2] *1988 Annual Report*, p. 3.

continued

EXHIBIT 24 ◆ 1

Merchandise net income of Wal-Mart, K mart, J. C. Penney, and Sears, 1983–89* ($ millions)

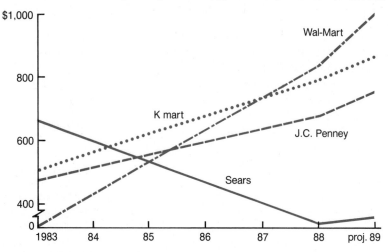

* Excludes foreign operations.

Source: John Huey, "Wal-Mart—Will It Take Over the World?" *Fortune,* January 30, 1989, p. 56. © 1989 The Time, Inc. Magazine Company. All rights reserved.

of stores and wholesale clubs it operates and the start-up of its hypermarts, its cost of sales has increased only 1.7 percentage points over 1986. This was due largely to the cost of sales in Sam's units, which is considerably higher than in the Discount City stores because of a lower markup on purchases. Reductions in operating, selling, and general administrative costs were 1.3 percentage points below 1986, and interest payments remained constant (see Exhibit 24–2). As a result, the company experienced record profits of $627 million in 1988, an increase of nearly 40 percent over 1987.

Wal-Mart's management emphasizes frugality—illustrated by the fact that its corporate headquarters in Bentonville

is often mistaken for a warehouse. Management regularly drives home the message that money is not well spent if it does not foster growth or lower costs. Wal-Mart is unique in the way it controls not only its expenses (down to a given department at the individual store level) but its merchandising activities as well. The essence of the company's success lies in its ability to couple state-of-the-art computer communications technology with hands-on management. Exhibit 24–3 illustrates how technology helps sell soap at Wal-Mart.

All of the company's regional vice presidents live in or near Bentonville.

continued

EXHIBIT 24 ♦ 2

Key operating percentages for Wal-Mart, 1986–88

	Percentage of sales Year ending January 31		
	1988	**1987**	**1986**
Sales	100.0%	100.0%	100.0%
Cost of sales	77.0	76.0	75.3
Operating, selling, and general and adminis- trative costs	16.3	16.9	17.6
Interest costs	.7	.7	.7
Provision for income tax	2.8	3.3	3.3
Net income	3.9	3.8	3.9

Source: Wal-Mart's 1988 Annual Report, p. 16.

Every Monday they and other management personnel, often including Walton and David Glass, president and chief executive officer, fly via corporate turboprops to stores in the various regions. There they talk with store managers, employees ("associates"), and customers. On Friday they return to Bentonville to share their findings with headquarters personnel and prepare for a Saturday merchandise meeting attended by the regional vice presidents, the chairman or vice chairman, the president, and 100 or more other employees.

This meeting is a no-holds-barred session concerned with moving merchandise. The participants use printouts of inventory levels and sales for key items. *Fortune* describes one such meeting—just before Christmas 1988—as follows:

For three hours, the managers pour over the printout. One is concerned that Wal-Mart has priced children's corduroy jeans at $3, while K mart is promoting them at two for $5; this is corrected. CEO Glass worries that a certain video game isn't moving in stores he has visited this week, and he wants orders cut off; the buyers have beaten him to it. Then a discussion ensures over knives, which the printout shows are heavily stocked in Wal-Mart's distribution centers. Quickly a senior manager orders a Christmas-gift knife display.[3]

These and similar decisions will reach all store managers by the following Monday at the latest. The company communicates all this by phone, but

_____

[3] Huey, "Wal-Mart—Will It Take Over the World?" p. 54.

continued

concluded

EXHIBIT 24 ♦ 3

Selling soap the high-tech way at Wal-Mart

SCANNERS TRACK SUDSY SALES AND MONITOR THE SUPPLY ON THE SHELVES.

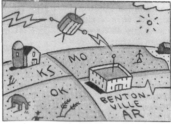

STORES BEAM ORDERS VIA SATELLITE TO AN IBM COMPUTER AT HEADQUARTERS.

SUDSY INC. SCHEDULES SHIPPING TO SATISFY WAL-MART'S NEEDS.

CARTONS OF SUDSY MOVE ON CONVEYORS INTO ONE OF WAL-MART'S 6,537 TRUCKS.

WITHIN 36 HOURS OF THE STORE'S ORDER, THE NEW SUDSY GOES ON SALE.

WAL-MART USES ITS SATELLITE TO TELL MANAGERS ABOUT A DISCOUNT ON SUDSY.

Source: John Huey, "Wal-Mart—Will It Take Over the World?" *Fortune,* January 30, 1989, pp. 56–57.

uses its satellite communications system for emergencies. This system's basic function is to transmit store data to the central computer, handle requests for credit-card approval from all stores, and track distribution activities. This communication network also informs lower-level managers at the individual store level how well their sections did the previous week and how they compare with similar sections in other stores. Managers seek causes for both good and bad performances. A department or section that consistently performs better than average receives monetary rewards—and recognition. Units doing less well are talked to in an effort to find out why and how to correct the problem.

The marketing management process consists of setting objectives, formulating strategies, implementing a plan of action, devising and controlling procedures, and reappraising the results. Because of its position in the process, the control and reappraisal steps monitor the extent to which the firm achieves its objectives. If it does not, this step finds out whether the reason lies in the environment, the strategies employed, the action plans, the way the plans were implemented, or some combination thereof. Thus, the control and reappraisal step is diagnostic; and it serves to start the marketing management process anew.

Because marketing control and reappraisal are involved with all the prior steps in the marketing management process, control processes correspond to the different organizational levels. Thus, corporate management is concerned with how well its various SBUs are performing relative to the opportunities and threats each faces as well as the resources given them. Control here would be environmentally oriented and, hence, strategic in nature. In addition, corporate management is concerned with how well each SBU is performing with regard to its various functional areas. In marketing, the control exercised by corporate is in the form of a **marketing audit.**

At the SBU level, concern is primarily with the unit's own strategy, especially as it pertains to its individual product-market entries. We will concentrate mainly on this level because it constitutes the bulk of any control system. The focus is on the **action (annual) plan** and especially on budget items and share determinants involving personal selling and advertising.

In this chapter, we discuss the control process first, followed by a section on profitability. We next examine strategic controls and marketing audits, which are activities undertaken by corporate but applied at the SBU level. The remainder of the chapter is devoted primarily to controls pertaining to individual product-market entries, particularly regarding their competitive position, their adherence to plan (including budget and share determinants), and the efficiency with which marketing manages its resources. The chapter ends with a discussion of global marketing control and contingency planning.

THE CONTROL PROCESS

The control process consists essentially of setting performance standards, specifying and obtaining feedback data, evaluating it, and taking corrective action (see Exhibit 24–4). Although the staff organization is largely responsible for generating the control data, the line organization administers the control process. Certainly, this is the case with Wal-Mart, as seen in the involvement of regional vice presidents, district managers, store managers, and department heads in obtaining and processing control data as well as taking corrective action.

EXHIBIT 24 ◆ 4

The control process

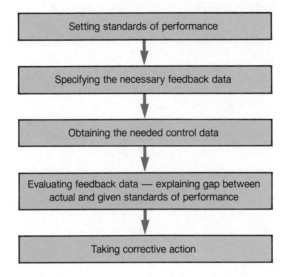

Setting standards of performance

The standards of performance derive largely from the objectives set forth at the corporate, SBU, and individual product-market entry levels. This generates a hierarchy of objectives stated in terms of profitability (say, return on equity or return on assets managed), market share, and sales. Standards of performance also include such sales and market-share determinants as percent effective distribution, relative shelf facings, awareness, consumers' attitude change toward a given product attribute, and the extent of price parity. And, finally, budget line items having to do with expenses such as the salesforce (salary payments) and advertising (cost of a specific campaign) also serve as standards of performance. Without a reasonable set of performance standards, managers could not know what results are being obtained or the extent to which the results are satisfactory. Nor could they gain insights into why the results obtained are or are not satisfactory.

To be of any value, performance standards must be measurable. Further, they must be tied to some specific time period. Generally speaking, control systems operate on a monthly, quarterly, and annual basis, with the monthly and quarterly data cumulated to present a current picture and to facilitate comparisons with prior years. In recent years, the trend has been for control systems to operate over shorter periods (weekly and even daily) and for control data to be more quickly available. Wal-Mart's inventory-control system, for example, provides instantaneous up-to-date data.

Specifying and obtaining feedback data

Once a company has established performance standards, the next step is to develop a system that provides feedback on actual performance. In most cases someone must gather and process considerable data to obtain the performance measures. For example, to determine profitability, accountants must construct a profit and loss statement for the time period. Feedback data must be usable and timely. The latter is important if management is to take corrective action before the situation suffers further deterioration.

Analysts obtain feedback data from a variety of sources, including company accounting records, syndicated marketing information sources such as A. C. Nielsen and Selling Areas-Marketing, Inc. (SAMI), and special marketing research projects. An example of data provided by a syndicated service is shown in Exhibit 24–5. It illustrates how SAMI data can be used to provide feedback on the competitive environment. The exhibit shows what happened to four established brands (A, B, C, D) when two brands (E, F) were introduced. The trend data show that one established brand (A) was not

EXHIBIT 24 ◆ 5

Example of feedback data obtained from a syndicated marketing research source concerned with brand-share trend data

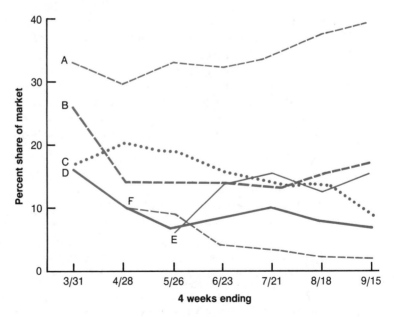

Source: Harper W. Boyd, Jr., Ralph Westfall, and Stanley F. Stasch, *Marketing Research: Text and Cases,* 7th ed. (Homewood, Ill.: Richard D. Irwin, 1989), p. 201. Chart presented through courtesy of Selling Areas-Marketing, Inc. (SAMI).

affected by the new introductions, brand E has benefited at the expense of C and D, and brand F is in serious trouble.

The sales invoice is the basic internal source of data because it provides a detailed record of each transaction. Invoices are the basis for measuring profitability, sales, and various budget items. They also provide data for analysis of the geographic distribution of sales and customer accounts by type and size.

The third source—and typically the most expensive and time consuming—involves undertaking one or more marketing research projects to obtain needed information. In-house research projects are apt to take longer and be more expensive than using an outside syndicated service. But there may be no alternative as, for example, in determining awareness and attitude changes. Exhibit 24–6 gives an example of how Wal-Mart uses in-house-generated marketing research to help maintain its low-price image.

Evaluating feedback data

Management evaluates feedback data to find out why the business unit or entry did or did not perform as expected; that is, why there was a deviation from plan. Wal-Mart does this by sending its regional vice presidents into the field on a regular basis to learn firsthand what's going on and why.

In any event, managers must use a variety of information to determine what the company's performance should have been under the actual market conditions that existed when the plan was executed. In many cases they may obtain the information in measured form—as, for example, a shift in personal disposable income (available from government sources); a change in demand for a product type (obtained in the process of measuring market share); or a change in price by a major competitor. In other cases, however, the explanation may have to rest on inferences drawn from generalized data. This would be the case in attempting to explain poor sales performance on the basis of an improvement in a competitor's salesforce.

EXHIBIT 24 ◆6

Wal-Mart uses marketing research to maintain price image

Wal-Mart makes every effort to keep its regular everyday prices lower than competitors on a set of critical products. These "image items" are thought to be the basis of a customer's perception of how expensive a store is. Every few weeks Wal-Mart undertakes research to determine the prices charged by K mart, Target, and Magic-Mart for these identical items. The company then makes sure that Wal-Mart has the lowest price. Even management—including Sam Walton—has been known to do comparison shopping.

Source: Case prepared by Clark Lawrence, College of Business, University of Arkansas at Little Rock, 1986.

Taking corrective action

The last step in the control process prescribes the action to correct the situation. At Wal-Mart, this is partly accomplished at the Saturday breakfast meeting, where managers decide what actions to take to solve selected problems. Success here depends on how well the evaluation step is carried out. When linkages between inputs and outputs are clear, a causal relationship is presumed and managers can specify appropriate action. For example, assume that inputs consisted of an advertising schedule that specified the frequency to air a given TV message. The objective was to change attitudes about a given product attribute (the output). If the attitude change did not occur, remedial action would start with an evaluation of the firm's advertising effort, particularly the advertising message and how frequently it was run.

Unfortunately, correcting a given situation is rarely this simple. Almost always, an interactive effect exists among the input variables. For example, advertisers can rarely separate out the effects of the message, the media, the frequency of exposure, and competitive responses. Sometimes the investigation requires that marketing research collect an array of data from the field. For example, to find out more about the success or failure of the advertising message, researchers could find out the extent to which the target audience recalled, understood, believed, and associated it with a given brand. They could determine much the same about the messages used by individual major competitors.

Even with a clear understanding of the problem, we face the difficulty of prescribing the specific, appropriate corrective action to take. If the advertising message needs to be changed, which phrases should the new one contain? If the message frequency needs to be increased, how much of an increase is needed? If price deals are needed, which deals should be made, and what specific programs are required to implement them?

As we have seen throughout this text, marketing management finds it difficult to perceive and formulate problems and to make decisions. There are many reasons for this, including the need to deal with the firm's external environment—something over which no executive has control. Further, because of delayed responses and carry-over effects, marketing executives find it difficult to predict outcomes for both the short and long terms. In addition, there are myriad ways to solve a marketing problem. And for each alternative, it is possible to vary the intensity with which specific resources are applied—making the problem that much more difficult to solve from an efficiency point of view.

Sometimes the outcome is greater or better than management had planned; for example, when sales and market share exceed the schedule. In such cases the marketers still need an evaluation to find out why such a variance occurred. Perhaps a more favorable environment evolved because demand was greater than expected and a major competitor failed to take advantage of it. Or perhaps the advertising message was more effective than expected. These different "reasons why" would call for different marketing responses to hold what had been obtained *and* to exploit the favorable situation.

The above process is sometimes referred to as the *traditional output-oriented management-control system*, which seems to work best in the short term for activities relating to well-defined management decisions. It has been criticized mainly because of its assumption that performance deviations can be corrected with any certainty and its failure to include behavioral assessment measures. The latter limits the system's ability to control the behavior of a higher-level marketing manager or situations in which quality needs to be assessed, as would be the case in service marketing.[4]

PROFITABILITY ANALYSIS

Regardless of the organizational level, control involves some form of profitability analysis. In brief, **profitability analysis** requires that analysts determine the costs associated with specific marketing activities to find out the profitability of such units of analysis as different market segments, products, customer accounts, and distribution channels (intermediaries). Wal-Mart does this analysis at department and store levels as well as for individual lines of goods within a department. More and more, management is attempting to obtain profitability measures pertaining to the linkage of individual products to each of its various markets.

Despite the fact that profitability is probably the single most important measure of performance, its limitations must be kept in mind. These are (1) many objectives can best be measured in nonfinancial terms (e.g., maintaining employment); (2) profit is a short-term measure and can be manipulated by taking actions that may prove dysfunctional longer term (e.g., reducing R&D expenses); and (3) profits can be affected by factors over which management has no control (e.g., the weather).[5]

Direct versus full costing

Analysts have the option of using direct or full costing in determining the profitability of a product or market segment. In **full costing,** analysts assign *both* direct or variable and indirect costs to the unit of analysis. **Direct costs**

---

[4] For a further discussion of these and related problems, see Bernard J. Jaworski, "Toward a Theory of Marketing Control: Environmental Context, Control Types, and Consequences," *Journal of Marketing*, July 1988, pp. 23–39.

[5] For further discussion, see John C. Camillus, *Strategic Planning and Management Control* (Lexington, Mass.: D. C. Heath & Company, 1986), pp. 170–73.

are directly associated with the unit of analysis. A product's direct *production* costs include direct labor and materials. Its direct *marketing* costs could include sales commissions, advertising, credit (cost of capital), bad debts, inventory, merchandising, and shipping. **Indirect costs** involve certain fixed joint costs that cannot be linked directly to a single unit of analysis. For example, the costs of occupancy, general management, and the management of the salesforce are all indirect costs for a multiproduct company. Those who use full costing argue that only by allocating all costs to a product or a market can they obtain an accurate picture of its value.

Direct costing involves the use of contribution accounting. Those favoring the **contribution margin** approach argue there is really no accurate way to assign indirect costs. Further, because indirect costs are mostly fixed costs, a product or market may make a contribution to profits even if it shows a loss. Thus, even though overhead must eventually be absorbed, the contribution method clearly indicates what is gained by adding or dropping a product or a customer. Exhibit 24–7 shows an example of full and direct costing. Note the substantial difference in the results obtained—$370,000 using full costing versus $650,000 with the contribution method.

Marginal analysis

Ultimately, the purpose of any profitability analysis is to help marketing managers decide how to better allocate their firms' marketing resources. Because the response to marketing effort varies by customer and by product, marketing managers must decide how to allocate their efforts (resources) across customers and products. Thus, they must know these things about each major account: its potential by product; whether the company receives a greater or lesser share of the account's business; and to what extent and in what form marketing effort is being applied to the account. Based on such knowledge and the past relationship between increases and decreases in effort and share, managers can estimate the results of applying more effort to customer accounts of certain sizes, given the share of the account's business the firm already has. For example, one company determined that for accounts with a $100,000+ annual potential, it could not obtain much more than a 50 percent share, regardless of the nature and magnitude of its efforts because most buyers wanted at least two major suppliers.

Contribution analysis is helpful in determining the yield derived from the application of additional resources. Using the data in Exhibit 24–7, we can answer the question, How much additional profit would result from a marginal increase in sales of $300,000—assuming the gross margin remains at 29.62 percent and the only cost is $35,000 more in sales commissions and expenses? As Exhibit 24–8 shows, the answer is an increase in profits before taxes of $53,000.

EXHIBIT 24 ◆ 7

Finding product or entry profitability with full costing and marginal contribution methods ($000)

	Full costing	Marginal contribution
Net sales	$5,400	$5,400
Less: Cost of goods sold—includes direct costs (labor, material, and production overhead)*	3,800	3,800
Gross margin	$1,600	$1,600
Expenses		
Salesforce—includes direct costs (commissions) plus indirect costs (sales expenses, sales management overhead)†	$ 510	$ 450
Advertising—includes direct costs (media, production) plus indirect costs (management overhead)	215	185
Physical logistics—includes direct costs (transportation) plus indirect costs (order processing, warehousing costs)	225	190
Occupancy—includes direct costs (telephone) plus indirect costs (heat/air, insurance, taxes, building maintenance)	100	25
Management overhead—includes direct costs (product/brand manager and staff) plus indirect costs (salaries, expenses, occupancy costs of SBU's general management group)	180	100
Total	$1,230	$ 950
Profit before taxes	$ 370	
Contribution to fixed costs and profits		$ 650

* Production facilities dedicated to a single product.
† Multiproduct salesforce.

STRATEGIC CONTROL AND MARKETING AUDITS

Strategic control procedures deal with the opportunities and threats pertaining to each SBU and the strategies adopted to exploit them. They, as well as marketing audits, are undertaken by the corporate level for each of its SBUs.

As for strategic control, the objective is to develop a continuous monitoring system that provides data designed to help answer the following questions.[6]

1. What changes in the environment have negatively affected the current strategy (interest rates, governmental controls, price changes in substitute products)?

---

[6] Glenn Boseman, Arvine Phatek, and Robert E. Schellenberger, *Strategic Management* (N.Y.: John Wiley & Sons, 1986), pp. 116–19.

EXHIBIT 24 ♦ 8

Effect of $300,000 increase in sales resulting from increased sales commissions and expenses of $35,000 (same data as in Exhibit 24–7)

Net sales	$5,700
Less: direct costs (29.62%)	4,012
	$1,688
Expenses	
Sales commissions and expenses	$ 485
Advertising	185
Physical logistics	190
Occupancy	25
Management	100
	$ 985
Contribution to overhead and profits	$ 703
Increase in profit (before tax) = $703 − $650 = $53	

2. What changes have major competitors made in their objectives and strategies?
3. What changes have occurred in the industry in such attributes as capacity, entry barriers, substitute products?
4. What new opportunities or threats have derived from changes in the environment, competitors' strategies, or the nature of the industry?
5. What changes have occurred in the industry's key success factors?
6. To what extent is the firm's current strategy consistent with the preceding changes?

General Electric monitors the performance of its individual SBUs on such criteria as profitability, cash flow, market/competitive position, and technological position. GE sets and weights criteria standards differently, depending on how it categorized the SBU based on its environment (market attractiveness) and business strengths; that is, whether the SBU is mandated to grow, remain as is, or be harvested. GE rewards its SBU managers according to a bonus schedule heavily influenced by the SBU's category. Thus, GE bases bonuses for managers of growth SBUs on factors reflecting current performance (40 percent), factors reflecting future performance (48 percent), and other factors (12 percent). This is in contrast to managers of harvest/divest SBUs, whose bonuses are weighted 72 percent on current performance, 16 percent on future performance, and 12 percent on other factors.[7]

---

[7] William K. Hall, "SBUs: Hot, New Topic in the Management of Diversification," *Business Horizons*, February 1978, pp. 17–25.

THE MARKETING AUDIT

At the corporate level managers conduct periodic comprehensive reviews of the company's total marketing effort, cutting across all products and business units. The mechanism for such an evaluation, called a **marketing audit,** involves an examination of an SBU's marketing objectives, strategy, plan of action, and personnel. It provides an assessment of each SBU's present competitive position plus insights into its marketing strengths and weaknesses. It requires an analysis of each of the marketing mix elements and how well they are being implemented. The audit must take into account environmental changes that impact the SBU's marketing activities. The audit should result in a plan of action designed to correct weaknesses and improve the SBU's marketing performance.

Conducting an audit

The firm's executives can perform the marketing audit. Some large companies use personnel from their corporate audit office to perform such work. Experienced, outside specialists produce the best results, however, because of their objectivity and independence in working with the SBU's marketing managers. The audit's value lies not only in its findings, but also in the process itself. Marketing managers study the firm's changing environment and evaluate company responses to these changes in the form of strategies and plans of action.

The audit procedure consists of specifying objectives, coverage areas, data to be gathered, data sources, and the time period involved; gathering and analyzing the data; and preparing the report. Rather than relying exclusively on company managers for information, the auditors should also interview customers and channel intermediaries.

Areas to be covered

An audit normally covers such major areas as the SBU's marketing environment, objectives, strategy, planning and control systems, organization, productivity, and individual marketing activities such as sales and advertising. These areas are shown in Exhibit 24–9, along with examples of the kinds of data needed and serve as the basis for the discussion that follows.

The **marketing environment audit** requires an analysis of the firm's present and future environment with respect to its economic, technological, political, and social components. The intent is to identify the more significant trends and to see how they affect the firm's customers, competitors, channel intermediaries, and suppliers. Thus, the analysis covers such areas as demographics, gross national product and disposable income, cost of alternative energy sources, technology, and legislation regarding pollution and product safety. It also covers consumer lifestyles, market growth, objectives and strategies of leading competitors, functions of channel intermedi-

EXHIBIT 24♦9

Major areas covered in marketing audit and questions concerning each for a consumer goods company

Audit area	Examples of questions to be answered
Marketing environment	What opportunities and/or threats derive from the firm's present and future environment; that is, what technological, political, and social trends are significant? How will these trends affect the firm's target markets, competitors, and channel intermediaries? Which opportunities/threats emerge from within the firm?
Objectives and strategy	How logical are the company's objectives given the more significant opportunities/threats and its relative resources? How valid is the firm's strategy, given the anticipated environment, including the actions of competitors?
Planning and control system	Does the firm have adequate and timely information about consumers' satisfaction with the products? With the actions of competitors? With the services of intermediaries?
Organization	Does the organization structure fit the evolving needs of the marketplace? Can it handle the planning needed at the individual product/brand level?
Marketing productivity	How profitable are each of the firm's products/brands? How effective are each of the major marketing activities?
Marketing functions	How well does the product line meet the line's objectives? How well do the products/brands meet the needs of the target markets? Does pricing reflect cross elasticities, experience effects, and relative costs? Is the product readily available? What is the level of retail stockouts? What percent of large stores carry the firm's in-store displays? Is the salesforce large enough? Is the firm spending enough on advertising?

aries, reliability of suppliers, transportation costs, interest rates, and, where applicable, foreign exchange.

Opportunities and threats come primarily from the external environment; but they can also emerge from *within* the firm. Examples of internal opportunities include new or improved products, unique advertising programs, or an ability to lower relative costs. Deteriorating product quality, high relative costs, high salesforce turnover, poor product availability, or a weak service program are strong internal threats to profitable growth.

The **objectives and strategy area audit** calls for an assessment of how appropriate these internal factors are, given current major environmental trends and any changes in the firm's resources. Questions asked here have to do with the logic of the company's objectives, given its competitive position, important trends, and available resources; the validity of the firm's strategy in light of the forecasted environment and the likely actions of major competitors; the targeting of market segments and the allocation of resources across them; and the positioning of products against competitors and the benefits wanted by the targeted consumers.

The unit's **planning and control system area audit** evaluates the adequacy of the systems that develop the firm's product-market entry action plans and the control and reappraisal process. This audit also evaluates the firm's new-product development procedures. The questions asked here pertain to the quantity and quality of the firm's information about customers and their satisfaction with the product; the actions of competitors and their success or failure; the extent to which channel intermediaries do a good job; the reliability of company forecasts and sales quotas; the appropriateness of the control measures in use and their reliability and timeliness; and the effectiveness of test and launch procedures for new products.

The **organization area audit** deals with the formal overall structure (can it meet the changing needs of the marketplace, especially the company's customers?); how the marketing department is organized (can it accommodate the planning requirements of the firm's assortment of brands?); and the extent of synergy between the marketing units (are there good relations between sales and merchandising?). At a higher level, the questions concern the relationship between functional areas such as marketing and production or marketing and R&D. This part of the audit throws considerable light on how well individual marketing managers perform.

The **marketing productivity area audit** evaluates the profitability of the company's individual products, markets (including sales territories), and key accounts. It also studies the cost effectiveness of the various marketing activities.

The **marketing functions area audit** examines, in depth, how adequately the firm handles each of the marketing mix elements. Questions relating to the *product* concern the attainability of the present product line objectives, the extent to which individual products fit the needs of the target markets, and whether the product line should be expanded or contracted. *Price* questions have to do with objectives, strategies, and implementation; price elasticity; experience effects, relative costs, and the actions of major competitors; and consumers' perceptions of the relationship between a product's price and its value. *Distribution* questions center on objectives, strategies, coverage, functions performed, and cost effectiveness. Questions about *advertising* focus on advertising objectives and strategies, media schedules, and the procedures to develop advertising messages. The audit of the salesforce covers its objectives, role, size, coverage, organization, and duties plus the quality of its selection, training, motivation, compensation, and control activities.

Recently a more focused type of audit has been suggested for consumer goods companies, one that involves the **product manager.** The product managers have a great deal to do with the success or failure of individual products, so higher-level managers are concerned about whether product

EXHIBIT   24 ♦ 10

Suggested interview subjects in a product manager audit

---

1. What percent of your time do you actually spend on each activity?
2. Rate how you like each of these activities (like, neutral, dislike, not applicable).
3. Rate the degree to which you expect to be supported in each activity (neither encouraged nor supported, officially encouraged but resources I need are inadequate, financial and technical resources I need are available but the time is not, financial and technical resources are available and I have enough time).
4. Rate the degree to which you expect to be rewarded for each activity (excellent performance is assumed and not rewarded, while failure to perform well gets me in trouble; excellent performance wins me a pat on the back but doesn't help me get a raise, a promotion, or more responsibility; excellent performance leads to one or more of these rewards).
5. What percent of your time would you ideally spend on each activity to build the business?
6. If you could free 10 hours each week of what is now busywork, to which activities would you reallocate them?
7. Rank the top five activities in which you would like training or coaching to help you do your job even better and prepare you for a higher level job.

Source: John A. Quelch, Paul W. Farris, and James M. Oliver, "The Product Manager Audit," *Harvard Business Review,* March–April 1987, p. 31.

managers are channeling their efforts in the best ways possible. Also, it would be important to find out how representatives of other departments (e.g., R&D and manufacturing) can be of greater help to a product manager.

Quelch et al. suggest an audit process that gets product managers to talk about what they're doing versus what they *ought* to be doing. (See Exhibit 24–10 for a listing of interview subjects.)[8] Respondents should also be asked to rate the extent to which various support groups, such as marketing research and management information systems, are helpful. Based on their research, these authors concluded product managers spend too much time on routine matters such as those relating to promotion execution and too little on product design and development.

PRODUCT-MARKET ENTRY ACTION-PLAN CONTROL

This control system is designed to ensure that the company achieves the sales, profits, and other objectives set forth in its annual product-market entry action plans. In the aggregate these plans represent the SBU's planning

---

[8] John A. Quelch, Paul W. Farris, and James M. Oliver, "The Product Manager Audit," *Harvard Business Review,* March–April 1987, p. 30.

efforts, which specify how resources will be allocated across products and markets. These entry plans include a detailed budget and the actions required of each organizational unit both inside and outside the marketing department to attain certain financial and competitive position objectives. In this section we discuss competitive position control, adherence to plan (both budget and sales/shares determinants), and sales analysis, which are designed to yield efficiency measures.

Competitive position control

Hulbert and Toy contend that in the main, most firms have not related marketing control procedures to such key strategy parameters as market share, market size, and market growth.[9] They propose a strategic framework for marketing control that evaluates marketing performance and includes **variance decomposition,** which attempts to isolate the causes for the deviations from plans. An example of their control procedure featuring an analysis of Product Alpha is shown in Exhibit 24–11.

In the exhibits, the unfavorable variance in contribution of $100,000 could develop from either the differences between planned and actual quantities and/or contribution per unit. The former could be due to differences between planned and actual market size and market share or penetration.

EXHIBIT 24 ◆ 11

Operating results for Product Alpha (000)

Item	Planned	Actual	Variance
Revenues			
Sales (pounds)	20,000	22,000	+2,000
Price per pound ($)	$0.50	$0.4773	$−0.227
Revenues	$10,000	$10,500	+$500
Total market (pounds)	40,000	50,000	+10,000
Market share	50%	44%	−6%
Costs			
Variable cost per pound ($)	$0.30	$0.30	—
Contribution			
Per pound ($)	$0.20	$0.1773	−$0.0227
Total ($)	$4,000	$ 3,900	−100

Source: James M. Hulbert and Norman E. Toy, "A Strategic Framework for Marketing Control," *Journal of Marketing,* April 1977, p. 13.

---

[9] James M. Hulbert and Norman E. Toy, "A Strategic Framework for Marketing Control," *Journal of Marketing,* April 1977, pp. 12–20. This section relies heavily on the contents of this article.

EXHIBIT   24 ◆ 12

Variance decomposition analysis for Product Alpha

$$\begin{matrix} \text{Market} \\ \text{volume} \\ \text{variance} \end{matrix} = \left(\begin{matrix} \text{Actual total} \\ \text{market} \\ \text{units} \end{matrix} - \begin{matrix} \text{Planned total} \\ \text{market} \\ \text{units} \end{matrix}\right) \times \left(\begin{matrix} \text{Planned} \\ \text{market} \\ \text{share} \end{matrix}\right) \times \left(\begin{matrix} \text{Planned} \\ \text{contribution} \\ \text{per unit} \end{matrix}\right)$$

$$= (50,000,000 - 40,000,000) \times (.50) \times (.20) \qquad = \$1,000,000$$

$$\begin{matrix} \text{Company} \\ \text{volume} \\ \text{variance} \end{matrix} = \left(\begin{matrix} \text{Actual} \\ \text{sales} \\ \text{in units} \end{matrix} - \begin{matrix} \text{Planned} \\ \text{sales} \\ \text{in units} \end{matrix}\right) \times \left(\begin{matrix} \text{Planned} \\ \text{contribution} \\ \text{per unit} \end{matrix}\right)$$

$$= (22,000,000 - 20,000,000) \times (.20) \qquad\qquad = \$400,000$$

$$\begin{matrix} \text{Company} \\ \text{share} \\ \text{variance} \end{matrix} = \left(\begin{matrix} \text{Actual} \\ \text{market} \\ \text{share} \end{matrix} - \begin{matrix} \text{Planned} \\ \text{market} \\ \text{share} \end{matrix}\right) \times \left(\begin{matrix} \text{Actual total} \\ \text{market} \\ \text{in units} \end{matrix}\right) \times \left(\begin{matrix} \text{Planned} \\ \text{contribution} \\ \text{per unit} \end{matrix}\right)$$

$$= (.44 - .50) \times (50,000,000) \times (.20) \qquad\qquad = -\$600,000$$

$$\begin{matrix} \text{Contribution} \\ \text{variance} \end{matrix} = \left(\begin{matrix} \text{Actual} \\ \text{contribution} \\ \text{per unit} \end{matrix} - \begin{matrix} \text{Planned} \\ \text{contribution} \\ \text{per unit} \end{matrix}\right) \times \left(\begin{matrix} \text{Actual} \\ \text{sales} \\ \text{in units} \end{matrix}\right)$$

$$= (.1773 - .20) \times (22,000,000) \qquad\qquad = -\$500,000$$

$$\begin{matrix} \text{Total} \\ \text{variance} \end{matrix} = \begin{matrix} \text{Market} \\ \text{volume} + \\ \text{variance} \end{matrix} \begin{matrix} \text{Company} \\ \text{volume} + \\ \text{variance} \end{matrix} \begin{matrix} \text{Company} \\ \text{share} + \\ \text{variance} \end{matrix} \begin{matrix} \text{Contribution} \\ \text{variance} \end{matrix}$$

$$= \$1,000,000 + \$400,000 - \$600,000 - \$500,000 \qquad = \$300,000$$

Thus, the potential sources of the $100,000 are the differences between planned and actual market size, market share, and price/cost per unit. The variance decomposition of each of these three variables, as shown in Exhibit 24–12, makes it possible to determine the origin of the variances.

The conclusions of the analysis showed:

1. The favorable volume variance of $400,000 was caused by two larger variances cancelling each other out—one positive and one negative, but neither desirable. By not achieving the planned share of market, the firm lost $600,000 in profit contribution. The loss of market share may have been due to poor planning and/or execution.

2. The $1 million positive contribution variance compensated for the unfavorable share variance because the market turned out to be much larger than forecasted. This represents a forecasting error.

3. The danger signal, strategy-wise, is clear—as the largest competitor the company lost market share in a fast-growth market.

4. The final variance component is the unfavorable price variance of − $500,000.

> To what extent did this lower price level expand the total market? Was the failure to hold price at the planned level a failure in tactics or planning, that is, inaccurate forecasts?

Hulbert and Toy conclude that this analysis "has limited potential for diagnosing the causes of problems. Rather, its major benefit is in the *identification* of areas where problems may exist. Determining the factors which have actually caused favorable or unfavorable variances requires the skill and expertise of the manager."[10]

Much along the same lines, Dearden notes that managers should be judged and compensated on their ability to manage and not on their ability to forecast. By evaluating the impact of the industry volume variable one can better evaluate whether the manager is gaining or losing market share—a measure of competitive position.[11]

Adherence to plan controls

Because budgets project revenues and expenses for a given time period, they are a vital part of the firm's planning and control activities. They provide the basis for a continuous evaluation and comparison of what was planned with what actually happened. In this sense, budgeted revenues and profits serve as objectives against which to measure performance in sales and profits as well as actual costs.

Budget analysis requires that managers continuously monitor marketing expenses to make certain that the company does not overspend in its effort to reach its objectives. They also evaluate the magnitude and pattern of deviations from the target ratios. Before taking corrective action, managers may need to disaggregate the data to help isolate the problem. For example, if total commissions as a percent of sales are out of line, analysts need to specify them for each sales territory and product (when possible) to determine exactly where the problem lies.

Sales/share determinants

Sales/market share are a function of primary determinants; for a consumer product these include effective distribution, relative price, attitude change toward one or more salient product characteristics relative to competition, and shelf facings. These, in turn, are a function of secondary determinants such as number and frequency of sales calls, trade deals, and the effectiveness of the advertising message with a given reach and frequency schedule. These determinants form a hierarchy of objectives ensuring that strategy is

---

[10] Ibid., p. 17.

[11] John Dearden, "Measuring Profit Center Managers," *Harvard Business Review*, September–October 1987, p. 84.

elaborated in specific measurable actions. Thus, the action plan provides the basis for the operational control system.

An analysis of the share determinants should provide insights into presumed linkages between the firm's inputs and its outputs; for example, number and frequency of sales calls and effective distribution. This, in turn, leads to a better understanding of the firm's marketing efficiency. Is the salesforce making as many calls per day as expected—*and* the right number of calls—on target accounts to obtain distribution?

Marketing research is usually required to ascertain the extent to which determinants are being attained. For example, a change in awareness and attitudes toward certain product characteristics would require the use of certain messages and an ad schedule with a certain reach and frequency. Interviewers would need to question the targeted audience to determine the message's success in communicating desired information. Analysts would use data from syndicated research services to obtain estimates of frequency of exposure and reach.

A control system must be flexible to be useful. This means that the data in the files must be in disaggregated form. Thus, data pertaining to products, territories, and accounts are rarely summed and entered in the data processing system. Rather, the sale of a particular product to a given customer is entered into the system, and the desired aggregations are made on demand using the decision support systems (DSS) we discussed in Chapter 9.

SALES ANALYSIS

Sales analysis is a generic term that describes ways of classifying, comparing, and evaluating company sales data. The general procedure is to divide aggregate sales data into certain breakdowns, such as products, end-user customers, channel intermediaries, sales territories, and order size. Then analysts make comparisons against other internal and external data.

The objective of sales analyses is to find areas of strengths and weakness; for example, products producing the greatest and least volume, customers accounting for the bulk of the revenues, and the prevailing order size. Thus, one of the more important benefits of even the most primitive sales analysis lies in identifying products, territories, and customers that account for the bulk of the company's sales. Such information enables a company to concentrate its resources where they provide the best yield.

Sales analysis recognizes that aggregate sales and cost data often mask the real situation sufficiently to allow a misdiagnosis of the real problem. For example, a firm marketing a line of male toiletries experienced an overall annual increase in dollar sales of 12 percent. In analyzing this increase, company executives were surprised to learn that the increase came primarily from two new products. Indeed, without the new products, overall sales would have declined 3 percent despite an inflationary factor of over 5 percent. Sales analyses not only help to evaluate and control marketing efforts; but they also help management better formulate objectives and strategies and administer nonmarketing activities like production planning, inventory management, and facilities planning.

Units of analysis

An important decision in designing the firm's sales analysis system concerns which units of analysis to use—that is, what levels of aggregation are important? Most companies assemble data in the following groupings:

1. Geographical areas—regions, counties, and sales territories.
2. Product, package size, and grade.
3. Customer—by type and size.
4. Channel intermediary—such as type and/or size of retailer.
5. Method of sale—mail, phone, channel, direct.
6. Size of order—less than $10, $10–$25, etc.

These breakdowns are not mutually exclusive. Most firms perform sales analyses hierarchically; for example, by county within a sales territory within a sales region. Further, they usually combine product and account breakdowns with a geographical one; say, the purchase of product X by large accounts located in sales territory Y, which is a part of region A. Only by conducting a sales analysis on a hierarchical basis using a combination of breakdowns can analysts be at all sure that they have made every reasonable attempt to locate the opportunities and problems facing their firms. We discuss different sales analyses briefly in the following sections.

Evaluation systems and sources of information

The two major evaluation systems are a simple sales analysis and a comparative one. In a **simple sales analysis,** the data are listed in tabular form with no effort to compare the figures against any standard. Sometimes referred to as a **performance analysis,** the **comparative analysis** uses comparisons between the facts and some set of standards.

Consider, for example, the data in Exhibit 24–13. A simple sales analysis would be restricted to the data in column 1, which suggests that White, who sold the most, was the best salesperson and Finch, who sold the least, was the worst. But the comparative analysis uses a performance standard consisting of a sales quota (column 2). It determines individual performance by dividing actual sales by the sales quota (column 4). On this basis White was not the best salesperson, but rather the worst with a performance index of 77 percent. Burrows' over-quota performance was best with an index of 104 percent. Other possible standards to use include last year's sales, average sales of the past three years, and forecasted sales.

EXHIBIT 24 ♦ 13

Sales analysis based on selected sales territories

Sales territory	Salesperson	(1) Company sales 1986	(2) Sales quota 1986	(3) Overage, underage	(4) Percent of potential performance
1	Barlow	$552,630	$585,206	− $ 32,576	94%
2	Burrows	470,912	452,800	+ 18,112	104
3	White	763,215	981,441	− 218,226	77
4	Finch	287,184	297,000	− 9,816	96
5	Brown	380,747	464,432	− 83,685	82
6	Roberts	494,120	531,311	− 37,191	93
7	Macini	316,592	329,783	− 13,191	96

Sources of information

Once managers have determined how many comparisons to make, they must choose which sources of information to use. Invoices are the major source. They contain data that form the essence of any sales analysis: The date; customer's name and location; products sold; quantity of each item sold; price per unit (including terms of sale and applicable discount); total dollar sales per product; total dollar amount; freight paid or collected; and salesperson. Sometimes the firm needs to add further information about the customer, such as size, type of business, and chain or independent. Other information sources include sales staff call reports and expense accounts; credit memos for returns and allowances; service costs for products under warranty; and data from syndicated subscription research firms such as A. C. Nielsen and Selling Areas–Marketing, Inc. (SAMI).

Sales analysis by territory

The first step in sales territory analysis is to decide which geographical control unit to use. The county is the typical choice; it can be combined into larger units such as sales territories, and it represents the smallest geographical unit for which many data items are available (such as population, employment, income, and retail sales). For these reasons, analysts often determine market potentials at the county level.

Analysts can compare actual sales by county against a standard such as the market potential or last year's sales adjusted for inflation. They can single out territories that fall below standard for special attention. Is competition unusually strong? Has less selling effort been expended there? Is the salesforce weak? Studies dealing with such questions help companies improve their weak areas and exploit the stronger ones.

Exhibit 24–13 illustrates a sales territory analysis. It shows that only one territory out of seven exceeded the 1986 quota or standard of performance. The amount of sales over quota was only $18,112. The other six territories accounted for a total of $394,685 under quota. Territory 3 alone accounts for 55 percent of the total loss. The sales and the size of the quota in this territory suggest the need for further breakdowns—especially by accounts and products. Such breakdowns may reveal that the firm needs to allocate more selling resources to this territory. In any event, the company needs to improve its sales primarily in territories 3 and 5. If it can reach its potential in these two territories, overall sales would increase by $301,911.

Sales analysis by product

Over time, a company's product line becomes overcrowded and less profitable unless management takes strong and continuous action to eliminate no-longer-profitable items. By eliminating weak products and concentrating on strong ones, a company can increase its profits substantially. Before deciding which products to abandon, management must study such variables as market-share trends, contribution margins, scale effects, and the extent of product complementarity with other items in the line.

A product sales analysis is particularly helpful when combined with account size and sales territory data. Using such an analysis, managers can often pinpoint substantial opportunities and develop specific tactics to take advantage of them. For example, one firm's analysis revealed that sales of one of its highest-margin products were down in all New England sales territories. Further investigation showed a regional producer aggressively promoting a recently modified product with reduced prices. An analysis of the competing product revealed questionable reliability under certain operating conditions. The salesforce used this information to turn around the sales problem.

Deciding what product units to use in a product analysis can be a problem. At one extreme a firm might classify its products by product class or in general groupings such as industrial, consumer, proprietary, or distributed. At the other extreme a firm might classify its products by color, size, or SKUs (stockkeeping units). Generally speaking, the brand is the best unit of analysis to use; but where considerable variation by package type and size exists, the SKU may be the best choice.

Sales analysis by order size

Sales analysis by order size may identify which dollar-size orders are not profitable. For example, if some customers frequently place small orders that require salesforce attention and need to be processed, order picked, and shipped as well, a problem of some importance likely exists. Using cost accounting data, managers can determine if such orders incur a loss.

Analysis by order size locates products, sales territories, and customer types and sizes where small orders prevail. Such an analysis may lead to setting a minimum order size, charging extra for small orders, training sales reps to develop larger orders, and dropping some accounts. An example of such an analysis involved a nationwide needlework product distributor, which found that 28 percent of all its orders were $10 and under. A study revealed that the average cost of servicing such an order was $12.82. The analysis also showed that the company did not break even until the order size reached $20. Based on these findings, the company installed a $35 minimum order, charged a special handling fee of $7.50 on all orders below $35, and alerted its field sales reps and telephone salespeople to the problem. The company generated $52,000 more in profits before taxes during the first year it operated with these new rules.

Sales analysis by customer

Analysts use procedures similar to those described earlier to analyze sales by customers. Such analyses typically show that a relatively small percentage of customers account for a large percentage of sales. For example, the needlework products distributor found that 13 percent of its accounts represented 67 percent of its total sales. Frequently, a study of sales calls shows that the salesforce spends as much time with the small accounts as with the larger ones. Shifting some of this effort to the larger accounts may well increase sales.

Analysis by customer combined with territorial and product analyses may be particularly helpful in identifying weak spots in the sales program. For example, some salespersons may fail to develop sales with certain customers and products that have proven successful elsewhere. When this is discovered, managers can take remedial action quickly, because they know the main cause of the weakness.

GLOBAL MARKETING CONTROL

There are many reasons why maintaining control over global marketing activities is more difficult than controlling domestic marketing. The major reason is the number of different environments in which the company is operating. Each country presents a unique set of opportunities and threats; and the rate at which they change makes it difficult to monitor the results of individual country plans—and to prescribe corrective action where appropriate. Differences in language and customs, accentuated by distance, futher compound the control problem.

Keegan recommends that global companies use essentially the same control system format for both their domestic and foreign operations.[12] Report frequency and extent of detail would vary by the subsidiary's size and environment uncertainties. The great advantage of using a single system is that comparisons between operating units are facilitated, as are communications between home office and local managers.

The extent of control exercised over an overseas subsidiary is largely a function of its size; differences in the environment, including its stability; and the extent to which the company employs a standardized rather than a localized strategy.[13] The larger a company's international operation, the greater the likelihood that staff personnel specializing in control activities will be on site—making the control system more elaborate and precise in its operation. Small overseas operations tend to have fewer specialists involved and a less intensive control system.

Another factor affecting the control system is the extent to which environmental differences exist. Ordinarily the greater the differences between the home country and the foreign subsidiary, the more decision-making authority is delegated. For example, a U.S. subsidiary in England would likely be given less autonomy than one in Spain. Large multinationals compensate for these differences by clustering countries with similar environments into regions that have sufficient revenues to permit the use of a headquarters staff. When considerable environmental instability is present, it is difficult to employ a formal control system; and the tendency then is to delegate to local management the authority to make decisions without review and approval by the home office.

A third major factor affecting the international control system is the extent to which a standardized strategy is used. The more standardized the strategy—especially with respect to the product—the greater the degree of control exercised by the home office over the individual foreign subsidiary. Control is essential over many activities, including the purchase of raw materials and components, manufacturing, and quality specifications. Ordinarily, control over marketing activities is far less stringent than with manufacturing.

Other factors affecting control are the success of the subsidiary (the greater the success, the less the home office interference); the physical distance separating the home office and the subsidiary (the greater the distance, the less frequently the subsidiary will be visited by home office personnel); and the availability of a satisfactory communication system in a subsidiary (the more primitive the system, the less control can be exercised). Rapidly improving voice and data communication systems throughout the world are fast negating this constraint.

---

[12] Warren J. Keegan, *Global Marketing Management* (Englewood Cliffs, N.J.: Prentice-Hall, 1989), chap. 4.

[13] Ibid.

CONTINGENCY PLANNING

Because all strategies and the action plans designed to implement them are based on assumptions about the future, they are subject to considerable risk. Too often, assumptions are regarded as facts; and little attention is paid to what action or actions can be taken if any or all of the assumptions turn out to be wrong.[14]

Managers thus follow a contingency planning process that includes the elements shown in Exhibit 24–14: (a) identifying critical assumptions, (b) assigning probabilities of being right about the assumptions, (c) ranking the importance of the assumptions, (d) tracking and monitoring the action plan, (e) setting the "triggers" that will activate the contingency plan, and (f) specifying alternative response options. We discuss these steps briefly below.

EXHIBIT   24 ♦ 14

The contingency planning process

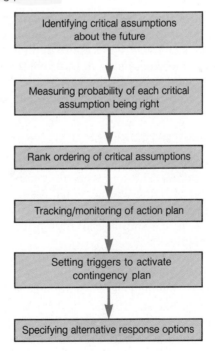

Identifying critical assumptions about the future

Measuring probability of each critical assumption being right

Rank ordering of critical assumptions

Tracking/monitoring of action plan

Setting triggers to activate contingency plan

Specifying alternative response options

---

[14] For a brief but insightful view of contingencies alert systems, see William E. Rothschild, *Putting It All Together* (New York: AMACOM, 1976), chap. 2.

Identifying critical assumptions

Since not all assumptions can be tracked—there are simply too many—contingency plans must cover only the more important ones. Assumptions based on events beyond the control of the individual firm but that strongly impact the entry's strategic objectives are particularly important. For example, assumptions about the rate of market growth coupled with the entry's market share will strongly affect the entry's profitability objectives. The effect of a wrong assumption here can be either good or bad; and the contingency plan must be prepared to handle both. If the market grows at a rate faster than expected, then the question of how to respond needs to be considered. Too often contingency plans focus only on the down side.

Another type of uncontrollable event that can strongly affect sales and profits is competitive action. This is particularly true with a new entry (when a competitor responds with its own new product), although it can apply with more mature products (competitor's advertising is increased). Assumptions about industry price levels must be examined in depth because any price deterioration can quickly erode margins and profits.

Assumptions about the effects of certain actions taken by the firm to attain its strategic objectives also need to be considered in depth. Examples include the firm's advertising objectives, which are based on assumptions about an improvement or maintenance of consumer attitudes toward the product's characteristics compared to competing brands; or the monies allocated to merchandising to improve the product's availability. Further, once the targeted levels of the various primary objectives are reached, there are assumptions about what will happen to sales and share.

Assigning probabilities

This step consists of assigning probabilities of being right to the critical assumptions. These probabilities must be considered in terms of the consequences of being wrong. Thus, assumptions that have a low probability of being wrong, but could affect the firm strongly, will need to be considered in depth (e.g., gas shortages or high prices or the demand for large-sized, luxury automobiles).

In discussing the selection and ranking of key assumptions, Rothschild uses the term *confidence*, which, he argues, involves more than probability. He states that managers "should also ask, 'Why do I think so?' Every assumption is based on either data from the past or analysis of the present, your intuition of how events will move, or your judgment of yourself or others. I have found it useful to record the source of each assumption, since the source may have a great bearing on how valid and reliable the prediction is."[15]

---

[15] Ibid., p. 225.

Rank ordering the critical assumptions

If assumptions are categorized on the basis of their importance, the extent to which they are controllable, and the confidence management has in them, then the basis for rank ordering the assumptions and drafting the contingency plan has been set forth. Ordinarily, these criteria will have screened out those assumptions that need not be included—those with a low impact on objectives and those about which there is a high confidence. Assumptions that relate to uncontrollable events should, however, be monitored if they strongly affect the entry's strategic objectives, because the firm can react to them. For example, if the assumption about the rate of market growth is wrong, then the firm can either slow or increase its investments in plant contruction.

Tracking and monitoring

The next step is to specify what information (or measures) are needed to determine whether the implementation of the action plan is on schedule—and if not, why. The contingency plan is, therefore, an early-warning system as well as a diagnostic tool. If, for example, the firm has made certain assumptions about the rate of market demand increase, then it would monitor industry sales on a regular basis. If assumptions were made about advertising and its effect on attitudes, then measures of awareness, trial, and repeat buying would likely be used. In any event, relevancy, accuracy, and cost of obtaining the needed measures must be examined in depth. Some of the information needed in the contingency plan might have been specified in the control plan, in which case it is already available.

Activating the contingency plan

This involves setting the "triggers" to activate the contingency plan. It requires a specification of both the level at which an alert will be called and the combination of events that must occur before the firm reacts. If, for example, total industry sales were 10 percent less than expected for a single month, this would not be likely to trigger a response, whereas a 25 percent drop would. Or a firm may decide the triggering would occur only after three successive months in which a difference of 10 percent occurred. Triggers must, therefore, be defined precisely and responsibility assigned for putting the contingency plan into operation.

Specifying response options

Actually, the term *contingency plan* is somewhat misleading. It implies that the firm knows in advance exactly how it will respond if one or more of its assumptions go awry. This implication is unrealistic because there are a great many ways for critical assumptions to turn out wrong. To compound the problem, the firm's preplanned specific responses can be difficult to implement, depending upon the situation and how it develops. This can lead to a *set of responses* that build in intensity. Thus, most firms develop a set of optional responses that are not detailed to any great extent, in an effort to provide flexibility and ensure further study of the forces that caused the alert.

SUMMARY

Marketing control and reappraisal is the final step in the marketing management process. Highly diagnostic, it starts the marketing management process anew. Marketing controls are necessary if the company is to operate profitably; and yet many, if not most, companies have poor control procedures. Much of the problem is a failure to set measurable objectives. When this is coupled with a weak plan of action, it becomes almost impossible to set up an effective control system.

Different control processes correspond to the organizational levels involved; that is, corporate, SBU, and product-market entry. Regardless of level, the control process sets standards of performance, specifies and obtains feedback data, evaluates it, and takes corrective action.

Control typically involves some form of profitability analysis. In these analyses, managers determine the costs associated with specific marketing activities to find out the profitability of such units of analysis as different market segments, products, customer accounts, and channel intermediaries. In performing such investigations, analysts have the option of using direct or full costing to determine the unit's profitability. In full costing, they assign both direct and indirect costs. Direct costing uses contribution accounting and is favored by those who argue that there is no really accurate way to assign indirect costs. It is also helpful in doing a marginal analysis study.

Strategic control is concerned with the opportunities and threats pertaining to each SBU, to each of their product-market entries, and with the strategies adopted to exploit them. A strategic control system should provide data to help answer questions about changes in the environment, strategies of major competitors, and the maturity of the industry—especially those changes in the industry's key success factors. From these answers, marketers can identify new opportunities and threats and determine whether the current strategy is still viable.

The marketing audit is the mechanism by which corporate management evaluates the company's total marketing effort. It involves an SBU's objectives, strategy, plan of action, and personnel. It provides an assessment of each SBU's present competitive position and insights into its marketing strengths and weaknesses.

Product-market entry control is concerned with the product's competitive position, adherence to plan, and sales analyses. The first has to do with such key parameters as market share, market size, and market growth. It is important to determine whether any deviation from plan is caused by errors in forecasting versus errors in management. A majority of most control systems are concerned with the extent to which the plan is adhered to—especially the budget. It is also important to determine whether the sales/share determinants have been attained.

Sales analysis involves dividing aggregate sales data into certain breakdowns such as those having to do with products, end-user customers, channel intermediaries, sales territories, and order size. Then analysts make comparisons against other data. The objective of such analysis is to find areas of strengths and weaknesses—products, territories, and customers that account for the bulk of the revenues. Sales analysis recognizes that aggregate sales and cost data may mask the situation sufficiently for a misdiagnosis of the problem. The two major evaluation systems are simple and comparative sales analyses.

Control over a firm's international operations is a difficult undertaking largely because of the number of different environments present. A firm should use the same control system for its international operations as it does for its domestic ones. The extent of control exercised over overseas units varies, depending upon the unit's size, whether a standardized or a localized marketing strategy is used, and the extent of environmental differences, coupled with the magnitude of risk present.

Contingency planning is concerned with the validity of the assumptions made in formulating strategy and developing action plans. The planning process consists of identifying and assessing the relative importance of assumptions made about the future, assigning probabilities that each is correct, rank ordering the critical assumptions, tracking the plan, indicating the triggers to activate the contingency plan, and specifying alternative responses.

QUESTIONS

1. MTS Systems, Inc., is a relatively small manufacturer of measurement instruments used to monitor and control automated production processes in a number of different industries, such as the automotive and aerospace industries. The firm has a company salesforce of 12 people, each of whom calls on companies in a particular user industry. While the firm's sales have increased steadily in recent years, its profits have been relatively stagnant. One problem is that the firm has no information concerning the relative profitability of the various products it makes or the different customers it sells to. MTS Systems has hired you as a marketing consultant to design a *control system* that will enable the firm to evaluate its performance across the various items in its product line and the various segments of its market. Outline the major steps or activities you would recommend including in such a control system.

2. What specific *types of information* would have to be collected and evaluated in order to implement the control system you outlined in your answer to question 1? What sources could be used to obtain each necessary type of information?

3. Discuss the relative advantages and limitations of the *full costing versus the contri-bution* margin approaches for determining the profitability of a specific item within a firm's product line. Which approach do you think is most commonly used by large, multi-SBU corporations? Why?

4. Using the data presented in Exhibit 24–7, suppose you believe the product's net sales could be increased by $250,000 by taking the following combined actions: (a) increase advertising by $45,000, (b) add one more salesperson at a total cost of $60,000, and (c) improve delivery time to customers by spending an additional $25,000 on order processing and warehousing for the product. Assuming the product's cost of goods sold does not change, what would be the effect of these actions on the product's *contribution margin*? What would be the *marginal effect* on pretax profits?

5. Another alternative to the actions described in question 4 would be to increase the advertising and promotion budget by $70,000 without making any changes in the salesforce or the logistics system. It is estimated that such an increase in advertising would generate an additional $130,000 in net sales. Which alternative would be most desirable: the one proposed in question 4 or the one proposed here?

6. You are a marketing manager in an SBU of a large consumer food manufacturer. The SBU's general manager has asked you to conduct a *marketing audit* of the SBU as a basis for evaluating its strategic and operational strengths and weaknesses. What issues or areas of concern should be covered by your audit?

7. For each set of issues to be included in the audit you designed in your answer to question 6, specify the kinds of information you would need to collect and the major sources you might use to obtain that information.

8. When they saw the results of the *sales territory analysis* presented in Exhibit 24–13, the firm's top managers concluded that Barlow in territory 1 was not devoting sufficient effort to her job, since her performance was more than $32,000 below her quota. They have asked you—the firm's sales manager—to have a talk with Barlow and suggest a way to improve her performance. Do you agree that Barlow's performance is probably the result of too little effort on her part? Why or why not?

9. What other causes might be responsible for Barlow's failure to make her quota? What additional information or analyses would you seek in order to determine what should be done to improve Barlow's future performance?

Epilog

Rubbermaid revisited

At the start of Chapter 1, Rubbermaid, Inc.'s success at selling an unexciting line of products in a mature industry illustrated the importance and competitive power of good marketing in today's economy. After reading the last 24 chapters, you should now have a greater appreciation for the magnitude of Rubbermaid's accomplishments over the past decade and a better understanding of how savvy marketing contributed to those accomplishments.[1]

Rubbermaid has not achieved success through unrelated diversification or far-flung acquisitions. It operates in a single industry, manufacturing plastic and rubber products for consumer and institutional markets. Nor can its success be attributed to a rapidly growing market. Most of the company's product line is targeted at consumer households, and new household formation in the United States has been limping along at about a 2 percent annual rate for the past decade. To make matters worse, Rubbermaid faces intense competition. More than 150 other firms make similar plastic household products; and nearly all of those competitors undercut Rubbermaid's prices.

Despite Rubbermaid's unencouraging environment, when Stanley Gault took over as the firm's chairman and chief executive in 1980, he specified an extremely ambitious set of corporate objectives for the next decade. He decreed the company would seek 15 percent average annual increases in sales, profits, and earnings per share. As Exhibit E–1 shows, the firm met or exceeded those objectives nearly every year during the 1980s. And for the last five years of that decade the company was ranked as one of America's 10 most admired corporations in *Fortune* magazine's annual survey of nearly 6,000 top executives and financial analysts.

How did Rubbermaid achieve such sparkling results in such a ho-hum business? It did this largely by gaining and sustaining an advantage over its many competitors through the effective planning and implementation of sound business strategies and marketing programs. Rubbermaid's road to success reflects a number of the major themes stressed throughout this book, including:

- Careful and continual monitoring of changes and trends in the environment, particularly those involving customers and competitors.
- Development of well-defined corporate, business-level, and marketing strategies that fit the firm's environment and its internal capabilities and are consistent with one another.
- Creation of marketing strategies targeted at clearly defined customer segments.
- Planning of marketing programs in which all of the 4 Ps are consistent with the firm's strategy of differentiating itself from competitors by positioning its products as the highest quality offerings in their markets.

---

[1] The following discussion is based on material found in Alex Taylor III, "Why the Bounce at Rubbermaid?" *Fortune*, April 13, 1987, pp. 77–78; *1987 Annual Report* (Wooster, Ohio: Rubbermaid, Inc., 1988); and Carol Davenport, "America's Most Admired Corporations," *Fortune*, January 30, 1989, pp. 68–75.

EXHIBIT   E ◆ 1

Rubbermaid's performance during the 1980s

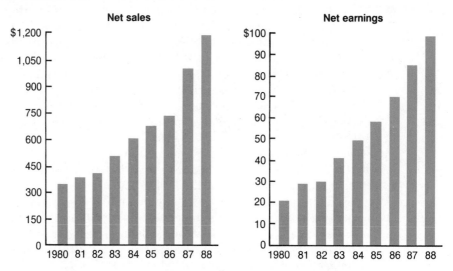

Source: 1987 Annual Report (Wooster, Ohio: Rubbermaid, Inc., 1988), pp. 3–4; and Carol Davenport, "America's Most Admired Companies," *Fortune,* January 30, 1989, p. 70.

◆ Ensuring effective implementation of marketing strategies and programs through an appropriate allocation of resources and the careful coordination of marketing with the firm's other functional departments.

Not surprisingly, the above list looks suspiciously like a capsule summary of the steps in the marketing management process we outlined in Exhibit 1–12 on page 26. A brief examination of Rubbermaid's actions in each of these areas will serve as a final review and reaffirmation of the importance of that process.

Market opportunity analysis

Rubbermaid's managers have paid close attention to many aspects of the firm's environment as a means of identifying both attractive opportunities for and potential threats against future growth. Because the company relies heavily on petroleum as the principle raw material for its products, managers pay particular attention to factors in both the natural and political environments that might affect future oil prices. Given the extremely competitive structure of the housewares industry, they also constantly analyze information about competitors' new-product introductions, production processes, pricing practices, and any other actions that might threaten Rubbermaid's position as the industry leader.

Most important, though, the company makes a fetish out of staying in close touch with its customers. For instance, it tests color preferences year-round through consumer focus groups in five cities, then confirms the results by surveying people in shopping malls. Company executives personally read letters from customers to find out how consumers like specific products and to gain ideas for improvements or new product offerings. However, to avoid tipping off competitors, Rubbermaid does not use full-scale test markets for its new products. Instead, it generates reams of research data from user panels, brand awareness studies, and customer diaries. All of this customer analysis has obviously paid dividends because the firm's success rate for new-product introductions over the past decade has been an outstanding 90 percent.

Well-defined and integrated strategies

As we mentioned earlier, Rubbermaid has avoided unrelated diversification. Instead, its corporate strategy has focused primarily on achieving internal growth within the rubber and plastics industry. While Rubbermaid has acquired some smaller firms over the years, those acquisitions added related product-markets to the Rubbermaid line and greater economies of scale and synergies in manufacturing and distribution. Thus, the company bought such businesses as Little Tykes, a manufacturer of plastic toys and children's play furniture, and MicroComputer Accessories, a maker of plastic computer accessories such as files for floppy discs.

Rubbermaid is organized into six divisions or SBUs, including an international division. Each SBU focuses on a set of related product-markets. Thus, the home product SBU incorporates products used by consumer households, such as dish drainers and microwave utensils; while the commercial SBU focuses on products for business markets, including a line of plastic office furniture. Most of Rubbermaid's SBUs can be characterized as pursuing *analyzer strategies*. That means they devote about equal effort to defending strong positions in established product-markets on the one hand and to prospecting for market growth through line extensions and new-product development on the other.

Careful market targeting

Much of Rubbermaid's volume growth over the last decade is the result of market expansion strategies pursued by the firm's various SBUs. Each SBU expends a great deal of money and time on marketing research aimed at identifying new applications for Rubbermaid products among current users and newly emerging customer segments with unique needs that might be satisfied with new Rubbermaid products. For example, the firm's research indicated the recent trend toward smaller households also meant more people were living in smaller apartments and condos with limited space.

Consequently, the firm introduced a line of space-saving products—such as a compact one-piece dish drainer—that was an immediate hit among members of that newly identified target segment.

Integrated marketing programs

Within its established product-markets Rubbermaid avoids direct confrontations with its many low-price competitors. Instead, it charges premium prices and relies on superior product quality and rapid new-product development to differentiate its offerings from those of its competitors.

The other elements of the firm's marketing programs are also consistent with such a "premium quality/premium price" competitive position. Rubbermaid uses some of the funds generated by its higher margins to support extensive advertising efforts in both broadcast and print media. That advertising informs target customer segments about new-product introductions and reinforces the high-quality image of Rubbermaid products. Because many of the company's products are low-involvement convenience goods, however, the firm also seeks extensive retail distribution through such mass merchandisers as K mart and Wal-Mart. To gain strong reseller support, the firm relies on extensive personal selling efforts and good service to the trade. For example, Rubbermaid has paid much attention to reducing delivery times to its retailers and providing good merchandising support. Such efforts have helped reduce retailers' investments in inventory and improved the turnover and profitability of Rubbermaid products in their stores.

Coordination of efforts across functions

As we have said many times throughout this text, marketing does not occur in a vacuum. Thus, Rubbermaid's marketing strategies and programs have been successful in part because they have been consistent with the firm's broader corporate focus and competitive positioning. Another part of the firm's success is due to effective implementation of those strategies and programs. For one thing, the firm has been careful to allocate sufficient resources to support all the functional activities necessary to carry out a strategy focused on high product quality and rapid new-product development. For instance, Rubbermaid's budgets for such activities as product R&D and market research are substantially greater than the average for its industry. And the firm has expanded its manufacturing and distribution facilities from 7 locations in 1980 to 25 locations in 1989 to keep pace with volume growth and to reduce delivery times and improve service to retailers and dealers in its distribution channels.

Of course, effective implementation also requires close coordination of efforts across the various functional departments within each SBU. Consequently, Rubbermaid relies on a combination of product managers and product development teams to provide that coordination. But while the firm's marketing managers bear the primary responsibility for analyzing target segments and developing programs to appeal to those segments, the company also realizes that it can continue to provide high-quality products and good service only if every employee in every functional area is market-oriented and dedicated to delivering desired benefits to the firm's customers. As CEO Gault declares: "Our formula for success is very open. We absolutely watch the market, and we [all] work at it 24 hours a day." That is not only a good formula for success in today's competitive marketplace, but it also provides a succinct summary of what this book has been all about.

Name Index

Subject Index